MEDICAL
BEHAVIORAL
SCIENCE

Edited and Introduced by

THEODORE MILLON, Ph.D.

PROFESSOR AND DIRECTOR, BEHAVIORAL SCIENCE PROGRAMS,
UNIVERSITY OF ILLINOIS COLLEGE OF MEDICINE,
CHICAGO, ILLINOIS

Foreword by MELVIN SABSHIN, M.D.
Medical Director, American Psychiatric Association

1975   W. B. SAUNDERS COMPANY · Philadelphia · London · Toronto

W. B. Saunders Company: West Washington Square
Philadelphia, PA 19105

12 Dyott Street
London, WC1A 1DB

833 Oxford Street
Toronto, Ontario, M8Z 5T9, Canada

Medical Behavioral Science   ISBN 0-7216-6387-7

Last digit is the print number: 9   8   7   6   5   4   3   2   1   •

Dedicated to

R.F. BADGLEY	DONALD A. KENNEDY	EVAN G. PATTISHALL
CLIFFORD BARNET	SOL KRAMER	EDWARD J. STAINBROOK
SAMUEL W. BLOOM	HANS O. MAUKSCH	JOSEPH STOKES III
LEON EISENBERG	IVAN N. MENSH	ROBERT STRAUS
C. RICHARD FLETCHER	RICHARD W. OLMSTED	NATHAN B. TALBOT
CHARLES C. HUGHES		ROBERT N. WILSON

Pioneers in Medical Behavioral Science
of the past decade

And to today's student-physicians and student-scientists
who will pioneer the next decade.

FOREWORD

Medical behavioral science was born at the very beginning of medicine's emergence as a viable entity. Unfortunately, its rate of maturation as compared to many other components of basic medical sciences has been slow. However, medical behavioral science is an idea whose time for tangible growth and development has now finally arrived. A wide variety of forces have retarded and inhibited previous efforts to integrate behavioral sciences into the central core of medicine. The hegemony of biological reductionism, prejudices against humanistic medicine, and the sheer overload of information and skills to be learned by students have all coalesced into resistances against the incorporation of behavioral sciences into medical curricula. Furthermore, serious questions have been raised periodically regarding the relevance of behavioral sciences to the actual range of activities conducted by modal physician populations.

Gradually, however, the advocates of behavioral science's significant role have become more persuasive; explicit resistance was slowly transformed into at least verbal consensus for change. Most medical schools began to include behavioral science content in their educational programs. Some schools organized divisions or even departments of behavioral sciences. National associations of behavioral science teachers emerged out of a complex, heterogeneous group of educators. The National Board of Medical Examiners reflected these developments by including questions on the subject in its Part I examination. Despite these significant changes, however, many thoughtful commentators have continued to raise serious questions about the relevant content for student learning in behavioral sciences as well as noting the lack of objectifiable goals associated with this learning process. During the last few years, coherent and systematic responses to these questions have begun to appear. Illustrative of this trend and at the vanguard of defining the content of medical behavioral science, Dr. Millon's sourcebook is an immense contribution toward elucidating this entire subject.

Sourcebooks vary considerably in their quality. Some are loosely organized conglomerations of heterogeneous perspectives; only a few reflect creativity in the author's blending of disparate elements into a coherent whole. Dr. Millon has demonstrated great skill in his categorization of medical behavioral science and in his selection of pertinent source material. Furthermore, his comments introducing each of the chapters provide a solid skeletal structure for this book.

The basic organizational structure employed by Dr. Millon involves the classification of medical behavioral sciences into Biobehavioral, Psychobehavioral, Interbehavioral, and Sociobehavioral foundations of medicine. Each of these units are subdivided into pertinent components including concepts and viewpoints which are then related to normal function and development, pathology, treatment, and implications for health care systems. A guiding principle in the book involves logical progression from the organism perspective to the person perspective, the relationship perspective, and the cultural perspective. Each of these areas is covered in depth but blended and orchestrated by the author's interstitial clarifications and bridges from perspective to perspective.

The first part of the book serves as an introduction in both a historical and a contextual sense. Medical student readers can find rational answers to their questions concerning why they should be interested in medical behavioral science. Furthermore, they are introduced to the general contours of the field and its pertinence to their personal development as physicians. The author was wise to include an introductory chapter on the behavioral environment of the student-physician, since each of the selected papers reaches out to the student to become a mature participant in the learning process. Indeed, the entire introductory section includes recent classics that encourage the reader to become interested in delving deeper into the subsequent chapters.

While the book has immediate pertinence to students and teachers of medical behavioral science, it can serve as a serious sourcebook for a wide variety of interested decision-makers and their constituents. Deans of medical schools, curriculum committees, practitioners of various medical and nonmedical specialties, and even critics of medical education will all find a great deal to learn in this source-book. Of course, some experts will question whether their particular field is presented in its most advanced state and others will criticize particular biases or emphases that inevitably enter a work of this kind. Hopefully, these concerns will not prevent the open-minded reader from learning more about those aspects of medical behavioral science that are not part of his expertise. Indeed, experts on hemispheric deconnection would do well to be interested in social modes of communication and vice versa.

Dr. Millon has not provided the last word on medical behavioral sciences. Certainly the field will change greatly in the coming decades. It will broaden in some respects while particularizing more sharply in other areas. Its relevance to physicians' role functions will become clearer but this too will change as more data become available and as medical practice itself changes. Recognizing the desirability and inevitability of this change, Dr. Millon has succeeded in meeting significant needs of the here and now. The time for tangible growth and development of medical behavioral science has indeed come, and this book is a fine reflection of substantive maturation.

Beyond reflection, however, the author has helped us to understand the terrain included within the subject. He has given us a detailed map with multiple guidelines if not directions to move from one part to another. By superb selection of original sources and his own integrating comments, he has also brought the subject to life at each of the hierarchical levels subsumed by the medical behavioral sciences.

MELVIN SABSHIN
Medical Director
American Psychiatric Association

PREFACE

Faced with the task of organizing a behavioral science curriculum for medical students some years ago, I was struck by the fact that no text had been published covering the broad scope of topics with which students are expected to be acquainted in this complex and wide-ranging field. Excellent works had been written and edited in relevant subjects — medical sociology, human development, biobehavioral processes, and health care delivery systems. Each of these texts, however, focused selectively on only one or another of the many varied components that make up the totality of medical behavioral science. In short, it seemed time to fill an important gap in our academic medical library, one that should have been filled years before.

The central purpose of a behavioral science text is to provide medical students with a guide to the psychosocial influences that shape the lives of their patients. Now, with growing success in the control of infectious diseases and marked advances in laboratory diagnosis and treatment, medicine has entered an era in which increasing attention is being given to behavioral events that promote and complicate physical illness, and which undermine the effective implementation of many remarkable technological advances. Of course, no book can fully convey to the student all the subtleties and information he needs and will ultimately acquire in this field. Nevertheless, his task can be greatly facilitated, particularly in the early phases of his student career, if he is sensitized, through text and lecture, to issues and concerns of relevance and if he is provided with an orderly framework of ideas and illustrations to guide his "real life" experiences.

Although this volume is primarily an anthology rather than a formal text, it is designed to be more than a compendium of miscellaneous topical readings. It was edited to achieve three major purposes.

First, its organization and content reflect an effort to define the scope and structure of a field that has only recently acquired the status of a formal course in the medical curriculum. Because of its newness, behavioral science has been taught in highly varied and often divergent ways. Developed by faculties with diverse professional and disciplinary backgrounds, the course material given students at different medical schools frequently has had no semblance of similarity in either content or goals. Fortunately, with the advent of new academic organizations such as the Association for Behavioral Sciences and Medical Education, conferences among concerned scientists and physicians have led to a growing consensus on the key topics that compose this field of study. Formerly disparate professionals have formed strong alliances, have learned to coordinate their expertise, and have begun to establish a common core of subject materials which have taken the shape of a well-structured "medical behavioral science" curriculum. No longer need this new science be taught with a limited focus or be presented as a potpourri of miscellaneous facts. Rather, it has taken the form of a separate and medically relevant discipline, cast in a framework of observations that are not fixed and immutable, but are sufficiently durable to serve as a guide to patient life for student-physicians. In line with this newly emerging consensus, the text format has been organized into four major areas: *biobehavioral foundations,* which provide the perspective of the "organism"; *psychobehavioral foundations*, oriented toward the perspective of the "person"; *interbehavioral foundations,* which focus on the "relationship" perspective and *sociobehavioral foundations*, to furnish the "cultural" perspective. Although the book can be used profitably in the sequence provided, it permits a good deal of flexibility among subject areas, encouraging both students and instructors to rearrange or select among chapters, topics and papers.

Readings have been carefully selected to fit the interests and needs of the medical student. Although behavioral science derives its scholarly principles from academic disciplines such as sociology and psychology, many of its concepts and findings are especially relevant to a medical curriculum and have clear implications for increasing the effectiveness of medical practice. If the format and selections included succeed in striking a proper balance between behavioral science principles and medical relevance, there is no reason why the text cannot serve with equal utility for behaviorally oriented and nonbehaviorally oriented students. It should whet the appetite and furnish some solid underpinnings for later work among those who plan a medical behavioral science career as well as expose a rich vein of patient-relevant information for those seeking breadth in the more narrowly focused aspects of their medical education. To create a sense of participation and intellectual challenge, complex and controversial issues have been presented in neither predigested nor oversimplified form. Moreover, by drawing upon original sources, students are furnished not only with each writer's distinctive way of stating his views but are exposed to a fully developed argument that can rarely be matched by secondhand summaries. With several authors often commenting on a single theme, the reader can participate in the interplay of contrasting views and convictions; such exposure not only enlivens the subject, but also alerts the student to logical shortcomings and to unsolved problems that remain a challenge to future investigators.

Most pragmatically, the text is intended to provide, in a single reference work, material useful in preparation for the new behavioral science section of the National Boards Examination, Part 1. As has been evident in discussions with students who anxiously ready themselves for this hurdle, there is great need for a single publication that not only covers the awesome scope of the behavioral sciences, but does so with a focus relevant to medical issues.

The present book is the first of two related volumes; the second, authored by this writer as an integrated text, will be published by the W. B. Saunders Company in the near future. Both have emerged directly from my involvement in a series of multidisciplinary courses in medical behavioral science at the University of Illinois. This still-developing curriculum reflects the shared efforts of several associates drawn from a number of different disciplines. The prime influence in this venture has been a good friend and colleague of mine, Melvin Sabshin. Not only was Mel instrumental in stimulating my interest in medical behavioral science, and not only has he been kind enough to write a thoughtful foreword for this book, but, most significantly, he has contributed his incisive intelligence, humane wisdom and unfailing integrity to all aspects of our department's work; his recent appointment to the medical directorship of the American Psychiatric Association will provide many others with the fruits of his notable talents. Many other colleagues associated with our behavioral science program have contributed immeasurably to its progress, particularly Pauline Bart, Rue Bucher, Louis Fourcher, Bob Meagher, and Hy Muslin. Thanks are also due my son Andy for the care with which he checked and corrected the text's bibliographic references. And, as I have noted many times before, a special word of appreciation is happily recorded for my most efficient and loyal secretary, Luberta Shirley.

The book has been dedicated, appropriately, I think, to those whose foresight and energy spurred the development of this new field of medical behavioral science. Without their efforts I could not have adhered to the sound advice of Sir Francis Bacon who, more than three centuries ago, wrote: "Books must follow sciences, and not sciences books."

THEODORE MILLON

CONTENTS

Part A

Introduction

I   BEHAVIORAL PERSPECTIVES IN MEDICINE

The attributes that define the "ideal" physician are neither universal nor permanent but differ from one culture to another, as well as from one historical period to the next. Given the fact that these ideal attributes are constantly evolving, it can never be said that medical education, the prime molder of society's physicians, has achieved a final or perfect curriculum. Rather, education is continually transformed to reflect the values and technology of the society it serves.

As Sigerist, the eminent medical historian, has written (1946):

Every society required of its physician that he have knowledge, skill, devotion to his patients and similar qualities. But the position of the physician in society, the tasks assigned to him and the rules of conduct imposed upon him by society changed in every period. The physician was a priest in Babylonia, a craftsman in ancient Greece, a cleric in the early Roman period and a scholar in the later Middle Ages. He became a scientist with the rise of the natural sciences, and it is perfectly obvious that the requirements put upon the physician and the tasks of medical education were different in all these periods.

We must keep in mind that the picture a society has of its ideal doctor—the goal of medical education—is determined primarily by two factors: the social and economic structure of that society and the technical means available to medical science at that time.

It was all but inevitable, given the remarkable growth in biologic knowledge since the turn of the century, that medical education would become increasingly dominated by the data and laboratory techniques of the natural sciences. Along with impressive medical breakthroughs such as asepsis, anesthesia and pharmacotherapy, there was a parallel and vigorous transformation in medical education, spurred largely by the publication of the Flexner Report in 1910. Sustained by the ever-growing accomplishments in physical diagnosis and treatment, Flexner's study was a powerful influence in moving medical schools toward their present technological orientation. And with each succeeding decade the curriculum for educating physicians was increasingly taken over by the methods and philosophies of the biological and physical sciences.

Despite the impressive achievements in human health produced by these technological advances, questions began to be raised in mid-century as to whether the pendulum toward laboratory science had swung too far from matters of patient care and society's needs. Many medical educators contended that students were losing the capacity to "see the forest for the trees," that they were forced to concentrate exclusively on the details of obscure disease mechanisms, and that they were taught, particularly in their first two years, to bypass the more human and everyday patient problems they would deal with as professional physicians. In the last decade students themselves began to question the utility of the rigid "scientific" curriculum to which they were exposed. As Pattishall, a distinguished physician and behavioral scientist, has recently noted (1972):

Medical educators are beginning to recognize and respond to overloaded and lopsided medical curriculum, the disciplinary bureaucracies, and the fragmentation and overspecialization of teaching time and patient care. The student is concerned because he sees himself being forced into an impossible learning situation often involving little relevance to the needs of a practicing physician. Also, he often sees himself being forced to participate in the perpetuation of priorities which seem to be incompatible with patient care and humanitarian concern.

Irrelevance is being challenged for the sake of relevance and meaning. With much student and faculty help, as well as help from some national commissions and public agencies, as medical educators we are being forced to recognize that the medical student is in medical school to become a physician and that he cannot continue to absorb the endless information explosion which has been superimposed upon the traditional courses of 10 to 20 years ago.

Nor can he achieve many of the fantasy notions that some basic scientists and academic physicians have structured for him. The simple reductionist model in the medical sciences has been accumulating an important, but often irrelevant, mountain of data in the name of education, professional standards, or understanding the scientific base of medical training and practice. Yet, we have little evidence to indicate that most of the mass of minutiae a medical student is forced to learn and regurgitate actually makes any difference in terms of improved patient care or physician performance. In fact, we have much reason to suspect that we have been fighting a losing battle, attempting to improve patient care by focusing on factual information rather than on problems of the patient and the patient care system.

An even stronger indictment of the dominant and narrow scientism that has become the standard of medical training is conveyed by the eminent internist George L. Engel (1973):

. . . For the past 40 years or more two dogmas have reigned supreme in medicine, physiochemical reductionism and technologic primacy. The dogma of physicochemical reductionism assumes that all activities of the living organism are ultimately to be explained in terms of its component molecular parts. All phenomena of life can be understood in the terms of chemistry and physics. The dogma of technologic primacy avers that all human problems are amenable to technologic solutions. . . . To achieve this they make use of the finest biochemists, the best molecular biologists, the most sophisticated technology, the most efficient computers, and the best equipped hospitals. But they, too, seem to have overlooked one thing, the human element. Medical education, after all, is meant to prepare physicians to serve the health needs of human beings. But where in our present day educational programs, graduate or undergraduate, is there genuinely serious attention devoted to preparing the student to deal with the human elements of medicine? That, I contend, is the missing dimension, the bog, of modern medical education. The triumphs of four decades of biomedical research, the unparalleled power of today's medical technology fall short of their real potential not only because of the defects of our systems of health care delivery, serious as they are, but also because modern medical education fails to equip the physician with the psychological knowledge and skills needed for his task. This is evident enough when one examines the deficiencies of what passes today as good medical care without considering the plight of those who receive no or only indifferent care.

To summarize the foregoing, "medical school admits incoming students who are interested in people and transforms them into doctors interested only in diseases."

In the three papers that comprise this introductory chapter we have chosen to present the views of several distinguished scientists. Each proposes antidotes to the pernicious effects of technological preoccupation and reductionistic scientism. To John H. Knowles, former medical director of Massachusetts General Hospital, the problem lies in the failure of the medical curriculum to provide the student with a thorough understanding of the social context of patient care; he contends that the values and economic institutions that influence the character of health delivery must be articulated and understood, and that the cultural forces shaping the incidence and course of physical disease must be made explicit. In the second, far-ranging and thoughtful essay, Roy R. Grinker, Sr., a distinguished medical researcher and teacher, presents a compelling argument for the synthesis of biological, psychological and sociological frames of reference; he points out, through numerous illustrations, the importance of teaching the fledgling physician to recognize that the interplay of influences from these three sources is a necessary step in achieving effective diagnosis and treatment. Focusing more sharply on the role of social factors, both in producing disease and in determining the quality of patient care, Professors David Mechanic, a medical sociologist, and Margaret Newton, a physician, outline, in a series of explicit examples, how behavioral science can lead the student to become a more efficient practitioner.

REFERENCES

Engel, G. L.: The best and the brightest: The missing dimension in medical education. Pharos. *10*:129-133 (1973).

Flexner, A.: Medical Education in the United States and Canada: A Report to the Carnegie Foundation for the Advancement of Teaching. New York, Carnegie Foundation, 1910.

Pattishall, E. G.: Curriculum trends in medical education and their implications for behavioral science. In Fletcher, C. R. (ed.): Behavioral Science Perspectives and Medical Education, Vol. 3. Rockville, Md., National Center for Health Service Research and Development, 1972.

Sigerist, H. E.: The University at the Crossroads. New York, Schuman, 1946.

1.   Medical Education and the Rationalization of Health Services

John H. Knowles

The formal years of education have been called a rehearsal for life, a preparation for the purposes of living. The individual should emerge, as Lionel Trilling has said, "at home in, and in control of the modern world." The aims of all forms of education are threefold: the development of the intellect; the acquisition of skills; and the passing on of the culture, its values and morals. Intellectual development brings flexibility to the individual to adapt to or solve the problems of his life. The acquisition of skills allows him to earn his living. The inculcation of cultural attitudes, beliefs, values, and morals allows him to participate fully as a social animal in the life of his community, state, and nation, and to strengthen the process of democracy thereby.

Undergraduate education in the university becomes differentiated into the special interests of natural and physical science and mathematics once the individual has declared himself a premedical student. There are at present no social science requirements for admission to medical school. There are two opposing views of this, expressed by well-intentioned educators, looking for the best balance between depth and breadth in college education. One view holds that breadth is particularly necessary for the would-be doctor and that the humanities and social sciences must receive their full measure of attention along with the biological and physical sciences. Sir Robert Platt has noted "the paradox that medicine has won its place in the university not through its

Knowles, J. H. (ed.): "Medical education and the rationalization of health services." *In* Knowles, J. H. (ed.): Views of Medical Education and Medical Care. Cambridge, Massachusetts, Harvard University Press, 1968.

humanism, but through becoming a science, and the influence of the university has been to put it further from and not nearer the humanities."[8]

The other view holds that the steadily increasing period of medical education must be reduced and that this can be accomplished by more intensive work in the "medical" sciences in college, which therefore will not be repeated in the first year or two of medical school.[4] There is merit here, but the intellectual acceleration and constriction of the student's interests may not be desirable. In this view, the humanities and social sciences become embroidery to the physical and biological sciences and mathematics.

Today, if the undergraduate wishes to leave little to chance on applying for admission to medical school, he must take science courses, not those in the humanities and social sciences. As the Assistant Dean for Admissions of the Faculty of Medicine of the Harvard Medical School stated in answer to the question of how best to gain entry, "the humanist dedicated to working with people but fearing mathematics, who hopes that science will be a minor part of his medical education, stands little chance of being accepted to medical school."[5]

There are two problems here. One is concerned with the too early acquisition of specialism and expertise, the other with the almost universally accepted notion that knowledge of the physical and biological sciences and mathematics (to the inevitable exclusion or competitive downplaying of the humanities and the social sciences) represents the best preparation for medical school and therefore one's life in medicine.

The hazards of specialism have been discussed by Harlow Shapley, himself a noted scientist, in a general criticism of the undergraduate curriculum: "Must we climb steeples? In other words, how far should we permit ourselves to go in specialism. Intellectual isolation may be an attempt to escape responsibility . . . The habit of steeple-climbing has, alas, helped to divert us from our civic duties. The intellectual, in spite of his specialization, should he not be a soldier in the army that makes democracy and Christian ethics work?"[10]

Shapley admits however that some steeple-climbing is necessary for the premedical student "unless the specialized professional training in medicine be prolonged still further toward middle life."

Jacques Barzun is more emphatic about the defects of specialism when, in referring to the "two cultures" dilemma, he speaks of "an endless separatism based on loyalty to the parish pump and linked with the unanimous desire to obliterate the mere observer by denying the validity of his role."[1]

Harold Laski has spoken of the lack of common sense in those who have sacrificed insight to the intensity of their experience. This naturally blends into my second question and that is, granted at least some necessary premedical steeple-climbing in the curriculum, is it necessarily true that the steeple to be climbed is the one built with the materials of physical and biological science? Can the medical intellect function only or best on a foundation of natural science? Certainly it is true for those who plan a career in medical research, but is mathematics necessary to the successful practice of medicine? Can intellectual development suitable for a doctor be developed other than through the study of the physical and biological sciences? Why did Virchow say that medicine is a social science and politics nothing but medicine on a large scale? Why did L. J. Henderson refer to the practice of medicine as "applied sociology"?[7] Could it be that man is, indeed, a social as well as biological animal? Is there *social* as well as biological ease and disease? And can disease in one system give rise to dis-ease in the other? The answers are obvious. The methods and content of scientific thought are vital disciplines for all educated men, but where does that leave the remainder of the liberal and general education? Is there anything in the humanities and social sciences which relates to medicine or more importantly to the well-educated man which we want our doctor to be? Does the following statement by President Pusey of Harvard relate in any way to our physician or say, his collective self, the American Medical Association? "The humanities have a very special place in a university, especially perhaps because of the pleasure they give, but also because of the heightened effects which experience of them can produce in individuals in terms of enlivened imagination, increased responsiveness, broadened interest, clarified purpose and in the end also, quickened ethical sense."[12]

My view is very simple: premedical education should be horizontal without steeples, broad without depth in any of the three areas; for I believe that medicine is a social as well as a physical and biological science, and that it needs the humanities and social sciences and the effects of their study as never before in the history of man. Premedical requirements should include all three areas, and not, as at present, just the physical and biological sciences. Let the differentiation occur in medical school and beyond but *educate* the man in college.

Science pervades all for the first two years in medical school, that is, biological and physical science. The last chance to treat of at least some of the aspects of medicine with the disciplines of the behavioral and social sciences is taken only in several of the present medical schools of this country. Why this exclusion? Not enough time in an already overcrowded curriculum? The "nonscientific" nature of their results? Perhaps it is all these reasons, but just as important has been the complete segregation of schools of public health from the mainstream of medicine. Such schools do utilize the social sciences when considering the subjects of medical administration and the formulation, organization, and implementation of public health programs. Quite clearly, human attitudes, beliefs, and values play a determining role in the utilization of health services by the recipient public as well as in the implementation of programs by the purveying members of the health profession. Sociological research in medical care has given us invaluable information in many spheres. A brief listing of such studies would include the analysis of health wants and needs of communities; the influence of prepaid insurance programs on the utilization of health services; the dynamics of solo versus the group practice

of medicine; role expectations among the various categories of health workers, including doctors, nurses, social workers, dieticians, and medical scientists; the influence of social and economic class on the receipt and utilization of services; the evaluation of types of organizations designed to give comprehensive, continuing medical care in ambulatory clinics; the internal organization of the hospital with its paradoxical arrangements of authority and responsibility; the public's attitude toward the general hospital, the mental institution, the public health unit, and so on; the assessment of medical-care programs for special population groups such as the medically indigent, dependents of military personnel, the chronic and mentally ill; the effect of cultural determinants on the utilization of health services; and the recruitment, development, organization, and retention of health personnel.

Clearly, the results of such studies have tremendous implications for all of us interested in the health of our communities, whether we be the professional purveyors or the nonexpert recipients of medical care. The rational organization, distribution, and utilization of limited and costly health resources is of central importance. The rationalization of the behavior of doctors, nurses, administrators, patients, and so on should facilitate the goal of high quality medical care for all the people.

I am perplexed and fascinated with the problem—or phenomenon—of why such intellectual activity is *not* an integral part of the medical school's program of teaching and research. As I have said elsewhere,[6] the medical school curriculum accelerates the constricting effect of premedical education by its complete emphasis on a foundation of biological science in the first two years of medical school. The opportunity still exists to study medicine from the viewpoint of the social sciences but it is not seized. The history of medicine, its people, its institutions, and its social setting is neglected, as are the political science, the cultural anthropology, and the economics of medicine. The student is relentlessly forced to focus on the individual doctor-patient relation and the science of disease as objects, and his own subjective self-understanding and his understanding of the world around him flags. At the end of four years, he is a highly individualistic person cloaked with the charismatic robes of the profession, trained to take immediate action with the individual patient and to expect immediate rewards, with his knowledge firmly grounded in science. The primary purpose of medical education, that is, to understand disease and to be able to comprehend and manage the problems of sick people from the perspective of biological science, has been fulfilled. But the broader issues of the physician's (as well as the patient's) place and problems in the world at large have been neglected. The world of the health profession and its institutions—the givers and the receivers of care—has been left undescribed and unstudied (and therefore will remain undisturbed by the profession). The social environment surrounding the sick person and its effects on the causation and/or course of disease is virtually unknown.

Why has this happened? Is the launching pad already too overcrowded with the physical and biological sciences to permit room for the social sciences? Is the inherently utilitarian nature of the social sciences incompatible with the truly scientific nature of present-day medical education? Do the social sciences really qualify as science, that is, hard, factual knowledge concerning predictable and reproducible natural phenomena?

Some of the confusion surrounding the social sciences should be dispelled. Popularly when one speaks of the social sciences, several points of view are conjured up in confused minds which hinder rational consideration. These are: (1) the confusion of the social science of medicine with *socialized* medicine and socialism, and the belief that social scientists advocate socialized medicine, particularly true of elements of the medical profession and the American Medical Association; (2) the quaint and misguided belief that knowledge of the medical social science is designed somehow to make the student more "humane," sympathetic, and tactful; (3) the idea that the intellectual development of the medical student would be

subverted and hindered by an overloading of vocational subjects with the misguided feeling that *medical* economics concerns itself mainly with the costs of starting an office practice and the pricing of drugs and is taught so that the student will be able to handle his *own* financial business; (4) the belief that social science (like social work) is concerned only with the impoverished, illiterate, and uneducated, in short, the disadvantaged individual; (5) the peculiar insistence that the same paradigm of evaluation be applied to the social sciences that is used in the biological and physical sciences, and the resulting hesitation of biologists to accept social sciences as "science"[8]; and (6) the confused idea that the study of traditional psychiatry includes the social sciences.

The idea of control and power over human behavior with improvement guaranteed as a result of social science study has been flagged, and I can do no better than to quote from a contemporary critic who notes the changeless hope that individuals can be guided for their own good by science when he says:

The underlying principles have not changed: man's acts in society are natural objects; these objects can be counted or their paths measured; and man's behavior can be improved by discovering its laws. It is this last, philanthropic purpose of behavioral science which marks it off from the pure curiosity-sating of natural science, but which also subjects it to public criticism proportional to public interest . . . "What can we do to make ourselves more practical and useful fellows?"

He then goes on to say:

The much more dangerous superstition abroad today is that if behavioral science did progress our problems could be solved. This plausible proposition is fraught with calamity. Our so-called problems are due in part to the willfulness, stupidity, greed, and fears of men; in part also to the presence in life of real choices and hence of ineducable conflicts! Washington in 1774 was not willful, stupid, greedy, or afraid; he simply preferred independence and was a problem to the British. He did not need to be cured or saved, but satisfied—like his opponents. How could behavioral science have helped—and on which side?"[2]

One should state here that the doctor, like Washington, prefers independence and seems to have become, at least collectively, a problem to the United States government, as he has at times to the governments of Belgium, Italy, Great Britain, and Saskatchewan.

Barzun sounds his final note of judgment with the following blast:

The social sciences today have yet to show one universal or controlling "law," one unit of measurement, one exactly plotted universal variable, or one invariant relation. The ologies in their latest avatar are not so much young as unborn. I am of course speaking of the social sciences as quantitative and predictive disciplines having general truth, not of the local descriptions and statistics found in sociology, economics, anthropology, and psychology, which were well-advanced in these ways as far back as 1890.[3]

Barzun calls the social sciences "not a pseudo-science . . . but an 'after-science.'"

All of these criticisms are important and should be understood by those who hope for the establishment of social science in medical education, if only to meet each criticism and either do away with it or do something about it. The arguments surrounding utility, pragmatism, and improvement in human behavior can be met simply. If the health profession understands as much of its history, economy, political science, social psychology, cultural anthropology, and behavioral psychology as is available, at least part of the behavior of doctors, patients, politicians, and so on can be understood, and rational choices for action or inaction can be taken on the basis of understanding through knowledge. Perhaps short-term, vested interest can be overcome more often by long-range decisions (or ideas, which ultimately are more powerful than vested interests) in the public, or over-all, interest through the moral suasion of knowledge. I must add, however, that I am still unable to answer in every instance Barzun's question of which side is right in the struggle for power. I am convinced that "the local descriptions and statistics found in sociology, economics, anthropology, and psychology" are central to the work of medicine and should be a part of the intellectual development of the doctor. The fact that it is not "science" and will not result necessarily in better behavior

disturbs me not one whit. I do believe that better understanding of this body of knowledge *will* help improve health services. I also believe (to paraphrase Brandeis and Santayana) that one page of history is worth a volume of logic and that he who knows no history is doomed to relive it. I also tend to agree with Keynes, who is quoted by Paul Samuelson in his textbook of economics, that "the ideas of economists and political philosophers, both when they are right and when they are wrong, are more powerful than is commonly understood. Indeed the world is ruled by little else. Practical men, who believe themselves to be quite exempt from any intellectual influences, are usually the slaves of some defunct economist."[10]

Can anyone argue that today the health profession and its various institutions is not being ruled by the ideas of economists and political philosophers? Is it not possible that the medical profession could play a larger, more constructive role in its future if it at least understood the issues and arguments?

Perhaps the crux of the situation is the necessity to bring the medical school and medical education back into the university, where the other university disciplines, and particularly the social sciences, can be used as powerful research tools in medicine and will be available to the intellectual development of the medical student. These needs for the social sciences are not peculiar to medical education. The graduate schools of business, law, education, and theology are also recognizing the need for a more complete approach to their highly specialized and vocational pursuits. They recognize the need for knowledge of human behavior and the social sciences for two reasons: (1) to increase the understanding of one's self and the professional socioeconomic system in which one works; and (2) to understand better the objects of one's professional work, be they patients, clients, employees, or students. More truly university work will further the aims of a true university education, and the social science disciplines can add much to the perspective of the student and to the development of knowledge in specialized areas.

REFERENCES

1. Barzun, J.: Science: The Glorious Entertainment. New York, Harper & Row, 1964, p. 27.
2. Barzun, J.: Science: The Glorious Entertainment. New York, Harper & Row, 1964, p. 186.
3. Barzun, J.: Science: The Glorious Entertainment. New York, Harper & Row, 1964, p. 185.
4. Cope, O., and Zacharias, J.: Medical Education Reconsidered. Philadelphia, J. B. Lippincott Co., 1966.
5. Culver, P. J.: What shall I tell my son or daughter? Harvard Medical Alumni Bulletin *38:*19 (Spring, 1964).
6. Knowles, J. H.: The balanced biology of the teaching hospital. N. Engl. J. Med. *269:*401–406, 450–455 (1963).
7. Henderson, L. J.: Practice of medicine as applied sociology. Trans. Assoc. Am. Physicians *51:* 8 (1936).
8. Merton, R. K.: Sociology of medical education. In Merton, R. K. et al.: The Student-Physician. Cambridge, Mass., Harvard University Press, 1957, pp. 3–79.
9. Platt, R.: Progress report to Thomas Linacre. Reflections on medicine and humanism. Linacre Lecture, 1963. Universities Quarterly *17:*327–340 (1963).
10. Samuelson, P. A.: Economics. 6th Ed. New York, McGraw-Hill Book Co., 1964, p. 12.
11. Shapley, H.: The View from a Distant Star. New York, Basic Books, Inc., 1963, p. 143.
12. The President's Report. Harvard University, 1961–1962. p. 21

2.   Biomedical Education as a System

Roy R. Grinker, Sr.

Currently, there is more than considerable dissatisfaction with our educational system, including its contents, teachers, and methods of teaching. Universities that in the past "taught how to think" have become more technically oriented, turning out products with limited capacities to live, play, love, and work well with hope for the future. Such technological education is time- and culture-bound, changing too fast for the stability necessary for contemplation.

In this essay I shall not consider the substantive content of education, student attitudes, or teacher capabilities. Instead I shall consider how we can teach the theories and methods of thinking that have more relevance to the current development of man.

NEED FOR CHANGE IN MEDICAL EDUCATION

In its long history, including much of the 20th century, medical education has been directed toward training practitioners to diagnose and treat diseases of the body. Students are taught the art of assembling diverse signs and symptoms into meaningful patterns or gestalts, called diseases, for which appropriate statements of course or prognosis can be made, and appropriate treatments prescribed when known. Gradually, interest intensified in causes and prevention determined by the recognition of natural sequences of events. Somewhere along the historical track medicine became recognized as scientific, facilitated in this country by the Flexner report of 1910.

Dependent on the so-called basic sciences of physiology, biochemistry, pathology, microbiology, etc., medicine at first was only an applied science. Yet the direct application of laboratory experimentation to clinical problems could not always be made. Gradually medicine became the empirical research arm of biological theory, receiving and giving to basic research in the natural harmony of theory and empiricism.

Nevertheless, something seems wrong about this simplistic notion and some

Grinker, Roy R., Sr.: Biomedical education as a system. Arch. Gen. Psychiatry *24:*291–7 (April, 1971).

things are missing. The scientific paradigm of holding dependent variables steady during experimentation created narrow foci in isolation from larger systems. Interests became polarized in the more and more "fundamental," reaching down to the physicochemical sciences as significant discoveries were made. Such "reductionism" squeezed the life of the larger biological organisms. If was then easier to become seduced into linear and single causal chains of events and to neglect the effects of early and later experiences on the form and function of the organism.

Since World War II, the pendulum has swung violently in the opposite direction with the development of intense interest in psychological and sociological factors that are capable of effectively altering biological functions either temporarily or permanently, depending on critical periods. This overreactive trend toward "humanism" and "behaviorism" resulted in ideological polarities and either/or antagonisms between reductionistic and humanistic thinking.

This dichotomy is one of the many examples of mankind's longstanding dualistic thinking. As a result contemporary science in general has failed to establish an adequate view of health and illness. As L. L. Whyte[20] states, our aim should be the search for "unity in diversity and for continuity in change" which emphasizes one general form beneath all dualisms. If this be an indictment of biomedical sciences mirrored in medical education—what I mean by "something is wrong"—it is only a special case of a general phenomenon.

The essential reason why a psychiatrist should be considering medical education in general, despite the fact that only lately has his discipline become one of the major departments in medical schools and hospitals, is that as a behavioral scientist he also has some grasp of what is missing. Mind-body relations have concerned philosophers since antiquity. Psychiatrists have translated this into the modern but still ambiguous term, psychosomatic, and have talked endlessly about the total personality or the patient as a person. Yet, we have gained little more knowledge than

the ancient philosophers such as Aristotle had, although we use different words. But psychiatric interest in both mentation and body has stimulated consideration of dualistic and unitary thinking in somewhat greater depth.

The psychiatrist focuses on human behavior in health and illness by observations, descriptions, and test challenges for both actions and verbalizations. He realizes that at a fictitious state of rest or idling he can observe few significant differences among people sick or well. He also realizes that a sophisticated mode of thinking views behaviors as a conglomerate of allocated functions designated and studied by several disciplines. Scientific psychiatrists, as contrasted with therapists, try to put all these together in a meaningful relationship or organization, striving toward establishing a unitary theory.[6]

No one knows how or why our thinking broke up the organism into levels. Paul Weiss states:

That strikes right home to a basic fallacy of our scientific development, namely, we have developed as atomists, which is an historical accident. It goes back to scientific history in antiquity, in the renaissance and after that, and we are still suffering from that history. What we are trying to do now, in the last twenty-five or fifty years, is to atone for our sins and repair the damage we have done by breaking up the universe into units, atoms of various degrees, and dealing with them as if they were really isolatable—as if they could be picked out and dealt with in a vacuum.[6](p114)

Thomas Mann, quoted in Grinker,[5] spoke these thoughts two decades ago in his beautiful prose:

"And yet, this is a time and world where it makes almost no difference what we talk about—we always talk about one and the same thing. Categories crumble, the borderlines between the different spheres of human thought become unessential. Everything is connected with everything else—and, in truth, it has always been so: only, we were not conscious of it. Once, it was possible to distinguish between a "purely esthetic," "purely philosophic," "purely religious" sphere and the sphere of politics, of human society, of national and international community life and to declare that we are interested in the one but not in the other. This is no longer possible. We are interested in the whole, or we are interested in nothing.

Medicine has obviously been most guilty in viewing the organism as composed of levels, parts, and isolated systems by its trend toward ever finer degrees of specialization, neglecting the human person as a total organization. The modern defensive response has blamed our "information explosion" as the primary cause of this atomistic focus. But the trend was obvious long ago, and explosion is not a completely accurate word. We are currently involved with more, but also changing information as past "facts" become untenable and new "facts" are temporarily substituted. Robert M. Hutchins said many years ago that what we need are not more facts, but attempts to find out what they mean. "Less facts and more philosophy." Paul Weiss states: "If we had come down from the universe gradually through the hierarchy of systems to the atoms we would be much better off. Instead, we now have to resynthesize the conceptual bonds between those parts which we have cut in the first place."[18]

I believe, however, that the atomistic approaches had to come first in order to contribute bit by bit to more general theory. The consideration of primary or primitive wholeness of structure-function which matures over time by differentiation, the development of control and regulation among these differentiated parts, the openness of the organism's boundaries, and the maintenance of exchange with its environment were, among many others, the necessary precursors of more general theory. Hopefully the times are ripe for synthesis, especially necessary for changes in our educational system.

DUALISTIC AND UNITARY THINKING IN EDUCATION

Probably the final evolutionary step that culminated in man was the development of language and the capacity for symbolic transformation. Infrahuman creatures were left far behind since they could only utilize signs and simple patterns of vocalization in communications. But symbols create serious difficulties in that they develop lives of their own and transcend their

functions as maps, and they become reified. Likewise combinations of symbols in so called rationalized ways of thinking compel men to follow where this logical process leads—often to personal destruction. Morison[13] quotes Dosteovsky's brilliant sentence demonstrating this: "Man would purposely become a lunatic in order to become devoid of reason and therefore able to insist on himself."

Factual language fragments the world into separate events and things, dissects and disintegrates experiences into categories and tends to become a language of permanence.[20] Over the centuries a few creative men were concerned with the insufficient, in fact deleterious, effect of such static kinds of thinking and attempted to develop a language of process. Heraclitus, Aristotle, Spinoza, and Goethe all understood the need to converge the language of permanence with the language of process, based on a unitary system of thinking. The influence of Descartes, however, whose dualistic system conceived of mind or consciousness without extension, and mathematics or objective science as extension without consciousness, harmonized by God, was too great. The Cartesian system has permeated western thought. Indeed, man seems to have separated himself from nature.

Watts[17] considers that myths developed as attempts at reconciling man and nature. Langer[10] sees various art forms as subserving a similar function—as a substitute for division that conscious thinking finds too difficult. Man has also attempted to develop organizing principles from worship of tradition, formal religions, humanism, technology, marxism, etc. But none has been successful.

There is a similarity, indeed sometimes identity, of thinking by a few philosophers and a handful of naturalists such as Whyte[20] and Coghill.[7,2] Thus, Whyte discusses forms of systems rather than parts, development prior to static permanence, and ultimately one general form of thought. Early wholeness followed by differentiation into parts that seem in conflict are controlled by supraordinate regulation (ego in psychological terms)[12] insuring survival behavior of the whole. Indeed, beyond such biological and psychological controls is a superimposed social system of control which in itself is a process developed and continuous with organic nature. The organism and its environment cannot as in the Cartesian system be separated into subjective purpose and objective material necessity, but each continually adjusts to each other in the process of attaining symmetrical form. Hierarchical structures under control in transaction with the environment (both open systems) are necessary for life, growth, and change.[1]

The search for "unity in diversity and for continuity in change" is reflected in personality with freedom of choice, limited by patterns of behavior to which it has to conform at least partially. This is what Florence Kluckhohn, quoted in Grinker,[6] calls the Being-in-Becoming value system and Charles Morris[14] calls the Buddhist component.

Throughout the world important changes are occurring in our social structures based on a discernable shift from dualistic toward unitary thought, language, and behavior. The outward appearance of this shift takes the form of dissent, protest, violence, and riots.[20] Many explanations have been proposed by psychologists, psychiatrists, social scientists, and even the participants which focus on the content rather than the form or which are based on biased projected conclusions. We hear that the student dissenters are paranoiacs, that American society is sick and naturally violent, or that poverty, poor housing, the war, etc., are the cause(s).

At least in this country two general conditions contribute to the weakening of dualism through vigorous challenge to it in the form of violence. The generality of these conditions is exemplified by those who wish to destroy the "establishment" but cannot offer a constructive suggestion for a new society. They do not realize that a new social system cannot replace an earlier one without systematic preparation. The two general conditions represent the increasing vigor of two components of dualistic thinking. One is the increasing pressure against conformity and rigidly constructed static rules for society. The

second reason is the increasing demands and opportunities for black individuality and black controls over their own community, education, and business, with increasing confidence and affluence. Furthermore, the white lower and middle classes also have more freedom and time to think and to consider values of life, future careers, and the stupidity of our military-industrial controls. In brief, the static dualistic forms involving conflict between excessive demands for social conformity and demands for the right of the individual to do his "thing" have reached the level of explosive change which must be endured optimistically for the sake of a better future.

As a subject, man strives to be free to choose in accordance with his own nature; as an observer he is required to recognize the necessity of nature which includes his society and culture. Those few who feel the former can only be achieved by revolutionary destruction of the latter, the older generation, which recognizes and endorses the necessity for change but is already anxious about the inevitability of its own death, resists. The wiser nonrevolutionary young adults, however, remain affiliated, realizing that although the community, of which they are part, is conservative, persistent, and an organizer of individual life, it is also subject to processes of change albeit slower.

When we turn from the philosophers to the naturalists such as Coghill, especially those of the first part of this century, we learn that by the very nature of their broad general interests in life processes and in the unity of nature, they also attempted to formulate unitary concepts. Among these were Hughlings Jackson[9] whose principles of evolution and dissolution of the central nervous system inspired Freud's ideas of psychological development and regression. Others, later, were Child,[1] Herrick,[8] and Lillie.[11] Later still came Werner[19] in psychology and Weiss,[18] a modern naturalist.

All this may seem far removed from the subject of medical and biological education, but indeed it is not. It is interesting to note that among the student rioters there were few from the medical schools, possibly because they had too much to lose or perhaps because they understood the principle of gradualism. But they have been and are continuing to dissent quietly against the form and content of their curricula. Some wise deans and teachers have experimentally increased the amount of time allotted to elective courses and clinical services. This is not much of a change. For example, one medical school after making the entire four years elective found that the students were still attending the previously required courses. Increasing the amount of elective opportunities changes nothing if the elective exercises contain the same contents and are taught in the same manner.

What is needed is change in our theoretical view of all behaviors, meaning biological, psychological, and social actions. A more general theory of human behavior that would move toward unitary thinking transcends the medical sciences. But pressures are increasing at a time when previous and existing attempts have only contributed to the fragmentation of human thinking. The current student unrest, protests, and riots cannot be understood on the basis of their specific contents or their rationalizations. They are symptoms against which tinkering with curricula only constitute temporary palliative measures. New and more general educational principles are needed.

UNITARY OR SYSTEMS THEORY

We now come to what has been a basic error in medical education, in fact with all thinking described as dualistic. More definitive knowledge about particular organs or systems of functions has increased specialization and isolation of professional groups. Medical education has become additive rather than integrated. A patient becomes a heart, kidney, or lung case and medicine has continued to be disease-oriented. What was, and, for that matter, still is missing constitutes the psychological realism of emotions and thinking, frustration, disappointment, and hopelessness. Recently the psychological and social have been included in the study of living functions. All this has required multidisciplinary

research groups, each component of which focuses on a part of the total. Separate disciplines or departments have at least entered into cooperation. We speak about this broader approach to problems of man in health and illness as biopsychosocial.

This has introduced complexities that have been denied and that have had even their language spurned. This is still the current error in biomedical thinking and education, understandable because an adequate theoretical umbrella has been ignored and obscured by pressing practical considerations, actually to their detriment. Some of us in the 1950's gathered in biyearly conferences to discuss a unified theory of human behavior where we recognized that analogies and homologies were not sufficient. We agreed that an overarching theory of systems was necessary.[6]

We used the term transactional as meaning a reciprocal relationship among all parts of the field and not simply as an interaction which is an effect of one system or focus on another. It is a philosophical or theoretical attitude and yet also a system of analysis. There is not a simple response to a stimulus, but a process occurring in all parts within the whole field. Any transactional study, of course, can be broken down into the interactional if observations are focused on two systems in order to see the isolated effect of one on the other.[3]

Since the early 1920's von Bertalanffy[15,16] has steadily progressed in his theoretical concepts to a unified theory called General Systems. For a long time his writings were unknown except to a handful of philosophers of science. During the war and its following space age, advancements in technology, radar computers, and automation forced both the military and industrial establishments to adopt systems designs. The biochemical fields of molecular biology, ethology, and physiology were the first to approach its use, and psychiatry the first in medicine (essentially because scientific psychiatry is an interdisciplinary field). General medicine has followed very slowly.

Science, like organisms, despite its analytic methods has a tendency toward the integration of its various disciplines into a whole governed by unitary abstract theory and unifying principles, from cell to society, what von Bertalanffy calls isomorphism. The trend of physical nature is toward increase in disorder and randomness while living systems organize, increase order, and maintain a steady state or negative entropy.

Control and regulation in open systems are achieved by means of communication, transmitting information within feedback arrangements but involving many complicated reverberatory cycles rather than simple linear chains. The living organism is not only reactive to its environment, but it also actively searches for changing goals by which it differentiates, grows, learns, and evolves. This proposition contradicts the robot model of man who supposedly searches for needs and relaxation of tension and achieves homeostasis because there is more to life than maintenance and survival. In fact, the human capacity for symbolic representation functions as a powerful force for change apart from biological evolution. New symbols are transmitted to other generations by means of language. Thus, symbols are the genes of culture.[6(p147)]

I have discussed some difficulties inherent in unitary thinking not all of which are personal to the observer or student. The essential problems include our habitual two-dimensional imagery. What is required is a three-dimensional spatial perception plus a recognition of temporal dimensions. Because this is so difficult I shall propose a model for the kind of imagery necessary. This is a transactional model that encompasses process and relationship.

The model would assume the form of a cylinder open at both ends. Height represents levels of complexity. At the bottom extension could occur to the physical world, at the top to the infinite cosmos. The depth of the cylinder represents the dimension of differentiation so that the center is least differentiated and the surface is the point of maximal differentiation equated with growth and decay or at least change in the life cycle.

On the surface of the cylinder would be three columns: (1) The first represents somatic variables such as physiological, biochemical, enzymatic, cardiovascular control, nervous systems, drives, and their regulatory and control systems. (2) The second represents the psychological variables such as memory, perception, cognition, motor behavior, and their controls. (3) The third represents environmental factors that surround the organism, stimulating growth and creating stresses and strains. These three columns also represent the traditional subsystems of the field designated as somatopsychosocial.

The model does not assume causal relationships between and within columns but assumes that a functional relationship does exist among and within the columns in any direction, giving rise to an infinite number of contingent variations depending both on heredity and experience which permit individual and patterned behaviors with specific meanings. At this point, I repeat that behavior is a term not only applicable to total movement but is also descriptive of somatic and psychological behaviors called mentation.

The model permits us to move in two directions: from trait to trait, or across systems, and across time in one system, permitting a longitudinal study of the changing nature of specific functions over time. It must be recognized that the designated systems are concepts whose relationships are descriptive and not explanatory. Subsequent explanations and attribution of cause or purpose in adaptation are permissable teleology based, however, on inferences. These are, then, hypotheses to be tested by means of appropriate designs.

LIFE CYCLE OF HEALTH AND ILLNESS

In its growing superspecialization or compartmentation medicine has early recognized that children were not small adults but have specific problems of their own; hence, they are allocated to a department of pediatrics. Even within this field divisions concerned with neonates, infants, toddlers, etc., are developing. Adolescence has become a demarcated area in medicine and is attracting great attention is psychiatry because of current social conditions. In psychiatry, at least, the young-adult age is beginning to be differentiated from middle-age, and gerontology and geriatrics have already been separated.

In biological research the phrase "critical period" indicates a border or boundary during which a jump-step is made and after which change, growth, etc., are difficult, if not impossible. Learning, socialization, and acculturalization in humans are profoundly altered after critical periods have been reached. Unfortunately, not enough attention has been paid to the significance of phasic divisions in life apart from their assignment to different specialties.

We do not know the boundaries or the timing (critical periods) of each phase and can only characterize them as development, growth, maturity, decline, illness, and death. Except for the last phase the others are reversible in that progression may be interrupted by regression to a previous temporal phase either temporarily or permanently.

The study of each phase requires specific kinds of multidisciplinary teams, not clinical specialties alone. This means the breaking down of departmental lines as early as the first year of medical school when each phase of the life cycle is recognized as having its own structure, function, susceptibilities, coping mechanisms, and predominate types of breakdown.

It is important to understand that movement in the cycle may occur in either direction, temporarily and permanently. This regression is usually partial and rarely complete except prelethally.[4]

I believe that this systematic way of relating medical sciences to the life cycle of health and disease could appropriately contribute to a logical organization of education. It is quite apparent that when we consider the growth and development of the human organism we can observe an increasing individuality and that this, despite stages or hierarchies of order, means that education about man contrasted with lower animals must be modified to include the complexities which accentuate individuality.

Genetics or constitution, heredity, etc., are the givens with which an organism is born, yet the genetic background cannot manifest itself except through transactions with environmental releasing mechanisms. Furthermore, genetic processes are not only apparent to some degree at birth but may influence the entire process of development, including the character and timing of aging and death. Thus, the genetic framework maintains its influence during all of life.

On the other hand, environments consisting of social and cultural processes are limiting factors. These are relatively constant, if one considers the social and cultural "surround" within civilization, as a *general* process, not including the specific ethnic and social groups.[2] The environment as an invarient is, however, slowly changing through social and cultural evolution on the one hand and, recently, rapidly through revolutionary changes on the other. Thus, the student protests in the colleges and the civil rights revolution are being effective in changing the entire sociocultural environment of our civilization.

We begin with the relatively undifferentiated infant who seems to be derived from a particular genetic background and born into a particular civilization. As a relatively undifferentiated organism its genetic differences are only partially revealed by morphological defects. Genetic variations such as potentialities or drive strengths can be surmised by the degree of activity and the complexity of the random motor movements of the infants. Secretory and endocrine differences of genetic origin are frequently only manifested when the organism is challenged later in life.

The second stage is one of considerable differentiation in which the organism has now incorporated within its psychosomatic systems memory traces derived from its experiences in its particular environment. Thus, the mother/child relations, the father/child relations, the child/child relations, the child/school, the child/church, experiences in the family as a unit, and many others serve to differentiate the organism. The resulting variables which are the subsystems of this stage may not all be fully developed but as variables they, in transaction, constitute the homeostatic processes within the systems and are the sources of possible compensations. Thus, if a mother/child relationship is defective, a child/peer relationship may compensate for that later. Differentiation in this stage is based upon learning and I speak here not only of cognitive and emotional learning but also *physical* learning. These may consist of reinforcement of conditioned reflexes, of releasing mechanisms of inate properties, of imitation, and of incorporation of memory images of both psychic and somatic experiences resulting in so-called identifications.

The third phase is the life style of the individual as expressed in adolescence. It includes his somatic behaviors, his personality, and his coping devices which are specific for him and remain relatively constant. One can surmise that new coping devices are rarely learned later in life. As a matter of fact it seems improbable that in the latter two stages there can be much reversibility or change in their components.

The fourth stage is more appropriate to adult life and is characterized by varying degrees of health and varying degrees of proneness to disintegrations or disease. The proneness or susceptibility requires suitable environmental agencies to bring it to an overt state of sickness. Health may persist in a relative sense until an aging process reveals the wearing out of certain tissues or systems (possibly genetically determined) in which case the system moves then to the phases of dying and death.

The fifth phase is the stage of aging with disease or illness characteristic of wearing processes. Disease is an expression of the effect of a particular environmental influence on the organism developed to this stage of life, influenced as it has been by its past experiences and its genetic background. In long-term illness the disease state manifests itself without much shift. The short-term phase may be transient and reversible to the prone condition but then greater degrees of reversibility are rarely possible.

In a later phase the person has assumed a career as a patient, whose only future is in dying, a death which ultimately has an effect on others, producing a mourning process.

One can diagram this series of events in the form of a semicircle in relation to gravity. Thus, the infant struggles against gravity and gradually moves upright into the erect posture of the adult. Slowly as he gets older he moves down again and finally gravity wins out and he is leveled to the ground. Of course, there are shortcuts to these phases of dying and death which can occur in any period of development. The schizophrenic might say that the life cycle is a journey from the womb to the tomb and he chooses not to go through all the viscissitudes of life and makes a direct journey by suicide. If we move from this brief description of phases of development and regression to the many disciplines involved in their study we find that they represent different methods of approach.

Supposing that, for the purpose of sound pedagogy and for a clearer understanding of process, we utilize not individual departments such as anatomy, physiology, biochemistry, or pathology but assign to the task multidisciplinary terms including appropriate clinicians and social scientists. For each phase of the life cycle the composition of these teams would be different. I shall not enumerate the disciplines involved in this study of health and illness within each phase. Neither the exact demarcation of phases (more or less may be included) nor the composition of the multidisciplinary teams need be standardized but can be tailored to the facilities and faculty of each school. But it is necessary that both university faculties of the social sciences and humanities and preclinical faculties of basic scientists become collaborators in education with appropriate clinicians in the medical school.

Presuming that the preceding educational opportunities have been initiated in the university in which the medical school is integrated and completed during the first year or two of the medical school, phases of the life cycle may now be studied from a more practical approach. Then prevention, diagnosis, therapy, and techniques for delivery of services can be learned by exposure to the actual operations of a different set of multidisciplinary teams. At this point many options are open to the student for concentration. More emphasis may be placed on ecology, epidemiology, public health, psychiatry, rehabilitation, etc.

The success of such learning experiences of course involves faculties willing to leave the confines of their departmental or specialty compounds and enter into a viable and effective transactional processes with new sets of colleagues.

The characteristics of this system of analysis indicates that in growth and development the trend is upward from relative undifferentiation to differentiation, toward greater refinement in development of control mechanisms, and toward decline in old age. There are also processes which push the organism back to a more undifferentiated state. This is perhaps more easily understandable when we speak of psychological regression, but it does occur as well in physical regression.

If we could get the student to recognize that there are not dichotomies between genetics and environment and no sharp differentiation between levels of development and no independence of any phases of the life cycle, I think that we will have accomplished what might be called the

philosophy of ontology in relation to scientific disciplines and to the therapeutic aspects of medicine.[5]

I believe this points to a new direction for a curriculum of education which, as can be seen from this outline, is multidisciplinary and not entirely medical. Some of it should be incorporated in the university, some in the premedical years, but much of it, however, is medical; at least it is a continuous process. The real purposes are to give to the student a concept of the totality of the life cycle, the transactional relationship among its parts, the components of the parts, and to avoid reductionism on the one hand and "existentionism" on the other. If we could give this full picture and then fill in the details, not only with contributions from scientific disciplines but also by the specialities of the applied medical sciences, then, even though there are a variety of approaches, and differences of methods, the total picture could give meaning to a concept of all of life, containing so-called healthy and sick components. This is an example of unitary thinking!

REFERENCES

1. Child, C. M.: Patterns and Problems of Development. Chicago, University of Chicago Press. 1941.
2. Coghill, G. E.: Anatomy and the Problem of Behavior. London, Cambridge University Press, 1929.
3. Dewey, J., and Bentley, S. F.: Knowing and the Known. Boston, Beacon Press, Inc., 1949.
4. Grinker, R. R., Sr.: Normality viewed as a system. Arch. Gen. Psychiatry 17:320-324, (1967).
5. Grinker, R. R., Sr.: The sciences of psychiatry: Fields, fences and riders. Am. J. Psychiatry 122:367-376, (1965).
6. Grinker, R. R., Sr. (ed.): Toward Unified Theory of Human Behavior. Ed. 2. New York, Basic Books, Inc., 1967.
7. Herrick, C. J.: George Elliott Coghill, Naturalist and Philosopher. Chicago, University of Chicago Press, 1949.
8. Herrick, C. J.: The Evolution of Human Nature. Austin, University of Texas Press, 1956.
9. Jackson, H.: Neurological Fragments. Oxford, England, Oxford University Press, 1925.

10. Langer, S.: Philosophy in a New Key. New York, Mentor Books, 1948.
11. Lillie, R. S.: General Biology and Philosophy of Organism. Chicago, University of Chicago Press, 1945.
12. Menaker, E., and Menaker, W.: Ego in Evolution. New York, Grove Press, Inc., 1965.
13. Morison, R. S.: Science and social attitudes. Science 165:150-55 (1969).
14. Morris, C.: The Open Shelf. New York, Prentice-Hall, Inc., 1948.
15. von Bertalanffy, L.: General Systems Theory. New York, George Braziller, Inc., 1968.
16. von Bertalanffy, L.: Robots, Men and Minds. New York, George Braziller, Inc., 1967.
17. Watts, A. W.: The Two Hands of God. New York, Collier Books, 1969.
18. Weiss, P.: Experience and experiment in biology. Science 136:468-471 (1962).
19. Werner, H.: Comparative Psychology of Mental Development. New York, International Universities Press, 1957.
20. Whyte, L. L.: The Next Development in Man. New York, Henry Holt Co., 1948.

3. Social Considerations in Medical Education

Points of Convergence between Medicine and Behavioral Science

David Mechanic and Margaret Newton

In recent years there has been growing interest in behavioral science among medical educators. This interest has been encouraged by the acute realization that medical institutions and American society in general are undergoing rapid technological and social change, and that the problems of accommodation between medical and other social insitutions are increasingly difficult. Interest has also been encouraged by the changing structure of disease patterns in American society and the growing relative importance of chronic, psychosomatic, and psycho-social problems. It is now commonplace to reflect on how the changing age-structure, the shorter work-week with increased leisure, increased geographic mobility, urban concentration and the like affect the kinds of problems the physician is called upon to deal with and the services he is expected to render. Associated with these changes are the tremendous changes in medicine itself: changing modes of rendering care, the growth of voluntary health insurance and group practice, increased specialization and the decline of the general practitioner, increased co-operation and coordination between medical institutions and other health professions, and many others.

The purpose of this paper is to discuss some of the points at which consideration of the behavioral sciences may contribute to medicine. Our basic premise is that if behavioral science is to be important in medical education, it must be taught to the prospective physician in a fashion which makes clear how such social considerations make him a better practitioner. Also, before behavioral science can be accepted as an intrinsic aspect of medical education, the relevance of such teaching for medical practice must be demonstrated. With the growth of medical knowledge and increasing specialization, there is deepening concern among medical educators as to how to best apportion the medical curriculum among competing subjects so that the medical student acquires the basic medical sciences and clinical techniques. Thus, in introducing any new area into the medical curriculum, the relevant question is not whether such learning may be valuable, but rather its relative value as compared with competing demands.

Perhaps this is not the time to be skeptical. But skepticism is realistic in that most medical schools view behavioral science and social considerations as relatively unimportant as compared with traditional medical sciences, except perhaps for departments of psychiatry and preventive medicine which themselves are often low in the medical status hierarchy. It should be clear that if behavioral science is to be accepted generally as basic to medicine, pediatrics, and other medical disciplines, demonstration is required that such teaching makes a difference in the kind and quality of physician produced by medical schools.

Mechanic, D., and Newton, M.: Social considerations in medical education: Points of convergence between medicine and behavioral science. J. Chron. Dis. *18:*291–301 (1965).

Thus, it seems important to discuss specifically the points at which convergence between behavioral science and medicine exists, and where behavioral science teaching is particularly likely to make a difference in the quality of medical practice. In this paper we shall draw largely on those areas where collaboration in teaching and research appear most fruitful.

Basic to both medicine and behavioral science is the statistical model as it relates to disease processes, patient selection, and medical decision-making. Probability theory is not only essential in understanding the course of disease, but also it is implicit in every treatment situation. *All medical decisions involve the weighing of probabilities.* Behavioral science enters the picture of disease and its treatment in that social, cultural, and psychological factors affect the probabilities of certain occurrences. Failure, therefore, to utilize such information produces certain biases in the predictions made in treatment situations. The points at which behavioral science can be most useful to the physician, consequently, are those where such considerations help him reduce bias or error in prediction. One of the major contentions of this paper is that if medical decisions are to be fully rational, they must take into consideration not only the salient medical facts but also the manner in which organizational contingencies have molded and, perhaps, even biased these facts. Thus, attention must also be focused on patient selection, the manner of eliciting medical information, and the prevalent medical and value assumptions affecting practice.

PATIENT SELECTION

The physician usually trained in medical schools, university hospitals, and various kinds of general hospitals sees a variety of patients with different diseases who have become patients through a process of selection, dependent not only on the severity of symptoms but also upon various social and cultural influences.[1] He is not usually attuned to the question of what kind of population his patients come from and what factors other than illness brought

them under his scrutiny. White, Williams and Greenberg[2] have estimated, on the basis of various data from the United States and Britain, that of an adult population of 1000 patients, 750 persons are likely to report one or more illnesses per month, 250 are likely to consult a physician, 9 patients are likely to be admitted to a hospital, 5 patients are likely to be referred to another doctor, and 1 patient is likely to find himself at a university medical center. Miller, Court, Walton and Knox[3] in their study of 847 children during their first five years in Newcastle-upon-Tyne, recorded 8467 significant incidents of illness of which 42 per cent were untreated. They report that untreated illness was not insignificant in that it included 1 in 5 attacks of bronchitis and pneumonia during the first year, and 2 of every 3 attacks of vomiting and diarrhea during the five-year period. Mechanic[4] in analyzing data relevant to a college student population, demonstrated that patients in various diagnostic categories constituted persons who were over-represented in respect to particular social variables which susggested biases in how patients with certain diseases became subjects for treatment.

These and various other studies suggest that there are various selective forces which influence how clinical populations arrive from a population at risk. They point very clearly to the importance of considering patterns of *illness behavior* (i.e., the ways in which different symptoms may be variously perceived, evaluated, or acted—or not acted—upon by different kinds of persons) in understanding why some persons suffering from particular diseases come under medical scrutiny while others fail to seek care. Thus, studies of social variables may serve as a focus for understanding patient-selection bias and its implications for medical care and medical investigation. They also serve to initiate discussion of the significance of *presenting symptoms* as an aspect of the treatment process. Relatively unimportant symptoms may be presented to the physician to justify a medical visit, while the major motivation for the visit becomes evident only after careful and skillful questioning.[5]

Statistical analysis of presenting complaints may also be illuminating. Physicians are frequently faced with symptoms which are relatively trivial from a medical standpoint, and which occur with very high prevalence among untreated populations. The fact that the patient presents a relatively simple and common symptom may be one indication of other problems in the patient's life which motivate the medical visit. To the extent that the physician directs himself only to manifest symptoms or views the patient as a hypochondriac, he fails to deal with the larger context of human *dis-ease.*

Patient selection and the catalog of ordinary human complaints that every practising physician hears also have implications for the effectiveness of medical education. As Huntley[6] points out, there may be vast discrepancies between the practice that a typical physician must deal with and the kind of practice for which he is prepared. In short, patient selection has implications for medical care, medical research, and medical education.

ELICITING MEDICAL INFORMATION

One of the most essential aspects of a medical examination is an adequate medical history. Although textbooks on medical diagnosis carefully discuss medical history-taking, they rarely utilize systematic research on interviewer effects and interview bias. Nor is the structure of questions, their order, and reliability discussed in a fashion which makes use of empirical studies of the interview. Cochrane and his associates[7] have demonstrated a considerable range of disagreement among competent physicians in the histories they elicit from patients even in fairly standardized interviews. Cobb and Rosenbaum[8] have shown differences in symptom data elicited by physicians and nonmedical interviewers with regard to joint pain, morning stiffness, and joint swelling. Various investigators studying general practitioners[9,10] have been dismayed at the quality of the examination

and history-taking procedure. All of these investigations suggest the importance of systematic study and teaching in this area.

In recent years interview bias has received considerable attention among survey analysts and other behavioral scientists. It is now widely recognized, for example, that slight wording variations in questions may elicit different response distributions; and at least one model of constructing attitude scales involves asking a similar question with slight variations in order to locate an individual's score on a particular attitude dimension as precisely as possible.[11] A great deal of research has been completed on the interview, the survey, and the questionnaire. Although it is sometimes difficult to generalize to the medical situation, which is unique in a variety of ways, consideration of such research does encourage more systematic work on the medical interview itself,[12] and existing studies can clearly sensitize the student to the various ways in which error may be introduced in the process of eliciting medical information. Hyman,[13] in an excellent introduction and summary of empirical research concerning the interview situation, discusses interviewer effects, respondent reactions, situational determinants of interviewer effect, interviewer effects under normal operating conditions, and the reduction and control of error. His approach is largely an empirical one, and data are presented that clearly show various ways in which bias may be introduced.

Careful attention to the medical interview—in addition to its apparent practicalities—is important also as an approach to the doctor-patient relationship as a social system. In 1935 Henderson[14] made a plea for the consideration of influence processes between doctor and patient, and its importance for medical practice. Various persons involved in research on medical care and medical education have continued to view the doctor-patient relationship as an important focus for analysis and concern. Freidson,[15,16] for example, has discussed the mutual influence of doctor and patient in solo and group practice, and Bloom[6,7] sees this as the focus for the behavioral scientist's major contribution to the medical setting.

How the social system aspects of the doctor-patient relationship can best be communicated to physicians is a matter of strategy. But we would contend that it must be taught within a framework meaningful for the doctor's practice; and careful evaluation of the medical interview is an excellent focus for developing an understanding of the nuances of the doctor-patient relationship. The consideration of the physician's biasing effects in the medical interview involves by necessity a consideration of doctor-patient transactions. The advantage of introducing social system considerations at this juncture is that its importance and practicality are clearly evident.

CONSIDERATION OF ASSUMPTIONS UNDERLYING MEDICAL ERRORS

Some errors are unavoidable; but they often occur because of carelessness, ignorance, and haste. Such errors are usually not difficult to identify by the experienced physician or in a medical auditing procedure. There are, however, a variety of possible errors which may result from the clinician's location in the patient-care system, and various implicit assumptions he holds. This type of error is usually more difficult to isolate and correct.

It has already been suggested that the physician finds his contacts with patients preceded by various selective influences. It is, thus, extremely difficult to generalize from such groups to larger populations at risk. The importance of the fact that different observer perspectives yield different impressions underlies the significance of controlled clinical trials and epidemiological methodology.[19] Even the most carefully controlled doubleblind, clinical trials involve difficult problems of inference and interpretation;[20] failure to view medical practice from a statistical as well as a clinical perspective is likely to give the physician an erroneous conception of the natural course of disease processes.

Another possible source of error may stem from the physician's assumptions of the risks involved in various aspects of

medical decision-making. Scheff[21] nicely illustrates this problem in his discussion of decision rules physicians use in deciding to treat or not to treat a patient. He argues that physicians usually adopt a conservative decision rule. He writes:

Do physicians and the general public consider that rejecting the hypothesis of illness when it is true, or accepting it when it is false, the error that is most important to avoid? It seems fairly clear that the rule in medicine may be stated as: "When in doubt, continue to suspect illness." ... most physicians learn early in their training that it is far more culpable to dismiss a sick patient than to retain a well one. This rule is so pervasive and fundamental that it goes unstated in textbooks on diagnosis.[21]

Scheff goes on to point out that there are various disease entities where the decision rule to continue to search for illness when disease is not apparent may be of greater harm to the patient than the possible risks of failing to provide treatment. Although various aspects of Scheff's viewpoint can be debated, his basic point is clearly important. The excellent physician must learn to weigh carefully the risks of diagnosis and treatment (whatever they may involve) with the anticipated risks of failure to pursue diagnosis and treatment. Such evaluations must involve not only medical considerations (such as the probability that a drug will prove useful as weighted against possible adverse effects) but also social considerations (the positive and unfortunate consequences of treatment for the patient in social, psychological, and economic terms). Of course, this is not an easy thing to do well; and every physician does it to some extent. But often the difference between an excellent and mediocre practitioner is his skill in making such difficult determinations.

A model which urges consideration of the probability of positive and adverse effects of various treatment alternatives and nontreatment is important also in light of the growing emphasis on computer technology and the likely significance of computer systems as future aids in medical diagnosis.[22-25] By sensitizing the prospective physician explicitly to the various components of medical decision-making, not only do we encourage sophistication about such processes, but also he becomes better prepared to understand and accept new technical aids in medical diagnosis and medical care based on similar logic.

CONSIDERATION OF THE CONTEXT OF MEDICAL ERROR AND VARIABILITIES IN PRACTICE

There are a number of studies and discussions concerning medical error,[26-29] and such papers should be valuable in familiarizing medical students with the many contexts in which such errors occur and possible means of avoidng them. Johnson[30] has discussed some of the perceptual factors which may affect observation and the possible role of considerations of observer errors in medical education. Most of the emphasis on medical error, however, concerns the personal, perceptual, and informational aspects of making medical judgments.

In addition to these types of factors, there are various organizational influences that may encourage particular forms of error in the optimal utilization of available medical resources. As Kilpatrick[26] observes, it is perhaps wiser not to think of errors *per se,* but rather of variabilities in medical practice. In this way, discussion is less threatening and physicians are more willing to participate in relevant investigations. The major question to be posed is this: Given various medical, laboratory, and hospital resources, how may they be utilized to produce optimal patient care. Thus, investigations can be posed in terms of how various resources are utilized under different prevailing forms of medical organization. Variabilities in practice, thus, call for careful investigation, evaluation, and discussion in medical education.

Assuming, for example, that the effective transmission of medical innovations is essential in good medical practice, *the social factors that hinder transmission* of information and *adoption* of new techniques can become sources of medical error. Coleman, Menzel and Katz[31-33] have carefully studied the social processes that differentiated physicians in four cities in terms of how quickly they adopted a

relatively important new drug placed on the market. They found considerable variability depending on the physician's exposure to certain information media and his relationships with his colleagues.

To take a somewhat different example, we can utilize some of the data reported by Meyers[34] on the use of antibacterial drugs in cases of simple and complicated inguinal hernia in various hospitals. He comments that:

It is well known that simple or uncomplicated inguinal hernia is one condition which should not be complicated by infection after herniorrhaphy, if the patients are properly selected and prepared for operation and if adequate surgical asepsis is observed during operation. Therefore, there is no need for anti-bacterials to be given routinely for prevention of infection following herniorrhaphy. Consequently, the indiscriminate use of these dangerous drugs is one indication of the quality of care of such patients.[34]

Myers finds a tremendous range of use of antibacterials in herniorrhaphy in data from 24 community hospitals, varying from 9.2 per cent to 100 per cent of all cases. What is particularly interesting is that he finds antibacterials used in 38.2 per cent of all simple cases, but not used if 47.8 per cent of all complicated cases. He further reports that 84 per cent of the patients with simple hernias who received antibacterials received them specifically for prophylactic use; what is particularly surprising is that the percentage receiving antibacterials for prophylactic use in complicated hernia ("in which the possibility of infection is greater") was almost identical. He concludes that inadequate clinical practices exist in the great teaching hospitals as well as the smaller hospitals, and that "regular, valid, and informative evaluations of the quality of care" are required. The factors underlying such variabilities, as described by Myers, appear to be more than personal factors since hospital patterns clearly emerge.

As the studies previously discussed suggest, the conditions of patient care are affected not only by the physician's competence and the quality of his training, but also by the organization of medical care. Although organization is often discussed in terms of moral imperatives, what is really needed is careful consideration of how various means of organizing medical care produce different pressures for physicians and patients. Friedson,[35] for example, in an analysis of the organizational contexts of 'solo' and 'group' practice, has pointed to the different degrees of influence patients and colleagues may have relative to the physician. He argues that physicians in group practice have greater protection against patient demands, and thus it is less difficult to practice good medicine at least in the respect that the physician can do what is medically indicated. However, he notes that the same organizational factors that produce the conditions for high professional quality may produce a certain rigidity in dealing with patient demands which can be disruptive to the doctor-patient relationship.

The financial arrangement for providing medical care also obviously affects decisions. It is well known that rates of hospitalization increase among persons carrying hospital insurance; although under comprehensive health insurance plans like the Health Insurance Plan of New York, rates of hospitalization and surgery appear to be less than among similar populations covered by less comprehensive Blue-Cross and Blue-Shield plans.[36-38] There are also some indications that lower rates of inpatient utilization occur under capitation plans as compared with fee-for-service plans, although at least one study suggests that the form of payment is not an important variable in the populations studied.[39]

In future years there will be increasing information available concerning the consequences of organizing and financing medical and hospital care in various ways. Data concerned with utilization, recommended hospitalization, and surgery are susceptible to varying interpretations. It is difficult, for example, to specify what is an optimal utilization rate for a particular population.[40] Although such uncertainties in interpretation exist, these data can be extremely useful for medical education. Obviously, various interpretations of the same data should be considered as well as the methodological aspects of the study which may be related to the reported

results. But it should also be clear that decisions can be evaluated in terms of the criteria and procedures used by the physician in making his decision. In addition, discussion of such data serves two broad purposes in medical education: it exposes the prospective physician to the organizational contingencies of his decisions; and it stimulates consideration and understanding of the advantages and problems of various organizational schemes for providing medical services and patient care.

What we wish to emphasize is that medical variabilities must be viewed within their largest context. The medical student must be attuned not only to his own mistakes and their possible consequences, but also he should have some understanding of the context of practice as it influences his alternatives and decisions.

THE ROLE OF VALUES IN MEDICINE

Values play an important part in medicine as in any other human endeavor, and it is particularly important that the physician recognize the points at which values influence medical decision-making. Values come into play in medical practice in two ways. Most simply, the physician's values may influence who receives treatments,[41, 42] the extent of treatment, how drugs are prescribed (generic *vs.* brand names), how medical procedures involving moral implications are dealt with (e.g., contraceptives), whether support is given to claims of disability, legal contests, etc.[43] More complex and subtle are those situations where medical decisions that are seemingly objective have moral, psychological, and social consequences for the patient's future. Thus, decisions about hospitalization may be influenced not only by the patient's illness and his finances but also considerations of the physician's convenience, the need for teaching material in some hospitals, etc. Although most physicians realize that delays in treatment and diagnosis or unnecessary periods of hospitalization often may have serious consequences for the patient in terms of his employment, family, or educational situation, one often wonders about how much more could be done to alleviate such consequences.

The typical physician is constantly faced with such dilemmas which involve values. To what extent should he seek to search for a definite diagnosis when the probability of finding a serious disease is low at increasing costs to patients with varying ability to finance such care? How long should a physician make 'heroic' efforts to keep patients with 'hopeless' outcomes alive—at great economic and social cost to others in his family?[44] How should the physical risks of a 'radical' as compared with a more 'conservative' approach to a particular illness be weighted against the social, psychological, and economic costs of these procedures for the patient? How much should the physician tell the patient? These and many other questions of a similar kind are typical for the practising physician.

There are no simple answers to such questions; they remain issues of individual judgment in particular situations. Not only do we know very little about what physicians as a group do in such situations, but also such matters are often outside the limits of polite discussion. Careful consideration of these issues as part of medical education will not provide answers, but it will make students more conscious of what it is they will be doing and the ramifications of the problems they will be faced with. To the extent that such matters become conscious, the physician is more likely to separate such judgments in his own mind from more specific medical judgments and, therefore, is more likely to allow patients to share in such judgments.

SOME FURTHER COMMENTS RELEVANT TO MEDICAL EDUCATION

We have considered five examples of areas where medical and behavioral science can collaborate fruitfully. In conclusion we shall consider some general points relevant to medical practice and medical education.

Patient care (which is usually used to refer to the quality of care rendered to a particular patient) is often viewed independently of medical care (the manner in which patient care is provided to various areas, groups, and persons). It is perhaps meaningful to view the quality of care a particular physician provides a particular patient independent of the larger medical system as a whole. But it should be clear that the organization of medical care in any community influences the kind and quality of services rendered, as well as the distribution of care. In this sense, at least, patient and medical care are inseparable. Thus concern with the quality of care must take into consideration how organizational influences affect it.

By medical organization we mean more than the formal means of rendering care. Medical care also includes the informal relationships among medical practitioners: the manner in which referrals occur, the forms of achieving status among colleagues, and the informal and subtle pressures that influence how a doctor practices.[45,46]

Such organizational problems also play some part in medical education. To what extent should the medical school be concerned with increasing specialization and the decline of the general practitioner?[47] Should the urban concentration of physicians and the failure to practice 'family medicine' be a concern?[48-51] It is perhaps reasonable to assume that the medical school has some role not only in training competent physicians but also in producing the type of physician who is willing to render the kinds of services the population needs and demands. Inaction on the part of the medical school is a form of action in that it has consequences for the manner in which physicians practice. One consequence, for example, of the medical school's orientation to a particular kind of quality care is the stimulation of urban concentration of physicians where medical centers, hospitals, and colleagues are available. It is increasingly difficult for a physician trained in a major medical center to return to a different pattern of medicine; even those medical schools attempting to counteract this trend are having their difficulties.

Medical educators are often amazed and concerned about the considerable deviation from good medical procedures taught by them, among practising physicians.[52] Often they seek to understand how they have 'failed' so badly in developing certain high standards. Practising physicians, in contrast, often feel that the medical school fails to understand them and regards them as second-class citizens. In the opinions of some, it is easy for medical faculty to talk about the complete work-up, the comprehensive history, and family and community considerations since such educators often do not find themselves faced with offices full of demanding patients, harassed mothers demanding house calls, and other pressures of a full-time general practice.

A dialogue of reciprocal indignation serves no useful purpose. There is some merit in the idea that medical schools should concern themselves to a greater extent with problems that the typical physician is likely to face in practice. To teach standards of high quality that are difficult to make operative within the usual practice encourages neither quality care nor good relationships between community physicians and the medical school. There is some merit in medical schools approaching the problem of high quality care with greater recognition and understanding of the pressures faced by the community practitioner.

This realization is becoming more widespread in respect to the context of medical education. There is now greater awareness that students tend to respond to the realities of the demands placed upon them as compared with the values expressed by the faculty.[53,54] If family and community medicine, for example, are to become viable aspects of medical education, it must be more than an expression of concern; it must be a working program in which the faculty are themselves involved. The medical educator who tells his students of the importance of community considerations and then retreats to his laboratory has no reason to expect any great exodus into 'community medicine.' Medical educators must take into consideration that the performance of physicians depends not only on their training but on the organization of medical practice, prestige and competition.

CONCLUSION

Although more good medical care in a technical-scientific sense is available to more people (who are continually increasing their level of utilization) than ever before, many of the economic, social, and organizational aspects of medical practice have become extremely complex. The success of medical practice at the community level is largely dependent on the organization of facilities, the distribution of services, and the effective utilization of practitioners. Moreover, as patients become more able to purchase medical services, and become more impressed with the medical products, they increasingly bring a variety of new complaints which are manifestations of an older population and new patterns of social life.

The physician operates within certain organizational, economic, and social forms. These boundaries of practice present many new opportunities for improved patient care; they also impose limits on what the physician can do. The physician—if he is to be effective—must understand and be able to utilize the advantages that complex medical organization provides and, similarly, he msut be vigilant so that he recognizes and takes into account the forces within social life and medical practice that may interfere with adequate diagnosis and care.

If the physician is to be a fine doctor in the most comprehensive sense, he must be trained to recognize social and psychological influences that affect his patients and influence the care he provides. Medical care—no matter how technically competent—is trivial unless the patient benefits. Thus, the physician's role obligates him to concern himself not only with the proper diagnosis and regimen, but also with the conditions that allow these to be translated into patient improvement.

In this paper we have suggested various examples of how a behavioral science perspective better allows the physician to perform his role. Perhaps one could choose many better examples than those presented here. The most important point, however, should be clear: social and psychological variables affect the probability of medically relevant occurrences, and thus must be taken into account in predicting and controlling such occurrences. Similarly, medical education would be more effective if medical educators took into account not only what is desirable but also

the social and organizational contexts which allow medically desirable practices to be successfully maintained.

In sum, medical educators must go beyond the attempt to teach the medical student lofty values and ideals. They must supplement such teaching by promoting the conditions of practice and patient care that allow lofty values to be implemented in practice.

REFERENCES

1. Mechanic, D.: Concept of illness behavior. J. chron. Dis. *15:*189 (1962).
2. White, K. L., Williams, T. F., and Greenberg, B. G.: The ecology of medical care. New Engl. J. Med. *265:*885, 1961.
3. Miller, F. J., Court, S. D. M., Walton, W. S., and Knox, E. G.: Growing Up in Newcastle upon Tyne. London, Oxford University press, 1960.
4. Mechanic, D.: Illness behavior and medical sampling. New Engl. J. Med. *269:*244 (1963).
5. Balint, M.: The Doctor, His Patient, and the Illness. New York, International Universities Press, 1957.
6. Huntley, R.: Epidemiology of family practice. J. Amer. Med. Ass. *185:*105 (1963)
7. Cochrane, A. L. et al.: Observer errors in taking medical histories. Lancet *1:*1007 (1951).
8. Cobb, S., and Rosenbaum, J.: A comparison of specific symptom data obtained by non-medical interviews and by physicians. J.Chron. Dis. *4:*245 (1956).
9. Peterson, A. L. et al.: Analytical study of North Carolina general practice. J. Med. Educ. *31:*(12), 1–165, Part 2, (1956).
10. Clute, K. F.: The General Practitioner. Study of Medical Education and Practice in Ontario and Nova Scotia. Toronto, University of Toronto Press, 1963.
11. Torgerson, W. S.: Theory and Methods of Scaling. New York, Wiley, 1958.
12. Feldman, J. J.: The household interview survey as a technique for the collection of morbidity data. J. Chron. Dis. *11:*535 (1960).
13. Hyman, H. H.: Interviewing in Social Research. Chicago, University of Chicago Press, 1954.
14. Henderson, L. J.: The patient and physician as a social system, New Engl. J. Med. *212:*819 (1935).
15. Freidson, E.: Client control and medical practice. Amer. J. Sociol. *65:*374 (1960).
16. Freidson, E.: Patients' Views of Medical Practice. New York, Russel Sage Foundation, 1961.
17. Bloom, S.: The role of the sociologist in medical education. J. Med. Educ. *34:*667 (1959).
18. Bloom, S.: The Doctor and His Patient. New York, Russell Sage Foundation, 1963.
19. Witts, L. J. (ed.): Medical Surveys and Clinical Trials. London, Oxford University Press, 1959.
20. Lasagna, L.: The controlled clinical trial: Theory and practice. J. Chron. Dis. *1:*353, 1955.
21. Scheff, T. J.: Decision rules, types of error, and their consequences in medical diagnosis. Behav. Sci. *8:*97, 99 (1963).
22. Lusted, L. B., and Ledley, R. S.: Mathematical models in medical diagnoses. J. Med. Educ. *35:*214 (1960).
23. Lusted, L. B., and Ludley, R. S.: Reasoning foundations of medical diagnosis. Science. *130:*9 (1959).
24. Lusted, L. B., and Ludley, R. S.: Medical diagnosis and modern decision making. Math. Problems Biol. Sci. *14:*117 (1962).
25. Lusted, L. B.: The proper province of automatic data processing in medicine. Ann. Intern. Med. *57:*855 (1962).
26. Kilpatrick, G. S.: Observer error in medicine. J. Med. Educ. *38:*38 (1963).
27. Garland, L. H.: Studies of the accuracy of diagnostic procedures. Amer. J. Roentgenol. *82:*25 (1959).
28. Fletcher, C. M.: The clinical diagnosis of pulmonary emphysema. Proc. Roy. Soc. Med. *45:*577 (1952).
29. Bakwin, H.: Pseudodoxia pediatrica. New Engl. J. Med. *232:*691 (1945).
30. Johnson, M. D.: Observer error: Its bearing on teaching. Lancet *2:*422 (1955).
31. Coleman, J., Menzel, H., and Katz, E.: Social processes in physicians' adoption of a new drug. J. Chron. Dis. *9:*1 (1959).
32. Coleman, J., Katz, E., and Menzel, H.: The diffusion of an innovation among physicians. Sociometry *20:*253 (1957).
33. Menzel, H.: Innovation, integration, and marginality. Amer. Sociol. Rev. *25:*704 (1960).

34. Myers, R. S.: Quality of patient care—Measurable or immeasurable. J. Med. Educ. *36:*776, 778–780 (1961).

35. Freidson, E.: Medical care and the public. Ann. Amer. Acad. Polit. Soc. Sci. *346:*57 (1963).

36. Anderson, O., and Feldman, J.: Family Medical Costs and Voluntary Health Insurance: A Nationwide Survey. New York, McGraw-Hill, 1956.

37. Densen, P. et al.: Prepaid medical care and hospital utilization in a dual choice situation. Amer. J. Publ. Hlth. *50:*1710 (1960).

38. Anderson, O., and Sheatsley, P. B.: Comprehensive Medical Insurance—A Study of Costs, Use, and Attitudes Under Two Plans. New York, Health Information Foundation Res. Ser. No. 9. Health Information Foundation, 1959.

39. Densen, P. et al.: Prepaid medical care and hospital utilization. Hospitals. *36:*62 (1962).

40. Health Information Foundation: Hospital use by diagnosis: A study in contrasts, Progr. Hlth Serv. *10:*1 (1961).

41. Hollingshead, A., and Redlich, F. C.: Social Class and Mental Illness. New York, Wiley, 1958.

42. Myers, J. K., and Schaffer, L.: Social stratification and psychiatric practice. Amer. Sociol. Rev. *19:*307 (1954).

43. Szasz, T. S.: Bootlegging humanistic values through psychiatry. Antioch Rev. *22:*341 (1962).

44. Fletcher, J.: The patient's right to die. Harper's *221:*139 (1960).

45. Hall, O.: The informal organization of the medical profession. Canad. J. Econ. Polit. Sci. *12:*30 (1946).

46. Hall, O.: The stages of a medical career. Amer. J. Sociol. *53:*327 (1948).

47. Bowers, A. D.: General practice—An analysis and some suggestions. New Engl. J. Med. *269:*667 (1963).

48. Silver, G.: The hospital and social medicine. New Engl. J. Med. *269:*504 (1963).

49. Silver, G.: Family practice: Resuscitation or reform. J. Amer. Med. Ass. *185:*188 (1963).

50. Haggerty, R. J.: Etiology of decline in general practice. J. Amer. Med. Ass. *185:*179 (1963).

51. White, R. L.: Family medicine, academic medicine, and the university's responsibility. J. Amer. Med. Ass. *185:*192 (1963).

52. Miller, G. E.: The continuing education of the physician. New Engl. J. Med. *269:*295 (1963).

53. Becker, H. S. et al.: Boys in White: Student Culture in Medical School. Chicago, University of Chicago Press, 1961.

54. Mechanic, D.: Students Under Stress: A Study in the Social Psychology of Adaptation, New York, Free Press of Glencoe, 1962.

II BEHAVIORAL ENVIRONMENT OF THE STUDENT-PHYSICIAN

There is no better way to introduce the role of behavioral factors in medicine than to include a set of papers dealing with student-physicians themselves, their varied origins and backgrounds, the individual differences in personality that typify them, the problems they experience as they progress through their four years, and the impact this first medical environment has upon their values and goals.

Before previewing the articles that comprise this chapter, it may be well to note some parallel changes that have recently taken place among students and society at large. Funkenstein reports that today's medical students differ significantly from their earlier counterparts. Not only are they more competent and aware of social problems by the time they complete their training, but they are more mature in these regards when entering as freshmen. Funkenstein lists several factors to which this greater sophistication can be attributed; most notable among them are the "revolutionary social changes which are sweeping our entire educational system." In another paper, Funkenstein (1971) observed that this evolution in student traits fully reflects the shift in our society's expectations for more equitable medical care. He notes that this transformation in student attitudes has precipitated conflicts within the medical profession, since students are much more in tune with social needs than are their "establishment" mentors. He states:

Changes in students are occurring at the same time that there is a crisis in the delivery of medical care. Both society and the Government are concerned about soaring costs and the failure of the profession to adequately supply medical care to all segments of society. Demands are being made on medical schools and the profession for change. Medical schools are urged to graduate more physicians as well as new types of physicians who will be chiefly interested in giving primary care. The students' demands in general correspond to those of society and the Government; most members of medical faculties and organized medicine are strongly opposed to changing the status quo.

The interaction of the "new" medical students with the medical school at this juncture in time, when there is already so much turmoil over the demands of society and the Government, can only result in many difficulties unless there is understanding by all sides in the controversy. The inadequate funding of medical schools at the very time they are being asked to take on new responsibilities is another major factor fueling the debate over the future of medicine.

Turning to the more specific themes of the three papers comprising this chapter, Thomas G. Webster, a prominent physician and education researcher, provides a thoughtful analysis of the diverse elements that contribute to effective medical training. Beginning with a basic examination of student personality types, he argues against the traditional model of medical education in which all students, despite their wide differences in background and interest, are forced into the same lockstep curriculum. Of particular interest is his account of three basic student types: the *student scientist,* who responds well to, and does well at, the rigorous laboratory courses that comprise the basic science years, but experiences considerable discomfort and uncertainty in clinical work; the *psychologically-minded student,* who frequently pursues a psychiatric career, struggles through, but does reasonably well in the basic sciences, and achieves best among all student types during the clinical years; and the *student practitioner,* who has as his goal the practice of one or another medical specialty, is primarily interested in direct work with patients and has minimal scholarly inclinations. Webster notes a feature in common among all student types. Perhaps as a consequence of the rigorous standards for achieving success in premedical curricula, those that survive exhibit strong compulsive traits and are highly organized in their work habits.

Along with Webster, Howard Becker and Blanche Geer, authors of the second paper and both distinguished medical sociologists, report on the processes by which student-physicians are inculcated into the attitude of "detached concern" that typifies the medical culture. The "cool cynicism" and seeming "loss of humanitarianism" that are increasingly evident as students progress through their four years is seen as a protective maneuver to maintain equanimity; this defensive facade serves to control against emotion-laden and psychologically painful experiences encountered in clinical work, and covers a deeper, but publicly embarrassing display of "naive idealism." Thus, in dealing with the weighty responsibilities and stressful adaptational problems that confront him daily, the fledgling physician acquires a veneer of human and personal indifference.

There are other aspects of the medical school experience which contribute to the loss of idealism, and quite often they have distressing behavioral consequences. Adding to the views of Becker and Geer, Daniel H. Funkenstein, an eminent physician and researcher into medical school life, points out in his informative paper that students express diverse and sound reasons for their frequently felt disillusionment and resentment. Dismayed, as they find the quality of their instruction falling quite short of their expectations, troubled by an atmosphere of intense competition, the scarcity of leisure time, the conflicting demands made of them, and the lack of relevance of much of what they are required to assimilate, students often lose faith in the highly vaunted ideals which they assumed characterized the profession they chose to enter. Given the sizable minority of students who exhibit serious adaptational stress in response to these difficulties, Funkenstein argues that complacency among the medical faculty cannot be tolerated. In the final section of his paper, he outlines a series of recommendations, not only for overcoming the status quo attitudes of faculty, but also for creating a more rewarding learning environment for students during this phase of their medical career.

REFERENCES

Funkenstein, D. H.: Medical students, medical schools, and society during three eras. In Coombs, R. H., and Vincent, C. E. (eds.): Psychosocial Aspects of Medical Training. Springfield, Ill. Charles C Thomas, 1971.

4.   Student Decisions and Self-images in Medical School

Thomas G. Webster

A. THE STUDENT AND MEDICAL SCHOOL SELECT EACH OTHER

Funkenstein[27] reported that some able students abandoned their plans for medical careers and decided not to enter medical school more because of their reluctance to become medical students than because of their lack of admiration for the career of the physician.

Aronson et al.[2] found that students select a medical school on the basis of its repute, its geographic location, and its teaching program. Advice and information from primary sources such as faculty, students, and catalogues of medical schools play a decisive role in the choice. To some degree students select schools near their home because more information is available and they wish to reside in the area.

Earley[18] states that "selection of the school is a complex, prejudiced, grapevine affair . . . Selection of a school near home is not only because of reasons which have to do with wishes of the students per se . . . In schools which are very near home, particularly those schools which are the university parts of a medical school, more students will be selected because more information is available on the student, and the selection committee is both consciously and unconsciously easier in making this selection because of the greater knowledge which is available to it. This plays an ongoing role over the years so that more students apply for that school because more are admitted, and at some point there comes a dynamic stability about the number who are admitted year after year."

According to a study by Aronson et al.,[2] a majority of students from 11 private medical schools were from the same geographic region as the school. In tax-supported medical schools students are even more apt to come from the same geographic area because of lower tuition fees and preference given by the school to students from the same state.

Eleven private medical schools (where location of hometown makes no different in tuition) and percent of entering freshmen from same geographic region, 1961 and 1962:[2]

Mid-Atlantic
  Columbia 67
  Cornell 64
  Rochester 55
Northeast
  Tufts 60
  Chicago, University of 55
  Northwestern 71
  Western Reserve 75
Southeast
  Duke 70
  Tulane 52
Southwest
  Baylor 63
West
  Stanford 67

During the application process, students apply to an average of 4.4 different medical schools.[45] This figure has increased from 3.7 to 4.4 during the last two available years, 1963-64 and 1964-65, after having fluctuated from 3.3 to 3.9 the preceding 10 years. The number of applicants per acceptance rose from 1.77 in 1962-63 to 2.12 in 1964-65. In 1964-65 there were 19,168 applicants of whom 9,043 (47.2 percent) were accepted.

Webster, T. G.: Student decisions and self-images in medical school. In Teaching Psychiatry in Medical School. American Psychiatric Association Publication, 1969.

The trend in mean MCAT scores of accepted applicants is as follows:

	Verbal Ability	Quantitative Ability	General Information	Science
1952–53	522	526	519	525
1961–62	533	538	522	537
1964–65	540	538	561	556

The average number of applicants per position varies from as low as 1.6 (U. of Arkansas) to as high as 10.4 (Albany). Generally the state university schools have the lowest number of applicants per position, which is usually associated with high preference being given to students from the same state.

Premedical academic performance is such a reliable predictor of success in medical school, especially for the first two years when most dropouts occur,[44] that structured tests and measurements take a secondary place. Of structured tests, the MCAT is relied on most heavily and is most available on a nationwide basis. However, interview impressions and personality ratings do have predictive value for the clinical years; information on their usefulness is available from individual schools rather than on a nationwide scale. Scholfield and Merwin[67] at the University of Minnesota reported "Premedical achievement contributes relatively more to prediction for students with questionable personality and interest scores than it does for applicants who are deemed to be favorable in these respects. It is of interest that junior-year (college) grades are more predictable for the questionable applicants than for those with personality and interests judged to be appropriate." What this seems to mean is that for students with questionable traits on the MMPI and Strong Vocational Interest Blank, schools should rely even more heavily on actual college performance, whereas the MCAT is at its best as a predictor for students who rate favorably on the MMPI and SVI.

Garfield and Wolpin[31] at the University of Nebraska reported on medical school dropouts: "Whereas the academic failure group appears to be below average, particularly on the Quantitative and Science Scales (MCAT), the group which drops out for emotional reasons shows no statistically significant inferiority on any of the MCAT Scales."

Because of the rise in medical school dropout rate from a low of seven percent of students admitted in 1950 to an estimated high of around 11 percent of those entering in 1961 the AAMC undertook a nationwide study.[40,44] The dropout rate was slightly higher in tax supported schools than private schools, in the South-Central states, in schools with lower total expenditures, in schools with a lower number of research dollars per faculty member, in schools which accept relatively lower proportion of students from outside the state, for older age students, and for female students. The average of nine percent student dropout rate consisted of five percent for primarily academic reasons and four percent for nonacademic reasons. It was noteworthy that 85 percent of "repeaters," i.e., students who repeated one or more years, ultimately got their M.D. degree. This compares favorably with the 92 percent graduation rate for all entrants.

Of interest to the present paper was the following: Students at low attrition rate schools showed significantly greater aesthetic value scores (Allport-Vernon-Lindsey Study of Values). High aesthetic value scores reflect a tendency to see value in form and harmony, an interest in people as objects of study, and a leaning toward individualism and self-sufficiency. Students at the low-attrition-rate schools also had higher average ratings on the "religious scale." This scale reflects the student's greater interest in continually trying to relate himself to the totality of life about him. The high-attrition-rate schools were producing a significantly larger proportion of students interested in general or straight specialty practice as opposed to careers having affiliation with academic medicine. The low-attrition rate schools "possess environments for learning which intrinsically motivate the student in his academic pursuits;" also their students rated higher on the science achievement variable of the scholastic aptitude test.

Case studies in greater depth were reported for two schools representing low and high dropout rates. The school with a high dropout rate was slightly atypical of such schools by virtue of the school's relatively high budget. There was evidence of poor faculty-student relations in the school with a high dropout rate, e.g., "Pass-or-else." "The student has an ax hanging over his head at all times," and "My first two years reminded me of basic training in the army ... We were belittled and reduced to nothing and then molded into a creature of their liking. There was no room for individualism." By contrast, the school with the low-attrition rate revealed evidence that "A good deal of mutual respect existed between the various departments ... All departments had a detailed knowledge of the student as an individual," and that consideration of the student encountering academic difficulty focused on the question, "How can we best help this individual?" A student from the latter school commented, "In medical school I found: (1) More independent study was required ... in constrast to spoon-feeding in college. (2) A more intellectual atmosphere than I had expected, and (3) An absolutely first-class faculty, class, and administration."

Funkenstein,[28] in an earlier study of school drop-outs, pointed to evidence of "increasing discrepancies between the preparation of students and the demands of medical schools on them;" 10–15 percent of students had psychosocial developmental problems which interfered with academic performance and students were sometimes in a particular medical school that seemed inappropriate for their aims. Other difficulties related to admissions criteria, finances, etc.

Earley[18] comments that, "There are some freshmen who quit because they 'gag' on what's done to them while they are in that year. They are not ignorant nor are they neurotic. They are simply those who emotionally and philosophically find ... the first year somewhat lacking in what they had hoped for." Earley perhaps overstates the case for point of emphasis. Such students are very exceptional, and first year hardships and disillusionment are usually contributing factors rather than primary reasons for major shifts in career decisions at this stage. The great majority of students enter the first year of medical school relatively well prepared to endure that which they cannot enjoy in order to achieve a more distant goal—albeit with their ego functions quite constricted and girded for the task, partly reinforced by their premedical experience. Earley's emphasis is that an able student who is not so prepared, nor so constricted, may choose to shift career plans rather than to endure the disillusionments and unpalatable experiences encountered after entering medical school, particularly if such experiences are extreme.

B. STUDENT CHARACTERISTICS AND TYPES

Kole and Matarazzo[46] reported that when compared with a variety of civil service occupational groups, such as firemen and policemen, medical students as an occupational group are relatively homogenous and in general have interests and attitudes which resemble those of successful practicing physicians. Medical students were found to be "intellectually superior, physically healthy, and emotionally stable," compared to the civil service occupational groups. They also express high motivation for achievement and express "a relative lack of need to depend on others for emotional support." While medical students as a group are characterized by a great deal of homogeneity compared to other occupational groups, individual students do differ considerably from one another. Naturally, there is considerable individual variation in the degrees of ''intellectual superiority, physical health, and emotional stability.''

Funkenstein[28] characterized three types of students on the basis of his studies of two classes of Harvard medical students:

1. *The student scientists:* majored in science and have as their goal teaching and research, demonstrate higher quantitative than verbal aptitudes on the MCAT, have studied much mathematics, have high MCAT science achievement scores, show the vocational interests of natural scientists, and are often not experienced in working with people or in the humanities. They have few difficulties during the first two years; they are apt to be the most content and successful of all three types during the first two

years; they are apt to have more problems than
the other two types during the last two years.
The latter difficulty is related to the greater
degree of uncertainty in clinical work coupled
with the necessity of making decisions on
incomplete evidence, difficulty working with
patients, and difficulties learning psychiatry.

2. *The psychologically-minded students:*
usually majored in the humanities and have as
their goal psychiatry in which they will function
principally as psychotherapists. Their verbal
aptitudes are highest of any group, but their
quantitative aptitudes are apt to be relatively
low. In secondary school they had difficulties
with mathematics and usually took only three
years of mathematics. They have worked with
people and have considerable skill in this area.
Science grades in college are often high but
represent a tremendous amount of work, and the
grades were achieved not because of interest in
the subject but in order to enter medical school.
On Strong Vocational Interest Blank they show
measured interests in the verbal-linguistics group.
Success in the first two years of medical school is
achieved by the great majority, although it is won
with some internal struggle. Their goal is psychiatry, and 50 percent of them made this decision
before entering college. They often have a
problem in learning science, since their goal is not
to use basic medical sciences in their future
careers. This is especially true if they have a
relatively low quantitative aptitude and less
preparation in mathematics.

They do well in the clinical years—often
making higher grades than the other two types of
students. This is related to the combination of
having learned enough science in the first two
years for clinical medicine and their ability to
understand behavior and to work with people.

3. *The student practitioners:* usually majored
in extracurricular activities and have as their goal
the practice of medicine, usually a specialty, in
which they will primarily work with people.
Their quantitative aptitudes are apt not to be as
high as those of the student scientist, and their
verbal aptitudes not as high as the psychologically-minded student. They may or may not have
studied mathematics at a high level, have science
achievement scores lower than the student
scientist, have some knowledge of the humanities, but have few intellectual interests. Strong
Vocational Interest Blanks show measured
interests in the service occupations.

Those student practitioners primarily interested
in people are apt to find the absence of patients
during their freshman and sophomore years a
problem. Their entire expectations of medical
school are different than that of learning basic
sciences. Their image of an M.D. is not met by
the study of science without patients. They will
begin to question their motivation and are apt to
spend so much time on this problem that they
will not do well, especially since their preparation
and basic intellectual interests are not so prominent as those of other students. Most of these
students do well, but some are unable to solve
these problems.

In the clinical years these students have everything in their favor. Having been able to get
through the preclinical years, they have learned
enough science to relate it to patients, and their
ability to relate to people comes to the fore.
Many have some difficulties in learning psychiatry, since they are not very introspective, but
these difficulties are apt to be minimal. Their
grades during these years may relate . . . more to
the quality of their work with patients than to
performance on written examinations.

Funkenstein elaborates very well, utilizing a flow chart, on the differences in these
types of students, their premedical preparation, and how they could be better
prepared for the hurdles of medical school.
He also makes clear how the first two years
of medical school are a narrow gate so far
as pursuing individual differences is concerned. After some wide variations in
major fields of college study (probably
considerably more variable at Harvard than
for many medical schools), they go
through two years where all are in the same
channel regardless of differences in backgrounds and interests, then they emerge
moving toward a differentiation on the
basis of medical specialties compared to
the differences in college majors which
earlier distinguished them. He points out
that each must have balance, possessing
both a high science ability and the ability
to relate to people, or they will flounder
despite very high ability in one of these
dimensions.

Except for the psychologically minded,
Funkenstein does not indicate any relation
between the three types of students and
their choice of specialty. While the distinction of the three types is very valuable, it
still leaves the great majority of medical
students—especially on a nation-wide
basis—in one large category. The "practitioner" group seems to be very similar to
the stereotype of the medical student and
physician in many other studies.

Funkenstein also categorizes types of
emotional problems of medical students on
the basis of severity: (1) Developmental
problems, which students usually handle
without professional help, 85 percent of
students. (2) Developmental problems for
which students frequently benefit from
professional help during medical school, 12
percent. (3) More severe emotional
problems, which may need one or two

years leave of absence in addition to psychiatric help, three percent.

Levitt[49] wrote a brief historical review spanning over 600 years and summarized recent psychiatric studies on the personality of the medical student. In summarizing recent studies he characterized "normal" or "successful" medical students as follows:*

These students are usually obsessive, compulsive, orderly, highly organized, responding primarily to the dictates of their own conscience. Their modes of functioning are rather basic attributes of what are called a "healthy" obsessive compulsive character. That is, productivity, achievement, isolation, denial, and repression serve to protect the student from disturbing intrapsychic and interpersonal conflicts. They tend to strive for mastery, control, and thoroughness along with safety and self-restraint. They put intellectual matters above emotions, security above pleasure, service to others above self-service, exactitude above fantasy. They work harder than most for good grades in subjects they care little about. Faculty members describe the typical medical student as a hard worker, extremely conscientious, a little shy and retiring, who doesn't let go of his feelings, and is somewhat hard to draw out. They have a balance between active and passive characteristics, indicating that there is an ability to shift defenses as the occasion arises. They suppress their aggressive and sexual impulses in the interest of satisfying conscience and need for security. Admission committees tend to select this type either because of a preference for this character or because of a preponderance of these students among the applicants. At any rate it is the self-disciplined and conscientious student who finds the going easier and who seems to adjust better to the stringent demands of the medical curriculum.

Levitt also summarized reports on the incidents of identifiable psychiatric disorders in medical students, different psychiatric studies finding from 18.3 percent to 46 percent of students—and a strong consensus in the range of 20 percent to 30 percent of students—with disorders. A study reported by King indicated that 50 percent of men and 64 percent of women students at the University of Toronto indicated they had worries for which they would like some kind of professional help.

A variety of studies in different medical schools describe from 10 percent to 30 percent of students receiving psychiatric help or counseling some time during their four years in medical school. It is suggested that schools with a low incidence of psychiatric consultation are probably those in which students are neglected. In his own series of 168 medical students seen for psychiatric help over a period of 15 years, Levitt reported the whole spectrum of psychiatric diagnoses from 1.2 percent psychosis to 51.7 percent "anxiety state."

Earley[19,20,21] from his vast experience with and study of medical students has characterized types of students and their types of problems from several different perspectives. Two types are "coarctation" and "hysterical character":

Especially challenging to us is the fact that the principal personality constellation is that of coarctation as described by Rorschach. Often this is a matter of a long-time, life adjustment which is closely related to the obsessive-compulsive, sometimes depressive adjustments. Our interviews and Thematic Apperception Tests support the view that over 25 percent of the students show a major coarctation. The fact that students with coarctation show relative poverty of production, a severe constriction of all emotional modalities in all three of these situations, suggests this adjustment as in some way definitive of a kind of "success" in being a medical student . . . this is in the general sense roughly coincidental with the quality of conformity.

A smaller group of students we not uncommonly find to have essentially 'hysterical' character organization, living principally by repression and frequently doing very well with respect to grades . . . not truly caring for people, but able to manipulate them skillfully . . . and able to live in a stereotyped, conventional manner.

In speaking of manifestations of identity crisis in medical students, Earley[21] describes their need to shift from being premedical biologists and chemists of sorts to mastering different types of intellectual and affective problems as medical students. These special tasks of the medical student, which interweave with this phase of his identity development, include mastering masses of material, devoting large amounts of time simply in classes, the shock of having a generally higher competitive level to meet, learning to deal with death in the form of a cadaver, and developing defenses

---

*Reprinted by permission of The Chicago Medical School Quarterly.

against the powerful imagery of mutilation. These crises, particularly when combined with a lack of firm commitment to medicine as a career, lead to dropouts from every first year medical class, according to Earley.

Earley also describes "some specific parts of the impact of the first year on identity or becoming a doctor":

(1) Students carry into this period a largely unconscious notion of what a physician is, based on variant mixtures of childhood fantasies, childhood models, adolescent ruminations, the demands of their premedical teachers, and that complex determinant the 'grapevine.' The heavy demands of the medical curriculum stir these elements and often call out all the individual's defensive system in energy-consuming activities which hardly necessarily relate to the tasks of learning. (2) A special instance of the identity problem with which all medical educators are familiar is the medical student whose father is a physician. The advantages of this in 'fitting in' are almost inevitably accompanied by other problems ranging from all degrees of true ambivalence and conflict to the more external problem that what physicians do now is quite different from a generation ago . . . Daughters of physicians pose a variation of this problem . . . but, I think I see a smaller percentage of diagnosable affective difficulty in these women than in their male counterparts. (3) The lock-step progress characteristic of many premedical and medical curricula tend to prevent the moratoria of identity choice which is helpful to many at this period of life.

In passing, I have never seen a freshman medical student in whom the career choice determinants were the major defining aspect of his need for affective help, where unconscious difficulties with the imagery of mutilation were not present in notable degree. There are in every class at least one or two of them in whom this conflict area is a major disabling aspect of their difficulties. These students can almost always be helped. After all, medicine has worked out over many centuries ritualistic, administrative, educational aids to deal with this problem which in most instances are effective.

Schlageter and Rosenthal,[66] on the basis of psychiatric interviews and psychological tests on 20 randomly selected Northwestern University freshmen medical students, reported that the "characteristic modes of operation" used by these students included the ego functions of "repression, isolation, productivity, and achievement; they fit the picture of an obsessive-compulsive personality type; and this is a type of organization probably

suited to the task before them at the time of the study." The authors felt that the strong "repression of growth and creativity"—also the relative lack of emotional concern, interest in others, fantasy life, and intellectual curiosity—may be partly an adaptation to the first year of medical school and that the students would show more release and humanitarian impulse in the fourth year. The authors considered this would be consistent with the "cynicism" observations of Becker and Greer.[5] Lief et al.[52] at Tulane University and Waggoner and Ziegler[78] at University of Michigan earlier reported studies in which student traits were quite consistent with those found in Northwestern students and in other studies cited.

Horowitz[37] was able to classify groups of students in his study according to "patterns of response to demands in learning": Students who had a clear purpose when they entered medical school; students without a clear purpose who enjoyed challenges of acquiring knowledge; students who lacked both enthusiasm and purpose but who eventually developed a commitment to patient care, and, a few, not readily classified in the first three categories, who usually had major motivation directed outside the medical school setting.

Coker et al.[13] using sociopsychological tests, classified students on scales of authoritarianism and Machiavellianism. They found that authoritarian students tend to prefer general practice and reject psychiatry and internal medicine, whereas Machiavellian students are more apt to prefer psychiatry.

Liske et al.[53] related students' performance ratings in providing comprehensive patient care to their perception of problems in the doctor-patient relation:

The student or faculty physician who receives lower performance ratings tends to see problems of the doctor-patient relationship in terms of the attributes and limitations of the patient. In the case of the student, he is also likely to have a father who is a professional man, and to view and deal with others impersonally, while expecting recognition and attention for himself.

In contrast, the physician or student who is rated as skillful in providing comprehensive care is one who tends to define problems in the doctor-patient relationship in terms of his own attributes and limitations. In the case of the student, he is also likely to have a non-professional father, and to exhibit humanitarian concern and accept responsibility in his relationship with others.

Ingersoll and Graves,[42] utilizing the California OPI, found the students' ability for "Yea-saying to what the teacher 'thinks' is right or wrong" was the most important factor in predicting success in the traditional first year program, while it was much less important in prediction of success in a modified liberal program. This and other studies, such as[5] and,[44] point out how *the success or failure of students in medical school is to some extent determined by the social climate of the school, especially student-faculty relations.* However, the characteristics of the students make up at least one-half of the issue.

Webster,[80] in a study of student learning processes of Harvard third-year medical students, found "the integration of new professional functions into the student's own evolving identity" to be one of "six major areas of student functioning which were significant to their learning and which distinguished the learning of one student from another." This learning task involves learning by doing and learning while doing; the new identity arouses within the student issues of activity vs. passivity during the learning process and in patient care.

(In the psychiatric clerkship) the students' emerging self-image as a doctor, and conflicts over this, can get involved. It is universal that the students have feelings such as "Do I call myself a medical student or tell the patient I am Doctor – – – ?" These are especially prominent early in the third year, their first year in clinical medicine, and in going to a new hospital setting. Problems are very apt to arise if this is not given attention by the instructor, but with rather minimal prior comment and discussion most students cope with it so that it is not a major obstacle to their learning with the patient. Two types of extremes would be: The student who depreciates and ingratiates himself to the patient, saying in effect, "I'm just a medical student, so I hope you will bear with me." (This student is more apt to be manipulated by the patient or not be sufficiently active in getting the information, making the observations and gaining the objective understanding which he needs as a doctor.) At the other extreme is the student who feels strongly that he should be recognized as the doctor, feels compelled to be of help in some specific way which the patient will recognize as his professional role (e.g., giving medical information

and advice or giving psychiatric interpretations), and is apt to compete with the patient's hospital doctors in looking after the "neglected" patient.

Often the process operates more subtly, and I have observed students with no unusual personal problem in this sphere who can have one stimulated by a specific patient, e.g., the paranoid patient who, aggressively puts the "medical student" on the defensive or the demanding patient who appeals directly for medical attention to his or her symptoms (thus appealing to the student's temptation to use his medical authority and action as a substitute for psychiatric understanding of the patient's underlying problem).

C. STUDENT ENVIRONMENT AND DEVELOPING PHYSICIAN-IMAGE

In order to become a physician the medical student must wrestle with not knowing all the answers as he learns the practical art of doctoring. While fulfilling many "doctor" fantasies he must at the same time partially surrender some of his unrealistic fantasies of "scientific medicine" and parts of his earlier idealized and largely unconscious fantasy of the omniscient and omnipotent healer. His peers know this struggle best and are a major source of support and temporary group identity during this phase of becoming a doctor. The following are examples of many studies which elaborate on this process.

In the already classic study of University of Kansas medical students, "Boys in White," Becker et al.[5] have provided valuable insight into many important aspects of student culture. For example, the investigators describe the great amount of effort which students devote to determining and adapting to the expectations of faculty members. The student culture also places high value on doing and on assuming clinical responsibility.

Interwoven into the school experience of all medical students is training for responsibility, autonomy, "uncertainty," "detached concern," etc., all of which is apart from curriculum content and is more specifically related to medical culture. The study of the learning of professional role and identity then lends itself particularly well to the methods of the sociologist and anthropologist.[26,51]   Tomich,[75] in a structured study of student self-concept, concluded "that the Home-Care Program is an effective technique for generating a professional identity in medical students." Students do not develop a professional identity as physicians until they begin to deal with patients. Ascribed, assigned, and perceived roles are congruent only when the student actually relates to patients.

The development of professional self-image is closely related to assumed roles. As Huntington's[38] report demonstrated, while the percent of students who thought of themselves "primarily as doctors" changed from 31 percent in the first year to 83 percent in the fourth year, this varied with different role relationships. See table below:

Self Images and Attributed Images of
First Year Students in Diverse Role
Relationships

In their dealings with	Percentages who thought of themselves as doctors	Percentages who thought others defined them as doctors
Faculty	2	2
Classmates . . .	3	0
Nurses	12	8
Patients	31	75

Number of students: 162

Valuable information can be gathered by intensive longitudinal studies of individual medical students, such as the study reported by Horowitz.[37] Such studies are especially useful in gaining insight, conceptualizing learning processes, and generating crucial questions for more definitive research. This type of data cannot in itself be readily generalized, but the deeper understanding of individual students helps to put other research results into appropriate perspective. Most of the factors discussed in the present paper are manifest in the students which Horowitz studied. A significant finding in his study of twenty students was that many students regarded personal growth as their main experience in medical school, and "all students identified some aspects of personal growth as among their significant achievements in (Western Reserve) medical school." Several students in the study indicated that illness in a family member

affected the decision to study medicine or the selection of specialty.

The finding of "cynicism" or "loss of humanitarianism" among medical students has been related to several factors, including the predominate attitude of faculty[47] and the stress of medical school.[32] One of the limitations of most sociological and psychological attitude scales is that the merits of statistical significance are gained without knowing just how or at what level an attitude is held. Earley[18] points out that the cynical attitudes of medical students conceal their underlying idealism. Applicants to medical school will often deny their idealism both directly and indirectly. "There is unwillingness in our culture on the part of these men to admit to soft attitudes. The idealism of many of them, however, is quite apparent—one only has to press this with them to find that it is really so." Further, there are sometimes cynical attitudes expressed by faculty, and students are very acute to pick this up and avoid embarrassment. Cynicism also functions as an unconscious defense to ward off the anxiety and discomfort of exposing more sensitive feelings to the stimuli encountered in medical school, let alone as an earlier established character trait.

Wolf[82] believes that the solution to the dilemma of humanizing the scientist practitioner lies in developing a codified set of behavioral patterns for dealing with the patient. Students would then be taught this codified information so that they would gradually develop a repertoire of therapeutic responses appropriate to the patient's needs without having to understand all of the psycho-dynamic reasons in each instance.

Training for what Fox has called "Detached Concern"[51] begins in the anatomy laboratory. Lief and Fox described how second year medical students learned from the prosector instructor to focus on the technical and scientific aspects of the autopsy. "Students are called upon to meet death and to watch the dissection of a human body with the relatively impersonal attitude of scientists. At the same time they are also expected to maintain some degree of sensitivity to the human implications of what they are doing." In the clinical years the students imitate the instructors but by the end of the junior year this role-playing has begun to become internalized as part of the student's own evolving identity as a doctor.

Study of changes in medical student attitudes by Pollack and Michael[59] indicated that students in all classes had much the same type of realistic appreciation of the limitations of medical care and medical science. Students in all classes also held the same measure of respect and esteem for doctors and the same degrees of approval of the policies and practices of the medical profession, so far as the study could determine. Freshmen medical students differed from seniors in only one dimension of doctor image in that freshmen felt that medical costs and doctor fees were less fair to the patient than did seniors. Medical students in all four years were reported to show the same strength of preference for personal and patient oriented medicine—seniors demonstrated no movement toward attitudes of impersonal symptom oriented medical practice, in contrast to a previous study of a group of practicing physicians. Medical students do hold attitudes and opinions which are similar to those which practicing physicians express. According to Scholten et al.,[68] student reactions to Medicare are apparently very similar to those expressed publicly by members of the medical profession.

Another type of study relating to the attitudes as well as the skills of the student is that conducted at the University of Colorado by Hammond & Kerns.[35] The study was designed to measure the effect of a particular curriculum change on the attitude of students. It demonstrated that authoritarian students tended to do less well in the comprehensive medicine clinic. In general, student attitudes toward medicine and the social psychological aspects of medicine changed in the direction for which the comprehensive medicine course was designed.

Some unexpected results have been reported when direct attempts have been made to change attitudes of students toward patients. A course designed to affect directly student attitudes toward patients may have complicating factors which push the attitudes in an opposite direction from that intended, as described by Mendel & Green.[56] Students obviously react to factors other than contentment. The reactions of teachers, patients, and other students all have a lasting effect on the medical student.

Faculty and students may perceive the role of the physician quite differently. Based on a study at University of Texas, Southwestern Medical School, Korman and Stubblefield reported:[47] "The faculty defines acceptability as a medical student in terms flattering to its own model, while the students endow the practicing, patient-oriented physician with many desirable personal and social characteristics."

An interesting finding by Coker et al.[13] based on a sample of 2548 medical students representing 90 percent of the student body of eight medical schools, was that authoritarian students tend to select general practice and Machiavellian students selected psychiatry. The study also showed the value climate of the school is apparently more important in the freshman designated choice of career than among seniors. During the course of medical school individual student considerations often counteract the stereotypes which the student culture carries concerning the desirability of medical fields.

Bruhn and Du Plessis made an interesting study of medical students' wives at University of Oklahoma.[10] The increasing number of wives play an important role in the medical school environment. The study revealed that the images of medical specialties as rated by wives were strongly positive and did not vary significantly between preclinical and clinical wives, whereas clinical medical students were more negative in specialty image scores compared to preclinical students.

McGuire[54] reviewed the literature on psycho-social studies of medical students. He summarized the reasons students choose medicine and pointed out a variety of conscious and unconscious factors which have been described in the present paper. He emphasized what he calls the students' "war with the faculty" as a source of stress and suggests that we need to know how this helps or hinders learning. Attitudes may affect how well the student does in medical school but in general determine quite independently the selection of specialty.

D. SPECIALTY CHOICE

The medical student is faced with a series of decisions about: (1) whether or not to specialize; (2) what type specialty; (3) what internship; and (4) the type of practice. Factors affecting such decisions will be discussed in the remainder of this section. Bruhn and Parsons[9] found that University of Oklahoma medical students tend to idealize the general practitioner as deeply interested in people, patient, friendly, sensitive, and full of energy. Students rated the internist as sensitive and interested in intellectual problems. The psychiatrist was also seen as interested in intellectual problems, but in addition he was seen as an emotionally unstable, confused thinker. Bruhn and Parsons summarized:

Medical students in both pre-clinical and clinical years show considerable agreement in their perceptions of traits salient to the surgeon, internist, psychiatrist, and general practitioner. Clinical students' specialty characterizations differ from the pre-clinical students only in the former group's changes in emphasis of certain traits. One would expect such changes as students have increasingly frequent and closer contact with faculty members in the various specialties and with patients. The implications of our data are that although students entering a particular specialty emphasize the positive traits of their specialty, their stereotype does not differ greatly from the stereotype of students not choosing that specialty. This study further implies that pre-clinical students' characterizations of medical specialties are not based on naive or distorted perceptions, but are in fact very similar to the specialty characterizations of clinical students electing these specialties.

A study was carried out by a nation-wide personal interview survey of 1,086 male medical students conducted in May and early June of 1956 by the National Opinion Research Center.[57] The average medical student appeared exceptionally well content with his choice of profession.

The principal satisfactions students anticipated achieving through their medical careers were related to doctor-patient relationships. To medical students financial returns, economic security, professional prestige, social position, and opportunity to conduct scientific research were secondary, even though expected income was thought to be rather high. Students expressed the usual physicians' complaints that are a "hallmark of the profession" rather than an indication of dissatisfaction with medicine as a career.

In career plans highly traditional preferences were predominant. Eighty-seven percent of medical students preferred non-salaried career and independent practice and individual practice with pooling of certain facilities with other physicians or group-practice in a partnership arrangement. The study showed most medical students to be more privileged in their family's economic and educational background than the population as a whole. Most medical students came from environments where relatively high income and living standards are likely to be taken for granted.

Even during the freshman year most medical students had in mind a specific preference for the type of career offered by a medical specialty. The reason for preferring private practice was based on a desire for independence and a chance of being one's own boss. Fifty-seven percent planned to continue their medical training through residency in some specialty. Those planning a general practice were more concerned about doctor-patient relationship, and specialists were more oriented toward such intellectual aspects of medicine as science, research, and teaching or meeting challenging diagnostic problems.

Based on the same study Kriesberg et al.[48] reported on career specification. The data indicated a decline of students who expected to enter general practice from 30 percent of freshmen to 21 percent of seniors, and an increase in students expecting to take a residency. Forty-six percent of freshmen, 53 percent of sophomores, 63 percent of juniors, and 66 percent of seniors expected to enter residency. There was definite evidence that interest in research declined over the four years; 27 percent of first year students were interested while only 16 percent of fourth year students were interested. It was found that students who had smaller debts, higher self-perceived scholastic standing, and who grew up in larger communities were more likely than other students to expect residency training and prefer to engage in research. It is interesting that while interests in specialty practice and research were closely related, students did not become more likely to wish to engage in research.

Specialization apparently served as a way to limit the fields of practice so that the student could master them better. Concerns about possible inadequacy seemed to be one element that encouraged some students to specialize. Students in the preclinical years who did *not* anticipate inadequacy were somewhat more likely to expect to enter specialty residencies, while in the clinical years the students who *did* anticipate feelings of inadequacy were more likely to expect to specialize. In both groups of students scholastic standing tended to be related to expectations to enter residency. In each category the percentage of students who expected to enter residency was greater in the clinical years than in the preclinical years with the significant exception of those who had debts of $2,000 or more and were in the lower half of their classes.

Similar findings are reported by Schumacher in a review of biographical data[69] on the same group of students. Those entering general practice came from families of lower socio-economic status, were married and had more children than those specializing or entering academic careers.

Factors such as the social climate in which the student expects to practice do have an effect on career choice. Approximately 18 to 25 percent of responding fourth year medical students (from four surveyed schools) stated that their career plans had been changed as a result of Medicare while only about 5 percent of first year students indicated any change. Students predicted that Medicare would

affect the least "three types of medical practice already supported to some degree by governmental funds."[68]

The study by Becker et al.[5] provides an excellent summary of the attitudes of Kansas University medical students toward types of medical practice and the relationship of these attitudes to the student culture.

Choice of type of practice is affected by the nature of the medical school. For example, in Hutchin's study[39] of high and low research emphasis institutions he found that a higher percentage of students from the former chose academic careers while a higher percentage of students from the latter schools chose general practice. For purposes of fostering research and academic careers, Hutchins reported "institutional climate in which original and independent work is highly valued" is more important than required student research. The demonstrable influence of an opportunity to pursue elective programs has been demonstrated in the report on the effect of NIMH student stipends on the selection of psychiatry as a specialty.[72]

The medical school emphasis on research and academic pursuits raises some serious questions despite laudable aims. Most students are in training for practice and will be in practice after completion of their training. Caughey's[12] report on student externships is quite revealing. Medical students have aims of their own, they are not simply "complacent sponges." A study of 3,275 completed questionnaires (representing) 47 percent of the 1961 graduating class of all U.S. medical schools showed that 70 percent were employed during the regular school term and 43 percent of them had clinical externships while enrolled as "full time" students. *Seventy-five percent of respondents would have chosen clinical externship in preference to a research fellowship if both included equal time and remuneration.* As he points out:

There is some reason to believe that the most influential members of the clinical departments of our medical faculties, absorbed in their own areas of professional activity—research, specialized graduate training and short term care of the complex cases referred to the university medical center—have allowed themselves to assume that all their students have abilities, interests and goals similar to those of the full-time faculty. This is clearly ridiculous in terms of the expressed career choices of medical students, the number of positions available for full-time clinical teachers, and the visible and predictable health needs of the community.[12]

REFERENCES

1. Albee, G. W.: Mental Health Manpower Trends, Monograph Series No. 3. Joint Commission on Mental Illness and Health. New York, Basic Books, Inc., 1959.
2. Aronson, J. M., Baumann, R. J., and Aronson, S. S.: Students select a medical school. J. Med. Ed. 40(2):155-60 (1965).
3. Axelrod, S., and Maury, L.: Identification as a mechanism of adaptation. In Wilbur, G., and Muensterberger, W. (eds.): Psychoanalysis and Culture. Section II. New York, International Universities Press, 1951, pp. 168-184.
4. Beardslee, D., and O'Dowd, D.: Students and the occupational world. In Sanford, R. N. (ed.): The American College. New York, Wiley and Sons, 1962.
5. Becker, H. S., Hughes, E. C., Greer, D., and Strauss, A.: Boys in White: Student Culture in Medical School. Chicago, University of Chicago Press, 1961.
6. Bienstock, H.: Some Facts Relating to Manpower Demands and Supply in the Next Decade. U.S. Dept. of Labor, September, 1965.
7. Boverman, H.: Senior student career choices in retrospect. J. Med. Ed. 40(2): 161-165 (1965).
8. Brode, W.: Approaching ceilings in the supply of scientific manpower. Science 143(3604): 313-324 (1964).
9. Bruhn, J. G., and Parsons, O. A.: Medical student attitudes toward four medical specialties. J. Med Ed. 39(1):40-49 (Jan., 1964).
10. Bruhn, J. G., and Du Plessis, A.: Wives of medical students: Their attitudes and adjustment. J. Med. Ed. 41(4):381-385 (April, 1966).
11. Cattell, R. B.: The concept of social stature. J. Social Psychol., 1942. Quoted in: McGuire, F. L.: Psycho-social studies of medical students: A critical review. J. Med. Ed. 41(5): 424-445 (May, 1966).
12. Caughey, J. L., Jr.: Selection of Students for Medical School. Preparatory Commission II, Conference on Psychiatry and Medical Education, 1966. Washington, D.C., American Psychiatric Association.
13. Coker, R. E., Greenberg, B. G., and Kosa, J.: Authoritarianism and machiavelianism among medical students. J. Med. Ed. 40(11):1074-1084 (1965).
14. Cole, C. C.: Encouraging Scientific Talent. College Entrance Examination Board, New York, 1956.
15. Davis, J. A.: Great Aspirations, Vol. I—Career Decisions and Educational Plans During College. Report No. 90, National Opinion Research Center, University of Chicago, March 1963. (NOTE: In 1965 Aldine Publishing Company, Chicago, Illinois, published Vol. I, Report No. 90, and a second volume by J. A. Davis called Undergraduate Career Decisions.)
16. Directory of Approved Internships and Residencies, 1965. Reprinted from the Education Number of the Journal of the American Medical Association, Vol. 194, No. 7, November 15, 1965.
17. Durnall, E. J. and Myer, J. C.: Attitudes of college preparatory seniors in york county, maine, toward medicine as a career choice. J. Maine Med. Assoc., 55:149-151 (Aug. 1964).
18. Earley, L W.: Personal Communication. (Nov., 1966).
19. Earley, L. W.: Selection of medical students. Mimeograph. 1948.
20. Earley, L. W.: Personal Factors in Withdrawal from Medical School. Mimeograph. 1960.
21. Earley, L. W.: The Care of the Emotional Problems of Medical students. Mimeograph. 1965.
22. Erikson, E.: Childhood and Society. New York, W. W. Norton Co., 1951.
23. Fishman, J.: Some social-psychological theory for selecting and guiding college students. In Sanford, R. N. (ed.): The American College, Chapter 19. New York, Wiley & Sons, 1962.
24. Flanagan, J. C. and Cooley, W. W.: Report of the Eleventh Grade—Follow-up Study—Project Talent-Identification and Utilization of Human Talents. Cooperative Research Project, No. 635. University of Pittsburgh (April, 1965).
25. Flanagan, J. C., Daley, Shaycroft, and Orr. Project Talent—Pittsburgh. Review in: Contemporary Psychology 9(8):312-313 (Aug., 1964) (NIMH).
26. Fox, R. C.: Training for uncertainty. In Merton, Reader, and Kendall (eds.): The Student-Physician. Cambridge, Mass., Harvard University Press, 1957.
27. Funkenstein, D. H.: A study of college seniors who abandoned their plans for a medical career. J. Med. Ed. 36(8):924-933 (Aug. 1961).
28. Funkenstein, D. H.: Failure to graduate from medical school. J. Med. Ed. 37(6):588-603 (June, 1962).
29. Funkenstein, D. H.: The Influence of Medical Schools on Their Graduates' Electing Careers in Psychiatry. Preparatory Commission VI, Conference on Graduate Psychiatric Education (background working paper). Mimeographed (October, 1962). Washington, D.C.: American Psychiatric Association.
30. Funkenstein, D. H.: The problem of increasing the number of psychiatrists. Am. J. Psychiatry, 121(9):852-863 (March, 1965).

31. Garfield, S., and Wolpin, M.: MCAT Scores and continuation in medical school. J. Med. Ed. *36*(8):888–891 (Aug., 1961).
32. Gee, H., and Glaser, R. (eds.): The ecology of the medical student. J. Med. Ed. *33*(10): Part 2, p. 253 (Oct., 1958).
33. Gray, R. M., Moody, P. M., and Newman, W. R. E.: An analysis of physicians' attitudes of cynicism and humanitarianism before and after entering medical practice. J. Med. Ed. *40*(8):760–766 (1965).
34. Greenhill, S., and Singh, H.: Comparison of the professional functions of rural and urban general practitioners. J. Med. Ed. *40*(9):855–861, (1965).
35. Hammond, K. R., and Kern, F.: Teaching Comprehensive Medical Care. Cambridge, Massachusetts, Harvard University Press, 1959.
36. Health Information Foundation (University of Chicago): Where Physicians Work. Progress in Health Services, Vol. XIII, No. 3. (Source data from American Medical Association Directory Report Service, Bureau of Census and Public Health Service), (May–June, 1964).
37. Horowitz, M. J.: Educating Tomorrow's Doctors. New York, Appleton-Century-Crofts, 1964.
38. Huntington, M. J.: The development of a professional self image. *In* Merton, Reader, and Kendall (eds.): The Student Physician. Cambridge, Massachusetts, Harvard University Press, 1957, pp. 179–187.
39. Hutchins, E. B.: The student and his environment. J. Med. Ed. *37*(12):67–82 1962.
40. Hutchins, E. B.: The AAMC study of medical student attrition: School characteristics and dropout rate. J. Med. Ed. *40*(10):921–927, (Oct., 1965).
41. Hutchins, E. B., and Gee, H. H.: The study of applicants 1959–60. J. Med. Ed. *36*(4):289–304 (1961).
42. Ingersoll, R. W., and Graves, G. O.: Predictability of success in the first year of medical school. J. Med. Ed. *40*(4):351–363 (1965).
43. Johnson, D. G.: Recruiting for medicine through the explorer movement. J. Med. Ed. *37*(1):50–53 (Jan., 1962).
44. Johnson, D. G.: The AAMC study of medical student attrition: Overview and major findings. J. Med. Ed. *40*(10):913–920 (Oct., 1965).
45. Johnson, D. G.: The study of applicants, 1964–65. J. Med. Ed. *40*(11):1017–1030 (Nov., 1965).
46. Kole, D. M., and Matarazzo, D. M.: Intellectual and personality characteristics of two classes of medical students. J. Med. Ed. *40*(12):1130–1144, Dec., 1965.
47. Korman, M., Stubblefield, R. L., and Martin, I. W.: Faculty and student perceptions of medical roles. J. Med. Ed. *39*(2):197–202, 1964.
48. Kriesberg, Louis, and Beale, Lathrop, V.: Career Specifications Among Medical Students. J. Health and Human Behavior *3*(3):204–212 (1962).
49. Levitt, L. P.: The personality of the medical student. The Chicago Medical School Quarterly *25*(4):201–214 (1966).
50. Lewis, J. C., and Rosenberg, H. H.: Planned Professional Activities of Medical Students. Resources Analysis Memo No. 8, Office of Program Planning, NIH, PHS, Department of Health, Education, and Welfare, July, 1966.
51. Lief, H. I., and Fox, R. C.: Training for Detached Concern in Medical Students. In Lief, Lief and Lief (eds.): The Psychological Basis of Medical Practice. New York, Harper & Row, 1963, pp. 12–35.
52. Lief, H., Young, K., Spruiell, V., Lancaster, R., and Lief, V.: A psychodynamic study of medical students and their adaptational problems. J. Med. Ed. *35:*696–704 (1960). Cited in Schlageter and Rosenthal: J. Med. Ed. *37*(1) (Jan., 1962).
53. Liske, R. E., Ort, R. S., and Ford, A. B.: Clinical performance and related traits of medical students and faculty physicians. J. Med. Ed. *39*(1):69–80 (1964).
54. McGuire, F. L.: Psycho-social studies of medical students: A critical review. J. Med. Ed. *41*(5):424–445 (1965).
55. Mawardi, B. H.: A career study of physicians. J. Med. Ed. *40*(7):658–666 (1965).
56. Mendel, W., and Green, G. A.: On becoming a physician. J. Med. Ed. *40*(4):266–272 (1965).
57. National Opinion Research Center (Chicago): Career Preferences of Medical Students in the United States. Study in conjunction with Office of the Surgeon General, Dept. of the Army, Publication No. DA49007MD719 (mimeographed), 1956.
58. Pennell, M. Y.: Career Patterns in Medicine. Public Health Report *80*(2):155–162, Feb., 1965. Department of Health, Education, and Welfare.
59. Pollack, S., and Michael, W. B.: Changes in attitudes of medical students toward psychological aspects of the doctor-image and the doctor-patient relationship. J. Med. Ed. *40*(12):1162–1165 (1965).
60. Powers, L., Whiting, J. F., and Oppermann, K. C.: Trends in medical school faculties. J. Med. Ed. *37*(10):1065–1091 (1962).
61. Public Health Service. Basic Reference Tables on Graduate Enrollment and Ph.D. Output in Selected Science Fields at 100 Leading Institutions, 1959–60 to 1963–64. Office of Program Planning, NIH, PHS, Department of Health, Education, and Welfare, April, 1965.
62. Public Health Service. Resources for Medical Research Report No. 9, Trends in Graduate Enrollment and Ph.D. Output in Scientific Fields at 100 Leading Institutions. 1963–64 to 1964–65. PHS Publication No. 1476, NIH, PHS, Department of Health, Education, and Welfare, May, 1966.
63. Rogoff, N.: The decision to study medicine. In Merton, R., Reader, G., and Kendall, P. (eds.): The Student Physician. Part II. Cambridge, Massachusetts, Harvard University Press, 1957, p. 115.

64. Sanford, R. N. (ed.): The American College, A Psychological and Social Interpretation of the Higher Learning. New York, Wiley, 1962.

65. Scantlebury, R. E.: Factors which influence youth to study medicine. J. Ed. Res. *42*(3):171–181 (Nov., 1948).

66. Schlageter, C., and Rosenthal, V.: What are "normal" medical students like? J. Med. Ed. *37*(1):19–27 (Jan., 1962).

67. Schofield, W., and Merwin, G.: The use of scholastic aptitude, personality and interest test data in the selection of medical students. J. Med. Ed. *41*(6):502–509 (June, 1966).

68. Scholten, J. R., Rubin, R., and Lewis, C. E.: Medicare and medical students. JAMA. *197*(5):333–338.

69. Schumacher, C. F.: The 1960 medical school graduate: His biographical history. J. Med. Ed. *36*(5):398–406 (1961).

70. Schumacher, C. F.: Interest and personality factors as related to choice of medical career. J. Med. Ed. *38*(11):932–942 (1963).

71. Severinghaus, A. E.: Distribution of graduates of medical schools in the United States and Canada according to specialties 1960 to 1964. J. Med. Ed. *40*(8):721–736 (1965).

72. Simon, R., and Shriver, B.: Impact of NIMH stipends on choice of specialty. J. Med. Ed. *39*(12) (Dec., 1964).

73. Stalnaker, J. M.: Attitudes of high school students toward higher education. J. Med. Ed. *38*(9):730–736 (Sept., 1963).

74. Stewart, W. H., and Pennell, M. Y.: U.S. medical school alumni. J. Med. Ed. *36*(11):1612–1616 (1961).

75. Tomich, J.: Home care: A technique for generating professional identity. J. Med. Ed. *41*(3):202–208 (1966).

76. Tucker, A. D., and Strong, E. K.: Ten year follow-up of vocational interest scores of 1950 medical college seniors. J. Applied Psych. *46*(2):81–86 (1962).

77. Umbarger, C., Dalsimer, J., Morrison, A., and Breggin, P.: College students in a mental hospital. New York, Grune and Stratton, 1963.

78. Waggoner, R., and Ziegler, T.: Psychiatric factors in medical students who fail. Am. J. Psychiatry *103*:369–76 (1946). Cited in Schlageter and Rosenthal: J. Med. Ed. *37*(1) (Jan., 1962).

79. Wartman, W. B.: Medical Teaching in Western Civilization. Chicago, Ill. Year Book Medical Publishers, Inc., 1961.

80. Webster, T. G.: Student Learning Processes. Part VI, Integration of new professional functions into the student's own evolving identity. Unpublished. 1962.

81. Weiskotten, H. G., Wiggins, W. S., Altenderfer, M. E., Gooch, M., and Tipner, A.: Changes in professional careers on physicians. An analysis of a resurvey of physicians who were graduated from medical college in 1935, 1940, and 1945. J. Med. Ed. *36*(11):1565–1586 (1961).

82. Wolf, G. A.: The Organization of medical practice in the United States: The specialist and the general practitioner. J. Med. Ed. *40*(8):737–741 (1965).

83. Wolfle, D.: Medicine's share in America's student resources. In Gee, H. H., and Cowles, J. T. (eds.): The Appraisal of Applicants to Medical Schools. Evanston, Ill. Association of American Medical Colleges, 1957.

84. Zabarenko, L.: Working Bibliography on Research in General Practice. Mimeograph. 1966.

5.   The Fate of Idealism in Medical School

Howard S. Becker and Blanche Geer

It makes some difference in a man's performance of his work whether he believes wholehartedly in what he is doing or feels that in important respects it is a fraud, whether he feels convinced that it is a good thing or believes that it is not really of much use after all. The distinction we are making is the one people have in mind when they refer, for example, to their calling as a "noble profession" on the one hand or a "racket" on the other. In the one case they idealistically proclaim that their work is all that it claims on the surface to be; in the other they cynically concede that it is first and foremost a way of making a living and that its surface pretensions are just that and nothing more. Presumably, different modes of behavior are associated with these perspectives when wholehartedly embraced. The cynic cuts

Becker, H., and Geer, B.: The fate of idealism in medical school. Am. Sociol. Rev. *23*:50–56 (1958).

corners with a feeling of inevitability while the idealist goes down fighting. *The Blackboard Jungle* and *Not as a Stranger* are only the most recent in a long tradition of fictional portrayals of the importance of this aspect of a man's adjustment to his work.

Professional schools often receive a major share of the blame for producing this kind of cynicism—and none more than the medical school. The idealistic young freshman changes into a tough, hardened, unfeeling doctor; or so the popular view has it. Teachers of medicine sometimes rephrase the distinction between the clinical and pre-clinical years into one between the "cynical" and "pre-cynical" years. Psychological research supports this view, presenting attitude surveys which show medical students year by year scoring lower on "idealism" and higher on "cynicism."[1] Typically, this cynicism is seen as developing in response to the shattering of ideals consequent on coming face-to-face with the realities of professional practice.

In this paper, we attempt to describe the kind of idealism that characterizes the medical freshmen and to trace both the development of cynicism and the vicissitudes of that idealism in the course of the four years of medical training. Our main themes are that though they develop cynical feelings in specific situations directly associated with their medical school experience, the medical students never lose their original idealism about the practice of medicine; that the growth of both cynicism and idealism are not simple developments, but are instead complex transformations; and that the very notions "idealism" and "cynicism" need further analysis, and must be seen as situational in their expressions rather than as stable traits possessed by individuals in greater or lesser degree. Finally, we see the greater portion of these feelings as being collective rather than individual phenomena.

Our discussion is based on a study conducted at a state medical school,[2] in which we carried on participant observation with students of all four years in all of the courses and clinical work to which they are exposed. We joined the students in their activities in school and after school and watched them at work in labs, on the hospital wards, and in the clinic. Often spending as much as a month with a small group of from five to fifteen students assigned to a particular activity, we came to know them well and were able to gather information in informal interviews and by overhearing the ordinary daily conversation of the group.[3] In the course of our observation and interviewing we have gathered much information on the subject of idealism. Of necessity, we shall have to present the very briefest statement of our

[2] This study was sponsored by Community Studies, Inc., of Kansas City, Missouri, and was carried on at the University of Kansas Medical School, to whose dean, staff, and students we are indebted for their wholehearted cooperation. Professor Everett C. Hughes of the University of Chicago was director of the project.

[3] The technique of participant observation has not been fully systematized, but some approaches to this have been made. See, for example, Florence R. Kluckhohn, "The Participant Observer Technique in Small Communities," *American Journal of Sociology,* 45 (November, 1940), pp. 331–343; Arthur Vidich, "Participant Observation and the Collection and Interpretation of Data," *ibid.,* 60 (January, 1955), pp. 354–360; William Foote Whyte, "Observational Field-Work Methods," in Maria Jahoda, Morton Deutsch, and Stuart W. Cook (editors), *Research Methods in the Social Sciences,* New York: Dryden Press, 1951, II, pp. 393–514; and *Street Corner Society* (Enlarged Edition), Chicago: University of Chicago Press, 1955, pp. 279–358; Rosalie Hankey Wax, "Twelve Years Later: An Analysis of Field Experience," *American Journal of Sociology,* 63 (September, 1957), pp. 133–142; Morris S. Schwartz and Charlotte Green Schwartz, "Problems in Participant Observation," *ibid.,* 60 (January, 1955), pp. 343–353; and Howard S. Becker and Blanche Geer, "Participant Observation and Interviewing: A Comparison," *Human Organization* (forthcoming). The last item represents the first of a projected series of papers attempting to make explicit the operations involved in this method. For a short description of some techniques used in this study, see Howard S. Becker, "Interviewing Medical Students," *American Journal of Sociology,* 62 (September, 1956), pp. 199–201.

[1] Leonard D. Eron, "Effect of Medical Education on Medical Students," *Journal of Medical Education,* 10 (October, 1955), pp. 559–566.

findings with little or no supporting evidence.[4] The problem of idealism is, of course, many-faceted and complex and we have dealt with it in a simplified way, describing only some of its grosser features.[5]

THE FRESHMEN

The medical students enter school with what we may think of as the idealistic notion, implicit in lay culture, that the practice of medicine is a wonderful thing and that they are going to devote their lives to service to mankind. They believe that medicine is made up of a great body of well-established facts that they will be taught from the first day on and that these facts will be of immediate practical use to them as physicians. They enter school expecting to work industriously and expecting that if they work hard enough they will be able to master this body of fact and thus become good doctors.

In several ways the first year of medical school does not live up to their expectations. They are disillusioned when they find they will not be near patients at all, that the first year will be just like another year of college. In fact, some feel that it is not even as good as college because their work in certain areas is not as thorough as courses in the same fields in undergraduate school. They come to think that their courses (with the exception of anatomy) are not worth much because, in the first place, the faculty (being Ph.D.'s) know nothing about the practice of medicine, and, in the second place, the subject matter

[4] A fuller analysis and presentation of evidence will be contained in a volume on this study now being prepared by the authors in collaboration with Everett C. Hughes and Anselm L. Strauss.

[5] Renee Fox has shown how complex one aspect of this whole subject is in her analysis of the way medical students at Cornell become aware of and adjust to both their own failure to master all available knowledge and the gaps in current knowledge in many fields. See her "Training for Uncertainty," in Robert K. Merton, George G. Reader, and Patricia L. Kendall, *The Student Physician: Introductory Studies in the Sociology of Medical Education*, Cambridge: Harvard University Press, 1957, pp. 207–241.

itself is irrelevant, or as the students say, "ancient history."

The freshmen are further disillusioned when the faculty tells them in a variety of ways that there is more to medicine than they can possibly learn. They realize it may be impossible for them to learn all they need to know in order to practice medicine properly. Their disillusionment becomes more profound when they discover that this statement of the faculty is literally true.[6] Experience in trying to master the details of the anatomy of the extremities convinces them that they cannot do so in the time they have. Their expectation of hard work is not disappointed; they put in an eight-hour day of classes and laboratories, and study four or five hours a night and most of the weekend as well.

Some of the students, the brightest, continue to attempt to learn it all, but succeed only in getting more and more worried about their work. The majority decide that, since they can't learn it all, they must select from among all the facts presented to them those they will attempt to learn. There are two ways of making this selection. On the one hand, the student may decide on the basis of his own uninformed notions about the nature of medical practice that many facts are not important, since they relate to things which seldom come up in the actual practice of medicine; therefore, he reasons, it is useless to learn them. On the other hand, the student can decide that the important thing is to pass his examinations and, therefore, that the important facts are those which are likely to be asked on an examination; he uses this as a basis for selecting both facts to memorize and courses for intensive study. For example, the work in physiology is dismissed on both of these grounds, being considered neither relevant to the facts of medical life nor important in terms of the amount of time the faculty devotes to it and the number of examinations in the subject.

A student may use either or both of these bases of selection at the beginning of

[6] Compare Fox' description of student reaction to this problem at Cornell (*op. cit.*, pp. 209–221).

the year, before many tests have been given. But after a few tests have been taken, the student makes "what the faculty wants" the chief basis of his selection of what to learn, for he now has a better idea of what this is and also has become aware that it is possible to fail examinations and that he therefore must learn the expectations of the faculty if he wishes to stay in school. The fact that one group of students, that with the highest prestige in the class, took this view early and did well on examinations was decisive in swinging the whole class around to this position. The students were equally influenced to become "test-wise" by the fact that, although they had all been in the upper range in their colleges, the class average on the first examination was frighteningly low.

In becoming test-wise, the students begin to develop systems for discovering the faculty wishes and learning them. These systems are both methods for studying their texts and short-cuts that can be taken in laboratory work. For instance, they begin to select facts for memorization by looking over the files of old examinations maintained in each of the medical fraternity houses. They share tip-offs from the lectures and offhand remarks of the faculty as to what will be on the examinations. In anatomy, they agree not to bother to dissect out subcutaneous nerves, reasoning that it is both difficult and time-consuming and the information can be secured from books with less effort. The interaction involved in the development of such systems and short-cuts helps to create a social group of a class which had previously been only an aggregation of smaller and less organized groups.

In this medical school, the students learn in this way to distinguish between the activities of the first year and their original view that everything that happens to them in medical school will be important. Thus they become cynical about the value of their activities in the first year. They feel that the real thing—learning which will help them to help mankind—has been postponed, perhaps until the second year, or perhaps even farther, at which time they will be able again to act on idealistic premises. They believe that what they do in their later years in school under supervision will be about the same thing they will do, as physicians, on their own; the first year had disappointed this expectation.

There is one matter, however, about which the students are not disappointed during the first year: the so-called trauma of dealing with the cadaver. But this experience, rather than producing cynicism, reinforces the student's attachment to his idealistic view of medicine by making him feel that he is experiencing at least some of the necessary unpleasantness of the doctor's. Such difficulties, however, do not loom as large for the student as those of solving the problem of just what the faculty wants.

On this and other points, a working consensus develops in the new consolidated group about the interpretation of their experience in medical school and its norms of conduct. This consensus, which we call *student culture,*[7] focuses their attention almost completely on their day-to-day activities in school and obscures or sidetracks their earlier idealistic preoccupations. Cynicism, griping, and minor cheating become endemic, but the cynicism is specific to the educational situation, to the first year, and to only parts of it. Thus the students keep their cynicism separate from their idealistic feelings and by postponement protect their belief that medicine is a wonderful thing, that their school is a fine one, and that they will become good doctors.

LATER YEARS

The sophomore year does not differ greatly from the freshman year. Both the work load and anxiety over examinations probably increase. Though they begin some medical activities, as in their attendance at autopsies and particularly in their introductory course in physical diagnosis, most

---

[7]The concept of student culture is analyzed in some detail in Howard S. Becker and Blanche Geer, "Student Culture in Medical School," *Harvard Educational Review, 28,* 70–80, 1958.

of what they do continues to repeat the pattern of the college science curriculum. Their attention still centers on the problem of getting through school by doing well in examinations.

During the third and fourth, or clinical years, teaching takes a new form. In place of lectures and laboratories, the students' work now consists of the study of actual patients admitted to the hospital or seen in the clinic. Each patient who enters the hospital is assigned to a student who interviews him about his illnesses, past and present, and performs a physical examination. He writes this up for the patient's chart, and appends the diagnosis and the treatment that he would use were he allowed actually to treat the patient. During conferences with faculty physicians, often held at the patient's bedside, the student is quizzed about items of his report and called upon to defend them or to explain their significance. Most of the teaching in the clinical years is of this order.

Contact with patients brings a new set of circumstances with which the student must deal. He no longer feels the great pressure created by tests, for he is told by the faculty, and this is confirmed by his daily experience, that examinations are now less important. His problems now become those of coping with a steady stream of patients in a way that will please the staff man under whom he is working, and of handling what is sometimes a tremendous load of clinical work so as to allow himself time for studying diseases and treatments that interest him and for play and family life.

The students earlier have expected that once they reach the clinical years they will be able to realize their idealistic ambitions to help people and to learn those things immediately useful in aiding people who are ill. But they find themselves working to understand cases as medical problems rather than working to help the sick and memorizing the relevant available facts so that these can be produced immediately for a questioning staff man. When they make ward rounds with a faculty member they are likely to be quizzed about any of the seemingly countless facts possibly

related to the condition of the patient for whom they are "caring."

Observers speak of the cynicism that overtakes the student and the lack of concern for his patients as human beings. This change does take place, but it is not produced solely by "the anxiety brought about by the presence of death and suffering."[8] The student becomes preoccupied with the technical aspects of the cases with which he deals because the faculty requires him to do so. He is questioned about so many technical details that he must spend most of his time learning them.

The frustrations created by his position in the teaching hospital further divert the student from idealistic concerns. He finds himself low man in a hierarchy based on clinical experience, so that he is allowed very little of the medical responsibility he would like to assume. Because of his lack of experience, he cannot write orders, and he receives permission to perform medical and surgical procedures (if at all) at a rate he considers far too slow. He usually must content himself with "mere" vicarious participation in the drama of danger, life, and death that he sees as the core of medical practice. The student culture accents these difficulties so that events (and especially those involving patients) are interpreted and reacted to as they push him toward or hold him back from further participation in this drama. He does not think in terms the layman might use.

As a result of the increasingly technical emphasis of his thinking the student appears cynical to the non-medical outsider, though from his own point of view he is simply seeing what is "really important." Instead of reacting with the layman's horror and sympathy for the patient to the sight of a cancerous organ that has been surgically removed, the student is more likely to regret that he was not allowed to

---

[8]Dana L. Farnsworth, "Some Observations on The Attitudes and Motivations of the Harvard Medical Student," *Harvard Medical Alumni Bulletin,* January, 1956, p. 34.

close the incision at the completion of the operation, and to rue the hours that he must spend searching in the fatty flesh for the lymph nodes that will reveal how far the disease has spread. As in other lines of work, he drops lay attitudes for those more relevant to the way the event affects someone in his position.

This is not to say that the students lose their original idealism. When issues of idealism are openly raised in a situation they define as appropriate, they respond as they might have when they were freshmen. But the influence of the student culture is such that questions which might bring forth this idealism are not brought up. Students are often assigned patients for examination and follow-up whose conditions might be expected to provoke idealistic crises. Students discuss such patients, however, with reference to the problems they create for the *student.* Patients with terminal diseases who are a long time dying, and patients with chronic diseases who show little change from week to week, are more likely to be viewed as creating extra work without extra compensation in knowledge or the opportunity to practice new skills than as examples of illness which raise questions about euthanasia. Such cases require the student to spend time every day checking on progress which he feels will probably not take place and to write long "progress" notes in the patient's chart although little progress has occurred.

This apparent cynicism is a collective matter. Group activities are built around this kind of workaday perspective, constraining the students in two ways. First, they do not openly express the lay idealistic notions they may hold, for their culture does not sanction such expression; second, they are less likely to have thoughts of this deviant kind when they are engaged in group activity. The collective nature of this "cynicism" is indicated by the fact that students become more openly idealistic whenever they are removed from the influence of student culture—when they are alone with a sociologist as they near the finish of school and sense the approaching end of student life, for example, or when they are isolated

from their classmates and therefore are less influenced by this culture.[9]

They still feel, as advanced students, though much less so than before, that school is irrelevant to actual medical practice. Many of their tasks, like running laboratory tests on patients newly admitted to the hospital or examining surgical specimens in the pathology laboratory, seem to them to have nothing to do with their visions of their future activity as doctors. As in their freshman year, they believe that perhaps they must obtain the knowledge they will need in spite of the school. They still conceive of medicine as a huge body of proven facts, but no longer believe that they will ever be able to master it all. They now say that they are going to try to apply the solution of the practicing M.D. to their own dilemma: learn a few things that they are interested in very well and know enough about other things to pass examinations while in school and, later on in practice, to know to which specialist to send difficult patients.

Their original medical idealism reasserts itself as the end of school approaches. Seniors show more interest than students in earlier years in serious ethical dilemmas of the kind they expect to face in practice. They have become aware of ethical problems laymen often see as crucial for the physician—whether it is right to keep patients with fatal diseases alive as long as possible, or what should be done if an influential patient demands an abortion—and worry about them. As they near graduation and student culture begins to break down as the soon-to-be doctors are about to go their separate ways, these questions are more and more openly discussed.

While in school, they have added to their earlier idealism a new and peculiarly professional idealism. Even though they know that few doctors live up to the standards they have been taught, they intend always to examine their patients

---

[9] See the discussion in Howard S. Becker, "Interviewing Medical Students," *op. cit.*

thoroughly and to give treatment based on firm diagnosis rather than merely to relieve symptoms. This expansion and transformation of idealism appear most explicitly in their consideration of alternative careers, concerning both specialization and the kind of arrangements to be made for setting up practice. Many of their hypothetical choices aim at making it possible for them to be the kind of doctors their original idealism pictured. Many seniors consider specialty training so that they will be able to work in a limited field in which it will be more nearly possible to know all there is to know, thus avoiding the necessity of dealing in a more ignorant way with the wider range of problems general practice would present. In the same manner, they think of schemes to establish partnerships or other arrangements making it easier to avoid a work load which would prevent them from giving each patient the thorough examination and care they now see as ideal.

In other words, as school comes to an end, the cynicism specific to the school situation also comes to an end and their original and more general idealism about medicine comes to the fore again, though within a framework of more realistic alternatives. Their idealism is now more informed although no less selfless.

DISCUSSION

We have used the words "idealism" and "cynicism" loosely in our description of the changeable state of mind of the medical student, playing on ambiguities we can now attempt to clear up. Retaining a core of common meaning, the dictionary definition, in our reference to the person's belief in the worth of his activity and the claims made for it, we have seen that this is not a generalized trait of the students we studied but rather an attitude which varies greatly, depending on the particular activity the worth of which is questioned and the situation in which the attitude is expressed.

This variability of the idealistic attitude suggests that in using such an element of personal perspective in sociological analysis

one should not treat it as homogeneous but should make a determined search for subtypes which may arise under different conditions and having differing consequences. Such subtypes presumably can be constructed along many dimensions. There might, for instance, be consistent variations in the medical students' idealism through the four years of school that are related to their social class backgrounds. We have stressed in this report the subtypes that can be constructed according to variations in the object of the idealistic attitude and variations in the audience the person has in mind when he adopts the attitude. The medical students can be viewed as both idealistic and cynical, depending on whether one has in mind their view of their school activities or the future they envision for themselves as doctors. Further, they might take one or another of these positions depending on whether their implied audience is made up of other students, their instructors, or the lay public.

A final complication arises because cynicism and idealism are not merely attributes of the actor, but are as dependent on the person doing the attributing as they are on the qualities of the individual to whom they are attributed.[10] Though the student may see his own disregard of the unique personal troubles of a particular patient as proper scientific objectivity, the layman may view this objectivity as heartless cynicism.[11]

Having made these analytic distinctions, we can now summarize the transformations of these characteristics as we have seen them occuring among medical students. Some of the students' determined idealism at the outset is reaction against the lay notion, of which they are uncomfortably aware, that doctors are money-hungry cynics; they counter this with an idealism

10 See Philip Selznick's related discussion of fanaticism in *TVA and the Grass Roots,* Berkeley: University of California Press, 1953, pp. 205-213.
11 George Orwell gives the layman's side in his essay, "How the poor Die" in *Shooting an Elephant and Other Essays,* London: Secker and Warburg, 1950, pp. 18-32.

of similar lay origin stressing the doctor's devotion to service. But this idealism soon meets a setback, as students find that it will not be relevant for awhile, since medical school has, it seems, little relation to the practice of medicine, as they see it. As it has not been refuted, but only shown to be temporarily beside the point, the students "agree" to set this idealism aside in favor of a realistic approach to the problem of getting through school. This approach, which we have labeled as the cynicism specific to the school experience, serves as protection for the earlier grandiose feelings about medicine by postponing their exposure to reality to a distant future. As that future approaches near the end of the four years and its possible mistreatment of their ideals moves closer, the students again worry about maintaining their integrity, this time in actual medical practice. They use some of the knowledge they have gained to plan careers which, it is hoped, can best bring their ideals to realization.

We can put this in propositional form by saying that when a man's ideals are challenged by outsiders and then further strained by reality, he may salvage them by postponing their application to a future time when conditions are expected to be more propitious.

6. Learning and Personal Development of Medical Students: Reconsidered

Daniel H. Funkenstein

Across the nation medical students are restless, unhappy, and markedly dissatisfied with the education they are receiving. They feel that medical school is a poor learning experience and that their personal development is being impeded. These future physicians are disenchanted with medical school policies, which they blame for the inadequacy of the health care delivery system. The majority of students complain that they experience constant anxiety and stress. A "dehumanizing experience" is their most frequent characterization of medical school. Other typical remarks—from a sophomore: "I was not sure the day after I entered whether I was in a prison or a kindergarten, and I still haven't made up my mind." From a junior: "Every day I like being a medical student less and a doctor more."

The reasons underlying the difficulties medical students report are complex but largely due to two factors: (1) the recent rapid social changes in our society have altered student's and society's demands on medical schools faster than the schools have been able to respond to them, and (2) medical schools have not applied the newer knowledge of the personal development and learning of students to the process of medical education.

Before discussing these two major factors in detail, it is important to realize that the difficulties experienced by students and their medical schools do not exist apart from the many vicissitudes now manifest in all areas of our society. Unfortunately, medical schools and the medical profession have always felt removed from the society which they serve. Felix Frankfurter[1] stated that he could never understand why physicians so often felt that they were above, outside, or beyond society, and why they did not understand that in every

Funkenstein, D. H.: The learning and personal development of medical students: Reconsidered. The New Physician *19*:740–755 (1970).

transaction between a doctor and his patient, society has an interest.

In addition to being part and parcel of society, medical schools are integral parts of universities, and, in considering the problems of medical students, the difficulties and institutions of higher learning must also be considered.

The rapid social changes of our time, with their attendant problems of the atom bomb, war, overpopulation, poverty, racism, pollution, and the failure of the health care delivery system, have resulted in a new generation of students with a different set of values from those of their parents' generation. This generation gap has resulted in a great deal of turmoil in all educational institutions.

In the medical schools, these differences in values between faculty and students manifest themselves in two major areas of contention: what the function of a medical school should be, and in career choice. Most faculty feel that the medical school's chief function should be biomedical research and the care of patients in teaching hospitals. Students feel the main emphasis should be place on the community, solving the problems of the delivery of primary health care to the poor, research on such commonly misunderstood problems as alcoholism, drug addiction, nutrition, massive venereal disease in teenagers, overpopulation, and action on social factors and environmental factors that breed disease and impede health.[2] Faculty wish to replicate themselves in the careers of their students; students plan to pursue careers in community medicine.

These fundamental differences between students and faculty make it unlikely that much time or energy will be devoted to improving the education of students in the near future. Preoccupation with the demands of society and the government, and the current financial restrictions leave little free energy to rethink the education of students, and to bring into medical schools the newer knowledge of learning and personal development necessary to improve the educational process.

Despite these major difficulties, which overshadow the education of the student, it is time to begin a discussion of those factors within schools which impede or facilitate the personal development and learning of medical students. Only by clarifying these issues can movement toward improving the educational process begin.

In 1957, I gave a paper at the Association of American Medical College's Institute on the Ecology of the Medical Student.[3] In this paper, many of the changes needed in medical education to facilitate the learning and personal development of medical students were discussed. In 1966 a paper dealing with this same subject, in the light of the changes during the previous nine years, was written.[4] This paper brings the two previous papers forward to early 1970. This is necessary because of the many changes during the past four years.

There are two important aspects in the education of future physicians; first, the actual learning of the body of knowledge of the profession—the technology of medicine—and second, facilitating the personal development of the student toward maturity so that he will become a physician possessing those personal characteristics so highly prized by patients. Among these are integrity, empathy and compassion for the patient, freedom from biases and prejudices, and social awareness and sensitivity to the whole spectrum of interpersonal relationships: with patients, other physicians, allied health personnel, and community members. Both aspects of the education of the student are of equal importance: without a knowledge of the scientific basis of medicine, the physician will be a failure, for nothing is so inhuman as incompetence; without maturity, the physician would be ineffective in applying his technological knowledge for the benefit of patients.

Fortunately or unfortunately, depending upon the situation, most of the same factors in the medical school environment that facilitate or impede the learning of the technology of medicine, also facilitate or impede the personal development of the student. For example, when learning is facilitated by good teaching and adequate "feedback" of performance, development is also expedited because of the feeling of mastery and independence that ensues.

When a student is respected as an individual and treated like an adult, his personal development moves toward maturity, and learning is thus expedited.

Although learning and personal development are intertwined and difficult to separate in real life, for the purposes of discussion each will be handled separately. The factors within medical school which directly affect each will be considered.

LEARNING THE TECHNOLOGY OF MEDICINE

The continuous, rapid accumulation of knowledge makes much of what the student learns soon obsolete. It is imperative that students be given a sound foundation of principles upon which they can build, that their capacity to learn be increased, and that they acquire a lifelong devotion to forwarding their own learning. Although the language of medicine must be learned, and a certain amount of data must be memorized, excessive passive memorization and excessive devotion to the lecture system are some of the chief causes of difficulties. Now that many students who have not had as good preparation as conventional students are being admitted, it is imperative that the eductional process be improved.

Certain principles of learning can be applied to the medical school situation.

Anxiety

Intense or prolonged anxiety impairs learning. Such anxiety can result from the learning situation itself or from failure to solve personal, developmental problems. On the other hand, if students do not experience some anxiety, learning is not facilitated. Athletes experience anticipatory anxiety before a contest; actors experience stage fright. Our own studies on the relationship of anxiety to learning confirm this, and may be seen in Figure 6-1.

Many factors in the learning situation such as excessive competition, lack of orientation including "feedback," failure to individualize learning, grading examinations, etc., all can cause undue anxiety. Two closely related emotions, hostility brought about by frustration, and guilt over failure, whether real or imagined, also increase difficulties in learning.

Challenge and Response

Before discussing the many factors increasing anxiety and making learning difficult for medical students, it is important to discuss the learning principle known as "Challenge and Response." This is closely related to the problem of the quality and severity of the anxiety produced in students. This principle can be

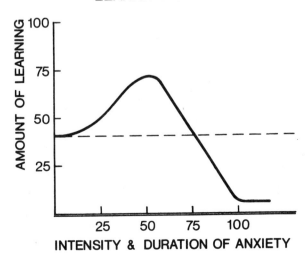

LEARNING & ANXIETY

(y-axis) AMOUNT OF LEARNING: 25, 50, 75, 100
(x-axis) INTENSITY & DURATION OF ANXIETY: 25, 50, 75, 100

Figure 6-1. From Funkenstein, D. H.: The learning and personal development of medical students. Reconsidered. The New Physician *19*:740–758 (1970).

stated as follows: If students are to learn optimally, they must be challenged enough to produce the degree of anxiety necessary to call forth new patterns of learning, but not so much that they become overanxious and fall back on older, less adequate techniques of learning such as passive memorization. The former is designated as adaptation, the latter as regression.

The core curricula in the basic sciences are usually too rigid to offer the appropriate degree of challenge to individual students. Frequently, biology and chemistry majors are not challenged sufficiently, while physical science, social science, and humanities concentrators are challenged beyond their ability to cope and understand. Different levels of the courses in the core curricula, or different core curricula depending upon the preparation of the students, would solve this difficulty. If a student is having difficulty in learning, he becomes anxious and regresses. Many experience intense guilt and hostility, which further interfere with learning and result in more regression.

Active versus Passive Learning

For learning to be optimal, it must be an active rather than a passive process. Medical schools are wedded to the lecture system in which the professor talks while the student listens passively and takes notes. In this situation, the huge amount of memorization required produces anxiety and an unreal learning experience. To overcome this passive memorization, facts or data must be linked to principles; seminars must be given in which students actively participate; laboratory exercises must be designed to require reasoning and ingenuity; basic sciences must be related to clinical medicine; opportunities must be provided to pursue one's own interests; and study must be carried out by active self-questioning. One reason computers and teaching machines are good teachers is because they promote the active engagement of the student in the learning process.

Orientation

Learning is facilitated when students are oriented in the following areas: to medicine, to the medical school environment, to what they are expected to learn, to their performance ("feedback").

Orientation to Medicine

Many students enter medical school with only a vague notion of what it means to be a physician in the modern world. They are surprisingly oblivious to the long hours of work and dedication required. At one end of the continuum, students are unaware of the problems of preventive medicine and health care delivery; at the other end, they are unaware of the importance of science and research. A particulr difficulty for students planning careers in community medicine is that "too few soldiers are as yet upon the battlefield" so they do not have role models to emulate and do not have a clear idea of the careers they will follow. Marked difficulties arise when the students who hold romantic illusions about medicine encounter the realities of the profession.

Orientation to the Medical School Environment

Bojar[5] has stated that a large number of entering medical students are well prepared for being medical school applicants, but not for being medical students or physicians. Many students hope to find medical education an experience quite different from college; above all, more satisfying. They expect that they will be able to realize their highest ideals about medicine and service to people; that the teaching will be of high caliber; that the courses, although difficult and time-consuming, will not be as abstract as college courses, but will be relevant to their life's work; and that they will have the opportunity to benefit from the wise counsel of an older generation.

These expectations are highly unrealistic. Compared to college, medical school offers less leisure time; less personal attention from the faculty; poorer teaching; and in many courses during the first two years, less relevance to the student's goals. Confronted with a situation even more difficult to cope with than that which they had encountered in college, the more naive students find their ideals crumbling.

Upon admission, students should be oriented to the medical school environment by their teachers and by students in the upper classes. Too often such orientation by teachers is too idealistic because they are unaware of the students' problems. The orientation by students is more apt to "tell it like it is." For example, the chairman of a department in a medical school that had upperclassmen orient the freshmen deplored the fact that the chief advice given by the upperclassmen was, "memorize the lecture notes, the rest doesn't matter." Many students go through medical school today reluctantly giving the faculty what they expect to acquire a union card (MD degree) so that the student can eventually realize his own career goal. It must be realized that most of medical school is unexciting, a poor educational experience, and irrelevant to many students' goals. Many years ago, I interviewed an applicant for admission to medical school who today is one of the outstanding scientists of our times. Inquiring about his college record, which contained only A's and D's, not B's or C's, he answered: "A's when I'm interested, and D's to give the bastards what they want to let me graduate." His medical school record was similar to his college one. Called in for an explanation of a "D" in pathology, the Dean of Students read him the department's comments: "Mr. _____ is very intelligent but he seemed uninterested in the course and did little work." The student replied, "All I can say is that the pathologists are very perceptive."

Orientation to What is Expected of Students

In every course, in every lecture, what the student is expected to learn must be exactly spelled out. Information he is not expected to remember should be so labelled.

Left to his own devices, the disoriented freshman student first tries to learn everything, which is impossible; then tries to learn what he thinks is relevant to clinical practice, of which he is ignorant; and finally settles on learning what is asked on examinations. He memorizes his lecture notes and does not explore material for his own interest and pleasure. Many students are able to orient themselves concerning what the instructor thinks is important and therefore know what will be asked on examinations. Students who are unable to do this often do poorly academically. They can improve their grades merely by asking a student making high grades what he considers important and what will be asked on the examination.

When individuals are forced to respond to conflicting demands, only a few handle the situation adequately. Many compensate by rigidly excluding responses to all but one demand; others experience great anxiety accompanied by reduced efficiency in learning. When instructors constantly tell students that minutiae are not important, that only general principles need be learned, and then ask for minutiae on examinations, students naturally become confused. Other difficulties arise when different instructors in the same course ask that conflicting things be learned, or when one course becomes so time-consuming that the only way the student can pass is to neglect another course.

Orientation to His Performance (Feedback)

To facilitate learning, nothing is more important for a student than to know how he is performing, so that he may correct himself. This is but part and parcel of a much larger subject, "The Evaluation of Students," which will now be discussed in considerable detail.

The Evaluation of Students

The evaluation of students by examinations and grading serves three purposes: (a) furthering the education of students, (b) furthering the education of teachers, (c) setting standards of competence.

Furthering the Education of Students

Exams can help students in two ways: by forcing them to review the course and by providing "feedback" on their performance.

Forcing a Review of the Course Material. Examinations make a student review course material. This is desirable because it puts the course in perspective, connects its various parts, and increases knowledge of the entire course. Review sessions give students the opportunity to ask questions, thus clarifying areas they do not understand.

Providing "Feedback" to Students. It is one of the cardinal principles of learning theory, backed by experimental evidence in both man and animals, that learning is severely impaired when there is no "feedback." It is absolutely necessary that the student know how well he is doing generally, and specifically the areas in which he is doing well, and the areas in which he is doing poorly. Possible ways to achieve this are:

Examinations which the student takes voluntarily. He does not hand in his blue book, but the exam is discussed in class, with the instructors giving the correct answers.

Sessions immediately following graded examinations in which the correct answers are gone over.

Prompt grading of examinations followed by a meeting between each student and instructor during which the examination is discussed, pointing out the student's areas of excellence and the areas in which he needs additional work. This must be done for *all* students regardless of how well they do, if all are to be brought to the highest level of which they are capable.

Grading of the exam by the teacher without his knowing whose exam he is grading.

Furthering the Education of Teachers

It is also important that teachers have "feedback" from their teaching. This can be acquired from student criticism of the course and by careful analysis of examinations to discover those areas the students are not learning well. Teaching in these areas should be revised and monitored by future examinations until this part of a course becomes a satisfactory learning experience. The National Board of Medical Examiners will supply a detailed breakdown of a class' performance in a particular school in various areas of each subject. On the basis of these data, teaching can be revised in the areas in which learning is below average.

Setting Standards of Competence

Standards of competence are determined for three reasons: (1) to inform outside institutions of the relative achievement of one student in relation to another, (2) to award honors, and (3) to set a minimal level of competence.

To Inform Outside Institutions. Most medical schools are primarily concerned with grades so that one student can be compared with another for securing entrance to the next higher rung on the educational ladder. Obviously students with high grades have a much better chance of acceptance at leading institutions than students with lower grades. Therefore, to get their graduates accepted, schools frequently grade their students on a curve that pits one against the other. In many instances, some students lose, no matter how much they know, since it is an arbitrary decision to give a certain number of students D's or E's. At some schools there are no automatic E's; at others, no automatic D's or E's. An example of the effects of grading on the curve is seen in the following letter actually received by a student who inquired about his mark in a college science course:

Dear Mr. _____ :
The reason that you made a D in your biology course is because the mean of the class was 450. We had decided that anyone whose mean was below 400 would receive a D. Your mean was 398, therefore we had no choice but to give you a D. If it makes you feel any better, if you had taken this same course when I last taught it two years ago, and had made 398, you would have made a B.

Sincerely yours,

_____

Signature

Grading on the curve causes great competition among students rather than fostering a cooperative spirit of learning. Excessive competition not only impedes learning by increasing anxiety, but plays a part in producing individuals who have difficulty in cooperating with others.

Another example of the unfairness of grading on the curve in medical school is the difference in preparation of students so that the examination may measure only preparation and ignore other aspects of the student's performance. For example, at Harvard Medical School, we found that the grade in genetics correlated 0.84 with having studied genetics in college.

Some schools attempt to lessen competition by not giving students back their grades unless they fail or are borderline cases. This device is not nearly as successful as most of its advocates believe. The student knows he is being graded; and he knows that his grade is important in applying for an internship. As stated earlier, the results of the examination must provide "feedback" to the student, not in terms of a letter or numerical grade, but in terms of his areas of competence and weakness.

Some schools pride themselves on their pass-fail system—letters of recommendation from the dean's office which are consolidated from a written comment from each instructor who has taught the student. These letters are often only substitutions for letter grades. In these letters students are classified into categories such as "outstanding," "excellent," "good," and "satisfactory." Even when a school does not resort to such a classification in a letter, it is easy to sort recommendations on a hierarchical basis. Too frequently, under the guise of doing something quite different, the consolidated letter of recommendation merely substitutes a "subjective" grading system for the old "objective" system of letter grades.

It is rather ironic that these letters are but a return to the system in vogue some 40 years ago, which was changed because it was considered undemocratic. The College Boards were founded to provide an "objective" measure of a student's academic ability regardless of his educational experience or geographic residence.

College admissions before this had been based on recommendations, social background, religious and ethnic factors, and school attended. College Boards resulted in a broadening of college opportunities to include the middle class. This was an advance, but a limited one. We know today that these tests excluded members of the lower social class and minority groups. If we now return to such subjective criteria as "recommendations" will they be used to exclude other groups? There is no grading or examination system that is truly "objective" and fair to all students and groups. It is important to understand the weaknesses of grades and exams. It is equally important to realize that this information can be abused in selection procedures and in comparing one student to another.

This brings up the entire question of whether it is the proper business of an educational institution to place its students in such a competitive situation, one against another, merely to inform the next higher institution about the student's performance in relation to another student. Perhaps the performance of the student should just be described; or perhaps the evaluation should be left to the institution to which he now seeks entrance.

To Award Honors. Comparing one student to another is the basis of awarding honors. Is this fair? Because different students excel in different fields, and because of the recent curricular changes that allow additional elective time to pursue individual interests, comparison of one student to another hardly seems valid.

To Set a Minimal Standard of Competence. Examinations are necessary to set a minimal standard of competence. It is necessary to achieve this standard if society is to be assured that graduating physicians are competent. The expected minimum should be carefully spelled out before the course begins, and it should be taught to achieve at least this level, although much more should be expected. When students fail to achieve the minimum, they should be quickly informed and given any necessary help. This requires a careful evaluation of the student from the standpoint of study skills, preparation, psychological problems, and personal difficulties such as family pressures or inadequate financing.

Final examinations are illogical in a pass-fail course with many subdivisions when students have already passed each component part. It is much better to suggest supplementary reading.

In summary, the evaluation of students by examinations should be used for "feedback," to enable students to review, and to establish minimal standards of competence. The question of honors and evaluating students for the next higher rung on the educational ladder by grading on the curve is debatable if the primary aim of the institution is the maximum education of students. Evaluation as currently practiced is often detrimental to the education of students because of the severe anxiety and resentment it produces. There is a need to establish minimal standards of competence, and evaluation must proceed in this direction. But a change in attitude toward the aim of helping students achieve competence and helping them correct their deficiencies would do much to reduce anxiety in medical schools.

Another area requiring careful scrutiny is grading in the clinical courses, where the student's willingness to do "scut work" for the house officer may be the chief factor in his grade.

Students must not be subject to arbitrary rules concerning promotion. Each case must be considered separately with a view toward the type of physician the student will become, rather than judged on a fixed grade point average.

There is fundamental dichotomy between evaluation and learning. This arises from the teacher's dual role: he is both the person who helps the student learn and the judge of the student's performance. This interferes with the student-teacher relationship. The student may not feel free to reveal his weakness by asking for the necessary help. American professors fail to perceive the difficulties of their dual role; at Oxford and Cambridge, tutors cannot understand how the same man could teach and evaluate at the same time, thus become judge and defense counsel, and often prosecutor as well. The tutor

teaches the student; evaluating is by an outside source. The tutor is the coach, trying to help the student learn and win by passing examinations. Failure is personal to both.

Integration

In recent years, much emphasis has been placed on integrated courses in the basic sciences with two, three, or more professors in different disciplines teaching a course together. These courses have the noble aim of helping students integrate material. There are also many drawbacks. They have worked well when the instructors planned the course with real enthusiasm and spent sufficient time beforehand to make sure it was integrated. Unfortunately, after the course is a year or two old and others teach it who did not originally plan it, instructors' meetings are few, and integration is lost. This creates considerable difficulty in learning. Students are presented with fragments of information bearing little relation to each other, which they must piece together as best they can. They must also attempt, on their own, to integrate the course into the general body of scientific knowledge.

Integration does not allow as much personal contact between students and teachers. When a subject is taught by one department over a concentrated period of time, professors get to know the students much better than they do when they see them at short intervals over a longer period of time.

Careful planning is needed to obviate these difficulties and facilitate the learning of students.

Individualization

To be effective, learning must be individualized. Students vary in their learning ability according to: (a) method of instruction and (b) interests, career plans, preparation, ability, and relevance.

Method of Instruction

Some students learn best by lectures, others by seminars, others by laboratories, others by reading. Wispe's studies[6] show that learning is facilitated when each student can use the method by which he learns most efficiently. Individualized instruction is more effective than teaching all students in the same manner.

By Interests, Career Plans, Preparation, Ability, and Relevance

Students learn best when their learning takes place in the context of their interests, career plans, and abilities. As courses in the basic medical sciences become more abstract and specialized, learning becomes progressively more difficult. Considerable discipline is needed to master material which is not perceived as relevant to one's life work. Medical students are well aware that much is taught during the first two years of medical school that has little application to medicine as it is currently practiced, and often even less application to their own career plans. For example, the student who expects to practice medicine in the community cannot see the relevance of a course in molecular biology, feeling that organ systems, ethology, psychology, and social sciences are more relevant for him. Nor can the future psychiatrist understand the part bacteriology will play in his practice. Students planning careers in biomedical engineering would like a more quantitative approach to the basic sciences.

In addition to the anxiety this creates in students, there is also a growing danger that material which is not yet applicable to medical practice may be crowding out more immediately useful material. Clinical faculty members in several schools have complained that when senior medical students are asked to report on the properties of a drug, they dwell on its exact mode of action in the cell and do not know its effects on organ systems. The token amount of social and behavioral science taught in medical school for those interested in public health and family medicine is another case in point.

Approximately 80 medical schools have changed their curricula in the direction of a core curriculum plus a year-and-a-half to two years of elective time. However, this still leaves a core curriculum which means that many students must learn a good deal of material not relevant to their careers. A multi-tracked curriculum with different core curricula is necessary. A start could be made by creating three basic science curricula: one more related to social factors, emphasizing ethology, ecology, psychology, and behavioral science; another with a quantitative basis; and one with the traditional biomedical, molecular basis. I have discussed this elsewhere.[7]

Unreasonable Work Loads and Unrealistic Standards

Students are often presented with unrealistic work loads and academic standards. These usually arise because of the specialization of faculty members. They often feel it necessary to cover their fields in the minutest detail and to conduct their classes as if all the student were Ph.D. candidates in their disciplines. Courses become boring and overloaded with factual material. Even though mastery of broad scientific principles is stressed during lectures, it is often the sheer memorization of minutiae that is rewarded during examinations.

Another aspect of the unreasonable work load is the large amount of scut work students in most schools are expected to do. Students start intravenouses, do laboratory work, and hold retractors—none of which have educational value. These tasks could easily be carried out by hospital personnel. Being on duty every other night and often losing sleep deprive the student of time to read and study. This is hardly educational. With tuition costs soaring, medical students feel great bitterness about such exploitation. This has had a damaging effect on their relationships with faculty members. They feel they are forced to subsidize the teaching hospital with their labor and their time.

Caliber of Teaching

The shift of faculty attention to research and consultation has also aggravated the learning problems of medical students by causing a decline in the quality of teaching. Most professors have no real knowledge of the pedagogical techniques taught in schools of education. Moreover, interest in teaching has waned considerably, not only because there is less time, but because, in comparison to other faculty activities, it is poorly rewarded and carries little prestige.

Teaching in the preclinical years generally takes the form of lectures. Reference has already been made to the difficulties in so-called integrated courses in which too often one professor does not know what the others are teaching.

In the clinical years, the situation is no better. Teaching is left largely to the overworked house officers who very often have only a minimal interest in pedagogy. With their heavy burden of patient care, they are even more exhausted and pressed for time than the professors.

How can excellence in teaching become the rule rather than the exception? First, medical schools must recognize that few faculty members are able to reach the high level of competence in all areas now demanded of them. In particular, *the myth that excellence in research makes for excellence in teaching must be discarded.* Diversity among faculty members should be recognized and encouraged so that some can devote themselves to full-time research, some to teaching, others to patient care and consultation with health agencies, and still others to various combinations of these. Merit in teaching, like merit in research, should be rewarded by promotion.

Teaching must also be professionalized with the help of consultants from schools of education. Together with students and competent faculty observers, these consultants should be responsible for the systematic evaluation of courses so that the poorer teachers can be relieved of their teaching duties. Courses must be carefully planned and constantly improved. Courses should emphasize general principles; well-motivated students can always learn on their own once they are given the proper foundation.

The new curriculum with its many electives gives students a weapon for forcing improvement in teaching. If an elective course is poorly taught, students should no longer take it, stating the reason to the instructor.

Technological Aids

Hardly a beginning has been made on the use of the teaching machine, computers, television, and movies as learning tools for the medical student. Refer to the Report of the Conference on a Biomedical Network by the Lister Hill Communications Center of the National Library of Medicine and the AAMC held in February of 1969.[8]

Professional Help as Needed

Students with emotional or academic problems or a combination of the two should be given appropriate assistance through counselling, tutoring, or psychotherapy. It is important that complete confidentiality be maintained between the student and the individual rendering the professional help. The student must also be assured that he will have comprehensive health care for himself and his family.

Financing

Adequate financing of medical students would allay a whole area of present anxieties and decrease the need of many students to work, thus increasing study time. This has now become a very acute problem with inflation sharply increasing the student's budget and the federal government unwilling to meet these costs. If more financial aid is not forthcoming in much larger amounts, students will have to work long hours in unrewarding jobs in order to stay in school. Even more alarming is the fact that under present financial conditions, the admirable programs for minority students may be stillborn.

THE PERSONAL DEVELOPMENT OF MEDICAL STUDENTS TO BECOME MATURE PHYSICIANS

Although the seeds of personal development of the student are planted long before he comes to medical school, too little attention is paid to the crucial factors in the medical school experience that contribute to the attributes of the mature physician. Since the extremely important developmental stages of infancy, childhood, and early adolescence are far behind, there is a tendency to forget that personality is a lifelong dynamic process. It is still in its very crucial stages during the medical school period, and a student's solutions to the conflicts of this period are of great importantce in determining the type of doctor he will become.

In discussing the personal development of medical students, many frames of reference are possible, but in my opinion Erikson's concepts of "stages of development,"[9] and White's "growth trends,"[10] give the clearest theoretical frames of reference. Their ideas of development in late adolescence and early adulthood will be modified to apply to the special situation of medical students in interaction with their schools. This material is derived from extensive studies of mine over a number of years.

Erikson states that from birth onward throughout life, man goes through a sequence of psychosocial developmental stages that parallel psychosexual development. Each individual goes through a series of crises in development as he solves the appropriate conflicts for each age level. In normal development they occur in a sequential pattern. As long as the conflicts for a particular level are not solved, a crisis exists. The conflicts of each stage are difficult to solve if adequate solutions were not reached in previous stages. This is not to imply that the origins of these developmental conflicts are recent; their roots go back to early childhood, but the problems of solving the conflicts become paramount at a particular time of life. However, it must be realized that individuals (and this is especially pertinent in the case of medical students) do not develop by any timetable, for all stages of development are seen in different individuals at different chronological ages. Individual students vary markedly in the time at which they solve these problems and in the duration and difficulties of the solution process.

Ideally, developmental tasks should be solved in sequence with sufficient time to consolidate the solutions to one developmental problem before moving on to the next. In the case of medical students, this is not possible; the unique characteristics and length of the medical school experience preclude this. Medical students are forced to work on developmental tasks long after their colleagues preparing for other careers have solved these problems, consolidated them, and moved on to other tasks of development. One example would be the choice of a career by medical students. This is spread over many years as they first make a choice to become a physician, then select a specialty, and finally decide what type of career they will have. i.e., academic medicine, practice, etc. The medical student's contemporaries preparing for other careers do not have to work over such a long period of time or on so many different aspects of professional identity. For example, if a student decides to go to graduate school to become an English scholar or physicist, he has a good idea of what the experience will be like from his college courses and there is a fairly straight line from college onward. They do not constantly have to reexamine their career commitments as medical students do. The uncertainty of admission to medical school, when so many qualified applicants are denied the opportunity to study medicine, is another factor making it difficult for the college student to consolidate his professional commitment. In all other careers, all qualified applicants secure entrance to some school.

In considering the personal development of medical students, four major developmental tasks will be described. Although emphasis will be placed on the effects of medical schools on the development of students, reference will also be made to the college premedical experience as well as the hospital training period, because they really represent one continuous process of education. These four major tasks at their zenith during medical school are: learning to accept responsibility, acquiring a sense of identity, developing mature interpersonal relationships, and preparing for marriage and parenthood.

Learning to Accept Responsibility

One of the chief qualities of the mature physician is the ability to accept responsibility. The main responsibility is directly for patients, but other important components are the responsibility of the doctor for his own ethical behavior, for calling in consultants, and for keeping up with expanding medical knowledge. This is especially important in view of the studies of Peterson, et al[11] which show that many physicians have not kept up. This points to the lack of controls by the profession or society in this area. The much discussed peer review is honored more in word than deed.

The roots of the ability to accept responsibility lie in adolescence as the student develops a sense of autonomy from his parents, entering a relationship of adult to adult, rather than parent to child. The long financial dependency of medical students on their parents, often extending into the residency period, makes this sense of autonomy difficult to achieve. The development of independence is hindered by the authoritarian aspects of medical schools where students are often treated as children, supervised too closely, not trusted to learn on their own, compelled to attend class, and examined too often. The exercise of *in loco parentis* in many subtle ways throughout the school results in students having little to say about their own destiny, little voice in their own education or in the policy decisions of the school. Such things do not encourage maturity. When the student becomes a house officer, his career very often depends upon the recommendation of one person, the chief of service. This does not make for independence. The inability to give students real responsibility for patients, although realistically related to legal restrictions, is often greatly exaggerated and makes responsibility difficult to achieve. If a student is financially dependent, whether on wife, scholarship, or loans, his sense of autonomy and his ability to accept responsibility in the broadest sense of the word are hindered.

Placing students on faculty committees with a voice and a vote in determining school policies would promote responsibility.

Sense of Identity

Although there are many aspects of identity, I will confine my remarks to the three that are of paramount importance to medical students: (a) professional, (b) values, (c) sense of self as man or woman.

Professional Identity

Students need to establish a sense of professional identity, and until this is achieved they can never be comfortable working with patients. For example, when sophomore medical students are asked to go on the ward, they quickly don white coats and let their stethoscopes dangle conspicuously from their pockets. Frequently they ask about their right to inquire into a patient's life history or their right to do physical examinations. Once they feel themselves physicians, they no longer need outside devices to establish their identity or inquire about their intrusion on patients.

Our studies show that although students begin working on their identity as a physician from early in life to the senior year in college, it is usually consolidated in the junior year in medical school. Although identity as a specialist is thought of as early as college, it becomes an intense problem during the junior year in medical school as soon as identity as a physician is established. For many, consolidation of specialty choice occurs after medical school, during the first year of residency, although it may occur during medical school or after several years of residency. A sense of career direction may emerge as early as entrance to college, but it usually becomes a pressing problem during residency training. While profession and specialty choice are difficult to change without the loss of much time, what the student does with his career is easily changed, less deeply established, and subject to many outside factors. The current cuts in research funds will cause many students to pursue a career in practice rather than in academic medicine. The long period of time over which a medical student must achieve these three aspects of professional identity means that he is never free from this problem and must constantly consider alternatives with the anxiety attendant upon making important decisions.

This is particularly difficult at the present time because many students do not want careers like today's faculty or practitioners. They do not have role models to emulate; they cannot see the kind of person they wish to become. At one end of the continuum, the uncertainty about postmedical school training and opportunities in public health make this career choice difficult. At the other end of the continuum, those planning careers in academic medicine are troubled by the cuts in funds which may make it difficult to pursue such a carrer.

Values

In acquiring a sense of identity, a student must develop a set of values that will guide him through life. Values, in Parson's definition, are deeply held beliefs that motivate to action. Students enter college with values learned at home and in their community. During college, they are faced with new values that often conflict with the old. The student must then acquire his own values. Within a continuum, there are three possible outcomes: to hold onto the old values and ignore the new, which results in a failure in growth; complete rejection of the old for the new; or a synthesis of the old and the new.

After college, students entering medical school must again alter their value system to incorporate the values that will guide their professional life. The process that went on in college must be repeated.

Difficulties in acquiring values appropriate for the future occur when social changes are so rapid that there is a marked discontinuity in value systems and when there are marked differences in values between parents and children, teachers and students, and practitioners and apprentices. Keenan[12] stated that to avoid the disruption of a society, social change should never be so rapid that the experiences of the fathers are irrelevant to the problems of the sons. This is now the situation in most educational institutions, including medical schools. Mead[13] states that the past is irrelevant, that we are now developing a prefigurative culture in which adults will have to learn the new values from their children. This is in contrast with the past when there were two kinds of culture—postfigurative, in which children learn from their forebears, or cofigurative, in which both children and adults learn from their peers.

There is a wide gap between the values of medical school faculties and those of their students. I have detailed these specific differences elsewhere.[14] These value differences generate the greates conflicts in two areas—career choices and the function of the medical school.

Faculty members' careers are entwined in the scientific era of medicine, and their interests are primarily in basic research or in the investigation and treatment of complicated problems in the teaching hospitals. Most students plan careers in the community era which will emphasize the delivery of health care to the community. They are more interested in working in community hospitals and neighborhood clinics or in becoming public health physicians.

Faculties take the stand that the medical school's function should be primarily to do biomedical research and to treat biomedical problems of a complicated nature. Only a minor effect is assigned to community problems. Interested in replicating themselves, they want students admitted who have similar values and whose careers will parallel their own. Most students, on the other hand, want the resources of the medical school devoted primarily to the community in solving the problems of health care delivery. They emphasize such commonly misunderstood problems as alcoholism and drug addiction. They want to develop a new preventive medicine that will take action on social factors that breed disease and impede health. They wish to resurrect the ' art of medicine and to educate more members of minority groups.

Although these two areas cause the greatest differences between students and faculty, there are two other sources of value conflict: the faculty emphasizes reasoned analysis of problems before action, while students demand action first, then trial by error; the faculty stresses competition, and the students emphasize cooperation.

Nothing is creating more strain among students and faculty than this difference in value systems. Until there can be some agreement about how the medical school should apply its resources, the conflict will continue, and no matter what is done in other areas, the learning and personal development of students will suffer. Faculty have a great deal to learn from students in living up to the new social responsibilities of our times; students have much to learn from faculty emphasis on scientific competence, even if they do not follow their careers.

Furthermore, students must be brought to the realization that they are but a small part of the total educational commitment of a medical school, which is also responsible for the education of house officers, Ph.D. students, postdoctoral fellows, and the continuing education of physicians in the community.

Identity

Although sexual identity as man or woman is established early and consolidated during adolescence, medical school with its stresses often produces problems in this aspect of identity.

For men, the long financial dependence on parents or wife, the lack of control over personal destiny, the authoritarian attitude of medical schools and hospitals, and the lack of responsibility make it difficult to feel mature in a manly way.

For women in medicine, the problem is even more difficult. First, women must find a means of combining a career and a family. They receive far too little support from their families, from society, and especially from male students and faculty members. Excellent positions as house officers are frequently difficult to come by. If a woman falters, she is counselled out of medicine; if a man falters, he is too long counselled in. The Pennsylvania College of Medicine (formerly Woman's Medical College) is the only school I know that will permit mothers to go through medical school on a part-time basis. Given these conditions, it is not surprising that developing the roles of physician, wife, and mother is extremely difficult.

Mature Interpersonal Relationships

Nothing is more important for the student than to develop mature relationships with others: with patients; with his colleagues; with older physicians in authority over him; with the myriad allied health personnel with whom he must work; and with members of the community with whom he must make a partnership in health matters.

The literature on the doctor-patient relationship is vast. The relationship should be characterized by empathy for, but not overidentification with, the patient, so that the physician's objectivity is not lost. He must remain sensitive to patient needs with an ability to respond to them in terms of the patient rather than the physician. Concern with the social and psychological aspects of the patient's illness is essential. Some other reasons for student anxiety in physician-patient relationships were described by Mudd and Siegel:[15] "... the pressure of grades and examinations, his incomplete mastery of knowledge and skills, his 'uncertainty,' his need to please his family, his contact with the mutilating procedures, pain and death, his concern for his own health, and his need to develop detached concern...." These same authors report on the importance of sexual conflict in students in producing anxiety in their relationships with patients.

Certain situations in medical school are particularly difficult for students. Our own studies show that problems arise principally in dealing with sick children, psychiatric patients, and sexual matters. Hostile, uncooperative, and elderly patients are also difficult, as is the dying patient. Opportunities should be provided for discussion of these problems, either with instructors or preferably in groups of medical students with trained professionals. It should also be realized that there are many other contacts with patients which are difficult for certain students, and they should have the opportunity to discuss their difficulties with a person skilled in teaching interpersonal relations.

Students in the future will need to become cooperative members of a team as they work with their colleagues and with allied health personnel. There is simply no other way of delivering adequate health care. A teaching hospital today is largely a team effort. Achieving the ability to have a cooperative relationship with others is difficult for today's physician who comes up through a college experience of intense competition for grades, then in medical school has to compete with his colleagues again to get the "best" internship. One of the top priorities of medical education should be to produce cooperative physicians rather than the highly competitive, individualistic ones of the past, who are anachronisms in the delivery of health care.

Another source of difficulty is between the student and the older physicians in authority over him. There is a long period when the student is under the authority of an older physician, in medical school, and as a house officer. This dependence upon authority is a delicate matter for students who have had difficulty in achieving autonomy from their parents. Contributing to these difficulties is the frequent, irrational use of authority by faculty members. An attitude of respect from the faculty would do much to alleviate this.

In the future, considerable skill in working with community members will be necessary for many physicians. This will require a knowledge of group dynamics and the social sciences, as well as practical training. Members of the community should become instructors in this aspect of human relations.

Developing a Readiness for Marriage and Parenthood

It is also necessary that the student be able to form a mature relationship with a person of the opposite sex so that he is ready for marriage, and beyond that, for parenthood. Unfortunately, the stresses and anxieties of medical school and the lack of time contribute to the difficulties in this area. Too often, marriages are difficult because of the reversal of roles with the wife supporting the student, the need to postpone a family, the absence of the student or house officer for days at a time, and the regressive nature of medical education in general. The Behavioral Science Center at Bowman Gray Medical School is studying medical marriages and the picture is not good. Fortunately, today's medical students are concerned with the conflict between professional demands and their families and are determined not to let the former interfere with the latter. Students desire to place their families ahead of their careers. They feel that faculty who spend 80-90 hours working are unsuitable role models because they are neglecting their families.

In summarizing learning and personal development, the chief impediments, beyond the preoccupation of faculty and students with the adjustment to rapid social change, are: the failure to apply modern knowledge of learning and personal development to the education of students; the long period of dependency in which students are kept; difficulties in financing a medical education; the absence of role models; the marked differences in values between faculty and students; and the educational philosophy of the faculty. Currently faculty have an industrial philosophy of education. They emphasize production and, as a mark of their own prestige, the number of students they can proselytize into their own disciplines. They feel that they can mold students on an assembly line into replications of themselves, who can be neatly packaged and marketed. Needed is an agrarian philosophy in which students are seen as growing plants, to be carefully nurtured, adequately fertilized, watered and given sunlight, protected from weeds, and allowed to grow into their own thing.

CONCLUSIONS

It is apparent from the previous discussion that there is a fundamental dichotomy between the current needs of medical education and the developmental needs of students. The rapid changes in colleges and medical schools have created serious problems for students in learning and personal development. These difficulties are now so widespread that the need for corrective measures has become urgent.

It is clear that medical schools cannot rely on the mere passage of time to resolve their dilemma. On the contrary, with further revolutionary social changes about to take place in the field of medicine, the disruptive pressures on students will, in all probability, intensify as time goes on.

Largely through preoccupation with other issues, inertia, and a lack of familiarity with the studies on learning and development carried out by many investigators, medical school faculties with few exceptions have resisted utilizing the findings of such studies to improve their own institutions.

It is to be hoped that this attitude will give way in the near future to a more productive approach. If medical schools would shift some of their attention from strictly academic considerations such as grades, examinations, and curriculum reform—important as they are—to the broader question of the schools' educational climate, they might learn what the disruptive features are and how they can be eliminated. This is not to suggest that academic standards should be lowered or less importance given to curricular matters, but rather that close attention must be paid to the nonacademic factors as well if medical schools are to graduate physicians not only with great technological skills, but with the maturity to use them wisely.

Above all, this is a time for positive action, not recrimination. Too many groups in the medical community—students, faculty members, private practitioners, medical school administrators— have tended to attribute their current difficulties to one another. Such mutual accusations are as groundless as they are destructive. It should be evident to all concerned that the difficulties we are encountering are not due to the failings of one or another group, but to the swift pace of change in society and in our educational system. Efforts at remedying these difficulties are sorely needed; they will have a far greater chance of succeeding if they can be carried out in an atmosphere of understanding and goodwill.

How can these major conflicts be reduced to a manageable level and a sense of community regained? Until such accommodation is reached, the learning and personal development of students will continue to have the lowest priority in medical schools.

How is it possible to get real dialogue going on these fundamental issues of how the financial and faculty resources of medical schools can be used to carry out its mission of acquiring and transmitting knowledge? Students have communicated their unhappiness with their situations, the overwhelming stress they experience, and the dehumanizing aspects of their education. The faculty and administration have not communicated to students their unhappiness and the strains under which they labor. Evidence of faculty and administrative stress can be seen in the fact that a very large number of deans have resigned during the past year, and the average tenure for deans is now less than three years. Departmental chairmen are also resigning in large numbers. The recent cuts in research funds coupled with inflation and inadequate reimbursement for patient services in medical school teaching hospitals are compounding the problems of faculty and deans.

The time has come for mutual understanding. Students have much to gain by acquiring some of the values of the faculty; but the faculty has even more to gain in aiding students to act upon their values, because it is upon them that the future depends.

Until the conflicts among all elements of the medical community become more manageable, so that mistrust is dispelled and a sense of community is regained, the education of students will continue to have a low priority, scientific research will suffer, and patient care, which is the chief reason for the existence of medical schools, will not be improved.

GUIDELINES

The following guidelines are suggested for facilitating the learning and personal development of medical students.

Planning and Evaluation. Each change, whether curricular or noncurricular, should be assessed in terms of its possible effects on the learning and personal development of students. When instituted, it should be made the subject of constant evaluation so that any unfortunate consequences can be detected and remedied without delay.

Knowledge of Learning and Personal Development. Modern knowledge of learning and personal development should be used to improve the educational process of medical school.

Proper Orientation. Entering students must be helped to learn what it means to be a medical student and a physician, beginning with an orientation period during the first week of medical school. Thereafter, they must have sufficient faculty feedback to know what they are expected to learn, the relevance of this material to medical practice, and the extent of their progress so that they can evaluate their own deficiences and competencies.

Excellent Teaching. Teaching must be professionalized and accorded the same prestige as other faculty activities. The myth that an excellent researcher makes an excellent teacher must be dispelled. Faculty must be evaluated as teachers. If they are not excellent, they must be educated to achieve a high standard or eliminated from teaching.

Work Loads and Academic Standards. Students must be presented with realistic work loads and academic standards. This means that professors must exercise selectivity in the topics they wish to cover and not expect students to master the volume of material that would be appropriate for a Ph.D. candidate specializing in one of the basic sciences. The challenge to the student must be great enough to produce the anxiety necessary to call forth new patterns of behavior, but not so overwhelming that it forces him to adjust passively or to fall back on previously learned behavior.

Respect for the Student. Faculty members must treat students as respected junior colleagues, expect them to succeed in medical school, listen with good will to their opinions, and take action on their suggestions about their education. They must also bear in mind that students have different abilities and not disparage those with talents unlike their own. Excessive proselytizing of students should likewise be avoided. Students must not be subjected to arbitrary rules concerning promotion or other aspects of their life or to the indignities of inadequate financing.

Professional Help as Needed. Students with emotional or academic problems or a combination of the two should be given appropriate assistance through counselling, tutoring, or psychotherapy. It is important in such cases that complete confidentiality be maintained between the students and the individual rendering professional help.

Interpersonal Relationships. The decline in student-faculty contact can be countered by providing each student with a faculty tutor. Students should also be helped to relate cooperatively rather than competitively with their classmates by eliminating such competitive situations as grading on the curve and ranking by grade-point average.

Adequate Health Services. The student must be assured of comprehensive medical care, including psychiatric help—for himself, his wife, and his children.

Control over His Own Destiny. The student should have the option of exercising some control over his own education. Instead of being forced to learn large amounts of material which have no relevance to his future career, he should be given a flexible education that is tailored to his academic background and specialty plans. Active participation in the learning process should be emphasized, not passive memorization from lecture notes. Students should also be allowed sufficient leisure time for pursuing their individual interests.

It is important that student representatives, duly elected by their peers, be allowed to sit on committees concerned with discipline and other aspects of student life. Representation or consultation privileges on curriculum and admission committees should also be granted to students.

Channels of Communication. Effective communication should be developed among students, administrators, and faculty members so that appropriate action may be taken to alleviate existing difficulties.

Financing. Scholarship funds should be greatly increased. A student's indebtedness should not be permitted to grow so large that it (a) becomes a source of great anxiety for him, (b) compromises his choice of a career, or (c) forces him to support himself while in medical school by taking nonmedical jobs which cut into his study time.

Dependency. If the preceding measures were adopted, the problem of enforced and prolonged dependency would be alleviated through assuring the student of adequate financing, encouraging him to engage in independent study, and allowing him more control over his own destiny.

REFERENCES

1. Frankfurter, F.: A lawyer's dicta on doctors. *Harvard Med. Alum. Bull.* (July) 1958.
2. Ford, A. B.: Casualties of our time: Social and technological changes produce new sources of death and disability which raise public issues. *Science* 167:256–263, 1970.
3. Funkenstein, D. H.: "The Implications of Diversity," in *The Ecology of the Medical Student,* a Report on the Fifth Teaching Institute, Association of American Medical Colleges, Evanston, Ill., 1958.
4. Funkenstein, D. H.: The learning and personal development of medical students and recent changes in universities and medical schools. *J. Med. Educ.* 43:883–897, 1968.
5. Bojar S.: "Psychiatric Problems of Medical Students," in Blaine, G. B., Jr., et. al. (ed.): *Emotional Problems of the Student.* New York: Appleton-Century-Crofts, 1961.
6. Wispe, S. G.: Evaluating section teaching methods in the introductory course. *J. Educ. Res.* 45:161, 1951.
7. Funkenstein, D. H.: Current changes in education affecting medical school admissions and curriculum planning. *J. Med. Educ.* 41:410–423, 1966.
8. Smythe, D. (ed.): *Potential Educational Services from a National Biomedical Communications Network.* Report of a Conference held

Feb. 25–26, 1969, National Library of Medicine, Bethesda, Md. Sponsored by the Council of Academic Societies of the Association of American Medical Colleges under Contract No. NLM 69–8 with the National Institutes of Health, Department of Health, Education, and Welfare, National Library of Medicine.
9. Erikson, E. H.: *Childhood and Society.* New York: W. W. Norton and Co., 1950.
10. White, R. W.: *Lives in Progress.* New York: The Dryden Press, 1952.
11. Peterson, O. L., et. al.: An analytical study of North Carolina general practice, 1953–1954. *JAMA* Part II, December, 1956.
12. Keenan, G. F.: *Realities of American Foreign Policy.* Princeton, N.J.: Princeton University Press, 1954.
13. Mead, M.: Youth revolt: The future is now. *Saturday Review* 43:23, 1970.
14. Funkenstein, D. H.: Medical students, medical schools, and society during three eras. *Proceedings of Conference on Medical Students* held at the Bowman Gray School of Medicine, Winston-Salem, N.C., June, 1969. (In Press).
15. Mudd, J. W. and Siegel, R. J.: Sexuality—the experience and anxieties of medical students. *New Eng. J. Med.* 25:1397, 1969.

Part B

Biobehavioral Foundations of Medicine: The Organism Perspective

III BIOBEHAVIORAL CONCEPTS AND VIEWPOINTS

Biobehavioral relationships have been speculated upon for centuries, yet the science that explores them is of recent origin. Ever since man began to ponder himself as an object of curiosity, he intuitively sensed that bodily processes were, in some fashion, associated with his moods, dreams, temptations and judgments. Although the interplay between body and mind is now a formal interest of professional philosophers and scientists, each one of us, in our everyday lives, experiences data that verify the intrinsic linkage between biological and behavioral events. As the well-known psychologist Harry Harlow has written (1958):

Every human being throughout his life has been a student of animal behavior, and the animal which he has most commonly studied is man. Furthermore, most human beings have studied, with varying degrees of interest and intensity, a generous sample of this species of mammal, and their behavioral studies have frequently taken interdisciplinary form as they correlated, often with more enthusiasm than accuracy, the observed behaviors with the anatomical and physiological variables of sex, facial form, body build, complexion, perspiration rate, and vasomotor patterns.

Not only is the study of behavior the common property of all men, but it approaches being the common property of all the disciplines forming the family of biological sciences. The pure behaviorist, the psychologist, studies behavior like the true artist studies art—for its own sake. Most biological scientists—the anatomists, physical anthropologists, zoologists, physiologists, and biochemists—correlate behaviors with other variables, and in so far as they work along these lines, they achieve interdisciplinary research. This does not mean, of course, that interdisciplinary research between or among biological sciences of necessity involves behavioral measures. Correlations between chemical and anatomical, chemical and physiological, and anatomical and physiological variables may be made without direct measures of, or reference to, behavior, but even in such studies the implications for behavior are frequently obvious and usually little distance removed. It is a safe generalization, I believe, to state that the universal common interest of the biological scientists is behavior, the single characteristic which best defines and differentiates the living animal.

As Harlow observes, the coalescence of biological and behavioral processes is necessary if man is to succeed in his efforts to reintegrate the separate disciplines created in the evolution of his sciences. Academic fields such as biology and psychology are only arbitrary divisions within the natural world, constructed by early scientists as a simplified means of ordering the universe in a logical manner. But "reality" is not in a *dis*solved state, and scientific man must, at some point, *re*solve what he has dismembered so as to bring his studies closer to the unity of natural phenomena; in effect, he must now take the step to create such "interdisciplinary" field as biobehavioral science. As the eminent biologist Paul Weiss has written (1939):

In breaking down the Universe into smaller systems, into the society, the group, the organism, the cells, the cellular parts, and so forth, we dissect the system: that is, we sever relations, and then we try awkwardly and clumsily to restore those relations systematically but frequently very inadequately . . . . If we had come down from the universe gradually through the hierarchy of systems to the atoms, we would be much better off. Instead we now have to resynthesize the conceptual bonds between those parts which we have cut in the first place.

But desire will not suffice for scientific progress. Efforts to bring together traditionally disparate fields require more than tender-minded speculation and theorizing. Fortunately, in the past thirty years, rigorous models and methodologies have been developed, spurred largely by the burgeoning technological revolution. Simple data-gathering instruments available to past generations of scientists have been replaced with sophisticated electronic hardware, and coarse methods of information analysis have been supplanted by modern computer procedures that rapidly describe and integrate awesomely complex networks of data.

Later chapters will detail the fruits of these advanced techniques of data analysis and synthesis. Here, in the first chapter of Part B, we have selected three papers addressed primarily to the broader implications of biological and behavioral integration.

Anne Anastasi, a distinguished psychologist, provides an insightful analysis of the intrinsic interplay of heredity and experience. Focusing on a central issue in the interpretation of hereditary influence, she states that too many scientists believe that their task is to answer the question of how much and in what spheres genetic and experiential factors contribute to human behavior; for her, the essential question to be answered is how these factors *interact.* She contends that each set of influences has previously been conceived as merely additive, when they should be seen as interdependent and reciprocal. Not only does Anastasi furnish a number of well-reasoned illustrations of faulty integrative thinking, but she formulates, in a persuasive way, her notion of a "continuum of indirectness" in the potency of hereditary control, noting several promising lines for future medical research.

The two papers by Leon Eisenberg and Seymour Kety, both distinguished professors and researchers at Harvard Medical School, describe a number of fascinating areas of research in which biological processes are shown to limit the range and shape the patterns of human behavior. In their separate presentations of these biobehavioral advances, they argue, both implicitly and explicitly for the rich possibilities of an interdisciplinary approach to physical disease and psychological behavior. Their lucid and erudite papers are exemplary as illustrations of the fruitfulness of this approach.

REFERENCES

Harlow, H. F.: Behavioral contributions to interdisciplinary research. In Harlow, H. F., and Woolsey, C. N. (eds.): Biological and Biochemical Bases of Behavior. Madison, University of Wisconsin Press, 1958.
Weiss, P.: Principles of Development. New York, Holt, 1939.

7   Heredity, Environment and the Question "How?"

Anne Anastasi

Two or three decades ago, the so-called heredity-environment question was the center of lively controversy. Today, on the other hand, many psychologists look upon it as a dead issue. It is now generally conceded that both hereditary and environmental factors enter into all behavior. The reacting organism is a product of its genes and its past environment, while present environment provides the immediate stimulus for current behavior. To be sure, it can be argued that, although a given trait may result from the combined influence of hereditary and environmental factors, a specific difference in this trait between individuals or between groups may be traceable to either hereditary or environmental factors alone. The design of most traditional investigations undertaken to identify such factors, however, has been such as to yield inconclusive answers. The same set of data has frequently led to opposite conclusions in the hands of psychologists with different orientations.

Nor have efforts to determine the proportional contribution of hereditary and environmental factors to observed individual differences in given traits met with any greater success. Apart from difficulties in controlling conditions, such investigations have usually been based upon the implicit assumption that hereditary and environmental factors combine in an additive fashion. Both geneticists and psychologists have repeatedly demonstrated, however, that a more tenable hypothesis is that of interaction.[15,22,28,40] In other words, the nature and extent of the influence of each type of factor depends upon the contribution of the other. Thus the proportional contribution of heredity to the variance of a given trait rather than being a constant, will vary under different environmental conditions. Similarly, under different hereditary conditions, the relative contribution of environment will differ. Studies designed to estimate the proportional contribution of heredity and environment, however, have rarely included measures of such interaction. The only possible conclusion from such research would thus seem to be that both heredity and environment contribute to all behavior traits and that the extent of their respective contributions cannot be specified for any trait. Small wonder that some psychologists regard the heredity-environment question as unworthy of further consideration!

But is this really all we can find out about the operation of heredity and environment in the etiology of behavior? Perhaps we have simply been asking the wrong questions. The traditional questions about heredity and environment may be intrinsically unanswerable. Psychologists began by asking *which* type of factor, hereditary or environmental, is responsible for individual differences in a given trait. Later, they tried to discover *how much* of the variance was attributable to heredity and how much to environment. It is the primary contention of this paper that a more fruitful approach is to be found in the question "How?" There is still much to be learned about the specific *modus operandi* of hereditary and environmental factors in the development of behavioral differences. And there are several current lines of research which offer promising techniques for answering the question "How?"

Anastasi, A.: Heredity, environment, and the question "How?" Psychol. Rev. *65*:197-208 (1958).

VARIETY OF INTERACTION MECHANISMS

Hereditary Factors

If we examine some of the specific ways in which hereditary factors may influence behavior, we cannot fail but be impressed by their wide diversity. At one extreme, we find such conditions as phenylpyruvic amentia and amaurotic idiocy. In these cases, certain essential physical prerequisites for normal intellectual development are lacking as a result of hereditary metabolic disorders.

A somewhat different situation is illustrated by hereditary deafness, which may lead to intellectual retardation through interference with normal social interaction, language development, and schooling. In such a case, however, the hereditary handicap can be offset by appropriate adaptations of training procedures. It has been said, in fact, that the degree of intellectual backwardness of the deaf is an index of the state of development of special instructional facilities. As the latter improve, the intellectual retardation associated with deafness is correspondingly reduced.

A third example is provided by inherited susceptibility to certain physical diseases, with consequent protracted ill health. If environmental conditions are such that illness does in fact develop, a number of different behavioral effects may follow. Intellectually, the individual may be handicapped by his inability to attend school regularly. On the other hand, depending upon age of onset, home conditions, parental status, and similar factors, poor health may have the effect of concentrating the individual's energies upon intellectual pursuits. The curtailment of participation in athletics and social functions may serve to strengthen interest in reading and other sedentary activities. Concomitant circumstances would also determine the influence of such illness upon personality development. And it is well known that the latter effects could run the gamut from a deepening of human sympathy to psychiatric breakdown.

Finally, heredity may influence behavior through the mechanism of social stereotypes. A wide variety of inherited physical characteristics have served as the visible cues for identifying such stereotypes. These cues thus lead to behavioral restrictions or opportunities and—at a more subtle level—to social attitudes and expectancies. The individual's own self-concept tends gradually to reflect such expectancies. All of these influences eventually leave their mark upon his abilities and inabilities, his emotional reactions, goals, ambitions, and outlook on life.

The geneticist Dobzhansky illustrates this type of mechanism by means of a dramatic hypothetical situation. He points out that, if there were a culture in which the carriers of blood group AB were considered aristocrats and those of blood group O laborers, then the blood-group genes would become important hereditary determiners of behavior.[12,p.147] Obviously the association between blood group and behavior would be specific to that culture. But such specificity is an essential property of the causal mechanism under consideration.

More realistic examples are not hard to find. The most familiar instances occur in connection with constitutional types, sex, and race. Sex and skin pigmentation obviously depend upon heredity. General body build is strongly influenced by hereditary components, although also susceptible to environmental modification. That all these physical characteristics may exert a pronounced effect upon behavior within a given culture is well known. It is equally apparent, of course, that in different cultures the behavioral correlates of such hereditary physical traits may be quite unlike. A specific physical cue may be completely unrelated to individual differences in psychological traits in one culture, while closely correlated with them in another. Or it may be associated with totally dissimilar behavior characteristics in two different cultures.

It might be objected that some of the illustrations which have been cited do not properly exemplify the operation of hereditary mechanisms in behavior development, since hereditary factors enter only indirectly into the behavior in question. Closer examination, however, shows this distinction to be untenable. First it may be noted that the influence of heredity upon behavior is always indirect. No psychological trait is ever inherited as such. All we can ever say directly from behavioral observations is that a given trait shows evidence of being influenced by certain "inheritable unknowns." This merely defines a problem for genetic research; it does not provide a causal explanation. Unlike the blood groups, which are close to the level of primary gene products, psychological traits are related to genes by highly indirect and devious routes. Even the mental deficiency associated with phenylketonuria is several steps removed from the chemically defective genes that represent its hereditary basis. Moreover, hereditary influences cannot be dichotomized into the more direct and the less direct. Rather do they represent a whole "continuum of indirectness," along which are found all degrees of remoteness of causal links. The examples already cited illustrate a few of the points on this continuum.

It should be noted that as we proceed along the continuum of indirectness, the range of variation of possible outcomes of hereditary factors expands rapidly. At each step in the causal chain, there is fresh opportunity for interaction with other hereditary factors as well as with environmental factors. And since each interaction in turn determines the direction of subsequent interactions, there is an ever-widening network of possible outcomes. If we visualize a simple sequential grid with only two alternatives at each point, it is obvious that there are two possible outcomes in the one-stage situation, four outcomes at the second stage, eight at the third, and so on in geometric progression. The actual situation is undoubtedly much more complex, since there will usually be more than two alternatives at any one point.

In the case of the blood groups, the relation to specific genes is so close that no other concomitant hereditary or environment conditions can alter the outcome. If the organism survives at all, it will have the blood group determined by its genes. Among psychological traits, on the other hand, some variation in outcome is always possible as a result of concurrent circumstances. Even in case of phenylketonuria, intellectual development will exhibit some relationship with the type of care and training available to the individual. That behavioral outcomes show progressive diversification as we proceed along the continuum of indirectness is brought out by the other examples which were cited. Chronic illness *can* lead to scholarly renown or to intellectual immaturity; a mesomorphic physique *can* be a contributing factor in juvenile delinquency or in the attainment of a college presidency! Published data on Sheldon somatotypes provide some support for both of the latter outcomes.

Parenthetically, it may be noted that geneticists have sometimes used the term "norm of reaction" to designate the range of variation of possible outcomes of gene properties.[cf. 13,p.161] Thus heredity sets the "norm" or limits within which environmental differences determine the eventual outcome. In the case of some traits, such as blood groups or eye color, this norm is much narrower than in the case of other traits. Owing to the rather different psychological connotations of both the words "norm" and "reaction," however, it seems less confusing to speak of the "range of variation" in this context.

A large portion of the continuum of hereditary influences which we have described coincides with the domain of somatopsychological relations, as defined by Barker et al.[6] Under this heading, Barker includes "variations in physique that affect the psychological situation of a person by influencing the effectiveness of his body as a tool for actions or by serving as a stimulus to himself or others."[6,p.1] Relatively direct neurological influences on behavior, which have been the traditional concern of physiological psychology, are excluded from this definition, Barker being primarily concerned with what he calls the "social psychology of physique." Of the examples cited in the present paper, deafness, severe illness, and the physical characteristics associated with social stereotypes would meet the specifications of somatopsychological factors.

The somatic factors to which Barker refers, however, are not limited to those of hereditary origin. Bodily conditions attributable to environmental causes operate in the same sorts of somatopsychological relations as those traceable to heredity. In fact, heredity-environment distinctions play a minor part in Barker's approach.

Environmental Factors: Organic

Turning now to an analysis of the role of environmental factors in behavior, we find the same etiological mechanisms which were observed in the case of hereditary factors. First, however, we must differentiate between two classes of environmental influences: (a) those producing organic effects which may in turn influence behavior and (b) those serving as direct stimuli for psychological reactions. The former may be illustrated by food intake or by exposure to bacterial infection; the latter, by tribal initiation ceremonies or by a course in algebra. There are no completely satisfactory names by which to designate these two classes of influences. In an earlier paper by Anastasi and Foley,[4] the terms "structural" and "functional" were employed. However, "organic" and "behavioral" have the advantage of greater familiarity in this context and may be less open to misinterpretation. Accordingly, these terms will be used in the present paper.

Like hereditary factors, environmental influences of an organic nature can also be ordered along a continuum of indirectness with regard to their relation to behavior. This continuum closely parallels that of hereditary factors. One end is typified by such conditions as mental deficiency resulting from cerebral brain injury or from prenatal nutritional inadequacies. A more indirect etiological mechanism is illustrated by severe motor disorder—as in certain cases of cerebral palsy—*without* accompanying injury to higher neurological centers. In such instances, intellectual retardation may occur as an indirect result of the motor handicap, through the curtailment of educational and social activities. Obviously this causal mechanism corresponds closely to that of hereditary deafness cited earlier in the paper.

Finally, we may consider an environmental parallel to the previously discussed social stereotypes which were mediated by hereditary physical cues. Let us suppose that a young woman with mousy brown hair becomes transformed into a dazzling golden blonde through environmental techniques currently available in our culture. It is highly probable that this metamorphosis will alter, not only the reactions of her associates toward her, but also her own self-concept and subsequent behavior. The effects could range from a rise in social poise to a drop in clerical accuracy!

Among the examples of environmentally determined organic influences which have been described, all but the first two fit Barker's definition of somatopsychological factors. With the exception of birth injuries and nutritional deficiencies, all fall within the social psychology of physique. Nevertheless, the individual factors exhibit wide diversity in their specific *modus operandi* —a diversity which has important practical as well as theoretical implications:

Environmental Factors: Behavioral

The second major class of environmental factors—the behavioral as contrasted to the organic—are by definition direct influences. The immediate effect of such environmental factors is always a behavioral change. To be sure, some of the initial behavioral effects may themselves indirectly affect the individual's later behavior. But this relationship can perhaps be best conceptualized in terms of breadth and permanence of effects. Thus it could be said that we are now dealing, not with a continuum of indirectness, as in the case of hereditary and organic-environmental factors, but rather with a continuum of breadth.

Social class membership may serve as an illustration of a relatively broad, pervasive, and enduring environmental factor. Its influence upon behavior development may operate through many channels. Thus social level may determine the range and nature of intellectual stimulation provided by home and community through books, music, art, play activities, and the like. Even more far-reaching may be the effects upon interests and motivation, as illustrated by the desire to perform abstract intellectual tasks, to surpass others in competitive situations, to succeed in school, or to gain social approval. Emotional and social traits may likewise be influenced by the nature of interpersonal relations characterizing homes at different socioeconomic levels. Somewhat more restricted in scope than social class, although still exerting a relatively broad influence, is amount of formal schooling which the individual is able to obtain.

A factor which may be wide or narrow in its effects, depending upon concomitant circumstances, is language handicap. Thus the bilingualism of an adult who moves to a foreign country with inadequate mastery of the new language represents a relatively limited handicap which can be readily overcome in most cases. At most, the difficulty is one of communication. On the other hand, some kinds of bilingualism in childhood may exert a retading influence upon intellectual development and may under certain conditions affect personality development adversely.[2,5,10] A common pattern in the homes of immigrants is that the child speaks one language at home and another in school, so that his knowledge of each language is limited to certain types of situations. Inadequate facility with the language of the school interferes with the acquisition of basic concepts, intellectual skills, and information. The frustration engendered by scholastic difficulties may in turn lead to discouragement and general dislike of school. Such reactions can be found, for example, among a number of Puerto Rican children in New York City schools.[3] In the case of certain groups, moreover, the child's foreign language background may be perceived by himself and his associates as a symbol of minority group status and may thereby augment any emotional maladjustment arising from such status.[34]

A highly restricted environmental influence is to be found in the opportunity to acquire specific items of information occurring in a particular intelligence test. The fact that such opportunities may vary with culture, social class, or individual experiential background is at the basis of the test user's concern with the problem of coaching and with "culture-free" or "culture-fair" tests[cf.1,2] If the advantage or disadvantage which such experiential differences confer upon certain indivduals is strictly confined to performance on the given test, it will obviously reduce the validity of the test and should be eliminated.

In this connection, however, it is essential to know the breadth of the environmental influence in question. A fallacy inherent in many attempts to develop culture-fair tests is that the breadth of cultural differentials is not taken into account. Failure to consider breadth of effect likewise characterizes certain discussions of coaching. If, in coaching a student for a college admission test, we can improve his knowledge of verbal concepts and his reading comprehension, he will be better equipped to succeed in college courses. His performance level will thus be raised, not only on the test, but also on the criterion which the test is intended to predict. To try to devise a test which is not susceptible to such coaching would merely reduce the effectiveness of the test. Similarly, efforts to rule out cultural differentials from test items so as to make them equally "fair" to subjects in different social classes or in different cultures may merely limit the usefulness of the test, since the same cultural differentials may operate within the broader area of behavior which the test is designed to sample.

METHODOLOGICAL APPROACHES

The examples considered so far should suffice to highlight the wide variety of ways in which hereditary and environmental factors may interact in the course of behavior development. There is clearly a need for identifying explicitly the etiological mechanism whereby any given hereditary or environmental condition ultimately leads to a behavioral characteristic—in other words, the "how" of heredity and environment. Accordingly, we may now take a quick look at some promising methodological appraoches to the question "how."

Within the past decade, an increasing number of studies have been designed to trace the connection between specific factors in the hereditary backgrounds or in the reactional biographies of individuals and their observed behavioral characteristics. There has been a definite shift away from the predominantly descriptive and correlational approach of the earlier decades toward more deliberate attempts to verify explanatory hypotheses. Similarly, the cataloguing of group differences in psychological traits has been giving way gradually to research on *changes* in group characteristics following altered conditions.

Among recent methodological developments, we have chosen seven as being particularly relevant to the analysis of etiological mechanisms. The first represents an extension of selective breeding investigations to permit the identification of specific hereditary conditions underlying the observed behavioral differences. When early selective breeding investigations such as those of Tryon[36] on rats indicated that "maze learning ability" was inherited, we were still a long way from knowing what was actually being transmitted by the genes. It was obviously not "maze learning ability" as such. Twenty—or even ten—years ago, some psychologists would have suggested that it was probably general intelligence. And a few might even have drawn a parallel with the inheritance of human intelligence.

But today investigators have been asking: Just what makes one group of rats learn mazes more quickly than the other? Is it differences in motivation, emotionality, speed of running, general activity level? If so, are these behavioral characteristics in turn dependent upon group differences in glandular development, body weight, brain size, biochemical factors, or some other organic conditions? A number of recent and ongoing investigations indicate that attempts are being made to trace, at least part of the way, the steps whereby certain chemical properties of the genes may ultimately lead to specified behavior characteristics.

An example of such a study is provided by Searle's[31] follow-up of Tryon's research. Working with the strains of maze-bright and maze-dull rats developed by Tryon, Searle demonstrated that the two strains differed in a number of emotional and motivational factors, rather than in ability. Thus the strain differences were traced one step further, although many links still remain to be found between maze learning and genes. A promising methodological development within the same general area is to be found in the recent research of Hirsch and Tryon.[18] Utilizing a specially devised technique for measuring individual differences in behavior among lower organisms, these investigators launched a series of studies on selective breeding for behavioral characteristics in the fruit fly, *Drosophila.* Such research can capitalize on the mass of available genetic knowledge regarding the morphology of *Drosophila,* as well as on other advantages of using such an organism in genetic studies.

Further evidence of current interest in the specific hereditary factors which influence behavior is to be found in an extensive research program in progress at the Jackson Memorial Laboratory, under the direction of Scott and Fuller.[30] In general, the project is concerned with the behavioral characteristics of various breeds and crossbreeds of dogs. Analyses of some of the data gathered to date again suggest that "differences in performance are produced by differences in emotional, motivational, and peripheral processes, and that genetically caused differences in central processes may be either slight or nonexistent."[29,p.225] In other parts of the same project, breed differences in physiological characteristics, which may in turn be related to behavioral differences, have been established.

A second line of attack is the exploration of possible relationships between behavioral characteristics and physiological variables which may in turn be traceable to hereditary factors. Research on EEG, autonomic balance, metabolic processes, and biochemical factors illustrates this approach. A lucid demonstration of the process of tracing a psychological condition to genetic factors is provided by the identification and subsequent investigation of phenylpyruvic amentia. In this case, the causal chain from defective gene, through metabolic disorder and consequent cerebral malfunctioning, to feeblemindedness and other overt symptoms can be described step by step.[cf.32;33 pp.389-391] Also relevant are the recent researches on neurological and biochemical correlates of schizophrenia.[9] Owing to inadequate methodological controls, however, most of the findings of the latter studies must be regarded as tentative.[19]

Prenatal environmental factors provide a third avenue of fruitful investigation. Especially noteworthy is the recent work of Pasamanick and his associates,[27] which demonstrated a tie-up between socioeconomic level, complications of pregnancy and parturition, and psychological disorders of the offspring. In a series of studies on large samples of whites and Negroes in Baltimore, these investigators showed that various prenatal and paranatal disorders are significantly related to the occurrence of mental defect and psychiatric disorders in the child. An important source of such irregularities in the process of childbearing and birth is to be found in deficiencies of maternal diet and in other conditions associated with low socioeconomic status. An analysis of the data did in fact reveal a much higher frequency of all such medical complications in lower than in higher socioeconomic levels, and a higher frequency among Negroes than among whites.

Direct evidence of the influence of prenatal nutritional factors upon subsequent intellectual development is to be found in a recent, well-controlled experiment by Harrell et al.[16] The subjects were pregnant women in low-income groups, whose normal diets were generally quite deficient. A dietary supplement was administered to some of these women during pregnancy and lactation, while an equated control group received placebos. When tested at the ages of three and four years, the offspring of the experimental group obtained a significantly higher mean IQ than did the offspring of the controls.

Mention should also be made of animal experiments on the effects of such factors as prenatal radiation and neonatal asphyxia upon cerebral anomalies as well as upon subsequent behavior development. These experimental studies merge imperceptibly into the fourth approach to be considered, namely, the investigation of the influence of early experience upon the eventual behavioral characteristics of animals. Research in this area has been accumulating at a rapid rate. In 1954, Beach and Jaynes[8] surveyed this literature for the *Psychological Bulletin,* listing over 130 references. Several new studies have appeared since that date.[e.g., 14, 21, 24, 25, 35] The variety of factors covered ranges from the type and quantity of available food to the extent of contact with human culture. A large number of experiments have been concerned with various forms of sensory deprivation and with diminished opportunities for motor exercise. Effects have been observed in many kinds of animals and in almost all aspects of behavior, including perceptual responses, motor activity, learning, emotionality, and social reactions.

In their review, Beach and Jaynes pointed out that research in this area has been stimulated by at least four distinct theoretical interests. Some studies were motivated by the traditional concern with the relative contribution of maturation and learning to behavior development. Others were designed in an effort to test certain psychoanalytic theories regarding infantile experiences, as illustrated by studies which limited the feeding responses of young animals. A third relevant influence is to be found in the work of the European biologist Lorenz[23] on early social stimulation of birds, and in particular on the special type of learning for which the term "imprinting" has been coined. A relatively large number of recent studies have centered around Hebb's[17] theory regarding the importance of early perceptual experiences upon subsequent performance in learning situations. All this research represents a rapidly growing and promising attack on the *modus operandi* of specific environmental factors.

The human counterpart of these animal studies may be found in the comparative investigation of child-rearing practices in different cultures and sub-cultures. This represents the fifth approach in our list. An outstanding example of such a study is that by Whiting and Child,[38] published in 1953. Utilizing data on 75 primitive societies from the Cross-Cultural Files of the Yale Institute of Human Relations, these investigators set out to test a number of hypotheses regarding the relationships between child-rearing practices and personality development. This analysis was followed up by field observations in five cultures, the results of which have not yet been reported.[cf.37]

Within our own culture, similar surveys have been concerned with the diverse psychological environments provided by different social classes.[11] Of particular interest are the study by Williams and Scott[39] on the association between socio-economic level, permissiveness, and motor development among Negro children, and the exploratory research by Milner[26] on the relationship between reading readiness in first-grade children and patterns of parent-child interaction. Milner found that upon school entrance the lower-class child seems to lack chiefly two advantages enjoyed by the middle-class child. The first is described as "a warm positive family atmosphere or adult-relationship pattern which is more and more being recognized as a motivational prerequisite of any kind of adult-controlled learning." The lower-class children in Milner's study perceived adults as predominantly hostile. The second advantage is an extensive opportunity to interact verbally with adults in the family. The latter point is illustrated by parental attitudes toward meal-time conversation, lower-class parents tending to inhibit and discourage such conversation, while middle-class parents encourage it.

Most traditional studies on child-rearing practices have been designed in terms of a psychoanalytic orientation. There is need for more data pertaining to other types of hypotheses. Findings such as those of Milner on opportunities for verbalization and the resulting effects upon reading readiness represent a step in this direction. Another possible source of future data is the application of the intensive observational techniques of psychological ecology developed by Barker and Wright[7] to widely diverse socioeconomic groups.

A sixth major approach involves research on the previously cited somatopsychological relationships.[6] To date, little direct information is available on the precise operation of this class of factors in psychological development. The multiplicty of ways in which physical traits—whether hereditary or environmental in origin—may influence behavior thus offers a relatively unexplored field for future study.

The seventh and final approach to be considered represents an adaptation of traditional twin studies. From the standpoint of the question "How?" there is need for closer coordination between the usual data on twin resemblance and observations of the family interactions of twins. Available data already suggest, for example, that closeness of contact and extent of environmental similarity are greater in the case of monozygotic than in the case of dizygotic twins.[cf.2] Information on the social reactions of twins toward each other and the specialization of roles is likewise of interest.[2] Especially useful would be longitudinal studies of twins, beginning in early infancy and following the subjects through school age. The operation of differential environmental pressures, the development of specialized roles, and other environmental influences could thus be more clearly identified and correlated with intellectual and personality changes in the growing twins.

Parenthetically, I should like to add a remark about the traditional applications of the twin method, in which persons in different degrees of hereditary and environmental relationships to each other are simply compared for behavioral similarity. In these studies, attention has been focused principally upon the amount of resemblance of monozygotic as contrasted to dizygotic twins. Yet such a comparison is particularly difficult to interpret because of the many subtle differences in the environmental situations of the two types of twins. A more fruitful comparison would seem to be that between dizygotic twins and siblings, for whom the hereditary similarity is known to be the same. In Kallmann's monumental research on psychiatric disorders among twins,[20] for example, one of the most convincing bits of evidence for the operation of hereditary factors in schizophrenia is the fact that the degrees of concordance for dizygotic twins and for siblings were practially identical. In contrast, it will be recalled that in intelligence test scores dizygotic twins resemble each other much more closely than do siblings—a finding which reveals the influence of environmental factors in intellectual development.

SUMMARY

The heredity-environment problem is still very much alive. Its viability is assured by the gradual replacement of the questions, "Which one?" and "How much?" by the more basic and appropriate question, "How?" Hereditary influences—as well as environmental factors of an organic nature —vary along a "continuum of indirectness." The more indirect their connection with behavior, the wider will be the range of variation of possible outcomes. One extreme of the continuum of indirectness may be illustrated by brain damage leading to mental deficiency; the other extreme, by physical characteristics associated with social stereotypes. Examples of factors falling at intermediate points include deafness, physical diseases, and motor disorders. Those environmental factors which act directly upon behavior can be ordered along a continuum of breadth or permanence of effect, as exemplified by social class membership, amount of formal schooling, language handicap, and familiarity with specific test items.

Several current lines of research offer promising techniques for exploring the *modus operandi* of hereditary and environmental factors. Outstanding among them are investigations of: (a) hereditary conditions which underlie behavioral differences between selectively bred groups of animals; (b) relations between physiological variables and individual differences in behavior, especially in the case of pathological deviations; (c) role of prenatal physiological factors in behavior development; (d) influence of early experience upon eventual behavioral characteristics; (e) cultural differences in child-rearing practices in relation to intellectual and emotional development; (f) mechanisms of somatopsychological relationships; and (g) psychological development of twins from infancy to maturity, together with observations of their social environment. Such approaches are extremely varied with regard to subjects employed, nature of psychological functions studied, and specific experimental procedures followed. But it is just such heterogeneity of methodology that is demanded by the wide diversity of ways in which hereditary and environmental factors interact in behavior development.

REFERENCES

1. Anastasi, A.: Psychological Testing. 2nd Ed. New York, Macmillan, 1961.
2. Anastasi, A.: Differential Psychology. 3rd Ed. New York, Macmillan, 1958.
3. Anastasi, A., and Cordova, F. A.: Some effects of bilingualism upon the intelligence test performance of Puerto Rican children in New York City. J. Educ. Psychol. *44:*1–19. (1953).
4. Anastasi, A., and Foley, J. P., Jr.: A proposed reorientation in the heredity-environment controversy. Psychol. Rev. *55:*239–249 (1948).
5. Arsenian, S.: Bilingualism in the post-war world. Psychol. Bull. *42:*65–86 (1945).
6. Barker, R. G., Wright, B. A., Myerson, L., and Gonick, M. R.: Adjustment to physical handicap and illness: A survey of the social psychology of physique and disability. Soc. Sci. Res. Council Bull. *55* (Rev.) (1953).
7. Barker, R. G., and Wright, H. F.: Midwest and Its Children: The Psychological Ecology of an American Town. Evanston, Ill., Row, Peterson, 1955.
8. Beach, F. A., and Jaynes, J.: Effects of early experience upon the behavior of animals, Psychol. Bull. *51:*239–263 (1954).
9. Brackbill, G. A.: Studies of brain dysfunction in schizophrenia. Psychol. Bull. *53:*210–226 (1956).
10. Darcy, N. T.: A review of the literature on the effects of bilingualism upon the measurement of intelligence. J. Genet. Psychol. *82:*21–57 (1953).
11. Davis, A., and Havighurst, R. J.: Social class and color differences in child rearing. Am. Sociol. Rev. *11:*698–710 (1946).
12. Dobzhansky, T.: The genetic nature of differences among men. In Persons, S. (ed.): Evolu-

tionary Thought in America. New Haven, Connecticut, Yale University Press, 1950, pp. 86–155.

13. Dobzhansky, T.: Heredity, environment, and evolution. Science. *111:*161–166 (1950).

14. Forgus, R. H.: The effect of early perceptual learning on the behavioral organization of adult rats. J. Comp. Physiol. Psychol. *47:*331–336 (1954).

15. Haldane, J. B. S.: Heredity and Politics. New York, Norton, 1938.

16. Harrell, R. F., Woodyard, E., and Gates, A. I.: The Effect of Mothers' Diets on the Intelligence of the Offspring. New York, Bureau of Publications, Teachers College, Columbia University, 1955.

17. Hebb, D. O.: The Organization of Behavior. New York, Wiley, 1949.

18. Hirsch, J., and Tryon, R. C.: Mass screening and reliable individual measurement in the experimental behavior genetics of lower organisms. Psychol. Bull. *53:*402–410 (1956).

19. Horwitt, M. K.: Fact and artifact in the biology of schizophrenia. Science *124:*429–430 (1956).

20. Kallmann, F. J.: Heredity in Health and Mental Disorder: Principles of Psychiatric Genetics in the Light of Comparative Twin Studies. New York, Norton, 1953.

21. King, J. A., and Gurney, N. L.: Effect of early social experience on adult aggressive behavior in C57BL10 mice. J. Comp. Physiol. Psychol. *47:*326–330 (1954).

22. Loevinger, J.: On the proportional contributions of differences in nature and in nurture to differences in intelligence. Psychol. Bull. *40:*725–756 (1943).

23. Lorenz, K.: Der Kumpan in der Umwelt des Vogels. Der Artgenosse als auslösendes Moment sozialer Verhaltungsweisen. J. Ornitholigie Leipzig, 289–413.

24. Luchins, A. S., and Forgus, R. H.: The effect of differential postweaning environment on the rigidity of an animal's behavior. J. Genet. Psychol. *86:*51–58 (1955).

25. Melzack, R.: The genesis of emotional behavior: an experimental study of the dog. J. Comp. Physiol. Psychol. *47:*166–168 (1954).

26. Milner, E.: A study of the relationships between reading readiness in grade one school-children and patterns of parent-child interaction. Child Dev. *22:*95–112 (1951).

27. Pasamanick, B., Knobloch, H., and Lilienfeld, A. M.: Socioeconomic status and some precursors of neuropsychiatric disorder. Am. J. Orthopsychiatry *26:*594–601 (1956).

28. Schwesinger, G. C.: Heredity and Environment. New York, Macmillan, 1933.

29. Scott, J. P., and Charles, M. S.: Some problems of heredity and social behavior. J. Gen. Psychol. *48:*209–230 (1953).

30. Scott, J. P., and Fuller, J. L.: Research on genetics and social behavior at the Roscoe B. Jackson Memorial Laboratory, 1946–1951—A progress report. J. Hered. *42:*191–197 (1951).

31. Searle, L. V.: The organization of hereditary maze-brightness and maze-dullness. Genet. Psychol. Monogr. *39:*279–325 (1949).

32. Snyder, L. H.: The genetic approach to human individuality. Sci. Monthly *68:*165–171 (1949).

33. Snyder, L. H., and David, P. R.: The Principles of Heredity. 5th Ed. Boston, D. C. Health, 1957.

34. Spoerl, D. T.: Bilinguality and emotional adjustment. J. Abnorm. Soc. Psychol. *38:*37–57 (1943).

35. Thompson, W. R., and Melzack, R.: Early environment. Sci. Am. *194*(1):38–42 (1956).

36. Tryon, R. C.: Genetic differences in maze-learning ability in rats. Yearbook National Social Studies Educ. *39:*Part I, 111–119 (1940).

37. Whiting, J. W. M., et al.: Field Guide for a Study of Socialization in Five Societies. Cambridge, Massachusetts, Harvard University (mimeograph).

38. Whiting, J. W. M., and Child, I. L.: Child Training and Personality: A Cross-Cultural Study. New Haven, Connecticut, Yale University Press, 1953.

39. Williams, J. R., and Scott, R. B.: Growth and development of Negro infants: IV. Motor development and its relationship to child rearing practices in two groups of Negro infants. Child Dev. *24:*103–121 (1953).

40. Woodworth, R. S.: Heredity and environment: a critical survey of recently published material on twins and foster children. Soc. Sci. Res. Council Bull. (1941).

8   Conceptual Problems in Relating Brain and Behavior

Leon Eisenberg

Each of the previous speakers at this morning's symposium has made experimental contributions to the exploration of the central nervous system. The inclusion of a mere clinician in this distinguished assemblage calls for some justification. If there be any, perhaps it lies in having a representative of the working audience participate from the platform, an orthopsychiatric everyman who might endeavor, in a tentative way, to view the biologic data from the vantage point of clinical practice.

Indeed, only if the findings of the laboratory can be incorporated into our thinking about patients are we likely to remember them for long. Purely academic studies may excite the intellectually adventuresome clinician. If they remain compartmentalized in a neat box labeled "basic science," they cannot fail to wither. When, a few years ago, I undertook to study for speciality certification, I acquired a respectable knowledge of formal neuroanatomy. The task was by no means a chore; it afforded aesthetic as well as intellectual delight, as any who have viewed Adolf Meyer's exquisitely stained brain sections will agree. Yet, but a few months later, what had been so diligently acquired had, to my dismay, largely effloresced, as imperceptibly as water from a crystal. Why? Apart from the fraility of a pedestrian memory, the explanation was to be found all too clearly in the lack of a frame of reference adequate to relate anatomic and physiologic facts to the concerns of daily practice. It was the search for this very conceptual framework that led to the suggestion of today's symposium, since I had reason to suppose that my distress was not unique. So much, then, for an Apologia.

The dilemma is not a new one. The relation between brain and mind concerned the ancient Greek philosophers. The gladiators and the battlegrounds have changed with the centuries, but the contending camps have continued to align themselves behind the selfsame banners of materialism and idealism. To the Ionian philosopher-scientists, mind resulted from the dance of atoms. This monistic view was shattered by Plato when he introduced the distinction between sensation and object. From his idealist and theocratic viewpoint, ideas could not be abstraction from their imperfect materialization in matter, but had to be immanent in mind. Knowledge of the true and the good was to be sought within, by recourse, to logic and reason, not by crude experiment. And how were the materialists to avoid the deterministic dilemma? People behaved as though they had a choice in what they did; indeed, ethics were only meaningful if choice was postulated. Lucretius, the faithful expositor of Epicurean materialism, sought a way out of the mechanistic universe through the doctrine of *clinamen* or swerve, a deviation from the atom's predestined course, in order to account for man's free will. But the nagging question was not to be so naïvely stilled.

Skipping a millenium and three quarters, we come upon Descartes trying to salvage the body from the theologians as an object of scientific study. In the corporeal automaton, where was there room for nonmaterial mind? He supposed that the nonextensible soul occupied a geometer's

Eisenberg, L.: Conceptual problems in relating brain and behavior. Am. J. Orthopsychiatry. *30:*37-48 (1960).

point in space. This he localized, elegantly enough, in the pineal body, unique in its central position in brain; soul now could influence body, free of somatic domination. The Cartesian dichotomy remains with us; witness the term psychosomatic with is conceptual pineal bridge.

Over the same span of time, the physician, less concerned with philosophic niceties, was daily confronted with the clinical fact that disease of the brain affected mental function. The Hippocratic physicians announced:

Men ought to know that from the brain, and from the brain only, arise our pleasures, joy, laughter, and jests, as well as our sorrows, grief, pain and tears. And by this, in a special manner, we get wisdom and knowledge, see and hear, and know what are foul and what fair, what bad and what good, and what sweet and what unsavory .... It is the same organ which makes us mad or delirious, inspires us with dread or fear by night or by day, and gives us dreams and untimely wandering, unsuitable cares, ignorance of present circumstances.... All these things we endure from the brain when it is not healthy. ....[1]

This Hippocratic dictum surely is, in itself, inadequate, though a progressive doctrine in its time. It epitomizes a point of view that Meyer termed the neurologizing trend in psychiatry. Can brain alone account for the differences in tongue, in habit, in values between one man and another? Man speaks only because he has fellows to whom he has something he must say; the symbols he employs are communal products. His behavior is comprehensible only in a social context, for which brain is a necessary but not a sufficient condition.

Moreover, Hippocrates' heroic affirmation was but a profession of faith. The complexity of human behavior far exceeded the subtlety of the brain models he or, for that matter, we could propose. I suspect that here has been one of the major stumbling blocks to the incorporation of physiologic data into psychologic theory. The analogy between the central nervous system and a telephone switchboard, on which most of us have been raised, left the necessity for a mentalistic demon, hermetically sealed in a pineal nose cone if you like, to plug in the proper connections. These A.T.&T. models were such inadequate objects of study as to foster the

development of psychologies of the empty organism. The CNS of the physiologist was far too crude to account for behavior. Besides, some argued, what difference did it make to the student of human behavior what went on under the calvarium? Could not the human organism be studied more profitably by the psychological engineer by prodding it with one or another stimulus and recording what ensued? Indeed, extremely useful data have been, and continue to be, accumulated in just such a fashion.

But, to physicians who concern themselves with restoring function when it is aberrant, it has always seemed germane to wonder what happened between stimulus and response, physiologically as well as psychologically. Would it not help to clarify the behavioral characteristics of the automobile to know what the motor is like? Agreed, I can drive a car without being a mechanic. But can I fix it?

We are in no danger of resolving the philosopher's dilemma. I urge only that, as physicians of the mind, we turn from metaphysical disputation to clinical issues. Confronted with disturbed behavior, we must, willy-nilly, try to understand its meaning. Conceptual clarification is necessary if we are to ask answerable questions.

The issue, for the clinician, is not whether brain and behavior are related, but how. Without the human brain, phylogenetically elaborated over hundreds of millenia, there could be no human behavior. Given the brain, however, the behavior of man is not sufficiently explained; it requires a social nexus. The central nervous system confers a multitude of potential behaviors. The actual behavior of a particular person is crystallized out of these multitudinous possibles during the highly specific ontogeny of individual experience, as the environment acts upon, and is in turn acted upon by, a particular central nervous system. It is not a question of heredity *or* experience, physiology *or* culture, but how much of the observed variance in specific behaviors is ascribable to each and how much to their interaction.

In a word, the biologic, social and psychologic levels of integration are phenomenologically distinct and have their own laws.[2] Each level of integration influences, and is influenced by, each other level. Psychologic phenomena are *not* reducible to biologic, any more than the behavior of an organism can be completely accounted for by summing the behavior of its individual cells. Once cells are joined in organs, and the organs in an organism, individual cell behavior, though still subject to the laws of cellular chemistry, is qualitatively altered by the group environment. Cells become "specialized"; that is, the products added, or the substrates removed, by other cells circumscribe the environment of the specialized cell in such a way that certain of its functions are augmented and the capacity for other functions may be totally lost. In turn, the new specialist exerts a reciprocal effect on its neighbors. New phenomena emerge when the now complete human organism interacts with the social fields of force. The potentialities are, to be sure, inherent in the physical structure but they do not manifest themselves until the group process supervenes. Social laws may entirely supersede individual dynamisms; the individual may sacrifice his life under the duress of social values, contrary to the biologic push for self-preservation. The emergence of such behavior would not be comprehensible from a study of neurophysiology alone, although the social forces will have produced detectable physiologic traces in the organism. The cause of the physiologic alterations remains inexplicable unless the investigator widens his horizons of study to include the social web in which the individual is imbedded. What we need to know are the "equations of transformation" which govern the translation from one level of integration to another; that is, from one set of phenomenologic coordinates to another.

This has been an overly long prologue to a discussion of contemporary neurophysiologic concepts. Yet it seemed necessary to make it clear that I do *not* regard behavior as solely explicable from physiologic study of what goes on inside the organism. Sociology and psychology are as vital as physiology for the comprehension of behavior; for the moment, I would agree

that they are of more immediate relevance to contemporary practice. I stress physiologic concepts because physiology is a discipline less familiar to our clinical thinking and one that can be ignored only at the price of an incomplete understanding of behavior.

One barrier to the acceptance of the classic physiologic models of the nervous system has been their static nature. The greatest neurophysiologist of all had focused upon the most stable characteristic of the nervous system, the reflex, as the basic unit of integration;[3] but, as Sherrington was to comment upon his own thesis, ". . . reflex action would go little way toward meeting the life of external relation of a horse or cat or dog, still less of ourselves."[4] Yet, beyond the temporary alteration in threshold that resulted from repetitive stimulation, the neurophysiologist had little to show for the consequences of previous experience in the central nervous system. Within the past decade, with Pavlovian methodology and refined electrical techniques, a vast revolution in the electrophysiology of learning has occurred. It has become possible to detect habituation and conditioning at so "elementary" a level as the cochlear nucleus.[5] Cortical rhythms have been shown to undergo major alterations under the influence of external driving, alterations which can be selectively conditioned.[6] Effects can be induced at initially indifferent cortical loci and can be inhibited at initially responsive areas.[7]

Still uncertain is the fundamental issue of where "closure" occurs. The decorticate preparation can be conditioned, but only in a crude, massive, and largely unadaptive fashion. Precision is only possible when cortical mechanisms are available.[8] It may nonetheless be true that cortex plays an increasingly less important role in a given task as it becomes progressively more automatized. That is, the more routine a task has become, the lower the centers capable of carrying it on, thus freeing the superordinate structures for new and more complex adaptations.

Of more immediate clinical interest may be the demonstration that a monkey with a discharging epileptogenic focus has great difficulty in establishing conditioned learning.[9] In the intervals between overt seizures, subliminal electrical storms, presumably by preempting cell groups necessary in learning, interfere with the conditioning process. This may account for the learning difficulties encountered by the poorly controlled epileptic.[9a] For precise adaptation, the organism must have available a multiplicity of channels.[10,11] for the simultaneous analysis of incoming information and the construction of appropriate behavior. If an irritable focus drives a significant number of cell groups into synchronous activity—activity which may have no clinical counterpart unless sensorimotor cortex is involved—then these cell groups, Gasser's "necessary internuncials," are simply unavailable for the transmission and integration of specific signals.[12] Hence, learning is impaired, just as if trauma or anesthesia had subtracted these cell groups.

The relations between cortical electrical activity and thought may be further illuminated by a clinical experiment. Efron[13,14] has reported a patient with uncinate fits who, upon perceiving the aura that signaled an impending seizure, was able to inhibit the evolution of the full seizure by inhaling a specific aroma. It may not seem remarkable that this inhibition was successfully transferred to a visual stimulus by classical conditioning methods. But the unity of body-mind is certainly apparent in the further finding that the patient became able to inhibit the fit after the aura had begun by *thinking* of the odor. The electrical correlates of the *idea* of the aroma were sufficient to block the abnormal discharge pathway, which otherwise would have seized control of cortex and have abolished consciousness.

The physiologic basis of consciousness itself has been reassessed as a result of the experimental studies of Magoun,[15] Moruzzi,[16] Bremer,[17] Penfield[18] and Jasper[19, 20] and the clinical reports of Cairns,[21,22] Brain[23] and others. The vast area known as the central reticular formation, centered in the brain stem but extending through thalamus to cortex, previously a little understood anatomic no-man's-land, has been shown to play a key role in relation to vigilance, attention and sleep. In this complex "system," better termed a system of systems, are located areas of facilitation and inhibition whose collaterals sweep up and down the neuraxis; its effects enhance or suppress activity from cortex to anterior horn cell. It modulates[24] the alerting or orienting response of Pavlov: the "readiness to respond" in the presence of novel stimuli from the environment.[25] It contributes to the background conditions necessary for learning through the focusing of attention selectively, a process in which appropriate cortical foci are put on the *qui vive* and areas irrelevant to the task inhibited.[26]

Sensory arousal from the electrical patterns of sleep has been shown to course through collaterals that leave the classic specific sensory pathways to terminate on cells of the "reticular activating system."[27,28] Cortical influences contribute specificity, for, in the encephale isole preparation, voice call results in "awakening" only so long as auditory cortex is intact.[17] The massive influence of the reticular formation has led to the term "nonspecific," but this fails to do justice to the precise sculpturing of three-dimensional electrical patterns coordinated in time sequences that are produced by reticular influences. Upon a single reticular cell impinge projections from peripheral, cerebellar, transreticular, and cortical sources;[16] thus, these cells constitute a uniquely placed neural mechanism for integration, as they express the algebraic sum of the excitatory and inhibitory influences sweeping over them. It would seem unwarranted to consider the reticular core as the "center of consciousness." As Bremer has stated, "A slackening of activity of any region of the brain must result in a lowering of excitatory state in areas or nuclei—including the reticular formation—with which the region in question has facilitating relationships, and so the whole of the synergic structures are gradually affected."[17] Whereas once the physiologist might have attempted to "localize" consciousness in cortex or, more recently, in reticular formation, it would now appear evident that consciousness is a physiologic state dependent upon the existing relations within the brain as a whole, though all areas are not equally prepotent. One might add that self-consciousness is a function of brain *and* environment as an interacting system.

A tentative basis for a physiologic carrier system for affect is emerging from studies on the phylogenetically ancient parts of the telencephalon. Anatomists had been confronted with the paradox that the rhinencephalon or olfactory brain continued to enlarge and elaborate complex interconnections in animals for whom smell had decreasing functional significance. Papez' intuition[29] that this system, more recently termed "limbic,"[30] might relate to emotion has proved extraordinarily fruitful. Nauta[31] has demonstrated major connections between the limbic lobe and nuclei interposed within reticular formation. Neuroanatomically, we have visualized for us reverberating long chain circuits within the limbic system which flow back and forth to neocortex, to hypothalamus and its endocrine satellites, and to midbrain activating centers. This provides an anatomic substrate for the clinical observations of aberrant attention, set and intellectual function in the presence of strong affect. Controversy still rages about the hierarchy of control over affective discharge. Is the rage induced by hypothalamic[32] or limbic stimulation "sham" or "real"?[33,pp.101-103] On clinical grounds, I would argue for the primacy of the cortical analyzer in normal man. The task of cortex lies in the assessment of the significance of complex environmental stimuli. It is the *meaning to the organism* that triggers the executive mechanisms of emotional display. In brain damage, severance of suppressor pathways may permit lower centers to fire with reckless disregard of cortical perception.[34] In neurosis, the pathologic affective charge assigned to the stimulus and stored in memory may interrupt orderly cortical analysis. But, however the hierarchy be established, the intimate interdependence between old and new brain demonstrated by the physiologist demands of the clinician a reexamination of ancient distinctions between cognition, conation and affect as compartmentalized psychic functions.[35]

Physiologic speculations from antiquity to the present have been circumscribed by contemporaneous anatomic models.[36] Psychologic speculations have been molded by available hypotheses in the physical and physiologic sciences. Freud's formulations on the pleasure principle and libido theory had their roots in nineteenth-century physics and physiology.[37] Pleasure was interpreted as the cessation of discomfort rather than as a positive state in itself, for which no physiologic basis seemed to exist. This constitutes a logical parallel to the search for constancy of the internal environment, Claude Bernard's inspired contribution to physiology. This has been the core of need reduction theories in psychology. Yet, it has become increasingly difficult to rationalize all of behavior within the framework of a theory that had the organism seeking only to avoid discomfort. Freud found it necessary to invent the repetition compulsion and the death instinct as *ad hoc* constructs.

It may be that the physiologic psychologist has come to our rescue with the discovery of what may be "pleasure centers" within the brain, though the evidence is far from conclusive on this issue. Olds and Milner[38] were the first to report that animals are rewarded by self-administered electrical stimulation of brain areas. Reward in this instance is operationally defined by the observation that the animal will seek to repeat the experience, at prodigious rates of activity,[39] even in the face of hunger, the need to traverse painful electrical grids, or the warning of impending shock to be delivered to the body, a warning which inhibits lever-pressing for food but not for brain reward. Miller[40] has extended the findings to indicate that the same stimulus which is avidly sought loses its "reward" as it continues and will be turned off by the animal who then again turns it on. Olds[41] has mapped the brain by his method and has found many areas with rewarding value, fewer with aversive effects, and others that are neutral. Moreover, he has found correlations between hunger, sex, and certain of the reward centers; strikingly, tranquilizing drugs affect these areas differentially.[41]

Are these, indeed, "pleasure" centers? The attribution of pleasure or pain to the psychic experience of animals is risky; the evidence from human experimentation is as yet inconclusive. Certainly, the predominance of unpleasant over pleasant features in epileptic aurae must give us pause,[42] though ecstatic states have been described.[43,pp. 258-259] Alternative explanations for the self-stimulation experiments are not difficult to construct. But classic theory has been struck a body blow. Desire, zest and adventure may have reentered psychology from physiology!

A final comment may serve to illustrate the convergence of physiologic and psychologic data to highlight the dynamic interaction between brain, mind and environment. Classic anatomic schemata have been limited to depicting the brain as the passive target of incoming stimuli, filtered only by the intrinsic qualities of the peripheral receptors. Recent experimental studies[44-48] have necessitated a drastic revision of this view of the central nervous system as the faithful but uncreative follower of what is fed into it. The brain, it is now clear, far from merely sounding to the sensory tunes played upon its end organs, in fact orchestrates its own intake. Centrifugal pathways to peripheral receptors and to sensory synaptic relays have been demonstrated, pathways which are capable of controlling the sensitivity of the receptors themselves and the amplitude of the impulses transmitted along sensory channels. The "central excitatory state," though responsive to the stimuli impinging upon the organism, in itself determines from moment to moment whether, how and in what pattern incoming messages are registered. At the same time, clinical experiments[49-51] have indicated that significant derangements of central function occur when the human organism is isolated from the kaleidoscopic patterns of sensory stimulation ordinarily encountered. The normal subject, deprived of variations in sight, sound and touch during an acute experiment, may show decrements in intellectual performance and may experience hallucinations. Normal mental function is evidently far more tenuous than previously suspected; like music, it must be continuously created; it emerges from the interaction between organism and environment. If we may reason from the sensory phenomena to social ones, there is in all this the suggestion that what we see in our patients is less explicable in terms of the past than we have been wont to consider. Contemporaneous reinforcement by social cues may account for much of what we take to be intrinsic consistency of personality molded by previous experience. This implies that, by emphasis on modification of current social environment rather than the uncovering of past memory traces, we may hope to alter disordered behavior.[52]

Taken together, the physiologic and psychologic lines of evidence lead to a considerably enriched conception of the relation between the central nervous sytem and its environment. Brain has been, on the one hand, freed of a parasitic dependence on the environment and, on the other, shown to be in obligatory symbiosis with it.

This has been, despite my original intention, a discursive presentation, with only fragmentary indications of the clinical relevance of the physiologic findings that have been so fascinating to me. It will have been successful only to the degree that it has aroused interest in studying the original literature and in approaching patients with the findings of the laboratory in mind. Such an orientation implies an enlarging of the frame of reference within which the meaning of disordered behavior is sought. Just as anatomic discoveries provide the spur for expanded physiologic generalizations, physiologic findings point to new directions for clinical theory. In turn, the clinical analysis of behavior pathology can continue to provide clues for the physiologist and anatomist.

We live in an exciting period of mental science. Studies pursued in isolation of one another are beginning to come together. This holds true for physiology itself as well as for its sister sciences. In the not too distant past, the neurophysiologist, in his endeavor to analyze unit activities, had limited himself to anesthetized or surgically mutilated preparations. The behaviorist, insisting that the adaptive aspects of behavior held the key to understanding, had focused upon the conscious organism in a laboratory or field environment and had disregarded the direct assessment of what went on inside the organism. Now, we find the neurophysiologist approaching the physiology of higher nervous activity with microelectrodes implanted in the waking brain while he manipulates the environment. The physiologic psychologist is no longer content to construct hypotheses about the central state in terms borrowed from physiology but endowed with special meanings.[53] From this marriage there have already emerged new conceptions of central function with immediate applicability to clinical problems. The very fact of today's symposium is an impressive indication of the search for a *rapproachement* between clinic and laboratory.

Perhaps you will permit me to close with a bit of poetry, chosen from an essay by Sir Charles Sherrington,[54] in which he portrays the awakening of brain, and with it, mind:

A Scheme of lines and nodal points, gathered together at one end into a great ravelled knot, the brain, and at the other trailing off to a sort of stalk, the spinal cord. Imagine activity in this shown by little points of light. Of these some stationary flash rhythmically, faster or slower. Others are travelling points streaming in serial lines at various speeds. The rhythmic stationary lights lie at the nodes. The nodes are both goals whither converge, and junctions whence diverge, the lines of travelling lights. . . .

Suppose we choose the hour of deep sleep. Then only in some sparse and out-of-the-way places are nodes flashing and trains of light points running. . . . The great knotted headpiece lies for the most part quite dark. . . . Occasionally at places in it lighted points flash or move but soon subside. Such lighted points and moving trains of lights are mainly far in the outskirts, and wink slowly and travel slowly. . . .

Should we continue to watch the scheme we should observe after a time an impressive change which suddenly accrues. In the great head end which had been mostly darkness spring up myriads of lights, as though activity from one of these local places suddenly spread far and wide. . . . The great topmost sheet of the mass, that where hardly a light had twinkled or moved, becomes now a sparkling field of rhythmic flashing points with trains of travelling sparks hurrying hither and thither. . . . It is as if the Milky Way entered upon some cosmic dance. Swiftly the head-mass becomes an enchanted loom where millions of flashing shuttles weave a dissolving pattern, always a meaningful pattern though never an abiding one; a shifting harmony of subpatterns. . . . The brain is waking and with it the mind is returning.

REFERENCES

1. Hippocrates: The sacred disease. Vol. XVII, pp. 1–16; cf. Jones, W. H. S.: Hippocrates. Vol. II. Cambridge, Mass., Harvard University Press, 1943.
2. Eisenberg, L.: Treatment of the emotionally disturbed pre-adolescent child. Proc. Child Res. Clin. Woods School. *35,* 30–41 (1953).
3. Sherrington, C.: The Integrative Action of the Nervous System. New York, Scribners, 1906.
4. Sherrington, C.: The Integrative Action of the Nervous System. New Haven, Conn., Yale University Press, 1947, Foreword, p. xvi.
5. Hernandez-Peon, R., et al: Modification of electric activity in cochlear nucleus during "attention" in unanesthetized cats. Science *123:*331 (1956).
6. John, E. R.: In Brazier, M. A. B. (ed.): The Central Nervous System and Behavior. New York, Josiah Macy, Jr., Foundation, 1959.
7. Morell, F.: In Brazier, M. A B. (ed.): The Central Nervous System and Behavior. New York, Josiah Macy, Jr., Foundation, 1959.
8. Gastaut, H.: Some aspects of the neurophysiological basis of conditioned reflexes and behavior. In Wolstenholme, G. E. W., and O'Connor, C. M. (eds.): Neurological Basis of Behavior. Boston, Little, Brown, 1958.
9. Morrell, F., et al.: Effect of focal epileptogenic lesions and their ablation upon conditioned electrical responses of the brain in the monkey. Electroenceph. Clin. Neurophysiol. *8:*217–236 (1956).
9a. Morrell, F.: Interseizure disturbances in focal epilepsy. Neurology *6:*327–344 (1956).
10. Lashley, K. S.: Brain Mechanisms and Intelligence: A Quantitative Study of Injuries to the Brain. Chicago, University of Chicago Press, 1929.
11. Wiener, N. S.: Cybernetics. New York, Wiley, 1948.
12. McCulloch, W. S., and Eisenberg, L.: Integrative aspects of the nervous system. In Basic Science Lectures. Washington, D.C., Walter Reed Army Research and Graduate School, 1949.
13. Efron, R.: The conditioned inhibition of uncinate fits. Brain *80:*251–262 (1957).
14. Efron, R.: The effect of olfactory stimuli in arresting uncinate fits. Brain *79:*267–281 (1956).

15. Magoun, H. W.: The ascending reticular activating system. Res. Publ. Ass. Res. Nerv. Ment. Dis. *30:*480–482 (1952).

16. Moruzzi, G.: Physiological properties of the brain stem reticular activating system. In Delafresnaye, J. F. (ed.): Brain Mechanisms and Consciousness. Sprinfield, Ill., Chalres C Thomas, 1954.

17. Bremer, F.: The neurophysiologic problem of sleep. In Delafresnaye, J. F. (ed.): Brain Mechanisms and Consciousness. Sprinfield, Ill., Charles C Thomas, 1954.

18. Penfield, W.: Epileptic automatism and the centrecephalic integrating system. Res. Publ. Ass. Res. Nerv. Ment. Dis. *30:*513–528 (1952).

19. Jasper, H. H., and Droogleever-Fortuyn, J.: Experimental studies on the functional anatomy of petit mal epilepsy. Res. Publ. Ass. Res. Nerv. Ment. Dis. *26:*272–298 (1947).

20. Jasper, H. H.: Diffuse projection systems: The integrative action of the thalamic reticular system. Electroenceph. Clin. Neurophysiol. *1:*405–419 (1949).

21. Cairns, H., et al.: Akinetic mutism with an epidermoid cyst of the third ventricle. Brain *64:*273–290 (1941)

22. Cairns, H.: Disturbances of consciousness with lesions of the brain stem and diencephalon. Brain *75:*109–146 (1952).

23. Brain, R.: The physiological basis of consciousness: A critical reivew. Brain. *81:*426–455 (1958).

24. Dell, P. C.: Some basic mechanisms of the translation of bodily needs into behavior. In Wolstezholme, G. E. W., and O'Connor, C. M. (eds.): Neurological Basis of Behavior. Boston, Little, Brown, 1958.

25. Pavlov, I. P.: Lectures on Conditioned Reflexes. Gantt, H. W. (trans.). New York, International Publishers, 1928.

26. Adrian, E. D.: The physiological basis of perception. In Delafresnaye, J. F. (ed.): Brain Mechanisms and Consciousness. Springfield, Ill., Charles C Thomas, 1954.

27. French, J. D., et al.: An activating system in brain stem of monkey. Arch. Neurol. Psychiatry *68:*577–590 (1952).

28. French, J. D.: An extra-lemniscal sensory system in the brain. Arch. Neurol. Psychiatry *69:*505–518 (1953).

29. Papez, J.: A proposed mechanism of emotion. Arch. Neurol. Psychiatry. *38:*725–743 (1937).

30. MacLean, P. D.: Some psychiatric implications of physiological studies on frontotemporal portions of limbic system (visceral brain). Electroenceph. Clin. Neurophysiol. *4:*407–418 (1952).

31. Nauta, W. J. H.: Hippocampal projections and related neural pathways and the mid-brain in the cat. Brain *81:*319–340 (1958).

32. Bard, P.: A diencephalic mechanism for the expression of rage with special reference to the sympathtic nervous system. Am. J. Physiol. *84:*490–513 (1928).

33. Masserman, J. H.: Principles of Dynamic Psychiatry. Philadelphia, W. B. Saunders Co., 1946.

34. Eisenberg, L.: Psychiatric implications of brain damage in children. Psychiat. Quart. *31:*72–92 (1951).

35. Eisenberg, L.: Emotional determinants of mental deficiency. Arch. Neurol. Psychiatry *80:*114–124 (1958).

36. Singer, C.: A Short History of Anatomy and Physiology from the Greeks to Harvey. New York, Dover, 1957.

37. Jones, E.: The Life and Work of Sigmund Freud. New York, Basic Books, Inc., 1953.

38. Olds, J., and Milner, P.: Positive reinforcement produced by electrical stimulation of septal area and other regions of rat brain. J. Comp. Physiol. Psychol. *47:*419–427 (1954).

39. Olds, J.: Self-stimulation of the brain. Science *127:*315–324 (1958).

40. Miller, N.: Experiments on motivation. Science *126:*1271–1278 (1957).

41. Olds, J.: Selective effects of drives and drugs on "reward" systems of the brain. In Wolstenholme, G. E. W., and O'Connor, C. M. (eds.): Neurological Basis of Behavior. Boston, Little, Brown, 1958.

42. Daly, D.: Ictal affect. Am. J. Psychiatry. *115:*97–108 (1958).

43. Dostoievsky, F.: The Idiot. Baltimore, Penguin Classics, 1955.

44. Granit, R., and Kaada, B. R.: Influence of stimulation of central nervous structures on muscle spindles in cat. Acta Physiol. Scand. *27:*130–160 (1952).

45. Granit, R.: Receptors and Sensory Perception. New Haven, Conn., Yale University Press, 1955.

46. Kuffler, S. W., and Hunt, C. C.: The mammalian small nerve fibres: A system for efferent nervous regulation of muscle spindle discharge. Res. Publ. Ass. Res. Nerv. Ment. Dis. *30:*24–47 (1952).

47. Walberg, F.: Corticofugal fibres to the nuclei of the dorsal columnis. Brain *80:*273–287 (1957).

48. Brodal, A., et al.: Corticofugal fibres to sensory trigeminal nuclei and nucleus of solitary tract. J. Comp. Neurol. *106:*527–555 (1956).

49. Hebb, D. O.: The mammal and his environment. Am. J. Psychiatry. *111:*826–831 (1955).

50. Lilly, J. C.: Mental effects of reduction of ordinary levels of physical stimuli on intact healthy persons. Psychiat. Res. Rep. *5:*1–9 (1956).

51. West, J. (Ed.): Symposium on hallucinations. A.A.A.S., in press.

52. Eisenberg, L., et al.: Diagnostic services for maladjusted foster children. Am. J. Orthopsychiatry *28:*750–763 (1958).

53. Konorski, J.: Trends in the development of physiology of the brain. J. Ment. Sci. *104:*1100–1110 (1958).

54. Sherrington, C.: Man on His Nature. New York, Doubleday, 1953.

9   A Biologist Examines the Mind and Behavior

Seymour S. Kety

I have given some thought to the question of whether, in an article such as this, it is better to present data or to discuss concepts, and have chosen to take the latter course. That is not entirely because the data are not so precise or so relevant as in some other fields; it is more because the knowledge of where to look, and how to look, and the meaning of what one finds may, in a field where the avenues to meaningful knowledge are uncertain or undiscovered, play a determining part in the productivity of men or movements.

It is no secret that psychiatry and behavioral science are such fields. There are well-ordered master plans in other branches of science, whose boulevards are already laid down, the trees pruned and the hedges clipped, and whose byways and alleys, even where they have not been broken through, have at least been indicated. In comparison with these, the territory of psychiatry and behavioral science is largely uncharted and unexplored, or spotted by primitive settlements trying to cut paths through the jungle between them. A creditable list of mental disorders have yielded their secrets to the pathologist or to the chemist, but the major psychoses taunt us today as they did the Hippocratic physicians.

It is easy to suppose, but difficult to demonstrate, that this state of affairs in psychiatry and behavioral science is to be ascribed to the ineptitude or indolence of its investigators, their lack of awareness of The Scientific Method, or their unwillingness to carry out research. A few direct encounters with some of the problems in the field are sufficient to convince one of the unparalleled intricacies of the nervous system and of the physical matrix which underlies behavior. If there is a more wonderfully complex structure in the universe, I do not know of it. One need not insist that psychiatry is not a branch of medicine to recognize that it is a superbly different one, nor deny the accomplishments and potentials of the physical sciences to recognize their limitations here.

PROMISE AND LIMITATIONS OF BIOLOGICAL SCIENCE

There are not many biological phenomena which tax the physicochemical complacency of the modern biochemist or biophysicist. The peculiar properties of protoplasm which formerly required the intervention of an *élan vital* seem almost comprehensible in terms of the versatilities of complex molecules; an understanding of the origin of life appears to have been made attainable through knowledge of viruses and bacteriophages which have filled the gulf between animate and inanimate matter, the deoxyribonucleic acid molecule appears capable of explaining genetic transmission, and concepts such as enzyme induction and biochemical specificity begin to provide models for the reduction of even the miracles of embryology to a self-determining series of physiocochemical events.

Machines are being built or can be designed which will evaluate and discriminate, learn from experience, and adapt to changing situations. No matter how complex each segment of human behavior, an electronic circuit can be designed to duplicate it, so that even though the cost in

Kety, S. S.: A Biologist examines the mind and behavior. Science.

resources and time would make such a construct unfeasible, the fact that physical models are conceivable does much to support what had previously been only a postulate of the mechanical basis of behavior.

THE PROBLEM OF CONSCIOUSNESS

There remains one biological phenomenon, more central to psychiatry and behavioral science than to other fields, for which there is no valid physicochemical model and (or so it seems to me) little likelihood of developing one; this is the phenomenon of consciousness—the complex of present sensations and the memory of past experiences which we call the mind.

When we look at the clear sky on a crisp autumn day, a remarkable sequence of physicochemical changes is set in motion, no less remarkable because it is commonplace. Today we can describe many of them, and we have every right to assume that some day we may be able to describe them all—from the light of a specific wavelength impinging on our retina, through the chemical and physical conversions there, to its emergence along the optic pathways as a series of specific signals in specific fibers. We shall trace these signals through the neuron pools in the great visual relay stations to certain portions of the visual cortex. We shall, I hope, someday be able to trace accompanying impulses through association pathways in the reticular system and in other areas of cortex, and if we are fortunate, we shall watch these ramifying impulses or their progeny converge in the motor centers of the brain in just the proper temporospatial arrangement to actuate the muscles which will say, "How blue the sky is today."

Where, pray, in that sequence is the sensation of blueness? It is neither wavelength, nor nerve impulse, nor spatial arrangement of impulses; it is not necessary to any of these processes and, though dependent on many of them, is explained or even described by none. It is richer and far more personal. One does not seem to get closer to its nature by increasing the complexity of its material counterpart—it is qualitatively and dimensionally different.

As I indicated above, a machine can be built to perform any function that a man can perform in terms of behavior, computation, or discrimination. Shall we ever know, however, what components to add or what complexity of circuitry to introduce in order to make it *feel*?

These are not new thoughts, and they were not new to Aristotle or Plato, nor to Spinoza, Leibnitz, Berkeley, Hobbs, or Mach, nor to the other dozens of great minds which contemplated them. Modern students of the nervous system, with all their knowledge of the mechanisms which may underlie consciousness, have been unable to explain it any more than did the philosophers who preceded them; some have, however, stated the problem quite cogently. Hughlings Jackson wrote: "We cannot understand how any conceivable arrangement of any sort of matter can give us mental states of any kind. . . . " C. Judson Herrick stated it more elegantly: ". . . . awareness is an intrinsic psychobiological event, self-centered and self-contained. It is a product of a bodily mechanism, but it must not be identified with the mechanism that makes it. It has an identity which is distinctive and unique, an identity with qualities which cannot be described in terms of the temporospatial relations of the mechanism employed." Sir Russel Brain has tried to come to grips with the problem by using the analogy of a pattern: "Not only are there twelve thousand million nerve cells out of which the patterns can be made, but nervous patterns exist in time, like a melody, as well as in space. If you look at a tapestry through a magnifying glass you will see the individual threads but not the pattern; if you stand away from it you will see the pattern but not the threads. My guess is that in the nervous system we are looking at the threads, while in the mind we perceive the patterns, and that one day we shall discover how the patterns are made of the threads." Fessard very succinctly spots the difficulty: "Momentary distributions or patterns of excitatory or inhibitory state . . . has been proposed . . . as the basis for conscious experience; but what makes a pattern 'conscious' of its own patterning remains an irritating problem."

But science has faced other "irritating problems" without becoming paralyzed, and scientists have treated the problem of consciousness in one manner or another which is satisfying to them and permits them to get on with their work. There are the materialists and their psychological counterparts, the behaviorists, who solve the problem of explaining consciousness by ignoring it or denying that it exists. Their ritualistic avoidance of what they call "mentalisms" and their clumsy and inappropriate use of "behavior" in those instances when they could more meaningfully say "sensation," or "feeling," or "consciousness" make their approach less satisfying than it otherwise might be, but none can deny its usefulness.

By emphasizing the objective and measurable aspects of psychiatry and the behavioral sciences, they have demonstrated their kinship with medicine and the natural sciences and have brought into them considerable rigor at the price of just a little rigidity. But in denying the existence or the importance of mental states merely because they are difficult to measure or because they cannot be directly observed in others is needlessly to restrict the field of the mental sciences and to curtail the opportunities for the discovery of new relationships. The remarkable hallucinogenic properties of lysergic acid diethylamide (LSD) are barely hinted at in behavior, and the behavioral disturbances in schizophrenia are a mere fragment of the entire picture. Nature is an elusive quarry, and it is foolhardy to pursue her with one eye closed and one foot hobbled.

Then there are the idealists and the extremists among them—the solipsists, who are so struck with the fundamental and undeniable reality of consciousness that they are led to deny any other existence than their own sensations, for they cannot conceive of what the material world would be like aside from them. It is possible and valid to construct an astronomy with the earth central and stationary; Aristotle showed that it was possible, and Einstein's theories supported its validity.

In the same way, the doctrine that my own consciousness creates and determines the universe is pleasant, if pretentious, and

quite unassailable. The real difficulty with egocentricity as with geocentricity is that it makes representation, comprehension, and prediction hopelessly complicated. The cosmogony, the physics, and the thermodynamics of a universe which is born each morning when I awake and annihilated when I fall asleep, which wobbles when I shake my head or have too much to drink, would make the complex equations of Ptolemaic astronomy a child's primer by comparison.

The glaring flaw in pure materialism and extreme idealism is that they are willing to entertain no inferences. And yet, science is born of inferences and thrives upon them. One may infer the existence of a universe of matter and energy outside of and quite independent of one's own consciousness and, by means of relatively simple generalizations called "laws of nature," render that universe and even consciousness itself more predictable and capable of description in parsimonious terms. One may also accept the direct and vivid testimony of the existence of one's own mental states and infer their existence in other beings similarly constructed.

Thus, one can acknowledge the existence of consciousness and of matter and energy without insisting that one must be reduced to the other. One can go further and study scientifically the relationships and correlations between them; one can without apology engage in a study of *psychopharmacology*, first describing the effects of drugs not only on behavior but also on mental state and then attempting to elucidate their actions on the brain. One can, as Penfield has done, study the particular sensations and mental states evoked from specific areas of the cortex; one can define a few of the correlates of sleep and attention in terms of the electroencephalogram or, as Evarts is doing, in the activity of single cortical neurons. One can seek the anatomical and pathological basis of coma and find that the regions essential for the maintenance of consciousness seem to lie in the brain stem. One can determine the metabolic requirements and the energy equivalence of consciousness.

This last function—the energy equivalent of consciousness—was vigorously speculated upon and pursued by the early materialists in the belief that its evaluation would somehow demonstrate that consciousness was a chemical process which adhered to the law of the conservation of matter and energy. Between 1945 and 1948, we were in the position of being able to make such measurements in conjunction with measurement of cerebral blood flow in normal, conscious young men. From these data the rate of energy utilization could be computed. Twenty watts provide the total power for the human brain—for all of its physicochemical processes, all of its thinking, all of its consciousness. What about the dependence of consciousness on the brain's power supply? If, as the result of circulatory insufficiency, substrate deficits, or derangements in metabolism, this continuous supply of energy becomes attenuated, consciousness begins to fail; the difference between full normal consciousness and the depths of coma is only a matter of seven or eight watts.

Now that we have an energy equivalent for thought (and it is a maximum figure, since the relevant processes may constitute only a small fraction of the total) I am not at all sure that this proves the physical nature of consciousness; what it does do, for me at least, is to demonstrate all the more what a remarkable mechanism the human brain is, which can correlate, discriminate, compute, effect behavior, and feel with such a trivial expenditure of energy.

By this time the biologist within me becomes impatient and says, "Enough of this prattle about consciousness, which I grant you exists, but which I can't dissect without losing it, and which I can never hope to understand. These are problems I worried about and resolved to my own satisfaction years ago. Let us talk about behavior, which is essentially nothing more than the contraction of muscles and the secretion of glands. That is the area which my physics and chemistry will someday understand quite completely."

THE MECHANISTIC VIEW OF LIFE AND BEHAVIOR

Most modern biologists enter their laboratories each day with an implicit assumption that the phenomena they are about to study are physical and chemical in nature and bound by the same laws which describe the behavior of matter and energy generally. This mechanistic treatment of life has had a long history, going back at least to Democritus. It was proclaimed heresy by the ecclesiasticism of the Middle Ages, to be reborn in the reaction of the Renaissance and nourished and invigorated by the materialism of the eighteenth century and beyond. But nowhere is the doctrine expressed more clearly than in the writings of Claude Bernard, the progenitor of modern physiology.

"In living bodies as in inorganic bodies, laws are immutable and the phenomena governed by these laws are bound to the conditions on which they exist by a necessary and absolute determinism . . . determinism in the conditions of vital phenomena should be one of the axioms of experimenting physicians. If they are thoroughly imbued with the truth of this principle, they will exclude all supernatural intervention from their explanations; they will have unshaken faith in the idea that fixed laws govern biological science. . . . Determinism thus becomes the foundation of all scientific progress and criticism."

Although I share this faith, I cannot avoid pointing out that it is in fact faith rather than proof which forms the basis of this Olympian generalization.

Of course, there have been arguments against mechanism, the most recent being based upon Heisenberg's principle of indeterminism, which rests upon our inability to study the motion of the tiny particles of which the world is constituted without disturbing them and harks back to Lucretius, who, with Epicurus, visualized atoms veering from their determined course "in uncertain position and indefinite time, by an amount so small as cannot be expressed . . . from which veering alone can come that freedom which is potent to subvert the bonds of fate, which alone need not follow the chain of cause on cause eternal." These arguments seem quite inapplicable. Those of Lucretius were based on the purest speculation, and even the Heisenberg principle, which is based upon the cold experience of modern physics, seems irrelevant. No mechanist ever expected to tally the position and motion of every particle in the universe, and being assured that one cannot do so is not much of a shock. It would seem that the concepts of freedom and purpose in the universe should be based upon nobler stuff than the clumsiness of our instruments.

The oldest argument against mechanism is the testimony of experience—we observe our will affecting our behavior in every moment of our waking lives. Against this the mechanist opposes a faith—but no demonstration—that the free choice was in fact an immutably determined event. Spinoza wrote, "Men think themselves free because they are conscious of their volitions and desires, but are ignorant of the causes by which they are led to wish and desire."

The modern mechanist can, moreover, correctly argue that no one has ventured to explain how a wish or desire in consciousness can move a muscle or activate a neuron. Clifford, who argued most convincingly for the reality of consciousness but also for its causal inefficacy, made this point: "the train of physical facts between the stimulus sent into . . . any one of our senses and the exertion which follows it and the train of physical facts which goes on in the train . . . these are perfectly complete physical trains and every step is fully accounted for by mechanical conditions. . . . If anybody says that the will influences matter, the statement is not untrue, it is nonsense. . . . It will be found excellent practice in the mental operations required by the doctrine to imagine a train, the forepart of which is an engine and three carriages linked with iron couplings, and the hindpart three other carriages linked with iron couplings: the bond between the two being made up of the feelings of amity subsisting between the stoker and the guard." And yet, even in classical Newtonian physics, we postulate and accept interactions for which there is no readily comprehensible model, explanation, or mechanism—for example, the gravitational "attraction" between two bodies across empty space.

Perhaps the most cogent argument for a mechanistic concept of the universe,

including animal and human behavior, is that is assumes and strives for predictability. And perhaps a need for predictability and a striving for it represent a primitive biological drive which the scientist in his laboratory shares with the young child or with the animal in the jungle, all of whom have learned that security in or mastery of their environments depends upon their ability to anticipate and predict its vicissitudes. Moreover, a mechanistic concept of the universe is heuristic. If productivity of a doctrine were the only proof necessary for its validity, the mechanistic concept would have been validated ten times over.

The mechanistic concept of behavior has sought and discovered a fascinating array of mechanisms which produce, determine, or modulate many aspects of behavior. The first two hundred years of the history of this search for a physiological basis of behavior was marked by a great debate over which was the organ of reason. The question appears to have been settled by the Hippocratic physicians who, around 400 B.C., wrote the final rebuttal of the Aristotelian notion that reason and feeling resided in the heart. I should like to quote their most succinct passage; even though it may have become quite familiar, its poetry and poignancy are nonetheless remarkable.

"And men should know that from nothing else but from the brain come joys, delights, laughter and jests, and sorrows, griefs, despondency and lamentations. And by this, in an especial manner, we acquire wisdom and knowledge, and see and hear and know what are foul and what are fair, what sweet and what unsavory. . . . And by the same organ we become mad and delirious and fears and terrors assail us, some by night and some by day, and dreams and untimely wanderings, and cares that are not suitable and ignorance of present circumstances, desuetude and unskillfulness. All these things we endure from the brain, when it is not healthy, but is more hot, more cold, more moist, or more dry than natural, or when it suffers any other preternatural and unusual affliction."

In the 23 centuries which have elapsed since those words were written, some progress has been made in postulating how the brain might perform certain of these functions and, to a more limited extent, in answering how in fact it does. Like the delusions of the paranoid psychotic, these designs for the brain have borrowed heavily from the technological developments of their times. We have seen first hydraulic, then mechanical, then crude electrical models of behavior. Cybernetics and computer and information theory, which in a sense emerged from efforts to understand the brain, have woven recently acquired anatomical and physiological information into a conceptual framework which electronics permits us to test in working models which perform useful functions.

CURRENT PHYSIOLOGICAL CONCEPTS OF BEHAVIOR MECHANISMS

Just as these electronic computers have tended to imitate the brain, so our concept of the nervous system has grown from what the computers have taught us. Instead of delineating a great sensory system and a great motor system feeding to and flowing from a massive memory and integrative system, one can view the nervous system as a decentralized organization of relatively autonomous functional units, each with its sensory, storage, and effector components and each with a built-in or acquired program.

Such systems could subserve practically all of our daily activities: standing, walking, shaving, driving our car, finding a parking space, pipetting, eating, playing the piano. A relatively small number, essential for immediate survival, such as breathing, sucking, and clasping, are probably laid down with the nervous system itself. Some are imprinted by early experience upon a genetically determined matrix, as exemplified in the lifelong postive tropism of the duckling for its mother but, equally, for any object which occupies its field of vision at a particular time after hatching. Some, such as sexual behavior, probably represent an acquired elaboration of an instinctive pattern. But many of the systems which mediate human behavior are experiential in origin, acquired by trial and error and by the persistence of the most successful or rewarding patterns.

There is remarkable economy in such a complex of semiautomatic sensory-motor programs to effect specific behavioral patterns. The cables actuating them can be relatively small, and the commands quite laconic, like "start; stop; slower; faster." These commands, in turn, can each be thought of as the result of a rigorous process of data reduction, whereby the tens of millions of impulses constantly pouring into the brain from all of the sensory receptors are sorted and compared against built-in or acquired master patterns to emerge as greatly condensed signals coded for destination and command or modulation.

These commands need not arise exclusively from the sensory systems; chemical changes arising from other regions of the body may operate at specific places to actuate appropriate sequences of behavior. Thus, dehydration sets off drinking by stimulation of specific osmoreceptors in the supraoptic nuclei of the hypothalamus, and certain of the sex steroids initiate appropriate sexual behavior in castrated animals when applied in infinitesimal amount directly to specific hypothalamic regions, and nowhere else. This study, reported only two years ago by Harris, Michael, and Scott, supports a remarkable speculation reached in 1905 by Freud: "We may now believe that in the interstitial tissues of the gonads special chemical substances are produced, which, when taken up in the bloodstream, charge definite parts of the central nervous sytem with sexual tension."

There is a further economy in the multiple utilization of the same component in many circuits. A network with a finite number of interstices may still provide an almost infinite number of separate pathways, and as the young brain is known to do, provide such pathways even after large segments are cut away.

Many have speculated that the cerebral cortex represents a great network where much of this storage, comparison, and coding occurs. The studies of Penfield who, by stimulation of the human cortex, is able to elicit crude sensations, or sometimes highly integrated memories of past experience, are compatible with such a function.

To this model of the nervous system there have been added, in recent years, the neurophysiological counterparts of attention and affect. The central reticular formation, rescued by Moruzzi and Magoun from the neglect which comes of ignorance, has been shown to have important relationships to sleep and wakefulness. This longitudinal network of short-branched interlacing neurons which taps the sensory systems and feeds into the motor outputs of other structures is strategically placed to intervene in the automaticity of the functional systems of which I spoke above. By selective facilitation, or by the inhibition of irrelevant activity, it can, so to speak, focus attention on a particular channel of sensory input or program of motor activity for the purpose of making and reinforcing new pathways. It appears that the anatomical substrate of consciousness resides here more than in any other place in the brain, not only because this seems reasonable but also because unconsciousness is most frequently associated with damage here. This remarkable ability to prevent the intrusion into consciousness of information irrelevant to the task in hand, which is so characteristic of alertness, appears to be accomplished through the reticular system not only by action at adjacent relay stations but also by newly elucidated sensory feedback systems which suppress the unwanted information at the peripheral receptors.

A system capable of representing affect or emotion is emerging from the imaginative speculations of Papez, substantiated by the functional studies of MacLean and the anatomical evidence of Nauta. The limbic system, corresponding to the rhinencephalon or olfactory brain, is richly connected with the reticular system, the neocortex, and, by way of the hypothalamus, modulates the endocrine and autonomic nervous systems. Specific areas of the hypothalamus which effect the release of the various trophic hormones of the pituitary have recently been elicited. Most interesting are the experiments of Olds and of others which suggest the presence of centers for reward as well as aversive centers in the brain. Animals with electrodes chronically implanted in various limbic areas and connected to a lever which, when pressed, will deliver a slight electrical stimulus will press the lever at extremely high rates, continuously for many hours. For the reward of stimulating these special areas, animals will run a maze or traverse an electrified grid with greater alacrity than will a hungry animal going after food. It is not unreasonable to suppose that such areas of affect enter into the sensory and motor programming circuits to facilitate or inhibit their establishment, and to compete for attention in terms of value to the animal.

GROWTH AND FLOURISHING OF NEUROCHEMISTRY

While the physics of the nervous system was being studied so productively by the neurophysiologists, an interest in its chemistry was developing, but much more slowly. Though derided by many of the powerful chemists of his day, Thudichum began a monumental program of extraction, purification, and analysis of the major chemical components of nervous tissue.

The next generation of neurochemists, influenced by the emphasis on cell respiration among the general biochemists, examined the energy metabolism of brain as exemplified by thin slices of that organ in a nutrient bath. Despite the liberties which they took with the functional integrity of their preparations, they learned a great deal about how the brain differed metabolically from muscle and liver: that the brain was the seat of a high metabolic rate; that its respiratory quotient was close to unity, indicating that carbohydrate was its main substrate for oxidation. These observations were later confirmed and extended in vivo, first in animals and finally in man. The latter studies, although they were, perforce, limited to the brain as a whole, had the unique advantage that all of the special features which characterize the function of that organ, including thought and consciousness, were preserved and could be correlated with cerebral oxygen consumption in normal man and in a variety of diseases.

In Table 9-1 are presented some of the data of my associates and myself, as well as those of others, relating the over-all oxygen consumption of the brain to presumed mental state. There is a rough progression downward in terms of the degree of interference with function, and it is clear that this interference with function is correlated with cerebral oxygen consumption. It is likely that these conditions have in common a primary interference with energy transfer in the brain, either through a circulatory embarrassment, which we know occurs in senile psychosis from concomitant cerebral blood flow measurement, or through some metabolic blockade, as with hypoglycemic, and possibly diabetic, coma, or by suppression of synaptic transfer of activity, as may occur in anesthesia. There is another condition, anxiety, whether endogenous or associated with epinephrine infusion, in which a significant increase in oxygen and energy utilization occurs (Table 9-2).

TABLE 9-1. CEREBRAL OXYGEN CONSUMPTION AND MENTAL STATE

Condition	Cerebral Oxygen Consumption (% of Normal)
Senile psychosis	82
Diabetic acidosis	82
Insulin hypoglycemia	79
Artificial hypothermia	67
Surgical anesthesia	64
Insulin coma	58
Diabetic coma	52
Alcoholic coma	49

But to me, the most interesting information contained in Table 9-2 is the finding that in a large group of mental states markedly different from normal there is no significant deviation in cerebral oxygen consumption. On the basis of the studies in sleep we were able to rule out the theory which attributed this state to the piling up of an unknown narcotic substance and to confirm certain neurophysiological interpretations. From the studies in schizophrenia we concluded that it requires just as much oxygen to think an irrational thought as to think a rational one. But we also derived some understanding along one

of the dimensions in which the brain is unique. "For it is neither a pump nor a motor and its current counterparts seem to be instruments of computation and communication. In such an instrument, although a defective power supply will produce dysfunction, meaningfulness of content and accuracy are by no means always correlated with the power used."

TABLE 9-2. CEREBRAL OXYGEN CONSUMPTION AND MENTAL STATE

Condition	Cerebral Oxygen Consumption (% of Normal or Control)
Normal sleep	97
Schizophrenia	100
LSD psychosis	101
Mental arithmetic	102
Anxiety	118
Epinephrine infusion	122

In recent years neurochemistry has moved into the large and challenging area which lies between oxidation and the specialized functions of the brain, and into another dimension which distinguishes the brain from every other organ—its magnificent organization. Some of our own studies on cerebral blood flow and metabolism have also moved toward the regional differentiation of these functions.

But regional neurochemistry has advanced far beyond oxidative metabolism. Lowry and his associates, by means of painstaking techniques by which it is possible to weigh individual neurons and analyze them for a variety of substrates and enzymes, are beginning to map the chemistry of the brain to its uttermost detail. In a number of laboratories a specific group of substances, the biogenic amines, have been demonstrated in relatively high concentrations and selectively distributed in the brain. The first of these to be studied was acetycholine, and in recent years, in staccato fashion, we have learned about norepinephrine, histamine, γ-aminobutyric acid, and serotinin.

Scientists at the National Institutes of Health, such as Brodie, Udenfriend, Axelrod, and their respective associates, have contributed much to our understanding of the distribution, synthesis and degradation, and pharmacological inter-relationships of these amines. The preferential distribution of some of them to the limbic system and the still crudely defined behavioral correlations of changes in their concentration in the brain suggest that they have important roles in behavior which remain to be defined. Udenfriend and his co-workers have shown that the enzyme for the synthesis of one of these amines, norepinephrine, exists in equal concentration in the caudate nucleus and in the adrenal medulla itself. It seems unlikely that these agents, pharmacologically active in other tissues, find themselves in the brain by sheer accident, and there is every reason to believe that neurochemistry, in association with precise psychological studies, will in the foreseeable future have a well-documented explanation of their presence in the brain.

The sensible and productive adolescence of neurochemistry portends a successful future, especially now that the earlier resistances of biochemistry to the field appear to be relaxing. That resistance was an interesting phenomenon and in marked contrast to the relationships of its parent discipline to neurophysiology. There were, of course, reasons for it.

The very origin of biochemistry from physiological chemistry—a handmaiden of clinical medicine—make it unduly defensive with respect to its interest in basic rather than applied research, forgetting all the while that biochemistry itself was an applied science, the application of chemistry to biology. But brain chemistry was looked upon as highly applied research—although I fail to see why the chemistry of neural transmission is less fundamental than the chemistry of fermentation or oxidation, or the chemistry of memory less interesting than chemical genetics. Then there was the doctrine of the "unity of biochemistry"—that all cells shared the same biochemical processes, so why gum up one's homogenizers with the mucky ointments of the brain when one could study bacteria. This doctrine, of course, emerged while biochemistry was pre-occupied with the common mechanisms for energy production by cells—oxidation

and phosphorylation—but it has always seemed to me like examining a tenement, the National Gallery of Art, and the White House, finding a furnace in the basement of each, and, without bothering to see what went on upstairs, declaring that they were all the same.

In a way this early provincialism served a useful purpose and perhaps contributed to the rich and rapid development of the field, and now that a point of diminishing returns appears to have been reached in the cataloging of enzymes and pathways of intermediary metabolism, biochemistry is moving upstairs, and the chemistry of differentiation and of genetics, chemical embryology, and even neurochemistry are becoming attractive areas. One can see a bright future in the study of the chemical processes in neural transmission—a work which has already begun; in the chemistry of memory, where interesting and heuristic hypotheses are being developed, centered on the coding possibilities which the protein molecule offers; in questions like neural specificity—how nerve fibers or neurons find their proper peripheral and central connections even when transplanted to unlikely places; and in the whole range of chemical processes in affect and behavior. For such work the biochemist will have to become interested in neurophysiology, in neuroanatomy, and in the behavioral sciences, and there is every indication that many are willing to do so.

So the sciences of biochemistry and biophysics have an assured and secure future in the study of the brain (and they were hardly waiting for me to point that out!). And if our assumption of the mechanistic nature of life and of behavior is correct, and man is nothing more than the most magnificent physicochemical engine which has ever been constructed, but an engine nevertheless, is it not obvious then that he or at least his behavior ought someday to be explained completely by physics and chemistry? If we believe that, and many do, then do not physics and chemistry and their sister biological sciences become the *real* sciences of behavior; while disciplines or bodies of knowledge and techniques like psychology, sociology, and psychoanalysis become merely empirical, descriptive, and derivative, to be tolerated as a sort of first-aid manual—what to do until the biophysicist or the biochemist arrives?

I should like to answer this question in the form of a parable; it is entitled "The True Nature of a Book."

THE TRUE NATURE OF A BOOK

Let us imagine a community with inhabitants who are of high intelligence and quite civilized except that they have never seen a book and have developed other means for the transmission of knowledge. One day a million books appear in their midst, an event which arouses so much curiosity and consternation that they decide to establish a scientific institute to study them. They set up this institute by disciplines and establish a policy that each scientist may examine these objects only with the tools and techniques and concepts of his discipline.

The first laboratory to be organized is the Laboratory of Anatomy. There the workers study these strange objects for a while, and their conclusion reads like this: "The specimen is a roughly rectangular block of material, covered ventrally and dorsally with two coarse, fibrous, encapsulated laminae approximately 3 millimeters thick. Between these lie several hundred white lamellae a fraction of a millimeter thick, all fastened at one end and mobile at the other. On closer inspection, these are found to contain a large number of black surface markings arranged in linear groupings in a highly complex manner."

By that time the chemists have appeared on the scene. The first chemist to get hold of a specimen burns it, and satisfies himself that it obeys the law of the conservation of matter and is therefore in his province; he may even compute the energy release per gram on complete oxidation. Next comes the analytical chemist, who discovers first its elementary composition but later breaks it down less completely into pure compounds; he also reports traces of elementary carbon, "which are probably impurities." Before I forget to mention it, one day a chemist accidentally drops a colored solution on one of the pages and by serendipity discovers paper chromatography, which lies around for 25 years before someone figures out what to do with it.

Then there are the biochemists, who slice the book and mince it and, best of all, homogenize it (because on the slices and the mince they can still see those black contaminants, while the homogenate can be centrifuged to remove them, permitting them to work with a Pure System). But all of these chemists have an uncomfortable feeling that though what they are doing is important, the real answers will come from the fellow down the hall who has just arrived and is still polishing his bright and expensive equipment—the molecular biologist.

With the self-confidence which comes from the adulation of the less fundamental sciences, he is anxious to begin work on the book he has selected because someone has told him that it is biased and distorted. Having hung a sign over his door which reads, "No twisted book without a twisted molecule," he proceeds to search for the molecule. By repeated extraction, centrifugation and ultracentrifugation, electrophoresis, hydrolysis, and repolymerization he finally isolates a pure substance, free of the carbon particles, and—what is even better—a macromolecule, and a twisted one at that.

Simultaneously, the physiologists have been attacking the subject. Unlike the biochemists, they have read the report from the anatomists and proceed to study and speculate upon why and how the pages are attached on one side. They study the movement of the pages as the book is riffled and derive complex equations to describe it. Then a biophysicist discovers that in an appropriate electrostatic field the graphite deposits produce discontinuities in potential. Fine microelectrodes are developed to pick these up, and amplifiers and oscilloscopes to display them. The biophysicists discover by sticking these electrodes into the book in various places that those which do not break off will pick up signals, some of which are reproducible.

They develop thousands of tracings of these signals and call in the cyberneticist to help uncode them. The signals are recorded on miles of magnetic tape and fed into huge computers. Excitement mounts when, in a particular region extending over a few millimeters in a certain book, one of them discovers on a particular day that, for a few minutes before he damaged the source of the signals, a tremendously complex pattern appeared which was reproducible but incomprehensible. This pattern is fed into the data reducers and the computers, which can generate and test thousands of hypotheses per minute. Finally, the electric typewriter begins to print; a meaning has been found in that complex pattern—it reads "THE."

By this time the behavioral scientists have been admitted to the institute and begin to study the problem. They are a strange lot. Some of them have read the reports of the anatomists, the chemists, and the physiologists, but many of them don't seem to care. Most will admit, if pressed, that the book is material in nature, that it obeys material laws, that it and its contents are nothing more than a highly specialized arrangement of chemical substances. But they don't slice the book, and they don't purify its chemical components—in fact, they seem to feel that it is improper to do so. Instead, they ask questions peculiar to their disciplines and look in the book for the answers. The first one likes to count, so he counts the number of letters in the words and comes up with a frequency distribution of the words by their length. He finds a preponderance of four-letter words, forms a hypothesis that the book is a modern novel, and ventures a prediction that it will be a best seller and also banned by the Postmaster General. Then he looks for particular words and counts them and confirms the hypothesis. His colleagues join him, asking other general questions and finding their answers in the content of the book. They learn a great deal about classes of books, how they differ from one another, and what their effects are on the community. Although the behavioral scientist has learned much about the nature of books—infinitely more, in certain areas,

than the physical scientist—his techniques falter in the area of the individual book, its characteristics, and his ability to make entirely reliable predictions about it. If it is important to learn something about the individual book, then there is need for a technique which can read it completely. Such a technique has not yet appeared, but some progress has been made in its development.

Finally, the book is brought in desperation to the psychoanalyst in the hope that he will be able to read it. That he does not do precisely, but instead asks the author to select portions and read them while he listens. Of course, the author is biased and reads what he wants to read, or, if there is "good transference," those passages which he thinks the analyst would like to hear. And the analyst himself doesn't always hear with equal acuity but, depending on his school or on his preconceived notions, is deaf to greater or lesser portions of the data.

Nonetheless, this anecdotal, biased, and selected patchwork may be the closest approximation which we have to the rich and almost inexhaustible fund of information which reposes in the individual human brain and, to a significant extent, determines individual behavior. Like all scientific methodologies this one was not born perfect and complete, and there are increasing numbers of analysts who recognize that. Many of the unavoidable biases in the data may not be all bad. To deal with all of the stored information would be impossible; some selection is clearly necessary, and there is some chance that the selection which the subject employs may have some relationship to the actual weightings of the data in his affect and behavior. Furthermore, this particular technique has been largely employed for therapeutic purposes, and clinical therapy in other branches of medicine has not always been characterized by the strictest adherence to scientific methodologies. There is increasing recognition of its unique values and limitations as an instrument of research, and its critical use in that connection by trained and qualified observers in a worth-while goal toward which perceptible progress is being made.

THE HIERARCHY OF THE
SCIENTIFIC DISCIPLINES

If I seem to have attached increasing values to the disciplines as I have enumerated them, I have done so only to counteract a hierarchical tendency in the opposite direction which I fear exists today. There are no higher or lower, better or worse, disciplines except with respect to their relevance to particular problems.

In the case of the brain, the biological disciplines have made and will continue to make remarkable progress toward understanding its structure, its metabolism, its functional interrelationships, and the mechanisms which underlie behavior, and they have solved or will solve those mental disorders which are primarily the result of disturbances there. But in the area of information, content, and experience, stored as it is in the complex interrelationships of 13 billion neurons, biology is extremely pretentious if it thinks that it can unravel them by means of its tools. There will, no doubt, someday be a biochemistry or a biophysics of memory—but not of memories.

Take the question of voting Republican or Democratic in a particular election. All of the experience and the biases and the motivation for doing one or the other are stored in the physical chemistry of the brain, but these cannot be reached by physics or chemistry. There are other, more appropriate, techniques for that.

But even in biochemistry, that approach is not the one always and uniquely adapted to yield truth, as DeWitt Stetten has so keenly pointed out: "Which of these many levels of disorganization is then to be recommended? The answer to this question is that unequivocal results as to what is happening in the intact mammal cannot be gleaned from studies conducted at any one level. Each level, considered separately, has led to unsatisfactory conclusions. We know of reactions catalyzed by isolated enzymes for which no counterpart in the intact animal has been discovered. We know of over-all conversions observed in the intact animal which have thus far defied study at subcellular levels and for which no enzymes have been unearthed. It is improper to hold that any one approach is in all cases superior to all others. Selection of level of disorganization, often in fact determined by the skills or prejudices of the individual investigator, should be based upon the nature of the specific question which is being asked." If this is true for metabolism, how much more true is it for behavior?

It has most certainly not been my intention to deny the tremendous importance and the major contributions which biochemistry and biophysics and the biological sciences generally have achieved within our lifetime. I have merely wanted to point out that we do not always get closer to the truth as we slice and homogenize and isolate—that what we gain in precision and in the rigorous control of variables we sometimes lose in relevance to normal function, and that, in the case of certain diseases or problems, the fundamental process may often be lost in the cutting. A Heifitz and a Rubinstein playing different sonatas at the same time will produce a cacophony which the most exhaustive study of either individually would never have revealed, and a truer picture of the nervous system and behavior will emerge only from its study by a variety of disciplines and techniques, each with its own virtues and its own peculiar limitations.

IV   BIOBEHAVIORAL ASPECTS OF BRAIN FUNCTIONING

Many aspects of the detailed structure and functional organization of the human brain are still unknown, forming a continuing puzzle that not only intrigues, but challenges the imagination and talents of scores of contemporary medical and behavioral scientists. Decades of work lie ahead before the intricate substrates that underlie behavior, emotion, and thought will be fully mapped. It is only within the realm of elementary sensory and motor functions that precise brain locales have been clearly identified. But sensory and motor regions compose but a small segment of that preeminent structure, the cerebral cortex. Activated in part by other brain structures, and transmitting its signals through myriad subcortical centers, the cortex is the hub of those highly developed capacities that distinguish man among the species. And it is here, within the cortex, where much of the mystery remains. As George W. Gray has described the cortex (1948):

> This roof brain is the supremely distinctive organ of the human species. What goes on within its network of cells makes the fundamental difference between man and brute. The functioning of the cerebral cortex not only distinguishes man from the animals, but more than any other faculty it distinguishes man from man. It marks the fateful difference between the meek follower and the dynamic leader, between the scholar and the artist, between the genius and the moron.
>
> If the proper study of mankind is man, surely the supreme biological interest of man is his brain, particularly the gray cortex of two billion cells without the orchestration of which "there can be no thought, no sweet sonnets of Shakespeare, no joy and no sorrow."

It is only in recent years that biobehavioral scientists have begun to decode such cortical processes as stimulus elaboration and information retrieval, as well the more elementary ways in which behavior and emotion are guided and integrated. As Eisenberg noted in his earlier essay, biobehavioral scientists no longer depict the brain as a passive target receiving and storing a barrage of incoming stimuli. We now know that it is not merely a faithful follower of what is fed into it from the environment. Not only does it maintain a rhythm and activity of its own, regardless of external stimulation, but it plays an active role in regulating the sensitivity, and in controlling the amplitude of what is picked up by the peripheral sense organs. Unlike a machine which passively responds to all sources of external stimulation, the brain has an orienting and directing function that determines substantially what, when and how events will be experienced. Each person's nervous system selects, transforms and registers the objective events of his life in accordance with distinctive biological sensitivities. Unusual sensitivities or gross abnormalities in this delicate orienting and selecting system can lead to marked distortions in perception and behavior. And any disturbance which produces a breakdown in the smooth integration of functions, or a failure to efficiently retrieve previously stored information, can create chaos and pathology.

The brain not only houses the higher centers of control and integration; it also contains the centers for such complex and diverse emotions as love and pleasure, and fear and pain. Until the past two decades, any serious scientist who thought that feelings could be stimulated directly by specific brain substrates would have been dismissed as foolish or naive, no more sophisticated than eighteenth century phrenologists with their crude notions. But in recent years there has been a spate of fascinating research that demonstrates the presence of relatively precise locales for activating a number of clearly differentiated emotions. Prompted by technical developments in fine needle electrodes which can be implanted within deeply recessed brain structures, numerous investigators have delineated specific anatomic regions underlying several emotional states. Caution is necessary, however, in interpreting these findings, as the editor has stated elsewhere (Millon, 1969):

> . . . psychological processes cannot be conceived as localized or fixed to one or another sphere of the brain. Rather, they arise from a network of interactions and feedbacks. All stimuli, whether generated externally or internally, follow long chains and reverberating circuits which modulate a wide range of other brain activities. Psychological functions must be conceived, therefore, as the product of a wide spread and self-regulating pattern of interneuronal stimulation.

Turning to the three articles of this chapter, Lawrence Kolb, author of a leading psychiatric text, provides a comprehensive review of the major concepts and findings researched in the past decade on brain-behavior relations. Ranging over topics such as information processing, arousal, sleep, and learning, his paper offers the reader a first-rate synopsis of current and ongoing work in the field.

Focusing more sharply on a single and specific biobehavioral phenomenon, the eminent neurosurgeon, Wilder Penfield, reports on his early and exciting encounter with the biophysical substrate of consciousness, a phenomenon that has for centuries been a most controversial topic among psychologists and philosophers. No one doubts that conscious self-awareness exists, but the question remains as to whether it can be categorized and measured scientifically. Penfield's work may serve as a foundation for empirical explorations of the concept.

Among the most intriguing studies of brain-behavior relations are those which derive from the laboratories of Roger Sperry, an eminent neuropsychological researcher. Like many other structures of the body, the brain is bilaterally symmetrical. Bands of neurons, known as commissures, interlace and connect regions making up the two halves of the cerebrum. Sperry has not only elucidated the important coordinating functions of the brain's commissural systems, but he has made the surprising discovery that when the commissures are cut, each hemisphere functions independently, that is, as if each were a complete brain. Studying hemisphere-deconnected neurologic patients, Sperry shows that the two halves exhibit slightly different functions. Most striking among his findings is that learning acquired in one hemisphere is not transferable to the other following deconnection.

REFERENCES

Gray, G. W.: The great ravelled knot. Sci. Am. *200:*10:66–79 (1948).
Millon, T.: Modern Psychopathology. Philadelphia, W. B. Saunders Co., 1969.

10.   The Brain and Behavior

Lawrence C. Kolb

The vast bulk of the earlier neurophysiologic studies have been directed on the one hand to examination of control of various systems or organs by the central nervous system and its spinal and peripheral extensions or systems, and on the other to examination of cognitive, perceptual, and volitional performances. Increasingly over the past two decades researchers have concentrated upon the structural-functional subsystems of the brain as they relate to behavior.

Inferences drawn from the study of clinical phenomena, commencing at the turn of the twentieth century, provided the impetus for the growth of physiology and behaviors and emotions which now has direct pertinence to functions significant in the daily living of the individual members of all species. Careful analysis of sequences or patterns of activity by ethologists and students of animal psychology, and their correlation with the activity of various portions of the nervous system as demonstrated during electrical or pharmacological stimulation or after ablations, have laid the groundwork for an expanding understanding of the dynamic structural-functional relationships within the nervous system which lead to arousal and execution of integrated goal-directed behaviors. Also, the empiric clinical discoveries of the powerful actions of the phenothiazines and, later, of the various antidepressant pharmaceuticals have stimulated much study. This study has in turn added to our capacity to formulate powerful new hypotheses of concern in understanding the process of synaptic transmission, particularly as related to the subsystems of the brain concerned with drives and affects.

By far the largest proportion of the observations on behavior and its relation to brain function reported in this chapter are derived from studies in animal species. Likewise, most of the hypotheses presented in this chapter are based on observations made by those whose principal concern is the study of nonhuman species. The extent to which one may extrapolate from the physiology of nonhuman species to that of man remains an open question. Yet those basic biological functions upon which the interest of neurophysiologists has focused are common to all species, including man. Furthermore, the majority of social drives recognized as essentially human are considered their derivatives. Finally, in the past there has been notable success in applying to human organ functioning the knowledge gained by physiologists from experimentation in animals. At best the information available today on brain function as it relates to behavior provides a structure for speculation upon the relationship between that function and its abnormal expressions in psychiatric disorder. At the least it has heuristic value.

The human brain differs from that of other mammalian species in the extent to which the cerebral cortex has expanded. Upon this growth rest the extensive cognitive functions of man: his capacities for language, elaborate communications systems, retention of information in memory, exquisitely discriminative and variable affective and conative sets, and the ability to solve problems and inquire. Man retains, however, the primitive brain structures found in subhuman species. Thus, the midbrain hypothalamic systems common to all vertebrates appear to control the regulating functions concerned with those

Kolb, L.: The Brain and behavior. In Kolb, L.: Modern Clinical Psychiatry. 8th Ed. Philadelphia, W. B. Saunders Co., 1973.

primary activities needed to sustain life: feeding, drinking, breathing, sexual activity, and thermal control. The limbic system, a paleocortical development, is conceived today to have emerged in the evolutionary process to function in connection with emotionally determined behaviors that MacLean hypothesizes are related principally to preservation of the self or the species. Thus, the human brain may be thought of as a hierarchical structure which, in effective functioning, demands the integration of each of the successively more complex systems extending from the hindbrain through the forebrain. Dysfunction at any level in the successively more complex structures and their interconnecting links, whether in the midbrain, the hypothalamus, the limbic system, or the various regions of the cortex, distorts behavior and in man may lead to symptoms impairing personality function.

Emotion is defined as those bodily processes and activities that are generated through threats to existence or frustration and delay in gratification of a drive state. These processes include the activation of organ systems by the involuntary nervous system as well as the associated subjective state denoted in psychiatry as an affect.

Direct attack induces the emotional states of rage or fear. Pain, hunger, and thirst, with their attendant drives and associated affects, may be regarded as primitive emotional states. Satiation of these needs—or expectation of satiation—leads to varying degrees of satisfaction or pleasure, another variety of affect with attendant emotional behavior. With the procreative drives (in man) painful and pleasurable emotional states are aroused in the seeking period, in copulatory and protective activities, and in the complexly organized rearing of the young characteristic of the mammalian species.

For the psychiatrist the most significant behaviors are those connected with the arousal of emotion, and particularly affect, and its variable modulation and control through a wide range of socially learned behavioral sequences. The mentally ill suffer as a consequence of their defective control of socially prohibited emotional expression, or their inept learning of defenses against it. Abnormalities in social functioning are seen in the senseless rages, the grotesque posturings, and the bizarre delusional and hallucinatory experiences of the psychotic, the seemingly irrational repetitions of the compulsive, or the sensorimotor inhibitions of the hysteric. In contrast to such behaviors there is the flexible and constructive expression of emotion displayed by those more fortunate in their growth and development. Owing to his development of a verbal communicative system, man alone of all the species is capable of reporting upon the variety of subjectively perceived affective states that attend the arousal of emotional behaviors. Tenderness and love, jealousy, anxiety, sadness and lonesomeness, guilt and shame, envy and hatred—all are shadings of the primitive affects of love, fear, and rage that may be defined only through the verbal reporting of the affective state in man: emotional states at best capable of inference in other mammalian forms.

Emotional behavior, then, is a complex organismal response to a perception of threat or of satiety. Such behavior represents a response to signals or cues sensed from either the internal or the external environment. Its expression may be examined in terms of the arousing percept, the goal-directed activity, or those associated subjective states capable of study only through man's verbal communications, his fantasy, and his thought. Thus, in man, one may examine the repetitive situations in which aggressive behavior occurs; the pattern of overt expression of aggressive behavior or its covert expressions in passivity and withdrawal, or, finally, the subjective accounts of perceived rage, jealousy, envy, fear, or anxiety that represent the many manifestations of human affect when the aggressive drive is stimulated.

Each emotional response varies quantitatively. The rage response may be intense or may be shown only through minor behavioral expression. The percept that calls out one emotion may be interrupted by another more prepotent for the organism's survival. Emotional behavior results from an infinity of triggering mechanisms: unfamiliar percepts, an inner awareness of lack of strength, a perceived threat. The same cause may produce differing reactions in the same subject at differing times. Each emotional state may be capable of expression in a number of behaviors. In the same subject these expressions change as the individual becomes habituated to the stimulating condition and learns different adaptations to the arousing stimulus situation.

ANALYSIS OF BEHAVIOR

For the understanding and evaluation of behavior one must comprehend not only the range and variety of pathological patterns but also the adaptive processes which maintain performance in the homeostatic state.

For the most part the physiological analyses of central nervous system function have been concerned with behaviors considered "instinctive." As defined by Tinbergen and other ethologists, instinctive behavior exists as innate hierarchically organized nervous mechanisms susceptible to certain priming, releasing, and directing impulses coming from both *within* and *without* the organism. In turn these mechanisms evince response by coordinated actions that contribute to the maintenance of the individual and the species. Such innate behavioral mechanisms are capable of discrimination in simpler vertebrate forms, as the stickleback fish or the herring gull. In mammalian forms, however, much of behavior is thought by animal psychologists to be derived from the innate drive states and learned. While the "instinctive" drives certainly exist in man, it is unknown whether innate stereotypes of behavior still exist. Because of the overriding importance of the learning capacity and opportunity inherent in the vast growth of the cerebral hemispheres and projected through the existing social systems, the analysis which might identify simple "instinctive" activity in man has as yet escaped accomplishment.

Study of submammalian species by ethologists has shown that in any sequence, whether it be to feed and relieve hunger, to find water and quench thirst, to obtain a mate and satisfy the sexual drive, or to progress through the successive states concerned with nuturing and preparing the young for independent growth, one may find "priming" and "releasing" mechanisms. The former consist of facilitating processes which build up the potential to act. Internally, the accumulation of appropriate hormonal agents sets the attention of the neuromuscular systems. The "releasing" mechanism initiates or triggers the sequence of acts which make up a coordinated series of behaviors leading to the achievement of the necessary goal. Such releasing mechanisms may come about by either the development of a certain intensity of tissue need or the perception of some stimuli in the environment facilitating the potential of the innate releasing mechanism.

In the sequence of behaviors considered instinctive the initial actions are "appetitive" or "exploratory"; they occur through the development of internal tensions. Following the preparatory appetitive and exploratory behaviors there follow the "consummatory" actions.

During the appetitive stage of a behavioral sequence, which may be very short or of prolonged duration, extending over days, the animal appears restless and agitated. Superficially, his actions sometimes appear aimless. He seems to have reserves of energy and strength, exposed in such aggressive actions as fighting to obtain food or gain a mate. Alertness to environmental stimuli is acute, and perceptual attentiveness is magnified toward those cues subserving the prepotent organismal goal, while sensitivity to other stimuli outside that urge is diminished. Organs concerned with the need demanding eventual gratification are placed in a state of readiness for functioning.

With the realization of the external goal—food, water, a sexual mate—there takes place the consummatory act, usually a stereotyped pattern of behavior. Satisfactory consummation is followed by a state of satiation accompanied by resting behavior, lessened alertness to and interest in the environment, and, as we know from man, a subjective state of satisfaction.

As the animal grows and records experience within his nervous system, his susceptibility to response through exposure to the releasing mechanisms is enhanced. Furthermore, the external releasing perceptions for particular behavior may assume a wider range of configurations or become more differentiated through learning processes. Without consummation for prolonged periods, actions directed toward certain goals may discharge spontaneously even though presentation of the external releasing stimulus has not taken place. Thus, it is apparent that innate behaviors constitute in themselves a sequence of complexly organized actions dependent upon the internal state of each organism and each species. Furthermore, such behaviors become subject to increasingly greater modifications through experience and learning according to the extent and the peculiar organization of the nervous system of the species. The components of a behavioral sequence may vary then in their capacity for arousal, in the intensity and complexity of response of the various perceptual motor components in appetitive, consummatory, and satiated states.

It seems from the analysis of behavioral sequences that the brain, as the integrative organ of each organism, must be so organized in all animal species as to assure sensitivity to environmental and internal stimuli, to effect arousal, with increased alertness and attentiveness, as well as rest and satiation. It must contain subsystems that establish the innate drives and in some species the stereotyped behaviors which take place without previous experience and learning. In other species there exist the cortical systems upon which the multivariate discrimination of sensory experiences develops as well as the encoding denoted as "memories" and upon which are based those highly discriminated learned patterns of perception, mediation, and action. From these derive the many flexible behavioral approaches available to man to serve his appetitive and consummatory drives.

INFORMATION PROCESSING

From the analytic descriptions of goal-seeking behavior as provided by ethologists, one must conceive of brain function in terms other than those offered earlier and derived from learning, theory and simple stimulus—response physiology. As an integrating organ, the brain must continuously process information registered upon the body from the exterior as well as the interior surfaces of the body, from the internal organ systems, and from its own structure. In this integrative process the brain utilizes systems which have laid down a record over time of past sensory experience and the recorded consequences of actions taken which succeeded or failed in goal-seeking or protective behavior. It must relate the incoming registrations to each other, collate them, and compare them with previous registrations.

The brain also serves a *mnestic function.* It must attend to those registrations that signal threat to the function of the organism as a whole or to any of its subsystems, and must determine the general or local response most likely to protect and preserve function. In carrying out the integrative and executive functions of the organism, brain subsystems sustain a constant watch to sense opportunity or threat and to attend to the stimulus. In so doing conscious percepts in man emerge from memories of the past.

So, too, in relation to the needs of the other major bodily systems concerned with energy processing and reproduction, man and other species, depending upon the selective needs deriving from the systems, variously attend to differing stimuli. When hungry, vigilance is intensified to cues indicating food. In man, only when the reproductive system has evolved to maturity is the brain alerted to attend to and enhance further behavior directed toward consummation with the sexual object.

AROUSAL AND SATIATION

The Reticular Activating System

Largely through the work of Magoun and his collaborators it is now recognized that within the central gray matter of the brain stem there exist cells with rich afferent and efferent connections with the spinal cord, hypothalamus, limbic system, and various areas of the cerebral cortex. Their activation is known to facilitate or inhibit the postural tonus of muscles throughout the body, to influence endocrine and visceral functions, and to be concerned as well with states of wakefulness, orienting, and attention. Thus stimulation of the cortico-parietal projections of the central reticular formations sets up the low-voltage frequencies in the electroencephalogram associated with states of attention and wakefulness. Similar behavior, with associated EEG patterns of arousal, follows stimulation in the sub and dorsal hypothalamus and the nonspecific thalamic nuclei as well as activation of the well-known specific afferent pathways in the brain stem. It appears from stimulation experiments in animals that arousal of the cortex may follow impulses reaching it from the midbrain by either of two routes: an extra-thalamic route, passing through the internal capsule from the subthalamic areas, or via the cortical projections of the nonspecific thalamic nuclei. Destruction of the central tegmental areas in animals leads to comatose behavior (high-voltage slow EEG patterns are seen in such states) even though the specific sensory pathways to the brain are intact, nor is it possible to bring about arousal even by the most intense stimulation thereafter.

That the reticular activating system is concerned with the modulations of consciousness and attention seems evident. Its activity now is known to be suppressed by general anesthetics, the barbiturates, the phenothiazines, reserpine, and other pharmacological agents. As we shall note in discussing innate alimentary, sexual, and aggressive behaviors, the electrical activity within the activating system is modified likewise by other metablic and endocrine imbalances.

ATTENTION AND VIGILANCE

The modifications of consciousness and attention to stimulations are not only dependent upon the afferent inflow to the midbrain activating system from the spinal and central sensory neurons but are also subject to "feedback" control from the cerebral cortex. Thus, electrical stimulation of diverse points in the cingulate, orbital, and lateral frontal areas, central and para-occipital areas, superior gyrus, and tip of the temporal lobe of the cortex leads to both augmentation and reduction of activity within the brain stem reticular system. It seems likely, then, that as facilitation of performance is brought about through cortical arousal by activity in the activating system, there occurs an inverse inhibitory corticoreticular discharge or feedback which obviates overexcitation and also dampens or inhibits sensory stimulation irrelevant to the prepotent behavioral sequence.

Little is known of the means by which the brain maintains its ability to attend selectively to one set of sensory registrations and not another. Acts of attention seem enormously different. On the one hand one may be struck by the precise visual attentiveness that must be exerted for an otherwise preoccupied man to suddenly catch a ball thrown past him by a playing child. Against this, one may conceive the narrowed attention of a microscopist as he focuses upon the tissue viewed through his scope. Then again there is the consciously determined scanning attention to a large stream of incoming registrations, such as might be given by a music critic while preparing to write his appraisal of the playing of a symphony orchestra, or that of the psychoanalyst attempting to discover a meaningful thread in scanning the sequence of the often apparently unrelated free association of his patient.

Arguing from a series of experiments, Pribram has suggested that attention derives from other than associations established by means of transcortical or cortico-cortical associations and that the brain's intrinsic processing system is other than a passive receptacle of information. He is of the belief that mnemic functions (memory) occur as active recoding and that the processing cortex regulates ongoing processes under the sensory system.

Thus from his work upon the association areas of the cerebral cortex concerned with recognition, we find it divisible into the posterior part, concerned with recognition, and the frontal part, concerned with recall. As for the latter, it is divided according to sense modality. Clinical studies and experiments over time indicate that the inferior temporal cortex functions in relation to visual recognition, the middle temporal to auditory recognition, the anterior temporal to gustation, and the posterior parietal to somesthesias. Pribram was struck with the anatomical fact that the aforementioned associative processing areas are separated by a considerable span from their related primary sensory systems. He found that one could remove the cortex between the primary cortical sensory receptive and the mnestic or associational cortex without loss of visual recognition of patterns in monkeys. What does take place is that impairment occurs in behaviors in which animals are required to process a number of visual cues in order to complete a task. Such animals fail, even though they "track" easily. Pribram states that behavioral learning (that is, identification) is based on a progressive differentiation and not on associative abstraction. He suggests the attention required in simple visual motor tracking as used in catching a fly depends only on the functioning of the primary sensory receptive cortex. Probably corticofugal impulses from that area to subthalamic system areas direct alerting. Scanning, requiring searching, relating and selection of a series of cues, comes about through actions of the primary intrinsic (associative) processing cortex. Here the scanning attention might be directed by corticofugal pathways to the subthalamic alerting spheres. Vigilance, the monitoring of external and internal registrations to determine their prepotency seems most likely the function of the limbic system. Cognitive factors, perhaps, are the consequence of diffuse corticocortical associational actions.

Physiologists have found that, just as the reticular activating system facilitates and inhibits sensory inputs from the spinal cord and brain stem, additional feedback control is exerted at peripheral sensory receptors outside the central nervous system, in the cochlea and retina. It is of interest that Freud predicted the existence of a *stimulus barrier* (reizschutz) to protect the organism from destructive and overwhelming stimulation. The discovery of the physiological arrangements within the nervous system preventing overactivation of sensory neurons and the excessive overload of the brain itself provides experimental support for his hypotheses.

The exigencies of life and adaptation to it have required the establishment of flexible gates excluding, reducing, or facilitating the inflow of sensory impressions from one or several sources, depending upon the immediate adaptive function demanded of the individual organism. That this protective barrier may fail to function, through maldevelopment or overload, and lead to disease is a distinct possibility. Such occurrences perhaps are exemplified in the sensory hypersensitivities noted in childhood schizophrenia, in such toxic states as delirium tremens, and in the stress reaction observed in man following prolonged battle exposure or after other catastrophes. The application of this knowledge to the clinic has suggested modulating the input of auditory stimulation to mask the pain incurred during dental procedures.

Still another characteristic of the activating system is its deactivation of the cortex on the presentation of repetitive, unvarying stimulation which may be interpreted as monotonous. Here the system functions by progressive reduction of electrocortical arousal even though the sensory input reaches the cortex. The system then is concerned with the process of habituation. Prolonged deprivation of cortical arousal now is known also to have deleterious effects.

Behavioral Reinforcement

While the activating systems in the brain stem and thalamus are concerned principally with alerting the organism and directing its attention to external or internal cues, there exist brain systems which reinforce sequences of behavior. These systems are concerned with emotional arousal and related affect. The anlages of the finely differentiated affective states of man rest upon primitive feeling states of pleasure and distress—states experienced first in the helpless dependency of infancy.

As with other brain systems, cellular interconnections are now understood to be made through electrochemical events taking place at the synaptic junctions between cells. The most popular of the current hypotheses relating to affect variability centers about presumed levels of concentration of the catecholamines at the synaptic junction, the cleft, and the post-synaptic receptor site.

Thus the passage of a nerve impulse from activated neurons across the synaptic junction to other nerve cells is considered to take place by discharge into the synaptic cleft of the biogenic amine norepinephrine. That substance is thought to activate the effector site of the host synaptic neuron.

Norepinephrine is found in highest concentration in the hypothalamus but is also present elsewhere, including the limbic system. The biogenic amine serotonin has a similar distribution. Dopamine, on the other hand, is concentrated highest in the basal ganglia. It has been suggested, but not yet proved, that all three of these biogenic amines may act as chemical transmitters. Some believe that one or more of these amines may act as modulators of synaptic transmissions that depend on other substances, perhaps acetylcholine.

Synthesized from tyrosine, norepinephrine is stored in intraneuronal granules at the presynaptic endings. When discharged into the synaptic cleft it is inactivated by conversion by the enzyme catechol-O-methyltransferase or is taken up again by the cell. Released within the cell it is inactivated by mitochondrial monoamine oxidase forming metabolites. The latter enzyme may then regulate the levels of norepinephrine within the cell. Epinephrine exists only in low concentrations in the brain. Peripherally it exists almost exclusively in the adrenal medulla. Serotonin synthesis takes place from 5-hydroxytryptophan by dicarboxylation. It, too, is metabolized by monoamine oxidase to form hydroxyindolacetic acid.

Earlier inference from clinical investigations related states of anger to the state of physiological arousal produced by injections of norepinephrine, whereas fear was thought to resemble those related to states induced by both norepinephrine and epinephrine injections. In monkeys in which blood levels of these amines may be measured, release of norepinephrine takes place with presentation of familiar and threatening stimuli. On the other hand, when the threatening situation is unknown or uncertain, epinephrine rises occur in the peripheral blood. So, too, improved performance with work under stress is associated with increased norepinephrine excretion. Exposure of men to emotionally arousing feelings leads to increased excretion of both norepinephrine and epinephrine; bland film exposure is followed by diminution.

It appears that the nature of differential perception of the external cues determines differentially the relative levels of excretion of these amines within the body. So, too, in animals decrements in brain norepinephrine take place with fear, immobilization, and even after intracerebral stimulation productive of heightened emotional arousal. Also, in animals adrenocorticosteroids enhance the activity of the enzymes that convert norepinephrine to epinephrine in the adrenal.

Experienced psychiatrists are highly impressed with the powerful effects of the new pharmaceuticals in modulating and changing pathologic affect and drive. The currently given biophysical interpretations of the actions by these drugs in terms of modifications of synaptic transmission must be recognized as oversimplified. Since synaptic transmission is involved in integration of all brain and peripheral neuronal interaction, one must realize that specificity as it relates to subsystem function must involve other variables. These may arise in either qualitative or quantitative production or depredation of transmitter substances. We remain far from a chemical control of man's affective state. The above work relates only to the primitive affects aroused in protective or agonistic behaviors to be described later. Yet there is physiological evidence for a central affective system within the brain.

Olds and Milner have found that animals with permanently implanted electrodes through which they might deliver stimuli to a portion of their own basal forebrains learned shortly to re-excite this brain area repeatedly and autonomously. When the electrodes were placed properly, rats stimulated themselves as often as 8000 times per hour.

Heath and his co-workers have reported pleasurable affects in some men with similar electrode placement carried out as a treatment of schizophrenia. When the electrode was placed in sites in the posterior hypothalamus or mid-brain, self-stimulation was much less frequent. Chlorpromazine and reserpine obliterate or inhibit self-stimulation in the latter sites but not in the more potently rewarding cephalic structures. The drive for autonomous self-stimulation can be modified by increasing the intensity of needs. In rats the drive for self-stimulation is much greater when they are exposed to the shocking pain of crossing an electric grid than when they are deprived of food for a day.

This system, with its capacity to reinforce behaviors, perhaps should be contrasted with the long-known sensory system concerned with pain—an emotional state which regularly leads to withdrawal behavior. Repetitive induction of this unpleasant emotion establishes behaviors of avoidance or aversion.

Cyclic Reinforcement

Many of the drive states which serve to maintain the health of man and other species and assure their procreative activities take place on time-fixed cycles of activity. Undoubtedly the most autonomous and least conscious cyclical activity is the spontaneously recurring movement of the chest cage and diaphragm concerned with the maintenance of respiration. In man this unconsciously maintained cyclical behavior is sometimes distorted in the form of respiratory tics, grunts, bouts of hyperventilation, and breath holding, or even in the disturbances of vocalization that take place in stuttering.

Equally important to the maintenance of health—and its disruption is so symptomatic of psychiatric disorder—is the sleep-wakefulness cycle. In procreative life, the estrous cycle represents a time-recurrent event as characteristic of woman as of the female of other mammalian species. Disruptions of this cycle, too, in women are among the most telling symptoms of personality disorder.

Time-bound behavioral sequences are less evident in the life of man than in his mammalian relatives. The flexibility with which he is endowed through his capacity for learning has detached him from the rigid behavioral cycles so characteristic of many simpler species. Yet evidence exists that he remains bound to behaviors determined by the function of "biological clocks." Disruption of these rhythmic functions by conflicting learned activities invariably indicates the presence of deep-seated and serious personality disorders.

Richter's studies of cyclical behaviors in man and animals have led him to hypothesize the presence of three types of "clocks": homeostatic, central, and peripheral. The estrous cycle represents a homeostatic "clock" wherein hormonal feedback mechanisms exist between distant target organs (in this case the ovary and uterus), an endocrine gland (the pituitary), and the hypothalamus. The timing systems of the central and peripheral clocks do not appear to be homeostatic and are capable of imposing recurrent behaviors through learning. Thus, one may learn to awaken at precise times; certain pathologic behaviors recurring in patients in regular time cycles appear to be learned. The anniversary reactions in connection with bereavements, are an example. While Richter states that the homeostatic systems are somewhat irregular, the central timing systems function with high constancy over long periods. The cellular timing devices exist outside the nervous system; they cycle certain phenomena of primary physical disease such as the regularly recurring fever of Hodgkin's disease. Such rhythms are thought to be ingrained into cellular and organ systems by the day-night and seasonal cycles which modify metabolic potentials and are modified in the evolutionary process.

Sleep-Wakefulness Behavior

For centuries the preservation of the regularly recurring sleep cycle has been recognized as imperative for the maintenance of health. Typical disruptions of the sleep cycle occur in depressive reactions and in various neurotic conditions and are represented as well by the somnambulistic trances seen most frequently in children. Less frequently met are those symptomatic eruptions of sleep which intrude upon the waking state: narcoleptic and hypersomniac attacks. The physiology of sleep has direct bearing upon the understanding of the clinical phenomenology just mentioned.

Both the sleeping and the waking states are associated with characteristic electroencephalographic patterns. The sleeping period is associated with at least two quite distinct types of brain activity. During 80 per cent of sleeping time there occurs an electroencephalographic pattern of large-amplitude slow waves and spindle bursts. This segment of sleep time is thought to represent inhibition of activity of the cerebral cortex. The other segment of sleep is characterized by an electroencephalographic pattern of low-voltage fast activity; this is thought to be a period in which subcortical function is predominantly impaired. It is now designated as "fast," "paradoxical," or "dreaming" sleep.

In the human adult, periods of dreaming sleep recur each night at intervals of approximately 90 minutes. Associated with the electroencephalographic pattern of dreaming sleep are bursts of rapid conjugate eye movements (REM). At times of such electroencephalographic and ocular activity, the awakened sleeper almost regularly reports dreaming, in contrast to his behavior when awakened during other periods of the sleep cycle. Other significant physiological changes also take place during REM sleep. Thus, respiration is irregular, heart rate and blood pressure are elevated, skin resistance is lowered, penile erection occurs, and there is a rapid and distinctive diminution in muscle tone as shown by the electroencephalograph.

Dreaming sleep occupies as much as 50 per cent of the sleep cycle in infants, decreasing in amount with aging. Similar cycles of REM sleep have been identified in many mammalian species other than man. One may infer from the periodic sleep activity of animals that they dream in association with this distinctive physiological phase of the sleep cycle.

Whether REM sleep is of greater or less depth or whether it represents a more primitive form of the dominant sleep periods remains a matter of discussion. While it has been assumed that dreaming sleep is light, at times the arousal threshold is higher during the REM period and at other times it is barely in excess of the waking threshold. Deprivation of REM sleep by awakening establishes a deficit which must be made up in subsequent sleep periods and may be associated with psychopathology.

Physiological studies have established the fact that the occurrence of the rapid low-voltage electrical activity depends upon the functioning of nuclear aggregations in the pontine reticular formations. REM records persist in mammals, including man, following decortication; they have been absent in several electroencephalographic recordings of patients with evidence of pontine damage. Even in decorticate animals, deprivation of "fast sleep" by repeated awakening leads to a pattern of sleep in which REM outbursts occur at increasingly frequent intervals. Cerebral tracts other than the ascending reticular formation are involved in the cortical driving mechanism in animals. "Fast sleep" disappears only with interruption of tracts in the ventral mesencephalon. It is of interest that there has been reported in men a syndrome of "peduncular hallucinosis" characterized by isolated visual hallucinations which occur at onset of sleep in those with lesions in the area of the ventral mesencephalon.

In the past five years much research has been done upon the effects of drugs in expressions of REM and nonREM sleep. Atropine reduces or abolishes REM sleep, whereas cholinergic agents such as eserine prolong its expression. It is of interest that atropine administered to cats just prior to the time of the expected circadian rise of 17-hydroxy steroids blocks that biological rhythmic activity. The barbiturates pentobarbital (Nembutal) and secobarbital (Seconal), glutethimide (Doriden), methyprylon (Noludar), and diphenhydramine (Benadryl) all reduce the amount of time spent in REM sleep. Of these drugs the barbiturates have the most effect. Dextroamphetamine, combined with pentobarbital, eliminates dreaming sleep. Following the withdrawal of the aforementioned drugs there occurs an increase in REM sleep in subsequent nights—a "rebound."

Particularly after the withdrawal of barbiturates and alcohol given over prolonged periods, the increased REM periods are punctuated by frightening nightmares. This is in contrast to deprivation of REM sleep by awakening; although increased REM sleep occurs on subsequent nights following interruption of REM by awakening, frightening dreaming is not usually reported.

The phenothiazines tend to change the electroencephalographic patterns of sleep toward that consistent with the state of coma. Antidepressants such as amitriptyline and imipramine decrease REM sleep activity, but over a few days of administration they expand the nonREM periods and lengthen the usual 90 minute cycles of REM expression up to 120 minutes. Their withdrawal is not followed by REM rebound.

〉 On the other hand reserpine and d-lysergic acid diethylamide (LSD) enhance REM sleep, as does L-tryptophan.

At this time it is hypothesized that depletion of the brain catecholamines, norepinephrine and dopamine, leads to a diminution of waking and REM sleep activity, whereas decrease of the brain indole amine serotonin is correlated with reduction in nonREM sleep activity. Others state it differently: the sleep-wakefulness cycle depends upon a complex balance of these amines in the brain subcellular structures.

"Napping" sleep apparently varies greatly with the time of day. Afternoon napping is associated with an earlier appearance and greater proportion of REM sleep than is evening napping. This observation suggests a greater potential for REM sleep expression during the daytime.

ENERGIC PROCESSING

Respiratory, Alimentary, and Excretory Behavior. All those functions directly concerned with the intake of substances and elimination of wastes occur in organs which embryologically are outgrowths of the alimentary tract. Accordingly, in this section are considered those physiologic processes concerned with respiration, feeding, and drinking, as well as the elimination of carbon dioxide, fecal matter, and urine.

Psychopathological disturbances of respiration were described earlier. Perverted eating and drinking behaviors are common symptomatic expressions of psychiatric disorders: prolonged anorexia, specific food aversions and obsessions, compulsive eating and drinking, constipation, and various diarrheas.

While the majority of the symptomatic disturbances of alimentation are learned to gratify symbolically some psychosocial need, they are mediated through and distort the functioning of related neuronal and organic systems. Others, however, are directly expressive of disturbances in the brain subsystem concerned with alimentary self-preservation.

The arousal of the need of oxygen, food, or fluids, recognized affectively as suffocation, hunger, or thirst, is mediated through the reticular activating system. In asphyxia, either a diminution in the oxygen in the blood or an increase in the carbon dioxide (the two components of asphyxia) powerfully stimulates the bulbar respiratory center as well as the mesencephalic reticular formation. During starvation, when the blood sugar level falls, there is an increase in circulating epinephrine which effects a compensatory release of glucose from glycogen. But as this latter process runs out, with depletion of glycogen stores, epinephrine may directly activate the ascending and descending reticular system, thereby facilitating cortical arousal and motor activity. Probably similar physiological processes lead to arousal in the face of emerging thirst, although there does not now exist experimental evidence for this assumption.

The innate processes which direct feeding behavior have been located in the hypothalamus and the limbic system (visceral brain). Thus, electrical stimulation of the lateral hypothalamus elicits feeding behavior in the satiated animal; its destruction causes aphagia. A dual control of eating seems probable, as stimulation of the hypothalamic ventromedial nucleus inhibits feeding and lesions in this area lead to hyperphagia and eventual obesity. Similarly, stimulation in the closely situated paraventricular nuclei elicits polydipsia, while electrical discharges related to fluid satiation have been observed in the supraoptic neurons following injection into animals of hypertonic solutions of saline and glucose.

Although it would seem that the hypothalamus is concerned solely with specifying the direction of the drive for food or fluid, shaping of the feeding behavior in mammals has been thought to depend upon the functioning of the rhinencephalon (the cerebral archicortex or limbic system, consisting of the olfactory bulb, septum pellucidum, cingulum, fornix, and amygdala). For many years clinicians have recognized that some epileptic seizures are initiated with one or several of the subjective experiences of hunger, thirst, choking, retching, or the wish to urinate or defecate, or by chewing or other oral activity, including automatisms of eating and drinking. In addition there may occur in such attacks manifestations of rage or fright expressed in screaming, running, or attack. It is known now that such convulsive seizures are due to focal lesions in the temporal lobe involving the structures of the limbic system. This system in turn projects to the hypothalamus and central gray matter of the mesencephalon through the median forebrain bundle. MacLean has found particularly that excitation in the amygdalar projections and ventral hypothalamus leads to oral activities; others have demonstrated that stimulation of the cingulate cortex in animals may inhibit feeding behaviors and related organ functions concerned with alimentation, including secretion of gastric juices.

REPRODUCTIVE BEHAVIOR

Arousal of the sexual drive, the finding of a mate, and the consummatory acts of copulation represent only the initial sequence of sexual behavior. Parturition in man, as well as other mammals, is followed by a long series of interdependent actions between the parents and the young designed to nurture the growth and development of the young. It is now recognized that the wide variety of behaviors evolved in reproduction of different species depend increasingly, as one ascends the evolutionary series, upon learned behaviors, particularly those concerned with socialization.

The midbrain activating system is known to become progressively more sensitive to electrical stimulation as estrous behavior evolves. In the period following coitus in female rabbits, when the animal relaxes, is inactive, or may sleep, the electroencephalographic recordings have shown spindle bursting, followed by REM sleep and hypersynchrony in limbic patterns.

Electrical stimulation of the tubular structures in animals induces ovulation. Lesions or implantations of estrogen in this area inhibit ovulation following coitus and later tend to cause atrophy of the ovary and reproductive tract. Similarly, testosterone implanted in this area in male dogs causes aspermia and testicular and prostatic atrophy. This system then responds to both neural influx and direct endocrine action as circulating gonadal hormones check pituitary gonadotropin secretion.

As for other components of the consummatory act, MacLean has found that in male monkeys penile erection and its modifications, pelvic movements, and ejaculation follow stimulation of the hippocampal projections, parts of the anterior and midline thalamic nuclei, and the hypothalamus, the septopreoptic and medial dorsal nuclei being the most sensitive areas.

Even more impressive is the enormous significance to sexual behavior in man of early experience in terms of learning patterns of socialization that lead to successful mating, copulation, and eventual child rearing. The thesis is now corroborated by a long line of experimental observations culminating in the reports of Harlow, who found that young monkeys that were isolated from a mother and contacted only an experimental wire frame for nutrition, or else were isolated from their peers, were defective in sexual approach, in the consummatory act, and in mothering behavior in adulthood. Here again the recording of experience over time is dependent upon the functioning of the cerebral cortex and allows the eventual patterning of the complex series of behaviors which determine the various phases of both procreation and child rearing. In man, particularly, each of these phases may be enhanced, distorted, or arrested through his extensive capacity for symbolizing during learning.

AGONISTIC SYSTEM

Expressions of and reactions to aggression—rage and fight, immobilization, flight, and fear—are the agonistic responses designed to protect each species from attack and also to facilitate alimentary and sexual activities.

Aggression, defined in the narrow sense of initiating attack, is a universal form of behavior in all classes of vertebrates and arthropods but rarely in lower invertebrates. In the animal kingdom fighting is common, useful, and apparently adaptive. The young of many mammalian species exhibit the beginnings of fighting behavior in their play. External and internal environment both influence the emergence of aggressivity and impulsivity. Hunger, territorial restriction, and increase in male sexual hormone increase fighting activity in various vertebrates.

Man alone resorts to violent aggressiveness with widespread maiming and killing of members of his own species. He alone has evolved exquisite means of cruelty and torture as well as equally subtle controls through social methods of inducing guilty and shameful affects and inhibiting ritualistic and expiatory behaviors. It has been said that the crowning achievement of man's evolution was the emergence of conscience—to control aggressivity. Man's aggressivity and the psychological control devices evolved for its control depend upon the vast growth of his cerebral cortex.

Perhaps because the socially feared and inappropriate aggressiveness of the psychotic has been most difficult to control, both clinical and laboratory studies of

the physiological processes related to the expression of rage preceded those of other forms of behavior. As early as 1892 Goltz reported upon the astounding behavior of his decorticated dog, which had displayed strong actions of growling, barking and biting on slight stimulation, actions expressive of the emotion of rage. Walter Cannon coined the term "sham rage" after he observed lashing of the tail, arching of the back, display of claws, biting, and panting respirations, behavior which showed the components of rage and attack, in acutely decorticated cats. A long series of arousal experiments by Bard and others demonstrated that "savage" behavior in cats followed precise lesions in the ventromedial nucleus of the hypothalamus. It is now known that removal of the neocortex alone, leaving the old brain rhinencephalic structures intact, leads to the behavioral expression of placidity—the obverse of rage. Rage reactions emerge spontaneously when both new and old cortices are removed or when the amygdala and pyriform cortex are resected, but not after damage to the hippocampus. The neocortex then appears to have both a facilitatory and an inhibitory influence on aggressive behaviors characterized by rage, and in addition influences the direction and timing of such behaviors. The inhibitory influence is dependent upon the cingulate gyrus and transmitted through the amygdala to influence the ventromedial hypothalamic nuclei.

It was the introduction of prefrontal lobotomy that established the relationship of function of brain to control of emotional behaviors. As the result of the many studies of psychiatrically ill persons treated by prefrontal lobotomy, the clinical indications for the procedure have been narrowed to the presence of certain symptoms which represent the expression of rage or related aggressive states. These are assaultive and destructive behavior, suicidal acts, chronic irascibility, agitation, undue anxiety, impulsiveness, and overactivity. Other behavioral symptoms often modified by lobotomy are depression, hypochondriasis, chronic pain, and refusal to eat—symptoms that often are recognized as symbolic of inhibition of rage or hostility. Lobotomy was found to offer little in terms of the social adaptation of the psychotic patient who showed apathy and indifference. It was found as well that prefrontal cortical resections made in a posterior plane which presumably damaged the amygdala induced apathy or placidity that mitigated against the social recovery of the patient.

COGNITIVE SYSTEM

The capacity to respond with increasingly effective goal-directed behavior to viable but previously unspecified circumstances defines adaptation. That capacity, in living systems, requires that incoming information be registered and encoded, that a memory of the experience be established. On the basis of the earlier memories presentation of information resembling that registered at any early time is recognized as familiar—is perceived. So, too, the responses to past experience are recorded, including those internal events which determine emotion and affect. With each succeeding experience of goal seeking or avoidance of threat, the organism learns by comparative analysis of the effectiveness of present with previous behaviors. It thus progressively discriminates the most significant cues in percepts, evolves more skillful and economical behavioral responses, and in the more complex mammalian species progressively analyzes and solves problems concerned with increasingly variable and complex environmental situations. Memory, perception, and cognition depend upon evolution of the brain.

Memory. It is now assumed that a series of electrochemical processes takes place to fix in the neuronal network of the brain those records of past sensory experiences which form the basis for perception and the development of motor and cognitive behaviors necessary for adaptation and defensive purposes. Much of what is written pertaining to these processes is highly speculative. Yet the mounting information and available hypothesis have heuristic value.

Memory processing is considered to be determined through two distinct but overlapping stages. The recall of immediately experienced events is recognized as different than that of past events. Electroshock shortly after experience will eradicate recall of recent events.

Clinical studies make it evident that extensive brain damage early in life impairs the storage of information and the potential for learning. With brain damage later in life specific deficits are noted in ability to retain recent percepts, while the memories encoded from the past are retained. Such impairment of storage or retention of experiences is a prominent symptom in certain of the alcoholic psychoses as well, and characterizes the psychosis associated with the senium. Similarly, during the induction of anesthesia and after electroshock therapy, memory processing is impaired. While immediate memory of short spans is possible, the recall of long-span percepts, which involves storage, is defective.

Within the past decade it has been observed that patients treated neurosurgically for epilepsy by bilateral temporal lobe resections lose their ability to process current experience into memory. Thus, retention of any cognitive material is severely impaired and there may occur as well impairment of recall extending backward for several years (retrograde amnesia). Retention of earlier memories is unaffected. The anterior mesial surfaces of the temporal lobe are significantly concerned with the processing of perceptions to become permanent memories, but such encoding of perceptions involves as well widespread processes throughout the cerebral cortex. DeJong has placed on record one human case in which precise bilateral localized necrosis of the hippocampi led to impairment of memory recording. Animal experiments have shown that bilateral hippocampal ablation is the significant lesion responsible for impairing acquisition of avoidance learning.

It has been suggested that in the processing of sensory experiences into the electrochemical mechanisms that establish permanent coding within the brain, both specific and nonspecific sensory pathways are activated, the latter discharging into the hippocampus via the fornix. In studies in animals of the electrical activity of the hippocampus, regularly recurring high-voltage theta rhythms are generally evoked in this structure. Such rhythms become localized when a learned behavioral response takes place as the result of conditioning. Early in the conditioned learning process the electrical activity in the hippocampus precedes that in the adjacent cerebral cortex. When conditioned learning is established, the electrical activity in the cortex appears to precede that in the hippocampus. It has been suggested that these shifting electrical wave changes between hippocampus and cortex which occur in the course of learning bring about enduring biochemical changes in the cytoplasm of fast synaptic neurons and related neuroglia upon which permanent registrations depend.

Since it is now known that the processes of the astrocytic glia are intimately applied to the neurons and seem to serve as metabolic bridges between them and the circulating blood, they may be implicated in any biochemical process which determines structural change related to acquisition of memory.

The permanent recording of sensory experiences—long-term memory—would seem to require the transformation of electrical energy generated in the neurons into some permanent changes in their structure or their relationship within the net. The analogy of the genetic code information processing through the template of RNA (ribonucleic acid) has been offered as a possible explanation for the structural change in the neurons which establishes the codes for a permanent memory. Yet in order to establish with certainty the evidence that one or another neurochemical process takes place to assure permanent encoding of an electroneural impulse and thus to demonstrate that a given molecule or set of molecules, or structure or set of structures, is specifically concerned in effecting a memory trace, a number of convincing demonstrations pertaining to that molecule or structure must be assured. Thus the molecule or structure must be shown to undergo a change of state in response to the experience to be remembered. That altered state must be shown to persist as long as the memory.

The disappearance of the alteration must coincide with the loss of the memory.

Today convincing evidence meeting the general criteria above does not exist to establish any protein, lipid, or other brain constituent as the substance involved in structural alteration related to memory storage.

Certainly the metabolism of RNA may relate to memory storage, as its major function is participation in the synthesis of proteins. Many are convinced that the structural changes related to storage do concern brain proteins, but point out that cellular metabolism is dynamic and not fixed, and that there are many regulatory mechanisms within the neuron and between the neuron, its processes, and its numerous synaptic functions. It has been suggested that coding then is not related to a permanently enduring state of change in the human. It occurs only when brain protein synthesis takes place above a certain critical rate. Experiments have shown that in small mammals (mice) interference with the rate of protein synthesis in the brain by such an inhibitor as the antibiotic puromycin prevents learning of new behavioral expressions and disrupts old learning as well. Flexner has suggested that the establishment of enduring memory traces depends upon the existence within the brain of a self-sustaining system for synthesis of necessary proteins. He suggests that in the evolution of the process of long-term memory the initial learning experience triggers the synthesis of one or more species of messenger ribonucleic acid (MRNA). This MRNA alters the synthetic rate of one or more proteins essential for structural change in various neurons. In turn, these proteins modify the characteristics of the synaptic network so as to variously effect the transmission of nerve impulses. Finally, the proteins or their products induce the related MRNA production to sustain a critical level of their synthesis. When the level of synthesis falls, there takes place a temporary memory failure. It is unlikely that this hypothesis alone is sufficient to explain either short-term or long-term memory.

Earlier theorists postulated memory as based upon the establishment of synaptic resistances or efficiency of reverberating electrical circuits. Probably in the future the electrochemical hypothesis will be related to the current fashionable molecular theories of memory. At any rate, at the moment the integrity of the hippocampal structures bilaterally seems necessary for the fixing of a trace event for immediate or long-term recall. Perhaps, as was discussed earlier under the subject of vigilance, this structure is concerned with the monitoring of meaningful internal and external information to determine its priority in terms of survival of the organism. High priority information is likely to be recorded. For a thorough examination of the past and present hypotheses and data relative to mnestic function, the reader is referred to Johns.

LEARNING

From both clinical and laboratory evidence there is reason to believe that the cerebral processes associated with learning in early life are fundamentally different from those which take place after maturation of the nervous system. For many years it has been known that children born blind because of corneal opacities do not develop good vision unless that defect is repaired by corneal transplant very early in life. Likewise the dreams of children born blind or deaf never contain visual or auditory images, presumably because the patterns of cerebral organization fail to evolve without early perceptual experience. The same holds true for the organization of the body percepts: children born without a limb do not experience a limb phantom as do adults who suffer amputations.

Hebb has suggested that early sensing is necessary for the establishment of perceptual functioning. Furthermore, all later learning depends upon the appropriate early experiencing which apparently stimulates the basic organization and integration of cerebral systems concerned with perception and cognition.

A long series of animal experiments now makes it clear that the organization of various sensory systems and behaviors depends upon experiencing at critical periods in the early life of each species. In the absence of the appropriate experiencing at the "critical time," the organism may be left with an enduring deficit in perception or behavior—an ego deficit, in psychoanalytic terms—a defect of personality functioning. The degree to which such deficits may be repaired by later experience is unknown.

"Imprinting," the specific emotional attachment of the young of some species to their parents, is a case in point. Discovered first in various birds, "imprinting" takes places when the young bird perceives a moving object during certain critical days following hatching. The attachment may be made to any moving object at this point in maturational development. Thus, when contact with man or some mobile inanimate object is substituted for contact with the parent, birds exposed to the substitute will thereafter follow that substitute when it is presented. From his observations on imprinting Hess points up the differences between *imprinting,* the early type of learning, and later *associational learning.* The former is dependent upon an experience that takes place at a critical period in early life. It is depressed by the prior administration of such pharmacologic agents as meprobamate or carisoprodol, and it is enhanced when painful stimuli occur with the visual percept. In contrast, later associational learning does not depend upon experience at critical periods in life, is not depressed by meprobamate, and leads to avoidance behaviors when associated with pain. In imprinting, the first percept is the most significant in the formation of the bond that leads to following behavior; in later associational learning the more recent learning has greater influence on behavior. Since this form of early learning, so important in establishing a social bond between young and their parents, may be adversely influenced by drugs which disturb electrochemical events in the brain,* we may generalize and assume that the electrochemical events of

---

*Whereas associational learning is not affected by such drugs.

learning differ in the nervous system of the immature as compared to the mature member of the species.

In the adult brain the evidence for the occurrence of electrochemical change comes from several sources. By using the Pavlovian technique of conditioning, the classic method of associational learning, it is possible to establish a blocking of the alpha rhythm of the electroencephalogram on presentation of a click as a conditional stimulus associated with eye opening that regularly acts in such a way as the unconditioned stimulus. In the initial stages of learning to respond to the click, the blocking of the alpha rhythm is generalized over the cortex; later it is localized to the occipital cortex, the projection site of the visual unconditioned stimulus. Other experiments in animals have shown that painful and pleasurable stimuli both augment the amplitude of cerebral electrical discharges and increase the distribution of afferent signals over the brain. As affective reinforcement is continued and learning occurs, the electrical discharges that were generally distributed initially are restricted to the site of projection of the unconditioned stimuli.

Learning theorists tend to distinguish between classical Pavlovian conditioning, associational learning, and instrumental conditioning. In the former an unconditioned stimulus, such as food which would lead a dog to salivate, when paired repeatedly with another signal such as a light or noise, would over a span of time bring an animal to salivate on presentation of the hitherto biologically unimportant but paired light or sound. Pavlov spoke of the latter as the conditioned stimulus and the salivation following its presentation as the conditioned response. So, too, he found it possible to pair signals with painful stimuli to produce conditioned evasive responses. Pavlov pointed out the necessity to assess the state of need or satiety of the animals he had under study. He came to know of the influence of the human experimenter upon the responsivity of his subjects and recognized that symbols could replace physical stimuli as signals for conditioned learning. To him sensations, perceptions, and direct impressions formed the primary

signals of reality for man. Words constituted the secondary signals, as abstractions of reality, that permitted generalizations. In this psychology the reflex concept is primary, but reflex here represents a behavior response with afferent, mediating central, and efferent portions. Pavlov conceived of processes of cortical excitation and inhibition, sleep and hypnosis representing inhibitory cortical states.

Instrumental learning differs from conditioned learning in the sense that the animal is rewarded when he performs a desired task. Thus an animal comes to learn that if he carries out such an action as striking a lever he will receive a food reward. So, too, he may learn to depress a lever in order to avoid a painful shock. In the course of instrumental learning, each time the correct response is given for either need reduction or escape the animal is rewarded. When he fails to carry out the desired behavior the positive reward is denied or the aversive stimulus is given. Such instrumental or operant conditioning is associated with the work of a long line of American psychologists, of whom Skinner is the best known current spokesman.

Doubt was expressed in the past that visceral responses could be "learned" through trial-and-error rewarding methods of instrumental conditioning. As DiCara reports, a long series of experiments by Neal Miller and his associates has demonstrated otherwise. Increase and decrease in heart rate, blood pressure, constriction and relaxation of the vascular bed, intestinal contraction, and rate of urinary secretions may all be influenced by such learning procedures. So, too, the learning is relieved by periodic reinforcement and extinguishes or disappears if the reinforcement is not provided. It is of interest that the same reward may be used to obtain learned visceral responses of opposing character. It seems from this experimental work that conditioning through the sympathetic nervous system may occur with a much greater degree of specificity than thought possible earlier. The work on visceral conditioning is of paramount significance in considering the operational forces concerned in the psychophysiological (psychosomatic) disorders.

While imprinting, conditioned, or instrumental learning paradigms are of importance in comprehending the evolution of adaptive and maladaptive (psychopathological) behavior on man, they have yet to explain many phenomena evident in his learning or creative conceptualizations. Thus many behaviors follow single exposures to stimulating events. Brilliant conceptualizations often appear to arise from sudden coalescence of internal associations.

Of immediate interest are the experiments of Hunt, who has found that a series of electroshocks attenuate a conditioned emotional response (CER) to a signal previously learned by rats in association with painful shocks given to their feet—but do not affect behavior learned in relation to a reward. Furthermore, amphetamine potentiates the attenuating effect of electroshock on the conditioned emotional response, while chlorpromazine given after electroshock strengthens the conditioned emotional response. So, too, learning theories relate directly to the now widely tried behavioral therapies.

In comparative psychopathology the paradigm of the CER in animals represents most closely the acute stress reactions or traumatic neuroses of men suffered immediately after threatening catastrophes —as in battle experiences in war time, or the multitude of sudden catastrophes of modern civil life. It is of interest, too, that the strength or acquired CER in animals varies in relation to the circadian rhythm. Thus if an animal is trained by an unavoidable shock at 8 A.M. daily, he will show the strongest response thereafter at the time of training and the weakest 12 hours later. So, too, this response is inhibited by adrenalectomy, or by suppression of adrenal function with methopyropine and phenothiazines.

Understanding the learning process is of paramount importance in man, since his large brain gives him a learning capacity far beyond that of other species. This capacity for learning new behaviors has made possible both the increased complexity of his intellectual creativeness and the extraordinary range of his socially maladjustive behavior and psychological defenses, described in later chapters. The gap remains great between the known physiology of behavior and the explanations it offers now of psychopathology.

While much of the investigation of these systems has been concerned with the discernment of their anatomical location and interpreted in electrophysiologic terms or in terms of neurohumoral transmission, it must be appreciated that the expanding knowledge of the ultrastructure of the cell and its intricate biochemical interchanges later may add an even more significant basis for understanding the regulatory systems of the brain and the influence of pharmacologic agents on behavior.

REFERENCES

1. Bliss, E. L., and Zwanziger, J.: Brain amines and emotional stress. J. Psychiat. Res. 4:189–198 (1966).
2. Cannon, W. B.: Wisdom of the Body. New York, Norton, 1939.
3. Collinson, J. B.: Ill-defined procedures in learing and growth. Arch. Gen. Psychiat. 19:298–299 (1968).
4. DiCara, S. V.: Learning in the autonomic nervous system. Sci. Am. 22:31–39 (1970).
5. DeJong, R. N., Habash, H. H., and Olson, J. R.: "Pure" memory loss with hippocampal lesions. Trans. Amer. Neurol. Assoc. 93:31–34 (1968).
6. Dell, P. C.: Some basic mechanisms of the translation of bodily needs into behavior. In Wolstenholme, G. E. W., and O'Connor, C. M. (eds.): Neurological Basis of Behavior. Boston, Little, Brown, 1958, pp. 187–201.
7. Harlow, H. F., and Harlow, M. K.: Social deprivation in monkeys. Sci. Am. 207:136–146 (1962).
8. Hartmann, E.: The Biology of Dreaming. Charles C Thomas, Springfield, Ill. 1967.
9. Heath, R. H. G.: Electrical self-stimulation of the brain in man. Am. J. Psychiat. 120:571–577 (1963).
10. Hebb, D. C.: The Organization of Behavior. New York, Wiley, 1949.
11. Hess, E. H.: Imprinting in birds. Science 146:1128–1130 (1964).
12. Hunt, H. F.: Electro-convulsive shock and learning. Trans. N. Y. Academy. Sc. 27:923–945 (1965).
13. Johns, E. R.: Mechanisms of Memory. New York, Academic Press, 1967.
14. Kales, H. (ed.): Sleep. Physiology and Pathology. Philadelphia, J. B. Lippincott Co. 1968.

15. Levine, R. (ed.): Endocrines and the central nervous system. Assoc. Res. Nerv. and Ment. Dis. *43*, 1966.

16. Lorenz, K.: On Aggression. New York, Harcourt, Brace & World, Inc., 1966.

17. Luce, G. G.: Biological Rhythms in Psychiatry and Medicine. National Clearing House for Mental Health Information, National Institute of Mental Health, Public Health Service. Publ. No. 2088. Washington, D.C., U.S. Government Printing Office.

18. MacLean, P. D.: Contrasting functions of limbic and neocortical systems of the brain and their relevance to psychophysical aspects of medicine. Am. J. Med. *25:*611–626 (1958).

19. Magoun, H. W.: The Waking Brain. 2nd Ed. Springfield, Ill. Charles C Thomas, 1963.

20. Miller, N. E.: Chemical coding of behavior in the brain. Science *148:*328–338 (1965).

21. Olds, J., and Milner, P.: Positive reinforcement produced by electrical stimulation of septal area and other regions of the rat brain. J. Comp. Physiol. and Psychol. *47:*419–429 (1954).

22. Pavlov, I. P.: Experimental Psychology and

Other Essays. New York, Philosophical Library, 1959.

23. Pribram, K. H.: Looking to see: Some experiments on the brain mechanisms of attention in perception. Res. Publ. Assoc. Nerv. and Ment. Dis. *48:*150–162 (1970).

24. Richter, C. P.: Biological Clocks in Medicine and Psychiatry. Springfield, Ill., Charles C Thomas, 1965.

25. Roizin, L.: A review of ultracellular structures and their functions with special reference to pathologenic mechanisms at a molecular level. J. Neuropath. and Exp. Neur. *19:*591–621 (1960).

26. Scott, J. P.: Critical periods in behavioral development. Science *139:*949–958 (1962).

27. Schildkraut, J. J., and Kety, S. S.: Biogenic amines and emotion. Science *156:*21–30 (1967).

28. Stroebel, C. F.: Behavioural aspects of circadian rhythms. In Zubin, J., and Hunt, H. (eds.): Comparative Psychopathology. Animal and Human. New York, Grune and Stratton, 1967.

29. Tinbergen, N.: The Study of Instinct. Oxford, Clarendon Press, 1951.

11. The Permanent Record of the Stream of Consciousness

Wilder Penfield

While considering how I might fortify my position before this Congress, composed as it is of leading psychologists from all the world, I took from my book shelves the two volumes of Psychology by William James.[1] I blew off the dust that had lain upon them, I fear, since my undergraduate days at Princton and read his classical chapter on The Stream of Thought.

Consciousness, he said, is a personal phenomenon. It deals with external objects, some of which are constant, and it chooses among them. But consciousness is never the same in successive moments of time. It is a stream forever flowing, forever changing.

It has fallen to my lot, during explorations of the cortex, to demonstrate a mechanism in the human brain which preserves the record of the stream of thought. When it becomes necessary to operate under local anesthesia and to stimulate the surface of one of the temporal lobes, it happens occasionally that small parts of that record are activated, bringing back a period of past experience with a startling degree of vividness and detail. The patient then reviews the sights and sounds and thinking of a previous period of time.

CORTICAL EXPLORATION

During the past twenty years of neurosurgical practice it has been necessary to expose the cerebral cortex under local anesthesia in a succession of patients. The reason for operation was that they were

Penfield, W.: The permanent record of the stream of consciouness. Acta Psychol. *11:*47–69 (1956).

afflicted by recurring attacks of focal epilepsy. Surgical excision of an abnormal area of cortex in which epileptogenic discharges arise may relieve such patients of their attacks in about fifty percent of cases.

But before excisions are carried out, it is our custom to explore the exposed cortex, applying a gentle electrical current to it from place to place. It is possible, thus, at times, to reproduce the beginning of a patient's attack in the form of a sensory aura or movement and, thus, to verify the position of the epileptogenic focus. Furthermore, stimulation is used to localize the functional areas of the cortex after which the excision can be carried out with a minimal sacrifice of function.

This practice made it possible to map out, in great detail, the motor representation in the cortex of man and the sensory areas—somatic, visual, auditory, etc. As years passed the supplementary motor area was demonstrated, hidden away in the sagittal fissure, and the second somatic sensory area within the fissure of Sylvius.

Two major areas of the human cortex remained, the anterior half of the frontal lobes and the enormously in-folded temporal cortex.*

From time to time over the years, stimulation has produced an astonishing result. Instead of movement or sensation, application of the electrode has caused the patient to report a psychical effect.**

In each case the location of stimulus was charted and a description immediately dictated to a secretary who sat in the "viewing stand" for the purpose. In such dictation the surgeon has always used the patient's own words as far as possible.

Positive psychical responses were obtained only from the previously unclaimed cortex of the temporal lobes and only then when that cortex had been rendered more responsive by long continued pre-operative epileptic conditioning. The responses, however, might bear no relationship to the content of the patient's seizures and they were produced without setting up epileptic after-discharge. Sensitization of the cortex, so that it reveals its function with greater ease when stimulated, is the common result of the presence of local epileptogenic process in other areas of cortex as well as in the temporal lobes. The stimulating electrode may imitate the effect of a local epileptic discharge but it does other things as well.

GENERAL STIMULATION RESPONSES AND THE MEANING OF CORTICAL LOCALIZATION

It was in 1870 that Fritsch and Hitzig applied an electrical current to a certain area of the cerebral cortex of a lightly anesthetized dog and produced movement in the opposite limbs. Previous to that time, the brain was considered to be the organ of the mind functioning somehow as a whole, although it is true that Hughlings Jackson had suggested some degree of localization and Broca had claimed a localized representation for speech.

The work of Fritsch and Hitzig, followed quickly by Ferrier, prepared the way for the great experimentalists to study the cerebral cortex. I refer to Sherrington and Pavlov and their pupils, but I should also mention many others, Luciani, Dusser de Barenne, Graham Brown, Adrian, Bard, Woolsey, Vogt, Lashley, to name only a few.

What can we say today about localization of function in the cerebral cortex of man? And in what sense can any function be said to have a localization? These questions have been discussed exhaustively elsewhere,[2,3,4] with references to literature. But a few words of interpretation may be useful here.

*A relatively small part of the first temporal convolution, the transverse gyrus of Heschl, was clearly devoted to auditory sensation and, perhaps adjacent to it, was some representation of labyrinthine sensation. The sense of smell has been given an ever smaller foothold in the region of the uncus. Otherwise the temporal cortex, which has enlarged so greatly in man, as compared with other mammals, represented a vast and unclaimed territory.

**It may be said at once that the word psychical is used in its original meaning, as Hughlings Jackson used it, to denote the more complicated mental phenomena made possible by final neuronal integration within the brain.

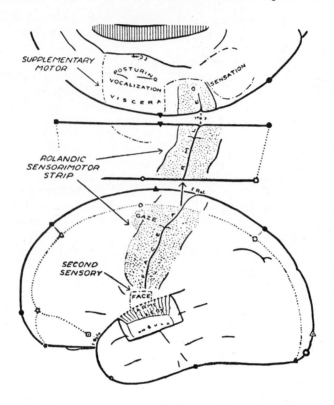

Figure 11~1. Somatic sensory and motor areas of the human cerebral cortex. As judged by the results of stimulation all three somatic areas (Rolandic, Supplementary, Second) are to some extent both motor and sensory. (From Penfield and Jasper, 1954.)

Stimulation of the motor cortex of conscious men produces movement (Figure 11-1), but the patient is always aware of the fact that he has not willed these movements. These movements are gross and uncomplicated with certain striking exceptions. The exceptions are motor performances which have a localization of mechanism elsewhere in the central nervous system, mechanisms which can be activated from a distance by the cortical stimulation. I refer to vocalization, mastication, swallowing, conjugate eye movements.

Stimulation of sensory areas causes the patient to experience only the elements of sensation. In the somatic area it is tingling, numbness, sense of movement of some part of the body; in the visual area, lights, shadows, colored forms usually moving; in the auditory area, a buzzing, humming, knocking or ringing sound.

Sensation (Figure 11-2) can not be said to be located in the cortex any more than it is in the peripheral receptor. Sensory areas of the cerebral cortex are way-stations in the current of afferent neuronal impulses. These impulses originate in the peripheral sense-organs and travel inward and upward to the cortex with ganglionic interruption in subcortical nuclei. From the cortex they pass inward again to the higher brain stem where the afferent stream from one field or body-half can join the others.* The most important, and the final, reorganization of sensory material must take place in the circuits of the higher brain stem rather than in the cerebral cortex.

The motor pathway, on the other hand, which subserves voluntary discriminative

_____

*Interference with this portion of the brain produces unconsciousness. [5]

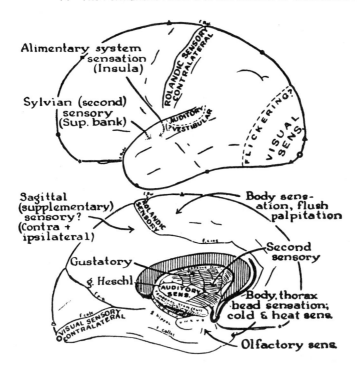

Figure 11-2. Sensory areas of the human cortex as judged by stimulation exploration in conscious patients. (The sensory area indicated in the anterior temporal region requires verification.)

movement originates in a central region between the hemispheres and passes out to the motor cortex of each hemisphere. After its ganglionic interruption in the precentral gyrus it descends to medulla and spinal cord and thence to the muscles.

Associative neuronal intercourse from one functional area of the cortex to another is of comparatively little importance. Integration of the function of the separate areas of the cortex by a subcortical centrencephalic system is of great importance.

It is the purpose of this address to discuss the ganglionic organization of an experiential recording mechanism, and to point out that there is some sort of representation of this mechanism in the temporal cortex. As time passes others will, no doubt, elucidate the nature of the role of the temporal cortex in this mechanism.

Case 1

T.S., Age 19

T. S. was a young man of 19 years. He had temporal lobe seizures that were sometimes precipitated by listening to music. He was fond of jazz and also symphonic music.

At the beginning of each attack he experienced what he called a "flash-back." *

He explained that this usually had to do with himself and his past but was "much more distinct" than anything he could summon to his memory.

At the time of operation, stimulation of a point on the anterior part of the first temporal convolution on the right caused him to say, "I feel as though I were in the bathroom at school." Five minutes later, after negative stimulations elsewhere, the electrode was reapplied near the same point. The patient then said something about "street corner." The surgeon asked him, "where," and he replied, "South Bend, Indiana, corner of Jacob and Washington." When asked to explain, he said he seemed to be looking at himself—at a younger age.

When the stimulation was repeated the response was quite different. This time he said, "that music, from 'Guys and Dolls.'" When asked which song in the play he referred to, he could not name it. "I was listening to it," he said. "It was an orchestration. . . ."

---

*Flash-back is an expression used by those familiar with moving picture techniques to describe the presentation of a scene that has occurred in the earlier history of one of the characters of the play.

Such results have been produced many times and we have used every practicable control and verification. The following case may be reported in greater detail.

Case 2
M.M., Age 26

The patient M. M. was a woman of 26 years who was afflicted by recurring cerebral seizures. The first manifestation of each attack was a sudden "feeling—as though I had lived through this all before." At times there was also a feeling of fear. On other occasions she experienced what she called a flash-back not unlike those just described in the case of T.S.

The initial feeling of familiarity she described as applying to the whole of any experience she might be having at the moment. On the other hand, the flash-backs were experiences from her earlier life. They came suddenly while she retained awareness of her actual surroundings. She gave the following example: Without warning she seemed to be sitting in the railroad station of a small town, which might be Vanceburg, Kentucky, or perhaps Garrison. "It is winter and the wind is blowing outside and I am waiting for a train." This was apparently an experience from her earlier life but it was one she had "forgotten."

These minor seizures (psychical seizures) were often followed by automatism, periods of irresponsible behavior of which she would have no memory. During these periods she might fall or walk about in a confused state, speaking unrelated and disjointed words and sentences.

Thus, in summary, the localized epileptic discharges in the right temporal lobe of this young woman were causing her to experience, from time to time: 1) a sense of false familiarity (déjà vu), 2) a feeling of fear, 3) reproductions of previous experience. This first was an illusion, the second an emotion, the third an hallucination. These are all to be considered psychical phenomena, any one of which the operator might hope to reproduce by stimulation.

Osteoplastic craniotomy (Figures 11–3 and 11–4) carried out under local anesthesia disclosed atrophy and sclerosis of the first temporal convolution, and the uncus and hippocampus as well. Electrographic recordings taken directly from the cortex by my associate, Dr. Herbert Jasper, showed spontaneous "spike" discharges from this area.

Electrical stimulation was carried out (Square wave generator, 60 cycles, 2 millisecond pulses). She was ordinarily warned by the operator each time the electrode was applied. But, as usual, at intervals the warning was given with no stimulus and at other times, stimulation without warning. This serves to eliminate with certainty false or imaginary responses.

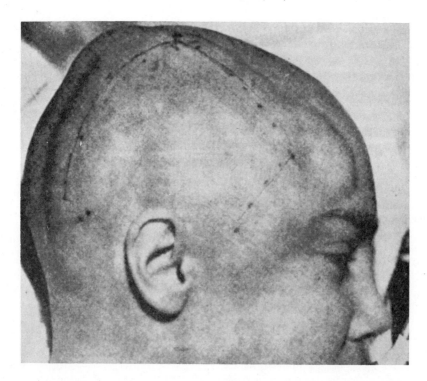

Figure 11–3. Prepared for operation. Incision marked on scalp after injection of nupercaine. Case M.M.

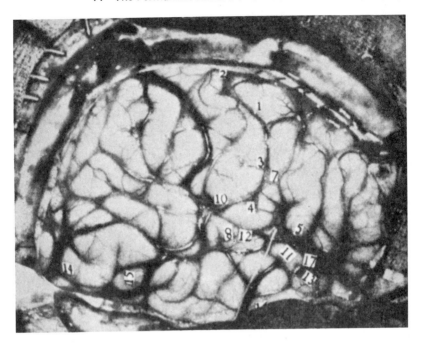

Figure 11-4. Photograph of brain after craniotomy. The paper tickets dropped on the cortex show points where stimulation produced positive responses, sensory, motor, or psychical. Case M.M.

Sensory and Motor Responses

A current of two volts proved to be the minimum threshold strength that would produce responses from the sensory and motor areas. See Figures 11-4 and 11-5.

Stimulation at point 2—sensation in thumb and index finger. She called it "quivering," "tingling."

3—"Same feeling on the left side of my tongue."

7—Movement of the tongue.

4—"Yes, a feeling at the back of my throat like nausea."

8—She said, "No." then she said, "Yes, I suddenly cannot hear." This is, obviously, the border of auditory sensory cortex.

The foregoing responses were motor and sensory in character much like those obtained routinely. They serve only to identify the Rolandic sensory and motor cortex and Heschl's auditory gyrus, a part of the first temporal convolution buried within the fissure of Sylvius.

Psychical Responses

The following effects are psychical. The strength of current was increased from 2 to 3 volts.

11—"I heard something familiar; I do not know what it was."

11 (repeated without warning)—"Yes, sir, I think I heard a mother calling her little boy

somewhere. It seemed to be something that happened years ago." When asked to explain, she said, "It was somebody in the neighborhood where I live." She added that it seemed that she herself "was somewhere close enough to hear."

Warning without stimulation—"Nothing."

11 (repeated)—"Yes, I hear the same familiar sounds, it seems to be a woman calling, the same lady. That was not in the neighborhood. It seemed to be at the lumberyard." Then she added reflectively, "I've never been around the lumberyard much."

This was an incident of childhood which she could never have recalled without the aid of the stimulating electrode. Actually she could not "remember" it but she knew at once, with no suggestion from us, that she must have experienced it sometime. The same incident was evoked again by another stimulation at approximately the same point. Then at a different point, 12, she had another experience but of a similar character. The ticket 12 was displaced before its position was recorded.

12—"Yes. I heard voices down along the river somewhere—a man's voice and a woman's voice calling."

When she was asked how she could tell that the calling had been "along the river," she said, "I think I saw the river." When asked what river it was, she said, "I don't know. It seems to be one I was visiting when I was a child."

Warning without stimulation—"Nothing."

Three minutes later without any warning stimulation was carried out again, probably near 13.

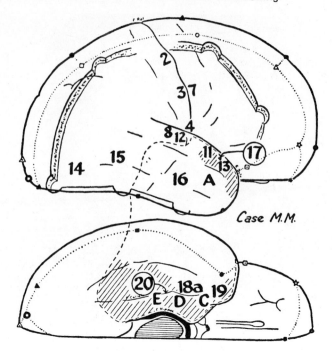

Case M.M.

Figure 11-5. Diagram of the operation. Broken line shows extent of removal of temporal lobe in treatment of the focal epilepsy and the shading indicates sclerosis and atrophy due to arterial compression associated with herniation of the hippocampus through the incisura of the tentorium, at the time of birth (incisural sclerosis).

While the electrode was held in place, she exclaimed: "Yes, I hear voices. It is late at night, around the carnival somewhere—some sort of travelling circus." Then, after removal of the electrode: "I just saw lots of big wagons that they use to haul animals in."

These simple re-enactments of experience had auditory and visual elements in them.

Eleven minutes later, stimulation was carried out without warning at a point just posterior to 11—"I seemed to hear little voices then," she said, "the voices of people calling from building to building somewhere—I do not know where it is but it is very familiar to me. I cannot see the buildings now but they seemed to be run-down buildings."

14 (just posterior to 15)—This stimulation caused her to say: "The whole operation now seems familiar."

Warning without stimulation—"Nothing."

15—"Just a tiny flash of familiarity and a feeling that I knew everything that was going to happen in the near future." Then she added, "as though I had been through all this before and thought I knew exactly what you were going to do next."

At point 17, an electrode, covered with an insulating coat except at its tip, was inserted to different depths and the current switched on so as to stimulate in various buried portions of the first temporal convolution and uncus.

17 (1 cm deep)—"Oh, I had the same very, very familiar memory, in an office somewhere. I could see the desks. I was there and someone was calling to me, a man leaning on a desk with a pencil in his hand."

Warning without stimulation—"Nothing."

11 (forty minutes after first stimulation of this point)—"I had a flash of familiar memory. I do not know what it was."

13 (repeated three times)—"Nothing."

11 (after four minutes)—"Nothing."

Conditions seemed to have changed and stimulation now would summon no experiences.

The plan of surgical excision had now been formulated. Accordingly the second and third temporal convolutions were removed, exposing the first temporal convolution and the uncus and hippocampal gyrus deep within the temporal fossa.

Stimulation near uncus or just lateral to it, at 18a—"I had a little memory—a scene in a play—they were talking and I could see it.—I was just seeing it in my memory."

Stimulation at a point nearby—"I feel very close to an attack—I think I am going to have one—a familiar memory."

20. (Stimulation of the lateral aspect of the hippocampal gyrus)—"Oh, it hurts and that feeling of familiarity—a familiar memory—the place where I hang my coat up, where I go to work."

The patient M. M., described in this case, was a good witness, self-critical, understanding, and tolerant. I have reported the features which are of psychological interest throughout the whole procedure of exploration and cortical excision, a three-hour period. But little reference is made to the pathological, surgical, and electrocortico-graphic details.

A zone of abnormality due to birth compression was found (shown by cross hatching in Figure 11-5). It was obvious that years of epileptic discharge arising in this zone had sensitized the temporal cortex so that stimulation could produce psychical responses. Stimulations elsewhere in the lobe were without positive effect even when a small increase was made in voltage.

The psychical hallucinations, thus produced, were experiences from this patient's past, not particularly important ones, and not ones that she could voluntarily remember with anything like the clarity of the hallucination. Yet she accepted them as part of her own past and she confessed that she was present in them. They brought to her the strong sense of familiarity that means recognition.

Case 3
N.C.

(Figures 11-6 and 11-7): This patient had seemed to be asleep on the operating table, but when the second temporal convolution on the left side was stimulated at point 19, she spoke as follows: "I had a dream, I had a book under my arm. I was talking to a man. The man was trying to reassure me not to worry about the book."

At 20, one cm distant, she said: "Mother is talking to me." Ten minutes later, point 20 was stimulated again and she laughed aloud. When asked to explain she said: "Well, it is kind of a long story but I will tell you." The stimulating electrode was then withdrawn. It seemed the occurrence took place at her home in Richmond, Washington. She said to her mother, "Don't forget the fabulous feeling." Her mother "mocked" her, she said, and she concluded the story, "I took my arm and brought it down on the plate and broke it all to pieces."

Stimulation was repeated at point 20 (Figure 11-7) without warning. While the electrode was kept in place the patient spoke quietly: "Yes, another experience, a different experience, a true experience. This man Mr. Meerburger, he, oh well, he drinks . . . ." The electrode was withdrawn and the patient continued to explain her experience. "I said, 'hmm, he is back,' meaning Mr. Meerburger's little boy, and the lady said, 'What is the matter,' etc. etc. etc." This was an experience she did remember.

At 23 on the first temporal convolution, stimulation caused her to hear music. Six times at intervals, stimulation was carried out here. She

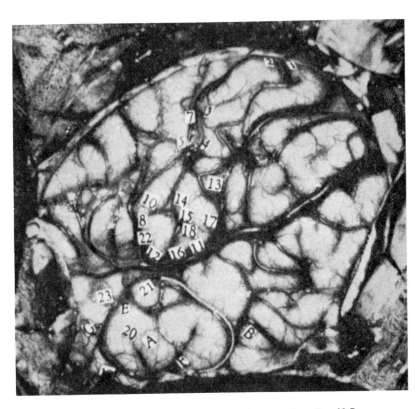

Figure 11-6.   Left hemisphere exposed at operation. Case N.C.

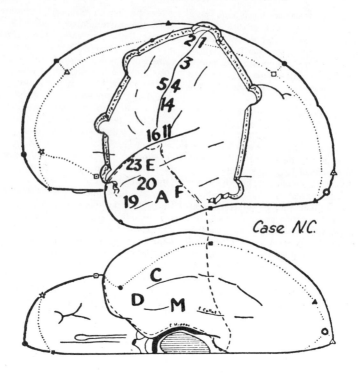

Figure 11-7. Diagram of operation. Case N.C.

heard first a "baby song" and later, what she called "The War March of the Priests."

On one occasion following stimulation which had been carried out with no warning, she said, "Yes. I was trying to identify the song." The surgeon asked her if she would like to have him stimulate again and she said, "yes." After the electrode was reapplied and while it was held in place she was quiet for a time. Then she began to hum and she hummed an air quite accurately. Finally she said, "Yes, it is 'The War March of the Priests.'" It was obvious that she had been accompanying the music with her humming.

Four minutes later, as a final test, she was asked to report just as soon as she heard music. After considerable delay the electrode was applied again at 23. Instantly she said, "There." It was the "War March" again. She explained that it was an orchestra playing each time, without any voice. She added that she had a phonograph record at home with the "Hallelujah Chorus" on one side and the "War March" on the other.

Case 4
R.M.

During stimulation of the superior surface of the left temporal lobe within the fissure of Sylvius, R. M. said: "A guy coming through the fence at the baseball game, I see the whole thing." Afterward he said, "I just happened to watch those two teams play when the fellow came through the fence. . . . That would be like the beginning of an attack, anything might come up." He went on to explain that such scenes from his past came to him suddenly at the beginning of a seizure, when he was thinking of something else, things he had forgotten all about.

One more example may be described. In this case the hallucination had to do with thoughts. It is difficult to discover whether in such cases the thought is divorced from any visual or auditory content or not.

Case 5
A.D.

This patient had temporal lobe seizures introduced by having what he called two thoughts simultaneously.

Stimulation in the first temporal convolution caused him to say, "My thoughts bounced together and I was mixed up for a second."

When the stimulation was repeated, he said, "The same two thoughts came together." After the electrode was withdrawn he explained that one of the thoughts was concerned with what was happening at the present time and the second thought was different but he could not recall it clearly.

When the same area was stimulated after an interval of time, he said, "This is it." When asked whether he had had a memory, he said, "No. It is the thought that crosses." But he could not explain and gave up the effort.

DISCUSSION

The foregoing examples demonstrate the nature of evidence upon which this discussion must be based. I have published other cases elsewhere and shall draw on our total experience in this argument.

Psychical Responses

From the patient's point of view there is a great difference between psychical responses and sensory responses to stimulation. When a sensory area is stimulated the patient never seems to feel an object. He does not hear words or music, nor see a person or building. In sensory responses there are no recollections of the past and the subject himself is usually clear that the sensation is not an ordinary experience at all.

What we have referred to as "psychical responses," on the other hand, include many different elements of thought, made up of auditory, visual, somatic, and labyrinthine information, as well as interpretations, perceptions, comparisons, emotions.

Under the heading of psychical, there are two types of response. One is a reproduction of past experience and the other is a sudden alteration in interpretation of present experience. Thus the psychical responses to stimulation, taken together, may be divided into two groups:

1. *Experiential.* This has to do with the past and includes past events and past interpretation.

2. *Interpretive.* This has to do with the present.

Experiential Responses

When these flash-backs, these short reproductions of past experience, occurred as epileptic phenomena, Jackson called them "dreamy states." They are the same when produced by stimulation—drawn from the patient's past experience. Let me use the words of the patient M. M. again: "I had a little memory—a scene from a play—they were talking and I could see it," and again, "Oh, . . . familiar memory, in an office somewhere. I could see the desks. I was there and someone was calling to me, a man leaning on a desk with a pencil in his hand."

All the detail of those things to which she had paid attention are still there. Perhaps the pencil in his hand had seemed important, but other images that must have reached her retina during the original experience are now lost, for they were ignored originally. Throughout all of these evoked experiences she continued to be aware of the fact that she was actually in the operating room.

It is clear that a flash-back response is usually completely experiential, including events and also the patient's interpretation. The patient feels the attendant emotion and understands the original meaning.

Interpretive Responses

As an example of interpretive responses, take again the case of M. M. When the electrode was applied to another area of the temporal lobe it produced a sudden sense of familiarity which she referred at once to her present experience. She felt the operation had happened before and that she even knew what the surgeon was about to do. This occurred independently of any recollection of the past.

When such interpretations have been described by temporal lobe epileptics, clinicians have long called them "déjà vu" phenomena. They are disturbances of the present process of interpretation. They are illusions, but these illusions take different forms. There may be a false sense of familiarity as already described; or, on the contrary, everything may seem strange or absurd. The relationship of the individual to his environment may seem to be altered. The distance from things seen or heard may seem to be increased or decreased. The patient may say he is far away from himself or from the world.

Allied to these altered interpretations is the production of emotions not justified by the experience. Fear is the commonest emotion produced by stimulation. It was reported as an epileptic aura 22 times out of 271 cases of temporal lobe epilepsy and was produced by stimulation 9 times.

All of these are interpretive responses. They correspond with the judgments which a normal individual is making constantly as he compares present experience with past experience. If a decision is to be made as to whether present experience is familiar or appropriate or menacing, the record of past experience must be available and the new record must be somehow classified with similar old records for the purposes of comparison.

Localization

Both types of response, experiential and interpretive, argue for the existence of a permanent ganglionic recording of the stream of consciousness. The record of that stream msut be preserved in a specialized mechanism. Otherwise experiential responses to an electrode applied locally would be impossible. It seems likely also that appropriate parts of this same record are somehow utilized when recurring judgments are made in regard to familiarity and meaning of each new experience.

These psychical responses were produced by stimulation of the temporal cortex, chiefly on the superior and lateral surfaces of both lobes and probably extending a

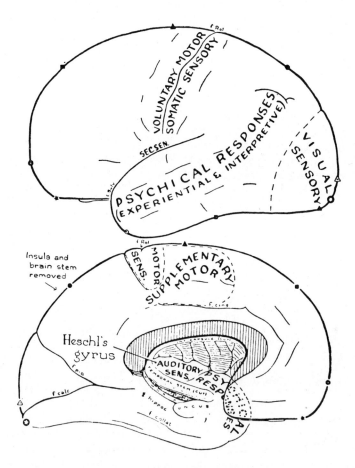

Figure 11-8. Area of cortex from which psychical responses are obtained. They may be experiential, recalling the experience of some past interval of time, or they may be interpretive and alter the patient's interpretation of present experience. The major sensory and motor areas are also indicated.

little way into the parietal lobe (Figure 11-8). None resulted from stimulation of other lobes. It seems fair to conclude, therefore, that these areas of cortex have a particular relationship to the formation of a record of experience and the preservation of that record. If this conclusion is correct, another important advance has been made in the evolution of our knowledge of cerebral localization.

Doubling of Conscious Experience

When stimulation produced an experiential response during operative exploration, the patient usually recognized that this was something out of his own past. At the same time he may have been acutely aware of the fact that he was lying upon the operating table. Thus he was able to contemplate and to talk about this doubling of awareness and to recognize it as a strange paradox.

A young man (J.T.)[3,p.36] who had recently come from his home in South Africa cried out when the superior surface of his right temporal lobe was being stimulated: "Yes, Doctor, yes, Doctor! Now I hear people laughing—my friends—in South Africa." After stimulation was over he could discuss that double awareness and express his astonishment, for it had seemed to him that he was with his cousins at their home where he and the two young ladies were laughing together. He did not remember what they were laughing at. Doubtless he would have discovered that also, if the strip of experience had happened to begin earlier, or if the surgeon had continued the stimulation a little longer.

This was an experience from his earlier life. It had faded from his recollective memory, but the ganglionic pattern which must have been formed during that experience was still intact and available to the stimulating electrode. It was at least as clear to him as it would have been had he closed his eyes and ears 30 seconds after the event and rehearsed the whole scene "from memory." Sight and sound and personal interpretation, all were re-created for him.

It is significant, however, that during the re-creation of that past experience he was not impelled to speak to his cousins. Instead he spoke to the "Doctor" in the operating room. Herein may lie an important distinction between this form of hallucination and the hallucinations of a patient during a toxic delirium or a psychotic state. In my experience (and relying only on my own memory!) no patient has ever addressed himself to a person who was part of a past experience, unless perhaps it was when he had passed into a state of automatism.*

As J. T. lay on the operating table two sets of ganglionic recordings were available to him for his conscious consideration, one that had been laid down during an interval of time that belonged to the past, and another that was being laid down during an equal interval of time in what we may call the present. He was evidently able to distinguish between the present experience and the past and so he addressed himself in astonishment to one of the actors in the present experience.

In the recording which he was then making of the present experience, he was including the experience that came to him from the past, together with the sensory information of his present environment in the operating room, and the results of his reasoning in regard to the two recordings.

When such states occurred in an epileptic attack, Hughlings Jackson spoke of a doubling of consciousness. But there is an important difference in the two experiences. Although the sensory elements may be as realistic in one as in the other, the interpretation in the flash-back was all finished while the interpretation of both experiences had to be made and recorded as a part of the present experience!

When we discussed the matter, the patient and I, during the period of convalescence which followed removal of a large portion of his right temporal lobe, he recalled the whole affair and also his own surprise that he should hear his friends so

---

*During automatism patients sometimes talk about unrelated matters, which might suggest that they were addressing someone, but they never describe hallucinations and there is complete subsequent amnesia.

far away and laugh with them while he faced such a serious situation here in Montreal.

One might suggest that, while the right temporal lobe under the influence of stimulation was engaged in the reproduction of the experience from the past, the left temporal lobe was being employed by the patient in the formation of the recording of the whole present experience. Such a suggestion is, of course, no more than a surmise. But that he did make a new record of both experiences somewhere is certain.

There are two elements in the experiential record, first, the sensory material of which the subject was originally aware and, second, the interpretation of the sensory material with a conclusion as to its significance. As already pointed out, in order to make the second, or interpretive, element possible, there must be comparison with past experience so that a conclusion may be drawn as to familiarity, strangeness, distance, danger, advantage, and necessity for action. It seems likely that under normal conditions the actual recording of the stream of consciousness may be utilized for the purposes of comparison long after it has been lost to voluntary recall.

Tempo of Action

I conclude that the interval of time involved in the past experience is the same as the time required for its subsequent re-enactment. The action or thought in the re-enactment progresses at the same speed as during the original experience. I make this conclusion about speed from consideration of the following evidence:

The patient N.C., whose case has been described, listened to an orchestra while the electrode was applied. When she hummed the air, accompanying thus the music, the tempo of her humming was the tempo that would be expected of an orchestra.

Let me give another similar example.

D.F.[3,p.128] was an intelligent young woman, a secretary and amateur musician. After the anterior end of her right temporal lobe had been amputated, the cut surface of the gray matter was stimulated at a point on the superior surface of the lobe. The stimulus caused her to say that she heard an orchestra playing and she asserted that we had turned on a phonograph. When she hummed the tune, Miss Phoebe Stanley, the operating nurse, recognizing the song, supplied the words of the lyric. The tempo of the patient's humming was certainly the tempo that would be expected of an orchestra playing that air.

And so, since the music is reproduced at a normal tempo regardless of the number of electrical impulses per second which may be varied from 30 to 100, I would conclude that the rate of movement in the recreated experience is the same as that of the original occurrence.

Further, and more important, verification of this conclusion is to be found in the fact that no patient has suggested that the people who walked or spoke or called during the hallucination did so at an unusual or unexpected rate of speed.

The Patient's Interpretation of an Experiential Response

Some patients call the response a dream. Others state that it is a flash-back from their own life history. All agree that it is more vivid than anything that they could recall voluntarily.

G.F.[3,p.137] was caused to hear her small son, Frank, speaking in the yard outside her own kitchen, and she heard the "neighborhood sounds" as well. Ten days after operation she was asked if this was a memory. "Oh, no," she replied. "It seemed more real than that." Then she added: "Of course, I have heard Frankie like that many, many times, thousands of times."

This response to stimulation was a single experience. Her memory of such occasions was a generalization. Without the aid of the electrode, she could not recall any one of the specific instances nor hear the honking of automobiles that might mean danger to Frankie, or cries of other children or the barking of dogs that would have made up the "neighborhood sounds" on each occasion.

The patients have never looked upon an experiential response as a remembering. Instead of that it is a hearing—and seeing—again, a living-through moments of past time. Do you remember Dickens' Christmas Carol, and how Old Scrooge seemed to re-live certain boyhood experiences under the strange spell of the "Spirit of Chirstmas Past"? It seems to be a little like that.

D.F. listened to an orchestra in the operating room but did not recall where she had heard it "that way." It was a song she had never learned to sing or play. Perhaps she had been oblivious of her surroundings while she listened to the orchestra in that previous period of time. T.S. heard music and seemed to be in the theatre where he had heard it. A.Br. heard the singing of a Christmas song in her church at home in Holland. She seemed to be there in the church and was moved again by the beauty of the occasion just as she had been on that Christmas Eve some years before.

Content of the Record

The nature of the contents of the record of the stream of consciousness may be guessed from the words of the patients that I have quoted tonight and of patients included in previous publications. It may be surmised also, by any clinician, from critical study of the content of the temporal lobe seizures which Hughlings Jackson called dreamy states. It may be guessed from the fact that when you meet a friend after many years you detect the little changes in him in a way that proves you had not lost the detail of original experiences. It may well be that seeing him renders details of the original record available for comparison, details which were lost to voluntary recollection.

The recording has strong visual and auditory components but always it is an unfolding of sight and sound and also, though rarely, of sense of position. The experience goes forward. There are no still pictures.

Curiously enough, no patient has yet reported pain or taste or smell during an experiential response. These sensations, without recollection of previous experience, were elicited by the electrode only from sensory areas. They were considered by the patient to be no more than present sensations, not elements in a past experience. It should be said, however, that the failure to get a response of any particular type has little statistical value, for the total number of patients from whom psychical responses have been elicited is, after all, small.*

One might seek to discover whether reasoning, which is divorced from awareness of sensory phenomena, finds any place in the cortical record. It is difficult for me to explore this possibility which involves certain questions of philosophical analysis. But it may be pointed out that patients do sometimes speak of unexpected thoughts coming into mind as a warning of the onset of a focal seizure. They usually report that this confuses them so that the account they give of the matter is not clear.

An example was presented above (Case A.D.) of the production of two thoughts by temporal stimulation. The patient said that one thought had to do with what was going on at the present time and the second thought was different, but the effect upon him was confusion and inability to explain. It might seem that two lines of reasoning or thinking could not co-exist without interference and that, if thoughts were really re-activated, they confused the patient's present effort to rationalize.

However that may be, it seems clear that the final interpretation and the understanding of any experience are recorded with the experience. This interpretation and understanding may be considered the end result or the conclusion of rationalization. Certainly, at the times of re-activation, the

---

*My associate Dr. Sean Mullan informs me that there have been 87 cases of temporal lobe epilepsy in which electrical exploration was carried out during the past three years. In only 22 of them did stimulation produce echoes of past experience. We have explored the cortex in 271 temporal lobe cases in all, which suggests that not over 60 patients had experiential responses. In no cases where the epileptogenic focus was located in central or frontal regions have there been such responses.

patient has no difficulty in perceiving his former understanding of a situation along with the objective aspects of the situation itself.

Memory Contrasted with the Record

It is clear that each successive recording is somehow classified and compared with previous recordings so that, little by little, each separate song is "learned" and becomes a unit in the memory, and all the familiar things in a man's life undergo the same change. A poem or an elocution may be "committed to memory." But memory, as we ordinarily think of it, is something more, and a great deal less, than any recording, unless that recording was made unusually vivid by fear or joy or special meaning. Then perhaps the detail of an original experience and the patient's memory of it might be identical.

The psychical responses of the "flash-back" variety were, for the most part, quite unimportant moments in the patient's life: standing on a street corner, hearing a mother call her child, taking a part in a conversation, listening to a little boy as he played in the yard. If these unimportant minutes of time were preserved in the ganglionic recordings of these patients, why should it be thought that any experience in the stream of consciousness drops out?

The evidence suggests that nothing is lost, that the record of each man's experience is complete. The time taken up by deep sleep or coma must drop out and it must be left an open question as to whether or not the time taken up by reasoning is included in the record.

CONCLUSION

In conclusion it is evident that the brain of every man contains an unchanging ganglionic record of successive experience. The psychical responses which have been produced by electrical stimulation, during craniotomy and cortical exploration, demonstrate that this record embraces and

retains the elements that once were incorporated in his stream of thought.

Simply expressed, the conditions which bring about these psychical responses, both experiential and interpretive, are these: The stimulating electrode, delivering for example 60 impulses per second, is applied to a point on the temporal cortex of a man who is fully awake. The ganglion cells of the cortex are hyper-irritable and ready to react because, for years, small electrical discharges have been playing over the cortical blanket day and night from a neighboring epileptogenic focus.

Thousands of these conditioned ganglion cells may well be reached directly by the stimulating current and they have neuronal connections that pass through the gray matter that covers the temporal lobe and also inward to the central integrating circuits of the brain stem. But instead of mass activity, a selective and highly patterned ganglionic action results.

Let me describe what seems to happen by means of a parable: Among the millions and millions of nerve cells that clothe certain parts of the temporal lobe on each side, there runs a thread. It is the thread of time, the thread that has run through each succeeding, wakeful hour of the individual's past life. Think of this thread, if you like, as a pathway through an unending sequence of nerve cells, nerve fibers, and synapses. It is a pathway which can be followed again because of the continuing facilitation that has been created in the cell contacts.

When, by chance, the neurosurgeon's electrode activates some portion of that thread, there is a response as though that thread were a wire recorder, or a strip of cinematographic film, on which are registered all those things of which the individual was once aware, the things he selected for his attention in that interval of time. Absent from it are the sensory impulses he ignored, the talk he did not heed.

Time's strip of film runs forward, never backward, even when resurrected from the past. It seems to proceed again at time's own unchanged pace. It would seem, once one section of the strip has come alive, that a functional all-or-nothing principle steps in so as to protect the other portions of the film from activation by the electric current. As long as the electrode is held in place, the experience of a former day goes forward. There is no holding it still, no turning it back. When the electrode is withdrawn it stops as suddenly as it began*

We have found a way of activating the anatomical record of the stream of consciousness. It is evident, therefore, that the ganglionic mechanism which preserves man's experiential record is either present, in duplicate, in the temporal cortex of each hemisphere, where stimulation produces these responses; or it is located in duplicate in the hippocampal zones of each side where direct stimulation does not produce the responses; or, finally, it is located more centrally in the brain where the closest functional connection is maintained with the stimulable zones of the temporal lobes.

However that may be, and whatever the mechanism involved, it is certain that in the temporal cortex lie the keys of activation of the record.

During any given period of waking time each individual forms a record of the stream of consciousness. The record is the final expression, and the outcome, of the action of central integration of nerve impulses. The formation of this record is subject to the selecting and limiting influences of attention. As the record is formed, it includes the elements of consciousness. Possibly, like a film, its contents are projected on the screen of man's awareness before it is replaced by subsequent experience. Thus it might seem that the record of the stream of consciousness is more than a record. It represents one of the final stages in the neuronal integration which makes consciousness what it is.

Probably no man can, by voluntary effort, completely re-activate any portion of the record of the stream of thought. Except for a few seconds or minutes after the event, he seems to have no voluntary mechanism that rivals the electrode. Memory, as ordinarily conceived, is quite a different phenomenon. It seems likely, however, that the original record continues to be available in some sort of way for the purposes of the comparison and interpretation of each new experience, as long as a man may live and keep his wits.

The stream of consciousness flows inexorably onward, as described in the words of William James. But, unlike a river, it leaves behind it a permanent record that seems to be complete for the waking moments of a man's life, a record that runs, no doubt, like a thread along a pathway of ganglionic and synaptic facilitations in the brain. This pathway is located partly or wholly in the temporal lobes.

There is hope in all this that physiology and psychology, and philosophy, too, may be drawn more closely together and that, with the opening of a new chapter of understanding of the localization of function within the human brain, some light may yet be thrown upon the mind of man.

REFERENCES

1. James, W.: The Principles of Psychology. New York, Holt & Co., 1910.
2. Penfield, W., and Rasmussen, T.: The Cerebral Cortex of Man. New York, Macmillan, 1950.
3. Penfield, W., and Jasper, H.: Epilepsy and the Functional Anatomy of the Human Brain. Boston, Little, Brown, 1954.
4. Penfield, W.: Mechanisms of Voluntary Movement. Brain 77: 1–17 (1954).
5. Penfield, W.: The cerebral cortex and consciousness. Arch. Neurol. and Psychiat. 40: 417–442 (1938. Also in French, Amnée Psychol. 39: 1 (1938).
6. Brown, G., Sherrington, T., and Sherrington, C.: On the instability of a cortical point. Proc. Roy. Soc. London, s.B. 85: 250–277.

---

*A particular strip can sometimes be repeated by interrupting the stimulation and then reapplying it at the same or a nearby point, for the threshold of evocation of that particular response is lowered for a time by the first stimulus. Graham Brown and Sherrington[6] described local facilitation and intensification of motor responses by repeated stimulation at a single point in the anthropoid cortex, and we have found the same to be true for man in motor and sensory areas of the cortex.[2]

12.   Hemisphere Deconnection and Unity in Conscious Awareness

R. W. Sperry

The following article is a result of studies my colleagues and I have been conducting with some neurosurgical patients of Philip J. Vogel of Los Angeles. These patients were all advanced epileptics in whom an extensive midline section of the cerebral commissures had been carried out in an effort to contain severe epileptic convulsions not controlled by medication. In all these people the surgical sections included division of the corpus callosum in its entirety, plus division also of the smaller anterior and hippocampal commissures, plus in some instances the massa intermedia. So far as I know, this is the most radical disconnection of the cerebral hemispheres attempted thus far in human surgery. The full array of sections was carried out in a single operation.

No major collapse of mentality or personality was anticipated as a result of this extreme surgery: earlier clinical observations on surgical section of the corpus callosum in man, as well as the results from dozens of monkeys on which I had carried out this exact same surgery, suggested that the functional deficits might very likely be less damaging than some of the more common forms of cerebral surgery, such as frontal lobotomy, or even some of the unilateral lobotomies performed more routinely for epilepsy.

The first patient on whom this surgery was tried had been having seizures for more than 10 years with generalized convulsions that continued to worsen despite treatment that had included a sojourn in Bethesda at the National Institutes of Health. At the time of the surgery, he had been averaging two major attacks per week, each of which left him debilitated for another day or so. Episodes of *status epilepticus* (recurring seizures that fail to stop and represent a medical emergency with a fairly high mortality risk) had also begun to occur at 2- to 3-month intervals. Since leaving the hospital following his surgery over 5½ years ago, this man has not had, according to last reports, a single generalized convulsion. It has further been possible to reduce the level of medication and to obtain an overall improvement in his behavior and well being.[3]

The second patient, a housewife and mother in her 30s, also has been seizure-free since recovering from her surgery, which was more than 4 years ago.[2] Bogen related that even the EEG has regained a normal pattern in this patient. The excellent outcome in the initial, apparently hopeless, last-resort cases led to further application of the surgery to some nine more individuals to date, the majority of whom are too recent for therapeutic evaluation. Although the alleviation of the epilepsy has not held up 100% throughout the series (two patients are still having seizures, although their convulsions are much reduced in severity and frequency and tend to be confined to one side), the results on the whole continue to be predominantly beneficial, and the overall outlook at this time remains promising for selected severe cases.

The therapeutic success, however, and all other medical aspects are matters for our medical colleagues, Philip J. Vogel and Joseph E. Bogen. Our own work has been confined entirely to an examination of the functional outcome, that is, the behavioral,

Sperry, R. W.: Hemisphere deconnection and unity in conscious awareness. Am. Psychol. *23:* 723-733 (1968).

neurological, and psychological effects of this surgical disruption of all direct cross-talk between the hemispheres. Initially we were concerned as to whether we would be able to find in these patients any of the numerous symptoms of hemisphere deconnection that had been demonstrated in the so-called "split-brain" animal studies of the 1950s.[12,15,16] The outcome in man remained an open question in view of the historic Akelaitis (1944)[1] studies that had set the prevailing doctrine of the 1940s and 1950s. This doctrine maintained that no important functional symptoms are found in man following even complete surgical section of the corpus callosum and anterior commissure, provided that other brain damage is excluded.

These earlier observations on the absence of behavioral symptoms in man have been confirmed in a general way to the extent that it remains fair to say today that the most remarkable effect of sectioning the neocortical commissures is the apparent lack of effect so far as ordinary behavior is concerned. This has been true in our animal studies throughout, and it seems now to be true for man also, with certain qualifications that we will come to later. At the same time, however—and this is in contradiction to the earlier doctrine set by the Akelaitis studies—we know today that with appropriate tests one can indeed demonstrate a large number of behavioral symptoms that correlate directly with the loss of the neocortical commissures in man as well as in animals.[4,15,16,19] Taken collectively, these symptoms may be referred to as the syndrome of the neocortical commissures or the syndrome of the forebrain commissures or, less specifically, as the syndrome of hemisphere deconnection.

One of the more general and also more interesting and striking features of this syndrome may be summarized as an apparent doubling in most of the realms of conscious awareness. Instead of the normally unified single stream of consciousness, these patients behave in many ways as if they have two independent streams of conscious awareness, one in each hemisphere, each of which is cut off from and out of contact with the mental

experiences of the other. In other words, each hemisphere seems to have its own separate and private sensations; its own perceptions; its own concepts; and its own impulses to act, with related volitional, cognitive, and learning experiences. Following the surgery, each hemisphere also has thereafter its own separate chain of memories that are rendered inaccessible to the recall processes of the other.

This presence of two minds in one body, as it were, is manifested in a large number and variety of test responses which, for the present purposes, I will try to review very briefly and in a somewhat streamlined and simplified form. First, however, let me take time to emphasize that the work reported here has been very much a team project. The surgery was performed by Vogel at the White Memorial Medical Center in Los Angeles. He has been assisted in the surgery and in the medical treatment throughout by Joseph Bogen. Bogen has also been collaborating in our behavioral testing program, along with a number of graduate students and postdoctoral fellows, among whom M. S. Gazzaniga, in particular, worked closely with us during the first several years and managed much of the testing during that period. The patients and their families have been most cooperative, and the whole project gets its primary funding from the National Institute of Mental Health.

Most of the main symptoms seen after hemisphere deconnection can be described for convenience with reference to a single testing setup—shown in Figure 12-1. Principally, it allows for the lateralized testing of the right and left halves of the visual field, separately or together, and the right and left hands and legs with vision excluded. The tests can be arranged in different combinations and in association with visual, auditory, and other input, with provisions for eliminating unwanted stimuli. In testing vision, the subject with one eye covered centers his gaze on a designated fixation point on the upright translucent screen. The visual stimuli on 35-millimeter transparencies are arranged in a standard projector equipped with a shutter and are then back-projected at $\frac{1}{10}$ of a second or less—too fast for eye move-

Figure 12-1. Apparatus for studying lateralization of visual, tactual, lingual, and associated functions in the surgically separated hemispheres.

ments to get the material into the wrong half of the visual field. Figure 12-2 is merely a reminder that everything seen to the left of the vertical meridian through either eye is projected to the right hemisphere and vice versa. The midline division along the vertical meridian is found to be quite precise without significant gap or overlap.[17]

When the visual perception of these patients is tested under these conditions the results indicate that these people have not one inner visual world any longer, but rather two separate visual inner worlds, one serving the right half of the field of vision and the other the left half—each, of course, in its respective hemisphere. This doubling in the visual sphere shows up in many ways: For example, after a projected picture of an object has been identified and responded to in one half field, we find that it is recognized again only if it reappears in the same half of the field of vision. If the given visual stimulus reappears in the opposite half of the visual field, the subject responds as if he had no recollection of the previous exposure. In other words, things seen through the right half of the visual field (i.e., through the left hemisphere) are registered in mental experience and remembered quite separately from things seen in the other half of the field. Each half of the field of vision in the commissurotomized patient has its own train of visual images and memories.

This separate existence of two visual inner worlds is further illustrated in reference to speech and writing, the cortical mechanisms for which are centered in the dominant hemisphere. Visual material projected to the right half of the field—left-hemisphere system of the typical right-handed patient—can be described in speech and writing in an essentially normal manner. However, when the same visual material is projected into the left half of the field, and hence to the right hemisphere, the subject consistently insists that he did not see anything or that there was only a flash of light on the left side. The subject acts as if he were blind or agnostic for the left half of the visual field. If, however, instead of asking the subject to tell you what he saw, you instruct him to use his left hand to point to a matching picture or object presented among a collection of other pictures or objects, the subject has no trouble as a rule in pointing out consistently the very item that he has just insisted he did not see.

We do not think the subjects are trying to be difficult or to dupe the examiner in such tests. Everything indicates that the hemisphere that is talking to the examiner did in fact not see the left-field stimulus and truly had no experience with, nor recollection of, the given stimulus. The other, the right or nonlingual hemisphere, however, did see the projected stimulus in this situation and is able to remember and recognize the object and can demonstrate this by pointing out selectively the corresponding or matching item. This other hemisphere, like a deaf mute or like some aphasics, cannot talk about the perceived object and, worse still, cannot write about it either.

If two different figures are flashed simultaneously to the right and left visual fields, as for example a "dollar sign" on the left and a "question mark" on the right and the subject is asked to draw what he saw using the left hand out of sight, he regularly reproduces the figure seen on the left half of the field, that is, the dollar sign. If we now ask him what he has just drawn, he tells us without hesitation that the figure he drew was the question mark, or whatever appeared in the right half of the field.

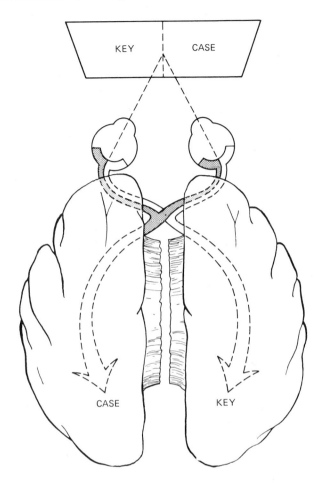

Figure 12-2. Things seen to the left of a central fixation point with either eye are projected to the right hemisphere and vice-versa.

In other words, the one hemisphere does not know what the other hemisphere has been doing. The left and the right halves of the visual field seem to be perceived quite separately in each hemisphere with little or no cross-influence.

When words are flashed partly in the left field and partly in the right, the letters on each side of the midline are perceived and responded to separately. In the "key case" example shown in Figure 12-2 the subject might first reach for and select with the left hand a key from among a collection of objects indicating perception through the minor hemisphere. With the right hand he might then spell out the word "case" or he might speak the word if verbal response is in order. When asked what kind of "case" he was thinking of here, the answer coming from the left hemisphere might be something like "in *case* of fire" or "the *case* of

the missing corpse" or "a *case* of beer," etc., depending upon the particular mental set of the left hemisphere at the moment. Any reference to "key case" under these conditions would be purely fortuitous, assuming that visual, auditory, and other cues have been properly controlled.

A similar separation in mental awareness is evident in tests that deal with stereognostic or other somesthetic discriminations made by the right and left hands, which are projected separately to the left and right hemispheres, respectively. Objects put in the right hand for identification by touch are readily described or named in speech or writing, whereas, if the same objects are placed in the left hand, the subject can only make wild guesses and may often seem unaware that anything at all is present. As with vision in the left field, however, good perception, comprehension, and memory can be demonstrated for these objects in the left hand when the tests are so designed that the subject can express himself through nonverbal responses. For example, if one of these objects which the subject tells you he cannot feel or does not recognize is taken from the left hand and placed in a grab bag or scrambled among a dozen other test items, the subject is then able to search out and retrieve the initial object even after a delay of several minutes is deliberately interposed. Unlike the normal subject, however, these people are obliged to retrieve such an object with the same hand with which it was initially identified. They fail at cross-retrieval. That is, they cannot recognize with one hand something identified only moments before with the other hand. Again, the second hemisphere does not know what the first hemisphere has been doing.

When the subjects are first asked to use the left hand for these stereognostic tests they commonly complain that they cannot "work with that hand," that the hand "is numb," that they "just can't feel anything or can't do anything with it," or that they "don't get the message from that hand." If the subjects perform a series of successful trials and correctly retrieve a group of objects which they previously stated they could not feel, and if this contradiction is then pointed out to them, we get comments like "Well, I was just guessing," or "Well, I must have done it unconsciously."

With other simple tests a further lack of cross-integration can be demonstrated in the sensory and motor control of the hands. In a "symmetric handpose" test the subject holds both hands out of sight symmetrically positioned and not in contact. One hand is then passively placed by the examiner into a given posture, such as a closed fist, or one, two, or more fingers extended or crossed or folded into various positions. The subject is then instructed verbally or by demonstration to form the same pose with the other hand, also excluded from vision. The normal subject does this quite accurately, but the commissurotomy patient generally fails on all but the very simplest hand postures, like the closed fist or the fully extended hand.

In a test for crossed topognosis in the hands, the subject holds both hands out of sight, forward and palm up with the fingers held apart and extended. The examiner then touches lightly a point on one of the fingers or at the base of the fingers. The subject responds by touching the same target point with the tip of the thumb of the same hand. Cross-integration is tested by requiring the patient to use the opposite thumb to find the corresponding mirror point on the opposite hand. The commissurotomy patients typically perform well within either hand, but fail when they attempt to cross-locate the corresponding point on the opposite hand. A crude cross-performance with abnormally long latency may be achieved in some cases after practice, depending on the degree of ipsilateral motor control and the development of certain strategies. The latter breaks down easily under stress and is readily distinguished from the natural performance of the normal subject with intact callosum.

In a related test the target point is presented visually as a black spot on an outline drawing of the hand. The picture is flashed to the right or left half of the visual field, and the subject then attempts as above to touch the target spot with the tip of the thumb. The response again is performed on the same side with normal facility but is impaired in the commissurotomy patient when the left visual field is paired with a right-hand response and vice versa. Thus the duality of both manual stereognosis and visuognosis is further illustrated; each hemisphere perceives as a separate unit unaware of the perceptual experience of the partner.

If two objects are placed simultaneously, one in each hand, and then are removed and hidden for retrieval in a scrambled pile of test items, each hand will hunt through the pile and search out selectively its own object. In the process each hand may explore, identify, and reject the item for which the other hand is searching. It is like two separate individuals working over the collection of test items with no cooperation between them. We find the interpretation of this and of many similar performances to be less confusing if we do not try to think of the behavior of the commissurotomy patient as that of a single individual, but try to think instead in terms of the mental faculties and performance capacities of the left and the right hemispheres separately. Most of the time it appears that the major, that is, the left, hemisphere is in control. But in some tasks, particularly when these are forced in testing procedures, the minor hemisphere seems able to take over temporarily.

It is worth remembering that when you split the brain in half anatomically you do not divide in half, in quite the same sense, its functional properties. In some respects cerebral functions may be doubled as much as they are halved because of the extensive bilateral redundancy in brain organization, wherein most functions, particularly in subhuman species, are separately and rather fully organized on both sides. Consider for example the visual inner world of either of the disconnected hemispheres in these patients. Probably neither of the separated visual systems senses or perceives itself to be cut in half or even incomplete. One may compare it to the visual sphere of the hemianopic patient who, following accidental destruction of an entire visual cortex of one hemisphere, may not even notice the loss of the whole half sphere of vision until this has been pointed out to him in specific optometric tests. These commissurotomy patients continue to watch television and to read the paper and books with no complaints about peculiarities in the perceptual appearance of the visual field.

At the same time, I want to caution against any impression that these patients are better off mentally without their cerebral commissures. It is true that if you carefully select two simple tasks, each of which is easily handled by a single hemisphere, and then have the two performed simultaneously, there is a good chance of getting better than normal scores. The normal interference effects that come from trying to attend to two separate right and left tasks at the same time are largely eliminated in the commissurotomized patient. However, in most activities that are at all complex the normally unified cooperating hemispheres still appear to do better than the two disconnected hemispheres. Although it is true that the intelli-

gence, as measured on IQ tests, is not much affected and that the personality comes through with little change, one gets the impression in working with these people that their intellect is nevertheless handicapped in ways that are probably not revealed in the ordinary tests. All the patients have marked short-term memory deficits, which are especially pronounced during the first year, and it is open to question whether this memory impairment ever clears completely. They also have orientation problems, fatigue more quickly in reading and in other tasks requiring mental concentration, and presumably have various other impairments that reduce the upper limits of performance in functions that have yet to be investigated. The patient that has shown the best recovery, a boy of 14, was able to return to public school and was doing passing work with B to D grades, except for an F in math, which he had to repeat. He was, however, a D student before the surgery, in part, it would seem, for lack of motivation. In general, our tests to date have been concerned mostly with basic cross-integrational deficits in these patients and the kind of mental capacities preserved in the subordinate hemisphere. Studied comparisons of the upper limits of performance before and after surgery are still needed.

Much of the foregoing is summarized schematically in Figure 12-3. The left hemisphere in the right-handed patients is equipped with the expressive mechanisms for speech and writing and with the main centers for the comprehension and organization of language. This "major" hemisphere can communicate its experiences verbally and in an essentially normal manner. It can communicate, that is, about the visual experiences of the right half of the optic field and about the somesthetic and volitional experiences of the right hand and leg and right half of the body generally. In addition, and not indicated in the figure, the major hemisphere also communicates, of course, about all of the more general, less lateralized cerebral activity that is bilaterally represented and common to both hemispheres. On the other side we have the mute aphasic and agraphic right hemisphere, which cannot express itself

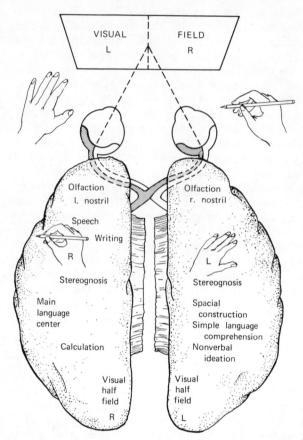

Figure 12-3. Schematic outline of the functional lateralization evident in behavioral tests of patients with forebrain commissurotomy.

verbally, but which through the use of nonverbal responses can show that it is not agnostic; that mental processes are indeed present centered around the left visual field, left hand, left leg, and left half of the body; along with the auditory, vestibular, axial somatic, and all other cerebral activities that are less lateralized and for which the mental experiences of the right and left hemispheres may be characterized as being similar but separate.

It may be noted that nearly all of the symptoms of cross-integrational impairment that I have been describing are easily hidden or compensated under the conditions or ordinary behavior. For example, the visual material has to be flashed at $\frac{1}{10}$ of a second or less to one half of the field in order to prevent compensation by eye movements. The defects in manual stereognosis are not apparent unless vision is excluded; nor is doubling in olfactory perception evident without sequential

occlusion of right and left nostril and elimination of visual cues. In many tests the major hemisphere must be prevented from talking to the minor hemisphere and thus giving away the answer through auditory channels. And, similarly, the minor hemisphere must be prevented from giving nonverbal signals of various sorts to the major hemisphere. There is a great diversity of indirect strategies and response signals, implicit as well as overt, by which the informed hemisphere can be used to cue-in the uninformed hemisphere.[11]

Normal behavior under ordinary conditions is favored also by many other unifying factors. Some of these are very obvious, like the fact that these two separate mental spheres have only one body, so they always get dragged to the same places, meet the same people, and see and do the same things all the time and thus are bound to have a great overlap of common, almost identical, experience. Just the unity of the optic image—and even after chiasm section in animal experiments, the conjugate movements of the eyes—means that both hemispheres automatically center on, focus on, and hence probably attend to, the same items in the visual field all the time. Through sensory feedback a unifying body schema is imposed in each hemisphere with common components that similarly condition in parallel many processes of perception and motor action onto a common base. To get different activities going and different experiences and different memory chains built up in the separated hemispheres of the bisected mammalian brain, as we do in the animal work, requires a considerable amount of experimental planning and effort.

In motor control we have another important unifying factor, in that either hemisphere can direct the movement of both sides of the body, including to some extent the movements of the ipsilateral hand.[10] Insofar as a response involves mainly the axial parts and proximal limb segments, these patients have little problem in directing overall response from sensory information restricted to either single hemisphere. Control of the distal limb segments and especially of the finer finger movements of the hand ipsilateral to the governing hemisphere, however, are borderline functions and subject to considerable variation. Impairments are most conspicuous when the subject is given a verbal command to respond with the fingers of the left hand. The absence of the callosum, which normally would connect the language processing centers in the left hemisphere to the main left-hand motor controls in the opposite hemisphere, is clearly a handicap, especially in the early months after surgery. Cursive writing with the left hand presents a similar problem. It

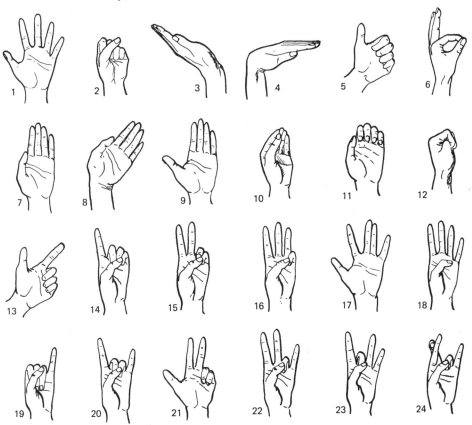

Figure 12-4. In tests for ipsilateral motor control, different hand postures in outline drawing are projected one at a time to left or right bisual field (see Figure 1). Subject attempts to copy the sample hand pose with the homolateral and the contralateral hand.

may be accomplished in time by some patients using shoulder and elbow rather than finger movement. At best, however, writing with the left hand is not as good after as before the surgery. The problem is not in motor coordination per se, because the subject can often copy with the left hand a word already written by the examiner when the same word cannot be written to verbal command.

In a test used for more direct determination of the upper limits of this ipsilateral motor control, a simple outline sketch of a finger posture (see Figure 12-4) is flashed to a single hemisphere, and the subject then tries to mimic the posture with the same or the opposite hand. The sample posture can usually be copied on the same side (i.e., through the main, contralateral control system) without difficulty, but the performance does not go so easily and often breaks down completely when the subject is obliged to use the opposite hand. The closed fist and the open hand with all fingers extended seem to be the two simplest responses, in that these can most often be copied with the ipsilateral hand by the more adept patients.

The results are in accord with the thesis[5] that the ipsilateral control systems are delicate and marginal and easily disrupted by associated cerebral damage and other complicating factors. Preservation of the ipsilateral control system in varying degree in some patients and not in others would appear to account for many of the discrepancies that exist in the literature on the sumptoms of hemisphere deconnection, and also for a number of changes between the present picture and that described until 2 years ago. Those acquainted with the literature will notice that the present findings on dyspraxia come much closer to the earlier Akelaitis observations than they do to those of Liepmann or of others expounded more recently.[8]

To try to find out what goes on in that speechless agraphic minor hemisphere has always been one of the main challenges in our testing program. Does the minor hemisphere really possess a true stream of conscious awareness or is it just an agnostic automaton that is carried along in a reflex or trancelike state? What is the nature, the

quality, and the level of the mental life of this isolated subordinate unknown half of the human brain—which, like the animal mind, cannot communicate its experiences? Closely tied in here are many problems that relate to lateral dominance and specialization in the human brain, to the functional roles mediated by the neocortical commissures, and to related aspects of cerebral organization.

With such in mind, I will try to review briefly some of the evidence obtained to date that pertains to the level and nature of the inner mental life of the disconnected minor hemisphere. First, it is clear that the minor hemisphere can perform intermodal or cross-modal transfer of perceptual and mnemonic information at a characteristically human level. For example, after a picture of some object, such as a cigarette, has been flashed to the minor hemisphere through the left visual field, the subject can retrieve the item pictured from a collection of objects using blind touch with the left hand, which is mediated through the right hemisphere. Unlike the normal person, however, the commissurotomy patient is obliged to use the corresponding hand (i.e., the left hand, in this case) for retrieval and fails when he is required to search out the same object with the right hand (see Figure 12-5). Using the right hand the subject recognizes and can call off the names of each object that he comes to if he is allowed to do so, but the right hand or its hemisphere does not know what it is looking for, and the hemisphere that can recognize the correct answer gets no feedback from the right hand. Hence, the two never get together, and the performance fails. Speech and other auditory cues must be controlled.

It also works the other way around: that is, if the subject is holding an object in the left hand, he can then point out a picture of this object or the printed name of the object when these appear in a series presented visually. But again, these latter must be seen through the corresponding half of the visual field; an object identified by the left hand is not recognized when seen in the right half of the visual field. Intermodal associations of this sort have been found to work between vision, hearing and touch,

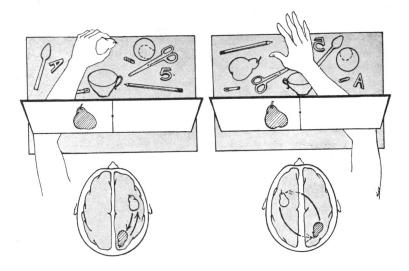

Figure 12-5. Visuo-tactile associations succeed between each half of the visual field and the corresponding hand. They fail with crossed combinations in which visual and tactual stimuli are projected into opposite hemispheres.

and, more recently, olfaction in various combinations within either hemisphere but not across from one hemisphere to the other. This perceptual or mnemonic transfer from one sense modality to another has special theoretical interest in that it is something that is extremely difficult or impossible for the monkey brain. The right hemisphere, in other words, may be animallike in not being able to talk or write, but in performances like the foregoing and in a number of other respects it shows mental capacities that are definitely human.

Other responses from the minor hemisphere in this same testing situation suggest the presence of ideas and a capacity for mental association and at least some simple logic and reasoning. In the same visuotactual test described above, the minor hemisphere, instead of selecting objects that match exactly the pictured item, seems able also to select related items or items that "go with" the particular visual stimulus, if the subject is so instructed. For example, if we flash a picture of a wall clock to the minor side and the nearest item that can be found tactually by the left hand is a toy wrist watch, the subjects significantly select the watch. It is as if the

minor hemisphere has an idea of a timepiece here and is not just matching sensory outlines. Or, if the picture of a dollar sign is flashed to the minor side, the subject searches through the list of items with the left hand and finally selects a coin such as a quarter or a 50¢ piece. If a picture of a hammer is presented, the subject may come up with a nail or a spike after checking out and rejecting all other items.

The capacity to think abstractly with symbols is further indicated in the ability of the minor hemisphere to perform simple arithmetical problems. When confronted with two numerals each less than 10, the minor hemisphere was able in four of six subjects so tested to respond with the correct sum or product up to 20 or so. The numbers were flashed to the left half of the visual field or presented as plastic block numerals to the left hand for identification. The answer was expressed by pointing to the correct number in columns of seen figures, or by left-hand signals in which the fingers were extended out of the subject's sight, or by writing the numerals with the left hand out of sight. After a correct left-hand response had been made by pointing or by writing the numeral, the major hemisphere could then report the same answer verbally, but the verbal report could not be made prior to the left-hand response. If an error was made with the left hand, the verbal report contained the same error. Two different pairs of numerals may be flashed to right and left fields simultaneously and the correct sum or products signaled separately by right and left hands. When verbal confirmation of correct left-hand signals is required under these conditions, the speaking hemisphere can only guess fortuitously, showing again that the answer must have been obtained from the minor and not from the major hemisphere. This has been demonstrated recently in a study still in progress by Biersner and the present writer. The findings correct an earlier impression[7] in which we underestimated the capacity for calculation on the minor side. Normal subjects and also a subject with agenesis of the callosum[13] were able to add or to multiply numerals shown one in the left and one in the right field under these conditions. The commissurotomy subjects, however, were able to perform such calculations only when both numerals appeared in the same half of the visual field.

According to a doctrine of long standing in the clinical writings on aphasia, it is believed that the minor hemisphere, when it has been disconnected by commisural or other lesions from the language centers on the opposite side, becomes then "word blind," "word deaf," and "tactually alexic." In contradiction to this, we find that the disconnected minor hemisphere in these commissurotomy patients is able to comprehend both written and spoken words to some extent, although this comprehension cannot be expressed verbally.[7,14,18] If the name of some object is flashed to the left visual field, like the word "eraser," for example, the subject is able then to search out an eraser from among a collection of objects using only touch with the left hand. If the subject is then asked what the item is after it has been selected correctly, his replies show that he does not know what he is holding in his left hand—as is the general rule for left-hand stereognosis. This means of course that the *talking* hemisphere does not know the correct answer, and we con-

cluded accordingly that the minor hemisphere must, in this situation, have read and understood the test world.

These patients also demonstrate comprehension of language in the minor hemisphere by being able to find by blind touch with the left hand an object that has been named aloud by the examiner. For example, if asked to find a "piece of silverware," the subject may explore the array of test items and pick up a fork. If the subject is then asked what it is that he has chosen, he is just as likely in this case to reply "spoon" or "knife" as fork. Both hemispheres have heard and understood the word "silverware," but only the minor hemisphere knows what the left hand has actually found and picked up. In similar tests for comprehension of the spoken word, we find that the minor hemisphere seems able to understand even moderately advanced definitions like "shaving instrument" for razor or "dirt remover" for soap and "inserted in slot machines" for quarter.

Work in progress shows that the minor hemisphere can also sort objects into groups by touch on the basis of shape, size, and texture. In some tests the minor hemisphere is found to be superior to the major, for example, in tasks that involve drawing spatial relationships and performing block design tests. Perceptive mental performance in the minor hemisphere is also indicated in other situations in which the two hemispheres function concurrently in parallel at different tasks. It has been found, for example, that the divided hemispheres are capable of perceiving different things occupying the same position in space at the same time, and of learning mutually conflicting discrimination habits, something of which the normal brain is not capable. This was shown in the monkey work done some years ago by Trevarthen[20] using a system of polarized light filters. It also required section of the optic chiasm, which of course is not included in the human surgery. The human patients, unlike normal subjects, are able to carry out a double voluntary reaction-time task as fast as they carry out a single task.[6] Each hemisphere in this situation has to perform a separate and different visual discrimination in order to push with the corresponding hand the correct one of a right and left pair of panels. Whereas interference and extra delay are seen in normal subjects with the introduction of the second task, these patients with the two hemispheres working in parallel simultaneously perform the double task as rapidly as the single task.

The minor hemisphere is also observed to demonstrate appropriate emotional reactions as, for example, when a pinup shot of a nude is interjected by surprise among a series of neutral geometric figures being flashed to the right and left fields at random. When the surprise nude appears on the left side the subject characteristically says that he or she saw nothing or just a flash of light. However, the appearance of a sneaky grin and perhaps blushing and giggling on the next couple of trials or so belies the verbal contention of the speaking hemisphere. If asked what all the grinning is about, the subject's replies indicate that the conversant hemisphere has no idea at this stage what it was that had turned him on. Apparently, only the emotional effect gets across, as if the cognitive component of the process cannot be articulated through the brainstem.

Emotion is also evident on the minor side in a current study by Gordon and Sperry (1968)[9] involving olfaction. When odors are presented through the right nostril to the minor hemisphere the subject is unable to name the odor but can frequently tell whether it is pleasant or unpleasant. The subject may even grunt, make aversive reactions or exclamations like "phew!" to a strong unpleasant smell, but not be able to state verbally whether it is garlic, cheese, or some decayed matter. Again it appears that the affective component gets across to the speaking hemisphere, but not the more specific information. The presence of the specific information within the minor hemisphere is demonstrated by the subject's correct selection through left-hand stereognosis of corresponding objects associated with the given odor. The minor hemisphere also commonly triggers emotional reactions of displeasure in the course of ordinary testing. This is evidenced in the frowning, wincing, and negative head shaking in test situations where the minor hemisphere, knowing the correct answer but unable to speak, hears the major hemisphere making obvious verbal mistakes. The minor hemisphere seems to express genuine annoyance at the erroneous vocal responses of its better half.

Observations like the foregoing lead us to favor the view that in the minor hemisphere we deal with a second conscious entity that is characteristically human and runs along in parallel with the more dominant stream of consciousness in the major hemisphere.[14] The quality of mental awareness present in the minor hemisphere may be comparable perhaps to that which survives in some types of aphasic patients following losses in the motor and main language centers. There is no indication that the dominant mental system of the left hemisphere is concerned about or even aware of the presence of the minor system under most ordinary conditions except quite indirectly as, for example, through occasional responses triggered from the minor side. As one patient remarked immediately after seeing herself make a left-hand response of this kind, "Now I know it wasn't me did that!"

Let me emphasize again in closing that the foregoing represents a somewhat abbreviated and streamlined account of the syndrome of hemisphere deconnection as we understand it at the present time. The more we see of these patients and the more of these patients we see, the more we become impressed with their individual differences, and with the consequent qualifications that must be taken into account. Although the general picture has continued to hold up in the main as described, it is important to note that, with respect to many of the deconnection symptoms mentioned, striking modifications and even outright exceptions can be found among the small group of patients examined to date. Where the accumulating evidence will settle out with respect to the extreme limits of such individual variations and with respect to a possible average "type" syndrome remains to be seen.

REFERENCES

1. Akelaitis, A. J.: A study of gnosis, praxis, and language following section of the corpus callosum and anterior commissure. J. of Neurosurg. *1:* 94–102 (1944).

2. Bogen, J. E., Fisher, E. D., and Vogel, P. J.: Cerebral commissurotomy: A second case report. J.A.M.A. *194:* 1328–1329 (1965).

3. Bogen, J. E., and Vogel, P. J.: Cerebral commissurotomy: A case report. Bull. Los Angeles Neurol. Soc. *27:* 169 (1962).

4. Gazzaniga, M. S.: The split brain in man. Sci. Am. *217:* 24–29 (1967).

5. Gazzaniga, M. S., Bogen, J. E., and Sperry, R. W.: Dyspraxia following division of the cerebral commissures. Arch. Neurol. *16:* 606–612 (1967).

6. Gazzaniga, M. S., and Sperry, R. W.: Simultaneous double discrimination following brain bisection. Psychonomic Sci. *4:* 262–263 (1966).

7. Gazzaniga, M. S., and Sperry, R. W.: Language after section of the cerebral commissures. Brain *90:* 131–148 (1967).

8. Geschwind, N.: Disconnexion syndromes in animals and man. Brain *88:* 237–294, 584–644 (1965).

9. Gordon, H. W., and Sperry, R. W.: Olfaction following surgical disconnection of the hemispheres in man. Proc. Psychonomic Soc. (1968).

10. Hamilton, C. R.: Effects of brain bisection on eye-hand coordination in monkeys wearing prisms. J. Comp. Physiol. Psychol. *64:* 434–443 (1967).

11. Levy-Agresti, J.: Ipsilateral projection systems and minor hemisphere function in man after neocommissurotomy. Anal. Rec. *160:* 384 (1968).

12. Myers, R. E.: Corpus callosum and visual gnosis. In Delafresnaye, J. F. (ed.): Brain Mechanisms and Learning. Oxford, Blackwell, 1961.

13. Saul, R., and Sperry, R. W.: Absence of commissurotomy symptoms with agenesis of the corpus callosum. Neurol. *18:* 307 (1968).

14. Sperry, R. W.: Brain bisection and mechanisms of consciousness. In Eccles, J. C. (ed.): Brain and Conscious Experience. New York, Springer-Verlag, 1966.

15. Sperry, R. W.: Mental unity following surgical disconnection of the hemispheres. The Harvey Lectures. Series 62. New York, Academic Press, 1967 (a).

16. Sperry, R. W.: Split-brain approach to learning problems. In Quarton, G. C., Melnechuk, T., and Schmitt, F. O. (eds.): The Neurosciences: A Study Program. New York, Rockefeller University Press, 1967 (b).

17. Sperry, R. W.: Apposition of visual half-fields after section of neocortical commissures. Anal. Rec. *160:* 498–499 (1968).

18. Sperry, R. W., and Gazzaniga, M.S.: Language following surgical disconnection of the hemispheres. In Milikan, C. H. (ed.): Brain Mechanisms Underlying Speech and Language. New York, Grune & Stratton, 1967.

19. Sperry, R. W., Gazzaniga, M. S., and Bogen, J. E.: Function of neocortical commissures: Syndrome of hemisphere deconnection. In Vinken, P. J., and Bruyn, G. W., (eds.): Handbook of Neurology. Amsterdam, North Holland, 1968.

20. Trevarthen, C. B.: Double visual learning in split-brain monkeys. Science *136:* 258–259 (1962).

V BIOBEHAVIORAL EFFECTS OF PHYSIOLOGIC PROCESSES

Biobehavioral science is a burgeoning field, establishing each year new frontiers of knowledge on the psychophysiologic basis of physical disease. Spurred by the work of interdisciplinary scientists drawn from formerly isolated fields such as endocrinology, ethology, biochemistry, psychology, neurology, neurophysiology, and pharmacology, we have progressed well along the road to solving problems that have puzzled philosophers and physicians for centuries. Using extraordinarily sophisticated tools for generating, probing, and analyzing data, the goal of deciphering the mechanisms of biobehavioral events is progressing at an unusually rapid rate. New areas of significant study, such as biological rhythms, sleep processes, pain, and the biochemistry of sexual behavior, have opened up and are now subject to the methods of systematic empirical research.

This revolution in interdisciplinary collaboration is not without its controversies. Few scientists would dissent from the thesis that psychological processes are dependent on a substrate of physiologic mechanisms. Yet there are those who claim that endeavors to integrate the biological and behavioral domains are premature and misdirected. Some contend that psychological and sociological scientists should remain "pure," that they should limit their efforts solely to relationships between overt behavioral responses and their observable environmental antecedents. To these more doctrinaire behaviorists, the study of "inner" organismic processes is best left to the anatomists, physiologists, and neurologists, asserting that efforts to create an interdisciplinary synthesis will sink in a sea of data that can be neither charted conceptually nor navigated methodologically. In rebuttal, those of an interdisciplinary persuasion point to the growing body of knowledge derived from collaborative studies. They contend that single discipline research will produce formulations that must inevitably be translated and coordinated into the language and theories of other disciplines. They assert, further, that the findings of a narrow and doctrinaire approach are simply incompatible with the fact that the world of natural phenomena is intrinsically unified. Given the availability today of an abundant supply of multidimensional diagnostic instruments, interdisciplinary scientists believe that it is both feasible and wise to devote their energies now to the solution of integrated rather than segmented biobehavioral problems.

There is a long history to man's belief in the central role of the nervous system as the primary coordinating agent for regulating and integrating behavior and thought. As described by Rickens (1972):

... control may be exerted directly via the peripheral nervous system or may have a more indirect pathway through the hypothalamus and/or medulla via the hormonal transmitters emanating from the pituitary. More recently, Sherrington has conceptualized a primary function of the brain as "the mover of the muscles," but even the ancients recognized the brain as the organ of the mind. That three principal functions of the brain, which we term *homeostasing, moving* and *minding,* are interdependent and covariant is axiomatic; but how they are interrelated has been a classical puzzle for theologians, philosophers and scientists. Neurophysiologists and neurologists have properly attacked the problems of homeostasing. Physiological psychologists aided by neurophysiologists and behaviorists have attempted to describe the natural laws governing moving functions. Phenomenologically oriented psychologists and philosophers have attempted to unravel the brain's minding behavior. To the psychophysiologist and the allied clinical field of psychosomatic medicine is left the Herculean feat of describing the interrelationships of these brain functions.

The fruits of intensive interdisciplinary studies into the medical and behavioral correlates of physiologic processes have multiplied at an astounding rate. Given the scope and space available in a text such as this, we can touch upon only a few topical areas, narrowing our selection to three themes of particular relevance to medical education: pain, sleep, and sex.

Pain is an almost universal element of physical disease, yet it is an entirely private experience whose definition, no less its essence, has never been adequately formulated. As Ronald Melzack has written (1961):

... When compared with vision or hearing, for example, the perception of pain seems simple, urgent and primitive. We expect the nerve signals evoked by injury to "get through," unless we are unconscious or anesthetized. But experiments show that pain is not always perceived after injury even when we are fully conscious and alert. Thus a knowledge of pain perception goes beyond the problem of pain itself; it helps us to understand the enormous plasticity of the nervous system and how each of us responds to the world in a unique fashion.

A vast amount of study has been devoted to the perception of pain, especially in the last decade, and from it is emerging a concept of pain quite different from the classical view. Research shows that pain is much more variable and modifiable than many people have believed in the past. Moreover, direct recordings of nerve signals are helping us to see, in physiological detail, why pain is such a complex experience.

Since his early writings on the nature of pain, Melzack and his colleague P. D. Wall have proposed a well-reasoned thesis as to the physiologic mechanisms involved in its perception. In their thoughtful and systematic paper, they outline alternate theories and articulate the rationale for their own view.

When the temperature drops and days grow shorter, birds migrate to warmer climes, plants become dormant, many animals develop a thick coat of fur, become fatter, and hibernate; the process reverses as days lengthen and temperatures rise. Animal biological rhythms approach the precision of clockwork, having followed a recurrent and predictable sequence since time immemorial. Of equal note are universal rhythms of arousal, activity and sleep which follow a fairly rigid daily or "circadian" sequence. A series of fascinating findings has emerged as investigators have brought the study of these biological clocks into the laboratory. It was once believed that environmental changes (e.g., seasonal shifts in temperature) supplied the necessary cues to activate changes in plant and animal behaviors. Today it is known that most species have an "internal clock" that exhibits cyclic behavior even when environmental forces are kept constant.

Among the most intriguing and thoroughly researched of these rhythmic sequences is the sleep and waking cycle. Milton Kramer's concise review of the literature summarizes a wide range of current findings. For example, two sleep states have been discovered: the deeper state, known as paradoxical sleep, associated with dreaming and characterized by rapid eye movements (REM), and a lighter state, lacking in REM and dreaming.

The third paper deals with the well known role that hormones play in the control of animal sexual behavior. Although the impact of the endocrines has been well established in laboratory research with lower species, questions have been raised as to its applicability to human sexuality. John Money, a distinguished researcher at Johns Hopkins, has investigated the basic physiological processes of human sexuality as well as the more practical issues of surgical therapy for those exhibiting sexual aberrations. In this carefully reasoned report of research, Money and his associate, A. A. Ehrhardt, elucidate the complex network of hormonal and experiential influences that contribute to the development of erotic behaviors in both men and women.

REFERENCES

Melzack, R.: The perception of pain. Sci. Am. *214:* 2:72-79 (1961).
Rickles, W. H.: Central nervous system substrates of some psychophysiological variables. In Greenfield, N. S., and Sternbach, R. A. (eds.): Handbook of Psychophysiology. New York, Holt, Rinehart and Winston, 1972.

13.   Pain Mechanisms: A New Theory

R. Melzack and P. D. Wall

INTRODUCTION

The nature of pain has been the subject of bitter controversy since the turn of the century.[1] There are currently two opposing theories of pain: (i) specificity theory, which holds that pain is a specific modality like vision or hearing, 'with its own central and peripheral apparatus',[2] and (ii) pattern theory, which maintains that the nerve impulse pattern for pain is produced by intense stimulation of nonspecific receptors since 'there are no specific fibers and no specific endings.'[3] Both theories derive from earlier concepts proposed by von Frey[4] and Goldscheider[5] in 1894, and historically they are held to be mutually exclusive. Since it is our purpose here to propose a new theory of pain mechanisms, we shall state explicitly at the outset where we agree and disagree with specificity and pattern theories.

SPECIFICITY THEORY

Specificity theory proposes that a mosaic of specific pain receptors in body tissue projects to a pain center in the brain. It maintains that free nerve endings are pain receptors[4] and generate pain impulses that are carried by A-delta and C fibers in peripheral nerves[6] and by the lateral spinothalamic tract in the spinal cord[2] to a pain center in the thalamus.[7] Despite its apparent simplicity, the theory contains an explicit statement of physiological specialization and an implicit psychological assumption.[8,9] Consider the proposition that the skin contains 'pain receptors'. To say that a receptor responds only to intense, noxious stimulation of the skin is a physiological statement of fact; it says that the receptor is specialized to respond to a particular kind of stimulus. To call a receptor a 'pain receptor', however, is a psychological assumption: it implies a direct connection from the receptor to a brain center where pain is felt (Figure 13-1), so that stimulation of the receptor must always elicit pain and only the sensation of pain. This distinction between physiological specialization and psychological assumption also applies to peripheral fibers and central projection systems.[9]

The facts of physiological specialization provide the power of specificity theory. Its psychological assumption is its weakness.

Melzack, R., and Wall, P. D.: Pain mechanisms: A new theory. Science *150:* 971-979 (1965).

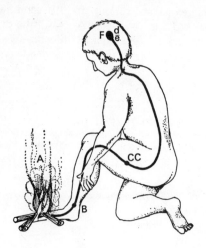

Figure 13-1. Descartes' (76) concept of the pain pathway. He writes: 'If for example fire (A) comes near the foot (B), the minute particles of this fire, which as you know move with great velocity, have the power to set in motion the spot of the skin of the foot which they touch, and by this means pulling upon the delicate thread CC, which is attached to the spot of the skin, they open up at the same instant the pore, de, against which the delicate thread ends, just as by pulling at one end of a rope one makes to strike at the same instant a bell which hangs at the other end.'

As in all psychological theories, there is implicit in specificity theory the conception of a nervous system; and the model is that of a fixed, direct-line communication system from the skin to the brain. This facet of specificity theory, which imputes a direct, invariant relationship between stimulus and sensation, is examined here in the light of the clinical, psychological, and physiological evidence concerning pain.

Clinical Evidence

The pathological pain states of causalgia (a severe burning pain that may result from a partial lesion of a peripheral nerve), phantom limb pain (which may occur after amputation of a limb), and the peripheral neuralgias (which may occur after peripheral nerve infections or degenerative diseases) provide a dramatic refutation of the concept of a fixed, direct-line nervous system. Four features of these syndromes plague patient, physician, and theorist.[8, 10]

1. Surgical lesions of the peripheral and central nervous system have been singularly unsuccessful in abolishing these pains permanently, although the lesions have been made at almost every level (Figure 13-2). Even after such operations, pain can often still be elicited by stimulation below the level of section and may be more severe than before the operation.[8, 10]

2. Gentle touch, vibration, and other nonnoxious stimuli[8, 10] can trigger excruciating pain, and sometimes pain occurs spontaneously for long periods without any apparent stimulus. The fact that the

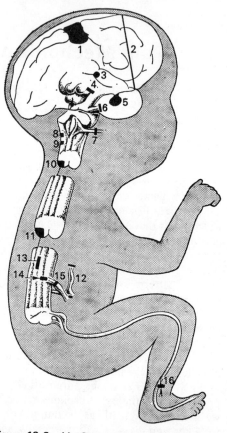

Figure 13-2. MacCarty and Drake's (77) schematic diagram illustrating various surgical procedures designed to alleviate pain: 1, gyrectomy; 2, prefrontal lobotomy; 3, thalamotomy; 4, mesencephalic tractotomy; 5, hypophysectomy; 6, fifth-nerve rhizotomy; 7, ninth-nerve neurectomy; 8, medullary tractotomy; 9, trigeminal tractotomy; 10, cervical chordotomy; 11, thoracic chordotomy; 12, sympathectomy; 13, myelotomy; 14, Lissauer tractotomy; 15, posterior rhizotomy; 16, neurectomy. McCarty, C. S., and Drake, R. L.: Proc. Staff Meetings Mayo Clinic *31:* 208 (1956).

thresholds to these stimuli are raised rather than lowered in causalgia and the neuralgias,[10] together with the fact that referred pain can often be triggered by mild stimulation of normal skin,[8] makes it unlikely that the pains can be explained by postulating pathologically hypersensitive 'pain receptors'.

3. The pains and new 'trigger zones' may spread unpredictably to unrelated parts of the body where no pathology exists.[8, 11]

4. Pain from hyperalgesic skin areas often occurs after long delays, and continues long after removal of the stimulus.[10] Gentle rubbing, repeated pin pricks, or the application of a warm test tube may produce sudden, severe pain after delays as long as 35 seconds. Such delays cannot be attributed simply to conduction in slowly conducting fibers; rather, they imply a remarkable temporal and spatial summation of inputs in the production of these pain states.[8,10]

Psychological Evidence

The psychological evidence fails to support the assumption of a one-to-one relationship between pain perception and intensity of the stimulus. Instead, the evidence suggests that the amount and quality of perceived pain are determined by many psychological variables[12] in addition to the sensory input. For example, Beecher[13] has observed that most American soldiers wounded at the Anzio beachhead 'entirely denied pain from their extensive wounds or had so little that they did not want any medication to relieve it,[13, p.165] presumably because they were overjoyed at having escaped alive from the battlefield.[13] If the men had felt pain, even pain sensation devoid of negative affect, they would, it is reasonable to assume, have reported it just as lobotomized patients[14] report that they still have pain but it does not bother them. Instead, these men 'entirely denied pain'. Similarly, Pavlov's[15,16] dogs that received electric shocks, burns, or cuts, followed consistently by the presentation of food, eventually responded to these stimuli as signals for food and failed to show 'even the tiniest

and most subtle'[15,p.30] signs of pain. If these dogs felt pain sensation, then it must have been nonpainful pain,[17] or the dogs were out to fool Pavlov and simply refused to reveal that they were feeling pain. Both possibilities, of course, are absurd. The inescapable conclusion from these observations is that intense noxious stimulation can be prevented from producing pain, or may be modified to provide the signal for eating behavior.

Psychophysical studies[18] that find a mathematical relationship between stimulus intensity and pain intensity are often cited[2,13,18,19] as supporting evidence for the assumption that pain is a primary sensation subserved by a direct communication system from skin receptor to pain center. A simple psychophysical function, however, does not necessarily reflect equally simple neural mechanisms. Beecher's[13] and Pavlov's[15] observations show that activities in the central nervous system may intervene between stimulus and sensation which may invalidate any simple psychophysical 'law'. The use of laboratory conditions that prevent such activities from ever coming into play reduces the functions of the nervous system to those of a fixed-gain transmission line. It is under these conditions that psychophysical functions prevail.

Physiological Evidence

There is convincing physiological evidence that specialization exists within the somesthetic system,[9] but none to show that stimulation of one type of receptor, fiber, or spinal pathway elicits sensations only in a single psychological modality. In the search for peripheral fibers that respond exclusively to high-intensity stimulation, Hunt and McIntyre[20] found only seven out of 421 myelinated A fibers, and Maruhashi et al.[21] found 13 out of several hundred. Douglas and Ritchie[22] failed to find any high-threshold C fibers, while Iggo[23] found a few. These data suggest that a small number of specialized fibers may exist that respond only to intense stimulation but this does not mean that they are 'pain fibers'—that they must always produce pain, and only pain, when they are stimulated. It is more likely that they represent the extreme of a continuous distribution of receptor-fiber thresholds rather than a special category.[24]

Similarly, there is evidence that central nervous system pathways have specialized functions that play a role in pain mechanisms. Surgical lesions of the lateral spinothalamic tract[2] or portions of the thalamus[25] may, on occasion, abolish pain of pathological origin. But the fact that these areas carry signals related to pain does not mean that they comprise a specific pain system. The lesions have multiple effects. They reduce the total number of responding neurons; they change the temporal and spatial relationships among all ascending systems; and they affect the descending feedback that controls transmission from peripheral fibers to dorsal horn cells.

The nature of the specialization of central cells remains elusive despite the large number of single-cell studies. Cells in the dorsal horns[24, 26] and the trigeminal nucleus[27] respond to a wide range of stimuli and respond to each with a characteristic firing pattern. Central cells that respond exclusively to noxious stimuli have also been reported.[28, 29] Of particular interest is Poggio and Mountcastle's[28] study of such cells in the posterior thalamus in anesthetized monkeys. Yet Casey,[30] who has recently confirmed that posterior thalamic cells respond exclusively to noxious stimuli in the drowsy or sleeping monkey, found that the same cells also signalled information in response to gentle tactile stimulation when the animal was awake. Even if some central cells should be shown unequivocally to respond exclusively to noxious stimuli, their specialized properties still do not make them 'pain cells'. It is more likely that these cells represent the extreme of a broad distribution of cell thresholds to peripheral nerve firing, and that they occupy only a small area within the total multidimensional space that defines the specialized physiological properties of cells.[9] There is no evidence to suggest that they are more important for pain perception and response than all the remaining somesthetic cells that signal characteristic firing patterns

about multiple properties of the stimulus, including noxious intensity. The view that only the cells that respond exclusively to noxious stimuli subserve pain and that the outputs of all other cells are no more than background noise is purely a psychological assumption and has no factual basis. Physiological specialization is a fact that can be retained without acceptance of the psychological assumption that pain is determined entirely by impulses in a straight-through transmission system from the skin to a pain center in the brain.

PATTERN THEORY

As a reaction against the psychological assumption in specificity theory, new theories have been proposed which can be grouped under the general heading of 'pattern theory'. Goldscheider,[21] initially one of the champions of von Frey's theory, was the first to propose that stimulus intensity and central summation are the critical determinants of pain. Two kinds of theories have emerged from Goldscheider's concepts; both recognize the concept of patterning of the input, which we believe[42] to be essential for any adequate theory of pain, but one kind ignores the facts of physiological specialization, while the other utilizes them in proposing mechanisms of central summation.

The pattern theory of Weddell[76] and Sinclair[61] is based on the earlier suggestion, by Nafe,[49] that all cutaneous qualities are produced by spatiotemporal patterns of nerve impulses rather than by separate modality-specific transmission routes. The theory proposes that all fiber endings (apart from those that innervate hair cells) are alike, so that the pattern for pain is produced by intense stimulation of nonspecific receptors. The physiological evidence, however, reveals[42] a high degree of receptor-fiber specialization. The pattern theory proposed by Weddell and Sinclair, then, fails as a satisfactory theory of pain because it ignores the facts of physiological specialization. It is more reasonable to assume that the specialized physiological properties of each receptor-fiber unit—such as response ranges, adaptation rates, and thresholds to different stimulus intensities—play an important role in determining the characteristics of the temporal patterns that are generated when a stimulus is applied to the skin[42]

Other theories have been proposed, within the framework of Goldscheider's concept, which stress central summation mechanisms rather than excessive peripheral stimulation. Livingston[36] was perhaps the first to suggest specific neural mechanisms to account for the remarkable summation phenomena in clinical pain syndromes. He proposed that intense, pathological stimulation of the body sets up reverberating circuits in spinal internuncial pools, or evokes spinal cord activities such as those reflected by the 'dorsal root reflex,'[2] that can then be triggered by normally non-noxious inputs and generate abnormal volleys that are interpreted centrally as pain. Conceptually similar mechanisms were proposed by Hebb[26] and Gerard,[20] who suggested that hypersynchronized firing in central cells provides the signal for pain.

Related to theories of central summation is the theory that a specialized input-controlling system normally prevents summation from occurring, and that destruction of this system leads to pathological pain states. Basically, this theory proposes the existence of a rapidly conducting fiber system which inhibits synaptic transmission in a more slowly conducting system that carries the signal for pain. These two systems are identified as the epicritic and protopathic,[7] fast and slow,[35] phylogenetically new and old,[36] and myelinated and unmyelinated[10] fiber systems. Under pathological conditions, the slow system establishes dominance over the fast, and the result is protopathic sensation,[7] slow pain,[35] diffuse burning pain,[36] or hyperalgesia.[10] It is important to note the transition from specificity theory[35, 36] to the pattern concept: Noordenbos[10] does not associate psychological quality with each system but attributes to the rapidly conducting system the ability to modify the input pattern transmitted in the slowly conducting, multisynaptic system.

The concepts of central summation and input control have shown remarkable power in their ability to explain many of the clinical phenomena of pain. The various specific theoretical mechanisms that have been proposed, however, fail to comprise a satisfactory general theory of pain. They lack unity, and no single theory so far proposed is capable of integrating the diverse theoretical mechanisms. More important, these mechanisms have not received any substantial experimental verification. We believe that recent physiological evidence on spinal mechanisms, together with the evidence demonstrating central control over afferent input, provides the basis for a new theory of pain mechanisms that is consistent with the concepts of physiological specialization as well as with those of central summation and input control.

GATE CONTROL THEORY OF PAIN

Stimulation of the skin evokes nerve impulses that are transmitted to three spinal cord systems: the cells of the substantia gelatinosa in the dorsal horn, the dorsal-column fibers that project toward the brain, and the first central transmission (T) cells in the dorsal horn. We propose that (i) the substantia gelatinosa functions as a gate control system that modulates the afferent patterns before they influence the T cells; (ii) the afferent patterns in the dorsal column system act, in part at least, as a central control trigger which activates selective brain processes that influence the modulating properties of the gate control system; and (iii) the T cells activate neural mechanisms which comprise the action system responsible for response and perception. Our theory proposes that pain phenomena are determined by interactions among these three systems.

Gate Control System

The substantia gelantinosa consists of small, densely packed cells that form a functional unit extending the length of the spinal cord. The cells connect with one another by short fibers and by the longer fibers of Lissauer's tract,[37, 38] but do not project outside the substantia gelatinosa. Recent evidence[39] suggests that the substantia gelatinosa acts as a gate control system that modulates the synaptic transmission of nerve impulses from peripheral fibers to central cells.

Figure 13–3 shows the factors involved in the transmission of impulses from peripheral nerve to T cells in the cord. Recent studies[39-41] have shown that volleys of nerve impulses in large fibers are extremely effective initially in activating the T cells but that their later effect is reduced by a negative feedback mechanism. In contrast, volleys in small fibers activate a positive feedback mechanism which exaggerates the effect of arriving impulses. Experiments[37, 39, 41] have shown that these feedback effects are mediated by cells in the substantia gelatinosa. Activity in these cells modulates the membrane potential of the afferent fiber terminals and thereby determines the excitatory effect of arriving impulses. Although there is evidence, so far, for only presynaptic control, there may also be undetected postsynaptic control mechanisms that contribute to the observed input-output functions.

We propose that three features of the afferent input are significant for pain: (i) the ongoing activity which precedes the stimulus, (ii) the stimulus-evoked activity, and (iii) the relative balance of activity in large versus small fibers. The spinal cord is continually bombarded by incoming nerve impulses even in the absence of obvious stimulation. This ongoing activity is carried predominantly by small myelinated and unmyelinated fibers, which tend to be tonically active and to adapt slowly, and it holds the gate in a relatively open position. When a stimulus is applied to the skin, it produces an increase in the number of active receptor-fiber units as information about the stimulus is transmitted toward the brain. Since many of the larger fibers are inactive in the absence of stimulus change, stimulation will produce a disproportionate relative increase in large-fiber over small-fiber activity. Thus, if a gentle pressure stimulus is applied suddenly to the skin, the afferent volley contains large-fiber impulses which not only fire the T cells but also partially close the presynaptic gate, thereby shortening barrage generated by the T cells.

If the stimulus intensity is increased, more receptor-fiber units are recruited and the firing frequency of active units is increased.[42, 72] The resultant positive and negative effects of the large-fiber and small-fiber inputs tend to counteract each other, and therefore the output of the T cells rises slowly. If stimulation is prolonged, the

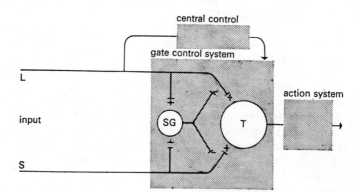

Figure 13–3. Schematic diagram of the gate control theory of pain mechanisms: L. the large-diameter fibers; S, the small-diameter fibers. The fibers project to the substantia gelatinosa (SG) and first central transmission (T) cells. The inhibitory effect exerted by SG on the afferent fiber terminals is increased by activity in L fibers and decreased by activity in S fibers. The central control trigger is represented by a line running from the large-fiber system to the central control mechanisms; these mechanisms, in turn, project back to the gate control system. The T cells project to the entry cells of the action system. +, excitation; –, inhibition (see text).

large fibers begin to adapt, producing a relative increase in small-fiber activity. As a result, the gate is opened further, and the output of the T cells rises more steeply. If the large-fiber steady background activity is artificially raised at this time by vibration or scratching (a maneuver that overcomes the tendency of the large fibers to adapt), the output of the cells decreases.

Thus, the effects of the stimulus-evoked barrage are determined by (i) the total number of active fibers and the frequencies of nerve impulses that they transmit, and (ii) the balance of activity in large and small fibers. Consequently, the output of the T cells may differ from the total input that converges on them from the peripheral fibers. Although the total number of afferent impulses is a relevant stimulus parameter, the impulses have different effects depending on the specialized functions of the fibers that carry them. Furthermore, anatomical specialization also determines the location and the extent of the central terminations of the fibers.[24,41,42]

There are two reasons for believing that pain results after prolonged monitoring of the afferent input by central cells. First, threshold for shock on one arm is raised by a shock delivered as long as 100 milliseconds later to the other arm.[43] Second, in pathological pain states, delays of pain sensation as long as 35 seconds after stimulation cannot be attributed to slow conduction in afferent pathways.[10] We suggest, then, that there is temporal and spatial summation or integration of the arriving barrage by the T cells. The signal which triggers the action system responsible for pain experience and response occurs when the output of the T cells reaches or exceeds a critical level. This critical level of firing, as we have seen, is determined by the afferent barrage that actually impinges on the T cells and has already undergone modulation by substantia gelatinosa activity. We presume that the action system requires a definite time period for integrating the total input from the T cells. Small, fast variations of the temporal pattern produced by the T cells might be ineffective, and the smoothed envelope of the frequency of impulses — which contains information on the rate of rise and fall, the duration, and the amplitude of firing — would be the effective stimulus that initiates the appropriate sequence of activities in the cells that comprise the action system.

Central Control Trigger

It is now firmly established[44] that stimulation of the brain activates descending efferent fibers[45] which can influence afferent conduction at the earliest synaptic levels of the somesthetic system. Thus it is possible for central nervous system activities subserving attention, emotion, and memories of prior experience to exert control over the sensory input. There is evidence[44] to suggest that these central influences are mediated through the gate control system.

The manner in which the appropriate central activities are triggered into action presents a problem. While some central activities, such as anxiety or excitement, may open or close the gate for all inputs at any site on the body, others obviously involve selective, localized gate activity. Men wounded in battle may feel little pain from the wound but may complain bitterly about an inept vein puncture.[13] Dogs that repeatedly receive food immediately after the skin is shocked, burned, or cut soon respond to these stimuli as signals for food and salivate, without showing any signs of pain, yet howl as normal dogs would when the stimuli are applied to other sites on the body.[16] The signals, then, must be identified, evaluated in terms of prior conditioning, localized, and inhibited *before* the action system is activated. We propose, therefore, that there exists in the nervous system a mechanism, which we shall call the central trigger, that activates the particular, selective brain processes that exert control over the sensory input (Figure 13-3). There are two known systems that could fulfill such a function, and one or both may play a role.

The first is the dorsal column-medial lemniscus system. The largest and most rapidly conducting A fibers which enter the spinal cord send short branches to the substantia gelatinosa, and long central branches directly to the dorsal column nuclei. Fibers from these nuclei form the medial lemniscus, which provides a direct route to the thalamus and thence to the somato-sensory cortex. The striking characteristics of this system are that information is transmitted rapidly from the skin to the cortex, that separation of signals evoked by different stimulus properties and precise somatotopic localization are both maintained throughout the system,[46] and that conduction is relatively unaffected by anesthetic drugs.[47] Traditionally, the dorsal column system is supposed to carry two-point discrimination, roughness discrimination, spatial localization, tactile threshold, and vibration.[48] Complex discrimination and localization, however, are not a modality; they represent decisions based on an analysis of the input. Indeed, the traditional view is questionable in the light of Cook and Browder's[49] observation that surgical section of the dorsal columns produced no permanent change in two-point discrimination in seven patients.

The second candidate for the role of central control trigger is the dorsolateral path,[50] which originates in the dorsal horn and projects, after relay in the lateral cervical nucleus, to the brain stem and thalamus. This system has small, well-defined receptive fields[51] and is extremely fast; in spite of having one additional relay, it precedes the dorsal column-medial lemniscus volley in the race to the cortex.[52]

Both these systems, then, could fulfill the functions of the central control triggers. They carry precise information about the nature and location of the stimulus, and they conduct so rapidly that they may not only set the receptivity of cortical neurons for subsequent afferent volleys but may, by way of central-control efferent fibers, also act on the gate control system. Part, at least, of their function, then, could be to activate selective brain processes that influence information which is still arriving over slowly conducting fibers or is being transmitted up more slowly conducting pathways.

Action System

Pain is generally considered to be the sensory adjunct of an imperative reflex.[53]

Pain, however, does not consist of a single ring of the appropriate central bell, but is an ongoing process. We propose, then, that once the integrated firing-level of T cells exceeds a critical preset level, the firing triggers a sequence of responses by the action system.

Sudden, unexpected damage to the skin is followed by (i) a startle response; (ii) a flexion reflex; (iii) postural readjustment; (iv) vocalization; (v) orientation of the head and eyes to examine the damaged area; (vi) autonomic responses; (vii) evocation of past experience in similar situations and prediction of the consequences of the stimulation; (viii) many other patterns of behavior aimed at diminishing the sensory and affective components of the whole experience, such as rubbing the damaged area, avoidance behavior, and so forth.

The perceptual awareness that accompanies these events changes in quality and intensity during all this activity. This total complex sequence is hidden in the simple phrases 'pain response' and 'pain sensation'. The multiplicity of reactions demands some concept of central mechanisms which is at least capable of accounting for sequential patterns of activity that would allow the complex behavior and experience characteristic of pain.

The concept of a 'pain center' in the brain is totally inadequate to account for the sequences of behavior and experience. Indeed, the concept is pure fiction, unless virtually the whole brain is considered to be the 'pain center', because the thalamus,[7, 25] the limbic system,[54], the hypothalamus,[55] the brain-stem reticular formation,[56] the parietal cortex,[57] and the frontal cortex[14] are all implicated in pain perception. Other brain areas are obviously involved in the emotional and motor features of the behavior sequence. The idea of a 'terminal center' in the brain which is exclusively responsible for pain sensation and response therefore becomes meaningless.

We propose, instead, that the triggering of the action system by the T cells marks the beginning of the sequence of activities that occur when the body sustains damage. The divergence of afferent fibers going to the dorsal horns and the dorsal column nuclei marks only the first stage of the process of selection and abstraction of information. The stimulation of a single tooth results in the eventual activation of no less than five distinct brain-stem pathways.[58] Two of these pathways project to cortical somatosensory areas I and II,[59] while the remainder activate the thalamic reticular formation and the limbic system,[60] so that the input has access to neural systems involved in affective[54] as well as sensory activities. It is presumed that interactions occur among all these systems as the organism interacts with the environment.

We believe that the interactions between the gate control system and the action system described above may occur at successive synapses at any level of the central nervous system in the course of filtering of the sensory input. Similarly, the influence of central activities on the sensory input may take place at a series of levels. The gate control system may be set and reset a number of times as the temporal and spatial patterning of the input is analysed and acted on by the brain.

ADEQUACY OF THE THEORY

The concept of interacting gate control and action systems can account for the hyperalgesia, spontaneous pain, and long delays after stimulation characteristic of pathological pain syndromes. The state of hyperalgesia would require two conditions: (i) enough conducting peripheral axons to generate an input that can activate the action system (if, as in the case of leprosy, all components of the peripheral nerve are equally affected, there is a gradual onset of anesthesia), and (ii) a marked loss of the large peripheral nerve fibers, which may occur after traumatic peripheral-nerve lesions or in some of the neuropathies,[61] such as post-herpetic neuralgia.[10] Since most of the larger fibers are destroyed, the normal presynaptic inhibition of the input by the gate control system does not occur. Thus, the input arriving over the remaining myelinated and unmyelinated fibers is transmitted through the unchecked, open gate produced by the C-fiber input.

Spatial summation would easily occur under such conditions. Any nerve impulses, no matter how they were generated, which converge on the central cells would contribute to the output of these cells. These mechanisms may account for the fact that non-noxious stimuli, such as gentle pressure, can trigger severe pain in patients suffering causalgia, phantom limb pain, and the neuralgias. The well-known enhancement of pain in these patients during emotional disturbance and sexual excitement[62] might be due to increased sensory firing as a result of an increased sympathetic outflow[63, 64] which is unchecked by presynaptic inhibition. Conversely, the absence of small fibers in the dorsal roots in a patient with congenital insensitivity to pain[65] suggests that the mechanisms for facilitation and summation necessary for pain may be absent.

Spontaneous pain can also be explained by these mechanisms. The smaller fibers show considerable spontaneous activity, which would have the effect of keeping the gate open. Low-level, random, ongoing activity would then be transmitted relatively unchecked (because of the predominant loss of A fibers), and summation could occur, producing spontaneous pain in the absence of stimulation. This is a possible mechanism for the pains of anesthesia dolorosa and the 'spontaneous' pains which develop after peripheral nerve and dorsal-root lesions. Because the total number of peripheral fibers is reduced, it may take considerable time for the T cells to reach the firing level necessary to trigger pain responses, so perception and response are delayed. This same mechanism can also account for post-ischemic pressure-block hyperesthesia and for the delays in sensation of as much as 10 seconds which occur when the large peripheral fibers fail to conduct.[66]

We propose that the A-fiber input normally acts to prevent summation from occurring. This would account for Adrian's[67] failure to obtain pain responses in the frog from high-frequency air blasts which fired peripheral nerves close to their maximum firing rate, in an experiment meant to refute the view that summation of the effects of noxious stimuli is important for pain. It is now clear that the air blasts would tend to fire a high proportion of the low-threshold A fibers, which would exert presynaptic inhibition on the input by way of the gate control system; thus the impulses would be prevented from reaching the T cells where summation might occur. The double effect of an arriving volley is well illustrated by the effects of vibration on pain and itch. Vibration activates fibers of all diameters, but activates a larger proportion of A fibers, since they tend to adapt during constant stimulation, whereas C-fiber firing is maintained. Vibration therefore sets the gate in a more closed position. However, the same impulses which set the gate also bombard the T cell and therefore summate with the inputs from noxious stimulation. It is observed behaviorally [26, 28] that vibration reduces low-intensity, but enhances high-intensity, pain and itch. Similar mechanisms may account for the fact that amputees sometimes obtain relief from phantom limb pain by tapping the stump gently with a rubber mallet,[69] whereas heavier pressure aggravates the pain.[8]

The phenomena of referred pain, spread of pain, and trigger points at some distance from the original site of body damage also point toward summation mechanisms, which can be understood in terms of the model. The T cell has a restricted receptive field which dominates its 'normal activities'. In addition, there is a widespread, diffuse, monosynaptic input to the cell, which is revealed by electrical stimulation of distant afferents.[41] We suggest that this diffuse input is normally inhibited by presynaptic gate mechanisms, but may trigger firing in the cell if the input is sufficiently intense or if there is a change in gate activity. Because the cell remains dominated by its receptive field, anesthesia of the area to which the pain is referred, from which only spontaneous impulses are originating, is sufficient to reduce the bombardment of the cell below the threshold level for pain. The gate can also be opened by activities in distant body areas, since the substantia gelatinosa at any level receives inputs from both sides of the body and (by way of Lissauer's tract) from the substantia gelatinosa in neighboring body segments.

Mechanisms such as these may explain the observations that stimulation of trigger points on the chest and arms may trigger anginal pain,[70] or that pressing other body areas, such as the back of the head, may trigger pain in the phantom limb.[11]

The sensory mechanisms alone fail to account for the fact that nerve lesions do not always produce pain and that, when they do, the pain is usually not continuous. We propose that the presence or absence of pain is determined by the balance between the sensory and the central inputs to the gate control system. In addition to the sensory influences on the gate control system, there is a tonic input to the system from higher levels of the central nervous system which exerts an inhibitory effect on the sensory input.[44, 71] Thus, any lesion that impairs the normal downflow of impulses to the gate control system would open the gate. Central nervous system lesions associated with hyperalgesia and spontaneous pain[7] could have this effect. On the other hand, any central nervous system condition that increases the flow of descending impulses would tend to close the gate. Increased central firing due to denervation supersensitivity[72] might be one of these conditions. A peripheral nerve lesion, then, would have the *direct* effect of opening the gate, and the *indirect* effect, by increasing central firing and thereby increasing the tonic descending influences on the gate control system, of closing the gate. The balance between sensory facilitation and central inhibition of the input after peripheral-nerve lesion would account for the variability of pain even in cases of severe lesion.

The model suggests that psychological factors such as past experience, attention, and emotion influence pain response and perception by acting on the gate control system. The degree of central control, however, would be determined, in part at least, by the temporal-spatial properties of the input patterns. Some of the most unbearable pains, such as cardiac pain, rise so rapidly in intensity that the patient is unable to achieve any control over them. On the other hand, more slowly rising temporal patterns are susceptible to central control and may allow the patient to 'think about something else' or use other stratagems to keep the pain under control.[73]

The therapeutic implications of the model are twofold. First, it suggests that control of pain may be achieved by selectively influencing the large, rapidly conducting fibers. The gate may be closed by decreasing the small-fiber input and also by enhancing the large-fiber input. Thus, Livingston[74] found that causalgia could be effectively cured by therapy such as bathing the limb in gently moving water, followed by massage, which would increase the input in the large-fiber system. Similarly, Trent[75] reports a case of pain of central nervous system origin which could be brought under control when the patient tapped his fingers on a hard surface. Conversely, any manipulation that cuts down the sensory input lessens the opportunity for summation and pain, within the functional limits set by the opposing roles of the large- and small-fiber systems. Second, the model suggests that a better understanding of the pharmacology and physiology of the substantia gelatinosa may lead to new ways of controlling pain. The resistance of the substantia gelatinosa

to nerve-cell stains suggests that its chemistry differs from that of other neural tissue. Drugs affecting excitation or inhibition of substantia gelatinosa activity may be of particular importance in future attempts to control pain.

The model suggests that the action system responsible for pain perception and response is triggered after the cutaneous sensory input has been modulated by both sensory feedback mechanisms and the influences of the central nervous system. We propose that the abstraction of information at the first synapse may mark only the beginning of a continuing selection and filtering of the input. Perception and response involve classification of the multitude of patterns of nerve impulses arriving from the skin and are functions of the capacity of the brain to select and to abstract from all the information it receives from the somesthetic system as a whole.[7-9] A 'modality' class such as 'pain', which is a linguistic label for a rich variety of experiences and responses, represents just such an abstraction from the information that is sequentially re-examined over long periods by the entire somesthetic system.

REFERENCES

1. Dallenbach, K. M.: Amer. J. Physiol. *52:* 331 (1939); Keele, K. D.: Anatomies of Pain. Oxford, Blackwell, 1957.

2. Sweet, W. H.: Handbook Physiol. *1:* 459 (1959).

3. Sinclair, D. C.: Brain *78:* 584 (1955).

4. von Frey, M.: Ber. Kgl. Sächs. Ges. Wiss. *46:* 185 (1894); ibid., p. 283.

5. Goldscheider, A.: Ueber den Schmerz in physiologischer und klinischer Hinsicht. Berlin, Hirschwald, 1894.

6. Bishop, G. H.: Physiol. Rev. *26:* 77 (1946); A-delta fibers are the smallest myelinated fibers and C fibers are the unmyelinated fibers, in the peripheral nerve.

7. Head, H.: Studies in Neurology. London, Keegan Paul, 1920.

8. Livingston, W. K.: Pain Mechanisms. New York, Macmillan, 1943.

9. Melzack, R., and Wall, P. D.: Brain, *85:* 331 (1962).

10. Noordenbos, W.: Pain. Amsterdam, Elsevier, 1959.

11. Cronholm, B.: Acta Psychiat. Neurol. Scand. Suppl. *72:* 1 (1951).

12. Livingston, W. K.: Sci. Am. *88:* 59 (1953); Melzack, R.: ibid. *204:* 41 (1961); Barber, T. X.: Psychol. Bull. *56:* 430 (1959).

13. Beecher, H. K.: Measurement of Subjective Responses. New York, Oxford Univ. Press, 1959.

14. Freeman, W., and Watts, I. W.: Psychosurgery in the Treatment of Mental Disorders and Intractable Pain. Springfield, Ill., Charles C Thomas, 1950.

15. Pavlov, I. P.: Conditioned Reflexes. Oxford, Milford, 1927.

16. Pavlov, I. P.: Lectures on Conditioned Reflexes. New York, International Publisher, 1928.

17. Nafe, J. P.: In Murchison, C. (ed): Handbook of General Experimental Psychology. Worcester, Mass., Clark Univ. Press. 1934.

18. Hardy, J. D., Wolff, H. G., and Goodell, H.: Pain Sensations and Reactions. Baltimore, Williams and Wilkins, 1952.

19. Morgan, C. T.: Introduction to Psychology. New York, McGraw-Hill, 1961.

20. Hunt, C. C. and McIntyre, A. K.: J. Physiol. London *153:* 88, 99 (1960).

21. Maruhashi, J., Mizaguchi, K., and Tasaki, I.: ibid. *117:* 129 (1952).

22. Douglas, W. W., and Ritchie, J. M.: ibid. *139:* 385 (1957).

23. Iggo, A.: ibid. *143:* 47 (1958).

24. Wall, P. D.: J. Neurophysiol. *23:* 197 (1960).

25. Mark, V. H., Ervin, F. R., and Yakovlev, P. I.: Arch. Neurol. *8:* 528 (1963).
26. Wall, P. D., and Cronly-Dillon, J. R.: ibid. *2:* 365 (1960).
27. Wall, P. D., and Taub, A.: J. Neurophysiol. *25:* 110 (1962); Kruger, L., and Michel, F.: Exp. Neurol. *5:* 157 (1962).
28. Poggio, G. F., and Mountcastle, V. B.: Bull. Johns Hopkins Hosp. *106:* 226 (1960).
29. Kolmodin, G. M., and Skoglund, C. R.: Acta Physiol. Scand. *50:* 337 (1960); Gordon, G., Landgren, S., and Seed, W. A.: J. Physiol. London *158:* 544 (1960); Eisenman, J. S., Landgren, S., and Novin, D.: Acta Physiol. Scand. Suppl. *214:* 1 (1963).
30. Casey, K. L.: A Search for Nociceptive Elements in the Thalamus of the Awake Squirrel Monkey, paper read at the 16th Autumn meeting of the American Physiological Society, Providence, R.I., 1964.
31. Weddell, G.: Ann. Rev. Psychol. *6:* 119 (1955).
32. Barron, D. H., and Matthews, B. H. C.: J. Physiol. London *92:* 276 (1938).
33. Hebb, D. O.: The Organization of Behavior. New York, Wiley, 1949.
34. Gerard, R. W.: Anesthesiology *12:* 1 (1951).
35. Lewis, T.: Pain New York, Macmillan, 1942.
36. Bishop, G. H.: J. Nerv. Ment. Dis. *128:* 89 (1959).
37. Wall, P. D.: Progr. Brain Res. *12:* 92 (1964).
38. Szentagothai, J.: J. Comp. Neurol. *122:* 219 (1964).
39. Wall, P. D.: J. Physiol. London. *164:* 508 (1964); Mendell, L. M., and Wall, P. D.: ibid. *172:* 274 (1964).
40. Wall, P. D.: J. Neurophysiol. *22:* 205 (1959); J. Physiol London *142:* 1 (1958).
41. Mendell, L. M., and Wall, P. D.: Nature *206:* 97 (1965).
42. Whitlock, D. G., and Perl, E. R.: Exp. Neurol. *3:*240 (1961).
43. Halliday, A. M., and Mingay, R.: Quart. J. Exp. Psychol. *13:* 1 (1961).
44. Hagbarth, K. E., and Kerr, D. I. B.: J. Neurophysiol. *17:* 295 (1954).
45. Kuypers, H. G. J. M., Fleming, W. R., and Farinholt, J. W.: Science *132:* 38 (1960); Lundberg, A.: Progr. Brain Res. *12:* 197 (1964).
46. Mountcastle, V. B.: In Rosenblith, W. A. (ed.): Sensory Communication. Massachusetts Institute of Technology, Cambridge, 1961.
47. French, J. D., Verzeano, M., and Magoun, W. H.: A.M.A. Arch. Neurol. Psychiat. *69:* 519 (1953); Haugen, F. P., and Melzack, R.: Anesthesiology *18:* 183 (1957).
48. Ruch, T. C., and Fulton, J. F.: Medical Physiology and Biophysics. W. B. Saunders Co., 1960.
49. Cook, A. W., and Browder, E. J.: Arch. Neurol. *12:* 72 (1965).
50. Morin, F.: Amer. J. Physiol. *183:* 245 (1955).
51. Oswaldo-Cruz, E., and Kidd, C.: J. Neurophysiol. *27:* 1 (1964).
52. Norrsell, U., and Voerhoeve, P.: Acta Physiol. Scand. *54:* 9 (1962).
53. Sherrington, C. S.: In Schäfer, E. A. (ed.): Textbook of Physiology. Edinburgh, Pentland, 1900.
54. Brady, J. V.: Handbook Physiol. *3:* 1529 (1960).
55. Hess, W. R.: Diencephalon: Autonomic and Extrapyramidal Functions. New York, Grune, 1954.
56. Delgado, J. M. R.: J. Neurophysiol. *18:* 261 (1955); Melzack, R., Stotler, W. A., and Livingston, W. K.: ibid, *21:* 353 (1958).
57. Schilder, P., and Stengel, E.: A.M.A. Arch. Neurol. Psychiat. *25:* 598 (1931).
58. Kerr, D. I. B., Haugen, F. P., and Melzack, R.: Amer. J. Physiol. *183:* 253 (1955).
59. Melzack, R., and Haugen, F. P.: ibid *190:* 570 (1957).
60. Nauta, W. J. H., and Kuypers, H. G. J. M.: In Jasper, H. H., et al. (eds.): Reticular Formation of the Brain. Boston, Little, Brown 1958.
61. Blackwood, W., McMenemey, W. H., Meyer, A., Norman, R. M., and Russell, D. S.: Greenfield's Neuropathology. London, Arnold, 1963.
62. Henderson, W. R., and Smyth, G. E.: J. Neurol. Neurosurg. Psychiat. *11:* 88 (1948).
63. Chernetski, K. F.: J. Neurophysiol. *27:* 493 (1964).
64. Doupe, J., Cullen, C. H., and Chance, G. O.: J. Neurol. Neurosurg. Psychiat. *7:* 33 (1944).
65. Swanson, A. G., Buchan, G. C., and Alvord, E. C.: Arch. Neurol. *12:* 12 (1965).
66. Sinclair, D. C., and Hinshaw, J. R.: Brain *74:* 318 (1951).
67. Adrian, E. D.: The Basis of Sensation: The Action of Sense Organs. London, Christophers, 1928.
68. Melzack, R., Wall, P. D., and Weisz, A. Z.: Exp. Neurol. *8:* 35 (1963); Melzack, R., and Schecter, B.: Science *147:* 1047 (1965).
69. Russell, W. R., and Spalding, J. M. K.: Brit. Med. J. *2:* 68 (1950).
70. Cohen, H.: Trans. Med. Soc. London *64:* 65 (1944).
71. Taub, A.: Exp. Neurol. *10:* 357 (1964).
72. Stavraky, G. W.: Supersensitivity Following Lesions of the Nervous System. University of Toronto Press, 1961; Sharpless, S. K.: Ann. Rev. Physiol. *26:* 357 (1964).
73. Melzack, R., Weisz, A. Z., and Sprague, L. T.: Exp. Neurol. *8:* 239 (1963).
74. Livingston, W. K.: Ann. N.Y. Acad. Sci. *50:* 247 (1948).
75. Trent, S. E.: J. Nerv. Ment. Dis. *123:* 356 (1956).
76. Descartes, R.: 'L'Homme' (Paris, 1644). Foster, M.: transl., in Lectures on the History of Physiology during the 16th, 17th and 18th Centuries. Cambridge University Press, Cambridge, England, 1901.
77. MacCarty, C. S., and Drake, R. L.: Proc. Staff Meetings Mayo Clin. *31:* 208 (1956).

14. Paradoxical Sleep

Milton Kramer

Throughout the ages man has been intrigued with the dream, that peculiar mental content that pervades his sleep each night. Physicians also have been interested in the dream, for many reasons. It has been suggested that the dream is the sane man's psychosis and that a study of the dream would help to unravel the mystery of psychosis, since hallucinated visual and auditory experiences are accepted as valid in both conditions. Patients' frequent complaints of sleep disturbances have been related to disturbing dreams, and if the dream could be altered by medical or psychologic treatment, the physician might be able to treat insomnia more effectively. A study of dreams also provides the physician with a significant insight into the psychology of men, which can assist in the psychologic understanding and treatment of his patients.

The absence of technics for signaling the occurrence of the dream had been one of the more serious obstacles to its study. Aserinsky and Kleitman's discovery in 1953 that dreaming sleep is accompanied by an observable phenomenon, conjugate rapid eye movement (REM), made it possible to study the process of dreaming with objective methods and to recover dream content almost at will. The availability of an objective indicator of dreaming has led to the elaboration of the sleep-dream cycle and to the detailed study of the paradoxical phase of sleep, in which each of us "turns on" four to six times a night without the assistance of psychedelic drugs.

We experience a state of total activation, of which the dream is the psychologic concomitant, about every 90 minutes during a night of sleep. The most frequently used of the 23 names assigned to this recurring period of activation are paradoxical sleep, dreaming sleep, emergent stage I, D state, REM state, and third organismic state. This peculiar recurring condition during sleep is characterized by conjugate rapid eye movements, autonomic irregularities in the cardiovascular and respiratory systems, elevated brain temperature, decreased postural muscle tone, penile erections, and a low-voltage fast electroencephalogram free of spindling. These dreaming episodes comprise 20 to 25 percent of the night's sleep in the young adult. They begin one to two hours after the onset of sleep, are each 15 to 60 minutes' duration, and become longer and more dreamlike as the night progresses. Subjects more often report dreaming when awakened from these periods than when awakened from other phases of sleep.

During paradoxical sleep the organism is neither awake nor asleep but is in some state in which functional relationships are uniquely integrated. The arousal threshold of the organism is generally higher during this REM state than during the other sleep phases. Yet the pattern of neuronal firing during this state is that of neither non-REM sleep nor waking, but is more like that of some hyper-alert state or seizurelike condition.

Both phylogenetic and ontogenetic studies support the concept that the dreaming phase of sleep is a third state of the organism, separate from both the waking state and nondreaming sleep. The REM state has been found in all mammalian species from the mouse to the elephant. It also has been observed in birds and probably in reptiles. The ontogenetic development of paradoxical sleep in the life cycle of a given species is remarkably consistent. The very young of any species

Kramer, M.: Paradoxical sleep. Postgrad. Med. *45:* 157–161 (1969).

spends fars more time in REM sleep than does the adult. In the human life cycle the newborn spends 50 percent of its sleep in the REM state while the aged person spends only 13 to 18 percent of his sleep in this state. The REM state is closely related to the waking state and it is at the expense of the REM state that waking develops, with the super-imposition of the 24-hour rest-activity cycle, since the amount of time spent in non-REM sleep changes little with age.

MECHANISMS OF REM CYCLE

How is such a basic, ubiquitous and recurrent state controlled? The periodicity of the sleep-dream cycle is under the control of nuclei in the pons, which have both anterior and posterior connections. Transection, coagulation and stimulation technics have shown that the anterior firing of the nucleus pontis caudalis accounts for the cortical desynchronization, the low-voltage fast electroencephalogram, which characterizes paradoxical sleep, while the posterior firing of a nucleus located in the roof of the fourth ventricle, the locus ceruleus, accounts for the motor inhibition that occurs during the REM state. The refractory period that follows electric stimulation of these nuclei has led investigators to explore the possibility that neurohumoral mechanisms are involved in the initiation and control of paradoxical sleep.

Cholinergic and adrenergic neurohumoral mechanisms are involved in the control of the REM-non-REM cycle. Special roles have been suggested for serotonin, norepinephrine and gamma aminobutyric acid, which have been shown experimentally to function as neuromodulators, if not neurotransmitters, in initiating the REM state.

The most promising hypothesis concerned with the neurochemical regulation of the REM cycle involves the interrelated effects of serotonin, norepinephrine and acetylcholine. This hypothesis states that increased "free" serotonin, or more probably a balance of serotonin and norepinephrine, in certain brain areas produces a tendency toward REM periods. When a certain level of serotonin is reached, it triggers a release of acetylcholine, which discharges the REM period, during which serotonin is metabolized, probably by monoamine oxidase.

The hormonal secretions of the anterior and posteriors pituitary gland and the gonads stimulate or prolong the REM cycle. The relationship of REM cycle length to the metabolic rate and the evidence for increased metabolic expenditure during the REM state strongly suggest a role for thyroid hormone in the process of paradoxical sleep.

SIGNIFICANCE OF REM STATE

The question arises as to the possible adaptive significance of paradoxical sleep to the organism. The functions which have been suggested for the REM state, none of which explains all of what is known and many of which are complementary rather than contradictory to one another, may be grouped under three headings: input theories, output theories, and theories that the function of REM sleep, at least in the adult human, is to permit psychologic dreaming to occur.

The input theories contend that REM sleep may permit (1) the periodic awakening of the organism to scan a potentially dangerous environment (a phylogenetic theory), (2) the reorganization of neuronal firing patterns that have become disorganized during non-REM sleep, (3) the periodic recovery from the sensory deprivation of deep sleep, or (4) the endogenous in utero stimulation of the developing nervous system to assist in the maturation and maintenance of function until external stimulation is available post partum (an ontogenetic theory).

The output theories maintain that the REM-state function may allow (1) the elimination of endogenous metabolites (such as serotonin) that have accumulated during the waking state and non-REM sleep, (2) the discharge of instinctual or drive energies (Freudian theory), (3) the discarding of unneeded information gathered during the day, or (4) the transference of recent memories to long-term memory systems.

The psychologic dreaming theories maintain that the REM state may permit (1) a disguised gratification of wishes (Freud), (2) the availability of the more universal truths of the unconscious (Jung), (3) a rehearsal for the events of waking life (Adler), or (4) the solution and integration of current emotional problems (French).

In pursuing the issue of the functional significance of the REM state, efforts have been made to deprive men and animals of this state by awakening them whenever they enter it. Depriving both men and animals of paradoxical sleep leads to an increased frequency of awakenings, to the onset of the REM-state electroencephalographic pattern immediately on returning to sleep, and on recovery nights to an almost quantitative increase in the percentage of the night's sleep spent in the REM phase.

In REM-deprived animals drive-oriented behavior (oral, aggressive and sexual) is intensified and thus may terminate in death. In some humans, REM-state deprivation leads to increased anxiety, irritability, hostility, appetite and difficulty in remembering, concentrating and motor coordination. These deprived subjects have a heightened susceptibility to hallucinations after photic stimulation. Subjects totally deprived of sleep report after 120 hours, especially at night, the cyclical intensification of hallucinations and delusions at about 90-minute intervals. Possibly, the hallucination is the breakthrough of the dream into waking life.

EFFECTS OF DRUGS ON DREAMS

If hallucinations are the breakthrough of dreams into waking life, it is intriguing to explore the effects of hallucination-stimulating drugs, such as the psychotogens (LSD) or alcohol, on the REM state, as well as the effects of the so-called anti-hallucinogenics such as the tranquilizers. In this attempt, one must focus on studies that have examined both the physiologic (dream time) and psychologic (dream content) effects of drugs on dreams.

The reports of the effects of drugs on REM time include an examination of the effects of psychotropics, psychotogens, alcohol, stimulants and depressants. With the possible exception of reserpine, chlordiazepoxide hydrochloride (LIBRIUM®), and related compounds (and one study of a tranylcypromine [PARNATE®] addict), all studies on the psychotropics, including major and minor tranquilizers and various types of antidepressants, report a decrease in REM time associated with taking these drugs. The work on the psychotogens is inconclusive, with a trend suggesting they cause an increase in REM time. Chronic alcoholics have shown extreme increases in REM time while having delirium tremens. Reports on such stimulants and depressants as caffeine, amphetamine, barbiturates and the opium derivatives generally show a decrease in REM time or no effect at all.

It has been aptly observed, "If we don't keep our attention on the psychology of the dream, we might find out a lot of biology without knowing what it is the biology of." The studies of the effects on dream content of various drugs have been extremely limited. Imipramine, an antidepressant, has been reported to stimulate the expression of hostility in the dreams of normal persons. In dreams of depressed patients, imipramine tends initially to increase hostility and anxiety, but taken on a long-term basis it tends to decrease hostility and anxiety and increase sexuality and motility. Meprobamate has been observed to lead to an increase in motility in dreams, phenobarbital to an increase in homosexuality, and prochlorperazine to an increase in heterosexuality. In general, drugs cause dreams that reflect an increase in anxiety and dependency and a decrease in intimacy.

RECOVERING DREAM CONTENT

A technic that detects the time of dreaming has contributed to our understanding of the psychology of the dream. It should be recognized that although mental content can be recovered from the non-REM phase of sleep, the dream as an intense, elaborated visual experience is most generally associated with the REM state. We have learned that the later in an

REM period or the later in the night the dream collection is made, the more visual and vivid is the dream report. The peripheral manifestations of paradoxical sleep (eye and limb movements) are indeed related to the content of the dream. The recall of dreams is higher if (1) a person is awakened from or just after an REM period, (2) he is awakened suddenly rather than gradually, and (3) he is stimulated to recall his dreams.

Interestingly, some emotional theme related to the previous day's experience rather than the experience itself is recalled in dreams. Tactile, auditory and visual stimuli presented concurrently with dreaming are incorporated 10 to 25 percent of the time. Tactile stimuli are the easiest and visual stimuli are the most difficult to incorporate into the dream content. Meaningful insights into personality-coping patterns can be gained from studying the interrelationships of the multiple dreams of a single night. However, because of difficul-ties in collecting the dream reports, the dream content of psychotic patients has only begun to be systematically examined.

COMMENT

Recent work on paradoxical sleep has stimulated a renewed interest in dreams. The delineation of a basic biologic cycle with a precise anatomic center and numerous neurohumoral and hormonal interrelationships has aroused hopes that a significant neurophysiologic basis for understanding nighttime and perhaps also daytime hallucinated states has at long last been realized. However, just as poetry will never be completely understood in electrophysical terms, dreams cannot be explained solely from a description of eye movements and activated REM-state electroencephalograms. We may some day have a biochemistry of dreaming but never of dreams.

REFERENCES

1. Dement, W. C.: Psychophysiology of sleep and dreams. In Arieti, S. (Ed.): American Handbook of Psychiatry. New York, Basic Books, Inc., 1966, Vol. 3, pp. 290–332.
2. Hartmann, E.: The biology of Dreaming. Springfield, Ill., Charles C Thomas, 1967.
3. Kety, S. S., Evarts, E. V., and Williams, H. L.: (eds.): Sleep and altered states of consciousness. Res. Publ. Ass. Res. Nerv. Ment. Dis. *45:* (1967).
4. Kleitman, N.: Sleep and Wakefulness. Chicago, University of Chicago Press, 1963.
5. Kramer, M., et al.: Pharmacology of dreaming. In Martin, C. J., and Kisch, B. (eds.): Enzymes in Mental Health. Philadelphia, J. B. Lippincott Co., 1966, pp. 102–116.
6. Kramer, M. (ed.): Dream Psychology and the New Biology of Dreaming. Springfield, Ill., Charles C Thomas, 1970.
7. Snyder, F.: The organismic state associated with dreaming. In Greenfield, N. S., and Lewis, W. C. (ed.): Psychoanalysis and Current Biological Thought. Madison, Wis. University of Wisconsin Press, 1965, pp. 275–315.
8. Witkin, H. A., and Lewis, H. B. (eds.): Experimental Studies of Dreaming. New York, Random House, Inc., 1967.

15. Pubertal Hormones: Libido and Erotic Behavior

John Money and Anke A. Ehrhardt

CASTRATION AND MENOPAUSAL EFFECTS

Mankind has known, apparently since time immemorial or at least since the discovery of animal husbandry, of the effects of castration on the mammalian male. The castration of captured enemies has long been recorded, as has the castration of youths assigned to be harem attendants. As late as the eighteenth century in Europe, boy soprano virtuosos were castrated to provide the opera with castrate sopranos for adult female roles, in an era when a stage career for a woman would have been morally vulgar. Even until the early twentieth century, there survived members of an obscure Russian sect, the Skoptsy, for whom removal of the testes, and preferably the penis also, was an article of faith and a badge of membership. Castration was part of the pseudomedical fake experimentation performed in Hitler's concentration camps, some of the survivors from which are still living as castrates on testosterone substitution therapy.

Castration is practiced in today's medicine chiefly for cancer of the testes, or as adjunctive therapy for cancer of the prostate. Rather rarely, it is also performed on transexuals who change their way of life from male to female. In some political jurisdictions, it has been possible, by court order, to castrate mental defectives and criminal sex offenders.[3] It is now realized, however, that vasectomy is sufficient to prevent a mentally defective youth from breeding, and that hormonal castration, which is reversible, is perhaps more effective than surgical castration, which is not, in the treatment of criminal sex offenders.[28]

The effects of castration on the body, when it is performed on a boy before puberty, are the same as complete testicular failure. The eunuch retains a soprano voice and grows no beard. His arms and legs grow disproportionately long, relative to the trunk. Pubic and axillary hair grows (presumably under the influence of adrenal androgens), but, along with body hair, is feminine in pattern. There is no masculine balding. Subcutaneous fat deposits are feminine in distribution.

There is an extraordinary lack of recorded information, from the time when prepubertal castrates were easy to find, concerning their sexual and erotic capacity.[24, 25] The older authorities, often with one eye on experimental animal evidence, generally claimed that prepubertal castrates showed no libidinal behavior. However, the evidence that prepubertal boys can easily get an erection and do sometimes, in prepubertal play, effect vaginal intercourse, contradicts this claim. Moreover, it is not unheard of for a teenaged castrate-equivalent, a boy with developmental anorchia, to marry[29] and by his own evidence and that of his wife have regular sexual intercourse accompanied by mutually satisfying erotic feeling. For the boy concerned, there was no ejaculatory discharge. It was not possible to calibrate and compare the orgasmic feeling he reported initially with the feeling he experienced following androgen treatment — except that the two were different.

Exceptional cases notwithstanding, it is probably true that prepubertal castration,

From Money, J., and Ehrhardt, Anke A., Man and Woman, Boy and Girl. Baltimore, The Johns Hopkins University Press, 1972.

without subsequent testosterone replacement therapy, is followed more often than not by sexual apathy in adulthood. Sexual apathy is not, of course, equivalent to effeminacy. If one judges from cases of anorchia (since prepubertally castrated normal males are almost nonexistent today), then lack of testes and testicular hormones does not, per se, dispose a boy to feminine emotionality, with lack of aggressive self-assertion and easy tears. He may be overcome by self-pity as he contemplates his nonvirilizing fate, but it is also likely that he will rile against his adversity, with defiance and determination to overcome it. Yet, even if he is disheartened and weepy as a teenager, it is because he strives to be a man, not because he is homosexually effeminate in wanting to be loved as a female.

The general and clinical wisdom of the ages, based on observation of human beings and of animal experiments, has long been that the effects of prepubertal and postpubertal castration are different. The difference in the postpubertally castrated male is that his genitalia, especially internally, have matured to full size, and his mind has accumulated the memory of sexual sensation and the feeling of ejaculatory orgasm. Animal and human evidence alike show that there is not only species variation, but also a wide range of individual variation. In human males, erection and ejaculation are both dependent on the central nervous system as well as the hormonal system. Ejaculation is more hormonally dependent, and so disappears first, but may be supplanted by a dry-run orgasm with corresponding feelings. Even when the feelings diminish in their peak of intensity, they may still be rewarding, so long as the erection is still potent and responsive to erotic stimuli. The length of time before erectile potency is eclipsed, after loss of the testes, is extremely variable. Some men lose it rapidly, within weeks, and others gradually, over months or years.

The same variability that relates to loss of erection relates also to emotional changes following castration. One man may be rapidly overtaken by almost catastrophic crying spells and depressions, whereas another finds himself sliding slowly, over a period of two years or more, into a state of reduced initiative, energy, and ability to assert himself socially and vocationally among his colleagues. One injection of long-acting testosterone enanthate, or a week of oral methyltestosterone, and the deleterious effects, emotional and erotic, are completely reversed.

As difficult as it is to find untreated eunuchs who were prepubertally castrated, it is virtually impossible to find their female counterpart. The removal of ovaries is surgically far more complex than the removal of testes, and there is no customary or legal tradition for doing so. In the rare case of a medical indication for prepubertal ovariectomy, replacement hormones are administered at the expected age of puberty. The most likely instance of the persistence of infantilism until late teenage generally proves to be diagnostically a case of Turner's syndrome. The growth defect of Turner's syndrome is incompatible with the eunuchoid increase in height that would otherwise accompany failure of ovarian puberty. Vaginally, however, there is the same failure of adult secretions as in castration. In both instances, if intercourse is attempted before hormonal replacement therapy and without application of an artificial lubricant, the vagina will be dry and painful.

Vaginal dryness is one of the chief sequelae of ovariectomy in adult women[7; 38] and also of the menopause.[13] It can be corrected by estrogen substitution therapy in small dosage, or by use of a lubricant.

Adult ovariectomy has been, and sometimes still is, recklessly included in surgery for hysterectomy. Usually it is unnecessary and undesirable and should be expressly forbidden by the patient when she signs the operative permit, particularly if she is not yet postmenopausal. Otherwise, unless she is put on replacement hormone, she will enter a postcastration menopause, with irregularities of vasomotor function, temperature, and perspiration control, emotional equilibrium, and sleep.

The symptoms of postcastration menopause are experienced by women with the androgen-insensitivity syndrome if their feminizing testes are removed after puberty and if replacement estrogen is not prescribed. Castration before puberty does not, however, induce such symptoms either at the time of the operation, or later, after the expected age of puberty. Girls with Turner's syndrome who have no ovaries do not exhibit castration symptoms if they remain untreated throughout teenage, nor if they later withdraw themselves from estrogen substitution therapy for a period of time. The same is true of hypopituitary dwarfs who have ovaries, but no gonadotropic hormones from the pituitary to stimulate the ovaries.

The equivalence of vasomotor postcastration symptoms in cases of the testicular-feminizing syndrome and in normal women, and their absence following castration in normal men, gives poor support to those who uphold the idea of a male climacteric as the equivalent of the female menopause. In normal male aging, there is a gradual quantitative tapering off of male hormone production, but no dramatic change, as in the cessation of hormonal cycling that heralds the finish of menstrual periods in the female. The older male is likely to find that his penis obliges with an erection less often than his libidinal desire would dictate, for he undergoes a slow diminution, in this repect, from the typical pneumatic-hammer insistence of the penis in early adolescence to its quietude in the eighth and ninth decades. The female may undergo a corresponding progressive libidinal quiescence, but her copulatory role is such that she possesses, mechanistically speaking, an orifice and a cavity that will awaken to their own feelings while they are in copulatory use, instead of as a prerequisite to their being put to such use, which is the way of the penis.

HORMONAL CASTRATION EFFECTS

In everyday usage, castration means surgical castration. The alternative of hormonal castration has been mentioned in connection with the estrogen treatment of male transsexuals. Functional castration with estrogen is familiar to livestock farmers for increasing the fat and weight of carcasses.

On a limited scale, estrogenic castration has sometimes been used as an attempted method of suppressing libido and sexual behavior in habitual sex offenders whose behavior otherwise would bring them excessively long or indeterminate jail sentences. The castrating effect is reversible. But, because estrogen promotes breast growth, its use is abhorrent to most men, irrespective of the nature of their sexual compulsion and the term of their prison sentence.

Like estrogen, progesterone also has a functional castration effect on the male.[5] By inhibiting spermatogenesis, it induces sterility, and by inhibiting androgen secretion by the testes, it induces a reduction of sexual activity. The testes become reduced in size. All these effects are reversible. There is no breast growth.

Within the past decade, hormones other than estrogen have been found to have nonfeminizing, androgen-depleting or antiandrogenic effects.[30; 5] They are synthetic hormones and they belong among steroids, as do also the naturally-occurring sex hormones. One is cyproterone acetate, a derivative of hydroxyprogesterone. The other is medroxyprogesterone acetate. Both of these nonestrogenizing hormones, when given to male sex offenders, have been discovered to have a favorable effect, at least in some cases, in lowering libido and facilitating better monitoring and regulation of sexual behavior so as to keep the offender out of jail.[15; 11; 34] Since the drug itself does not have an androgenizing effect, it thus acts as a chemical castrating agent for as long as it is administered. The effect is reversible. Its efficacy, while being administered, may conceivably be due also in part to a direct, inhibiting action on sex-organizing centers of the brain, for it is one of the progesterones that, in large enough doses, is known to have an anesthetic effect on the central nervous system.

It is probable that the beneficial effect of androgen antagonists is not simply a matter of their hormonal action alone, but also of a psychic realignment[28] made possible by reason of the life crisis commonly responsible for the initiation of treatment.

Medroxyprogesterone acetate administered to very young girls with idiopathic precocious puberty suppresses breast enlargement and suppresses menstruation. Since these young girls, if untreated, do not show overt sexual behavior to any significant degree, one has as yet no way of knowing whether the hormone may also reduce sexual behavior in the female. At the present time, as a matter of fact, there is no pharmacologic agent known specifically to suppress libido and sexual behavior in the female.

When androgen is given to women, it does not have a counteractive but an augmentive effect on sexual desire and the potential initiation of sexual behavior. One may, indeed, make a case for the proposition that androgen is the libido hormone in both sexes[24] — in woman, for the initiative phase versus the acceptive phase of her menses-cycle of erotism. (See also the section on primate experiments, below.)

WOMAN'S SEXUAL CYCLE

In the male, androgen is secreted by the Leydig cells of the testes either at a steady rate or, possibly, with episodic peaks related to sexual activity.[1] The possibility of a peak derives from the evidence that the shaved beard grows faster the day before intercourse is expected following a period of forced sexual isolation and inaction. In the female by contrast, the hormonal secretions of the ovary are cyclic, in synchrony with the menstrual cycle. At the completion of the phase of menstrual bleeding, a new egg-containing follicle takes its turn at enlarging, and secreting estrogen. At mid-point in the new cycle, ovulation occurs: the follicle ruptures and releases its egg. Estrogen production then diminishes during the succeeding week, while progesterone, the pregnancy hormone (also referred to as a progestin or a gestagen), increases. It is the withdrawal of estrogen that induces the uterus to shed its unoccupied endometrial lining and to menstruate, as is evident in all cases requiring replacement therapy: it is sufficient to prescribe estrogen for three weeks on, and one week off, to induce regular menstruation. Progesterone (gestagen) is literally a gestation hormone, its initial gestational function being to facilitate nidation of the egg in the uterine wall, should it have encountered spermatozoa and have become fertilized by one of them.

The hormonal events that lead up to menstruation are not restricted to the ovaries and uterus. Because the delivery system for all hormones is the bloodstream, all cells of the body are potentially involved. This is the physiological fact that underlies the phenomena of premenstrual tension and/or menstrual cramps. Some women will frankly describe themselves as cranky, bitchy, and impossible to live with, in spite of their own best intentions, during the days of premenstrual tension. Others will not even be aware that their cycle has revolved full turn, unless they look at the calendar. And some, because of negative attitudes instilled into them in childhood, will transform a mild malaise into a major hypochondriachal illness.

There is no satisfactory explanation as to why some women are afflicted with particularly difficult premenstrual tension and irritability. The fact that they are is important, however, in any study of the female's peak period of sexual desire, because these women may feel too miserable to be bothered with sexual intercourse. These are women who are more likely to say that their period of maximum interest in sex is around the mid-cyclic time of ovulation.

Other women will say that their period of maximum desire corresponds with the menstrual phase of their cycle — even though they may not be able to do much about it, if they (or the partner) live with a taboo against menstrual blood.

Few studies have been done on the cyclicity of woman's sexual desire. [13; 36; 8] These studies have produced confusing or contradictory results because they did not clearly distinguish between the quality of sexual desire that woman may experience at the ovulatory versus the menstrual phase of the sexual cycle. At the ovulatory period, her feeling of sexual desire is likely to be a desire to surrender and to be occupied sexually. At the menstrual period it is likely to be a feeling of desire to capture and envelop. The accomplishment of this desire requires taking the erotic initiative, or, in the standard jargon of sex, being aggressive — which conventionially is supposed to be the prerogative of the male. The man who adheres scrupulously to the outmoded convention that a woman always is and should be erotically and sexually passive is wrong. Not only is he wrong, but he also doesn't know what he is missing — nor does the female. She too has the capacity and feeling for taking the sexual initiative. This is the feeling that seems to be enhanced if, for some or other therapeutic reason, a woman is given androgen in amounts abnormally high for a female.

The cyclic change in the nuance of woman's sexual desire, from being more receptive to more assertive, may manifest itself not only in her sexual behavior but also in her dreams. Van de Castle and Smith (1971, personal communication) studied 50 women student nurses, collecting their dreams over the course of the menstrual cycle, an average of nine dreams per person (range, 4 to 16). With reference to aggression in general, not specifically sexual aggression, they found a significant increase of dreams of aggression toward males, but not females, during the menstrual phase as compared with the nonmenstrual phase of the cycle. During the nonmenstrual phase, there were more dreams than during the menstrual phase of the female being the recipient of male aggression, but not of aggression from other females.

Friendliness toward both sexes was higher during the menstrual then the nonmenstrual phase, but only in the nonmenstrual phase were men in the dreams more frequently friendly toward a woman dreamer than were women. Friendliness initiated by other women was the same in both phases of a woman's dreams, but friendliness initiated by men increased significantly during the nonmenstrual phase.

Adding together dreams of either aggression or friendliness initiated, versus those of aggression or friendliness received, the menstrual phase emerged as the one when

more interaction is initiated with either sex in dreams; and, conversely, the nonmenstrual phase as the one when there is more dream interaction received from either sex, but especially from men. In both phases men figure more frequently than do women in dreams as initiators or recipients of either aggression or friendliness. The additive effect reaches higher statistical significance in the nonmenstrual than the menstrual phase, which obviously is the phase when a woman dreams predominantly of encounters with men, whether positively or negatively.

Van de Castle and Smith did not make a study specifically of the approach-receive dimension in the sexual interactions represented in their subjects' dreams. The ratio of dreams with sex to total dreams during the menstrual phase was .105, and .111 during the nonmenstrual phase, the difference not being statistically significant. The total number of dreams in each phase was 114 and 352, respectively.

Human females are not alone in having two peaks or phases of sexual desire per cycle of menstruation. Loy[17] studied free-ranging rhesus monkeys on Cayo Santiago, Puerto Rico, and found that nonpregnant females showed a phase of sexual behavior at midcycle, and another phase of similar behavior perimenstrually or during menstruation.

PRIMATE EXPERIMENTS ON HORMONES AND MATING CYCLICITY

Because of the convenience of their size, rodents have been favorite laboratory animals on which the effects of hormones on mating behavior have been tested. For those who are interested in human sexual behavior, however, these animals are not so valuable: they are an estrous species and we, with other primates, are a menstrual species. Moreover, rodents, as well as annually seasonal mammals, exhibit certain components of copulatory dimorphic behavior only if the necessary and appropriate hormones activate them. By contrast, many components of sexual behavior in the human and other higher primates are not exclusively hormone-dependent, even if hormonally influenced, for their release. The most valuable animal experiments for human beings interested in themselves are, therefore, experiments on higher primates.

Michael[22] and Herbert[10] and their collaborators have directed research expressly to the determinants of sexual behavior related to the sexual cycle of the female rhesus monkey. Their experiments are all carefully designed, with all the necessary cross-checks and controls, so that their findings are clear and not contaminated with doubt. Their studies make clear that the female's hormonal cycle influences not only her own behavior, but that of her male partner also. The hypothesis, namely that the male's sense of smell is influenced by odor [40; 10; 21] emanating from the vagina has been conclusively demonstrated by Michael, Keverne, and Bonsall.[22] They isolated the odiferous substance from the vagina, that is to say the pheromone, named copulin, which is at its peak level at the time of ovulation. It proved to be constituted of short-chain aliphatic acids. The strength or level of this pheromone in the vagina is at its height at the time of ovulation. Then, when the cells lining the vagina are cornified, the male rhesus finds the female most attractive, and he initiates sexual activity more persistently. The amount of time from first mount to ejaculation is shortened, and the mounting rate and number of thrusts per mount increases.

The rhesus male typically mounts once or twice a minute, and after inserting the penis makes up to ten thrusts in 1½ to 2½ seconds before dismounting. The number of mounts may be half a dozen or more before ejaculation occurs. After dismounting, the animals sit together and may groom each other. In her estrogenic phase, the male grooms the female more than she him, whereas at other times, she is likely to groom him more.[20] He is then likely to be inattentive if he has access to another female who is at the ovulatory point of her cycle, even though this female would normally be low on his list of preferred females.

Sexual preference exists among rhesus monkeys, apparently in much the same way as it does in human beings. It can be easily tested by putting two females and one male together. One becomes his favorite, and the other a lonely outcast, unless she is ovulating or estrogenized by injection while the other female is not. Though the basis of preference is known not to be hormonal, its actual basis has not been discovered. It may bear some relationship to dominance hierarchy, for when raised in a troop, an infant monkey's subsequent dominance is affected by its mother's own dominance position; and the dominance position of the mother herself reflects the favoritism accorded her by the dominant male of the group. By contrast, a monkey raised in isolation, with no mother and no playmates, is unable to be sexually receptive and to position itself correctly for coitus in adulthood.[9]

When a female is at her maximum attractiveness to the male, either because she is at the ovulatory phase of her cycle or because she has been experimentally estrogen treated, the male usually makes his mounts without any visible invitation from her in the form of a sexual presentation. Such signaling is not necessary to stimulate the male at this time, though it may help to arouse his interest later in the cycle.

The various experiments of Michael, Herbert and their co-workers leave no doubt that the female's attractiveness to the male is estrogen determined. If she is ovariectomized, it disappears. Likewise, if she is injected with progesterone, it disappears. At the same time, her own receptivity and interest in sex, as indicated by her standard gesture of presenting her hind end in sexual presentation, does not disappear. Obviously, sexual attractiveness and sexual receptiveness are not synonymous in monkeys (nor are they in human beings!). Herbert addressed himself to this issue and approached it specifically in consideration of the human clinical evidence that androgen is the libido hormone in women as well as men.[24] He administered a small dose of testosterone (1 mg/day) to ovariectomized females and found that it greatly increased the number of times they presented sexually to males. The behavior of the males was unaffected. Larger doses of testosterone did not increase sexual behavior in the females, but diminished it by inducing aggressiveness in their behavior. The males did not retaliate.

The crucial question remaining was whether the female monkey's own endogenous production of androgen affected her sexual drive or receptivity.[6] The adrenal cortex is the principal source of androgen in females.[2] Herbert's next experiment, in collaboration with Everitt was one utilizing the drug, dexamethasone sodium sulphate (0.5 mg/kg/day), to suppress the production of hormones by the adrenal cortex. As expected, androgen levels fell, as did the levels of other adrenocortical hormones. At the same time, sexual receptivity also fell, as indicated by reduced presentations to invite the male to mount, or by outright rejection of his attempts to mount. This loss of receptivity was not responsive to any type of hormone treatment except treatment with minute amounts of testosterone (100 or 200µg/day). Receptivity was then completely restored. Moreover, treatment with testosterone before dexamethasone prevented the dexamethasone suppressive effect on sexual receptivity.

Herbert's experiments suggest that knowledge of human sexuality can be expanded by studying patients undergoing special treatments or tests — the dexamethasone test of adrenocortical function for example. Waxenberg[38] and coworkers gathered psychosexual information on women undergoing ovariectomy first and then adrenalectomy, as part of a radical treatment for breast cancer. They found that only after the adrenals as well as the ovaries had been removed did libidinal feeling disappear.

More needs to be done also on the sense of smell in relationship to sexuality in men and women: It is known that women's smell acuity is, in general, superior to that of men, and that this superiority is lost if estrogen levels fall, after ovariectomy, for example.[26] Smell acuity also varies with the menstrual cycle. There is lesser acuity during the menstrual phase, and greater acuity at the ovulatory phase when the level of estrogen reaches a peak.

With respect to the male, one wonders whether the avid interest of some men in cunnilingus may not be related to an odiferous arousal or enhancement of sexual enthusiasm, but there is no experimental evidence one way or the other at the present time.

PUBERTAL HORMONES AND HOMOSEXUALITY, BISEXUALITY, AND HETEROSEXUALITY

The ordinary heterosexual man or woman is unable to reconcile his or her own common sense expectations with the phenomenon of an anatomic male who behaves with the mannerisms of a female, and is capable of a love affair and sexual relationship only with another anatomic male. Conversely, the same irreconcilability holds with respect to the masculine-behaving lesbian. The evidence of common sense is still further challenged, if the homosexual male or female also dresses as an impersonator of the opposite sex, and passes maritally, socially, and occupationally as a member of the opposite sex.

Impersonative homosexuality can be perhaps an obvious travesty, or else so convincing that writers of social, psychologic, or medical texts have fallen easily into the trap of reiterating a venerable shibboleth, namely, that homosexuality in one of its forms is innate and in its other form is acquired. Shibboleths, by their very nature, don't need proof. There is, as yet, no currently acceptable evidence of an innate form of homosexuality.[27] There is also no evidence of an exclusively acquired form of homosexuality, as traditionally defined, for the so-called "acquired form" is actually a manifestation of bisexuality. Permanent or exclusive homosexuality will most likely be eventually explained as the product of interaction between prenatal and postnatal determinants.

All discussions of homosexuality become wasteful word games unless, at the outset, a differentiation is established between homosexuality defined as a behavioral act, versus homosexuality defined, by inference, as a permanent state of erotic disposition and preference. Any mammal is capable of homosexual behavior, in the sense of performing part or all of the act of mounting on a member of the same sex. In the case of males, intromission per rectum may also occur, and has been proved, in the ram, one mode of infectious sterility. This kind of behavior is widespread in the animal kingdom, though the evidence is transmitted, often by oral tradition in anecdotal accounts, rather than systematically observed and reported in writing. Mounting and smelling behavior is probably the most common homosexual behavior in the lower animals, and licking of the genitals of a same-sex partner less common than intromission between males.

Farm animals or wild animals observed in homosexual behavior are, almost without exception, also able to breed. In other words, they are bisexual. When in season, they copulate with alacrity if the opportunity provides for it. They exhibit homosexual behavior more often in childhood than in adulthood, and more often when sex-segregated than not. Housebound animals raised as pets and wild animals raised or held in captivity are more likely to show such long-term deviations from heterosexual behavior as preferential homosexuality.

Among human beings, facultative (optional; essentially bisexual) homosexual behavior sometimes occurs as part of the sexual play of childhood and prepuberty, or part of the sexual exploration of puberty and adolescence. Facultative homosexuality in the early years of sexual maturity may be in part a by-product of sexual segregation and cultural injunctions against boy-girl relationships. In some societies, indeed, adolescent homosexuality is a prescribed instead of a proscribed way of life. After adolescence, facultative homosexuality may be a product of enforced sexual segregation, as in prison or military service.

In our own society, the phenomenon of facultative homosexuality is nowhere better illustrated than when men or women are segregated in jail.[4] In a men's prison, some men are of a sexual type known, in some insitutions, by the nickname of "gorilla." The gorillas are men whose sexual activity on the outside is, by strong preference, heterosexual. They are not so moralistically and inhibitedly heterosexual, however, as to be incapable of achieving erection and orgasm by means of oral or

anal insertion, whereas there are some men who are unable to hold an erection for oral or anal insertion. The gorillas, while they are incarcerated, therefore, seek opportunities for oral or anal sexual liaison with other male prisoners. There are certain rare institutions which permit cell-mate arrangements between such men and essential or obligative homosexual male prisoners who want to be the sexual partner of an otherwise heterosexual male. Other institutions segregate obligative (non-bisexual) homosexuals in a special tier or cell block. These are the institutions in which the gorillas earn their nickname. With no willing homosexuals available as partners, they test all newcomers of slight build to see if they have the will, the power, or the weapon (sharp objects are traded among prisoners) of self-defense. If the newcomer qualifies as timid, then he is slated to become the victim of repeated homosexual anal rape, in the shower room or in the cell block. It is perilous for him to lodge a complaint. Since the problem is frequent, the authorities do not have facilities to deal with it. A complainant is, therefore, subject to severe retribution from the gorillas against whom he has lodged a complaint.

Sexual relationships in a woman's prison are somewhat similar, except that the dominant and demanding partner, the "bull" or "stud", is one who is either lesbian or bisexual by preference on the outside and, in prison, tries to establish a relationship with a fellow prisoner who would, by preference, be heterosexual.

The male prisoner who is subjugated by the gorilla, and the female prisoner who is subjugated by the bull, do not develop a long-term pattern of homosexuality as a result of their experiences. The influence of experience in prison is, in fact, more likely to be that it exposes potentially bisexual people to the example of how to be gorillas or bulls, until they are released. Training in bisexuality of this type is, indeed, one of the indictments that may be brought against our juvenile detention institutions.

Imprisonment is not, of course, the sole source of facultative homosexuality — it is simply an exceptionally clear illustration of the difference between the extremes of obligative heterosexuality, facultative heterosexuality-homosexuality, and obligative homosexuality. The origin of these three different conditions in human psychosexuality is still without a definite explanation. The new science of cytogenetics gives no answer, for the majority of homosexuals and bisexuals have the same number of chromosomes as obligatively heterosexual people. Whether there may be not a chromosomal but a genic difference between the three psychosexual types is an open question for which no answer is available at the present stage of the development of genetic science.

The science of endocrinology also gives no clear clue as to the origin of the three psychosexual types — homosexual, bisexual, and heterosexual. In the 1940s, there were a few studies of the urinary output of metabolites of the sex hormones in homosexuals versus controls, but the methods were crude, and the results equivocal.[24] Interest in this particular type of investigation lapsed until 1970, when two new publications appeared.[18; 16] Both used improved, modern methods of estimating sex-hormone production by measuring hormonal metabolites in urine. This is an acceptable procedure, but one that yields no precision of information regarding the level of biologically active sex hormones in the blood stream. The metabolic breakdown products of sex hormones get into the urine by way of the liver and the kidneys. Urinary levels of these metabolites often tell more about the functional efficiency of the liver than they do about the amount or type of sex hormone actually released by the gonads and the adrenal cortices into the bloodstream. Hormone release is best determined by directly measuring hormone levels in the blood's plasma.

Both of the 1970 studies claim to find different proportions of various selected metabolic products of sex hormones in the urine of homosexuals — females are included in the sample of Loraine and coworkers — as compared with heterosexual controls. Both are pilot studies with too few subjects from which to formulate any statistical conclusions with confidence. There are various weaknesses in experi-

mental design, such as not controlling for age, nor for amount or frequency of sexual deprivation or activity, which might be important, nor for general health status.

The only safe inference to make at the present stage of history is that, if indeed there are differences between homosexuals and heterosexuals or bisexuals in urinary excretion of sex-hormone metabolites, then there is such extreme variation in the amount excreted by heterosexual controls, that the number of homosexuals tested will need to be much greater than in the samples of two, four, and fifteen so far reported. If the reported differences should hold up when larger samples are tested, then their origin and significance will remain to be explained, for they may prove to be related to homosexuality only secondarily or derivatively.

The more exact and newly developed method of measuring sex hormone levels by direct blood plasma determinations of hormones circulating in the blood stream was first applied specifically to the homosexual-bisexual-heterosexual issue in 1971.[14] They found no difference in the distribution of plasma testosterone levels between a control group of heterosexual college men and approximately 75 percent of a group of bisexual and homosexual college men. The remaining 25 percent, who ranked among the most extreme on Kinsey's six-point rating scale for homosexuality, had levels of plasma testosterone lower than those of the lowest normal controls. These same homosexual men also manifested an excess of low sperm counts, including four with no sperm count at all. It seems likely that these men, low in sperm count and plasma testosterone, may represent an as yet unidentified syndrome, perhaps of prenatal origin (see reference to Ward, 1972) in which a homosexual gender identity differentiates more easily than in the population at large. If so, then the syndrome would have a parallel in the XXY and the XYY syndromes, in both of which homosexuality tends to appear rather frequently.

An earlier study of homosexual plasma testosterone levels[23] had as its subjects five male transsexual patients awaiting hormonal (estrogen) therapy and sex-reassignment surgery. These patients may be regarded as being at the extreme of the homosexual spectrum, since they seek a partnership with a male after surgery, if not before. All five patients had plasma concentrations of the androgens testosterone, androstendione, and dehydroisoandrosterone that were within normal limits. These same five patients also proved to be within normal limits in urinary excretion of steroids measured as 17-ketosteroids, 17-hydroxy-corticosteroids, pregnanediol, pregnanetriol, and estrogens. They were also within normal limits of urinary gonadotropin secretion.

Corresponding to the report of Migeon and associates on male-to-female transsexuals, there is one report on hormonal levels in three female-to-male transexuals.[12] Utilizing gas-liquid chromatographic methods, he determined plasma testosterone concentrations in the three female patients. In two cases, additional determinations were done in conjunction with gonadotropin and ACTH suppression and stimulation.

The baseline plasma testosterone concentrations were within the normal female range in two patients (0.02–0.04 mg/100 ml plasma) and in the range found in the androgenizing-ovary (Stein-Leventhal) syndrome in the third patient (0.05–0.08 mg/100 ml plasma). In no case did the baseline concentrations of testosterone approximate the normal male range, and they were not as high as the concentrations found in the testicular feminization syndrome or in female patients with a masculinizing tumor of the ovary (arrhenoblastoma). The suppression-stimulation studies generally indicated that approximately 50 percent of circulating testosterone was of ovarian origin and 50 percent of adrenal origin, a finding consistent with control studies in normal females.

There is another approach to the hypothesis of a hormonal effect on homosexuality, bisexuality, or heterosexuality in adolescence or adulthood, namely, by way of patients whose proper hormonal balance is upset by developmental malfunction or disease. For example, a boy at adolescence may undergo breast enlargement (for reasons not yet

scientifically explainable) similar to that of an adolescent girl. He may wonder whether fate has destined him to turn into a female, or a half-female freak, but the very thought mortifies him, because he does not feel like a female and does not want to be one. Medically, his only ambition, judging by the majority of cases, is to be rid of the deformity on his chest, so that he can be normal as a young man. So strong is the desire to be heterosexually normal that one young man, who wanted very much not to be drafted for the Vietnam war, was totally unable to entertain the idea that, if he had had but one homosexual experience, he would be ineligible.

The converse of the estrogenized boy is the adolescent girl who virilizes because of an adrenal or ovarian malfunction or tumor. Such a girl wants only to be rid of her hairy disfigurement, and to get her menstrual periodicity reestablished. She may wonder whether fate is turning her into a circus freak. If she does, she resents the idea totally and longs to be told that she can be restored to morphologic normalcy.

The lack of a relationship between postpubertal androgen or estrogen levels and homosexuality, bisexuality, or heterosexuality is further indicated by the fact that injections of hormone are used therapeutically in vain, if the intention is to make homosexuals heterosexual, heterosexuals homosexual, or bisexuals monosexual. The effects of such injections are only that androgen, within limits, increases libido in both sexes, and estrogen has a functional castrating effect on the male.

The most likely source of hormonal difference between homosexual, bisexual, and heterosexual people, if there is one, will not be found at puberty, but prenatally. Prenatal hormonal differences between the three types, if they in fact exist, are not at present known. Nonetheless, an open mind is in order, in view of such evidence as that of Gorski and his associates on the effect of prenatal drugs that counteract prenatal hormones. These researchers found that they could prevent the well-known masculinization of a female fetus under the influence of excess male hormones injected into the pregnant mother animal, if they simultaneously injected either a barbiturate (phenobarbital or pentobarbital), or an experimental antibiotic (puromycin or actinomycin-D). The daughter fetuses then were protected against the expected masculinizing influences of the male sex hormone injections, presumably because the second injection competed with the first and cancelled its action on the chemistry of the genetic code within the body's cells.

Nothing at present is known concerning a possible prenatal drug effect that might predispose toward the later differentiation of a homosexual as compared with a bisexual or heterosexual gender identity. In fact, very little is known about the effect on the fetus of medications taken by the pregnant mother, especially if the effect should be delayed and manifested not in anatomy but only in temperament or behavior. Conceivably, not only medications, but also foodstuffs might be implicated, or even the hormones produced by the mother's own placenta or other endocrine organs, if one builds a conjecture on the basis of the competitive-uptake, radioactive-hormone studies of Stern and Eisenfeld.[35]

The possibility that an endogenous substance produced by the mother might have a predisposing effect on the psychosexual differentiation of the offspring is given more credence than would otherwise be the case by the experiment of Ward,[37] which showed that stress of the pregnant mother rat had a transmitted effect, presumably hormonally mediated, on the fetus, rendering the sons deficient in masculine behavior in adulthood. Not only the hormonal effect of the mother's stress may be implicated, but also a hormonal effect from brothers or sisters in the uterus, according to the evidence of Clemens. Surprisingly, a presumed hormonal effect may be transmitted from the grandmother: Wehmer, Porter, and Scales[39] found that stress of the pregnant mother increased not only the exploratory behavior of her daughters, but also that of the daughter's offspring in the next generation.

Since there are no systematic data relative to a possible relationship, either direct or indirect, between prenatal stress, prenatal medication, or prenatal hormonal functioning and the subsequent development of homosexuality, bisexuality, and heterosexuality in adulthood, an open mind obviously is in order. Nonetheless, in view of the fact that the incidence of homosexuality and bisexuality crosses many ethnic barriers into cultures that have entirely different traditions of food, medications, and stress conditions in pregnancy, the hypothesis of prenatal effects will need to be tested very rigorously.

The concept of a prenatal hormonal component in the eventual differentiation of homosexuality is difficult to sustain also because the phenomenon of obligative homosexuality, to say nothing of facultative homosexuality or bisexuality, is by no means uniform in its manifestations. The erotic preferences and activities, and the general everyday behavior of one obligatively homosexual person (male or female) may differ so widely from that of another homosexual as the behavior of an obligatively heterosexual woman differs from that of an obligatively heterosexual man. Thus, whereas one obligative homosexual male may impersonate a female in dress, daily living, and sexual relationships with men, another may be indistinguishable among his heterosexual colleagues, except in the general context of his private life and sexual activities. The same holds true, obversely, for the obligative homosexual female.

Despite the nonuniformity of traits in the homosexual personality, there is one that tends to be shared by obligative homosexual males: as boys, they were not fighters. They avoided challenges to compete for dominance in the dominance hierarchy of boyhood. Like girls, they remained low in the pecking order of their respective childhood groups. The obligative homosexual female, by contrast, is likely to have competed for dominance as a child, and to have been weak in maternalistic play interests.

Competitive dominance-aggression and maternalism are both traits that might conceivably be subject to prenatal hormonal influences on the brain. Their presence or absence need bear no fixed relationship to psychosexual differentiation on the homosexual-bisexual-heterosexual continuum. Nonetheless, atrophic competitive dominance-aggression in a boy, or its hypertrophy in a girl may, dependent on other developmental experiences, be a contributing influence in the psychosexual differentiation of obligative homosexuality. Lack of maternalism may have a parallel influence. Though the hypothesis is an attractive one, the idea of a prenatal hormonal influence on the brain is not integral to it. Lack of dominance-aggression or maternalism, or too much of either, may equally well be conceived of as having a postnatal origin either in bodily size, health and strength, or in social contingency learning. In male rhesus monkeys, a correlation has been found between dominance hierarchy ranking, assertive aggressiveness, and blood-testosterone level.[33] In the hamster, assertive aggressiveness is a trait of the female, the larger sex, in interaction with the male, and correlates with blood levels of progesterone, not testosterone.[32]

There is no more convincing evidence of the power and importance of social contingency learning in the establishment of homosexuality, bisexuality, and heterosexuality than that offered in matched pairs of hermaphrodites. Such cases show that gender identity can differentiate discordantly with chromosomal sex, prenatal hormonal sex, and even postnatal hormonal sex and secondary sexual body morphology. The discordance is so complete and predictable that one can actually make therapeutic plans for its occurrence in cases of a genetic male, born with a microphallus too miniscule ever to function as a copulatory organ, who is assigned and surgically and hormonally corrected for life as a female. The same applies, for example, to the case of a normal boy who suffers complete accidental ablation of the penis in infancy as the result of a circumcision accident, and is immediately rehabilitated as a female. These cases represent what is, to all intents and purposes, experimentally planned and iatrogenically induced homosexuality. But homosexuality in these cases must be qualified as homosexuality on the criterion of genetic sex, gonadal sex, or fetal hormonal sex. Postsurgically, it is no longer homosexuality on the criterion of the external sex organs nor of the sex of replacement hormonal puberty.

The most likely explanation of the origins of homosexuality, bisexuality, and heterosexuality of gender identity is that certain sexually dimorphic traits or dispositions are laid down in the brain before birth which may facilitate the establishment of either of the three conditions but are too strongly bivalent to be exclusive and invariant determinants of either homo- or heterosexuality, or of their shared bisexual state. The primary origins of the three conditions lie in the developmental period of a child's life after birth, particularly during the years of late infancy and early childhood, when gender identity differentiation is being established. The state of knowledge as of the present does not permit any hypotheses (many psychodynamic claims to the contrary) that will predict with certainty which biographical conditions will ensure that an anatomically normal boy or girl will become erotically homosexual, bisexual, or heterosexual. Once the pattern is established in the early development years, however, it is remarkably tenacious. The hormones of puberty bring it into full expression.

REFERENCES

1. Anon. 1970. Effects of sexual activity on beard growth in man. Nature 226:869–70

2. Baird, D., Horton, R., Longcope, C., and Tait, J. F.: 1968. Steroid prehormones. Perspectives in Biology and Medicine 11:384–421.

3. Bremer, J. 1959. Asexualization. A follow-up study of 244 cases. New York, Macmillan.

4. Davis, A. J. 1969. Report on Sexual Assaults in the Prison System and Sheriff's Vans. Philadelphia, District Attorney's Office and Police Department.

5. Diamond, M. 1966. Progestagen inhibition of normal sexual behavior in the male guinea-pig. Nature 209:1322–24.

6. Everitt, B. J., and Herbert, J. 1969. Adrenal glands and sexual receptivity in female rhesus monkeys. Nature. 222:1065–66.

7. Filler, W., and Drezner, N. 1944. Results of surgical castration in women over forty. American Journal of Obstetrics and Gynecology 47:122–24.

8. Hampson, J. L., and Hampson, J. G. 1961. The ontogenesis of sexual behavior in man. In Young, W. C., (ed.): Sex and Internal Secretions, 3rd ed. Baltimore, Williams and Wilkins.

9. Harlow, H. F., Joslyn, W. D., Senko, M. G., and Dopp, A. 1966. Behavioral aspects of reproduction in primates. Journal of Animal Science 25:49–67.

10. Herbert, J. 1970. Hormones and reproductive behavior in rhesus and talapoin monkeys. Journal of Reproduction and Fertility (Supplement) 11:119–40.

11. Hoffet, H. 1968. Ueber die Anwendung des Testoseronblockers Cyproteronazetat (SH 714) bei Sexualdelinquenten und psychiatrischen Anstaltspatienten. Praxis 7:221–30.

12. Jones, J. R. 1972. Plasma testosterone concentrations in female transexuals. Archives of Sexual Behavior, in press.

13. Kane, F. T., Lipton, M. A., and Ewing, J. A. 1969. Hormonal influences in female sexual response. Archives of General Psychiatry 20:202–9.

14. Kolodny, R. C., Masters, W. H., Hendryx, J., and Toro, G. 1971. Plasma testosterone and semen analysis in male homosexuals. The New England Journal of Medicine 285:1170–74.

15. Laschet, U. 1969. Die Anwendbarkeit von Antiandrogenen in der Humanmedizin. Saarlaendisches Aerzteblatt 22:370–71.

16. Loraine, J. A., Ismail, A. A. A.; Adamopoulos, D. A., and Dove, G. A. 1970. Endocrine function in male and female homosexuals. British Medical Journal 4:406–9.

17. Loy, J. 1970. Perimenstrual sexual behavior among rhesus monkeys. Folia Primatologica 13:286–97.

18. Margolese, M. 1970. Homosexuality: a new endocrine correlate. Hormones and Behavior 1:151–55.

19. Michael, R. P. 1971. Neuroendocrine factors regulating primate behavior. In Martini, L., and Ganong, W. F. (eds.), Frontiers in Neuroendocrinology, 1971. New York, Oxford University Press.

20. Michael, R. P., and Herbert, J. 1963. Menstrual cycle influences grooming behavior and sexual activity in the rhesus monkey. Science 140:500–1.

21. Michael, R. P., and Keverne, E. B. 1968. Pheromones in the communication of sexual status in primates. Nature 218:746–49.

22. Michael, R. P., Keverne, E. B., and Bonsall, R. W. 1971. Pheromones: isolation of a male sex attractant from a female primate. Science 172:964–66.

23. Migeon, C. J., Rivarola, M. A., and Forest, M. G. 1968. Studies of androgens in transsexual subjects. Effects of estrogen therapy. Johns Hopkins Medical Journal 123: 128–33.

24. Money, J. 1961a. Components of eroticism in man: I. The hormones in relation to sexual morphology and sexual desire. Journal of Nervous and Mental Disease, 132:239–48.

25. Money, J. 1961b. Components of eroticism in man: II. The orgasm and genital somesthesia. Journal of Nervous and Mental Disease 132:289–97.

26. Money, J. 1965a. Influence of hormones on sexual behavior. Annual Review of Medicine 16:67–82.

27. Money, J. 1970b. Sexual dimorphism and homosexual gender identity. Psychological Bulletin 74:425–40.

28. Money, J. 1970C. Use of an androgen-depleting hormone in the treatment of male sex offenders. Journal of Sex Research 6:165-72.

29. Money, J., and Alexander, D. 1967. Eroticism and sexual function in developmental anorchia and hyporchia with pubertal failure. Journal of Sex Research 3:31–47.

30. Neumann, F., and Elger, W. 1965. Proof of the activity of androgenic agents on the differentiation of the external genitalia, the mammary gland and the hypothalamic-pituitary system in rats. In Androgens in Normal and Pathological Conditions, International Congress Series No. 101. Proceedings of the Second Symposium on Steroid Hormones. Amsterdam, Excerpta Medica.

31. Neumann, F., Steinbeck, H., and Hahn, J. D. 1970. Hormones and brain differentiation. In Martini, L., Motta, M., and Fraschini, F. (eds.), The Hypothalamus. New York, Academic Press. Pp. 569–603.

32. Payne, A., and Swanson, H. H. 1971. Hormonal control of aggressive dominance in the female hamster. Physiology and Behavior 6:355–62.

33. Rose, R. M., Holaday, J. W., and Bernstein, I. S. 1971. Plasma testosterone, dominance rank and aggressive behaviour in male rhesus monkeys. Nature 231:366–68.

34. Seebandt, G. 1968. Gedanken und Überlegungen zur Behandlung sexualtriebabartiger

Psychopathen mit Antiandrogenen. Das oeffentliche Gesundheitswesen: Monatsschrift für Gesundheitsverwaltung und Sozialhygiene 30:66–71.

35. Stern, J. M., and Eisenfeld, A. J. 1971. Distribution and metabolism of 3H-testosterone in castrated male rats; effects of cyproterone, progesterone and unlabeled testosterone. Endocrinology 88:1117–25.

36. Udry, J. R., and Morris, H. M. 1968. Distribution of coitus in the menstrual cycle. Nature 220:593–96.

37. Ward, I. 1972. Prenatal stress feminizes and demasculinizes the behavior of males. Science. 175:82–84.

38. Waxenberg, S. E. 1963. Some biologic correlates of sexual behavior. In Winokur, G. (ed.), Determinants of Sexual Behavior. Springfield, Ill, Charles C Thomas.

39. Wehmer, F., Porter, R. H., and Scales, B. 1970. Pre-mating and pregnancy stress in rats affects behavior of grandpups. Nature 227:622.

40. Wiener, H. 1966. External chemical messengers. I. Emission and reception in man. New York State Journal of Medicine 66:3153–70.

VI BIOBEHAVIORAL FACTORS IN PHYSICAL ILLNESS

The notion that emotional and social events affect the course of medical disease has intrigued physicians since ancient times. Although lacking the definitive data of experimental research, Daniel Hack Tuke, a noted nineteenth century English physician, was able to compile an impressive body of anecdotal material on the biobehavioral aspects of physical illness. In the summary of his exhaustive work, entitled Illustrations of the Influence of the Mind on the Body. Tuke concluded as follows:

We have seen that the influence of the mind upon the body is no transient power; that *in health* it may exalt the sensory functions, or suspend them altogether; excite the nervous system so as to cause the various forms of convulsive action of the voluntary muscles, or to depress it so as to render them powerless; may stimulate or paralyze the muscles of organic life, and the processes of Nutrition and Secretion — causing even death; that *in disease* it may restore the functions which it takes away in health, reinnervating the sensory and motor nerves, exciting healthy vascularity and nervous power, and assisting the *vis medicatrix Naturae* to throw off disease action or absorb morbid deposits.

Stewart Wolf is perhaps the most prolific and creative contemporary investigator of the role of behavioral factors in physical illness. In the following quote, he recounts the experiences of Louis Pasteur to illustrate that nineteenth century scientists were fully aware of the fact that medical pathology, precipitated initially by an infectious agent, cannot be explained by the effects of the precipitant alone (1971):

Since the days of Pasteur and until recently, medical thinkers have been preoccupied with the need to establish a single cause for disease processes. Such a concern has tended to obscure the evidence relating to the modulating power of the central nervous system on all sorts of noxious and potentially noxious experiences. In fact, the weakness of the single-cause idea was recognized by some of the members of the French academy who had blocked Pasteur's appointment to that august body. One of his opponents, Pidoux, expressed it thus: "Disease is the common result of a variety of diverse external and internal causes [that] bring about the destruction of an organ by a number of roads which the hygienist and the physician must endeavour to close." Thus, a rational concept of disease would hold that illness and incapacity arise from efforts on the part of the body to deal with adverse forces in the environment more frequently than they arise from the direct effect or intrinsic nature of the adverse stimulus itself. In a sense, disease is a reaction to, rather than an effort of, noxious forces. As each human organism may respond slightly differently, depending on genetic equipment, previous experience with disease, conditioning effects, and so forth, the manifestations of the same disease in different individuals will be variable.

The most persuasive proponent of the "multifactorial" approach to illness is the eminent internist and psychiatrist, George Engel, author of the first paper of this chapter. Engel emphasizes that physical disease is *not* a thing in itself, unrelated to the patient as a unified whole, his personality, bodily constitution, or mode of life. He rejects the language habit of physicians who speak of their patients as "having a disease" or of their practice of "treating a disease." Although specific microorganisms may be necessary ingredients in producing an infection, it is by no means the exclusive or even major determinant of the patient's condition. "Disease" explanations, which may include the most refined specification of biochemical or molecular components, reflect the persistence of mechanistic concepts that typified medical thinking in the first half of this century; the identification of disease entities is no longer the exciting and fruitful innovation in thinking that it was 50 years ago but an aged obstacle to the full understanding of pathology.

Turning from Engel's broad considerations of the nature of health and disease to more specific factors in the etiology of physical illness, the second paper of this chapter, by R. W. Olmsted and D. A. Kennedy, focuses on the most prevalent problem of modern medicine, that of athersclerosis. In their summary report of a conference on behavioral science in medical education, they illustrate that man's psychosocial environment and life style are as important as causal factors in producing this clinical entity as are bacteria, viruses, and noxious chemicals. Of particular note is their concern with issues of prevention and early identification, supplemented by a list of specifiable psychosocial risk factors associated with increased athersclerotic complications. According to Olmsted and Kennedy, physicians must recognize that the mere presence of coronary difficulties among their patients signifies a medical failure on their part; unless they acknowledge such cases as failures, they are not likely to develop a preventive attitude and take the necessary steps to decrease the incidence of this and similar ailments.

The most striking demonstration of the impact of behavioral factors on physical health can be seen in the field of psychosomatic medicine. The article by Theodore and Renée Millon provides a comprehensive overview of the history, theories and contemporary findings of this increasingly important sphere of general medical practice.

REFERENCES

Wolf, S.: Patterns of social adjustment and disease. In Levi, L. (ed.): Society, Stress and Disease. Vol. 1. New York, Oxford, 1971.

16.   A Unified Concept of Health and Disease

George L. Engel

We shall examine some of the ways in which development, adaptation and adjustment may be disturbed or interfered with and some of the expressions thereof. Our preoccupation will be with the psychological and social aspects, but it is first necessary that we consider such disturbances or derangements in terms of the total organization of the human being as a biological, psychological and social organism. These encompass the deviations referred to as disease, the proper subject of medicine.

UNITARY CONCEPT OF DISEASE VERSUS UNIT-CAUSES

Medicine is concerned in the broadest sense with the problems of health and disease and, more specifically, with the mechanisms and the processes whereby health is maintained or disease develops. Health and disease are relative concepts which do not easily lend themselves to simple definition. Life itself involves a series of adjustments within the environment, and therefore, health and disease may be seen as phases of life. [1, 2, 3, 8] We may speak of the organism as a whole (or of organs or systems within the organism) as being in a state of health (healthy) when functioning effectively, fulfilling needs, successfully responding to the requirements or demands of the environment, whether internal or external, and pursuing its biological destiny, including growth and reproduction. Disease, on the other hand, corresponds to failures or disturbances in the growth, development, functions and adjustments of the organism as a whole or of any of its systems. Clearly, such a definition is too broad to be of much practical value. Still, it is useful as a starting point, since it does not restrict us to any one parameter. It is to be contrasted, for example, to the cellular concept of disease which, by focussing primarily on changes within the cell as the basic component of disease, is reductionistic and tends to restrict attention to only one aspect of disease, and one which is not necessarily always present. This broader formulation tries to get away from the substantive assumption that disease is a thing in itself, unrelated to the patient, the patient's personality, bodily constitution or mode of life, a concept of antiquity which repeatedly reasserts itself even in our language, as when we say that a patient *has* a disease or that we treat a disease.[6] The broad definition of disease does not confine our attention to any single system or organization of the body. It permits us to conceptualize disturbances or failures at all levels of organization — biochemical, cellular, organic, psychological, interpersonal or social — and to consider their interrelationships. Further, it does not restrict us to any single etiological concept but permits the application of a multifactor concept.

An important aspect of many concepts of disease in the past has been the tendency to think of disease primarily in terms of a "bad" influence, usually conceived of as something external which gets into the body and thereby causes the disease. This theme characterizes most primitive and prescientific views of disease, and has reappeared repeatedly in various

---

Engel, G. L.: A unified concept of health and disease. In Engel, G. L.: Psychological Development in Health and Disease. Philadelphia, W. B. Saunders Co., 1962.

guises in the scientific era. To be able to think of disease as an entity, separate from oneself and caused by an identifiable agent seems to have great appeal to the human mind. Perhaps this reflects the operation of the mechanism of projection, whereby what is felt or experienced as uncomfortable, painful or dangerous is ascribed to the outside. In prescientific medicine such psychological processes achieved expression in the form of demonological concepts, according to which disease resulted from the malevolent influence of demons, ancestor or animal spirits, spirits of the dead, revengeful ghosts, mystical object intrusion, loss of soul, taboo violation, sorcery, or witchcraft.[11] A man became ill because he had an enemy who cast a spell or because he was being punished for a transgression or for breaking a taboo. Essentially similar psychological concepts have continued to influence many interpretations of scientific medicine. Patients certainly, regardless of their level of education and sophistication, prefer to blame their illness on something they "caught," or ate or that happened to them, and consequently to think of disease as something apart from themselves. Many in one way or another formulate it in terms of punishment. Physicians also find attractive such ways of thinking, particulary if they can see the "cause" of disease as something which they can attack and destroy. Indeed, that which can be so attacked is often considered by physician and patient alike as the "cause" rather than as one element or aspect of the disease process. Thus, the tubercle bacillus is the cause of (rather than a necessary condition for) tuberculosis; insufficient insulin is the cause of (rather than a mechanism involved in) diabetes, etc. The thoughtful physician, of course, immediately sees the inadequacy of such formulations. But because such ideas have strong psychological appeal, new scientific contributions repeatedly tend to be translated into such terms, essentially the terms of demonology and of the universal introjection-projection schema of early childhood. A germ theory of disease which identifies a particular micro-organism as *the* cause of a disease is reformulated in terms of demonology to the extent that it

postulates an invisible, omnipresent agent which, if it gains access to the body, invariably produces disease. Actually, when it was first proposed, the very physicians who were most vigorous in attempting to introduce scientific methods and concepts into medicine saw the germ theory as a revival of ancient demonology and opposed it on that ground. But when it was demonstrated that certain micro-organisms did indeed bear an etiological relationship to certain disease processes, there quickly developed the expectation that a different germ would be found to account for each and every disease, including mental disease. So attractive psychologically was this idea of the "bad" germ that the emphasis of early workers on factors within the host was often ignored or minimized. In general, lay people and many physicians readily embraced the concept of a single external cause of disease. Certain patients even developed their own idiosyncratic germ theories, suffering from obsessional fears or paranoid delusions about germs, contagion or dirt.

Another tendency is to equate an anatomical lesion with the disease. With the development of pathology and the increasing refinement of techniques whereby deviations from the normal structure can be identified, the temptation has been to consider these findings as the explanation for the disease rather than as manifestations of the disease state. Under such circumstances the disease then tends to be considered in substantive terms, and it is believed that the patient can be cured if the diseased ("bad") part is removed. The fact that such measures often do prove therapeutic, as attested to by the success of surgery, is actually not evidence for the general validity of such a point of view.

The failure of morbid anatomy to explain more than some mechanisms of disease now is leading to the concept of the biochemical defect as underlying disease. Again, the search is for the single defect, an abnormal enzyme or biochemical system, as the explanation for the disease. There are some who even go so far as to anticipate a single biochemical defect for each disease, an idea reminiscent of those advanced in the early days of the germ theory. Regardless of whether disease is equated with an anatomical, a physiological or a biochemical lesion, such concepts again involve the idea of a discrete "thing" inside the body, an entity having an existence of its own, apart from the patient, who is the victim.

Still another variation on this theme is the mechanistic concept, which sees the body as a machine and disease as a condition due to a defective part. In modern medicine this takes the form of the mechanism (the "how") being used as the explanation of the disease state. For example, one is told that peptic ulcer is "due" to overactivity of the vagal outflow. Why the vagus is "overactive" is ignored. In this approach a misbehaving organ or system again fulfills the psycho-economic requirement of the disease as a thing apart. Even the patient who says, "It's my nerves," often is thinking in terms of something wrong with "the telephone wires." Some of the "stress" theories currently popular have also tended to emphasize "stress" as some kind of "bad" force to which the person falls helpless victim. Others formulate "stress" in terms of evil psychological or social influences which cause the person to break down. A variation of this sees the bad influence as inside – for example, the "bad" emotions, such as rage, fear, envy, greed or disgust, which "cause" the patient to fall ill. Physicians thinking in such terms are likely to exhort their patients not to get angry or excited, as if the bad affect or behavior itself would cause illness. Some physicians and laymen have distorted the concepts of psychoanalysis so that instincts or drives are spoken of as evil and dangerous forces which exert a destructive influence on the body or mind. Characteristic of all these concepts of disease, as well as many others not mentioned, is the tendency to concentrate on a single factor which qualifies for condemnation as "bad," and which is then to be attacked (or exorcised). Whatever qualities permit it to be so designated result in its being given a degree of exclusive importance which rarely is justified.

NOSOLOGY AS A CIRCUMSCRIBING FACTOR

Another difficulty in formulating a general concept of disease has been the inhibiting influence of nosology. Valuable as it is to be able to classify and categorize the phenomena of disease, the application of a name also may have the effect of over-emphasizing one aspect of the process at the expense of others or of implying a degree of certainty of our knowledge not actually justified. Names for diseases often have originated from the more obvious, rather than the more important, characteristics of the condition or from some etiological factors. Thus, pernicious anemia is not specifically a disease of the blood and it is no longer pernicious; lupus erythematosus disseminatus is not a skin disease and it is not disseminated. Hypertension refers to the physiological parameter which can be most easily measured. The names used generally reflect the state of knowledge of the conditions at the time they were identified; although names are rarely changed, our understanding of the processes involved is constantly changing. But the name often continues to exert a weighty influence on the physician's concepts, at times completely blocking any approach contrary to what is implied by the name. A classic example is hysteria, so named because the Greeks attributed its manifestations to disorder of the uterus. Obviously, therefore, it could not occur in men and in the last century Freud was ridiculed when he demonstrated some cases of male hysteria before the medical society of Vienna.

What do our diagnostic names tell us? Diagnostic labels are ways of indicating categories of information about our patient. A diagnostic label rarely, if ever, fully defines the illness. Rather it has statistical and predictive value. Thus, if we are told that a man has tuberculosis, we assume that he harbors the tubercle bacillus and we can predict the probability of his having certain signs and symptoms. On the other hand, we cannot assume that he has any or all of these signs and symptoms nor can we assume that he does not have other signs and symptoms which are not statistically related to the diagnostic term "tuberculosis." Nor can we even assume, if the patient does have the predicted signs and symptoms, that all or any of them are necessarily related to tuberculosis. In practice, of course, we begin with signs and symptoms and attempt to reach a diagnosis. We listen to the patient's story and we subject him to various types of examinations and then we attempt to categorize the areas of the patient's illness in which we feel we have understanding and we represent these by the appropriate diagnostic terms. In the course of study of a patient, a great deal of other information is revealed, some of which may and some of which may not bear on the decision about diagnostic categories, but much of which does not lend itself to any such categorization. Yet this unclassifiable information is also essential for the physician's understanding of how, and perhaps also of why, the patient is sick. Thus, with respect to any patient, although the physician's obligation is to establish the clinical diagnosis(es), this is not an end in itself but is the physician's way of indicating those aspects of the patient's illness which he knows and is able to identify, as established by experience and convention. Such diagnostic terms, however, do not include other important aspects or other important knowledge about the patient, nor do they exclude other diagnostic categories or even other phenomena which have not yet been categorized in diagnostic terms.

TUBERCULOSIS AS AN EXAMPLE

Having considered some of the factors that subtly influence how physicians view disease, we are now ready to examine the application of the broad concept of disease. As a hypothetical example, we might postulate the various possible relationships between man and the tubercle bacillus. The tubercle bacillus has the potentiality of producing disease in man in a number of ways:

1. It is a parasite that competes with certain tissues of the body for nutriment and elaborates certain materials which are damaging to cellular systems. It may thereby produce tissue changes which the pathologist identifies as "tuberculosis."

2. The concept of tuberculosis as a known contagious disease may have certain symbolic meaning to a person and may mobilize, or be utilized for, certain phobic or delusional processes.

3. The presence of tuberculosis in one person may alter his relationships with another person in such a way that the latter is frustrated or that certain needs remain unfulfilled. Failure to adjust successfully to this new situation may be expressed as illness in the second person.

Whether or not disease will develop in any of these situations depends upon a number of circumstances. Clearly, only in the first situation is the tubercle bacillus directly involved and is the diagnostic category "tuberculosis" justified. But everything that develops in this first situation will not be understandable exclusively in terms of the relationship between the tubercle bacillus and the cells and organs of the host. Under any of these circumstances, whether or not disease develops will depend upon a variety of factors. Various theoretical possibilities may be summarized:

1. The virulence or number of the organisms may be low. Although inhaled or ingested, they do not have the capacity to penetrate the cellular barrier and gain access to the interior of the body. They are dealt with as inert foreign bodies. No disturbance of existing defenses occurs; no mobilization of new defenses of sufficient magnitude to alter the bodily state is necessary. There is no disease.

2. The organisms are virulent but the resistance of the host is adequate to circumscribe and destroy the organisms locally. This may involve a local tissue change, including the formation of a Ghon tubercle, but no change in the total body economy is subjectively experienced by the person in whom this process is taking place. From his point of view, no illness is experienced. However, an x-ray examination or a tuberculin test may reveal to the physician that this process of adaptation has taken place. This may constitute

one of many successful adaptations experienced by this one individual, but it does not constitute a disease. As a result of this adaptation, the person now has a different and usually an enhanced capacity to deal with further exposures to the same organism.

3. In contrast to the previous example, the primary lesion of tuberculosis may be apparent to the person, as when it develops in the skin as a result of a penetrating injury by a contaminated instrument. The development of a painless, indolent skin nodule or ulcer may pass unnoticed by some people or may arouse only slight curiosity. Others may experience considerable concern and may feel it necessary to consult a doctor. A medical student or a pathologist, knowing that he has incurred this injury in the course of autopsying a cadaver with tuberculosis, will most likely experience considerable concern and may have a variety of symptoms, including some that simulate tuberculosis. But such clinical manifestations are largely psychological and have no direct relationship to the activity of the tubercle bacillus per se. Even though this local infection heals spontaneously with minimal tissue change, the patient's total illness experience will be quite different from that occurring when the primary infection is in the lung and runs its course silently, without ever becoming known to the person.

4. Virulent organisms may gain access to the lung and overcome local defenses. This may occur on first exposure or, as is more often the case, when a change takes place in the resistance to organisms already present. In either case we must assume that the capacity of the host to resist the virulent organisms either was inadequate to begin with or that it changed. A series of events is set in motion, some of which are experienced by the patient as symptoms, some of which are manifest to the physician-observer as signs, and some of which are detectable only by special laboratory or other techniques of examination. In the aggregate, these represent the various ways in which the patient responds to the virulent organism as well as to the situation of reacting to it. These processes are taking place simultaneously at many different levels of organization:

(a) There is a local tissue process which results from the destructive effects of the tubercle bacilli on the lung tissue and from the various attempts of the body to overcome and confine the invaders locally, to protect tissues from further damage, and restore damaged tissue. These include the variety of biochemical and cellular responses of inflammation, alterations in local blood and lymph flow, mobilization of phagocytes and other local immune processes, disposal of dead tissue by lysis, phagocytosis, coughing, etc., alteration in the local activity of the lung, and so on.

(b) General biochemical and physiological processes are set in motion as part of the "behind the line" activity to support these local processes. These include shift of circulation to the advantage of the local area, modifications of the ventilatory activity of the lung to protect the damaged part, the formation in and supply from distant organs of chemical and cellular material involved in defense against the microorganism, etc. Some of these are reflected in such manifestations as increased metabolism, fever, sweating, loss of weight, altered respiration, changes in circulating white cells, plasma proteins, etc.

(c) As various systems of the body are brought into action to cope with the local process, the total behavior of the person must eventually be influenced. Central neuro-humoral systems will already have been activated and must eventually have an impact on systems of internal perception of the mental apparatus, indicating changes in the bodily status. This changing status may first be experienced as a general sense of malaise, fatigue, restlessness, uneasiness, vague anxiety, decreased interest in activity, etc., and only a little later may more specific symptoms, such as cough, sputum, etc., be noted by the patient. The former manifestations are nonspecific. They represent the activation of the signal functions of ego, essentially affects indicating a change from the existing dynamic steady state. Such manifestations vary from individual to individual as determined by past psychological experience. They indicate only that the patient is sick. The more specific symptoms — cough, fever, sputum, etc. — are more indicative of the local pathological changes and provide the clues for the diagnosis of the specific infection. Yet since one is dependent upon the patient's report of how he experiences these changes, his psychological development may be crucial in determining what manifestations he presents to the physician and how he does so. From the point of view of the psychic reality of the patient, the general as well as the specific manifestations of his illness will be related to his own personal experience, which may or may not include the concept of tuberculosis. The affective responses to the perception of the pathological changes going on in his body are linked with other past experiences associated with similar affects and not necessarily with past experiences associated with similar pathological processes. The defenses that are mobilized to deal with these unpleasant feelings will also be an expression of the person's usual way of dealing with such feelings and they will be highly individual. Thus, one person may focus quickly on a specific manifestation, such as cough, pain or sputum, whereas another may minimize such specific manifestations and present mainly the more general phenomena. Another may need to deny weakness or disability because of his psychological background and hence may acknowledge no symptoms until the tissue changes are far advanced; in such a case it may be a family member who is the first to call attention to the cough or the weight loss. Still another person may respond to the specific symptoms with overwhelming anxiety or depression.

(d) Social and cultural factors will also influence how the disorder is experienced by the patient, by the environment and by the physician. Such factors may determine what symptom the patient selects to present to his family or to his physician and what symptom he may elect to minimize or conceal. Different cultures have different standards as to what is acceptable and what is grounds for shame and concealment. Such factors may also determine when, how and where the patient goes for help. In some social settings and cultural groups, the expected behavior is to seek medical help early; in others, one goes only

as a last resort. The various techniques that the person uses to help himself or to get help from others constitute another level of the total behavioral expression of being ill for each individual.

5. Once a person has had active tuberculosis, the degree of recovery may not be uniform in all systems involved. In some patients there may be complete healing of the local process; they may be left with no demonstrable deficiency in respect to pulmonary or other functions, and they may be able to return successfully to their previous level of adjustment, occupation, etc., and to function effectively thereafter. Yet in many respects they are different by virtue of having experienced this illness. In other patients, the tubercle bacillus may be eliminated as an active pathogenic agent, but varying degrees of irreversible damage to the lung or other structures may remain, resulting in some decrement in functional ability. This may require a psychological and social adjustment which he may or may not succeed in achieving. Still other patients may have complete healing of the local tubercular process and no residual anatomical defect and yet may continue to have a variety of symptoms, sometimes the same as those experienced with tuberculosis, sometimes different. Or patients may be improving or even symptom-free until the time of discharge from the hospital, only then to develop new symptoms. In the last two examples the pathological process at the cellular and organ level has been successfully resolved, but a disturbance in psychological adjustment remains. This is no less an illness than the tuberculosis and may, indeed, prove to be even more disabling or incapacitating.

6. The occurrence of active tuberculosis in one member of the family may contribute to the development of illness in other members of the family. The disruption in a family unit, the loss of an object (husband, wife, mother, father, child, as the case may be), the increased burdens or the deprivations imposed upon the other members of the family, the mobilization of ambivalent feelings toward the sick person — all of these may constitute significant psychological decompensating factors which may in the

susceptible individual eventuate in illness. The nature of the illness so precipitated cannot be predicted. One person may decompensate in a largely psychological fashion and manifest neurotic, psychotic, or behavioral disturbances. Another, decompensating with feelings of helplessness or hopelessness in relation to what he is experiencing, may prove susceptible to a pre-existing or an intercurrent process which is eventually manifested somatically, such as diabetes, an infection, cardiac decompensation, etc. A great number of factors will determine whether a person falls ill and if so, when and in what way. In this example, the tubercle bacillus and tuberculosis are only indirectly involved. The stress is primarily psychological and the immediate response is psychological. Whether there will also be decompensation involving somatic symptoms is determined by other factors, some somatic and some psychological.

7. The concept of the tubercle bacillus as a dangerous agent or of tuberculosis as an internally destructive process may become the content of a phobic or delusional system. (In current clinical practice, cancer is the disease which is most commonly used for such phobic or delusional ideas. In times past, tuberculosis and syphilis were more commonly used. However, to preserve the uniformity of our examples, we shall apply this concept to tuberculosis.) In this type of situation the tubercle bacillus and/or tuberculosis is a symbolic expression of some fearful feeling or idea of the patient. As such, it is generally a substitute for some unacceptable aggressive or sexual impulses or may represent his way of dealing with an ambivalent object whom he experiences as actually inside him and destroying him. The fear of contamination, perhaps taking the form of contamination by the tubercle bacillus, again may represent the projection to the outside of the patient's own feared or unacceptable impulses.

These examples are intended to illustrate in broad terms the many levels of behavior and response characteristic of any disease process. Whether or not the tubercle bacillus is actively involved, the response of the host takes place simultaneously at many different levels. Not all of these responses are adaptive; particularly are they not necessarily adaptive in respect to the interaction with the tubercle bacillus. Thus, both the psychological and the social responses may in some instances help and in other instances hinder successful coping with the pathogenic micro-organism. Not all the varieties of responses are to the tubercle bacillus as a parasite; some may also, or instead, be to the concept of the tubercle bacillus or of tuberculosis. These examples also tell us something of the relativity of the manifestations of disease. At certain times and under certain circumstances, the success or failure of adaptive processes may be of quite a different order in one system as compared to another.

DISEASE AS A NATURAL PHENOMENON

Health and disease have been defined in relative terms. When the organism is successfully adjusting in its environment and is able to maintain this state free of undue excitation, capable of growth, development and activity in an integrated and effective sense, a state of health may be said to exist. This is an active, dynamic process taking place in the face of an ever changing environment. There is continued need for adjustment and adaptation to maintain this state in the face of tasks imposed from the outside and from within the organism itself. When adaptation or adjustment fail and the pre-existing dynamic steady state is disrupted, then a state of disease may be said to exist until a new balance is restored which may again permit the effective interaction with the environment. Obviously there is no sharp dividing line between health and disease, nor are all parameters of the adaptive process necessarily equivalently involved. A person may satisfy all the criteria of health at any point in time simply because the adaptive capacity of a defective system, be it biochemical, physiological, or psychological, has not been exceeded. This may be a matter of fortunate circumstances or of the infrequency or limited intensity of the factors which would put the system under strain. It may also be a matter of time; eventually the system will break down under the impact of accumulated and repeated small stresses. This principle is best illustrated in relation to some genically determined defects which may eventuate in manifest disease only after a lapse of time or under particular circumstances — or perhaps never at all, as will be described later. Another possibility is that, after a disease experience, a limitation in adaptive capacity may result, but the person may be healthy in all other respects unless or until he strains the capacity of the system beyond its limits of adjustment. A mitral valve damaged in the course of rheumatic fever may impose a limitation on the range of possible circulatory adjustment, but this may be inapparent for many years, during which the person "enjoys good health." The physician's knowledge of the presence of such a potential limitation and the likelihood of eventual breakdown does not alter the fact of relatively good health over a certain span of time, especially when we realize how many persons carry potential limitations completely unknown to themselves or to physicians. But even when there is gross and manifest disability, we must recognize the relative integrity of other systems or modes of function, permitting us to refer quite accurately to the "more healthy" parts of the body or the person.

Such considerations naturally raise the practical question of how we know that someone is sick. We need not concern ourselves with the deviations in structure, performance or behavior that are so gross as to be obvious even to an untrained person. Rather, we need to examine some generalizations that will enable us to identify the state of disease regardless of its severity, etiology or the particular systems involved. We must also be able to identify the potential for breakdown in the apparently healthy person. As a starting point, we can say that the presence of a complaint must be regarded as *presumptive* evidence of disease. It indicates that there is a disturbance in the dynamic steady state, and that this disturbance is now being consciously experienced as unpleasant. The complaint itself does not

necessarily give any information as to the severity or nature of the process. The complaint may be to a physician or a member of an allied profession, a member of the family, or a friend, or it may be kept to oneself. This is a *symptom* — something subjectively and privately experienced which may or may not be communicated to someone else in the form of a complaint. It may also involve something apparent to an outside observer, such as a swelling, a mass, or peculiar behavior, in which case it is also a *sign.* Whether or not it is communicated depends on a great number of factors, some personal, some social and some cultural. For example, it may depend on what the person considers to be the proper domain of the physician, a perspective which changes as views of medicine change.

On the other hand, the absence of a complaint (a symptom) cannot be equated with the absence of disease. As will be detailed later, significant disturbances involving physical as well as psychological processes may be kept out of consciousness so successfully that patients may show the grossest defects or changes in parts of the body, in their physical functioning, in their behavior, or in their thinking processes and yet may deny the fact that any change has taken place. An observer, lay or professional, may immediately recognize that the person is ill. This circumstance, however, differs from the situation already alluded to in which some technique of examination, physical, psychological or laboratory, reveals to the physician a defect which is at the moment compensated for or is simply not involved in the person's current function. The latter conditions fall in the borderland between health and disease, involving as they do relative or potential disability but adequate function under most circumstances. (These may be regarded as belonging more in the domain of preventive medicine than to therapeutic medicine.) Asymptomatic or latent syphilis revealed by a positive serological test would be an example. These considerations should make it clear that health and disease are relative processes in a variety of respects.

The perspective presented here is, of

course, much broader than the conventional. It is customary in medicine at the present time, when attempting to establish whether or not a person is ill, to place the greatest emphasis on that which can be determined objectively, i.e., by the physician rather than the patient, often preferably by some impersonal instrument, such as by a laboratory procedure. Regardless of the nature and the severity of a patient's complaint, the failure to discover an abnormality on physical or laboratory examination means to many physicians that there is "nothing wrong." (How this influences what patients feel they must tell physicians in order to be accepted as patients and receive help will not be discussed here.) The common slang is that the patient has "no pathology," and it carries the double implication that he is not sick and often also that he is not worthy of help or that he is "fooling" the physician. If the patient responds favorably to the simple reassurance of "There is nothing wrong" (as some patients do), this may be regarded simply as a demonstration that there really was nothing wrong rather than that the patient had been experiencing some kind of disturbance which was alleviated by this type of reassurance. Another aspect of this is that when some type of objective pathological change is demonstrated, the correction of the abnormality may be equated with cure regardless of the patient's subjective experience. The extreme of this is the not-so-humorous statement, "The operation was a success but the patient died."

Some may argue that this concept of disease is so broad as to be essentially valueless. Experience refutes this argument. The traditional attitude toward disease tends in practice to restrict what is categorized as disease to what can be understood or recognized by the physician and/or what he notes can be helped by his intervention. This attitude has plagued medicine throughout its history and still stands in the way of physicians fully appreciating disease as a natural phenomenon. Disease cannot be defined simply on the basis of the function of physicians, who are changing variables in a social and institutional context. The scientific attitude requires

that a clear distinction be made between the study and understanding of disease as a natural phenomenon and the categorization of disease in terms of the function and role of the physician in a society. Only the first is relevant to a scientific concept of disease. The latter changes with time and circumstance. Actually, the patient himself is not always able to make such a distinction and he brings a wide variety of symptoms and problems to his physician, hoping and looking for help. The fact that a physician arbitrarily excludes certain categories of complaints or signs as not appropriate is a reflection of his concept of his role as a physician and does not necessarily bear any relationship to the scientific question of what is disease. Nor does the fact that some patients may use other personal, social or institutional devices to achieve the same end bear on the definition of disease.

Viewing disease from such a naturalistic rather than institutional perspective means that many kinds of processes or experiences may be thought of in terms of disease or related to disease even though they are not currently so regarded. For example, the experience of grief, which ordinarily follows the loss of a loved person, a valued possession or an ideal, fulfills all the requirements of a disease process as we have defined it.[4] The usual arguments to dispute such a point of view are as follows: First, even though everyone recognizes the magnitude of suffering and disability accompanying grief, this is regarded as "natural" and expected, meaning that anyone who suffers a loss would be expected to experience grief. But it is also "natural" for an orderly sequence of events to take place in the tissues following a blow, a thermal injury or the ingestion of virulent typhoid bacilli. And as is also true of exposure to a blow, heat or the ingestion of typhoid bacilli, not everyone experiences grief following a loss and, among those who do experience grief, not all experience it in exactly the same way. A pugilist will have a lesser reaction to a blow that a fragile old man, a dark-skinned person will tolerate the infra red rays of the sun better than a blonde, and a person immunized by a previous exposure to typhoid bacilli will resist the effect of ingested organisms more effectively than a person not so immunized. A second argument is that grief is a self-limited process from which one can expect to recover without help. Even when this is so (and it is not always) the same may be said of many situations which are commonly categorized as disease. Wounds also may heal and infections run their course without any intervention by a physician, but this does not make such processes any the less disease experiences. A third argument (which is not usually verbalized, but which nonetheless influences opinions) is that a person suffering a loss is not usually expected to consult a physician for the diagnosis and treatment of the ensuing grief. If the physician is to consider him as a patient, convention dictates that the patient present with a "legitimate" complaint (e.g., a physical symptom), not with grief. Indeed, this is what usually happens. The grieving patient brings a physical complaint and the physician may never even learn of the bereavement. If he does learn of it, he regards it as "natural" and irrelevant, or "noncontributory," as current medical slang puts it, ignorning the fact that the basis for this judgment was never examined, much less established. Many other types of examples could be given. What I wish to emphasize is that many phenomena of everyday life which are considered natural are not customarily regarded in terms of disease, but nevertheless they involve processes which basically do not differ from those which are involved in disease. The term "pathological" is a relative one and is set by medical, scientific and even social convention. Conventions change, so that what may be considered as illness or disease at one time or by one person may not be so considered at another time or by another person. Epilepsy, drug addiction and psychosis are examples of disease processes which have been variously regarded at different times and by different people. That such conventions have value and use does not bear on the validity of this point of view. The heuristic value of differentiating between normal and pathological should not blind us to the fact that this is a relative matter

based on ever-changing criteria.

The main advantage of this point of view is that it helps to focus on natural processes which may then be evaluated in terms of their success or failure in assuring adjustment. Our concepts of etiology need not be dependent on whether or not the end result is designated as "pathological." We are thus free to study any natural phenomenon in its own right and to evaluate its meaning in relationship to success or failure of adjustment, regardless of whether or not convention has established this to be concerned with disease. An anxiety experience is a natural phenomenon justifying our attention whether it involves a student before an examination, a pilot before a bombing mission, a businessman before a law suit, a housewife before an operation, a woman in a crowded elevator, a son opposing his father — regardless of whether or not the person actually comes to us for help and whether or not we can help him. Yet the need for help, whether it is perceived by the person himself or by an outside observer, and whether it is solicited from a physician or from someone else, will provide one of the important criteria of success or failure of adjustment and, hence, of health and disease.

ETIOLOGICAL CONSIDERATIONS: THE NECESSARY AND SUFFICIENT CONDITIONS

We now turn our attention to the factors concerned in the genesis of disease, the etiological factors. *We define etiological factors as factors which either place a burden on or limit the capacity of systems concerned with growth, development or adaptation, or as factors which, by virtue of their physical or chemical properties have the capacity to destroy cells or parts of the body.* They may operate through the impact of something added to or impinging on the system as well as through a deficiency, as when something necessary is taken away, is insufficient or is unavailable. They may originate within the organism as well as in the environment. No etiological factor can be considered in the abstract, but only in relationship to the system or systems upon which it is operating. Further, factors which have etiological significance in respect to a disease process at one time or under one circumstance may at another time or under other circumstances not have such implication. One never deals with a single etiological factor in the genesis of a disease state, although one factor may be more important than others or there may be practical advantages in paying more attention to one factor than to others. To quote Shimkin,[9] "There are few, if any, simple or single causes in biology; there are instead complex situations and environments in which the probability of certain events is increased." The scientific approach to disease assumes multiple factors, some more proximate, some more distant in time; some more specific, some more general in their effects; some necessary, but not in themselves sufficient to bring about the condition of disease. We may qualify the role of any factor by such adjectives as "precipitating", "conditioning", "predisposing", "permissive", "specific", or by indicating its mode of action, viz., genic, biochemical, physiological, psychological, social, etc. Postdictively we seek to identify the conditions necessary and sufficient to bring about a particular constellation of signs and symptoms. As physicians we intervene where we can to aid in the restoration of a state of health. As medical scientists we study these factors in terms of their qualifications as necessary and/or sufficient conditions, and attempt to predict the probability of occurrence of a particular constellation of manifestations characterizing a disease state. Again, as physicians we attempt to prevent the occurrence of the disease state by interfering with the operation of one or more factors before the necessary *and* sufficient conditions have been achieved. The scientific attitude can permit no restriction as to the category of natural phenomena investigated; the scientist's first obligation is to his data, wherever or however they present.

In any consideration of etiology it is necessary to take into account both the *"how"* and the *"why"* (Mayr[6]). The mechanistic tradition of medicine has led to an emphasis on the *"how."* The *"how"* refers to the manner in which things operate. It is essentially a description in dynamic terms of what is happening or what has happened in whatever system one might be examining, cellular, organ, total organism, psychic apparatus, social system, etc. In pneumococcal pneumonia, for example, the "how" will focus attention on the sequence of changes that take place in the lung after the pneumococcus has gained access to it. The question "why" has two possible meanings: *"How come?"* and *"What for?"* The former concerns the conditions which permitted the pneumococcus to gain access to the body in the first place — in other words, *"How come* the person got sick when he got sick?" and *"How come* it was pneumonia?" "What for?" focusses attention on the purpose or functions of the changes which take place after the micro-organism has gained entry. What function, if any, in the person's adjustment or attempt at adjustment to the "invasion" by the pneumococcus is served by leukocytosis, fever, phagocytosis, cough, etc.? All three perspectives must be kept in mind in considering the etiology of any disease process.

Let us now examine more closely some categories of etiological factors. The strictures of speech prevent us from discussing more than one at a time but this does not obviate the fact that in nature many processes will be operating simultaneously.

Factors Which Determine the Capacity of the Organism to Grow, Survive and Adapt.

Genic Factors [5, 10]

These are factors which are to be understood exclusively in biochemical terms, referring to the chemical composition of the body as determined by genic inheritance. They include factors underlying the individual chemical characteristics of the cells of each person and as such contribute to the basic chemical structure underlying the capacity for growth and development of every cell and system. We may presume that a normal distribution curve will describe the ranges and the capacities of each biochemical system in the population and, hence, the limit of functional or structural potential of the system for each individual. This refers to what we may speak of as the "biochemical universals," those systems which occur in all humans and which are generally regarded as "normal." This perspective emphasizes the genically determined variance within the normal biochemical systems of the body. This variance will describe one of the categories of factors concerned both with the potential for growth and development and with the capacity to adjust to changes imposed from without or from within. It will be a remote factor, one in a chain of events which may prove critical in a breakdown at some later date. Its influence may range all the way from the activity of enzyme systems to what people look like (e.g., pigmentation or body configuration). The influence of skin pigmentation on susceptibility to sunburn or on adjustment in a social group provides a whole range of examples of the remote operation of a genic factor as a determinant of health and disease. It is reasonable to assume that such molecular factors also may circumscribe the limits of operation of the brain and of the mind in any individual (e.g., the presence and activity of certain biochemical systems in the brain may be a limiting factor in determining what kinds or ranges of mental or psychic processes are possible in any individual).

In addition, genic factors play a role in the transmission of abnormal or defective biochemical systems responsible for the variety of so-called inborn errors. These may include factors which are incompatible with fetal survival, factors which produce or are responsible for major developmental defects, and factors which may become manifest only under particular circumstances and at particular times in development. Among some of the better studied examples are such conditions as sickle cell trait, glycogen storage disease, hereditary phenylpyruvate oligophrenia, congenital galactosemia, gout, porphyria, etc. These relatively rare conditions lend themselves to study because the defect represents such a striking deviation from the normal. Yet it seems likely that many other more common conditions, such as diabetes, pernicious anemia or celiac disease, for example, will prove to involve similar factors. Whether or not genically-transmitted inborn errors become manifest in the form of a recognizable disease state depends on nonspecific as well as highly specific factors having to do with the particular defect as well as with developmental processes. Phenylpyruvate oligophrenia, a form of mental deficiency of infancy, for example, depends on the presence of phenylalanine in the diet for the cerebral metabolic defect to be expressed. Galactosemia, a disorder of infants, becomes manifest only with galactose ingestion. The intestinal malabsorption of the celiac syndrome apparently requires the presence of wheat protein in the diet. These are examples of conditions in which substances normal to the diet are harmful to those individuals who carry the enzyme defect, with a consequent biochemical disturbance involving important body systems. Other types of defects, such as those underlying gout, pernicious anemia and porphyria, may become manifest only after many years, presumably because other factors may be involved and/or because of the length of time necessary for the process to evolve.

The genic determination of the chemical composition of the body is, then, a basic factor in the specific strengths and vulnerabilities of the individual. It plays a role not only in the vulnerability to breakdown but also in the nature and type of development of various systems including the psychic system. It is very probable that some of the factors which determine the strength or character of instinctual drives are, in part at least, genically determined. The sense of taste, for example, which is known to be determined by genic factors, could be a significant influence in the early oral experience of the infant and its relation to the mother. Genic factors are probably important also in the specific development and organization of the brain and hence in certain capacities for mental functioning. There is the challenging possibility that the biochemical characteristics of individuals can some day be established and from this may be anticipated certain potential lines of development, including eventual pathological changes. Beginnings in this direction are to be found in Mirsky's[7] success in predicting peptic ulcer and pernicious anemia on the basis of high and low pepsinogen concentrations in blood. However, such new knowledge of biochemical determinants does not justfiy a regression to concepts of "molecular diseases," a reversion toward a single cause-effect relation reminiscent of the oversimplified germ theory.

Developmental Factors Other than Genic

These include all the factors, from conception on, which influence developmental and adaptational capacities favorably or unfavorably. This developmental perspective takes into account all the ways in which the organism and its component parts in the course of development "learn" to secure needs and to adjust to strains, including those provoked by deprivation or insufficiences. We postulate that within the framework provided by the genically determined structure, the nature and variety of experiences during life will determine the specific ways of development, the particular variety of techniques utilized to relate effectively to the external environment, and the particular varieties of defense, ranging from cellular to psychosocial. The concept of biological and psychological assimilation and accommodation is important here. A wide variety of external things or processes must be taken in physically or psychically and become part of the organism, ranging from molecules to percepts of persons, ideals, etc., and then are utilized in the service of further adjustment and development. All individuals share the need for certain essential elements, but each individual will, in addition, evolve a particular variety necessary for his survival, growth and development, depending on the nature of his individual experience. Thus, at the level of cellular function we note the capacity of the cell to "recognize" and select what it needs for its own development and to reject or actually defend itself against damaging molecules. After a particular micro-organism or foreign

protein has gained access to the body, the body may thereafter be permanently changed so that the cells thereafter "recognize" this foreign substance and react differently to it. Some such change may be permanent (e.g., immunity) while others may develop slowly and last only as long as the substance is present (e.g., tolerance and addiction).

At the level of the organism as a whole we note the variety of influences, notably persons and situations, which the individual comes to experience as providing something necessary for continued effective functioning, and the absence of which may be experienced as a loss requiring some type of adjustment. This has been discussed in the sections on development in terms of object relations and psychic object representations. We emphasize here the highly individual nature of such object relationship capacities and how they help to determine what constitutes the strengths and weaknesses of the individual, what he comes to need from his environment in order to remain comfortable, to grow and to function effectively. These phenomena of assimilation and accommodation are basically biological, their psychological expression being found in terms of objects, object relations, object representation and in learning.

In considering the gamut of developmental factors it is important to emphasize the concept of critical periods, both somatic and psychological. For example, only during a very specific interval in fetal life may virus infections in the mother (e.g., rubella) damage the fetus. Similary, the susceptibility to certain types and modalities of psychic stress is very different at different ages. The consequences of separation from the mother are vastly different at three months, three years and 30 years. A host of processes occurring at a biochemical, cellular or psychological level early in life may be critical in determining the capacity of a person to develop certain pathological changes later in life, but the age at which these occur may be the factor determining whether or not there will be an effect and if so, what it will be. Thus, at any later point in time, what constitutes a stress to any individual will be determined to a large degree by the nature of his past experience (as well as by the character of his genic endowment). This will apply to the nature of the response to micro-organisms as well as to the loss of a love object. By virtue of what has gone before, the person may be more or less able to cope with ingested typhoid bacilli and more or less able to tolerate the death of his mother.

Factors Which Strain Current Capacities

Having emphasized the influence of past experiences on determining both the capacities for adjustment and the specific vulnerabilities and tolerances, we can now consider the varieties of processes which can put such capacities under strain. Because such factors are usually more obvious and certainly more proximate, they are often erroneously designated as "the cause" of the disease process. Not only is this incorrect and misleading, but also at times it tends to exclude other more important considerations.

For convenience we divide such factors into a number of categories:

Factors Which Injure by Virtue of Their Physical and/or Chemical Properties

These include all the varieties of physical and chemical noxae which may impinge upon man from the external environment, (e.g., mechanical forces, poisons, heat, cold, radiation, electricity, etc.) as well as substances which are formed or forces which may develop within the body which injure by virtue of inappropriate quantity or location (e.g., excess insulin, action of gastric juice on the esophagus, increased intracranial pressure). Such internal factors are almost always secondary to other factors, but nonetheless may bring consequences (signs and symptoms) which are specific and not necessarily related to the predisposing factors.

The external noxae come the closest to constituting absolute causes in the sense that beyond a certain degree they will be damaging or lethal to everyone. Even here, however, there are important predisposing considerations. Persons differ in respect to the magnitude of a blow or the dose of a poison that they can tolerate. Further, many other factors of psychological and/or social importance may be critical in determining the circumstance of the exposure in the first place, including suicidal intent, accident proneness, impulsivity, industrial exposure, ignorance, mental confusion, pure coincidence, and so on. Some of these agents, as, for example, carcinogenic substances or radiation, do not necessarily produce their effects immediately or in all who are exposed. In general, the longer the time lapse between exposure and the development of patho-logical tissue changes, the more complex and multiple are the other conditions necessary for such developments. Some molecular substances achieve a noxious quality by virtue of the host's capacity or tendency at certain times and under certain conditions to develop a specific sensitivity response, the allergic reaction. Such reactions may also take place in response to substances which are part of the person's own cell composition (auto-immune reactions).

Physical Factors Which Lead to Injury or Impairment of Function When Insufficient or Unavailable

In this group we restrict ourselves to the essential chemical elements (oxygen, water, electrolytes, nutriments, vitamins, etc.) which the organism must obtain from the enviornment (deficiency states) and the essential substances formed in the body, such as hormones (insufficiency states). Again, we must keep in mind the predis-posing conditions which determine "how come" the deficiency or insufficiency occurred in the first place as well as the magnitude and character of the resulting reaction. Here again the less immediately or less consistently developing reactions either involve less critical substances or require the operation of multiple predis-posing or intervening processes before the conditions necessary and sufficient for manifest disorder have been achieved. We can contrast the relatively narrow range of resistance to oxygen lack and the more variable response to lack of a single nutritional element, or the pronounced response to insulin or adrenal steroid insufficiency compared to the minor effects, if any, of gastric hydrochloric acid insufficiency. The availability of alternative mechanisms or the capacity for compensatory internal rearrangements are important in determining whether or not deficiency or insufficiency actually will become manifest.

Micro-organisms and Parasites

These deserve a special category in the etiology of disease because they involve the interrelations between two or more living systems (more than two if intermediary vectors are included). In the case of each agent there are highly specific as well as nonspecific factors which determine (1) whether it gains entry to the body; (2) whether it exists there in a harmless parasitic or a helpful or neutral symbiotic relationship, or whether it damages or destroys its host; (3) in what particular locus, i.e., cell, tissue, organ or body fluid, it can live. The fields of microbiology, parasitology and immunology are devoted to the elucidation of such factors. Suffice it to say that multiple factors in the natural history of the micro-organism and in the host are involved. There are some micro-organisms to which humans are almost universally susceptible on first exposure (e.g., the viruses of measles and smallpox) so that the most significant factor determining susceptibility to infection (though not capacity for survival) may be a previous exposure and the development of immunity. Other micro-organisms may be capable of infecting only a small proportion of people, and others may at some point in the life of the host or of the micro-organism change from a harmless guest to a destructive agent. Here may be involved multiple factors in the host, ranging from fixed (genic or constitutional) biochemical structure to general or local changes associated with other stresses or responses to stresses. As examples of the latter may be cited the clinical observation of an apparent increased tendency to certain infections in diabetes or during certain kinds of psychological decompensation. Some consequences of infection with micro-organisms may be indirect and dependent on the characteristics and condition of the host, so that only certain individuals at certain times may so react (e.g., the relation between hemolytic streptococcus infection and later rheumatic fever or hemorrhagic nephritis).

Factors Which Operate Through Their Effect on the Central Regulating System (Brain and Mental Apparatus)

All the factors so far listed are of such a nature that they *may* exert their influence directly at the level of cells, tissues or organs, involving the central regulating systems only secondarily, if at all. However, if the central nervous system and the mental apparatus are indeed the systems whereby the organism maintains adjustment of its internal environment in relation to the external environment (physical, interpersonal and social) and thereby maintains growth, development and organism integrity, we must anticipate that some factors which determine health or disease are mediated in one way or another through this system.

REFERENCES

1. Dubos, R.: The Mirage of Health. New York, Harper & Brothers, 1950.
2. Engel, G. L.: A unified concept of health and disease. Perspect. Biol. & Med. *3:* 459 (1960).
3. Engel, G. L.: Homeostasis, behavioral adjustment, and the concept of health and disease. In Grinker, R. (ed.): Mid-Century Psychiatry. Springfield, Ill. Charles C Thomas, 1953.
4. Engel, G. L.: Is grief a disease? A challenge for medical research. Psychosom. Med. *22:* 18 (1961).
5. Kalckar, H. M.: Some considerations regarding biochemical genetics in man. Perspect. Biol. & Med. *1:* 3 (1957).
6. Mayr, E.: Cause and effect in biology. Science *134:* 1501 (1961).

7. Mirsky, I. A.: Physiologic, psychologic and social determinants in the etiology of duodenal ulcer. Am. J. Digest. Dis. *3:* 285 (1958).

8. Romano, J.: Basic orientation and education of the medical student. J.A.M.A. *143:* 409 (1950).

9. Shimkin, M. B.: Hormones and neoplasia. In Raven, R. W. (ed.): Cancer. Vol. 1. London, Butterworth & Co., 1952.

10. Snyder, L. H.: Fifty years of medical genetics. Science *129:* 1 (1959).

11. Veith, I.: Psychiatric nosology: From Hippocrates to Kraepelin. Am. J. Psychiat. *114:* 385 (1957).

17.   Atherosclerosis: Behavioral Science Components of Prevention and Control

R. W. Olmsted and D. A. Kennedy

In the United States, one in every five men develops coronary disease, and one in every 15 dies of it before the age of 65. Atherosclerosis, the form of coronary disease which involves the blocking of the arteries by fatty deposits, has reached epidemic proportions.

Because such a large part of the practice of many physicians involves the care of patients with atherosclerosis, and because it is a disease which has such far-reaching behavioral and social effects on the lives of patients and their families, this disease is a particularly good model for behavioral sciences in a medical context. During the conference, Dr. Joseph Stokes III, Dr. William B. Kannel, and Dr. S. Leonard Syme discussed the characteristics of this disease, its epidemiology and risk factors related to it. The panel and other participants then explored the ways that the social and behavioral sciences are involved in such solutions as development of preventive programs for atherosclerosis, and the implications of these relationships for medical education.

Atherosclerosis is a disease so big, so generalized and so common that it took a long time for pathologists or anyone else to recognize it as a disease at all, said Dr. Joseph Stokes III, Professor and Chairman, Department of Community Medicine, San Diego School of Medicine of the University of California. For a long time, atherosclerosis was considered to be a natural process of aging. This is a great way to obscure ignorance about any disease — and it did, even though defining atherosclerosis is not really particularly difficult. It has many analogies to problems of plumbing. Basically, the disease relates to the function of a pipe and the fluid that flows through it. As any housewife who regularly puts grease down a drain knows, sooner or later the pipe will become clogged and she will have trouble.

Atherosclerosis is slow to develop and requires a long period of time. It begins in childhood with fatty streaks on the large arteries of the body. Serum lipids are also involved, because cholesterol, which has a lot to do with arterial blood pressure, is carried on a lipoprotein fraction in the blood.

Clinical manifestations caused by interference with organ blood flow do not appear until late in the disease process. We have poor tools to measure its early development, and those to measure the secondary stage are also clumsy. Inability to diagnose the disease in its early stages is one of the problems that makes definition and management difficult.

Study of the circumstances under which

Olmsted, R. W., and Kennedy, D. A.: Atherosclerosis: Behavioral science components of prevention and control. In Behavioral Sciences and Medical Education. Public Health Service of N.I.M.H., H.E.W. Publication (NIH) 72–41, 1972.

coronary disease arises, evolves and terminates fatally in the general population has shown that the only strategy that is likely to have a major impact on coronary mortality is primary prevention, said Dr. William B. Kannel, Medical Director of the Framingham, Massachusetts Study of the National Heart and Lung Institute. Mortality cannot be reduced by focusing on persons in whom symptoms have already appeared, since about 20 percent of all first coronary attacks present as sudden, unexpected death. The entire course of the illness from start to finish is over within a matter of minutes. More than half of all coronary deaths occur this way, and two-thirds of these were unheralded by prior symptoms or overt evidence of coronary disease.

The bulk of coronary deaths occur outside the hospital, out in the community. Only about 40 percent are hospitalized and only 12 percent of the sudden deaths occur in hospitals. Even in patients with prior coronary disease, only 15 percent of the deaths occur in hospitals.

This indicates that the problem of coronary deaths — both initial attacks and recurrences in patients with established coronaries — must be solved out in the community, not in the hospital. The only road to substantial reduction in coronary mortality is the prevention of sudden death. This, obviously, requires identification of potential sudden death victims and the factors which make them vulnerable.

The background of the sudden death victim is virtually identical to that of the potential candidate for any coronary attack, fatal or not. It is well known from clinical and prospective studies such as those at Framingham, where research has been in progress since 1948. The attributes of potential coronary victims have been established by studies of more than 5000 men and women classified according to suspected precursors. These findings have been confirmed in other studies.

Two factors which need further clarification are family history and stress in life style. Persons who have close relatives who develop some manifestation of atherosclerosis early in life seem to have an increased risk of developing a coronary

event themselves. Families share more than genes, and these phenomena could be due to shared environmental factors. For example, the spouses of subjects who develop coronary disease show an increased propensity to do so also. It is evident that something these spouses share is not good for them. As might be expected, they share a number of things. They share eating habits. They share obesity. The "Jack Spratt could eat no fat" adage does not really apply. Fat men tend to have fat wives and vice versa. Husbands and wives share the cigarette habit. They even share blood pressures to some extent. More research needs to be done on familial aggregation and its environmental and behavioral determinants.

Stress in life style is hard to pin down. What is stressful to one individual may be enjoyable to another, or at least not traumatic; and the way a person perceives and copes with stress is as important as the traumatic experience itself. People react to stress in different ways — some with their gut, some with their bronchial tubes, some with emotional outbursts against their families.

Each of a number of risk factors has been shown to at least double the risk of a coronary event. Among these, four stand out as being readily and simply measured, common in the population, and avoidable or correctable. These include hypertension, hypercholesteremia, the cigarette habit and obesity.

In considering risk associated with any factor, one must consider related factors as well. For example, while hypertensive blood pressure levels are associated with substantial risk, the probability of coronary attack in a hypertensive is also related to the cholesterol value. A cholesterol level which constitutes no more than the standard risk of the population in normal tensives may be a formidable risk in hypertensives. The presence of multiple risk factors has an additive effect which mounts progressively in proportion to the number of categorical risk factors present.

Correction in the general population of the faulty living habits contributing to coronary risk, such as too rich diet, too much food, sedentary living and cigarette smoking could lower the overall level of coronary proneness. Although the potential reduction in coronary morbidity and mortality that could be achieved through application of current knowledge to the task cannot be estimated precisely, data from Framingham suggest that a change in these four risk factors could reduce the coronary incidence in highly vulnerable young men by 90 percent. A lesser impact would be expected in older persons; but even there, the potential for salvage is great.

Public health action in the form of environmental control which does not require individual initiative or motivation will be required to reduce the large reservoir — probably a quarter of the adult population — of undetected or potential coronary disease. This is not a simple matter. Our therapeutically oriented medical care system is already overburdened caring for those who are ill and makes little provision for preventive efforts. One stumbling block is the attitude of physicians. Prevention of cardiovascular disease requires attention to what many physicians regard as medial trivia. Both doctors and patients prefer pills rather than recommendations like, "Lose weight, change your diet, give up smoking, get more exercise." Why should a patient pay $25 for that advice when he is getting it free from his mother-in-law?

These attitudes need to change. Physicians must come to regard the occurrence of strokes, coronary attacks, congestive failure and peripheral vascular disease as medical failures rather than as the starting point for medical management.

Detecting and coping with the precursors of disease is properly a community concern. Primary preventive efforts need to be integrated into the medical care system through industries and labor unions, the armed forces medical establishment, school health programs, state, university and veterans hospital systems, and public health facilities. Resources must be developed for coping with the preventive care needs of high risk individuals who are identified. It will do no good to uncover hordes of coronary-prone people if they will then be sent to physicians who cannot

or do not care to provide preventive management.

For an effective, sustained preventive effort, a team approach is needed. Physicians, public health nurses, nutritionists, physical culture experts, sociologists, and other behavioral scientists all need to be involved in developing screening and diagnostic facilities which are linked to community resources for prevention and care.

There is much that we need to learn about coping with risk factors, and it is here the behavioral scientist is particularly needed as a member of the team. He can help determine what features of the life style of individuals promote risk, and he can help identify ways that the biochemical and physiological precursors of atherosclerotic disease can be avoided and corrected.

The behavioral scientist can also illuminate the social and psychological concepts which relate to the problems of various diseases, said Dr. Leonard Syme, a sociologist and professor of epidemiology at the University of California School of Public Health. For example, the behavioral scientist can study the relationship between coronary heart disease or ulcers or arthritis and phenomena like mobility or anxiety.

Within the United States, there are tremendous differences in death rates from coronary disease in different parts of the country. The rates are two or three times higher in the eastern and western industrial states that in the rural midwestern states. North Dakota, for example, has a very low rate; New York a very high rate. The difference is so extreme that the rate of deaths from all causes in North Dakota is not as high as the coronary mortality rate alone in New York State. This is not just a difference in diagnostic customs and certifications.

Facts like these suggest that there may be something about urbanization that is involved. This hypothesis is supported by the findings of a study in North Carolina which focused on the change in coronary death rates in various counties — all of them originally rural — as some became urbanized over a 10 year period. Among the originally rural residents, the highest coronary rates were in the counties that had experienced the most dramatic urbanization.

However, urbanization is not the whole story, and other contributory factors need to be identified. One investigator explored psychological patterns in men who had not had heart attacks, giving special attention to a pattern in which anxiety, hostility and aggression were combined. No association between this pattern and the later occurrence of heart attacks could be found, although this pattern appeared frequently in men who had already suffered an attack.

There are at least five types of studies through which social and behavioral scientists can contribute significantly to medical knowledge and medical education in relation to coronary disease. These are:
- descriptive or demographic studies
- studies of personality or psychological traits
- studies of life's dissatisfactions
- studies of mobility or incongruity of status
- studies of coronary-prone behavior patterns

Retrospective and prospective studies in the fifth category, coronary-prone behavior patterns, have divided people into Types A and B. Type A people have more coronary heart disease than Type B people. Type A people behave in competitive, time-oriented, goal-directed ways. They are ambitious, restless and have a profound sense of time urgency. The show such somatic and motor manifestations as fist clenching, desk pounding, facial grimacings and keyed up body movements. They move rapidly and attempt to condense or hurry the speech of others. Although suggestive data have emerged from some of these studies, many of the findings are ambiguous and need to be tested more fully if they are to provide reliable guidelines for physicians. We need to get past clichés and euphemisms and measure risk factors in ways that make it possible to assess the difference that different factors make in the incidence and prevalence of disease.

If the epidemic of atherosclerosis is to be halted, Dr. Stokes said, first priority should be given to a large cooperative trial project on primary prevention. High risk individuals should be identified by screening for hypertension, hyperlipidemia and other factors. Those so identified should be divided into two groups. One would serve as control. With the other, there would be systematic intervention. The rates of morbidity and mortality from atherosclerosis would be followed for a period of five to seven years.

We know that systematic intervention is going to be necessary for control and prevention of this disease. As long as we must rely on individual response, results will be minimal, because it is difficult to get patients to follow their doctors' advice unless their problems are acute and they are motivated by fear of the consequences. As long as they are asymptomatic, they will not be inclined to follow a regimen that involves no more beef steaks, cutting out cigarettes, jogging every day and spending $10 a week on anti-hypertensive drugs. What sort of intervention program can be devised that will get patients to accept restriction over a long period of time in order to avoid some future event?

This is an area in which social and behavioral scientists need to be involved. We need sophisticated motivational studies to determine how we can get patients to adhere to the desirable regimen over a long period of time; and we need to develop programs of environmental manipulation which do not rely on individual initiative or response. These changes are going to have to be equally drastic as those which enforce environmental sanitation for the control of typhoid fever and other diseases. These changes can only be brought about through the efforts of many groups — the medical profession, the consumers, the behavioral scientists and the political, social and economic decision makers of the country.

This public health effort will have to involve battles with the food industry, the tobacco industry, the Food and Drug Administration and the Department of Agriculture. The present system of rating meat, for example, encourages development of meats which have a high fat content. The same is true of dairy products; grading is based on butterfat, which is one of the most unhealthful fats in the food we customarily consume each day. Non-dairy cream substitutes are another example. These are made from coconut oil, which is worse for people than real cream. This should be pointed out to consumers in many ways, including proper labelling.

We should not underestimate the size of these battles, Dr. Stokes said. At the present time the medical establishment does not have enough political sophistication, economic sophistication, or general understanding of human behavior to fight the problem effectively. This is why it needs help from other professions, and it is why medical education needs to give more attention to preparing physicians for preventive medicine.

There are those who believe that a private physician should not bear any more responsibility for preventive medicine than a garage mechanic or auto body repairman has for automobile design and highway safety. His own belief, Dr. Stokes said, is that certainly selected, and probably all, physicians have some responsibility to play a role in prevention.

The behavioral sciences tie into atherosclerosis as a topic of medical education in a number of specific ways, other participants said. Because it is a long-range, life-span experience, atherosclerosis is a valuable model for demonstrating both the behavioral aspects of disease and the characteristics of the social institution of medicine which attempts to treat the disease. This material might be included either in a behavioral science course, when an atherosclerotic patient is being presented to students, or when atherosclerosis is the subject being covered by clinical medical faculty or basic scientists in biochemistry, pathology, physiology, etc. Appropriate content areas include:

Distribution of Disease

We have enough data on atherosclerosis so that it could be used as a basis for teaching students about the cultural, ethnic and national bases of disease.

Death Occurring Outside the Hospital

Medical Students tend to assume that most people die in hospitals in the presence of doctors. Since 60 percent of the people who die of coronary disease are not in the hospital, atherosclerosis is an excellent model for helping the student understand the death process as it affects both the patient and his family.

Family Structure

The importance of family structure versus a gene pool is one element to be considered here.

Relationship of Culture to Disease

An important behavioral science concept that bears upon medicine comes out of anthropology: the concept that culture produces disease. The behavioral sciences can help the student understand that a society which is moving rapidly into urbanized, technological forms will manifest certain kinds of disorders such as heart disease and mental disorders.

Interaction of Life Style and Technology

This relates specifically to history-taking. The behavioral sciences can help the student understand that by examining the economic, social, cultural, historical and political factors in the history of a coronary-prone patient, he may be able to intervene as a physician in constructive ways.

Values as They Relate to Health and Disease

Medical students need to recognize that each patient has a value system and makes behavioral choices on the basis of this system. He may elect a life style that includes smoking heavily, eating a lot of saturated fat and getting very little exercise. The behavioral scientist can explicate how such consequences as atherosclerosis flow from this value system.

Dynamics of Changing Life Style

Students need to know that it is not enough to tell a patient to change his life style or to refer him to someone else. They need to learn how behavioral change can be induced.

Personality Attributes of Coronary-prone Individuals

Much of the data on the relationships of personality types to specific diseases has been discredited, but some good data is being developed on personality attributes of this high risk population group.

Stress

The student needs to understand the many ways this term is used and what it has to do with physiology and biochemistry as well as with the emotions. He needs to know how to define and analyze different types of stress that may affect what he, as a physician, can do for a patient with atherosclerosis.

The Interrelationship of Biochemistry and Behavior

The student needs to know that biochemical changes may be a result of behavior as well as a cause of behavior, and that behavior may be a result as well as a cause of biochemical change. This is an intriguing notion to many students because they have usually learned it only one way around: that biochemistry and molecules dictate behavior. They are often not aware that behavior alters and prescribes biochemical and molecular reactions.

Relevance of Animal Studies

By learning how important animal studies are to understanding atherosclerosis in humans, students also become aware of some of the ethical and practical problems of human research and the value of animal research as an alternative approach.

The Role of the Physician in Prevention

Because atherosclerosis demonstrates the need to go beyond the classic dyad of physician and patient in a one-to-one relationship and reconstruct the very role of the physician, it has profound implications for medical education. If the concern for maintenance of health as opposed to treatment of disease becomes a fundamental focus in medical education, it will greatly change the students' perception of the role of the physician.

Amassing Political Support to Bring About Health Improvements

Medicine has a lot of political power, especially through the American Medical Association; and this should be used for constructive causes. Students should learn how medicine can enlist lobbyists, the lay public, politicians and others to bring about prevention and control of disease.

Quality of Life as a Major Goal of Medical Advances

We tend to talk as if the goal of medicine is to make people live forever. We talk in terms of life expectancy when we should, perhaps, talk in terms of life span, with a concept that there ought to be graceful ways of exiting at the end of that time. A happy, productive life of 75 or 80 years with an individual dying quietly in his sleep can be a beautiful thing. Sudden death from coronary disease is a much pleasanter way to go than lingering illness, so it is not in itself undesirable. What we need to get across to medical students is that people should not die *prematurely* of atherosclerosis, and that they should live in a state of health rather than in a state of incapacity.

18.   Psychophysiologic Disorders

Theodore Millon and Renée Millon

INTRODUCTION

It is at times of illness or under conditions of excitement and stress that we become aware of many of the bodily functions we normally take for granted. If we stop to think for a moment we will recognize that each of the several systems which comprise our biophysical make-up — cardiovascular, gastrointestinal, respiratory, genitourinary and so on — is quietly carrying out a variety of functions requisite to organic survival.

Faced with threat, these systems are quickly activated to release and regulate energies which prepare the organism to cope efficiently with danger. Most frequently, the energy and tension that build up in response to these threats are discharged in the coping process. At other times, however, these physiological energies mount and persist since the individual is unable or unwilling to vent them. For example, fear and anger precipitate, among other things, a sharp rise in blood pressure, which normally will subside if tension is expressed in the form of a rapid flight or a direct attack upon the threatening source. If fear or anger persists and tension is restrained and undischarged, a state of chronic high blood pressure may ensue, with eventual permanent tissue or organ damage.

Circumstances such as these are referred to as psychophysiologic or psychosomatic disorders; the persistence of unrelieved physiological energies, precipitated initially by psychogenic agents, ultimately results in a fundamentally altered biological state. The central feature of these disorders, then, is the buildup of unexpressed protective physiological reactions. This upsets normal homeostatic balance and leads to irreversible organic diseases such as ulcer, hypertension and asthma. Thus, individuals who are subjected to persistent environmental stress or who are unable to resolve basic conflicts, may be afflicted with bodily ailments that are no less severe than many that are caused by hereditary defects and infectious agents.

CLINICAL PICTURE

More than twenty psychosomatic disorders have been ascribed, at least in part, to psychologic causes. Which ones are influenced substantially by emotional factors remains a matter of dispute to be decided by future research. In the following paragraphs we shall list and briefly describe the symptoms of six psychophysiologic disorders which have been subjected to numerous theoretical and research studies.

1. The *gastrointestinal system* is a frequent locale for psychophysiologic impairment.

Particularly common are *peptic ulcers* in which the patient exhibits a crater-like lesion in the stomach or the upper part of the small intestine. Normally, a mucous lining protects the surface of these organs by blocking the corrosive effects of acid secretions that are requisite to digestion. However, should the lining be perforated or should excess secretions be produced, the patient will experience "burning" sensations, nausea and vomiting about one or two hours following meals. In these cases, the corrosive action of acids continues to dissolve the unprotected stomach and intestinal tissue. When large open

Millon, T., and Millon, R.: Psychophysiologic disorders. In Millon, T., and Millon, R.: Abnormal Behavior and Personality. Philadelphia, W. B. Saunders Co., 1974.

perforations are present there may be severe internal bleeding that may result in death. The following case history illustrates life history data for a typical peptic ulcer patient.*

Case 1
Frederick B., Age 46, Married, Three Children

This man was admitted to a psychiatric hospital immediately after having been discharged from a senior executive position in a large company because of excessive drinking and unreliability in keeping appointments. Apart from a few years in military service Fred had been with this company for the preceding 25 years, had worked extremely hard, and felt personally responsible for much of the company's growth and expansion during the preceding 15 years. He had spent much time away from home traveling on company business and had worked evenings and weekends, and had not taken a vacation with his family for some years. However, Fred had come to feel that his talents and dedication were not appreciated or adequately rewarded. During the preceding five years he had perceived his future as bleak, with little or no opportunity for further advancement financially or in terms of prestige. Every morning he would feel sick over the dismal prospect of another day's exhausting demands. He would not express his feelings of frustration and resentment directly at work, but became increasingly irritable at home with his family. Fred started to drink excessively to relieve his tension and he developed peptic ulcers which were treated medically. He was given some sedative medication, but remained dependent on alcohol and became increasingly depressed, although he never reached the point of considering suicide.

Fred was born the fourth child in a family of five boys, and his father was an unsuccessful farmer whom he never respected and disliked from an early age. He felt much closer to his mother, who was nervous and physically frail, with numerous chronic bodily complaints that the family regarded as 90 percent emotional. This hypochondriacal mother, however, dominated her husband, criticized him, and nagged her sons into striving for the success that their father had never achieved.

Poverty and small physical stature contributed to making Fred feel inferior to other children in the neighborhood, but he overcompensated for this by striving for academic distinction. In spite of having to work in a store during noon hours, after school, and on Saturdays, he remained at the top of his class in school and graduated as valedictorian. He left home soon afterward, worked in an office during the daytime, and attended night school, where he claimed to have

*From Gregory, I.: Fundamentals of Psychiatry. 2nd edition. Philadelphia, W. B. Saunders Co., 1968. p. 383.

completed four years of college work, including two years of law school, although he never obtained a degree. At the age of 24 he married, and subsequently had three children, who he hoped would all go to college. It was a bitter blow to Fred when his eldest daughter got married shortly after leaving high school. Although his work always came ahead of his family, there was little conflict between him and his wife until the last few years during which he had been resentful, depressed, irritable, and drinking excessively.

At the time Fred was admitted to hospital after losing his job he was angry, tense, tremulous, and unhappy, but he showed no evidence of organic intellectual impairment, was in good contact with reality, and his depression appeared to be of neurotic intensity. For several years he had been dissatisfied with his way of life, and the loss of his job freed him from its obligations and confronted him with the necessity of reevaluating his patterns of behavior and goals in life. Fred participated actively in individual and group psychotherapy, and rapidly acquired considerable insight into developmental psychodynamics. His tension and depression diminished, his excessive smoking decreased, and he gained about seven pounds in weight. Fred was given a mild tranquilizing drug and after six weeks he left hospital much improved. There was no recurrence of his former symptoms during the next two years.

A similar disease, known as *colitis*, represents an inflammation of the colon (large intestine) and is typically accompanied by severe cramps and diarrhea.

2. *The cardiovascular system* exhibits two prominent psychophysiological disorders.

Essential hypertension consists of chronically elevated blood pressure, without organic cause, often resulting in serious circulatory and kidney ailments.

Migraine refers to repeated headaches, lasting several hours, attributable to arterial spasms; it is characterized by severe throbbing or pressure on one side of the head, and frequently is accompanied by nausea and other gastrointestinal upsets.

3. Certain *respiratory system* disorders are attributed in part to psychogenic influences.

Bronchial asthma is characterized by episodic attacks of wheezing, panting, gasping and a terrifying feeling of imminent suffocation. These symptoms reflect marked contractions or spasms in the bronchial muscles which cause the passages of the bronchi (lung tubes) to shrink, thereby creating a severe reduction in air intake. The background and experiences of an asthmatic woman with depressive inclinations are illustrated in the following history.*

Case 2
Leah V., Age 34, Married, Four Children

This woman was admitted to a psychiatric hospital with a history of asthmatic attacks which had been increasing in frequency and severity during the preceding twelve years, together with feelings of fatigue, insomnia, and depression which had been increasing progressively over the preceding three months. She reported that her maternal grandmother and one maternal aunt had suffered from severe asthma, and she claimed that she was allergic to several fruits and vegetables. However, she had had extensive medical investigations and sensitivity tests but no program of desensitization had ever been recommended by the physicians caring for her, and her asthmatic attacks tended to be precipitated and aggravated by emotional stress.

Leah was the eldest of eight children and her mother was pregnant with her at the time of her marriage. This probably led to unconscious resentment and partial rejection of the patient by her mother who appeared to discriminate against the patient and favor some of the younger children. She perceived no such discrimination or favoritism on the part of her father who was a conscientious man, regularly employed, and well liked by everyone. In this home, however, he was rather passive and ineffectual, whereas the mother was dominant and aggressive. Leah described her mother as being moody and "a martyr type" who was critical and demanded high standards of behavior from all members of the family. During her childhood, Leah was given a great deal of responsibility in caring for her younger siblings and during adolescence she was frequently deprived of social activities with her friends in order to help at home. The patient was never able to express anger as a child and at the age of 34 she still felt that the opinion of her parents was as important as when she was a child.

Leah obtained little sexual information from her mother but started dating about the age of 15 and had a number of boy friends. During her junior year in high school she started going steady with a boy slightly older than herself and within six months she began a pregnancy which led to a forced marriage. Her parents disapproved of her husband, who was not a Catholic, but after marriage he changed his religion and their children were raised in this faith. During the first 12 years of her marriage the patient was pregnant 11 times. Six of these pregnancies terminated in spontaneous abortions and one child died a few days after birth, so that she was left with four living children. Pregnancy was always stressful for her and her first attack of asthma occurred shortly after the birth of her second child. The attacks became more frequent and severe during subsequent pregnancies, and after 12 years of marriage she submitted to a sterilization operation which freed her from this particular source of stress. However, a couple of years prior to this Leah became aware that her husband was going out with another woman. This made her feel nervous and angry inside, but she never confronted him with the fact or expressed her anger directly. Instead she punished him by denying him sexual relations, which she had in fact feared from the time of her first spontaneous abortion. Her husband's interest in the other woman was of very brief duration, but she continued to deny him sexual relations until about two years after her sterilization operation at which time he was involved in an automobile accident and sustained a whiplash injury to his neck. He felt unable to work and began drawing regular unemployment insurance which probably prolonged his disability. In addition, Leah became more solicitous of him and went out to work to supplement the family income. When the husband's insurance payments ran out, he looked for work sporadically but remained unemployed. He visited various employment offices and was offered several jobs, but turned them down for various reasons such as poor wages, no chance for getting ahead, or simply because he did not feel he would like the work.

In this situation Leah was unable to express resentment directly to the husband, but felt obliged to continue providing for the family and became increasingly worried about their financial situation. She became tired, had difficulty in sleeping, lost interest in her usual recreations, lost her appetite and some weight, and felt miserable. At interview she was in good contact with reality, and projective tests indicated neurotic constriction of personality with some hysterical denial and evidence of depression. Leah maintained that her husband and children were wonderful and initially she denied the marital conflict already outlined. During several weeks of psychotherapy, however, she was able to verbalize freely her sources of frustration and conflict and to gain considerable insight into previously unconscious psychodynamics. She also received antidepressive medication and gained about ten pounds in weight. Her husband was seen on several occasions, and eventually found employment. Leah left hospital much improved and was felt to be somewhat less vulnerable to developing overt psychopathology than formerly.

4. The *skin* is a major system of bodily functioning, centrally involved in mediating the organism's contact with the environment. As such, it is highly reactive not only to physical stimuli but to a whole range of psychologically significant events

*From Gregory, I.: Fundamentals of Psychiatry. 2nd edition. Philadelphia, W. B. Saunders Co., 1968, p. 380.

(e.g., blushing in embarrassment or blanching in fear).

Among the more prominent psychophysiologic skin disorders is *neurodermatitis,* a chronic and nonallergenic inflammation accompanied by severe itching.

All psychophysiologic symptoms mimic diseases that can be ascribed entirely to physical causes; thus, bronchial asthma or peptic ulcer may have its basis in hereditary defects or infectious agents. Many theorists contend that even where known psychogenic factors operate as causal agents, they merely aggravate and make manifest a latent biological vulnerability. Regardless of cause, the final clinical picture is essentially the same, making the task of differential diagnosis an extremely difficult one at best. We label these diseases as psychophysiologic when psychogenic factors are considered to play a significant role.

Let us next turn to some of the historical ideas which have shaped our understanding of the psychogenic roots of these disorders.

THEORETICAL VIEWS

The label "psychosomatic" was first applied to cases of insomnia by Heinroth in 1818. This term remains a common synonym for psychophysiologic disorders. Until the early twentieth century, however, little was known about the psychological mechanisms involved in these ailments, other than the fact that they appeared to be related to emotional stress.

Early Psychoanalytic Concepts

Current thinking about psychophysiologic disorders may be traced to two notions first formulated by Freud.

In the concept of the "actual neuroses," Freud spoke of symptoms which were a direct consequence of the "damming up" of body energies. Here he included anxieties, neurasthenia and hypochondriasis, viewing them to be the simple result of a failure to discharge physiological sexual instincts. Although the three ailments he specified as resulting from this damming up process do not correspond to our present day list of psychophysiologic disorders, the notion that they reflect a blockage of physiological tensions may clearly be traced to Frued's "actual neurosis" hypothesis.

Several of Freud's disciples utilized the symbolism which he observed among the neurotic conversion disorders as a means of explaining psychosomatic symptoms, or what they called the "organ neuroses." To them, these symptoms symbolized, through a form of "body language," the character of the patient's repressed intrapsychic conflicts. For example. Ferenczi considered diarrhea to be an aggressive form of giving to others which substituted for real performance, and Garma conceived peptic ulcers to be symbolic attacks upon the mucous lining by the patient's hostile mother. This symbolic conversion hypothesis for psychophysiologic disorders has been seriously questioned. It has been believed in the past that the visceral organs, from which these symptoms arise, may not be connected to higher cortical processes, and therefore do not lend themselves to the expression of symbolic ideas. Recent work by Miller and DiCara does suggest, however, that visceral organs can be "conditioned" psychologically. Should their work be verified and extended, it is possible that symbolic learning can take place in these organs, thereby making the psychoanalytic conversion hypothesis at least a tenable one.

Dunbar's Personality Profile Theory

The conversion model utilized by Freud's disciples attempted to account for the "specificity" of the symptom, that is, why patients with specific types of psychological problems developed certain psychophysiologic disorders rather than others. Since it was believed that the conversion model of symbolic symptom expression was inapplicable to the visceral organs, alternate hypotheses had to be devised. This seeemed necessary since many investigators had observed a correlation between particular experiences and particular somatic disorders.

The first of these alternative models was provided by Flanders Dunbar. As a consequence of her exhaustive studies of psychosomatic diseases, she was led to conclude that there was a direct correspondence between *personality types* and specific psychophysiologic symptoms. For example, she proposed that ambitious and hard-driving executive personalities were especially vulnerable to coronary artery disease. Other personality profiles were found according to Dunbar to correlate specifically with migraines, peptic ulcers and so on.

Despite the plausibility and superficial validity of her thesis, subsequent evidence has indicated that there is no simple one to one correspondence between specific personality types and specific psychophysiologic disorders. Each psychosomatic symptom has been found in a variety of different personality profiles.

Alexander's Conflict-Regression Theory

Franz Alexander agreed with Dunbar that psychophysiologic disorders should not be conceived as symbolic conversions, but disagreed with her view that direct correlations existed between particular personality types and specific somatic diseases. Instead, Alexander proposed that each psychosomatic disorder reflected a *specific* type of *unconscious conflict,* which could be found not in one but in a variety of different personality types.

Central to his thesis was the belief that a specific and different configuration of physiological reactions was activated in conjunction with each of several types of emotional states, e.g., rage was specifically associated with cardiovascular responses, dependency needs characteristically stimulated gastrointestinal activity and respiratory functions was notably involved in problems of communication. To Alexander, then, whatever correspondence existed between specific organs and specific psychological difficulties reflected neither a symbolic conversion process nor a personality style, but rather the presence of a specific emotional conflict. Since certain physiological responses are correlated with these emotions, patients with particular conflicts will, according to Alexander, suffer corresponding physiological disorders.

In attempting to explain how the psychophysiological symptom arose in particular patients, Alexander invoked the Freudian concept of "regression," stating that psychosomatic patients had experienced traumatic conflicts in childhood which were "fixated," persist and are reactivated in the present. Current threats that stir up these fixated unconscious conflicts not only set into motion the person's "immature" psychological defenses, but in addition activate the *specific* physiological reactions that had been associated with these conflicts in childhood. Thus, to Alexander, adult psychophysiologic disorders reflect the consequence of chronic reactivations of the physiological reactions of childhood. For example, ulcer patients ostensibly suffered fixated dependency conflicts during the oral stage of psychosexual development. When present events reactivate this conflict, the patient's body responds with the same physiological reaction as when the conflict originally occurred in infancy. Specifically, these reactions took the form of excess gastrointestinal secretions since these occurred as a consequence of the infant's search for the security provided through maternal nutrition. Since "mother's milk" is not forthcoming in adulthood, the stomach and upper intestine are subjected, as a consequence of these physiological reactions, to a repeated flooding of gastric acids, causing the destruction of mucous lining and eventuating in a peptic ulcer.

Table 18-1 provides a summary of some of the psychogenic causes, personality characteristics and coping aims which theorists have proposed as correlated with the six psychophysiologic disorders described earlier. We will comment on the validity of these hypotheses following our presentation of a number of alternate theories which reject the notion that psychosomatic symptoms are correlated with *specific* psychological needs or experiences.

TABLE 18-1.   SOME HYPOTHESIZED PSYCHOLOGICAL CORRELATES OF
PSYCHOPHYSIOLOGIC DISORDERS

Disorder	Psychogenic Causes, Personality Characteristics and Coping Aims
Peptic Ulcer	Feels deprived of dependency needs; is resentful; represses anger; cannot vent hostility or actively seek dependency security; characterizes self-sufficient and responsibile "go-getter" types who are compensating for dependency desires; have strong regressive wish to be nurtured and fed; revengeful feelings are repressed and kept unconscious.
Colitis.	Was intimidated in childhood into dependency and conformity; feels conflict over resentment and desire to please; anger restrained for fear of retaliation; is fretful, brooding and depressive or passive, sweet and bland; seeks to camouflage hostility by symbolic gesture of giving.
Essential Hypertension	Was forced in childhood to restrain resentments; inhibited rage; is threatened by and guilt-ridden over hostile impulses which may erupt; is a controlled, conforming and "mature" personality; is hard-driving and conscientious; is guarded and tense; needs to control and direct anger into acceptable channels; desires to gain approval from authority.
Migraine	Is unable to fulfill excessive self-demands; feels intense resentment and envy toward intellectually or financially more successful competitors; has meticulous, scrupulous, pefectionistic and ambitious personality; failure to attain perfectionist ambitions results in self-punishment.
Bronchial Asthma	Feels separation anxiety; was given inconsistent maternal affection; has fear and guilt that hostile impulses will be expressed toward loved persons; is demaninding, sickly and "cranky" or clinging and dependent; symptom expresses suppressed cry for help and protection.
Neurodermatitis	Has overprotective but ungiving parents; has craving for affection; has conflict regarding hostility and dependence; demonstrates guilt and self-punishment for inadequacies; is a superficially friendly and over-sensitive personality with depressive features and low self-image; symptoms are atonement for inadequacy and guilt by self-excoriation; displays oblique expression of hostility and exhibitionism in need for attention and soothing.

Nonspecificity Theories

A number of theorists state that there is insufficient evidence to warrant acceptance of any of the various "specificity" models that have been proposed. Despite impressive and intriguing theorizing, no clear-cut empirical relationship has been found to indicate that specific psychogenic factors are correlated with specific forms of psychophysiologic disorder.

The nonspecificity theorists offer an alternative. *First,* they contend that all sources of psychogenic stress, ranging from external realistic events (e.g., face to face warfare) to unconscious conflicts (e.g., repressed childhood hostilities), produce essentially similar *diffuse* physiological reactions. *Second,* should these generalized

physiological states be prolonged or frequently repeated, one or several of a number of psychosomatic ailments may ensue. *Third,* the particular ailment that the patient finally displays *cannot* be predicted by reference either to the content or to the source of the precipitant.

The nonspecificity model has been criticized by many clinicians on the grounds that it fails to correlate psychosomatic disorders with psychological difficulties. This criticism is inaccurate. The model claims merely that the *specific* form of the psychophysiologic disorder cannot be predicted by the *specific* type of emotional difficulty experienced. The nonspecificity model asserts, quite clearly, that psychosomatic ailments *in general* are found to be associated with psychogenic problems. More specifically, its proponents claim that patients who are chronically unable to reduce anxiety are strongly disposed to exhibit *some form* of psychophysiologic disorder. This aspect of the nonspecificity view is nicely summarized in the following:

We believe that as long as a patient can deal with unpleasant emotions and with the anxiety engendered by his conflicts by means of various psychological defenses and mechanisms, there will be no abnormal psychogenic physical functioning nor resultant psychosomatic illness. If, however, a patient's psychological defenses are inadequate to reduce his excited or anxious state of emotional tension, then a variety of psychosomatic diseases may be produced in constitutionally susceptible individuals as a result of the physiological concomitants of chronic tension. According to this view, many psychosomatic diseases are a consequence of the *breakdown* of psychological defenses. It should be added that we do not consider the aforementioned mechanism to account for all instances of psychosomatic illness; other mechanisms, such as conditioning, may play a role in certain diseases. Nor do we believe that there is sufficient evidence to indicate that the nature of the psychological stimulus setting off the emotional tension determines the type of disease that develops. The problem of "organ selection," i.e., what accounts for the type of disease suffered by a particular patient, is unsolved as yet.*

Constitutional Specificity Theories

The criticism that most psychological models fail to take account of constitutional differences as a factor in psychophysiologic disorders has led a number of researchers to propose the following alternate hypothesis: although specific psychogenic factors have not been shown to correlate with specific psychosomatic ailments, patients with distinctive and different physiological reaction patterns are disposed to develop specific types of ailments. This proposal may be spoken of as a "response specificity" thesis, resting on the well-accepted notion of intrinsic constitutional differences among individuals.

*Kaplan, H. I., and Kaplan, H. S.: Current theoretical concepts in psychosomatic medicine. Am. J. Psychiat. *115:* 1091–1096 (1959).

It was Adler, Freud's early disciple, who first spoke of the role of "organ inferiorities" in psychological illness. However, Adler did not concern himself particularly with psychosomatic ailments; rather, he drew upon the notion of bodily weaknesses to demonstrate mechanisms of compensatory striving.

It has only been in recent years, through the systematic experimental research of several investigators, that evidence has accrued to show that individuals exhibit rather distinctive and stable types of physiological reactions to stress. For example, it has been shown that some individuals characteristically react with muscular rigidity to such varied conditions as embarrassment, pain and frustration whereas others react to the same variety of stressful events with intense gastrointestinal upsets. According to this thesis, the dominant sphere of physiological reactivity in an individual will dispose him to develop a specific type of correlated psychosomatic disorder; for example, "cardiovascular reactors" tend to experience heart palpitations and chest pains whereas "muscle reactors" are inclined to develop severe headaches.

The question may be posed as to whether these physiological reactivity patterns are acquired as a consequence of social learning or whether they are inborn. Studies indicate that distinctive autonomic behavioral patterns are exhibited shortly after birth and persist for many years thereafter. Since these styles of responding were evident prior to the effects of socialization, it would appear safe to assume that later patterns of reactivity are *in part* attributable to intrinsic constitutional tendencies.

Among the virtues of the constitutional specificity theory is that is rescues the notion of "symptom choice" from oblivion. Rather than depending on unverified clinical hypotheses, this theory is based on experimentally validated research, although much remains to be done in correlating physiological reaction patterns and vulnerabilities to particular psychosomatic ailments. It should be noted, further, that the constitutional thesis does not preclude the role of social learning influences. Combined with certain social learning hypotheses, it can account for which patients experience psychosomatic ailments in the first place, and which specific ailments they eventually will display. In short, psychophysiologic disorders are likely to reflect the interaction of both psychological experience and constitutional vulnerabilities; more on this point will be discussed in the following theory.

Autonomic Response Learning Theory

Lachman has recently published a model of psychosomatic development based essentially on social learning theory. He does not depreciate the significance of constitutional specificity, that is, organ vulnerability but gives it a secondary role to social reinforcement history. His view is that when positive reinforcements become associated with responses of the autonomic nervous system, the probability is increased that these autonomic responses will, in similar situations, be produced again. The following quote summarizes Lachman's thesis well:

Not only are autonomic responses learned on the basis of their being conditioned to new stimuli, but also particular autonomic responses are selectively learned on the basis of differential reward or reinforcement. A specific rewarded autonomic response tends to be differentiated out of the emotional response constellation and to be selectively strengthened. Thus, the individual who is rewarded for his expression of gastrointestinal pain by being permitted to stay home from school or from work and who is given special attention, consideration, and love under those circumstances is likely to have strengthened gastrointestinal reactions that led to the gastrointestinal pain, that is, increased gastric acid secretion. This is a statement of the idea that *rewarded autonomic responses may be selectively learned.*

The concept of *vicious-circle effects* is also necessary to understand certain psychosomatic phenomena. Once initiated, a psychosomatic event may produce stimuli that lead to implicit reactions, which rearouse or intensify the psychosomatic event, and so on. For example, the noxious stimulation from a gastric ulcer may elicit implicit reactions including facilitated stomach-acid secretion, which intensifies that ulcerous condition, which leads to further emotional reaction and further irritation of the ulcer.*

SUMMARY COMMENT

What conclusions can we draw concerning the determinants of psychophysiologic disorders from the many alternate theories and data just reviewed?

1. Although the issue is not a closed one and is awaiting further and more detailed investigations for final judgment, the greater body of research evidence to date indicates that the *specific* type of psychophysiologic disorder exhibited by a patient *cannot* be predicted from the *specific* character of his psychological problem.

2. A fairly substantial body of data has accrued to the effect that psychosomatic disorders, *in general,* arise as a consequence of the failure to dissipate tensions, regardless of the content or source of these tensions. Individuals whose personality styles lead them into repeated tension producing situations or prevent them from discharging the cumulative build up of tensions, are likely to succumb to one or several of a number of different psychophysiologic disorders.

3. Essentially identical difficulties have been postulated as the cause of a wide variety of psychosomatic problems. A review of the literature, as summarized in Table 18-1, indicates that diverse psychosomatic disorders such as hypertension, ulcers, asthma and neurodermatitis, appear to derive from a single basic conflict, i.e., suppressing hostile impulses for fear that they may endanger dependency security. It is extremely difficult to uncover different etiologies among these disorders. The conflict between dependency security and hostile assertion seems to apply to all. This uniformity leads us to conclude that most psychosomatic patients are trapped in an unresolvable dependency-independency ambivalence. They are unable to express

---

*Lachman, S. J.: Psychosomatic Disorders: A Behavioristic Interpretation. New York, John Wiley, 1972.

feelings associated with one part of their conflict without increasing tensions in the other. As a consquence, their overall level of tension continues to mount and churn internally until it finally results in an irreversible psychophysiologic disorder.

4. Recent research indicates that the specific type of psychosomatic symptom the patient develops is likely to depend either on constitutional vulnerabilities or on his dominant physiological reaction pattern.

5. We are led to conclude that the pathway which leads to a psychophysiologic disorder derives from both social learning and constitutional influences. We must envision, then, a sequence of interactions in which the individual's learned instrumental behaviors *either* produce autonomic disturbances to gain support, attention, and so forth, *or* fail to dissipate physiological tensions. A constitutionally predisposed individual will develop a specific type of psychosomatic disorder since his psychological problems, whatever their source or content, will have a selective physiological effect upon certain vulnerable organ systems.

6. Definitive conclusions concerning the specific interplay of social learning and physiogenic factors must await further empirical research. Most of what has been published in the field of psychosomatic medicine can be faulted on a number of methodological grounds. At the very best, these studies provide some rough guidelines for future systematic research.

PERSONALITY AND INSTRUMENTAL BEHAVIOR

It may be possible from what we have reviewed thus far to deduce which of the various personality patterns are most susceptible to psychophysiologic disorders. Toward this end, it will be useful to examine first the various instrumental functions that underlie psychosomatic symptom formation.

One purpose of the psychosomatic patient's strategy is to block from awareness the content and source of his tensions. This aim, however, is neither distinctive to psychophysiologic disorders nor to any particular personality type. Since it is a basic instrumental function of most disorders, we must look to other factors to account for the psychosomatic symptom and its personality correlates.

Two other coping functions fulfilled by the psychosomatic symptom are the control or inhibition of hostile impulses and the eliciting of attention, sympathy and nurture. These instrumental functions are also found in neurotic disorders, and are characteristic of the personality patterns that are subject to these disorders. Since various instrumental functions are found in common among these personality patterns, we are led to believe that psychosomatic symptoms would covary with neurotic symptoms. Further, we would hypothesize that neurotic and psychosomatic symptoms will coexist or fluctuate interchangeably in the same patient. This latter finding has regularly been reported in the literature, but has not been systematically researched. It may reflect the fact that neurotic disorders often only partly discharge physiological tensions, therefore leaving a residue which may take the form of a psychosomatic ailment.

We believe that psychophysiologic disorders will arise most frequently in passive and active-ambivalent personalities. Ample evidence exists for this view in the literature, but let us examine our reasons for believing it.

Among the central features of psychosomatic etiology are repetitive upsets of the body's physiological balance and a chronic failure to dissipate physiological tensions. These events will arise most often in patients who repeatedly find themselves in conflict situations, especially those in whom the discharge of tensions created by one side of the conflict will increase tensions created by the other. This state of affairs describes, in effect, the experiences of ambivalent personalities; they are trapped between acquiescent dependency on the one hand, and hostile or assertive independence on the other. When they allow themselves to submit to the wishes of others, they experience deep resentments and angers for having displayed weakness and given up their independence. Conversely, if they assert their independence and feelings of hostility, they experience intense anxieties for fear they will have further endangered their tenuous dependency security.

Let us next examine how this conflict develops into psychophysiologic disorders in each of the two major ambivalent personality patterns.

The *passive ambivalent* keeps under close wraps most of the tensions generated by his dependence-independence conflict. His resentments and anxieties are tightly controlled and infrequently discharged. As a consequence, his physiological tensions are not dissipated, tend to cumulate and result in frequent and persistent psychophysiological ailments, as illustrated in the following brief sketch.

Case 3
Peter S., Age 23, Married, No Children

This passive-ambivalent graduate student was admitted to the college infirmary following a recurrence of an old ulcer ailment. Peter's early history showed intense rivalries with an alcoholic but "brilliant" father who constantly 'demanded superior performances on the part of his son in both academic affairs and athletics. However, no matter how well Peter would perform, his father demonstrated "how much better he could do it now — or did it when he was young." Although Peter "quietly hated" his father, he dared not express it for fear of "being publicly humiliated by him."

In recent weeks, Peter's thesis proposal had been severely criticized by his departmental advisor. Peter believed that the professor was completely wrong in his judgments and suggestions, but dared not express these thoughts for "fear of further condemnation." Unable to vent his resentments, which were so much like those he felt toward his father, Peter's repressed emotions churned away inside and resulted in a flareup of his ulcer.

The precipitants and sequence of physiological tensions take a somewhat different turn in the *active-ambivalent*. Here, the patient periodically discharges his tensions, but because of his hypersensitivities and irritable behaviors, he creates an endless sequence of one troublesome problem after another. In other words, he accumulates tension faster than he dissipates it. Moreover, because of his fretful and contentious behaviors, his body is subject to constant vacillations in mood and emotion. As he swings erratically from one intense feeling to another, his homeostatic equilibrium, so necessary for proper physiological functioning, is kept constantly off balance. Not only is he likely to experience, then, an excess of chronic or repeated tension, but his system rarely settles down into a smooth and regularized pattern. As a consequence, the active-ambivalent is kept churning and sets himself up for a variety of psychosomatic disorders.

In conclusion, then, both personalities are disposed to psychosomatic disorders, the specific form of which appears to depend on their particular constitutional vulnerabilities and social learning experiences. The two ambivalent types seem especially susceptible to these disorders since their dependent-independent conflict disposes them to tensions which cannot either readily be resolved or easily be dissipated through behavioral discharge.

TREATMENT APPROACHES

Of all the abnormalities described we can see most clearly the close interweaving of biological and psychological functions in the psychophysiologic disorders. Of course, every abnormality derives in part from the operation of both psychic and somatic factors. Psychophysiologic disorders are notable in this regard only because they give evidence of this inseparable fusion in manifest physical form.

Therapeutic attention must be directed first to remedying whatever physical impairments have occurred in conjunction with the disorder. Body pathology, as in ulcer perforations or severe hypertension, should be dealt with promptly by appropriate medical, nutritional or surgical means. When the physical disease process is under adequate control, attention may be turned to the management of environmental stresses and to the modification of detrimental attitudes and habits.

As we have said, psychosomatic symptoms arise as a consequence of the patient's instrumental learning and/or his inability to resolve conflicts and discharge tensions. Because of the patient's fear that these emotions will overwhelm him if released, the therapist must move slowly before exposing these conflicting attitudes or "opening the floodgates" to the onrush of these feelings. Quite evidently, the patient has been willing to suffer considerable physical discomfort as the price for achieving his instrumental goals and containing his unacceptable impulses. The danger of precipitating a crisis is great if the patient gains insight too quickly or if his previously hidden feelings are uncovered and unleashed too rapidly. Such exposure and release must be coordinated with a parallel strengthening of the patient's capacity to cope with these feelings.

The warning just noted points to the important role of supportive techniques in the early stages of treatment. At first, care should be taken to diminish tension and to help dissipate the cumulation of past tensions. Psychopharmacological tranquilizers may be useful in softening the response to tension precipitants. In addition, arrange-ments should be made where feasible to have the patient avoid those aspects of everyday living which prompt or aggravate unresolvable anxieties and conflicts.

Turning to the formal psychotherapeutic measures, behavior modification approaches may be used to extinguish attitudes and habits which have generated tensions, and to build in new ones which may help in discharging, avoiding or otherwise coping with them. Group therapy often serves as a valuable adjunct to help the patient explore his feelings, learn methods of resolving conflicts and liberate tensions. The probing and uncovering methods of psychoanalytic therapy should not be utilized in the early phases of treatment since they may prompt the surge of severely upsetting forbidden thoughts and impulses. However, should other procedures prove unsuccessful in alleviating tension or in diminishing the disturbing symptomatology, it may be necessary to employ this technique and to begin a slow and long-term process of reconstructing the patient's personality pattern.

Part C

Psychobehavioral Foundations of Medicine: The Person Perspective

VII PSYCHOBEHAVIORAL CONCEPTS AND VIEWPOINTS

The interdependence of medical and psychological sciences was well understood by physicians of earlier centuries. However, as both fields fragmented into smaller units and subdisciplines, investigators turned their attention to isolated topics, of interest only to their immediate professional colleagues. Fortunately, as the papers of this chapter demonstrate, the period of disciplinary isolation is drawing to a close. Psychological and medical researchers have begun the task, as Weiss has put it, of "resynthesizing the conceptual bonds between those parts which we have cut in the first place."

There are many threads that bind psychological and medical science. Each is anchored firmly to foundations in biological theory, recognizing that all human processes, be they normal or abnormal, are grounded ultimately in the physical properties of the organism. Along similar lines, each appreciates that these processes derive their special human character from the impact of social and cultural forces. Another parallel feature is their joint tradition of research, technology, and instrumentation, as is evident in their rigorous methodologies and empirically based investigations. But the attribute that links them most closely is their shared clinical tradition, that is, the assumption of a caretaking role designed to improve the health and well-being of others.

On a narrower scale, studies of the "learning" process have become directly applicable to medical problems. For example, methods of "behavior modification" — techniques of therapy based on principles of learning and unlearning — have proved to be especially efficient in extinguishing troublesome psychiatric symptoms (e.g., phobias) and assisting in the acquisition of adaptive behaviors (e.g., eliciting speech in withdrawn or autistic children). The most exciting use of learning principles in dealing with medical problems has been the application of conditioning techniques in the control of such psychosomatic ailments as essential hypertension. The following quote refers to several physical disorders that have been subjected to these methods (Kamiya et al., 1971):

... Experiments show that humans can train themselves to control their own heart rates voluntarily. The technique uses a device that is a sort of "physiological mirror." The heart rate is detected by an electronic device and fed back to the experimental subject through a signal. This keeps him continuously informed of even the slightest beat-to-beat variations in the heart rate. He tries various "internal experiments" on how to control the feedback signal and gradually achieves partial control. He may sometimes describe the "method" in terms of thoughts, feelings, and emotions; but he may also be totally unable to provide any clear verbal description of his new skill.

In other studies subjects train themselves to enter a kind of relaxed but alert mental state with the aid of a tone signal controlled by their brainwaves; or they can overcome chronic tension headaches by learning to relax their scalp muscles with the aid of a muscle tension monitor. In work with animals it has been shown that the rate of kidney output and rate of salivation can be increased by rewarding the animals whenever they spontaneously show such increases.

What these studies suggest is exciting indeed: With modern technological devices man may be able to exercise direct voluntary control over many body and brain functions that had been considered as being totally beyond such control. The range of physiological functions that can possibly be controlled is wide. Trained voluntary control of excessive sweating, high blood pressure, stomach acidity, migraine headaches and insomnia, and many other symptoms of nervous tension come to mind.

The range of medical problems to which these feedback-learning procedures can be fruitfully applied continues to grow at a rapid pace. As Neal Miller, the distinguished experimental psychologist notes in the first article of this chapter, a wide band of autonomically controlled visceral responses can now be modified through the use of operant conditioning techniques. In this detailed review of research carried out at his Rockefeller University laboratory, Miller reports on the efficacy of biofeedback training in moderating not only cardiovascular disorders, but a whole host of individual differences in homeostatic functioning. Other investigators, stimulated by Miller's illuminating work, have demonstrated the utility of his methods in controlling such diverse somatic responses as EEG waves, muscle tension, cardiac rates and arrhythmias, skin temperature, peristaltic movement, electrodermal activity, and so on. Long term biofeedback training to achieve psychosomatic changes, however, is often time-consuming and expensive. Hence, a number of investigators have proposed the development of commercial feedback devices which can be distributed for home use by patients; at home, on their own time, these patients can employ the instrument on a daily or other routine basis, reporting in periodically for medical checkups by their attending physician.

Along more conventional lines, Melvin Goldstein furnishes a scholarly review of the concept of emotion, thoughtfully summarizing a number of classical physiological theories and their behavioral counterparts. Because of the difficulties they have had in finding a simple way to describe or categorize its diverse qualities, the concept of emotion is often referred to by psychobehaviorists as "the whale among the psychological fishes." Goldstein's paper provides a glimpse into the reasons for the troublesome nature of this deceptively complex phenomenon.

In the final paper, Lewis Wolberg, author of a definitive psychotherapeutic text, explores the techniques employed by psychoanalysts in uncovering the anxieties and eliciting the defensive maneuvers patients conceal within their unconscious. He provides two clinical examples and illuminates with extraordinary sensitivity the processes involved in analyzing the elements of this deeply recessed sphere of psychological functioning.

REFERENCES

Kamiya, J., et al.: Biofeedback and Self-Control. Chicago, Aldine, 1971.

19   Learning of Visceral and Glandular Responses

Neal E. Miller

There is a strong traditional belief in the inferiority of the autonomic nervous system and the visceral responses that it controls. The recent experiments disproving this belief have deep implications for theories of learning, for individual differences in autonomic responses, for the cause and the cure of abnormal psychosomatic symptoms, and possibly also for the understanding of normal homeostasis. Their success encourages investigators to try other unconventional types of training. Before describing these experiments, let me briefly sketch some elements in the history of the deeply entrenched, false belief in the gross inferiority of one major part of the nervous system.

HISTORICAL ROOTS AND MODERN RAMIFICATIONS

Since ancient times, reason and the voluntary responses of the skeletal muscles have been considered to be superior, while emotions and the presumably involuntary glandular and visceral responses have been considered to be inferior. This invidious dichotomy appears in the philosophy of Plato,[1] with his superior rational soul in the head above and inferior souls in the body below. Much later, the great French neuroanatomist Bichat[2] distinguished between the cerebrospinal nervous system of the great brain and spinal cord, controlling skeletal responses, and the dual chain of ganglia (which he called "little brains") running down on either side of the spinal cord in the body below and controlling emotional and visceral responses. He indicated his low opinion of the ganglionic system by calling it "vegetative"; he also believed it to be largely independent of the cerebrospinal system, an opinion which is still reflected in our modern name for it, the autonomic nervous system. Considerably later, Cannon[3] studied the sympathetic part of the autonomic nervous system and concluded that the different nerves in it all fire simultaneously and are incapable of the finely differentiated individual responses possible for the cerebrospinal system, a conclusion which is enshrined in modern textbooks.

Many, though not all, psychiatrists have made an invidious distinction between the hysterical and other symptoms that are mediated by the cerebrospinal nervous system and the psychosomatic symptoms that are mediated by the autonomic nervous system. Whereas the former are supposed to be subject to a higher type of control that is symbolic, the latter are presumed to be only the direct physiological consequences of the type and intensity of the patient's emotions.[4]

Similarly, students of learning have made a distinction between a lower form, called classical conditioning and thought to be involuntary, and a superior form variously called trial-and-error learning, operant conditioning, type II conditioning, or instrumental learning and believed to be responsible for voluntary behavior. In classical conditioning, the reinforcement must be by an unconditioned stimulus that already elicits the specific response to be learned; therefore, the possibilities are quite limited. In instrumental learning, the reinforcement, called a reward, has the property of strengthening any immediately preceding response. Therefore, the possi-

Miller, N.: Learning of visceral and glandular responses. Science. *163*:434–445 (1969).

bilities for reinforcement are much greater; a given reward many reinforce any one of a number of different responses, and a given response may be reinforced by any one of a number of different rewards.

Finally, the foregoing invidious distinctions have coalesced into the strong traditional belief that the superior type of instrumental learning involved in the superior voluntary behavior is possible only for skeletal responses mediated by the superior cerebrospinal nervous system, while, conversely, the inferior classical conditioning is the only kind possible for the inferior, presumably involuntary, visceral and emotional responses mediated by the inferior autonomic nervous system. Thus, in a recent summary generally considered authoritative, Kimble[5] states the almost universal belief that "for autonomically mediated behavior, the evidence points unequivocally to the conclusion that such responses can be modified by classical, but not instrumental, training methods." Upon examining the evidence, however, one finds that it consists only of failure to secure instrumental learning in two incompletely reported exploratory experiments and a vague allusion to the Russian literature.[6] It is only against a cultural background of great prejudice that such weak evidence could lead to such a strong conviction.

The belief that instrumental learning is possible only for the cerebrospinal system and, conversely, that the autonomic nervous system can be modified only by classical conditioning has been used as one of the strongest arguments for the notion that instrumental learning and classical conditioning are two basically different phenomena rather than different manifestations of the same phenomenon under different conditions. But for many years I have been impressed with the similarity between the laws of classical conditioning and those of instrumental learning, and with the fact that, in each of these two situations, some of the specific details of learning vary with the specific conditions of learning. Failing to see any clear-cut dichotomy, I have assumed that there is only one kind of learning.[7] This assumption has logically demanded that instrumental training procedures be able to produce the learning of any visceral responses that could be acquired through classical conditioning procedures. Yet it was only a little over a dozen years ago that I began some experimental work on this problem and a somewhat shorter time ago that I first, in published articles,[8] made specific sharp challenges to the traditional view that the instrumental learning of visceral responses is impossible.

SOME DIFFICULTIES

One of the difficulties of investigating the instrumental learning of visceral responses stems from the fact that the responses that are the easiest to measure — namely, heart rate, vasomotor responses, and the galvanic skin response — are known to be affected by skeletal responses, such as exercise, breathing, and even tensing of certain muscles, such as those in the diaphragm. Thus, it is hard to rule out the possibility that, instead of directly learning a visceral response, the subject has learned a skeletal response the performance of which causes the visceral change being recorded.

One of the controls I planned to use was the paralysis of all skeletal responses through administration of curare, a drug which selectively blocks the motor end plates of skeletal muscles without eliminating consciousness in human subjects or the neural control of visceral responses, such as the beating of the heart. The muscles involved in breathing are paralyzed, so the subject's breathing must be maintained through artificial respiration. Since it seemed unlikely that curarization and other rigorous control techniques would be easy to use with human subjects, I decided to concentrate first on experiments with animals.

Originally I thought that learning would be more difficult when the animal was paralyzed, under the influence of curare, and therefore I decided to postpone such experiments until ones on nonparalyzed animals had yielded some definitely promising results. This turned out to be a mistake because, as I found out much later, paralyzing the animal with curare not only greatly simplifies the problem of recording visceral responses without artifacts introduced by movement but also apparently makes it easier for the animal to learn, perhaps because paralysis of the skeletal muscles removes sources of variability and distraction. Also, in certain experiments I made the mistake of using rewards that induced strong unconditioned responses that interfered with instrumental learning.

One of the greatest difficulties, however, was the strength of the belief that instrumental learning of glandular and visceral responses is impossible. It was extremely difficult to get students to work on this problem, and when paid assistants were assigned to it, their attempts were so half-hearted that it soon became more economical to let them work on some other problem which they could attack with greater faith and enthusiasm. These difficulties and a few preliminary encouraging but inconclusive early results have been described elsewhere.[9]

SUCCESS WITH SALIVATION

The first clear-cut results were secured by Alfredo Carmona and me in an experiment on the salivation of dogs. Initial attempts to use food as a reward for hungry dogs were unsuccessful, partly because of strong and persistent unconditioned salivation elicited by the food. Therefore, we decided to use water as a reward for thirsty dogs. Preliminary observations showed that the water had no appreciable effects one way or the other on the bursts of spontaneous salivation. As an additional precaution, however, we used the experimental design of rewarding dogs in one group whenever they showed a burst of sponteneous salivation, so that they would be trained to increase salivation, and rewarding dogs in another group whenever there was a long interval between spontaneous bursts, so that they would be trained to decrease salivation. If the reward had any unconditioned effect, this effect might be classically conditioned to the experimental

situation and therefore produce a change in salivation that was not a true instance of instrumental learning. But in classical conditioning the reinforcement must elicit the response that is to be acquired. Therefore, conditioning of a response elicited by the reward could produce either an increase or a decrease in salivation, depending upon the direction of the unconditioned response elicited by the reward, but it could not produce a change in one direction for one group and in the opposite direction for the other group. The same type of logic applies for any unlearned cumulative aftereffects of the reward; they could not be in opposite directions for the two groups. With instrumental learning, however, the reward can reinforce any response that immediately precedes it; therefore, the same reward can be used to produce either increases or decreases.

The results are presented in Figure 19-1, which summarizes the effects of 40 days of training with one 45-minute training session per day. It may be seen that in this experiment the learning proceeded slowly. However, statistical analysis showed that each of the trends in the predicted rewarded direction was highly reliable.[10]

Since the changes in salivation for the two groups were in opposite directions, they cannot be attributed to classical conditioning. It was noted, however, that the group rewarded for increases seemed to be more aroused and active than the one rewarded for decreases. Conceivably, all we were doing was to change the level of activation of the dogs, and this change was, in turn, affecting the salivation. Although we did not observe any specific skeletal responses, such as chewing movements or panting, which might be expected to elicit salivation, it was difficult to be absolutely certain that such movements did not occur. Therefore, we decided to rule out such movements by paralyzing the dogs with curare, but we immediately found that curare had two effects which were disastrous for this experiment: it elicited such copious and continuous salivation that there were no changes in salivation to reward, and the salivation was so viscous that it almost immediately gummed up the recording apparatus.

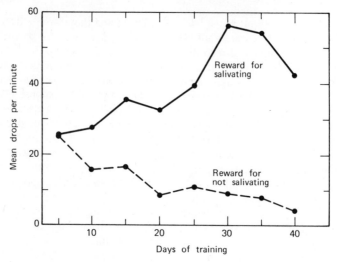

Figure 19-1. Learning curves for groups of thirsty dogs rewarded with water for either increases or decreases in spontaneous salivation. (From Miller and Carmona (10). Copyright 1967 by the American Psychological Association. Reprinted by permission.)

HEART RATE

In the meantime, Jay Trowill, working with me on this problem, was displaying great ingenuity, courage, and persistence in trying to produce instrumental learning of heart rate in rats that had been paralyzed by curare to prevent them from "cheating" by muscular exertion to speed up the heart or by relaxation to slow it down. As a result of preliminary testing, he selected a dose of curare (3.6 milligrams of a-tubocurarine chloride per kilogram, injected intraperitoneally) which produced deep paralysis for at least 3 hours, and a rate of artificial respiration (inspiration-expiration ratio 1:1; 70 breaths per minute; peak pressure reading, 20 cm-H_2O) which maintained the heart at a constant and normal rate throughout this time.

In subsequent experiments, DiCara and I have obtained similar effects by starting with a smaller dose (1.2 milligrams per kilogram) and constantly infusing additional amounts of the drug, through intraperitoneal injection, at the rate of 1.2 milligrams per kilogram per hour, for the duration of the experiment. We have recorded, electro-myographically, the response of the muscles, to determine that this dose does indeed produce a complete block of the action potentials, lasting for at

least an hour after the end of infusion. We have found that if parameters of respiration and the face mask are adjusted carefully, the procedure not only maintains the heart rate of a 500-gram control animal constant but also maintains the vital signs of temperature, peripheral vasomotor responses, and the pCO_2 of the blood constant.

Since there are not very many ways to reward an animal completely paralyzed by curare, Trowill and I decided to use direct electrical stimulation of rewarding areas of the brain. There were other technical difficulties to overcome, such as devising the automatic system for rewarding small changes in heart rate as recorded by the electrocardiogram. Nevertheless, Trowill at last succeeded in training his rats.[11] Those rewarded for an increase in heart rate showed a statistically reliable increase, and those rewarded for a decrease in heart rate showed a statistically reliable decrease. The changes, however, were disappointingly small, averaging only 5 percent in each direction.

The next question was whether larger changes could be achieved by improving the technique of training. DiCara and I used the technique of shaping — in other words, of immediately rewarding first very small, and hence frequently occurring, changes in the correct direction and, as soon as these had been learned, requiring progressively larger changes as the criterion for reward. In this way, we were able to produce in 90 minutes of training changes averaging 20 per cent in either direction.[12]

KEY PROPERTIES OF LEARNING: DISCRIMINATION AND RETENTION

Does the learning of visceral responses have the same properties as the learning of skeletal responses? One of the important characteristics of the instrumental learning of skeletal responses is that a discrimination can be learned, so that the responses are more likely to be made in the stimulus situations in which they are rewarded than in those in which they are not. After the training of the first few rats had convinced us that we could produce large changes in heart rate, DiCara and I gave all the rest of the rats in the experiment described above 45 minutes of additional training with the most difficult criterion. We did this in order to see whether they could learn to give a greater response during a "time-in" stimulus (the presence of a flashing light and a tone) which indicated that a response in the proper direction would be rewarded than during a "time-out" stimulus (absence of light and tone) which indicated that a correct response would not be rewarded.

Figure 19-2 shows the record on one of the rats given such training. Before the beginning of the special discrimination training it had slowed its heart from an initial rate of 350 beats per minute to a rate of 230 beats per minute. From the top record of Figure 19-2 one can see that, at the beginning of the special discrimination training, there was no appreciable reduction in heart rate that was specifically associated with the time-in stimulus. Thus it took the rat considerable time after the onset of this stimulus to meet the criterion and get the reward. At the end of the discrimination training the heart rate during time-out remained approximately the same, but when the time-in light and tone came on, the heart slowed down and the criterion was promptly met. Although the other rats showed less change than this, by the end of the relatively short period of

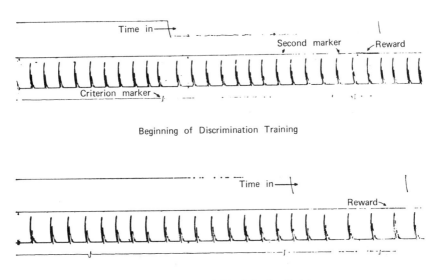

Beginning of Discrimination Training

After 45 Minutes of Discrimination Training

Figure 19-2. Electrocardiograms at the beginning and at the end of discrimination training of curarized rat rewarded for slow heart rate. Slowing of heart rate is rewarded only during a "time-in" stimulus (tone and light). (From Miller and DiCara (12). Copyright 1967 by the American Psychological Association. Reprinted by permission.)

discrimination training their heart rate did change reliably ($P < .001$) in the predicted direction when the time-in stimulus came on. Thus, it is clear that instrumental visceral learning has at least one of the important properties of instrumental skeletal learning — namely, the ability to be brought under the control of a discriminative stimulus.

Another of the important properties of the instrumental learning of skeletal responses is that it is remembered. DiCara and I performed a special experiment to test the retention of learned changes in heart rate.[13] Rats that had been given a single training session were returned to their home cages for 3 months without further training. When curarized again and returned to the experimental situation for nonreinforced test trials, rats in both the "increase" and the "decrease" groups showed good retention by exhibiting reliable changes in the direction rewarded in the earlier training.

ESCAPE AND AVOIDANCE LEARNING

Is visceral learning by any chance peculiarly limited to reinforcement by the unusual reward of direct electrical stimulation of the brain, or can it be reinforced by other rewards in the same way that skeletal learning can be? In order to answer this question, DiCara and I[14] performed an experiment using the other of the two forms of thoroughly studied reward that can be conveniently used with rats which are paralyzed by curare — namely, the chance to avoid, or escape from, mild electric shock. A shock signal was turned on; after it had been on for 10 seconds it was accompanied by brief pulses of mild electric shock delivered to the rat's tail. During the first 10 seconds the rat could turn off the shock signal and avoid the shock by making the correct response of changing its heart rate in the required direction by the required amount. If it did not make the correct response in time, the shocks continued to be delivered until the rat escaped them by making the correct response, which immediately turned off both the shock and the shock signal.

For one group of curarized rats, the correct response was an increase in heart rate; for the other group it was a decrease. After the rats had learned to make small responses in the proper direction, they were required to make larger ones. During this training the shock signals were randomly interspersed with an equal number of "safe" signals that were not followed by shock; the heart rate was also recorded during so-called blank trials — trials without any signals or shocks. For half of the rats the shock signal was a tone and the "safe" signal was a flashing light; for the other half the roles of these cues were reversed.

The results are shown in Figure 19-3. Each of the 12 rats in this experiment changed its heart rate in the rewarded direction. As training progressed, the shock signal began to elicit a progressively greater change in the rewarded direction than the change recorded during the blank trials; this was a statistically reliable trend. Conversely, as training progressed, the "safe" signal came to elicit a statistically reliable change in the opposite direction, toward the initial base line. These results show learning when escape and avoidance are the rewards; this means that visceral responses in curarized rats can be reinforced by rewards other than direct electrical stimulation of the brain. These rats also discriminate between the shock and the "safe" signals. You will remember that, with noncurarized thirsty dogs, we were able to use yet another kind of reward, water, to produce learned changes in salivation.

TRANSFER TO NONCURARIZED STATE: MORE EVIDENCE AGAINST MEDIATION

In the experiments discussed above, paralysis of the skeletal muscles by curare ruled out the possibility that the subjects were learning the overt performance of skeletal responses which were indirectly eliciting the changes in the heart rate. It is barely conceivable, however, that the rats were learning to send out from the motor

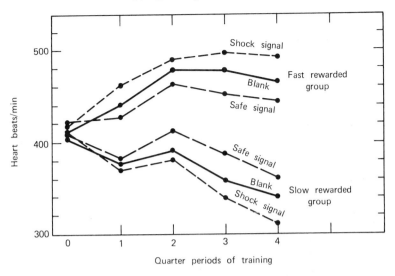

Figure 19-3. Changes in heart rate during avoidance training. (From DiCara and Miller (14). Copyright 1967 by the American Psychological Association. Reprinted by permission.)

cortex central impulses which would have activated the muscles had they not been paralyzed. And it is barely conceivable that these central impulses affected heart rate by means either of inborn connections or of classically conditioned ones that had been acquired when previous exercise had been accompanied by an increase in heart rate and relaxation had been accompanied by a decrease. But, if the changes in heart rate were produced in this indirect way, we would expect that, during a subsequent test without curare, any rat that showed learned changes in heart rate would show the movements in the muscles that were no longer paralyzed. Furthermore, the problem of whether or not visceral responses learned under curarization carry over to the noncurarized state is of interest in its own right.

In order to answer this question, DiCara and I trained two groups of curarized rats to increase or decrease, respectively, their heart rate in order to avoid, or escape from, brief pulses of mild electric shock.[15] When these rats were tested 2 weeks later in the noncurarized state, the habit was remembered. Statistically reliable increases in heart rate averaging 5 percent and decreases averaging 16 percent occurred. Immediately subsequent retraining without curare produced additional significant

changes of heart rate in the rewarded direction, bringing the total overall increase to 11 percent and the decrease to 22 percent. While, at the beginning of the test in the noncurarized state, the two groups showed some differences in respiration and activity, these differences decreased until, by the end of the retraining, they were small and far from statistically reliable ($t = 0.3$ and 1.3, respectively). At the same time, the difference between the two groups with respect to heart rate was increasing, until it became large and thus extremely reliable ($t = 8.6$, $df = 12$, $P < .001$).

In short, while greater changes in heart rate were being learned, the response was becoming more specific, involving smaller changes in respiration and muscular activity. This increase in specificity with additional training is another point of similarity with the instrumental learning of skeletal responses. Early in skeletal learning, the rewarded correct response is likely to be accompanied by many unnecessary movements. With additional training during which extraneous movements are not rewarded, they tend to drop out.

It is difficult to reconcile the fore-going results with the hypothesis that the differences in heart rate were mediated primarily by a difference in either respiration or amount of general activity. This is especially true in view of the research, summarized by Ehrlich and Malmo,[16] which shows that muscular activity, to affect heart rate in the rat, must be rather vigorous.

While it is difficult to rule out completely the possibility that changes in heart rate are mediated by central impulses to skeletal muscles, the possibility of such mediation is much less attractive for other responses, such as intestinal contractions and the formation of urine by the kidney. Furthermore, if the learning of these different responses can be shown to be specific in enough visceral responses, one runs out of different skeletal movements each eliciting a specific different visceral response.* Therefore, experiments were performed on the learning of a variety of different visceral responses and on the specificity of that learning. Each of these experiments was, of course, interesting in its own right, quite apart from any bearing on the problem of mediation.

SPECIFICITY: INTESTINAL VERSUS CARDIAC

The purpose of our next experiment was to determine the specificity of visceral learning. If such learning has the same properties as the instrumental learning of skeletal responses, it should be possible to learn a specific visceral response independently of other ones. Furthermore, as we have just seen, we might expect to find that, the better the rewarded response is learned, the more specific is the learning. Banuazizi and I worked on this problem.[17] First we had to discover another visceral response that could be conveniently re-

corded and rewarded. We decided on intestinal contractions, and recorded them in the curarized rat with a little balloon filled with water thrust approximately 4 centimeters beyond the anal sphincter. Changes of pressure in the balloon were transduced into electric voltages which produced a record on a polygraph and also activated an automatic mechanism for delivering the reward, which was electrical stimulation of the brain.

The results for the first rat trained, which was a typical one, are shown in Figure 19-4. From the top record it may be seen that, during habituation, there were some spontaneous contractions. When the rat was rewarded by brain stimulation for keeping contractions below a certain amplitude for a certain time, the number of contractions was reduced and the base line was lowered. After the record showed a highly reliable change indicating that relaxation had been learned (Figure 19-4, second record from the top), the conditions of training were reversed and the reward was delivered whenever the amplitude of contractions rose above a certain level. From the next record (Figure 19-4, middle) it may be seen that this type of training increased the number of contractions and raised the base line. Finally (Figure 19-4, two bottom records) the reward was discontinued and, as would be expected, the response continued for a while but gradually became extinguished, so that the activity eventually returned to approximately its original base-line level.

After studying a number of other rats in this way and convincing ourselves that the instrumental learning of intestinal responses was a possibility, we designed an experiment to test specificity. For all the rats of the experiment, both intestinal contractions and heart rate were recorded, but half the rats were rewarded for one of these responses and half were rewarded for the other response. Each of these two groups of rats was divided into two subgroups, rewarded, respectively, for increased and decreased response. The rats were completely paralyzed by curare, maintained on artificial respiration, and rewarded by electrical stimulation of the brain.

---

*"It even becomes difficult to postulate enough different throughts each arousing a different emotion, each of which in turn innately elicits a specific visceral response. And if one assumes a more direct specific connection between different thoughts and different visceral responses, the notion becomes indistinguishable from the ideo-motor hypothesis of the voluntary movement of skeletal muscles." James, W.: *Principles of Psychology*. New York; Dover, New Ed., 1950, Vol. 2, Chap. 26.

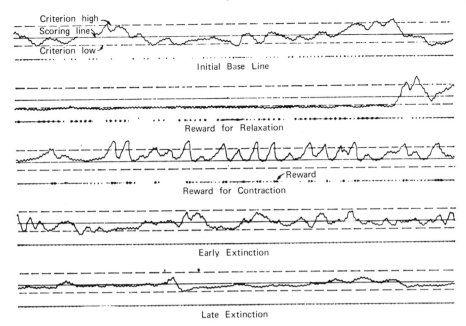

Figure 19–4. Typical samples of a record of instrumental learning of an intestinal response by a curarized rat. From top to bottom: Record of spontaneous contraction before training; record after training with reward for relaxation; record after training with reward for contractions; record during nonrewarded extinction trials. (From Miller and Banuazizi (17). Copyright 1967 by the American Psychological Association. Reprinted by permission.)

The results are shown in Figures 19-5 and 19-6. In Figure 19-5 it may be seen that the group rewarded for increases in intestinal contractions learned an increase, the group rewarded for decreases learned a decrease, but neither of these groups showed an appreciable change in heart rate. Conversely (Figure 19-6), the group rewarded for increases in heart rate showed an increase, the group rewarded for decreases showed a decrease, but neither of these groups showed a change in intestinal contractions.

The fact that each type of response changed when it was rewarded rules out the interpretation that the failure to secure a change when that change was not rewarded could have been due to either a strong and stable homeostatic regulation of that response or an inability of our techniques to measure changes reliably under the particular conditions of our experiment.

Each of the 12 rats in the experiment showed statistically reliable changes in the rewarded direction; for 11 the changes were reliable beyond the $P < .001$ level,

while for the 12th the changes were reliable only beyond the .05 level. A statistically reliable negative correlation showed that the better the rewarded visceral response was learned, the less change occurred in the other; nonrewarded response. This greater specificity with better learning is what we had expected. The results showed that visceral learning can be specific to an organ system, and they clearly ruled out the possibility of mediation by any single general factor, such as level of activation or central commands for either general activity or relaxation.

In an additional experiment, Banuazizi[18] showed that either increases or decreases in intestinal contractions can be rewarded by avoidance of, or escape from, mild electric shocks, and that the intestinal responses can be discriminatively elicited by a specific stimulus associated with reinforcement.

KIDNEY FUNCTION

Encouraged by these successes, DiCara and I decided to see whether or not the

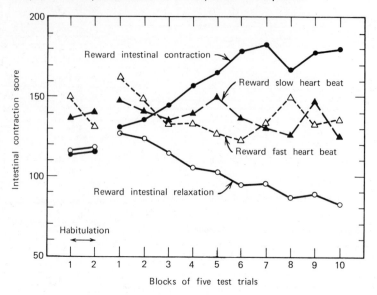

Figure 19-5. Graph showing that the intestinal contraction score is changed by rewarding either increases or decreases in intestinal contractions but is unaffected by rewarding changes in heart rate. (From Miller and Banuazizi (17). Copyright 1967, American Psychological Assoc. Reprinted by permission.)

rate of urine formation by the kidney could be changed in the curarized rat rewarded by electrical stimulation of the brain[19]. A catheter, permanently inserted, was used to prevent accumulation of urine by the bladder, and the rate of urine formation was measured by an electronic device for counting minute drops. In order to secure a rate of urine formation fast enough so that small changes could be promptly detected and rewarded, the rats were kept constantly loaded with water

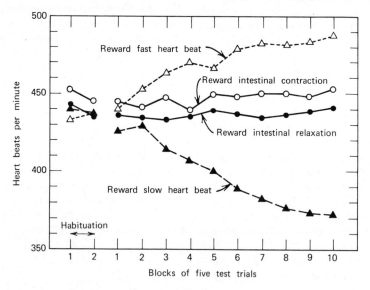

Figure 19-6. Graph showing that the heart rate is changed by rewarding either increases or decreases in heart rate but is unaffected by rewarding changes in intestinal contractions. Comparison with Figure 5 demonstrates the specificity of visceral learning. (From Miller and Banuazizi (17). Copyright 1967 by the American Psychological Association. Reprinted by permission.)

through infusion by way of a catheter permanently inserted in the jugular vein.

All of the seven rats rewarded when the intervals between times of urine-drop formation lengthened showed decreases in the rate of urine formation, and all of the seven rats rewarded when these intervals shortened showed increases in the rate of urine formation. For both groups the changes were highly reliable ($P < .001$).

In order to determine how the change in rate of urine formation was achieved, certain additional measures were taken. As the set of bars at left in Figure 19-7 shows, the rate of filtration, measured by means of ^{14}C-labeled inulin, increased when increases in the rate of urine formation were rewarded and decreased when decreases in the rate were rewarded. Plots of the correlations showed that the changes in the rates of filtration and urine formation were not related to changes in either blood pressure or heart rate.

The middle set of bars in Figure 19-7 shows that the rats rewarded for increases in the rate of urine formation had an increased rate of renal blood flow, as measured by ^{3}H-p-aminohippuric acid, and that those rewarded for decreases had a decreased rate of renal blood flow. Since these changes in blood flow were not accompanied by changes in general blood

pressure or in heart rate, they must have been achieved by vasomotor changes of the renal arteries. That these vasomotor changes were at least somewhat specific is shown by the fact that vasomotor responses of the tail, as measured by a photoelectric plethysmograph, did not differ for the two groups of rats.

The set of bars at right in Figure 19-7 shows that when decreases in rate of urine formation were rewarded, a more concentrated urine, having higher osmolarity, was formed. Since the slower passage of urine through the tubules would afford more opportunity for reabsorption of water, this higher concentration does not necessarily mean an increase in the secretion of antidiuretic hormone. When an increased rate of urine formation was rewarded, the urine did not become more diluted — that is, it showed no decrease in osmolarity; therefore, the increase in rate of urine formation observed in this experiment cannot be accounted for in terms of an inhibition of the secretion of antidiuretic hormone.

From the foregoing results it appears that the learned changes in urine formation in this experiment were produced primarily by changes in the rate of filtration, which, in turn, were produced primarily by changes in the rate of blood flow through the kidneys.

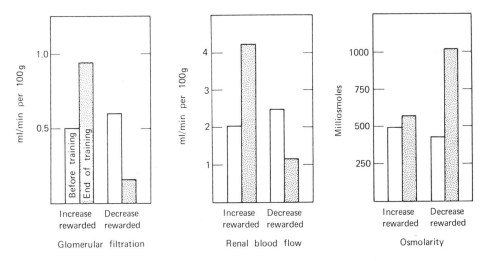

Figure 19-7. Effects of rewarding increased rate of urine formation in one group and decreased rate in another on measures of glomerular filtration, renal blood flow, and osmolarity. (From data in Miller and DiCara (19).)

GASTRIC CHANGES

In the next experiment, Carmona, Demierre, and I used a photoelectric plethysmograph to measure changes, presumably in the amount of blood, in the stomach wall.[20] In an operation performed under anesthesia, a small glass tube, painted black except for a small spot, was inserted into the rat's stomach. The same tube was used to hold the stomach wall against a small glass window inserted through the body wall. The tube was left in that position. After the animal had recovered, a bundle of optical fibers could be slipped snugly into the glass tube so that the light beamed through it would shine out through the unpainted spot in the tube inside the stomach, pass through the stomach wall, and be recorded by a photocell on the other side of the glass window. Preliminary tests indicated that, as would be expected, when the amount of blood in the stomach wall increased, less light would pass through. Other tests showed that stomach contractions elicited by injections of insulin did not affect the amount of light transmitted.

In the main experiment we rewarded curarized rats by enabling them to avoid or escape from mild electric shocks. Some were rewarded when the amount of light that passed through the stomach wall increased, while others were rewarded when the amount decreased. Fourteen of the 15 rats showed changes in the rewarded direction. Thus, we demonstrated that the stomach wall, under the control of the autonomic nervous system, can be modified by instrumental learning. There is strong reason to believe that the learned changes were achieved by vasomotor responses affecting the amount of blood in the stomach wall or mucosa, or in both.

In another experiment, Carmona[21] showed that stomach contractions can be either increased or decreased by instrumental learning.

It is obvious that learned changes in the blood supply of internal organs can affect their functioning — as, for example, the rate at which urine was formed by the kidneys was affected by changes in the amount of blood that flowed through them. Thus, such changes can produce psychosomatic symptoms. And if the learned changes in blood supply can be specific to a given organ, the symptom will occur in that organ rather than in another one.

PERIPHERAL VASOMOTOR RESPONSES

Having investigated the instrumental learning of internal vasomotor responses, we next studied the learning of peripheral ones. In the first experiment, the amount of blood in the tail of a curarized rat was measured by a photoelectric plethysmograph, and changes were rewarded by electrical stimulation of the brain.[22] All of the four rats rewarded for vasoconstriction showed that response, and, at the same time, their average core temperature, measured rectally, decreased from 98.9° to 97.9°F. All of the four rats rewarded for vasodilatation showed that response and, at the same time, their average core temperature increased from 99.9° to 101°F. The vasomotor change for each individual rat was reliable beyond the $P < .01$ level, and the difference in change in temperature between the groups was reliable beyond the .01 level. The direction of the change in temperature was opposite to that which would be expected from the heat conservation caused by peripheral vasoconstriction or the heat loss caused by peripheral vasodilatation. The changes are in the direction which would be expected if the training had altered the rate of heat production, causing a change in temperature which, in turn, elicited the vasomotor response.

The next experiment was designed to try to determine the limits of the specificity of vasomotor learning. The pinnae of the rat's ears were chosen because the blood vessels in them are believed to be innervated primarily, and perhaps exclusively, by the sympathetic branch of the autonomic nervous system, the branch that Cannon believed always fired nonspecifically as a unit.[3] But Cannon's experiments involved exposing cats to extremely strong emotion-evoking stimuli, such as barking dogs, and such stimuli will also evoke generalized activity throughout the skeletal musculature. Perhaps his results reflected the way in which sympathetic activity was elicited, rather than demonstrating any inherent inferiority of the sympathetic nervous system.

In order to test this interpretation, DiCara and I[23] put photocells on both ears of the curarized rat and connected them to a bridge circuit so that only differences in the vasomotor responses of the two ears were rewarded by brain stimulation. We were somewhat surprised and greatly delighted to find that this experiment actually worked. The results are summarized in Figure 19-8. Each of the six rats rewarded for relative vasodilatation of the left ear showed that response, while each of the six rats rewarded for relative vasodilatation of the right ear showed that response. Recordings from the right and left forepaws showed little if any change in vasomotor response.

It is clear that these results cannot be by-products of changes in either heart rate or blood pressure, as these would be expected to affect both ears equally. They show either that vasomotor responses mediated by the sympathetic nervous system are capable of much greater specificity than has previously been believed, or that the innervation of the blood vessels in the pinnae of the ears is not restricted almost exclusively to sympathetic-nervous-system components, as has been believed, and involves functionally significant parasympathetic components. In any event, the changes in the blood flow certainly were surprisingly specific. Such changes in blood flow could account for specific psychosomatic symptoms.

BLOOD PRESSURE INDEPENDENT OF HEART RATE

Although changes in blood pressure were not induced as by-products of rewarded changes in the rate of urine formation, another experiment on curarized rats showed that, when changes in systolic blood pressure are specifically reinforced, they can be learned.[24] Blood pressure was recorded by means of a catheter permanently inserted into the aorta, and the reward was avoidance of, or escape from, mild electric shock. All seven rats rewarded for increases in blood pressure showed further increases, while all seven rewarded for decreases showed decreases, each of the changes, which were in opposite directions, being reliable beyond the $P < .01$ level. The increase was from 139 mm-Hg, which happens to be roughly comparable to the normal systolic blood pressure of an adult

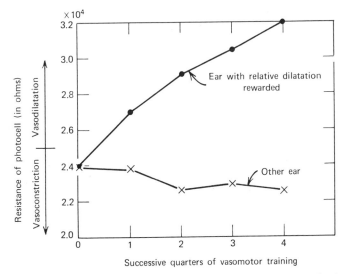

Figure 19-8. Learning a difference in the vasomotor responses of the two ears in the curarized rat. (From data in DiCara and Miller (23). Copyright 1968 by the American Association for the Advancement of Science.)

man, to 170 mm-Hg, which is on the borderline of abnormally high blood pressure in man.

Each experimental animal was "yoked" with a curarized partner, maintained on artificial respiration and having shock electrodes on its tail wired in series with electrodes on the tail of the experimental animal, so that it received exactly the same electric shocks and could do nothing to escape or avoid them. The yoked controls for both the increase-rewarded and the decrease-rewarded groups showed some elevation in blood pressure as an unconditioned effect of the shocks. By the end of training, in contrast to the large difference in the blood pressures of the two groups specifically rewarded for changes in opposite directions, there was no difference in blood pressure between the yoked control partners for these two groups. Furthermore, the increase in blood pressure in these control groups was reliably less ($P < .01$) than that in the group specifically rewarded for increases. Thus, it is clear that the reward for an increase in blood pressure produced an additional increase over and above the effects of the shocks per se, while the reward for a decrease was able to overcome the unconditioned increase elicited by the shocks.

For none of the four groups was there a significant change in heart rate or in temperature during training; there were no significant differences in these measures among the groups. Thus, the learned change was relatively specific to blood pressure.

TRANSFER FROM HEART RATE TO SKELETAL AVOIDANCE

Although visceral learning can be quite specific, especially if only a specific response is rewarded, as was the case in the experiment on the two ears, under some circumstances it can involve a more generalized effect.

In handling the rats that had just recovered from curarization, DiCara noticed that those that had been trained, through the avoidance or escape reward, to increase their heart rate were more likely to squirm, squeal, defecate, and show other responses

indicating emotionality than were those that had been trained to reduce their heart rate. Could instrumental learning of heart-rate changes have some generalized effects, perhaps on the level of emotionality, which might affect the behavior in a different avoidance-learning situation? In order to look for such an effect, DiCara and Weiss [14] used a modified shuttle avoidance apparatus. In this apparatus, when a danger signal is given, the rat must run from compartment A to compartment B. If he runs fast enough, he avoids the shock; if not, he must run to escape it. The next time the danger signal is given, the rat must run in the opposite direction, from B to A.

Other work had shown that learning in this apparatus is an inverted U-shaped function of the strength of the shocks, with shocks that are too strong eliciting emotional behavior instead of running. DiCara and Weiss trained their rats in this apparatus with a level of shock that is approximately optimum for naive rats of this strain. They found that the rats that had been rewarded for decreasing their heart rate learned well, but that those that had been rewarded for increasing their heart rate learned less well, as if their emotionality had been increased. The difference was statistically reliable ($P < .001$). This experiment clearly demonstrates that training a visceral response can affect the subsequent learning of a skeletal one, but additional work will be required to prove the hypothesis that training to increase heart rate increases emotionality.

VISCERAL LEARNING WITHOUT CURARE

Thus far, in all of the experiments except the one on teaching thirsty dogs to salivate, the initial training was given when the animal was under the influence of curare. All of the experiments, except the one on salivation, have produced surprisingly rapid learning — definitive results within 1 or 2 hours. Will learning in the normal, non-curarized state be easier, as we originally thought it should be, or will it be harder, as the experiment on the noncurarized dogs suggests? DiCara and I have started to get additional evidence on this problem. We have obtained clear-cut evidence that rewarding (with the avoidance or escape reward) one group of freely moving rats for reducing heart rate and rewarding another group for increasing heart rate produces a difference between the two groups. [25] That this difference was not due to the indirect effects of the overt performance of skeletal responses is shown by the fact that it persisted in subsequent tests during which the rats were paralyzed by curare. And, on subsequent retraining without curare, such differences in activity and respiration as were present earlier in training continued to decrease, while the differences in heart rate continued to increase. It seems extremely unlikely that, at the end of training, the highly reliable differences in heart rate ($t = 7.2; P < .0001$) can be explained by the highly unreliable differences in activity and respiration ($t = .07$ and 0.2, respectively).

Although the rats in this experiment showed some learning when they were trained initially in the noncurarized state, this learning was much poorer than that which we have seen in our other experiments on curarized rats. This is exactly the opposite of my original expectation, but seems plausible in the light of hindsight. My hunch is that paralysis by curare improved learning by eliminating sources of distraction and variability. The stimulus situation was kept more constant, and confusing visceral fluctuations induced directly by skeletal movements were eliminated.

LEARNED CHANGES IN BRAIN WAVES

Encouraged by success in the experiments on the instrumental learning of visceral responses, my colleagues and I have attempted to produce other unconventional types of learning. Electrodes placed on the skull or, better yet, touching the surface of the brain record summative effects of electrical activity over a considerable area of the brain. Such electrical effects are called brain waves, and the record of them is called an electroencephal-ogram. When the animal is aroused, the electroencephalogram consists of fast, low-voltage activity; when the animal is drowsy or sleeping normally, the electroencephalogram consists of considerably slower, higher-voltage activity. Carmona attempted to see whether this type of brain activity, and the state of arousal accompanying it, can be modified by direct reward of changes in the brain activity. [27,28]

The subjects of the first experiment were freely moving cats. In order to have a reward that was under complete control and that did not require the cat to move, Carmona used direct electrical stimulation of the medial forebrain bundle, which is a rewarding area of the brain. Such stimulation produced a slight lowering in the average voltage of the electroencephalogram and an increase in behavioral arousal. In order to provide a control for these and any other unlearned effects, he rewarded one group for changes in the direction of high-voltage activity and another group for changes in the direction of low-voltage activity.

Both groups learned. The cats rewarded for high-voltage activity showed more high-voltage slow waves and tended to sit like sphinxes, staring out into space. The cats rewarded for low-voltage activity showed much more low-voltage fast activity, and appeared to be aroused, pacing restlessly about, sniffing, and looking here and there. It was clear that this type of training had modified both the character of the electrical brain waves and the general level of the behavioral activity. It was not clear, however, whether the level of arousal of the brain was directly modified and hence modified the behavior; whether the animals learned specific items of behavior which, in turn, modified the arousal of the brain as reflected in the electroencephalogram; or whether both types of learning were occurring simultaneously.

In order to rule out the direct sensory consequences of changes in muscular tension, movement, and posture, Carmona performed the next experiment on rats that had been paralyzed by means of curare. The results, given in Figure 19-9, show that both rewarded groups showed changes in the rewarded direction; that a

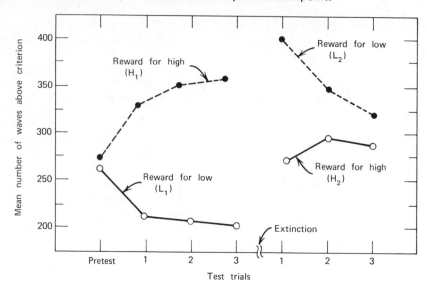

Figure 19-9. Instrumental learning by curarized rats rewarded for high-voltage or for low-voltage electroencephalograms recorded from the cerebral cortex. After a period of nonrewarded extinction, which produced some drowsiness, as indicated by an increase in voltage, the rats in the two groups were then rewarded for voltage changes opposite in direction to the changes for which they were rewarded earlier. (From Carmona (28).)

subsequent nonrewarded rest increased the number of high-voltage responses in both groups; and that, when the conditions of reward were reversed, the direction of change in voltage was reversed.

At present we are trying to use similar techniques to modify the functions of a specific part of the vagal nucleus, by recording and specifically rewarding changes in the electrical activity there. Preliminary results suggest that this is possible. The next step is to investigate the visceral consequences of such modification. This kind of work may open up possibilities for modifying the activity of specific parts of the brain and the functions that they control. In some cases, directly rewarding brain activity may be a more convenient or more powerful technique than rewarding skeletal or visceral behavior. It also may be a new way to throw light on the functions of specific parts of the brain. [29]

HUMAN VISCERAL LEARNING

Another question is that of whether people are capable of instrumental learning of visceral responses. I believe that in this respect they are as smart as rats. But, as a recent critical review by Katkin and Murray [30] points out, this has not yet been completely proved. These authors have comprehensively summarized the recent studies reporting successful use of instrumental training to modify human heart rate, vasomotor responses, and the galvanic skin response. Because of the difficulties in subjecting human subjects to the same rigorous controls, including deep paralysis by means of curare, that can be used with animal subjects, one of the most serious questions about the results of the human studies is whether the changes recorded represent the true instrumental learning of visceral responses or the unconscious learning of those skeletal responses that can produce visceral reactions. However, the able investigators who have courageously challenged the strong traditional belief in the inferiority of the autonomic nervous system with experiments at the more difficult but especially significant human level are developing ingenious controls, including demonstrations of the specificity of the visceral change, so that their cumulative results are becoming increasingly impressive.

POSSIBLE ROLE IN HOMEOSTASIS

The functional utility of instrumental learning by the cerebrospinal nervous system under the conditions that existed during mammalian evolution is obvious. The skeletal responses mediated by the cerebrospinal nervous system operate on the external environment, so that there is survival value in the ability to learn responses that bring rewards such as food, water, or escape from pain. The fact that the responses mediated by the autonomic nervous system do not have such direct action on the external environment was one of the reasons for believing that they are not subject to instrumental learning. Is the learning ability of the autonomic nervous system something that has no normal function other than that of providing my students with subject matter for publications? Is it a mere accidental by-product of the survival value of cerebrospinal learning, or does the instrumental learning of autonomically mediated responses have some adaptive function, such as helping to maintain that constancy of the internal environment called homeostasis?

In order for instrumental learning to function homeostatically, a deviation away from the optimum level will have to function as a drive to motivate learning, and a change toward the optimum level will have to function as a reward to reinforce the learning of the particular visceral response that produced the corrective change.

When a mammal has less than the optimum amount of water in his body, this deficiency serves as a drive of thirst to motivate learning; the overt consummatory response of drinking functions as a reward to reinforce the learning of the particular skeletal responses that were successful in securing the water that restored the optimum level. But is the consummatory response essential? Can restoration of an optimum level by a glandular response function as a reward?

In order to test for the possible rewarding effects of a glandular response, DiCara, Wolf, and I[31] injected albino rats with antidiuretic hormone (ADH) if they chose one arm of a T-maze and with the isotonic saline vehicle if they chose the other, distinctively different, arm. The ADH permitted water to be reabsorbed in the kidney, so that a smaller volume of more concentrated urine was formed. Thus, for normal rats loaded in advance with H_2O, the ADH interfered with the excess-water excretion required for the restoration of homeostasis, while the control injection of isotonic saline allowed the excess water to be excreted. And, indeed, such rats learned to select the side of the maze that assured them an injection of saline so that their glandular response could restore homeostasis.

Conversely, for rats with diabetes insipidus, loaded in advance with hypertonic NaCl, the homeostatic effects of the same two injections were reversed; the ADH, causing the urine to be more concentrated, helped the rats to get rid of the excess NaCl, while the isotonic saline vehicle did not. And, indeed, a group of rats of this kind learned the opposite choice of selecting the ADH side of the maze. As a further control on the effects of the ADH per se, normal rats which had not been given H_2O or NaCl exhibited no learning. This experiment showed that an excess of either H_2O or NaCl functions as a drive and that the return to the normal concentration produced by the appropriate response of a gland, the kidney, functions as a reward.

When we consider the results of this experiment together with those of our experiments showing that glandular and visceral responses can be instrumentally learned, we will expect the animal to learn those glandular and visceral responses mediated by the central nervous system that promptly restore homeostasis after any considerable deviation. Whether or not this theoretically possible learning has any practical significance will depend on whether or not the innate homeostatic mechanisms control the levels closely enough to prevent any deviations large enough to function as a drive from occurring. Even if the innate control should be accurate enough to preclude learning in most cases, there remains the intriguing possibility that, when pathology interferes with innate control, visceral learning is available as a supplementary mechanism.

IMPLICATIONS AND SPECULATIONS

We have seen how the instrumental learning of visceral responses suggests a new possible homeostatic mechanism worthy of further investigation. Such learning also shows that the autonomic nervous system is not as inferior as has been so widely and firmly believed. It removes one of the strongest arguments for the hypothesis that there are two fundamentally different mechanisms of learning, involving different parts of the nervous system.

Cause of Psychosomatic Symptoms

Similarly, evidence of the instrumental learning of visceral responses removes the main basis for assuming that the psychosomatic symptoms that involve the autonomic nervous system are fundamentally different from those functional symptoms, such as hysterical ones, that involve the cerebrospinal nervous system. Such evidence allows us to extend to psychosomatic symptoms the type of learning-theory analysis that Dollard and I [7,32] have applied to other symptoms.

For example, suppose a child is terror-stricken at the thought of going to school in the morning because he is completely unprepared for an important examination. The strong fear elicits a variety of fluctuating autonomic symptoms, such as a queasy stomach at one time and pallor and faintness at another; at this point his mother, who is particularly concerned about cardiovascular symptoms, says, "You are sick and must stay home." The child feels a great relief from fear, and this reward should reinforce the cardiovascular responses producing pallor and faintness. If such experiences are repeated frequently enough, the child, theoretically, should learn to respond with that kind of symptom. Similarly, another child whose mother ignored the vasomotor responses but was particularly concerned by signs of gastric distress would learn the latter type

of symptom. I want to emphasize, however, that we need careful clinical research to detemine how frequently, if at all, the social conditions sufficient for such theoretically possible learning of visceral symptoms actually occur. Since a given instrumental response can be reinforced by a considerable variety of rewards, and by one reward on one occasion and a different reward on another, the fact that glandular and visceral responses can be instrumentally learned opens up many new theoretical possibilities for the reinforcement of psychosomatic symptoms.

Furthermore, we do not yet know how severe a psychosomatic effect can be produced by learning. While none of the 40 rats rewarded for speeding up their heart rates have died in the course of training under curarization, 7 of the 40 rats rewarded for slowing down their heart rates have died. This statistically reliable difference ($X^2 = 5.6, P < .02$) is highly suggestive, but it could mean that training to speed up the heart helped the rats resist the stress of curare rather than that the reward for slowing down the heart was strong enough to overcome innate regulatory mechanisms and induce sudden death. In either event the visceral learning had a vital effect. At present, DiCara and I are trying to see whether or not the learning of visceral responses can be carried far enough in the noncurarized animal to produce physical damage. We are also investigating the possibility that there may be a critical period in early infancy during which visceral learning has particularly intense and long-lasting effects.

Individual and Cultural Differences

It is possible that, in addition to producing psychosomatic symptoms in extreme cases, visceral learning can account for certain more benign individual and cultural differences. Lacey and Lacey [33] have shown that a given individual may have a tendency, which is stable over a number of years, to respond to a variety of different stresses with the same profile of autonomic responses, while other individuals may have statistically reliable tendencies to respond with different profiles. It now seems possible that differential conditions of learning may account for at least some of these individual differences in patterns of autonomic response.

Conversely, such learning may account also for certain instances in which the same individual responds to the same stress in different ways. For example, a small boy who receives a severe bump in rough-and-tumble play may learn to inhibit the secretion of tears in this situation since his peer group will punish crying by calling it "sissy." But the same small boy may burst into tears when he gets home to his mother, who will not punish weeping and may even reward tears with sympathy.

Similarly, it seems conceivable that different conditions of reward by a culture different from our own may be responsible for the fact that Homer's adult heroes so often "let the big tears fall." Indeed, a former colleague of mine, Herbert Barry III, has analyzed cross-cultural data and found that the amount of crying reported for children seems to be related to the way in which the society reacts to their tears. [34]

I have emphasized the possible role of learning in producing the observed individual differences in visceral responses to stress, which in extreme cases may result in one type of psychosomatic symptom in one person and a different type in another. Such learning does not, of course, exclude innate individual differences in the susceptibility of different organs. In fact, given social conditions under which any form of illness will be rewarded, the symptoms of the most susceptible organ will be the most likely ones to be learned. Furthermore, some types of stress may be so strong that the innate reactions to them produce damage without any learning. My colleagues and I are currently investigating the psychological variables involved in such types of stress. [35]

Therapeutic Training

The experimental work on animals has developed a powerful technique for using instrumental learning to modify glandular and visceral responses. The improved training technique consists of moment-to-moment recording of the visceral function and immediate reward, at first, of very small changes in the desired direction and then of progressively larger ones. The success of this technique suggests that it should be able to produce therapeutic changes. If the patient who is highly motivated to get rid of a symptom understands that a signal, such as a tone, indicates a change in the desired direction, that tone could serve as a powerful reward. Instruction to try to turn the tone on as often as possible and praise for success should increase the reward. As patients find that they can secure some control of the symptom, their motivation should be strengthened. Such a procedure should be well worth trying on any symptom, functional or organic, that is under neural control, that can be continuously monitored by modern instrumentation, and for which a given direction of change is clearly indicated medically — for example, cardiac arrhythmias, spastic colitis, asthma, and those cases of high blood pressure that are not essential compensation for kidney damage.* The obvious cases to begin with are those in which drugs are ineffective or contraindicated. In the light of the fact that our animals learned so much better when under the influence of curare and transferred their training so well to the normal, nondrugged state, it should be worth while to try to use hypnotic suggestion to achieve similar results by enhancing the reward effect of the signal indicating a change in the desired direction, by producing relaxation and regular breathing, and by removing interference from skeletal responses and distraction by irrelevant cues.

Engel and Melmon [36] have reported encouraging results in the use of instrumental training to treat cardiac arrhythmias of organic origin. Randt, Korein, Carmona, and I have had some success in using the method described above to train epileptic

_____

*Objective recording of such symptoms might be useful also in monitoring the effects of quite different types of psychotherapy.

patients in the laboratory to suppress, in one way or another, the abnormal paroxysmal spikes in their electroencephalogram. My colleagues and I are hoping to try learning therapy for other symptoms – for example, the rewarding of high-voltage electroencephalograms as a treatment for insomnia. While it is far too early to promise any cures, it certainly will be worth while to investigate thoroughly the therapeutic possibilities of improved instrumental training techniques.

REFERENCES

1. The Dialogues of Plato. Jowett, B.: (transl.) London, University of Oxford Press. ed. 2, 1875, Vol. 3, Timaeus.
2. Bichat, X.: Recherches Physiologiques sur la Vie et le Mort. Paris, Brosson, Gabon, 1800.
3. Cannon, W. B.: The Wisdom of the Body. New York. Norton, 1932.
4. Alexander, F: Psychosomatic Medicine: Its Principles and Applications. New York, Norton, 1950, pp. 40–41.
5. Kimble, G.A.: Hilgard and Marquis' Conditioning and Learning. ed. 2, New York, Appleton-Century-Crofts, 1961, p. 100.
6. Skinner, B.F.: The Behavior of Organisms. New York, Appleton-Century, 1938; Mowrer, O.H.: Harvard Educ. Rev. *17*:102 (1947).
7. Miller, N. E., and Dollard, J.: Social Learning and Imitation. New Haven, Yale University Press, 1941, Dollard, J., and Miller, N.E., Personality and Psychotherapy. New York, McGraw-Hill, 1950; Miller, N.E.: Psychol. Rev., *58*:375 (1951).
8. Miller, N.E.: Ann. N.Y. Acad. Sci. *92*:830 (1961); in Jones, M.R., Nebraska Symposium on Motivation. (ed.): Lincoln, University of Nebraska Press, 1963; in Proc. 3rd World Congr. Psychiat., Montreal, 1961. *3:* p. 213 (1963).
9. Miller, N. E.: In Proceedings, 18th International Congress of Psychology. Moscow, 1966. in press.
10. Miller, N. E., and Carmona, A.: J. Comp. Physiol. Psychol. *63*:1 (1967).
11. Trowill, J.A.: J. Comp. Physiol. Psychol. *63*:7 (1967).
12. Miller, N.E., and DiCara, L.V.: J. Comp. Physiol. Psychol. *63:* 12 (1967).
13. DiCara, L.V., and Miller, N.E.: Commun. Behav. Biol. *2*:19 (1968).
14. DiCara, L.V., and Miller, N.E.: J. Comp. Physiol. Psychol. *65:* 8 (1968).
15. DiCara, L.V., and Miller, N.E.: J. Comp. Physiol. Psychol. *68*:159 (1969).
16. Ehrlich, D.J., and Malmo, R.B.: Neuropsychologia, *5*:219 (1967).
17. Miller, N. E., and Banuazizi, A.: J. Comp. Physiol. Psychol., *65*:1 (1968).
18. Banuazizi, A: Thesis. Yale University, (1968).
19. Miller, N. E., and DiCara, L. V.: Amer. J. Physiol., *215*:677 (1968).
20. Carmona, A., Miller, N.E., and Demierre, T.: in preparation.
21. Carmona, A: in preparation.
22. DiCara, L. V., and Miller, N. E.: Commun. Behav. Biol. *1:* 209 (1968).
23. DiCara, L.V., and Miller, N.E.: Science *159*:1485 (1968).
24. DiCara, L.V., and Miller, N.E.: Psychosom. Med. *30*:489 (1968).
25. DiCara, L. V., and Weiss, J. M.: J. Comp. Physiol. Psychol., in press.
26. DiCara, L.V., and Miller, N.E.: Physiol. Behav., in press.
27. Miller, N.E. Science, *152*:676 (1966).
28. Carmona, A.: Thesis. Yale University, (1967).
29. For somewhat similar work on the single-cell level, see Olds, J., and Olds, M.E., Delafresnaye, J., Fessard, A., and Konorski, J. (eds.): In Brain Mechanisms and Learning. London, Blackwell (1961).
30. Katkin, E.S., and Murray, N.E.: Psychol. Bull. *70*:52 (1968) for a reply to their criticisms, see Crider, A., Schwartz, G., and Shnidman, S.: Psychol. Bull., in press.
31. Miller, N. E., DiCara, L. V., Wolf, G.: Amer. J. Physiol., *215*:684 (1968).
32. Miller, N.E., Byrne, D., and Worchel, P. (eds.): In Personality Change. New York, Wiley, p. 149 (1964).
33. Lacey, J.I., and Lacey, B.C.: Am. J. Psychol. *71*:50, (1958) Ann. N.Y. Acad Sci., *98*:1257 (1962).
34. Barry, H.III: Personal communication.
35. Miller, N.E.: Proc. N.Y. Acad. Sci., in press.
36. Engel, B.T., and Melmon, K.T.: Personal communication.

20   Physiological Theories of Emotion: A Critical Historical Review from the Standpoint of Behavior Theory

Melvin L. Goldstein

The concept of emotion has been reformulated by several psychological (Brown & Farber,[5] Duffy,[9] Leeper,[25] Miller,[32] Webb,[42] Young,[44]) and physiological (Arnold,[1] Freeman[11] Hebb,[18] Lindsley,[27] Wenger[43]) theorists. Their efforts have tended to clarify research ideas in this area of investigation. The present paper analyzes several traditional and more recent physiological theories of emotion from the viewpoint of behavior theory and shows how several theoreticians approach the basic problem of the definition of emotion. To further such an analysis, certain general criteria for a meaningful definition of emotion and for the use of theoretical constructs in behavior theory are considered before the physiological theories themselves are examined. Comprehensive reviews of empirical findings within the area of emotion are available by Brady,[4] and Grossman,[17] Morgan,[33] and Ruch, Patton, Woodbury, and Towe.[36]

TOWARD AN OPERATIONAL DEFINITION OF EMOTION

Meaningful definitions of emotion, whether behavioral, physiological, or clinical, must fulfill at least the requirements of *verifiability* and *significance*. These two criteria of acceptability of any scientific concept have been emphasized in psychology by Spence[40] and others. The criterion of verifiability could be satisfied by defining the concept so that the laboratory manipulations could be repeated by any qualified investigator. The definition must then specify the relevant environmental, organismic, and response variables. This first criterion is the procedure for defining scientific concepts "operationally" that has been agreed upon by most behavior theorists. It corresponds to the criterion of intersubjective testability of scientific constructs as formulated by Feigl.[10] Such an operational definition, or set of definitions, would tend to decrease the ambiguity that characterizes the concept of emotion and would remove the vague connotations that such terms as "emotion," "feeling," "pleasantness," "hedonic tone," "anxiety," "fear," and "rage" have accumulated through years of common usage. This type of redefinition would avoid the implicit introduction of unspecified meanings into the definition of the concept. Formulation of such redefinitions should lead to *quantifiable*, replicable results.

Operational definitions are admittedly of little value if they cannot be employed to integrate data or to formulate laws. The second criterion of an adequate definition mentioned above, that is, significance, refers to just such a possible objection. The significance of a concept is, according to Spence,[40] "measured in terms of the extent to which [the concept] leads to the formulation of laws about the phenomena. . . ."

The approach to the problem of emotion that has been outlined above is in general agreement with the suggestions of Brown and Farber[5] that emotions be defined as intervening variables.

The empirical referents of theoretical constructs may be behavioral, physiological, or neurophysiological events. Level

Goldstein, M. L.: Physiological theories of emotion: A critical historical review from the standpoint of behavior theory. Psychol. Bull. *69:* 23–40 (1968).

of description in itself should presuppose nothing at all about the sophistication of a particular theory. Whether a behavioral or neurophysiological construct is used depends, primarily, upon the kinds of data with which the individual scientist deals. The behavioral scientist sometimes has greater success with his type of construct than does the neurophysiologist, perhaps because behavioral events are at a much simpler operational level than are neurophysiological events. For example, the latency of a rat jumping a hurdle in the classical aversive or fear conditioning situation[13, 25] is a much simpler event, operationally, than electroencephalographic recordings taken in conjunction with such an event in an attempt to trace the particular neural pathways that might be involved. A behavioral event is also much simpler than tracings of the somatic sensory afferent pathways in the immobilized animal using the evoked response technique in a search for "pain" pathways or centers.

The possibility of reductive explanations of behavioral phenomena depends, in the first instance, upon the establishment of a number of empirical behavior laws, upon the degree to technological sophistication within a particular research area, and upon the ability of the theoretician to make coordinating definitions among the various levels of observable events. Adequate reductive explanations of behavioral phenomena do not seem likely unless *quantifiable* statements can be made at each level, that is, the behavioral, physiological, and neurophysiological. Within the area of emotion, such an approach is being attempted by the behaviorists, notably by Miller[32] and Grossman.[17] Nonbehavioristic workers in the area of neural mechanisms of emotion generally use nonquantifiable terminology such as "hiss," "growl," and "purr" rather than objective behavioral tests, so that any kind of reductionism does not seem possible.

THE CONCEPT OF EMOTION IN BEHAVIOR THEORY

Before examining physiological theories of emotion, several attempts of behavior

theorists to systematize emotion within a nonphysiological framework are reviewed. This enables evaluation of the extent to which the two approaches conform with the criteria for formulation of theoretical constructs and the extent to which they have led to the formulation of empirical laws.

Miller's and Mowrer's Concepts of Fear

Miller's[30,31,32] use of fear as an inferred motivational concept can serve as an example of one behavior theorist's efforts to deal with emotion. This is one of several attempts to include emotion under the category of motivation.[9, 24, 42] According to Miller,[31] fear consists of "an innate [internal] response to certain stimuli, such as pain, and the fear response innately produces the fear stimulus, just as electric shock produces pain." Responses that are instrumental in reducing the strength of the fear stimulus will be reinforced. The fear response can be conditioned to various stimulus aspects of the environment. After conditioning has occurred, the originally neutral stimulus elicits the fear response in the absence of the noxious stimulus. A well-known experiment by Miller[30] illustrates the operation of these principles. Miller trained rats to fear a white compartment by shocking them in it and allowing them to escape into an adjoining black compartment. He then placed the rats into the white compartment without administering the electric shock and found that the animals continued to run into the black compartment. He next changed the conditions so that the animals could escape from the white compartment only by learning to turn a small wheel. Most of the animals learned this new response. The previously acquired drive of fear was the only relevant drive present during these learning trials, the electric shock having been eliminated after the original fear acquisition trials. The stages of learning involved in this experiment and the theoretical constructs employed are summarized in Figure 20-1, which illustrates Miller's theory of fear conditioning. During the first stage, pairing of the unconditioned stimulus (S_u) with the conditioned stimu-

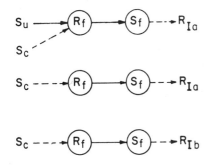

Figure 20-1. Miller's conceptualization of fear (after Miller, 1951). (S_u = unconditioned stimulus, a shock; S_c = conditioned stimulus, the white compartment; R_f = fear response; S_f = fear stimulus; R_{1a} = instrumental response, running into black compartment; R_{1b} = instrumental response, turning the small wheel. Unlearned connections are indicated by solid lines, learned connections by dotted lines. Theoretical constructs are encircled.)

lus (S_c) elicits an innate "fear" response (R_f) which in turn elicits the fear stimulus (S_f) which can be conditioned to the instrumental response (R_{1a}). During the second stage, S_c elicits the sequence leading to R_{1a}. The third stage involves substitution of one instrumental response (R_{1a}) for another (R_{1b}). It should be recognized, of course, that the fear response is not directly measurable. Its strength is inferred from the vigor of wheel turning[30] or from latency of hurdle jumping.[13, 28]

Mowrer's[35] treatment of this problem, although similar to Miller's, is presented in different terminology and has led to the development of various avoidance conditioning techniques. According to Mowrer, the conditioned stimulus serves as a "danger signal" and elicits a state which has been variously termed "fear," "anxiety," "expectancy," and "set." In addition to these minor differences, Mowrer postulated two learning processes to account, respectively, for the conditioning of the fear response to the conditioned stimulus and for the learning of responses that are instrumental in reducing the fear state. Mowrer has attempted to specify at least the gross neurological mechanisms involved in these two learning processes. He has speculated that, in a general

fashion, fear conditioning depends upon the autonomic nervous sytem, while the learning of instrumental responses is mediated by the central nervous system. Solomon and Wynne[39] have made a test of this hypothesis by attempting to condition sympathectomized and normal dogs in an avoidance situation. They found that although both normal and operated animals could be trained in the problem, the operated animals required more than twice as many trials as the normal subjects to learn. Sympathectomized animals were extinguished after 650 trials. It was concluded that although the autonomic nervous sytem is not absolutely necessary for avoidance conditioning, it does play some role.

The Miller-Mowrer analysis of fear is far from a comprehensive one, although it has led to much research. The systematic contribution to the measurement of the fear response of such variables as the strength of the unconditioned stimulus, the time relationships between the conditioned and unconditioned stimuli, the number of reinforcements, the presence of irrelevant drives, and various extinction procedures have yet to be determined precisely, although much progress has recently been made.[13, 23, 26, 28]

Miller and Mowrer have attempted to integrate the concept of fear, or acquired motivation, with primary motivation and learning. Until such a redefinition has been more completely demonstrated experimentally, the concept of fear is limited directly to descriptions of those few experimental situations that employ classical conditioning and must exclude much relevant work on avoidance and escape behavior. A step in this direction is the notion that several of the differences between classical aversive conditioning and shuttle-box avoidance conditioning may include control of the duration of the unconditioned stimulus in the former situation and the relative incidence and type of response competition in the two situations.[16] The investigation of the relative contribution of limbic system structures, such as the amygdaloid nuclei, to classical aversive conditioning has only just begun.[15] The contribution of specific neural structures to the different types of avoidance conditioning and to the conditioned emotional response has attracted much more research effort, recently reviewed by Grossman [17] and McCleary. [29]

Brown and Farber's Theory of Frustration

The importance in theory construction of specifying functional relations between concepts as well as employing strictly operational definitions of these concepts has been emphasized by Brown and Farber.[5] They have presented the beginnings of a theory of frustration in which emotional concepts, such as "frustration" and "competitive tendency," are used as intervening variables that are defined operationally and are related to other Hullian theoretical constructs such as habit strength, drive, irrelevant drive, and excitatory potential. Figure 20–2 illustrates the essentials of Brown and Farber's theory of frustration. In general, antecedent conditions of blocking, nonreinforcement of an ongoing response tendency, or competition between two response tendencies (sEr_0, sEr_c) results in the frustration state (F). This frustration state in turn generates an irrelevant drive (D) and frustration stimuli (S_F) which combine with the original excitatory tendencies to produce the observed responses.

Comparison of Brown and Farber's approach to frustration with Miller and Mowrer's formulation of fear reveals certain differences in the use of theoretical constructs. The most important of these differences is the tendency of Brown and Farber to relate emotional constructs to *a variety* of nonemotional behavior constructs. Miller and Mowrer also employ this procedure, but their efforts are restricted to a simple equation of fear with secondary drive, and possibly with habit strength.

The types of intervening variables used by the two sets of theorists also differ. Miller's "fear as a response-produced stimulus" may be classified as an intervening process variable defined behaviorally. This construct can acquire empirical status only if the relationships between the internal fear response and the fear stimulus it

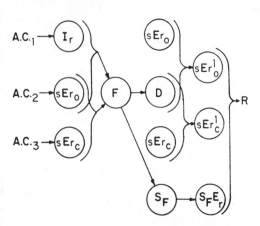

Figure 20–2. Brown and Farber's theory of frustration ($A.C._1$ = antecedent manipulable conditions of blocking, nonreinforcement, and work; $A.C._2$, $A.C._3$ = antecedent manipulable conditions of number of reinforcements, hours of deprivation, noxious stimulation, etc., that is, the variables commonly included in the Hullian constructs of drive and habit stength; I_r = competitive inhibitory tendency; sEr_0 = initial excitatory strength of ongoing response tendency; sEr_c = initial excitatory strength of competing tendency; F = frustration state; D = irrelevant drive due to frustration; S_F = frustration-generated stimuli; sEr'_0 = final excitatory strength of initially dominant response tendency; sEr'_c = final excitatory strength of initially competing response tendency; $S_F E_r$ = strength of excitatory tendency, either innate or learned, associated with frustration; R = observable responses. Theoretical constructs are encircled.)

produces are established. The construct will then no longer be necessary, for it will have been replaced by a set of empirical laws. Brown and Farber also employ intervening process variables, for example, "frustration stimulus," but, in contrast with Miller and Mowrer, they make some attempt to specify the innate and learned referents of this concept. Their basic emotional construct "frustration state" is an intervening state variable, a type of variable which Miller and Mowrer do not employ in their discussions of fear.

PHYSIOLOGICAL THEORIES OF EMOTION

The remainder of this paper examines the use of theoretical constructs in physiological theories of emotion. No attempt is made to present a complete survey of such theories since there are already adequate summaries in the literature.[17, 27, 44] Instead, the theoretical structure of traditional peripheral and central theories and some more recent attempts to systematize the concept of emotion are described.

William James's Peripheral Theory

James's[20, 21] theory of emotion is important primarily for its emphasis on physiological variables as opposed to the analysis of emotion as an element of consciousness. The physiological research that the theory has stimulated suggests that it may be recast into a more objective terminology that will permit experimental verification. This reformulation has been accomplished, implicitly, by several investigators who have tested various implications of the theory. James's theory of emotion, although untestable in its original form, is represented by the following quotation:

An object falls on a sense-organ and is apperceived by the appropriate cortical center.... Quick as a flash, the reflex currents pass down through their pre-ordained channels, alter the condition of muscle, skin, and viscus, and these alterations, apperceived like the original object, in as many specific portions of the cortex, combine with it in consciousness and transform it from an object-simply-apprehended into an object-emotionally-felt. ... My thesis ... is that *the bodily changes follow directly the* Perception *of the exciting fact, and that our feeling of same changes as they occur* Is *the emotion.*[20, p. 190]

There are certain assumptions in this statement, and in James's more complete elaboration of his theory, that must be considered in greater detail:

1. There are both afferent and efferent neural pathways (reflex connections) between unspecified cortical centers and the muscles, skin, and viscera.

2. This mechanism is "innate" and "anticipatory of the specific features of the environment in which [the organism] is to live."[20]

3. By a process similar to association, previously neutral situations can acquire the power to elicit this mechanism. This assumption is implied in James's[20] state-

ment that "a nervous tendency to discharge being once there, all sorts of unforseen things may pull the trigger and let loose the effects."

4. The mechanism is similar to a reverberating circuit in that once excited it is self-perpetuating. According to James,[20] "each fit of sobbing makes the sorrow more acute, and calls forth another fit stronger still, until at last repose only ensues with lassitude and with the apparent exhaustion of the machinery."

5. Each emotional experience can be identified with a unique pattern of bodily change. James's[20] description of this correspondence is apparently inconsistent with his main thesis concerning the sequence of emotional behavior and emotional experience, for he said that "the various permutations and combinations of which ... organic activities are susceptible, make it ... possible that no shade of emotion, however slight, would be without *a bodily reverberation* as unique, when taken in its totality, as is the mental mood itself."

6. There are no special or separate centers for emotion in the cortex. "The emotional brain-processes not only resemble the ordinary sensorial brain-processes, but in very truth, are nothing but such processes variously combined."[20] This appears to contradict Point 2 and James's statement to the effect that bodily sensations combine in consciousness with the original perception of the object with the result that the "object is emotionally felt."

7. Emotional experience may be inferred from verbal reports in emotional situations. James was not altogether clear on this point. In his 1948 discussion of actors' reports of experienced emotion he apparently accepted the verbal report as an indicator of emotional experience, but in his description of a case of pathological anaesthesia he seemed to confuse emotional experience with emotional behavior, for he described the patient as "tranquil ... not irritable, not quarrelsome" and emotionally apathetic. These are generally thought of as signs of emotional behavior, not of emotional experience. Figure 20-3 illustrates James's theory of emotion. S_c,

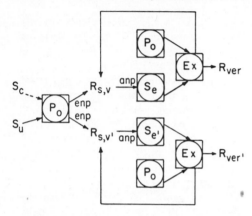

Figure 20-3. Conceptualization of James's theory of emotion. (S_c = "neutral situation," or conditioned stimulus; S_u = "emotion eliciting situation," or unconditioned stimulus; P_o = "object-simply-apprehended"; enp = efferent neural pathways; $R_{s,v}$ and $R_{s,v}^1$ = somatic and visceral responses, or emotional behavior; anp = afferent neural pathways; S_e and S_e^1 = "apperception of body changes," or proprioceptive stimuli; Ex = "object-emotionally-felt," or emotional experience; R_{ver} and R_{ver}^1 = verbal report. Learned connections are indicated by dotted lines, unlearned connections by solid lines. Theoretical constructs are encircled. Symbols enclosed in rectangles refer to cortical states or processes.)

the "neutral situation" combines with S_u "the emotion eliciting situation" to produce the "object-simply-apprehended," P_o. This results in somatic and visceral responses, or emotional behavior, which in turn lead to "apperception of bodily changes," or proprioceptive stimuli. This leads to emotional experience which results in a verbal report (R_{ver}).

One can now determine the kind of experiments that should yield information relevant to James's theory. A comprehensive review of published experiments will not be attempted here; instead, the types of investigations that have been stimulated by the theory are discussed. Much of this research, although valuable in itself, does not offer evidence relevant to the theory because of certain misunderstandings concerning the nature of the assumptions and theoretical constructs. The types of research are as follows:

1. *Determination of the afferent and efferent connections between the cortex and the muscles, skin, and viscera.* This is

perhaps the most obvious approach, since absence of afferent or efferent connections would exclude the possibility that the emotional mechanism is as James described it. There is some evidence [22] that afferent visceral impulses reach the cortex and that afferent somatic impulses also terminate in cortical tissue. [34]

2. *Investigation of the innate and learned characteristics of response patterns in emotional situations.* Evidence bearing on this question would not necessarily be relevant to James's main thesis since it does not matter whether conditioned or unconditioned stimuli arouse the emotional mechanism. The effects, and causal sequence, should be the same in either case.*

3. *Determination of specific neural centers whose removal or activation will influence emotional behavior.* Reference to Figure 20-3 shows that according to James, destruction of the cortex should result in the elimination of both emotional behavior and emotional experience since the neural processes mediating these effects are triggered by the cortex. Bard's[3] localization of this neural process in the hypothalamus rather than the cortex emphasizes James's inability to specify in detail the important neural mechanisms involved in emotion. It is questionable, however, whether the "sham rage" described by Bard is the same class of response as the "emotional behavior" described by James.

4. *Determination of the physiological correlates of emotional experience.* This kind of experimentation is especially difficult because it involves an introspective differentiation of emotional experience into mutually exclusive states. Verbal reports could, however, be correlated with various visceral and somatic patterns of behavior, and if a relationship were discovered between these variables the results would have some bearing on the theory. Cannon[7] presented evidence which indicates that there is no differentiation of visceral responses in the various emotional states, but that the sympathetic nervous

---

*Compare Landis and Hunt[24] on the startle pattern and Watson[41] on innate emotional responses.

system is dominant in all emergency situations. He apparently correlated visceral and somatic response patterns since he was dealing with animals that are unable to introspect. Cannon's confusion of emotional experience with emotional behavior is discussed below. Arnold,[1] on the other hand, claimed to have distinguished at least two patterns of autonomic response in emotional situations.

5. *Determination of the effect of experimental destruction of neural connections with the viscera.* Sherrington's much quoted experiment[7] in which he denervated the viscera of an animal is sometimes used as evidence against James's theory. Sherrington's animals showed signs of emotional expression. Cannon[6] concluded that this evidence was detrimental to James's theory since, according to Cannon, the theory should have predicted that with central nervous connections to the viscera severed, emotional behavior could not occur. Cannon[6] admitted that he could have no knowledge of the animals' emotional experience, but then went on to say that

James attributed the chief part of the felt emotion to sensations from the viscera. . . . According to [James] . . . the felt emotion should have largely disappeared. . . . . The animals *acted* however . . . with a lessening of the intensity of emotional display. In other words, operations which, in terms of the theory, largely or completely destroy emotional feeling, nevertheless leave the animals behaving as angrily, as joyfully, as fearfully as ever [p. 120].

Reference to Figure 20-3 shows that Cannon missed the point. James differentiated between emotional behavior and emotional experience. Cannon believed that he did not and that, according to his interpretation of James, one could not occur in the absence of the other. According to the conceptualization represented in Figure 20-3, emotional behavior involving skeletal muscles can occur as long as the connections from the cortex to the muscles remain intact. The effect on emotional behavior of severing the neural connections to the viscera is therefore irrelevant to James's theory of emotion. Cannon apparently inferred emotional experience from the presence of emotional behavior, as

James sometimes did. Figure 20-3 indicates that emotional experience can be inferred only from the verbal report and not from skeletal muscle or visceral responses.

6. *Determination of the effects of artificial induction of visceral changes.* Several experimenters,[8] following James's suggestion that voluntary control of emotional behavior should affect emotional experience, have attempted to produce emotional experience artificially by administering adrenalin to human subjects. The results have been equivocal. Some subjects reported that they experienced "real" emotional states while others reported that the felt "as if" they were afraid. Assuming for the moment that subjects' reports of conscious states can be compared with one another and that one person's report of "fear" refers to the same state as a similar verbal report by another individual, the discrepancy between reports of "real" and "pseudo" emotional states is still to be explained. Figure 20-3 indicates that one should not expect reports of "real" emotion in laboratory situations where the unconditioned or conditioned emotional stimuli are absent. Under such conditions, the verbal report would be mediated by the construct S_e and not by the construct Ex. One might expect such a response to differ from reports of "real" emotion, at least with respect to object reference. Subjects reporting "real" emotion may do so because the experimenter inadvertently introduces conditioned emotional stimuli into the situation. These stimuli, broadly defined, might include the needle used to administer adrenalin as well as other less obvious aspects of the laboratory situation.

This review of James's theory of emotion and of the research it has generated suggests certain conclusions concerning its testability and its value in explaining various experimental results. The theory as formulated by James is untestable, since hypotheses derived from its postulates must be formulated in mentalistic, introspective terminology. The theory as reformulated in the present paper (Figure 20-3) can be tested experimentally, but only with human subjects. The large amount of subhuman experimentation on emotion, although valuable in itself, is irrelevant to the theory, since verbal reports cannot be obtained from animals and emotional experience should be inferred only from verbal reports.

Wenger's Peripheral Theory

Wenger[43] has described a theory of emotion based upon visceral responses which is supposed to be an extension of Lange's position. In an attempt to purify introspective accounts of emotion, Wenger equated visceral response with emotion and showed how this mechanism would function in a "hypothetical robot." Wenger decided, in effect, to deal with emotional behavior and to disregard emotional experience. Wenger's approach is illustrated by the following quotation:

In order to put emotion into a machine I concluded that it would have to be *reaction and nothing else but reaction;* and the next question became — reaction of what? In the literature I could find only two cores of agreement: 1. Emotional behavior involves changes in activity of the autonomic nervous system. 2. Emotional behavior is related to frustration, anticipated frustration, satisfaction, or anticipated satisfaction of a need. It was a simple matter to provide the hypothetical robot with a set of drive switches related to its needs . . . and to provide it with a pair of reverberating circuits which influenced its overt behavior and were particularly sensitive to its drive stimuli. . . . For me, then, emotion became inner motion, i.e., visceral action, as elicited by these reverberating circuits — the autonomic nervous system.[43,p.4]

Wenger further suggested that states which are ordinarily termed "emotions" are really "emotional complexes" and that there is no adequate terminology to describe "emotions per se."

Such terms as "fear," "anger," or "jealousy" imply not only an emotion, but also the external stimulus situation, the perception of that stimulus, the perception of visceral action, overt expression, and related ideation. Fear, then, is not simple emotion, but organismic reaction. It is emotion plus, and we might better refer to it, as to other organismic reactions involving marked visceral change, as emotional complexes.[43,p.8]

Figure 20-4 illustrates Wenger's theory of emotion. Conditioned stimuli paired with unconditioned stimuli lead to perception of the external stimulus situation. Arousal

of the autonomic nervous system leads to visceral responses, which in turn lead to drive stimuli or "perception of visceral action." These drive stimuli eventuate in skeletal muscle responses and the verbal report.

Wenger's theory of emotion is similar in certain respects to the kind of reformulation of the problem proposed by the behavior theorists. The discussion of fear as an "emotional complex" involving both stimulus and response variables is similar to Webb's[42] statement that emotion should be defined as an intervening variable. The two approaches differ, however, in that Wenger considers the S-R relationship and its intervening processes as the "emotional complex," for example, fear, and reserves the term "emotion" for visceral action — the intervening processes — while Webb would call the intervening processes the "emotion," for example, fear. This may be nothing more than a semantic difference. Wenger and Webb are probably referring to similar mechanisms and the important point, upon which they agree, is that emotion should be inferred from observations of both stimulus and responsive

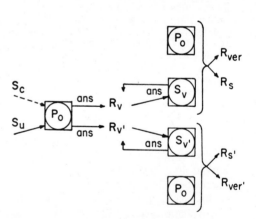

Figure 20-4. Conceptualization of Wenger's theory of emotion. (S_c = conditioned stimuli; S_u = unconditioned stimuli; P_o = "perception of the external stimulus situation"; ans = autonomic nervous system; R_v and R_v^1 = visceral responses; S_v and S_v^1 = drive stimuli or "perception of visceral action"; R_s and R_s^1 = skeletal muscle responses; R_{ver} and R_{ver}^1 = verbal report. Learned connections are indicated by dotted lines, unlearned connections by solid lines. Theoretical constructs are encircled. Symbols enclosed in rectangles refer to cortical states or processes.)

variables and not from observations of one or the other variable alone.

Comparison of James's and Wenger's theories reveals several interesting differences between the two approaches. James formulated his theory in introspective terminology that made it untestable. Animal experiments are irrelevant with respect to its major assumptions. Wenger's theory, on the other hand, can be subjected to test by both animal and human experimentation. This results from Wenger's emphasis on emotional behavior rather than emotional experience and from his classification of skeletal response and the external signs of visceral action — but not visceral action itself — as emotional behavior. Wenger's major theoretical construct, that is, drive stimulus, might be labeled an intervening process variable defined in psychological terms. There is still, however, a remnant of introspectionism in the theory, since the drive stimulus can determine both emotional behavior (skeletal responses) and the verbal report, from which Wenger infers "feeling." However, Wenger's theory can be employed to set up objective animal experiments. One could simply ignore the verbal response and search for relationships between observable S-R variables.

Wenger [43] has presented several suggestions for research that stem from his theoretical position:

1. *Investigation of "differential patterns of autonomically innervated activity."* Information with respect to this problem would be important for both James's and Wenger's theories, since they both assume that differential patterns of activity, somatic or visceral, are in some way responsible for various emotional experiences and responses.

2. *Investigation of "stimuli originally effective for different patterns of emotion."* This would involve the determination of the relationships between verbal responses and "drive stimuli" (see Figure 20-4).

3. *Investigation of "overt and covert reaction patterns in striate musculature that occur with changes in visceral activity," or determination of the relationships between R_s and R_v.* See Figure 20-4.

4. *Investigation of "perceptions . . . concurrent with emotional change," or determination of the relationship between S_v and R_v.* See Figure 20-4.

5. *Investigation of "thought processes concurrent with emotional change," or determination of the relationship between $P_o + S_v$ and R_v.* See Figure 20-4.

Of these five types of research proposed by Wenger, only the last two need involve verbal reports or human experimentation. The first three could be performed quite adequately with animals. Wenger's theory shows a marked advance over James's in both testability and in relevance to animal research in this area.

Cannon's Central Theory

The distinction between central and peripheral theories of emotion is based primarily upon the relative importance assigned to central neural mechanisms. Some of the criticisms of James's peripheral theory advanced by Cannon have already been discussed. Cannon's theoretical position is now examined in greater detail.

Cannon[6, 7] emphasized the role of the thalamus and other subcortical centers in emotion. His view was that the release from cortical inhibition of neural impulses originating in the thalamus was the basis for both emotional experience and emotional behavior.

Cannon[6] has described his theory as follows:

An external situation stimulates receptors and the consequent excitation starts impulses towards the cortex. [These impulses are] associated with conditioned processes which determine the direction of the response. Either because the response is initiated in a certain mode or figure and the cortical neurones therefore stimulate the thalamic process, or because on the centripetal course the impulses from the receptors excite the thalamic processes, they are roused and ready for discharge . . . [The thalamic] neurones do not require detailed innervation from above in order to be driven into action. Being *released* for action is a primary condition for their service to the body — they then discharge precipitately and intensely. . . . When these neurones discharge in a particular combination, they not only innervate muscles and viscera but also excite afferent paths to the cortex by direct connection or by irradiation. . . . *The peculiar quality of the emotion is added to simple sensation when the thalamic processes are roused* (p. 120).

Figure 20-5 illustrates Cannon's theory of emotion. Conditioned stimuli combine with unconditioned stimuli to lead to the perception of the object, or simple sensation, which results in a pattern of neural discharge in the thalamus. Conduction over afferent and efferent nerve paths leads to the verbal report and somatic and visceral responses (emotional behavior).

Figure 20-5 reveals several important features of Cannon's theory:

1. Emotional experience and emotional behavior are for the first time *explicitly* differentiated.[7]

2. Thalamic impulses may be aroused directly through cortical mediation.

3. The thalamus is recognized as a neural center that both receives and transmits impulses.

4. Emotional experience is still referred to as the result of the combination of simple sensations with "a peculiar quality," or type, of sensation.

5. Emotional experience is inferred from the verbal report.

6. Emotional experience is not the result

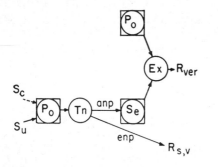

Figure 20-5. Conceptualization of Cannon's theory of emotion. (S_c = conditioned stimuli; S_u = unconditioned stimuli; P_o = perception of the object, or "simple sensation"; Tn = pattern of neural discharge in the thalamus; anp = afferent nerve paths; enp = efferent nerve paths; S_c = emotional stimuli produced by thalamic discharge; Ex = emotional experience; R_{ver} = verbal report; $R_{s,v}$ = somatic and visceral responses, or emotional behavior. Learned connections are indicated by dotted lines, unlearned connections by solid lines. Theoretical constructs are encircled. Symbols enclosed in rectangles refer to cortical states or processes.)

of emotional behavior, but is independently aroused by thalamic processes.

Although Cannon's major theoretic constructs, that is, Tn and S_e, are defined in neurological terms, he has endowed them with different degrees of empirical content. The construct S_e — "the peculiar quality of the emotion" — is as meaningful as James's "apperception of bodily changes." Both James and Cannon attempted to infer this construct from introspective accounts or from emotional behavior, although it was at times described in pseudoneurological terminology. Cannon made an effort to specify the neurological mechanisms identified by the constructs P_o and Tn. He stated that the cortex exercises an inhibitory function over the thalamus and that the thalamus is the origin of neural patterns which contribute the emotional quale to perception. This dichotomy is reminiscent of the time-worn distinction between "higher intellectual" and "lower emotional" processes, and it would be an anachronism were it not for Bard's[3] investigations of cortical and subcortical mechanisms in emotion.

Cannon[7] presented experimental and clinical evidence in support of his theory that serves the additional function of identifying the areas of research where new relevant information might be found. Some of the evidence for his belief that "the thalamic region is a coordinating center for so-called 'emotional' reactions" is as follows:

1. Bard's[3] findings that decorticate cats exhibit "sham rage" and that this reaction disappears when the thalamus is removed.

2. Cannon's[7] finding that "a tumor affecting one side of the thalamus in man results in unilateral laughter or the grimace of pain ... although *cortical* control of the same muscles is bilateral."

3. Cannon's[7] finding that "temporary impairment of cortical control centers in light anesthesia or permanent impairment by disease releases free and often prolonged weeping or laughing."

Bard[3] has summarized attempts to specify the cortical and subcortical mechanisms in emotion. Once these mechanisms have been identified, the theoretical constructs employed by Cannon should no longer be necessary. Neurophysiological correlates would take their place. Cannon's relatively naïve notion of cortical inhibition has already been modified as the result of experiments that have attempted accurate localization of neural mechanisms in the cortex, hypothalamus, and lower centers. It has been found, for example, that the telencephalon not only inhibits thalamic discharges, but that it also "increases the excitability of specific brainstem mechanisms, augments the range of rage-provoking stimuli, and renders aggressive behavior more effective in respect to each adequate stimulus."[3] Bard removed the neocortex in cats, leaving the rhinencephalon intact. This operation resulted in a state of "placidity" that could be changed to one of "ferocity" by removal of the amygdaloid complex of the rhinencephalon. Bard[3] concluded from these and other experiments that

normally the neocortex tends to lower the threshold of rage reactions. . . . The inhibitory influences [of the rhinencephalon] become dominant when the neocortex is removed. [In addition] there originates from or passes through the region of the amygdala an influence which powerfully inhibits the brain-stem mechanisms in the execution of angry behavior [p. 235].

Bard has also shown that removal of the amygdala and pyriform cortex in cats, leaving the neocortex intact, results in angry behavior which is object-directed and can be "evoked by stimuli, e.g., visual, that are ineffective in wholly decorticate animals." In contradistinction to these findings, however, are the more recent results of Schreiner and Kling[37, 38] and Gastaut,[12] who have described taming and refractoriness to rage-producing stimuli following amygdala and pyriform lobe lesions in the cat. Resolution of these discrepancies, which may be due to differences in operative techniques and to different observational criteria, awaits further research.

Bard's extensive work on cortical and subcortical mechanisms in emotion makes it possible to modify Cannon's theory so that it can be applied more adequately to expression of emotion in intact, healthy animals. These experiments help to define the relationships between neural structures and emotional behavior.

Arnold's Theory

Arnold[2] has proposed an "excitatory" theory of emotion, in reply to Cannon's "inhibitory" theory, that is apparently little more than a revision of James's theory. According to Arnold, "Emotion seems to be an excitatory phenomenon which is not unitary but can be analyzed into at least two divisions, fear and anger, which are transmitted over separate cortico-thalamic pathways, touching off different hypothalamic effector systems, and producing different physiological effects." The thalamus is thought of as a "motor relay station to the hypothalamic effectors" and a "sensory relay station to the cortical areas where peripheral changes is one of the bases for emotional experience."

According to this theory, the sequence of events in an emotional situation would be as follows: Incoming sensory stimulation is "evaluated" in the cortex (or, in decorticate animals, in the thalamus). This process of evaluation results in an emotional attitude, or feeling, for example, fear or anger, which

initiates nerve impulses from the cortex to centers in the thalamus-hypothalamus, which touch off the appropriate pattern of emotional expression [or emotional behavior] as well as the corresponding peripheral changes. The autonomic effects thus produced . . . are then reported back to the cortex via the afferent sensory pathways.[2,p.28]

A "secondary evaluation" then occurs which adds a "secondary feeling," that is, "I am afraid," to the original perception. Figure 20-6 illustrates Arnold's rather complicated theory of emotion. Sensory stimulation (S) leads to emotional "attitudes" which activate the thalamus. Conduction over efferent nerve pathways leads to autonomic responses and emotional behavior, or somatic responses. Somatic responses eventually lead to the verbal report.

Figure 20-6 shows that the primary difference between James and Arnold is the latter's more detailed speculation regarding central mechanisms. Both theories consider emotional experience as essentially based upon skeletal muscle and visceral

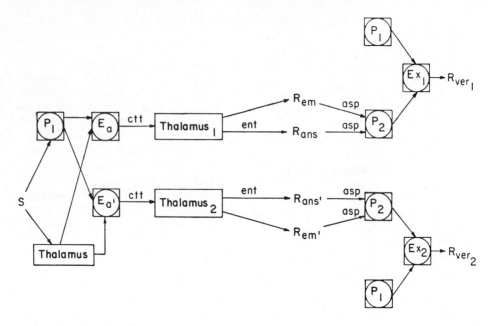

Figure 20-6. Conceptualization of Arnold's theory of emotion. (S = sensory stimulation; P_1 = evaluation of stimuli; E_a and $E_a{}^1$ = emotional attitudes, that is, fear and anger; ctt = cortico-thalamic tract; $Thalamus_1$ and $Thalamus_2$ = thalamo-hypothalamic centers; ent = efferent nerve pathways; R_{ans} and $R_{ans}{}^1$ = autonomic responses; R_{em} and $R_{em}{}^1$ = emotional behavior, or somatic responses; asp = afferent sensory pathways; P_2 = secondary evaluation; Ex_1 and Ex_2 = emotional experience or "secondary feeling"; R_{ver_1} and R_{ver_2} = verbal report. Theoretical constructs are encircled. Symbols enclosed in rectangles refer to cortical states or processes.)

responses, although Arnold's theory is more explicit concerning the cortical processes which generate the appropriate neural patterns mediating emotions. Arnold's use of the terms "feeling" and "secondary feeling" is, however, somewhat ambiguous. These concepts are apparently used to refer to feeling resulting from evaluation of the external stimuli and evaluation of the bodily states, respectively. James, on the other hand, reserved the term "feeling" for the simple perception of bodily changes. Perception of the external situation was, for him, merely a cold, intellectual experience.

Arnold collected a variety of experimental and clinical evidence to support the theory and to demonstrate its superiority to Cannon's theory of cortical inhibition. According to Arnold, the fact that sham rage is not always "more intense, or more frequent, or more lasting than rage in normal animals" suggests that removal of the cortex does not result in disinhibition or in a gain in function, as Cannon believed

it did. If Cannon's theory of cortical disinhibition is valid, then "an emotion once aroused should . . . go on until the animal is completely exhausted." Arnold is apparently unaware that particularly in a decorticate animal, external stimuli must be present for a response to occur. In an intact animal, cortical mediation might prolong the effects of a stimulus, but it is difficult to see how this could occur in a decorticate preparation. Bard[2] has shown, in fact, that lasting and object-oriented sham rage can be elicited in a cat with neocortex intact but with lesions in the amygdaloid complex. (Arnold's point that "removal of the cortex does not result in an increase of fear or other emotional reactions" is, however, well taken.)

Arnold's interpretation of sham rage is that it results from the "short-circuiting" of sensory impulses in the thalamus and the subsequent shunting of these impulses to the "hypothalamic effector centers which mediate the expression of rage." Explosive rage reactions are supposedly due to acute irritation caused by scar tissue. Normal rage responses in decorticate cats should occur in the absence of such irritation. In the intact animals, on the other hand, "the annoying situation will be perceived cortically, and from the cortex excitatory impulses [will] touch off the hypothalamic effector pattern."

Evidence that prefrontal lobotomy reduces fear was presented by Arnold in support of this view. She believes that since the "perception of fear" (P_1) is eliminated by the operation, the hypothalamic mechanism mediating fear responses cannot be activated. One wonders, however, why impulses could not be "short-circuited," or "shunted" directly to the hypothalamus, and be "perceived subcortically" as are stimuli which produce rage in decorticate cats. According to Arnold, anger persists in lobotomies because "anger stimulates primarily the parasympathetic nervous system," while fear stimulates the sympathetic nervous system, and it is the cortico-thalamic sympathetic pathways that are divided in this operation. Why, then, one might ask, can anger be aroused in decorticate cats?

What type of evidence could possibly refute such a theory? To what does the term "subcortical perception" refer, and how do cats perceive and "evaluate" external stimuli? These concepts were introduced in a vague and uncritical manner by Arnold and serve merely to confuse the issue. Indiscriminate application of the theory to both human and cat behavior is one of its fundamental inadequacies.

Freeman's Dynamotor Theory

Freeman[11] has proposed a theory that accounts for emotion in terms of "neuromuscular homeostasis." Emotional experiences are described as "perceptual meaning-structures" resulting from cortical interaction between exteroceptor impulses, "proprioception from learned reactions made to [external stimuli] on previous occasions, and backlash from unlearned thalamic motor discharge." Emotional behavior apparently consists of primitive,

unlearned thalamic motor discharges and learned reactions. This process is described in greater detail in the following quotation from Freeman: [11]

Excitation from exteroceptors and interoceptors is normally carried to cortical centers where highly differentiated patterns of neuromuscular discharge are developed. However, such excitation will break over and influence subcortical motor centers if it is too intense, or if a competition or "conflict" of excitation within the cortical centers causes the release of lower centers from inhibitory control. . . . Widespread motor processes of a non-discriminatory character are aroused, and backlash effects therefrom flood the cortex with a mass of diffuse interoceptive excitation which interacts with the exteroceptive excitation to produce the emotional experience (p. 287).

Figure 20-7 illustrates Freeman's theory of emotion. External stimuli combine with conditioned stimuli to produce a pattern of neuromuscular discharge, conflict of discharges, and, by way of the thalamus, somatic and visceral responses which lead to the verbal report.

Figure 20-7 shows that Freeman has attempted a reconciliation of peripheral and central theory. Both proprioceptive stimulation and hypothalamic processes are

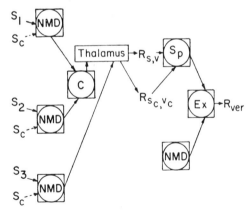

Figure 20-7. Conceptualization of Freeman's theory of emotion. (S_1 and S_2 = external stimuli; S_3 = intense external stimuli; S_c = conditioned stimuli; NMD = pattern of neuromuscular discharge; C = conflict of NMDs; $R_{s,v}$ = somatic and visceral responses; R_{s_c,v_c} = conditioned responses; S_p = proprioceptive stimulation or "backlash"; Ex = emotional experience or "perceptual meaning-structure"; R_{ver} = verbal report. Theoretical constructs are encircled. Symbols enclosed in rectangles refer to cortical-subcortical states or processes.)

considered to be responsible for emotional experience. In this respect there is disagreement with Cannon, who believed that emotional experience results entirely from afferent thalamic impulses. Cannon realized the necessity for differentiating between emotional behavior and emotional experience, and he apparently believed that the most appropriate way to accomplish this would be to postulate mutually exclusive physiological correlates for the two. Freeman has demonstrated, on the other hand, that it is possible to admit the experiential effects of proprioceptive stimulation and still maintain the essential distinction between the two aspects of emotion. It has already been shown that Arnold attempted a similar integration — although she denied the mechanism of cortical inhibition — but that she was unsuccessful because of her ambiguous use of hypothetical constructs denoting mentalistic cortical processes. Freeman has avoided this error by defining most of his hypothetical constructs in neurophysiological terminology. The one outstanding exception to this statement is, of course, "perceptual meaning-structure," which we have equated with emotional experience.

If one were not interested in emotional experience but simply wished to study emotional behavior in animals, one could still proceed within the general framework of Freeman's theory by disregarding emotional experience and concentrating instead on the behavior produced by intense stimulation, stimulation requiring conflicting response patterns, or neutral stimuli presented under these conditions. Freeman's theory might well be employed to supplement Brown and Farber's theory of frustration, since the latter's approach is also based upon the effects of conflicting response tendencies. If one felt the need to postulate the existence of neurophysiological processes in Brown and Farber's rats, Freeman's concepts might perhaps be the most appropriate to us.

Hebb's Central Theory

Hebb [18] has proposed a provocative theory of behavioral organization that includes certain observations relevant to the neural basis of emotion. The theory is impressive primarily because of the wide range of phenomena it seeks to integrate and because it gives some indication of being testable. It has reversed the trend toward the empirical determination of neural correlates of emotional behavior that has been seen in Bard's work. It consists, essentially, of a set of hypotheses concerning vaguely defined cortical mechanisms. These hypotheses are discussed briefly here, and some attempt is made to discover the kind of evidence that is relevant to the theory.

Hebb [18] asserted that he was not interested in emotional experience but rather in emotional behavior, or, more specifically, in "emotional disturbance" and "emotion." Emotional disturbance refers to the "violent and unpleasant emotions, roughly, and to the transient irritabilities and anxieties of ordinary persons as well as to neurotic and psychotic disorder." The term emotion refers to "the hypothetical neural processes that produce emotional behavior." Emotions may be organizing or disorganizing, depending upon their "tendency to maintain or increase original stimulating conditions (i.e., pleasure) or their tendency to abolish or decrease the stimulus (i.e., rage, fear, disgust)." We shall be concerned primarily with Hebb's treatment of emotion as emotional disturbance, although emotions as organizing tendencies will also be considered.

Hebb's major theoretical constructs are the "cell assembly" and "phase sequence." A cell assembly consists of "a diffuse structure comprising cells in the cortex and diencephalon . . . capable of acting briefly as a closed system, delivering facilitation to other such systems and usually having a specific motor facilitation." A phase sequence consists of a series of such cell assemblies and is equivalent to the thought process. The formation of cell assemblies depends primarily upon past experience which alters synaptic connections by a process involving the growth of synaptic end knobs. Hebb's use of such broadly defined concepts in a discussion of emotion may be explained as an attempt to integrate emotion with learning, perception, and thought, and to deal with the problem on the level of the primates.

The major aspects of emotional disturbance for which Hebb attempted to account are as follows:

1. "The great variety of causes of disturbance," for example, fear of the strange, interruption of sleep, hunger, nutritional deficiency, withdrawal of a drug from the addict.

2. "The fact that a single cause may produce anger, fear, or nausea and faintness, in the same subject at different times, or in different subjects."

3. "The great variety of expression even of a single emotion."

4. "The different ways in which the expression of emotion changes, as the subject is habituated to the stimulating conditions."

Hebb's primary assumption is that "emotional disturbance is . . . a disruption of the timing of neuronal activity in the cerebrum." This disruption of the phase sequence may be caused by any of three conditions, namely:

1. *Conflict of phase sequences.* "A familiar attendant A, wearing the equally familiar coat B of another attendant, may arouse the fear of the strange in an infant chimpanzee just as a complete stranger would. A causes no disturbance, B causes none, A and B together cause a violent emotional reaction.

2. *Lack of "sensory support" for the phase sequence.* Examples are "fear of the dark, fear of solitude, fear aroused by loss of support . . ." and fear aroused by experimental deafness or sudden loss of sight.

3. *Metabolic changes.* Examples are "the effects of chemical changes in the nutrient fluids that bathe the neural cell" and any condition that changes "the amount of oxygen in the blood or the amount of blood that is supplied to neural tissues. . . ."

The emotional disturbance is at first an innate disruptive response. Learning enters the picture in at least two ways. Although the immediate results of the disruption of the phase sequence depend upon innate response mechanisms, the phase sequence itself must first be learned before it can be

interfered with. Learning also modifies the nonspecific emotional disturbance and transforms it into various organized patterns of emotional behavior. For example, the emotional disturbance modified by an avoidance tendency constitutes the fear response; the disturbance plus a tendency toward approach or aggression results in a rage response. The particular phase sequence that is disrupted also influences the kind of emotional behavior that results. Hebb suggested that the milder degrees of disruption may innately lead to aggression (approach) while stronger degrees of disruption may lead to avoidance. Hebb's theory of emotion is summarized in Figure 20-8. In general, antecedent conditions that produce phase sequences can lead to conflict of phase sequences and emotional disturbance. These conditions are reflected in electroencephalogram patterns.

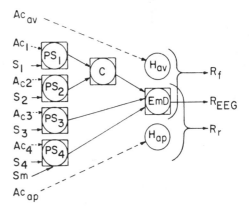

Figure 20-8. Conceptualization of Hebb's theory of emotion ($Ac_{1 \to n}$ = antecedent conditions that produce phase sequences; S_{1-n} = sensory support; Ac_{av} = antecedent conditions leading to avoidance tendencies; Ac_{ap} = antecedent conditions leading to approach tendencies; Sm = metabolic changes; $PS_{1 \to n}$ = phase sequences; C = conflict of phase sequences; H_{av} = avoidance tendencies; H_{ap} = approach tendencies; EmD = emotional disturbance; R_f = fear response; R_{EEG} = Electroencephalogram patterns; R_r = rage response. Lack of sensory support is indicated by the two vertical lines interrupting the connection between S_3 and PS_3. Theoretical constructs are encircled. Symbols enclosed in rectangles refer to cortical-subcortical states or processes. Learned connections are indicated by broken lines, unlearned connections by solid lines.)

Figure 20-8 shows that there is a surprising similarity between Hebb's and Brown and Farber's theories. The most obvious point of agreement is the introduction of theoretical constructs relating to conflict between response tendencies. Hebb introduced constructs in terms of *hypothetical* neural processes that direct the normal behavior of the organism but that, when antagonistic, result in emotional behavior. Brown and Farber introduced their construct referring to conflict, that is, "frustration state," in terms of antagonistic response tendencies that are in turn defined by *specific* antecedent conditions. Hebb's "emotional disturbance" which may be induced by the conflict of phase sequences is quite similar to Brown and Farber's "irrelevant drive due to frustration" and "frustration stimulus" in that both sets of constructs may, when combined with previous response tendencies, produce the observed emotional behavior.

The two theories differ in the empirical nature of their respective constructs and in the testability of hypotheses derived from the theories. Hebb's constructs are defined in terms of hypothetical neural mechanisms whose antecedent determining conditions are not clearly specified. Hebb asserted that differences in phase sequences, and their disruption, produce different electroencephalographic patterns. Hebb's theory of emotion might be tested by determining whether such differential EEG patterns can be obtained under the various conditions that supposedly disrupt phase sequences. Whether or not the individual phase sequences themselves can be demonstrated by means of the EEG is not clear. Brown and Farber, on the other hand, defined their concepts in terms of specific *manipulable* antecedent conditions and observable responses. A test of hypotheses generated from their type of theory would involve a series of experiments in which antecedent conditions were systematically varied and the effects on behavior were observed.

Although Hebb has disregarded much of the experimental evidence on hypothalamic and cortical mechanisms in emotion, his theory, in retrospect, probably represents an advance — at least with

respect to theory construction — over the previous physiological theories that have been considered.

Lindsley's Activation Theory

Lindsley's [27] activation theory of emotion is an attempt to integrate the findings of electrophysiology and investigations of cortical and subcortical interaction with emotional behavior. The theory approximates a summary of empirical relationships between two classes of response (i.e., electroencephalogram and emotional behavior) more closely than any theory previously considered. In this respect it lacks the theoretical content of the previous approaches considered here. Lindsley did not present as comprehensive an account of emotional behavior as did Hebb, Cannon, or James. Lindsley admitted that his "theory" can best explain the extremes of emotional behavior (ie., the coordinated patterns of maximal excitement in fear, rage, startle responses, and the relaxed states of sleep and the milder or pleasant emotions), but that it cannot account for "intermediate and mixed states."

Lindsley presented the following "postulates" of his theory. They are not really postulates since each statement is supported by experimental evidence. They represent, rather, statements of empirical relationships.

1. The electroencephalogram in emotion presents an activation pattern characterized by reduction or abolition of synchronized (alpha) rhythms and the induction of low-amplitude fast activity.

2. The activation pattern in the EEG can be reproduced by electrical stimulation of the brainstem reticular formation extending foward into the basal diencephalon through which its influence projects to the thalamus and cortex.

3. Destruction of the basal diencephalon . . . abolishes activation of the EEG and permits restoration of synchronized rhythmic discharges in thalamus and cortex.

4. The mechanism of the basal diencephalon and lower brainstem reticular formation, which discharges to motor outflows and causes the objective features of emotional expression, is either identical with or overlaps the EEG activating mechanisms, described under point 2, which arouses the cortex. [27,p. 505]

Figure 20-9*A* illustrates Lindlsey's theory of central neural mechanisms in emotion excitement. Antecedent emotional stimuli and electrical stimulation (S_e) activate the brain stem, which in turn sends impulses to the thalamus and cortex. These impulses are transformed by the hypothetical activating mechanism into responses characterized by emotional excitement and into the activation pattern of the EEG. Figure 20-9*B* illustrates Lindsley's theory of central neural mechanisms in emotional apathy. Antecedent emotional stimuli elicit responses in the thalamus and cortex, which in turn lead to hypothetical synchronized discharges that result in synchronized EEG rhythms.

Figures 20-9*A* and 20-9*B* show that Lindsley is in essential agreement with both Hebb and Cannon, except that emotional experience is disregarded completely. Lindsley is concerned, instead, with the neural mechanisms mediating emotional behavior. His major contribution is the correlation of these mechanisms with EEG patterns, a procedure previously suggested by Hebb. He differs from Hebb in the specificity with which he discusses these relationships.

It might be profitable to consider in greater detail the subcortical projections to the various areas of the cortex responsible for different EEG patterns or differentiation of EEG patterns within the subcortical region. Evidence of this sort could be used to achieve a closer integration of Bard's and Lindsley's results.

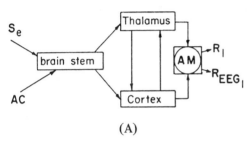

(A)

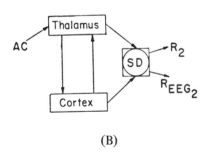

(B)

Figure 20-9A. Central neural mechanisms in emotional excitement according to Lindsley's theory of emotion. (S_e = electrical stimulation; AC = antecedent emotional stimuli; AM = activating mechanism; R_1 = emotional behavior characterized by excitement; R_{EEG_1} = "activation pattern" of EEG, characterized by low-amplitude fast activity. Cortical and subcortical structures are enclosed in rectangles. Theoretical constructs are encircled. Solid lines represent major neural pathways.) **B.** Central neural mechanisms in emotional apathy according to Lindsley's activation theory of emotion. (SD = synchronized discharges; R_2 = emotional behavior characterized by apathy; R_{EEG_2}= synchronized EEG rhythms. Other symbols same as in Fig. 9A.)

Summary of the Major Differences Between Brown and Farber's, Hebb's, and Lindsley's Theories

Brown and Farber, and Hebb both introduced theoretical constructs relating to conflict between response tendencies. Hebb used constructs introduced in terms of hypothetical neural processes that are not directly observable while Brown and Farber introduced their construct referring to conflict in terms of antagonistic response tendencies that are defined by specific antecedent conditions. Lindsley's theory is almost devoid of theoretical content. It approximates, instead, a summary of empirical relationships between two classes of response, the electroencephalogram and emotional behavior.

CONCLUSIONS

Several theoreticians have failed to recognize that animal experimentation cannot be employed to test the major theories of emotion as they were originally formulated. This has resulted from a misunderstanding of the essential distinction between emotional behavior and emotional experience and the use of anthropomorphic terminology to describe animal behavior. Theories that consider emotional experience in their major postulates cannot be tested by animal experimentation.

Some theoreticians have incorrectly inferred emotional experience from emotional behavior. Such a practice adds little to one's understanding of emotion, since emotional experience or emotional states are not *necessarily* correlated with overt emotional behavior. In any case, there is no method by which such inferences could be checked with animals. Emotional experience could be included in the theories as a construct inferred from verbal reports. Such a procedure could lead to fruitful research.

REFERENCES

1. Arnold, M. B.: Physiological differentiation of emotional states. Psychol. Rev. *52:* 35–48 (1945).
2. Arnold, M. B.: An excitatory theory of emotion. In Reymert, M. L. (ed.): Feelings and Emotions: The Mooseheart Symposium. New York, McGraw-Hill, 1950, pp. 11–33.
3. Bard, P.: Central nervous mechanisms for the expression of anger in animals. In Reymert, M. L. (ed.): Feelings and Emotions: The Mooseheart Symposium. New York, McGraw-Hill, 1950, pp. 211–237.
4. Brady, J. V.: Emotional behavior. In Handbook of Physiology. Section I. Neurophysiology. Vol. 3. Baltimore, American Physiological Society, 1960, pp. 1529–1552.
5. Brown, J. S., and Farber, I. E.: Emotions conceptualized as intervening variables – With suggestions toward a theory of frustration. Psychol. Bull. *48:* 465–495 (1951).
6. Cannon, W. B.: The James-Lange theory of emotions: A critical examination and an alternative theory. Am. J. Psychol. *39:* 106–124 (1927).
7. Cannon, W. B.: Again the James-Lange and the thalamic theories of emotion. Psychol. Rev. *38:* 281–295 (1931).
8. Cantril, H., and Hunt, W. A.: Emotional effects produced by the injection of adrenalin. Am. J. Psychol. *44:* 300–307 (1932).
9. Duffy, E.: Leeper's motivational theory of emotions. Psychol. Rev. *55:* 324–328 (1948).
10. Feigl, H.: Operationism and scientific method. In Feigl, H., and Sellars, W. (eds.): Readings in Philosophical Analysis. New York, Appleton-Century-Crofts, 1945, pp. 498–509.
11. Freeman, G. L.: Physiological Psychology. New York, Van Nostrand, 1948.
12. Gastaut, H.: Corrélations entre le systèm nerveux végétatif et le systèm de la vie de relation dans le rhinencéphalon. J. Physiol. Pathologique Général. *44:* 431–470 (1952).
13. Goldstein, M. L.: Acquired drive strength as a joint function of shock intensity and number of acquisition trials. J. Exp. Psychol. *60:* 349–358 (1960).
14. Goldstein, M. L.: Aversive conditioning methodology in animal research. Psychol. Rep.

11: 841–868 (1962).
15. Goldstein, M. L.: Effects of hippocampal, amygdala, hypothalamic, and parietal lesions on a classically conditioned fear response. Psychol. Rep. *16:* 211–219 (1965).
16. Goldstein, M. L.: Some methodological considerations in physiological research on aversive behavior. J. Genet. Psychol. *109:* 47–55 (1966).
17. Grossman, S. P.: A Textbook of Physiological Psychology. New York, Wiley, 1967.
18. Hebb, D. O.: Organization of Behavior. New York, Wiley, 1949.
19. Hull, C. L.: Principles of Behavior. New York, Appleton-Century, 1943.
20. James, W.: What is emotion? Mind. *9:* 188–204 (1884).
21. James, W.: Psychology. New York, World, 1948.
22. Kaada, B. R.: Somato-motor, autonomic, and electrocorticographic response to electrical stimulation of rhinencephalic and other structures in primates, cat, and dog. Acta Physiol. Scand. *24* (monogr. Suppl. 83) (1951).
23. Kalish. H. I.: Strength of fear as a function of the number of acquisition and extinction trials. J. Exp. Psychol. *47:* 1–10 (1954).
24. Landis, C., and Hunt, W. A.: The Startle Pattern. New York, Farrar & Rinehart, 1939.
25. Leeper, R. W.: A motivational theory of emotion to replace "Emotion as disorganized response." Psychol. Rev. *55:* 2–21 (1948).
26. Ley, R.: Effects of food and water deprivation on the performance of a response motivated by acquired fear. J. Exp. Psychol. *69:* 583–589 (1966).
27. Lindsley, D. B.: Emotion. In Stevens, S. S. (ed.): Handbook of Experimental Psychology. New York, Wiley, 1951, pp. 473–516.
28. McAllister, W. R., and McAllister, D. E.: Variables influencing the conditioning and the measurement of acquired fear. In Prokasy, W. F. (ed.): Classical Conditioning: A Symposium. New York, Appleton-Century-Crofts, 1965. pp. 172–191.
29. McCleary, R. A.: Response-modulating functions of the limbic system: Initiation and suppression. In Stellar, E., and Sprague, J. M.

(eds.): Progress in Physiological Psychology. Vol. I. New York, Academic Press, 1966, pp. 210-272.

30. Miller, N. E.: Studies of fear as an acquirable drive: I. Fear as motivation and fear-reduction as reinforcement in the learning of new responses. J. Exp. Psychol. *38:* 89-101 (1948).

31. Miller, N. E.: Learnable drives and rewards. In Stevens, S. S. (ed.): Handbook of Experimental Psychology. New York, Wiley, 1951, pp. 435-472.

32. Miller, N. E.: Liberalization of basic S-R concepts: Extensions to conflict behavior, motivation and social learning. In Koch, S. (ed.): Psychology: A Study of a Science. Study I. Conceptual and Systematic. Vol. 2. General Systematic Formulations, Learning, and Special Processes. New York, McGraw-Hill, 1959, pp. 196-292.

33. Morgan, C. T.: Physiological Psychology. New York, McGraw-Hill, 1965.

34. Mountcastle, V. B.: Somatic functions of the nervous system. Ann. Rev. Physiol. *20:* 471-508 (1958).

35. Mowrer, O. H.: Learning Theory and Personality Dynamics. New York, Ronald Press, 1950.

36. Ruch, T. C. Patton, H. D., Woodbury, J. W., and Towe, A. L.: Neurophysiology. Philadelphia, W. B. Saunders Co., 1965.

37. Schreiner, L. H., and Kling, A.: Behavioral changes following rhinencephalic injury in cat. J. Neurophysiol. *16:* 643-659 (1953).

38. Schreiner, L. H., and Kling, A.: Rhinencephalon and behavior. Am. J. Physiol. *184:* 486-490 (1956).

39. Solomon, R. L., and Wynne, L. C.: Avoidance conditioning in normal dogs and in dogs deprived of normal autonomic functioning. Am. Psychol. *5:* 264 (1950).

40. Spence, K. W.: The methods and postulates of "behaviorism." Psychol. Rev. *55:* 67-78 (1948).

41. Watson, J. B.: Psychology from the Standpoint of a Behaviorist. Philadelphia, J. B. Lippincott Co., 1919.

42. Webb, W. B.: A motivational theory of emotions. Psychol. Rev. *55:* 329-335 (1948).

43. Wenger, M. A.: Emotion as visceral action: An extension of Lange's theory. In Reymert, M. L., (ed.): Feelings and Emotions: The Mooseheart Symposium. New York, McGraw-Hill, 1950, pp. 3-10.

44. Young, P. T.: Emotion in Man and Animal. New York, Wiley, 1943.

45. Young, P. T.: Emotion as disorganized response — A reply to Professor Leeper. Psychol. Rev. *56:* 184-191 (1949).

21   Unconscious Material

Lewis Wolberg

The bringing of the patient to awareness of certain aspects of his unconscious is an integral part of all insight therapy. Where treatment is geared toward reeducative goals, this uncovering process need not be too ambitious. On the other hand, the achievement of reconstructive goals may require extensive exposure of segments of the inner psychic life which have been isolated from consciousness by repression, and which serve as actual or potential sources of conflict.

The "depth" of exploration of repressed conflictual foci will vary according to the needs of the patient. It is doubtful that a total divulgence of unconscious material is ever required. Nor is it possible, through the use of any of the techniques known today — focused interviewing, free association, dream and fantasy interpretion, exploration of transference, hypnoanalysis, narcoanalysis, art therapy and play therapy — to uncover the unconscious completely. There are some repressions that seem to remain insoluble in the face of the most skilled therapeutic handling. Fortunately, however, most people may be helped sufficiently through the gaining of insight into merely some of their unconscious conflicts.

Among repressed and repudiated aspects of psychic activity are fears and fantasies

Wolberg, L.: Unconscious material. In Wolberg, L.: Technique of Psychotherapy, New York, Grune & Stratton, 1967.

associated with the various bodily functions, particularly eating, excretion, and sexuality. There are hostile and destructive impulses directed toward other persons and toward the self. There are traumatic memories and experiences too painful to be recalled in consciousness. There are incestuous desires and other unresolved Oedipal elements. There are impulses toward sadism, masochism, voyeurism, exhibitionism and homosexuality. There are such normal strivings as desires for love, companionship, recognition, self-esteem, independence, and creative self-fulfillment, which have developed incompletely, or, for anxiety reasons, been abandoned. There are, in addition, rejected neurotic drives for affection, dependence, superiority, dominance, ambition, power, and detachment, as well as the conflicts that these drives initiate.

The individual, while often partially aware of his unconscious strivings, usually does not understand their meaning or how they act to create his symptoms. For example, he may know that he has had certain damaging experiences, and that he has tried to banish from his mind some painful events in his life; yet he does not fully appreciate the important hold they have on him. He may be aware of murderous aggression or perverse sexual impulses, and he may feel repulsed by these. However, the determining influence that such impulses have on his behavior is outside the range of his understanding. He may, from time to time, realize how his character drives operate; for instance, he may recognize how dependent he is in one or another relationship, but he may not know how dependency acts as a key motif of his life. He does not understand the extent to which it saps his self-esteem and renders him helpless and without energy. Nor does he see how it clashes with such coexistent drives as those for independence and power, generating tension and anxiety.

The specific psychic elements that are repressed are dependent upon the unique experiences of the individual. Any aspect of feeling or thinking or behaving may be subject to repression if it conflicts with social standards, as transmitted to the patient by the parent through disciplines.

These injunctions, incorporated into the superego, continue to exert pressure on the person. In our culture such impulses as sexuality, hostility and assertiveness are particularly subject to repression. Also commonly repudiated are impulses toward dependency and passivity, as well as compulsive drives for power and independence.

In spite of deflection from the mainstream of the individual's thinking, repressed material may gain access to awareness in the form of highly symbolized and distorted derivatives. It is through detection and translation of such derivatives that awareness of the deeper content becomes possible.

THE SYMBOLISM OF THE UNCONSCIOUS

Thus, the patient's dreams, fantasies, free associations, symptoms and behavioral tendencies may reflect extremely primitive or childish symbols. Often, expression is couched in terms of various organ functions. Simple activities, such as sucking, eating, excreting, and sexual functioning may represent a host of attitudes and strivings. The form of expression may seem bizarre, senseless, and without rational design. A need for security and dependency may thus appear as a desire to suck the breast, penis or nipple. All parts of the body, including the genital organs, may be implemented in this sucking process. Dependency may also be expressed by fantasies of cannibalistic incorporations of a real or nonexistent person. The amalgamation may be achieved by other means, as by entering the body of the person through any of the various orifices, by sexual intercourse, or by changing into a phallus and being sucked up into the vagina and womb. There may be a peculiar extension in which the person on whom the subject wishes to depend is identified with the fecal mass, with resultant overvaluation of excretory products and activities.

Hostile attitudes toward women may be represented by the biting and destroying of a female figure, or of a woman's body contents, breasts, or nipples, or of a fantasied penis within her abdomen. This attack may be attempted with the mouth, anus, or penis, or with excretory products. Destructive feelings toward males may be symbolized by impulses to castrate, or to devour or incorporate the penis or the body conceived as a penis. Fantasies of eating or of expelling loved or hated persons in the form of feces may occur.

Guilt feelings and fears of retaliation may be symbolized by fantasies of being eaten or castrated by devouring animals, ghouls, monsters, or witches, of being absorbed into a vagina for purposes of destruction, of being attacked by a male sexual organ, a female organ, or an imagined intravaginal penis. There may be fears of being penetrated anally by the penis of a strong man, or of being injured and killed by feces. A loss of aggressiveness and intactness may be designated by a fear of castration; this in males may be accompanied by reparative attempts, and in females by a denial of the fact that there is no penis, or by frenzied attempts to secure one in fantasy from a paternal, fraternal, or maternal person in whose body a penis may be imagined to exist.

Phallic symbolism is extraordinarily common in unconscious ideation. Some persons are more prone than others to use it to express basic needs and attitudes. Sexuality here becomes a magical short cut to close relationships with people and the nucleus around which the individual's thoughts and symptoms are oriented.

Possession of an intact male organ is frequently utilized to represent a sense of aggressiveness and power. It may become the symbol of the chief values and goals in life. Strivings for strength, activity, and dominance may thus be symbolized unconsciously by a desire for a penis in a female, who may believe that possession of a penis would be a magical solution for all her problems, including the fear of functioning as a female. The same impulses may also bring about a wish for a larger and more powerful penis in a male. Submission, passivity, and subordination may be signified in a woman by the lack of a penis, and in a man by desires for breasts, castration and homosexuality. Where security is sought through dependency and subordination, castration may also be a goal which is usually countered by a desire for activity and a fear of castration.

FORGOTTEN MEMORIES AND EXPERIENCES

In the course of exploring the unconscious, the patient is apt to revive experiences in his past that have been traumatic to him. Forgotten memories may be remembered of which the patient may have been relatively or completely unaware. The importance of this material constantly comes up for appraisal.

There are those who believe that the recall of forgotten traumatic incidents in the developmental history is essential for cure in reconstructive therapy, since repressed memories are fountainheads of conflict. A criterion of cure set by Freud was a removal of the amnesia of the third and fourth years, and a recovery of memories during this period that are associated with the patient's neurosis. There are other authorities who tend to disagree with this standard, believing that therapy, focused on immediate interpersonal relationships, can change personality without the need for probing into the past.

The mechanism associated with the repression of early experiences is organized around the need to avoid anxiety. In early childhood, inimical happenings are extremely traumatic. One reason for this is that the child feels relatively helpless in a world, the manifestations of which are a constant source of mystery to him. Relations between cause and effect are indeterminate, and he is menaced by many inscrutable events over which he has no control. One way of coping with childhood anxieties is to project them in the form of phobias. Another way of dealing with anxiety that threatens to overwhelm the immature ego is through processes of repression and dissociation. These phobic and repressive defenses continue to function far beyond the period of childhood, and the ego reacts to the original traumatic events as if it still were too weak and too vulnerable to deal with them. This is possibly the reason why many adults feel that there is something buried deep within themselves so terrifying that they cannot bear to bring it up.

An important question is whether early traumatic experiences are universally damaging. It is difficult to provide a complete answer to this question. All children undergo traumatic experiences of one sort or another during the period of socialization. A cataclysmic happening, however, can bring the effects of minor experiences to a head and can embody the accumulated emotions of all past inimical events.

Traumatic experiences in early childhood thus act upon a sensitized soil at a time when ego resources are relatively limited. Often these experiences, when uncovered, appear so insignificant that one might doubt their potency in evoking such disproportionate emotional responses. Yet, if one considers that the traumatic experience is a condensation of a series of damaging events, and that it comes to stand symbolically for all of them, one may appreciate that it can be greatly overvalued.

As a general rule, early traumatic experiences are of two types. In one type, the events are so devastating or destructive that no child could be expected to cope with them. This occurs where the child is severely injured physically, or witnesses an incident so horrible that the experience takes away his security. The other type of traumatic experience can in no way be considered extraordinary, since it is part of the normal growth process. Growing up involves the capacity to abandon narcissistic and omnipotent strivings, to tolerate frustration, to channelize aggression into socially accepted outlets, to control sexual impulses, and to develop independence and self-assertiveness. In the course of his development, the child is subjected to many frustrations that involve abandonment of selfish strivings in favor of those that will bring him into cooperative relationships with the group. Most children are capable of handling such frustrations without too great difficulty. However, an insecure child, and particularly one who has been rejected and denied legitimate demands for love and support, will be so overwhelmed by feelings of helplessness that he will be unable to tolerate frustration and to withstand traumatic experiences that are a usual component of growing up. Such an individual is likely to react catastrophically to relative normal hardships as are imposed on every child. In him certain events like the birth of a sibling, the discovery of the genital difference between the sexes, the witnessing of parental intercourse ("primal scene") or exposure to any bloodshed and cruelty, may mobilize inordinate anxiety.

The insecure child may feel so threatened by rejection or punishment that he will find it necessary to repress such impulses as hostility toward his parents and siblings, masturbatory desires, sexual curiosities, and strivings for mastery, independence and self-assertion. The repression of these impulses involves much experiment. The child for a long time defies the parents, even at the risk of incurring retaliatory punishment. Gradually, however, he may yield to parental discipline. Frequently repression occurs dramatically following a particularly traumatic incident that convinces the child that danger can be real. For instance, an insecure child who retains within himself certain rebellious tendencies may witness the flogging of a dog that has done something to offend its master. He may be frightened by this brutal treatment, and he may unconsciously identify himself with the animal, fearing that he will be injured in the same way if he persists in defying his parents. The result may be a phobia in regard to dogs, the dynamic purpose of which is to insulate himself against fear of his own aggressive impulses. The event comes to constitute a traumatic experience that may be repressed in an effort to avoid any reminder of pain. The dog phobia will nevertheless persist, aiding the repressive process.

During later life, too, even in adulthood, intensely traumatic experiences may shock the organism into a revival of the mechanism of repression. This move is motivated by a need to ward off a threat to the ego. There are no better examples of this than those seen in the neuroses of war in which traumatic incidents may be blotted from the mind.

In the course of therapy, the recovery of

repressed traumatic experiences may ameliorate or dissipate certain symptoms, especially those that serve the function of keeping these memories repressed. Many compulsions, obsessions, and conversion symptoms fall into this category. The most dramatic results occur in simple conditioned fears and in amnesias of recent origin such as hysterical amnesias, trauma of the skull, and exposure to unbearable stresses like those during disasters and war. Where the personality is relatively intact, and the individual has, prior to the traumatic event, functioned satisfactorily in his interpersonal relationships, the recall of forgotten events may restore the previous status.

Theoretically, all symptoms have an historical origin. It may be argued that were we capable of probing deeply enough into the past, of penetrating the myriad conditionings, of reviewing every stimulus that ever invaded the senses and every idea that entered the mind, of peering into all influences, pleasurable and inimical that have impinged on the patient, we might be able to demonstrate to him how each of his symptoms came into being. This task, however, is impossible, for many vital early experiences that have molded the personality are not accessible to recall, having occurred prior to the phase of mnemonic accessibility, or having been subjected to a practically impenetrable sealing-off process of repression. In spite of a most extensive analysis one is able to recapture only a fragment of the total of life experiences. Even where we have not laid out for ourselves so ambitious a task, and are satisfied with reviewing the most important experiences in the patient's development, we find these so numerous as to defy recapitulation.

However, to indulge our imagination, we may conjure up a situation in which we track down the origin of each of the patient's symptoms. Having done this, we should probably find, in most cases, that the symptoms themselves would not vanish. The expectation that recovery of traumatic experiences will invariably produce an amelioration or cure of the patient's neurosis is founded on a faulty theoretic promise. Even though the individual's character structure is in large measure developed from the bedrock of past experiences and conditionings, and even though damage of his personality has resulted from untoward happenings in his early interpersonal relationships, it does not follow that a recall of these experiences will correct the existing condition.

As an analogy, we may consider a focus of infection that operates insidiously over a period of years. The original source of the individual's physical disability is this infective focus, but by the time it is discovered, it has already influenced other bodily structures. It may have produced kidney damage or acted as a stimulus of secondary foci of infection. The removal of the primary focus will leave the body still suffering from the effects of the original infection, and it will be essential to cure these secondary effects before the patient can be pronounced cured. A single catastrophic experience or a series of harmful experiences can likewise act as a focus, engendering in an insecure person the conviction that the world is menacing and that the people in it are not to be trusted. The experience may influence him in forming decisive attitudes and reaction patterns. By the time he enters adulthood, however, his manner of dealing with his conflicts will have been structuralized into behavior so ingrained that the recall of the original trauma will have little effect upon his habitual responses. Therapy will involve tedious reeducation and reconditioning long after the recall of the initial traumatic memories.

Often during therapy a patient may recover the memory of a forgotten traumatic happening, and through this recall he may experience considerable abreaction. He may even liberate himself from certain associated symptoms. However, the essential difficulty will probably remain. The patient will still be insecure. The circumstances that sensitized him to the original traumatic scene will continue to plague him in his daily interpersonal relationships. The essential task in therapy, therefore, would seem to lie not only in recovery of early traumatic experiences, but also in ascertaining the reasons why the experiences became so catastrophic as to necessitate repression.

It must always be remembered that a neurosis is not a fortuitous happening dependent exclusively upon early traumatic events. It is rather a form of adaptation to, and defense against a world that is regarded by the child and later by the adult as potentially hostile and menacing. Current reaction patterns and attitudes, while derived from past experiences, are not an automatic repetition of infantile modes in an adult setting. They are forms of behavior motivated by a desire to escape helplessness, to gratify vital needs, and to allay tension, anxiety and hostility. The individual reacts to the present with characterologic machinery that is rooted in his past experiences; but his present-day problems are the immediate result of conflicts deriving from demands, fears and resentments that arise also from his current interpersonal relationships.

Overemphasis on the part played by the past may produce certain unfortunate effects during therapy. The patient may utilize his inimical childhood experiences as a justification for his neurosis and for resistance to change. His therapy may bog down in a compulsive historical review of his past, a definite cleavage developing to isolate it from the present. Some patients who have familiarized themselves with early theories of psychoanalysis are led to believe that awareness of their past conditionings will magically dissolve their problems and reintegrate them in their dealings with the world. Consequently, the analysis becomes a stereotyped search for an illusory pot of gold at the end of a mnemonic rainbow.

While an exclusive preoccupation with the past imposes definite limitations in therapy, one must not be won over to the fallacious notion that the historical experience can be entirely meaningless. Tendencies in this direction are apparent in certain present-day insight therapies, and foster a concentration on relatively superficial material. There is in this approach a dichotomization of the personality, as though the individual had two parts — an important present, and a past that has little bearing upon prevailing attitudes, values and goals.

Knowledge of the historical roots of a disorder is in itself not sufficient to produce cure, but it is of tremendous value in establishing continuity in the individual's life, from infancy to adulthood. It points to weakness and sensitivity of the ego at the time of a particularly traumatic experience. It demonstrates how repetitive happenings in the present are a reflection of the same problems that existed in childhood. Of particular therapeutic benefit is the ability of the ego to withstand the emotions liberated by the recall of early traumatic incidents. The neurotic individual often has little respect for himself because he has to yield to his fear of the past. To be able to master this fear, and to tolerate the anxiety that previously caused him to cringe, has an enhancing effect on ego strength.

The relationship with the therapist acts as an important tool in the recall of buried memories. In the transference the patient will be stirred up emotionally and will experience attitudes and impulses that have a potent effect in reviving mnemonic prototypes of what he is undergoing in the present. The transference will frequently touch off patterns that cannot be uprooted by any other method.

During therapy the patient may, however, for some reason be incapable of remembering any traumatic experiences. This failure need not necessarily block the therapeutic process, and important changes in the dynamic structure of the personality can occur with little recall of the past. Interpretation of the transference and the establishing of an unambivalent relationship with the therapist may enable the individual to function on better terms with himself and with others. It is possible also that he may give up infantile defenses without recalling the specific traumatic memories or experiences that inspired them.

On the other hand, analysis of the transference, and interpretation of dreams, free associations, and material elicited through interviewing, may, in themselves, fail to produce change. The patient seems to be stymied by a stubborn amnesia relating to vast segments of his childhood or later life. The inability to recall vital situations of the past may represent resistance to accepting the implications of certain drives and defenses and they reveal themselves in the relationship with the therapist.

Obdurate resistance to recall frequently constitutes a means of avoiding anxiety of a sort that initially fostered the repression. In some patients it serves to retain the secondary gain inherent in their neurosis. The amnesia affecting recall may be so stubborn that even the most concerted effort will fail to bring the repressed material to the surface. Where, with extensive probing the patient is unable to recover damaging traumatic experiences — although one is reasonably certain that such experiences have occurred — it is probable that the amnesia protects the ego from anxiety that it would be unable to handle if the experiences were recalled. Here the reasonable ego is still too weak to absorb anxiety and to reconsider the experience in a factual light. The ability to recall early traumatic experiences, and to reevaluate them, requires considerable ego strength. In a number of conditions, for example hysterical disorders, sufficient ego intactness exists so as to make possible the handling of fears and conflicts associated with an inimical past. In these ailments the recovery of repressed experiences may suffice to produce a cure of specific symptoms.

In other conditions, however, such as certain personality disorders and psychoses, the ego is so vulnerable and weak that it cannot tolerate either the repressed memories or their implications. Therapy may fail to break down the resistances to recall, or the traumatic experience may be remembered with a peculiar dissociation of its emotional content. The forgotten event may be remembered as a vague experience with emotional implication, what is recalled being enough to satisfy the rational demands of the individual. The damaging emotions and the significance of the experience itself are, however, repressed. The individual reacts to devastating childhood incidents or fantasies in an apathetic manner, as if they were somehow detached from himself. There is no abreactive process. It is almost as though the patient, by his recall, seeks to fulfill a dual purpose; first, to retain the good will of the therapist by remembering things, and, second, to hold on to his resistance by repressing the emotional meaning of the traumatic event.

Failure to uncover buried memories may be due to the fact that therapy has not bolstered the ego to a point where it can absorb the anxiety liberated by the recall of early experiences.

HYPNOTIC RECALL OF FORGOTTEN MEMORIES

In some cases, hypnosis may uproot unconscious memories. One may question the efficacy of such a process, for it is axiomatic that a premature confrontation of the ego with unconscious material merely serves to create anxiety and to enhance resistance. Yet hypnosis need not have this effect, providing the recall is adroitly handled. Instead of battering down the patient's resistances by forcing him to remember things, it is best to give him full freedom to recall when he feels himself able to handle his memories. During deep hypnosis the patient may be told that there are certain experiences and memories that are quite important, and that, because of their painful nature, they have been forgotten. He may be assured that it is not necessary to remember all details of such memories at once, but that he will be able to reveal and to tolerate isolated fragments of these memories and experiences as time goes on. Under the influence of such suggestions the patient will bring out those elements of a forgotten memory or experience that he can tolerate, and as he becomes stronger and realizes that he is not injured by the recall, more and more material will be available to him, until finally he can reconstruct the fragments into a consistent whole.

Piecemeal recovery of a forgotten memory or conflict may be furthered by employing such techniques as dream induction, automatic writing, regression and revivification, dramatics, drawing and mirror gazing. The evidence elicited by all these procedures may make the meaning of the experience increasingly clear to the patient. As a general rule, the implications of the memory will not be accepted by the patient until he himself realizes its importance and presents the interpretation as a product of his own efforts and conviction. Reconstructing the patient's memory for him in the waking state, from material uncovered during hypnosis, may rob the recall of its therapeutic effect.

One. of the best methods of handling material which is recalled in hypnosis is to instruct the patient to forget a revived memory until he feels that he is convinced of the truth of the memory and understands it thoroughly. It may be weeks before the patient is capable of bringing up portions of the material spontaneously, with corresponding insight. Even where the patient recalls in the waking state memories recovered in a recent hypnotic session, he will usually be unable to integrate their meaning until his ego has had time to prepare itself.

THE HANDLING OF UNCONSCIOUS MATERIAL

The actual handling of derivatives of the unconscious depends upon the projected goals in treatment. In supportive therapy, one may totally disregard unconscious outpourings. In reeducative therapy, the more manifest eruptions are selected for exploration. Thus, immediate character distortions and the surface conflicts these initiate may be a chief focus. The less manifest, more repressed aspects of the unconscious, are usually deliberately avoided. In reconstructive therapy, various strata may be explored, from topical spontaneous unconscious manifestations to those that are so deeply repressed that they require mobilization through the dissolution of repressive barriers.

Among the techniques employed to stir up unconscious activity and to remove repression are: employing a passive role in the therapeutic relationship; focusing on dreams, fantasies, past experiences and early relationships with parents; increasing the frequency of sessions; and using the couch position and free association. These activities may lead to a transference neurosis. Sometimes narcoanalysis, hypnoanalysis, art analysis and play analysis are utilized as adjuncts for the probing of unconscious material. Of all measures, the provocation of a transference neurosis is perhaps most effective.

Unless the therapist is trained to do reconstructive psychotherapy, it is unwise and even dangerous to stir up unconscious material. Explosive forces may be liberated by a lifting of repressions with which the untrained therapist may be ,incapable of coping. Where, in the course of supportive or reeducative therapy, disturbing unconscious material spontaneously appears, the therapist may strive to help repression by avoiding discussion of the material, by dealing with it reassuringly, by focusing the interview on reality matters, and by the use of greater activity in the relationship.

There are a number of ways in which unconscious feelings and attitudes can be expediently brought to the patient's attention. Some activities employed during interviewing are: restating, reflecting and interpreting whenever the therapist recognizes an unconscious trend in the patient's verbalizations, dreams, fantasies, slips of speech, free associations or transference reactions. These activities at first register themselves only minimally on the patient's mind, since acknowledgment of unconscious trends is laden with much anxiety. Incredulity or polite acceptance without conviction may mark the first reactions of the patient to the disclosures.

As has been indicated, a patient may be helped to accept repudiated aspects of his psyche by the recollection of early traumatic experiences and memories. The realization that he has been repressing traumatic memories, and the understanding of their symbolic significance may provide him with a wedge with which he can penetrate into his unconscious conflicts and gain insight into their significance.

In presenting interpretations to the patient, it may be important to recast the wording of early memories or experiences in the very terms utilized by the patient, even though these parallel the expressions used by him as a child.

Case 1

The following excerpt illustrates the verbalization in transference of unconscious sexual impulses on the part of a male patient toward his father. The material was expressed explosively with great anxiety, following a prolonged period of silence. This is from a session in which free association was employed.

Pt. My God. I feel I'm in love with you. I can't break away from you, but I want to come. I want to come here every day.

Th. Every day?

Pt. I'm afraid of you. You are so high and I am so low. I'm afraid of my feelings for you. Oh, God, as I talk I think of your penis. It's in my mouth. Oh, Oh . . . it makes me afraid. It makes me so afraid . . . oh, oh. [*The patient seems to be in a transference neurosis.*]

Th. Why?

Pt. You're so big and I'm so little. I'm down on the floor. Oh God, I'm frightened . . . oh, oh. I'm afraid you'll stick it up. This is awful. Please don't. I have to do what you want me to do. I want you to put me down on the floor. I want you to be powerful like my father. I want you to tell me what to do. I want to love you and I want you to love me. I don't want you to hurt me or kill me.

Th. You feel I may hurt you?

Pt. I know this isn't real, but I have a feeling you are my father. I want to reach out and grab my father. He is sitting there, gentle and strong. I want to scream and cry. I want you to come to me. Father, come to me! Please come to me! I want you to kiss me and hold me close. Everything is whirling around. I can't stand it. I see myself nude. You are standing over me Oh, God, please give it to me.

Th. What is it that you want?

Pt. Don't get near. Oh God, don't kill me. I'll do anything you say. I feel so little when I talk. I'm afraid to be big. I can't be the same as you. I don't want to, I don't want to. (*cries*) I don't want to . . . no, no, no. (*cries*)

Th. Why don't you want to?

Pt. I don't want to grow up. I can't fight like the other boys. I never could. I love you. I want to wear your suit, but I can't wear it. I can't touch it, anything you wear. (*continues crying and then begins to act more cheerful*)

Th. Well, how do you feel now?

Pt. God, that was a horrible experience. It was like I was a little boy again. I can't understand why I said the things I said. I remember father. He never let me do anything. I always thought I hated him and was afraid to do anything, not even shovel the snow. He acted like he always had to be the boss. Kind of hard on me, I can see it now. I always felt that I never wanted to grow up; I wanted to be a little boy. Maybe I wanted to be punished because I felt guilty about not liking my father. Even now, when I am near him, I am afraid he will hit me. He goes into such a rage. I wonder what would happen if I hit him back. I felt the same way about you, but I never realized

these sexual feelings. It scares me to think about that (*pause*)

Th. It scares you?

Pt. It's funny I never wanted you to touch me. It scares me. It scared me suddenly to realize I want you to treat me like a woman. On the other hand, I want you to touch me. I was afraid for father to touch me. Maybe I felt the same way toward him as toward you. This whole thing must be some way connected with my fear of homosexuality.

Th. And with fantasies about your father.

Pt. I just remembered a dream I had last night. I'm at home, the house we had when I was little. There is a bed against the wall. Father is there in the room. He is undressing. I wonder if he is approaching me. I'm in bed. There is a funny excitement, repulsion and fear. His body is big. It has a nauseating smell. His penis is enormous, big and red, fearful. I feel repelled by his body. I know he wants to stick his penis up my rectum. This I realize will kill me. I grab a gun and shoot at him, but it doesn't go off. I keep firing, but the bullets shoot out a couple of inches and fall on the floor. Father comes closer. I want to scream and can't. I then woke up screaming and found I had an ejaculation.

Th. What do you think this means?

Pt. It must be connected with what we've been talking about — my fear of women, my fear that they'll reject me. I must be scared of being rejected or even killed for my interest.

Case 2

The following interview illustrates the use of hypnosis in recovering the memory of a traumatic incident, in the form of a "primal scene," which engendered an hysterical conversion symptom. The patient, a woman of twenty-eight, came to therapy because of anxiety that was so severe that it absorbed all of her attention and energy. It had its inception in a particularly violent quarrel with her boy friend, with whom she had expressed growing dissatisfaction. The imminence of a rupture in her relationship with her friend caused the patient to respond with panic, since she was devoted to the man, and marriage had been contemplated in the near future. She was aware of the fact that she was repeating a pattern, because all of her relationships with men had terminated in the same kind of violent disagreement. During one interview, while working on her sexual attitudes, the patient complained of a blurring of vision. She confided that this symptom had appeared on certain occasions when she looked into a mirror. She then searched the room intently with her eyes, and asked if a mirror were present. The following is an excerpt of the recorded interview, during which the meaning of the eye symptom becomes apparent. The patient is in a waking state at the start of the session.

Pt. (*panic in voice*) I have that funny feeling again about a mirror — looking at it, (*pause*) and everything is blurred.

Th. You act somewhat upset by this.

Pt. Everything is upside down.

Th. Upside down?

Pt. Not really, but it seems like it. (*pause*) Do you have a mirror here? I don't see one, but it feels like it.

Th. What does it feel like?

Pt. I . . . don't . . . know . . . An upside down feeling . . . I'm doing something with a mirror reflection . . . a reflection.

Th. Tell me about it.

Pt. It's like last night. The same thing happened. I was at a friend's house, thinking of coming here. There was a mirror table in front of the sofa, when I was sitting there . . . I looked in the mirror and everything I saw in the mirror began to look more real than the women in the room. And I thought, that's strange, and it looked like I could walk right into the room . . . the mirror room.

Th. Almost as if it were a different world?

Pt. Well . . . well, it didn't seem to be upsetting anyhow. (*pause*) It looked very inviting.

Th. You were not afraid to walk into that mirror room?

Pt. Now, it looks very frightening, but I have been dreaming about a mirror. (*pause*)

Th. Tell me more.

Pt. Upside down, backwards, and all the letters and all . . . (*pause*) everything you say — everything has to be read backwards. I used to do mirror writing when I was little.

Th. What about your writing; you say it was mirror writing?

Pt. Oh! I wrote quite a lot.

Th. What did you write?

Pt. Oh, just the way I felt, and whatever I did when I was a child. I sometimes would doodle something about a mirror. A mirror of some kind seemed to be on my mind.

Th. You did write about a mirror?

Pt. Well, sometimes.

Th. Do you remember seeing anything unusual in a mirror?

Pt. I can't think . . . I can't remember.

Th. Maybe I will put a pen in your hand, and we'll see. Let your hand just do what it wants [*I try to induce automatic writing in the waking state which may be possible in patients suffering from hysterical reactions. This may reveal repressed material.*]

Pt. I use the typewriter.

Th. You can write freehand pretty well, can't you?

Pt. I guess so.

Th. Just let your hand move along as it wishes. Just let it do as it wishes, and pay no attention to what it writes. Just put the pen right down, and don't look at it as you talk to me; just let your hand travel along as it wishes. You will notice that it will be almost as if an outside force pushes your hand along without paying any attention to what your hand writes. Just talk to me. You acted a little bit nervous when you walked in here today.

Pt. Yes.

Th. Are you any less panicky than you were?

Pt. Well . . . it isn't panic exactly.

Th. What is it then?

Pt. I don't know.

Th. Like something deep down underneath that bothers you?

Pt. Uh huh.

Th. Are you now aware of what that something is?

Pt. Oh! It's disgusting — something I saw, I guess.

Th. Something you saw?

Pt. Uh huh.

Th. What?

Pt. I don't know.

Th. There was something you saw?

Pt. Uh huh.

Th. Put your pen down and maybe your hand will tell us more about what you saw — what it actually was that you saw. (*The patient's hand scribbles a few words.*) Can I see that? I mean the sheet you wrote on. Your hand seemed to scribble something while we talked. Now let's see what your hand wrote. [*The patient responded to the suggestion to write automatically.*]

Pt. It says, "You used to have a mirror to write in when you were a girl."

Th. You used to write in a mirror?

Pt. Yes, it was a mirror with a barricade in front of it, and when you put the paper down, you couldn't see what you were writing, but you had to look in the mirror and then you could see. That was the mirror writing.

Th. I see. How old were you then?

Pt. I guess around eight, seven or eight.

Th. Around seven or eight?

Pt. Uh huh.

Th. It would seem that perhaps around that period of your life something quite significant happened to you.

Pt. Yes, I guess so.

Th. Do you know what that was?

Pt. (*pause*) I can't remember.

Th. Now I would like to have you sit just exactly as you are. [*Hypnosis is induced at this point.*] And I want you today to bring your hands up, this way — clasp them together closely. I want you to watch them — watch your hands. I am going to count from one to five. You are going to notice when I count from one to five that your hands will become pressed together, the muscles will stiffen, your hands will get tighter, tighter and tighter, so that at a count of five, it will be difficult or impossible for you to open them. Keep gazing at them. One, tight; two, tight, tight; three, tighter and tighter; four as tight as a vise; five, so tight now that when you try to separate them, you cannot. (*pause*)

You notice now that your eyelids will get very heavy, that they close, they shut, they feel as if little steel bands are pulling them together. Your breathing gets deep and automatic, and you go into a deep, deep sleep. You are very, very drowsy; you are very tired — very, very sleepy, you are going to get drowsier, drowsier and drowsier. You are going to fall asleep now, and you will stay asleep until I give you the command to awaken. You'll stay asleep until I give you the command to awaken. You feel very relaxed. Let your breathing become regular and deep. You feel more comfortable and relaxed. You are very, very sleepy. I am going to unclasp your hands now — just like this. I am going to bring them right down to your sides.

I am going to take this arm and stretch it out in front of you now, and as I do this, the arm is going to get very stiff and rigid. The arm will get stiff and heavy and rigid, heavy and stiff like a board. I am going to count from one to five. At the count of five, the arm will have got so firm, stiff and heavy and rigid, that it will be difficult or impossible to bend it. One, firm; two, heavy; three, firmer; four, just as firm and stiff and rigid as a board; five, just as firm and stiff and rigid as a board. Notice how stiff it is. The harder you try to bend it, the heavier and stiffer it becomes, until I push it back the other way, and then it loosens up. Bring it down, bring your head down this way. Relax yourself and go to sleep. Go to sleep, deeply asleep, very deeply asleep. Just relax all over. (*pause*)

Now I am going to give you a suggestion that you begin to enter into a deep sleep, so deep that you don't keep anything back from me. I am going to help you to a point where you will be able to see what it is that is behind the mirror. (*pause*) I want you to start getting very, very little. I want you to start feeling very, very little. Your head is getting smaller, your arms and legs are getting smaller. You are going back, back, back to the time when you had that mirror. You are going right back to the time of the mirror. Your feet are getting tiny, you are shrinking, you are getting little, you are getting very small, you are shrinking, you are getting very, very small, you are getting very tiny. You are very, very small and tiny as if you are little again, just the way you were then. You are little, you are tiny. How old are you? How old are you?

Pt. Eight.

Th. You are eight years old. (*Patient appears to be trembling with fear.*) Are you afraid? You look afraid. Tell me what you are afraid of. What are you afraid of? Tell me.

Pt. (*panicky*) Of myself.

Th. Anything else?

Pt. I don't know. It's a secret.

Th. You are afraid of yourself, afraid of yourself. Now listen carefully to me. I am going to ask you now to make your mind a blank; I am going to ask you now to make your mind a mirror. You are a little girl and you are looking in a mirror. In your mind, you will see a letter that will appear in the mirror. Every time when I clap my hands together, you will see a letter. It will appear in the mirror. The letters all put together, in whatever order they may come, will spell a word. That word holds the secret of what frightens you. One, two, three, four, five — watch the mirror. (*clap*)

Pt. K.

Th. K — one, two, three, four, five — watch the mirror. (*clap*)

Pt. F.

Th. F — one, two, three, four, five — watch the mirror. (*clap*)

Pt. U.

Th. Now, when I clap my hands together, see the entire word.

Pt. F-U-C-K.

Th. F-U-C-K. Now watch that mirror again — watch that mirror, and when I clap my hands together, you will see that secret, you will see that secret. Don't be afraid now . . . One, two, three, four, five. (*clap*) (*pause*) Tell me about it.

Pt. Woman up on top of a man. (*Patient is panicky as she talks.*)

Th. Who? (*Patient moans in a distressed manner.*) You see a woman on top of a man All right now, watch that mirror. Watch that mirror. I am going to clap my hands together, and then, all of a sudden, the face of the woman in the mirror becomes clear. As soon as I clap my hands together, it will be as if you see the face, you see the features. Watch carefully. (*clap*)

Pt. Mother!

Th. Your mother! Now watch carefully. I am going to clap my hands together. The minute I do, you will be drawn right into the mirror, and the man's face will become clear.

Pt. (*with fright*) My father.

Th. Your father. Are you afraid? What do you think is happening?

Pt. I'm afraid.

Th. Now listen carefully. If this is an actual scene — an actual memory — you finally will be able to understand it. Your fear is getting less now; you are beginning to get less and less fearful. Don't be afraid, don't be afraid. Good. I want you to sit here for a while, then I'm going to help you start growing up to your present adult age. If you like, you can remember what you saw, remember everything that happened, when you awaken. After that, you can talk to me; we can talk this thing out. You would like to be well, completely well and unafraid, wouldn't you?

Pt. Uh huh.

Th. Good. In a moment I am going to wake you up. (*pause*) Now listen carefully to me. When you awaken, I want you to begin talking. Try not to be afraid even If you remember an actual memory. If you remember all the details, I want you to remember also the reasons you became afraid and had to forget them. I want you, if you can, to remember your fears, whatever they were. When you talk to me, the thing may come back as it happened, just exactly as it happened with all details. If you remember, tell me exactly how it happened. You have spent your life running away — hiding. You may not want to hide now. I am going to count from one to five, and, on the count of five, open your eyes suddenly and talk to me rapidly. One, two, three, four, five. (*patient awakens*) How do you feel?

Pt. (*mumbles*)

Th. I can't hear you.

Pt. Very funny.

Th. Tell me all about it.

Pt. I don't know. What shall I do now?

Th. Do you remember what happened here?

Pt. Yes.

Th. What happened?

Pt. (*somewhat fearful*) The mirror writing happened . . . and then mother and father vanished.

Th. Are you afraid now?

Pt. Yes.

Th. Did you ever see your mother and father together — intimately?

Pt. I know I did. It's all been in the mirror writing.

Th. Do you recall the incident when you saw your mother and father together?

Pt. My father's dresser with the mirror was next to the door, and that was reflected then. I was outside and I saw it all. [*It would seem that the image inspired such anxiety in the patient, that she attempted to repress it. Yet the mirror image also caused great excitement. The consequence of this conflict was mirror writing and blurring of vision.*]

Th. I see. So you stood outside there, and you saw the mirror reflection?

Pt. I saw mother on top of father.

Th. So you saw your mother on top of your father?

Pt. I think so.

Th. A child, when she perceives these things, thinks of them in different terms than an adult. What might you have thought as a child, what could have been going through your mind? What do you think was happening? You must have thought something. (*pause*)

Pt. They keep turning around.

Th. Do you see the two of them now?

Pt. Yes, when I close my eyes.

Th. Do they keep turning around?

Pt. Yes.

Th. Describe to me what they do.

Pt. First father is on top, and then mother is on top now. First mother is on top, and then father is on top. (*There is fear and excitement in the patient's voice.*)

Th. Now what's happening?

Pt. Upside down.

Th. Do you remember the first few weeks when you came to see me? You were so upset, you said everything was upside down.

Pt. Uh huh . . . upside down.

Th. Perhaps you were excited by what you saw?

Pt. Yes, yes.

Th. Do you have any thoughts of upside down?

Pt. I don't like it upside down. (*pause*)

Th. Why?

Pt. I feel as if it's been killing me.

Th. You feel what?

Pt. As if it's been killing me.

Th. What's been killing you?

Pt. It isn't real, like in the mirror.

Th. Now keep your eyes closed, and when I count from one to five, you will be asleep.

[*Hypnosis is reintroduced here.*] One, go to sleep; two, sleepier and sleepier; three, go to sleep, deeply; four, deeply asleep; five, deeply asleep. (*pause*) How did you feel about your mother, when you saw that thing? What did you think about your father when you saw a thing like that?

Pt. I don't know. [*It is possible that the patient has repressed some of her feelings in relation to this memory.*]

Th. Now listen carefully. I want you to sit there. I am going to count from one to five, and then clap my hands together. When I do, you are going to have the same emotion that you had when you looked into that mirror, if you actually did look into that mirror. You won't be able to keep it back. Just let it come out spontaneously. As soon as I clap my hands together, tell me the emotions that you feel. One, two, three, four, five, as soon as I clap my hands together, tell me the emotion. (*clap*)

Pt. Anger.

Th. You feel anger? Listen to me now. When I count from one to five, and clap my hands together, you will see who it is that you are angry at. One, two, three, four, five. (*clap*)

Pt. (*pause*) Mother.

Th. Mother. You were angry at mother; at what you saw?

Pt. Yes, but I always try to see backwards.

Th. Why?

Pt. I was angry at father, too. She didn't really want him.

Th. She didn't want him?

Pt. No.

Th. Why?

Pt. Mother didn't seem to want to bother with him, I guess.

Th. Did you love your father?

Pt. Yes.

Th. You did love him?

Pt. Uh huh, very much, but I stopped loving him.

Th. What made you stop loving him? How old were you when you stopped loving him?

Pt. I don't know. Maybe I didn't love father because of mother.

Th. Did you feel that you would eventually like to find a man like your father?

Pt. Oh, I did in my teen age, yes. Father is quick — he used to be very clever and funny. Once he got angry with mother, and he didn't speak to her for a long time. He was very jealous. He was very cross with me.

Th. He was very cross with you?

Pt. Yes, father was, when I started going out with boys.

Th. He did not like to have you go out with boys?

Pt. He was always . . . (*pause*) jealous.

Th. He was jealous.

Pt. Yes, he was.

Th. What was his name?

Pt. Lewis (*laughs*).

Th. Why did you laugh when you said Lewis?

Pt. 'Cause your name is Lewis.

Th. 'Cause my name is Lewis?

Pt. Uh huh.

Th. Do I in some way resemble your father?

Pt. Not very much. I got awfully upset when I saw that mirror thing.

Th. What sort of person was your father?

Pt. He was very determined.

Th. Determined?

Pt. Uh huh. Maybe I liked him too much.

Th. Most little girls love their father. Little girls often get infuriated with their mother for having father; but they finally decide that they will find a man of their own, that they don't have to have father.

Pt. Mother was always like that, telling me that too.

Th. Did she want you to go out with men?

Pt. Yes, she did (*pause*), oh, yes; but I think she turned me against them.

Th. What did she do to turn you against them?

Pt. Oh, always blazed at me; she's always blazed at me. I think she really hated men.

Th. She really hated men?

Pt. Uh huh.

Th. How did you learn that?

Pt. I . . . I . . . I just felt it.

Th. Now I am going to wake you up. When you feel you understand the meaning of what we have been discussing, you will remember what is necessary. I will count from one to five. At the count of five, open your eyes and wake up. One, two, three, start waking up, four, five.

This excerpt has illustrated the use of hypnosis for the recovering of a traumatic memory by employing hypnoanalytic techniques of regression and revivification, along with a counting procedure. These adjuncts are of aid in circumventing repression. Because repression is sponsored by anxiety which the patient is yet unable to control in the waking state, she is given a suggestion at the end of the session to remember the incident only when she has worked through its implications. In this particular case she was able to understand in a short while the significance of her mirror fixation and eye symptom, and to integrate her reaction to the traumatic scene of childhood. She was also able, with further therapy, to resolve her difficulty in her relationships with men.

VIII PSYCHOBEHAVIORAL SIGNIFICANCE OF HUMAN DEVELOPMENT

Throughout the eighteenth century most leading biologists agreed that reproductive cells contained preformed miniatures of the human body which evolved inexorably into predetermined adult shapes. There were vigorous debates among them, however, as to whether the location of this microscopic homunculus resided in the ovum or the spermatozoa. Because of technological limitations and theological prejudgments, the complex process of development from a fertilized germ cell to a fully mature organism could be neither observed nor even faintly grasped. Other technical inadequacies and preconceptions limited the ability of early biologists to conceptualize the inordinately intricate steps involved in postnatal physical maturation and psychological development. In fact, until recent decades, most scientists believed that human growth — from diffusion to differentiation to integration — arose exclusively from templates fixed within the structure of the genes. Accordingly, development evolved in terms of a preset timetable, completely autonomous of environmental influences.

This view of predetermined growth is no longer tenable. Maturation does follow an orderly progression, but the sequence and the ultimate character of the person's biological and psychological equipment is substantially dependent on both the quantity and quality of environmental experience to which he is exposed. Development does not progress on a fixed course that reaches a predestined level, but is subject to the impact of numerous experiential influences. Of course, some features of maturation are experienced in common by all humans, since we share many elements of biological structure and societal life. The extended dependency of infancy, the transformations of puberty, the acquisition and use of communicative language, the indoctrination into family roles and cultural values all lead to parallels in the lives of men and to relatively predictable stages through which these experiences progress.

That the topic of human development is especially relevant to medicine should be self-evident, since almost half of the patients a general practice physician will assume responsibility for are under the age of 21. Knowledge of age-related growth norms will enable the physician to identify developmental deviations such as muscular deficiencies, intellectual deficits, language dysfunctions, and so on. It is important for the physician to know also that the effects of particular diseases will vary considerably if they occur at different developmental periods. Similarly, the impact of separation from family upon hospitalization will be strikingly dissimilar for young as opposed to older children. At the other end of the life cycle, the problems of the aged have become especially significant to physicians, given the marked increase in the population now living well into their later years. Since difficulties stemming from personal and social dislocation complicate the medical status of elderly patients, physicians have found it necessary to become acquainted with both physical *and* psychosocial methods of diagnosis and treatment.

The first article of this chapter by Jane Kessler, a well-known child psychologist, describes the effects of a wide range of familial and social influences upon the development of the young child, with special reference to the impact of these forces on the maturation of intellectual functions. In her thoughtful and comprehensive essay, Kessler addresses numerous questions about the special role of early maternal care and cultural deprivation. Although the central thrust of her argument is directed toward issues of cognitive development, much of what she concludes has obvious applicability to other spheres of psychobehavioral growth.

The second paper, by Theodore Millon, presents an outline of the significant stages of early development. In his "neuropsychological" model, he notes the particular stimulus experiences all individuals face at three critical early developmental stages. In a manner similar to the views of Erik Erikson, the eminent psychoanalyst, these age-related periods are characterized by a specific task to which solutions must be found if the person is to progress toward greater maturity and health. Satisfactory solutions prepare the person to deal effectively with the problems of the next stage; unsuccessful solutions lead to cumulative adaptive difficulties. Erikson has proposed a parallel series of developmental stages encountered by those in adulthood and old age. According to his thesis, each young adult must interweave the characteristics of his personal identity with a significant other person if he is to acquire the capacity for genuine *intimacy;* failure to do so leads to what Erikson speaks of as "self-absorption." In the mid-phases of adulthood, the task to be solved is that of achieving *generativity,* a process of laying the foundations for effective functioning of the part of one's children; a negative outcome during this stage, that is, a failure to achieve generativity, is characterized by what Erikson terms "stagnation." The final phase of Erikson's model concerns the acceptance of one's life's achievements, that is, attaining mature dignity or what he terms *integrity;* the feeling that one's life has been wasted or worthless signifies the presence of what Erikson calls the "despair" of old age.

Robert Havighurst, a distinguished scholar and educator at the University of Chicago, furnishes a detailed review of the biological and psychological changes associated with the aging process. Here he summarizes numerous studies of these two stages of life, providing a thoughtful analysis of many of the factors that the student-physician should be thoroughly acquainted with as he approaches his work with more mature and older patients.

22.   Environmental Components of Measured Intelligence

Jane W. Kessler

The fact that there are significant individual differences in intelligence is undisputed, and no one advances a single-cause explanation for this fact. It is customary to speak of intelligence as the product of the interaction of environment and genetic potentiality. A small minority of psychologists, for example, Burt and R.B. Cattell, prefer to restrict the term intelligence to inborn capacity. Objection to this view is taken on the basis that inborn capacity is of necessity a hypothetical construct, something which can be inferred but never directly measured. Even before birth, there are factors operating to influence the genetic potential, and it is several years *after* birth and exposure to environment before one can get reliable measures of intelligence. For these reasons, among others, it is impossible to measure inborn potential. Intelligence is better and more commonly used to describe mental functioning which can be observed in home life, at school, at work, and which is sampled by standardized psychological tests.

Since the genetic components of intellectual ability have been well covered in other articles, this paper attempts an analysis of four factors which can be subsumed under the broad heading of "environment": (1) prenatal and paranatal conditions; (2) early maternal care; (3) sociocultural influences; and (4) individual personality characteristics. The paper concludes with a discussion of the validity of IQ tests and the proper use of their results.

ENVIRONMENT

Prenatal and Paranatal Conditions

At birth babies are already different. Experimental studies of such behavior as spontaneous motor activity in the first week of life[4] and changes in skin temperature and cardiac rate in response to stimulation in three-day-old neonates[33] show differences falling into the normal distribution curve. Although heredity undoubtedly contributes a large share to these constitutional differences, the effects of the fetal environment and process of birth are perhaps equally important. Ashley-Montague reviewed the many kinds of prenatal influences possible and concluded, contrary to the traditional view, that the placenta is apparently a highly permeable filter through which almost anything can be transferred to the fetus.[1] Abundant evidence has shown the effects of maternal nutrition upon the physical development of the fetus. There is also some evidence to show that the intelligence of the offspring, as measured by performance in later life, may be affected by the mother's nutrition during pregnancy. Harrell, Woodyard, and Gates reported the results of a study in Kentucky and Virginia concerning the influence of vitamin supplementation of the diets of pregnant and lactating women on the intelligence quotients obtained by their children at three to four years of age.[15] A

Kessler, J. W.: Environmental components of measured intelligence. The School Rev. *73:* 339–353 (1965).

statistically significant difference of 3.7 points was found between the Binet IQ's of the children whose mothers had had the vitamin supplements and those children whose mothers had received placebos during pregnancy and lactation. Since inadequate maternal nutrition is more prevalent in conditions of poverty, this provides a partial explanation for the lower mean IQ's in children from poor socioeconomic backgrounds.

Another possible influence on fetal reactions and development is the mother's emotional state, Sontag noted that bodily movements of fetuses increased several hundred percent while their mothers were undergoing emotional stress.[39] When the mother's emotional upset lasted several weeks, fetal activity continued at an exaggerated level throughout the entire period. Other more recent studies have confirmed the general idea that the mother's emotional attitudes are reflected in the newborn.[6] It is hard to evaluate the long-range effects of prenatal influences because of the overlay of later events, but it was Sontag's contention that prolonged maternal emotional stress during pregnancy may have enduring consequences for the child.

Pasamanick and his co-workers have reported a number of retrospective investigations in which the pregnancy and birth histories of children with physical and mental problems are compared with the early case histories of "normal" children. They concluded that there is a continuum of reproductive casualty resulting from prematurity and complications of pregnancy. In the extreme, these complications resulted in death, but there were many survivors with lesser degrees of brain damage who subsequently developed a series of disorders extending from cerebral palsy, epilepsy, and mental retardation through all types of behavioral and learning disabilities.[26] An important part of the Pasamanick studies is the association of pregnancy abnormalities with certain life experiences related to socioeconomic status. It is not only possible, but highly probable that the poor physical health and stressful emotional state of the pregnant mother in economically deprived circumstances put her baby at a significant disadvantage from the moment he is born.

Early Maternal Care

The lasting importance of the maternal care provided the baby in the first years of life is highlighted by noting the serious consequences of deprivation. The publication which most forcefully draws attention to this is that of Bowlby.[3] Bowlby reviews direct studies of the development of children living in institutions and hospitals, retrospective studies investigating the early histories of adolescents or adults who developed psychological problems, and follow-up studies of children who had no consistent mother figure during the first year. The most frequently quoted follow-up study is that of Goldfarb [11] in which he compared fifteen adolescents, who had lived in an institution for the first three or four years of life, with fifteen adolescents, supposedly of similar genetic background, who had lived in foster homes since infancy. The mean Wechsler IQ of the institution children was 72.4 and of the group living in foster homes, 95.4. Along with the mental retardation of the "ex--institution" children, there were distinct emotional trends; chiefly, the absence of a normal capacity for inhibition. The institution group showed extremely difficult behavior with symptoms of hyperactivity, restlessness, inability to concentrate, and unmanageability. Furthermore, they seemed to have no genuine attachments to people although they were indiscriminately and insatiably demanding of affection.

A more recent study of infants in institutions was made by Provence and Lipton.[31] They examined 75 children placed in an institution, 75 children with similar backgrounds placed in foster homes, and 75 children who remained with their own families. Although there were individual differences, the institutional children were significantly retarded in general development compared to both other groups. Language development was the first area revealing retardation, and it showed the greatest amount of retardation. It also took a longer period of family living for significant improvement to take place.

Studies with animal subjects also show that early experience influences adult problem-solving capacity. A classic experiment relating to this ability is that of Thompson and Heron who used dogs as subjects.[43] Some were reared under isolation in laboratory cages from the time of weaning to eight months of age. Their litter mates were reared for this same period in homes as pets. The cage-reared and pet-reared dogs were put together in a dog pasture for ten months; then, at eighteen months of age, their ability to solve mazes was tested. The pet-reared dogs were clearly superior to their cage-reared litter mates, indicating the permanent importance of the environmental differences in their early infancy.

In the face of such clear evidence concerning the effects of maternal care deprivation, the amount of misunderstanding has been surprising. First, some clinicians understood "maternal deprivation" to include *any* separation of the infant from the mother. This is not true; it is only prolonged separation with inadequate substitute mother care for which serious consequences may be expected. Second, many have thought that the dire consequences were inevitable and universal; that all children undergoing early institutionalization or other sorts of gross maternal deprivation develop an "affectionless character" or suffer retarded mental development. This is also untrue; but the fact that there are differences in vulnerability does not destroy the causal connections. In physical medicine not every individual exposed to a particular virus falls ill of the disease. Third, the inference has been made by some that every child of psychopathic disposition or with mental retardation has had this pathogenic experience in infancy. This also is not logical; many kinds of pathogenic factors can have the same end result. In this respect there is a difference between physical and mental illnesses. Physical illnesses are likely to be more specific in their symptomatology and be

the result of more specific antecedent conditions. Psychological problems are less sharply delineated and may result from multiple rather than single causes.

Oversimplification of the maternal deprivation concept has had its effects on clinical opinion and practice. Concern about maternal care tends to exaggerate the role of the mother in the development of any and all psychological difficulties of her children. Prevention is conceived solely in terms of maternal love and attention, and the cause of psychological difficulties is automatically attributed to "maternal rejection." Another misinterpretation has arisen from the issue of the possible irreversibility of damage done by early deprivation. Somehow the evidence showing the lasting effects of early deprivation despite improved environmental opportunities has been taken by some to mean that the personality is fixed by the age of three years and that no further changes are possible. On the basis of common sense and ordinary observation, this stand is obviously untenable. In normal development, the child of three years is reasonably plastic, having a potential for a great deal of further learning and development. It is only in abnormal conditions that the capacity for change is lost. A child who has been exposed to pathogenic deprivation and reacted to it in a sensitive way is in some ways "scarred for life." Depending on circumstances and the endowment of the child, these scars may be barely noticeable or may be severely handicapping. But the results of the special conditions of maternal deprivation cannot be generalized to children under normal environmental conditions.

In terms of clinical practice, Prugh and Harlow object to the current tendency to believe that separation of the child from his mother is to be avoided at all costs. [32] They point out that there can be "masked deprivation" where the infant's needs are unfulfilled even though he remains at home. After clinical study of the parents of mentally retarded children who were in the IQ range from 50 to 80 and had no history of birth injury or demonstrable organic pathology, Goshen suggests that mental retardation can occur as the by-product of certain types of maternal attitudes.[13] Specifically, he suggests that neurotic maternal attitudes which are characterized by a failure to stimulate and evoke meaningful signals during critical periods of life can result in the child's failure to grasp the significance of language. This failure may proceed to a state recognizable as mental retardation. Goshen was concerned with mothers who were ordinarily capable and conscientious but temporarily unable to give more than perfunctory physical care to their infants. He concluded with the excellent recommendation that "when a mother develops a deep psychological depression during the first year of a child's life, it would seem to be an urgent necessity to place the child in the care of a healthy adult until the mother comes out of the depression."[14]

There is nothing mystical about the importance of "mother love" in the first year of life. Biological motherhood does not guarantee maternal devotion, and the baby will accept a substitute mother if one is provided. It is not the existence of the person that counts, but the part that she plays in the infant's daily life. The relationship with a single person is the key factor in the infant's development. The gratifications provided by the mother draw the baby's attention to the outside world and serve as a bridge to other objects external to himself. After the baby has come to know her and to attach some importance to her, he becomes aware of her absences, and this helps him in differentiating between self and not-self. Inevitably, the mother frustrates the baby at times, and this adds further impetus to the baby's drive to gain independence and control over the outside world. By virtue of the coincidence of neural maturational changes, the baby acquires at the same time new powers of perception, memory, discrimination, motor coordination, and immitation which create some new problems for him, but, at the same time, new ways of solving them. Thus, we see that during the first year the baby is normally in an ideal educational situation where ability, opportunity, and motivation combine in the service of a common goal-development.

Sociocultural Influences

Although there is some connection between low socioeconomic status and (a) poor prenatal condition and (b) inadequate maternal care in the first year of life, the impact of these conditions on mental development is even greater at later ages. For many years there has been cogent evidence attesting to the effects of environment on measured intelligence. Skeels and Dye showed that the IQ's of retarded children in institutions could be raised by "differential stimulation";[37] Skodak and Skeels studied the effects of adoptive homes in raising IQ's,[38] and Klineberg reported the effect of environment on Negro children who had moved from the South.[23] The lowest scores were obtained by the groups most recently arrived from the South, with a close correlation between the length of time lived in New York and intelligence test scores. The improvement seemed to take place almost entirely in the first five or six years; those children who had lived in New York for a longer period showed little further improvement, and those Negroes who had moved to the North were, as a group, approximately at the average of the whole Negro school population of their original home cities.

Other studies, conversely, show the deteriorating effect of cultural impoverishment. Gordon, for instance, studied a group of children who grew up on canal boats in England.[12] At young ages, the average IQ of these children was about 90 (low average) but when the children were older the IQ dropped consistently, so that in their teens it was well below the average for the general population. Sherman and Key studied some communities located in Appalachia and reported similar findings.[36] The lowering of IQ in the older children was related to the varying degrees of isolation and opportunities for schooling that were provided in the areas studied This is similar to the "cumulative deficit phenomenon" recently described by Deutsch as taking place between the first- and fifth-years in lower-class children attending New York City schools.[7]

Although the importance of environment on measured intelligence has been well substantiated for some period of time, very little was done with this knowledge. Attempts were made to construct "culture-free" tests of intelligence to get at the "underlying potential" but none was successful. For example, Rosenblum, Keller, and Papania tried the Davis-Eells ("Culture-Fair") test with a group of mentally handicapped school-aged boys of lower social-class standing and found that the mean score was not significantly higher than the mean IQ's obtained on the Binet, which is highly verbal in content.[35] The authors commented that, though the Davis-Eells test may not contain culturally biased items, the conditions under which the test was administered cannot be said to have been completely free of middle-class overtones. Although it was presented to the children as a series of games, the children were not fooled and revealed by their comments that they knew from the outset that they were taking a test. A "good" test-taking attitude is dependent on cultural factors insofar as the child has been schooled to think it is important and profitable to try to do one's best.

In the 1960's, many people began to take a new, hard look at the old knowledge. The new questions asked were, "In what ways does culture affect intelligence?" and "What can be done about it?" It was soon obvious that many children came to school ill-prepared for academic work, and attention was focused on the preschool years. The role of maturation in early child development was re-examined. The work of Gesell and his colleagues provided normative pictures of children at different ages and stressed the orderly sequence of behavioral changes with increasing age. The developmental principles that Gesell offered as explanations were couched in terms of embryology[9] and stressed *intrinsic* factors rather than external, environmental factors. His dictum that "training does not transcend maturation"[10] implied a passive approach to early child care. Not only was early training considered futile, it was viewed as dangerous to "pressure" a child before he reached the point of optimum "readiness." According to this philosophy the young child should be left alone as much as possible in order that intrinsic

growth processes take their natural course of progression.

In some quarters there was question about this assumption of automatic growth in the young child. For one thing, the observations of the results of early maternal deprivation indicated the importance of the environment in stimulating and supporting the very beginnings of mental development. Animal experiments showed permanent loss of function without proper stimulation. By keeping chimpanzee babies in total darkness for varying lengths of time, Riesen and others found that certain anatomical structures of the retina were permanently damaged.[34] With a very different approach, namely, the study of mental development in young children in normal circumstances, Piaget came to the similar conclusion that nothing was so automatic that it did not require practice. Talking about the sucking reflex, Piaget stated that only practice leads to normal functioning.[28]

That is the first aspect of accommodation: contact with the object modified, in a way, the activity of the reflex, and, even if this activity were oriented hereditarily to such contact, the latter is no less necessary to the consolidation of the former. This is how certain instincts are lost or certain reflexes cease to function normally, due to the lack of a suitable environment.[29]

The new thought that "readiness" is in part an acquisition of experience rather than solely a development of time prompted an analysis of the environmental conditions in which culturally disadvantaged children spent their first five years. Even more specifically, attention was drawn to the role of social class in language development (Deutsch).[8] Children in the lower socioeconomic groups start to talk, on the average, at a later age than do children in higher socioeconomic groups. In the lower income groups, verbal productions from the child are likely to be ignored as of little value. It is regarded as more important that the child take care of himself and achieve independence from the mother as early as possible so she can turn her attention to other babies, earn extra money, or maintain the household. In contrast, parents of middle and high socioeconomic status are more likely to talk to their children and to listen with pride and pleasure to what their children have to say. Irwin demonstrated that talking *to* children from an early age (twelve months and up) increases the verbal productivity of the child.[19] He explained this in two ways. First, in classical learning terms, a certain behavior, that is, verbalization, is positively rewarded by the mother's attention. Second, in psychodynamic terms, the child normally identifies with his mother, and if she talks, so does he.

There have been efforts to pinpoint the language deficiencies prevailing in lower-class families. Errors in enunciation and grammatical syntax have been analyzed. Perhaps even more important than the quality of language is its use. John and Goldstein report that children from low-income homes have relatively little opportunity to engage in active dialogue when learning labels,[22] and Bernstein points out that in poorer homes language is used in a restrictive fashion rather than in an explanatory one.[2] If the child asks for something, the parental response is an abbreviated acknowledgment rather than a complete sentence or thought which elaborates on the child's utterance. The feedback does not provide the child with more information than that with which he started. The parents, setting little store by words, are content with approximations and imprecise labels where "flower" covers "tree," "bush," "weed," and so on. As pointed out by John and Goldstein,[22] it is only by corrective feedback that the child learns that a "dog" is not a horse or cat or some other four-legged object (discrimination). By the same process he learns that "dog" is not only the white Spitz but also the black police dog, the brown stuffed animal, and the picture of "Spot" in a book.

There are many theories regarding the intimate connections between language and thought. Piaget emphasizes the importance of language in the socialization process. Progression from primitive modes of thinking requires that the child become aware of himself as thinking, feeling, seeing, hearing, from a point of view unique to himself. He needs a dual perspective whereby he not only perceives reality but is aware of himself perceiving and is thus able, within limits, to discount and compensate for his own biases, blind spots, and restricted vision. He can only require his kind of awareness of self in contrast to something else, namely, the point of view of others. To see the world as it appears to someone else can only be done through the medium of language.

> Intelligence, just because it undergoes a gradual process of socialization, is enabled through the bond established by language between thoughts and words to make an increasing use of concepts; whereas autism, just because it remains individual, is still tied to imagery, to organic activity, and even to organic movements. The mere fact, then, of telling one's thought, of telling it to others, or of keeping silence and telling it only to oneself must be of enormous importance to the fundamental structure and functioning of thought in general, and of child logic in particular.[27]

Others have studied children's ability to solve complex problems as related to the use they make of language in verbal mediation. Jensen defines verbal mediation as "verbal behavior which facilitates further learning, which controls behavior and which permits the development of conceptual thinking."[21] It appears that children who receive insufficient verbal stimulation in early childhood develop deficiencies not only in spoken language but also in verbal mediational behavior so that they are handicapped in the concept formation and problem-solving abilities required in the school learning situation.

The facts about early language development and later intellectual ability have given renewed impetus to preschool education. Hunt has proposed preschool enrichment as an antidote for cultural deprivation and social disadvantage.[16] In accordance with these new ideas, preschools in underprivileged, urban neighborhoods have been mushrooming in an effort to fill in the gaps, particularly in language, which are left by the parents. One hopes that the parents will not be forgotten in all the flurry. It is unlikely that the preschool teacher can equal the parent as an identification figure for the child. It would be profitable to give the parents the opportunity to identify with the teacher so that the parents in turn can serve as models for the child and support the educational efforts.

Individual Personality Characteristics

The influence of sociocultural factors on intelligence development is usually considered in terms of group trends with little attention to the individual variations. The emphasis is on environmental conditions insofar as they provide the child with an opportunity to learn. There is less thought given to the role of motivation for learning; there is an assumption that if the proper opportunities are provided at the crucial times, the child will "naturally" seize upon these opportunities because of some intrinsic growth motivation. In Hunt's words,

the problem for a teacher endeavoring to keep children interested in intellectual growth is one of providing circumstances so matched, or mismatched, to those with which her pupils are already familiar that an interesting and attractive challenge is continually provided.[17]

Hunt feels that there is a "kind of intrinsic motivation which is inherent in information processing and action" and that "an opportunity to see and hear a variety of things is more important than the fate of instinctual needs and impulses."[18]

There is a tendency for exciting new ideas to be taken as a replacement for what went before. There is no fundamental conflict between the psychoanalytic ideas concerning the transformation of basic drives in the stimulation of intelligence and Hunt's suggestions regarding the importance of environmental stimulation for promoting intelligence. Early maternal deprivation has its devastating effect on intelligence not only because of lack of environmental stimulation but also because of the lack of emotional attachments. To put it simply, the child must care for a person before he really cares about things. Without an emotional attachment he tends to be either apathetic and disinterested in his environment, or he takes an obsessive interest in objects and things excluding those stimulations emanating from people. Such an exclusion has a disastrous effect on language development and eventually on the whole of mental development. This distortion is seen most clearly in autistic children, though other forms of childhood psychosis also block intellectual development as a by-product of the disturbed social relationships. Without help on the social score, these children are unable to take advantage of environmental opportunities for learning and remain fixed at primitive levels of thinking.

There are less pathological conditions where one also sees the interaction of personality factors and the development of intelligence. Learning requires activity, and if the parents keep the child dependent and in a state of enforced passivity, mental growth is often stunted as a consequence. An interesting study that corroborates this thesis was done by Sontag, Baker, and Nelson.[40] They compared the personalities of children who showed increases or decreases in measured intelligence over a period of years. According to their observations, the "passive, infantile dependent pattern" led to a decreasing level of Binet performance, whereas, "aggressive, self-reassuring mastery of tasks, competitive independent patterns" led to progressively advanced performance. Child therapists (for instance, Sperry, Ulrich, and Staver[42]) have noticed that therapy for learning problems is more effective with aggressive children than with passive, compliant children. Regardless of socioeconomic status, the drive for mastery is not the same in all children. This may in part be determined by inborn constitution, but it is also affected by parental attitudes toward the child's early strivings for independence and autonomy.

A second important connecting link between personality, and intelligence is the fate of early childhood curiosity. During the age period of one to two years, curiosity finds expression primarily through physical acts. From the age of two years on, curiosity becomes increasingly intellectual. Although curiosity is generally thought of as a desirable characteristic, this holds true only for impersonal topics. Questions about God, death, sex differences, the origin of babies are often shunted aside by the nervous parent. Individual families may have special secrets which are constantly in evidence, but which at the same time are taboo for discussion. Forbidden secrets exist in families of all cultural descriptions but are perhaps more frequent in disorganized families of low socioeconomic level. For instance, a family forced to make repeated, surreptitious moves in order to "jump the rent" will not prepare the child in advance or explain it after the move. If the child cannot ask (and receive an answer) about such vital questions as to where he will sleep, where is Daddy, who is that man (or woman), he is not going to venture questions about the moon and stars. Anxiety is one powerful incentive for wonderment. The child wants to know what is going to happen and why, in order to avoid surprises and prepare himself. If curiosity does not help to relieve anxiety, it has little value. Curiosity cannot be compartmentalized or restricted only to safe subjects.

A corollary to this problem of forbidden curiosity is the problem of forbidden knowledge. By independent observation the child may learn something about which he later feels guilty or anxious. Inner conflict may motivate the child to repress or hide his knowledge from others. This is one of the dynamic mechanisms involved in the oft quoted case of "pseudoimbecility" published by Mahler.[24] Many times the repressed or hidden knowledge is of a sexual nature because sexuality is commonly an emotionally charged topic, though any subject can be equally taboo in specific family circumstances. In these cases where the retardation is a defense against the anxiety of knowing, the child acts out the aphorism, "Where ignorance is bliss, it's folly to be wise."

There are many other possible points of connection between personality and mental development based on the mechanism of displacement. For example, conflicts in infantile feeding experiences do not inevitably result in symptoms of an oral nature only. Eating is a form of incorporation, a process of taking in from the outside world. Difficulties in taking in by mouth may spread to the perceptual processes of taking in through the eyes and ears. The possible connection is shown in everyday idioms such as "drinking in with the eyes,"

"devouring the sight," "digesting information," "a voracious reader," "hunger for knowledge," and so on. There is more than a similarity in process. The carry-over from eating to learning may stem from the repetition of a specific interpersonal relationship as well. A child who has been fed against his will, for instance, is likely to have residual feelings about superior, strong persons who force things on him. Learning requires the gracious acceptance of someone's superiority (at least on a pro tem basis) and can be blocked by unconscious feelings against someone who knows more than the learner. The neurotic children in whom eating conflicts have been displaced to the intellectual sphere, show poor absorption, appear not to understand what they are taught, and seem to forget from one time to the next.[41]

Another kind of displacement is from genital conflicts. Here the child's major concern is with the genital differences between the sexes and his feelings about his own genital adequacy. Visual experience is important in learning about the sex difference. Jarvis, in an article on visual problems in reading disabilities, linked neurotic conflicts in looking with fantasies which deny the fact of castration in women.[20] A child warding off the anxiety caused by looking at one thing avoids looking at anything with close attention. For example, at the age levels of four and a half and five years, there are several items on the Stanford-Binet test which require comparison of visually presented objects in terms of their likenesses and differences. Occasionally a child will refuse to look at them, saying flatly, "They are all the same." If a child will not look for fear of seeing differences, he will have considerable difficulty in learning to read.

One could give other examples where the acquisition, retention, and/or demonstration of knowledge are blocked because of anxiety about one or another aspect of "knowing." When stupidity serves a defensive purpose to reduce anxiety, the child is immune to environmental stimulation no matter how well it is planned. Throughout a child's life there is constant interaction between mental and emotional development, and difficulties on the one side usually affect the other. Under normal conditions there is no incompatibility; affective and cognitive lines of development proceed together. In the absence of conflict there is indeed pleasure in "knowing" because it gives a sense of mastery and relieves the anxiety of helplessness.

MEASUREMENT OF INTELLECTUAL FUNCTIONING

In talking about intelligence and the factors that influence its development, it is important to consider how intelligence is measured. Intelligence is judged by overt behavior. Some use diffuse standards of "adaptive" behavior, such as getting along well with people and meeting the demands of school and work. Quantification of individual differences, however, demands the use of more limited, rigid criteria provided by intelligence-test performance. As measuring tools, IQ tests have much less reliability than tools of physical measurements. The probabilities of IQ changes over a period of time have been well researched. Pinneau prepared a series of tables which give the changes in Binet IQ's in individuals tested and retested at various ages.[30] One study showed that in a group of children first tested at six years and retested at twelve years, 50 per cent showed IQ changes of 8 points or more, with 25 per cent changing 13 points or more. The accumulation of such figures has completely destroyed the myth of IQ constancy. The changes are in part errors of measurement, and in part changes in the individual being tested.

The changes in the person can come about for many reasons. The opportunities the child has for experience is one possible causal factor. Psychologists do not hesitate to say that intelligence tests measure the results of learning and that no sharp distinction can be made between intelligence and attainment. In the words of Cureton:

It is obvious that every test of intelligence, as well as every test of school achievement, is a measure of a set of developed abilities. The difference lies in the choice of abilities to be measured and in the method of devising items to measure them. The general intelligence test, as its name implies, tries to measure general ability. To do this, it must include a variety of mental tasks, including samples of the more important types of mental operations and of symbolic content. The achievement test, on the contrary, limits the range of sampling to a relatively narrow and specific set of abilities. The symbolic content covered is fairly definite, and the range of mental operations called for is well-defined and not extremely extensive.[5]

More recently, Vernon arrived at a similar conclusion. "There is no essential difference between the acquisition of, say, reading skills and the acquisition of reasoning or other capacities which would be conventionally regarded as part of intelligence."[44]

Environment is filtered through the individual's screen of perceptual styles, interests, ego ideals, and prejudices. Neurotic conflicts with their subsequent defenses, characterological traits, and specific anxieties all affect efficiency of intellectual functioning, sometimes serving to heighten it. It has been proposed that intelligence be regarded as a dynamic aspect of personality, and suggestions have been made regarding the analysis of intelligence-test behavior for such personality features as "coping styles."[25]

Considering errors of measurement and the effects of learning and personality on intelligence-test scores, one can appreciate that we are very far from measuring anything like "inborn potential." This does not render the intelligence test meaningless. The intelligence test is useful for short-range predictions of scholastic ability. The score is not an attribute of the child; by itself it does not explain why the child is the way he is. A good intelligence test gives important information about present functioning. When combined with an evaluation of the history and total situation of the child, it may provide the basis for remediation of deprivation and/or psychological conflict. The information from careful tests should not be brushed aside as irrelevant because it is environmentally produced. The term "pseudo-retardation" is a misnomer in that it implies retardation on a familial or organic basis. "Pseudo-retardation" may be less permanent but it is no less real at the moment. Intelligence tests (assuming that they have been carefully administered) are valid in describing present level, which is of necessity the starting point for therapists or teachers. Just as a child cannot jump from primer reading to Shakespeare, he cannot jump from magical thinking to an understanding of the principle of number equations. IQ results cannot be projected backward to evaluate genetic potentiality nor can they be projected into the future to determine the ceiling of achievement possibilities. It is quite sufficient that they be used for current planning.

REFERENCES

1. Ashley-Montague, M. F.: Prenatal Influences. Springfield, Ill., Charles C. Thomas, 1962.
2. Bernstein, B.: Language and Social Class. Brit. J. Soc. 271–76 (1960).
3. Bowlby, J.: Maternal Care and Mental Health. World Health Organization Monograph, Series No. 2, 1951.
4. Brownfield, E. D.: An Investigation of the Activity and Sensory Responses of Healthy, Newborn Infants. Unpublished doctoral dissertation, Cornell University, 1956.
5. Cureton, E. E.: The Accomplishment quotient technique. J. Exp. Educ. 5: 315-26 (1937).
6. Davids, A. S., and Talmadge, M.: Anxiety, pregnancy, and childbirth abnormalities. J. Consult. Psychol. 25: 74-77 (1961).
7. Deutsch, M.: Facilitating development in the preschool child: Social and psychological perspectives. Merrill-Palmer Quarterly. 0: 249–63 (1964).
8. Deutsch, M.: The Role of Social Class in Language Development and Cognition. Institute for Developmental Studies, Department of Psychiatry, New York Medical College, April, 1964. (mimeographed).
9. Gesell, A.: Infant Development: The Embryology of Early Human Behavior, New York, Harper & Bros., 1932.
10. Gesell, A.: The Developmental Psychology of Twins. In Murchison, C. (ed.) Handbook of Child Psychology, Worcester, Mass., Clark University Press, 1931, p. 189.
11. Goldfarb, W.: The effects of early institutional care on adolescent presonality. J. Exp. Educ. 12: 106-29 (1943).
12. Gordon, H.: "Mental and scholastic tests among retarded children: An enquiry into the effects of schooling on the various tests", Education Pamphlet. London, Board of Education, No. 44 (1923).
13. Goshen, G. E.: Mental retardation and neurotic maternal attitude. Arch. Gen. Psychia. 9: 168-75 (1963).
14. Goshen, C. E.: Mental retardation and neurotic maternal attitudes. Arch. Gen. Psychiat. 9: 174 (1963).
15. Harrell, R. F., Woodyard, E., and Gates, A. I.: The Effect of Mothers' Diets on the Intelligence of the Offspring, New York, Teachers College Press, 1955 VII.
16. Hunt, J. McV.: The psychological basis for using pre-school enrichment as an antidote for cultural deprivation. Merrill-Palmer Quarterly 10: 209-248 (1964).
17. Hunt, J. McV.: The psychological basis for using pre-school enrichment as an antidote for cultural deprivation. Merrill-Palmer Quarterly 10: 209-248 (1964).
18. Hunt, J. McV.: The psychological basis for using pre-school enrichment as an antidote for cultural deprivation. Merrill-Palmer Quarterly 10: 209-248 (1964).
19. Irwin, O. C.: Infant speech: The effect of systematic reading of stories. J. Speech Hearing Res., pp. 187-90 (1960).
20. Jarvis, V.: Clinical observations on the visual problem in reading disability. Psychoanalytic Study of the Child. Vol. XIII, New York, International Universities Press, 1958.
21. Jensen, A.: Learning in the pre-school years. J. Nursery Educ. 133-39 (1963).
22. John, V. P. and Goldstein, L. S.: The social context of language Acquisition. Merrill-Palmer Quarterly. 10: 265-76 (1964).
23. Klineberg, O.: Negro Intelligence and Selective Migration. New York, Columbia University Press, 1935.
24. Mahler, M.: Pseudo-imbecility: A magic cap of indivisibility. Psychoanal. Quart. 11: 149-64 (1942).
25. Moriarty, A. E.: Coping patterns of pre-school children in response to intelligence test demands. Genet. Psychol. Monog. 64:1 3-127 (1961).
26. Pasamanick, B., and Knobloch, H.: Epidemiologic studies on the complications of pregnancy and the birth process. In Caplan, C.: Prevention of Mental Disorders in Children, New York, Basic Books, Inc., 1961.
27. Piaget, J.: Language and Thought of the Child, New York, Meridian Press, 1955, p. 64.
28. Piaget, J.: The Origin of Intelligence in the Child, Trans. Margaret Cook. New York, International Universities Press, 1952.
29. Piaget, J.: The Origin of Intelligence in the Child. Trans. Margaret Cook. New York, International Universities Press, 1952, p. 30.
30. Pinneau, S. Changes in Intelligence Quotient. Boston, Houghton Mifflin Co., 1961.
31. Provence, S. and Lipton, R. C.: Infants in Institutions. New York, International Universities Press, 1962.
32. Prugh, D. C., and Harlow, R. G.: Masked deprivation in infants and young children. In

Depreviation of Maternal Care: A Reassessment of Its Effects. Geneva, World Health Organization, Public Health Papers, No. 14, 1962.

33. Richmond, J. and Lustman, S.: Autonomic function in the neonate: Implications for psychosomatic theory. Psychosom. Med. *17:* 269-275 (1955).

34. Riesen, A. H., Harlow, H. F., and Woolsey, C. N. (eds.): "Plasticity of behavior: Psychological aspects. In Biological and Biochemical Bases of Behaviors, Madison, University of Wisconsin Press, 1958, pp. 425-50.

35. Rosenblum, S., Keller, J. E., and Papania, N.: Davis-Eells ("Culture-fair") test performance of lower class retarded children. J. Consult. Psychol. *19:* 51-54 (1955).

36. Sherman, M. and Key, C. B.: The intelligence of isolated mountain children. Child Dev. 3:279-290 (1932).

37. Skeels, H. M. and Dye, H. B.: A study of the effects of differential stimulation on mentally retarded children. Proc. Am. Assoc. Men. Defic. *40:* 114-36 (1939).

38. Skodak, M. and Skeels, H. M.: A final follow-up study of one hundred adopted children. J. Genet. Psychol. *75:* 85-129 (1949).

39. Sontag, L. S.: The significance of fetal environmental differences. Am. J. Obstet. Gynec. *42:* 996-1003 (1941).

40. Sontag, L. S., Baker, C. T. and Nelson, V. P.: Personality as a determinant of performance. Am. J. Orthopsychiat. *25:* 555-62 (1955).

41. Sperry, B., Staver, N., and Mann, H.: Destructive fantasies in certain learning difficulties. Am. J. Orthopsychiat. *22:* 356-366 (1952).

42. Sperry, B., Ulrich, D. N., and Staver, N.: The relation of motility to boys' learning problems. Am. J. Orthopsychiat. *28:* 640-646 (1958).

43. Thompson, W. R., and Heron, W.: The effects of restricting early experience on the problem-solving capacity of dogs. Can. J. Psychol. *8:* 17–31 (1954).

44. Vernon, P. E.: Intelligence and Attainment Tests. New York, Philosophical Library, 1960, p. 39.

23.   Neuropsychological Stages of Development

Theodore Millon

A major theme of this chapter is that development progresses as a result of an intimate interplay of intraorganismic and environmental forces; such interactions start at the time of conception and continue throughout life. Individuals with similar biological potentials emerge with different personality patterns depending on the environmental conditions to which they were exposed. These patterns unfold and change as new biological maturations interweave within the context of new environmental encounters. In time, these patterns stabilize into a distinctive hierarchy of behaviors which remain relatively consistent through the everchanging stream of experience.

To state that biological factors and environmental experiences interact is a truism; we must be more specific and ask how, exactly, these interactions take place.

Before we begin, let us discount questions about the proportionate contribution of biological factors as contrasted to environmental learning. The search to answer such questions is not only impossible from a methodological point of view, but is logically misleading. We could not, given our present state of technical skill, begin to tease out the relative contribution of these two sources of variance. Furthermore, a search such as this would be based on a misconception of the nature of interaction. The character and degree of contribution of either biogenic or psychogenic factors are inextricably linked to the character and degree of the contribution of the other. For example, biological influences are not uniform from one situation to the next but vary as a function of the environmental conditions within which they arise. The position we take, then, is that both factors

Millon, T.: Modern Psychopathology. Philadelphia, W. B. Saunders Co., 1969.

contribute to all behavior patterns and that their respective contributions are determined by reciprocal and changing combinations of interdependence.

Let us return now to the question of how, exactly, biogenic and psychogenic factors interact in development.

Biological factors can shape, facilitate or limit the nature of the individual's experiences and learning. For example, the same objective environment will be perceived as different by individuals who possess different biological sensibilities; people register different stimuli at varying intensities in accord with their unique pattern of alertness and sensory acuity. From this fact we should see that experience itself is shaped at the outset by the biological equipment of the person. Furthermore, the constitutional structure of an individual will strengthen the probability that he will learn certain forms of behavior. Not only will his body build, strength, energy, neurological make-up and autonomic system reactivity influence the stimuli he will seek or be exposed to, but they will determine, in large measure, which types of behaviors he will find are successful for him in dealing with these encounters.

We must recognize further, that the interaction between biological and psychological factors is not unidirectional such that biological determinants always precede and influence the course of learning and experience; the order of effects can be reversed, especially in the early stages of development. From recent research we learn that biological maturation is largely dependent on favorable environmental experience; the development of the biological substrate itself, therefore, can be disrupted, even completely arrested, by depriving the maturing organism of stimulation at sensitive periods of rapid neurological growth. The profound effect of these experiences upon biological capacities will be a central theme in this chapter; we will contend that the sheer quantity as well as the quality of these early experiences is a crucial aspect in development.

Beyond the crucial role of these early experiences, we will argue further that there is a circularity of interaction in which initial biological dispostions in young children evoke counterreactions from others which accentuate their disposition. The notion that the child plays an active role in creating environmental conditions which, in turn, serve as a basis for reinforcing his biological tendencies is illustrated well in this quote from Cameron and Magaret (1951):

> ... The apathy that characterizes an unreactive infant may deprive him of many of the reactions from others which are essential to his biosocial maturation. His unresponsiveness may discourage his parents and other adults from fondling him, talking to him, or providing him with new and challenging toys, so that the poverty of his social environment sustains his passivity and social isolation. If such a child develops behavior pathology, he is likely to show an exaggeration or distortion of his own characteristic reactions in the form of retardation, chronic fatigue or desocialization.

This thesis suggests, then, that the normally distributed continuum of biological dispositions which exists among young children is widened gradually because initial dispositions give rise to experiences that feed back and accentuate these dispositions. Thus, biological tendencies are not only perpetuated but intensified as a consequence of their interaction with experience.

Despite the fact that there are cases in which later experience can reverse early behavior patterns, we cannot understand these cases fully without reference to the historical background of events which precede them. We assert that there is an intrinsic continuity throughout life; thus, the present chapter has been organized to follow the sequence of natural development. Furthermore, not only do we contend that childhood events are more significant to personality formation than later events, but we also believe that later behaviors are related in a determinant way to early experience. Despite an occasional and dramatic disjunctiveness in development, there is an orderly and sequential continuity, engendered by mechanisms of self-perpetuation and social reinforcement, which links the past to the present. Moreover, certain forms of behavior appear immutable and resistant to change.

Such deeply rooted traits need not signify the presence of an innate disposition, nor need they stem from the effects of a biological trauma or disease. Embedded patterns of behavior may arise entirely as a product of psychological experience, experience which shapes the development of biological structures so profoundly as to transform it into something substantially different from what it might otherwise have been.

Under what circumstances can psychological experience exert so profound an effect?

An answer that enjoys a great degree of acceptance is experience during infancy and early childhood. The major impetus for this view can be traced to the seminal writings of Freud at the turn of this century. The observations of a number of eminent European ethologists on the effects of early stimulation upon adult behavior in animals have added substantial naturalistic evidence to support this position in the past twenty years. Experimental work during this period has shown more precisely that environmental stimulation is crucial to the maturation of several psychological functions.

The thesis that early experience has a paramount effect upon personality formation is taken for granted by many theorists and researchers; this consensus is not reason enough, however, to accept it without further elaboration. We must ask why early experience is crucial, and, more specifically, how this experience shapes the biological substrate of personality.

Several answers advanced in response to these questions will be elucidated throughout the chapter. For the moment we will concentrate on one: the dependence of maturation on early environmental stimulation. The thesis may be stated simply: certain biological capacities will fail to develop fully as a result of impoverished stimulation; conversely, these same capacities may be overdeveloped as a consequence of enriched stimulation.

PLASTICITY OF THE MATURING BIOLOGICAL SUBSTRATE

Maturation refers to the intricate sequence of ontogenetic development in which initially diffuse and inchoate structures of the body progressively unfold into specific functional units. Early stages of structural differentiation precede and overlap with more advanced stages in which lower level units interweave and connect into a complex and integrated network of functions displayed only in the adult organism.

It was once believed that the course of maturation — from diffusion to differentiation to integration — arose exclusively from inexorable forces laid down in the genes. Maturation was thought to evolve according to a preset timetable that operated autonomously of environmental conditions. This view no longer is tenable. Maturation follows an orderly progression, but the developmental sequence and level of the organism's ultimate biological equipment are substantially dependent on a variety of stimuli and nutritional supplies from the environment. Thus, maturation progresses not in a fixed course leading to a predetermined level, but is subject to numerous variations which reflect the character of the organism's environment.

The answer to why early experiences are more crucial to development than later experiences derives in part from the fact that the peak period of maturation occurs from the prenatal stage through the first years of postnatal life. Granting that experience can influence the course of maturation, it is reasonable to conclude that the organism is subject to more alteration in the early, or more plastic years, than when it has fully matured. An example in the sphere of body structure may illustrate this point well. Inadequate nutrition in childhood may result in stunted bone development, leading to a permanently shortened stature; no amount of nutrition in adult life can compensate to increase the individual's height. However, had adequate nutrition been given during the formative or maturing years, the child might have grown to his full potential. Similarly, in the nervous system, prenatal deficiencies in nutrition will retard or arrest the differentiation of gross tissue into separable neural cells; early postnatal deficiencies will deter or preclude the proliferation of neural collaterals and their integration. However, deficiencies arising later in life will have little or no effect on the development of these neural structures.

Concept of Stimulus Nutriment

The concept of nutrition must be viewed more broadly than we commonly view it if we are to understand its role in the development of biological maturation. Nutrition should be conceived as including not only obvious supplies such as those found in food, but in what Rapaport had termed "stimulus nutriment" (1958). This notion of nutrition suggests that the simple impingement of environmental stimuli upon the maturing organism has a direct bearing on the chemical composition, ultimate size and patterns of neural branching within the brain. Stated simply, the sheer *amount* of stimulation to which the child is exposed has a determinant effect on the maturation of his neural capacities. (We are bypassing, for the moment, any reference to the effects of the timing or quality of the stimulative source, factors which also have a bearing on development.)

The notion that degree of stimulation can produce changes in neural development is not new. Spurzheim, in 1815, proposed that the organs of the brain increase by exercise. Ramon y Cajal suggested in 1895 that since neural cells cannot multiply after birth, cerebral exercise will result in the expansion of neural collaterals and in the growth of more extended intercortical connections. For more than fifty years, experimental biologists have reported that the development and maintenance of neural connections are dependent on periodic stimulus activation. As early as 1915, Bok showed that nerve fibers grow out along the path of repeated stimuli; he termed this phenomenon *stimulogenous fibrillation.* Similar observations in the 1930's led Kappers to formulate the concept of *neurobiotaxis.* Valid criticisms have been leveled at certain features of these concepts, but there appears to be considerable support from recent research that neurochemical processes, essential to the growth and branching of neural structures, are activated by stimulation; extremes of stimulus impoverishment or enrichment appear to prompt an under or overdevelopment of neural connections and patterns

(Conel, 1939, 1955; Pasamanick et al., 1956; Scheibel and Scheibel, 1964; Eisenberg, 1967).

The belief that the maturing organism must receive periodic stimulus nutriments for proper development has led some theorists to suggest that the organism actively seeks an optimum level of stimulation. Thus, just as the infant cries out in search of food when deprived, or wails in response to pain, so too may it display behaviors which provide it with sensory stimulation requisite to maturation. Murphy (1947) and Butler and Rice (1963), for example, have proposed that the maturing organism possesses a series of "adient drives" or "stimulus hungers." They note that although infants are restricted largely to stimulation supplied by environmental agents, they often engage in what appears to be random exercises, exercises which, in effect, furnish them with the stimulation they require. Thus, in the first months of life, infants can be seen to track auditory and visual stimuli; as they mature further, they grasp incidental objects, and then mouth, rotate and fondle them. Furthermore, we observe that the young of all species engage in more exploratory and frolicsome behavior than adults. These seemingly "functionless" play activities may not be functionless at all; they may be essential to growth, an instrumental means of self-stimulation that is indispensable to the maturation and maintenance of biological capacities.

Implicit in the above is the view that the organism's partly matured capacities enable it to provide for itself sources of stimulation necessary for further maturation; according to this thesis, each stage of maturational development establishes a foundation of capacities which are prerequisites for, and conducive to, the development of more advanced stages of maturation. For example, a child with deficient sensory capacities such as vision may be unable to maneuver within its environment, and consequently may be delayed in the development of motor capacities such as walking and running. Similarly, a child with a marked hearing loss may develop inarticulate speech since he is unable to discriminate sounds.

Consequences of Early Stimulus Impoverishment

It should be evident from the foregoing, that unless certain chemicals and cells are activated by environmental stimulation, the biological substrate for a variety of psychological functions may be impaired irrevocably. Furthermore, deficiencies in functions which normally mature in early life may set the stage for a progressive retardation of functions which mature later.

What evidence is there that serious consequences may arise from an inadequate supply of early stimulation?

Numerous investigators have shown that an impoverished environment in early life results in permanent adaptational difficulties. For example, experimental animals reared in isolation tend to be markedly deficient in such traits as emotionality, activity level, social behavior, curiosity and learning ability. As adult organisms they possess a reduced capacity to manipulate their environments, to discriminate or abstract essentials, to devise strategies and to cope with stress.

Comparable results have been found among humans. Children reared under unusually severe conditions of restriction, such as in orphanages, evidence deficits in social awareness and reactivity, are impulsive, deficient in solving intellectual problems, susceptible to sensorimotor dysfunctions and display a generally low resistance to stress and disease. These consequences have double-barreled effects. Not only is the child hampered by the specific deficiency he suffers, but each of these deficiencies yields progressive and long-range consequences in that they preclude or retard the development of more complex capacities. Thus, early deficits may precipitate a whole series of stunted or distorted adaptive capacities.

Consequences of Early Stimulus Enrichment

Intense levels of early stimulation also have effects. Several investigators have demonstrated among animals that an enriched environment in early life results in measurable changes in brain chemistry and brain weight. Others have found that early stimulation accelerates the maturation of the pituitary-adrenal system, whereas equivalent stimulation at later stages was ineffective. On the behavioral level, enriched environments appear to enhance problem-solving abilities and increase the capacity of the organism to withstand stress. Comparable data among humans is either lacking or equivocal. Nevertheless, several theorists have proposed that enriching experiences can foster the development of higher intellectual abilities and adaptive coping behaviors.

There has been little systematic exploration of the potentially detrimental effects of environmental enrichment, since researchers and clinicians alike are inclined to assume that the opposite side of the coin, that of impoverishment, is more conducive to pathological consequences. This assumption probably is correct, but it should not lead us to overlook the possibility that excessive stimulation can lead to an overdevelopment of certain biological capacities which may prove disruptive to effective psychological functioning. Thus, just as excessive food nutrition leads to obesity and physical ill health, so too may stimulus enrichment produce unhealthy psychological growth. For example, the enhancement or strengthening of certain neural patterns, such as those associated with emotional reactivity, may dispose the organism to overreact to social situations. The predominance of any biological response tendency may throw off key what would otherwise have been a normal or more balanced pattern of psychological functioning. Clearly then, the enrichment of biological capacities does not produce beneficial consequences only; whether enhanced functions prove advantageous or disadvantageous to the individual depends on which of the many and diverse capacities have been enriched, and whether the resultant pattern is balanced or unbalanced.

NEUROPSYCHOLOGICAL STAGES OF DEVELOPMENT

The previous section focused only on the determinant effects of *volume* of early stimulation. Our attention now will turn from the issue of "how much" to that of "when"; here we will explore the view that the specific time of stimulation has a direct relationship to its effect. The question can be raised: are the effects of extremes in stimulation greater at certain periods of early maturation than others? Interest will be directed and limited to the *interaction* of volume and timing, not to the content or quality of the stimulative source. Questions about the effects of different kinds of stimuli will be discussed in the next section; for the present, we shall deal only with the interplay between "how much" and "when," not with "what." In reality, of course, these three elements are not separable. We distinguish among them, however, not only for pedagogic purposes; we believe that each of these variables can produce different and specifiable effects upon the development of personality; they should be distinguished, therefore, for theoretical clarification and research execution as well.

Two kinds of relationships may be observed between the effect of a stimulus and the time of its occurrence; we may term these *recurrent periods* and *sensitive developmental periods.*

The first relates to recurrent tissue needs, best illustrated in periodic deficit conditions known as hunger and thirst. At various times each day, the depletion of certain nutritional substances leads to increased levels of neurological activation and the selective focusing of sensory receptors. As a consequence, stimuli to which attention is not ordinarily given become dominant and have a marked impact upon the organism. For example, while driving along a road, we tend to notice signs pertaining to food if we are hungry; after a good meal, however, these signs pass by in a blur. The role of these recurrent periods will be elaborated when we discuss, in a later section, the operation of what is known as "motivation" in learning.

The second, and less obvious, relationship between timing and stimulus impact will be our principal focus in this section. It refers to the observation that certain types of stimuli have an especially pronounced effect upon the organism at par-

ticular and well-circumscribed periods of maturation. At these periods or stages, the organism is unusually responsive to and substantially influenced by the action of these stimuli.

Concept of Sensitive Developmental Periods

The contention that stimuli produce different effects at different ages can scarcely be questioned, e.g., the shapely legs of an attractive girl catch the eye of most young and middle-aged men but rarely draw the attention of preadolescent boys and senile men. The concept of sensitive or critical periods of development states more than this, however. It argues, first, that there are limited time periods during which particular stimuli are necessary for the full maturation of an organism and, second, that if these stimuli are experienced either before or after the sensitive period, they will have minimal or no effects. Thus, if critical periods pass without proper stimulus nourishment, the organism will suffer certain forms of maldevelopment which are irremediable, that is, cannot be compensated for by the presentation of the "right" stimuli at a later date.

The rationale for the sensitive period concept was presented initially in the field of experimental embryology. One of the early researchers, Child (1941), found that rapidly growing tissues of an embryo are especially sensitive to environmental stimulation; the morphological structure of proliferating cells was determined, in large part, by the character of the stimulus environment within which it was embedded. At later stages, where growth had slowed down, these same cells were resistant to environmental influences. These embryological findings suggested that the effects of environmental stimuli upon morphological structure are most pronounced *when tissue growth is rapid.*

It is unclear as to what mechanisms operate to account for the special interaction between stimulation and periods of rapid neural growth. *First,* there is evidence that stimulation itself promotes a proliferation of neural collaterals, and that this effect is most pronounced when growth potential is greatest. *Second,* early stimulation may result in a selective growth process in which certain collaterals establish particular interneuronal connections to the exclusion of others. *Third,* we may hypothesize that once these connections are embedded biologically, the first set of stimuli which traverse them preempt the circuit and thereby decrease the chance that subsequent stimuli will have comparable effects. Whatever the sequence and mechanisms may be, it appears clear that the effects of stimulation are maximal at periods of rapid tissue growth; at this point in our knowledge we only can speculate on the apparatus involved.

The notion that brief early experiences may produce a permanent modification of functions has been theorized by scientists in fields other than embryology. Lorenz (1935), the eminent European ethologist, has discovered critical periods during which primary social bonds are permanently established in birds. In human research, McGraw (1943) demonstrated the existence of peak periods for learning specific motor skills, and illustrated the resistance of these skills to subsequent extinction. Murphy (1947) reports a number of studies to support the concept of canalization, a notion signifying an irreversible initial learning process.

Developmental theorists have proposed, either by intention or inadvertently, schemas based on a concept of sensitive periods. Few, however, have formulated this notion in terms of neurological growth stages.

Heinz Werner, for example, has proposed a comparative-developmental approach in which he coordinates the total behavior of organisms in accord with a basic set of developmental principles. His central thesis is that development proceeds from an initially undifferentiated and diffuse state to one that is progressively refined and differentiated. As the organism matures further, these differentiated functions intermesh and become integrated into smoothly coordinated higher capacities.

The theories and studies of Piaget (1952) provide us with an insightful picture of the invariable and hierarchic order in the developmental progression; he demonstrates

how each progressively more complex stage is based on foundations established in preceding stages, and prepares the groundwork for succeeding ones. Pertinent to our own formulations is Piaget's sequence of intellectual development which he divides into several major periods; the first of these is known as "reflexive," the second as "sensorimotor" and the third through fifth are abbreviated as "representational-conceptual"; these periods correspond closely to the three major neuropsychological stages to be presented later in this chapter.

The brilliant speculations of Hebb (1949), phrased according to developmental concepts such as cell-assemblies and phase-sequences, may be viewed as parallel to the neurological orientation proposed here. More recently, Milner (1967) has furnished a carefully detailed review and theory of maturation with explicit reference to the interrelationships of neural and behavioral development; although the theory is presented in sketchy form, she coordinates the impact of experience on neurological growth with a model similar to that formulated in this chapter.

Freud's theory of discrete stages of psychosexual development, in which particular early experiences at specified times in development have deeply etched and lasting effects, may be viewed as the first major theory based on a concept of sensitive periods. Despite Freud's early training as a neurologist, his schema was founded *not* in terms of internal neurological maturation, but in terms of a peripheral sphere of maturation, that of sexual development. His concern lay with variations in external sensory erogenous zones (e.g., oral, anal and genital), not with the more central neurological structures which underlie and are basic to them.

It would appear from recent neurological and behavioral research that a more profitable basis for organizing a system of developmental periods would be in terms of internal neurological growth potentials. Relationships certainly will exist between these inner variables and other less centrally involved variables, such as Freud's concept of erogenous zones. But to focus on peripheral spheres of maturation as did

Freud, is, from our view, to put the proverbial "cart before the horse."

Other theorists have organized the stages of personality development in accord with interpersonal experience. First among these is Harry Stack Sullivan, whose developmental notions stress the progressive capacity of the child to understand and communicate with others. The first stage of infancy represents a period of preverbal and primitive imagery in which generalized feelings of trust and security are the primary features of interpersonal communication. The second stage is characterized by the emergence of verbal communication; communication at this point is highly idiosyncratic, however, and often is illogical and confused. In the final stage, the child's capacities have matured sufficiently to enable him to grasp the consensually validated, that is, the shared meanings of language and communication. Psychopathology arises, according to Sullivan, when the child fails to receive proper experiences requisite to the progressive development of consensually validated communication. Anxiety-producing or deficient and confusing communications lead to distortions in the development of communication capacities, and result in an inability to maintain adequate interpersonal relationships.

As with Freud, Sullivan's schema tends to be somewhat narrow in scope. To Freud, the sexual variable was central to each of the successive periods of development. Sullivan opts for a single and primary variable also, that of interpersonal communication. No doubt, both Freud and Sullivan are correct in specifying two of the crucial elements operative in the developmental sequence; the question that arises, however, is whether the foundation of a comprehensive theory of stages should be constructed from either of the two "peripheral" variables they espouse or from a more central neurological process.

Erikson has formulated an important synthesis of both Freud's and Sullivan's proposals, one enriched further by adding to them the contribution of the "ego" theorists. Erikson extends Freud's focus on childhood psychosexuality, that is, the development of id energies, by adding to them the role of constructive sensorimotor and cognitive capacities, that is, the development of ego energies. These two sources of energy are interconnected within the maturing infant and provide him with a "succession of potentialities for significant interaction with those who tend him." Thus, Erikson attempts to bring together within a single conception of developmental stages the previously separate spheres of sexuality, ego capacity and interpersonal relatedness. Furthermore, he relates this developmental progression to a series of personal and interpersonal crises. At each step in maturation, the child faces a new and decisive encounter with the environment in which his maturing capacities are tested and refined before he progresses toward the realization of his full potentials.

Erikson's theory is the most comprehensive formulation for organizing the varied dimensions of personality growth. Furthermore, his recognition of the crises encountered during each epigenetic period makes his schema relevant to an understanding of development. In presenting the neuropsychological stages of development that have been formulated for this chapter, we will draw freely upon Erikson's seminal ideas; his views owe, in turn, a special indebtedness to Freud, Sullivan and his fellow ego theorists.

Despite the scope and relevance of Erikson's theory to development, it is not coordinated directly to the notion of neurological growth and maturation. As stressed earlier, the central logic for a conception of sensitive periods is founded on evidence that environmental stimuli have their most pronounced effects at times of potentially rapid neural growth. It would seem reasonable, therefore, to revise Erikson's synthesis in line with this neurological viewpoint. Recast in this fashion, it will have a firmer basis as a theory of sensitive periods, and will be formulated in terms consonant with our growing knowledge of the neurological substrate of development.

It is appropriate, before we progress further, to ask a simple but important question: how precise is our knowledge of the character and sequence of neurological maturation? The simplest and most direct answer, given our present state of empirical research, is that we have little knowledge that is clear and relevant; we grasp only the barest outline of the diverse and intricate features which unfold in the developing nervous system. At best, we can make only a few rough distinctions for separating the developmental sequence into identifiable periods of rapid neurological growth. These neurologically sensitive periods must be inferred from sketchy odds and ends gathered from fields as diverse as embryology, neurophysiology, ethology, behavior development and childhood psychopathology. The framework we shall employ to divide these neurological stages will be revised, no doubt, as research progresses.

How shall we divide the maturational sequence, given the sketchy knowledge we possess today?

Keeping in mind the tentative nature of the proposed divisions, and the substantial overlapping which exists between successive stages (all aspects of growth occur simultaneously, though in varying degrees), current theory and research suggests three broad periods of development in which an optimal point of interaction occurs between neurological maturation and environmental stimulation:

1. The first stage, extending in its peak period from birth to 18 months of age, evidences a rapid maturation of sensory receptors, and is characterized by a substantial dependency of the infant upon others. This stage will be termed the period of *sensory-attachment.*

2. The second period, beginning roughly at 12 months and extending in its peak development through the sixth year, is characterized by a rapid differentiation of motor capacities which combine and corrdinate with developed sensory functions; this integration enables the young child to locomote, manipulate and verbalize in an increasingly skillful way. This stage will be referred to as the period of *sensorimotor -autonomy.*

3. The third and final period of maturation begins at about four to five years of age and continues through adolescence; it is characterized at first by the rapid development of higher cortical connections and in its later phases by the turbulent effects of rapidly maturing sexual hormones. These advances enable the child to reflect, plan and act independent of parental supervision. We shall call this stage the period of *intracortical-initiative.*

Obviously, this simple tripartite schema does not differentiate the manifold and detailed substages of neurological development; that task awaits future research. We have referred to these periods as the "neuropsychological stages of development" because they group together and summarize what we believe are the psychologically relevant features of neurological growth, that is, they focus on those neurological capacities that are both sensitive to environmental influence and crucial to the individual's capacity to cope with his social environment. Let us keep in mind that although these stages reach their peak periods at different ages, they extend through the entire course of development. As maturation progresses from one stage to the next, the sensitivities of preceding stages do not cease, but merely become less prominent.

Comment. Let us note a number of qualifications upon the generalizations we shall be making before we elaborate the features and consequences associated with each of these stages.

1. During the sensitive developmental stages, minimal external stimulation produces maximal neuronal patterning; subsequent neural growth, such as in adulthood, requires considerably greater external stimulation. One of the distinguishing features of man's immense brain is that it contains a tremendous number of surplus neural fibers which can be stimulated to develop collaterals throughout adulthood. Thus, inadequate neuronal connections, especially in the higher cortical areas, may be strengthened after maturity.

2. It is erroneous to assume that children of the same chronological age are comparable with respect to the level and character of their biological capacities. Not only does each infant start life with a distinctive pattern of neurological, physiochemical and sensory equipment, but he progresses at his own maturational rate toward some ultimate but unknown level of potential. Thus, above and beyond

initial differences and their not insignificant consequences, are differences in the rate with which the typical sequence of maturation unfolds. Just as some youngsters grow in rapid spurts, reaching their full height by 13, while others progress slowly and steadily until 19 or 20, so too may children follow different courses in the maturational speed and pattern of their neurological substrates. Furthermore, different regions in the complex nervous system within a single child may mature at different rates. To top it all, the potential or ultimate level of development of each of these neurological capacities will vary widely, not only among children but within each child. Thus, a youngster may have a constitutional disposition to mature a sparse neurological substrate for sensory functions, and a dense and well-branched substrate for intracortical or integrative functions. A brief summary of the rationale of the neuropsychological stages and their relation to psychopathology may be useful before we furnish a detailed description of their separate developmental features and consequences.

The initial capacities of each organism are established by genetic factors. The sequences in which these capacities mature follow a general species-specific order. However, the rate and level to which these capacities develop are determined in large measure by the amount of stimulation the organism experiences at certain peak periods of neural growth. During growth, the organism utilizes its established capacities as a means of providing itself with the stimulus nutriment required for further development. Despite these efforts, the developing organism usually is dependent upon others to supply its nurturant needs. Failure in stimulus nourishment leads to an undermaturation or a retarded progression in development; overstimulation leads to overdevelopment or unbalanced development. When the peak or sensitive period of neural growth has passed, further development is low and arduous; for all essential purposes, the organism's neuropsychological capacity has reached its likely upper limits. Continued stimulus nutriment is required, however, to sustain this level of development. Following the peak period,

therefore, the organism will continue to engage in activities which provide a level of stimulation consonant with its capacities; undeveloped, that is, previously impoverished individuals, *once past the peak period of neural growth,* will require a lower level of stimulus maintenance than overdeveloped or previously enriched individuals. Each individual will seek to maintain an optimum level of stimulus activation, that is, a level that corresponds to his developed neuropsychological capacities.

Let us now turn to the stimulus characteristics and consequences of the three principal stages of neuropsychological development.

Stage 1: Sensory-Attachment

The first year of two of life is dominated by *sensory* processes; these functions are basic to subsequent development in that they enable the infant to construct some order out of the initial diffusion and chaos he experiences in his stimulus world. This period has also been termed that of *attachment* because the infant cannot survive on his own, and must affix himself to others who will provide the protection, nutrition and stimulation he needs.

Development of Sensory Capacities

The early neonatal period has been characterized as one of undifferentiation. This descriptive term suggests that the organism behaves in a diffuse and unintegrated way; perceptions are unfocused and behavioral responses are gross. Recent research indicates that certain sensory functions are well matured at birth and that they progress rapidly in their development shortly thereafter.

One of Freud's signal achievements was his recognition that the mouth region was a richly endowed receptor system through which the neonate establishes his first significant relationship to the stimulus world. It is evident, however, that this oral unit is merely the focal point of a more diverse system of sensory capacities in the infant. Freudians have focused on this well-circumscribed region to the exclusion of other less clearly defined spheres of sensitivity; we now know that it is not only through oral contacts that the infant establishes a sense or "feel" of his environment.

Despite the paucity of knowledge about early receptor sensitivities, experimental studies support the view that the near receptors, involving touch, taste, smell and temperature, are dominant in the neonate. This evidence is not inconsistent with Freud's belief in the importance of the oral region, since the mouth, lips and tongue are especially rich in several of these receptor capacities. However, tactual and kinesthetic sensitivities pervade the entire body, and there is every reason to believe that the infant can discriminate and respond to subtle variations in temperature, texture and general physical comfort.

According to the theory espoused earlier, we would expect that the amount and quality of tactile stimulation to which the neonate is exposed will contribute significantly to his neuropsychological development. Not only may extremely low levels of stimulation result in developmental retardations, but the quality and pattern of this stimulation may lead him to experience generalized feelings of isolation, tension or pleasure. (Parenthetically we might note that care must be taken not to attribute subtle or cognitively complex attitudes to the infant; for example, it is unlikely that a two month old can discern the difference between a rough rejecting mother and one that is clumsy and inexperienced.)

The primacy in the first months of life of touch, taste, temperature and smell recedes as distance receptors of vision and audition come to the foreground. Whereas the near receptors are limited to bodily contact stimuli in the immediate environment, the distance receptors expand the scope of the infant's experiences by enabling him to survey and explore a far-ranging and infinitely more elaborate sphere of stimuli. Here again, variations in the quantity and quality of his stimulus world can have profound effects on his neuropsychological development.

Development of Attachment

The neonate does not differentiate between objects and persons; both are experienced simply as stimuli. How does this initial indiscriminateness become transformed into specific attachments to particular stimuli, especially the stimulus of the mother? Phrased less abstractly, we may ask why the two month old infant is intrigued and soothed by most forms of stimulation, the five month old by the behavior of certain toys and the antics of most humans, and the 12 month old only by a special blanket and the presence of mother.

A few words should be said first about what appears to be an innate tendency on the part of infants to turn toward and be soothed by stimulation. Soviet psychologists refer to this attraction to stimuli as the "orienting reflex"; Goldstein (1939) has described it simply as a "turning toward the stimulus." For example, normal infants will automatically close their fists when their palm is stroked, and turn their heads toward shimmering leaves, rather than stare at a blank wall. We know also that stimulation-producing activities and devices (e.g., rocking, wheeling, mobiles and radios) are commonly employed by mothers as a means of capturing the attention and calming the discomforts of their infants. Any one of a number of currently popular terms can be applied to describe this behavior — orienting reflex, stimulus hunger, arousal seeking, exploratory curiosity. Whatever, the label, it simply signifies that the newborn organism seems intrinsically attracted and responsive to stimulation.

Let us now return to the main question: how does the neonate's diffuse orientation to stimuli become progressively refined into specific attachments? This process can best be described in terms of concepts and mechanisms utilized in the field of learning; in the next major section of this chapter, we will elaborate the process in a detailed manner; the sequence will briefly be described here.

The newborn, for all essential purposes, is helpless and dependent on others to supply its needs. Separated from the womb at birth, the neonate has lost its "attachment" to the mother's body, and the nurturance it provided. It now must turn toward other sources of attachment if it is to survive, be comforted and obtain the requisite stimulation for its further development. The infant's stimulus seeking and attachment behavior may be viewed, albeit figuratively, as an attempt to reestablish the intimate and gratifying unity lost at birth. Since it will be some years before it can provide these needs on its own, the infant progressively discriminates, through its developing sensory capacities, those objects which have a high nurturant and stimulus value. Attachments may occasionally be made to inanimate objects, such as the odor of a doll's hair or the texture of a favorite blanket, but the infant, under normal conditions, will center his attachments to the complexly stimulating and rewarding object of his mother. Gradually distinguishing her as a stimulus source providing warmth, softness, food and comfort, he begins to seek her touch, her odors and her soothing voice. Thus, his attachment to her.

What systematic evidence is there to support the view that sensory processes play a central role in the development of specific attachments? In large measure, this support is obtained from research on subhuman avian and mammalian species; these data are extrapolated or analogized then to similar behaviors displayed among humans.

One body of animal research deals with what has been referred to as "imprinting" behavior; young birds and sheep, for example, are first attracted to the sight of moving objects, then track or follow them as they locomote (Lorenz, 1935; Hess, 1959; Moltz, 1968). The second body of research, referred to as "the establishment of primary affectional and social bonds," has concentrated on the early behaviors of dogs and monkeys (Scott, 1960, 1968; Harlow, 1960, 1963, 1965); for example, these animals demonstrate attachments to surrogate mother objects who provide soft tactual stimulation.

Research on early social bonds points up the primacy of sensory stimulation over conventional rewards. Harlow, for example, found that "ungiving" surrogate mothers covered with a soft terry cloth were preferred to food-nourishing mothers constructed of wire. Furthermore, he showed that young monkeys cling to terry cloth rather than wire mothers when faced with novel and upsetting objects; thus reassured, they venture forth to explore the initially frightening object. If no mother, or if only the wire mother is present under these conditions, the infant displays continued fear and anxiety. In other studies, noxious air blasts were vented from the terry-cloth mother after the primary bond of attachment was established; following the infliction of this pain, the infant monkey, rather strikingly, clung even more tightly to his "unworthy" terry-cloth mother. According to traditional notions of reward and punishment, we would expect the monkey to have avoided the painful terry-cloth mother. However, if we interpret this finding as evidence of an attachment to the cloth mother, or as a sign of the primacy of sensory stimulation over all other rewards or punishments at this stage, then this seemingly paradoxical result becomes more understandable. In short, these studies support the view that early sensory stimulation gives rise to the development of strong attachment behaviors.

Attachment behavior studies with humans lean heavily on naturalistic evidence. Ribble (1943), Spitz (1965), Bowlby (1952), Gewirtz (1963) and Rheingold (1963), though differing in their interpretation of the mechanisms involved, all conclude that the tactile and kinesthetic stimulation provided by the mother serve as the basis of the infant's attachment. Aspects of their work will be elaborated more fully in later sections.

Maladaptive Consequences of Impoverishment

What we have stressed thus far is that the simple volume of sensory stimulation is a significant part of the child's environmental experience; let us be mindful, however, that the character or quality of that stimulation is of equal importance; that topic will be dealt with fully in another section in this chapter.

A wealth of clinical evidence is available to show that humans, deprived of adequate maternal care in infancy, display a variety of pathological behaviors. Of course, we cannot design studies to tease out precisely which of the complex of variables that comprise maternal care account for these irreparable consequences; the lives of babies cannot be manipulated to satisfy our scientific curiosity. The value of animal research is clear here since it is possible in these studies to arrange conditions necessary for a more precise analysis of the problem.

Riesen (1961) and Beach and Jaynes (1954) have provided extensive reviews of the consequences in animals of early stimulus impoverishment. Briefly, sensory neural fibers atrophy and cannot be regenerated by subsequent stimulation. Almost any means of stimulation (e.g., stroking tossing, shaking or shocking) will provide the necessary activation for neural development. Inadequate early stimulation in any of the major receptor functions results in marked decrements in the capacity to utilize these and other sensory processes in later life.

Assuming the infant animal has an adequate base of *physical* stimulation, what consequences will follow if it is deprived of *social* stimulation?

The profound effects of social isolation have been studied most thoroughly by Harlow and his associates (1960, 1963, 1965). In a series of studies in which monkeys were totally or partially deprived of social contact, they found that the longer and more complete the social isolation, the more devastating were the behavioral consequences. Deprived monkeys were incapable at maturity of relating to their peers, of participating effectively in sexual activity and of assuming adequate roles as mothers.

Many theorists have sought to relate stimulus impoverishment in human infants to aberrations in later behavior. Most notable in this regard are the views of Bowlby (1952), Goldfarb (1955) and Spitz (1965). According to their observations, an inadequate supply of stimuli from a caretaking environment results in atypical response patterns to nonsocial stimuli and marked deficits in social attachment behaviors; quite often, these are gross developmental retardations, limited capacities for human relationships and a pervasive apathy and depression. These children display inadequate use of their visual and auditory functions; for example, experimenters ofter are unable to achieve visual contact with these youngsters, and they appear to "look through" observers when approached frontally.

The disorder known as *infantile autism* provides an interesting case in point. These children display excessive preoccupations with inanimate objects, engage in repetitive "self-exercising" activities and seem oblivious to the presence and communications of other humans. Kanner (1949) has suggested that these youngsters received "impersonal" care during infancy, that the warmth and direct human contact requisite to the development of specific human attachment behaviors were denied them either through parental rigidity, remoteness or incompetence. Without cuddling, warmth and a soothing voice, so necessary in the early stages of new receptor development, these infants failed to identify the mother as a stimulus object able to supply their diverse needs. As a result, these youngsters developed a series of diffusive or undifferentiated attachments to random and essentially inanimate objects which, as they mature, they continue to fondle and manipulate to provide themselves with the warmth and stimulation they need. To illustrate, a nine year old "autistic" boy seemed totally oblivious of the presence of other humans, exhibiting no seeming awareness of and response to them, even when efforts were made to intrigue him with comic antics, a soothing voice or the display of bright noise-producing toys; rather, his interest was focused on a few colorless blocks and a misshapen doll to which he had become attached in infancy, and which he fondled and smelled nearly all of his waking time. We might note parenthetically that autistic behaviors have been attributed by other theorists to constitutionally defective sensory or arousal systems; thus the child is viewed to be biologically incapable of responding to most stimulative sources and, thereby, cannot become attached to specific stimulus objects. This formulation runs into difficulty, however, since many autistic children do form attachments to inanimate objects; if their defect arose from a generalized sensory or arousal deficiency, any form of attachment would appear unlikely. A more narrowly circumscribed biological deficiency, such as a "social-affect" deficit, seems rather far fetched, but would obviate this inconsistency.

Observers with diverse theoretical views concur on the consequences of inadequate early care; not all agree, however, that it is simply the deficit volume, apart from the nature, of stimulation which is crucial to these aberrations. According to the thesis presented here, variations in the amount of stimulation are more significant during the early neonatal period than is the nature of that stimulation, although both are important. As the infant matures into his second and third year, the nature or quality of the stimulative source becomes the more significant dimension of environmental experience.

Little has been said in the literature about the potential effects of less severe degrees of early sensory impoverishment. We should not overlook the fact that degree of sensory impoverishment is a gradient or continuum, not an all-or-none effect. There is every reason to believe that children who receive less than an optimum degree of sensory stimulation (an amount that will vary, no doubt, in accord with individual differences) will grow up to be less "sensory oriented" and less "socially attached" than those who have experienced more.

Maladaptive Consequences of Enrichment

What are the consequences of too much early sensory stimulation? Unfortunately, data and theories on this score are few and far between; researchers have been preoccupied with the effects of deficit sensory stimulation rather than excess sensory stimulation. There is a substantial body of theory, but little research, describing the process of overattachment.

It is not unreasonable to hypothesize that excess stimulation in the sensory-attachment stage would result in an overdevelopment of associated neural structures. The work of Rosenzweig et al. (1962), for example, has shown that enriched early environments produce increments in certain neurochemicals. It would not be implausible to hypothesize, further, than an abundance of these chemicals would prove detrimental to subsequent development. Thus, just as too little stimulation may lead to deficit sensory capacities, so too may superfluous stimulations lead to receptor oversensitivities and, in turn, to a maladaptive dominance of sensory functions.

In this vein, Freud hypothesized that excessive indulgence at the oral stage was conducive to fixations at that period; he referred to adult individuals who underwent this childhood experience as "oral characters." According to psychoanalytic theory, these individuals display a life-long pattern of socially gregarious and dependent behaviors. We will reformulate this conception, eschewing both oral and fixation notions, in terms of the effects of an overdevelopment of early sensory functions. Specifically, we propose that excessive sensory development in childhood would require a high level of stimulus maintenance in adulthood; these maintenance needs would be displayed in persistent sensory activation behavior. Thus, these individuals might be characterized by their seeking of sensory stimulation, their boredom of routine and their capricious searching for excitement and adventure. They would have, in Murphy's terms, an overenriched adient drive or, as Riesen might put it, a need to sustain their established level of neural sensory development. For example, a 14 year old hyperactive girl seemed incapable of "being satisfied" and made inordinate demands upon her parents to "take me here" and "take me there" and "buy me this" then "buy me that"; no sooner would she go somewhere or get something than she would be bored and want to do or get something new. A review of her early history showed that she was a "happy and good baby," but indulged excessively with warm affection and playful stimulation by doting parents and grandparents.

Exactly what neural or chemical mechanisms account for this stimulus-seeking pattern is a matter for speculation: perhaps sensory tissue abundance leads to a rapid adaptation to stimuli; since the effects of stimuli would "wear off" rapidly under these circumstances, the need for new stimulation would build up quickly again. Whatever the mechanisms may be, it appears plausible neurologically, and consistent with clinical observation, to conclude that overenriched early stimulation can result in pathological stimulus-seeking behavior.

Turning briefly to attachment behaviors, it would seem reasonable to assume that excess stimulation, anchored exclusively to the mother, would result in an overattachment to her. This consequence is demonstrated most clearly in the pathological disorder known as the *symbiotic child*, where we find an abnormal clinging by the infant to the mother, an unwillingness to leave or allow her out of sight and a persistent resistance to stimulation from other sources (Mahler, 1952). Feelings of catastrophe, isolation and panic often overtake these children if they are sent to nursery school, or "replaced" by a newborn sibling.

The need to sever the ties of early attachments, so deeply troubling for the symbiotic child, is experienced in some measure by all children. The progression from the first to the second neuropsychological stage is a gradual and overlapping one; a progressive unfolding of newly matured capacities facilitate the shift, however. We next will turn to the characteristics and consequences of this second stage.

Stage 2: Sensorimotor-Autonomy

All infants possess the rudiments of certain motor capacities at birth; however, it is not until the end of the first year that they are sufficiently matured to engage in actions independent of parental support. A holding of the drinking cup, purposeful crawling, the first few steps or a word or two, all signify a growing capacity to act autonomously of others.

As the child develops the functions which characterize this second stage, he has begun to comprehend with some clarity the attitudes and feelings communicated and intended by stimulative sources. No longer is rough parental handling experienced merely as excess stimulation, undistinguished from the playful tossing of an affectionate father; the child now can discern the difference between parental harshness and good-natured roughhouse. As the meaning or quality of stimulating experiences begins to take on primacy, the importance of pure volume of stimulation itself becomes less significant than it was in the first stage of development. For this reason, discussions regarding the role of psychogenic influences in the second and third stages must focus primarily on the intricate processes and consequences of learning, rather than on the more diffusive processes of neurological growth. Nevertheless, a brief presentation of the overall role of under or overstimulation during these two periods will be instructive.

Development of Sensorimotor Capacities

The unorganized gross movements of the neonate progressively give way to differentiated and focused muscular activity. As the neural substrate for muscular control unfolds, the aimless and groping motor behavior of the infant is supplanted by focused, voluntary movements. These newly emergent functions coordinate with previously matured sensory capacities to enable the child to explore, manipulate, play, sit, crawl, babble, throw, walk, catch and talk.

The innately maturing fusion between the neurological substrates of sensory and motor functions is strengthened by the child's exploratory behavior. His absorption in manipulative play, or the formation of babbling sounds, are methods of self-stimulation which facilitate the growth of interneuronal connections; he is building a neural foundation for progressively more complicated and refined skills such as running, handling utensils, controlling sphincter muscles and articulating precise speech. His intrinsic tendency to "entertain" himself is not merely "something cute to behold," but a necessary step in establishing capacities that are more substantial than maturation alone would have furnished. Stimulative experiences, either self-provided or through the actions of others, are requisites then for the development of normal sensorimotor skills. Unless retarded by environmental restrictions, by biological handicaps or by deficits in early sensory development, the toddler's growing sensorimotor capacities prepare him to cope with his environment with increasing competence and autonomy.

Development of Autonomy

Perhaps the most significant aspect of sensorimotor development is that it enables the child to begin to do things for himself, to exert an influence upon his environment, to free himself from parental domination and to outgrow the attachment and dependencies of his first years — in other words, to develop a range of competencies by which he can master his world and establish a feeling of autonomy.

This developmental progression can be seen in many spheres of behavior. With his growing skill in locomotion, he can explore new environments. With the advent of speech, he can engage in new social relationships, challenge the thoughts and desires of others, pronounce his own directives, resist, entertain, cajole and manipulate his parents. He becomes aware of his increasing competence and seeks to test his mettle in new ventures. Needless to say, conflicts and restrictions inevitably arise as he asserts himself. These may be seen most clearly during the period of toilet training when youngsters often resist submitting to the demands and strictures of their parents. A delicate exchange of power and cunning ensues. Opportunities arise for the child to manipulate his parents and to extract promises or deny wishes; in response, parents may mete out punishments, submit meekly, register dismay or shift inconsistently among all three. Important precedents for attitudes toward authority and feelings of power and autonomy

are generated during this and other periods of parent-child conflict.

Maladaptive Consequences of Impoverishment

Most of the consequences of this period reflect the quality or kind of stimulation to which the child is exposed, rather than the simple amount of stimulation he experiences. Certain consequences, however, may be attributed primarily to impoverishment.

The failure to encourage and stimulate sensorimotor capacities can lead to serious retardations in functions necessary to the development of autonomy and initiative. This may be seen most clearly in children of overprotective parents. Spoon-fed, helped in dressing, excused from "chores," restrained from exploration, curtailed in friendships and protected from "danger," all illustrate controls which restrict the growing child's opportunities to exercise his sensorimotor skills and develop the means for autonomous behavior. A self-perpetuating cycle may unfold. The child may not be able to abandon his over-learned dependency upon his parents since he is ill-equipped to meet other children on their terms. He is likely to be timid and submissive when forced to venture out into the world, likely to avoid the give and take of competition with his peers, likely to prefer the play of younger children and likely to find an older child who will protect him and upon whom he can lean. Each of these adaptive maneuvers intensifies his established sensorimotor retardations since it prevents him from engaging in activities that will promote catching up with his peers. He may become progressively more unfit for autonomous behaviors and social competition, and eventually, may display the features of a submissive and dependent adult.

Maladaptive Consequences of Enrichment

The consequences of excessive enrichment of the second neuropsychological stage are found most often in children of lax, permissive or overindulgent parents. Given free rein to test new skills with minimal restraint, stimulated to explore at will and to manipulate things and others to his suiting without guidance or control,the child will soon become irresponsibly narcissistic and undisciplined in his behaviors. When carried into the wider environment, however, these behaviors normally will run up against the desires of other children and the restrictions of less permissive adults. Unless the youngster is extremely adept, or the larger community unusually lax, he will find that his self-centered and free-wheeling tactics fail miserably. For the few who succeed, however, a cycle of egocentrism, unbridled self-expression and social arrogance may become dominant. To illustrate, a seven year old boy was completely unmanageable both in kindergarten and first grade, talking aloud while the teacher spoke, telling her that he knew "the answers" better than she, intruding and disrupting the play of other children, who referred to him as a "pest" and "bully"; from the family history it was learned that this youngster's parents not only believed in "total permissiveness" but encouraged their son to "speak up and disagree with them" and to "do whatever he wished, short of physically hurting others." The majority of these youngsters will fail to gain acceptance by their peers and will never acquire the give-and-take skills of normal social relationships. In the long, run, many of them learn to remain aloof from social activities; the fact that their "talents" have not been esteemed by the wider community is too painful an experience. In general, they come to be characterized by their haughty independence, and maintain their childhood illusions of self-importance through the fanciful workings of their imagination.

Stage 3: Intracortical-Initiative

By the time the major features of this stage begin to unfold, the role played by the amount of stimulus experience, apart from its content, has receded in significance. Volume of stimulation, per se, no longer is as crucial as it was in the first stage when the meaning of incoming stimuli was dimly perceived. Its relevance, at this third stage, serves to remind us that the peak periods of neurological maturation for certain psychological functions occur between the years of four and 18, and that the total amount of environmental stimulation at these times of rapid growth will have a strong bearing on the *degree* to which these functions mature. Thus, the volume of stimulus experience will influence not the character or content of these functions but their magnitude; weak or infrequent stimulation will result in capacity deficits, whereas intense or frequent stimulation will lead to exaggerated capacities.

What capacities unfold during this intracortical and initiative stage, and what consequences can be attributed to differences in the magnitude of relevant stimulus experience?

Development of Intracortical Capacities

Progressively complex arrangements of neural cells become possible as the infant advances in maturation. Although these higher order connections begin as early as four to six months of age, they do not form into structures capable of rational foresight and planning until the youngster has fully developed his more basic sensorimotor skills. With these capacities as a base, he is able to differentiate, arrange and control the objects of his physical world. As his verbal skills unfold, he learns to symbolize these concrete objects; soon he can manipulate and coordinate these symbols as well as, if not better than, the tangible events themselves. Free now of the need to make direct reference to the concrete world, he can recall past events and anticipate future ones. As more cortical connections are established, higher conceptual abstractions are formulated, enabling him to transfer, associate and coordinate these symbols into ideas of increasingly finer differentiation, greater complexity and broader integration. it is his own internal representations of reality, his own patterns of symbolic thought and his own constructions of events — past, present and future — which take over as the primary units of his stimulus world.

This process of neural growth toward higher forms of cortical integration depends on, and is stimulated by, both his own growing capacity to fantasize, and the evergrowing diversity of his environmental experiences. Without an increase in the complexity in his stimulus environment, and without his own inner symbolic manipulations, the major steps in the growth of potentially more elaborate intracortical connections will fail to materialize.

Somewhere between the eleventh and fifteenth years a rather precipitous series of hormonal changes unsettle the level of intracortical integration so carefully constructed in preceding years. These changes mark the onset of puberty — the emergence of strong sexual impulses and adult-like features of anatomy, voice and bearing. Erratic moods, changing self-images, new urges and hopeful expectancies and a growing physical and social awkwardness, all upset and challenge the relative equanimity of an earlier age. Disruptive as it may be, this turbulent stage of neural and physical growth activates and ties together the remaining undeveloped elements of the youngster's biological potential; it is a preparatory phase for the soon forthcoming independence from parental domination and direction. With it are called forth secretive self-stimulating activities and fantasies; for example, the typical adolescent promotes through masturbation the development of his adult sexual potentials. Once this last of his undeveloped capacities blossoms forth and is coordinated with other more developed functions, he is fully prepared, biologically, to assume the responsibilities of initiating an independent adult course.

Development of Initiative

When the inner world of symbols is mastered, giving the diverse elements of objective reality an order and integration, the growing youngster is able to create some consistency and continuity in his life. No longer is he buffeted from one mood or action to another by the swirl of rapidly changing events; he now has an internal anchor, a nucleus of stable cognitions which serves as a base, and which imposes a sameness upon an otherwise fluid environment. Increasingly, as he grows in his capacity to organize and integrate his symbolic world, one configuration predominates. Accrued from his experiences with others and from his effects upon them and their reactions to him, an image of the self-as-object takes shape. This highest order of abstraction, the sense of individual identity, becomes the core of personality functioning, the dominant source of stimuli which guides and influences the individual's style of behavior. External sources of stimulation no longer have the power they once exerted; the youngster now has an everpresent and stable sphere of internal stimuli which governs his course of action — he has an established inner base from which *he* initiates events.

It is through fantasy and reflection that the youngster plans goals and devises means of attaining them. Through prior experience he has developed a "conscience" by which he judges the appropriateness of his relations with others; past remembrances provide him with a reservior from which he can gauge the dangers and values of one course of behavior versus another. He now has the wherewithal to establish the boundaries of self-restriction and constructive action; he now has the anchor of a personal self from which he initiates new directions for growth and adult independence.

Maladaptive Consequence of Impoverishment

The task of attaining integration is not an easy one in a world of changing events and values. What is best? What is right? How shall I handle this or think about that? Questions such as these plague the growing child at every turn. How can the diverse and everchanging guidelines for behavior be fashioned into a well-integrated system of beliefs and actions? From what source can a consistent image of self be consolidated?

The fabric of organized society is designed to indoctrinate and inculcate the young. Family, school, church and industry set implicit values and explicit rules by which the child is guided to find means of behaving and thinking that is consonant with those of others. The youngster not only is subject to cultural pressures but requires them to give structure and direction to his rapidly proliferating capacities and impulses. Without them, his maturing potentials may become overly diffuse and scattered; conversely, too much guidance may narrow the scope of his potentials and restrict their flexibility and adaptiveness. Once his basic pattern of thought is shaped during this crucial growth period, it is difficult to alter or reorient it toward new pathways.

Let us elaborate the consequences of understimulation. Erikson (1959) has formulated the concept of *identity diffusion,* a notion we will borrow to represent the effects of inadequate or erratic stimulation during the peak years of intracortical integration. Without direct tuition from his elders, a youngster will be left to his own devices to master the complexities of a varied world, to control intense aggressive and sexual urges which well up within him, to channel his fantasies and to pursue the goals to which he aspires. He may become a victim of his own growth, unable to discipline his impulses or fashion acceptable means for expressing his desires. Scattered and unguided, he cannot get hold of a sense of personal identity, a consistent direction and purpose to his existence. He becomes an "other-directed" person, one who vacillates at every turn, overly responsive to fleeting stimuli and who shifts from one erratic course to another. Ultimately, without an inner core or anchor to guide his future, he may flounder or stagnate. The so-called "hippie" characterizes in mild form this state of diffusion; his aimlessness and disaffiliation from the mainstream of traditional American life may be traced, in part, to the failure of contemporary society to provide a coherent set of values around which he can focus his life and orient himself toward a meaningful future.

From the foregoing, it is evident that the impoverishment of integrative stimuli, regardless of their kind or quality, will have a profound effect. Fortunately, there is a superabundance of untapped cortical cells in the adult brain; thus, the "immaturity and irresponsibility" of many adolescents who have suffered prolonged identity diffusion may be salvaged in later years. But for others, the inability to settle down into a well-defined and consolidated path becomes a problem of increasingly severe proportions. Given the demands of an overly organized society, the perennially unintegrated adult will find himself ostracized, stereotyped and relegated to progressively inferior positions of responsibility.

Maladaptive Consequences of Enrichment

The negative consequences of overenrichment at the third stage usually occur when parents are controlling and perfectionistic. The overly trained, overly disciplined and overly integrated youngster is given little opportunity to shape his own destiny. Whether by coercion or enticement, the child who, too early, is led to control his emergent feelings, to focus his thoughts along narrowly defined paths and to follow the prescriptions of parental demands, has been subverted into adopting the identities of others. Whatever individuality he may have acquired is drowned in a model of adult orderliness, propriety and virtue. Such oversocialized and rigid youngsters lack the spontaneity, flexibility and creativeness we expect of the young; they have been trained to be old men before their time, too narrow in perspective to respond to excitement, variety and the challenge of new events. Overenrichment at this stage has fixed them on a restrictive course, and has deprived them of the rewards of being themselves.

Evaluative Comments

The developmental theory outlined in the preceding pages provides a plausible model for the successive stages of neuropsychological growth. But the model, and several of its particulars, is unproven. Many of the assertions made are based on extrapolations from animal research; what data exist at the human level are founded on naturalistic studies, most of which produce equivocal results, or on findings of undetermined reliability. Moreover, knowledge is sorely lacking of the precise maturational sequence of most of the neurological mechanisms which underlie psychological functions. In short, the empirical verification of relevant biophysical and behavioral variables through careful research remains a task for the future.

REFERENCES

1. Beach, F., and Jaynes, J.: Effects of early experience upon the behavior of animals. Psychol. Bull. *51:* 239–262 (1954).
2. Bowlby, J.: Maternal Care and Mental Health. Geneva: World Health Organization, 1952.
3. Butler, J. M., and Rice, L. N.: Adience, self-actualization and drive theory. In Wepman, J., and Heine, R. (eds.): Concepts of Personality. Chicago, Aldine, 1963.
4. Child, C. M.: Patterns and Problems of Development, Chicago, University of Chicago Press, 1941.
5. Conel, J. L.: The Postnatal Development of the Human Cerebral Cortex. Five Volumes. Cambridge, Mass., Harvard University Press, 1939–1955.
6. Eisenberg, L.: Normal child development. In Freedman, A., and Kaplan, H. (eds.): Comprehensive Textbook of Psychiatry. Baltimore, Williams and Wilkins, 1967.
7. Erikson, E. H.: Growth and crises of the healthy personality. In Klein, G. S. (ed.): Psychological Issues. New York, International University Press, 1959.
8. Gerwitz, J. L.: A learning analysis of the effects of normal stimulation upon social and exploratory behavior in the human infant. In Foss, B. M. (ed.): Determinants of Infant Behavior II. New York, Wiley, 1963.
9. Goldfarb, W.: Emotional and intellectual consequences of psychologic deprivation in infancy: A reevaluation. In Hoch, P., and Zubin, J. (eds.): Psychopathology of Childhood. New York, Grune and Stratton, 1955.
10. Goldstein, K.: The Organism. New York, American Book Co., 1939.
11. Harlow, H. F.: Primary affectional patterns in primates. Am. J. Orthopsychiatry. *30:* 67–84 (1960).
12. Harlow, H. F.: The maternal affectional system. In Foss, B. M. (ed.): Determinants of Infant Behavior II. New York, Wiley, 1963.
13. Harlow, H. F., and Harlow, M. K.: The affectional systems. In Schrier, A., et al. (eds.): Behavior of Non-Human Primates. Vol. 2 New York, Academic Press, 1965.
14. Hebb, D. O.: The Organization of Behavior. New York, Wiley, 1949.
15. Hess, E. H.: Imprinting. Science *130:* 133–141 (1959).
16. Kanner, L.: Problems of nosology and psychodynamics of early infantile autism. Am. J. Orthopsychiatry *19:* 416–426 (1949).
17. Lorenz, K.: Der Jumpan in der Umwelt des Vogels. Der Artgenosse als auslosendes Moment Socializer Verhaltungsweissen. J. orn. Ipz. *83:* 137–213; 289–413 (1935).
18. Mahler, M. S.: On child psychosis and schizophrenia: Autistic and symbiotic infantile psychosis. In Psychoanalytic Study of the Child. Vol. 7. New York, International University Press, 1952.
19. McGraw, M. B.: The Neuromuscular Maturation of the Human Infant. New York, Columbia University Press, 1943.
20. Milner, E.: Human Neural and Behavioral Development. Springfield, Ill., Charles C. Thomas, 1967.
21. Moltz, H.: An epigenetic interpretation of the imprinting phenomenon. In Newton, G., and Levine, S. (eds.): Early Experience and Behavior. Springfield, Ill., Charles C. Thomas, 1968.
22. Murphy, G.: Personality: A Biosocial Approach to Origins and Structures. New York, Harper, 1947.
23. Pasamanick, B., et al.: Socioeconomic status: Some precursors of neuropsychiatric disorders. Am. J. Orthopsychiatry. *26:* 594–601 (1956).
24. Piaget, J.: The Origins of Intelligence in Children. New York, International University Press, 1952.
25. Rapaport, D.: The theory of ego autonomy: A generalization. Bull. Menninger Clin. *22:* 13–35 (1958).
26. Rheingold, H. L.: The effect of environmental stimulation upon social and exploratory behavior in the human infant. In Foss, B. M. (ed.): Determinants of Infant Behavior II. New York, Wiley, 1963.
27. Ribble, M. A.: The Rights of Infants. New York, Columbia University Press, 1943.
28. Riesen, A. H.: Stimulation as a requirement for growth and function in behavioral development. In Fiske, D., and Maddi, S. (eds.): Functions of Varied Experience. Homewood, Ill., Dorsey, 1961.
29. Rosenzweig, M. R., et al.: Effect of environmental complexity and training on brain chemistry and anatomy: A replication and extension J. Comp. Physiol. Psychol. *55:* 429–437 (1962).
30. Scott, J. P.: Comparative social psychology. In Waters, R. H. (ed.): Principles of Comparative Psychology. New York, McGraw–Hill, 1960.

31. Scott, J. P.: Early Experience and the Organization of Behavior. Belmont, Calif., Brooks-Cole, 1968.
32. Scheibel, M. E., and Scheibel, A. B.: Some neural substrates of postnatal development. In

Hoffman, M., and Hoffman, L. (eds.): Review of Child Development Research. Vol. 1. New York, Russel Sage, 1964.
33. Spitz, R. A.: The First Year of Life. New York, International University Press, 1965.

24.   Adulthood and Old Age

Robert J. Havighurst

The long segment of the human life span after adolescence is not very well known to science. In spite of a considerable amount of research in the current century, we cannot claim to have gone far beyond Shakespeare's insight by which he was able to describe the seven ages of man.

BODY CHANGES IN THE ADULT LIFE CYCLE

Physical strength and speed of body movement reach a peak at about 30 years of age, after which there is a slow decline. Between 40 and 50 there is a noticeable loss in attractiveness of the body, because of skin wrinkles, fat around the middle of the body, and thinning hair. The eye lens slowly loses elasticity until in the forties many people must use reading glasses in order to see fine print clearly. Also, as people go into their sixties, they lose acuity of vision at night. The sense of hearing holds out without loss until the sixties, generally, though men tend to lose their hearing earlier than women do.

The sex glands of women atrophy around the age of 50, at the time of the menopause. In men, there is a gradual reduction in glandular activity after about 50. Both sexes continue sexual activity after this age, but there is a substantial decrease in the frequency of sexual intercourse.

There is loss of teeth throughout the adult years for some people, and in the 1950's in the United States, a dental survey found that 56 percent of people aged 65-74 had no natural teeth. There is also a shrinkage of most muscles, possibly due to disuse.

Thus, the middle and later years bring insults to the body, but a very large proportion of people maintain robust health in spite of them. The variability of the population increases with age. That is, the range of health status becomes broader and broader with time, and people are more "spread out" on a health scale.

Studies of the extent of illness and the number of days of disability due to illness show a sharp increase of disability after age 50, but the great majority of people feel quite well and go about their work quite actively.

The average person in the United States lives to the age 70, according to the mortality rates of the 1960's. The average 60-year-old lives for another 18 years, and the average 70-year-old lives another 11 years. There is some evidence that those who survive beyond 70 are especially "hardy" and have less illness than those who die in their fifties and sixties.

There is a relatively high incidence of mental disease loosely called "senility" after about age 70.

After about 50, the death rate due to chronic and degenerative diseases goes up, while that due to acute diseases does not change very much. Heart disease and cancer are the two principal causes of death

Havighurst, R.J.: Adulthood and old age. In Encyclopedia of Educational Research. 4th Ed., New York, Macmillan Co., 1969.

after age 50. Not until medical science gains control over these diseases will the death rate be appreciably reduced.

Thus, the general picture of the changes undergone by the body during the adult life cycle of present-day Americans is one of decrement; but the great majority of people live in fairly good health and feel physiologically comfortable throughout their adult years. They adapt easily to the physiological changes of maturing and aging.

The biological aspects of aging are summarized in several handbooks, the most complete and authoritative being that of Birren,[1] while the chapter by Confrey and Goldstein[7] on health status gives a convenient overview.

BODY, SELF, AND SOCIETY

The behavior of children and adolescents is very closely tied to the development of their bodies. Their maturation gives them new powers and opens up new aspects of life to them as they grow older. But the behavior of adults is much less defined and limited by their physical and physiological condition. Charlotte Buehler pointed this out more than 30 years ago in her book on the course of human life.[5] She distinguished between the "biological" curve of the life span and the "biographical" or "psychological" curve.

The biological life curve rises steeply in childhood and adolescence to a peak at about 30, when the biological resources of the body are at a maximum. After a plateau lasting about 20 years, this curve slopes downward from age 50, reflecting the decreasing physical vigor and decreasing body efficiency. Manual workers have a biographical life curve very similar to this. However, people who work with their brains and many highly skilled craftsmen start slowly in the biographical curve because they have a long period of preparation, and then their biographical curve stays on a high plateau after the biological curve commences to decline. In other words, the curve of functioning as workers and citizens and social beings builds to its adult maximum after the structure of the body begins to decrease its effectiveness

and power. Havighurst[15] has described this as the principle of the separation of function from structure in the later part of life. The older person is able to function efficiently through his stored-up experience and knowledge in spite of his loss of physical strength and skill.

What the older person accomplishes is determined by his self-concept, his aspirations, and by the society around him, which encourages him in certain activities and discourages him in others. His body is a limiting factor, particularly if he is in poor health. But self and society are more influential in his behavior than body is.

Even in such a biological event as the menopause in women, the self seems to determine the reaction of the woman. Kraines,[25] in studying women who had recently passed through the menopause, found that those who complained of body tensions and other symptoms of malaise at the time of the menopause were less well-adjusted socially and personally than women who took the menopause in their stride and reported minimal ill effects. In other words, one could predict with considerable confidence that women who before the menopause were well adjusted to their lives would have less difficulty with body symptoms at the time of the menopause than women who had been relatively poorly adjusted.

The relation of the state of the body to the state of the self is not at all clear, nor has it been clarified much by recent research. All we can say for certain is that drastic changes in the body — such things as heart attacks, crippling illness, and profound loss of physical vigor have some influence on the self-concept of a person, or on his personal-social adjustment. On the other hand, a person's self-concept tends to determine his reaction to physical disability.

In this connection an interesting set of researches has been reported on the relation of illness to aging. One speculative hypothesis is that aging is a kind of illness, and illness is a kind of aging. If this is so, then middle-aged people who are sick should feel old and appear old, while old people who are in good health should feel young and appear young. In order to test this hypothesis, Schwartz and Kleemeier[42] compared a group of healthy men in the adult range with another group who were in a hospital for acute (not chronic) conditions such as fractures, ulcers, and back trouble. The two groups were given tests of their feelings about themselves (self concept). The two groups were divided again into two groups by age. It was hypothesized that the chronologically old but well men would see themselves in a more favorable light than the chronologically old but ill men. Similarly, the young ill men would have less favorable self concepts than the young and well men. There was some tendency in this direction, but it was not statistically significant. And the young but ill men had more favorable self-concepts than the old but well men. Evidence on this matter was also obtained by Birren and his colleagues[3] in a comparison of older men (65 to 90) in average health with older men in very good health. The older men in very good health did act and feel as though they were younger than the older men in average health. The men in very good health showed low or negligible correlations between age and intelligence, and between age and symptoms of senility; but the old men of only average health did show decreased intellectual efficiency with greater age. Birren wrote that "health status is more significant in determining various aspects of functioning than the unspecified consequences of advanced chronological age."

ABILITIES AND THE LIFE CYCLE

The abilities and skills that are measured by psychologists have been explored through the adult years for a number of variously selected samples. Sampling is a weakness of research in this area, since the researcher did not make repeated studies of the same persons but compared people of diverse ages, assuming that his sample of a given age was equivalent to his samples of other ages and that therefore the observed age changes were truly changes that occur in people as they grow older. However, in a cross-sectional research, the group which is older in age is generally a "better" group than one which is younger in average age, because the older group has already lost some of its "weaker" members by death. Furthermore, the psychological tests of ability have generally been made on samples of people who were in relatively good health. Thus, those who are in poor health are left out, and there are more of these in the older groups.

Nevertheless, there are some facts about changes of ability with age which are quite thoroughly documented in spite of the sampling problem just mentioned. For instance, acuity of hearing, seeing, feeling, and tasting all decrease after middle age. The decrease is not extremely rapid or severe in most people, and they adjust to this decline with relatively little difficulty. The range of performance and the standard deviation generally increase with increasing age of the group. This seems to mean that there is a more rapid and extended decrease in some people than in others.

The scientific studies of human ability have been well organized and summarized by seven or eight people in Birren's Handbook.[1] Each person reviewing his own area of special competence as a psychologist. Welford[46,47] has established the fact that sensorimotor performance decreases in speed and accuracy with greater age in the adult period of life. He interprets this to mean that as impulses come into the central nervous system from the sense organs, the central mechanisms take longer to act in older than in younger people. If the older person is not forced to hurry but can take his time, his accuracy is not impaired. The more complex the task is, the more fully this finding of Welford applies. Jerome[18] has demonstrated that the performance of people in situations where they need to learn is poorer in older people than in younger ones. He is not sure whether there is something about the aging process per se that reduces learning ability or whether the reduction is due to decreased speed, decreased motivation, or decreased health.

Creativity

One quality which may not be generally considered an "ability" is that of creativity. Since Lehman's monumental work,[28] there have been other studies in this field, with somewhat contradictory results. Lehman, studying the ages at which prominent people have done their best work, found that the decades from 20 to 40 were far more productive than those from 40 to 60. Artists, poets, and mathematicians were earlier in reaching their creative peaks than philosophers, historians, and social scientists. But Dennis[9] has used a different method of study and believes that Lehman has exaggerated the relation of age and creativity. For instance, if only people who lived to be 75-80 are studied, the inverse relation of age and quality of creative work is much less marked than when the work of people who died rather young is included. Obviously, those who died young must have done their best work while they were young. There is some reason to accept Lehman's findings in general, after applying Dennis' critique. If this is done, it appears likely that one cause for decreasing productivity and creativity after age 40 is the fact that many successful leaders in the arts and sciences accept positions of administrative power and responsibility as they grow older, and they have less time to devote to their own scholarly and artistic work.

Sexual Power

Another area of "ability" is that of sexual activity. Not much had been known scientifically about the relation of sexual activity to age until the publications of Kinsey's books.[22,23] Males and females decrease in their frequency of achieving physical sexual outlet after their early adult years. Men decrease more rapidly than women after the age of 50. The fact that women also decrease after the age of 50 may be attributed to the fact that male sexual partners are less active and less available to women after this age. In any case, it is generally believed that sexual activity decreases substantially in both sexes after 70, but the samples of people studied in that age group are small, and the evidence is scanty. It is supposed that the decrease of sexual activity after about age 50 may be due partly to decreased physio-logical (gonadal) activity, but also partly to a kind of satiation, and, to quote Kinsey,[22] "by psychological fatigue, a loss of interest in repetition of the same sort of experience, an exhaustion of the possibilities for exploring new techniques, new types of contacts, new situations."

Capacity to Learn

There has been a dramatic change in our notions of the capacity of adults to learn. Until as recently as 1950 it was generally supposed that people lost much of their learning ability after age 40 and that 50 was nearly the limit for useful learning. Yet since that time the Federal Aeronautics Authority decided to permit commercial airline pilots up to the age of 55 to shift from flying piston airplanes to jet planes — a formidable learning task.[2] Professor Ross McFarland of the Harvard University School of Public Health says, "In general, it may be concluded that the older pilots can be utilized very effectively until they reach 60 years of age. This observation would not have been acceptable or predictable in the earlier history of the air transport industry."[31]

Learning the new skills that go with automation in industry has been studied with respect to age of employees in several industries. When the level of education is taken into account, there is very little difference in learning ability related to age among adult employees. Birren[32] summed up the evidence on learning ability of adults within the 25-65 age range with the conclusion that there is very little relation to age. For many if not for most tasks, the amount of education a person has is more significant than his age in predicting his ability to learn a new job.

The data on the relation of intelligence-test scores to age show decreases with age in scores on tests that require speed and perception, while tests which allow for accumulated experience such as vocabulary show increasing scores with age.

The longitudinal studies of mental ability which have included people over 60 generally show a significant decline beginning about 70 years of age.

From the longitudinal study by Owens[38]

of men from about 20 to 60, it appears that there is no appreciable change of intelligence with age until after 60.

PERSONALITY AND MOTIVATION

The motives, or needs and values, of people change through their adult years. These changes reflect changes in the life situation rather than changes in basic personality. The interests and choices of where to focus one's energy and how to allocate one's time depend on such matters as marriage, the birth of children and their presence in the home, the possibility of advancement in one's work career, the possession of a nice home, the existence of a group of congenial friends, the opportunity to take a responsible role in local civic affairs, the existence of a local theater group, the existence of good hunting or camping nearby, and so on.

There are two broad types of motivation in adult life. One is a *growth-expansion* motive and the other, opposed to it, is a motive resulting from *anxiety and sense of threat.* These have been summarized by Kuhlen.[26] There seems to be a continuing need for expansion, through achievement, power, self-actualization, and generativity in Erikson's sense.[10] This need continues at least until age 60 in most people but may die down in some toward the close of middle age and decrease even more later on. Family and work constitute the major areas of expansion in the first half of adult life. Then civic activity, home beautification, sociability, and various forms of creativity may become the theater for these needs in the latter half of adult life, after 50 or 55.

The opposite form of motivation, due to anxiety, presumably arises from the inevitable losses of physical strength and attractiveness after 40 or 50, coupled with increasing responsibilities and commitments to family and work. Thus, in a national interview study on mental health status, Gurin and others[13] found the following five factors of subjective maladjustment: (1) felt psychological disturbances, (2) unhappiness, (3) social inadequacy, (4) lack of identity, and (5) physical distress. Both sexes showed the first four factors, but women did not show the physical-distress factor. There are losses in these areas in the middle and later years.

Incidentally, how one classifies oneself with respect to age appears to be a reflection of good and poor self-concept. Studies made by several different researchers indicate that many people over 70 or 75 classify themselves as middle-aged when asked on a questionnaire "In which age group do you feel that you belong — elderly, young, or middle-aged?" As many as 50 percent of persons over 65 rate themselves as middle-aged, and one study found that this sub-group was better adjusted in measure of personal-social adjustment than those who rated themselves in the other two groups.[17]

There is a socioeconomic factor in the way people perceive the appropriate ages for such concepts as "prime of life," "good-looking" (for women), "most competent," "middle-aged," and "old." People in the upper middle class place these at later ages than do people of working-class status. This is probably related to the actual fact that working-class people are more dependent on physical strength and physique for competence in their lives than are middle-class people. It may also be due to a tendency for middle-class people to have a more favorable perception of middle age and old age than working-class people have.

There is really no integrated body of psychological theory concerning the development of human personality during the adult years, as Neugarten has pointed out.[36] However, there are orderly and sequential changes that occur with the passage of time as individuals move from adolescence through adulthood, and students of adult psychology are beginning to trace these changes. We shall look at the research and the findings when we come to the subject of stages or phases in the adult life cycle.

COMPETENCE

"Competence" is a global term which denotes and contains much of what we consider desirable in human behavior. It includes skill, determination, and judgment. It is what Buehler[5] intends to discuss when she differentiates between the biographical curve and the biological curve of adult life. It is what the adult brings to bear on the tasks and roles of his life, and it is measured in terms of his effectiveness.

Wilensky[48] made a study of what he called "orderly careers," in relation to the extent and quality of social-civic participation of people. He found that people who were competent in their work careers were more active in social and civic roles in the community than were those who had less "orderly" work careers. This finding of a kind of *g* factor of adult competence has been confirmed in other studies. For instance, in the Kansas City Study of Adult Life, Havighurst[14] rated people aged 40 to 70 on their competence in performing nine common social roles: worker, parent, spouse, homemaker, citizen, club and association member, church member, friend, and user of leisure time. He found a positive intercorrelation among all the roles, which was taken as evidence of a *g* competence factor. He also found no change with age up to 65, when certain roles, such as spouse and worker, are often lost to a person through no act of his own. Some people compensate for these losses by increasing their activity in other roles. Other people simply drop these roles and carry on the other roles with relatively little change.

Subgroups of people move up or down the socioeconomic scale during their adulthood. This motion might be interpreted as competence or incompetence. Coleman and Neugarten[6] reported on the social mobility of a sample of men in Kansas City, aged 40 to 70. Compared with the socioeconomic status of their fathers, 36 percent had moved up at least one step on a five-class scale, and 13 percent had moved down.

SOCIETY AND THE ADULT LIFE CYCLE

Up to this point, attention has here been directed to the individual as he progresses through the life cycle. Although it is understood that society and its social institutions form the framework within which a person lives his life, very little attention is paid to the influence of society in the psychological and biological analyses of the life cycles that have been reported. Now the focus will be shifted to the society which surrounds the individual and to the ways by which it shapes the adult life cycle.

The Economy

The economy or the system of producing and distributing goods and services provides employment, purchasing power, and income during retirement. The economy also deprives a person of employment under certain conditions. The economy is the principal source of nonfinancial as well as financial rewards to the person who is employed. As noted by Friedmann and Havighurst,[11] work gives people a sense of achievement, a feeling of being creative, a feeling of being of service, and a place to make good friends and to enjoy human companionship. At the very least, the economy structures many of the waking hours and helps the person without much individual initiative to organize his life and to make time pass in a tolerable way.

In return, the economy asks the adult as a worker to do his job conscientiously and to support the economic system intelligently and critically. The economy also asks the worker to give up his life work and accept retirement status, generally in his mid-sixties, whether he likes it or not.

For women the American economy has been increasingly hospitable during the twentieth century. Most young women are employed before their marriages. After age 45, women enter or reenter the labor force in large numbers. In effect, a woman makes a choice, after her childbearing and child-rearing years are over, whether she will take on a worker role or will put more time and energy into various social-civic roles outside the family and outside the economy.

The trend of retirement policy and practice is toward earlier retirement. While rules for compulsory retirement in most large organizations have not been changed in the past decade, there has been a policy of encouraging voluntary retirement for wage workers through liberalized pension plans on the part of many large enterprises, and this has been supported by most labor unions. The reason for this is that industry and commerce have been using automated production and service machinery to an increasing degree, thus eliminating certain jobs and forcing the necessity of reducing the working force. In order to protect jobs for younger and middle-aged workers, older workers have been encouraged to retire voluntarily.

In connection with the tendency toward earlier retirement, employers have given more attention to the preparation of their employees for retirement through counseling and through short educational courses on preparations for retirement.

The State

The government differentiates with regard to age in its relations with adult citizens perhaps less than most other social institutions do. The right and the obligation to vote is independent of age in adults. Certain government offices have minimum ages attached to them, but very few have compulsory retirement related to age. Taxes are assessed independent of age, except for minor concessions to people over 65. Military service is related to age and to sex.

Through government-operated social security and medical-care programs, the government pays special attention to the economic and health needs of its older citizens. This is balanced, partially at least, by the provision of education at state expense which goes mainly to young adults.

For all ages the government increasingly supplies such cultural goods as subsidized theater and music, recreation in national parks, and educational television.

The Church

The role of the church member changes very little through the adult life cycle. Those who do not invest much of themselves in this role may attend church services more or less regularly and send their children to church school. Those who are more involved in this role may take positions of responsibility open to laymen, and they may continue in these positions generally beyond the normal age of retirement from employment. Some elderly people increase their church activities as they become free of other responsibilities, and they get great satisfaction from active church work.

The church itself recognizes some of the special needs of old age and attempts to give assistance. Many clergymen study problems of the aging so as to be able to counsel their older parishioners. Most church groups provide homes for elderly members whose families cannot look after their welfare.

The Family

While people's participation in most social roles tends to decrease as they get older, the family roles generally increase in importance for them. The role of parent is central throughout adulthood but takes somewhat less time and energy after about the age of 50. However, the man or woman of 50 to 60 generally finds himself involved in assisting his aging parents to work out some of their problems. Also the role of grandparent enters and provides many satisfactions together with responsibilities, especially for women. The role of homemaker continues in full force for most women and many men become more involved in the physical upkeep of their houses and gardens as they grow older. Studies of family interaction through the life cycle[43] indicate that the relations among the generations in the family are active and well maintained in the contemporary urban family, much more than would be expected from some of the sociological essays which portray a decrease of family activity and a narrowing of family function in this century.

The Social Environment

There are fairly definite expectations on the part of society concerning the social behavior of people at various stages of the adult life cycle. People in their thirties and forties are expected to be most interested in their children, in schools, and in the building of a secure and stable family. In their fifties they are expected to extend their interests to the wider community since their children are now growing up and leaving home. In their sixties, and more in the seventies, they are expected to "slow down," to take life more easily. In their personal-social lives they are expected to become less active — to go out less often at night, to be less interested in the opposite sex, and to exert less authority over others in their family, at their place of work, and in other roles where they have been leaders.

These expectations on the part of society are documented in several studies of what people expect of other people at various age periods.[36,17] People thus know in a general way what is expected of them by society, and they may conform to these expectations or they may resist them more or less successfully.[27]

The social policy with respect to adult behavior is mainly implicit in these general social expectations but becomes more explicit in such things as the age of eligibility for social security benefits, the age of eligibility for private company pensions, and for government pensions, the age of eligibility for membership in retirement communities, etc. In general, this social policy seems to be based more on the needs and convenience of the American economy than on the biological capability of the individual or any kind of ideology about what is good or bad for the human personality.

ADULT EDUCATION AND THE ADULT LIFE CYCLE

In 1962 about 15 percent of the adult population took part in some formal adult education program. What kinds of people are these "volunteers for learning," to use the phrase of Johnstone and Rivera?[19] Their study and two others (Knox & Videbeck, 1963; London & others, 1963) give a good idea of the characteristics of adult education students. They cluster

mainly in the age group 25 to 45, with relatively few over 50. They tend to be middle-class rather than working-class people. The people with most education are likely to continue with adult education, and those who participate after age 50 are definitely higher in educational level than the average of those who participate below this age.

Until now the stress in adult education has been upon *instrumental* rather than *expressive* educational activity. The instrumental educational activity has as a goal something beyond the immediate activity. That is, it may lead to a better job, to better cooking on the part of a young wife, to better care of children, etc. The expressive educational activity is largely done for its own sake. It is done for the value of the immediate experience. Courses in painting, art, foreign language, "great books," photography, etc., are in the expressive category for most people, though they may also have an instrumental value for a minority of students.

The older people in adult education tend to elect expressive activities aimed at helping them enjoy leisure time more fully. An example of the trend to be expected is the programs of the Institute for Lifetime Learning, in Washington, D.C. Affiliated with the American Association of Retired Persons, the Institute in 1966 offered about 50 courses, most of them of an expressive type. This may herald a major development of expressive forms of adult education as more people have more leisure time at all ages. It may also foretell an increase in the proportion of students past 50 years of age.

STAGES AND DEVELOPMENTAL PHASES OF THE ADULT LIFE CYCLE

Considering the normal progression in the situation of adults in a modern society, with concomitant changes in their social roles, the expectations that society lays upon them, and their expectations of themselves, a scheme of three stages with transition periods preceding each stage seems to fit the facts reasonably well.

Transition period from adolescence to

(1) *early adulthood* (20-30 to 40-45). Duration of stage: 15 years.

Transition period to (2) *plateau of adulthood* (40-45 to 60-70). Duration of stage: 25 years.

Transition period to (3) *later maturity* (60-70 to 85-90). Duration of stage: 20 years.

The transition periods vary in length for different persons. For example, a young man who enters college and then goes on to medical school and to a hospital residency in a specialty requires a full ten years to make the transition into early adulthood. By contrast, a young man who goes right to work upon graduation from high school, gets married at once, and starts a family requires only two or three years to make the transition. Also, a person who tapers off from full-time employment to a leisurely retirement by working part-time for several years during his sixties may take eight or ten years for the transition to later maturity.

Generally, people of lower socio-economic status make the transitions at younger ages than those of higher socio-economic status.

Each stage of the adult life cycle has its characteristic developmental tasks. For *early adulthood* these are finding a mate; and getting well established in an occupation. The tasks of the *plateau of adulthood* are setting adolescent children free; establishing a comfortable home; maintaining a peak of occupational effectiveness; adjusting to unfavorable changes in body status; and (for women who have concentrated on raising children) working into new civic-social-occupational roles. For *later maturity* the developmental tasks are working out a new pattern of social roles that suits one's personality; accepting one's personality; accepting one's status as an elderly person; adjusting to loss of employment and/or loss of spouse; relating to one's grown children on an adult-to-adult level; finding satisfactory housing and living arrangements.

Stage or Phase Theories

Several students of adult psychology have defined stages or phases of adult life.

Erikson[10] has proposed that the ego or self goes through eight stages of development from birth to death. The last three stages are similar in timing to the three stages noted above. Dominating the stage of early adulthood is the psychosocial need for *intimacy* — the ability to merge one's own self with that of another person, to share love and life intimately with another person. Next comes the phase of *generativity*. This is investment in the next generation and in the community. It is an altruistic preoccupation. Normally it involves getting children ready for their adult life, and it may also consist of improving one's land and one's house and working for the betterment of one's community.

Finally comes the stage of *integrity*. One's active life has nearly been completed; one looks over it and accepts it as meaningful and in a sense inevitable. One does not make excuses for it, even though it has not been all that one hoped for. Therefore one has no fear of death, because one does not feel a need to make something different of one's life.

Other formulations of adult life in terms of stages have been given by Buehler[5] and by Havighurst.[16] Buehler organized the total life cycle into ten stages and applied a theory of *basic tendencies* to the description of these stages. Havighurst took each decade of life as a unit and described its "dominant concerns."

LONGITUDINAL STUDIES OF ADULT LIFE

All of these stage or phase theories suffer from the lack of evidence provided by longitudinal studies — studies of one and the same person through an extended period of time. This kind of study has given us our most valuable information on childhood and adolescence. Longitudinal studies of children and adolescents have established the fact that while all persons go through the stages of development, the actual timing and the detailed characteristics of each person's career are unique to him. Thus, it is not sufficient to study groups of people at various ages on the supposition that each person at a given age will be like the others at that age.

The life career is the proper subject of study if we are to learn the most about adulthood and old age. There are several semilongitudinal studies in existence. The study of gifted children started by Terman about 1920 has been continued with a publication by Terman and Oden,[44] when the subjects were in their forties. The University of California Study of Adolescents, which began in 1932 with a sample of ten-year-olds, has been continued with reports by Jones and others,[20] Mussen,[32] and Tuddenham[45] when the subjects were in their thirties. A biological study of men in their early middle age was commenced by Keys in 1947, with a psychological panel which has been reported from time to time by Brozek.[4] Specific studies made on a group of subjects at a given time have been repeated on the same subjects as far as possible at later times. One of the most valuable of these is the study of intelligence of men averaging about 21 who were inducted into the Army in World War I. A substantial number of these men have been retested twice by Owens and Charles,[38] the latest study being made when the men were an average of 61 years old. Useful as these studies are, none of them has been continued long enough with the kind of measurements and assessments that can answer the most interesting question of all — to what extent is human personality constant through time?

Studies of this question can start with the personality in childhood or adolescence and trace it into adulthood, or they may start in early or middle adulthood and follow through a decade or more of adult life.

In the studies made at the Institute of Human Development at the University of California at Berkeley it proved very difficult to predict personality characteristics of young adults from data obtained about them in their adolescence. Jones and his associates[20] concluded that the myriad changes in life situations to which the adolescents were exposed as they grew older would produce changes in behavior that would be difficult to predict from the kinds of information obtainable about personality in childhood and adolescence.

This view was also confirmed by Rohner and Edmonson[41] in their study of 20 young Negro adults who had been studied 20 years earlier and described by Davis and Dollard in their book *Children of Bondage*.[8]

A study made by Kelly[21] reported on a group of 300 young couples engaged to be married who were studied in the 1930's and then retested with many of the same instruments about 1955 when they were in their forties. Kelly found correlation coefficients of about .50 in the areas of values and vocational interests and coefficients of about .30 on paper-and-pencil tests of personality between scores in the 1930's and those in 1955. He concludes: "Our findings indicate that significant changes in the human personality may continue to occur in the years of adulthood."

From middle to old age there have been no longitudinal studies reported, but there have been several studies of personality of middle-aged and older people in which age was treated as a variable. Among these studies the Kansas City Studies of Adult Life are especially useful because they were made with normal people, drawn by random-sampling techniques from the community at large. There were three main lines of study. The first dealt with social competence and social interaction. Havighurst's study[14] dealt with competence in the common social roles. He found that the quality of role performance did not vary with age between 40 and 65. At about 65, there was indication of gross changes in social interaction.

The second dealt with personal-social adjustment or life satisfaction. Peck and Berkowitz[39] rated 120 persons in the Kansas City sample, aged 40 to 64 and from all social class levels, and found no relationship to chronological age. Similarly, Neugarten and her associates[37] rated more than 200 persons, aged 50 to 85, on life satisfaction, and found no correlation with age.

The third type of study concentrated on the "inner personality and was made with projective tests. Here it was found that there are changes with age in the modes of dealing with impulse life and of relating in fantasy to the environment.[34] Beginning as early as age 40, there is a decrease in active manipulation and attempts to dominate the environment. The person is seen increasingly as a passive object manipulated by the environment. By the sixties the heroes in the Thematic Apperception Test are conforming, meek, and friendly. They no longer try to dominate the situation by taking the initiative through aggressive action. In another study using the Thematic Apperception Test, the amount of "ego energy" was measured, defined as energy available to the self to respond to events in the outer world. Scores on ego energy decreased regularly with age from 40 to 71. These studies do not necessarily mean that people become overtly more passive as they grow older, although they would be expected to change in this direction eventually. Rather, it means that people become more preoccupied with themselves, more concerned with the control or satisfaction of their personal needs, and more likely to take a reflective stance with respect to the world around them.[34]

PERSONALITY AND PATTERNS OF AGING

It appears, from the best evidence we have today, that there are no gross changes in personality after the individual reaches the plateau of adulthood which are attributable to the process of aging alone. Such changes as do take place are at the covert level. The observable life style of the individual persists with relatively little change as long as he maintains the physical and mental ability to look after his personal needs.

Consequently, the patterns of behavior in the latter half of life should be systematically related to personality. There should be distinct personality types which lead to distinct behavior patterns. A search for such personality types was made at the University of California at Berkeley by Else Frenkel-Brunswik and her colleagues, who studied a group of 87 elderly men, 42 of them retired and 45 not retired. They reported finding five personality types[40] which were systematically related to patterns of successful and unsuccessful aging.

The Kansas City Study of Adult Life made a study of 159 men and women aged 50 to 90, who were interviewed a total of seven times between 1956 and 1962. They were rated on 45 personality variables reflecting both the cognitive and the affective aspects of personality. Types of personality were extracted from the data by means of factor analysis. There were four major types, which were called the integrated, armored-defended, passive-dependent, and unintegrated personalities.

Patterns of behavior were defined on the basis of a rating of *activity* in 11 common social roles: worker, parent, grandparent, kin-group member, spouse, homemaker, citizen, friend, neighbor, club and association member, and church member. Ratings were made by judges on each of the 11 roles, based on a reading of the seven interviews with each person. The sum of the role-activity scores was used to divide the respondents into three activity levels, high, medium, and low.

A third component of the patterns of aging was a measure of *life satisfaction* or psychological well-being, which was a composite rating based on five scales recording the extent to which a person (1) finds gratification in the activities of his everyday life (2) regards his life as meaningful and accepts both the good and the bad in it, (3) feels that he has succeeded in achieving his major goals, (4) has a positive image of himself; and (5) maintains happy and optimistic moods and attitudes. Scores on life satisfaction were grouped into high, medium, and low categories.

The analysis based on these three dimensions (personality, role activity, and life satisfaction) was applied to the 59 men and women in the study who were aged 70 to 79. This is the group in which the transition from middle age to old age has presumably been accomplished. Fifty of these people fell clearly into one or another of eight patterns of aging, which are presented in the following scheme.[35]

A. integrated personality, high role activity (RA), high life satisfaction (LS); 9 persons.

B. integrated personality, medium RA, high LS; 5 cases.

C. integrated personality, low RA, high

LS; 3 cases.

D. armored-defended personality, high or medium RA, high LS; 11 cases.

E. armored-defended personality, low or medium RA, high or medium LS; 4 cases.

F. passive-dependent personality, high or medium RA, high or medium LS; 6 cases.

G. passive-dependent personality, low RA, medium or low LS; 5 cases.

H. unintegrated personality, low RA, medium or low LS; 7 cases.

Group A, called the *reorganizers,* are competent people engaged in a wide variety of activity. They are the optimal agers in terms of the American ideal of "keeping active, staying young.: They reorganize their lives to substitute new activities for lost ones.

Group B were called the *focused.* They are well-integrated personalities with medium levels of activity. They tend to be selective about their activities, devoting their time and energy to gaining satisfaction in one or two role areas.

Group C were called the *successful disengaged.* They have low activity levels and high life satisfaction. They have voluntarily moved away from role commitments as they have grown older. They have high feelings of self-regard, with a contented "rocking-chair" position in life.

Group D exhibit the *holding-on* pattern. They hold as long as possible to the activities of middle age. As long as they are successful in this, they have high life satisfaction.

Group E are *constricted.* They have reduced their role activity, presumably as a defense against aging. They constrict their social interactions and maintain a medium to high level of satisfaction. They differ from the focused in having less-integrated personalities.

Group F are *succorance-seeking.* They are successful in getting emotional support from others and thus maintain a medium level of role activity and of life satisfaction.

Group G are *apathetic.* They have low role activity combined with medium or low life satisfaction. Presumably, they are people who have never given much to life and never expected much from it.

Group H are *disorganized.* They have deteriorated thought processes and poor control over their emotions. They barely maintain themselves in the community and have low or at the most medium life satisfaction.

These eight patterns of aging probably are established and predictable by middle age, though we do not have longitudinal studies to prove this proposition. It seems reasonable to suppose that a person's underlying personality needs become consonant with his overt behavior patterns in a social environment that permits wide variation.

ORGANIZATIONS FOR SCIENTIFIC STUDY OF ADULTHOOD

There are several organizations intended primarily to study adulthood or to promote education for adults. The Adult Education Association has become an effective organization for the promotion and improvement of educational practices and has sponsored a number of useful researches and reports on the status of adult education. The Division on Maturity and Old Age of the American Psychological Association has been a stimulant to psychological research. The Gerontological Society is an interdisciplinary group consisting of psychologists, sociologists, social workers, and medical and biological scientists devoted to the study of aging. The International Gerontological Association has held congresses every third year since 1948, to bring together representatives of gerontological societies from about twenty countries.

REFERENCES

1. Birren, J. E.: Handbook of Aging and the Individual. Chicago, University of Chicago Press, 1959.
2. Birren, J. E.: Adult capacities to learn. In Kuhlen, R. G. (ed.): Psychological Backgrounds of Adult Education. Center for the Study of Liberal Education for Adults, 1963.
3. Birren, J. E., et al: Human Aging: A Biological and Behavioral Study. U. S. Public Health Service, National Institutes of Mental Health, 1963.
4. Brozek, J.: Personality changes with age. J. Geront. *10:* 194–206 (1955).
5. Buehler, C.: Der menschliche Lebenslauf als psychologisches Problem, 2d Ed. Verlag für Psychologie, 1959. For an English version see Buehler, C. The course of life as studied in biographies. J. Applied Psychol. *19:* 405-9 (1933).
6. Coleman, R., and Neugarten, B. L.: Social mobility in a midwestern city. In Havighurst, R. J., et al (eds.): Society and Education. Boston, Allyn and Bacon, 1967, p. 38-49.
7. Confrey, E. A., and Goldstein, M. S.: The health status of aging people. In Tibbits, C. (ed.): Handbook of Social Gerontology. Chicago, University of Chicago Press, 1960, p. 165-207.
8. Davis, A. and Dollard, J.: Children of Bondage. New York, Ace, 1940.
9. Dennis, W.: Creative productivity between ages of 20 and 80 years. J. Geront. *21:* 1–8, (1966).
10. Erikson, E. H.: Identity and the life cycle: Selected papers. Psychol. Issues *1:* (1959).
11. Friedmann, E., and Havighurst, R. J.: The Meaning of Work and Retirement. Chicago, University of Chicago Press, 1954.
12. Gordon, M. S.: Work and patterns of retirement. In Kleemeier, R. W. (ed.): Aging and Leisure. Oxford U. Press, 1961, p. 15-53.
13. Gurin, G., et al: Americans View Their Mental Health. New York, Basic Books, Inc., 1960.
14. Havighurst, R. J.: The social competence of middle-aged people. Genet. Psychol. Monogr. *56:* 297-375 (1957).
15. Havighurst, R. J.: The sociological meaning of aging. *Geriatrics 13:* 43–50 (1958).
16. Havighurst, R. J.: Dominant concerns in the life cycle. In Gegenwartsprobleme der Entwick-lungspsychologie: Festschrift für Charlotte Buehler. Verlag für Psychologie, 1964.
17. Havighurst, R. J., and Albrecht, R.: Older People. New York, McKay, 1953.
18. Jerome, E. A.: Age and learning — Experimental studies. In Birren, J. E. (ed.): Handbook of Aging and the Individual. Chicago, U. of Chicago Press, 1959, p. 655–99.
19. Johnstone, J. W. C., and Rivera, R. J.: Volunteers for Learning. Chicago, Aldine Publishing Co., 1965.
20. Jones, H. E., et al.: Progress report on growth studies at the University of California. Vita Humana *3:* 17-31 (1960).
21. Kelley, E. L.: Consistency of the adult personality. Am. Psychol. *10:* 659-81 (1955).
22. Kinsey, A. C., et al: Sexual Behavior in the Human Male. Philadelphia, W. B. Saunders Co., 1948.
23. Kinsey, A. C., et al: Sexual Behavior in the Human Female, Philadelphia, W. B. Saunders Co., 1953.
24. Knox, A. B., and Videbeck, R.: Adult Education and the adult life cycle. Adult Educ. *13:* 102-21 (1963).
25. Kraines, R.: The Menopause and Evaluations of the Self: A Study of Women in the Climacteric Years. Unpublished doctoral dissertation. U. of Chicago, 1963.
26. Kuhlen, R. G.: Motivational changes during the adult years. In Kuhlen, R. G. (ed.): Psychological Backgrounds of Adult Education. Center for the Study of Liberal Education for Adults, 1963, p. 77-113.
27. Kuhlen, R. G.: Developmental changes in motivation during the adult years. In Birren, J. E. (ed.): Relations of Development and Aging. Springfield, Ill. Charles C Thomas, 1964, p. 209-46.
28. Lehman, H. C.: Age and Achievement. Princeton, N.J. Princeton U. Press, 1953.
29. London, J., et al.: Adult Education and Social Class. Survey Research Center, U. of California, 1963.
30. Maves, P. B.: Aging, religion, and the church. In Tibbitts, C. (ed.): Handbook of Social Gerontology. Chicago, U. of Chicago Press, 1960, p. 698-749.
31. McFarland, R. and O'Doherty, B.: Work and occupational skills. In Birren, J. E. (ed.): Handbook of Aging and the Individual. Chicago, U. of Chicago Press, 1959, p. 477.
32. Mussen, P.: Some antecedents and consequents of masculine sex typing in adolescent boys. Psychol. Monogr. *75:* (Whole No. 506) (1961).
33. Neugarten, B. L.: Personality Changes during the adult years. In Kuhlen, R. G. (ed.): Psychological Backgrounds of Adult Education. Center for the Study of Liberal Education for Adults, 1963, p. 43-76.
34. Neugarten, B. L.: Personality Change over the Adult Years. In Birren, James E. (Ed.) Relations of Development and Aging. Charles C Thomas, Publisher, 1964. p. 176-208.
35. Neugarten, B. L.: Personality and patterns of aging, Gawein *13:* 249-56 (1965).
36. Neugarten, B. L.: Adult personality: Toward a psychology of the life cycle. Paper presented at annual meeting of the APA. New York, September, 1966.
37. Neugarten, B. L., et al.: The measurement of life satisfaction. J. Geront. *16:* 134-43 (1961).
38. Owens, W. A., and Charles, D. C.: Life

History Correlates of Age Changes in Mental Abilities. W. Lafayette, Ind., Purdue U. Press, 1963.

39. Peck, R. F., and Berkowitz, H.: Personality and adjustment in middle age. In Neugarten, B. L. (ed.): Personality in Middle and Late Life. Chicago, Atherton Press, 1964, p. 15-43.

40. Reichard, S. et al.: Aging and Personality. New York, Wiley, 1962.

41. Rohner, J. H., and Edmonson, M. S. (eds.): The Eighth Generation. Harper, 1960.

42. Schwartz, A. N., and Kleemeier, R. W.: The effects of illness and age upon some aspects of personality. J. Geront. *20:* 85-91 (1965).

43. Shanas, E., and Streib, G. F.: Social Structure and the Family: Generational Relations. Prentice-Hall, 1965.

44. Terman, L., and Oden, N. H.: The Gifted Group at Mid-Life, Stanford U. Press, 1959.

45. Tuddenham, R. D.: Constancy of personality ratings over two decades. Genet. Psychol. Monogr. *60:* 3-29 (1959).

46. Welford, A. T.: Psychomotor performance. In Birren, J. E. (ed.): Handbook of Aging and the Individual, Chicago, U. of Chicago Press, 1959, p. 562-613.

47. Welford, A. T.: Skill and Age. London, Oxford U. Press, 1961.

48. Wilensky, H.: Orderly careers and social participation. Am. Sociol. R. 26: 521-39 (1961).

IX PSYCHOBEHAVIORAL APPROACHES TO PERSONALITY

Personality theories are abstractions created by working scientists to guide them as they explore the intricacies of the natural world. Theories are not to be confused with reality; they are symbolic systems which represent certain features of the objective world. We must recognize at the start, therefore, that theories are merely optional intellectual tools which focus observations and serve as provisional means for understanding a delimited sphere of experience. Theorists have free rein to select whatever facets of experience they wish to focus upon and to construct the propositions and concepts of their theories in any of several different ways.

The most crucial problem a personality theorist faces is choosing what kinds of empirical data he will use as his raw material. Data are the basic ingredients of his concepts, as they are of the theories that will coordinate these concepts. The choice of data is guided first, of course, by common sense; for example, no one interested in the laws of chemistry will spend his professional time exploring the cultural rites of a primitive society. Generally, scientists within the same discipline agree on which kinds of data are likely to prove relevant to the questions they pose in common.

At some point, however, consensus breaks down. Within the circumscribed sphere of their common interests, theorists begin to display differences over which particular events or processes are the most fruitful for attaining their goals. It is here that we uncover substantive differences among theorists of the same discipline. For example, certain physicists believe that astronomical observations will provide the most fruitful data for explaining the origins of the universe; other physicists, seeking an answer to the same problems, will opt for an experimental study of elementary particles. Similarly, some sociologists contend that the institutional patterns of natural societies provide the most relevant data for understanding group behavior; others assert with equal conviction that experimental methods of small-group interaction will prove more fruitful in this quest.

What basic differences in data exist among personality theorists?

Essentially, the data of personality may be differentiated into any of several categories, and theorists may be divided according to which one of these they emphasize for their observations and concepts. Each of these categories of data represents one facet of personality functioning only. No one, in itself, covers the entire range of relevant events. Taken together, however, they comprise the primary elements traditionally included in the study of personality. For example, theorists oriented toward biological data focus on the neurological and physiochemical substrata of human functioning. Psychoanalytic theorists, in contrast, concern themselves with processes that operate without the individual's awareness, that is, in his unconscious. Those who are geared to a behavioristic level deal essentially with the data of overtly observable actions.

No theoretical level can be viewed as reducible to the others since each can provide a complete and internally consistent set of propositions about those specific features of personality to which it attends. However, no one level of data encompasses all of the myriad functions and processes relevant to personality study. Each provides a systematic and necessary, but not a sufficient and complete, representation of the overall picture.

Theories often contradict one another, but comparisons of alternate propositions should be made only of theories that utilize the same class of data. For example, it would be incorrect, philosophically speaking, to say that a theory in physics contradicts a theory in biology, since they concern themselves with different kinds of data. In this same sense, theories that deal with overt behavior should not be compared with theories that utilize unconscious processes or neurophysiological functions. The mistaken belief that these theories are contradictory arises in large measure from the fact that theorists use the same terms when they are referring to substantially different empirical phenomena. For example, laws derived to explain the "learning" of overt behavior need not necessarily be the same as laws describing the "learning" of cognitive processes, since behavior and cognition refer to different kinds of empirical phenomena. An example from nonbehavioral fields may be instructive: in chemistry, laws concerning the "bonding" of complex molecules are not the same as those in physics for the "bonding" of particles within single atoms. Certain similarities exist, of course, but there are differences as well.

In the following papers, theories which focus on different levels of personality data are presented and their rationales described. Keep in mind while reading them that the alternative approaches presented are not necessarily inconsistent. Rather, they represent complementary ways of investigating different facets of personality functioning and organization.

The first article summarizes the basic concepts of Freudian psychoanalysis, an approach to personality that stresses the processes and influences of the unconscious. Roger J. Williams, author of the second reprint and a distinguished biochemist, proposes an alternative model that emphasizes the role of physiological elements in the development of personality. The third paper, presented by the editor of this volume, attempts to synthesize the many determinants and data of personality functioning in his biosocial-learning model.

25   Concepts of Freudian Psychoanalysis

Theodore Millon

It would not be misleading to say that Sigmund Freud was the most influential psychologist and physician of the twentieth century. Along with Copernicus, who forced man to accept his peripheral place in the universe, and Darwin, who forced him to accept his nonunique and animalistic origins. Freud forced man to recognize that his rational superiority over other animals was but another of his delusions.

A proper understanding of Freud's ideas cannot be achieved without knowing the cultural and intellectual environment within which they developed. The latter half of the nineteenth century was a period of tremendous progress in the world of science: the theory of evolution; the chemistry of metabolism; the cell doctrine; the microbial origin of infection; quantum theory; the rediscovery of Mendelian heredity; and the integration of the nervous system.

Freud was born in Moravia in 1856, moving shortly thereafter to Vienna where he resided for 80 years until Austria was overrun by the Nazis. Antisemitism flourished in Austria throughout his lifetime; Freud may have developed much of his skill for originality by being forced into the role of an outsider from early life. Despite this "outsider's" orientation, three major influences can be seen clearly to have shaped the course of his ideas: the physiological energy theories of Helmholtz, Brücke, and Meynart; the concepts of Darwin as elaborated by Jackson; and finally the studies of hypnosis and hysteria initiated by Charcot, Bernheim and Breuer.

Freud's ideas are often dated from his contact with Charcot, Bernheim and Breuer. Crucial as these experiences may have been, it is evident that the principles upon which he constructed his theories were first shaped when he was a medical student under Ernst Brücke and elaborated soon thereafter when he was a research associate in the neuroanatomical laboratories of Theodore Meynart. The physicalistic physiology formulated by Helmholtz and taught by Brücke and Meynart influenced both the language and the concepts Freud was to develop in his own psychodynamic theories. Brücke's lectures on physiology in the 1880's note the following (Jones, 1953):

Real causes are symbolized in science by the word "force" . . . Knowledge reduces them to two — attraction and repulsion. Freud, characterizing his own views in 1926, wrote " . . . forces assist or inhibit one another, combine with another, enter into compromises with one another. . ."

Freud's concepts were consistently organized as energies interacting in a dynamic play of forces and counterforces. *Libido* was a life force struggling against *thanatos,* a death force; the *id* was an instinctual force regulated by the *ego,* a regulating and controlling force. Freud's entire metapsychology with its mental apparatus, regulating mechanisms and dynamic, topographic and economic modes of description, shows striking parallels with the tenets of his early neurological training. Although he gave up his early efforts to find a physiological basis for mental processes, he was never fully emancipated from the Helmholtzian energy model.

A second and often unrecognized influence upon Freud, came from Darwin's theories of evolution. Hughlings Jackson, the great English neurologist, extended Darwin's basic observations by proposing

Millon, T.: Concepts of Freudian psychoanalysis. In Millon, T.: Modern Psychopathology. Philadelphia, W. B. Saunders Co., 1969.

that the symptoms of brain disorders reflect the emergence of primitive brain functions which had been submerged during evolution. Freud, borrowing this notion, formulated the idea that emotional traumas lead to the loss of mature capacities and are followed by "regression" to more primitive childhood behavior. Jackson further espoused the view that organisms compensate for the loss of a biological function. He viewed these substitutive behaviors as clinically useful signs of an unobservable disease. Freud drew upon this idea, first to formulate his concept of adaptive defense mechanisms, and second, for this view that mechanisms are a sign of an unobservable or unconscious disturbance. Jackson's comments on the diagnostic value of dreams were also adapted by Freud. Although Freud elaborated each of these ideas in an original and insightful manner, it is obvious that as a young neurologist he was fully acquainted with the speculations of Jackson, the most eminent theoretical neurologist of his day.

As early as 1880, Joseph Breuer, a well-known Viennese internist, observed that the recall of early traumatic experiences during hypnosis often resulted in therapeutic relief for hysterical patients. Freud first became acquainted with the relationship between hypnosis and hysteria in 1885 when received a fellowship to study diseases of the nervous system with Charcot in Paris. Upon Freud's return to Vienna he learned from Breuer, who had been an associate of his in Meynart's laboratory, that emotional catharses among hysterics during hypnosis appeared to benefit these patients. In order to understand this unusual phenomenon better, Freud returned to France in 1889, to study with Bernheim.

After availing himself of Bernheim's psychological interpretations of hysteria, Freud returned to Vienna and adopted the hypnotic-cathartic method of Breuer. After an intensive treatment of several cases of hysteria by this technique, Freud and Breuer reported their studies in an article in 1893, and more fully in their epochal book *Studies of Hysteria* published in 1895. In contrast to the biologically oriented theories of Janet, which failed to explain the personal meaning of hysterical symptoms, the formulations of Freud and Breuer specified the logical relationship of the symptom to the experiences and strivings of the patient. Their thesis was that painful thoughts and feelings were repressed into an unconscious force which exerted powerful pressures within the patient. This pressure expressed itself in symptoms which symbolically represented the repressed thoughts and feelings. Emotional catharsis, known as *abreaction*, relieved the unconscious pressure and, in turn, eliminated the symptom that the pressure had created.

Soon after their joint publication, Breuer gave up his research and left Freud to explore its further development alone. Freud soon found that hypnosis was of limited value. Some patients could not be hypnotized and symptoms often returned after the hypnotic trance. Freud devised an original technique to meet these problems. The technique, called *free association,* consisted merely of requiring that the patient speak aloud every thought and feeling, inhibiting nothing that came to his mind. This method, together with reports of dreams, provided Freud with all the clinical data he needed to build a new system of psychology which he named *psychoanalysis.*

Despite the lonely years following Breuer's withdrawal, Freud remained fascinated by the obscure labyrinths of human thought and emotion. His relentless search into these mysterious and hidden processes proved to be a perilous journey professionally. That he stumbled into blind alleys and held tenaciously to fruitless and obscure concepts does not diminish the courage and inventiveness of his efforts. With rare brilliance he uncovered the inner world of man's psychological makeup.

Freud was not the first to uncover the role of unconscious processes. Perceptive men have known it for ages. But Freud was the first to trace the complex manner in which unconscious motives and conflicts weave into intricate and distorted patterns of overt behavior. As he learned to unfold the strategies for self protection and conflict resolution, such seemingly purposeless behavior as dreams, phobias, compulsions and even everyday slips of the tongue took on meaning and clarity. Freud argued that the individual unconsciously adopted extreme defensive maneuvers to deny, falsify or distort the pain of unfulfilled strivings and fears. He recognized clearly that these unconscious processes occurred in normal and abnormal individuals alike. This realization helped close the gap between the study of normal behavior and psychopathology.

In his early writings, Freud believed that disorders resulted primarily from traumatic childhood experience. His later work minimized the importance of trauma and stressed that indulgence or frustration during any of the crucial early stages of development was the major cause of disorders. The remnants of these early experiences were deeply imbedded within the unconscious and were not accessible to the modifying influence of changing circumstance. As the pressure of these memories persisted, the individual anticipated and recreated new experiences similar to those of his childhood. Freud specified different forms of psychopathology depending on the intensity and the stage when these difficulties arose first. From this notion he derived such disorders as the oral and anal characters.

Personality structure was conceived by Freud to consist of three major components – id, ego and superego – interacting in dynamic tension and balance. These concepts were merely convenient ways of describing processes involved in personality functioning and were not viewed by Freud as things or entities.

The id represented inborn and unmodifiable instinctual strivings within the individual; these strivings seek expression unmindful of reality. The similarities Freud observed between the instinctual behavior of infants and the expression of adult sexuality led him to speak of infantile strivings as sexual in nature; the sequence through which these early instinctual drives unfolded were termed the psychosexual stages. The second component of personality, referred to as the ego, represented processes geared to reality adaptations. These processes – judgment, memory, knowledge, anticipation and the uncon-

scious mechanisms of defense – controlled the instinctual drives of the id and directed their expression within the boundaries of practical reality. The third personality structure, the superego, consisted of internalized social prohibitions that inhibited instinctual impulses; these took the form of guilt feelings and fears of punishment. Practical compromises between the impulses of the id and the inhibitions of the superego are a primary function of the ego; a failure to reconcile these opposing forces led inevitably to tension and emotional disorder.

The emphasis given to early childhood experience by Freudian theorists represents their contention that disorders of adulthood are a direct product of the continued and insidious operation of past events. To them, knowledge of the past provides information indispensable to understanding adult difficulties. To the question, "what is the basis of adult disorders?" they would answer: "the anxieties of childhood and the progressive sequence of defensive maneuvers which were devised to protect against a recurrence of these feelings".

Freudian theorists contend that these two determinants of adult behavior, childhood anxieties and defensive maneuvers, are unconscious, that is, cannot be brought to awareness except under unusual conditions. It is the search for these unconscious processes which is the distinguishing feature of the intrapsychic approach. The obscure and elusive phenomena of the unconscious are the data which they uncover and use for their concepts. These data consist first, of repressed childhood anxieties that persist within the individual and attach themselves insidiously to ongoing experiences, and second, of unconscious adaptive processes which protect the individual against the resurgence of these anxieties.

How is the unconscious manifested? Essentially, through indirect methods. Since the unconscious cannot be seen by direct means, it must be inferred.

Unconscious processes are revealed most often when we let down our guard, as in "slips of the tongue," or when we put aside the controls of wakeful activity, as in sleep, or when we relinquish our contact with reality, as in serious mental disorders.

Unconscious data may be obtained also in specially designed clinical settings. The technique of *free association*, where the patient is asked to relax his usual controls and to verbalize every passing thought or emotion, often elicits unconscious processes which are not evident in daily life. The seemingly unrelated fragments of free association — memories, hopes and casual commentaries — turn out to be neither random nor irrelevant, but display a pattern of repetitive themes. These themes are interpreted as evidence for the existence of unconscious forces which underlie and direct conscious behavior. *Dream analysis* is another clinical method of uncovering unconscious processes. In sleep, without the controls of reality and responsibility, unconscious processes display themselves freely in symbolic dream imagery. The method of *projective tests* is another clinically created procedure for inferring the unconscious. Here, ambiguous stimuli are presented to the subject and he is forced to draw upon his own inner resources in order to make a response. Idiosyncratic responses result and unconscious processes often are displayed.

Questions have been raised as to whether or not scientific concepts can be founded on unconscious data. Freudian theories have been criticized as unscientific mixtures of metaphorical analogies, speculative notions and hypothetical constructs because their data are anchored so tenuously to the observable world.

Added to this rather harsh judgment is the equally critical view that the methods of collecting unconscious data are both unreliable and imprecise. How can concepts of the unobservable unconscious be empirically anchored? Can one accept what the patient says without having it corroborated by external evidence? Is the patient an unbiased judge, or is he motivated to agree with his all-knowing therapist? Are free associations really free, or do patients produce what their therapists implicitly suggest?

These and many other questions have been raised about the subjective and methodologically uncontrolled procedures used for the development of psycho-

analytic theories. Without tools such as tape recorded therapeutic interviews, corroborative data from relatives and experimentally controlled longitudinal studies, the probability of objectifying the concepts and propositions of intrapsychic theories is highly unlikely. To critics, the ingenious speculations of intrapsychic theorists are, at best, a starting point, a preliminary set of propositions which must be articulated into clearly specifiable behaviors which can be confirmed or disproved.

Despite these criticisms, many of which are equally applicable to other theoretical approaches, unconscious processes are a necessary part of the study of man's functioning. Although these processes are difficult to formulate according to the tenets of scientific objectivity, their existence cannot be denied or overlooked. Efforts to unravel them will fall prey inevitably to theoretical obscurity and methodological difficulty, yet the search is mandatory.

FREUD'S PSYCHOSEXUAL CONFLICT THEORY

Freud's theory of psychopathology was developed over a 50-year professional career. Its essential features may be summarized as follows: Man possesses basic biological instincts, the most important of which are the sexual or life-propelling energies known as the *libido*. These energies, together with aggressive death-energies, compose the *id*. A maturational sequence unfolds in which these libidinous energies shift in their primary locus from one organ or zone of the body to another; this sequence is referred to as the stages of *psychosexual development*. Biological instincts must find outlets of expression. In attempting to gain these outlets the child runs into conflict with reality limitations and societal prohibitions. Frustration or conflict associated with these biological drives leads to anxiety. The child learns a variety of techniques to relieve his anxiety and to gratify his instinctual needs; these protective and need-gratifying techniques are referred to as the processes of the *ego*. Ego processes which develop in response to particularly intense infantile anxieties become *fixated* and may persist as lifelong *character disorders*. Experiences in later life which threaten to reactivate these repressed and unconscious anxieties lead to pathological symptoms; these symptoms represent, in symbolic form, both the repressed anxieties and the defensive techniques learned to control them.

Subsequent theorists extended and modified these basic notions. Those features of Freud's theory which characterize his position in distinction to those of his followers will be detailed next.

The Instincts

Freud believed that the root of all psychopathology could be found in the frustration of certain basic biological instincts. Instincts were viewed as inborn biological energies which excite and direct behavior. They could be satisfied, as can hunger and thirst, by a variety of instinct-gratifying activities. Two major energy sources were proposed by Freud, the life and the death instincts. Because the value of the death instinct as an explanatory concept has been almost universally rejected, we will bypass this concept and deal only with his views regarding the life instinct.

The energies of the life instinct, called the libido, were manifested in what Freud referred to as sexual excitations. To Freud, all of man's interests, tastes and behaviors were but surface expressions or substitutions for more direct gratifications of these excitations. Freud's entire system assumed that "civilized" and social phenomena could be reduced ultimately to the basic biological instincts. Mental disorders, according to Freud, arose as a result of conflicts and frustrations of these instincts.

Psychosexual Stages

Direct gratification of sexual excitation can be obtained by the manipulation of extremely sensitive surface areas of the body. The primary bodily region of maximal sexual excitation shifts, however, as

the individual matures. This progression of *erogenous zones* was termed the psychosexual stages.

In the first year and a half of life, the lips and mouth region are the primary locus of libidinal excitation; during this period sucking and eating behavior produce pleasure and gratification. This *oral* period is followed by a libidinous centering in the *anal* region which lasts about a year; it is replaced, in turn, by an erogenous *phallic* stage in which rubbing and massaging of the genitals serves as the basis of pleasure. These three *pregenital* stages are followed by a *latency* period which lasts until puberty, following which the mature *genital* stage unfolds in preparation for normal adult sexuality.

The three pregenital periods were seen by Freud as prone to conflict and frustration. In early life the young child's needs are entirely dependent upon and subject to the attitudes and whims of his parents. Second, there is a rapid shift in the bodily zones of gratification, leaving little opportunity for resolving or working through whatever frustrations and conflicts arose. To Freud, then, the first few years of life were especially susceptible to unresolved anxiety and defective adaptation.

During the latency period the child learns to accept the restrictions and prohibitions of his parents, establishing thereby what Freud termed the *super-ego*. Henceforth, the child restrains direct gratification of his instinctual impulses by his own volition. Conflicts arise now between the youngster's "ideals" and his instinctual drives. If the prohibitions of the super-ego are too restrictive, however, the individual may be unable to gratify normal adult sexual needs when they emerge during the genital stage. Thus, numerous children have been led by parental teachings and religious admonishments to believe that it is "immoral" to engage in "sex"; the impact of this belief may be so deeply ingrained that they continue to experience feelings of tension and guilt even when sexual activities are fully sanctioned, as in marriage.

Psychosexual Character Types

Each stage of psychosexual development produces a distinctive set of anxieties and defenses resulting from instinct frustration and conflict. Psychopathological character traits arise from the persistence into adulthood of these distinctive childhood anxieties and defenses. For example, a child may have experienced oral gratification only when he submitted to a rigid feeding schedule imposed by his parents. Anxious lest he lose parental support and fearful of deviating from parental regulations, he may become a cautious and acquiescent person unable to take any step toward adult independence. This pattern of early oral frustration would dispose the individual to retreat or *regress* to this fixated pattern of early adaptation whenever he is faced with anxiety. As a freshman college student, he might develop a psychosomatic ailment if he failed to be accepted into a fraternity and return to the "security" of his parental home; faced with marital or vocational difficulties, he might turn to excessive eating or drinking as a regressive mode of oral gratification.

Freud differentiated the oral period into two phases: the *oral-sucking* phase, in which food is accepted indiscriminately, followed by the *oral-biting* period, in which food is accepted selectively, occasionally rejected and aggressively chewed. Excessive gratifications, conflicts or frustrations associated with each of these phases establish different patterns of adult personality. For example, an overly indulgent sucking stage may lead to imperturbable optimism and naive self-assurance. An ungratified sucking period may lead to excessive dependency and gullibility; for example, the deprived child may learn to "swallow" anything in order to ensure that he will get something. Frustration experienced at the biting stage might lead to the development of aggressive oral tendencies such as sarcasm and verbal hostility in adulthood.

Difficulties associated with the anal period likewise lead to distinctive modes of adult personality. Toilet training occurs in the second year, a time when the child can both control his sphincter muscles and comprehend the desires of his parents. For the first time in his life, he has the power to actively and knowingly thwart his parents' demands; he has the option now of pleasing or foiling their desires. A battle of wits often arises. Depending on the outcome, the child will adopt a pattern of attitudes toward authority which will have a far-reaching effect in shaping his adult traits. If, for example, the child's pleasure in defecation is punished and condemned, his assertive tendencies may be shattered, leading him to become a compliant and conforming person, fearful of expressing independent thoughts. Conceivably, he might accept parental condemnations of his soiling behavior as "right," and thereby attempt to show them how "worthy and clean" he is. He may, in time, become not only compulsively clean and orderly, but may display harsh attitudes toward those who fail to be like him. Thus, he may seek to control others with rules and principles as severe and arbitrary as those his parents imposed upon him. Other reactions to parental severity in toilet training are possible. To avoid toilet training conflict he may learn to hold back his feces; as a result, he may become a retentive, parsimonious and constricted individual, who forever procrastinates and always saves "for a rainy day." As another possibility, harsh training procedures might lead to rage and anger; this may result in a withdrawal of parental demands. Finding himself successful in this maneuver, the child may develop a lifelong pattern of self-assertion, disorderliness and negativism.

Conflicts during the phallic stage were viewed by Freud to be crucial to the development of psychopathology. In the third and fourth year, libidinous energies center upon the genitals, and are manifested in masturbation, sexual curiosity and exhibitionism. At this time there is a shift in the child's attitude toward his parents. Feelings toward the opposite sex become tinged with sexual desire; this is paralleled by jealousy and hostility toward the same-sex parent. A struggle ensues between the child and the same-sex parent for the affection of the opposite-sex parent; this Freud termed the *oedipus complex*. Freud considered his observation of this conflict to be a major discovery and viewed it as the ."nucleus" of neurotic disorders. In the young boy this conflict eventuates in an intense fear that his more powerful and jealous father will punish him for his lustful feelings. Anxieties of castration become so intense that he represses his incestuous desire for his mother and denies his hostile feelings toward his father.

If the oedipal conflict is resolved adequately, the boy will not experience a feeling of defeat and humiliation. He will learn to transform his incestuous desire into a more acceptable expression of affection. He will have learned to control his envy and hostility toward his father. He will identify with his father's powerful masculinity and channel his struggle for mastery into acceptable activities such as athletic and social competitions. In brief then, he will transform his sexual and aggressive urges into more realistic modes of expression. In a manner similar to the boy, the young girl will learn to renounce her attraction to the father and her hostile attitudes toward her mother. In healthy resolutions, both boy and girl emerge with a strengthened pattern of ego capacities and an undiminished feeling of self-esteem.

Should the entanglements of the oedipal period be unresolved, the child will forever handle sexual and aggressive impulses in a troubled manner. Sexuality may remain in a conflict between seductive thoughts, on the one hand, and guilt and fear of punishment, on the other. Faulty identification with the same sex parent may lead to a homosexual pattern. Aggressive impulses may persist, turning the individual into a bully and obstructionist.

To Freud, early instinctual frustrations and conflicts remain deeply anchored within the person. Although the anxieties and adaptive reactions they produce are unconscious, they persist as a mold that shapes the entire course of life.

Mechanisms

Drives must be gratified and conflicts must be resolved if the individual is to avoid anxiety and disintegration. Under persistent or extraordinary stress, the individual may be forced to deceive himself and to distort reality in order to mitigate the tensions he experiences. To some de-

gree, all of us avoid conflicts, turn from anxiety and soften blows to our self-image. The mechanisms we adopt to avoid the strains of life often are maladaptive. Self-deception and reality-distortion can interfere with effective functioning and may result in a cycle of events that intensifies the very problems supposed to be circumvented. The more ingrained these mechanisms of self-deception become, the more they will function indiscriminately and the less apt they will be in dealing with reality.

Mechanisms of self-protection and need-gratification may be conscious, of course. Conscious mechanisms can be appraised and adjusted so as to successfully alleviate stress. Mechanisms which operate unconsciously, however, are not subject to reflective appraisal; unaware of their existence, the individual continues to use them even though they may fail to fulfill his needs adequately or appropriately. They are more self-defeating than conscious mechanisms, therefore not for any intrinsic reason, but because they are less likely to be abandoned if they prove maladaptive.

Two broad classes of unconscious mechanisms may be differentiated. The first group, noted as the *denial mechanisms,* represents the banishing from consciousness of intolerable memories, impulses and conflicts. By various maneuvers, the patient disavows these feelings and thoughts, and thereby avoids acknowledging their painful nature. The second class of defenses, noted as *distortion mechanisms,* represents the misinterpretation of painful thoughts and feelings in order to minimize their impact. A discussion of these mechanisms follows.

Denial Mechanisms

These concepts represent unconscious processes in which the individual denies the existence of painful or irreconcilable thoughts.

1. *Repression* is the most common of the mechanisms and is a prerequisite to other denial mechanisms. It involves the simple but involuntary process of excluding one's undesirable thoughts and feelings from consciousness; in this way, the indi-

vidual keeps inaccessible what would otherwise be unbearable.

2. The mechanism known as *isolation* represents a segmented or limited repression; here the painful association between a thought and its emotional counterpart is disconnected. By repressing the feeling associated with a painful event, the individual prevents this feeling from upsetting his equilibrium. For example, a prisoner may isolate his emotional feelings from thoughts about his impending execution; in response to questions about his fate, he may shrug his shoulders and say, "well, that's the way the cookie crumbles." He detaches feeling from the event to protect himself against overwhelming anxiety.

3. *Projection* represents first, a repression of one's own objectionable traits and motives and second, an attribution of these characteristics to others. The failing college student may claim that "his school has a lousy curriculum and stupid professors"; the tax-dodging businessman may state that he was driven to do it by "mercenary union leaders" and "dishonest government investigators"; the sexually driven patient may accuse the object of his advances as having seduced him.

Projection may allow the individual to vent as well as disclaim his unacceptable impulses. For example, by attributing hostile motives to others, he may claim the right to be hostile to them. Since they have engaged in shameful misdeeds, and he is their victim, he feels justified in seeking retribution.

4. In *reaction-formation* the individual represses his undesirable impulses and assumes a diametrically opposite conscious attitude. A hostile patient may display a façade of exaggerated amiability; a rebellious youngster may become scrupulously polite and gracious; a socially insecure woman puts forth a blasé attitude and gregarious manner.

Reaction-formations not only maintain repression, but strengthen the patient's control over his unconscious tendency, e.g., by being scrupulously polite, the youngster is able to keep his rebellious inclination under constant check. Reaction-formations may also give vent to the repressed desire. Thus, leaders, in condemning public immorality, devote their spare time to "investigating" obscene literature, burlesque houses and neighborhood brothels. They may be gratifying their own unconscious, lascivious desires, while consciously decrying the shameful state of our society.

5. *Undoing* is a self-purification mechanism in which the individual attempts to repent for some misdeed or counteract a repressed "evil" motive. Avaricious financiers donate their fortunes to charity; miserly husbands, unable to tolerate their niggardliness, give exorbitant tips to bellhops and waitresses. In more pathological form, undoing may be displayed in bizarre rituals and "magical" acts. The patient who compulsively washes his hands may symbolically be "cleansing his dirty thoughts"; his intolerable feeling of moral impurity is kept unconscious and counteracted by his ritual. Although his compulsion may cause him considerable discomfort, and consciously may be acknowledged as absurd, he neither has the power to control it nor can he recognize its unconscious significance.

6. *Fixation* denotes the repression of maturing impulses and capacities. The individual refuses to "grow up" and acknowledge feelings and responsibilities appropriate to his age. This attempted cessation of psychological growth stems usually from a fear of adult impulses and responsibilities, or an unwillingness to forego the security of childhood relationships. Thus, in a rather unusual case, an otherwise fully developed and highly intelligent 12 year old boy never learned to drink liquids by any means other than through a nipple; moreover, he refused to wear undershorts, insisting that his parents purchase diapers that fit him.

7. *Regression* is similar to fixation; it differs in that it represents a retreat to an earlier level *after* normal development has progressed. Unable to face the anxieties and conflicts of adult existence, the individual reverts to immature and even infantile behaviors. Thus, disturbed adolescents, fearful of heterosexual impulses and competition, or anxious about their ability to be independent of their parents, often retreat to the safety of an infantile depen-

dency. Their regressive mechanisms may be observed in signs such as incontinence, baby talk, thumbsucking and womb-like postures.

Distortion Mechanisms

These concepts represent processes that misinterpret distressing experiences and feelings in order to make them more bearable.

1. *Fantasy* is a semiconscious process of imagination serving to gratify wishes that cannot be fulfilled in reality. Thus, the musings of a shy and withdrawn 15 year old served to "transform" him into an admired and powerful figure, on some occasions, and a noble sufferer whose unjust plight would be redeemed, on others; his fantasies occupied much of his wakeful time and thereby precluded opportunities for realistic gratification.

2. *Rationalization* is the most common mechanism of reality distortion. It represents an unconscious process in which the individual excuses his behavior or relieves his disappointments with reasons that are plausible but not "true." Rational explanations are concocted to cloak unrecognized and unacceptable motives. Thus, the businessman may justify hostility toward his wife by claiming "a hard day at the office"; the failing college student assuages his self-esteem by attributing his failure to "merciless freshman grading"; the spinster aunt alters her feelings of frustration and loneliness by pointing out how much better her life is than that of "those bickering Smiths next door."

3. *Identification* signifies a distortion of self-image in which the individual assigns to himself the power, achievements and stature of those with whom he associates. In this way he experiences vicariously gratifications which otherwise are not available to him. An alumnus may identify with his college's football team in order to bask in the glory of its athletic victories; an insignificant clerk may read biographies of great men and revel in minor similarities he finds between them and himself. Identification serves important developmental functions in the young, but it may lead to self-repudiation and identity confusion among adults. The belief that one is someone else is a sign of serious pathology; thus, every large mental hospital has one or two patients who claim they are "Napoleon," "Jesus Christ" or some other figure of historical eminence.

4. *Compensation* represents a less pathological attempt to disguise one's deficiencies, frustrations or conflicts. In this mechanism, the individual overcomes his weakness by counteracting it or developing substitute behaviors. Short men may counter their feelings of insignificance by aggressive attention-getting behavior; physically unattractive girls may become preoccupied with their academic studies, and thereby cultivate respect for their "brains"; wives who have been cast aside by their husbands may gratify their need for love symbolically by insatiable appetites for sweets and drink. Well-known examples of successful compensation may be found throughout history. Demosthenes surmounted his early stuttering and became a great orator; Theodore Roosevelt overcame his sickly childhood by turning to feats of physical vigor and courage.

5. *Sublimation* usually is a healthy form of self-distortion. It represents the gratification of unacceptable needs by socially approved substitutes. Through this process the individual keeps his selfish and forbidden impulses out of awareness, yet finds acceptable channels for their expression. An aggressive individual may find gratification in an athletic, military or surgical career; unconscious strivings for power may form the basis of a political or business career; unacceptable desires for recognition may underlie success in science, teaching or acting. In none of these does the person consciously recognize that his occupation is a disguised outlet for unattractive needs or motives.

6. *Displacement* signifies the transfer of negative emotions from one object onto a more neutral or safe object. Through this mechanism, the individual maintains the illusion that his feelings toward the first object do not exist; moreover, he minimizes the risk of counteraction from that object. For example, the professor who displaces upon his students the hostility he experiences at home, protects himself from

recognizing his hostile feelings toward his wife and gives vent to his emotions safely; his anger is dissipated in this manner, he maintains the illusion that his marital relations are ideal and he avoids the possibility of retribution from his wife.

26   The Biological Approaches to the Study of Personality

Roger J. Williams

The study of personality logically involves trying to answer three questions: First, of what is personality composed; e.g., if two people have differing personalities, in what specific ways do they or may they differ? Second, how do distinctive personalities arise? Third, how can improvement or modification of personality be brought about?

The first question, of what is personality composed, is a difficult and complicated one, and the answers to the second and third questions hinge upon the answer to it. Our discussion in this paper will be a contribution toward the answering of all these questions. Our approach is in a sense not new, but it is largely unexplored, and, we believe, rich in potentialities. It has the advantage that it can be used to supplement all other approaches; it does not require the rejection of older insights regardless of their origin or how time-honored they may be.

Certainly one of the earliest attempts to account for personality differences was made by the astrologers who recognized that people differed one from another and sought to explain these differences on the basis of the influence of the heavenly bodies. The hypothesis of the astrologers has not stood up well in scientific circles, but there are numerous citizens who still believe in horoscopes and many magazines and newspapers that publish them. The tenacious belief rests, I believe, on a fundamental failure of real scientists to come up with other reasons and explanations which satisfy.

In the beginning of the nineteenth century, Gall and Spurzheim developed phrenology which was destined to be in public vogue for a number of decades. This purported to be a science essentially concerned with the relation between personality traits and the contours of people's heads. Partly because it lacked scientific validity and partly because its implications were fatalistic and deterministic, the fundamental idea has largely been discarded.

In the middle portion of the nineteenth century the possible importance of heredity as a factor in the production of personality differences was brought to the fore by the investigations and writings of Darwin and his nephew Galton. Galton, the founder of eugenics, had none of our modern information as to how complicated heredity is; his emphasis on "good" and "bad" heredity (his own, of course, was "good") was misleading and his ideas of improving the race not only flew in the face of religious teachings but were so oversimplified that they came to be regarded as unsound scientifically. The eugenic view also had the disadvantage from the standpoint of public acceptance of being impregnated with determinism.

Before the end of the nineteenth century, Freudianism came into being and has subsequently received such wide acceptance that it has dominated the field of psychiatry for several decades. Funda-

Williams, R.J.: The biological approach to the study of personality. From a paper presented at the Berkeley Conference on Personality, May, 1960.

mentally, Freudianism is a system of surmises of such a nature that they have not and cannot be tested by controlled experiments. These surmises appear so implausible as to demand rejection. Controlled experiments are quite outside the routine thoughts and discussions of adherents of the Freudian school.

The surmises which form the basis of the Freudian doctrine include the essential idea that personalities are built during the lifetime of the individual and that the prime factors which enter are the environmental happenings beginning on the day of birth — possibly even before — and the thoughts that are developed as a result of these happenings. Therapeutic psychoanalysis is based upon the idea that if an individual can come to understand how the events of his earlier life have developed his present unfortunate attitudes, his personality difficulties tend to evaporate. Inherent in this approach is the idea that minds are much more complex than they superficially appear to be; they are like icebergs in that there is much more "out of sight" than there is in open view.

That the Freudian approach to personality has elements of strength is so obvious as not to require argument. It leaves room for the unknown and unexpected in human behavior (which is needed), it emphasizes the dynamic aspects of personality, and strongly encourages the belief that human beings are not powerless to change and modify their personalities and that parents have tremendous potentialities in developing the lives of their children. The wide acceptance of Freudian ideas bears out the thought that the public, including the physicians, are first people and second, if at all, scientists. Certainly a cold-blooded scientific approach would never have developed and fostered the Freudian concepts.

Freudian doctrine tacitly assumes that at the beginning of their lives individuals are substantially duplicates of one another. This doctrine is almost, if not wholly, universalized; that is, its pronouncements apply to everyone alike. Freud himself wrote, "I always find it uncanny when I can't understand someone in terms of myself."

To be sure, people develop later in life very diverse personalities, but the observed differences are, according to the Freudian school, essentially environmentally induced and the laws of development are the same for all. Freud and his followers sometimes make references to tendencies which are inherited by the human race as a whole but it is the consistent practice to disregard or minimize individual differences in heredity as a potential source of personality differences. Certainly Freudians as such have not fostered research in this area.

The neglect of hereditary factors among those who are concerned with personality disorders is so pronounced that the veteran physician, Walter C. Alvarez, has recently complained "in most of the present day books on psychiatry, there is not even a short section on heredity. The book resembles a text on paleontology written for a fundamentalist college, with not one word on evolution!"[1] Of course, the dilemma of developing environmentalist doctrine while paying some attention to heredity is a real one. If one begins to allow heredity to make inroads and demand attention, there is no telling where the process will end; the whole structure of environmentalistic Freudianism might come tumbling down.

On hard-nosed scientific ground one does not escape from determinism by adopting an environmentalist point of view, though many seem to think so. They resist considering the importance of heredity for this reason. Rigorous scientific thinking leads us to conclude that environmentalism is just as deterministic in its implications as is hereditarianism. People say, "If we don't like one environment we can move to another," but scientific reasoning if followed implicitly leads to the conclusion that we cannot move to a new environment unless there is some stimulus in the old or the new environment which *makes us* move.

This subject is much too large to discuss in detail in this paper, but as a prelude to further discussions I will briefly state my position. In the first place I have not the slightest doubt that heredity has a great deal to do with personality development. I do not resist this idea. I do not believe this recognition leads inevitably to determinism. I do not know how or why intelligence originated on earth; I do not understand how or why free will originated or just how it works. But there are many other questions to which scientific reasoning gives me no answer. I do not even know why positive electricity attracts negative or why every particle of matter in the physical universe exerts an attractive force on every other particle. I do accept the idea of free choice, with limitations imposed by laws, as a fundamental premise. With the acceptance, as a background for my thinking, of the exercise of intelligence and free choice as prime factors in life, I do not resist the recognition of hereditary influences. Their recognition does not pin me down to determinism.

Behavioristic psychology which at its inception was *completely* environmentalistic has bolstered the environmental approach of Freudianism. This school of psychology has a fundamental basis the facts discovered by Pavlov using dogs and commonly designated as conditioned reflexes. The development of personality thus becomes a pyramiding conditioning process whereby the developing infant is continuously modified in his responses by the stimuli he or she received.

What was not quoted by the behavioristic school were correlative findings by Pavlov which are highly pertinent. Pavlov found as a result of extensive study of many dogs that they often exhibited innate tendencies to react very differently to the same stimulus. He recognized in his dogs four basic types: (1) excitable, (2) inhibitory, (3) equilibrated, and (4) active, as well as intermediate, types.[2] He recognized enormous differences in dogs with respect to their condition-ability and was by no means inclined to focus his attention solely upon the behavior of the *"the* dog." Scott and others have in more recent times found ample justification for Pavlov's concern over the fundamental differences between dogs of different breeds and between individual dogs within each breed. These differences, which can be studied under controlled conditions in dogs vastly easier than in human beings, are *not* the result of training.

It is beyond dispute, of course, that dogs, cats, rats, and monkeys, for example, show species differences with respect to their patterns of conditionability. Stimuli which are highly effective for one species may be of negligible importance for another. If hereditary factors make for inter-species differences, it is entirely reasonable to suppose that intra-species differences would exist for the same reason.

Before we proceed to the principal part of our discussion it should be pointed out that the pronouncements of men whose memories we may revere must be taken in their historical context. Freud, for example, developed most of his fundamental ideas before there was any knowledge of hormones, indeed before the term "hormone" was coined. He had at this time no knowledge of present-day biochemistry; the chemical factors involved in nutrition were almost wholly unknown; and he certainly had no knowledge of the close ties which exist between biochemistry and genetics. It can safely be assumed that if the youthful Sigmund Freud were reincarnated today, he would include these vast developments in endocrinology, biochemistry, and genetics in his purview, and that his thinking would follow quite different paths from those which it followed about the turn of the century.

A parallel case has existed in the field of medicine with respect to the monumental work of Louis Pasteur. Pasteur's thrilling contribution may be summarized in a single sentence: "Disease is caused by microorganisms." To convince his contemporaries of this fact Pasteur had to overcome terrific resistance. Once established, however, the next generation not only accepted the idea but was strongly inclined to go even further and assert that disease is caused *exclusively* by microorganisms. After Pasteur's death substantial evidence began to accumulate that disease could be caused by malnutrition. This idea in turn met with terrific resistance, possibly because this was considered a slur on Pasteur's memory. Actually, however, if the youthful Pasteur could have been reincarnated about 1900 he probably would have been one of the first to recognize the importance of malnutrition — an importance which many physicians even today do not fully recognize nor welcome with open arms.

The parallel between the two cases may be discerned if we summarize Freud's contribution thus: "Personality disorders result from infantile conditioning." It appears that many followers of Freud tend to insert the word exclusively and to say "Personality disorders result exclusively from infantile conditioning." It seems an extremely doubtful compliment to Freud's memory to follow slavishly doctrines which he — if he were alive and in possession of present-day knowledge — would repudiate or radically modify.

A biological approach to personality should seek to bring from biology *everything* that can help to explain what personality is, how it originates and how it can be modified and improved. Biology has much to contribute, particularly in an area of biology which has received relatively little attention; namely, that involving anatomical, physiological, biochemical (and psychological) individuality.

It seems indefensible to assume that people are built in separate compartments, one anatomical, one physiological, one biochemical, one psychological, and that these compartments are unrelated or only distantly related to each other. Each human being possesses and exhibits unity. Certainly anatomy is basic to physiology and biochemistry, and it may logically be presumed that it is also basic to psychology.

Let us look therefore in the field of anatomy for facts which are pertinent to our problem.

Anatomists, partly for reasons of simplicity, have been prone in centuries past to concentrate on a single picture of the human body. Obvious concessions are made, when necessary, in considering the male and the female of the species, and always anatomists have been aware that within these two groups there are variations and anomalies. Only within the past decade,[3] however, has comprehensive information been published which indicates how great these inter-individual variations are and how widespread they are in the general population.

For example, normal stomachs vary greatly in shape and about sixfold in size.

Transverse colons vary widely in the positions at which they cross over in the abdomen and pelvic colon patterns vary widely. Arising from the aortic arch are two, three, four, and sometimes five and six branch arteries; the aorta itself varies greatly in size and hearts differ morphologically and physiologically so that their pumping capacities in healthy young men vary widely. The size of arteries and the branching patterns are such that in each individual the various tissues and organs are supplied with blood unequally well, resulting in a distinctive pattern of blood supply for each.

Morphological differences in the respiratory systems of normal people are basic to the fact that each person exhibits a distinctive breathing pattern as shown in the spirograms of different individuals made under comparable conditions.

Each endocrine gland is subject to wide variation among "normal" individuals. Thyroid glands vary in weight about sixfold,[4] and the protein-bound iodine of the blood which measures the hormonal output varies to about the same degree.[8] Parathyroid glands also vary about six fold in total weight in so-called "normal" individuals, and the number of lobes varies from 2-12.[5] The most prevalent number of lobes is four, but some anatomists estimate that not over fifty percent of the population have this number. The number of islets of Langerhans, which are responsible for insulin production, vary over a tenfold range in diabetes-free individuals.[9] The thickness of the adrenal cortex, where the critical adrenal hormones arise, is said to vary from 0.5 mm to 5 mm (tenfold).[10]

The morphology of the pituitary glands, which produce about eight different hormones is so variable, when different healthy individuals are compared, as to allow for several-fold differences in the production of the individual hormones. [11,12,13] The male sex glands vary in weight from 10 to 45 grams[6] in so-called "normal" males and much more than this if those with "subnormal" sex development are included. The female sex glands vary in weight over a fivefold range and the number of primordial ova present at the birth of "normal" female infants varies over a thirteenfold range.[7] It is evident that all individuals possess distinctive endocrine systems and that the individual hormonal activities may vary over a several-fold range in individuals who have no recognized hormonal difficulty.

The nervous system is, of course, particularly interesting in connection with the personality problem, and the question arises whether substantial variations exist. The classification of the various kinds of sensory nerve endings, for example, is by no means complete nor satisfactory, and the precise function of many of the recognized types is unknown. Investigations involving "cold spots," "warm spots," and "pain spots" on the skin indicate that each individual exhibits a distinctive pattern of each. In a relatively recent study of pain spots in twenty-one healthy young adults, a high degree of variation was observed.[14] When subjected to carefully controlled test conditions the right hand of one young man "A" showed seven per cent of the area tested to be "highly sensitive," while in another, "B," the right hand showed one hundred per cent "highly sensitive" areas. On A's hand, forty-nine per cent of the area registered "no pain" under standard pain producing test conditions. On B's hand, however, there was no area which registered "no pain."

It is evident that there is room for wide variations with respect to the numbers and distributions of sensory nerve endings in different individuals. That such differences exist is indicated by the extreme diversity in the reactions of individuals to many stimuli such as those involving seeing, hearing, and tasting. An entire lecture could be devoted to this subject alone.

The branching of the trunk nerves is as distinctive as that of the blood vessels.[3] Anson, for example, shows eight patterns of the branching of the facial nerve, each type representing, on the basis of examination of one hundred facial halves, from five to 22 per cent of the specimens. About 15 per cent of people do not have a direct pyramidal nerve tract in the spinal column; an unknown percentage have three splanchnic nerves as compared with the usual two; recurrent laryngeal nerves may be wholly unbranched or may have as many as six branches;[15] the termination of the spinal cord varies in different individuals over a range of three full vertebrae.[3]

Variations in brain anatomy have received little attention. Thirteen years ago, however, Lashley in a review wrote:[16] "The brain is extremely variable in every character that has been subjected to measurement. Its diversities of structure within the species are of the same general character as are differences between related species or even between orders of animals . . . Even the limited evidence at hand, however, shows that individuals start life with brains differing enormously in structure; unlike in number, size, and arrangement of neurons as well as in grosser features."

Unfortunately, partly due to the complexity of the problem, there is no information whatever available as to how these enormous anatomical differences are related to the equally striking personality differences which are commonplace. Recently there has been published, primarily for the use of surgeons, an extensive study of differences in brain anatomy.[17]

Up to the present in our discussion we have paid attention only to certain facts of biology — those in the field of anatomy. Before we consider other areas — physiology, biochemistry, and psychology — it seems appropriate to note whether we have made any progress in uncovering facts that have important implications for personality development.

Consider the fact (I do regard it a fact and not a theory) that every individual person is endowed with a distinctive gastrointestinal tract, a distinctive circulatory system, a distinctive respiratory system, a distinctive endocrine system, a distinctive nervous system, and a morphologically distinctive brain; furthermore that the differences involved in this distinctiveness are never trifling and often are enormous. Can it be that that fact is inconsequential in relation to the problem of personality differences?

I am willing to take the position that this fact is of the *utmost* importance. The material in the area of anatomy alone is sufficient to convince anyone who comes upon the problem with an open mind that here is an obvious frontier which should yield many insights. Those who have accepted the Freudian idea that personality disorders arise from infantile conditioning will surely be led to see that, *in addition,* the distinctive bodily equipment of each individual infant is potentially important.

The failure of psychologists — and of biologists, too — to deal seriously with innate individual differences in connection with many problems probably has deep roots.

McGill has said, "Experimental psychologists . . . ignore individual differences almost as an item of faith."[18] The same statement holds, in the main, for physiological psychologists, physiologists, and biochemists. Anatomists have adopted in the past (and some do even at present) the same attitude. Generally speaking, individual differences are flies in the ointment which need to be removed and disregarded. Every subject becomes vastly simpler and more "scientific" when this is done.

If one is pursuing knowledge about personality, however, neglect of innate individual differences is fatal. All of biology and all of psychology have suffered, in my opinion, from at least a mild case of "universalitis," an overruling desire to generalize immediately — oftentimes long before sufficient facts are gathered to give the generalization validity. This desire to generalize is of itself laudable, but the willingness to do so without an adequate background of information is unscientific and has devastating effects in the area of personality study.

The most treacherous type of premature generalization is the one that is not stated, but is merely accepted as obvious or axiomatic. Such a generalization is hidden, for example, in the famous line of Alexander Pope: "The proper study of mankind is man." This common saying *assumes* the existence of a meaningful prototype, *man,* a universalized human being — an object of our primary concern. From the standpoint of the serious realistic study of personality, I object to this implied generalization. If we were to alter Pope's line to read "The proper study of mankind is men," we would have detracted from its poetic excellence but we would

have added immeasurably to its validity in the area of personality study.

"Universalitis" is probably born of fundamental egotism. If one can make sweeping generalizations, they are self-gratifying, they can be readily passed on to disciples, the atmosphere seems to clear, life becomes simple, and we approach being gods. It is more pleasant often to retain one's conceit than it is to be realistically humble and admit ignorance. "Universalitis" is thus a sign of immaturity. When personality study has grown up it will recognize realistically the tremendous diversity in personalities, the classification of which is extremely difficult and must be based upon far more data than we now have.

With these ideas as additional background for our thinking let us consider some of the other aspects of biology. Physiologically and biochemically, distinctiveness in gastrointestinal tracts is just as marked as is the distinctiveness in anatomy. The gastric juices of 5,000 individuals free from gastric disease were found to contain from 0–4300 units of pepsin.[19] The range of hydrochloric acid in a smaller study of normal individuals was from 0.0 to 66.0 milliequivalents per liter.[20] No one can deny the probability that large variations also exist in the digestive juices which cannot be so readily investigated. Some "normal" hearts beat more than twice as fast as others,[21] some have pumping capacities at least three times as large as others,[22] and the blood of each individual is distinctive. The discovery of the existence of "blood groups" was just the beginning of our knowledge of the individuality of the blood. Enzyme levels in the blood, which are a reflection of fundamental biochemical differences, vary from one well individual to another over substantial ranges, sometimes tenfold or even thirtyfold or more.[23]

Our neuromuscular systems are far from assembly line products as can easily be demonstrated by a study of motor skills and by a large number of physiological tests. Our senses are by no means identical, as has been made clear by taste tests for PTC and many other substances,[24] by tests involving sense of smell (verbenas,[25] hydrocyanic acid[26]), sense of sight (peripheral vision, foveal size, flicker fusion, and related phenomena, eighteen types of color "blindness"), sense of balance, pitch discriminations, and hearing acuities at different frequencies, etc., etc. From the tremendous variation in the action of specific drugs and chemicals on different individuals, we gain further evidence of fundamental differences in physiology and biochemistry.[27]

Thurstone's pioneering work on primary mental abilities called attention to the fact that human minds have different facets, and that some individuals may be relatively well endowed with respect to arithmetical facility, for example, while being relatively deficient in word familiarity or spatial imagery. Others may be strong in the area of word familiarity but weak in rote memory or arithmetic. Guilford has more recently suggested that there are at least forty facets to human minds, involving a group of memory factors, four groups of thinking factors, the latter involving abilities relating to discovering, evaluating, and generating ideas.[28] All of this leaves room for a multitude of mental patterns (patterns of conditionability) which it seems reasonable to suppose must be related to the enormous variation in the anatomy of human brains. People even when confronted with the same facts, do not think alike, and this appears to have a sound anatomical as well as psychological basis.

Those social anthropologists and other social scientists, who regard culture as the one factor which determines what an individual will be like, often say, or imply, that adult members of a society bear a very great resemblance to each other because of the similarities of their upbringing. In view of this common implication it may be well to ask whether inborn differentness and distinctiveness fades out as a result of the adjustment of the individuals to the culture to which they are exposed.

That this is not the case is indicated by the results of a game played anonymously with a group of 140 adults. They were given the following list of twenty desirable items, each of which was to be rated 0, 1, 2, 3, 4, or 5 depending on its satisfaction-giving value for the individual making the anonymous rating.

1. Animals, pets of all kinds
2. Babies, enjoyment of
3. Bargaining, buying and selling
4. Beauty, as seen through the eyes
5. Conversation, all kinds
6. Creative work
7. Exploring, travel
8. Food, eating of all kinds
9. Gardening
10. Medical care
11. Music, all kinds
12. Nature, enjoyment of
13. Odors, perfumes, etc.
14. Ownership of property
15. Reading, all kinds
16. Religious worship
17. Routine activities
18. Self-adornment
19. Sex
20. Shows, all kinds

The results showed clearly that every individual was distinct and different from every other individual. No two patterns were alike even with respect to a half-dozen items; no pattern had a faint resemblance to the average for the group. Furthermore, the distinctiveness of each was not based upon minor differences in ratings; every item was rated 5 by some individuals. In fact every item received, by members of this group, every possible rating from 0 to 5.

At the risk of being naive, it appears that the whole story we have been unfolding hangs together. Individual infants are endowed with far-reaching anatomical distinctiveness; each has a distinctive endocrine system, a highly distinctive nervous system, a highly distinctive brain. The same distinctiveness carries over into the sensory and biochemical realms, and into their individual psychologies. It is not surprising therefore that each individual upon reaching adulthood exhibits a distinctive pattern of likes and dislikes not only with respect to trivialities but also with respect to what may be regarded the most important things in life.

That culture has a profound influence on our lives no one should deny. The serious question arises, however, as to the relative postion that different factors occupy in producing distinctive personalities. To me it seems probable that one's distinctive endocrine system and one's distinctive brain morphology are more important factors than the toilet training one receives as an infant.

We cannot state as a demonstrated fact that differences in brain morphology or in endocrine systems have much to do with personality differences. On the other hand we have no rigorous scientific proof that toilet training has any substantial effect on personality development. We can only surmise. In one sense, personality study is in its very early infancy.

Another pertinent question — simple but important — awaits a clear answer: Are patterns of brain morphology inherited? On the basis of what is known about the inheritance of other morphological features including fingerprints and the branching of blood vessels in the chest, etc., it may be *inferred* that specific morphological features in the brain are handed down by inheritance, but we do not have definite proof.

A fact which makes the study of the inheritance of such morphological features difficult is that expressed by geneticists David and Snyder.[29] "It has become more and more widely recognized that single-gene differences which produce readily distinguishable discontinuities in phenotype variation are completely non- representative of the bulk of genetic variability in any species." Multiple-gene effects are extremely common and in many cases, because of the complexity of the inheritance process, it is impossible to trace them in families or to know when and where such effects may be expected to arise. This complication is not the only one which exists; there is also the possibility (and certainty in some species) of maternal influence (cytoplasmic) which does not follow the rules of gene-centered genetics, and can thus throw one's calculations off.[30]

The complications of broad genetic study are so great that closely inbred animals, which, according to the simpler concepts of genetics, should be nearly identical in body makeup, are often relatively far from it. Even within relatively closely inbred groups of animals each has a distinctive pattern of organ weights, a distinctive excretion pattern, and at the same time a distinctive pattern of behavioral responses.

The technique of twin studies also has its pitfalls. Monozygotic twins have, according to the simpler concepts of Mendelian genetics, identical inheritance. Actually, however, because of cytoplasmic factors or other unknowns, they appear not to have. It is a common observation that so-called "identical" twins vary markedly in their resemblance to each other. Sometimes they have almost indistinguishable facial features and very similar temperaments. In other cases, however, they are readily distinguished one from another by facial features and/or by temperaments. Our study of excretion patterns suggests that these show in monozygotic twins a high degree of similarity but not an identity. Kallmann states, "Discordance between them [monozygotic twins] is not, as is commonly assumed, a measure merely of postnatal or even prenatal development; it may also have a genetic component."[31]

Consideration of the available facts leads me to suppose in the absence of completely definitive information, that differences in brain morphology, in endocrine patterns, in digestive, circulatory, muscular, and nervous systems, etc., have important roots in heredity. It is difficult to see how such differences as exist could arise independent of heredity. The exact mechanisms whereby all these differences are inherited will probably be obscure many decades hence.

The recognition of hereditary factors does not, by any means, exclude from consideration the dynamic aspects of personality development. Potentialities and conditionabilities are inherited, not fixed, characteristics. The widespread idea that personalities are developed from early childhood is fully in accord with an appreciation of the hereditary factors. Conditioning still takes place but the recognition of innate biological differences calls attention to distinct makeup that each newborn baby possesses. Conditioning does not take place starting with assembly line babies, each one, according to Watson, possessing exactly the same potentialities to develop into a "doctor, lawyer, artist, merchant, chief, and yes, even beggar man and thief."

We have two choices in personality study: one is to neglect hereditary factors as we have done in the past decades, in which case progress will come to a full stop; the other is to recognize the numerous individual differences to be observed in the various areas of biology and study them intensively and ascertain their pertinence.

If we adopt the latter course this means the cultivation of spontaneity in research and perhaps a de-emphasis on theory until some valuable data are collected. Hebb has recently called attention to the weakness of the "design of experiment" approach.[32] "It assumes that the thinking is done in advance of experimentation, since it demands that the whole program be laid out in advance; it tends also, in its own procrustean way, to confirm or deny the ideas with which one began the experiment, but its elaborate mathematical machinery is virtually certain to exclude the kind of unexpected result that gives one new ideas . . . . We must not let our epistemological preconceptions stand in the way of getting research done. We had much better be naive and productive than sophisticated, hypercritical and sterile."

To tackle in one giant undertaking the problem of understanding, characterizing, and cataloguing all personalities from the biological or any other point of view seems hopeless. A strategy which seems far from hopeless, however, involves studying *one at a time* various personality characteristics to ascertain what biological roots they may have. The personality characteristics to be chosen for investigation should, obviously, be as definite as possible. They might include not only matters of temperament or emotion but also the ability to perform specialized types of mental processes, or they might include personality problems of numerous types.

Studying even one particular personality characteristic to ascertain its biological roots is a large undertaking and might involve making scores, possibly hundreds, of measurements on every individual subjected to study. If one has some rational basis for selecting wisely the measurements to be made, the number of desirable measurements might be reduced. This fact would constitute an argument for selecting as the "personality problem" to be investigated, one for which the type of biological roots *might be* successfully guessed in advance. Such might include hyper- or hyposexuality, homosexuality, obesity, depressions, alcoholism, insomnia, accident proneness, etc. When one after another of personality disorders have been studied from this standpoint, it seems very likely that the whole picture will begin to clear and that the study of specific personality characteristics and problems will become successively easier the farther it progresses. What I am considering is obviously a relatively long-range proposal.

Such a type of study as I am suggesting is not in line with the vast amount of experimentation which is currently fashionable. It is very common, for example, to develop a measurement and then apply it to large numbers of people. It is almost or totally unheard of to apply a large series of measurements to a relatively few individuals to determine their individual distinctive patterns. This must be done if we are to find the biological roots of personality characteristics, and psychologists should be warned that the major part of the work must be done in the area of biology, and the biological scientists concerned cannot be looked upon as minor contributors.

Digressing for a moment, it has been with this thought in mind that I have objected strenuously to the current widespread implication that "behavioral sciences" constitute a distinct group including psychology, sociology, and social anthropology and excluding the biological sciences. Hidden in this classification is the *assumption* that biological factors are of no importance in behavior and that conditioning is the whole story. It actually may well be, however, that anatomy, physiology, and biochemistry are, from the standpoint of the practical potentialities, the most important behavioral sciences at our disposal.

In connection with tracing the biological roots of personality characteristics or problems, a highly important part of the strategy is to recognize what I have elsewhere called "disconformities" in the various measurements that are made.[33] High or low values within the so-called "normal range," for example, are disconformities. Such values are abundant and may be highly meaningful, and more important (because of their wider occurrence) than "abnormalities," especially when, as is often the case, the adopted "norms" are selected arbitrarily and without any rational basis whatever.

One of the most encouraging aspects of this type of study is the potential application of high-speed computers to study biological disconformity patterns, and their pertinence to particular personality characteristics or personality problems. Techniques for studying patterns are in their infancy, but the possibilities are most alluring. It may spur our interest in these possibilities to know that, according to recent reports from the Soviet Medical Academy, an electronic diagnosing machine has been constructed. This utilizes, no doubt, some of the mathematical principles and techniques that would be useful in personality study.

Parenthetically, but very briefly, it may be stated that a study of disconformity patterns such as we have suggested is also urgent for reasons other than those involving personality study. These patterns constitute the basis for the complex patterns of innate susceptibilities which all individuals have for all types of diseases.

Space will not permit a discussion of the numerous ways in which my own discipline, biochemistry, impinges on personality problems.[34] The effects of various chemicals on personality behavior, the correlations between brain metabolism and behavior, the effects of various hormones on personality characteristics are all well recognized. What is not so well recognized is that each individual's body chemistry is distinctive and different, and that complex biochemical roots of personality characteristics are likely to be found when we look for them with due care and thoroughness.

Before I close this discussion, I want to stress a most important environmental factor which is capable of contributing enormously to healthy personality development.

The monumental work of Beadle and Tatum[35] demonstrated for the first time the vital connection between genes and enzymes, and, in effect, between heredity and biochemistry. Their work made clear the inevitable basis of individual body chemistry. As a direct consequence of this finding, it becomes inevitable that the nutritional needs of genetically distinctive individuals are quantitatively not the same. Carrying the idea still further it becomes inescapable that the brain cells of individual people do not have quantitatively identical nutritional needs.

It has been amply demonstrated that malnutrition of various kinds can induce personality disorders. This was observed in the starvation studies of Keys and associates,[36] in thiamin deficiency studies,[37] in amino acid deficiency studies,[38] and perhaps most notably in pellagra where unequivocal insanity may result from niacin deficiency and can be abolished promptly by administration of the missing vitamin. It has also been shown repeatedly that inadequacy of prenatal nutrition can cause all sorts of development difficulties and abnormalities in the growing fetus.

One of the most obvious environmental measures that can be taken to insure favorable personality development is to see, for example, that the nervous system of each distinctive individual, with his distinctive needs, receives prenatally and postnatally the best possible nourishment. Nourishment of brain cells like the nourishment of other cells throughout the body can be maintained at many levels of excellence, and of course achieving the best is no small order.

Serious attention to nutrition which must involve the utilization of substantial manpower and a great deal of human ingenuity and persistence can, I believe, make tremendous contributions to our knowledge of personality states and personality disorders, and to the alleviation and prevention of personality difficulties.

In conclusion I would emphasize that the biological approach to personality, outstandingly important as I believe it to be, is not a substitute for all other valid approaches. Whatever we may know or may be able to accomplish by other approaches, if valid, is not lost. Consideration of the biological approach expands our horizon and gives us a much broader view. In my opinion the insight we may gain from this approach will be most valuable and produc-

tive. I should reiterate also what I have said before, that personality study is in its early infancy.

REFERENCES

1. Alvarez, W.C.: Practical Leads to Puzzling Diagnoses. Philadelphia, J.B. Lippincott, 1958, p. 181.
2. Malorov, F.P.: History of Study on Conditioned Reflexes. 2nd rev. and completed ed. Moscow and Leningrad, U.S.S.R. Academy of Sciences, 1954, p. 190. In Russian.
3. Anson, B.J. Atlas of Human Anatomy. Philadelphia, W.B. Saunders Co., 1951.
4. Grollman, A.: Essentials of Encocrinology. 2nd Ed. Philadelphia, J.B. Lippincott Co., 1947, p. 155.
5. Ibid., p. 247.
6. Ibid., p. 460.
7. Ibid., p. 497.
8. Williams, R.J.: Biochemical Individuality. New York, Wiley, 1956, p. 53.
9. Pincus, G., Thimann, K. (eds.): The Hormones. Vol. I. New York, Academic Press, 1948, p. 303.
10. Goldzieher, M. A.: The Endocrine Glands. New York and London, Appleton-Century-Crofts, 1939, p. 589.
11. Rasmussen, A.T.: American Journal of Anatomy, 1928, *42:* 1-27 (1928).
12. Rasmussen, A.T.: Endocrinology, 1924, *85* 24 (1924).
13. Rasmussen, A.T.: Endocrinology, 1928, *12:* 129-150 (1928).
14. Tindall, G.T., Kunkle, E.C.: A.M.A. Archives of Neurology and Psychiatry, 1957, *77:* 605-610 (1957).
15. Rustad, W.H.: Journal of Clinical Endocrinology and Metabolism, 1954, *14:* 87-96 (1954).
16. Lashley, K.S.: Psychological Review, 1947, *54:* 333-334 (1947).
17. Schattenbrand, G., Bailey, P.: Introduction to Stereotaxis, With an Atlas of the Human Brain. Stuttgart, Georg Thiene, Verlay; New York, Grune & Stratton, 1959, 3 vols.
18. McGill, W.J.: Behavior, genetics and differential psychology. Symposium presented at the American Psychological Association, New York, September 4, 1957.
19. Osterberg, A.E., Vanzant, F.R., Alvarez, W.C., Rivers, A.B.: American Journal of Digestive Diseases. *3:* 35-41 (1936).
20. Bernstein, R.E.: Journal of Laboratory and Clinical Medicine, 1952, *40:* 707-717 (1952).
21. Heath, C. W., et al. What people are. Cambridge, Mass., Harvard University Press, 1945, p. 126.
22. King, C. C., et al.: Journal of Applied Physiology, 1952, *5:* 99-110 (1952).
23. Williams, op. cit., pp. 6979.
24. Ibid., pp. 127–130.
25. Blakeslee, A. F.: Proceedings of the National Academy of Sciences, 1918, *48:* 298-299 (1918); Journal of Heredity, 1932, *23:* 106, (1923).
26. Kirk, R.L., Stenhouse, N.S.: Nature, 1953, *171:* 698-699 (1953).
27. Williams, op. cit., pp. 106-*118.*
28. Guilford, J. P. Science, 1955, *122:* 875 (1955).
29. David, P.R., Snyder, L.H.: Social Psychology at the Crossroads. New York, Harper & Row, 1951, pp. 61-62.
30. Williams, R. J.: Journal of Heredity, 1960, *51:* 91–98 (1960).
31. Kallmann, F.J.: American Journal of Human Genetics, 1954, *6:* 157-162 (1954).
32. Harlow, H.F., Woolsey, C.N. (eds.): Biological and Biochemical Bases of Behavior. Madison, Wisc., University of Wisconsin Press, 1958, p. 464.
33. Williams, R.J.: Texas Reports on Biology and Medicine, 1960, *18:* 168-185 (1960).
34. Williams, R. J.: Texas, op, cit., pp. 197–209.
35. Beadle, G. W., Tatum, E. L.: *Proceedings of the National Academy of Sciences, 1941, 27:* 499-506 (1941)
36. Keys, A.: Experimental induction of neuropsychoses by starvation. In Biology of mental health and disease. New York, Paul R. Hoeber, 1952, pp. 515-525.
37. Wilder, R.M.: Experimental induction of psychoneuroses through restriction of intake of thiamine. In Biology of mental health and disease. New York, Paul D. Hoeber, 1952, pp. 531-538.
38. Rose, W.C.: Personal communication.

27.   A Biosocial-Learning Model of Personality and Psychopathology

Theodore Millon

As the title of this paper suggests, an attempt will be made to formulate a schema that is neither doctrinaire nor loosely eclectic in its approach; rather, the theory presented is intended to be both broad in scope and sufficiently systematic in its application of principles to enable the major varieties of personality and psychopathology to be derived logically and coherently. In the following sections a few of the major themes of the model will be provided in condensed form.

DEVELOPMENT: AN INTERACTIONAL VIEW

A. For pedagogical purposes, it is often necessary to separate biogenic from psychogenic factors as influences in personality development; this bifurcation does not exist in reality. Biological and experiential determinants combine and interact in a reciprocal interplay throughout life. This sequence of biogenic-psychogenic interaction evolves through a never-ending spiral; each step in the interplay builds upon prior interactions and creates, in turn, new potentialities for future reactivity and experience. *Etiology in personality and psychopathology may be viewed, then, as a developmental process in which intraorganismic and environmental forces display not only a reciprocity and circularity of influence but an orderly and sequential continuity throughout the life of the individual.*

The circular feedback and serially unfolding character of the developmental process defy simplification, and must constantly be kept in mind when analyzing the etiological background of personality. There are few unidirectional effects in development; it is a multideterminant transaction in which a unique pattern of biogenic potentials and a distinctive constellation of psychogenic influences mold each other in a reciprocal and successively more intricate fashion.

B. Each individual is endowed at conception with a unique set of chromosomes that shapes the course of his physical maturation and psychological development. The physical and psychological characteristics of children are in large measure similar to their parents because they possess many of the same genetic units. Children are genetically disposed to be similar to their parents not only physically but also in stamina, energy, emotional sensitivity and intelligence.

Each infant displays a distinctive pattern of behaviors from the first moments after birth. These characteristics are attributed usually to the infant's "nature," that is, his constitutional makeup, since it is displayed prior to the effects of postnatal influences.

It is erroneous to assume that children of the same chronological age are comparable with respect to the level and character of their biological capacities. Not only does each infant start life with a distinctive pattern of neurological, physiochemical and sensory equipment, but he progresses at his own maturational rate toward some ultimate but unknown level of potential. Thus, above and beyond initial differences and their not insignificant consequences, are differences in the rate with which the typical sequence of maturation unfolds. Furthermore, different regions in the complex nervous system within a single child may mature at different rates. To top it all,

Millon, T.: A biosocial-learning approach. In Millon, T.: Theories of Psychopathology and Personality. Philadelphia, W. B. Saunders Co., 1973.

the potential or ultimate level of development of each of these neurological capacities will vary widely, not only among children but within each child.

C. The maturation of the biological substrate for psychological capacities is anchored initially to genetic processes, but its development is substantially dependent on environmental stimulation. The concept of *stimulus nutriment* may be introduced to represent the belief that the quantity of environmental experience activates chemical processes requisite to the maturation of neural collaterals. Stimulus impoverishment may lead to irrevocable deficiencies in neural development and their associated psychological functions; stimulus enrichment may prove equally deleterious by producing pathological overdevelopments or imbalances among these functions.

D. The notion of sensitive developmental periods may be proposed to convey the belief that stimuli produce different effects at different ages, that is, there are limited time periods during maturation when particular stimuli have pronounced effects which they do not have either before or after these periods. It may be suggested, further, that these peak periods occur at points in maturation when the potential is greatest for growth and expansion of neural collaterals.

Three neuropsychological stages of development, representing peak periods in neurological maturation, may be proposed. Each developmental stage reflects transactions between constitutional and experiential influences which combine to set a foundation for subsequent stages; if the interactions at one stage are deficient or distorted, all subsequent stages will be affected since they rest on a defective base.

The first stage, termed *sensory-attachment,* predominates from birth to approximately 18 months of age. This period is characterized by a rapid maturation of neurological substrates for sensory processes, and by the infant's attachment and dependency on others.

The second stage, referred to as *sensori-motor-autonomy,* begins roughly at 12 months and extends in its peak development through the sixth year. It is characterized by a rapid differentiation of motor capacities which coordinate with established sensory functions; this coalescence enables the young child to locomote, manipulate and verbalize in increasingly skillful ways.

The third stage, called the period of *intracortical-initiative,* is primary from about the fourth year through adolescence. There is a rapid growth potential among the higher cortical centers during this stage, enabling the child to reflect, plan and act independent of parental supervision. Integrations developed during earlier phases of this period undergo substantial reorganization as a product of the biological and social effects of puberty.

Maladaptive consequences can arise as a result of either stimulus impoverishment or stimulus enrichment at each of the three stages.

From experimental animal research and naturalistic studies with human infants, it appears that marked stimulus impoverishment during the sensory-attachment period will produce deficiencies in sensory capacities and a marked diminution of interpersonal sensitivity and behavior. There is little evidence available with regard to the effects of stimulus enrichment during this stage; it may be proposed, however, that excessive stimulation results in hypersensitivities, stimulus seeking behaviors and abnormal interpersonal dependencies.

Deprived of adequate stimulation during the sensorimotor stage, the child will be deficient in skills for behavioral autonomy, will display a lack of exploratory and competitive activity and be characterized by timidity and submissiveness. In contrast, excessive enrichment and indulgence of sensorimotor capacities may result in uncontrolled self-expression, narcissism and social irresponsibility.

Among the consequences of understimulation during the intracortical-initiative stage is an identity diffusion, an inability to fashion an integrated and consistent purpose for one's existence and an inefficiency in channeling and directing one's energies, capacities and impulses. Excessive stimulation, in the form of overtraining and overguidance, results in the loss of several functions, notably spontaneity, flexibility and creativity.

E. There has been little systematic attention to the child's own contribution to the course of his development. Environmental theorists of psychopathology have viewed disorders to be the result of detrimental experiences that the individual has had no part in producing himself. This is a gross simplification. Each infant possesses a biologically based pattern of reaction sensitivities and behavioral dispositions which shape the nature of his experiences and may contribute directly to the creation of environmental difficulties.

The biological dispositions of the maturing child are important because they strengthen the probability that certain kinds of behavior will be learned.

Highly active and responsive children relate to and learn about their environment quickly. Their liveliness, zest and power may lead them to a high measure of personal gratification. Conversely, their energy and exploratory behavior may result in excess frustration if they overaspire or run into insuperable barriers; unable to gratify their activity needs effectively, they may grope and strike out in erratic and maladaptive ways.

Adaptive learning in constitutionally passive children also is shaped by their biological equipment. Ill-disposed to deal with their environment assertively and little inclined to discharge their tensions physically, they may learn to avoid conflicts and step aside when difficulties arise. They are less likely to develop guilt feelings about misbehavior than active youngsters who more frequently get into trouble, receive more punishment and are therefore inclined to develop aggressive feelings toward others. But in their passivity, these youngsters may deprive themselves of rewarding experiences and relationships; they may feel "left out of things" and become dependent on others to fight their battles and to protect them from experiences they are ill-equipped to handle on their own.

It appears clear from studies of early patterns of reactivity that *constitutional tendencies evoke counterreactions from others which accentuate these initial dispositions. The child's biological endowment shapes not only his behavior but that of his parents as well.*

If the child's primary disposition is cheerful and adaptable and has made his care easy, the mother will tend quickly to display a positive reciprocal attitude; conversely, if the child is tense and wound up, or if his care is difficult and time consuming, the mother will react with dismay, fatigue or hostility. Through his own behavioral disposition then, the child elicits a series of parental behaviors which reinforce his initial pattern.

Unfortunately, the reciprocal interplay of primary patterns and parental reactions has not been sufficiently explored. It may prove to be one of the most fruitful spheres of research concerning the etiology of psychopathology and merits the serious attention of investigators. The *biosocial-learning-approach* presented in this paper stems largely from the thesis that the child's constitutional pattern shapes and interacts with his social reinforcement experiences.

F. The fact that early experiences are likely to contribute a disproportionate share to learned behavior is attributable in part to the fact that their effects are difficult to extinguish. This resistance to extinction stems largely from the fact that learning in early life is presymbolic, random and highly generalized.

Additional factors which contribute to the persistance and continuity of early learnings are social factors such as the repetitive nature of experience, the tendency for interpersoanl relations to be reciprocally reinforcing and the perseverance of early character stereotypes.

Beyond these are a number of self-perpetuating processes which derive from the individual's own actions. Among them are protective efforts which constrict the person's awareness and experience, the tendency to perceptually and cognitively distort events in line with expectancies, the inappropriate generalization to new events of old behavior patterns and the repetitive compulsion to create conditions which parallel the past.

Children learn complicated sequences of attitudes, reactions and expectancies in response to the experiences to which they were exposed. Initially, these responses are specific to the particular events which prompted them; they are piecemeal, scattered and changeable. Over the course of time, however, through learning what responses are successful in obtaining rewards and avoiding punishments, the child begins to crystalize a stable pattern of instrumental behaviors for handling the events of everyday life. These coping and adaptive strategies come to characterize his way of relating to others, and comprise one of the most important facets of what we may term his personality pattern.

CONCEPT OF PERSONALITY PATTERNS

A. As noted above, in the first years of life children engage in a wide variety of spontaneous behaviors. Although they display certain characteristics consonant with their innate or constitutional dispositions, their way of reacting to others and coping with their environment tends, at first, to be capricious and unpredictable; flexibility and changeability characterize their moods, attitudes and behaviors. This seemingly random behavior serves an exploratory function; each child is "trying out" and testing during this period alternative modes for coping with his environment. As time progresses, the child learns which techniques "work," that is, which of these varied behaviors enable him to achieve his desires and avoid discomforts. Endowed with a distinctive pattern of capacities, energies and temperaments, which serve as base, he learns specific preferences among activities and goals and, perhaps of greater importance, learns that certain types of behaviors and strategies are especially successful for him in obtaining these goals. In his interaction with patents, siblings and peers, he learns to discriminate which goals are permissible, which are rewarded and which are not.

Throughout these years, then, a shaping process has taken place in which the range of initially diverse behaviors becomes narrowed, selective and, finally, crystallized into particular preferred modes of seeking and achieving. In time, these behaviors persist and become accentuated; not only are they highly resistant to extinction but they are reinforced by the restrictions and repetitions of a limited social environment, and are perpetuated and intensified by the child's own perceptions, needs and actions. Thus, given a continuity in basic biological equipment, and a narrow band of experiences for learning behavioral alternative, the child develops a distinctive pattern of characteristics that are deeply etched, cannot be eradicated easily and pervade every facet of his functioning. In short, these characteristics *are* the essence and sum of his personality, his automatic way of perceiving, feeling, thinking and behaving.

When we speak of a personality pattern, then, we are referring to those intrinsic and pervasive modes of functioning which emerge from the entire matrix of the individual's developmental history, and which now characterize his perceptions and ways of dealing with his environment. We have chosen the term pattern for two reasons: first, to focus on the fact that these bahaviors and attitudes derive from the constant and pervasive interaction of both biological dispositions and learned experience; and second, to denote the fact that these personality characteristics are not just a potpourri of unrelated behavior tendencies, but a tightly knit organization of needs, attitudes and behaviors. People may start out in life with random and diverse reactions, but the repetitive sequence of reinforcing experiences to which they are exposed gradually narrows their repertoire to certain habitual strategies, perceptions and behaviors which become prepotent, and come to characterize their distinctive way of relating to the world.

B. We stress the centrality of personality patterns in our formulations in order to break the long entrenched habit of thinking that all forms of psychopathology are diseases, that is, identifiable foreign entities or intruders which attach themselves insidiously to the person, and destroy his "normal" functions. The archaic notion that all forms of illness are a product of external intruders can be traced back to such prescientific ideas as demons, spirits and witches, which ostensibly "possessed" the person and cast spells upon him. The recognition in modern medicine of the role of infectious agents has re-awakened this archaic view; no longer do we see "demons," but we still think, using current medical jargon, that alien, malevolent and insidious forces undermine the patient's otherwise healthy status. This view is a comforting and appealing simplification to the layman; he can attribute his discomforts, pains and irrationalities to the intrusive influence of some external agent, something he ate or caught or some foreign object he can blame that has assaulted his normal and "true" self. This simplification of "alien disease bodies" has its appeal to the physician as well; it enables him to believe that he can find a malevolent intruder, some tangible factor he can hunt down and destroy.

The disease model carries little weight among informed and sophisticated psychiatrists and psychologists today. Increasingly, both in medicine and psychiatry, disorders and disturbances are conceptualized in terms of the patient's *total capacity to cope* with the stress he faces. In medicine, it is the patient's overall constitution – his vitality and stamina – which determine his proclivity to, or resistance against, ill health. Likewise, in psychiatry, it is the patient's personality pattern, his coping skills, outlook and objectivity, which determines whether or not he will be characterized as mentally ill. Physical ill health, then, is less a matter of some alien disease than it is an imbalance or dysfunction in the overall capacity to deal effectively with one's physical environment. In the same manner, psychological ill health is less the product of an intrusive psychic strain or problem than it is an imbalance or dysfunction in the overall capacity to deal effectively with one's psychological environment. Viewed this way, the individual's personality pattern becomes the foundation for his capacity to function in a mentally healthy or ill way.

C. Normality and pathology are relative concepts; they represent arbitrary points on a continuum or gradient. Psychopathology is shaped according to the same processes and principles as those involved in normal development and learning; how-ever, because of differences in the character, timing, intensity or persistence of certain influences, some individuals acquire maladaptive habits and attitudes whereas others do not.

When an individual displays an ability to cope with his environment in a flexible and adaptive manner and when his characteristic perceptions and behaviors foster increments in personal gratification, then he may be said to possess a normal and healthy personality pattern. Conversely, when average responsibilities and everyday relationships are responded to inflexibly or defectively, or when the individual's characteristic perceptions and behaviors foster increments in personal discomfort or curtail his opportunities to learn and grow, then a pathological personality pattern may be said to exist. Of course, no sharp line divides normality and pathology; not only are personality patterns so complex that certain spheres of functioning may operate "normally" while others do not, but environmental circumstances may change such that certain behaviors and strategies prove "healthy" one time but not another.

Despite the tenuous and fluctuating nature of the normality-pathology distinction, it may be useful to note three criteria by which it may be made: *adaptive inflexibility,* that is, the rigid use of a limited repertoire of strategies for coping with different and varied experiences; *vicious circles,* that is, possessing attitudes and behaviors which intensify old difficulties, and which set into motion new self-defeating consequences; and *tenuous stability,* that is, a susceptibility and lack of resilience to conditions of stress. Together, these three features perpetuate problems and make life increasingly difficult for the unfortunate individual.

COPING STRATEGIES AND PATHOLOGICAL PERSONALITIES

A. Coping strategies may be viewed as complex forms of instrumental behavior, that is, ways of achieving positive reinforcements and avoiding negative reinforcements. These strategies reflect what reinforcements the individual has learned to seek or avoid, where he looks to obtain these reinforcements and how he performs in order to elicit or escape them.

It would be extremely useful if a consistent theoretical framework were provided to coordinate the various syndromes into a coherent classification system. Toward this end, we will describe briefly how eight coping strategies that are conducive to pathological personality functioning can be derived essentially from a 4 x 2 matrix combining two basic variables: (a) the patient's interpersonal style; and (b) the nature and source of the reinforcements he seeks, and the instrumental acts he utilizes to achieve them.

a. Interpersonal behaviors are considered important for several reasons. Most notably, they alert the clinician to significant relationships in the patient's developmental history, and provide suggestive leads for treatment. Moreover, interpersonal factors are especially relevant in the case of the mild personality patterns since these patients maintain active contact with others, meeting and interacting with people in normal everyday life. The character of the interpersonal behaviors they exhibit in these relationships will shape the kinds of reactions they evoke from others, and these reactions, in turn, will influence whether the patient's present degree of pathology will remain stable, improve or become worse.

b. The other major feature guiding our analysis relates to: the kinds of reinforcements the patient seeks (positive or negative); where he looks to find them (self or others): and how he behaves instrumentally to acquire them (active or passive).

Those patients who fail to seek positive reinforcements are referred to as *detached;* within this category are those who seek neither to gain positive reinforcements nor to avoid negative reinforcements (passive-detached or asocial personality), and those who do not seek positive reinforcements but do seek to avoid negative ones (active-detached or avoidant personality). All the other personality syndromes seek both to gain positive reinforcements and to avoid negative reinforcements.

Those who experience reinforcements primarily from sources other than themselves are referred to as *dependent;* within this group are those who wait for others to provide these reinforcements (passive-dependent or submissive personality), and those who manipulate and seduce others to provide reinforcements for them (active-dependent or gregarious personality).

Patients who experience reinforcements primarily from themselves are referred to as *independent;* within this category are those who are self-satisfied and content to leave matters as they are (passive-independent or narcissistic personality), and those who seek to arrogate more power to themselves (active-independent or aggressive-personality).

The fourth major category, referred to as *ambivalent,* is composed of patients who have conflicting attitudes about dependence or independence; some submerge their desire for independence and behave in an overly acquiescent manner (passive-ambivalent or conforming personality) whereas others vacillate erratically from one position to another (active-ambivalent or negativistic personality).

B. Before we outline the principal personality syndromes, let us be mindful that the classification schema is merely a theory-derived synthesis, a set of "armchair" prototypes drawn from diverse sources such as hospital psychiatry, multivariate cluster studies, learning research and psychoanalytic theory, It is a typology documented only in part by systematic empirical research; it is a theory, a provisional tool which hopefully will aid us in organizing our subject more clearly and with greater understanding, a convenient format designed to focus and systematize our thinking about psychopathology.

1. The *passive-deteached* strategy is characterized by social impassivity; affectionate needs and emotional feelings are minimal, and the individual functions as a passive observer detached from the rewards and affections, as well as from the dangers of human relationships.

2. The *active-detached* strategy represents an intense mistrust of others. The individual maintains a constant vigil lest his impulses and longing for affection result in a repetition of the pain and anguish he has

experienced previously; distance must be kept between himself and others. Only by an active detachment and suspiciousness can he protect himself from others. Despite desires to relate to others, he has learned that it is best to deny these desires and withdraw from interpersonal relationships.

3. The *passive-dependent* strategy is characterized by a search for relationships in which one can lean upon others for affection, security and leadership. This patient displays a lack of both initiative and autonomy. As a function of early experience, he has learned to assume a passive role in interpersonal relations, accepting whatever kindness and support he may find, and willingly submitting to the wishes of others in order to maintain their affection.

4. In the *active-dependent* strategy we observe an insatiable and indiscriminate search for stimulation and affection. The patient's gregarious and capricious behavior gives the appearance of considerable independence of others, but beneath this guise lies a fear of autonomy and an intense need for signs of social approval and affection. Affection must be replenished constantly and must be obtained from every source of interpersonal experience.

5. The *passive-independent* strategy is noted by narcissism and self-involvement. As a function of early experience the individual has learned to overvalue his self-worth; however, his confidence in his superiority may be based on false premises. Nevertheless, he assumes that others will recognize his worth, and he maintains a self-assured distance from those whom he views to be inferior to himself.

6. The *active-independent* strategy reflects a mistrust of others and a desire to assert one's autonomy; the result is an indiscriminate striving for power. Rejection of others is justified because they cannot be trusted; autonomy and initiative are claimed to be the only means of heading off betrayal by others.

7. The *passive-ambivalent* strategy is based on a combination of hostility toward others and a fear of social rejection and disapproval. The patient resolves this conflict by repressing his resentment. He overconforms and overcomplies on the surface;

however, lurking behind this front of propriety and restraint are intense contrary feelings which, on rare occasion, seep through his controls.

8. The *active-ambivalent* strategy represents an inability to resolve conflicts similar to those of the passive-ambivalent; however, these conflicts remain close to consciousness and intrude into everyday life. The individual gets himself into endless wrangles and disappointments as he vacillates between deference and conformity, at one time, and aggressive negativism, the next. His behavior displays an erratic pattern of explosive anger or stubbornness intermingled with moments of hopeless dependency, guilt and shame.

C. A major theme stressed in the theory is the intrinsic continuity of personality development. Granting the validity of this assertion, it is proposed that the more severe forms of psychopathology are elaborations and extensions of a patient's basic personality style, and that a successful analysis of his decompensated state rests on a thorough understanding of his basic personality. Severe states are viewed, then, as logical outgrowths of one of the basic eight styles of coping seen under the pressure of intense or unrelieved adversity. No matter how dramatic or maladaptive a patient's behavior may be, it is best understood as an accentuation or distortion that derives from, and is fully consonant with, his personality coping pattern.

A MILD PATHOLOGICAL PERSONALITY PATTERN

One of the eight basic personality patterns (active-ambivalent) will be described in detail in the following sections to provide the reader with an in-depth view of the theory-generated syndromes.

The *active-ambivalent pattern* or negativistic personality is perhaps the most frequent of the milder forms of pathological coping; it arises in large measure as a consequence of inconsistency in parental attitudes and training methods, a feature of experience that is not uncommon in our complex and everchanging society. What distinguishes life for the active-ambivalent child is the fact that he is subject to appreciably more than his share of contradictory parental attitudes and behaviors. His erraticism and vacillation, his tendency to shift capriciously from one mood to another, may be viewed as mirroring the varied and inconsistent models and reinforcements to which he was exposed.

There are two diagnostic syndromes in the DSM-II* that relate to the principal clinical features of the active-ambivalent pattern: the *explosive personality* and the *passive-aggressive personality*. The characteristics described under these separate labels represent, we believe, the same basic coping pattern, and should be combined, therefore, into one syndrome. Excerpts from the DSM-II are quoted below; the first paragraph describes the "explosive" type, and the second that of the "passive-aggressive." Together, they provide a brief portrait of the typical behavior of the active-ambivalent pattern as we have conceived it.

This behavior pattern is characterized by gross outbursts of rage or of verbal and physical aggressiveness. These outbursts are strikingly different from the patient's usual behavior, and he may be regretful and repentant for them. These patients are generally considered excitable, aggressive and over-responsive to environmental pressures. It is the intensity of the outbursts and the individual's inability to control them that distinguishes this group.

The aggressiveness may be expressed passively, for example by obstructionism, pouting, procrastination, intentional inefficiency or stubbornness. This behavior commonly reflects hostility which the individual feels he dare not express openly. Often the behavior is one expression of the patient's resentment at failing to find gratification in a relationship with an individual or institution upon which he is overdependent.

As we perceive it, the active-ambivalent displays an everyday "passive-aggressive" style, punctuated periodically by "explosive" outbursts, for which he is subsequently regretful and repentant.

_____

*The DSM-II refers to the official psychiatric classification system adopted in 1968 by The American Psychiatric Association.

Clinical Picture

A. The negativistic person displays a rapid succession of moods and seems restless, unstable and erratic in his feelings. These persons are easily nettled, offended by trifles and can readily be provoked into being sullen and contrary. There is a low tolerance for frustration; they seem impatient much of the time and are irritable and fidgety unless things go their way. They vacillate from being distraught and despondent, at one time, to being petty, spiteful, stubborn and contentious, another. At times they may appear enthusiastic and cheerful, but this mood is short-lived. In no time, they again become disgruntled, critical and envious of others. They begrudge the good fortunes of others and are jealous, quarrelsome and easily piqued by indifference and minor slights. Their emotions are "worn on their sleeves"; they are excitable and impulsive and may suddenly burst into tears and guilt or anger and abuse.

The impulsive, unpredictable and often explosive reactions of the negativist make it difficult for others to feel comfortable in his presence, or to establish reciprocally rewarding and enduring relationships. Although there are periods of pleasant sociability, most acquaintances of these personalities feel "on edge," waiting for them to display a sullen and hurt look or become obstinate and nasty.

B. The active-ambivalent can be quite articulate in describing his subjective discomfort, but rarely does he display insight into its roots. In speaking of his sensitivities and difficulties, he does not recognize that they reflect, in largest measure, his own inner conflicts and ambivalence.

Self-reports alternate between preoccupations with their own personal inadequacies, bodily ailments and guilt feelings, on the one hand, and resentments, frustrations and disillusionments with others, on the other. They voice their dismay about the sorry state of their lives, their worries, their sadness, their disappointments, their "nervousness" and so on; they express a desire to be rid of distress and difficulty, but seem unable, or perhaps unwilling, to find any solution to them.

Cognitive ambivalence characterizes the thinking of negativistic persons; no sooner do they "see" the merits of solving their problems one way than they find themselves saying, "but . . . ." Fearful of committing themselves and unsure of their own competencies or the loyalties of others, they find their thoughts shifting erratically from one solution to another. Because of their intense ambivalences, they often end up acting precipitously, on the spur of the moment; for them, any other course would lead only to hesitation, vacillation and immobility.

The negative personality often asserts that he has been trapped by fate, that nothing ever "works out" for him and that whatever he desires runs aground. These persons express envy and resentment over the "easy life" of others; they are critical and cynical with regard to what others have attained, yet covet these achievements themselves. Life has been unkind to them, they claim. They feel discontent, cheated and unappreciated; their efforts have been for naught; they have been misunderstood and are disillusioned.

The obstructiveness, pessimism and immaturity which others attribute to them are only a reflection, they feel, of their "sensitivity," the pain they have suffered from persistent physical illness or the inconsiderateness that others have shown toward them. But here again, the negativist's ambivalence intrudes; perhaps, they say, it is their own unworthiness, their own failures and their own "bad temper" which is the cause of their misery and the pain they bring to others. This struggle between feelings of guilt and resentment permeates every facet of the patient's thoughts and feelings.

C. A distinguishing clinical feature of the active-ambivalent is his paucity of intrapsychic controls and mechanisms. His moods, thoughts and desires rarely are worked out internally; few unconscious processes and maneuvers are employed to handle the upsurge of feelings; as a consequence, these emotions come directly to the surface, untransformed and unmoderated. Thus, negativistic personalities are like children in that they react spontaneously and impulsively to events on the

passing scene; each new stimulus seems to elicit a separate and different emotion; there is no damping down, no consistency and no predictability to their reactions.

D. Negativistic personalities do not exhibit a distinctive or characteristic level of biological activation or energy. However, there is some reason to believe that they may possess an intrinsic irritability or hyper-reactivity to stimulation. These patients seem easily aroused, testy, highstrung, thin-skinned and quick-tempered. All sorts of minor events provoke and chafe them; they get inflamed and aggrieved by the most incidental and insignificant behaviors on the part of others. Be mindful, however, that this hypersensitivity may result from adverse experiences as well as constitutional proclivities.

Note should be made here of the high frequency of psychophysiological disorders found among these personalities. In addition to specific ailments, many negativistic individuals complain of ill-defined physical discomforts and generalized states of fatigue.

In summary, four major characteristics distinguish the personality type under review. Several of these have been described in the "clinical picture"; others will be developed in later sections. These characteristics have been labeled as follows: *irritable affectivity* (is moody, high-strung and quick-tempered), *cognitive ambivalence* (holds incompatible ideas and shifts erratically among them), *discontented self-image* (feels misunderstood, disillusioned, a failure) and *interpersonal vacillation* (is impatient and unpredictable with others; switches from resentment to guilt).

Etiology and Development

A. Fretful and "nervous" youngsters are good candidates for the negativistic pattern because they are likely to provoke bewilderment, confusion and vacillation in parental training methods. Such "irregular" children may set into motion erratic and contradictory reactions from their parents which then serve, in circular fashion, to reinforce their initial tendency to be spasmodic and variable.

Children who mature in an unbalanced progression, or at an uneven rate, are more likely to evoke inconsistent reactions from their parents than normally developing children. Thus, a "very bright" but "emotionally immature" youngster may precipitate anger in response to the "childish" dimensions of his behavior, but commendation in response to the "cleverness" he displayed while behaving childishly. Such a child will be confused whether to continue or to inhibit his behavior since the reactions it prompted were contradictory. Additionally, such children may possess "mature" desires and aspirations but lack the equipment to achieve these goals; this can lead only to feelings of discontent and disappointment, features associated with the active-ambivalent pattern.

Conceivably, the affective excitability of the negativistic personality may arise in part from a high level of reticular activity or a dominance of the sympathetic division of the autonomic nervous system.

Equally speculative, but plausible, are hypotheses which implicate segments of the limbic system. Anatomically dense or well-branched centers subserving several different, and irreconcilable, emotions such as "anger," "sadness" and "fear" could account for the ambivalent behavioral proclivities seen in this pattern. Of interest in this regard is the recently uncovered "ambivalence" center in the limbic region; hypotheses concerning this area may also be considered as plausible.

Active-ambivalent personalities develop with appreciably greater frequency among women than men. Conceivably, many negativistic women may be subject to extreme hormonal changes during their menstrual cycles, thereby precipitating marked, short-lived and variable moods. Such rapid mood changes may set into motion sequences of erratic behavior and associated interpersonal reactions conducive to the acquisition and perpetuation of this pattern. Let us caution the reader that these hypotheses are merely unconfirmed speculations.

B. The central role of inconsistent parental attitudes and contradictory training methods in the development of the negativistic personality has been referred to repeatedly in our discussions. Although every child experiences some degree of parental inconstancy, the active-ambivalent youngster is likely to have been exposed to appreciably more than his share. His parents may have swayed from hostility and rejection, at one time, to affection and love another; and this erratic pattern has probably been capricious, frequent, pronounced and lifelong.

These children constantly are forced into what are termed approach-avoidance conflicts. Furthermore, they never are sure what their parents really desire, and no matter what course they take, they find that they cannot do right. This latter form of entrapment has been referred to as a double-bind; thus, the child is unable not only to find a clear direction for his behavior but to extricate himself from the irreconcilable demands that have been made of him. The double-bind difficulty is often compounded by the fact that the contradictions in the parental message are subtle or concealed. Thus, he cannot readily accuse his parents of failing to mean what they overtly say since the evidence for such accusations is rather tenuous; moreover, the consequences of making an accusation of parental dishonesty or deception may be rather severe. Unable to discriminate, and fearful of misinterpreting, the intent of these communications, the child becomes anxious, and may learn to become ambivalent in his thinking and erratic in his own behavior.

Paradoxical and contradictory parental behaviors often are found in "schismatic" families, that is, in families where the parents are manifestly in conflict with each other. Here, there is constant bickering, and an undermining of one parent by the other through disqualifying and contradicting statements. A child raised in this setting not only suffers the constant threat of family dissolution, but, in addition, often is forced to serve as a mediator to moderate tensions generated by his parents. He constantly switches sides and divides his loyalties; he cannot be "himself" for he must shift his attitudes and emotions to satisfy changing and antagonistic parental desires and expectations. The different roles he must assume to placate his parents and to salvage a measure of family stability are markedly divergent; as long as his parents remain at odds, he must persist with behavior and thoughts that are intrinsically irreconcilable.

This state of affairs prevents the child from identifying consistently with one parent; as a consequence, he ends up modeling himself after two intrinsically antagonistic figures, with the result that he forms opposing sets of attitudes, emotions and behaviors. As is evident, schismatic families are perfect training grounds for the development of an ambivalent pattern.

We may summarize as follows. *First,* the child learns vicariously to imitate the erratic and capricious behavior of his parents. *Second,* he fails to learn what "pays off" instrumentally; he never acquires a reliable strategy that achieves the reinforcements he seeks. *Third,* he internalizes a series of conflicting attitudes toward himself and others; for example, he does not know whether he is competent or incompetent; he is unsure whether he loves or hates those upon whom he depends. *Fourth,* unable to predict the consequences of his behaviors, he gets "tied up in emotional knots," and behaves irrationally and impulsively.

Coping Strategies

It would appear from first impressions that the erratic course of the active-ambivalent pattern would fail to provide the individual with reinforcements; if this were the case, we would expect these persons to quickly decompensate into severe forms of pathology. Obviously, most do not, and we are forced to inquire, then, as to what gains, supports and rewards an individual can achieve in the course of behaving in the erratic and vacillating active-ambivalent pattern.

The strategy of negativism, of being discontent and unpredictable, of being both seductive and rejecting and of being demanding and then dissatisfied, is an effective weapon not only with the intimidated or pliant but with people in general. Switching back and forth among the roles of the martyr, the affronted, the aggrieved, the misunderstood, the contrite, the guilt-ridden, the sickly and the overworked, is a clever tactic of interpersonal behavior which gains the active-ambivalent the attention, reassurance and dependency he craves, while at the same time, it allows him to subtly vent his angers and resentments. Thus, for all the seeming ineffectuality of vacillation, it recruits affection and support, on the one hand, and provides a means of discharging the tensions of frustration and hostility, on the other. Interspersed with periods of self-deprecation and contrition, acts which relieve unconscious guilt and serve to solicit forgiveness and reassuring comments from others, this strategy proves *not* to be a total instrumental failure.

In an earlier section we noted the paucity of controls which characterize the active-ambivalent personality, the muddle and confusion of feelings that active-ambivalents experience prompt a variety of erratic and contradictory intrapsychic mechanisms. Thus, sometimes the negativist will turn his externally directed, hostile feelings back toward himself, a mechanism termed by some theorists as introjection, the converse of projection. For example, hatred felt toward others is directed toward the self, taking the form of guilt or self-condemnation. But, true to form, the active-ambivalent often alternates between introjection and projection. Thus, at one time, by projection, he ascribes his own destructive impulses to others, accusing them, unjustly, of being malicious and unkind to him. At other times, by introjection, he reverses the sequence, and accuses himself of faults which, justifiably, should be ascribed to others.

Thus, even in the use of unconscious mechanisms, the active-ambivalent behaves in an erratic and contradictory manner. Those at the receiving end of these bizarre intrapsychic processes cannot help but observe their irrationality, uncalled for outbursts and peculiar inconsistency.

Self-Perpetuation

The mere process of behaving erratically, of vacillating from one course of action to another, is a sheer waste of energy. By attempting to secure his incompatible goals, the negativistic personality scatters his efforts and dilutes his effectiveness. Caught in his own cross currents, he fails to commit himself to one clear direction; he swings indecisively back and forth, performs ineffectually and experiences a paralyzing sense of inertia or exhaustion.

In addition to the wasteful nature of ambivalence, the negativistic person may actively impede his own progress toward conflict resolution and goal attainment. Thus, active-ambivalents often undo what good they previously have done. Driven by contrary feelings, they may retract their own "kind words" to others and replace them with harshness, or contaminate and undermine achievements they struggled so hard to attain. In short, their ambivalance may rob them of the few steps they secured toward progress.

The inconstant "blowing hot and cold" behavior of the active-ambivalent precipitates other persons into reacting in a parallel capricious and inconsistent manner; thus, by prompting these reactions he recreates the same conditions of his childhood that initially fostered the development of his unstable behavior.

People weary quickly of the moping, sulking, manipulative, stubborn and unpredictable explosive behaviors of the active-ambivalent. They are goaded into exasperation and into feelings of confusion and futility when their persistent efforts to placate the negativist invariably meet with failure. Eventually, these persons express hostility and disaffiliation, reactions which

then serve to intensify the dismay and anxiety of the negativistic personality.

Not only does the active-ambivalent precipitate real difficulties through his negativistic behaviors, but he often perceives and anticipates difficulties where none in fact exist. He has learned from past experience that "good things don't last," that the pleasant and affectionate attitudes of those from whom he seeks love will abruptly and capriciously come to an end, and be followed by disappointment, anger and rejection.

Rather than be embittered again, rather than allowing himself to be led down the "primrose path" and to suffer the humiliation and pain of having one's high hopes dashed, it would be better to put a halt to illusory gratifications, to the futility, deception and heartache of short-lived pleasures. Protectively, then he refuses to wait for others to make the turnabout; he "jumps the gun," pulls back when things are going well and thereby cuts off experiences which may have proved gratifying, had they been completed. His anticipation of being frustrated and of being set back and left in the lurch prompts him into creating a self-fulfilling prophecy. Thus, by his own hand, he defeats his own chances to experience events which may promote change and growth.

These crushing experiences recur repeatedly, and with each recurrence, the negativist further reinforces his pessimistic anticipations. And in his effort to overcome past disillusionments, he throws himself blindly into new ventures that lead inevitably to further disillusion.

X   PSYCHOBEHAVIORAL CONSIDERATIONS IN PATIENTHOOD

Studies of "illness behavior" and "patienthood" are among the most useful contributions of behavioral science to medicine. Illness behavior refers to the way in which a person reacts to the experience of physical pain or other signs of organic malfunction. Patienthood pertains to the experience of being in the role of a sick person, with its special responsibilities and expectations. Several medical and sociological scientists have proposed theoretical models of the phases of illness behavior and patienthood; two such proposals have been especially fruitful, the "stages of transition" model formulated by Edward Suchman (1965) and the "sick role sequence" presented by Talcott Parsons (1964).

Suchman divides the transition from health to illness as progressing through five stages. The first, termed the *symptom experience stage,* is characterized by three aspects: the recognition of physical pain, the interpretation of the discomforting symptom, and the anxiety it evokes. Patients typically make one of two constrasting responses at this point. Either they attempt to deny the possibility of illness and delay seeking treatment or they become extremely concerned and decide immediately to search some form of assurance or medical guidance. The second phase, according to Suchman, is called the *assumption of the sick role stage* and refers to the decision that one, in fact, is sick and needs physical care. Typically, the person employs palliative drugs for symptom alleviation at this point and seeks advice as to the character of his illness from family and friends. In turning to "lay" guidance the person attempts not only to obtain information as to the possible severity of his difficulty, but is implicitly asking them for permission to assume the sick role, that is, to suspend his normal activities. The *medical care contact stage,* the third phase in Suchman's sequence, is noted by the person's decision to seek professional assistance. Here, he is provided with a medical rather than a "lay" diagnosis and receives a prescribed and formal course of treatment. By consulting a physician, he has also sought "legitimate" sanction either for assuming the role of a sick person or for returning to his normal functions. The fourth step in the sequence, the *dependent-patient role stage,* is noted by a decision to put one's welfare in the hands of a physician, with its attendant responsibility to follow the prescribed treatment plan. At this stage the sick person becomes a formal "patient." While viewing the dependent-patient role with a measure of ambivalence, he is likely to conclude that it is the only way to regain his health and resume normal activities. The *recovery* or *rehabilitation stage,* the last of Suchman's five steps, is noted by a decision to relinquish the role of being a patient. Medical treatment has come to a close because the patient has either been dismissed as healthy or has chosen to withdraw from active medical care.

Parsons' formulation of the "sick role" overlaps in several respects with Suchman's. It differs in that its focus is on the "deviant status" of the patient and the consequent social expectations and prerogatives that flow from that status. Kessebaum and Baumann (1965) summarize the central features of Parsons' thesis as follows:

According to Parsons, sickness produces a temporary disturbance in the individual's capacity to fulfill his usual roles. It is a conditionally legitimate state, which has the effect of insulating the individual from certain types of mutual influence with other persons, and of alienating him from certain norms obtaining in the "well" population; in particular, those which value independent achievement. He is regarded as not responsible for having incurred his condition, which is by definition undesirable, and therefore he is motivated to "get well." Since he is incapable of achieving this end through volition alone, he has an inherent right to receive care, and, indeed, is obligated to seek and accept professional help. For the duration of his illness, "the element of exemption from ordinary role-obligations may be interpreted as permissive for temporary relief from the strains of trying hard to achieve. The patient is permitted to indulge his dependency needs under strictly regulated conditions, notably his recognition of the conditional legitimacy of his state, and exposure to the therapeutic task." Thus, the normative expectations do not preclude the fact that a patient may enjoy various secondary gains due to illness, but these are purchased at a steep price, and accompanied by the obligation to cooperate actively toward his cure and subsequent resumption of usual role-obligations.

Parsons' proposal has been criticized for its failure to recognize the disparate ways in which different persons and social classes assume the sick role. His formulation does convey, however, the double-edged character of this deviant status. On the one hand, the patient is allowed a measure of freedom from his normal social functions; but on the other, he is expected to seek professional assistance so that he will return, as soon as possible, to resume his responsibilities in family and work.

The stages of patienthood have psychobehavioral consequences also for the physician. Physicians lament the fact that patients delay excessively in seeking professional care following their initial symptoms. Dismay and annoyance are also expressed at the frequent failure of patients to appear for necessary appointments. Most distressing is the unwillingness of patients to follow the prescribed course of medication or to return for check-up examinations after crisis care. Above and beyond the strictly physical aspects of illness, then, numerous psychological and social factors are involved in shaping the course of a patient's reaction to illness.

The first paper of this chapter, a particularly thorough study by the distinguished medical sociologist David Mechanic, provides a scholarly review of the many response factors to illness. Professor Mechanic organizes his presentation into a number of subcategories, making special reference to the culturally learned aspects of attentiveness to symptomatology, and to the psychological use of illness as a method of coping with everyday situational difficulties.

In the second paper, a lucid and insightful discourse on "how the sick view their world," Henry Lederer describes the myriad events, attitudes, and feelings that patients experience as they move from a state of health to one of illness. Of particular value is his thoughtful advice to physicians concerning ways in which they can make this transition less painful and less anxiety producing.

Rose Laub Coser extends a number of the themes touched upon by Lederer in her report on hospitalized patients. Through a careful procedure based on standardized interviews, she elicited detailed information concerning the fears and preoccupations of these patients. Her quantitative study is enriched with numerous quotes and vignettes, making her paper all the more effective as a guide to the student-physician.

REFERENCES

Parsons, T.: The Social System. New York, Free Press, 1964.
Suchman, E. A.: Stages of illness and medical care. J. Hlth. Hum. Behav. 6: 114–128 (1965).

28   Response Factors in Illness: The Study of Illness Behavior *

David Mechanic

Medicine has three principal tasks — to understand how particular symptoms, syndromes or disease entities arise either in individuals or among groups of individuals; to recognize and cure these or to shorten their course and minimize any residual impairment; and to promote living conditions in human populations which eliminate hazards to health and thus prevent the occurrence of disease. Each task can only be pursued with maximal effectiveness if the *integral* importance of social and psychological, as well as biological, factors is appreciated.

Much medical activity — whether in research, clinical practice, or preventive work — requires an understanding of the cultural and social pressures which influence an individual's recognition that he needs advice, his decision whether to seek it, his choice of counsellor, his cooperation in carrying out any measures that are

suggested and his willingness to remain in contact should there by any recommendation that further supervision is needed. Unless our knowledge of these processes is taken into account in training doctors, dealing with patients and designing sociomedical services, we shall continue to make grave errors in all three fields.

In this paper, I shall consider only one aspect of these problems: that concerning response factors in illness. Although there is a good deal to learn in this area, considerable knowledge is already available.

Data about illness, whether clinical or epidemiological, usually contain two kinds of information: one on the state of the patient (for example, a description of symptoms or dysfunctions); and the other on his reactions to his condition. The physician's diagnosis is influenced by each of these kinds of information. He obtains data from physical examination and laboratory studies and also from a clinical history, which usually includes the patient's reactions to his condition. Within the traditional medical model, the patient lodges a complaint and the physician attempts to account for, explain, or find justification for it through his inves-

*This work was supported in part by a Public Health Service Special Fellowship (MH-8516) from the National Institute of Mental Health. During the period of the fellowship the author was affiliated with the Medical Research Council Social Psychiatry Research Unit, Maudsley Hospital. The author is indebted to Dr. John Wing for his helpful comments.

Mechanic, D.: Response factors in illness: The study of illness behavior. Soc. Psychiat. 1: 11–20 (1966).

tigation. Logically, if not empirically, the diagnostic situation involves two sets of facts: historical data and symptoms reported by the patient or other informants about his condition, and data obtained by the physician through a systematic examination for abnormal signs and through laboratory investigation if necessary. Thus it is logically possible for physicians to hypothesize that some patients are hypochondriacs or malingerers if they note substantial discrepancies between the patient's complaints and other findings elicited through an independent investigation of the complaints.

However, it is often very difficult in the process of medical (and particularly of psychiatric) diagnosis to make an objective and independent examination of the patient's state of health. So much depends upon information provided and processed by the patient and other informants, and colored by their needs and reactions, that the study of these responses becomes a central concern of medicine itself. It is these "secondary" psychological and social processes, as contrasted with the "primary" biological ones usually considered by doctors, that I refer to under the heading of "illness behavior." The term "illness" has always been used in two ways in medicine. On the one hand it has referred to a limited scientific concept (with which I am not here specifically concerned) and, on the other, to any condition which causes, or might usefully cause, an individual to seek advice from a doctor. "Illness Behavior" is any behavior relevant to the second, more general, interpretation. It is therefore necessary to consider what goes on even before a person sees a doctor. I also wish, in this paper, to illustrate how the importance of "reaction" components in illness has been independently recognized and explored in a number of different areas of medical and sociomedical investigation.

On the most simple and obvious level, the extent to which symptoms are differentially perceived, evaluated and acted (or not acted) upon by different kinds of people and in different social situations is obvious. Whether because of earlier experiences with illness, because of differential training in respect to symptoms, or because of different biological sensitivities, some persons make light of symptoms, shrug them off, and avoid seeking medical care. Others will respond to little pain and discomfort by readily seeking care, by releasing themselves from work and other obligations, and by becoming dependent on others.[23] Thus, the study of illness behavior involves the study of attentiveness to pain and symptomatology, the examination of processes affecting how pain and symptoms are defined, accorded significance and socially labelled, and the consideration of the extent to which help is sought, change in life regimen affected, and claims on others made.

The study of illness behavior by its very nature requires an epidemiological model. Since illness behavior affects the utilization of medical care, choice of paths to possible advisers, and responses to illness in general, the selection of patients who seek help from general practitioners, from clinics, or even from hospitals is usually biased. Groups of patients with a particular disease, selected from such populations, will usually be biased compared with those in the general population with the same disease, but untreated, and this is particularly true for illness of high prevalence which are easily recognized by the public and known to have a benign course.[25]

Approximately, only one in three persons who report illnesses in a household interview seek a physician's advice, and in any given month only nine of 750 persons who report illnesses will be hospitalized.[49]

Different patterns of illness behavior may be viewed from at least three general perspectives. First such patterns of behavior may be seen as a product of cultural and social conditioning, since they may be experienced and enacted naturally in the social contexts within which they appear relevant. Secondly, illness behavior may be seen as part of a coping repertoire — as an attempt to make an unstable, challenging situation more manageable for the person who is encountering difficulty. Thirdly, illness behavior may be analyzed in terms of its advantages for the patient in seeking and obtaining attention, sympathy and material gain.

ILLNESS BEHAVIOR AS A CULTURALLY AND SOCIALLY LEARNED RESPONSE

Cultures are so recognizably different that variations in illness behavior in different societies hardly need demonstration. The idea implicit in much of the anthropological work is that primitive conceptions of illness are part of a learned cultural complex, and are functionally associated with other aspects of cultural response to environmental threat. Some of the earlier investigations of illness behavior in America were based on the same idea — that different patterns of response to illness are culturally conditioned and functionally relevant. Thus Koos[20] observed that upper class persons were more likely than lower class persons to view themselves as ill when they had particular symptoms and when they were questioned about specific symptoms, they reported more frequently than lower class persons that they would seek the doctor's advice. Illness responses were described in this study as part of a constellation of needs including those associated with work, family and finances. Saunders[37] described in some detail the differences between "Anglos" and Spanish-speaking persons in the American southwest in attitudes and responses toward illness and in the use of medical facilities. Whereas the Anglos preferred modern medical science and hospitalization for many illnesses, the Spanish-speaking people were more likely to rely on folk medicine and family care and support which was more consistent with their cultural conceptions. More recently, Clark[8] has described how Mexican-Americans view various life situations and symptoms as health problems in contrast to physicians who do not view these problems with similar seriousness and alarm. Other problems among these people which are ignored and undefined are seen by physicians as serious health problems. Similar observations have been made concerning various American Indian groups, and in a variety of other cultural contexts.

The role of cultural differences in illness behavior was nicely described by Zborowski[53] who, in a study of ethnic reactions to pain in a New York City hospital, observed that while Jewish and Italian patients responded to pain in an emotional fashion, tending to exaggerate pain experiences. "Old Americans" tended to be more stoical and "objective," and Irish more frequently denied pain. Zborowski also noted a difference in the attitude underlying Italian and Jewish concern about pain. While the Italian subjects primarily sought relief from pain and were relatively satisfied when such relief was obtained, the Jewish subjects were mainly concerned with the meaning and significance of their pain, and the consequences of pain for their future welfare and health. In trying to explain these cultural differences, Zborowski reports that Jewish and Italian patients related how their mothers showed over-protective and over-concerned attitudes about the child's health, and participation in sports, and how they were constantly warned of the advisability of avoiding colds, fights, and other threatening situations. Zborowski reports that: "Crying in complaint is responded to by parents with sympathy, concern and help. By their over-protective and worried attitude they foster complaining and tears. The child learns to pay attention to each painful experience and to look for help and sympathy which are readily given to him. In Jewish families, where not only a slight sensation of pain but also each deviation from the child's normal behavior is looked on as a sign of illness, the child is prone to acquire anxieties with regard to the meaning and significance of these manifestations." Although Zborowski presents something of a caricature, it is clear that he viewes the etiology of these behavioral patterns and attitudes as inherent in the familial response to the child's health and illnesses.

Zborowski's observations concerning ethnic differences in illness behavior have been supported in a variety of other studies. Croog[9] administered the Cornell Medical Index to 2,000 randomly chosen army inductees. He found that Italian and Jewish respondents reported the greatest number of symptoms of illness. He further found that although the Italian response was associated with low educational status, reports of symptoms among Jewish respondents were not affected by the educational variable. Mechanic,[26] studying 1,300 students at two American universities, found that Jewish students reported higher illness behavior patterns than either Protestant or Catholic students. Since income was also found to be related to illness behavior reports, and since Jewish students were also more likely to be represented in the higher income groups, the analysis was repeated, controlling income. The differences in illness behavior reports between Jewish and other students were only significant for the high income group. Mechanic also attempted to test the hypothesis that use of medical services was an alternative among several possible modes of dealing with stress, and that the difference in reports of illness behavior between Jewish students and Catholic and Protestant students could be explained by the relatively limited involvement in religious activities among Jewish students. This hypothesis was not confirmed. The observed differences in illness behavior patterns has persisted in other studies. Segal (unpublished paper), in a study of student clinic facilities, found that Jewish students used such facilities somewhat more than Catholic or Protestant students. Similarly, several studies of the use of psychiatric facilities have shown a higher receptivity and utilization rate among Jewish subjects.[21,40,42,44]

Suchman[46,47] in a recent study of 5,340 persons in different ethnic groups in New York City found that the more ethnocentric and socially cohesive groups included more persons who knew little about disease, who were skeptical toward professional medical care, and who were dependent during illness. He found that the Jewish respondents were more likely to report a high or moderate pattern of "preventive medical behavior" and "acceptance of the sick role" as compared with respondents from the other groups studied, but that they were not particularly different from other groups on the scale dealing with dependency during illness.

The studies described above suggest considerable consistency in ethnic variations in illness behavior. Although such trends are clear, the variation within groups is much greater than it is between groups. In any case, it is important to note that illness behavior patterns can have both healthy and unhealthy consequences. For example, the traditional concern about health among Jewish persons — especially the health of children — can under some circumstances lead to over-concern and can encourage doubts and anxiety. Such concern and attention can also encourage a high standard of infant rearing and caring as suggested by an early study of infant mortality among immigrants to America which showed that although the Jewish group was foreign born, had just as many children, and had an income which was much lower than that of native-born whites, this group had the lowest rate of infant mortality of all of the groups studied, including the native-white population.[1]

Although it is fairly clear that culturally learned differences in illness behavior are important to some extent, such differences explain only a small proportion of the total variation in behavior. Moreover, the contribution of other factors is not well understood. Mechanic,[27] in a study of 350 mother-child pairs, attempted to investigate the relationship between maternal attitudes and maternal illness behavior, and between these and the illness behavior of their children. The sample chosen from a relatively homogeneous population in the Midwest of America did not include any substantial ethnic diversity. Data were obtained from both mother and child independently, as well as from teachers, school records, and a daily illness log maintained by the mother. Mechanic found that the mother's attitudes toward illness and illness behavior were rather poor predictors of the attitudes of their children. Maternal attitudes however played a more important role in determining whether medical aid would be sought for the child when ill.

In this study of the illness behavior of children, the two best predictors of children's reports of "fear of getting hurt" and attention to pain" were the child's age and sex. Boys were more stoical than girls, and older children were more stoical than younger children. These findings support the idea that age and sex role learning is important in illness behavior and attitudes toward health risks. The results are consistent also with a number of other observations such as the higher utilization of medical facilities among women compared with men,[2] and the higher rate of accidents among boys compared with girls of the same age. Similarly, in another study of reported responses to illness, Mechanic [28] found that respondents expected women to be less stoical than men when ill.

In summary, it seems fair to conclude that cultural and social conditioning play an important though not an exclusive role in patterns of illness behavior, and that ethnic membership, peer pressures, and age-sex role learning to some extent influence attitudes towards risks and towards the significance of common threats.

LINKS BETWEEN REACTION PATTERN AND PHYSIOLOGICAL RESPONSE

It is interesting to note that, in general, observations from field studies concerning ethnic differences in the perception of pain have withstood not only repeated study, but also more detailed scrutiny under laboratory conditions. Sternbach and Tursky,[45] for example, brought Irish, Jewish, Italian and "Yankee" housewives into a psycho-physiological laboratory where they administered pain by electric shock, recording skin potential responses. Their findings tend to support some of the observations made by Zborowski. They found, for example, that Italian women showed significantly lower upper thresholds for shock, and fewer of them would accept the full range of shock stimulation used in the experiment. The investigators believe that this response is consistent with the Italian tendency to focus on the immediacy of the pain itself as compared with the future orientation of the Jewish response tendency. Similarly, they believe that the finding that "Yankee" housewives had faster and more complete adaptation of the diphasic palmar skin potential has an attitudinal correlate to their "matter of fact" orientation to pain. As they note: "This is illustrated by our Yankee subjects' modal attitude toward traumata, as they

verbalized it in their interviews: 'You take things in your stride.' No such action-oriented, adapting phrase was used by the members of the other groups. The similarly undemonstrative Irish subjects may 'keep a tight upper lip' but 'fear the worst,' a noxious stimulus being a burden to be endured and suffered in silence."

However, we must be careful in generalizing conclusions from laboratory pain situations to pathological pain experiences. Henry Beecher,[4] an eminent researcher and Anesthetist-in-Chief at the Massachusetts General Hospital, has reported the failure of fifteen different research groups to establish any dependable effects of even large doses of morphine on pain of experimental origin in man, although the effect of morphine on pathological pain is substantial. He has found it necessary to distinguish between pain as an *original sensation* and pain as a *psychic reaction*. As Beecher notes, one of the difficulties with most forms of laboratory pain is that they minimize the psychic reaction which plays an essential role in pain associated with illness. For example, in a comparative study of pain, he asked a group of wounded soldiers and a group of male civilian patients undergoing major surgery the same questions about their desire for pain medication. While only one-third of the soldiers wanted medication to relieve their pain, 80 per cent of the civilians wanted such pain relief although they were suffering from far less tissue trauma. He explains the variation in terms of differing definitions of pain in the two circumstances. The soldier's wound, Beecher explains, was an escape from the battlefield and the possibility of being killed; to the civilian surgical pain was viewed as a depressing, calamitous event. Beecher reports that the civilian group reported strikingly more frequent and severe pain and he concludes that there is no simple, direct relationship between the wound *per se* and the pain experienced. He further concludes that morphine primarily acts on the reactive component of the pain experience, largely through a process of "mental clouding."

The reactive or definitional component in illness has long been recognized as a significant aspect not only in defining the condition but also in the patient's response to treatment. Physicians working with the severely ill are often impressed by the attitudinal component and its influence on the patient's condition. In its extreme form, physicians have commented on the importance of the patient's "will to live" although it has been difficult to quantify this phenomenon or to present clear evidence in support of its importance. At best, we have anecdotal reports of preparation for death and actual death following witchcraft, and some physiological explanations have been offered to explain the mechanisms involved in such impressive happenings.[11] But if we are to integrate such events with our common conceptual schemes we require a better understanding of such phenomena as they occur in more subtle but more observable forms.

Models for the experimental study of the psycho-physiology of stress that more closely take into account the reactive or definitional components are beginning to be developed. It has long been recognized that difficult life circumstances or experimentally constructed "stress situations" lead to varied physiological and social responses. It is believed that these differences are due to subjects' differing definitions and capacities to cope with these stimuli, and genetic differences. Until recently, psychophysiological investigations have not taken into consideration differing definitions of experimental "stressors" and the differing capacities of subjects to deal with them. Recently, Lazarus and his colleagues[43] have developed a method for inducing different psychological sets in subjects who are viewing the same threatening films, and they have demonstrated the importance of the definitional set in the reactions of subjects to the experimental films. They as well as others have also observed that, as subjects are exposed over many trials to the threatening films, they appear to develop orientations or adaptations which allow them to experience the same stimulus more calmly. In sum, the reactive component is obviously important and manipulation of "reactive sets" in experiments appear to affect physiological response.

The definitional components in response to difficult circumstances have also been observed in natural situations where physiological response has been studied. Friedman and his colleagues[12, 13] in making observations of parents anticipating the death of their children who were suffering from neoplastic diseases found that urinary 17-hydroxycorticosteroid levels in parents would vary from one parent to another, and from one period in the child's illness to another. The period of highest "distress" as measured physiologically occurred for most parents well before the death of the child, the most common situation being when the child was put on the critical list for the first time. For some of the parents the death of the child seemed to be a relief, and it appears as if they had already worked through a substantial part of their grief prior to the death of the child. Other parents, however, who maintained hope despite evidence to the contrary, and who showed little marked acceleration in 17-hydroxycorticosteroid levels at crucial points during the illness, seemed to experience a marked acceleration after the child died. The study illustrates both the tremendous variability in response to difficult circumstances, and the probable link between coping reactions and physiological responses under "stress."

ILLNESS BEHAVIOR AS A COPING RESPONSE TO SITUATIONAL DIFFICULTIES

The idea that illness is "stressful" and that it may engender further life difficulties is sufficiently obvious to require no elaboration. What is interesting to the behavioral scientist, however, is the tremendous variability in response to what is presumably the same illness condition. While one person will hardly acknowledge a condition and refuse to allow it to alter his life, another with a more mild form of the same condition will display profound social and psychological disabilities.

An emotional component has often been seen in the etiology or precipitation of illness.[17,19,36,52] What is often less appreciated is the importance of life difficulties in influencing illness behavior. Indeed, it appears from a careful scrutiny of psychosomatic evidence that "distress" is often more influential in its effects on seeking help and on the expression of illness, than it is on the actual occurrence of the condition. Balint[3] has argued, for example, that the presentation of somatic complaints often masks an underlying emotional problem which is frequently the major reason why the individual has sought advice. Certainly, what little evidence we have on this point suggests that a complaint of trivial illness may be one way of seeking reassurance and support through a recognized and socially acceptable relationship when it is difficult for the patient to present the underlying problem in an undisguised form. In such circumstances the real problem may not even be consciously recognized. The emphasis Balint places on emotional factors in the utilization of the general practitioner appears, nevertheless, to be oversimplified since it fails to take into account the more complex relationship between life difficulties and social and cultural patterns.

Mechanic and Volkart[31] have attempted to examine this problem through an investigation of more than 600 students at a major university. One of the major concerns of the study was the relationship between measures of "stress," and measures of illness behavior, and their joint effect on the use of medical facilities. Analysis of the data showed that perceived stress (as measured by indices of loneliness and nervousness) and illness behavior (as measured by several hypothetical items concerning the use of medical facilities) were clearly related to the use of a college health service during a one-year period. Among students with a high inclination to use medical facilities and high "stress," 73 per cent were frequent users of medical services (three or more times during the year), while among the low inclination-low "stress" group, only 30 per cent were frequent users of such services. Our attention, however, centered on the interaction between our measure of "stress" on the one hand, and illness behavior on the other, in encouraging a person to present a complaint. When illness behavior patterns

were statistically controlled, we found that the influence of "stress" was somewhat different among persons with a high receptivity to medical services than among those who were less inclined to favor medical services. In the high inclination group, "stress" was a rather significant influence in bringing people to the physician. Thus among those with high "stress," 73 per cent used facilities frequently, while only 46 per cent did so among those with low "stress." Although the same trend was observed among those who were less inclined to seek advice from a doctor, the relationship was subantially smaller, and not statistically significant. Thus our data support the interpretation that "stress" leads to an attempt to cope; those who are inclined to adopt the patient role tend to adopt this particular method of coping more frequently than those who are not so inclined.

As I have already noted, the reactive component in illness is clearly relevant to treatment response. Beecher,[4] for example, has collected considerable data to show that the effectiveness of a placebo is very much greater when the patient is distressed than when he is not. Placebos, for example, have very little effect on relieving pain inflicted in the laboratory but they are impressive in relieving pain following surgery. Beecher has accumulated data from several laboratories which show placebos effective in relieving pain of angina pectoris, seasickness, headache, cough and so on. In reviewing fifteen studies totalling 1,082 patients he found an average of 35.2 (plus or minus 2.2) per cent relieved by placebo. In contrast, Beecher calculates the effectiveness of placebos in relieving experimentally contrived pain as 3.2 per cent; thus the placebo is ten times as effective in relieving pain of pathological origin (where distress is an important factor) than it is in relieving pain of experimentally contrived origin.

Studies in social psychology have shown that under situations that are difficult, usual habits and problem-solving patterns may be disrupted and behavior may become disorganized. Under these conditions the directions which coping attempts take depend on the one hand on external influences and stimuli which serve to define circumstances and their meaning, and on the other on past experience and preparation. We will discuss each of these in turn.

In a recent ingenious experiment, Schachter and Singer[39] have shown how external cues influence behavior and feeling states under conditions of altered physiology. They demonstrated that whether subjects experienced anger or euphoria when injected with epinephrine was dependent on whether they had (i) an *appropriate explanation* for their altered physiological state and (ii) *directive external cues*. When the individual had an appropriate explanation for his feelings, he had little need for evaluating himself in terms of environmental stimuli and was not very much affected by them. However, when individuals had no immediate explanation for their altered feelings, external cues became important and, in the experimental situation, determined the emotional state. The same type of altered physiological experience was variously interpreted as happiness or anger depending on cues determined by stooges of the experimenter who were playing the role of subjects. Thus we see that, when persons lose their bearings, environmental cues play an important part in helping the person make sense of his subjective state. Placebos may determine cues in a similar way during illness.

Several studies similarly reflect the importance of cultural and developmental experiences in reactions to threatening circumstances. Schachter[38] in another set of impressive experimental studies, showed that first-born and only children were more likely to affiliate when threatened in adult life than other adults. Schachter believes that the attention given to the first child, and the inexperience of parents, is likely to instill a greater dependence on others in first and only born children as compared with later born children. Although birth order has not been studied directly in illness behavior studies, several other investigations support the idea that past experience, habits, and social values help define — consciously and unconsciously — the alternatives that will be utilized in challenging circumstances.

Phillips,[35] for example, in a recent study has shown that attitudes of self-reliance and health values both affect the willingness of people to report that they would seek help when ill. Many studies of delay in treatment reflect the same tendency for delay to be related to a constellation of ingrained sociomedical habits[16] which tend to be typical — at least in the United States — of the lower socio-economic groups. Suchman[46,47] found, for example, that both individual medical orientation (an index based on knowledge about disease, on skepticism about medical care, and on dependency in illness) and social group organization (an index based on ethnic exclusiveness, friendship solidarity, and family orientation to tradition and authority) were related to socio-economic status. A "parochial" as compared with a "cosmopolitan" social structure and a "popular" as compared with a "scientific" orientation to medicine were both linked with lower socio-economic status. Similarly, persons of higher socio-economic status were more likely to buy health insurance, to get a periodic medical check-up, to receive polio immunization, to eat a balanced diet, and they more frequently had eye examinations and dental care.

Under conditions of manageable difficulties, persons have a tendency to normalize or ignore symptoms that do not become too severe. For example in our study discussed earlier[32] we found that when illness is of a kind that is common and familiar, and the course of the illness is predictable, the presentation of the illness for medical scrutiny is substantially related to the inclination to use medical services as measured by hypothetical illness situations. As symptoms become more atypical, less familiar, and less predictable in their course, the role of social and situational factors in bringing a person for medical attention becomes less important. Similarly, Scheff and Silverman,[40] in a study of the use of a college psychiatric clinic, found social and demographic factors to be better predictors of the use of such facilities than the "seriousness" of the patient's condition. However, when they stratified their psychiatric cases into those more serious and those less serious, it became clear that while social and demographic factors were crucial in the presentation of "moderate psychiatric problems," they were relatively unimportant in predicting use of such facilities among those with "severe psychiatric problems."

If we are to make progress in the study of illness behavior, it becomes necessary to move beyond gross cultural and social differences in illness patterns toward the development of a social-psychological model which gives a clear conception of the processes involved when someone seeks help. From our various studies, we are able to suggest a working model which describes some of the contingencies relevant to illness behavior.[24, 29] Seven groups of variables appear to be particularly important: (I) the number and persistence of symptoms; (II) the individual's ability to recognize symptoms; (III) the perceived seriousness of symptoms; (IV) the extent of social and physical disability resulting from the symptoms; (V) the cultural background of the defining person, group or agency in terms of the emphasis on tolerance, stoicism, etc.; (VI) available information and medical knowledge, and (VII) the availability of sources of help and their social and physical accessibility. Here we include not only physical distance and costs of time, money and effort, but also such costs as "fear," stigma, social distance, feelings of humiliation, and the like.

When we inspect these seven groups of variables, it becomes clear that what may appear salient to the definer may not appear relevant to the physician. For example, the recognizability of symptoms is not necessarily correlated with medical views of their seriousness. Similarly, some symptoms which are, for example, disfiguring or disruptive or which bring about work disability may be self-limited and medically trivial while other symptoms (such as signs of cancer) may have no disruptive effects at all. Yet one of the major cues patients use in deciding to seek help is the disruption of their activities. Illness behavior and the decision to seek medical advice frequently involves, from the patient's point of view, a rational attempt to make sense of his problem and cope with it within the limits of his

intelligence and his social and cultural understandings.

Zola[55] has attempted to delineate five timing "triggers" in patient's decision to seek medical care. The first pattern he calls "interpersonal crisis" where the situation calls attention to the symptoms and causes the patient to dwell on them. The second "trigger" he calls "social interference"; in this situation the symptoms do not change, but come to threaten a valued social activity. The third "trigger" – "the presence of sanctioning" – involves others telling him to seek care. Fourthly, Zola discusses "perceived threat" and, finally, "nature and quality of the symptoms." The latter "trigger" involves similarity of symptoms to previous ones or to those of friends, and the like. Zola reports the impression that these "triggers" have different effects in various social strata and ethnic groups.

The difficulty in preventive medicine is that commonsense models of health and coping with disease do not necessarily conform to scientific models, yet it is usually commonsense models that determine the use of medical facilities. Similarly, a frequent problem faced by the physician in providing care is the failure of the patient to conform to medical advice and most typically this occurs when the patient fails to take his drugs or return for follow-up because, subjectively, he feels well. From the patient's commonsense perspective, to stop medication or cancel a follow-up visit when he is feeling well, is logical.

ILLNESS BEHAVIOR AS AN ATTEMPT TO SEEK SECONDARY ADVANTAGES

Since illness is recognized as an acceptable cause for withdrawing from certain role obligations, social responsibilities, and expectations, persons may be drawn to the patient role in order to obtain secondary advantages, to make claims on others for care and attention, and to provide an, acceptable reason for social failure. Thus individuals may be motivated to adopt the "sick role,"[34] and others may be anxious to accord people the status of sickness in order to avoid embarrassment and social difficulties. The interpenetration between medical and other social institutions is quite complex, and often these relationships are not fully appreciated.

In the final analysis, illness and social disability are socially defined and somewhat arbitrary.[22] The problem of mental subnormality, for example, is a greater problem in a highly developed industrial nation requiring a high level of skills than it is in a communal agrarian community; and if we had no schools most of the mildly subnormal would be unrecognized and undefined. Similarly, the extent to which people are to be held accountable for fulfilling responsibilities regardless of health status involves a compromise between personal and community needs. The need to minimize the consequences of ill health as a practical or a humanitarian gesture is theoretically only one value to be weighed against other personal and social goals, and the limits and scope of the definition of illness may serve different needs and different agencies, depending on social, political, and historical contingencies.

Since a discussion of problems of the definition of "illness," as distinct from "illness behavior," will take us too far afield, I will not develop the topic here.[30] It should, however, be noted that the concept of illness can be used to support humanitarian values in the face of moral and legal sanctions.[48] Thus, illness concepts are used to overcome restrictive laws on abortion, or on criminal responsibility, as an excuse for academic failure, and so on. On other occasions, the concept of illness may be used to discredit people's views and actions, and to undermine their integrity. The use of illness labels may differ depending on who controls medical institutions, and the goals they are meant to serve.[10] Medical independence of political control is of obvious importance here as is the necessity for medical decisions affecting the community to be reviewed by expert laymen. In a free society the value and functions of medicine have primary relevance from a social standpoint in that they can enhance or retard the ability of

the individual to fulfill personal and social choices. Physicians, on the whole, have been very successful in protecting medical systems from external manipulation for non-medical purposes. For the most part, even in this complicated age, the doctor serves as the patient's agent, and often even as his advocate.

As society becomes more humanitarian, and as illness becomes not only an excuse for social failure and neglect of social responsibilities but also cause, in and of itself, for monetary and social compensation, the realtionship between illness as a physical state and as a secondary coping technique becomes even more difficult. It is fairly obvious that under some circumstances desire for compensation for injury and disability may encourage persons to exaggerate their inabilities to perform routine tasks, and discourage attempts to cope with the disability.

DISCUSSION: IMPLICATIONS OF ILLNESS BEHAVIOR FOR MEDICAL CARE

The value of a medical perspective which takes into account illness behavior can be illustrated by a study at the Massachusetts General Hospital.[54] The hypothesis was that the patient's cultural background would influence how the patient presented his symptoms, and thus, how the doctor evaluated them. The analysis was undertaken because the investigator had the impression that more Italian than Irish or Anglo-Saxon patients were being labelled as psychiatric problems although there was no objective difference in the extent to which members in these groups reported psycho-social problems. Zola selected a group of 29 patients who presented themselves at the Medical and Ear, Nose and Throat clinics but for whom no medical disease was found. There was good reason to believe that these groups of patients did not differ in the extent of their life difficulties. But it was clear that their mode of cultural expression was very different. Italians are more emotional in the presentation of symptoms, and give more attention and expression to pain.

Zola found psychogenesis was implied in the medical reports of 11 of the 12 Italian cases, and only in four of thirteen remaining cases. Although this was not a well-controlled study, the results strongly suggest that the patient's cultural mode of expression affected how the doctor viewed him and how he was medically evaluated.

The place of illness behavior is particularly important in disorders that are largely diagnosed through behavioral manifestations and the patient's social history. For it is particularly difficult to separate symptoms from sub-cultural patterns of expression and affect, and different behavioral patterns among the various social strata. Similarly, it is in such disorders that symptoms and etiological factors are more frequently confused with factors which may differentially lead to social intervention and the seeking of care.

The provision of care depends to a considerable extent on the social and cultural processes that lead particular people to define themselves as requiring care, or that lead others to define them as targets for community action. Many factors unrelated to the severity of illness and incapacity may assist in the selection of patients for care, while other persons requiring attention to a greater extent go unnoticed.

We all recognize that there are many persons in the general population who require care and treatment and who can benefit by it but do not come to the attention of care facilities. Conversely, there are some who have developed an over-dependence on the physician, psychiatrist, or social agency who can be adversely affected by particular kinds of intensive care and attention. Although psychiatrists, especially those more dynamically oriented, often work under the assumption that all persons can benefit from therapy — or at least, that it will not harm them — and although the plea for help is usually taken on pragmatic grounds as proof for the need for psychiatric assistance, it is important to consider the counterproposition — that certain kinds of assistance, however well-meaning, can be detrimental for certain patients. There are those, for example, for whom excessive focus on symptoms and life difficulties

may reinforce an already hypochrondrial pattern, induce or encourage further displays of illness behavior, and bring about reduced coping effectiveness. As we have already noted, illness is one of the few widely recognized and acceptable reasons for failing to meet social responsibilities and obligations and thus the sick role often carries advantages for those who wish to escape the difficulties of meeting social expectations without incurring disapproval. The improper use of the sick role and the willingness to encourage persons to assume the role of the patient without careful consideration of its implications involves serious dangers. The improper use of the sick role under some circumstances can reinforce "immature" and "irresponsible" patterns of behavior. Military psychiatrists have learned — and this is consistent with the observations of Beecher we discussed earlier — that under military conditions where persons often wish to evade responsibilities and dangers, the sick role may offer clear advantages. This is one of the reasons military organizations often make it so difficult to be sick, and similarly totalitarian governments have done so during periods of labor shortage. During the second world war, it was observed that when troops became upset under combat stress and were evacuated for treatment it was extremely difficult to return these men as functioning soldiers. When these men were brought back to the hospital, and when their problems were defined as having roots in their early years, the men had an acceptable reason for failure which could be viewed as beyond their control and it was difficult to mobilize them.[14] In contrast, during the Korean war, when such problems were defined as problems of mastery of common fears shared by many others, it was possible to encourage men to make instrumental efforts to cope with the extreme difficulties in their situation.[18]

The issue is not, of course, whether we should adopt a permissive approach to illness or on the other hand subjugate health organizations to other social institutions. From the perspective of a free medical system (that is, one where the doctor acts primarily as the patient's agent and on his behalf), the doctor-patient relationship is one where the doctor has considerable influence in affecting the patient's feeling state and behavior. As we have noted, patients often seek care when they are distressed; and there is a large amount of evidence that distressed persons are highly suggestible and open to influence.[11] Thus, the doctor's attitude toward the patient and his illness are important forces which can be used to support coping efforts, or they can encourage an elaboration of the disability.

There are factors which affect illness behavior perhaps less visibly but which strongly influence coping efforts and the nature of disability. It is now well recognized that particular hospital environments can have deleterious effects on the patient.[15,50] Patients who are cared for in environments which fail to stimulate them may deteriorate. Wing and Brown[5,51] showed that in the case of schizophrenia, in socially poor hospitals, pateints are more withdrawn and have more symptoms such as poverty of speech. Similarly, Brown and his associates found that schizophrenic patients have poor outcome in family environments characterized by "high emotional involvement."[6] Through well planned programs encompassing community care and "social treatment," the advantages of more limited medical treatments and procedures can be realized without incurring inactivity, separation from social ties, loss of confidence and skills, and other liabilities associated with long-term patient roles.

As we noted at the beginning of this discussion, the problems of separating out "primary" biological from "secondary" psychological and social factors in conditions such as "institutionalism" are enormously complex, though perhaps easier with some physical diseases than with psychiatric disorders.[7,50] In research efforts, attempts to reliably separate these components is an important and necessary endeavor. In the practice of clinical medicine and psychiatry, however, concern with social and psychological disabilities may achieve results comparable, and under some circumstances superior, to those gained by directing attention to the "primary" disorder.

We often tend to forget that our language and the professional stances we take have a moral as well as a scientific and practical importance. And since our orientation toward patients implies a vocabulary of motives, it is not surprising that it has effects on their future motives and efforts. Over the years there has been an increasing tendency to view problems of living within a deterministic model of illness, and there is no question but that this tendency has served a valuable social function in perpetuating the humanitarian perspective which it encompassed. But as we increasingly recognize the social influences of the labelling process and of environmental contexts, it is important to consider how iatrogenic disability may be avoided without abandoning the human values to which medicine and psychiatry have made so important a contribution.

REFERENCES

1. Anderson, O.: Infant mortality and social and cultural factors: Historical trends and current patterns. In Jaco E. G. (ed.): Patients, Physicians and Illness 1st ed. New York; The Free Press, 1958.
2. Anderson, O.: The utilization of health services. In Freeman, H. et al. (eds.): Handbook of Medical Sociology. Englewood Cliffs, N.J., Prentice Hall, 1963.
3. Balint, M.: The Doctor, His Patient, and the Illness, New York, International Universities Press, 1957.

4. Beecher, H.: Measurement of Subjective Responses, New York, Oxford University Press, 1959.
5. Brown, G. W., and Wing, J. K.: A comparative clinical and social survey of three mental hospitals. Soc. Rev. Monogr. 5, Sociology and Medicine. Studies Within the Framework of the British National Health Service, Keele, 1962.
6. Brown, G. W., et al.: Influence of family life on the course of schizophrenic illness. Brit. J. Prev. Soc. Med. *16:* 55–68 (1962).
7. Brown, G. W., et al.: Schizophrenia and

Social Care. London, Oxford University Press, 1966.

8. Clark, M.: Health in the Mexican American Community. Berkeley, University of California Press, 1959.

9. Croog, S. H.: Ethnic origins, educational level, and responses to a health questionnaire. Hum. Org., *20:* 65–69 (1961).

10. Field, M.: Doctor and Patient in Soviet Russia, Cambridge, Harvard University Press, 1957.

11. Frank, J.: Persuasion and Healing. Baltimore, John Hopkins Press, 1961.

12. Friedman, S. B. et al.: Behavioral observations on parents anticipating the death of a child. Pediatrics *32:* 610-625 (1963).

13. Friedman, S. B., *et al.:* Urinary 17-hydroxy-corticosteroid levels in parents of children with neoplastic disease. *Psychosom. Med. 25;* 364–376 (1963).

14. Glass, A. J.: Psychotherapy in the combat zone. In Symposium on Stress. Washington, D.C.: Army Medical Service Graduate School, Walter Reed Army Medical Hospital, 1953.

15. Goffman, E.: Asylums, New York, Double-day-Anchor, 1961.

16. Goldsen, R.: Patient delay in seeking cancer diagnosis: Behavioral aspects, J. Chron. Dis., *16:* 427–436 (1963).

17. Graham, D., et al.: Physiological response to the suggestion of attitudes specific for hives and hypertension. Psychosom. Med. *24:* 159–169 (1962).

18. Group for the Advancement of Psychiatry: Preventive psychiatry in the armed forces: with some implications for civilian use. Report no. 47, New York, 1960.

19. Hinkle, L. E., and Wolff, H. G.: Health and the social environment: Experimental investigations. In Leighton, A. H. et al., (eds.): Explorations in Social Psychiatry. New York, Basic Books, Inc., 1957.

20. Koos, E.: The Health of Regionsville: What the People Thought and Did About It. New York, Columbia University Press, 1954.

21. Linn, L.: Social Characteristics and Social Interaction in the Utilization of a Psychiatric Outpatient Clinc.

22. Mechanic, D.: Illness and social disability: Some problems in analysis. Pacific Soc. Rev. *2:* 37–41 (1959).

23. Mechanic, D.: The concept of illness behavior. J. Chron. Dis. *15:* 189–194 (1962).

24. Mechanic, D.: Some factors in identifying and defining mental illness. Ment. Hyg., *46:* 66–74 (1962).

25. Mechanic, D.: Some implications of illness behavior for medical sampling. New Engl. J. Med., *269:* 244–247 (1963).

26. Mechanic, D.: Religion, religiosity, and illness behavior. Human Org., *22:* 202-208 (1963).

27. Mechanic, D.: The influence of mothers on their children's health attitudes and behavior. Pediatrics, *33:* 444-453 (1964).

28. Mechanic, D.: Perception of parental responses to illness. J. Hlth. Hum. Behav.,*6:*

253–257 (1965).

29. Mechanic, D.: The sociology of medicine, viewpoints and perspectives. J. Hlth. Hum. Behav. *7:* 237–248 (Winter, 1966).

30. Mechanic, D.: Community psychiatry: Some sociological perspectives and implications. In Roberts, L. et al. (eds.): Community Psychiatry. Madison, Wisc., University of Wisconsin Press, 1966.

31. Mechanic, D., and Volkart, E. H.: Illness behavior and medical diagnoses., J. Hlth. Hum. Behav. *1:* 86-94 (1960).

32. Mechanic, D., and Volkart, E. H.: Stress, illness behavior, and the sick role. Amer. Sociol. Rev. *26:* 51–58 (1961).

33. Meyer, R. J., and Haggerty, R. J.: Streptococcal Infections in Families, Pediatrics *29:* 539–544 (1962).

34. Parsons, T.: The Social System. New York, The Free Press, 1951.

35. Phillips, D.: Self-reliance and the inclination to adopt the sick role. Social Forces *43:* 555–563 (1965).

36. Roessler, R., and Greenfield, N. (eds.): Physiological Correlates of Psychological Disorders. Madison, Wisc., University of Wisconsin Press, 1962, pp. 257-267.

37. Saunders, L.: Cultural Differences and Medical Care. New York, Russell Sage Foundation, 1954.

38. Schachter, S.: The Psychology of Affiliation. Palo Alto, Stanford University Press, 1959.

39. Schachter, S., and Singer, J.: Cognitive, social, and physiological determinants of emotional state. Psychol. Rev. *69:* 379–399 (1962).

40. Scheff, T. J., and Silverman, A.: Users and non-users of a student psychiatric clinic, J. Hlth. Hum. Behav. *7:* 114–121 (1966).

41. Segal, B.: Scholars and patients: Religion, academic performance, and the use of medical facilities by male undergraduates. Unpublished paper. Department of Sociology, Dartmouth College.

42. Segal, B., et al.: Emotional adjustment, social organization and psychiatric treatment rates. Amer. Sociol. Rev. *30:* 548–556 (1965).

43. Speisman, J. C., et al.: Experimental reduction of stress based on ego-defense theory. J. Abnorm. Soc. Psychol. *68:* 367–380 (1964).

44. Srole, L., et al: Mental Health in the Metropolis. New York, McGraw-Hill, 1962.

45. Sternbach, R. A., and Tursky, B.: Ethnic differences among housewives in psychophysical and skin potential responses to electric shock. Psychophysiology *1:* 241–246 (1965).

46. Suchman, E.: Sociomedical variations among ethnic groups. Amer. J. Sociol. *70:* 319–331 (1964).

47. Suchman, E.: Social Patterns and medical care. J. Hlth. Hum. Behav. *6:* 2–16 (1965).

48. Szasz, T. S.: Bootlegging humanistic values through psychiatry. Antioch. Rev. *22:* 341–349 (1962).

49. White, K. L., et al.: The ecology of medical care. New Engl. J. Med. *265:* 885–892 (1961).

50. Wing, J. K.: Institutionalism in mental

hospitals. Brit. J. Soc. Clin. Psychol. *1:* 38–51 (1962).

51. Wing, J. K., and Brown, G. W.: Social treatment of chronic schizophrenia: A comparative survey of three mental hospitals. J. Ment. Sci. *107:* 847–861 (1961).

52. Wolff, H.: Stress and Disease. Springfield, Ill., Charles C. Thomas, 1953.

53. Zborowski, M.: Cultural components in responses to pain. J. Soc. Issues. *8:* 16–30 (1952).

54. Zola, I.: Problems of communication, diagnosis and patient care. J. Med. Educ. *10:* 829–838 (1963).

55. Zola, I.: Illness behavior of the working class. In Shostak, A., and Gomberg, W. (eds.): Studies of the American Worker. Englewood Cliffs, N. J., Prentice Hall, 1964.

29   How the Sick View Their World

Henry D. Lederer

The experience of illness is a complex psychological situation. To clarify the responses of the sick to this experience it is necessary to consider three main time periods, each of which has a characteristic orientation.[1] These stages of the experience of illness are: (1) the transition period from health to illness, (2) the period of "accepted" illness and, (3) convalescence.

THE ORIENTATIONS OF THE SICK IN THE TRANSITION PERIOD FROM HEALTH TO ILLNESS

Upon falling ill most persons become aware of undesirable, unpleasant, and painful sensations; of a disturbing reduction in strength and stamina; of a diminution in ability to perform habitual acts. For example, at the onset of virus pneumonia, the patient experiences headaches, vague chest pains, tightness of the skin. He fatigues easily, desires more than usual rest, and "plays out" quickly on prolonged tasks. In addition, he finds the performance of his daily routine of work and play tiring and aggravating to his discomforts.

One finds certain definite patterns of response to these initial events. Some degree of apprehension or anxiety is felt as in any situation in which a painful, unpleasant, and threatening circumstance is encountered.[2] Consequently the pattern of response to the initial symptoms is often the characteristic mode of reaction to anxiety whenever it arises. Many persons attempt to ignore this threat and through such a denial of the frightening experience to allay their anxieties. This denial may be reinforced by a "plunge into health" through engaging in more than routine activity. In this manner the patient seems to be reassuring himself by saying, "If I can manage to be so very active there is nothing to fear — the whole affair is an illusion." Another form of denial is to minimize the importance of the symptoms by identifying them with symptoms of benign or trivial indispositions. Thus the "coronary vascular accident" symptoms are identified with "an upset stomach" and the chest pains of lobar pneumonia with a "touch of pleurisy."

Still further, one observes other patients who meet anxiety aggressively and such persons in the initial stages of illness are irascible, querulous, and ill-humored. Conversely, others allay anxiety by passivity and behave in a compliant, obsequious, and pitiable manner.

The ordinary day-to-day life routines of most persons constitute a source of satisfaction of various needs and defenses against anxiety. Since illness renders painful and tiring participation in such gratify-

Lederer, H. D.: How the sick view their world. J. Soc. Issues *8:* 4–15 (1952).

ing and reassuring activities, anxiety is compounded and frustration of many needs is felt.[3] Thomas Mann has written humorously and understandingly of this experience in *"The Magic Mountain."* His hero, Hans Castorp, in the early febrile stage of an activated tuberculosis tries to preserve his daily rituals which have formerly proven gratifying and soothing. One of these practices is the smoking of the after dinner cigar, a luxury of great importance to Castorp; but now he finds an evil taste and light-headedness in the place of a delightful aroma and general feeling of well-being.[4]

Certain men become especially anxious when they find themselves having to restrict their activities and to admit the existence of their discomforts.[5] To these persons, manliness depends on being active and never yielding to physical discomfort; to them, passivity and any intolerance of pain are equated with femininity. Consequently, becoming ill is viewed as an emasculating process and, thereby, highly provocative of anxiety. There may be a dangerous denial of symptoms in such a person through his abortive attempts to reassert his masculinity in sports, late hours, heavy work, etc.

For many persons, parts of their bodies or certain bodily functions have been invested with intense emotion. The skin, the facial structures, the head, the genitals, the breasts are examples of bodily parts often intensely loved by the patient. Obviously great apprehension is experienced when symptoms seem to indicate dysfunction of these treasured parts.

There is a continuing folk tradition in some areas that suggests that illness is the just desert of the sinner. Persons holding to this misconception feel guilty when developing an illness and may even be impelled to malinger health rather than appear with the stigma of immorality.

Specific illnesses exhibiting a familial occurrence are particularly alarming since most persons do not want to discredit the purity of their families. This attitude has been one of the impedances to early diagnosis of such illnesses as carcinomata and tuberculosis. Often the afflicted person has great anxiety because of the uncon-

scious fantasy of rejection and wrath by other members of the family. Most physicians have had contact with patients who are deeply shamed by symptoms which they interpret as a possible disgrace to their family lines.

Many persons, who because of emotional immaturity and stressful living have been reduced to a psychoneurotic level of functioning, may react paradoxically to the advent of physical illness. Often there is an amelioration of the neurotic symptoms and the patient seems to welcome the concrete threat of physical illness which can divert his attention from his neurosis. With some neurotic persons, physical illness may actually bring emotional relief through its symbolic meaning as a penalty for unconscious guilt feelings. Moreover, the anticipated care and consideration as well as release from social responsibilities can be highly appealing to a neurotic patient. His feelings of guilt and shame for his withdrawing, dependent, and infantile wishes are relieved by the occurrence of physical sickness which "legitimizes" these claims. "The individual with a relatively weak ego may find an escape from his (neurotic) anxieties in the less demanding situation that illness provides."[6]

An example of this type of response to physical illness was observed in a young, single woman who was undergoing psychotherapy for severe phobias. Her neurosis developed in reaction to the stress of her approaching marriage for which her previous psychosocial growth had not prepared her. In the midst of this emotional distress, she developed visual and gait disturbances which were definitely diagnosed as symptoms of multiple sclerosis. At the onset of these grave symptoms and her entrance into the hospital, she announced with elation that her phobic obsessions had departed and that she was entirely rid of anxiety.

To recapitulate, in the initial symptom phase of many illnesses, one may encounter evidence of anxiety, guilt, and shame as well as the many personality defenses against these disagreeable affects. Moreover, in certain neurotic patients there may be a paradoxically positive acceptance of illness.

The continuing pressure, and often the increase, of symptoms forces the patient into another psychologically difficult set of experiences — those of diagnosis and the beginning of therapy. At this time the former habitual patterns of health still exert a powerful attraction on the patient whereas his submission to diagnostic and therapeutic procedures involves entering an unknown area. But in order to be rid of his discomforts and dysfunctions he must face this unknown situation.

(It is important to note that at this point another crucial factor is met which influences the orientation of the patient — this factor is the behavior of the medical personnel who are responsible for his diagnosis and therapy.)

Whenever one enters an unknown or partially understood situation, he exhibits fairly typical responses. Once again anxiety is aroused because of fantasied dangers and because of unfamiliarity with what one may expect. Under these circumstances there is much indecision reflected in vacillating behavior. For example, urgent requests for diagnostic examinations are rapidly alternated with failure to appear for examination. Physicians must learn to expect such vacillating and indecisive behavior and not to be angered or disgusted by it. The firm, patient, and understanding attitude of the physician will help in allaying the patient's anxiety.

The highly scientific nature of medical diagnosis places these affairs beyond the full understanding of the average layman. The physical paraphernalia of many diagnostic processes are awesome to many persons. In addition, the technical language of medicine is an unknown tongue to the layman who can only hope that what he overhears is an optimistic statement rather than a pronouncement of doom or further pain for him. When these mystifying matters are coupled to the impersonality of diagnostic activity in many modern hospital and clinics, it is easy to empathize with the mounting anxiety of the patient and his problem of cooperating in diagnosis.

Much attention in recent years has been centered upon ways of cushioning the effects of these experiences by the attitude of the physician. The awe and fear of the cold, aseptic, impersonal atmosphere of the clinic can be considerably diminished by attitudes of personal interest in, and exhibitions of respect for, the patient in his contacts with medical personnel.[7] A concise but specific and clear-cut explanation of diagnostic procedures can undercut most of the mystery of diagnosis. Excluding all but the necessary equipment from the examination room is still another aid in this direction. Many clinics are now furnishing waiting rooms in styles which lessen their resemblance to operating rooms or laboratories and consequently are reassuring.

Unnecessary repetitions of diagnostic examinations and tests should be avoided because any signs of indecision or insecurity shown by the physician augment the patient's apprehension. When the doctor demonstrates his skill by his determination and decisiveness, the patient is usually grateful for such real reassurance; then he is sure he is in capable, trustworthy hands. There is much wisdom in the old medical dictum that "in any contact between doctor and patient there is room only for one anxious person — the patient."

The future course of the patient's behavior often depends upon the manner in which his diagnosis is presented to him. If the doctor speaks simply and forthrightly, in most instances anxiety is relieved. Clouding the issue in technical jargon or discussing equivocal findings usually increase the patient's emotionality. For example, nothing is gained and much may be lost by announcing "borderline" findings to a patient. It is easy to imagine the confusion aroused by informing a person: "I don't think you have much to worry about. Your heart seems O.K. but we want to watch your electrocardiogram because it was a little abnormal." After this report the patient is in a dilemma about understanding himself, his physical limits, and what, if any, dangers confront him.

Experienced physicians expect a possible distortion of facts when interviewing patients about their symptoms and the histories of their illnesses. These distortions stem from the patient's anxiety and his defenses and should be taken with a benevolent skepticism. Some of the art of interviewing rests on the doctor's recognition of these unconscious distortions. If the doctor behaves like a detective in pursuing facts, the patient is made even more tense.[3]

Most persons view with conflicting, mixed feelings the start of therapy. Actually, some therapeutic maneuvers do cause discomfort and pain so that the patient has to accept a paradox — that is, to be relieved of discomfort, he must at times submit to a transistory increase in it. Usually a sick person anticipates far more discomfort than is involved in most treatments. This gloomy expectation is a reflection of his apprehensive state and calls for an equivocal frankness from the doctor for correction. Again, a concise, unambiguous description of the therapy and the rationale for it alleviates anxiety and goes far toward gaining the patient's cooperation.[9] Vagueness about details of therapy must be avoided in order to reduce the opportunities for the patient to imagine the worst. Whenever possible, impersonal contact between the patient and his therapist should be reduced. For example, a visit by the anesthetist before an operation neutralizes some of the fear that most patients entertain about general anesthesia.

When treatment requires a hospital setting, the doctor and his aides have the responsibility for explaining hospital procedures to the patient. The patient is able to cooperate more easily when he knows about such routine matters as the duty hours of the floor nurses, when meals are served, visiting rules, the names of his internes, etc. Often antagonistic, belligerent behavior can be charged to negligence in clarifying the hospital situation when the patient was admitted — it is his way of aggressively resolving his anxiety. The rate of "sign-out against medical advice" is inversely related to the success of the medical personnel in their handling of these problems.

THE STAGE OF "ACCEPTED" ILLNESS

When the patient has accepted diagnostic and initial therapeutic procedures, he enters another distinct time period in his experience of illness. Now, he views himself as ill and abandons pretenses of health. In our society, accepting illness includes accepting help from physicians and their aides. He temporarily withdraws from his adult responsible activities and, cooperating with his doctor, dedicates himself to the problem of getting well; he substitutes preoccupation with his symptoms and illness for the many concerns of mature life. Whereas in health he has made his own decisions, he now transfers this right to his physician, nurse and other attendants. These changes in orientation are reinforced by the doctor's prescription that he not pursue his work, his usual recreations, nor his responsibilities. Society as a whole also frees him for the duration of his illness from the discharge of ordinary duties and obligations.

All of these changes determine the structure of the patient's world which can be described as a simpler, more childish, constricted life. His illness has led him into a social setting which is similar to his childhood.[10] Therefore, one can refer to this arrangement as being very regressed and infantile.

To such a regressed social situation the patient now reacts with behavior used earlier during his childhood. His actions, thoughts, and feelings are regressive in response to the childlike world of illness. The main features of this behavior are: (1) egocentricity, (2) constriction of interests, (3) emotional dependency, (4) hypochondriasis.[11]

Charles Lamb, in his essay, "The Convalescent," accurately described the egocentricity of the sick when he wrote, "How sickness enlarges the dimensions of a man's self to himself! He is his own exclusive object. Supreme selfishness is inculcated upon him as his only duty."[12] Like a child the patient is concerned with the selfish matters of satisfying simple needs for rest, food, absence of pain, physical comfort, and relief of bodily tensions such as the urge to urinate, defecate, pass flatus, or to belch. Satisfaction of these needs assumes precedence over more social ones. The patient presumes that his attendants share in these preoccupations and he feels resentful or hurt if the doctor or nurse is distracted by other concerns.

His egocentricity renders him provincial and highly subjective, like a child, in his judging the events occurring around him. If the nurse frowns for a moment, he is worried that she has taken a dislike to him; if she does not respond to his ring, she is damned as lazy and uninterested in his welfare.

Often the patient becomes a sick-room tyrant, dominating others and intolerant or often unaware of their rights and needs. "If there be a regal solitude, it is a sick bed. How the patient lords it there" — "He keeps his sympathy, like some curious vintage, under trusty lock and key, for his own use only." This egocentric despotism frequently disturbs the friends and relatives of the patient who are accustomed to his former consideration and objectivity.

Dynamically related to his egocentricity is the constriction of interests of the sick person. The narrowing follows partially from the reduced scope of the patient's world and partly from his regressed narcissism. The ill person shows an often amazing disinterest or even apathy toward the impersonal events of the day. He has abandoned his concern for politics, business, social events and will not persist in discussion of these matters.

Lamb outlines this constriction of interest as follows: "A little while ago he was greatly concerned in the event of a lawsuit, which was to be the making or the marring of his dearest friend. He was to be seen trudging about upon this man's errand to fifty quarters of the town at once. The cause was to come on yesterday. He is absolutely as indifferent to the decision as if it were a question to be tried at Pekin . . . he picks up enough to make him understand that things went cross-grained in the court yesterday, and his friend is ruined. But the word 'friend' and the word 'ruin' disturb him no more than so much jargon. He is not to think of anything but how to get better."

The protection and devotion accorded the patient by his medical attendants relieve him of adapting himself to interests other than his own and thereby increase his provincialism. There is often little or no

check to his regressive, constricted, and narcissistic behavior so that apathy appears.

Dependence on others is imposed by the physical helplessness stemming from illness and by the psychological inadequacy secondary to egocentricity and constricted interests. The patient's physical weakness, like that of the child, requires the strength of other persons to meet his needs. His regression into a self-centered, subjective world demands that healthier persons apply their more mature and objective judgment to his affairs — again parallcling the experience of the child whose parents assume responsibility for most important matters. With this dependency, one observes much ambivalence toward the benefactors. Like a child the patient often exhibits an uncritical "love" and admiration for his benefactors, but at the same time resentment toward them because of his weak and inferior relation to them. All persons working with the sick should anticipate and learn to recognize this ambivalent dependency and neither be flattered, nor offended, by it.

The unpleasant sensations of illness, in combination with the reduced regressive world and perceptions of the patient, lead to a great concern with the functioning of the body. There is usually much hypochondrical worry over medical matters such as pulse rate, temperature, bowel movements, weight changes, etc., all of which may dominate the patient's thoughts and conversations. This hypochondriasis resembles in some ways the curiosity and exploration of the body and its functions undertaken normally by all children.

The attitudes and behavior of the medical personnel can limit or extend the emotional regression of the patient. The appearance of apathy as a response to over-pretection has already been cited.[13] In recent years, many warnings have been sounded against unnecessary restriction of patient's activities.

The indiscriminate prescription of prolonged bed-rest has been demonstrated as a cause of invalidism out of proportion to actual physical incapacity. The current practice of encouraging patients to get on their feet as early as possible following operations has proven both physically and emotionally beneficial; it has prevented lengthy convalescence. It seems that the best course for the physician is to encourage the minimum amount of regression necessitated by the physical limitations of the patient and to avoid any unnecessary infantilizing.

The regression, during illness, is adaptive and often significant for survival. It is conceivable that through social and emotional regression the sick person redistributes his energies to facilitate the healing process or possibly that the regressive integration is in itself an essential factor in the healing process. The biological task of the sick is to get well and this work is furthered by the focussing of personality energies on the self and withdrawing them from other uses and purposed.[14] Recognition of this utility in the regression of the sick should make medical attendants welcome it rather than deplore it.

In persons, whose general character development has led to elaborate behavior defenses against regression and the expression of dependency, there is little or no phase of "accepted illness." Denial of physical limits and symptoms continues to some extent; the advice and ministrations of medical personnel are challenged and not followed; hospital care may be refused. All in all the neurotic defenses of such a patient militate against the healing benefits of regression and the course of his illness may be worsened or fatal. His behavioral adjustment to his neurosis takes precedence over adaptive regression during physical illness.

To illustrate: A physician, in middle age, sustained an acute coronary heart attack. His professional colleagues, who diagnosed his illness, advised immediate and absolute bed rest, quiet, and heavy sedation, all of which the patient stoutly refused on the grounds of his heavy schedule of work with his own patients. He persisted in his medical work and died suddenly in his office twenty hours later. This patient's personality was structured largely to deny any dependent emotional trends. He was a "self-made" man who had labored hard to graduate from medical school. He steadfastly pursued his career, never permitting

himself a vacation. In his personal life he lavished gifts on his family, but was Spartan in any self-indulgence. It can be conjectured that his neurotic character was a considerable factor in his early death.

Under those conditions, the total medical management must include measures to aid the patient in accepting regression and dependency. At times a psychiatrist or psychiatric social worker must be included in the therapeutic team to contribute their skills in meeting this neurotic complication of a physical illness.

The period of "accepted illness" gradually ends after optimal regression and medical therapy have reversed or arrested the pathogenic process. The patient then enters the convalescent period of his experience of illness.

THE STAGE OF CONVALESCENCE

Convalescence is the time period of transition from illness back into a state of health. This recovery of health involves a return of physical strength and a reintegration of the personality of the patient who has been living, feeling, and thinking in a regressed, more or less infantile way.

The return of physical strength and health is usually an automatic process but it is not necessarily paralleled by a restoration of "healthy," adult behavior; getting well physically must be associated with the patient's relinquishing his dependent, egocentric and provincial reactions.[15]

Many students of convalescence have recognized its structural and dynamic similarities to adolescence. This analogy is instructive in understanding the problems of the convalescent and suggests many techniques for helping the convalescent "grow up" again into adult health.[16]

The convalescent, like the adolescent, has to leave a protected world in which responsibilities were minimal and the satisfaction of his self-centered needs the major concern of himself and those attending him. These pleasant aspects of illness attract the convalescent so that he wants to remain in his "regal home" of regression. It is hard for one to give up the attentions, protection, and kindnesses of doctors and nurses and to fend once more for oneself. "Farewell with him all that made sickness prompous — the spell that hushed the household — the mute attendance — the inquiry by looks — the still softer delicacies of self-attention — what a speck is he dwindled into (by his physical recuperation).[17]

If the patient has suppressed his resentful hostility toward his medical attendants during the preceding phase, he frequently remains regressed because of a guilty overdependence upon them. Recent studies on polio-myelitis patients who require respirators have shown that the patients who are slowly weaned from the "artificial lung" are those who have been unable to express openly any negative feelings toward their doctors and nurses.[18]

Convalescence is often prolonged in persons whose previous state of health did not provide them with sufficient gratifications and relief from anxiety. Examples of this situation are seen in military service where full recovery from illness means re-entering a hazardous and depriving existence.

Fortunately, for most convalescents, the broader scope of their "healthy" worlds is more attractive than the regressive pleasures of illness. In such persons the stronger motive is toward health but may be impeded by continuing feelings of inadequacy. Like adolescents who yearn for adult life but feel unsure of themselves, these convalescents wistfully long for health but are afraid to try it. These fears may be related to neurotic self-depreciation which was part of the original behavior pattern in childhood, reactivated during the period of regression.

Certain convalescents repeat their adolescent method of "growing up" by rebelliously wrenching themselves loose from dependency. These persons are in a tremendous hurry to get well, often prematurely dismiss their physicians, and over-step their physical strengths.

Again one realizes that the participation of the physician and his aides can profoundly affect the course of convalescence. Under these conditions the medical personnel occupy roles similar to those of the

parents and counselors of adolescents; the successful medical management of convalescence is the analogue of proper parenthood during adolescence.

To illustrate: The parent who gradually and progressively relaxes his protection and instead offers guidance and advice is encouraging the adolescent toward adulthood. He quietly retires to the side-lines ready to reassure but willing to let his child experiment with new strengths. Only stepping in when gross errors of judgment may arise. The adolescent senses the confidence of the parent and is reassured by it, especially when immediately perfect or ideal results are not demanded. Moreover, the helpful parent is not threatened by his child's interest in other persons or new activities.

Convalescence can be promoted and enhanced by similar attitudes on the part of the doctor. Physicians must have the courage to recommend more activity and to lift the restrictions on the patient's behavior. Some physicians, like parents, are unconsciously gratified by the dependency of others upon them; this narcissistic pleasure must be abandoned by no longer encouraging regressive dependency through protection. The physician sometimes is loath to risk his reputation through the possibility of a relapse and thereby continues to treat the convalescent with great caution; this is frequently the event when the patient is a person of some prominence in the community so that his illness has been under a public scrutiny which makes the physician uneasy.

The rehabilitation of the convalescent has become a matter of growing medical concern, research, and progress. During the war the military medical services were alert to these problems and contributed many important findings to this aspect of medical management.[19] Since the war some of the medical colleges have established departments of rehabilitation as integral basic training units.

Offering the convalescent stimulation for re-integration is stressed. Increasing visiting privileges, permitting the wearing of ordinary rather than hospital clothes, providing radio and television, permitting trial leaves overnight from the hospital are examples of opportunities which may stimulate the patient toward a state of health. Transferring the convalescent to a special rehabilitation center or ward has been recommended as an aid in helping him relinquish the regressive patterns of life followed on ordinary hospital wards.

The modern physician is urged to lead a team of therapists in the guidance and support of the convalescent just as the wise parent welcomes the contributions of the teacher, youth leader, student counselor, etc. who promote the growth of the adolescent. Social workers, occupational therapists, vocational counselors, recreational therapists, etc. can broaden the scope of the convalescent's world, encourage him and help reestablish his self-confidence and self-sufficiency.

While the patient is still in the state of "accepted illness," the caseworker may have discovered sources of tension and dissatisfaction in his family, home, work situations and can initiate changes which will make the return to health more attractive. In addition the cooperation of the family in the management of convalescence is often won by a skillful caseworker.

Much attention has been given to occupational therapy through which the patient is gently led into a more self-assertive, creative life. Moreover, he is given the opportunity to re-exercise rusty talents and techniques in an experimental setting. Here he can regain self-confidence through a series of progressive "successes."

Well-planned recreational therapies provide practice in socializing and engaging in gradual competition. Here again the success in group living encourages the patient to re-enter the large arena of adult "healthy" society.

The expanding use of vocational counseling is an indication of its value to the convalescent. Many patients cling to regressed behavior because they cannot engage further in past occupations. For example, convalescent tuberculous patients frequently must find less strenuous jobs to protect them from relapses. In such a situation, hopeful and realistic planning can be constructed through consultations with a competent vocational counselor. The convalescent, like the adolescent, is less afraid of his future when his vocational potentialities are clear to him.

In addition to the special services each member of the therapeutic team has to offer, there is the over-all benefit of providing the patient contact with many mature, healthy persons with whom he can emotionally identify. This process is similar to the identification of the adolescent with key adult persons in his environment. Both the convalescent and adolescent find such identification a most positive aid in accepting an adult status. Conversely, emotionally immature persons serving on therapeutic teams can seriously retard the convalescent's recovery by not providing the bridge of a healthy identification.

All of these various services and stimuli can be offered to a patient but it is necessary to realize, no one can force him to use them constructively. For the majority of persons "health" is preferred to regression. With the few patients who cannot respond positively to planned convalescence, one usually finds that an earlier neurosis has been revived by the trauma of illness; these persons should be offered psychotherapy to resolve the neurotic difficulties prolonging their full recovery.

To summarize: The state of convalescence is structurally and dynamically similar to adolescence. The behavior of the convalescent is analogous to that of the adolescent. The success of helping the patient is dependent on the recognition of his "adolescent" emotional status which then should call forth from his medical attendants attitudes similar to those of the parent who encourages and aids the growth of his adolescent child. Opportunities must be provided for re-establishing self-confidence through graded "successes" in groups and in the exercise of one's returning physical strengths. The convalescent phase of illness terminates with the parallel recovery from physical limitations and psychological regression.

REFERENCES

1. Barker, R. G., *et al.:* Social psychology of acute illness. In *Adjustment to Physical Handicap and Illness. (Rev. ed.)* New York, Social Science Research Council, 1953.
2. Binger, C.: *The Doctor's Job.* New York, Norton, 1945.
3. Upham, F.: *A Dynamic Approach to Illness.* New York, Family Service Association of America, 1949.
4. Mann, T.: *The Magic Mountain.* New York, Knopf, 1945.
5. Barker, *et al., op. cit.*
6. Upham, *op. cit.*
7. Barker, *et al., op. cit.*
8. Levine, M.: *Psychotherapy in Medical Practice.* New York, Macmillan, 1942.
9. *Ibid.*
10. Conference on Convalescent Care. New York Academy of Medicine, 1940.
11. Barker, *et al., op. cit.*
12. Lamb, C.: *Essays.* New York, Viking, 1949.
13. Barraclough, W.: Mental reactions of normal children to physical illness *Am. J. Psychiat. 93:* 865–877 (1937).
14. Ferenezi, S.: Disease or pathoneurosis. In *Further Contributions to the Theory and Technique of Psychoanalysis.* London, Hogarth, 1926.
15. Romano, J.: Emotional components of illness. *Conn. State Med. J. 7:* 22–25 (1943).
16. Barker, *et al., op. cit.*
17. Lamb, *op. cit*
18. Unpublished data from studies in progress. Department of Psychiatry, College of Medicine, University of Cincinnati.
19. Watson-Jones, R.: Rehabilitation in the Royal Air Force. *Brit. Med. J. 1:* 403–407, Wilson, E. H.: Rehabilitation in war-time Britain. *Arch. Surgery. 46:* (1943), and Thorndike, A.: Convalescent recondition. *J. A. M. A. 126:* 773 (1944).

30　　A Home away from Home*

Rose Laub Coser

The sick person who is admitted to the hospital ward is frequently overcome by anxiety to such an extent that he is likely to suffer from a partial blurring of his self-image because of the actual and symbolic threat to his body. His forced passivity, his horizontal pose, the removal of his own clothes and belongings, the fact that doctors and nurses, persons hitherto unknown to him, have full access to his body, and the fact that he cannot anticipate what will happen to him — all these factors contribute to a loss of ego identity.[1] The threat he experiences and the concomitant loss of ego strength are likely to bring with them a partial regression[1] to a stage in childhood when the outer world was preceived as but an extension of the self, having as its sole function providing satisfaction to the child. The outer world, at that stage, was not seen as reality separate from the self to be acted *upon,* but rather as a source of intake and

---

*This paper is based on some findings from a study of the role of the patient in the ward of a general hospital. The hospital is situated in a metropolitan area in the Eastern United States and serves as a teaching hospital to several medical schools. The research consisted of participant observations of the medical and surgical wards, as well as of standardized interviews given to patients at discharge. The 51 patients interviewed at discharge were chosen at random from the female and male surgical wards and female and male medical wards, each of about 25 beds. The following is a qualitative analysis of some interview data.

---

[1] The term "regression" is here used as defined by Kurt Lewin. It refers to a "primitivization of behavior, a 'going back' to a less mature state which the individual has already outgrown." Lewin goes on to say: "A temporary regression frequently occurs in tense emotional situations with normal adults and children, particularly if these emotions are unpleasant ... Fatigue, oversatiation and sickness often cause temporary regression."[4]

Coser, R. L.: A home away from home. Soc. Problems *4:* 3–17 (1956).

security. Similarly, many patients seem to find in the hospital sources for the satisfaction of their primary needs.

After recovering from their initial fears after admission, many patients felt protected and taken care of; many of them said that "this is as good as" or "better than" home. Their meals were brought to them, their beds were made, their hygiene was supervised. Their health was the concern of doctors and nurses and not their own responsibility. The legitimate passivity in which they could now indulge constituted a gratification of desires which in ordinary life they would have had to repress in order to live up to their everyday obligations.

Moreover, relationships among patients in the ward were characterized by a high degree of sociability and the formation of friendship ties. These ties suggested to the patient something akin to "home," as they themselves expressed it. Mr. Golder,[2] to cite just one example, felt, "It's wonderful here, it's a regular party . . . . it seems home to everybody."

Thus the hospital was often seen as "home away from home." It was experienced as a source for the satisfaction of primary needs; primary relationships established there were sufficiently similar to those that characterize family life: the relationships were considered ends in themselves and very frequently outlasted the time and the place in which they were first formed.[3]

Several factors combined to make patients feel "at home" in the hospital, in addition to the ones mentioned above. For some, there was a traditional element, as for Mrs. Lee, who said proudly: "I knew this place when you weren't even born," or Mrs. Brown, who, when admitted for the second time, explained: "I have been here once before, but when I came here, I knew the place. My mother had been here several times and my husband, he was both on the medical and the surgical wards. My father died here. *This is like home for me.*" For

others, the hospital was a substitute for the family because they had nobody to take care of them. Mrs. Norstin, for example, did not want to go home when discharged: "I'm surprised my doctor sends me home . . . I'm helpless when I go home . . . ." Mr. Morris felt the same way: "The trouble is this, I have nobody to take care of me . . . . It's only a week and here they discharge me."

But even to many who had families, the care in the hospital seemed preferable; Mr. Drake, asked whether he would rather be home or in the hospital, in case of illness, replied: "I'd rather come to the hospital, get more attention . . . " or Mr. Fazzio: "This hospital is very nice; they're courteous and meet every wish and you don't get your every wish at home, so if I had to be sick I'd rather be here."

The hospital was considered frequently a source for the maintenance of the patients' security rather than a physical setting in which specific,well-defined tasks had to be accomplished. This became evident in the patient's answers to the question, "When you're sick, would you rather be home or in the hospital?" This question gave the patients the opportunity to elaborate on what they thought about hospital life. We were interested in their comments about the hospital rather than in their statements of preference.

Some patients felt that the hospital was better equipped to do a specific job. Miss Peterson, who said that she preferred the hospital to home, explained: "They are more equipped, their research is further advanced, there is always something new coming into a hospital, you are not in the care of any one person but of the whole staff . . . " Patients like this one saw the functions of the hospital as *limited* and *instrumental*.

Other patients felt that "care and attention" were the main aspects of hospital life. Their response indicated that they saw the hospital as a source for the gratification of *primary* needs.[4]

---

[2] All names are fictitious.

[3] The term "primary" is here used to indicate total rather than segmental involvement of the personality, and affective and diffuse rather than affectively neutral and specific attitudes.[2, 9]

[4] Eleven out of the 51 patients failed to make any comments in addition to their straight answer about preference; their answers were classified as "not applicable" to the categories discussed here.

Of the 40 patients who at discharge disclosed the meaning that the hospital had for them, 21 felt that receiving "care and attention" was the most important aspect of hospital life.

If the dichotomy that emerges here is actually indicative of the patients' differential orientations toward hospital life, their desires for primary satisfactions should appear in other responses dealing with relationships in the hospital structure. In other words, if the above categories are meaningful for the testing of patient orientation, the desire for the satisfaction of primary needs, on the one hand, and the instrumental attitudes, on the other, should manifest themselves in the patients' relationships with the hospital personnel.

For the patient the most important person in the hospital is the doctor. He is the one who is responsible for the medical care for which the person entered the hospital. It seems justified to ask: "What does the patient expect from the doctor?"

Two basically different images of the doctor emerge from the patients' responses to the question, "What is your idea of a good doctor?" – (a) the professional man, and (b) the omnipotent figure, or the dispenser of protection and love.

When answering this, 22 patients gave instrumental criteria for judging a good doctor, i.e., somewhere in their answers they pointed to the necessity of scientific and professional competence. For example: "He should be understanding, polite and know what he studied, what his profession is, that he understands what he is trying to diagnose." "A bad one is careless, independent, he thinks his reputation makes up for him. A good doctor don't overlook much, weighs things carefully."

Twenty-seven patients, however, saw in the doctor a gratifier of primary needs, either through the provision of kindness and love or through his inherent omnipotence. "The main thing: talks nice to me, gives me hope ... "; "when the doctor takes interest. A smile doesn't cost nothing ... A student may be a better doctor ... A smile cost no money." Trying to give me his idea of a good doctor, Mr. Rubin related his experience with two private doctors: "He is not too good a doctor, he is a Harvard graduate, a sporty guy, gave me a speech, that's all. There was another one, he was good, he was a sociable and talkative man, he used to talk to me nice." These patients felt that a "good doctor" was one who "talks nice," who makes them "feel good"; they did not answer in terms of skillful medical practice. In this category belong the patients who expected from the doctor omnipotence and omniscience. The most striking description of the magical medicine man came from a 70-year-old arthritic lady:

A good doctor is when I came to this country 50 years ago. When people came to him they went back happy. He just looked at a patient, they make him talk, people went back all cured. He didn't even give them medicine, and people went back, happy and so cured. If a patient came to him he write everything on a postal card and he kept it for years. He didn't have any equipment like they have now and every patient was cured.

Not all those who expected omnipotence from the doctor went to these extremes. Some simply said that all doctors "know more, know better," or, "In my whole life I've never known a doctor to be wrong."

The patients' definitions of a "good doctor" correlate significantly with the definition of the hospital's function (Table 30-1). Patients who felt that the hospital needed to do an efficient job were more likely to expect the doctor to display professional competence while those who expected "care and attention" tended to expect solace or omnipotence from the doctor.

The fact that of the 19 patients who had an instrumental attitude toward the hospital, 16 had a similar attitude toward the doctor, and of the 21 who had a primary attitude toward the hospital, 19 gave a similar response with regard to the doctor, seems to indicate that the instrumental-primary dichotomy is significant.

We feel that we are justified, therefore, in classifying the patients into *three* types:

I. *Instrumental:* Those who were instrumental in both responses, or whose response to only one question was instrumental while that to the other was not applicable to our categories.

TABLE 30-1. PATIENTS' ATTITUDE TOWARD HOSPITAL
BY ATTITUDE TOWARD DOCTOR

Attitude Toward Doctor	Attitude Toward Hospital			
	Instrumental	Primary	N.A. (or not applicable)	Total
Instrumental	16	1	5	22
Primary	3	19	5	27
N.A.	0	1	1	2
Total	19	21	11	51

II. *Primary:* Those who manifested a primary orientation in both answers or whose answer in one only was primary while that to the other was not applicable to our categories.

III. *Mixed:* Patients who were "mixed" in their orientation, i. e., who gave one primary and one instrumental answer.

We must now ask whether there is a significant difference in the adaptation to hospital demands between the patients who had a primary and those who had an instrumental orientation with regard to such demands.

The following seem to be some important conditions imposed on the patient:

a. That he forfeit his reliance on family and friends in the matter most important to him at the moment, his health. From the time he enters the hospital, those who have been closest to him will be "vistors," i. e., strangers, and those who are strange to the patient will have control over his person.

b. That he accept the "routine" and "order" of the hospital as defined by nurses and doctors and that he accept the hospital setting *as is,* i. e., as something that is not subject to his interference.

c. That he attempt to be a "good patient." This means, in terms of doctors' and nurses' expectations, that he not complain, that he submit to rules and regulations without making any personal claims.

We shall now examine some ways in which the three types of patients differ with regard to the three "adaptability factors" discussed above.

We shall try to show that with regard to these three demands made on the patients,

those who have a primary orientation toward the hospital or the doctor are more likely to comply, at least to judge from their responses to the formal interview, than those who have an instrumental orientation. The primary orientation is functional, it will be seen, for responding to hospital authority.

In order to find out whether some patients forfeited their reliance on family and friends and gave up, generally, their non-patient role, we shall consider the patients' answers to the question: "What do you miss most while you're in the hospital?"

To find out whether patients accepted the hospital setting as something that was defined by others and was not subject to their own interference, we shall consider the patients' responses to the question: "Are there any suggestions that you would care to make for a possible improvement of the patients' comfort?"

Finally, we shall examine the patients' images of a "good patient," to find out whether they agree that patients should submit to rules and regulations without making any personal claims.

If we analyze the answers to the question, "What do you miss most while in the hospital?" we find that the responses can be classified into the following types:

a. Twenty-four patients missed those things or people that determined their roles in their non-hospitalized condition. Mrs. Thompson said that she missed her "freedom." Miss Terrini, who lived at home with her mother and supported her, said that she missed her mother, and Mr. Thomas, a father, missed his "little boy, eight and one-half." Mrs. Miller, a mother, missed husband and daughter; 68-year-old grandmother Mann missed her grandchildren. The high-school girl, Miss Bluestein, missed her friends, and the homemaker, Mrs. Wood, missed "husband, child, household," and said "work is waiting for me; I wasn't relaxed enough to look at television."

b. Eleven patients missed things that assured their own bodily comfort, such as food, liquor, smoking, and things that can be considered "body extensions," i. e., belongings and especially clothes. Mrs. Stephanos missed food. Mrs. Goldman, age 51, said that she missed "nothing more than what I have here. I mean I like nice clothes to wear . . . " Mr. Finkelstein, who lived with his daughter and her family, seemed to exemplify the type of person whose primary concern is his body when he explained what he missed most: "First thing, I have a good bed [i. e., at home]. Second thing, I got a bathroom next to me. Third thing, I eat too much in the hospital. Today they had some kind of lamb, that's all I ate, meat, vegetables, bread, a cup of tea, that's all."

As Table 30-2 indicates, the differential awareness of wants is related to the patients' differential orientation toward hospital or doctor.

Patients whom we have called "instrumental" in their orientations toward hospital or doctor were more likely to miss people or activity while in the hospital than patients whom we have called "primary" in their attitudes.

We have reason to suspect that the patient who enjoyed the "care and attention" in the hospital and expected solace from doctors was better able to meet the demand that he "forget about" his former duties and responsibilities and forfeit his reliance on relatives and friends.

We should now try to ascertain whether the patients who were interviewed accepted the hospital setting as given, whether they accepted rules and regulations not so much because they were forced to but because they considered the rules "good," whether they questioned the daily routine of the hospital or whether, in Erich Fromm's words, they *"wanted* to do what they *had* to do."[5] We will now

TABLE 30-2.   ATTITUDE TOWARD HOSPITAL OR DOCTOR
BY REPORTED DEPRIVATION

	Attitude Toward Hospital or Doctor				
Miss Most:	*Instrumental*	*Mixed*	*Primary*	*N.A.*	*Total*
People, activity	14	2	8	0	24
Belongings, intake, nothing	4	2	13	1	20
N.A. (not applicable)	3	0	4	0	7
Total	21	4	25	1	51

Nine patients simply said that they didn't miss anything. When Mrs. Kit was asked whether there was anything she missed while in the hospital, she said, "No, I don't miss nothing," and Mr. Goldman, who lived with his wife and was a foreman in a bakery, said "I got everything, I don't need nothing, you press the button, the nurse is right there."

The answers to these questions were therefore divided into two main groups: (a) those who express the need for activity or interaction, and (b) those who express no such need or are concerned with bodily and passive gratification.

consider the answers to the question: "Do you have any suggestions for the improvement of the patient's comfort?"

Two types of patients emerge: those who had nothing to suggest as improvements for

---

[5] Cf. Bettelheim, who says that in a concentration camp (which has in common with the hospital that it is a restrictive community, that the residents do not leave the confines, that basic things, such as food and shelter, are provided without the subjects' initiative, and that the residents live in fear of their well-being), the inmates after some time accept the norms of those in command.[1]

TABLE 30-3. ATTITUDE TOWARD HOSPITAL OR DOCTOR
BY WILLINGNESS TO MAKE SUGGESTIONS

Made Suggestions	Attitude Toward Hospital or Doctor				
	Instrumental	Mixed	Primary	N.A.	Total
Yes	14	2	7	0	23
No	4	2	16	1	23
N.A.	3	0	2	0	5
Total	21	4	25	1	51

the patients' comfort, even after being probed;[6] and those who, often after being probed, made some suggestions for a change in routine. The suggestions range from "larger washroom," "better television set," "more visiting time," to "less talk among nurses," "brighter coloring on the walls," "waking at a later hour."

As Table 30-3 shows, respondents who had no suggestions to make for the improvement of the patients' comfort were likely to have a primary attitude toward hospital or doctor, while those who made some suggestion tended to have an instrumental approach.

Out of the 18 instrumentally oriented patients who answered the question about suggestions, 14 had a concrete suggestion to make, while out of the 23 primary-oriented patients who answered this question, only 7 had a suggestion to make. Mr. Flowerman seems to be representative of the patient who had a primary orientation and identified with those in authority. He enjoyed the attention he received in the hospital, expected the "good doctor" to "talk nice," missed "smoking," and had

this to say: "I would like to smoke. But it wouldn't be right. If I were in charge, I wouldn't let anybody smoke, either." Mr. Flowerman, when asked whether he had any suggestions for improvement of the patients' comfort, gave indication of not understanding the question. When he was probed — "Suppose you were on the board of directors of the hospital, could you think of any recommendations?" — he said, "Everything is as it should be. They have a television here, of course now it's out of order. What more could they do? They have a waiting room. What more could you want? They change beds for me . . . At home you can't get that attention, you can't change your bed every day."

It is worthy of note that, in answer to this question, six patients stated their identification with hospital authority in the following terms: "The hospital is being run how they see fit," "Patients shouldn't talk," "I don't think a patient should make suggestions," "Everything is as it should be," "The doctors know what's best," and "[Patients have] to obey orders." *All of these patients were of the primary type.*

We have implied that the patient's inability to make suggestions for the improvement of hospital routine is an indication of his acceptance of the hospital's norms. However, we would feel on surer grounds if we could discover yet another manifestation of the patient's identification with those in authority.

The responses to the question, "What makes a good patient?" may serve us well here.

In the analysis of the answer to this question, we want to find out whether the respondents have expectations as to the behavior of patients that are similar to the

---

[6] It is interesting to note that the idea that the patient has no say is often so internalized that, more frequently than not, the interviewer's question about suggestions was not understood. The respondent had a questioning look, or simply said "everything is all right," but he indicated that this is something he had never even thought about. Therefore, a probe was attempted whenever the patient seemed not to understand. The probe consisted in asking specifically about those things which were objects of gripes on the ward, like not sleeping enough, being awakened early, inadequate food, etc. If even after probing, the patient did not say that changes in hospital routine would be desirable, he was classified as having nothing to suggest.

expectations of doctors and nurses. In our interviews with nurses and doctors, we found that the latter, for the most part, expected the patients "to be quiet," "not to ask" and "not to complain." We now want to find whether the patients themselves, in their evaluations of patients' behavior, use criteria of submission to rules and regulations rather than criteria indicating concern for "self-determination." In other words, we are interested in finding out whether the respondent granted the patient in the hospital ward some degree of "autonomy" or whether he considered hospital rules as absolutes to which the patient must submit unquestioningly.

The concept of autonomy is here used in the sense in which Jean Piaget first defined it. In his *The Moral Judgment of the Child* [10], Piaget distinguishes between "heteronomous" and "autonomous" authority. People who have a heteronomous conception of authority feel that rules and regulations emanate from a power *outside* of the social relations within which they are applied. They hold that rules cannot be changed and must be accepted *in toto* without questioning. On the other hand, persons who have an autonomous conception of authority feel that rules are made by people who interact with each other and can be changed, through agreement, by those who participate in the "game." According to these persons, rules can be judged and evaluated and changed by those who comply with them.

Piaget shows that, in order to be autonomous, individuals must develop a sense of "reciprocity."[8,10] They must be able to put themselves, in their imagination, in the position of the other participants, in the interaction. Two corollaries derive from this: (1) The autonomous judgment of "good" or "bad" derives from the consideration of the point of view of the actor;[7] good and bad are not absolute standards, but are relative to the actor's intention and to his ability to assume responsibility (2) Social interaction can proceed smoothly only if each party organizes his own behavior in accordance with his expectations of the other party in the "game."[8]

Autonomous behavior, then, according to Piaget's theory, consists in self-sufficiency of the individual, his ability to judge "good" and "bad" deeds from the point of view of the actor, and his ability to interact with others on the basis of their positions and intentions.

These criteria of autonomy may serve us well in the classification of the responses to the question, "What makes a good patient?" The concern for "autonomy" on the part of the respondents in their answers to this question was expressed in different ways.

a. Some respondents felt that "you got to help yourself," that a patient should be "self-sufficient as much as possible." Mrs. Hardman felt that "the patient has to do a lot himself. Patients should help themselves. They can't follow completely ... " Mrs. Bowman felt that a good patient is one who "understands the doctor ... [he must] know what it's all about."

b. The autonomous approach to the patient's role may be expressed in an indirect way. Some respondents claimed that the attribute of "goodness" makes sense only if considered from the point of view or the condition of the individual patient. Thus, Mr. Hailos felt that "that depends on the age ... it also depends on their education .... " Mrs. Nathan stated:

I say this much, the patient can be good, she wants relief and I can't blame her. I've seen some pesty patients, they holler and yell but they feel that someone can help them. If there's any spark of life in you, you try to fight, but if you are desperately ill you can't fight.

Mr. Geoffrey also felt that the patient's "goodness" depends on his own ability to make judgments. He said,

If a patient knows what's the matter, if they take off a piece from his finger [shows his finger

---

[7] This philosophy is the basis of modern criminology.

[8] George Herbert Mead has elaborated especially on this aspect of reciprocity in social relations: "The child who plays in a game must be ready to take the attitude of everybody else involved in that game ... The child taking one role must be ready to take the role of everyone else ... [6]

which was partially amputated previously], he knows what's wrong, he can be a good patient; but if his stomach hurts him and it's inside and he doesn't know what's going on, he can't be a good patient.

c. Finally, some respondents expected of the patient that he be "considerate," "cooperative," etc. Although at first sight these answers seem to belong to a different dimension of classification, we feel reasonably justified in interpreting them as an expectation of an attitude of reciprocity in Piaget's sense discussed above. Thus, if Mrs. Smith felt that a patient should be "nice ... it takes two to be nice, it takes two to make the bargain, you got to be understandable that a person can do only so much," she implied that a patient, to be good, must put himself, in his imagination, in the position of the other partners in the relationship. We have therefore decided that answers of respondents who consider the patient "good" if he is "cooperative," "considerate," etc., should be classified together with the two first types of responses as "autonomous." Although we are very well aware of the fact that, in everyday language, "cooperation" is an undefined term and may often be a polite term for "obedience," we still felt that these responses differed significantly from those of some patients who felt that a good patient is one who "keeps quiet," who "keeps his mouth shut,"etc.

Indeed, in contradistinction to the three types of responses outlined above, there was another type of answer, which revealed that the interviewees did not allow for any leeway in the decision-making of the patient himself. Thus, Mrs. Cherry felt that patients are good "when they lie in bed and keep their mouth shut . . . . "; Mrs. Norman said that a patient should "do what he is told"; Mrs. Kane thought a good patient "is one who keeps his mouth shut"; Mr. Walnut felt that he must "just behave himself." These respondents implied that nothing but the most submissive behavior is appropriate for the patient.

If we divide our respondents into two groups, those who expected some degree of autonomy of the patient and those who expected complete submission, and compare these two groups with respect to their expectations of hospital or doctor, we find that those who were instrumental in their orientation toward hospital or doctor were more likely to grant some degree of autonomy to patients than were those whose attitude toward doctor or hospital was primary (Table 30-4).

Respondents who granted some autonomy to patients were more likely to consider the hospital as a place to "do a job" or to judge the doctor from the point of view of his professional competence than were respondents who expected patients to be submissive to hospital demands. The latter were more likely to expect from the hospital or the doctor gratification of primary needs of attention, care, or fatherly behavior.

In the preceding pages we have tried to throw some light on the question of whether the patients' attitudes toward doctor and hospital generally were related to their acceptance of deprivation and restrictions imposed by the hospital structure. More specifically, we found that patients who had primary orientations toward the hospital or doctor were more likely to accept hospital norms.

TABLE 30-4. ATTITUDES TOWARD HOSPITAL OR DOCTOR BY CONCEPTION OF THE GOOD PATIENT

| A Good Patient Should Be: | Attitude Toward Hospital or Doctor | | | | |
	Instrumental	Mixed	Primary	N.A.	Total
Autonomous	17	2	8	0	27
Submissive	3	2	15	0	20
N.A.	1	0	2	1	4
Total	21	4	25	1	51

In response to all these questions — "What do you miss most while in the hospital?" "Do you have any suggestions to make for the improvement of patients' comfort?" and "What is your idea of a good patient?" — patients who expected gratification of primary needs were more likely to answer in terms of adaptation to the demands of the hospital structure than patients who considered hospital or doctor from an instrumental point of view. Patients with a primary orientation more frequently said that they did not miss anything in the hospital or that they missed objects for bodily and passive gratification; they tended to accept the hospital setting as "given" and not to have any suggestion to make for the improvement of the patient's comfort; and they more often than not expected patients to be submissive to the demands of doctors and nurses.

While patients' primary orientations toward hospital or doctor seem to be associated with adaptability to their sick role in the ward, we should now like to turn our attention to some dysfunctional consequences of such adaptability.

For the definition of the patient's social role, we have accepted Parsons' analysis of the sick role: the patient is exempted from usual responsibilities, he is in a condition that must be "taken care of." The sick person is not, by institutional definition, competent to help himself. He is generally in a position in which he cannot do what is to be done, and more specifically, he does not know what is to be done. He must follow doctors' orders and must let others in his environment make decisions about him.[9]

As Parsons also points out, however, one element of the definition of the patient's role is its "undesirability," with its "obligations to want to get well."[9] Inherent in the patient role, then, is also its negation. What Everett Hughes has to say about some occupational roles applies here: frequently in the occupational realm, the success of a role performance consists precisely in the eventual abandonment of that very role.[3] If this is true in some occupations whose exercise is a necessary social activity, it is even more true in the case of the patient, whose condition is considered socially undesirable. In the hospital structure, where the doctor is endeavoring to be "more of a doctor" and the nurse tries to be "more of a nurse," the patient is expected to be "less of a patient" as hospitalization draws nearer to the end. It is for the sake of his speedy recovery, i.e., for the creation of a situation in which the sick role can be abandoned, that the restrictions imposed on the sick person are given justification. A good patient, as defined in society, is not only one who submits to medical and nursing authority, but one who gets well quickly and then is ready to take up his everyday activities.

In the hospital (as elsewhere in our culture), a patient who makes a speedy recovery is praised as being a "good girl" or "good boy," not only because his getting well is an indication of his obedience to doctors' instructions, but because he gets ready to move out of the patient's role and to assume again a life of social usefulness. Getting ready to abandon the patient role is inherent in this role, and someone who "refuses to get better" is considered a bad patient. Thus, a patient whose relapse prevented him from being discharged on the expected day greeted me one morning with the following words: "I was a bad boy today. Three days ago the doctor said I can go home in a few days. Today I started bleeding again."

We are justified in wondering whether complete adjustment to the requirements of the hospital structure makes it more difficult for patients to move out of their sick role. This patient, who had a relapse after hearing of his oncoming discharge, had made a "good adjustment" to the hospital in the estimation of doctors and nurses. He felt that "the doctors know best what is good" and that it is not up to the patient to make suggestions, and that the patient should be submissive. While he was hospitalized, he described the process of his adaptation in the following words:

The first two weeks I was here, I was very impatient to go home. But now, I figure it's better to be here; this way, I'll really get better. After all, *they* have so much experience, *they* know better, *they* are running the hospital.

This patient accepted the norms of the hospital. But it is significant that at discharge he said with a smile: [At home] my wife has my bed all made for me," thus indicating that he relished the idea of continuing to play the sick role.

We don't know whether this patient's relapse was the result of his psychological unwillingness to leave the sheltered hospital atmosphere. But there certainly were patients in the ward of whom the doctors said, "He likes it here too well," or "This patient has hospitalitis; each time we tell her she can go home; her blood pressure shoots up sky-high." Although such patients were generally liked by doctors and nurses because, they said, "she is so sweet," or "he's a really good patient, he never complains," such liking of the patient was never without ambivalence.

A patient who "enjoys it here too much" was looked at with suspicion because he contradicts the cultural definition of the patient, which is a suffering role, as the etymology of the word indicates. Moreover, the sick person allows both doctors and nurses to do a job: to get him better. If the patient refuses to move out of his sick role, however, or comes back again and again, doctors and nurses are robbed of the satisfaction of a job well done.

The patient who likes the ward is easily suspected of not being very sick. This suspicion is sometimes justified. As one patient put it:

I just came in because I wanted a checkup. From time to time I want my diet straightened out. It gives me a fresh start. As a matter of fact, I don't mind going to the hospital, I like the ward.

These patients are getting a free ride, so to speak; they are getting something for nothing, and, what is more, they hurt the self-esteem of doctors and nurses, whose efforts to cure them seem to be in vain. One nurse expressed well the staff's concern about the patient who "likes" the hospital. She said "[The patients] should have more diversional therapy . . . . but when you make things too pleasant they won't want to go home."

In order to shed some light on the problem of the patient's readiness to assume again his non-patient role, we asked at discharge at the end of the formal interview, when the patient was in his own street clothes and ready to go home, "Now what will be the first thing you're going to do when you get home?"

The patients' answers to this question were classified into categories similar to those used in classifying the answers to "What do you miss most while in the hospital?" Some patients wanted, first of all, to be with family or friends, or to *do* things they had neglected while sick. Thus, Mr. James said, "Look around at my things . . . . I'll try and get myself a good stick so I can go out in the yard [to see how the beans and tomatoes are growing]," Mrs Brown, a mother of two children, said, "Kiss my son and squeeze him. He's three . . . . I have another one who's only one," and Mrs. Peterson "will make different arrangements around the house so that things will be organized."

Other patients answered in terms of bodily gratification or complete passivity. Mrs. Abrams was going to "take a bath." Mr. Roth said proudly, "My wife has my bed all made for me." Mr. Finkelstein was going to "lie down," and Mrs. Stephanos will "rest, feel everything I have."

According to the criteria of anticipated interaction or action, on the one hand, and bodily gratification or complete passivity on the other, it turned out that more than one-half of the patients interviewed (29 out of 51) did not anticipate resumption of their relations with family or friends. These were the patients who were more likely than the others to consider hospital or doctor as gratifiers of primary needs (Table 30-5).

Patients who considered hospital or doctor in their instrumental functions were more ready to think of some activity or some interaction with those from whom they were separated during hospitalization. On the other hand, the seeking of gratification of primary needs seemed to be associated with the patients' lack of readiness to leave the patient role.

It will be remembered that the latter patients tended to be better adapted to hospital life, since they more frequently than the others did not miss anything pertaining to their everyday life outside the

TABLE 30-5. ATTITUDE TOWARD HOSPITAL OR DOCTOR
BY ANTICIPATED POST-HOSPITAL EXPERIENCE

Anticipated Post-Hospital Experience	Attitude Toward Hospital or Doctor				
	Instrumental	Mixed	Primary	N.A.	Total
Interaction or action	15	1	2	0	18
Bodily gratification or passivity	5	3	20	1	29
N.A.	1	0	3	0	4
Total	21	4	25	1	51

hospital, felt no desire for improvements for patients' comfort, and seemed to identify with the authority in the hospital structure.

Thus, while acceptance of the passive role and the concomitant primary orientation toward the hospital and the doctor seem to be functional for ward adaptation, they are dysfunctional for preparing the patients to leave the sick role and orient themselves toward a life of work and other-directedness.[9]

The apparent contradiction, that patients who adjust better to the demands of hospital efficiency tend to be less prepared than others to take up again activities and intercourse pertaining to their normal lives, seems, at first glance, to be due to the fact that the patients' role obligations are contradictory in themselves. It would seem that the demand that the sick person should let others care for him induces him to passivity, to a state of mind which he might not be ready to abandon for psychological reasons when his physical condition permits him to do so.

We don't think that the problem can be reduced to such simple terms. Rather, we feel that the contradiction inherent in the role of the patient, especially when hospitalized, is only one example — dramatic though it may be — of more general role contradictions in "rational" types of social organization.

We have purposely avoided using, in the construction of the typology in the preceding pages, the term "rational" as denoting a means-ends approach to action. The orientation which we have called "instrumental" is one that might be called "rational," in that it is concerned with the effective means to the end of a cure.

However, the ambiguity of the term led us to abandon it in the preceding presentation. This ambiguity is not a mere semantic one; rather, it expresses the ambiguity of the orientation that the term is supposed to explain. And it is precisely this ambiguity that seems to us to be at the source of the apparently contradictory aspects of patient adaptations.

We can hope to shed some light on the problem if we differentiate, with Karl Mannheim, between substantial and functional rationality. "We understand as substantially rational," says Mannheim, "an act of thought which reveals intelligent insight into the inter-relations of events in a given situation."[5, p. 53] Patients whom we have called "instrumental" in their orientation showed some insight into the inter-relations between means of hospitalization and competence and the desired result of a medical cure. They tended to be "substantially rational."

However, we have seen that these patients were less ready than the non-instrumental patients to accept the demand that they relinquish autonomous judgment of hospital procedure. Complete subordination of patients' judgment to the demands of the organization is, in Mannheim's definition of the term, "functionally rational," in that it leads to optimum

---

[9] "Function" and "dysfunction" are here used in terms of Merton's distinction: functions are those observed consequences which make for the adaptation or adjustment of a given system; and dysfunctions, those observed consequences which lessen the adaptation or adjustment of the system.[7]

adaptation to the demands of a structure which is recognized as effective in bringing about the desired cure. "Everything that breaks through and disrupts this functional ordering is functionally irrational." [5, p. 54] A patient who wants to make suggestions to hospital staff and organization, who feels that a sick person must maintain his self-sufficiency, may contribute to the disruption of the functional ordering of hospital procedure. It may be said that patients who attempt to maintain their substantial rationality in the hospital setting are, more than other patients, likely to introduce some disturbance into the functional rationality of the organization.

Mrs. Thompson, a 50-year-old black woman in the surgical ward, is an example in point. She felt that a good doctor would be one "who can tell you what's wrong instead of running back and forth." She said that she "got stuck here for six weeks" and missed her "freedom, and home-made cooking. In a place like this you get mad and have to do things whether you want to or not, abide by rules, accustom to new habits, they take your freedom away from you." Her suggestion was that they get "first of all a new cook. And some doctors who handle you easy and not as if you're made out of iron." The doctors said about her that she "had the whole floor upset," that "she's making trouble for the nurses." The nurse felt that "she's a troublemaker, she's giving the doctor a hard time."[10] At discharge, she talked to me about her work – she was an operator in a factory – and felt that it was a nuisance to have to go to a convalescent home. She added, "I'm not used to anybody waiting on me, fussing over me."

The demands made on the patient seem to be logically consistent. He is asked to relate means to ends; if sick, he should let

others take care of him as a means to getting better. At the same time, he should, as soon as possible, be self-sufficient, so as to be able to carry out his obligations in normal life. The difficulty is, however, that as he gives up his substantial rationality he may not be able to recapture it when his health is restored.

It might be claimed that, in modern society, everybody must, at all times, face such apparently contradictory demands. Moving from one sphere of activity to another – the family, the job, voluntary associations, etc. – individuals must alternate between situations in which they must make their own decisions on the basis of their weighing the relations between means and ends, and situations in which they must conform to decisions made by others in order to maintain or strengthen the functional rationality of the whole. But the very fact that individuals shift rapidly from one attitude to another – a shift which is accompanied by a change of social environment at the same time – puts them in a position, at least for a small part each day, to have to reflect about the consequences of choices that they themselves have to make. This is a situation quite different from the one we are dealing with here. The patient is not expected to make substantially rational choices during the whole length of his stay in the hospital, i.e., as long as he is defined as "sick," so that he may have "unlearned" to make such choices upon discharge. Motives, once internalized, may continue to operate when they are no longer functionally adequate. As Mannheim says,

It is clear that persons who are confronted more frequently with situations in which they cannot act habitually and without thinking and in which they must always organize themselves anew will have more occasion to reflect on themselves and on situations than persons who have adapted themselves once and for all.[5, p. 57]

Corroborative evidence comes from another type of social organization whose members are expected to relinquish autonomous judgment and decision-making for twenty-four hours each day, namely, the army. Willard Waller provides useful insight into the difficulty the soldier faces once he

---

[10] The intern who was in charge of this patient had this to say a week after her discharge: "Did you see Mrs. Thompson coming back for a checkup? You know it's funny, for all the trouble she gave me, I was glad when I saw her. I said 'hello' to her like to an old friend. I kind of miss her on the ward. She sure kept me on my feet."

has to "organize himself anew" in civilian life:

The regimentation of the lives of millions of men involves . . . . some damage to their sense of self and to their power to think for themselves; it involves a redirection of their emotional life into channels acceptable to the military system. The soldier must form a soldier's habit . . . . learn to eat, sleep, dress, bathe – as a soldier, adjust his sex life to the soldier's necessities. Necessarily, he loses the sense of self-direction. A personality formed by such a milieu is thereby to some extent unfitted for civilian life.[11]

Organizations like the army, the orphanage, the prison, the hospital, have in common the facts that they provide for their members a *home away from home,* that they relieve their members from the burden of decision-making twenty-four hours a day, and that they demand that their members give up substantial rationality in practically all aspects of life in favor of the functional rationality of organizational life.

All such institutions [Waller says] rob the individual of his sense of self-direction and ultimately damage the capacity for it. Virtue in such institutions consists in having no preference about many things; in eating whatever is put on the table, in wearing what one is told to wear, in going to bed and rising again according to instructions, in making the best of things. The

good institution member does not make choices or decisions. He submits and permits himself to be carried along, as it were, in a "moral automobile." When he returns to civilian life, his suddenly uncorseted soul seems flabby and incapable of standing alone.[11]

Mannheim's insight quoted above, that a person's ability to "organize himself anew" is related to the *degree* to which he is exposed to an environment which demands unquestioning and unreflective behavior, introduces the problem of *intensity* as well as *length of time* of regimentation. There doubtless is a difference in the intensity of regimentation between an army and a general hospital, as well as a difference in the duration of the individual's exposure; in the army, the individual spends a larger part of his life than does the patient in the ward of a general hospital.[11]

Further research is indicated to ascertain the effects of different degrees of regimentation (in different types of wards, for example) as well as the consequences of variations in its duration or frequency. In this way, one might hope to throw further light on the differential adaptation of patients to hospital demands as well as on their differential re-adaptation to their non-patient roles.

REFERENCES

1. Bettelheim, Bruno: "Individual and Mass Behavior in Extreme Situations," *Journal of Abnormal and Social Psychology, 38:* 417–452, 1943.
2. Davis, Kingsley: *Human Society,* The Macmillan Company, New York, 1949, pp. 295–297.
3. Hughes, Everett C.: seminar notes, University of Chicago, 1949.
4. Lewin, Jurt: *Field Theory in Social Science,* Harper & Brothers, New York, 1951, p. 87.
5. Mannheim, Karl: *Man and Society in an Age of Reconstruction,* Routledge & Kegan Paul, Ltd., London, 1940.
6. Mead, George Herbert: *Mind, Self, and Society,* University of Chicago Press, Chicago, 1934, p. 151.
7. Merton, Robert K.: *Social Theory and Social Structure,* Free Press, Glencoe, Ill., 1949, p. 50.
8. Odier, Charles: *L'Angoisse et la pensée magique,* Delachaux et Niestle, Neuchatel-Paris, 1947.
9. Parsons, Talcott: *The Social System,* Free Press, Glencoe, Ill., 1951.
10. Piaget, Jean: *The Moral Judgment of the Child,* Free Press, Glencoe, Ill., 1948.
11. Waller, Willard: *The Veteran Comes Back,* The Dryden Press, New York, 1944, p. 191.

[11] On the other hand, the hospital patient is less mobile than the soldier. He can never leave the building and is bedridden during at least the largest part of his stay.

Interbehavioral Foundations of Medicine: The Relationship Perspective

XI INTERBEHAVIORAL CONCEPTS AND VIEWPOINTS

As we turn to the study of interbehavioral processes we begin to approach the core of our subject. Despite the diverse character of much that typifies the work of the medical behavioral scientist, he must always connect these activities to the web of relations that men weave with one another. It is within this sphere of interpersonal behavior that medical and behavioral science are most closely linked.

Interbehavioral events exist whenever people are mutually aware of or directly interact with one another; such relations are the essence of our everyday social activities. The physician engaged in examining his patient, the intern issuing orders and the nurse obeying them, the clinic consultant evaluating student diagnostic procedures — all of these, if studied in terms of how each member of the pair behaves towards the other, are interbehavioral events.

Interbehavioral processes are given their structure by socially accepted customs and traditionally defined rights. These customs and rights are implicitly shared or explicitly acknowledged by the participants. The professional relation between a doctor and his patient can be viewed as a traditional interbehavioral system since it is determined by well established customs concerning the roles and duties each is expected to perform, be it in the office, clinic, or hospital.

The concept of communication represents the medium through which interbehavioral events occur. At the most basic level, communication serves the function of conveying information between persons, such as when a patient asks his physician for an appointment and receives a schedule of alternative times. For the greater part, however, communications of interest to the behavioral scientist and physician are more subtle or complex than merely transmitting information.

Among the more interesting functions of communication is that of creating an impression upon others, such as acting poised and self-assured or weak and sickly. Interbehavioral communication is also employed to achieve control over others; for example, when a physician recommends optional surgery, the patient either follows this advice with its attendant life adjustments or decides not to pursue the recommendation with the usual anxieties as to future consequences.

Interbehavioral events are transmitted through several communication channels other than direct verbal message. Even within the voice channel itself such dimensions as tone, inflection, and silence play a role in conveying intentions and moods beyond the mere words themselves. Body language, as expressed in gestures, posture, eye contact, and facial expression, is another major form of communication; to illustrate, tensely suspicious patients can often be observed to sit in a rigid posture while scanning the environment with quick, darting eye movements. Not to be overlooked are other visual communication cues such as those of dress and grooming; for example, a 50 year old female patient who wears a seductive dress more suitable on a 20 year old actress is conveying aspects of her idealized self-image and social needs to the observant physician; conversely, an attractive 20 year old who dresses in an overly plain manner is telling quite a different story about herself. There are other nonverbal forms of interbehavioral communication that transmit clear messages of intent; the eye-wink, the authoritative handshake, the shaken fist, the affectionate arm about the shoulder, all convey attitudes and other intimations that are "read" by alert observers and create a mood for interpreting more explicitly phrased verbal messages. Another, essentially implicit form of communication is imparted through status symbols such as the physician's white coat, the policeman's uniform, or the wealthy person's limousine. These obvious but unspoken symbols carry a message or establish a hierarchy in the relationship that is well understood by all involved.

The first paper of this chapter, by Tannenbaum, Wechsler, and Massarik, presents a comprehensive analysis of the process of "understanding people." Their carefully reasoned study focuses on the interaction of the perceiver and perceived, with special attention paid to a phenomenon of critical significance to the physician — empathy. The concept of empathy is derived from the German word *Einfühlung* and literally means "feeling oneself into another person." The capacity to sense the inner thoughts and feelings of one's patients is an extremely important trait among young physicians. However, as one acquires a measure of poise in the process of learning to comfort and treat painfully ill or dying patients, medical students often become hardened to human suffering, the antithesis of empathic sensitivity. Fortunately, with increased experience and maturity, a proper balance usually emerges between these contrasting characteristics.

The second paper, by Leonard Schatzman and Anselm Strauss, two distinguished medical sociologists, reports on their research into divergent styles of communication that typify persons from different socioeconomic classes. Extrapolating from their work, it would seem wise that physicians become sensitive to the often contrasting styles of thought and communication of patients from diverse social strata. Knowledge of these qualities is particularly relevant since physicians and patients often come from markedly different economic classes and minority group backgrounds.

The final paper recounts the findings of a study carried out with hospitalized patients by a distinguished nursing educator, Ruth G. Elder. She reports that most patients fail to adequately communicate their needs for assistance to hospital personnel. The reasons proposed for this difficulty are many and varied. Serious medical students would do well to recognize these constraints upon patient communications so as to fulfill their roles and responsibilities more effectively.

31   The Process of Understanding People

Robert Tannenbaum, Irving R. Weschler, and Fred Massarik

Mike Corey walked into his office, fifteen minutes behind schedule. Through the glass partition Mike caught a glimpse of his boss. Arthur Blick looked up briefly as Mike slid into his chair. A number of signs obscured the full view: "Tomorrow We Finally Have to Get Organized," "THIMK," "Wait Till Next Time — You Have Done Enough Damage for Now." Mike tried to look inconspicuous, though his mind was working rapidly. He was late for the third straight day. Oh, there were good reasons all right . . . one day his wife needed to be driven downtown and *she* wasn't ready — one day he had a terrible headache . . . and then . . . today . . . His thoughts shifted abruptly — it really didn't matter as long as Blick was in a good mood. Mike had some very definite ideas about what kind of guy his boss was. Usually he wasn't a bad sort; businesslike, but human too. If you had a big problem, he probably would listen. Still he was so darn changeable, and you had to hit him "just right" if you wanted to get along. This morning Blick seemed preoccupied . . . he looked up as if he hardly saw you, yet the way he spun back to his desk telegraphed "bad news."

This was Jean Krugmeier's first day on her job. She liked being an employment interviewer. People were interesting, and it would be a novel experience to sit behind a desk all day. The initial two interviews proceeded uneventfully. The third applicant wanted to be foreman of the shipping gang. He was a young, burly 250-pounder who said that he used to work in the steel mills near Gary. He spoke loudly, with much self-assurance. "Some sort of a bully — a leering Casanova of the hot-rod set," Jean thought. Jean always did dislike guys like this, especially this sort of massive redhead. Just like her kid brother used to be — "a real pest!" The more he bragged about his qualifications, the more Jean became annoyed. It wouldn't do to let her feelings show; interviewers are supposed to be friendly and objective. She smiled sweetly, even if she did have a mild suspicion that her antagonism might be coming through. "I am sorry, we cannot use you just now," she said. "You don't seem to have the kind of experience we are looking for. But we'll be sure to keep your application in the

active file and call you as soon as something comes up. Thank you for thinking of applying with us."

LOOKING AT SOCIAL PERCEPTION

These anecdotes serve to illustrate the all-pervasive role that *social perception* plays in our lives. Forming impressions of people is a part of our daily experience, yet we rarely single out the process for explicit consideration.[1]

Mike Corey was very much concerned with making the correct perceptual assessment of Arthur Blick's mood for the morning. Of course, he reacted without specifically worrying about his *empathy*.[2] He did what came naturally. The physical

---

[1] The area covered by this chapter has been subject to systematic study only in very recent years. It is still much in flux, and few findings of certainty are as yet available. As we seek to lay out some of the problems, methods, and results with which this research is concerned, we are much aware of the tentative nature of our comments. The technically inclined reader is urged to examine Tagiuri, R., and Petrullo, L.: *Person Perception and Interpersonal Behavior.* Stanford, Calif.; Stanford University Press, 1958; Heider, F.: *Psychology of Interpersonal Relations.* New York; John Wiley and Sons, Inc., 1958; and Bronfenbrenner, U., Harding, J., and Gallwey, M. The measurement of skill in social perception. In McClelland, D. C. et al.: *Talent and Society.* Princeton, N. J., D. Van Nostrand Company, Inc., 1958.

[2] In this context, we shall treat as synonymous the concepts *empathy, understanding of people, social sensitivity,* and *accuracy in social perception.*

Tannenbaum, R., Weschler, I. R., and Massarik, F.: The process of understanding people. In Tannenbaum, R. et al.: Leadership and Organization: A Behavioral Science Approach. New York, McGraw-Hill, 1961.

obstructions in the glass partition between the two offices were not the only barriers between these men. Mike's own views, attitudes, and feelings contributed to the difficulties, and so in turn did Blick's behavior, which provided Mike with only a limited amount of information (or *cues*). The fact that the entire relationship was set in the context of a given office situation both aided and impeded the extent to which Mike Corey could accurately perceive the relevant aspects of his boss's personality.

Jean Krugmeier probably does not think of herself as a prejudiced person. She may associate the term "prejudice" primarily with racial intolerance. She argues vociferously that people must have an "open mind." Still, like all of us, she too has "blind spots" and uses "shortcut thinking," which gives her a distorted picture of reality. Her feelings about burly redheaded men are very much like any other prejudice. They are supported by a *stereotype* that, in essence, says: "All of them are alike!" Thus, Jean's feelings may be irrational, her mind may be closed, and her social perception less than accurate because she subconsciously prevents relevant information about people "of this sort" from reaching her.

The Illusion of Objectivity

Most of us pride ourselves on our ability to look at people in a dispassionate, objective manner. Yet the psychological realities are that every time we have a personal contact we *do* form favorable or unfavorable impressions that influence our social behavior. We all have some positive or negative feeling in our interpersonal experiences. We *do* like or dislike in varying degrees, even if we are not always willing or able to recognize our true feelings.

Social perception is the means by which people form impressions of and, hopefully, understand one another. *Empathy,* or *social sensitivity* is the extent to which they succeed in developing *accurate impressions,*

or actual understanding, of others.[3] Social perception is not always rational or conscious; thus it follows that empathy is not necessarily the result of conscious, rational effort. For some, it may just seem to "happen," while others may develop it only after much training, and living experience.

Three basic aspects of social perception must be considered: (1) *the perceiver,* the person who is "looking" and attempting to understand; (2) *the perceived,* the person who is being "looked at" or understood; and (3) *the situation,* the total setting of social and nonsocial forces within which the act of social perception is lodged. We have already encountered "perceivers" Mike Corey and Jean Krugmeier, and their respective "perceived" counterparts, Arthur Blick and the burly job applicant.

The Perceivers and the Perceived

Perceivers and perceived need not be single individuals. Entire *social groupings* may do the "looking" or may be "looked at." We can, for example, conceive of the social perceptions existing between two rival departments of a corporation, with each department viewing the other with possible hostility or competitive jealousy. Similarly, we may distinguish social perceptions among small work groups, among large companies, and even among nations. Indeed, any group of people, as well as any given person, can be a principal participant in the process of social perception.

The perceiver and perceived are not billiard balls on a flat table top. Their

---

[3] Many complexities are involved in the actual measurement of social sensitivity. The definition given here is a kind of practical short cut, useful for most everyday applications. For a consideration of the conceptual issues, see, for example, Gage, N. L. and Cronbach, L. J.: Conceptual and methodological problems in interpersonal perception. *Psychol. Rev.* 62: 411-22 (1955), and Cronbach, L. J.: Processes affecting scores on understanding of others' and assumed similarity. *Psychol. Bull.,52:* 177-93 (1955).

interactions do not usually produce obvious one-to-one cause-and-effect relations, for the perceived and the perceiver both possess personalities of great complexity. Social perception develops in the give and take among these *personalities in action.*

What is termed "personality" for the individual may be viewed as a unique pattern of "group characteristics" for the social grouping, be it work group, department, company, or nation. This pattern does not result from a simple addition of the personalities of individual members, although these individual personalities do have an impact. Rather, the social grouping's "personality" results from its formal and informal traditions, and from its accepted ways of "doing things." For example, some groups operate rigidly "according to the book"; others are more flexible and freewheeling. Some groups are highly integrated, with close and supportive relationships existing among their members; others are torn by antagonistic cliques and by intense rivalries. Some groups set high and constant standards for the admission of new members; others are more open and lax in their membership requirements.[4]

Patterns of Perceiving

The process of social perception can be graphically portrayed in a variety of ways. If I stands for "individual," and G for any "grouping" of individuals (and if the arrow stands for the act of perceiving), we may consider such relations as the following:

Type		Perceiver to perceived
A	I → I	(individual to individual)
B	I → G	(individual to grouping)
C	G → I	(grouping to individual)
D	G → G	(grouping to grouping)

---

[4] Among the better-known approaches to the analysis of the personality of a group is that of Hemphill, J. K. and Westie, C. M.: The measurement of group dimensions. *Journal of Psychol. 29:* 325–42 (1950). Many sociologists have also made important contributions in this area; see, for example, Dubin, R.: *The World of Work.* Englewood Cliffs, N.J., Prentice-Hall, Inc., 1958, and Dalton, M.: *Men Who Manage.* New York, John Wiley and Sons, Inc., 1959.

Our anecdotes were of the type A variety — one individual perceiving another individual. Jean Krugmeier's perception of the job applicant, however, was influenced by a type B perception, her view of all burly, red-headed men — a view that she as an individual held for a broader (though tenuous) grouping of persons. Under conditions beyond those already described, Mike Corey may be perceived in a type C relationship by his fellow employees, a grouping that may view him with envy and anger because of his ability to get away with lateness without apparent untoward consequences.

Type D perceptions become important particularly in attempts to analyze the nature of complex organizations, such as large sections or departments, entire firms, or other entities composed of various subgroups.

The four types of perceptual processes noted so far are relatively straightforward: type A, interindividual perception; type B, an individual's perception of a grouping; type C, a grouping's perception of an individual; and type D, intergroup perception. Yet in each type countless obvious as well as hidden distortions can and do occur which prevent the perceiver from obtaining a faithful image. These breakdowns in communications, which we shall need to explore further at a later point, magnify their effects when we consider what might be termed *higher-order perception.*

As Mike Corey, for instance, forms his perceptions of Arthur Blick, he also considers the way in which Blick reciprocates. In other words, Corey is very much concerned to know how Blick feels about him. Corey makes assumptions about Blick's view of him which may or may not be correct. He may "think" that Blick hardly saw him, when — if he were to probe Blick's true reaction — he might learn that Blick saw Corey very well indeed and was actively annoyed with his repeated tardiness. The extent to which one accurately recognizes someone else's reactions to oneself defines a special kind of social sensitivity — the ability to assess correctly what another person "thinks" about you.

Above, we are dealing with a "perception of a perception." We may conceive of a theoretically infinite series of social perceptions that begin as follows:

1. First-order perceptions: how the perceiver views the perceived (as illustrated by types A, B, C, and D).
2. Second-order perceptions: how the perceiver "thinks" the perceived views the perceiver.
3. Third-order perceptions: how the perceiver "thinks" the perceived views "the perceiver's perception of the perceived," etc.

By the time we reach third-order perceptions, the pattern has become immensely problematical. Any further higher order adds to the complexity. Fortunately, most of our actual perceptions governing interactions with others probably do not get more involved than those defined by the first or second order.

One Empathy — or Many?

There may be several different "empathies." Some perceivers seem more skillful in seeing beneath the surface and in ferreting our correct perceptions from vast networks of superficial psychological defenses. Others are more capable in hurdling the abyss that separates their actual observations of cues from the more remote recesses of behavior that they are seeking to understand. Some excel in painstakingly accumulating fragments of perceptual evidence and piecing them together. Others have a unique capacity for the elegant sweep that pulls together quickly and accurately a broad complexity of social phenomena.

Understanding social groupings rather than individuals involves unique problems and may require different skills of perception from those needed in understanding individuals. The talent for sizing up group opinion is probably different from the "diagnostic skills" needed for understanding a specific employee. An executive of a large corporation, for instance, may excel in accurately assessing opinions and attitudes of union and work force, but he may need to sharpen his skills in empathizing with his fellow corporate officers.

The probable existence of several "empathies" is not surprising if we consider the diversity of the factors at work. We have available a tremendous variety of cues that we may draw on in order to understand how another person thinks or feels, and these make differential demands upon our skills to draw inferences that will yield accurate perceptions.

Cues: Raw Material of Perceiving

Cues are often direct: through words, gestures, facial expressions, and specific behavioral acts, they are transmitted to the perceiver (interpreter) directly by the perceived (communicator), sometimes consciously, sometimes subconsciously. At other times, the perceiver gets his insights secondhand — as by gossip, through reference letters, or by comments overheard during a coffee break.

Some cues are more obvious in their apparent meaning. A broad smile and a friendly hello usually reflect a clear expression of personal warmth, while a vague wave of the hand is considerably more ambiguous and thus more difficult to interpret.

Some cues are more clear-cut than others. A girl's approximate age — the beautician's art notwithstanding — is likely to be more easily assessable than the meaning of a Mona Lisa-like smile; and despite best intentions, it may be virtually impossible to base an analysis of a person's basic psychological motivations on a casual martini-clouded social contact.

The psychological leap to be made from the cues available to what we seek to understand presents another consideration. As Mike Corey viewed his boss Blick, he had knowledge of Blick's customary office behavior. He had observed Blick before and under roughly similar conditions. Past cues provided a good base of present generalizations. On the other hand, Mike Corey might want to join Blick's country-club set. There he would need some insights into the latter's social behavior. Corey would search for some implicit theory, derived from Blick's on-the-job reactions, the only reactions with which he is actually familiar. He would try to extrapolate from Blick's available pattern of cues into a relatively distant and different situation, and risk empathic failure in the process.

The Perceiver's Background

The perceiver brings to the task of understanding others two sets of inter-related characteristics: (1) his general background, *demographic characteristics;* and (2) his unique self, *personality characteristics.*

Demographic characteristics are those broad sociological aspects of the individual which, for the most part, are easily defin-able, specific, and outside the more subtle ebb and flow of personality as such. Age, sex, nationality, religion, number of siblings, occupation, and economic level are illustrative.

When the psychologist Ronald Taft[5] reviewed studies on the relation of certain demographic attributes to social perceptual skill (especially empathy for individuals rather than for social groupings), he formed conclusions such as the following: (1) ability to judge emotional expression in others increases with age in children, but does not seem to increase further with age in adulthood; (2) sex differences in empa-thy are negligible, but there may be a very slight edge in favor of women.

Thus it seems that when dealing with adults, such as those encountered in busi-ness, age alone provides no free ticket to social perceptual wisdom. Although — hopefully — age may bring increases in some areas of technical knowledge, the process of getting older in and of itself does not lead to heightened empathy. Further, there does not seem to be much substance to the widely held assumption that women are "better judges" of people than men; the controversy on this point is not fully resolved.

More significant relationships emerge from an analysis of dynamic personality characteristics. Taft's attempt to find com-mon threads in the web of available re-search leads him to postulate rather sub-stantial association between emotional adjustment and empathy. A person's emo-tional adjustment hinges primarily on how he sees himself and how he feels about himself — it is closely linked to his *self concept.*

One's self concept provides a kind of psychological "base of operations" that inevitably affects relations with family, friends, business associates, and strangers. Some aspects of the self concept are at the surface of personality; these are the *publicly held attitudes* — the things we don't mind telling other people about ourselves and our views of the world. And there are some feelings about the self of which we are aware, but which we do not want to share with others — these are the *privately held attitudes* to the self. And buried still deeper are the *subconscious and unconscious aspects* — feelings about "who" we are and "what" we are that somehow we cannot face up to, even to ourselves. The theories of psychoanalysis and depth psychology deal at length with these "dissociated" parts of the self, which as subtly disturbing, often powerful sources of internal turmoil may affect and hinder a person's effective functioning.

BARRIERS AND AIDS TO EMPATHY

The individual who has resolved most of his internal conflicts appears in a better position to direct his energies to the understanding of others. He is likely not to meet "booby traps" of his own uncon-scious devising that prevent accurate per-ception. *The healthy personality* is based upon a fundamental self-acceptance at all levels — public to unconscious. It relies on an openness to experience, a willingness to respond realistically to relevant cues; it exhibits a lack of dogmatism and a capa-city for responding to the world flexibly and dynamically. When we are under pres-sure, or in a state of anxiety, we are less likely to perceive accurately the motives and actions of those about us. It is only when we have reached a fair give-and-take balance between ourselves and the world that we are in a secure position to venture important human relations judgments.

---

[5] See Taft, R.: The ability to judge people. *Psychol. Bull. 52:* 1–23 (1955).

In light of this, is it likely that in a nirvana of perfect psychological equilibrium all social perceptions would be accurate? On the basis of what we know, the answer is no. In order to understand others, there must be some driving force, some motivation, some problem. Such cause or problem implies the existence of some tensions within the perceiver. In a fully tensionless state — in a hypothetical state of perfect adjustment — there could be no reason to care about understanding anything or anybody. As a result there would be little meaningful social perception or social interaction. As too many cooks are said to spoil the broth, too many tranquilizers seem to spoil the wellsprings of human understanding. While excess tension reduces empathy, its complete absence induces a state of apathy.

The Special Case of Self-Insight

Empathy and self-insight tend to go hand in hand, although the evidence is by no means all in.[6] Fortunate, they say, is the individual who knows how much or how little he truly knows about himself — who is aware of his own capacities, limitations, motivations, and attitudes.

The sole tool that we bring to the task of understanding others is our own personality. The cues we receive from the outside must be processed through the perceptual equipment that is "us" — through lenses of our own background and expectations. If we are to be successful in assessing the meaning of cues that impinge on us, we must become aware of the distortions that may be introduced by our "built-in" perceptual equipment.

A realistic view of our perceptual limitations, and of the kinds of aberrations we tend to introduce in what we see and hear, should help us to make allowances in interpreting the world around us. If, for instance, we are aware that people who

seem to be weak and submissive make us irrationally angry, we may be able to develop safeguards against our own unreasonable anger and ultimately gain a more realistic understanding of the motivations of the other person.

Self-insight does not come easy. Many factors mitigate against it. Central among these is our system of *psychological defenses* — the ways in which we systematically and subconsciously protect ourselves from facing what might be real or imagined threats to our personal security.

These protective distortions — which frequently concern our perceptions of others — help us make reality more palatable. There is no human being alive who is without some pattern of psychological defenses. Unfortunately, the cost of excessive utilization of defenses is the progressive removal from reality. Without some controlled and mild forms of self-delusion, adjustment of the ordinary everyday sort may be difficult. Yet the defenses that we bring into play as we seek to understand ourselves and others seduce us into various states of unreality; they make us see that which is *not* there, and hide that which might be apparent.

The Force of Attitude

One particularly pervasive pattern of personal defenses which interferes with the process of understanding others is characterized by a high degree of *authoritarianism,* with concurrent *rigidity in perception* and *intolerance for ambiguity.* The authoritarian person seems to need to view the world in clearly defined segments, some strictly black, others strictly white. He does not make much room for gradations — things that are clearly good or abominably bad, people friendly or hostile, nations with us or against us. Thus, the authoritarian unconsciously fails to recognize subtle but significant interpersonal phenomena, because he is unable to evaluate shades of gray for what they are.[7]

---

[6] See, for example, Bruner, J. S., and Tagiuri, R.: The perception of people. In Lindzey, G. (ed.): *Handbook of Social Psychology.* Reading, Mass., Addison-Wesley Publishing Company, 1954, Vol. 2, pp. 645–46.

[7] See Adorno, T. W., Frenkel-Brunswik, E. Levinson, D. J., and Sanford, R. N.: *The Authoritarian Personality.* New York, Harper & Brothers, 1950.

Extreme nonauthoritarian personalities — "nothing is definite, all is a matter of shading" — also encounter difficulties in understanding others since they too have a singularly single-minded view of what the world and its inhabitants are like.

The attitudes with which we approach the task of understanding others, then, do a great deal to determine just what we will be able to see. Attitudes basically serve as organizing forces that order in some preliminary manner the potential chaos and complexity confronting us. They give meaning to what we are prepared to see and hear. As such, they serve a necessary and useful function.

"Playing the Odds"

The question of whether the holding of stereotypes is necessarily detrimental to accurate social perception deserves consideration. If we define a "stereotype" as an *inaccurate perception* of a given grouping, it follows logically that stereotypes are hindrances. But, more generally, we *do* need to be able to type people by means of broad and flexible generalizations. In that sense, a realistic view of a group of individuals (a kind of "accurate stereotype") may increase the odds for accuracy in our perception of others. This kind of "typing" while based upon prior perceptions of individuals and groups, necessarily is a kind of oversimplification; still its use in a consciously wary manner is a constant nececessity if we are to relate to people.

Since understanding people involves relative probabilities of being right, caution is always in order. We must ever attempt to remain open to a constant flow of new information which may help us alter our perceptions in the light of changing circumstances. It is the danger of fossilization — the pitfall of "hardening" perceptions irrationally — that needs to be avoided.

Link between Perceiver and Perceived

The personality of the perceived also determines the success of social perception.

Ultimately it is the relationship that emerges between perceiver and perceived which becomes crucial, *Communication* linking the two — the sending and receiving of messages (involving feelings as well as content) — becomes raw material underlying the process of understanding others. Cues are messages from the perceived to the perceiver. In each instance, the perceiver "samples" certain small units of behavior that come from the perceived. While these samples in a statistical sense are neither random nor necessarily representative, they form the basis for generalizations that constitute predictions about the behavior of others. As communications develop, a person becomes both perceiver and perceived — sending and receiving cues of great variety and with high speed.

In the relationship between perceiver and perceived it becomes important for the perceiver to elicit cues from the perceived which will do the most to reveal, on a sample basis, the relevant aspects of the perceived's feelings, thoughts, and potential behavior. This ability to break through a person's outer veneer, to penetrate false fronts, has two facets: (1) the perceiver's *skill in facilitating the sending of cues* by the perceived, and (2) the perceiver's *skill in picking up and interpreting properly* the cues that have been sent.

Jean Krugmeier, for example, by eliciting fully the attitudes and aspirations of her job applicant might have succeeded in bringing to the surface relevant cues that might have made possible a more sensible evaluation of his potential. She might have reduced the applicant's defensiveness by proving herself receptive to his comments and accepting of him as a person, by listening for his feelings as well as meaning, and by communicating to him her understanding of his point of view.

As we engage in the process of understanding people, our hope for ever-increasing accuracy rests partially with our ability to get *feedback* on how others view the accuracy of our perceptions. We must remain in tune with the reactions of others — not in order to become blind automata, but rather to double check and review the validity of our own perceptions.

The Danger of Expertise

Usually we receive feedback from members of our own *reference groups* — our families, friends, and business associates. These are the people whose opinions about us usually matter to us. Parents and close relatives especially, who have provided us with experiences which make us what we are, often continue to give us, as Robert Burns so aptly put it, "the giftie . . . . to see oorsels as ithers see us."

At times, the validity of our insights and understanding of people is assessed by experts, by psychiatrists or psychologists who have been trained in personality diagnosis and behavior prediction. Unfortunately, research has shown that some of these experts, in spite of their intellectual grasp of interpersonal relations, are rather inept judges of people. This startling paradox has some rather persuasive explanations to account for it. First, intellect alone — though a slight help — does not guarantee empathy. More importantly, for some people too much knowledge is a dangerous thing! For them, there exists the danger of *overreaching*. They are confronted with the ever-present temptation to read into cues complex "deeper" meanings which in reality may not be there at all. This is the pitfall of imagining psychological ghosts behind each casual remark, simply because of some intellectual predisposition to make interpretations at more esoteric levels.

For experienced clinicians, the process of feedback here again proves to be a partial safeguard. If all too often our views of others, though psychologically "sophisticated," find no confirmation, either by the subject of our perception or through the perceptions of other observers, we may suspect that we are overreaching in our search for perceptual accuracy.

The Role of Feelings

Regardless of the specific situation in which social perception takes place, some positive feelings of varying intensity will be exchanged between perceiver and perceived. These feelings condition the process of social perception. They set up *halos,* which reduce the accuracy of empathic judgments. If we believe that some persons "can do no wrong," if we are enamored of their righteousness and virtue, if we blindly approve of everything they do — we will be unable accurately to assess their less desirable characteristics or behaviors. The inverse is equally true: pervasive hostility and prejudice also obliterate any chance for a realistic appraisal of people's positive characteristics.

A more subtle manifestation of the impact of feelings on perceptual accuracy can be found in the process of *naive projection* (assuming similarity), the attributing by the perceiver of his own characteristics to the perceived. If few cues are available to the perceiver, if he is unable to utilize those that are available, or if his feelings toward the other person are in fact similar to those he has about himself, projection may become his significant *modus operandi*. The vacuum that might be filled by meaningful cues is taken up by assumptions implying that the perceived resembles the perceiver.

Assuming similarity to another person is intrinsically neither a barrier nor a block to accurate social perception. If the perceived really *is* much like the perceiver with respect to the characteristics involved in the judgment, assuming similarity is clearly warranted. Although some unique psychological perceptual skill may or may not have been at work, accurate social perception will result.

One can visualize an extreme situation in which the major prerequisite for social perceptual accuracy is the knack for picking out associates who resemble us with regard to relevant personality dimensions. If we succeed in this selection, be our choice conscious or unconscious, all we may need in order to understand them is to assume that they are, more or less, replicas of ourselves. Obviously, reality rarely permits this uncritical, though convenient, approach. More likely we may find that we assume similarity where none exists, thus hindering social sensitivity by the unwarranted assumption.

A blind assumption, on the other hand, that we do *not* resemble others (or a particular "other") can also lead to misperception. In most cases, the perceiver and the perceived do share in common some attitudes, feelings, and similar personality characteristics. The challenge confronting us is to recognize those elements that we have in common with other individuals, while at the same time noting the differences that make us unique. Likewise, when dealing with many people, we need to learn to discriminate the relevant differences among them, while remaining aware of the similarities which they, as a group, share. Thus, as a particular boss considers a group of subordinates, he must ask — and answer — these four questions:

1. In what respects is each of these persons like me?
2. In what respects does each of these persons differ from me?
3. In what ways do all these people resemble one another?
4. In what ways is each of these people unique from every other?

Clearly, this is a large order.

The *relative stress* with which people relate to one another also influences their ultimate empathy toward each other. As superiors, for instance, we may find it relatively easy to size up properly the feelings and attitudes of our subordinates; as subordinates our anxieties may becloud our perceptions of our superiors' intent and attitudes. The well-known phenomenon of "seeing red" when angered and the notion that "love is blind" represent classic illustrations of the befogging effect of strong emotions on social perception. Most accurate social perception, it seems, occurs under conditions which do not involve extremely charged feelings.

Because each individual approaches the task of social perception in his own particular situation, his personal receptivity will be influenced by the nature of this situation. An executive who operates in an environment of "yes men" may come to be attuned to hearing "yes," even if the real sound is more like "maybe." An amusing cartoon series of medical specialists on vacation shows a plastic surgeon fascinated by the Sphinx in Egypt, a urologist intrigued by the shapes of swimming pools, and a gynecologist marveling at the fertile life in the farm's pigsty.

The *broader culture,* too, provides certain expectations and highlights specific types of cues. The "man in the gray flannel suit," the "rate buster," the "organization man," the "huckster," the "tycoon" — all these are cultural types which are readily found on the American business scene, and whose existence is typically recognized by those of us who share a common cultural heritage.

Pay-off for Empathy

Whatever its correlates and roots, empathy provides a road map, defining properly the social world confronting the perceiver. There is no guarantee, however, that even the most understanding perceiver will be able to behave appropriately, even if his road map is clear and accurate. He further requires an adequate repertory of behaviors — *behavioral flexibility* — to provoke the kinds of action that will most effectively attain the goals he seeks.

Social sensitivity and social effectiveness do not necessarily go hand in hand. In *The Outsider,* Colin Wilson[8] draws the portrait of the cultural hero who sees too much, whose perceptions penetrate all too well, but who tragically lacks the customary social skills for functioning within the reality that he perceives.

"Seeing too much," if not buttressed by an appropriate range of available behaviors, can indeed prove a threat to self and others and thereby reduce ultimate social effectiveness. In terms of actual pay-off, having too much empathy may well be as detrimental as having too little. Seeing the surrounding social world in proper perspective is useful only if knowledge can be successfully implemented by action.

Social effectiveness can be developed. For some people, dealing with feelings is as easy as recognizing and manipulating facts.

---

[8] Wilson, C.: *The Outsider.* Boston, Houghton Mifflin Company, 1956.

For others, the world of emotions is mysterious indeed. The improvement of social skills is a many-sided challenge. Neither intellectual learning nor emotional experience alone suffice. Nor is the heightening of social sensitivity the sole sacrosanct cure-all. Experiences are needed that reach the full personality. Increased social effectiveness depends on a "tool kit" of appropriate behaviors, in addition to enhanced understanding of social situations. Special clinically oriented training experiences hold promise to bring about integrated intellectual, emotional, and behavioral learnings that can make for greater effectiveness in dealing with others.

32 Social Class and Modes of Communication

Leonard Schatzman and Anselm Strauss

Common assumptions suggest that there may be important differences in the thought and communication of social classes.[1] Men live in an environment which is mediated through symbols. By naming, identifying, and classifying, the world's objects and events are perceived and handled. Order is imposed through conceptual organization, and this organization embodies not just anybody's rules but the grammatical, logical, and communicative canons of groups. Communication proceeds in terms of social requirements for comprehension, and so does "inner conversation" or thought. Both reasoning and speech meet requirements of criticism, judgment, appreciation, and control. Communication across group boundaries runs the danger — aside from sheer language difficulties — of being blocked by differential rules for the ordering of speech and thought.[2]

If these assumptions are correct, it follows that there should be observable differences in communication according to social class and that these differences should not be merely matters of degree of preciseness, elaboration, vocabulary, and literary style. It follows also that the modes of thought should be revealed by modes of speaking.

Our data are the interview protocols gathered from participants in a disaster. The documents, transcribed from tape, contain a wealth of local speech. Respondents had been given a relatively free hand in reporting their experiences, and the interviews averaged twenty-nine pages. These seemed admirably suited to a study of differences between social classes in modes of communication and in the organization of perception and thought. We used them also to explore the hypothesis that substantial intraclass differences in the organization of stories and accounts existed; hence low-class respondents might fail to satisfy the interviewer's canons of communication.

Approximately 340 interviews were available, representing random sampling of several communities ravaged by a tornado. Cases were selected by extreme position on educational and income continuums. Interviewees were designated as "lower" if education did not go beyond grammar school and if the annual family income was considered at the poverty level. The "upper" group consisted of persons with

---

[1] The writers are greatly indebted to the National Opinion Research Center in Chicago, which allowed them to use data gathered during a study of responses to disaster. The disaster occurred as the result of a tornado which swept through several small Arkansas towns and adjacent rural areas.

[2] Cf. Cassirer, E.: *An Essay on Man.* New Haven, 1944; Langer, S.: *Philosophy in a New Key.* 1948, New York, Lindesmith, A. R., and Strauss, A.L.: *Social Psychology New York, 1949,* pp. *237*–52; Mead, G.,: *Mind, Self, and Society* Chicago, 1934; Mills, C.W.: Language, logic, and culture. *Am. Sociol. Rev. 1:*(1939). 670–80.

one or more years of college education and annual incomes in the mid and upper levels. These extremes were purposely chosen for maximum socioeconomic contrast and because it seemed probable that nothing beyond formal or ritual communication would occur between these groups.

Cases were further limited by the following criteria: age (twenty-one to sixty-five years), race (white only), residence (native of Arkansas and more than three years in the community), proximity (either in the disaster area or close by), good cooperation in interview (as rated by interviewer), and less than eight probes per page (to avoid a rigid question-answer style with consequent structuring of interview by the interviewer's questions). The use of these criteria yielded ten upper-group cases, which were then matched randomly with ten from the lower group.[3]

DIFFERENCES BETWEEN CLASSES

Differences between the lower and upper groups were striking; and, once the nature of the difference was grasped, it was astonishing how quickly a characteristic organization of communication could be detected and described from a reading of even a few paragraphs of an interview. The difference is not simply the failure or success — of lower and upper groups, respectively — in communicating clearly and in sufficient detail for the interviewer's purposes. Nor does the difference merely involve correctness or elaborateness of grammar or use of a more precise or colorful vocabulary. The difference is a considerable disparity in (1) the number

and kinds of perspectives utilized in communication; (2) the ability to take the listener's role; (3) the handling of classifications; and (4) the frameworks and stylistic devices which order and implement the communication.

PERSPECTIVE OR CENTERING

By perspective or centering is meant the standpoint from which a description is made.[4] Perspectives may vary in number and scope. The flexibility with which one shifts from perspective to perspective during communication may vary also.

Lower Class. Almost without exception any description offered by a lower-class respondent is a description as seen through his *own* eyes; he offers his own perceptions and images directly to the listener. His best performance is a straight, direct narrative of events as he saw and experienced them. He often locates himself clearly in time and place and indicates by various connective devices a rough progression of events in relation to his activities. But the developmental progression is only in relation to himself. Other persons and their acts come into his narrative more or less as he encountered them. In the clearest interviews other actors are given specific spatial and temporal location, and sometimes the relationships among them or between them and himself are clearly designated.

The speaker's images vary considerably in clarity but are always his own. Although he may occasionally repeat the stories of other persons, he does not tell the story as though he were the other person reconstructing events and feelings. He may describe another person's act and the motive for it, with regard to himself, but this is the extent of his role-taking — he does not assume the role of another toward still others, except occasionally in an implicit fashion: "Some people was helping other

[3] Each document was scrutinized by both authors, and comprehensive notes were taken to help establish categories descriptive of the communicative style and devices of each respondent. From these notes profiles of respondents were constructed. From the notes and case profiles, there emerged the separate profiles for lower and upper groups that will be described. We had expected to code the documents to bring out the degree of overlap between groups, but it turned out that there was literally no overlap; nevertheless, each reader coded separately as he went along. Agreement upon coding scores between readers was virtually perfect.

[4] Cf. Piaget, J.: *The Psychology of Intelligence.* London, 1950. See also a suggestive treatment of inadequate thinking analyzed in terms of centering in Wertheimer, M.: *Productive Thinking.* New York, 1945, pp. 135–47.

people who was hurt." This limitation is especially pronounced when the behavior of more than two or three persons is being described and related. Here the description becomes confused: At best the speaker reports some reactions, but no clear picture of interaction emerges. The interaction either is not noticed or is implicitly present in communication ("We run over there to see about them, and they was alright"). Even with careful probing the situation is not clarified much further. The most unintelligible speakers thoroughly confound the interviewer who tries to follow images, acts, persons, and events which seem to come out of nowhere and disappear without warning.

Middle Class. The middle class can equal the best performance of the lower class in communicating and elaborating a direct description. However, description is not confined to so narrow a perspective. It may be given from any of several standpoints: for instance, another person, a class of persons, an organization, an organizational role, even the whole town. The middle-class speaker may describe the behavior of others, including classes of others, from their standpoints rather than from his, and he may include sequences of acts as others saw them. Even descriptions of the speaker's own behavior often are portrayed from other points of view.

CORRESPONDENCE OF IMAGERY BETWEEN SPEAKER AND LISTENER

Individuals vary in their ability to see the necessity for mediating linguistically between their own imagery and that of their listeners. The speaker must know the limits within which he may assume a correspondence of imagery. When the context of the item under discussion is in physical view of both, or is shared because of similarity of past experience, or is implicitly present by virtue of a history of former interaction, the problem of context is largely solved.[5] But when the context is

neither so provided nor offered by the speaker, the listener is confronted with knotty problems of interpretation. In the accounts of the most unintelligible respondents we found dreamlike sets of images with few connective, qualifying, explanatory, or other context-providing devices. Thus, the interviewer was hard pressed to make sense of the account and was forced to probe at every turn lest the speaker figuratively run away with the situation. The respondents were willing and often eager to tell their stories, but intention to communicate does not always bring about clear communication. The latter involves, among other requirements, an ability to hear one's words as others hear them.

Lower Class. Lower-class persons displayed a relative insensitivity to disparities in perspective. At best, the respondent corrected himself on the exact time at which he performed an act or became aware that his listener was not present at the scene and so located objects and events for him. On occasion he reached a state of other-consciousness: "You can't imagine if you wasn't there what it was like." However, his assumption of a correspondence in imagery is notable. There is much surnaming of persons without genuine identification, and often terms like "we" and "they" are used without clear referents. The speaker seldom anticipates responses to his communication and seems to feel little need to explain particular features of his account. He seldom qualifies an utterance, presumably because he takes for granted that his perceptions represent reality and are shared by all who were present. Since he is apt to take so much for granted, his narrative lacks depth and richness and contains almost no qualifications and few genuine illustrations. The hearer very often is confronted with a descriptive fragment that supposedly represents a more complete story. The speaker may then add phrases like "and stuff like that" or "and everything." Such phrasing is not genuine summation but a substitute for detail and abstraction. Summary statements are virtually absent, since they signify that speakers are sensitive to the needs of listeners. Certain phrases that appear to be summaries — such as "That's all I know" and

---

[5] For a good discussion of this see Malinowski, B.: The problem of meaning in primitive language. In *Magic, Science and Religion and Other Essays.* Boston, 1948, pp. 228–76.

"That's the way it was" — merely indicate that the speaker's knowledge is exhausted. Other summary-like phraseologies, like "It was pitiful," appear to be asides, reflective of self-feeling or emotion rather than resumes of preceding detail.

Middle Class. The middle-class respondent also makes certain assumptions about the correspondence of the other's images with his own. Nevertheless, in contrast with the lower group, he recognizes much more fully that imagery may be diverse and that context must be provided. Hence he uses many devices to supply context and to clarify meaning. He qualifies, summarizes, and sets the stage with rich introductory material, expands themes, frequently illustrates, anticipates disbelief, meticulously locates and identifies places and persons — all with great complexity of detail. He depends less on saying "You know"; he insists upon explaining if he realizes that a point lacks plausibility or force. Hence he rarely fails to locate an image, or series of images, in time or place. Frequent use of qualification is especially noteworthy. This indicates not only multiple centering but a very great sensitivity to listeners, actual and potential — including the speaker himself.

In short, the middle-class respondent has what might be called "communication control," at least in such a semiformal situation as the interview. Figuratively, he stands between his own images and the hearer and says "Let me introduce you to what I saw and know." It is as though he were directing a movie, having at his command several cameras focused at different perspectives, shooting and carefully controlling the effect. By contrast the lower-class respondent seems himself more like a single camera which unreels the scene to the audience. In the very telling of his story his is more apt to lose himself in his in his imagery. The middle-class person — by virtue, we would presume, of his greater sensitivity to his listener — stands more outside his experience. He does not so much tell you what he saw as fashion a story about what he saw. The story may be accurate in varying degrees although, in so far as it is an organized account, it has both the virtues and the defects of organization.

The comparative accuracies of middle- and lower-class accounts are not relevant here; the greater objectivity of the former merely reflects greater distance between narrator and event.[6]

In organizing his account, the middle-class respondent displays parallel consciousness of the other and himself. He can stop midstream, take another direction, and, in general, exert great control over the course of his communication. The lower-class respondent seems to have much less foresight, appearing to control only how much he will say to the interviewer, or whether he will say it at all, although presumably he must have some stylistic controls not readily observable by a middle-class reader.

CLASSIFICATIONS AND CLASSIFICATORY RELATIONS

Lower Class. Respondents make reference mainly to the acts and persons of particular people, often designating them by proper or family names. This makes for fairly clear denotation and description, but only as long as the account is confined to the experiences of specific individuals. There comes a point when the interviewer wishes to obtain information about classes of persons and entire organizations as well as how they impinged upon the respondent, and here the lower-class respondent becomes relatively or even wholly inarticulate. At worst he cannot talk about categories of people or acts because, apparently, he does not think readily in terms of classes. Questions about organizations, such as the Red Cross, are converted into concrete terms, and he talks about the Red Cross "helping people" and "people helping other people" with no more than the crudest awareness of how organizational activities interlock. At most the respondent categorizes only in a rudimentary fashion: "Some people were running;

---

[6] Our discussion of objectivity and of mediation between self and image in communication is reminiscent of some of the literature on child, schizophrenic, and aphasic thought.

other people were looking in the houses." The interviewer receives a sketchy and impressionistic picture. Some idea is conveyed of the confusion that followed upon the tornado, but the organizing of description is very poor. The respondent may mention classes in contrasting juxtaposition (rich and poor, hurt and not-hurt), or list groups of easily perceived, contrasting actions, but he does not otherwise spell out relations between these classes. Neither does he describe a scene systematically in terms of classes that are explicitly or clearly related, a performance which would involve a shifting of viewpoint.

It is apparent that the speakers think mainly in particularistic or concrete terms. Certainly classificatory thought must exist among many or all the respondents; but, in communicating to the interviewer, class terms are rudimentary or absent and class relations implicit: relationships are not spelled out or are left vague. Genuine illustrations are almost totally lacking, either because these require classifications or because we — as middle-class observers — do not recognize that certain details are meant to imply classes.

Middle Class. Middle-class speech is richly interlarded with classificatory terms, especially when the narrator is talking about what he saw rather than about himself. Typically, when he describes what other persons are doing, he classifies actions and persons and more often than not explicitly relates class to class. Often his descriptions are artistically organized around what various categories of persons were doing or experiencing. When an illustration is offered, it is clear that the speaker means it to stand for a general category. Relief and other civic organizations are conceived as sets or classes of co-ordinated roles and actions; some persons couch their whole account of the disaster events in organizational terms, hardly deigning to give proper names or personal accounts. In short, concrete imagery in middle-class communication is dwarfed or overshadowed by the prevalence and richness of conceptual terminology. Organization of speech around classifications comes readily, and undoubtedly the speaker is barely conscious of it. It

is part and parcel of his formal and informal education. This is not to claim that middle-class persons always think with and use classifactory terms, for doubtless this is not true. Indeed, it may be that the interview exacts from them highly conceptualized descriptions. Nonetheless, we conclude that, in general, the thought and speech of middle-class persons is less concrete than that of the lower group.

ORGANIZING FRAMEWORKS AND STYLISTIC DEVICES

One of the requirements of communication is that utterances be organized. The principle of organization need not be stated explicitly by the speaker or recognized by the listener. Organizing frames can be of various sorts. Thus, an ordering of the respondent's description is often set by the interviewer's question, or the speaker may set his own framework ("There is one thing you should know about this"). The frame can be established jointly by both interviewer and respondent, as when the former asks an open-ended question within whose very broad limits the respondent order his description in ways that strike him as appropriate or interesting. The respondent, indeed may organize his account much as though he were telling a special kind of story or drama, using the interviewer's questions as hardly more than general cues to what is required. The great number of events, incidents, and images which must be conveyed to the listener may be handled haphazardly, neatly, dramatically, or sequentially; but, if they are to be communicated at all, they must be ordered somehow. Stylistic devices accompany and implement these organizing frames, and the lower and upper groups use them in somewhat different ways.

Lower Class. The interviewer's opening question, "Tell me your story of the tornado," invites the respondent to play an active role in organizing his account; and this he sometimes does. However, with the exception of one person who gave a headlong personal narrative, the respondents did not give long, well-organized, or tightly knit pictures of what happened to them during and after the tornado. This kind of general depiction either did not occur to them or did not strike them as appropriate.

The frames utilized are more segmental or limited in scope than those used by the middle class. They appear to be of several kinds and their centering is personal. One is the personal narrative, with events, acts, images, persons, and places receiving sequential ordering. Stylistic devices further this kind of organization: for instance, crude temporal connectives like "then," "and," and "so" and the reporting of images or events as they are recollected or as they appear in the narrative progression. Asides may specify relationships of kinship or the individuals' location in space. But, unless the line of narrative is compelling to the speaker, he is likely to wander off into detail about a particular incident, where the incident in turn then provides a framework for mentioning further events. Likewise, when a question from the interviewer breaks into the narrative, it may set the stage for an answer composed of a number of images or an incident. Often one incident becomes the trigger for another, and, although some logical or temporal connection between them may exist for the speaker, this can scarcely be perceived by the interviewer. Hence the respondent is likely to move out of frames quickly. The great danger of probes and requests for elaboration is that the speaker will get far away from the life-line of his narrative — and frequently far away from the interviewer's question. As recompense the interviewer may garner useful and unexpectedly rich information from the digressions, although often he needs to probe this material further to bring it into context. General questions are especially likely to divert the speaker, since they suggest only loose frames; or he may answer in general, diffuse, or blurred terms which assume either that the listener was there too or that he will put meaningful content into the words. If a question is asked that concerns abstract classes or is "above" the respondent — a query, say, about relief organizations — then very general answers or concrete listing of images or triggering

of images are especially noticeable. When the interviewer probes in an effort to get some elaboration of an occurrence or an expansion of idea, he commonly meets with little more than repetition or with a kind of "buckshot" listing of images or incidents which is supposed to fill out the desired picture. The lack of much genuine elaboration is probably related to the inability to report from multiple perspectives.

One requirement of the interview is that it yield a fairly comprehensive account of the respondent's actions and perceptions. With the lower-class respondent the interviewer, as a rule, must work very hard at building a comprehensive frame directly into the interview. This he does by forcing many subframes upon the respondent. He asks many questions about exact time sequence, placement and identification of persons, expansion of detail, and the like. Especially must he ask pointed questions about the relations of various personages appearing in the account. Left to his own devices, the respondent may give a fairly straightforward narrative or competently reconstruct incidents that seem only partially connected with each other or with his narrative. But the respondent seldom voluntarily gives both linear and cross-sectional pictures.

The devices used to implement communication are rather difficult to isolate, perhaps because we are middle class ourselves. Among the devices most readily observable are the use of crude chronological notations (e.g., "then, . . . and then"), the juxtaposing or direct contrasting of classes (e.g., rich and poor) and the serial locating of events. But the elaborate devices that characterize middle-class interviews are strikingly absent.

Middle Class. Without exception middle-class respondents imposed overall frames of their own upon the entire interview. Although very sensitive generally to the needs of the interviewer, they made the account their own. This is evidenced sometimes from the very outset; many respondents give a lengthy picture in answer to the interviewer's invitation, "Tell me your story." The organizing frame may yield a fluid narrative that engulfs self and others in dense detail; it may give a relatively static but rich picture of a community in distress; or, by dramatic and stage-setting devices it may show a complicated web of relationships in dramatic motion. The entire town may be taken as the frame of reference and its story portrayed in time and space.

Besides the master-frame, the middle-class respondent utilizes many subsidiary frames. Like the lower-class person, he may take off from a question. But, in doing so — especially where the question gives latitude by its generality or abstractness — he is likely to give an answer organized around a subframe which orders his selection and arrangement of items. He may even shift from one image to another, but rarely are these left unrelated to the question which initially provoked them. He is much more likely also to elaborate than to repeat or merely to give a scattered series of percepts.

One prerequisite for the elaboration of a theme is an ability to depart from it while yet holding it in mind. Because he incorporates multiple perspectives, the respondent can add long asides, discuss the parallel acts of other persons in relation to himself, make varied comparisons for the enrichment of detail and comprehension — and then can return to the original point and proceed from there. Often he does this after first preparing his listener for the departure and concludes the circuit with a summary statement or a transitional phrase like "well — anyhow" that marks the end of the digression.

The stylistic devices utilized by any respondent are many and varied. But each speaker uses some devices more frequently than others, since certain ones are more or less appropriate to given frames. There is no point in spelling out the whole range of devices; they are of the sort used in any clear detailed narrative and effective exposition. If the respondent is pressed to the limit of his ability in explaining a complex point or describing a complicated scene, he calls into play resources that are of immensely high order. Sometimes a seemingly simple device will turn out on closer inspection to demand a sophisticated handling of communication — for instance, the

frequent and orderly asides that break into exposition or narrative and serve with great economy to add pertinent detail.

INTRACLASS DIFFERENCES

Middle Class. Although all middle-class accounts were informative, there were considerable differences of construction among them. The frames utilized by any respondent are multiple, but respondents tend to use either a frame emphasizing sequence, human drama, and personal incident or one stressing interlocking classes of civic acts. Each orientation is implemented by somewhat different stylistic techniques. There are of course different ways of narrating; thus one can dwell more upon conditions for activity than upon the acts themselves. Similarly, accounts focused upon town organization vary in such matters as the scope of description and the degree of emphasis upon temporal sequence. Both frameworks are interchangeable, and their use is a function either of the speaker's habitual orientation or of his definition of the interview situation rather than of his ability to use one or the other mode.

Lower Class. Lower-class persons can best be distinguished in terms of ability to meet the minimum requirements of the interview. Some literally cannot tell a straight story or describe a simple incident coherently. At the other extreme we find an adequate self-focused narrative, with considerable detail tightly tied to sequential action, including retrospective observation about the narrator's facts as he develops them. Midway between these extremes are the people who can tell portions of narrative but are easily distracted: either an image suggests some other image, or the interviewer asks a question focusing interest and concentration elsewhere than upon the narrative or he calls for some expansion of detail. Then the interviewer must remind the speaker of the break in narrative. The interviewer constantly must be on the *qui vive* to keep the story going and to fill in gaps.

In the best accounts, also, competent description is handled by linking a variety of perceptions to the narrative. Images then appear to the listener to be in context and thus are fairly comprehensible. At the other extreme, images and incidents are free-floating. Probing improved the quality of this sort of interview but slightly. More frequently, the interviewer was confronted with fragments of the narrative and its related imagery. Then he had to piece together the general lineaments of the story by a barrage of probes: "Who?" "When?" "Where?" Even then the reader of these interviews will come across stray images and be hard pressed to fit them into the context. Competence in recounting narrative generally is accompanied by competence in making understandable departures from the narrative itself, and, lacking both skills, some lower-class respondents gave quite baffling and unintelligible reports. The best accounts are moderately clear, although subject to all the limitations already discussed.

DISCUSSION

Only if the situation in which the respondent spoke is carefully taken into account will we be on safe ground in interpreting class differences. Consider, first, the probable meaning of the interview for the middle-class respondents. Although the interviewer is a stranger, an outsider, he is a well-spoken, educated person. He is seeking information on behalf of some organization, hence his questioning not only has sanction but sets the stage for both a certain freedom of speech and an obligation to give fairly full information. The respondent may never before have been interviewed by a research organization, but he has often talked lengthily, fairly freely, and responsibly to organizational representatives. At the very least he has had some experience in talking to educated strangers. We may also suppose that the middle-class style of living often compels him to be very careful not to be misunderstood. So he becomes relatively sensitive to communication per se and to communication with others who may not exactly share his viewpoints or frames of reference.

Communication with such an audience requires alertness, no less to the meanings of one's own speech than to the possible intent of the other's. Roletaking may be inaccurate, often, but it is markedly active. Assessing and anticipating reactions to what he has said or is about to say, the individual develops flexible and ingenious ways of correcting, qualifying, making more plausible, explaining, rephrasing – in short, he assumes multiple perspectives and communicates in terms of them. A variety of perspectives implies a variety of ways of ordering or framing detail. Moreover, he is able to classify and to relate classes explicitly, which is but another way of saying that he is educated to assume multiple perspectives of rather wide scope.

It would certainly be too much to claim that middle-class persons always react so sensitively. Communication is often routinized, and much of it transpires between and among those who know each other so well or share so much in common that they need not be subtle. Nor is sensitive roletaking called forth in so-called "expressive behavior," as when hurling invective or yelling during a ball game. With the proviso that much middle-class speech is uttered under such conditions, it seems safe enough to say that people of this stratum can, if required, handle the more complex and consciously organized discourse. In addition to skill and perspicacity, this kind of discourse requires a person who can subtly keep a listener at a distance while yet keeping him in some degree informed.

Consider now, even at risk of overstating the case, how the interview appears to the lower group. The interviewer is of higher social class than the respondent, so that the interview is a "conversation between the classes." It is entirely probable that more effort and ability are demanded by cross-class conversation of this sort than between middle-class respondent and middle-class interviewer.[7] It is not surprising that the interviewer is often baffled and that the

---

[7] Somewhat like this is the I.Q. testing session which involves a middle-class test (and tester) and a lower-class subject. The many and subtle difficulties in this situation are analyzed by Davis, A.: In *Social Class Influences upon Learning.* Cambridge, Mass., 1951.

respondent frequently misinterprets what is wanted. But misunderstanding and misinterpretation are only part of the story.

Cross-class communication, while not rare, probably is fairly formalized or routinized. The communicants know the ritual steps by heart, and can assume much in the way of supporting context for phrase and gesture. The lower-class person in these Arkansas towns infrequently meets a middle-class person in a situation anything like the interview. Here he must talk at great length to a stranger about personal experiences, as well as recall for his listener a tremendous number of details. Presumably he is accustomed to talking about such matters and in such detail only to listeners with whom he shares a great deal of experience and symbolism, so that he need not be very self-conscious about communicative technique. He can, as a rule, safely assume that words, phrases, and gestures are assigned approximately similar meanings by his listeners. But this is not so in the interview or, indeed, in any situation where class converses with class in nontraditional modes.

There still remains the question of whether the descriptions of perceptions and experiences given by the lower-class respondent are merely inadequate or whether this is the way he truly saw and experienced. Does his speech accurately reflect customary "concrete" modes of thought and perception, or is it that he perceives in abstract and classificatory terms, and from multiple perspectives, but is unable to convey his perceptions?[8] Unless one assumes that, when talking in familiar vein to familiar audiences, speech and gesture incorporate multiple perspectives, which is, as we have already indicated, improbable, one concludes that speech does in some sense reflect thought.

The reader is perhaps best left at this point to draw his own conclusions, although we shall press upon him certain additional evidence and interpretation arising from examination of the interviews.

In any situation calling for a description of human activities it is necessary to utilize motivational terminology, either explicitly or implicitly, in the very namings of acts.[9] In the speech of those who recognize few disparities of imagery between themselves and their listeners, explicit motivational terms are sparse. The frequent use among the lower class of the expression "of course" followed by something like "They went up to see about their folks" implies that it is almost needless to say what "they" did, much less to give the reason for the act. The motive ("to see about") is implicit and terminal, requiring neither elaboration nor explanation. Where motives are explicit ("They was needin' help, so we went on up there"), they are often gratuitous and could just as well have been omitted. All this is related to preceding discussions of single centering and assumed correspondence of imagery. To the speaker it was quite clear why people did what they did. There was no need to question or to elaborate on the grounds for acts. Under probing the respondent did very little better: he used motivational terms but within a quite narrow range. The terms he used ordinarily reflected kinship obligations, concern for property, humanitarian ("help") sentiments, and action from motives of curiosity ("We went down to see"). Such a phrase as "I suppose I went to her house because I wanted reassurance" would rarely occur.

Middle-class persons exhibit familiarity with a host of distinct "reasons" for performing particular acts. Their richness in thinking allows activities to be defined and described in a great variety of ways. Here, indeed, is an instrument for breaking down diffuse images ("They was runnin' all over") into classes of acts and events. The middle-class person is able to do this, for one thing, because he possesses an abstract motivational terminology. Then, too, the

---

[8] "The lower class is even more concrete in its outlook than the lower-middle class. For example, a question . . . where chewing gum is usually purchased will be answered by an upper-middle person: 'At a cashier's counter or in a grocery store.' By the lower-middle: 'At the National or the corner drugstore.' By the lower class: 'From Tony.' Marketing Chewing Gum in New England: A Research Study. Chicago, Social Research, Inc., 1950.

[9] Cf. Burke, K.: *Grammar of Motives.* New York, 1945.

fine and subtle distinctions for rationalizing behavior require devices for insuring that they will be grasped by the hearer. In a real sense the need to explain behavior can be linked with the need to communicate well — to give a rational account as well as to be objective. Hence, there is a constant flow of qualifying and generalizing terms linked with motivational phraseology ("I don't know why, but it could be he felt there was no alternative . . . ").

It is not surprising to find the middle class as familiar with elements of social structure as with individual behavior. Assuredly, this familiarity rests not only upon contact with institutions but upon the capacity to perceive and talk about abstract classes of acts. The lower-class person, on the other hand, appears to have only rudimentary notions of organizational structure — at least of relief and emergency agencies. Extended contact with representatives of them, no doubt, would familiarize him not only with organizations but with thinking in organizational, or abstract, terms. The propensity of the lower class to state concretely the activities of relief organizations corroborates the observation of Warner that the lowest strata have little knowledge or "feel" for the social structures of their communities.[10] It also suggests the difficulty of conveying to them relatively abstract information through formal media of communication.

It may be that rural townspeople of the lower class are not typical of the national or urban low strata. This raises the question — vital to urban sociology but to which currently there is no adequate answer — of whether pockets of rural-minded folk cannot live encapsulated in the city[11] and, indeed, whether lower-class persons have much opportunity to absorb middle-class culture without themselves beginning the route upward, those remaining behind remaining less urban.[12]

---

[10] Warner, W. L.: *American Life: Dream and Reality.* Chicago, University of Chicago Press, 1953, pp. 193–94.

[11] Riesman, D.: Urbanity and the urban personality. In *Proceedings of the Fourth Annual Symposium, The Human Development Bulletin.* Chicago: University of Chicago, 1953 p. 37.

[12] William Henry, of the University of Chicago, has conveyed his impression to us that urban lower-class and middle-class people perform on Thematic Apperception Tests much as our Arkansas respondents did in the interview.

We have also examined interviews about disasters in Brighton, N.Y., a middle-class suburb of Rochester, and Elizabeth, N.J., an urban community near New York City. There are no observable differences between the middle-class respondents of these areas and those of Arkansas. Four interviews with Elizabeth lower-class respondents paralleled the modes of the Arkansas lower class. A fifth exhibited considerable middle-class characteristics

33   What Is the Patient Saying?

Ruth G. Elder

A young nursing student in the psychiatric setting was heard to say, "I'm so glad to be going back to the general hospital where patients tell you what they want when they want it and that's all there is to it!"

How often do we take it for granted that patients in general hospitals can clearly communicate their needs with little or no help from the personnel? The numerous requests, questions, and comments from

---

Elder, R. G.: What is the patient saying? Nurs. Forum *2:* 25–37 (1963).

patients that we hear as we make rounds, respond to the executone, and give treatments and medication would seem to indicate that patients are able to make their needs known. But is this true?

THE MOTIVATING INCIDENT FOR THE STUDY

An experience on a surgical unit focused my attention on the patient's initial communication to nursing personnel. While I was working with one patient, I heard another patient in the room — a young woman with a puzzled frown who was sitting up in bed — ask a nurse when her operation was scheduled. The nurse told her it was scheduled for the "day after tomorrow" and then went on her way. A few minutes later, I was surprised to hear Miss X ask the identical question of another member of the staff. She received a similar answer. Almost on the heels of this brief encounter, her physician entered the room, and she asked the same question of him. Apparently she had asked him this before because he said, "Now don't you worry about a thing. I've told you it's the day after tomorrow and there's nothing to worry about." He, too, left.

Puzzled and concerned, I then approached the young woman only to be greeted by the same query. I responded by sharing with her my puzzlement, telling her that I had heard her ask the same question of a number of people and that I felt that somehow their answers did not seem to satisfy her. I wondered what it was she really wanted to know. She looked extremely miserable as she said, "Yes, I know that's what I've been doing, but ... " her voice trailed off. As I carefully encouraged her and clarified the words she was using, it gradually emerged that she was extremely frightened of the proposed operation on her leg. She had been hospitalized a few months before, following an accident in which she had received head injuries, and for a few days had been "out of her mind." She vaguely remembered the terror of this period, but more important, she had the feeling that the same thing would happen again after the operation on her leg. No

wonder she was so frightened! As she talked and we outlined the vast differences between these two hospitalizations, she seemed to relax; she heaved a deep sigh and smiled for the first time since I had begun observing her.

After telling Miss X that I would see her the next day, I went to the head nurse to report what had occurred. The nurse broke into my narrative to tell me that this patient was "crazy." She had been asking everyone the same question about her operation; obviously she was confused and didn't remember the previous answer. I wasn't to let her upset me. I agreed that I, too, had wondered if the patient was unable to remember what had been told her and recounted my experience of that morning. The nurse immediately commented sympathetically and expressed her amazement at how "mixed up" Miss X was about the operation.

Then I spoke with the physician, who said that he knew something was worrying Miss X but had had no idea that that was what it was. After hearing my story, both the nursing personnel and the physician rallied to the patient's support, encouraging her to relate her doubts and misgivings about the operation and explicitly outlining what she might realistically expect.

I continued working with this patient throughout her hospital stay. Her progress presented many interesting facets, but the aspect that I wish to examine here is her initial communication to the staff — her questions and her furrowed brow. Both the nurses and the physician had observed this behavior and had come to a conclusion about its meaning. Their actions from this point on did not seem to be helpful to Miss X. Yet each had had thoughts evoked by Miss X's behavior which, if directly utilized to gain more information about how the patient was thinking and feeling, might have been of benefit. For instance, the nurse might have asked Miss X if she realized that she had asked the same question several times before. Or, if the patient sounded confused to her, she might have attempted to sort out with her exactly what it was that was confusing in the situation. Then both she and Miss X would have been at least one step closer to finding out what was so upsetting. By the same token, the doctor might have asked Miss X what was worrying her, instead of attempting a blanket reassurance. One thing was certain: this patient was not communicating clearly and she certainly needed some help to do so.

THE STUDY OF SIXTY NURSE-PATIENT CONTACTS

As I became more intrigued with patients' communications, I began to examine more closely their initial communication to the nursing personnel. I was particularly interested in their verbal and non-verbal behavior as a nurse approached them. I wanted to determine how clearly or adequately this behavior expressed their state of comfort or discomfort, or their need for nursing assistance. To collect data of this type I became a nurse participant-observer, working with patients on a semi-private, surgical unit. This was not rigidly controlled research, but rather a beginning, exploratory study. My sample was made up of patient contacts similar to those the nurse on the floor was encountering. All patients to whom I responded, whether they were directly assigned to me or not, were included in the study. Some patients were encountered more than once, but only the first interaction on any day was included in the sample. In all, the study included a total of sixty contacts with forty-one patients.

As I came in contact with patients, I noted their verbal and non-verbal behavior and then responded to them in accord with some aspect of the thoughts, feelings, or questions that their behavior evoked in me. This response was made in an exploratory and non-judgmental manner so that the patients were encouraged to confirm, deny, or elaborate upon my perception of their behavior or situation. The ensuing interaction was directed toward a mutual understanding of their present condition and their areas of discomfort or distress. If they were experiencing discomfort, I then focused on ways to alleviate it or to enhance their ability to cope more adequately with their current concerns, using

whatever nursing skills were required. The data thus collected included (1) the verbal and non-verbal behavior manifested by patients as the nurse observer approached (overt behavior), (2) the state of comfort, discomfort, concern, or distress revealed by patients during the nurse-patient interaction (aspects of covert behavior) and (3) the type of nursing assistance that the patients required to attain a more satisfactory adjustment to their current situation if they were experiencing some degree of distress.

THE FINDINGS OF THE STUDY

The results of the study offer implications for nursing practice as well as ideas for further research. First and foremost was the finding that the patients in this study did not adequately communicate their needs for nursing assistance as the nurse initially approached them. In forty-seven of the sixty contacts, the patients expressed no aspect of their needs clearly in their presenting behavior. In an additional eleven contacts, the patients did not express their needs fully. Over 40 per cent of these patients had received either "routine morning care" or "routine evening care" immediately prior to their contact with the nurse observer — a fact that offered further support to the hypothesis that patients do not communicate their needs clearly or adequately to nursing personnel. Presumably, if the patients had been able to express their needs for nursing assistance clearly, they would have been met during the evening or the morning care period.

In the eleven instances in which the patients did express their needs in part, an interesting phenomenon occurred. Each of these patients requested some concrete item of physical assistance, such as a bedpan, an adjustment in the height of the bed, or a glass of water. As I met these requests satisfactorily, other needs emerged. The patients tended to move from expressing needs which involved concrete help to the expression of those which are frequently categorized as emotional. Some of the patients were confused and apprehensive about their illness or treatment to the point where they were experiencing severe emotional tension, yet they initiated communication with a relatively minor request for assistance.

One of the patients in this group had already acquired the title of "demander," although she had been in the hospital for only a few hours. As I passed her room she called to me, "Nurse, will you put down this window? I'm in a draft." She was a thin, middle-aged woman, with a pale, pinched, birdlike face and restless, fluttering hands. Before I finished adjusting the window, she asked if I would find out when her doctor was coming to see her. I later learned that she had just asked this question of the nurse who had given her evening care. Instead of immediately going to find out, I wondered aloud if there were some particular reason for her wanting to see him. With this slight bit of encouragement, she poured out her tale of how she happened to be in the hospital, of the scheduled operation, of her many fears and concerns about what was going to happen to her. I encouraged her to talk. Many of her fears were unrealistic, based on misconceptions and misinformation about hospital procedures in the postoperative period. I carefully clarified with her what she might expect and the specific questions she had yet to ask her doctor. As she talked, her facial expression changed, the muscles around her mouth and eyes seemed to relax, and her hands quietly came to rest. She verified my impression that her excess tension was abated by commenting on how anxious she had felt before and how much better she felt now. Like many patients, this woman was unable to say directly to any of the nursing personnel, "I am so anxious, frightened, and confused about this operation scheduled for me. I need desperately to talk to someone and see if I can't get a few things sorted out." Instead, she manifested her intense anxiety by requesting small individual items of care or service from the staff.

In the forty-seven contacts in which patients were not clear in communicating any aspect of their need as the nurse approached them (including thirty in which the patients' behavior was coded as "non-verbal only"), the patients followed a variety of patterns when their behavior was explored. Some needed physical assistance first, and then as they became more comfortable through this means, began to discuss their concerns, worries, and fears. Others reversed this pattern; only as they began to feel some relief from their pent-up emotions did they seem to become aware of specific areas of bodily discomfort. For example, a man who was suffering from severe postoperative gas pains angrily berated the staff and complained about the service he had been receiving. I listened to him and expressed my concern for his discomfort, and we gradually clarified his misunderstandings about the physician's orders and his plan of treatment. He responded to this discussion by relaxing, releasing flatus, and then feeling relief from pain.

In most situations, however, there was no clear-cut demarcation between the two types of approach — physical and emotional. As I was bathing perspiring bodies, changing damp, wrinkled linen, adjusting bandages or dressings that were either too tight or too loose, massaging aching backs, and helping patients to shift into more comfortable positions, I was also listening and responding to their reactions to their current situations. It was difficult, if not impossible, to ascertain which specific intervention, response, or action met a particular need. In other words, it was impossible to separate *psyche* from *soma*.

A second finding of my study was that the form of behavior initially exhibited by a patient was not a reliable basis for assessing his degree of discomfort. The thirty patients who were experiencing severe discomfort at the beginning of my contact with them manifested a wide range of observable behavior. The largest single group (fourteen patients) said nothing, but their tense facial expressions and contorted body positions indicated that something was amiss. At the opposite extreme were those who at first glance seemed relaxed and comfortable, sitting quietly in their beds and appearing to observe the passing scene. Some patients initiated interaction with requests, others asked for information, and still others merely made a comment — for example, "I find it difficult to sleep in hospitals." One man was steadfastly pacing the hall, head down, hands behind his back. With all of these patients an investigative approach was essential to find out how severe their distress was and how they could be helped to relieve it.

IMPLICATIONS OF THE STUDY

As I have stated, my main finding was that the patients in this study did not communicate their needs for assistance adequately. Is this a universal phenomenon, or was it peculiar to this ward milieu? Descriptions of patient behavior in nursing literature indicate that this finding is not atypical of other settings, other classes of patients, or other parts of this country.[1,2] Nevertheless, further study is needed to ascertain the degree to which the findings are replicated in other settings and the effects that such factors as age, social class, and racial origin have on a patient's ability to communicate clearly.

The reasons patients do not communicate more clearly are probably multiple and varied and involve cultural, psychological, and physiological factors. Initially, both patient and nurse are strangers to each other. In our culture, we hesitate to reveal our thoughts and feelings and more intimate personal needs until we have a sense of trust in or safety with the other person involved. One patient expressed it this way: "It's sort of a sizing up of the nurse. What is she going to be like with me? Can I talk to her and is she going to try to understand, or is she going to make me feel like an idiot? Or is she in a hurry; will she have time?" This patient went on to say that he could do this "sizing up" in a minute in some cases. "It isn't so much what she says as how she says it . . . how she looks at you. Does she really hear you and really see you, or is she thinking of something else?"

In addition to the possible effect of this cultural factor, some patients are only vaguely aware of what is making them feel uncomfortable. They do not really know what assistance they really need. Occas-

sionally medications interfere with the patients' ability to think clearly, or the disease and recovery process may leave them little energy for assessing their situation realistically. They frequently require a nurse with considerable skill in responding to the nuances of their verbal and nonverbal behavior before the immediate sources of distress can be identified and the specific means to alleviate it provided.

Those of us who have been patients ourselves may recognize another factor which can enter into the situation. Even persons who pride themselves on their communications skills and who are familiar enough with hospitals not to have the extra burden of strangeness find that the stress of hospitalization, illness, or uncertain diagnosis renders them astonishingly inept at expressing themselves. Anxiety can interfere with a patient's ability to communicate, although he may know within himself exactly what he wants to say.

The ward social system may also have an effect on patients' communications. Even though it is acknowledged that it is desirable to meet patient needs, it is obvious that in many hospitals the primary focus of the administrative and ward personnel is on the general management of the unit, on "getting the work done." Moreover, there are few concrete rewards by way of status or financial recognition for those who might be interested in developing their skill in working more effectively with patients.[3] Consequently, the very structure of the work situation discourages patients from communicating clearly. Frequently we hear nurses criticizing the physician who hurriedly makes rounds, leaving the patient little opportunity to air his concerns. Not as many nurses seem aware that they do precisely the same thing. Patients realize it, however, as is indicated by their frequent comment, "The nurses are so busy."

Is the nurse really so busy that she does not have time to respond effectively to patients? On the unit on which I made my study, she was. She was involved in a multitude of nursing, administrative, and organizational tasks. As one nurse expressed it, "I don't even have time to get that medication to him within a reasonable period after he asks for it, let alone stop and talk." This is one aspect of the problem. Reorganization must occur in our hospitals if the nurse is to be freed to respond to the needs of patients and develop the potential of her staff to do likewise. Yet lack of time is not the total answer, as research by Aydelotte and by New, Nite, and Callahan has so dramatically demonstrated. Both of these studies indicate that even when the nurse does have time, she does not use it in direct patient-care activities. In the New study, patients expressed no increased satisfaction with nursing care as the staffing pattern increased, contrary to expectations.[4] Aydelotte found no improvement in patient welfare with increases in staffing.[5]

No doubt effective nursing care does require more time at specific stages in a patient's illness and hospitalization. However, this factor may be balanced by the time subsequently saved. To answer a patient's light every few minutes may require a great deal of time and energy on the part of both nurse and patient. If some extra minutes of exploration are allowed when the call light first flashes, other trips may not be necessary, and the satisfaction of both the nurse and the patient may be increased. Many nurses who worked twelve-hour shifts learned through experience that a few minutes spent with patients in the evening saved many minutes later in the night. Relaxed, satisfied patients meant fewer sleeping and pain medications, fewer post-operative catheterizations, and fewer complications, as well as greater satisfaction for all concerned. It appears that the old adage, "a stitch in time saves nine" can be applied to the nurse as well as to the housewife. It is an adage worth testing by research.

In any event, the time, though short, must be utilized effectively. If patients do not express their needs adequately on initial contact, it is the nurse's responsibility to initiate activity toward the discernment of need. Clarity of purpose and skill in communicating are fundamental to this end. The nurse must have access to the patient's frame of reference, taking into consideration his perception of his plight and his feelings, concerns, and desires before she acts or even assesses the situation with any degree of validity.

In initiating activity, the separation of pateints' needs into physical and emotional categories can lead to several dilemmas. One is illustrated by the nurse who attempts to investigate a patient's emotional needs and considers that the only way to fulfill this function is through interviewing techniques and verbal interaction. Her efforts may be doomed to failure if her patient's first concern is with matters which require physical activity on her part. On the other hand, the nurse who limits herself to physical activities may find her efforts ineffective with patients whose discomfort is primarily caused by their reactions to their illness, treatment or environment.

Despite the inaccuracy and inadequacy of the patient's presenting behavior as an index of his total need, it has an essential place in the establishment of a free flow of communication. Ruesch[6] notes that "cooperative abilities begin with the acknowledgment of the participants' perceptions of each other; this marks the opening signal for subsequent communicative exchanges." If the nurse responds to the patient by expressing aspects of the perceptions, thoughts, or feelings evoked in her by his initial behavior, several objectives are accomplished immediately. The patient has the impact of a nurse, who actually sees him, is aware of him, is interested in him, and is implicitly or explicitly asking him to verify, correct, or elaborate on her perceptions. He is thus encouraged to reveal what he is experiencing, thinking, or attempting to communicate in the situation. His responses, verbal and non-verbal, stimulate new thoughts and feelings in the nurse, aspects of which she may continue to express or utilize in an effort to understand with the patient his present situation. This ongoing communicative process sets the stage for nursing as a cooperative endeavor.

REFERENCES

1. VanSan, Genne "Patients' Problems Are Not Always Obvious. *American Journal of Nursing,* April 1962, p. 59.

2. McCabe, Gracia, "Cultural Influences on Patient Behavior," *American Journal of Nursing,* August 1960.

3. Brown, Esther Lucile, *Newer Dimensions of Patient Care,* Part II, Introduction and Chapter I, Russell Sage Foundation, New York, 1962.

4. New, P. K.; Nite, Gladys and Callahan, Josephine M., *Nursing Service and Patient Care: A Staffing Experiment,* Community Studies, Inc., Kansas City, Missouri, November 1959, pp. 73ff.

5. Aydelotte, Myrtle K., *An Investigation of the Relation Between Nursing Activity and Patient Welfare,* State University of Iowa, 1960.

6. Ruesch, Jurgen and Kees, Weldon, *Nonverbal Communication,* University of California Press, Berkeley and Los Angeles, 1956, p. 82.

BIBLIOGRAPHY

Brown, Esther Lucile, *Newer Dimensions Of Patient Care,* Part I and II, Russell Sage Foundation, New York, 1962.

Orlando, I.J., *The Dynamic Nurse-Patient Relationship,* G. P. Putram's Sons, New York, 1961.

Peplau, Hildegard, *Interpersonal Relations in Nursing,* G. P. Putnam's Sons, New York, 1952.

XII INTERBEHAVIORAL DIMENSIONS OF THE PATIENT-PHYSICIAN RELATIONSHIP

Medicine today is focused sharply on the laboratory methods of biological technology; as a consequence, the education of physicians tends to overlook the fact that health delivery occurs essentially in a relationship between a patient and his physician. As Sigerist, the eminent medical historian has written (Marti-Ibanez, 1960):

> In every medical action there are always two parties involved, the physician and the patient or, in a broader sense, the medical corps and society. Medicine is nothing else than the manifold relations between these two groups. The history of medicine, therefore, cannot limit itself to the history of the science, institutions and characters of medicine, but must include the history of the patient in society, that of the physician, and the history of the relations between physician and patient.

All of the chapters of this volume are geared to achieve one primary purpose: to educate the medical student in ways that will maximize his competence in the patient-physician relationship. Be it the study of the socialization of the student-physician, the biobehavioral factors in physical illness, the crises of human development, or the experience of patienthood, each of these earlier topics, as well as future ones, is designed to contribute to the effective practice of general medicine. The patient-physician relationship is not merely one of many co-equal topics in the study of behavioral medicine; rather, it lies at the heart of all fields of medicine.

Despite the diverse streams of knowledge and experience that have an ultimate bearing upon the patient-physician relationship, there is need, at some point, to bring it into clear focus, that is, to concentrate on the study of the relationship itself. This focus is especially justified with first year medical students, for as Pollack and Manning have noted (1967):

> ... Although freshman students seem to be sentitive to the patients' problems, as they progress through school to senior status, they apparently show less interest and proficiency in relating to patients as persons. This purported change is ascribed to a complex of reasons:
> ... 1. The freshman is introduced to patients within a framework of organic pathology, and there is great emphasis on organic disease throughout the years of medical school.
> ... 2. Increasing interest and attention is directed toward highly specialized laboratory procedures necessary for the technical treatment of diseased organ systems.
> ... 3. Emphasis on scientific scrutiny and objective inquiry tends to "dehumanize" the patient.

Although relationships between patients and physicians differ in significant ways from other forms of social interaction, they do share a number of features in common. In all relationships there is a process of mutual influence in which each member assumes that what he does or says will affect the actions of the others. A breakdown in this sequence of the reciprocal impacts will destroy the character of the interaction, e.g., a physician who fails to acknowledge a patients' complaints, appearing preoccupied with matters elsewhere, is likely to lose the confidence required to maintain the relationship. Social interactions of this nature will also involve sequential interpretations, that is, each participant conveys meaning in his behaviors and simultaneously analyzes the intent or reason for the actions of the other. To guide the interpretive process, that is, to make it more communicative, each participant creates an image that reflects his status, mood, or purpose. Thus, through body language or other nonverbal cues, a patient may establish an image of his present state of health, e.g., rather than walking into the doctor's office at a brisk pace with a bright and cheerful smile, he drags in slowly, looking exhausted and morose.

Despite the many interbehavioral features that the physician-patient relationship shares with other forms of social interaction, there are several characteristics that set it apart and distinguish it. In discussing the views of the prominent sociologist, Talcott Parsons, Bloom and Wilson comment as follows (1972):

> The Parsonian assertion that the roles of treater and client must be mutually understood and mutually rewarded does not at all mean that practitioners and patients are equals in the therapeutic situation. In the nature of the case, it is calculated that some significant change is to be promoted in the behavior, the total state of health, of the patient. As the skilled person meets the unskilled and tries to alter the latter, the parties can no more be equals than are parent and child or teacher and student. The helping agent, it is asserted, must have leverage to induce change; this leverage is generated by over-all circumstances, notably the *professional prestige* and *situational authority* of the health agent and the *situational dependency* of the patient.

The three papers comprising this chapter deal with different aspects of the patient-physician relationship. The first, by C. Allen Haney, a medical sociologist, concerns a major role assumed by the physician, that of decision maker. As Haney notes, most faculty conceive medical decision-making as an "art," one that can be acquired by mere observation and osmosis, rather than by systematic study. Recent studies of how medical decisions are made indicate that it is an intricate form of probability analysis in which the physician sifts through the data available to him and assigns the patient to one or another disease category. Haney contends that medical decisions of the probability type are determined in great measure by factors other than the physical signs of the illness alone. In his discussion, he notes a variety of determinants that derive from the social background of the patient, the value system of the physician, and the interaction of these behavioral determinants. Most useful to the student is Haney's schema for learning effective decision-making and for predicting such matters as the choice of future specialities.

Haney's article illustrates trends in a movement that is now two decades old, a movement that seeks to study the physician-patient relationship in a formal and systematic manner, rather than in a cursory way. An early original analysis in accord with this newer approach was proposed in the mid-1950's by two prominent medical scholars, Thomas Szasz and Marc Hollender. Their paper, the second article of the chapter, deserves special attention, since it presents a careful exposition of several "relationship models" established between physicians and patients. Szasz and Hollender organize these models into three categories: active-passive, guidance-cooperation, and mutual participation. As suggested in their paper, certain relationships are suitable for particular types of problems; others may not be as conducive to optimal care. Not only do some patients seek or create relationships that are inappropriate to their physical needs, but physicians themselves may unconsciously eliminate from their active practice those patients who fail to adopt the type of relationship they find congenial to their professional image.

The third article of the chapter, by the sociologist Morris J. Daniels, addresses itself to another aspect of the patient-physician interaction, that of "affect and its control." Relationships between doctors and their clients are characterized by a balance between psychological empathy and interpersonal distance. A problem that often arises, particularly among medical students and young physicians, is that they feel removed or indifferent with certain patients, and overinvolved or deeply affected by others. Although it is quite natural for the medical student to empathize with the plight of those with whom he works, he must, at the same time, protect himself from the emotional strains and entanglements that this can engender. Daniels describes the elements of this struggle with great clarity and offers some guidance as to how the dilemma might be resolved.

REFERENCES

Marti-Ibanez, Felix (ed.): *Henry Sigerist on the History of Medicine.* New York, MD Publications, 1960.

Pollack, S., and Manning, P. R.: An experience in teaching the doctor-patient relationship to first-year medical students. *J. Med. Educ. 42:* 770–774 (1967).

34   Psychosocial Factors Involved in Medical Decision Making

C. Allen Haney

In this book are described a variety of trends and developments in medical education and practice that are associated with the search for more efficient ways of delivering medical services. These developments and innovations — most of them spurred by the increasing shortage of medical manpower — range from increased use of computers for diagnosis to programs for training "medical associates" or "medical assistants"* to perform such time-consuming tasks of the physician as taking histories and conducting routine physical examinations.

Like most of the approaches to solving the medical manpower shortage, the deferring of activities to paramedical personnel increases the number, if not the complexity, of the doctor's decisions. And it is probably safe to say that no single aspect of medical education is so important and yet has received so little attention as the

---

*At present there are probably less than ten such training programs. The developers of these programs agree that the new practitioner will have a range of responsibilities broader than that of a nurse but narrower than that of a physician.

The stated goal of these programs is to train individuals to handle a great many routine, time-consuming tasks, so that the physician will be free to make the actual medical judgments and to diagnose, treat, and manage problem cases.

Haney, C. A.: Psychosocial factors involved in medical decision making. In Coombs, R., and Vincent, C. (eds.): Psychosocial Aspects of Medical Training. Springfield, Ill., Charles C Thomas, 1971.

decision-making process. Whatever else a physician may be, he is a decision maker. An increasing proporation of his time is required for this task which, as an extremely subjective endeavor, is most likely to generate anxiety and uncertainty.

The medical decision-making process has been neglected for a long time. Neither the Flexner Report nor the Coggeshall Report[1] recognized the significance and need of systematic training for decision making. Perhaps because of the difficulty and complexity of such training, the implicit assumption has been that medical students have been left to learn decision making by osmosis rather than by systematic study. It frequently is written off as "that element of medical science which is more appropriately considered art," and dismissed as a function of intuition or "clinical judgment." The minimum attention given medical decision making implies that the process is either so straightforward as to make a study of the factors influencing the process unnecessary or so subjective and specific to a given situation as to make such a study useless.

What does the physician mean when he states that his decisions are based on "clinical evidence?" Studies in tuberculosis hospitals indicate that such "clinical evidence" is obtained not only from reading the reports of x-ray examinations and bacteriological studies, but from a consideration of such factors as who took and who interpreted the x-rays, who examined the slides, how long the patient has been in the hospital, and also what circumstances await the patient upon discharge.[2]

Consciously or subconsciously, the physician uses a highly complicated process for weighing and evaluating all the evidence relevant to the decisions he must make daily. If it is not fully understood, this process may ill serve his medical practice and personal life. Increases in his patient load, in paper work, and in medical knowledge make ever increasing demands on the physician and leave him with all too little time and energy for the really difficult and critical decisions. This situation is compounded by the patient's age-old concept of the physician as a "counselor and advisor" on nonmedical problems. As if this were not enough, the physician also is expected to make an increasing number of medicolegal decisions regarding certain drastic treatment regimens, abortions, and mental incompetence. All of these decisions involve not only his medical knowledge but his values, his attitudes, and his decision-making "set," i.e. his view of his role as a decision maker.

Regrettably, we have only a modicum of empirical data regarding this role.* Through the years it has been assumed that somehow in the course of medical education or during the early years of practice the young physician will automatically absorb the inclinations, attitudes, values, and skills necessary for decision making. He does, of course, but not always in the proper proportion.

Ideally, the physician's decision-making set must be rigid enough to protect him from the anxiety that would otherwise be engendered by constant and crucial decision making and at the same time flexible enough to prevent the various contingencies of a given case from becoming paralyzing barriers to action. Much of the existing literature relevant to this rigidity-flexibility continuum tends to assume that the physician has a very limited, undimensional philosophic orientation.[4,5]

Lusted has defined diagnosis, and thereby, medical decision making as a special type of probability analysis. In this process the task is one in which the clinician sifts through the data available to him and assigns the patient, on the basis of probability statements, to a taxonomic category.[3] The contention in this chapter is that the assessment of probabilities and ultimately the assignment of the patient to a category is influenced by a host of

---

*One notable exception to this general tendency to neglect medical decision making is the body of material most clearly and concisely coordinated and organized by Lee B. Lusted. It is his contention, and conceded here, that there have been two major foci in the study of medical decision making. One of these has been the concern with attempts to develop techniques and computer aids to assist in medical decision making. The other has been the tendency to examine the physician as the occupant of a decision-making role. See Lusted.[3]

contingencies which reside not only in the illness, but in the patient, the operating philosophy of the physician, and in the interaction of these contingencies.

In the remainder of this chapter I will try to make explicit some of the factors that influence decision making and to demonstrate the dimensions along which these influences operate. I will also attempt to provide some theoretical schemata for teaching decision making and for predicting the choice of a specialty. Before proceeding with these tasks, it is necessary to make explicit some of the tacit assumptions that underlie medical decision making.

IMPLICIT ASSUMPTIONS IN DECISION MAKING

One primary assumption is that the physician must always suspect illness. Although few empirical studies are available to document this assertion, Bakwin's study of medical decisions regarding the need for tonsillectomy in children and Garland's studies of diagnostic error in roentgenology both indicate that the pervasive attitude among physicians is that "it is better to suspect illness than not — better safe than sorry."[6,7]

It would seem that the traditional injunction, *primum non nocere* ("first do no harm"), is suspended in favor of the rule, "first do something." This unwritten rule stems partially from the public's typical overevaluation of treatment: when a patient has a complaint and consults a physician, he usually expects some form of treatment. Aware of this expectation, the physician responds by "doing something." The decision to do something is perhaps so automatic a response that is rarely even recognized as a decision. Two basic and quite pervasive assumptions which bolster this response, and thereby preclude critical questioning of the decision to "first do something," have been made explicit by Scheff.[5]

The first assumption is that disease is an inevitably unfolding process which will, if undetected and untreated, increase in severity until it reaches threatening propor-

tions. Although this is an oversimplified statement of the assumption, the point is simply that the rule to "first do something" is supported by the assumption of a deterministic process in disease.

The second assumption is that medical diagnosis is in itself neutral and innocuous in comparison to the dangers resulting from disease.[5] Medical diagnosis or observation, even though it may involve pain, inconvenience, or expense, is not seen as capable of doing appreciable damage to the patient.

These two assumptions which buttress the rule or decision to do something are consistent with ethical standards and are highly functional. They facilitate such results as satisfying patients and providing legal protection:

> ... A physician who dismisses a patient who subsequently dies of a disease that should have been detected is not only subject to legal action for negligence and possible loss of license for incompetence, but also to moral condemnation from his colleagues and from his own conscience for his delinquency.[5]

Most medical decisions, however, are not as automatic and simple as is the decision to do something, nor as well supported by other working assumptions. Even casual observations of medical practice reveals a host of complex factors and value hierarchies which influence medical decision making. In addition, a wide variety of implicit assumptions and biases derive from the conflict between the scientific and the humanistic approach to illness, from the selective perceptions in physician-patient interaction, and from the social, occupational, and familial expectations arising outside the treatment relationship but impinging on it.

To illustrate this point, I will discuss several sources of bias in medical decision making and then examine some implications for the teaching of decision making. The kind and degree of bias associated with these sources, while not unique to a given physician, are not necessarily recurrent. They may change over time and may show variations related to the nature of the illness, the patient, and the treatment setting. The bias arising from any of these sources does not always take the same direction, and it is probably more pronounced in some specialties than in others, and among physicians trained in some schools than among those trained in other schools. Moreover, the direction and degree of bias are also a function of the physician's experience. The fact remains, however, that these sources of bias can be observed in any setting with relative ease.

SELECTED SOURCES OF BIAS IN MEDICAL DECISION MAKING

Recruitment to the Profession

The very nature of medical education is such that students must have a background in the basic sciences in order to master the material. Hence, medical schools give preference to applicants with a more scientific background over those with a humanistic background. The extension of this point is that, throughout the premedical and preclinical years of training, students are molded into disease-oriented "scientists," trained to make objective, clear-cut decisions (frequently in areas where the issue is dichotomized). When the clinical years begin, however, the emphasis is on the "whole man" concept, and nonscientific contingencies are introduced into the decision-making process. The student is asked to become patient-oriented, capable of making decisions in unstructured and ambigious situations in which pain and discomfort take on more than abstract meaning.

A student with an extremely good record in the preclinical years may lose his ability and even his inclination to make decisions when faced with "flesh and blood" patients. The problem centers on the fact that he has been selected and trained to be concerned primarily with intellectual matters rather than human-relation ones. He has, in a sense, been expected to obtain great knowledge, often at the expense of understanding.* Yet medical educators

---

*This point has been elaborated by A. Steiger, and V. A. Hansen, Jr., in their book *Patients and You.*[32]

hopefully assume that, through experience, the physician will learn to reconcile the two viewpoints so that his decision making will not be impaired by inability to maintain a balance between the disease-oriented scientist and the patient-oriented humanitarian.

Transactions Between Physicians and Patients

Another source of bias influencing decision making derives from the transactions that inevitably take place between doctor and patient. These transactions have been the object of research in psychiatric treatment settings, but they have received minimum attention in the context of other medical decisions.

Balint,[8] Coleman,[9] and Frank[10] have documented the transaction (offer and response) which occurs between the physician and the patient at the time of diagnosis. They have noted that patients may overstate their subjective symptoms in an attempt to justify their presence in the doctor's office. The hypochondriac's purely imaginary ailments are an extreme example, but even the genuinely ill individual may use overstated symptoms as "tickets to treatment" or as justification for any number of other problems attributed to "not feeling well."[9] Other patients will minimize the magnitude of their problems in order to appear stoic.[11] I am not concerned here with the psychodynamics which prompt the patient to take one or the other of these approaches but simply want to point out that the patient may, for conscious or subconscious reasons, modify the information he shares with the physician in an attempt to alter the latter's evaluation of him.

Another complicating factor is that symptoms and signs normally associated with disease have been found to exist in a high proporation of the "normal" population. There is a rapidly expanding group of studies showing that the significance of many common signs of disease is somewhat less straightforward than was previously thought. For example, Schwartz and Baum[12] have found that histoplasmosis, once thought to be a rare tropical disease with a uniformly poor prognosis, is widely prevalent and well tolerated in some populations. The same kind of evidence exists regarding such physical diseases as high blood pressure as well as some mental disorders.[13-16]

Some symptoms reported by patients can be quickly and accurately verified by objective means. In other cases, however, test results may conflict with what the patient reports. Symptoms such as pain, furthermore, are highly subjective. Before making any diagnostic decision, the physician must decide which, if any, of the patient's complaints are valid and significantly beyond those expected in the normal population. This process involves a series of decisions dependent upon his ability to weigh and sift through the patient's information.

Where decisions regarding treatment are concerned, the problem is somewhat more straightforward. In diagnosis, the patient offers symptoms and the physician responds with a diagnosis. After that, the situation is reversed. The physician offers a treatment regimen and the patient responds with either acceptance or rejection (partial or complete). At this point, bargaining must take place. The physician evaluates the situation from the point of view of caution, effectiveness, and accuracy: the patient, on the other hand, considers expense, pain, inconvenience, and his evaluation of the physician. The physician, with justification (since patients are seldom ideal), often overstates the importance of directions for treatment in order to make sure that at least the minimum requirements will be met.

In tuberculosis hospitals, for example, one of the key areas of bargaining is over a "timetable."[2] Patients attempt to put pressure on the physician for more activities, to get surgery if they feel they need it, and ultimately to be discharged. The physician and the patient both develop norms about the time required for treatment. The patient has his future in mind; the physician is concerned with a complete recovery. Often the patient considers time of more crucial importance than pain or expense. When there is marked conflict between physician and patient, the two must bargain; unless the difference can be resolved, the realtionship must be terminated. The weapons used by the patient in the bargaining process may include arguments, threats, name calling, and tears. The physician, on the other hand, must rely on communicating his greater knowledge, on his personal charisma, and, as a last resort, on institutional red tape and formal policy statements.

Thus, the physician's decision making will be influenced by his own feelings of security in his profession as well as by his assessments of the patient's attitudes toward medicine, his desire for recovery, and other contingencies influencing his response to treatment.

The Physician's Concept of the Sick Role

Related to the idea of offer and response outlined above is the concept of the "sick role."[17, 18] The sick role in our society is a conditionally legitimate[19] role whereby the sick person is temporarily exempted from his normal work and from social and personal responsibilities and is not blamed for being ill. The sick role remains legitimate, however, only if the patient satisfies two conditions or obligations: (1) that he seek help, and (2) that he try to get well as rapidly as possible.

The physician's decision making will be influenced by the extent to which he is aware of and believes in the process of sick-role behavior. Scheff[5] pointed out how easy it is for a person to enter the sick role or take on symptoms in circumstances where no serious health problem would have arisen if a physician had not confirmed the patient's suspicion of illness. Trained to find signs of disease if they are present, the physician searches diligently through the information he has about the patient; at the same time the patient, who has defined himself as needing treatment, is searching through his subjective repertoire of feelings, impulses, and sensations for symptoms. In the process, an assessment of the situation which pleases both may be uncovered.[5]

There is a growing body of literature to support the belief that symptoms can become fixated by hasty diagnosis in questionable cases; "iatrogenic" heart disease is a case in point. Warren and Wolter[20] state that the physician, "by calling attention to a murmur or some cardiovascular abnormality, even though functionally insignificant, may precipitate" symptoms of heart disease. Eichorn and Anderson[21] report evidence that people with an iatrogenic syndrome make more changes in their lives than patients with the actual disease.

So great is the power of suggestion that the patient may sometimes be influenced by reactions from the doctor, of which the latter is completely unaware. Research has indicated that a patient who is inclined to adopt the sick role can get "hooked" on chronic illness by such unintentional validation as the look on a physician's face. Such subtle clues may also influence the patient's response to the physician's search for information and may significantly alter the flow of valid information.

If he is to minimize distortion in decision making, the physician needs to remain constantly alert for secondary gains that might accrue to the patient, to members of the patient's family, or even to the medical or nursing staff from a diagnosis of chronic illness. Exemption from work and responsibility and from blame for his condition is often the goal that the patient is seeking, consciously or not. In some cases, however, the patient's family, the medical staff, and even fellow patients[19] can gratify certain needs through the patient's sickness. In cases where the illness brings a pension or compensation, the secondary gains are obvious. Less obvious gains that may be sought include removal of the patient from a family or from a personal crisis. Bursten and D'Esopo[19] have reported cases in which problems were solved by the patient's illness.

Secondary gains for the medical and nursing staffs are occasionally responsible for the fact that "good" patients become fixtures on the ward. Certain procedures, phrases, or even nonverbal clues, used intentionally or inadvertently, can convey to the patient the expectation that he will remain chronically ill. This expectation can be conveyed by the withdrawal of a medication that the patient has been told was very effective, or by the failure to grant certain privileges at the time the patient expects them.

Prognosis, Responsibility, and Stigma

Closely related to the concept of the sick role is a cluster of three factors which are a source of bias and which influence not only the finding of illness but also the severity of the diagnosis and the choice of treatment: (1) the prognosis for the condition, (2) the patient's responsibility for his illness, and (3) the stigma which may be attached to a given diagnosis or treatment.[22]

The influence of possible prognosis on decision making can be seen most clearly in situations where the suspected illness will have a sweeping effect on the patient's life. The more damning the diagnosis, the more hesitant the physician will be to name the disease without careful consideration of all contingencies. The more serious the possible outcome, the more careful and comprehensive will be the data collection. The physician's difficulty is greatest in the extreme situation where the only alternatives available involve treatments nearly as dangerous as the disease and entail devastating social and emotional consequences.

At the other extreme is the situation in which a child has symptoms suggesting a minor illness that is "all over town." The physician may not even feel that it is necessary to see the patient but may simply prescribe by telephone, having decided that the prognosis is of such a nature that this casual management is all that is required.

The second factor in this cluster refers to the patient's real or presumed part in "causing" his condition. The responsibility the physician himself may feel, because of failure to see the patient promptly, inaccurate diagnosis, or improper treatment, may also contribute to the nature of his decision making; but we are concerned here only with the patient's responsibility. In considering the concept of the sick role, we noted that the patient has an obligation to try to get well. The social mores concerning this obligation are very viable; if there is any evidence that the patient has failed to comply with the physician's instructions or in other ways has not tried his best to get well, he is considered at least partially responsible for his condition and therefore not worthy of the same consideration as more conscientious patients.

In the extreme, this attitude is illustrated by Sudnow's study of cases in which the admitting diagnosis was "dead on arrival."[23, 24] He reported that efforts at resuscitation, and even the tests used to confirm death are apt to be cursory in the case of patients sent to the hospital as a result of their own drunken driving. When a "wino" is brought to the hospital with no respiration or pulse, he is likely to be pronounced dead, with no attempt at resuscitation, after a stethoscopic examination shows no heartbeat. A child or an apparently well-to-do businessman with the same outward signs of death is more likely to be the subject of dramatic efforts at restimulation.

As this illustration suggests, one of the key features by which responsibility for one's condition is determined is the smell of alcohol on the breath. To quote Sudnow:[23]

The alcoholic patient is treated by hospital physicians, not only when the status of the body as alive or dead is at stake, but throughout the whole course of medical treatment, as one for whom the concern to treat can properly operate somewhat weakly.

Sudnow contends that this decision is based on the physician's evaluation of the patient's moral worth. I would argue, however, that the crucial determinant is instead the physician's assignment of blame or responsibility for the condition. In general, more perfunctory examinations and more apathetic care are the lot of all patients who, according to public opinion, could have avoided their present condition. These include victims of attempted suicide, dope addicts, known prostitutes, assailants in crimes of violence, and vagrants.

The third source of bias in decision making is stigma, which is inextricably bound up with the two foregoing factors.

The diagnosis of schizophrenia provides an illustration of how stigma may serve as a source of bias in medical decision making. The decision to enter this diagnosis on a patient's record is influenced by the physician's concern over the extent to which it will alienate the significant people in the patient's life and will prejudice other physicians and health-related professionals who may deal with the patient in the future. In some cases the physician's concern may be great enough to cause him to withhold an official diagnosis of schizophrenia, even though he may treat the disease as such. The factor of stigma also affects the physician's decisions regarding the formal diagnosis of diseases such as syphilis, leprosy, and tuberculosis in a highly regarded patient. The physician often feels that the loathing, fear or disgust associated with these diseases would be extremely destructive to the patient's self-concept. Certain surgical procedures and treatment regimens also fall into this category.

Third-Party Intervention

The diagnosis and treatment of disease may often be complicated by a conflict of interests, especially if the doctor is serving as the agent of somebody other than the patient.[25] For example, he may be employed by an insurance company, appointed by a judicial body, returning a favor for a colleague by treating a member of his family, or delivering a baby born out of wedlock to the fourteen-year-old daughter of one of his long-time patients. In each case where the physician does not have a direct and exclusive relation to the patient as a client, he must continually clarify for himself his responsibility to the patient and the way in which his relationship to a third party may be influencing his decisions concerning what he reports to whom. These complex situations with potential conflicts of interest include not only involvements with courts, insurance companies and minors, but the day-to-day relationships with other doctors that occur in teaching hospitals and partnerships.

The Physician's Values

Finally, decision making is inevitably influenced by the values and value hierarchies of the physician. The death or impending death of a patient is particularly revealing of a physician's values. Under what conditions are heroic livesaving procedures undertaken? Some of the unique contingencies which can influence decision making are illustrated when the dying patient is a particularly important person. Note the following report made by an attending physician about the treatment of President Kennedy after his assassination:[26]

Medically, it was apparent the President was not alive when he was brought in. There was no spontaneous respiration. He had dilated, fixed pupils. It was obviously a lethal head wound. Technically, however, by using rigorous resuscitation, intravenous tubes and all the supportive measures, we were able to raise the semblance of a heart beat.

As indicated above, contingencies residing in the patient can call into play certain of the physician's values. Contingencies which stem from the treatment setting can also raise value questions for the physician. Values in a teaching hospital, for example, are often different from those in an institution concerned only with healing. When the physician is also teacher and scientist, it may be difficult for him to put the interests of the patient first in all cases. Is the patient's discomfort relieved immediately, or is the teaching value of the case considered first? Is the patient's discharge sometimes delayed while tests are run for purposes of research instead of treatment?

The important role of values in medical decision making has not escaped critical consideration. It has received recurring attention because biomedical advances continue to bring new problems along with scientific gains. Stickel contends that the most perplexing of these value questions have emerged in the wake of tissue and organ transplantation. It is his belief that values both tangible (that is, those which can be ranked in some monetary or numerical scale) and intangible (those which cannot be so ranked) all must be weighted together in the decision process.[27] By their nature some values, the tangible ones, can

be communicated in the form of broad guidelines. Other values, the intangible, can only be determined by the observation of the decision-making process of other physicians. The implication of importance here is that each physician must come to grips with his personal values as well as institutionalized ones. To the extent that a balance can be achieved early in his career, the decision-making biases to which these values contribute can be recognized and compensated for, if not eliminated.*

In institutions where new doctors are learning their professions and research is being carried out, decision making is influenced by the tendency to regard patients less as people needing treatment than as means to the end of collecting "experience-related" information. In such a situation the administration and physicians themselves can legitimately institute a wide variety of practices and procedures which may be unrelated to the strict interests of the patient or even in conflict with his interests. The activities associated with teaching, research, and treatment will always influence the decision-making processes of those who work within a teaching hospital; when the values underlying these different spheres of activity are conflicting and even contradictory, decision making will be that much more complex and time consuming.

The extent to which the physician's decision making is influenced by the foregoing sources of bias is quite variable. This fact is hardly surprising in view of the wide variability in the personal dynamics of the physician and his patients, in diseases, treatments, and sites of surgery, and in institutions and institutional policies. The fact remains that, as the physician becomes more and more a decision maker and less and less a technician, increasing attention should be directed toward teaching and training related to decision-making processes. The foregoing discussion of factors and sources of bias influencing medical decision making is but an exploratory probe down

_____

*At this point, a discussion of the situation ethic could be introduced but it would add little to the main thesis of this chapter.

what should become a long road of research, teaching, and training in this increasingly important area of the physician's professional life. Continuing in this exploratory spirit, I will now attempt to provide some heuristic schemas related to decision making and the choice of a medical specialty.

IMPLICATIONS FOR DECISION MAKING AND IN THE SELECTION OF A SPECIALTY

A number of common themes run throughout the foregoing discussion of the sources of bias in decision making. These themes and their interaction are here translated into several dimensions which, in my opinion, can be used to clarify the decision-making skills required in certain specialties. Perhaps, with refinement, these dimensions might be used to predict the student's choice of a specialty and even the satisfaction he would find in a particular speciality.

The Treatment Mode: An Active-Passive Continuum

The first dimension is the treatment mode, which comprises an active-passive continuum. At one end of this continuum is the situation in which the patient is totally inactive. At the opposite end is the situation in which the patient is actively engaged in working with the physician toward his own cure. Midway between these extremes is the situation in which the physician gives guidance and the patient cooperates. This continuum, first developed by Szasz and Hollender,[28],[29] can be used heuristically to identify several different pure or ideal types of physician-patient interaction.

In the treatment mode characterized by an active physician and a passive patient, things are done to the patient whose cooperation is unnecessary. This is the mode used during surgery and in cases where the patient is unconscious for any reason. At the other extreme is the treatment mode most often used in chronic illness when the patient conducts his own treatment with only occasional consultations with the physician. This mode is clearly illustrated in illnesses such as diabetes. In the middle of this continuum is the mode characterized by a relationship in which the patient comes seeking treatment, usually for an acute illness. Because such a patient is most often in need of relief from some distress or discomfort, he or she is usually cooperative and willing to follow instructions.

The skills needed for the physician to operate effectively are different for each of these modes of treatment, and decision making in each is biased by influences inherent in that mode. It should be noted that the treatment mode appropriate at admission may undergo changes during the course of treatment. To use Hollender's example:[29]

When a patient with diabetes mellitus is brought to the hospital in coma, the relationship must be based on the activity-passivity [physician active, patient passive] model. The physician must do something to the patient who is completely helpless (unconscious). Later the patient has to be educated (guided) and during this stage must cooperate. Finally, ideally, he is treated as a full fledged partner in the management of his own health (mutual participation).

The Physician's Personal Orientation: An Intervention-Maintenance Continuum

As if the treatment mode were not sufficient to complicate the decision-making process, the physician's personal orientation toward the maintenance-intervention continuum must be added to the equation. This personal orientation may be derived from the physician's early personal-belief systems or may emerge during his training; in either event, it is likely to be modified by his experience in medical practice. The physician's personal orientation determines, at least in part, his approach to medicine, his definition of disease, and even his determination of good and bad treatment.

The interventionist is more likely to be disease oriented, whereas the physician characterized by a tendency toward maintenance is more likely to be patient oriented. Generally the interventionist is inclined toward immediate action. He considers it more culpable to dismiss a sick patient than to retain a well one. The strong pressures encouraging the interventionist perspective were noted earlier in the discussion of the rule, "First, do something."*

The influence of the physician's personal orientation on decisions he makes is obviously qualified by a number of factors.[30] The first is the nature of the disease, discussed in the foregoing section. Some diseases or ailments demand a specific type of response. Coma, for example, dictates a mode of treatment in which the physician is active and the patient passive. Similarly, certain diseases dictate intervention rather than maintenance. When the disease is such that the outcome is uncertain and treatment is costly, painful, protracted, and of questionable value, intervention may be so obviously inappropriate that the physician, regardless of his personal orientation, is forced to settle for maintenance.

The physician's assessment of the many nonmedical aspects of the patient's personality and life situation can also influence the personal-orientation dimension of decision making. The patient defined as a "crock" will undoubtedly not warrant the same degree of intervention as the stoic who minimizes serious symptoms.

Finally, the degree of responsibility the physician feels toward the patient influences his place in this dimension. This feeling of responsibility, or the lack of it, can have many sources. Some of these stem from the unique characteristics of the case; others are determined by the treatment setting; and still others reside in the personality of the physician.

The Physician's Philosophic Orientation: A Scientistic-Humanistic Continuum

A third dimension involved in medical decision making is the physician's philosophic orientation toward the scientistic-

---

*Scheff refers to this tendency to treat illness when it is only suspected as "conservatism."

humanistic continuum. This dimension is difficult to conceptualize. It is partially evident in the tendency for one physician to call for tests while another relies on experience or "hunches." In this context, the dimension might be polarized into a scientistic-experiential continuum. The present discussion, however, is focused more on the conflict seen especially in teaching hospitals between scientific pursuits and the interests of the patient. The relative merits of the scientistic versus the humanistic orientation have been debated for some time, and as yet no consensus has been reached.[31] This fact makes it even more important that the physician attempt to clarify this dimension of the decision-making process by examining his own value priorities. These may be revealed in his answers to questions such as, Whose agent am I? Am I primarily a researcher in a medical school, a teacher, a healer of the sick? His answers to these and related questions can enhance his awareness of his philosophic orientation and its influence upon his medical decisions.

The humanist is more inclined to view the administering of medical care as a special form of psychosocial interaction. Implicit at this pole of the dimension is the assumption that medical care relies to a great extent on the physician's perceptual and communication skills and his ability to draw inferences and to make judgments and decisions in keeping with the patient's entire life situation. This assumption has been examined in a different context by John Romano,[4] who contends that the art of medicine (humanism) is based on intuition because it is gained in human interaction; most physicians, he believes, consider it basically different from knowledge gained by the conscious, systematic pursuit of information (scientism).

Three Dimensions Combined

Although other dimensions enter into the decision-making process, the three just discussed are considered basic in structuring the physician's decision-making set. When there is unresolved conflict within or between these dimensions, the result may be considerable personal distress for the physician. Conversely, a physician who has a harmonious combination of attitudes within and between these dimensions derives great support and defense against the anxiety produced by the constant need to make literally vital decisions in situations of uncertainty.

At the onset of this paper it was asserted that the physician uses a complicated weighing system in reaching decisions. These dimensions of decision making, as well as the others not dealt with, provide the basis for this weighing system. The combined operation of these three dimensions is shown in Figure 34-1. It should be noted that since the dimensions considered are as yet unmeasured, the location assigned to each medical specialty is more approximate than exact. Furthermore, a bar is used for each specialty to indicate that there is variation from one member of a speciality to the next. Of more vital imporatnce to the present discussion however is the implication that with each combination of locations on the three dimensions, the contingencies of a given case (or type of case) could be given a specific weight. For example, a physician

characterized by a personal orientation toward maintenance, a desire to treat in the mode of mutual participation, and a humanistic philosophy will give greater weight to the nonmedical contingencies.

If the dimensions just discussed are measurable, they might be used to predict the best choice of a specialty for a given medical student. Skills and knowledge from the field of behavioral science are more appropriate in some specialties (psychiatry, in particular) than in others, of which pathology is the extreme example. Decision making in psychiatry can be characterized as toward the extremes of humanism rather than scientism, of mutual participation rather than activity on the part of the physician, and of maintenance rather than intervention; hence it relies heavily upon the behavioral sciences. Decisions in the surgical specialities, which are generally the reverse on all three dimensions, are concerned less with nonmedical contingencies. The obvious implication is that a medical student who is most comfortable with patients that are passive, who defines himself as a scientist, and whose inclination is toward more intervention in the disease

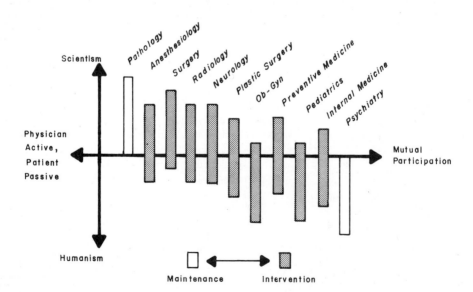

Figure 34-1. Hypothesized location of selected medical specialties on three dimensions of decision making.

process would be better satisfied in a specialty such as surgery than in psychiatry.

SUMMARY AND CONCLUSION

Decision making is rapidly becoming a primary task and responsibility of the physician. Decision making is subject to bias and distortion from many sources, of which some reside in the very nature of medical practice and some in the process of medical education. Others are inherent in human personality and human interaction. In an attempt to find classes or categories of contributing factors that influence the physician's decision-making set and thereby bias his decisions, I have posited three psychological dimensions which, both single and in combination, can affect the decisions made by a physician.

In conclusion, let me urge medical educators to turn their attention to ways of training physicians to recognize and compensate for those factors in themselves, in their patients, and in the setting of their practice which might bias the decisions they make concerning diagnosis and treatment. As a sort of byproduct of such training, the medical student might be aided in selecting the specialty for which he is best suited by virtue of his decision-making set.

REFERENCES

1. Coggeshall, L. T.: *Planning for Medical Progress Through Education.* Evanston, Association of American Medical Colleges, 1965.
2. Roth, J. A.: *Timetables: Structuring the Passage of Time in Hospital Treatment and Other Careers.* Indianapolis, Bobbs, Merrill, 1963.
3. Lusted, L. B.: *Introduction to Medical Decision Making.* Springfield, Charles C Thomas, 1968.
4. Romano, J.: Requiem or Reveille: The Clinician's Choice. *J Med Educ, 38:* 584–590, 1963.
5. Scheff, T. J.: Decision Rules, Types of Error, and Their Consequences in Medical Diagnosis. *Behavioral Science, 8:* 97–107, 1963.
6. Bakwin, H.: Pseudocia Pediatrica. *New Eng J of Med, 232:* 681–697, 1945.
7. Garland, L. H.: Studies of the Accuracy of Diagnostic Procedures. *Amer J Roentgen, 82:* 25–38, 1959.
8. Balint, M.: *The Doctor, His Patient and the Illness.* New York, International University Press, 1957.
9. Coleman, J.: Social Factors Influencing the Development and Containment of Psychiatric Symptoms, read before the First International Congress of Social Psychiatry. Reprinted in Scheff, T. (Ed.): *Mental Illness and Social Processes.* New York, Harper and Row, 1967, pp. 110, 158–168.
10. Frank, J. S.: The Dynamics of Psychotherapeutic Relationship. *Psychiatry, 22:* 17–34, 1959.
11. Koos, E.: *The Health of Regionville: What People Thought and Did About It.* New York, Columbia University Press, 1954.
12. Schwartz, J., and Baum, G. L.: The History of Histoplasmosis, *New Eng J Med, 256:* 253–258, 1957.
13. Plunkett, R. J., and Gordon, J. E.: *Epidemiology of Mental Illness.* New York, Basic Books Inc., 1961.
14. Dunn, J. P., and Etter, L. E.: Inadequacy of the Medical History in the Diagnosis of Duodenal Ulcer, *New Eng J of Med, 266:* 68-72, 1962.
15. Rautahargu, P. M., Karvonen, M. J., and Keys, A.: The Frequency of Arteriosclerotic and Hypertensive Heart Disease in Ostensibly Healthy Working Populations in Finland, *J Chron Dis, 13:* 426–439, 1961.
16. Stokes, J., and Dawber, T. R.: The "Silent Coronary"; The Frequency and Clinical Characteristics of the Unrecognized Myocardial Infarction in the Framingham Study. *Ann Intern Med, 50:* 1359-1369, 1959.
17. Parsons, T.: Illness and the Role of the Physician. *Amer J Orthopsychiat, 21:* 452–460, 1950.
18. Parsons, T.: The Social System. Glencoe, The Free Press, 1951, pp. 436–437.
19. Bursten, B., and D'Esopo, R.: The Obligation to Remain Sick, *Arch Gen Psychiat, 12:* 402–407, 1965.
20. Warren, J. V., and Wolter, J.: Symptoms and Diseases Induced by the Physician. *Gen Practitioner, 9:* 77–84, 1954.
21. Eichorn, R. L., and Anderson, R. M.: Changes in Personal Adjustment to Perceived and Medically Established Heart Disease: A Panel Study, presented in Washington, D. C. to the American Sociological Association, 1962.
22. These three concepts have been most clearly outlined in regard to rehabilitation; see,

Freidson, E.: Disability as Social Deviance. In Sussman, M. B. (Ed.): *Sociology and Rehabilitation.* Washington, American Sociological Association, 1965, pp. 71–99.

23. Sudnow, D.: Dead on Arrival. *Transaction, 5:* 36–43, 1967.

24. Sudnow, D.: *Passing On: The Social Organization of Dying.* Englewood Cliffs, Prentice Hall, 1967.

25. Szasz, T. S.: *Law, Liberty, and Psychiatry.* New York, MacMillan, 1963.

26. *The New York Times* (November 13, 1963).

27. Stickel, D. L.: Ethical and Moral Aspects of Transplantation. *Monogr Surg Sci, 3:* 267–301, 1966.

28. Szasz, T. S., and Hollender, M. H.: A Contribution to the Philosophy of Medicine – The Basic Models of the Doctor-Patient Relationship. *Arch Intern Med, 97:* 585–592, 1956.

29. Hollender, M. H.: *The Psychology of Medical Practice.* Philadelphia, W. B. Saunders Co., 1958, p. 8.

30. "Genetics and Ironing" or the Two Cultures and the Physician. Editorial, *Ann Intern Med, 52:* 523–524, 1962.

31. Wood, W. B.: *From Miasmas to Molecules.* New York, Columbia University Press, 1961, pp. 85–86.

32. Steiger, W. A., and Hansen, A. V., Jr.: *Patients and You.* Boston, Little, Brown, 1964.

35   A Contribution to the Philosophy of Medicine:

The Basic Models of the Doctor-Patient Relationship

Thomas S. Szasz and Marc H. Hollender

INTRODUCTION

When a person leaves the culture in which he was born and raised and migrates to another, he usually experiences his new social setting as something strange – and in some ways threatening – and he is stimulated to master it by conscious efforts at understanding. To some extent every immigrant to the United States reacts in this manner to the American scene. Similarly, the American tourist in Europe or South America "scrutinizes" the social setting which is taken for granted by the natives. To scrutinize – and criticize – the pattern of other peoples' lives is obviously both common and easy. It also happens, however, that people exposed to cross cultural experiences turn their attention to the very customs which formed the social matrix of their lives in the past. Lastly, to study the "customs" which shape and govern one's day-to-day life is most difficult of all.[1]

In many ways the psychoanalyst is like a person who has migrated from one culture to another. To him the relationship between physician and patient – which is like a custom that is taken for granted in medical practice and which he himself so treated in his early history – has become an object of study. While the precise nature and extent of the influence which psychoanalysis and so-called dynamic psychiatry have had on modern medicine are debatable, it seems to us that the most decisive effect has been that of making physicians explicitly aware of the possible significance of their relationship to patients.

The question naturally arises as to "What is a doctor-patient relationship?" It is our aim to discuss this question and to show that certain philosophical preconceptions

Szasz, T., and Hollender, M.: A contribution to the philosophy of medicine: The basic models of the doctor-patient relationship. Arch. Intern. Med. *97:* 585–592 (1956). Copyright 1956. American Medical Association.

associated with the notions of "disease," "treatment," and "cure" have a profound bearing on both the theory and the practice of medicine.*

WHAT IS A HUMAN RELATIONSHIP?

The concept of a relationship is a novel one in medicine. Traditionally, physicians have been concerned with "things," for example, anatomical structures, lesions, bacteria, and the like. In modern times the scope has been broadened to include the concept of "function." The phenomenon of a human relationship is often viewed as though it were a "thing" of a "function." It is, in fact, neither. Rather it is an abstraction, appropriate for the description and handling of certain observational facts. Moreover, it is an abstraction which presupposes concepts of both structure and function.

The foregoing comments may be clarified by concrete illustrations. Psychiatrists often suggest to their medical colleagues that the physician's relationship with his patient "per se" helps the latter. This creates the impression (whether so intended or not) that the relationship is a thing, which works not unlike the way that vitamins do in a case of vitamin deficiency. Another idea is that the doctor-patient relationship depends mainly on what the physician does (or thinks or feels). Then it is viewed not unlike a function.

When we consider a relationship in which there is joint participation of the two persons involved, "relationship" refers to neither a structure nor a function (such as the "personality" of the physician or patient). It is, rather, an abstraction embodying the activities of two interacting systems (persons).[5]

---

*In our approach to this subject we have been influenced by psychologic (psychoanalytic), sociologic, and philosophic considerations. See in this connection References 2-4 and Szasz, T. S.: On the Theory of Psychoanalytic Treatment, read before the Annual Meeting of the American Psychoanalytic Association, Atlantic City, N.J., May 7, 1955; Internat. J. Psychoanal., to be published.

THREE BASIC MODELS OF THE DOCTOR-PATIENT RELATIONSHIP

The three basic models of the doctor-patient relationship (see Table 35-1), which we will describe, embrace modes of interaction ubiquitous in human relationships and in no way specific for the contact between physician and patient. The specificity of the medical situation probably derives from a combination of these modes of interaction with certain technical procedures and social settings.

1. The Model of Activity-Passivity

Historically, this is the oldest conceptual model. Psychologically, it is not an interaction, because it is based on the effect of one person on another in such a way and under such circumstances that the person acted upon is unable to contribute actively, or is considered to be inanimate. This frame of reference (in which the physician does something to the patient) underlies the application of some of the outstanding advances of modern medicine (e.g., anesthesia and surgery, antibiotics, etc.). The physician is active; the patient, passive. This orientation has originated in — and is entirely appropriate for — the treatment of emergencies (e.g., for the patient who is severely injured, bleeding, delirious, or in coma). "Treatment" takes place irrespective of the patient's contribution and regardless of the outcome. There is a similarity here between the patient and a helpless infant, on the one hand, and between the physician and a parent, on the other. It may be recalled that psychoanalysis, too, evolved from a procedure (hypnosis) which was based on this model. Various physical measures to which psychotics are subjected today are another example of the activity-passivity frame of reference.

2. The Model of Guidance-Cooperation

This model underlies much of medical practice. It is employed in situations which are less desperate than those previously mentioned (e.g., acute infections). Although the patient is ill, he is conscious

TABLE 35-1   THREE BASIC MODELS OF THE PHYSICIAN-PATIENT RELATIONSHIP

Model	Physician's Role	Patient's Role	Clinical Application of Model	Prototype of Model
1. Activity-passivity	Does something to patient	Recipient (unable to respond or inert)	Anesthesia, acute trauma, coma, delirium, etc.	Parent-infant
2. Guidance-cooperation	Tells patient what to do	Cooperator (obeys)	Acute infectious processes, etc.	Parent-child (adolescent)
3. Mutual participation	Helps patient to help himself	Participant in "partnership" (uses expert help)	Most chronic illnesses, psychoanalysis, etc.	Adult-adult

and has feelings and aspirations of his own. Since he suffers from pain, anxiety, and other distressing symptoms, he seeks help and is ready and willing to "cooperate." When he turns to a physician, he places the latter (even if only in some limited ways) in a position of power. This is due not only to a "transference reaction" (i. e., his regarding the physician as he did his father when he was a child) but also to the fact that the physician possesses knowledge of his bodily processes which he does not have. In some ways it may seem that this, like the first model, is an active-passive phenomenon. Actually, this is more apparent than real. Both persons are "active" in that they contribute to the relationship and what ensues from it. The main difference between the two participants pertains to power, and to its actual or potential use. The more powerful of the two (parent, physician, employer, etc.) will speak of guidance or leadership and will expect cooperation of the other member of the pair (child, patient, employee, etc.). The patient is expected to "look up to" and to "obey" his doctor. Moreover, he is neither to question nor to argue or disagree with the orders he receives. This model has its prototype in the relationship of the parent and his (adolescent) child. Often, threats and other undisguised weapons of force are employed, even though presumably these are for the patient's "own good." It should be added that the possibility of the exploitation of the situation — as in any relationship between persons of unequal power — for the sole benefit of the physician, albeit under the guise of altruism, is ever present.

3.   The Model of Mutual Participation

Philosophically, this model is predicated on the postulate that equality among human beings is desirable. It is fundamental to the social structure of democracy and has played a crucial role in occidental civilization for more than two hundred years. Psychologically, mutuality rests on complex processes of identification — which facilitate conceiving of others in terms of oneself — together with maintaining and tolerating the discrete individuality of the observer and the observed. It is crucial to this type of interaction that the participants (1) have approximately equal power, (2) be mutually interdependent (i.e., need each other), and (3) engage in activity that will be in some ways satisfying to both,

This model is favored by patients who, for various reasons, want to take care of themselves (at least in part). This may be an overcompensatory attempt at mastering anxieties associated with helplessness and passivity. It may also be "realistic" and necessary, as, for example, in the management of most chronic illnesses (e.g., diabetes mellitus, chronic heart disease, etc.). Here the patient's own experiences provide reliable and important clues for therapy.

Moreover, the treatment program itself is principally carried out by the patient. Essentially, the physician helps the patient to help himself.

In an evolutionary sense, the pattern of mutual participation is more highly developed than the other two models of the doctor-patient relationship. It requires a more complex psychological and social organization on the part of both participants. Accordingly, it is rarely appropriate for children or for those persons who are mentally deficient, very poorly educated, or profoundly immature. On the other hand, the greater the intellectual, educational, and general experiential similarity between physician and patient the more appropriate and necessary this model of therapy becomes.

THE BASIC MODELS AND THE PSYCHOLOGY OF THE PHYSICIAN

Consideration of why physicians seek one or another type of relationship with patients (or seek patients who fit into a particular relationship) would carry us beyond the scope of this essay. Yet, it must be emphasized that as long as this subject is approached with the sentimental viewpoint that a physician is simply motivated by a wish to help others (not that we deny this wish), no scientific study of the subject can be undertaken. Scientific investigation is possible only if value judgment is subrogated, at least temporarily, to a candid scrutiny of the physician's actual behavior with his patients.

The activity-passivity model places the physician in absolute control of the situation. In this way it gratifies needs for mastery and contributes to feelings of superiority.[6,7] At the same time it requires that the physician disidentify with the patient as a person.

Somewhat similar is the guidance-cooperation model. The disidentification with the patient, however, is less complete. The physician, like the parent of a growing child, could be said to see in the patient a human being potentially (but not yet) like himself (or like he wishes to be). In addition to the gratifications already mentioned, this relationship provides an opportunity to recreate and to gratify the "Pygmalion Complex." Thus, the physician can mold others into his own image, as God is said to have created man (or he may mold them into his own image of what they should be like, as in Shaw's "Pygmalion"). This type of relationship is of importance in education, as the transmission of more or less stable cultural values (and of language itself) shows. It requires that the physician be convinced he is "right" in his notion of what is "best" for the patient. He will then try to induce the patient to accept his aims as the patient's own.

The model of mutual participation, as suggested earlier, is essentially foreign to medicine. This relationship, characterized by a high degree of empathy, has elements often associated with the notions of friendship and partnership and the imparting of expert advice. The physician may be said to help the patient to help himself. The physician's gratification cannot stem from power or from the control over someone else. His satisfactions are derived from more abstract kinds of mastery, which are as yet poorly understood.

It is evident that in each of the categories mentioned the satisfactions of physician and patient complement each other. This makes for stability in a paired system. Such stability, however, must be temporary, since the physician strives to alter the patient's state. The comatose patient, for example, either will recover to a more healthy, conscious condition or he will die. If he improves, the doctor-patient relationship must change. It is at this point that the physician's inner (usually unacknowledged) needs are most likely to interfere with what is "best" for the patient. At this juncture, the physician either changes his "attitude" (not a consciously or deliberately assumed role) to complement the patient's emergent needs or he foists upon the patient the same role of helpless passivity from which he (allegedly) tried to rescue him in the first place. Here we touch on a subject rich in psychological and sociological complexities. The process of change the physician must undergo to have a mutually constructive experience with the patient is similar to a very familiar process: namely, the need for the parent to behave ever differently toward his growing child.

WHAT IS "GOOD MEDICINE"?

Let us now consider the problem of "good medicine" from the viewpoint of human relationships. The function of science is not to tell us what is good or bad but rather to help us understand how things work. "Good" and "bad" are personal judgments, usually decided on the basis of whether or not the object under consideration satisfies us. In viewing the doctor-patient relationship we cannot conclude, however, that anything which satisfies — irrespective of other considerations — is "good." Further complications arise when the method is questioned by which we ascertain whether or not a particular need has been satisfied. Do we take the patient's word for it? Or do we place ourselves into the traditional parental role of "knowing what is best" for our patients (children)?

The shortcomings and dangers inherent in these and in other attempts to clarify some of the most basic aspects of our daily life are too well known to require documentation. It is this very complexity of the situation which has led, as is the rule in scientific work, to an essentially arbitrary simplification of the structure of our field of observation.*

Let us present an example. A patient consults a physician because of pain and other symptoms resulting from a duodenal ulcer. Both physician and patient assume that the latter would be better off without these discomforts. The situation now may

be structured as follows: healing of the ulcer is "good," whereas its persistence is "bad." What we wish to emphasize is the fact that physician and patient agree (explicitly or otherwise) as to what is good and bad. Without such agreement it is meaningless to speak of a therapeutic relationship.

In other words, the notions of "normal," "abnormal," "symptom," "disease," and the like are social conventions. These definitions often are set by the medical world and are usually tacitly accepted by others. The fact that there is agreement renders it difficult to perceive their changing (and relativistic) character. A brief example will clarify this statement. Some years ago — and among the uneducated even today — fever was regarded as something "bad" ("abnormal," a "symptom"), to be combated. The current scientific opinion is that it is the organism's response to certain types of influences (e. g., infection) and that within limits the manifestation itself should not be "treated."

The issue of agreement is of interest because it has direct bearing on the three models of the doctor-patient relationship. In the first two models "agreement" between physician and patient is taken for granted. The comatose patient obviously can not disagree. According to the second model, the patient does not possess the knowledge to dispute the physician's word. The third category differs in that the physician does not profess to know exactly what is best for the patient. The search for this becomes the essence of the therapeutic interaction. The patient's own experiences furnish indispensable information for eventual agreement, under otherwise favorable circumstances, as to what "health" might be for him.

The characteristics of the different types of doctor-patient relationships are summarized in Table 35-2. In this connection, some comments will be made on a subject which essentially is philosophical but which continues to plague many medical discussions; namely, the problem of comparing the efficacy of different therapeutic measures. Such comparisons are implicitly based on the following conceptual scheme: We postulate disease "A," from which

---

*We omit any discussion of the physician's technical skill, training, equipment, etc. These factors, of course, are of importance, and we do not minimize them. The problem of what is "good medicine" can be considered from a number of viewpoints (e.g., technical skill, economic considerations, social roles, human relationships, etc.). Our scope in this essay is limited to but one — sometimes quite unimportant — aspect of the contact between physician and patient.

many patients suffer. Therapies "B," "C," and "D" are given to groups of patients suffering with disease "A," and the results are compared. It is usually overlooked that, for the results to be meaningful, significant conceptual similarities must exist between the operations which are compared. The three categories of the doctor-patient relationship are concretely useful in delineating areas within which meaningful comparisons can be made. Comparisons between therapies belonging to different categories are philosophically (and logically) meaningless and lead to fruitless controversy.

To illustrate this thesis let us consider some examples. A typical comparison, with which we can begin, is that of the various agents used in the treatment of lobar pneumonia: type-specific antisera, sulfonamides, and penicillin. Each superseded the other, as the increased efficacy of the newer preparations was demonstrated. This sort of comparison is meaningful because there is agreement as to what is being treated and as to what constitutes a "successful" result. There should be no need to belabor this point. What is important is that this conceptual model of therapeutic comparisons is constantly used in situations in which it does not apply; that is, in situations in which there is clear-cut disagreement as to what constitutes "cure." In this connection, the problem of peptic ulcer will exemplify a group of illnesses in which several therapeutic approaches are possible.

This question is often posed: Is surgical, medical or psychiatric treatment the "best" for peptic ulcer?* Unless we specify conditions, goals, and the "price" we are willing to pay (in the largest sense of the word), the question is meaningless. In the case of peptic ulcer, it is immediately apparent that each therapeutic approach implies a different conception of "disease" and correspondingly divergent notions of "cure." At the risk of slight overstatement, it can be said that according to the surgical viewpoint the disease is the "lesion," treatment aims at its eradication (by surgical means), and cure consists of its persistent absence (nonrecurrence). If a patient undergoes a vagotomy and all evidence of the lesion disappears, he is considered cured even if he develops another (apparently unrelated) illness six months later. It should be emphasized that no criticism of this frame of reference is intended. The foregoing (surgical) approach is entirely appropirate, and accusations of "narrowness" are no more (nor less) justified than they would be against any other specialized branch of knowledge.

To continue our analysis of therapeutic comparisons, let us consider the same patient (with peptic ulcer) in the hands of an internist. This specialist might have a somewhat different idea of what is wrong with him than did the surgeon. He might regard peptic ulcer as an essentially chronic disease (perhaps due to heredity and other "predispositions"), with which the patient probably will have to live as comfortably as possible for years. This point is emphasized to demonstrate that the surgeon and the internist do not treat the "same disease." How then can the two methods of treatment and their results be compared? The most that can be hoped for is to be able to determine to what extent each method is appropriate and successful within its own frame of reference.

If we take our hypothetical patient to a psychoanalyst, the situation is even more radically different. This specialist will state that he is not treating the "ulcer" and might even go so far as to say that he is not treating the patient for his ulcer. The psychoanalyst (or psychiatrist) has his own ideas about what constitutes "disease," "treatment," and "cure."[9],[10]

CONCLUSIONS

Comments have been made on some factors which provide satisfactions to both patient and physician in various therapeutic relationships. In conclusion, we call attention to two important considerations regarding the complementary situations described.

First, it might be thought that one of the three basic models of the doctor-patient relationship is in some fundamental (per-

---

*Such a question is roughly comparable to asking, "Is an automobile or an airplane better?" – without specifying for what. See Rapoport.[8]

TABLE 35–2.—ANALYSIS OF THE CONCEPTS OF

Doctor-Patient Relationship	The Meaning of "Treatment"	The "Therapeutic Result"
1. Activity-passivity	Whatever the physician does; the actual operations (procedures) which he employs	Alteration in the structure and/or function of the patient's body (or behavior, as determined by the physician's judgment); the patient's judgment does not enter into the evaluation of results; e. g., T & A is "successful" irrespective of how patient feels afterward
2. Guidance-cooperation	Whatever the physician does; similar to the above	Similar to the above, albeit patient's judgment is no longer completely irrelevant; success of therapy is still the physician's private decision; if patient agrees, he is a good patient, but if he disagrees he is bad or "uncooperative"
3. Mutual participation	An abstraction of one aspect of the relationship, embodying the activities of both participants; "treatment" cannot be said to take place unless both participants orient themselves to the task ahead	Much more poorly defined than in the previous models: evaluation of the result will depend on both the physician's and the patient's judgments and is further complicated by the fact that these may change in the very process of treatment

haps ethical) way "better" than another. In particular, it might be considered that it is better to identify with the patient than to treat him like a helplessly sick person. We have tried to avoid such an inference. In our opinion, each of the three types of therapeutic relationship is entirely appropriate under certain circumstances and each is inappropriate under others.

Secondly, we will comment on the therapeutic relationship as a situation (more or less fixed in time) and as a process (leading to change in one or both participants). Most of our previous comments have dealt with the relationship as a situation. It is, however, also a process in that the patient may change not only in terms of his symptoms but also in the way he wishes to relate to his doctor. A typical example is the patient with diabetes mellitus who, when first seen, is in coma. At this time, the relationship must be based on the

activity-passivity model. Later, he has to be educated (guided) at the level of cooperation. Finally, ideally, he is treated as a full-fledged partner in the management of his own health (mutual participation). Confronted by a problem of this type, the physician is called upon to change through a corresponding spectrum of attitudes. If he cannot make these changes, he may interfere with the patient's progress and may promote an arrest at some intermediate stage in the evolution toward relative self-management. The other possibility in this situation is that both physician and patient will become dissatisfied with each other. This outcome, however unfortunate, is probably the commonest one. Most of us can probably verify it first-hand in the roles of both physician and patient.[11]

At such juncture, the physician usually feels that the patient is "uncooperative" and "difficult," whereas the patient regards

"DISEASE," "TREATMENT," AND "THERAPEUTIC RESULT"

The Notions of Disease and Health	In Medicine (Illustrative Examples)	In Psychiatry (Illustrative Examples)
The presence or absence of some unwanted structure or function The actual state of affairs / The same state without the disability	1. Treatment of the unconscious patient; for example, the patient in diabetic coma; cerebral hemorrhage; shock due to acute injury; etc. 2. Major surgical operation under general anesthesia	1. Hypnosis 2. Convulsive treatments (electroshock, insulin, etc.) 3. Surgical treatments (lobotomy, etc.)
The presence or absence of "signs" and "symptoms"; the physician's particular concept of "Disease" (e. g., infection) / "Health" (usually, no disease; e. g., no infection)	Most of general medicine and the postoperative care of surgical patients (e.g., prescription of drugs, "advice" to smoke less, etc.)	1. "Suggestion," counseling, therapy based on "advice," etc. 2. Some modifications of psychoanalytic therapy 3. So-called psychotherapy "combined" with physical therapies (e. g., electric shock)
The notions of disease and health lose most of their relevance in this context; the notions of more-or-less successful (for certain purposes) modes of behavior, adaptation, or integration take the place of the earlier, more categorical concepts	The treatment of patients with certain chronic diseases or structural defects; for example, the management of diabetes mellitus or of myasthenia gravis; "rehabilitation" of patients with orthopedic defects, such as learning the use of prostheses, etc.	1. Psychoanalysis 2. Some modifications of psychoanalytic therapy

the physician as "unsympathetic" and lacking in understanding of his personally unique needs. Both are correct. Both are confronted by the wish to induce changes in the other. As we well know, this is no easy task. The dilemma is usually resolved when the patient seeks another physician, one who is more attuned to his (new) needs. Conversely, the physician will "seek" a new patient, usually one who will benefit from the physician's (old) needs and corresponding attitudes. And so life goes on.

The pattern described accounts for the familiar fact that patients often choose physicians not solely, or even primarily, on the basis of technical skill. Considerable weight is given to the type of human relationship which they foster. Some patients prefer to be "unconscious" (figuratively speaking), irrespective of what ails them. Others go to the other extreme.

The majority probably falls somewhere between these two polar opposites. Physicians, motivated by similar personal "conflicts" form a complementary series. Thus, there is an interlocking integration of the sick and his healer.

SUMMARY

The introduction of the construct of "human relationship" represents an addition to the repertoire of fundamental medical concepts.

Three basic models of the doctor-patient relationship are described with examples. The models are *(a)* Activity-passivity. The comatose patient is completely helpless. The physician must take over and do something to him. *(b)* Guidance-cooperation. The patient with an acute infectious process seeks help and is ready and willing to cooperate. He turns to the physician for guidance. *(c)* Mutual participation. The patient with a chronic disease is aided to help himself.

The physician's own inner needs (and satisfactions) form a complementary series with those of the patient.

The general problem usually referred to with the question "what is good medicine?" is briefly considered. Different types of doctor-patient relationships imply different concepts of "disease," "treatment," and "cure." This is of imporatance in comparing diverse therapeutic methods. Meaningful comparisons can be made only if interventions are based on the same frame of reference.

It has been emphasized that different types of doctor-patient relationships are necessary and appropriate for various circumstances. Problems in human contact between physician and patient often arise if in the course of treatment changes require an alteration in the pattern of the doctor-patient relationship. This may lead to a dissolution of the relationship.

REFERENCES

1. Ruesch, J., and Bateson, G.: Communication: The Social Matrix of Psychiatry, New York, W. W. Norton & Company, Inc., 1951.
2. Dewey, J., and Bentley, A. F.: Knowing and the Known, Boston, Beacon Press, 1949.
3. Russell, B.: Power: A New Social Analysis, New York, W. W. Norton & Company, Inc., 1938.
4. Szasz, T. S.: Entropy, Organization, and the Problem of the Economy of Human Relationships, Internat. J. Psychoanal. 36: 289, 1955.
5. Dubos, R. J.: Second Thoughts on the Germ Theory, Scient. Am. 192: 31, 1955.
6. Jones, E.: The God Complex, in Jones E.: Essays in Applied Psychoanalysis, London,
Hogarth Press, 1951, Vol. 2, p. 244.
7. Marmor, J.: The Feeling of Superiority: An Occupational Hazard in the Practice of Psychotherapy, Am. J. Psychiat. 110: 370, 1953.
8. Rapoport, A.: Operational Philosophy, New York, Harper & Brothers, 1954.
9. Zilboorg, G.: A History of Medical Psychology, New York, W. W. Norton & Company, Inc., 1941.
10. Bowman, K. M., and Rose, M.: Do Our Medical Colleagues Know What to Expect from Psychotherapy? Am. J. Psychiat. 111: 401, 1954.
11. Pinner, M., and Miller, B. F., Editors: When Doctors Are Patients, New York, W. W. Norton & Company, Inc., 1952.

36   Affect and Its Control in the Medical Intern

Morris J. Daniels

In any system of roles a crucial area of social control centers about the expression of attitude and intent by one person toward another. These may be communicated by ordinary verbal and non-verbal symbols, by special patterns of symbolism, or through instrumental actions which are interpreted as having expressively symbolic overtones. The particular form which such expressive behavior takes will have a significant effect upon the values, objectives, and functional problems faced by social systems. In an analogous manner, the way an individual controls his expressive behavior will affect his fate within an organization in important ways. For this reason, we would expect one aspect of the organization of both social groups and personalities to be expressive patterns and controls congruent with their dominant objectives.

Daniels, M. J.: Affect and its control in the medical intern. Am. J. Sociol. *66:* 259–267 (1960).

The major focus of attention of this paper will be upon the explicit positive and negative controls of expressive behavior built by the medical system into the role of the physician in general and that of the medical intern in particular, although some attention will also be given to certain indirect controls. Consideration not only will be limited to one segment of the medical career, that of the intern, but will be further restricted to the interaction between the intern and his patient.

The modes of affective involvement and other propositions concerning their control stated here emerged from mechanically recorded interview material with forty-six interns in two hospitals in a metropolitan area in Tennessee. Thirty-five of the interns were specialty oriented and eleven were in rotating internships. Considerable time was also spent in observation while accompanying the interns on their hospital rounds.

MODES OF AFFECTIVE INVOLVEMENT AND THEIR CONTROL

The following propositions seem to reflect the variations in the attitude of the interns toward broad categories of patients as well as gradations in the intensity of the affective involvements with them:

A. When based upon some aspect of the illness itself, affective involvement of the intern with his patient varies in content and intensity from (1) an almost complete lack of any affective involvement with the patient as of intrinsic value; to (2) a somewhat intellectualized understanding of the problem of his pateint, an appreciation of his intrinsic value and the personal implications of his illness and suffering, together with a commitment to disinterested service on behalf of all whose illness leads them to need help; to (3) a complete emotional identification in which the intern emphatically suffers a great deal.

B. A qualitatively different type of affective involvement emerges in the positive and negative responses of the intern to the patient's personality.

We maintain that A(2) is explicitly prescribed by the medical system; that A(1) is permitted; that A(3) is controlled in an indirect way by normative, instrumental, and situational influences; and that B is explicitly proscribed.

POSITIVELY SUPPORTED PATTERNS

Of interest, first of all, is the support provided by the medical system for certain expressive patterns which are prescribed and encouraged. The first generalization, therefore, deals with the positive encouragement given the intern to become involved expressively with the patient in a certain way.

I. The approved type of affective involvement and expression is the intermediate one — A(2). It combines the personal and impersonal in inexactly determined proportions, the balance tipping frequently either toward a profound affective involvement with the patient or toward indifference.

In its intermediate form, compassion is a mixture of impersonality and warm human interest. In the relationship between intern and patient, characterized by a minimum of uniqueness and particularity, there is still, ideally, a profound mutual sense of the common-human. Whatever compassion emerges may focus upon a particular person, but it is only a manifestation of a general disinterested and universalized compassion for all persons with similar problems. One intern put it as follows:

As a student in medical school, I tended to become more emotionally identified with the patient, or at least with those who were the loved ones of the patient. I had to learn to restrain myself, to see that this is just another case of something that will go on and on and never end completely as long as there is human life and death . . . There emerges an increasing interest in other problems and in knowledge for the sake of knowledge. Through a process that becomes somewhat automatic, you become so detached that you can see death at one moment and sleep soundly the next, because you have done the best you can and know you cannot stop the inevitable.

Even the interest that you continue to show in the patient as a person becomes somewhat detached. You learn to talk a lot to the patient because you know he needs this support. You know, intellectually, what it must feel like to be facing death or for the loved ones to know this fact, but you don't, except in a few cases, feel the deep sorrow — this you reserve for your own loved ones... You are interested in human welfare and the alleviation of suffering, but this interest is directed to one patient at one moment and another later. Today, for instance, there was a man admitted with cancer of the larynx. He will never talk again after it is removed. Today and tonight he chatted cheerfully with his family. Tomorrow night, his speech will be gone forever. You can say, "I am sorry, old chap," or something of that nature, or think the same, but inwardly you cannot become too personally involved.

Though expressed in many ways, there was a general awareness among most of the interns that a certain amount of compassion and concern in its milder and more universalized form, as stated here, represented the type of affective involvement most consistently experienced. Also, this type of affective involvement and its expressive manifestation seems to be the basic one supported by the system.

PERMISSIVE ATTITUDE TOWARD INDIFFERENCE

Deviation from morally supported expressive behavior may occur in either of two directions. It may move in the direction of a further intensification of compassion and concern for particular categories of patients. Insofar as this degree of uncalled-for involvement occurs, inhibiting controls are evoked. On the other hand, deviation may move toward a state of indifference to the patient as a person. Here, neither explicit proscriptions nor the more indirect instrumental controls are operative. Rather, a certain *value emphasis* tends to stifle even the morally indicated concern. We may state this as follows:

II. A permitted direction of deviance from the preferred pattern of affective involvement is toward a problem-centered interest.

The interns were generally aware of the emotional abstraction and hardening that increases with clinical experience and leads them to overlook the intrinsic value of the patient and perhaps repress compassion. One pediatrics intern noted that he and his friends had called to one another's attention the fact that they had begun to look more and more upon each illness and injury as just another case and less and less

as something in which they got emotionally involved:

The very same things that we once could feel deeply for and perhaps shed an inside tear — we now regard with objective and analytical eyes. Everything becomes cases and we become hardened to the feelings we once had. That is, I suppose, partly the result of the massive problem of getting around to everyone. Even so, I get attached to some of the chronically ill older children.

When developed to an extreme, this attitude becomes indifference; there is no compassion, but, instead, intense attachment to the case as a problem. There is still affective involvement with the patient, but it is focused on him as a case, that is, as a means to something else. The indifference, therefore, pertains to the absence of affective involvement along one morally approved axis. It is a change of emphasis and, since the direction of it is in itself approved, is not strongly disapproved. According to twelve of the interns, in a great many cases they regarded the other staff and private physicians as treating the patients as if "interested in the patients as pathological specimens only," with little interest in their intrinsic worth. This is the antithesis of the mild compassion which the profession thinks essential to disinterested service. After expressing his concern for his patients, an intern remarked:

We don't usually hash this over. It certainly is true with some of the fellows I work with, and I'm sure it is with most everybody. But some of the fellows, well, they treat patients as cold blocks of disease. They don't appear emotionally concerned or upset about it. And I think that is not the way I react.

Though not approved, a problem-centered orientation with its resultant indifference to the patient does not seem particularly disapproved in the medical system. A surgeon with little compassion, for example, who regards his cases primarily as little more than pathological specimens is not regarded as extremely deviant. The patient, if he senses it, might conceivably exert certain types of sanctions. Given the conditions of specialization and the elements of chance in the selection of a physician, however, it may be as difficult for the specialist to develop or manifest a great deal of concern for the patient as it is for the patient to be aware that he is concerned. Sanctions of the medical system seem more concerned with overt conduct and efficiency than with basic attitudes toward patients, which are difficult to establish and more difficult to weight.[1]

CONTROL OF INTENSE INVOLVEMENT

The most intense and prolonged experiences and expressions of compassion and concern are focused upon particular groups of patients whose illnesses are inappropriate to their age or may perhaps bring untimely death. Expressions such as the following are typical:

I do think that young patients who are hopelessly and incurably ill certainly kind of make your heartstrings draw a bit. I think that, with children and young people who are hopelessly ill, you are inclined to regard it as particularly tragic, whereas, in the case of another person who has reached the end of his expected life span and has something which is very common and which we see time after time, certainly you don't have the same feeling. At least I don't think so.

Yes, probably such things as the deforming diseases of childhood and cancers of young women. With the extremely old, it is more expected and less emotionally provoking. I really think it is more what the normal outcome of disease will be. If you see a guy's life cut short sixty years by a disease he has, that's pretty bad, whereas if you see someone who has lived his expected number of years, why, the feeling is less.

---

[1] Other professionalized helping roles, such as those of the minister, social worker, and psychiatrist, do not appear to provide the same opportunity for unsanctioned development of the type of affective indifference described above. In the case of the minister and the social worker, there are probably extremely strong ideological commitments to service. How strong these are in the service motivation of the medical student has not been assessed. [See Howard S. Becker and Blanche Geer, "The Fate of Idealism in Medical School," *American Sociological Review*, XXIII (February 1958), 50–56.] For the minister and the social worker, however, commitments are not coupled with an equally valued "problem" and "skill" orientation rooted in science and capable of providing a rationale for those who are seemingly indifferent.

The length of time spent with the patient enters into the intern's attitude, according to a few of the informants:

I think by and large the ones you get more interested in are the ones you spend more time with. These are also the ones with whom I get more emotionally involved. In other words, a patient who is very seriously ill — you spend an awful lot of time with him as an intern, and the ones that you really work with and strive to improve and no improvement occurs and they expire — that sort of patient is the one that gets you emotionally. It is partly a matter of time spent in which you get to know the patient.

Concerning the time at which the emotional impact may be felt, one intern notes:

By the time one is an intern, this process [emotional detachment] has developed to the point where "the case" looms as the crucial thing. Even then, however, there are times when I feel emotionally shaken up concerning events which happen. For instance, when I have to tell a husband sitting in the lobby that his wife has died in childbirth or from cancer, I may in a matter of fact way say, "Sorry, old boy," or something like that and go on. But recently, while seeing the movie, *The Four Poster,* the flashbacks there reminded me of similar episodes I had seen many times on the faces of husbands to whom I had to convey the bad news of death of their wives. These came so rapidly that I had to get up and leave. I just couldn't stand it any more. I almost cried. But this isn't a problem in practice. You can't afford to get too emotionally involved with any patient. There have to be emotional reservations which are part of one's professional attitude.

Given all this, we would expect mild compassion occasionally to develop into more intense involvement and inhibitive controls to appear. We propose:

III. Controls on intensive affective involvement arising from apsects of the illness itself are negative. They emerge primarily from three sources: (1) an interpretation by the interns of certain highly general professional norms as calling for inhibition; (2) situational pressures; and (3) conviction of the interns that such controls are conducive to the patient's welfare.

Many interns recognized as controls the implications of certain general norms pertaining to their role in the hospital system: technical efficiency and the professional self-image of the physician as poised and rational in medical crises. Seeking technical efficiency, many interns recognized that they would be incapacitated should they indulge in excessive and intense identification with their patients. Second, both the interview material and the ward observations indicated that the situation prevented the emergence of intense involvement by reducing the circumstances which were most likely to produce them: a heavy patient load, specific contact, and the brevity of the inter-patient relationship.

Lastly, the interns themselves realized the deleterious effect of profuse sympathy upon the patient's welfare. As one intern suggested, "When sympathy is too profuse, the patient becomes suspicious that that is all you have to offer." Here explicit proscription or prescription by the medical system is not at issue. Rather, control comes from the realization by the interns that, given certain professional objectives, inhibition is desirable.

PROSCRIPTION OF PERSONALITY-BASED INVOLVEMENT

Unlike the controls on intense affective involvement discussed above, the control over differential treatment by interns of patients based on the personalities of the latter is an explicit proscription. Concerning reactions to it, we propose the following:

IV. The interns' like or dislike of patients affects the quality of treatment provided them. There may be minimum adequate treatment for all, with an increment of better treatment for the more favored or substandard care for those who are not liked.

With few exceptions the interns agreed that whether they liked a patient or not *did* make a difference in the caliber of care. The following responses were typical:

I think it is only natural that any patient who for some reason or other antagonizes you, whether he does it willingly or not, will become the object of your dislike. I'm sure that there have been patients I have come across I have disliked and, as a consequence, I don't take quite the interest in them as a pathological specimen.

Yes, certainly! One develops positive and negative attitudes towards his patients.

One of the two directions in which such attitudes can make a difference in treatment is toward provision of superior care to the better liked, with a minimum but adequate care to those not liked. Thus, in answer to inquiry as to whether personal attitudes influence treatment, thirty of the interns answered in a fashion of which the following is typical:

I think that it is true and I think it will always be true. You have to watch it. You have to fight it all the time. I do myself . . . For example, when you have a patient you like, you will stop if you walk by his door. On the other hand, if it is the other kind of patient who tends to be complaining and uncooperative, unless you stop and make yourself conscious of the situation, you won't. In my own experience, I have spent less time with some patients for this reason. They get adequate care, but not the extra, unless it is on a conscious level, when I make myself go by the same number of times to see them all.

Well, it probably does. I don't mind going by to see the patients I like. You don't mind taking a little extra time with them, doing little things for them . . . they are people you like to help a little bit more. On the other hand, those people who nag you every time you go into the room about what their doctor thinks, this and that, you learn to avoid the embarrassing and difficult situations of this type which keep you busy without any response from them. I think that if the patients appreciate what you do for them, you will spend more time with them.

I think the fact of liking a patient or not liking him will have no effect on the quality of medical care given to them, but I'm sure I like to go to greater lengths to do little things for one of them when I like them, such as arranging for getting telephone calls out and getting cigarettes for them . . . small personal favors.

Yet another direction in which affective involvement can affect the caliber of treatment is that of substandard care which may be given to unpopular patients:

I know it is true of myself. You get a patient that comes in whom you like a lot — you are going to want to spend more time with those patients and thereby you give better care. I feel quite sure about this. I know it's come up several times that you make special diagnoses of persons you like and people you don't like — well, sometimes you overlook things like gall-stones and laugh off their complaints.

Q: Ideally, are supposed to do this?

A: No, no, but, frankly, it enters in.

Controlling the feelings in the interest of professional considerations sometimes proves a rather difficult task, and constant vigilance is necessary: "You have to fight it all the time." In answer to the inquiry as to whether he ever had any difficulty in avoiding this sort of behavior, another intern observed:

Well, what you do and what you should do are sometimes different. I know. I recognize the fact that whenever a patient gets me upset at him, he's one up on me. He's got me to do something I should not do. A doctor should never let his patient get him upset.

The provocations are usually the patient's unco-operativeness, his inability to express needs, or his excessive demands and complaints:[2]

---

[2] See Patricia Kendall and Robert Merton, "Medical Education as Social Process," in E. Gartly Jaco (ed.), *Patients, Physicians and Illness* (Glencoe, Ill.: Free Press, 1958), pp. 342–343, for a condensed description of similar problems of affect control faced by the undergraduate medical student. For related problems faced by the psychiatrists see August Hollingshead and Frederick Redlich, *Social Class and Mental Illness* (New York: John Wiley & Sons, 1958), Chap. ix.

I think that the way you feel about the patient as a person has a great deal to do with the treatment he receives. I think that, if there is a little hostility, say you are very tired, and you have to get up at four to see a patient and ask them what's wrong and they say, "I don't know, but I have a funny feeling," you are very likely to feel hostile toward them. Actually I know everybody does. I certainly do.

That positive or negative attitudes develop almost universally among the interns toward patients seen over some length of time seems likely. That they are expressed in action was also found to be prevalent. While there may be some question as to whether the existence of the attitudes themselves is proscribed by the medical profession, their expression in differential treatment is. There is evidence here of the conscious attempt by the intern not to let it influence treatment, although he often fails in it. Substandard care, given to patients who are obnoxious, may be rationalized as due to the unco-operativeness of the patient — yet not completely so, for the realization of its unethical nature was present.

XIII INTERBEHAVIORAL DIFFICULTIES IN PATIENT MANAGEMENT

Many a student-physician has fantasized donning the cloak of a Dr. Kildare or a Dr. Welby, that is, becoming a medical hero who ingeniously diagnoses and dramatically cures grateful patients. Unfortunately, students quickly learn that their first clinical efforts are viewed as neither ingenious nor dramatic, and that the reception patients give to these efforts is not nearly as favorable as they would hope. Medical care infrequently meets with enthusiastic or appreciative responses since clinicians only rarely are able to provide for all the physical and psychological needs of their patients. To their dismay, student-physicians come to recognize that patients make demands that exceed not only physicians' medical competencies, but their emotional capacities, as well.

Protected from direct clinical responsibilities in the first year or two, medical students often find themselves thrust into a patient-care unit with but minimal preparation for the realities of daily clinical work. In a brief period they become aware of the marked disparity that exists between the research orientation of their academic professors and the service mentality of the clinical staff. This conflict may lead a student to an "identity crisis." Should he ally himself with the intellectual subtleties that characterize the training faculty or should he adopt the down-to-earth, pragmatic attitudes that characterize the crisis-oriented ward staff? This self-cleaving dilemma of contrasting ideologies between his professional superiors is but the first of many parallel struggles that the student will experience before he can achieve an identity as a physician.

Among other realizations that flow from direct patient service is a profound change in the student's self-image. Not only is he cast in the role of an adult for the first time, leaving behind his adolescent student status, but he is catapulted into tasks that make him responsible for the health and welfare of other, often older adults. To complicate this dramatic shift in self-image, the student is forced hourly to switch back and forth in a psychological no man's land. At one moment, he anxiously seeks the guidance and approval of his professional superiors; minutes earlier or later, he is expected to assume an air of self-assurance when relating to his patient charges.

Compounding this inner disharmony and identity cleavage, most students have not been prepared to deal with the emotional needs for support and reassurance demanded by their patients. Although the curriculum of the basic sciences may have armed them with first rate academic knowledge, it is the rare student who approaches the hospital bedside for the first time with the interpersonal tools required to handle both his patient's psychological needs and his own psychological reactions to them. For many, the tasks of completing a physical examination, probing into the intimacies of a patient's life history and providing emotional reassurance, that is, routine aspects of daily clinical service, are so humbling that they begin to ask themselves "what they're doing there" and "whether they've made the right choice" in selecting a medical career. Many experience an urge to flee, to run from the anger, embarrassment, anguish, or heartbreak that faces them daily. And this revelation can prove all the more shattering in that it signifies, not only a desire for flight, but an end to a career they struggled to achieve, perhaps since childhood.

In a study based on experiences in teaching the doctor-patient relationship during the first year of medical school, Pollack and Manning report a number of psychological "defenses" that students employ in coping with the stresses of patient contact (1967):

1. Early termination of interview because of anger or annoyance with the patient.
2. Excessive defensiveness.
3. Marked directiveness in the interview situation. (In the early years of the course, a few students tried to limit or direct personal interviewing of the patient by obtaining significant material from the case history on the chart. This was specifically forbidden.)
4. Excessive time spent in getting the patient's life history.
5. Obsessive approach to certain content of the interview despite the patient's attempt to avoid these topics.
6. Almost complete avoidance of topics or life experiences of emotional significance for the patient.
7. Detachment from the patient.
8. Over-involvement with the patient and the patient's life history (that is, excessive identification with the patient).
9. Using the interview as an occasion for solving own problems.
10. Discussion of own problems or interests as a means of avoiding talking with or listening to patient.

Following their study, Pollack and Manning were able to identify several patient management problems that students find particularly difficult. Among them are: embarrassment with frank displays of sexuality, trouble with morally repugnant behavior patterns, hesitancy at intruding into the personal life of patients, problematic feelings toward minority group patients, and an inability to relate when a patient's death is imminent.

The papers comprising this chapter focus on three problems of patient management. The first, by a distinguished medical educator, Harold I. Lief, addresses the psychological issues involved in discussing sex. Discomfort about sexual matters is one of the most commonly voiced concerns of fledgling physicians. Even mature medical students, otherwise poised and self-assured, exhibit a marked hesitancy when inquiring into the more intimate details of a patient's sex or married life. Dr. Lief provides the student, through numerous case vignettes, with insight into the emotional sources of these problems. The student-physician would do well to develop a measure of comfort in this sphere and to engage in his inquiries without communicating embarrassment or without displaying a brusque or tactless attitude. Judiciously probing questions are not only necessary medically but are fully sanctioned in the public's eye.

The second article, by the prominent research psychologist Irving Janis, reports on an extensive and detailed study of emotional stress among surgical patients. Student-physicians will spend much of their clinical work-up time with surgical patients. Not inappropriately, their primary preoperative concern should be with matters of surgical feasibility such as the patient's general physical state or other issues which might complicate the procedure or the postoperative recovery phase. In many surgical cases, however, the major issue is not the physical, but the psychological, state of the patient. Despite the frequency with which emotional difficulties occur, physicians too often are inclined to overlook these problems or to believe that they require the talents of an experienced psychiatric consultant. Janis's article furnishes a thoughtful analysis of these potentially troubling emotional factors. As will be evident from his presentation, Janis sees no reason why a general physician could not acquire the necessary skills for dealing with these matters on his own.

No more difficult task faces the student-physician than disclosing to his patient that he has a terminal illness or that death is imminent. With insight and sensitivity, Barney Glaser, a distinguished medical sociologist, presents in the third article of the chapter the problems of disclosure and the typical sequence of responses that patients exhibit. Glaser's paper is an extremely useful guide to procedures that may be followed in dealing with this distressing task.

REFERENCE

Pollack, S. and Manning, P. R.: An experience in teaching the doctor-patient relationship to first-year medical students. *J. Med. Educ. 42:* 770–774 (1967).

37   Sex Education of Medical Students and Doctors

Harold I. Lief

GENERAL CHARACTERISTICS OF SEX BEHAVIOR

Examining a representative cross-section of medical students as we did in our study, we found a striking absence of "far out" aberrant behavior. There are very few students who would be willing clients for the sort of activities sponsored by Dr. Ward and Christine Keeler. Although there are homosexual students and homosexual doctors, and almost every class has at least one, more exceptional behavior, such as fetishism, exhibitionism, peeping, cross-dressing, true sexual sado-masochism, or the use of more than one mate at a time occurs only sporadically. For every student whose sexual behavior is undercontrolled, there are 5 students who are overcontrolled and sexually inhibited. From the standpoint of behavioral characteristics alone, the majority of medical students fall in the usual or "normal" (where "normal" is used in a statistical sense) range. Using the two most general categories of undercontrol and overcontrol, it might be useful to cite a few examples of each.

A student we shall call Arthur had a contemptuous disregard for the opposite sex. He took great delight in the conquest of girls and became an expert seducer. Needless to say, he had little ability to love, for sex and love were not fused as they are in a healthy person. He could never experience the complete enjoyment from coitus available to the person who can feel the full rapture of a relationship in which the mate's pleasure is as important as his own. Arthur enjoyed his reputation as a reprobate and lady-killer among his classmates even though his fellow students, almost to a man, detested and shunned him.

Another student, whom we shall call Bernard, had a similar attitude and approach to women but disguised it under a facade of being a clean-cut and righteous youth, giving altogether the impression of

Lief, H. I.: Sex education of medical students and doctors. *Pacific Med. and Surg. 73:* 54–58 (1965).

being an "All-American Boy." Only a few of his close friends recognized the real character of this student. Bernard was married to an older woman who played a maternal role to her youthful husband. This is a variant of the madonna-prostitute theme, in which the man experiences sexual pleasure only with "degraded" women. A degraded woman, in the eyes of men like Bernard, is any woman who has sexual relations outside the marital bed. Behind this viewpoint is the attitude that sex is nasty and "dirty." One can enjoy sex only with "dirty" women, not with one's wife, who, like mother, is "clean" and "pure." Accordingly, Bernard tried to seduce the nurses who had a reputation around the hospital for being easy marks or "push-overs."

A third medical student, whom we shall call Caesar, came from a Latin American country in which the double standard of morality is even more in evidence than in the United States. In that culture it is expected that a man proves himself by having affairs and by having a mistress even after his marriage. This cult of *machismo* or masculinity regards a man as weak who is celibate or who remains faithful to his wife. Caesar firmly believed in this value system and spent a lot of time that should have been devoted to his studies pursuing and seducing women in order to reassure himself that he was a man.

Dan is a pseudonym for a medical student whose father was aggressive, domineering, and sadistic. Dan felt intense hatred for his father and acted out his unconscious desires for revenge upon him by attempting to seduce as many married women as possible. After he succeeded in making one his mistress, he would abruptly leave her to begin the cycle over again with another married woman. Most of the time the women were the wives of his "friends." He carried out the pattern with another medical student and his wife. The latter, deeply depressed after Dan's desertion, had a severe psychotic reaction. Remorse over this caused Dan to seek psychiatric treatment.

From the viewpoint of the medical educator, the significant aspect of these case vignettes is not the abberrant sexual be-havior *per se* but its effect on the doctor-patient relationship. How will these four men deal with the sexual problems of their patients? Before discussing this question, let us first turn to the much more frequently found type of medical student, the student who is overcontrolled and sexually inhibited.

Among medical students we find a surprising number of men who had not had coitus before marriage. Sometimes this is based on religious grounds; more frequently it is based on sexual fears and consequent internal restraints. An extreme example of the latter was described to me by a urologist. He reported that, in his hospital, 2 interns (of the opposite sex, of course) fell in love and wanted to get married. When they came to him for advice it turned out that neither of them had any idea of how to proceed with the sexual act. In retrospect, he feels that coming to him for advice was a courageous act on their part, since most students are deeply ashamed of admitting their ignorance of sex, so aware are they of the expectation of the public that they are experts in this field.

Let us call another student Edward. He got married when he was in college to a girl in a neighboring school. He had been very shy and had found it difficult to make friends with girls before he met his wife. Happily married, he nevertheless keeps on wondering whether he has missed something in life. He tries to bury these thoughts; when questioned he states that he feels it is wrong to have a different standard for men than for women. If he expected his wife to be a virgin (as he did) it was mandatory that he be one. He would expect that of any man in similar circumstances.

Fred was adversely affected in a somewhat different fashion by his sexual fears. Burdened by a chronic illness in childhood, and overprotected and dominated by his mother, he could never quite trust a woman. Each girl was unconsciously seen as a spider attempting to trap him in her web. He had no trouble finding girls, but each time it became serious he would find some excuse for leaving her, usually by provoking the girl into a fight or into the arms of another man. Sexual relations were too dangerous, for then he would be under the spell of the woman. It was not until he was far along in his residency training that he was able to have sexual relations; even then he was emotionally detached. The first time that he thoroughly enjoyed coitus was with a married woman. When she declared her love for Fred and her intention of seeking a divorce from her husband in order to marry him, he turned her down, saying that he would like to carry on the sexual affair with her but could not countenance divorce because of his Catholicism. He did have strong religious beliefs, but it is not surprising that they fitted in with his emotional needs and were used to rationalize them.

George was so guilty about sexual activities that he had enormous remorse after petting. On several occasions he was certain that the girl would become pregnant if an accidental ejaculation occurred while he was fully clothed and there was no chance that the seminal fluid could come into contact with the girl's vagina. He was also afraid that he would contract syphilis or develop a cancer of the penis. These fears are quite common among adolescents, and it may be surprising to some to realize that they are present in medical students as well, but they are not uncommon. Guilt over masturbation is so frequent as to be rather commonplace in the experience of psychiatrists treating medical students.

There are even more extreme cases of overcontrol. One student had so much guilt over self-stimulation that he clamped off his penis to prevent ejaculation. He developed a prostatitis. Still terribly guilty, he told his roommate that he had to masturbate several times weekly in order to drain the prostate. Sexual pleasure was permissible as long as it was a treatment not a treat.

Guilty fears, with or without religious scruples, make many students adopt a moralistic attitude toward others. A professor in the department of public health and preventive medicine gave a lecture on health practices of certain preliterate societies; he included examples of their sexual behavior, e.g., polygamy. On an examination, the students accurately described this

behavior, but many appended notes such as "this is morally wrong" or "this is indecent."

IMPACT UPON LEARNING

How do the responses of students affect learning about sex and marriage? After all, this is the major reason for being interested in this side of the student's life, for the graduate physician's competence in this area is bound to be an amalgam of his own life experiences modified by what he has learned in medical school, in internship, in residency, and finally, in practice.

Anxieties about sex are ubiquitous among medical students. Even mature students, otherwise self-confident and poised, are hesitant about discussing the intimate details of a patient's sex or married life. Some degree of embarrassment is found in each student, no matter how stable or integrated his personality, because our Hollywood-Madison Avenue culture overstimulates sexual appetites and, especially for our young people, surrounds it with tantalizing mystery creating strong tendencies toward exhibitionism and peeping, the end result of which is a feeling of shame. (Shame is even more frequent than guilt; the Victorian era of repression produced guilt; the modern era of sexual expression and performance evokes shame and humiliation, although the two effects are overlapping.)

He has to learn, through practice, that his role as physician requires his obtaining sex information and that his efforts in this direction are sanctioned by the public. He has to learn through experience that these interviewing technics are not akin to the furtive whisperings of adolescents behind closed doors. The student who is uncomfortable with his own feelings, has even more discomfort with such material, especially in interaction with patients. He would be happier if he could deal with each patient as if the patient were a machine, rather than a person with feelings. This student, while demonstrating the outward poise and grace of good personal relations with his patients, often has trouble acquiring the proper amount of "detached concern"[9] and, hence, is troubled by the show of emotions frequently evoked in patients during discussion of their marital and sexual lives. The range of reactions among emotionally disturbed students is great — from relatively mature responses when dealing with sex to the most disturbed. Extreme pathologic reactions are generally found in this group.

In any event, nearly every student has some anxiety when dealing with sexual material, especially in taking a history from a patient. This often becomes most noticeable in the clerkship in psychiatry. "The initial encounter with psychiatry," states Miller,[10] may trouble a student deeply as he is led to introspection about his own emotional problems and conflicts. It may become particularly evident as he meets the open expression of sexual problems that are found so frequently in disturbed psychiatric patients. This causes at least some discomfort to almost any student, and may produce great anxiety in the one who has some sexual problems of his own."

Sexual anxieties may make medical interviewing difficult. The student may communicate his own embarrassment to the patient, increasing the patient's own feelings of shame, making rapport difficult to establish or maintain, and he may never obtain information vital to the understanding of the patient's complaints.

More disturbed students, usually those with undercontrol of their sex drives, may be very brusque and tactless. Their questions may probe too far, too fast, and, by increasing the patient's anxiety, interfere with rapport and with communication. One student would steer every interview around to sex and, even in the first interview, ask for detailed descriptions of sexual behavior. His patients would squirm like fish at the end of a hook; many became enraged.

Such unusual interest is, in reality, a defense against sexual fears, as are certain emotional reactions to patients' sexual behavior. Disgust, contempt, and sarcasm are out of place in a physician's response; yet, strong anxiety may produce such untoward emotional reactions, which are, in other circumstances, not evoked or are easily controlled.

Some of the defenses against sexual anxiety have been mentioned in passing, such as emotional isolation and grandiose attempts at repairing masculine pride. Other prominent defenses employed by students and physicians are overidentification (or introjection) and projection. In the former, the doctor sees the patient's problems as his own and may lose his capacity for objectivity; in the latter, he sees his own problems and the patient's as being similar and may even suggest his own solutions to the patient. For example, it is not surprising to find that those with overcontrol of their sexual drives restrict the sexual activity of patients with coronary heart disease and healed tuberculosis far more than is necessary.[12] The failure to release sexual tensions and the loss of the opportunities to share mutual pleasure with a loved person may be much more dangerous than the added "work" and expenditure of energy in coitus.

Another danger lies in the possibility that the student or doctor may suggest, either directly or by innuendo, his own distorted values to the patient. Fortunately, most value systems dealing with sex are long held and deeply entrenched by the constant reinforcement of the original conditioning stimuli and are given up, if at all, slowly over a long period of time. Thus, most patients are protected from any ill-considered or impulsive suggestions.

The examination of patients provides additional sources of stress for students. Breast and pelvic examinations are not learned without blushes and trembling, fumbling hands. Despite these anxieties, all students learn these mechanical skills quite readily and it is a rare physician who is troubled by the physical examination, though there are a few who are not quite as "detached" as they should be.

Another indication that the topic of sex elicits anxiety is in the frequency with which humor is employed to deal with it. One junior student, an older man, put it this way:

The only way sex is discussed by the class is to make a joke of it. No one can be serious about it except when he is by himself. A student bought the book, *Sexual Deviants;* when a number of students were looking at it they could only joke about it. That was their way of responding to it. The private beliefs of students about sex are really not known because they won't be serious about it. No one in the class has discussed sex, that is, no lecturer has discussed it, except in anatomy. Oh yes, Dr. B. gave us a lecture on the physiology of sex, but it turned into a big laugh session. I thought it was immature. The students' ignorance of sex is colossal. Only in jokes will they consider sexual deviations. What you know from years of experience is unknown to them. They think that you put words in the patients' mouths by your manner of interviewing. They don't realize that it is experience that led you to ask questions in certain directions. The students can't act shocked, although they are; so they respond with humor.

Students tend to over-react, as well, to the teaching of sexual material. They may show great interest, even become absorbed, but in large groups they are afraid to reveal what they consider to be undue concern so they pretend to be casual or "sophisticated." Actually, they may be shocked by information new to them because of their lack of experience but are careful not to "let on" that they feel the way they do.

At other times they demonstrate strange resistances; they may claim that a relatively normal or frequent form of sex behavior is perverse or that a genuine perversion is normal, depending on the relative strength of their beliefs and guilty fears. They may object to case presentations of sexual materials because they feel the presence of a patient before a medical group is damaging or "traumatic" to the patient. In one such instance, in a 17 year old boy with delayed sexual maturation, the students thought that a testicular biopsy was preferable to a case presentation in which the boy's feelings about his "small penis" would be revealed, completely disregarding the potential reassurance that could be given the patient by the psychiatrist. The discussion with the students in this and in a very similar incident indicated that their resistances could be attributed to an over-identification with the patient.

Resistances decrease sharply in small group discussions and in informal bull sessions in which the students feel less threatened and defensive are reassured by finding that their areas of ignorance, doubts, and fears are shared by others.

During internship and residency young doctors are more open to experience than are students, but, since there are practically no formal programs of sex education for them, their experiences are extremely varied. Only in psychiatry and in obstetrics and gynecology do the majority of residents obtain enough instruction and experience to make them feel competent to deal adequately with their patients' sexual and marital problems.

REFERENCES

1. Lief, Harold I.: What Medical Schools Teach About Sex, Bull. Tulane Med Fac., 22: 161–168,1963.
2. Lief, Harold I.: Orientation of Future Physicians in Psychosexual Attitudes, in Manual of Contraceptive Practice, edited by Mary S. Calderone, Williams & Wilkins, Baltimore, 1963, pp. 104–119.
3. Lief, Harold I.: Sexual Attitudes and Behavior of Medical Students: Implications for Medical Practice, in Marriage Counseling in Medical Practice, edited by Ethel M. Nash, Lucie Jessner and D. Wilfred Abse, University of North Carolina Press, Chapel Hill, 1964, pp. 301–318.
4. Herndon, C. and Nash, Ethel M.: Premarriage and Marriage Counseling, J. A. M. A., 180: 395–401, May 1962.
5. Rubin, Isadore: Marital Sex Behavior: New Insights and Findings, Med. Times, March 1964.
6. Kavinoky, Nadina R.: The Premarital Medical Examination, J. A. M. A., 156: 692–695, October 1954.
7. Greenbank, Richard K.: Are Medical Students Learning Psychiatry? Pennsylvania Med. J., 64: 989–992. 1961。
8. Lief, Harold I.: A Psychodynamic Study of Medical Students and Their Adaptational Problems. J. Med. Educa., 35: 696–704, 1960.
9. Lief, Harold I. and Fox, Renee C.: Training for "Detached Concern" in Medical Students, in The Psychological Basis of Medical Practice, edited by Harold I. Lief, Victor F. Lief and Nina R. Lief, Hoeber Medical Division, Harper & Row, New York, 1963. pp. 12–35.
10. Miller, George E.: Teaching and Learning in Medical Schools, Harvard University Press, Cambridge, Massachusetts, 1961.

38   Psychological Stress Among Surgical Patients

Irving L. Janis

The method of controlled comparisons was used in analyzing the observational data from the case study series as well as from the questionnaire survey in order to assess the following general hypothesis:

Hypothesis 1. Persons who display a moderate degree of anticipatory fear before being exposed to physical stress stimuli (pain, bodily discomforts, and severe deprivations) will be less likely to develop emotional disturbances during or after the stress exposure than those persons who display either a very high degree or a very low degree of anticipatory fear.

According to this hypothesis, postoperative adjustment can be predicted from the level of anticipatory fear, but the relationship is a curvilinear one. Reactions of anticipatory fear are assumed to form a continuum ranging from almost complete absence of any fear symptoms ("low" level of fear) through a wide band of intermediate degrees of fear ("moderate" level of fear) to an extreme state of agitated apprehensiveness ("high" level of fear). In Hypothesis 1, the term "emotional disturbances" refers to any form of maladjustive reaction to stress such as: *(a)* demoralization; *(b)* reactive depression; *(c)* acute anxiety symptoms; and *(d)* hostility or resentment. The latter two categories appeared to constitute the most frequent types of manifest "problem" behavior among convalescing surgical patients and were investigated in relation to the two extremes of the anticipatory fear continuum. The available observational data on postoperative anxiety and hostility were used to test the following two descriptive hypotheses, which supplement Hypothesis 1 by specifying more precisely what is

likely to happen when a person displays either very low or very high anticipatory fear:

Hypothesis 2. Persons who display an extremely high level of anticipatory fear or anxiety during the "threat" period will be more likely than others to display intense fear of body damage during the subsequent crisis period, when exposed to actual stress stimuli.

Hypothesis 3. Persons who display an extremely low degree of anticipatory fear or anxiety during the "threat" period will be more likely than others to display reactions of anger and resentment toward danger-control authorities during the subsequent crisis period, when exposed to actual stress stimuli.

The findings from the case studies and the survey research support the three hypotheses. It was found to be necessary, however, to specify a proviso for Hypothesis 3, namely that persons with low anticipatory fear will tend to display a higher incidence of subsequent reactions of anger and resentment only if they are exposed to relatively *severe* stress stimuli, such as intense pain or an accumulation of harassing deprivations. It was observed that when postoperative stress stimuli turn out to be comparatively mild (as is usually the case with those "minor" surgical operations which do not require opening the abdomen or the chest wall), patients displaying a low level of preoperative fear do not differ appreciably in their subsequent postoperative behavior from those displaying a moderate level of preoperative fear. However, for "major" surgery cases, large and consistent differences were observed, indicating that patients who are relatively free from fear before the operation are

Janis, I. L.: Psychological stress among surgical patients. In Janis, I. L.: Psychological Stress. New York, Wiley, 1958.

more likely than others to become angry and resentful during the recovery period after the operation.

In the following sections, a detailed summary is presented of the main findings and inferences concerning the overt behavior and psychological mechanisms of patients with low, moderate, and high anticipatory fear.

For each group, the generalizations will be classified into the following categories: (1) preoperative behavior; (2) postoperative behavior; (3) reassurance mechanisms; (4) major causal factors; and (5) problems of psychological preparation. No attempt will be made, however, to repeat the statements already made concerning the nature of the evidence bearing on each conclusion. Suffice to say, the statements in all five categories are to be regarded as more or less tentative conclusions, none of which have as yet been rigorously verified. The first two categories deal with preoperative and postoperative behaviors that are directly observable, and the findings are based on relatively systematic comparative data. The findings in these two categories may therefore be regarded as the most reliable ones. Somewhat less dependable are the generalizations in the third category, which state inferences about intervening reassurance mechanisms derived from: *(a)* a content analysis of the men's comments in the survey questionnaires, and *(b)* qualitative features of the intensive interviews which provide suggestive leads as to how different individuals attempt to cope with their fears at times of crisis. Most tentative of all are the statements in the last two categories, dealing with causal factors and problems of psychological preparation. A few of the conclusions are supported by a systematic correlational data showing that the absence of preoperative information is related to postoperative disturbances. Most of the propositions, however, are speculative inferences based on an attempt to piece together a coherent explanation from the over-all array of case study and survey findings. Such propositions are offered merely as suggestive hypotheses which are capable of being tested — and which warrant being tested — by means of longitudinal "panel" studies, systematic correlational research, and controlled experiments.

LOW ANTICIPATORY FEAR

Preoperative Behavior

A surgical patient is said to have a "low" degree of anticipatory fear if he displays practically no perceptible signs of fear or emotional disturbance during the period when he knows that he is scheduled to have an operation. Thus the patients in the low fear group are those who remain consistently calm and unperturbed while receiving routine preoperative care. They have no special sleeping disturbances at night. When interviewed, they report feeling quite unworried about the impending surgical operation and show no symptoms of emotional tension. In response to intensive questioning, they will at most admit being mildly concerned about their financial affairs or about other extraneous matters, but they will deny any apprehensiveness about the potential dangers or deprivations that may ensue from undergoing surgery. Consistent with their subjective reports is the fact that they make little or no effort to seek information about the operation, although when authoritative information is offered, they do not ignore it. By and large, these patients appear to spend little time thinking or fantasying about the operation. In so far as their physical condition permits, they engage in their usual daily activities with no apparent loss in mental efficiency and without noticeable changes in their everyday social behavior.

Postoperative Behavior

Upon being subjected to the pains and other stresses of the postoperative period patients in the low anticipatory fear group tend to react with angry resentment, combined with varying degrees of anxiety and depression. They are more likely than others to display a prolonged mood of irritable grouchiness along with occasional outbursts of belligerent protest. Although it rarely happens that a surgical patient refuses to conform with the postoperative medical procedures administered by nurses or physicians, a uniquely high incidence of such refusals occurs among patients in the low fear group. Moreover, this group of patients is more likely than others to express complaints against the hospital staff, including serious charges that doctors, nurses, and orderlies are deliberately sadistic, grossly negligent, or wholly incompetent. The strongly negative attitudes which develop during the stressful recovery period persist long after convalescence is over. These patients look back upon the operation as having been an unnecessarily disturbing experience and they retain an attitude of relatively low confidence in the surgeon.

Reassurance Mechanisms

While awaiting the operation, the dominant mode of reassurance of patients with low anticipatory fear consists of optimistic denial of potential dangers and deprivations. Their view of what is in store for them seems to be quite different from that of patients with moderate fear, most of whom develop a rather differentiated conception of their personal invulnerability, involving the expectation of surviving intact *despite* undergoing pain and suffering. In contrast, the patients with low anticipatory fear tend to feel convinced that they will remain wholly unaffected by the surgical experience, and sometimes also expect to obtain unusual gratifications. They are apt to adopt a joking or facetious attitude and often make use of simple slogans, such as "there's nothing really to it," to bolster their belief that the stressful occurrences will prove to be of a very trival nature. When actual suffering occurs, it comes as a somewhat shocking surprise and is frequently interpreted as meaning that someone has failed to treat them properly. The usual pains, discomforts, and unpleasant postoperative treatments tend to be regarded as unnecessary accidents caused by the hospital staff. Thus, instead of regarding their suffering as an unavoidable conse-

quence of surgery, they are inclined to place the blame upon danger-control personnel, who are now apperceived as being inept, unprotective, or malevolent. By becoming distrustful and resistant toward danger-control personnel, these patients may succeed in warding off apprehensiveness to some degree, but their level of postoperative emotional disturbance nevertheless tends to be comparatively high, the symptoms of which include low frustration tolerance and externalized rage, as described in the above section on postoperative behavior.

MAJOR CAUSAL FACTORS

Among patients in the low fear group there are marked individual differences in the degree to which emotional reactions are determined by predispositional and situational factors. In some surgical patients, low anticipatory fear seems to be largely attributable to personality predispositions which incline the person to deny signs of impending dangers and to ignore the explicit as well as the implicit warnings made by medical authorities. This subgroup probably includes a variety of severe neurotics and prepsychotics — severe obsessionals, withdrawn schizoidal characters, and patients with related types of disorders who are chronically disposed to use denial and isolation mechanisms for warding off disturbing affect. But there are other patients in the low fear group who appear to be relatively normal personalities, highly responsive to emotional stimulation from the environment. For such persons, exposure to specific information about unpleasant aspects of impending surgical experiences has a marked influence, shifting them from a calm, unworried attitude to a moderate degree of apprehensiveness. However, if given no such information, these same patients are likely to remain free from preoperative fear. Thus, a tentative answer can be given to the question: Do environmental factors play a significant role in causing the presence or absence of anticipatory fear? In a sizeable minority, if not in the majority of cases, the relative absence of preoperative fear is partly attributable to environmental circumstances which prevent the person from being exposed to impressive information about the impending stresses of surgery.

It is a separate question whether low anticipatory fear plays any causal role in producing postoperative reactions of anger and resentment. The available evidence suggests that a major consequence of low anticipatory fear is a general lack of psychological preparation for coping with subsequent episodes of stress. This generalization may apply to the entire low fear group, whether the patient's lack of fear is attributable primarily to predispositional or to situational factors. The unworried person is inclined to develop spontaneously a sense of *blanket immunity* which is readily shattered by the impact of actual stress stimuli; whereas, if motivated by anticipatory fear, he is more likely to develop *partial immunity* reassurances which take account of the actual dangers to which he expects to be exposed. The latter type of reassurances continues to be effective in preventing feelings of helplessness at moments of acute crisis, thereby reducing the probability of emotional shock and aggrievement reactions when personal suffering subsequently occurs. A low degree of anticipatory fear can, therefore, be regarded as *pathogenic* in that subsequently, if exposed to severe stress stimuli, the unworried person tends to lose emotional control and becomes adversely sensitized because of his lack of effective inner defenses.

Problems of Psychological Preparation

The evidence bearing on the relationship between preoperative information and postoperative emotional reactions forms the basis for the following inferred generalization concerning the probable effects of preparatory communications: If a person's anticipatory fear is stimulated to a moderate degree by impressive warnings or by other forms of information, the probability that he will subsequently overreact emotionally to actual stress stimuli and develop sustained attitudes of resentment toward

danger-control authorities will be markedly lower than if his anticipatory fear is not at all stimulated during the precrisis period.

For the purpose of conceptualizing the normal processes of inner preparation, the "work of worrying" has been introduced as a construct which is analogous to the "work of mourning." The prophylactic goal of preparatory communications can be described in terms of guiding the surgical patient's affective processes as well as his thought sequences in such a way that he will carry through the "work of worrying" to completion before being exposed to the actual stresses of the postoperative period. Carefully planned communications, individually "hand-tailored" in private interviews conducted by the patient's physician or by a professional counselor, will probably be required in order to take account of individual differences in personality tendencies which make for evasion of the "work of worrying."

The problem of devising effective preparatory communications to *initiate* the work of worrying applies most directly to the low anticipatory fear group and especially to that subgroup which consists of chronic, overcontrolled neurotics who rigidly defend themselves against affect and, hence, remain unresponsive to authoritative communications about impending dangers. For such persons, it may be essential to develop quasi-therapeutic techniques to reduce internal resistances to the point where the person will begin thinking over the implications of the threatening situation, become affectively involved, and, hence, be motivated to replace his blanket immunity expectations with reality-oriented reassurances.

Within the low anticipatory fear group there is probably also a sizeable subgroup of more or less normal personalities who will spontaneously develop and cling to pathogenic attitudes of denial unless their anticipatory fears are deliberately stimulated by impressive communications. For such persons, no special psychological devices may be necessary for successful emotional inoculation beyond conveying purely factual statements from a prestigeful source. In order to guide the work of worrying in such a way that the person will end up with an effective set of reality-oriented reassurances, it will probably prove to be advantageous to present well-balanced communications with respect to two general types of content: *(a)* fear-arousing statements which describe the impending dangers and deprivations in sufficient detail so as to evoke a vivid mental rehearsal of what the crisis situations will actually be like, thus reducing the chances that subsequent adverse events will be frighteningly ambiguous or surprising; and *(b)* fear-reducing statements which describe realistically the favorable or mitigating aspects of the threat situation, calling the person's attention to the ways the authority figures will help him and to the things he can do for himself.

MODERATE ANTICIPATORY FEAR

Preoperative Behavior

Surgical patients with a *moderate* degree of anticipatory fear have minor symptoms of emotional tension but do not display outbursts of acute, paniclike apprehensiveness. They appear to be "part-time worriers," occasionally preoccupied with fretful forebodings but quite capable of suppressing disquieting thoughts about the dire crises that may be in store for them. At night they sometimes suffer from insomnia but usually respond well to a mild dose of a sedative. During the day, their outward manner is relatively calm and well-controlled, punctuated only infrequently by visible signs of inner agitation. These patients generally engage in their usual daily tasks and recreational activities, if circumstances allow them to do so; but they are likely to become restless from time to time. Their work efficiency is occasionally reduced as a result of sporadic episodes of heightened uneasiness, usually precipitated by external signs which remind them of the grim events ahead.

Postoperative Behavior

Although they appear to be experiencing just as much postoperative pain and depri-vation as those in the other two groups, the patients in the moderate fear group show a relative absence of emotional disturbance throughout the entire recovery period. Rarely, if ever, do these patients display any overt signs of resentful attitudes, anger, depression, or apprehensiveness during their convalescence. Many of them are regarded as "model" patients by the hospital staff because they are so affable, cooperative, and conscientious. They generally conform uncomplainingly to all authoritative demands.

Reassurance Mechanisms

During the preoperative period, patients in the moderate fear group generally ask for and pay attention to information about the nature of their impending surgical experiences. They use the information available to them to develop a set of reassuring concepts which take into account some of the objective characteristics of the dangers and deprivations to which they will be exposed. Their reassuring concepts frequently include references to mitigating features of the stress situation, focusing especially on the skill and availability of the surgeon and other members of the hospital staff who are regarded as protective authority figures. In arriving at these reassuring notions, the patients seem first to have a few disquieting fantasies about being physically helpless and being at the mercy of the powerful authority figures who may inflict hazardous procedures or withhold essential aid. Their imaginative rehearsal of these and other potential dangers leads them to counteract the frightening features of the impending stress situation by arriving at plausible fear-reducing anticipations to the effect that: The authorities have genuinely benign intentions; effective aid will be available; the intensity and duration of pain will be within tolerable limits; and some compensatory gains or rewards will ensue from undergoing suffering. Thus, as a result of taking account of available information and "working through" the impending dangers in advance, the patients develop some reality-tested reassurances.

Such reassurances continue to function effectively in warding off disturbing feelings of helplessness when the objective stress situation actually materializes.

Major Causal Factors

Persons who react with a moderate level of anticipatory fear are less likely to have a history of psychoneurotic disorder than those who react with low or high anticipatory fear. They appear to be normal personalities whose emotions are highly responsive to external stimulation. Thus, when facing a threat of body damage, their level of anticipatory fear is markedly influenced by the information available to them. The mere knowledge that an operation is scheduled may produce very little fear in such persons if they are led to believe that it is a safe, routinized procedure; but additional information about the temporarily distressing effects of the surgery will tend to increase anticipatory fear to a moderate level. The arousal of anticipatory fear plays a causal role in the development of psychological stamina because, when the person pictures himself in the danger situation, blanket immunity concepts are recognized to be inadequate and lose their capacity to reduce emotional tension; the person then seeks to discover more convincing sources of reassurance which take into account objective features of the danger situation. The learning process whereby blanket immunity concepts are gradually replaced by a more effective set of danger-contingent reassurances tends to be facilitated when the person is given concrete information concerning: *(a)* the nature of the potential dangers; *(b)* how the dangers can be surmounted; and *(c)* the mitigating or protective features of the environment.

Problems of Psychological Preparation

Although surgical patients in the moderate fear group develop more adequate defenses for coping with the crisis phases than those in the low or high fear groups,

their psychological preparation may, nevertheless, be incomplete in various ways. During the postoperative period, isolated episodes of fright or emotional agitation occasionally occur among patients in this group, despite the fact that they are reasonably well prepared for the main sources of stress. Disruptive episodes seem to occur mainly when there is a gap in the patient's knowledge about postoperative occurrences (e.g., the patient may be surprised to find that he is required to swallow a stomach tube shortly after awakening from the anesthetic). Thus, systematic efforts to give comprehensive information covering as many distressing events as possible may have the effect of minimizing the subsequent occurrence of fright reactions within the moderate fear group.

In addition to personal somatic experiences of suffering and discomfort, there are numerous other unpleasant events which should be mentally rehearsed beforehand. For example, unless specifically informed in advance, a naive surgical patient is apt to become upset and temporarily demoralized by the "gruesome" sights and sounds of mutilation or agony among other patients on the surgical ward. A subsidiary goal of psychological preparation may be that of building up tolerance for the large series of ambiguous, annoying, and mildly threatening events that occur every day during the recovery period. Thus, it may be useful to let the patient know beforehand about various minor discomforts, restrictions of movement, and unfamiliar body sensations which he will experience during convalescence, even though none of these occurrences are apt to be acutely frightening or severely frustrating. There are some indications that even when stressful events are only mildly unpleasant, if there is a large *accumulation* occurring unexpectedly, the patient tends to lose confidence in the protective capabilities of the danger-control authorities. At the same time, he may find his own psychological capacity for controlling emotional behavior gradually diminishing with each new onslaught of unexpected stimulation. Hence, the lower the incidence of minor surprises, the higher the chances of being able to ward off overwhelming fright or aggrievement when a major danger episode occurs.

However, if vivid descriptions are given of a large variety of potentially frightening and distressing stimuli, the person may develop an exaggerated anxiety-laden conception of the danger situation which interferes with the normal work of worrying. Accordingly, it may be essential to present the fear-arousing material in small doses, and also to encourage the patient to ventilate his fears so as to devise supplementary communications which will help to correct his mistaken notions about the extent to which he might be victimized.

Since a person's stress tolerance depends to a considerable degree upon his ability to maintain high confidence in protective authority figures, preparatory communications could present some additional contents especially for this purpose. In this connection, it has been suggested that confidence may be fostered whenever a representative of the authorities makes a series of correct predictions, even if they refer to relatively unimportant events. Thus, the communications designed for the psychological preparation of patients may be more effective if they include, along with statements about the major and minor unpleasant occurrences that are to be anticipated, a series of predictions concerning relatively neutral aspects of the daily convalescent routines. In a new environment, such predictions may have an especially reassuring effect by reducing the ambiguity of unfamiliar stimuli and, at the same time, fostering the view that the seemingly strange things which happen are well understood by the authorities.

In general, the "work of worrying" in surgical patients is facilitated by information which conveys a concrete picture of what the patient will himself *perceive.* There is probably little gain from didactic explanations of the nature of surgical procedures or from comments about those surgical risks which will not be directly perceived by the patient. Such material may do more harm than good, and probably should be omitted, except when specifically needed to clear up a patient's misconceptions about what is going to happen.

HIGH ANTICIPATORY FEAR

Preoperative Behavior

Surgical patients with high anticipatory fear display overt symptoms of sustained emotional tension with occasional outbursts or affect spells characterized by trembling, flushing, and agitated weeping. Throughout the day, they are markedly restless and have difficulty concentrating on normal activities; at night they complain about insomnia or other sleep disturbances, and usually require relatively heavy sedation. These patients report feeling continually "jittery" or "nervous" about the impending operation. Sometimes the intense motivation to escape from the threatening situation breaks through into overt action, as when a hyperanxious patient seeks to postpone or cancel the scheduled operation, or actually leaves the hospital against medical advice.

Postoperative Behavior

Patients with a high level of fear before the operation continue to display a relatively high level of fear after the operation. According to their own reports, they frequently feel apprehensive during the convalescent period, lack confidence about fully recovering from the operation, and are often preoccupied with reminiscences of one or another event that distressed or frightened them. Nevertheless, their attitudes toward the hospital staff tend to be extremely positive and they frequently express gratitude and admiration. These patients make strong efforts to be in frequent contact with members of the hospital staff and to obtain their attention. They also make a strong effort to comply with the demands made upon them in connection with routine convalescent procedures. However, from time to time, they involuntarily delay the administration of injections and other such treatments because of their intense fear of being injured. In general, their convalescence is characterized by friendly and cooperative relationships with physicians and nurses, punctuated by occasional disruptive incidents, stemming from the patient's excessive timidity or hypochondriacal attitudes.

Reassurance Mechanisms

Surgical patients with high anticipatory fear make repeated efforts to gain reassurance, but are unsuccessful at putting aside frightening anticipations of being mutilated or killed by the operation. They seem to be more likely than others to make deliberate efforts to: (a) engage in distracting mental activities; (b) think about the personal gains that will ensue from undergoing the ordeals of surgery; and (c) adopt an attitude of resignation or fatalism. But none of these self-initiated efforts at reducing fear are successful for more than a very short period, and the patients repeatedly turn to authority figures for emotional support. They ask many questions about what will happen to them but, even when given highly optimistic answers, their emotional relief is shortlived. It appears that whether the reassurances come from others or are selfdelivered, these patients cannot sustain a conception of themselves as being safe and physically intact; any optimistic picture of the future is rapidly replaced by an involuntary image of being helpless and overwhelmed by catastrophic danger. When contemplating the implications of undergoing surgery, these patients are much more likely than others to dwell upon improbable dangers — such as the possibility that the surgeon's knife may make a fatal slip — which appear to be the product of inner conflicts. Thus, although strongly motivated to build up reassuring concepts beforehand, these patients enter into the postoperative phase without any highly effective defenses with which to reduce their emotional tension. They have a low capacity for gaining reassurance when they encounter frightening stimuli during the postoperative period, just as during the preoperative period.

Major Causal Factors

The most important single factor in accounting for extremely high preoperative and postoperative fear appears to be a chronic psychoneurotic predisposition. The case history data available for the small sample of patients in this group suggest that, prior to the present hospitalization, most of these individuals had suffered from severe neurotic symptoms, including acute anxiety reactions in response to a vareity of major and minor danger experiences in the past. Thus the excessive apprehensiveness and timidity displayed before the operation and then again afterwards may be attributable to an underlying neurotic predisposition.

The basic predisposition to overreact to surgery is probably not present in all chronic psychoneurotics, but, rather, may be limited to those for whom threats of body damage arouse certain types of intense psychosexual conflicts. The unconscious symbolic significance of the threat may be either of a castration punishment or of a temptation to satisfy latent masochistic strivings. The anticipated dangers of surgery are symbolically elaborated in the patients' horror fantasies of being mutilated or annihilated, which they know are irrational, but which they cannot dispel. Thus, the fact that repressed inner dangers are touched off by the external threat may be responsible for preventing the person from gaining any effective reassurances from factual knowledge about protective features of the environmental situation, and may also account for the person's subsequent inability to correct his exaggerated fears, despite favorable opportunities for emotional relearning provided by successful surgical experiences.

In a minority of patients in the high fear group, the overreactive tendency may be very narrowly confined to only one specific type of threat which happens to resemble a past traumatizing situation; in such instances, the predispositional factor may involve a special vulnerability which does not necessarily imply a chronic neurotic disorder.

Because of the predominance of one or another type of predispositional factor, variations in situational factors play only a limited or subsidiary role as determinants of a high level of fear. Nevertheless, certain features of the threat situation appear to influence the over-all incidence of high fear reactions. Surgical operations are more likely to evoke a sustained high level of fear if the patient knows that: *(a)* the risk of suffering pain, permanent injury, or death is relatively high rather than low; and *(b)* the incision will be near the genital region rather than in the upper part of the abdomen or the chest. Cognitive factors involving detailed knowledge about the potential complications and risks of surgery may also augment the chances of intractable fear reactions. However, the majority of patients in the high fear group tend to be relatively uninfluenced by the authoritative information they are given. Although preoperative information was found to be related to the relative incidence of moderate as against low fear, such information did not have any relationship to the incidence of high fear. Thus, it appears that once a person is aware of the fact that he is required to have a certain type of operation, further information about the nature of the surgical situation probably plays only a small causal role, if any, in determining whether or not he will react with an excessively high level of fear.

Problems of Psychological Preparation

For excessively fearful persons, the central problem is not that of stimulating the work of worrying but, rather, of reducing emotional excitement to a moderate level so that the work of worrying can be carried out more effectively and brought to successful completion. When a very high level of anticipatory fear persists it implies an inability to develop adequate inner defenses with which to cope with the situation; the person remains in a state of hyper-vigilance, involving a loss of mental efficiency, lowering of reality-testing capacities, and reduced tolerance for subsequent stress.

In some cases, excessive fear may be evoked primarily because of misleading information or cognitive errors concerning the severity and magnitude of the impending danger. Whenever misinformation plays a major role, the disruptive effects of acute anticipatory fear may be somewhat lessened by means of corrective communications which convey a realistic and concrete picture of the danger situation, with special emphasis on those positive features and protective resources that warrant a more optimistic attitude concerning the chances of surviving intact. However, such information is probably of little value for the majority of high fear cases who react to anticipated surgery and to other external threat situations with paniclike affect spells, severe hypochondria, phobic avoidance reactions, obsessional ruminations about anticipated catastrophe, or related types of acute anxiety symptoms. In so far as these psychoneurotic reactions are attributable to repressed psychosexual conflicts, surgical patients who display such symptoms during the preoperative period cannot be expected to benefit very much from any program of psychological preparation on the part of professional counselors, unless some form of therapy can be included to decrease the pathogenic influence of repressed sources of fear. Perhaps a brief form of psychological treatment can be developed which will help the overreactive patient to gain emotional control by confining his neurotic fantasies to other spheres; so that, even though the underlying neurosis is not "cured," it encroaches to a lesser extent upon his apperception of surgical experiences and no longer blocks so completely the development of reality-based reassurances.

In many normal persons, certain types of information about impending dangers may be capable of evoking excessive fear reactions, i. e., when frightening events are depicted which stimulate fantasies associated with repressed conflicts or which reactivate memories of past traumatic experiences. It may be necessary, therefore, to design preparatory communications for surgical patients in such a way as to avoid giving overdoses of fear-arousing material, especially by eliminating those horror elements which lend themselves most readily to autistic, anxiety-arousing elaborations. This is one reason why preparatory communications should be carefully pretested with a pilot group and rigorously assessed by means of systematic research studies.

The above summary, which emphasizes

the major differences between low, moderate, and high anticipatory fear groups, should not be construed as an attempt to formulate a typology. Anticipatory fear, like any other emotional response, should be conceptualized as a continuum ranging from zero intensity to very high intensity. The characteristics specified for each group should, therefore, be regarded as behavioral tendencies or trends that predominate within a given region of the continuum. On every aspect of postoperative adjustment, it was observed that the three groups showed considerable overlap; hence any predictions based on the level of anticipatory fear must be expected to have a wide margin of error. The most that can be claimed for any of the observed relationships between preoperative and postoperative behavior is that they may enable one to predict significantly better than chance.

39   Disclosure of Terminal Illness

Barney G. Glaser

One of the most difficult of doctor's dilemmas is whether or not to tell a patient that he has a terminal illness. The ideal rule offered by doctors is that they should decide for each patient whether he really wants to know and can "take it." However, since, depending on the study, 69 to 90 per cent of doctors favor not telling their patients about terminal illness,[1] rather than making a separate decision for each patient, it appears that most doctors have a general standard from which the same decision flows for most patients – that he should not be told. This finding also indicates that the standard of "do not tell" receives very strong colleagueal support.

Many conditions reduce a doctor's inclination to make a separate decision for each case. Few doctors get to know each terminal patient well enough to judge his desire for disclosure or his capacity to withstand the shock of disclosure. Getting to know a patient well enough takes more time than doctors typically have. Furthermore, with the current increase of patient loads, doctors will have less and less time for each patient, which creates the paradox; with more patients dying in hospitals, more will not be told they are dying. Even when a doctor has had many contacts with a particular patient, class or educational differences or personality clashes may prevent

[1] Feifel, H., "Death," in N. L. Farberow (ed.), *Taboo Topics,* New York: Atherton Press, 1963, p. 17.
This paper derives from an investigation of terminal care in hospitals supported by N. I. H. Grant NU00047. I wish to thank Anselm Strauss for helpful comments and criticisms on an earlier draft. Other papers from this study are: A. Strauss, B. G. Glaser and J. Quint, "The Nonaccountability of Terminal Care," *Hospitals, 36:* 73-87, January 16, 1964; B. G. Glaser and A. Strauss, "The Social Loss of Dying Patients," *Amer. J. Nursing, 64:* 119-121, June, 1964; B. G. Glaser and A. Strauss, "Awareness Contexts and Social Interaction," *Amer. Soc. Rev., 29:* 669-678, October, 1964; B. G. Glaser and A. L. Strauss, "Temporal Aspects of Dying as a Non-scheduled Status Passage," *Amer. J. Sociology,* July, 1965; B. G. Glaser and A. L. Strauss, "Discovery of Substantive Theory: A Basic Strategy Underlying Qualitative Research," *Amer. Behav. Scientists, 8:* 5-12, February, 1965; J.C. Quint and A. Strauss, "Nursing Students, Assignments and Dying Patients," *Nursing Outlook,* Vol. 12, January, 1964; B. G. Glaser, "The Constant Comparative Method of Qualitative Analysis, *Social Problems 12:* 436-445, Spring, 1965; two books, B. G. Glaser and A. Strauss, *Awareness of Dying,* Chicago: Aldine Press, 1966, and B. G. Glaser and A. Strauss, *Discovery of Grounded Theory,* Chicago: Aldine Press, 1970.

Glaser, B. G.: Disclosure of terminal illness, J. Hlth. Hum. Behav. *7:* 83-91 (1966).

effective communication. Some doctors simply feel unable to handle themselves well enough during disclosure to make a complicated illness understandable. If a doctor makes a mistake, he may be liable for malpractice. Some doctors will announce an impending death only when a clear-cut pathologist's report is available. Others do not tell because they do not want the patient to "lean" on them for emotional support, or because they simply wish to preserve peace on the ward by preventing a scene.

Similarly, a number of conditions encourage disclosure of impending death regardless of the individual patient's capacity to withstand it. Some doctors disclose to avoid losing the patient's confidence should he find out indirectly through other sources, such as changes in his physical condition, accidentally overhearing the staff discuss his case or comparing himself with other patients. Telling also justifies radical treatment or a clinical research offer; it also reduces the doctor's need to keep up a cheerful but false front. Some tell so that the patient can put his affairs in order, plan for his family's future or reduce his pace of living; others, because family members request it. Of course, if the chances for recovery or successful treatment are relatively good, a doctor is naturally more likely to disclose a possibly terminal illness; disclosing a skin cancer is easier than disclosing bone cancer.

little information, it is almost always easier and safer to not act.[2]

RESPONSE TO DISCLOSURE

The intent of this paper is to formulate a descriptive, process model for understanding disclosure of terminal illness. This model combines *both* (1) the stages typically present in the response process stimulated by such disclosure *and* (2) the characteristic forms of interaction between the patient and staff attendant to each stage of the response process. Thus the focus in the following pages is just as much upon how hospital staff initiates, and attempts to guide and control the response process through interaction with the patient as upon the patient's responses per se.

First, the response process is stimulated by a doctor's *disclosure* to the patient. The patient's initial response is almost invariably *depression,* but after a period of depression he either *accepts* or *denies* the disclosure, and his ensuing behavior may be regarded as an affirmation of his stand on whether he will, in fact, die. Acceptance may lead to active preparation, to passive preparation or to fighting the illness. A particular patient's response may stop at any stage of the process, take any direction, or change directions. The outcome depends on the manner in which he is told, and then managed by staff, as well as his

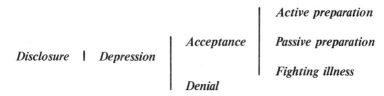

Figure 39-1.   The response process.

The combined effect of these conditions — some of which may induce conflicting approaches to the same patient — is to make it much easier for doctors to apply to all patients a flat "no, he should not be told." For when people are in doubt about an action, especially when the doubt arises from inability to calculate the possible effects of many factors on which there is

own inclinations. The response process is diagrammed in Figure 39-1, and the characteristic forms of staff-patient interaction

[2] For a conceptual analysis that applies to why there is less risk for doctors in not disclosing terminality, see T. J. Sheff, "Decision Rules, Types of Error, and Their Consequences in Medical Diagnosis," *Behavioral Science, 8:* 97–107, April 1963.

that occur at each stage, often precipitating advance to the next stage, are discussed in the remaining pages.

METHOD AND RESEARCH SITE

This conception of the characteristic stages of a patient's response to disclosure of terminal illness is based largely on field observations and interviews with patients, doctors, nurses and social workers on the cancer wards of a Veterans' Administration Hospital in the San Francisco Bay Area. In this hospital the normal procedure is to disclose the nature of his illness to every patient; as a result, many patients are told of a fatal illness.[3]

By and large, the patients in these wards are in their middle or late years and in destitute circumstances. Since their care is free, they are captive patients — they have little or no control over their treatment, and if they do not cooperate, their care may be stopped. If a man goes "AWOL," the hospital is not obliged to re-admit him, or it can re-admit him but punish him by denying privileges. Because the patients lack financial resources, they typically have no alternative to their current "free" care, and their lower-class status accustoms them to accepting or to being intimidated into following orders from people of higher status. Since these captive lower-class patients are unable to threaten effectively the hospital or the doctors, disclosure of terminal illness occurs regardless of the patient's expected reaction.

These patients seemed to exhibit a full *range* of responses to disclosure of impending death, which it is our only purpose to set forth here. (How differently, if at all, from higher socio-economic patients they might be distributed throughout the response process is unascertainable with the collected data.) So many cases of direct disclosure and the consequent variety of response patterns made this hospital a highly strategic research site for studying the problem. In other hospitals we found only a few cases of direct disclosure of terminal illness and the general aspects were the same as those of the VA cases.

DISCLOSING TERMINAL ILLNESS

Disclosure of terminal illness to patients in this hospital has two major characteristics. First, the patient is told that he is certain to die, but not when he will die. Expectations of death have two dimensions: *certainty* and *time* of demise, and the first is the more readily determined in advance.[4] As one doctor put it: "In my opinion, however, no doctor should take it upon himself to say to a patient, 'You have ten weeks to live' — or three months, or two years or any time whatsoever." And another doctor said: "Doctors simply do not know when patients are going to die." Stopping short of full disclosure tends to soften the blow to the patient and reduces chances of error for the doctor.

Second, the doctors typically do not give details of the illness, particularly mode of dying, and the type of patient under consideration usually does not ask for them. Primarily, this is a problem of communication: a doctor finds it hard to explain the illness to a working-class patient, while lack of familiarity with the technical terms, as well as a more general deference to the doctor, inhibits the patient's impulse to question him. In addition, not giving details is a tactic doctors use to cut down on talk with the patient and to leave him quickly.

In combination, these two characteristics of disclosure often result in *short, blunt announcements* of terminal illness to the patient. Even the nurses are often shocked by the doctor's bluntness. Nevertheless, they often feel that the patient is better off for being told because, as one nurse put it, he "becomes philosophical in a day or two."

[3] This norm may be considered an aspect of "batch" treatment of captive inmates of a total institution. It is also the procedure on the medical ward of the state penitentiary in California. See E. Goffman, "Characteristics of Total Institutions," in A. Etzioni (ed.), *Complex Organizations,* New York: Holt, Rinehart and Winston, 1961, pp. 312–340.

[4] See Glaser and Strauss, "Temporal Aspects . . . ," *op. cit.,* for a full discussion of death expectations.

A short, blunt announcement may be softened, however, in various ways. One way is to add a religious flavor: "You've had a full life now, and God will be calling you soon." This manner is perhaps most appropriate for older patients. Another is to muffle the language. To the patient's question, "Is it cancer, Doc?" the doctor responds, "We don't call it that . . ." and then gives it a technical name that the patient can understand only vaguely. The "suspicion" announcement also dulls the blow: "There is a high clinical suspicion that the tumor removed was cancer. However, we won't have a pathological report on it for ten days." The announcement that there is "nothing more to do" (to cure the patient) can be muffled with a hopeful lie such as by adding "but then who knows, next week, next month or maybe next year there may be a drug that will save you," or by suggesting to the patient that he join an experimental program that may help him, as well as mankind.[5] Finally, there is the important statement that softens any form of disclosure: "We can control the pain."

In some forms, the blunt announcement *sharpens* the blow of disclosure by forcing a *direct confrontation* of the truth with little or no preamble. The doctors are quite aware of, and favor the use of, this approach by colleagues. One doctor says, "With average patients, we tell them what they got." Another says, "I don't think the staff as a whole goes along with the hard-boiled approach, but me, I try to tell them the truth." The "hardboiled" announcement is often linked with a report to the patient of the results of his surgery. In this hospital, patients are customarily told, two or three days after surgery for cancer, whether they will die. For example, one doctor walks into the patient's room, faces him, says, "It's malignant" and walks out. To be sure, this tactic also eliminates having to answer the patient's questions. Another rather

direct confrontation is, "We weren't able to get it (the malignant tumor) all out." Another form of sharp announcements is the *direct retort:* when a patient asks, "Doctor, do I have cancer?" the doctor replies, "Yes, you do." (One doctor commented, "If they ask directly, we answer as directly as possible.") Lastly, the *implied, but sharp, confrontation* of terminal illness is exemplified by the doctor who greeted a patient returning to the hospital with the order to sell her house and all her things, for she would not leave the hospital again.

In this group of doctors who favor the short, blunt disclosure there is one who does not. He refuses to disclose in this fashion because he has had previous experience with errors due to changing pathology reports, and because he tries, through surgery, to make the patient's last weeks more comfortable. Other doctors tend to disagree that his "comfort surgery" is useful, but he continues because sometimes he actually saves the patient for years. This doctor, continually maintains a cheerful and optimistic manner, never directly disclosing to the patient that he will die. What actually occurs when he offers the patient comfort surgery or participation in a clinical experiment is *silent disclosure:* both doctor and patient know of the latter's fatal illness, and both know the other knows, but they do not talk to each other about it.[6] The doctor reveals the patient's fatal illness by oblique references to it in proposing comfort surgery or experimental participation, the meaning of which the patient clearly understands. The patient thus begins his process of response-to-disclosure without the customary stimulus of direct disclosure.

DEPRESSION

The initial response of the patient to disclosure is depression. The large majority

---

[5] If the patient takes the experimental drug, he continually checks his condition by asking the doctor: "What next, Doc?" "What now?" "Am I better?" "Am I getting well?" When the experiment is over and the patient is still going to die, he must start through the response process again with a depressing "now what" feeling.

[6] See Glaser and Strauss, "Awareness Context . . .," *op. cit.,* for a discussion of the "mutual pretense awareness context" which silent disclosure institutes.

of patients come to terms with their depression sufficiently to go on to the next stage of the response process. A few do not. Their depression precipitates a *withdrawal* from contact with everyone, and they remain in a state of hopelessness. In this limiting sense they become non-interacting, non-cooperative patients; the nurses can not "reach" them. Depression is usually handled by staff with sedation until the patient starts relating to them again. In one case a nurse observed that a patient visibly shortened his life because of his period of anxiety and withdrawal.

ACCEPTANCE OR DENIAL?

After the initial period of acute depression, the patient responds to the announcement by choosing either to accept or to deny the imminence of his death. In effect, he takes a stand on whether and how he will die, and this stand profoundly affects his relations with the staff from that time on.

In general, sharp, abrupt disclosure tends to produce denial, and dulled disclosure, acceptance.[7] When the disclosure is sharp, the depression is more immediate and profound, and denial starts right in as a mechanism to cope with the shock.[8] To predict an individual's response, however, one needs the kind of intimate knowledge of the patient that doctors would prefer to have. Without it, it is very difficult to say which path to death a patient will take, or for how long. In some cases, the patient's response changes; he cannot hold out against accumulating physical, social and

---

[7]These hypotheses complement the discussion by Feifel on the importance of "how telling is done" (*op. cit.*)

[8]For another discussion of denial of illness upon disclosure, see H. D. Lederer, "How the Sick View Their World," in E. Gartly Jaco (ed.), *Patients, Physicians and Illness,* New York: Free Press, 1958, pp. 247–250. Denial of dying is characteristic of our society as shown by R. Fulton's data: see "Death and the Self," *Journal of Religion and Health, 3:* 359–368, July, 1964. See the analysis of denial of death in American Society by T. Parsons, "Death in American Society," *Amer. Behav. Scientist,* May, 1963, pp. 61–65.

temporal cues. The usual change is from denial to acceptance, though when patients improve briefly before growing worse or a new drug helps for a few days, acceptance may change, for a time, to denial. The direction an individual takes depends not only on how he is told, but also on a variety of social and psychological considerations impinging on the passage from life to death.

Acceptance

Patients may demonstrate acceptance of impending death by actively preparing for death, passively preparing, or fighting against it. *Active preparation* may take the form of becoming *philosophical* about dying, death and one's previous life; patients review and discuss how full their life has been with family, nurses, social workers and chaplain. They may pose the destiny question: "Why me?" and try to work through it with the philosphical help of others. This approach leads the patients to draw the nurses into the discussion which can be very difficult for them. Nurses are still only trained by and large to help motivate patients to live, not to die! If a nurse is to help a patient prepare himself she too must accept his impending death and refrain from chastising him for not fighting to live. Otherwise she is likely to consider the patient "morbid" and tends to avoid his invitations to help him face death squarely. She will usually try to transfer the burden to the social worker, sister or chaplain when they are available.

Some patients start immediately to prepare themselves for death through religion. For others it is an easy transition to slip from philosophical to religious terms, a transition often aided by the chaplain, who then helps the patient prepare himself.

Another form of active preparation for death is to *settle social* and *financial affairs,* perhaps linking this effort with philosophical or religious preparation. The typical helpers in settling affairs are family members and social workers. For example, upon learning that he was going to die, the patient turned to his wife and said, "Well, we've got to get everything lined up; I promised (so and so) my . . ." This immediate getting down to the provisions of a will was considered abnormal by one nurse who said, "I've never seen a reaction like that, it was almost morbid." Another patient began discussing with the social worker the various veteran's benefits they could obtain for his wife, and another tried to marry his wife, who was emotionally very dependent on him, to a hospital corpsman. One patient gave up his pain medication long enough to put his financial affairs in order with the aid of a social worker, for he knew that as soon as he was too drugged to operate effectively, his family would try to take over his estate.

To give the patient a chance to settle his affairs, to plan for the future of his family, is, of course, an important consideration when a doctor decides whether to disclose terminal illness. He can seldom be sure, however, that the patient's response will take this direction or advance so far. Moreover, some affairs to be settled are less important than social or financial ones, though they do allow patients to pick up loose ends or accomplish unfinished business. For example, before entering the hospital for cancer surgery one woman said, "I am going to do three things before I enter the hospital — things I've been meaning to do for a long time. I'm going to make some grape jelly. I've always dreamed of having a shelf full of jelly jars with my own label on them. Then I'm going to get up enough nerve to saddle and bridle my daughter's horse and take a ride. Then I'm going to apologize to my mother-in-law for what I said to her in 1949." Another patient with leukemia quit work and bought a sail boat. He planned to explore the delta region of the Sacramento and San Joaquin rivers until his last trip to the hospital.

Another form of active preparation is to attempt a *"full life"* before death.[9] This pattern is characteristic of younger patients (in contrast to older patients who review the fullness of their life) like the 22-year-old who, when told he had three months to

three years to live, married a nurse. "If we have only two months," she said, "it will be worth it." The patient lived two years and had a son. Faced by certain death, he had achieved the most he could from life.

Auto-euthanasia (suicide) is another way of actively preparing for death.[10] It eliminates the sometimes very distressing last weeks or days of dying. One patient, who had no friends to visit him, felt that he was very alone and that no one in the hospital cared, so he tried to hasten his death by suicide. Some patients try to end their lives while they are physically presentable, not wanting their families to see their degeneration. Other stresses that encourage auto-euthanasia are unbearable pain and the discipline imposed by a clinical experiment to which one may be irrevocably committed. Others decide to end their life when they can no longer work.[11] Still others prefer auto-euthanasia as a way of controlling their dying as they controlled their living, thus wresting this control from the hands of the staff and the rigors imposed by hospital routine.[12]

Passive preparation for death, among patients who accept their terminal illness, also has some characteristic forms. One is to take the news in a *nonchalant* manner. Nurses sometimes find this response disturbing; one put it: "But some take it quite nonchalantly. We've had several very good patients — right to the end. One that upset me was here when I came. He was the hardest for me to see die — he was young

---

[9] This form of active preparation is appropriate in American society which stresses the value that death is unacceptable until one has had a full life; see: Parsons, *op. cit.*

[10] Shneidman feels a question deserving of research is "why so many cancer patients, *do not* commit suicide." E. S. Shneidman, "Suicide," in Farberow, *op. cit.*

[11] For an account of a cancer patient who planned to commit auto-euthanasia after he could no longer work, see L. Wertenbaker, *Death of a Man,* New York: Random House, 1957.

[12] A growing problem that medical staff and hospitals must face is that people wish to control their own way of dying; they do not want it programmed for them by medical staff and hospital organization. To achieve this end, many patients also wish to die at home. (Fulton, *op. cit.,* pp. 363-364); see the analysis of this problem in J. Quint, "Some Organizational Barriers to Effective Patient Care in Hospitals," paper given at the American Medical Association convention, June 24, 1964.

and not only that — such a wonderful fellow. Even as sick as he was, he was always kind and courteous." Apart from the social loss factor — "young" and "wonderful" — which usually upsets nurses,[13] this nurse also found such a passive outlook on death rather disquieting.

Nurses, however, are grateful to patients who approach death with *calm resignation.* This response relieves them of the responsibility for cheering up the patient and improves their morale, too. Since it would not do for a nurse to be less calm or resigned than her patient, a patient who responds in this fashion raises and supports the nurse's morale. The *nonverbal* patient, who simply accepts his fate and does not talk about it, also relieves the nurse of possible stress in having to talk, as she often does with the more actively preparing patient. He makes few or no demands on nurses or social workers. A disquieting aspect of this response is the loss of contact with the patient: "It is very hard for us 'well people' to really grasp how they feel." One social worker bridges this gap by sitting with the patient for a time each day. She reports, "Sometimes it's a matter of just touching their hand — whatever is natural — to make them feel that you understand and care." Another version of the passive response is expressed by the patient who emerges from his depression only to turn his face to the wall, "the spirit drained out of him," and "passively wait to die."

Some patients accept their terminal illness but decide to *fight* it. Unlike denial behavior, this fight indicates an initial acceptance of one's impending death together with a positive desire to somehow change it. Three forms of fighting behavior are *intensive living, going to marginal doctors or quacks,* and *participating in an experiment.* One patient, for example, started going out on passes, and living it up, asserting, "I'll beat it," as if he could hold death off by living life to the full. He kept getting thinner and eventually died. This mode of fighting off death can be readily transformed into active preparation

for death if it increases the patient's fullness of life before death.

Taking an outside chance with quacks or marginal doctors[14] gives some patients a feeling that they are actively combatting the disease. A regular physician usually permits his patient to go to a marginal doctor, since the visits keep the patient hopeful and busy and his permission allows the physician to see that the marginal treatments do not injure his patient. Denied this permission, a patient who wants to fight his disease in some way may break off relations with his physician, so that the physician loses control over both the patient and the marginal doctor. A rupture like this makes it difficult for the patient to return to the original doctor when, as is typical, the marginal treatment fails.[15]

The search for a way to fight the fatal illness can also lead a patient into a clinical experiment. If he does not win his own battle, he at least may help future patients with theirs. The chance to contribute to medical science does not, however, sustain the motivation of *all* research patients.[16] Some, when they see it is hopeless for themselves and find the experimental regime too rigorous to bear, try to extricate themselves from the experiment. If the doctors will not let them off, these patients sometimes interfere with the experiment by pulling tubes out, by not taking medicine or by taking an extra drink of water. Some attempt auto-euthanasia. Doctors may carry on the fight regardless of the patient's desire to give up. One nurse, at least, feeling that the lives of research patients are excessively prolonged, bitterly said: "They (doctors) keep them alive until the paper (the research report) is written."

---

[14] In this connection see B. Cobb, "Why Do People Detour to Quacks?" in Jaco, *op. cit.*

[15] For an illustration of how the doctor allowed, hence could control, a dying patient's submission to the rigorous treatment of a marginal doctor, see J. Gunther, *Death Be Not Proud,* New York: Harper Bros., 1949.

[16] Cf. R. Fox, *Experiment Perilous,* New York: Free Press, 1959. One gets the feeling that the patients in Fox's sample were all highly motivated to go on with the experiments to the bitter end.

---

[13] Glaser and Strauss, "The Social Loss...," *op. cit.*

Denial

Some patients deny they are approaching death and proceed to establish this stand in their interaction with staff members. Typical denying strategies are juggling time, testing for denial, comparing oneself to other patients, blocking communication, becoming intensely active, emphasizing a future orientation, and forcing reciprocal isolation. In the cancer ward, it is relatively easy to deny impending death by *juggling time*, for, as we have noted, disclosure implies certainty that death will occur, but no assurance as to *when* it will occur. Patients can therefore invent a time, and this becomes a way of denying that one is truly dying.[17] Some literally give themselves years. But even when a denying patient is given a time limit, he is still likely to start thinking, as one nurse said, "in terms of years, when it really is a matter of a month or two."

A patient can *test* the staff in various ways *to establish* his *denial*. A negative way is not to test, by failing to ask the questions called for. For example, the doctor who tells the patient he has a tumor adopts a grave manner, indicating that the tumor is malignant, and expects the patient to try to verify it. The patient never asks the doctor or anyone else. Other patients test the nurses, indirectly, by asking. "Why aren't I feeling better?" "Why aren't I gaining weight?" Since these patients can be assumed to know why, the nurse understands that they want these physical cues interpreted in such a way as to deny that they indicate impending death. Patients often ask nurses to manage temporal cues in the same way, by interpreting extended stays in the hospital or slow recuperation in ways that point away from death.

Another form of testing for denial is the *polarity game*. By questioning a nurse or social worker about the most extreme

[17] That in the case of dying, patients will tend to give themselves *more* time than they actually have, contrasts with studies of recovery which show that patients are likely to give themselves *less* time than it takes to recover. See F. Davis, *Passage Through Crisis*, Indianapolis: Bobbs-Merrill, 1963, and J. Roth, *Timetables*, Indianapolis: Bobbs-Merrill, 1963.

living or dying implications of his illness, the patient forces her to give a normalizing answer, which usually locates him a safe distance from death. For example, focusing on the dying implications, the patient asks, "Am I getting worse? The medicine isn't helping." The forced answer is, "Give yourself a chance — medicine takes a long time." Or focusing on the living implications, to a social worker trying to figure out his VA benefits for his family a patient replies, "Well, all right — but it won't be for long, will it?" Since the social worker cannot confront the patient with coming death if he "really doesn't know," she in effect denies it for him by classifying him with the living but disabled. "This is what welfare is for — to help the families of men who are disabled and can't work." Here, the social worker understood the patient's words as a request "for assurance that he wasn't going to die," and she responded appropriately.

Patients may deny their fate by using other patients as *comparative references*. Two common types of comparison are the exception and the favorable comparison. A patient using the first approach becomes very talkative about other patients with the same disease. He adopts a manner, or style, like that of staff members, that is, people who do not have the illness. In the end this borrowed objectivity and immunity leads him to conclude that he is an exceptional case, that somehow the illness that caused so many others to die will not kill him: he will be cured. The favorable comparison is a distorted effort to include one's illness in a non-fatal category: one patient said, "The doctor says I *only* have a (severe illness)." Another literally dying patient said, "Thank God, I am not as bad off as (another patient near death)."

Some patients try to prove they are not terminal by *engaging in strenuous activities*. One patient, having been told he had a bad heart, left the hospital and started spading up his garden to prove the doctor wrong, that is, his denial correct. Another patient wouldn't stick to his diet. The death impending in the present can also be denied through *future-oriented talk* with the nurses. One patient began making plans to buy a chicken farm when he left the hospital — as soon as he learned he was going to die. *Communication blocks* of various sorts aid denial. Some patients simply don't hear the doctor, others refuse to admit it, others cannot use the word "cancer" in any verbal context, and still others avoid any discussion of the nature of their illness or the inevitability of death.

A denying patient can start an accumulating process of *reciprocal isolation* between himself and nurses, doctors, family members and social workers. After disclosure, others expect him to acknowledge his impending death, so they attempt to relate to him on this basis. Doctors speak to him and nurses give treatment on the understanding that his impending demise can be mentioned, or at least signaled. Family members and social workers may refer to plans for his burial and his finances. A patient who avoids the subject when he is not expected to avoid it forces others to avoid it, too, and thus renders them unable to help and prepare the patient. One social worker said, hopelessly, about a denying patient, "There was nothing I could do for him." At this first stage of the isolation process, the patient has forced an implicit agreement between himself and others that the topic of his illness will not be discussed.[18] In the next stage, some of these people may avoid all contact with the patient because he has frustrated their efforts to help him. Nurses, doctors and social workers tend to spend their time with patients they can help, to prevent the feeling of helplessness that often overcomes them while engaged in terminal care. As a result, the patient finds himself alone, apart from receiving the necessary technical care to insure painless comfort, thus his isolation is complete.

Avoidance of the denying patient occurs because he refuses to act as a dying patient, although it has been clearly pointed out to him that this is exactly what he is. In contrast, an unaware patient, who is not expected to act like a dying patient, will not be avoided on these grounds. Rather, he is likely to attract others who will

gather around him in silent sympathy, wishing they could tell him and help him. In the end, both the denying patient and the unaware patient may die without preparation for death. But a denying patient had the chance to accept his impending death and prepare himself with the help of others, while the unaware patient's chances for preparation are mostly dependent on his doctor's decision not to disclose his terminal illness.

IMPLICATIONS FOR DISCLOSURE

Many of the standard arguments given by doctors for and against disclosure anticipate a single, permanent impact on the patient.[19] The patient is expected to "be brave," "go to pieces," "commit suicide," "lose all hope," or to "plan for the future" and such. But the impact is not so simple. Since disclosing the truth sets off a response process through which the patient passes, to base the decision as to whether to disclose on a single probable impact is to focus on only one stage in the response process, neglecting the other stages and how each stage may be controlled through appropriate forms of interaction by hospital staff. For example, to predict that the patient will become too despondent is to neglect the possibility that he will overcome this despondency and with the aid of a nurse, chaplain, social worker or family member prepare adequately for his death and for his family's future. Or, to expect a patient simply to settle his affairs is to fail to evaluate his capacity for overcoming an initial depression, as well as the capacity of the staff to help him at this stage.

A doctor deciding whether to tell the patient therefore should consider not a single impact as a desiderata, but how, in what direction and with what consequences the patient's response is likely to go, and what types of staff are available and how will they handle the patient at

---

[18] Thus, instituting a "mutual pretense awareness context" is part of this process: see Glaser and Strauss, "Awareness Contexts . . .," *op. cit.*

[19] For an illustration of this kind of argument, see the discussion between two doctors in "How Should Incurably Ill Patients Be Dealt with: Should They Be Told the Truth," *Parent's Magazine, 71:* 196–206, January, 1963.

each stage. A doctor who says "no" to disclosure because the patient will "lose hope" need not be in conflict with one who says "yes," to give the patient a chance to plan for his family. Each is merely referring to a different stage of the same process. For both, the concern should be to judge whether the patient can achieve the acceptance-active preparation stage.

Once again, the benefits and liabilities of unawareness (non-disclosure) as opposed to disclosure and the possibilities for acceptance or denial, depend on the nature of the individual case. But on the whole, there is much to recommend giving more to patients than are presently given an opportunity actively to manage their own dying and prepare for death. As a strong controlling factor, staff members in interaction with the patient could self-consciously soften the disclosure, handle the depression so as to encourage acceptance, and guide the patient into active preparations for death. They could also find interaction strategies that would convert a patient's denial to acceptance. Yet staff members may hesitate to tamper with a patient's choice of passage to death. For example, one social worker said of a denying patient, "I'm loathe to play God on this. Unless it

could serve a useful purpose — would it really be helpful. Where a man shies away from something — maybe you should let him — why make him face this most terrible reality?"

The understanding that the descriptive model presented here affords will, we trust, give doctors as well as other parties to the dying situation, such as family members, nurses, social workers and chaplains, a perspective that is of use in deciding the advisability of disclosing terminal illness to a patient, and if advisable, how best it might be done, and how to guide the patient through the response process. Thus perhaps this understanding will reduce some of the current reluctance of medical staff to disclose and to tamper with patients' responses to disclosure. This model also provides sociologists with a beginning basis both for entering into, as consultants, the discussion on whether or not to disclose and for the needed social psychological research on the problem. For instance, further research could specify what types of terminal patients follow what kinds of patterns of movement through the response process under what conditions of patient-staff interaction — a problem only hinted at in this paper.

XIV INTERBEHAVIORAL CHARACTERISTICS OF HOSPITAL SYSTEMS

It is only in modern times that the delivery of medical care has shifted from the patient's home to the physician's office and, more recently, to the hospital center. In the past, the typical doctor's daily routine included traveling from one patient's home to the next. This peripatetic style has proved to be not only wasteful of time and an inefficient use of talent and energy, but has been increasingly difficult to carry on, given the expanding need for cumbersome and expensive laboratory apparatus. All but the most routine aspects of medical care require technical procedures available only in well equipped offices or modern hospital centers. John Knowles, distinguished physician and author of the first article of this volume, outlines this progression from home service to hospital care, noting a number of its less attractive social consequences (1973):

In its present form the hospital has been shaped by the needs of society and reflects not only its attitudes, beliefs and values but also its economy. In the past half-century scientific and technological developments have contributed so heavily to the diagnosis, treatment and prevention of disease that it is no longer possible for the physician to work effectively without the modern apparatus and the specialists and technicians centralized in the hospital. As in so much of modern institutional and technology-based life, the threat of dehumanization of personal relationships — here between the physician and the patient — has in many instances become a reality.

The fact remains that the steady expansion of knowledge has necessitated specialization and the housing of advanced technology within the walls of the modern hospital and that these developments have been of pronounced benefit to mankind. Progress in medical science and in the specialized division of medical skills has changed medicine from an individual, intuitive enterprise into a social service. The hospital is the institutional form of this social service. It has evolved from a house of despair for the sick poor to a house of hope for all social and economic classes in just the past 60 years.

Hospitals have not only taken over procedures that formerly were performed in the home or office, but now offer services that were provided only rarely in earlier days. Among these newer programs are crisis care centers. Emergency facilities such as these have grown as a consequence of the availability of rapid transportation and the centralizing of complex laboratory equipment staffed by skilled medical personnel. By concentrating a vast network of technical instruments that can be adapted for a wide range of emergencies, the crisis physician has ready access to high-powered resources that maximize the recovery prospects of his patient.

Graham, in the following quote, describes several additional benefits of the hospital center in optimizing both clinical service and medical training (1968):

Other conveniences provided by the hospital to the physician and parenthetically to his patient, arise from the centralization of patients in the hospital, which enables the practitioner to treat many more persons on a given day than he could by extensive home visits. The hospital also furnishes a centralization of physicians of various specialities, and physicians are often quick to take advantage of the resulting opportunities for consultation. Finally, the concentration of patients and of physicians of various specialties makes the hospital a valuable teaching ground. Traditionally, medical training was carried out through a master apprentice relationship. The hospital now allows apprentices to group together and learn from each other; it allows them to observe the techniques of a variety of physicians; it allows them to see various kinds of patients in their training years, and to observe certain illnesses which they otherwise might not see during many years of practice.

Superbly equipped and staffed modern hospitals are not without their share of problems. To enable such institutions to function adequately requires the coordination of diverse personnel such as dieticians, x-ray technicians, admitting clerks, accountants, and janitors, as well as nurses, orderlies, social workers, residents, interns, and, of course, physicians. Overseeing, and occasionally engulfed by this huge bureaucracy is an administrative staff with its own hierarchy and goals, most notably those of ensuring the continued solvency of the institution they run.

As a hospital grows and flourishes it becomes transformed into a complex community with a structure and internal life of its own. These institutions are not only organized along traditional clinical services such as medicine, surgery and psychiatry, but they formalize other occupational functions into departments such as nursing, nutrition, records, maintenance, and so on. Professional "lay" administrators come into being, gradually replacing the older practice of employing experienced physicians as hospital directors. This new class of administrators, many of whom have been trained at a professional or graduate level, compete for authority with the senior medical staff in running the institution. Among the thorniest of difficulties are the power struggles that emerge between medical specialty chiefs, each jealously guarding against infringements upon his sphere of influence and prestige.

Robert Wilson, distinguished medical sociologist and author of the first paper of this chapter, provides a comprehensive analysis of the structure, functions, and goals of the modern general hospital. He describes the awesome task involved in coordinating an institution that is, at once, a hotel, a treatment center, a laboratory, and a university. Special problems surround the physician who, though merely a "guest" utilizing the hospital's facilities, is the only member of the staff possessing the legal authority and clinical skills to enable the institution to meet its prime function of medical care. Despite his essential, if not vital, role, the physician finds himself today with less status than in the past, encountering increasing pressures from the hospital to fit into a limited niche within the bureaucracy. These complexities and tensions notwithstanding, the phrase employed by Hans Mauksch for the title of a paper, "It defies all logic — but a hospital does work," still holds.

In the second article of the chapter, by Leonard Stein a recognized medical researcher, the interbehavioral features of the physician-nurse relationship are described with clarity and insight. Characterizing the interplay of these two key professional groups as a "game," Stein notes the way in which nurses successfully carry on major functions while feigning humility. Most learn to assume a subservient public role, always deferring to the doctor as the authority for patient-care decisions while, in reality, often making these judgments for him.

The final paper, by distinguished educator and social scientist Esther L. Brown, portrays the many psychological and social needs of patients that must be met by the hospital staff. She notes that patients enter the hospital with anxieties other than those directly connected to their illness, particularly those generated by family, occupational, and financial concerns. She takes great pains to point out the importance of helping the patient accommodate to the alien hospital environment and overcome the feelings of loneliness and isolation this experience creates.

REFERENCES

Graham, S.: Sociological Aspects of Health and Illness. In Faris, R. E. L. (ed.): Handbook of Modern Sociology. Chicago, Rand McNally, 1968.

Knowles, J. H.: The hospital. Sci. Am. 299:3: 128–137 (1973).

40   The Social Structure of a General Hospital

Robert N. Wilson

Dr. Harvey Cushing, pioneer surgeon and philosopher of medicine, speaks in his *Consecratio Medici* of the "personality" of a hospital. He had observed that each institution seems distinguished by a style of its own, a tempo of work and an emotional atmosphere peculiar to a given hospital, its traditions, its community of staff and patients. When we turn from the single hospital's unique organizational life toward a more general formulation, toward recurrent features of social structure, it is important to note that the flavor and tone of the individual institution are blunted. The personality which is thus left out, and must be, may be precisely the most significant element determining the shape and satisfactions of life for the persons involved as treaters or clients. But, because generalization is essential to the scientific enterprise, we shall focus on the typical environs of institutional personality; in this effort, the model of organization will be the large general hospital, urban and voluntarily supported, responsible for the three major hospital functions of care, teaching, and research.

We thus neglect many features unique to government institutions, small or rural hospitals, or the common run of hospitals which focus almost solely on patient care. The justification for selecting the major medical center as our model is that such organizations are most sharply exemplary of modern medical trends; further, although there is no more a "typical" hospital than there is a "typical" individual, most of the issues characteristic of metropolitan hospitals are largely shared by other varieties of organization.

Hospitals, like universities, often seem to place an inordinate emphasis on physical plant, on the bricks and glass which embody a viable social organization. Perhaps this is because buildings are a tangible symbol of stability and vigor for institutions which have no "product" in the usual sense; the human being who is educated or healed is not a thing but a process, and it is difficult to point to him as the concrete output of a work pattern. Perhaps, too, the vocations which minister to mind and body are reluctant or inarticulate when they come to speak of their central values. In any case, it is clear that, although architecture and human relations interpenetrate, the crucial features of an organization are manifest in social, rather than physical, structure. The social structure of a hospital consists of patterned relationships among people. It is the moving configuration of individuals joined together in the repeated performance of certain activities directed toward certain goals. For convenience and

Wilson, R. N.: The social structure of a general hospital. Ann. Amer. Acad. Polit. Soc. Sci. *346:* 67–76 (1963).

simplicity, it is probably best to think of social structure in terms of various clusters of role relationships, of those recurring nexuses of interpersonal action which center around some desired end. In the general hospital, the major role relationships are ordered to staff-staff and staff-patient activities. In contrast to the mental hospital, where lengthy sojourns generate a sense of community among patients, the relation of patient to patient is not often seen as a very important aspect of life in the general hospital.

As a social organization, the modern hospital is one of the most complicated enterprises in our civilization; partly by rational design, partly by the inheritance of historical accident, the hospital entails a multiplicity of goals, a riotous profusion of personnel, and an extremely fine-grained division of labor. Although it is intimately attached to its community setting — and the manifold relations between the institution and the surrounding society are one of the more inviting fields for social research — a general hospital is, to a considerable extent, a self-contained social universe. Because its work goes on around the clock and its life-sustaining goals demand a maximum of self-sufficiency, the hospital constitutes an internally diverse society within a society. This very complex and enveloping character of the institution is at once perhaps the first thing to know about it and a primary reason why it fascinates the social researcher. The sociologist, whether his interest is in social roles, professional organization, status and stratification, the administration of large institutions, or whatever, finds here a compelling scene for the study of behavior.

Historically, the hospital was more nearly a place of refuge than a place for medical treatment. A haven for the weary and ill on the routes of medieval crusades and pilgrimages, it has roots deep in religion and altruistic hospitality. Over the long centuries of medical ignorance, centuries in which the homeless and impoverished were many and were unsupported by schemes of social welfare, the hospital was the charitable last resort of the ill pauper. It was where one went to die, rather than to be cured; mortality rates among patients *and* staff were of a magnitude we would today think astronomical. Anybody who could afford to be cared for at home stayed there, for one's own house was a far safer place to be in the days before asepsis and sophisticated medical technique. The rise of scientific medicine in the late nineteenth and early twentieth centuries transformed the hospital from a sanctuary of simple food and warmth into a workshop of the physician and an accepted destination for the ill of diverse ailments and social standings. As recently as the 1920's, many hospitals were still construed as primarily charitable organizations for individuals who could not arrange proper treatment at home. Only in the last few decades, and especially with the burgeoning of hospitalization insurance, has the hospital come to be routinely used by the bulk of the population as the appropriate setting for surgical intervention or medical care.

The large general hospital is the prototype of the multipurpose organization; it is a hotel and a school, a laboratory and a stage for treatment. All these purposes, their attendant values and specialized personnel, must be somehow articulated into a going concern. Co-ordination of specialized activity into a whole that makes organizational sense is the huge and delicate task of the administrator, a task that is never completed to anyone's entire satisfaction. Underlying the disparate goals of patient care, teaching, and research is that first necessary aim of any institution: self-maintenance, or corporate survival, with its human and economic imperatives. If it is not quite all things to all men, the hospital is very many things to very many different kinds of people. Occupational specialization, the compounding of professional groups, the demands of patients, physicians, trustees, or whomever, all imply that the organization is likely to be marked by conflict and confusion. Yet there is a vital focusing element which serves to pull together individuals and techniques: the presence of the patient and his need. In a real sense, the patient is the implicit director of activity, his need for care setting the direction and pace of work. And the goal of treatment unifies separate parts of the hospital, centering them on the prepotent value of health. Indeed, patient care is a master value even for those whose work seldom brings them into direct contact with ill people. The administrator has, then, this ally, this overriding appeal to counter the extraordinary difficulties of medical organization.

In a curious fashion, the two most significant actors in the hospital plot – the patient and the physician – are "guests" of the organization. The patient, who has the distinction of being simultaneously the hospital's client and its product, is, hopefully, just passing through. His identity and his basic loyalties obviously lie elsewhere. The physician, with the exception of department heads, students, and the house staff of doctors-in-training, is also one who uses the organization without fundamentally belonging to it. His membership is nominal and his physical habitation transitory. Thus, these two chief figures are in the organization but not of it; without them there is no meaning in the medical process, yet with them comes a "disturbance" with which the institution must strenuously cope.

PATIENTS AND DOCTORS

The patient comes unbidden to a large organization which awes and irritates him, even as it also nurtures and cures. As he strips off his clothing, so he strips off, too, his favored costume of social roles, his favored style, his customary identity in the world. He becomes subject to a time schedule and a pattern of activity not of his own making. The patient's expectations are relatively vague; most of the initiative in social intercourse passes to the staff, which is exceedingly ready to exercise it in the service of expert knowledge and mundane convenience. Ill persons have to learn how to be patients, for being sick and performing adeptly in the role of hospital patient are not at all the same thing. Patients are passive creatures for the most part, and their passivity is linked to an understandable dependency which is inseparable from illness; pain and fear have a well-recognized tendency to reduce the mature human being toward the childlike.

This very regression acts to afford the treater a necessary leverage on which he capitalizes in manipulating the patient. One of the most interesting current developments in nursing care, however, is an attempted partial reversal of the habit of staff initiative and patient receptivity; it involves a radical fixing of attention on patients' felt needs, together with an encouraging posture aimed at eliciting expression of those needs. [1]

Although the patient's expectations are vague in detail with respect to hospital procedures, he and his relatives faithfully anticipate miracles of medical care. Medical services must forever fall short of the proficiency which Americans, for a variety of reasons, increasingly tend to demand. The belief that all ailments can be diagnosed and rapidly repaired is a naive but understandable assumption rooted in the achieved excellence of scientific medicine and our traditional philosophy of environmental mastery. As patients, we cherish the notion that everything is known, or can be; we grow restive under delay in cure and unwilling to accept chronicity. The client nourishes the fallacy, intrinsic to our cultural propensity for problem-solving and for dominating the natural world, of believing "that all good things can be deliberately achieved." His impatience is exacerbated by the overwhelming importance we attach to health; physical well-being, tied to the cult of youth and the virtue of efficiency, is something of a secular religion. From the size of legislative appropriations to the medical content of the mass media, there is a good deal of evidence that health and medical research are among the few things everyone can be for, and no one against, in our national life.

An increased demandingness on the part of patients may also be stimulated by the heightened medical sophistication which now characterizes some sectors of the public and by the insured patient's feeling that, as a paying client, he is fully entitled to maximum service.

---

[1] Ida J. Orlando, *The Dynamic Nurse-Patient Relationship: Function, Process and Principles* (New York: G. P. Putnam's Sons, 1961).

There has been surprisingly little social psychological research which holds patient care as such, or the patient's role in the hospital organization, as its central object. This neglect has been partly a matter of availability; patients in the general hospital do not usually stay very long, and their treatment clearly has priority over their subjection to the inquiring sociologist – to say nothing of the fact that they may be extremely ill. Another probable reason why the patient is the forgotten man of hospital research is that the social scientist does not ordinarily feel equipped to gauge either the quality of care or the patient's medical status. Treatment is, furthermore, at the core of the doctor's technical preserve and at the core of the hospital administrator's managerial competence. It may often be neither penetrable nor safe territory for the innocent researcher. A few current studies do focus on the patient's hospital experience – as mental hospital research has nearly always done – and their results promise great value to the student of the hospital as a social institution.*

If the patient has been *terra incognita*, the other "guest" of the hospital – the physician – has been almost too well known for the comfort of some hospital administrators. The medical staff is essentially an intrusion, albeit a profoundly necessary one, into the organized structure of authority and assigned tasks. A hospital without decisive *medical* excellence has been described as "just a hotel for sick people"; yet the administrator must run a hotel, among many other things, and doctors are traditionally the mavericks who make his life uneasy. The basic problem is the existence of two broad sets of activities, the general administrative and the technical medical, which are manned in overlapping fashion and which generate something close to two lines of authority.

Moreover, although the administrator obviously heads one line, the other is captained in fragments by a changing guard of physicians who happen to be involved in a given case. Doctors are fiercely independent professionals who control expert knowledge; administrators are nascent professionals who are, in Chester Barnard's phrase, "specialists in generalities" but have not the cachet in the medical world that executives in other organizations possess.[2] Since physicians are only minimally subject to the hospital administrator's direction, it is apparent that, to some extent, the social structure of a hospital is inherently divisive. Clashes between administrative and medical desiderata are among the most disruptive of hospital conflicts; like other conflicts we shall rehearse, notably in the area of interprofessional competition, they are truly structural and thus only very partially dependent on the personal idiosyncrasies of specific doctors or administrators.[3]

THE FORMAL STRUCTURE

At the top of the hospital's social blueprint stand three dominant forces: the administrator, the trustees or board of managers, the medical staff. Well below them in formal power, but in effect the day-to-day decision-makers who fix the hospital's image, is the nursing staff. The nurse is, of course, traditionally subordinate to the physician, and she is a paid employee amenable to routine administrative strictures, yet she wields immense influence because of sheer weight of numbers and closeness to the central job of healing. It is fair to assume that the picture of a hospital held by its clients and its surrounding community is pre-eminently based on nurses' behavior; they are the persons the patient sees, the persons who

---

*For instance, there is a study in progress at Grace-New Haven Hospital, New Haven, Connecticut, under the direction of Raymond Duff, M. D., and August B. Hollingshead which attempts to explore the meaning of the hospital stay to different types of patients.

[2] Harold L. Wilensky, "The Dynamics of Professionalism: The Case of Hospital Administration," *Hospital Administration*, Vol. 7, No. 2 (Spring 1962), pp. 6–24.

[3] Harvey Smith, "Two Lines of Authority Are One Too Many," *Modern Hospital*, Vol. 85 (1955), pp. 48–52.

express the guiding spirit of the institution in the minutiae of action. Paralleling the nurse there is a variety of professional groupings, including such specialties as social work, dietetics, pharmacology, and other vocations. These groupings possess very narrowly circumscribed authority, and they stand in a no man's land of prestige and control vis-à-vis the nurse. The "strictly administrative" staff, again, such as fiscal and clerical personnel of various grades and functions, is more or less parallel to nursing, depending on just who is involved in what context of decision. With the exception of the lowest categories of hospital worker, orderlies and aides, the general principle is that prestige hinges on the extent to which an individual's work entails direct patient care; in contrast to most other types of large organization, the hospital ranks a certain kind of manual labor — the "production" job on the "assembly line" — above almost all sorts of white-collar jobs. The surgeon, for instance, is at the peak of the prestige hierarchy, and he works with his hands.

There is no way to summarize the social structure of a general hospital in concise form; there are simply too many relationships, and the universe of action is too diffuse.[4] Two master themes, however, may help one comprehend the major contingencies of interpersonal behavior. These are, first, the diffusion of authority, and, second, the excruciating struggle for occupational prestige. Returning to the troika at the top, there is no doubt that ultimate legal authority and responsibility are vested in the trustees. But, like most trustees, these august individuals cannot exercise daily detailed supervision; they occasionally attempt to do so, capriciously, but then the administrator's essential minimum of operating autonomy is perilously undercut. The hospital administrator, the creature of his board, has directive control of the formal organization. However, because administration is a relatively new specialty in hospitals, having been conventionally performed by former doctors, nurses, or business managers, it does not have the prestige or professional stature of medicine. Indeed, one of the critical changes in the modern hospital is just the move toward professional administration, replete with master's degrees and graduate courses, and the upgrading of the administrator. The third arm of top command, the medical staff, represents the hospital's largest concentration of prestige and expert skill. It exercises absolute *medical* authority but is only tangentially involved in administration of the total organization. Again and again, however, the medical and the "strictly administrative" interpenetrate and overlap. A typical instance might be a decision on recruitment and compensation of nursing staff, which is a clear prerogative of the administrator but obviously has potent implications for the pattern of patient care and for the close working relationship between doctor and nurse.

If authority is diffuse because of the nature of medical work and the history of hospital organization, it is also complicated by the peculiar urgency of patient need. When the patient's condition dictates action, there is no time to resolve a jurisdictional dispute or to refer the matter to higher authority. Necessary things must be done, although, in doing them, the nurse or other staff person may be confusedly vulnerable to what Jules Henry has called "multiple subordination," taking orders, sometimes opposing ones, from a plethora of sources.

The uncertain distribution of higher authority is matched as one goes down the formal hierarchy. Such pairings as nurse-dietitian or nurse-social worker are often engaged in situations of unclear power, in which resolutions can only be hammered out on an *ad hoc* basis. Granted that it is sometimes hard to tell by formal criteria who should exert what leverage in a given case, the plain fact is that the hospital's functions do get performed, for the most part with admirable dispatch. This is so because what would be a nightmare to the theorist of formal bureaucratic organization is transformed by several factors into a viable scheme of work. One of these factors is the informal organization, the

---

[4] A very general, primarily descriptive account is essayed in Temple Burling, Edith M. Lentz, and Robert N. Wilson, *The Give and Take in Hospitals* (New York: G. P. Putnam's Sons, 1956).

network of relationships that develops over time in any human enterprise. Any hospital is characterized by innumerable groupings that spring up in the natural course of events, that cross the barriers of specialization and status in order to get jobs done and to meet the social needs of the staff. These informal ties are far from being diversions or obstacles in the pursuit of organizational goals; although they may be conceptually untidy, they are the flesh and blood of an institution as the formal blueprint is the skeleton. Another element promoting cohesion is, of course, patient need and the humane response to it. Few people in a hospital have to be convinced that their work is significant; the ill person is a magnet drawing forth unusual resources of energy and devotion and helping personnel transcend disparities of aim.

A struggle for a place in the hospital sun is unremittingly waged by most of the myriad occupational groups, especially those most closely tied to therapeutic tasks. Precisely because systems of authority are unclear, there is often a premium on flexible, not to say opportunistic, behavior. The hospital is the scene of very rapid change in the techniques of medicine and slower but still substantial change in the patterns of social organization. Because the model of occupational prestige and autonomy is the physician, other personnel strive to become similarly professionalized, with concomitant independence, corpus of technical knowledge, standards of competence, and pride in craft. Each yearns for a sphere of effort in which he and he alone can be a proficient actor. The professionalization of work has many implications, from the deleterious consequences of departmental infighting to the beneficent results of enhanced competence. Unfortunately, the patient is often the battleground of professional competition; his body, mind, and purse are scarred by the zealous attempts to do for him what each staff member's specialty dictates. The hospital, too, is a battleground, often ripped by a cross fire of prefessional purposes. Yet there is an increasing emphasis on the patient as a whole being, and the specialty groups are

engaged in serious exploration of ways to co-ordinate their work. Further, if professionalization insures that the hospital work flow cannot be quiet or routine, it also insures the existence of a reservoir of initiative and responsibility. Professional élan, the morale-enhancing properties of "the religion of competence," lends stability and direction to a system which might otherwise resemble organized chaos.

At heart, the hospital is more like a federal system than a monolithic entity; its organization takes the form of a federation of departments, each department enjoying considerable autonomy and discretion in its management of work. The great challenge is, then, one of co-ordination, of somehow knitting these special excellences into a comprehensive framework of care. We have seen that the patient, by his very presence, is a co-ordinating force. But the needs of the ill are not enough and are today progressively supplemented by the shaping patterns of rational bureaucracy.

With its history of altruistic and undifferentiated caretaking, and under the dominion of a free-wheeling medical corps, the hospital grew in haphazard fashion. It is probably the last major institutional complex in the modern West to accede to the bureaucratic patterning of work which has long characterized government, big industry, and other large organizations. There are two persistent reasons why the hospital can perhaps never approach the degree of formal controllability, of symmetrical power and task arrangements, which distinguishes industry and government. One is the nature of the work flow, the temporal and ethical constraints imposed by intractable human material: the patient. The other is the nature of the medical profession, which resists bureaucratization and is the unchanging repository of certain fundamental decisions about the care of the ill. Despite these strictures, however, the hospital is now exhibiting many more of the faces of bureaucracy. Specifically, it is becoming rationalized and specialized to an unprecedented extent. Rationality is expressed in such features of the modern hospital as cost accounting and written personnel policies, quality control, and job descriptions; a loose benevolence is yielding to calculated, planful organization of services. Specialization, already acute in medicine itself, is now seen in administrative as well as technical guises. Task assignments and spheres of discretion are increasingly narrowed and legitimized in formal rather than accidental ways. Most hospital jobs are increasingly constricted as the assumed prerogatives of general helping roles are replaced by the deliberate mandates of announced organizational functions.

SOME ENDURING ISSUES

One key problem for the future of hospital organization is the juxtaposition of this rising tide of bureaucracy and the free professional. The physician's case is the most obvious, but many elements are common to the other hospital groups. Certainly, the doctor is bound to reshape his role in a manner more congruent with bureaucratic organization than had been true in the past; from a wise healer who often possessed charismatic qualities and enjoyed a very generalized respect, he is becoming more nearly a technical specialist who works as part of a close-knit medical team.[5] As team member, the physician sacrifices at least a certain portion of the autonomy of action and the unique prestige which have been traditionally attendant on his role. George Rosen has commented perceptively on the change:[6]

Sociologically viewed and interpreted, the behavior of organized medicine represents the reaction of a segment of the older middle class to the process by which it is being shifted and adjusted to the modern urbanized, industrialized society characterized by a high degree of social complexity, integration, division of labor and bureaucratization. To use an analogy, one may say that the Industrial Revolution has finally caught up with medicine, and that the medical practitioner is being brought into the "factory"

(the hospital and the whole bureaucratic complexity of the provision of medical care) where he is being subjected to the necessary "labor disciplines."

If "labor disciplines" are applied to the professional, the critical question becomes one of limits: how far may the professional be bureaucratized and yet retain the distinguishing talents and bear the distinguishing responsibilities of a true professional?

Akin to this issue is the conundrum of the power balance between expert and lay authority, what Sir Alfred Zimmern termed "the right relation between knowledge and power." The hospital trustees and the administrator are, in some sense, lay figures coping with a manifold of expert specialists; they must take many things on faith, must render unto experts the matters that are technical, yet, at the same time, exercise the vigilance of informed citizenship. An administrator vis-à-vis doctors, nurses, social workers, and a range of technicians recapitulates the alignment, of, say, the American legislator confronting Pentagon officialdom. Hospital social structure, marked as it is by a peculiar urgency of task and a highly refined division of labor, is a vivid illustration of those power accommodations which are insistently demanded by our thoroughly expert but rootedly populist society.

Many students of hospital organization have remarked on both the complexity of the internal hierarchy of task and prestige and the extent to which the hierarchy is frozen to seal off individual movement within the structure. Again, largely due to the intense specialization of medical craft, hospital jobs do not admit of very much interchangeability of personnel and do not foster many paths for smooth progression along a skill hierarchy. Thus, the hospital is a classic illustration of "blocked mobility." With the exception of a few opportunities for movement within a job category (usually at lower levels of responsibility, such as the shift from one classification of aide to another) medical advancement depends upon technical training which can only be secured through formal schooling in a setting outside the organization itself. Although varieties of in-service

---

[5] Robert N. Wilson, "The Physician's Changing Hospital Role," *Human Organization,* Vol. 18, No. 4 (1959).

[6] George Rosen, "Notes on Some Aspects of the Sociology of Medicine with Particular Reference to Prepaid Group Practice" (Unpublished manuscript), pp. 4–5.

training schemes exist, individuals can seldom make a change of real magnitude through on-the-job education or superior performance in some parochial task: no nurse works up to surgeon; no orderly cultivates his talents in hope of becoming a hospital administrator. The relatively frozen contours of organization then create a severe problem of morale and motivation. Once more the hospital may perhaps be seen as a specific instance of a more general dilemma in the social organization of work: the provision of job satisfactions for people below the professional or managerial level. A much-simplified but germane conception of American social stratification might indeed lead one to think of the hospital as an example of our division into "two nations": the college-trained professional or executive, and all others.

It is difficult to prophesy the future of hospital social structure in clear-cut terms. Such pervasive innovations as the automation of work are not susceptible of easy analysis. Surely the automated hospital will, to some extent, lighten the problem of blocked mobility for lower-level personnel, because fewer strictly routine chores will need doing and there will, thus, be fewer employees with extremely shallow job horizons. On the other hand, automation may exacerbate the already serious problems of staff-patient relationships. The warmth and intimacy of "tender loving care," a closeness which many believe to be already greatly attenuated by professional specialization, will presumably be still less readily apparent under automation.

Other issues are equally obscure. For example, the renewed emphasis on home care of the ill, together with the unsuitability of the general hospital for sustained treatment of those chronic diseases which are an increasing part of the load of American illness, might dispose one to think that hospital use might decline — proportionately, not absolutely, of course — over the next generation. Yet there are vast sectors of the population relatively newly covered by hospitalization insurance and newly attuned to the habit of recourse to the hospital, so that hospital use seems destined to rise sharply in these sectors.

Another cloudy area is that of hospital-community relationships. Wilensky[7] predicts that these relationships will be increasingly important and that they may well become a primary sphere for the activities of the hospital administrator. Can communities be educated to more appropriate use of the hospital, especially of out-patient facilities? Will increased federal financing of hospital construction, medical research, and so on mean a decreased feeling of community identity with "its" voluntary institution? How may political debate about the role of government in medical care affect the organization and economics of the general hospital?

It seems apparent that the social structure of the general hospital is not a single inherent pattern, an unchanging pyramid of organization. Patients, staff, and the techniques of medical care are in flux. Although human relations in the hospital are subject to certain imperatives of decision-making and patterned skill, notably in surgical operations,[8] there is room for considerable maneuver and for entertaining alternative structures. The pace of change in hospital organization is far less accelerated than in medical technology itself, but there are indications that an attitude of social experiment may begin to parallel the propensity to scientific experiment. Research into social structure is undoubtedly as important to the future of medical care as is research into cell structure. Patient care is, after all, the crux, the point of application for the virtuosities of medical science.

---

[7] Harold L. Wilensky, *op. cit.*
[8] Robert N. Wilson, "Teamwork in the Operating Room," *Human Organization,* Vol. 12, No. 4 (1954).

41   The Doctor-Nurse Game

Leonard I. Stein

The relationship between the doctor and the nurse is a very special one. There are few professions where the degree of mutual respect and cooperation between co-workers is as intense as that between the doctor and nurse. Superficially, the stereotype of this relationship has been dramatized in many novels and television serials. When, however, it is observed carefully in an interactional framework, the relationship takes on a new dimension and has a special quality which fits a game model. The underlying attitudes which demand that this game be played are unfortunate. These attitudes create serious obstacles in the path of meaningful communications between physicians and nonmedical professional groups.

The physician traditionally and appropriately has total responsibility for making the decisions regarding the management of his patients' treatment. To guide his decisions he considers data gleaned from several sources. He acquires a complete medical history, performs a thorough physical examination, interprets laboratory findings, and at times, obtains recommendations from physician-consultants. Another important factor in his decision-making are the recommendations he receives from the nurse. The interaction between doctor and nurse through which these recommendations are communicated and received is unique and interesting.

THE GAME

One rarely hears a nurse say, "Doctor I would recommend that you order a retention enema for Mrs. Brown." A physician, upon hearing a recommendation of that nature, would gape in amazement at the effrontery of the nurse. The nurse, upon hearing the statement, would look over her shoulder to see who said it, hardly believing the words actually came from her own mouth. Nevertheless, if one observes closely, nurses make recommendations of more import every hour and physicians willingly and respectfully consider them. If the nurse is to make a suggestion without appearing insolent and the doctor is to seriously consider that suggestion, their interaction must not violate the rules of the game.

Object of the Game

The object of the game is as follows: the nurse is to be bold, have initiative, and be responsible for making significant recommendations, while at the same time she must appear passive. This must be done in such a manner so as to make her recommendations appear to be initiated by the physician.

Both participants must be acutely sensitive to each other's nonverbal and cryptic verbal communications. A slight lowering of the head, a minor shifting of position in the chair, or a seemingly nonrelevant comment concerning an event which occurred eight months ago must be interpreted as a powerful message. The game requires the nimbleness of a high wire acrobat, and if either participant slips the game can be shattered; the penalties for frequent failure are apt to be severe.

Rules of the Game

The cardinal rule of the game is that open disagreement between the players

Stein, L. I.: The doctor-nurse game. Arch. Gen. Psychiat. *16:* 699–703 (1967).

must be avoided at all costs. Thus, the nurse must communicate her recommendations without appearing to be making a recommendation statement. The physician, in requesting a recommendation from a nurse, must do so without appearing to be asking for it. Utilization of this technique keeps anyone from committing themselves to a position before a sub rosa agreement on that position has already been established. In that way open disagreement is avoided. The greater the significance of the recommendation, the more subtly the game must be played.

To convey a subtle example of the game with all its nuances would require the talents of a literary artist. Lacking these talents, let me give you the following example which is unsubtle, but happens frequently. The medical resident on hospital call is awakened by telephone at 1 AM because a patient on a ward, not his own, has not been able to fall asleep. Dr. Jones answers the telephone and the dialogue goes like this:

This is Dr. Jones.
(An open and direct communication.)
Dr. Jones, this is Miss Smith on 2W — Mrs. Brown, who learned today of her father's death, is unable to fall asleep.
(This message has two levels. Openly, it describes a set of circumstances, a woman who is unable to sleep and who that morning received word of her father's death. Less openly, but just as directly, it is a diagnostic and recommendation statement; i.e., Mrs. Brown is unable to sleep because of her grief, and she should be given a sedative. Dr. Jones, accepting the diagnostic statement and replying to the recommendation statement, answers.)
What sleeping medication has been helpful to Mrs. Brown in the past?
(Dr. Jones, not knowing the patient, is asking for a recommendation from the nurse, who does know the patient, about what sleeping medication should be prescribed. Note, however, his question does not appear to be asking her for a recommendation. Miss Smith replies.)
Pentobarbital mg 100 was quite effective night before last.
(A disguised recommendation statement. Dr. Jones replies with a note of authority in his voice.)
Pentobarbital mg 100 before bedtime as needed for sleep, got it?
(Miss Smith ends the conversation with the tone of a grateful supplicant.)
Yes, I have, and thank you very much doctor.

The above is an example of a successfully played doctor-nurse game. The nurse made appropriate recommendations which were accepted by the physician and were helpful to the patient. The game was successful because the cardinal rule was not violated. The nurse was able to make her recommendation without appearing to, and the physician was able to ask for recommendations without conspicuously asking for them.

The Scoring System

Inherent in any game are penalties and rewards for the players. In game theory, the doctor-nurse game fits the nonzero sum game model. It is not like chess, where the players compete with each other and whatever one player loses the other wins. Rather, it is the kind of game in which the rewards and punishments are shared by both players. If they play the game successfully they both win rewards, and if they are unskilled and the game is played badly, they both suffer the penalty.

The most obvious reward from the well-played game is a doctor-nurse team that operates efficiently. The physician is able to utilize the nurse as a valuable consultant, and the nurse gains self-esteem and professional satisfaction from her job. The less obvious rewards are no less important. A successful game creates a doctor-nurse alliance; through this alliance the physician gains the respect and admiration of the nursing service. He can be confident that his nursing staff will smooth the path for getting his work done. His charts will be organized and waiting for him when he arrives, the ruffled feathers of patients and relatives will have been smoothed down, his pet routines will be happily followed, and he will be helped in a thousand and one other ways.

The doctor-nurse alliance sheds its light on the nurse as well. She gains a reputation for being a "damn good nurse." She is respected by everyone and appropriately enjoys her position. When physicians discuss the nursing staff it would not be unusual for her name to be mentioned with respect and admiration. Their esteem for a good nurse is no less than their esteem for a good doctor.

The penalties for a game failure, on the other hand, can be severe. The physician who is an unskilled gamesman and fails to recognize the nurses' subtle recommendation messages is tolerated as a "clod." If, however, he interprets these messages as insolence and strongly indicates he does not wish to tolerate suggestions from nurses, he creates a rocky path for his travels. The old truism "If the nurse is your ally you've got it made, and if she has it in for you, be prepared for misery," takes on life-sized proportions. He receives three times as many phone calls after midnight than his colleagues. Nurses will not accept his telephone orders because "telephone orders are against the rules." Somehow, this rule gets suspended for the skilled players. Soon he becomes like Joe Bfstplk in the "Li'l Abner" comic strip. No matter where he goes, a black cloud constantly hovers over his head.

The unskilled gamesman nurse also pays heavily. The nurse who does not view her role as that of a consultant, and therefore does not attempt to communicate recommendations, is perceived as a dullard and is mercifully allowed to fade into the woodwork.

The nurse who does see herself as a consultant but refuses to follow the rules of the game in making her recommendations, has hell to pay. The outspoken nurse is labeled a "bitch" by the surgeon. The psychiatrist describes her as unconsciously suffering from penis envy and her behavior is the acting out of her hostility towards men. Loosely translated, the psychiatrist is saying she is a bitch. The employment of the unbright outspoken nurse is soon terminated. The outspoken bright nurse whose recommendations are worthwhile remains employed. She is, however, constantly reminded in a hundred ways that she is not loved.

GENESIS OF THE GAME

To understand how the game evolved, we must comprehend the nature of the doctors' and nurses' training which shaped the attitudes necessary for the game.

Medical Student Training

The medical student in his freshman year studies as if possessed. In the anatomy class he learns every groove and prominence on the bones of the skeleton as if life depended on it. As a matter of fact, he literally believes just that. He not infrequently says, "I've got to learn it exactly, a life may depend on me knowing that." A consequence of this attitude, which is carefully nurtured throughout medical school, is the development of a phobia: the overdetermined fear of making a mistake. The development of this fear is quite understandable. The burden the physician must carry is at times almost unbearable. He feels responsible in a very personal way for the lives of his patients. When a man dies leaving young children and a widow, the doctor carries some of her grief and despair inside himself; and when a child dies, some of him dies too. He sees himself as a warrior against death and disease. When he loses a battle, through no fault of his own, he nevertheless feels pangs of guilt, and he relentlessly searches himself to see if there might have been a way to alter the outcome. For the physician a mistake leading to a serious consequence is intolerable, and any mistake reminds him of his vulnerability. There is little wonder that he becomes phobic. The classical way in which phobias are managed is to avoid the source of the fear. Since it is impossible to avoid making some mistakes in an active practice of medicine, a substitute defensive maneuver is employed. The physician develops the belief that he is omnipotent and omniscient, and therefore incapable of making mistakes. This belief allows the phobic physician to actively engage in his practice rather than avoid it. The fear of committing an error in a critical field like medicine is unavoidable and appropriately realistic. The physician, however, must learn to live with the fear rather than handle it defensively through a posture of omnipotence. This defense markedly interferes with his interpersonal professional relationships.

Physicians, of course, deny feelings of omnipotence. The evidence, however, renders their denials to whispers in the wind. The slightest mistake inflicts a large narcissistic wound. Depending on his underlying personality structure the physician may obsess for days about it, quickly rationalize it away, or deny it. The guilt produced is usually exaggerated and the incident is handled defensively. The ways in which physicians enhance and support each other's defenses when an error is made could be the topic of another paper. The feelings of omnipotence become generalized to other areas of his life. A report of the Federal Aviation Agency (FAA), as quoted in *Time Magazine* (Aug. 5, 1966), states that in 1964 and 1965 physicians had a fatal-accident rate four times as high as the average for all other private pilots. Major causes of the high death rate were risk-taking attitudes and judgments. Almost all of the accidents occurred on pleasure trips, and were therefore not necessary risks to get to a patient needing emergency care. The trouble, suggested an FAA official, is that too many doctors fly with "the feeling that they are omnipotent." Thus, the extremes to which the physician may go in preserving his self-concept of omnipotence may threaten his own life. This overdetermined preservation of omnipotence is indicative of its brittleness and its underlying foundation of fear of failure.

The physician finds himself trapped in a paradox. He fervently wants to give his patient the best possible medical care, and being open to the nurses' recommendations helps him accomplish this. On the other hand, accepting advice from nonphysicians is highly threatening to his omnipotence. The solution for the paradox is to receive sub rosa recommendations and make them appear to be initiated by himself. In short, he must learn to play the doctor-nurse game.

Some physicians never learn to play the game. Most learn in their internship, and a perceptive few learn during their clerkships in medical school. Medical students frequently complain that the nursing staff treats them as if they had just completed a junior Red Cross first-aid class instead of two years of intensive medical training. Interviewing nurses in a training hospital sheds considerable light on this phenomenon. In their words they said,

> A few students just seem to be with it, they are able to understand what you are trying to tell them, and they are a pleasure to work with; most, however, pretend to know everything and refuse to listen to anything we have to say and I guess we do give them a rough time.

In essence, they are saying that those students who quickly learn the game are rewarded, and those that do not are punished.

Most physicians learn to play the game after they have weathered a few experiences like the one described below. On the first day of his internship, the physician and nurse were making rounds. They stopped at the bed of a 52-year-old woman who, after complimenting the young doctor on his appearance, complained to him of her problem with constipation. After several minutes of listening to her detailed description of peculiar diets, family home remedies, and special exercises that have helped her constipation in the past, the nurse politely interrupted the patient. She told her the doctor would take care of the problem and that he had to move on because there were other patients waiting to see him. The young doctor gave the nurse a stern look, turned toward the patient, and kindly told her he would order an enema for her that very afternoon. As they left the bedside, the nurse told him the patient has had a normal bowel movement every day for the past week and that in the 23 days the patient has been in the hospital she had never once passed up an opportunity to complain of her constipation. She quickly added that if the doctor wanted to order an enema, the patient would certainly receive one. After hearing this report the intern's mouth fell open and the wheels began turning in his head. He remembered the nurses comment to the patient that, "the doctor had to move on," and it occurred to him that perhaps she was really giving him a message. This experience and a few more like it, and the young doctor learns to listen for the subtle recommendations the nurses make.

Nursing Student Training

Unlike the medical student, who usually learns to play the game after he finishes medical school, the nursing student begins to learn it early in her training. Throughout her education she is trained to play the doctor-nurse game.

Student nurses are taught how to relate to physicians. They are told he has infinitely more knowledge than they, and thus he should be shown the utmost respect. In addition, it was not many years ago when nurses were instructed to stand whenever a physician entered a room. When he would come in for a conference the nurse was expected to offer him her chair, and when both entered a room the nurse would open the door for him and allow him to enter first. Although these practices are no longer rigidly adhered to, the premise upon which they were based is still promulgated. One nurse described that premise as, "He's God almighty and your job is to wait on him."

To inculcate subservience and inhibit deviancy, nursing schools, for the most part, are tightly run, disciplined institutions. Certainly there is great variation among nursing schools, and there is little question that the trend is toward giving students more autonomy. However, in too many schools this trend has not gone far enough, and the climate remains restrictive. The student's schedule is firmly controlled and there is very little free time. Classroom hours, study hours, meal time, and bedtime with lights out are rigidly enforced. In some schools meaningless chores are assigned such as cleaning bed springs with cotton applicators. The relationship between student and instructor continues this military flavor. Often their relationship is more like that between recruit and drill sergeant than between student and teacher. Open dialogue is inhibited by attitudes of strict black and white, with few, if any, shades of gray. Straying from the rigidly outlined path is sure to result in disciplinary action.

The inevitable result of these practices is to instill in the student nurse a fear of independent action. This inhibition of independent action is most marked when relating to physicians. One of the students' greatest fears is making a blunder while assisting a physician and being publicly

ridiculed by him. This is really more a reflection of the nature of their training than the prevalence of abusive physicians. The fear of being humiliated for a blunder while assisting in a procedure is generalized to the fear of humiliation for making any independent act in relating to a physician, especially the act of making a direct recommendation. Every nurse interviewed felt that making a suggestion to a physician was equivalent to insulting and belittling him. It was tantamount to questioning his medical knowledge and insinuating he did not know his business. In light of her image of the physician as an omniscient and punitive figure, the questioning of his knowledge would be unthinkable.

The student, however, is also given messages quite contrary to the ones described above. She is continually told that she is an invaluable aid to the physician in the treatment of the patient. She is told that she must help him in every way possible, and she is imbued with a strong sense of responsibility for the care of her patient. Thus she, like the physician, is caught in a paradox. The first set of messages implies that the physician is omniscient and that any recommendation she might make would be insulting to him and leave her open to ridicule. The second set of messages implies that she is an important asset to him, has much to contribute, and is duty-bound to make those contributions. Thus, when her good sense tells her a recommendation would be helpful to him she is not allowed to communicate it directly, nor is she allowed not to communicate it. The way out of the bind is to use the doctor-nurse game and communicate the recommendation without appearing to do so.

FORCES PRESERVING THE GAME

Upon observing the indirect interactional system which is the heart of the doctor-nurse game, one must ask the question, "Why does this inefficient mode of communication continue to exist?" The forces mitigating against change are powerful.

Rewards and Punishments

The doctor-nurse game has a powerful, innate self-perpetuating force — its system of rewards and punishments. One potent method of shaping behavior is to reward one set of behavioral patterns and to punish patterns which deviate from it. As described earlier, the rewards given for a well-played game and the punishments meted out to unskilled players are impressive. This system alone would be sufficient to keep the game flourishing. The game, however, has additional forces.

The Strength of the Set

It is well recognized that sets are hard to break. A powerful attitudinal set is the nurse's perception that making a suggestion to a physician is equivalent to insulting and belittling him. An example of where attempts are regularly made to break this set is seen on psychiatric treatment wards operating on a therapeutic community model. This model requires open and direct communication between members of the team. Psychiatrists working in these settings expend a great deal of energy in urging for and rewarding openness before direct patterns of communication become established. The rigidity of the resistance to break this set is impressive. If the physician himself is a prisoner of the set and therefore does not actively try to destroy it, change is near impossible.

The Need for Leadership

Lack of leadership and structure in any organization produces anxiety in its members. As the importance of the organization's mission increases, the demand by its members for leadership commensurately increases. In our culture human life is near the top of our hierarchy of values, and organizations which deal with human lives, such as law and medicine, are very rigidly structured. Certainly some of this is necessary for the systematic management of the task. The excessive degree of rigidity, however, is demanded by its members for their own psychic comfort rather than for its utility in efficiently carrying out its mission. The game lends support to this thesis. Indirect communication is an inefficient mode of transmitting information. However, it effectively supports and protects a rigid organizational structure with the physician in clear authority. Maintaining an omnipotent leader provides the other members with a great sense of security.

Sexual Roles

Another influence perpetuating the doctor-nurse game is the sexual identity of the players. Doctors are predominately men and nurses are almost exclusively women. There are elements of the game which reinforce the stereotyped roles of male dominance and female passivity. Some nursing instructors explicitly tell their students that their femininity is an important asset to be used when relating to physicians.

COMMENT

The doctor and nurse have a shared history and thus have been able to work out their game so that it operates more efficiently than one would expect in an indirect system. Major difficulty arises, however, when the physician works closely with other disciplines which are not normally considered part of the medical sphere. With expanding medical horizons encompassing cooperation with sociologists, engineers, anthropologists, computer analysts, etc., continued expectation of a doctor-nurselike interaction by the physician is disastrous. The sociologist, for example, is not willing to play that kind of game. When his direct communications are rebuffed the relationship breaks down.

The major disadvantage of a doctor-nurselike game is its inhibitory effect on open dialogue which is stifling and anti-intellectual. The game is basically a transactional neurosis, and both professions would enhance themselves by taking steps to change the attitudes which breed the game.

42   Meeting Patients' Psychosocial Needs in the General Hospital

Esther Lucile Brown

Patients who enter hospitals are frequently, if not generally, people in trouble. There is "something wrong" with them that requires diagnosis, treatment, or both. That very fact, even though they may not be in pain, is often sufficient to arouse anxiety about their imminent hospital experience, what the diagnostic tests will show, and whether they will be really cured, left with physical disabilities, or faced with the likelihood of too early a death.

In addition, there are other kinds of troubles, which concern family, work, and financial matters, that patients take with them to the hospital. How will the family get along in the absence of the mother or the father; how will the bills be paid even though there be hospital insurance; will the breadwinner find his job waiting for him on his return, will he be able to do the kind of work he has always done, or will he be incapacitated? How long will it be before the mother and housewife is able to resume her indispensable role in the family? Sometimes there is the nagging question of whether the marital partner can be left foot-loose with safety for more than a day or two, or whether the children's affection will not be weaned away from the sick parent or grandparent.

These troubles differ, of course, according to the life circumstances and the basic personality structure of the particular individual. His socioeconomic background, education, and cultural attitudes and values are important determinants of how he will react to sickness and hospitalization. Many of his worries are neurotic in origin. A recent study, for example, suggested that no fewer than half of the eighty patients admitted to one hospital with a diagnosis of appendicitis experienced neurotic anxiety. That some of the fears about minor surgery, financial difficulties, or the infidelity of a spouse may have little basis in reality does not make the discomfort less pronounced.

ADMISSION TO THE HOSPITAL

It is against this background of diversified troubles that the admission of patients to the hospital must be viewed. At the moment when most persons probably want individualized attention and sympathetic understanding, they are likely to find themselves confronted with a clerk who asks, in a matter-of-fact manner, for information that they may even resent as trespassing upon their private lives. Discussion of how the hospital bill is to be paid is often particularly disturbing not only to persons with limited economic resources but to those in favored circumstances who consider it a serious breach of etiquette to discuss money matters at so inappropriate a time.

Once the admission data have been obtained, the clerk calls an aide who, almost without comment, bustles the patient off, generally accompanied by an adult relative or friend, to an undesignated floor of the institution. In some hospitals, the patient is taken to his room in a wheel chair even though he arrived on two good feet. If he is not accustomed to hospital mores, this unexpected act is likely to raise the question in his mind of whether he is more sick than he realized. He discovers

Brown, E. L.: Meeting patients' psychosocial needs in the general hospital. Ann. Amer. Acad. Polit. Soc. Sci. *346:* 117–125 (1963).

later in such hospitals that he is sent to X-ray or elsewhere in a wheel chair or perhaps strapped on a stretcher, as if he were likely to lose consciousness. At discharge, he will again be wheeled to the outer door of the institution, where the hospital's legal responsibility for him ends.

Although impersonal admission procedures have come to characterize most large hospitals, many attempts have been made, often with temporary or limited success, to introduce some amelioration. Small hospitals are generally able to preserve more friendliness and informality. Unusual indeed, however, is the Community Hospital in Waterville, Maine, where the writer saw families received as guests by the nurse in charge of admissions or the nurse director of the hospital. Both women wore their white uniforms, hopefully as visible symbols of warmth, interest, and understanding. After a visit in a pleasant lounge designed to reassure the family, one of the two nurses escorted the family to the appropriate floor where she introduced them to the head nurse as if they were her personal friends. Opportunity was provided for them to examine the patient's room and the layout of the area and to learn something of how patient care was organized. If it seemed desirable, the suggestion was made that a member of the family might like to stay at least overnight and sleep on a folding cot readily at hand. When the patient left the hospital, a group of staff gathered at the door to wave a friendly good-by to him and his relatives.

The admission procedure is only the first of a long series of initiation rites into an institution that is differently organized and operated than any other with which the patient is familiar. In the usual hospital, the patient discovers that a bed has been assigned for his use, but, if he is the average patient, he will have no effective voice in deciding where the bed will be placed, how the room will be arranged or perhaps even ventilated, whether he can have quiet and privacy if he wishes and who his roommates will be. Instead, a member of the nursing service will promptly suggest that he give her his money and any valuables to be locked in the safe. Unless he has the luxury of at least a semiprivate room,

street clothes will also be taken away and carefully checked.

THE LOSS OF SELF-IDENTITY

Simultaneously, he is expected to check most of his individualized wants and desires and his long-standing habit of making decisions for himself and others. It is assumed that he will place himself implicitly in the hands of the medical and hospital staff and co-operate with them in what they are doing for his good. However, as the stripping process continues and its effect on him becomes cumulative, he often feels as if he were losing one layer after another of his self-identification. The patient is frequently not known as a college professor, an expert steel riveter, and exceptionally fine homemaker, or a champion fisherman; he is the occupant of the second bed in Room 34, or the patient with gallstones, a broken hip, "Ca," or "CVA." The individual has been reduced to the anonymity of a horizontal figure between white sheets. In his own estimation, he may be scarcely better off than the patient undergoing surgery of whom T. S. Eliot remarks in *The Cocktail Party:*

All there is of you is your body
And the "you" is withdrawn.

For some patients, this loss of self-identity is one of the most difficult aspects of hospitalization. The greater the degree to which a person has formerly been able to maintain himself as "the subject, the centre of reality," to quote Eliot again, the more he is likely to suffer from role deprivation and lack of recognition.

THE LOSS OF HOME

This loss of self-identity is closely related to and exacerbated by the alien physical environment in which the patient finds himself. Unless his life has been deviant from that of most other persons, he has spent much of it within the setting of a home, where both people and things have given him some sense of rootedness, where the *he* that he has become is in no small part the product of these associations.

Whether he be conscious of it or not, his clothes and other possessions, his work and play, as well as his family and friends, form an enveloping and generally supporting environment.

Just when patients tend to be most in need of this environment, they are deprived of many of its significant symbols. They are deprived, perhaps, of items of food that have been their cultural heritage for generations, of their early-morning coffee and their regular meal hours; they are deprived of the particular furnishings, gadgets, or knickknacks that give them a peculiar sense of comfort; they discover that, in a society as compulsive about time as is the United States, the hospital has provided the rooms with neither clock nor calendar. Their possible craving for the companionship of a much loved dog or even bird will be unsatisfied, and — most unfortunate of all — they will have to forego seeing their children or grandchildren unless the youngsters are more than twelve or fourteen years of age. In spite of the progressive liberalization of visiting hours for adults, other members of their family may still visit them only at specified times and rarely are permitted to stay with them at night.

These deprivations would not be so burdensome if ample provision were made to keep the patient occupied and entertained to the extent that his condition permitted. Except for pediatric, psychiatric, and rehabilitation services, however, recreational facilities at best are often limited to books and magazines, radio or television, and perhaps, "canned" music. Rarely is there provision for meals to be served to ambulatory patients in small dining areas on the patient floors, for moving pictures to be shown, or for occupational therapists to engage at least a few bed patients in engrossing manual skills. Some hospitals do not even have cards, games, and drawing paper and crayons to distribute on adult medical and orthopedic floors where statistics show that a considerable proportion of patients are in residence for several weeks. Under such circumstances, is it remarkable that patients are bored, strained, querulous, and that time seems almost endless?

LACK OF INDIVIDUALIZED ATTENTION

Above all else perhaps, most patients hope that physicians and nurses will not only give them competent medical attention but will spend time with them, listen to their troubles, and comfort them. They often assume that they will be able to adjust reasonably well to the role deprivations, the unfamiliar routines, the sometimes alarming or painful treatments, and the lack of recreational facilities if only "their doctor" and "their nurse" explain things to them in language they can understand, give them a chance to talk about themselves, and show interest in them.

Unfortunately, in this era of rapid advances in the science and technology of medicine, this kind of service appears to be in increasingly short supply. This seems to be true even though much is heard about the necessity for "treating the entire person" and not simply the disease entity. If a patient is fortunate enough to have a private physician whom he already knows and who is his doctor in the hospital, the likelihood is good that he will receive some individualized attention. However, the frequent absence of the physician and the possibility in teaching hospitals that he will be accompanied by house staff, often deprive the patient of those few minutes with "his doctor" to which he looks forward from one day to the next. The average patient, moreover, does not have a private physician in attendance but must rely on members of the medical staff assigned him.

The nurses on the staff of the hospital are often heard to remark: "The nurse is with the patient twenty-four hours a day." In reality, this statement only means that the patient floors are under nursing supervision around the clock; it does not mean that each patient has "a nurse" unless he is ill enough to require private-duty nursing. During the three shifts of duty, several graduate nurses will give the prescribed medications and carry out the treatments and technical procedures that supposedly require more skill and judgment than practical nurses and aides possess. An even larger number of auxiliary nursing personnel will provide the routine care. With nursing so subdivided among many persons and so technically oriented, and with few graduate nurses trained as yet in the exacting task of encouraging patients to talk about their feelings and needs, it may be almost impossible for a particular patient to find a nurse to whom he can relate himself. Instead, he is likely to find himself bereft of the comfort of a mother figure that his illness may have caused him to want or need.

No fewer than twenty or thirty different staff persons may well go in and out of his room during the course of a day. Each has a small, sharply defined duty to perform such as drawing blood for laboratory tests, bringing the food trays, filling the thermos bottle with fresh water, mopping the floor. Duties may be as circumscribed as in instances where the man from the food service puts the tray on the patient's dresser but is not expected to roll up the bed and place the tray on the table over the bed. Many a meal has waited until cold, beyond the reach of a patient, because of an emergency that kept the appropriate nursing aide from checking the tray and moving it from dresser to table.

Some of the persons who go in and out of the rooms rarely speak to the patients, some appear unaware of their presence. The patient in turn knows few of these persons by name, and sometimes he does not even recognize the category of personnel to which they belong, so bewildering are the different uniforms. A few patients find welcome distraction in the frequent appearance of different members of the staff; often there is one person, perhaps the woman who mops the floor with whom spirited conversation is exchanged. More often patients complain to their visitors that the room is like a railroad station; the continuous coming and going is exhausting and annoying, and, instead of feeling less lonely, they feel psychologically deserted.

PATIENT-STAFF PERCEPTIONS

The foregoing pages described a few of the representative perceptions of patients about their hospital experiences as re-

ported by them and their families, by staff, or by those social scientists who have recently begun to make studies of the hospital as a social institution. The growing body of evidence suggests more strain and stress within that institution than either it or the community it serves would like to admit. The picture presented here suffers from the distortion that occurs in most reports based on broad generalization without opportunity for extended qualifications. We think it safe to conclude, however, that, although some patients are well satisfied with and appreciative of the care they have received, many are not only dissatisfied but disturbed by the way in which patient care is organized and administered.

Although the hospital is also frequently disturbed by the quality of patient care provided, its staff have a set of perceptions, which are the product of their training and experience, that are sometimes very different from those of their patients. Often the divergencies are so great that it is difficult for doctors and nurses to understand why the sick person is critical, withdrawn, or depressed unless they can find the cause in the illness itself. It should be noted, however, that, when staff members become patients, their vision often undergoes rapid change. Some of the most illuminating comments the writer has heard have come from physicians and nurses who had vigorously disagreed with her statements about patient care until they themselves were ill.

SOCIALIZATION OF STAFF

Doctors and nurses undergo a long process of conditioning — or socialization, to use the terminology of behavioral scientists — to the hospital as a place for the practice of medical and nursing knowledge and skills. When they are first introduced to clinical training, they must have something of the sense of strangeness and apprehension that patients experience, but in time the hospital becomes so familiar an environment that they may not even recall how they felt initially. Occasionally, one hears members of the staff admit privately that *they* are afraid of some of the new machines and new forms of radical treatment, but they often fail to realize that large X-ray equipment and oxygen masks or tents that have long been familiar to them can create fear for patients, particularly those with limited education and life experience.

Staffs have seen hospitals undergo a radical transformation in physical appearance since World War II. The pleasant architecture, the often fashionable lobbies and visiting rooms, the cheerful colors in patients' rooms — these are changes that have relieved the hospital of its formerly cold and sterile atmosphere. Great efforts have been made, moreover, to provide staff with functional work areas and with time- and energy-saving equipment. Is it any wonder that they take it for granted that patients will find the results impressive? What they may not note is that many of the most impressive changes have occurred in the greatly increased space and facilities for diagnostic tests and treatments, nursing stations, administrative offices, laboratories, classrooms, and an auditorium for educational and research purposes, and lounges and coffee shops for visitors.

Except for the elimination of large open wards and the creation of more cheerful rooms, the modification of the patient units has not been comparable. Only now is the concept of comprehensive patient care beginning to be reflected in greater variation in construction and furnishing of these units. And, as yet, this variation rests scarcely at all on any systematic examination of how the physical environment can be utilized to meet the psychological needs of patients. So little attention has been paid to this subject in the clinical training of physicians, nurses, and hospital administrators that it is surprising that departments of pediatrics, psychiatry, and rehabilitation have sometimes been able to initiate conspicuous changes. Such departments often make use of an abundance of things and activities symbolic of normal recreation and work and of life outside the hospital. It is in the adult medical and surgical departments, which serve a large proportion of all patients, that staff find the greatest difficulty in perceiving that

their patients, too, may need symbols of home, health, and community living.

STAFF RELIANCE ON DIAGNOSIS

From careful observation of the behavior of diseases and of surgical intervention, it has been possible to assemble statistical data predicting probable outcome. Once a diagnosis has been established, therefore, doctors and nurses know, at least in a general way, what to expect. If the diagnosis indicates that the disease or accident is of relatively minor importance and recovery is almost certain, staff write off the need for any apprehension on their part. This perception may be greatly at variance, however, with that of the patient who often does not know what his prognosis is and, hence, relies upon how he feels and on his frequently incorrect assumptions. Many a person has suffered unnecessary anxiety because staff failed to tell him that his chances for a successful recovery were good. Later, if staff discover that he is apprehensive, they may remark that they can not understand why Mr. B is "so worried when there is no reason for it."

The case of a woman who was to undergo surgery for a ruptured vertebral disc illustrates the degree to which long reliance upon scientific prediction may restrict the therapist's ability to foresee probable causes of patient anxiety. In this instance, the woman dreaded the acute pain that she assumed would result from the surgical wound. To her relief, she found that she had only slight discomfort from stiffness in the lower back. When she told the neurosurgeon, he showed surprise that she should have expected pain. At least half the patients on whom he performed this type of surgery, said he, did not have more than minor discomfort afterwards. Again he appeared surprised when the patient suggested that she would have been greatly reassured had he told her in advance that she had a fifty-fifty chance of escaping acute pain subsequent to the surgery.

THE PATIENT'S VIEWPOINT

Staff often take it for granted that patients think and feel much as they do about many matters. This is an error with unfortunate consequences. They forget that they are not only accustomed to the hospital and have the knowledge requisite for predicting the probable outcome of disease but also that they are well, fully occupied, often young, and generally interested in what they are doing. These factors are such important determinants of their attitudes and reactions that many experience difficulty in looking at situations from the point of view of patients and families whose orientation and experience are very different.

Staff personnel see themselves "running all day," as the nurses say, "to make the patients comfortable." So busy and often harried are they that they find themselves annoyed by the patient's many complaints about time dragging, the quality of the coffee, dinner at five o'clock, noise in the corridor, and so on. They are likely to dismiss these seemingly petty inconveniences with a curt, "Well, I guess Mrs. C can put up with things for a few days." Were they to listen to what patients are trying to tell them, they might conclude that the Mrs. C's are not so inflexible as it appears; what patients are perhaps doing, consciously or unconsciously, is using situations about which they feel free to complain as symbolic of deep-seated and significant protests.

Many psychiatrists, psychiatric nurses, and social workers are distressed by the failure of staff to see more clearly the patients' point of view, and they have succeeded in introducing some consideration of the psychological needs of patients into professional training. However, like so many efforts that are largely verbal, these discussions — unless accompanied by supervised practice in listening and interpretation — are likely not to have the emotional impact necessary to assure change in perceptions and attitudes. Perhaps, if medical and nursing students and prospective hospital administrators were given a ten-day experience as bed patients, they would be better able to recall later how patients feel; perhaps they could express more understanding and interest themselves in making changes wherever possible that might reduce patients' boredom, frustration, and worry.

LACK OF COMMUNICATION

One of the chief reasons why differences in perception go unrecognized and consequently produce misunderstanding both for patients and staff is the paucity of conversation, about other than strictly medical matters, between clinicians and patients, clinical nurses and patients, and between these doctors and nurses about the patients. Inasmuch as the medical history rarely gives staff a sufficiently inclusive picture of the patient's life background, one might assume that doctors and nurses would utilize every possible opportunity to get acquainted with their patients and to exchange information, clues, and suggestions with each other. In actuality, doctors and nurses appear too busy to carry on extended conversations with patients, and communication between the two professions is limited primarily to written doctors' orders and doctors' and nurses' progress notes about each patient.

Although lack of time is the reason usually given, many less obvious but perhaps more compelling reasons contribute to the inadequacy of communication. As seen in social-science perspective, they are the product of the organizational structure of the hospital, the attitudes inculcated by professional schools and associations, and certain insufficiently cultivated areas in the training of health personnel.*

Within the hierarchical organization of the hospital, communication moves primarily from top to bottom within each professional or service group; horizontal communication between the several health professions is sharply restricted. Every

---

*The writer has attempted to discuss these subjects in some detail in *Newer Dimensions of Patient Care: Improving Staff Motivation and Competence in the General Hospital* (New York: Russell Sage Foundation, 1962).

system of professional education attempts to develop knowledge and skills that are largely exclusive to it, and the professional associations promote the idea of "uniqueness." As a consequence, the professions are not greatly encouraged to share this heritage with patients or each other. Because of the long history of medicine as compared with that of the other health professions, physicians still view the newer groups primarily as their assistants. Thus, they see themselves in the role of giving orders and directing action. This attitude is reflected in their failure to initiate the exchange of more information with nurses about the welfare of their patients and in the seeming inability of nurses to insist upon needed discussions of patient care.

Most important, perhaps, among the causes of paucity of communication, is the fact that doctors and nurses are still trained almost exclusively to treat disease and to make patients physically comfortable. The concept of "total patient care" is extensively promoted, but it is only in the initial stage of becoming an operational concept. Behavioral scientists would probably question whether it can become more fully operational until communication between staff and patients is greatly increased. And such communication can scarcely be achieved until all doctors and nurses have had training similar to what psychiatrists, social workers, and clinical psychologists are now receiving in listening and talking to patients and to staff. To be able to use both verbal and nonverbal communication therapeutically is a skill of a high order. Without training in its use, staff will continue to find reasons for not permitting patients to talk about their troubles; the reason closest at hand is lack of time. Sometimes, however, physicians and nurses glimpse the probability that, had the patient been given the opportunity to pour out his feelings initially, or had they discussed with each other the planning and co-ordination of his care, time might ultimately have been saved and his recovery might have been more rapid.

Part E

Sociobehavioral Foundations of Medicine: The Cultural Perspective

XV SOCIOBEHAVIORAL CONCEPTS AND VIEWPOINTS

The notion that medicine and social science have similar, if not identical goals has been a long held view. Referring to a European thesis of a century earlier, in which medicine was considered in its "very bone and marrow" a social science, Henry Sigerist, the patriarch of American medical historians, commented (1946):

> That medicine is a social science sounds like a truism, yet it cannot be repeated often enough because in medical education we still act as if medicine were a natural science and nothing else. There can be no doubt that the target of medicine is to keep individuals adjusted to their environment as useful members of society, or re-adjust them when they have dropped out as a result of illness. It is a social goal. Every medical action, moreover, presupposes a relationship between at least two individuals, the patient and the physician, or between two groups, society on the one hand, and the medical corps, in the broadest sense of the word, on the other hand.

Rudolf Virchow, the distinguished medical scientist, wrote in the mid-19th century that public health issues required the study of the social and political sciences and, therefore, were legitimate aspects of the training of physicians. Despite strenuous efforts by forward-looking physicians to make "social medicine" a full-fledged subject for professional study, the increasing complexity and heterogeneity of society, combined with the burgeoning of biologic knowledge and technology, served to preclude the development of these topics. Noting societal changes that have caused a retrogression in the study of "society and health," Straus and Clausen wrote (1963):

> It is important to remember that, during the period when physicians were commonly oriented to the social and cultural implications of disease, the dimensions of the community were relatively limited and the relationship of the physician to his patients more intimate. However, with industrialization and urbanization came an increase in the size and complexity of communities and in the degree of impersonalization in human relationships. As a result, the physician has found himself less well equipped to understand the nonphysical aspects of illness.

Nevertheless, in the past two decades, there has been a resurgence of interest in the social aspects of health care. As Straus and Clausen note further (1963):

> ... there has been a growing interest in medicine on the part of society at large in the United States and in other areas of the Western world. At the same time, there has been a rebirth of interest on the part of the formal medical professions in the social and cultural aspects of health and medical care. These trends are reflected in the popularization of information about medical science, in the growing public expectations directed toward organized medicine for the prevention and alleviation of human misery, and in the increased demand for medical care coming from all segments of the population. They are reflected in the increased role of government in providing controls to safeguard the public health, in supporting programs of health education and research, in providing direct medical services for large segments of the population, and in adopting legislation concerned with the economic barriers to medical care. They are also reflected by an expansion in the horizons of medical research to include studies of social, cultural, and psychological factors in the course of human disease and by the introduction of social- and behavioral-science content and concepts to programs of education for health personnel.

Despite this resurgence in sociobehavioral medicine, John Knowles, commenting on the delivery of health services to society's disadvantaged, writes rather vexingly that "the medical ostrich has buried its head in the sands of biology and turned its backside to the major issues of medical care." Expanding on this intentionally provocative statement, Knowles notes (1973):

> Let us look further at the present scene. The preamble to the constitution of the World Health Organization defines health *comprehensively* as a "state of complete physical, mental and social well-being, and not merely the absence of disease and infirmity." So be it! Medicine has a long list of triumphs in the cure, containment or amelioration of established disease. It is doing much better in some areas of mental health, but it knows almost nothing of social, as opposed to biological, well-being.
>
> Little attention is paid by the medical world to such causes of social disease as parental inadequacy, overcrowding, the oppressive threat of scientific war, poverty, inadequate educational opportunities, the nontherapeutic uses of leisure, the misuse of the mass media or the suppression and persecution of minority groups. Yet, medicine today, with its successes, its problems and the demands it faces, has become inextricably a part of larger social concerns.

As is evident from the above quotes, sociobehavioral medicine is in a state of flux, a reflection no doubt of the cross currents that inevitably arise when an established profession expands its frontiers in response to the demands of the larger society.

Public health physicians in the early decades of this century were concerned with finding engineering solutions to achieve better sanitation and with developing different methods for the quarantine control of infectious diseases. This public health emphasis has shifted in recent years. With the advent of antibiotics, quarantine is only rarely employed and prevention is now achieved through massive inoculation programs. More notably, health resources are increasingly devoted to retarding the development of noninfectious chronic illnesses such as atherosclerosis and cancer. Sanitation engineering has likewise broadened its concerns, moving from its early preoccupation with waste elimination and water purification to the vigorous solution of problems such as air pollution, radioactivity, drug efficacy, and food toxicity.

The three papers that comprise this chapter focus on a number of significant issues in medicine as a sociobehavioral science. Kerr White, a prominent physician at Johns Hopkins, provides a thorough analysis of epidemiological data, particularly those relevant to the problem of establishing priorities in allocating health care resources. The second paper, by the distinguished Harvard sociologist, Lee Rainwater, offers astute observations and insights into social class differences among patients. Rainwater furnishes a clear and thoughtful review of the contrasting medical care experiences that distinguish "middle" from "lower" class groups. The final article, by a prominent behavioral scientist, Clark Vincent, stresses the often overlooked role of the family, both as an influence in determining disease and as a resource for providing significant sick-care functions.

REFERENCES

Sigerist, H. E.: *The University at the Crossroads.* New York, Schuman, 1946.

Straus, R., and Clausen, J. A.: Health, society and social science. Ann. Am. Acad. Polit. Soc. Sci. 346: 1–8 (1963).

43   Life and Death and Medicine

Kerr L. White

Why, at this time, are medicine and the provision of health care rapidly becoming a major focus of debate in almost every industrialized society?

The most obvious reason has to do with the dramatic rise in recent years in the cost of supporting a health-care establishment. The governments and people of the developed countries are understandably becoming concerned about the prospect of spending 8 percent or more of their gross national product on health services. Investments of this magnitude inevitably give rise to questions concerning the relation of value to money: the universal formula for balancing the exchange of energy and resources for benefits.

Part of the reason, however, is to be found in a larger context. A decade of international strife and cultural conflict has challenged the entire spectrum of individual and collective values and has forced the reappraisal of many goals, particularly as they relate to the impact of science and technology on human welfare. The issues of personal accountability and social responsibility, the problems of governance not only of society as a whole but also of its institutions, and the increasingly evident need to establish priorities for allocating energy and resources in all sectors of the economy now dominate discussions of public policy. Medicine is only one arena in which these issues are being debated with growing insight and involvement by concerned consumers, politicians, professionals and scholars.

Two decades of social experimentation promise a more rational basis, derived from the social sciences, for deploying, financing and managing health-care systems more efficiently. So far, however, we have not been outstandingly successful in applying this new knowledge and experience to the problems of organizing health care in the U.S. Inequities and inadequacies in the provision of health care are increasingly apparent, and the burden of health-care expenditures continues to grow.

Three decades of intensive biomedical research have provided a more rational basis for certain elements of medical practice, and as a result there are now many forms of clinical intervention that are clearly more beneficial than they are either harmful or useless. Nonetheless, although disease patterns have changed significantly in the U.S., in part as a result of biomedical advances, there has been little or no improvement in life expectancy for adults since the 1920's. In particular, effective means have not been found for coping with the stubborn complex of chronic and social illnesses that now predominate in the economically advanced countries.

Under these circumstances it is inevitable that society in a period of instability and change should raise basic questions about the contribution of medicine to the quality of personal existence as it is experienced between birth and death. In this introduction I shall try to clarify the issues that must be identified, debated and resolved if modern medicine is to make its most beneficial impact on the human condition. The issues themselves are not new; only the urgency with which we now perceive them in the U.S. is new.

On what basis does a society assign priorities for medicine? Whose values are expressed in the allocation of a nation's energy and resources to improve the quality of life for all its citizens? At the

White, K. L.: Life and death and medicine. Sci. Am. *229:* 22–33 (1973).

heart of any consideration for medicine's place in contemporary society are the underlying models that give rise to both assumptions and expectations — assumptions on the part of the health-care establishment about the role of science and technology in the provision of health services, and expectations on the part of consumers about what medicine can accomplish and what they must achieve for themselves by modifying their personal behavior.

Should diseases be likened to ivy growing on the oak tree or are they part of the oak tree itself? Should diseases be regarded as human analogues of defects in an internal-combustion engine or a Swiss watch, or should they be regarded as psychobiological expressions of man evolving within the constraints and potentials contributed from his aliquot of society's gene pool. Are diseases "things" that "happen" to people, or are they manifestations of constructive or destructive relations of individuals in their social and physical environment? Depending on our views about the relevance of these contrasting models for understanding health and disease, we modify our behavior, change our expectations, deploy our resources and measure our accomplishments. By resolving these conflicting views we strike a balance in undergraduate medical education between the biological and the social sciences, in graduate medical education between the preparation of technologically based specialists and psychobiologically trained generalists, in medical organization between solo entrepreneurial practice and multispecialist corporate or group practice, and in medical insurance between "catastrophic" coverage of major medical illnesses and "first dollar" coverage of early ambulatory care, anticipatory medicine and counseling.

In the absolute sense there are no right or wrong resolutions of these issues. It is rather the counterbalance of our individual positions as citizens that must determine the social policies affecting the kinds and numbers of health professional we prepare, the facilities and organizations we create and the way we use and finance health care. Above all our collective position on these issues must determine the contribution of medicine to the quality and duration of our lives and perhaps of our society.

Unwritten social contracts between society and its health-care establishment provide the mandate for physicians and others to minister to individual and collective health needs. In return for the benefits medicine bestows, society accords the health professions substantial power, prestige and pecuniary rewards. Traditionally the overt expression of these contracts has embodied unrealistic promises and expectations. Both parties become increasingly realistic in their renegotiations as they are provided with information about the health needs of people, about the clinical efficacy of preventive and therapeutic procedures, and about the effectiveness and efficiency of different organizational arrangements for providing health care.

Progress in the "old" basic sciences of medicine — anatomy, biochemistry, pathology, pharmacology and physiology — makes it increasingly difficult today for clinical practitioners to invoke tradition and authoritarian pronouncements in support of medical decisions. Progress in the "new" basic sciences of medicine — biostatistics, epidemiology, medical economics and medical sociology — makes it increasingly possible to identify and measure the health problems of individuals and populations and to evaluate the impact of health services on those problems. Both biomedical and health-services research create new insights that reshape our social policies for medical education and medical practice and in turn give rise to another set of issues for research, debate and resolution.

Given the present state of medical science and technology in the context of contemporary industrial communities, what should be the objectives of medical education and medical care? Should medicine adopt the posture that it "fixes" illnesses and "cures" diseases, or should it adopt the posture that it helps people to identify their individual and collective health problems and assists them to resolve or contain them? Should the health-care establishment be judged more on its capacity to investigate and treat abnormal pathology than on its accomplishments in helping patients and their families to understand and manage their problems? What social or even medical utility is to be accorded diagnostic ability if it is not accompanied by effective action and an acceptable outcome? Because we have mastered some procedure, does it follow that society should make it available to all who seek it? To all who can pay for it? To all who need it? Is the new procedure to be preferred over some other form of intervention for the same health problem?

For example, should we concentrate on perfecting coronary-artery bypass operations or on improving early detection and better medical management for patients with coronary-artery insufficiency? Should we concentrate on dialysis and transplants for chronic kidney disease or on early detection, coordinated medical management and follow-up of initial urinary-tract infections? In short, should we continue to develop and rely heavily on complex medical technology for the treatment of acute or life-threatening diseases and conditions? Or would we be better advised to broaden our approach and devote more of our efforts to identifying, containing or resolving the health problems that have major impact on the quality of our lives?

What proportions of society's health-care resources should be directed to the "curing," in contrast to the "caring," components of medical practice? Should resources currently expended on pills, potions and procedures whose benefits or efficacy have never been objectively evaluated be shifted to the provision of personnel and services to make living with chronic disability more comfortable and dying more dignified? How much responsibility has medicine for the terminally ill? What are the limits of these responsibilities, and who decides? Are the decisions determined by scientific knowledge and available technology, or by ethical, social and humanitarian considerations, or by a mixture of both? To what extent should the doctor, in the original sense of the word, be a teacher of patients and of populations? Is it enough to tell the patient that he has chronic heart failure and prescribe a suitable regimen, or should he and his family be taught to manage the problem so that he can live a satisfying life within the limits of his own capacity without restricting unduly the rights and independence of his family and his community? To what extent should the doctor be responsible for educating his community so that its members can better cope with current epidemics of accidents, alcoholism, delinquency, drug dependency, deprivation, inadequate "parenting," loneliness, occupational boredom and suicide?

Current systems for acquiring and organizing health statistics provide the only available quantitative basis for resolving these issues about the allocation of health resources, and indirectly they condition our basic views on the task of medicine in society. Health and disease are manifested idiosyncratically for each individual as he traverses the hazardous course of life from birth to death. Collectively these experiences with health and disease, with living and dying, find expression as statistics — "people with the tears wiped off," as the medical statistician A. Bradford Hill used to say.

Although imperfect in validity, classification and timeliness, the real limitations of current statistical approaches are associated as much with their orientation and emphasis as with their quality. The problem is best exemplified by the traditional preoccupation of compilers of vital statistics with death rates (and perhaps in a related way of physicians with dying and postponement of death). Without detracting from the importance of classifying and counting the dead, we should recognize that society is increasingly concerned with the problems of living, the quality of life and the burden of disability, distress and dependency.

For example, even the concept of "disease," based on an anatomical and clinical classification introduced a century and a half ago, may be disappearing. The more we learn about the genetic and molecular substrates of disease and the interacting forces arising from within and without the individual, the harder it becomes to classify ill health into discrete categories. The International Classification of Diseases, developed under the auspices

DISEASE CATEGORIES

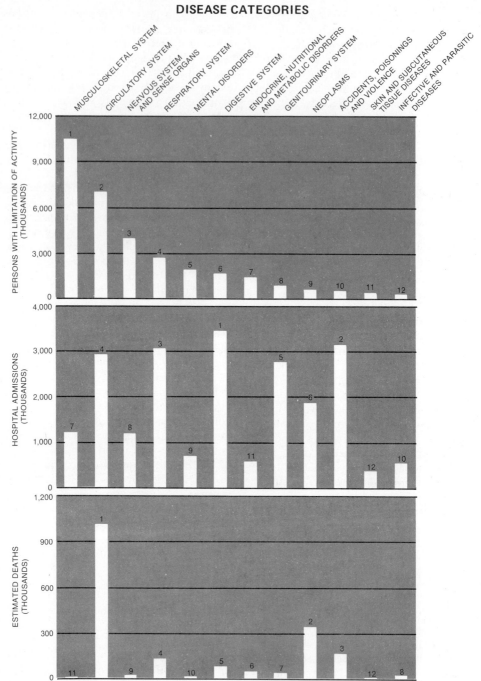

Figure 43-1. STATISTICAL AMBIGUITY at the root of the problem of trying to establish priorities for the allocation of health-care resources in the U.S. is graphically demonstrated in the three bar charts on this page, which rank 12 principal disease categories (as defined by the World Health Organization) according to three different measures of ill health. The three measures, all of which are expressed in terms of the number of people affected per year in the U.S., are limitation of activity *(top),* hospital admissions *(middle)* and estimated deaths *(bottom).* The lack of correlation between the respective rank orders is evident. The data on which the illustration is based are for 1971, the latest year for which usable figures for the 12 WHO categories are available from the U.S. National Center for Health Statistics.

of the World Health Organization and adapted for use in the U.S. by the National Center for Health Statistics, is devoted primarily to classifying and coding causes of death rather than categorizing illness. It has limited utility for hospital care and is largely unsuited for classifying health problems associated with ambulatory care, limitation of activity or bed disability. Patients describe complaints, problems and symptoms, not diseases, when they first perceive themselves to be ill and seek care. "Disease" and its classification are professional constructs, whereas "health problems and complaints" are lay constructs, and we need to recognize the differences in developing our health-information systems.

The problem of relating health-care priorities and resources to the relative impact of disability, disease and death can be illustrated by referring to the latest available data on three parameters of health and disease for 12 of the 17 principal WHO categories for which usable figures are available. (Figure 43-1). The illustration ranks the causes of limitation of activity, as perceived by respondents to a national household-interview survey. "Limitation of activity" is defined as inability or decreased ability to carry on the usual activities for one's age-sex group, such as working, keeping house, going to school and participating in civic, church and recreational activities. It is largely a measure, from the individual's point of view, of the long-term burden of chronic disease and impairment, and indirectly of morbidity in relation to the quality of life. "Hospital admissions" are probably the best currently available measure of disease as recognized and defined by the medical profession; since only a small proportion of the population have more than one admission a year, these figures essentially represent people with hospital admissions in 1971. The rank orders for these two measures bear little relation to each other. When compared with the rank order for "Deaths," the third and most widely used measure, there is even less correlation; many categories that generate substantial volumes of disability and disease produce comparatively few deaths.

The allocation of health-care resources should be related to two additional measures. "A day of bed disability" is one during which a person stays in bed for more than half of the daylight hours because of a specific acute or chronic illness or injury. "Days of hospital care" are a subset of bed-disability days and reflect the intensity of demand for health services.

Let us now consider the 12 principal conditions for which comparative data are available on days of bed disability and days of hospital care (Figure 43-2). These conditions constitute a more refined classification than the 12 principal disease categories in Figure 43-1 and reflect more specifically the relative impact of ill health on productivity and the quality of daily life. Apart from funds devoted to fundamental laboratory research, which is a priceless prerequisite for most advances in medical science, figures for money spent on clinical research and care for each of these conditions are not available. If they were, however, they should reflect some coherent relation between health resources needed or consumed and disability and disease experienced by the citizens of the U.S. For example, if we accord relief of disability, disease and death about equal priority, we would allocate more money to heart disease than to cancer (malignant neoplasms). If disability alone had a high priority, arthritis and the musculoskeletal category could be near the top.

None of these measures is entirely satisfactory in orientation, quality, definition or classification if our object is to improve the decision-making process for the allocation of resources, and particularly if we give priority to the problems of living in contrast to those of dying. Conspicuously lacking, for example, is reliable information about the number of people seeking ambulatory care for their health problems. Here the contrast between the problems of daily living and the problems of dying is undoubtedly more pronounced.

The most reliable information available on this question is a compilation of the 12 most common conditions treated by 171 general practitioners in England and Wales in 1958 (Figure 43-3). Problems of classifi-

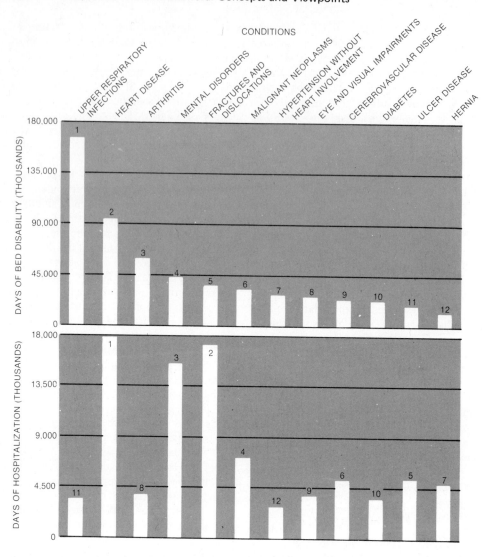

Figure 43–2. TWO ADDITIONAL MEASURES of the nationwide demand for health services — days of bed disability *(top chart)* and days of hospitalization *(bottom chart)* — focus more specifically on the relative impact of ill health on productivity and the quality of daily life. The 12 principal conditions for which comparative data are available for the U.S. from the National Center for Health Statistics in this case constitute a more refined classification than the 12 WHO disease categories used as the basis of the illustration on page 502.

cation make it difficult to relate these conditions to the major causes of death, but we can at least say that the common cold is not one of them and very few of the general practitioner's patients will die of the conditions for which they visit him most frequently.

Similar data for the U.S. are not available, but that deficiency is being remedied by the National Center for Health Statistics. A national probability sample of physicians in office-based practice, who will fill out short encounter forms on their patients for a period of one week, will relate problems, complaints and symptoms to diagnoses, tests, treatments, referrals and disposition. The importance of this annual survey for defining the objectives of undergraduate and graduate medical education, of health-manpower training and of supporting facilities, equipment and services can hardly be overemphasized.

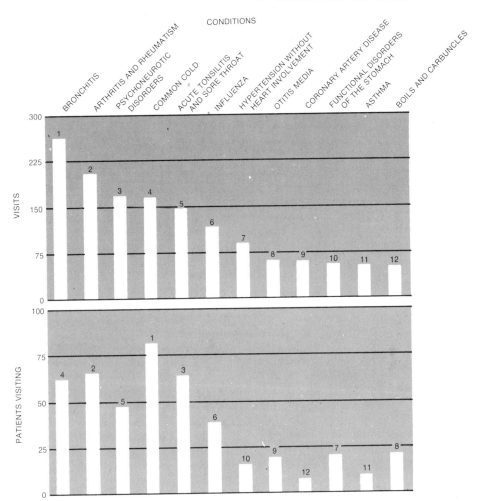

Figure 43-3. THE MOST RELIABLE INFORMATION available about the number of people seeking ambulatory care for their health problems is represented by this compilation of the 12 most common conditions (per 1,000 people) treated by 171 general practitioners in England and Wales in 1958. Such health data, which give priority to the problems of living in contrast to those of dying, are not available for the U.S. but are clearly needed if the decision-making process for the allocation of health-care resources is to be improved.

Health data for small areas such as counties, standard metropolitan statistical areas and even states are also largely lacking, but this too is being tackled through the development of cooperative statistical systems involving Federal, state and local participation. In both the short run and the long we cannot make sensible decisions about professional education and the cost-benefit ratio of medical services and research without vastly improved health information on the problems of living as well as the probabilities of death.

Many of these issues concerning the priorities of medicine are finding contemporary expression in the growth, even renaissance, of primary care and the general practitioner, or family doctor, in North America and Europe. As we have seen, no reliable estimates are available on the distribution in populations of health problems, symptoms and complaints brought to physicians at the initial time of contact, and only limited estimates are available on the medical reasons for using hospitals or long-term-care facilities. In the absence of such elementary "marketing" information it is virtually impossible to define the overall objectives of medical education, to apportion opportunities for training physicians of all types in accordance with need, or to determine the best balance of health-care facilities and services. There is a growing consensus, however, that in the U.S. primary care has been largely neglected in favor of specialty care, that in the United Kingdom the quality of primary care needs substantial improvement, and that in many other European countries the coordination of primary care with other levels of care in some viable form of regionalization is essential to achieve optimal use of all resources. This is particularly true of expensive, technologically based resources provided by hospitals and other health-care facilities that need to be used prudently, promptly and appropriately.

In many ways the need for primary medical care can be considered the central problem facing American medicine today. Two schools of thought illustrate the issues. The first sees the physician's task as being concerned essentially, if not solely, with diseases for which there are recognized treatments or palliative measures (or diseases that, if they were investigated more intensively, might eventually be better understood and treated). The trivial, commonplace, chronic and terminal problems should be identified and managed by other health personnel. These "physician-extenders" (physician assistant, nurse practitioner and health associate are among the titles currently used) should have largely technical training, be supported by technological devices and be guided by prescribed instructions telling them how to make decisions. They should receive various degrees of supervision and surveillance by a physician. This physician's own training in primary medical care is as a rule only vaguely specified, and potential students are usually described as not finding the problems of primary care very interesting. (Presumably patients find them more so.) Patients should be referred to the supervising physician or to a specialist if the primary-care physician-extender is unsuccessful (according to his own lights) in identifying or managing the patient's

problems. This scheme for the provision of primary care was conceived and is being advocated by the leadership of the American academic medical community and by hospital-based, technologically oriented specialists. Few advocates of these arrangements have themselves had any direct, extensive experience with the provision of continuing primary care to general populations.

The second school sees the task of medicine as being concerned with helping patients and families to identify and manage their own health problems, indeed to work toward the full achievement of their own potential for personal growth. Health problems in this context are regarded as essentially problems of living constructively and dying more comfortably without imposing intolerable burdens on oneself and others. They constitute the vast bulk of medical problems presented by patients to sources of primary care and are regarded as responses to the stresses and strains of domestic, occupational and social life and such potentially noxious contemporary accompaniments of industrialized societies as foul air, noise, cigarette smoking, chemical contaminants, constant residential mobility, jet-travel fatigue, radiation hazards, urban crowding and traffic congestion.

Most of these problems have a behavioral component and tend to be observed first by the pediatrician, for whom they constitute the majority of contemporary complaints. They are viewed as requiring a broadly educated physician, selected initially for his interest in people, his "caring" qualities, his capacity for integrating a vast array of usable knowledge from the biomedical and social sciences, his interest in resolving problems as well as in analyzing their genesis, his ability to tolerate anxiety and to make decisions in the face of uncertainty and his capacity for working with the open-ended nature of the problems of living and dying that most patients present most of the time.

This primary-care physician should be well trained scientifically, particularly in the behavioral sciences. He should know the limits of his capabilities and have access to teams of highly trained subspecialists supported by ancillary personnel, by technologically sophisticated equipment and particularly by on-line computer regimes that provide timely information about the distribution of clinical manifestations and the efficacy of treatments. This scheme has its origins in the efforts of the academic and professional societies that have rejuvenated primary medical care under the aegis of family medicine in the U.S. and general practice in the United Kingdom, the Netherlands and Canada. Most advocates of this definition of medicine's task have had experience in the practice of primary care, and some have done extensive research in the field. Until recently few such people have been regarded as acceptable candidates for medical-school faculties in any country.

These two schools represent polar views of medicine's task and illustrate the basic issues at stake in the current process of redefining medicine's mandate. The first is unlikely to be successful because it confuses the nature of the medical-care process and the characteristics of the information needed for most clinical decision making. At the level of primary care decisions about the severity, complexity and urgency of the patient's illness are based on a probablistic system, not a deterministic one. The decision maker needs to be skilled in eliciting information from the patient and in interpreting vast amounts of data on the prevalence and patterns of clinical manifestations in general populations. The best that contemporary medical science can offer requires that these two sets of information be put together intelligently. At this juncture the task of the primary physician requires judgment, wisdom, compassion, patience and common sense, not more hardware. Decision making in medicine is rarely simple even in so-called simple cases. To assume otherwise is to misjudge the task of medicine and the power of organized medical knowledge and medical care. It is rare that specific decisions for individual patients can be found in books or made by computers.

Resolution of these conflicting viewpoints poses a major challenge to the medical profession. In the final analysis the terms of the unwritten contract depend largely on the profession's own capacity for generating new knowledge about health problems and for providing new forms of leadership on behalf of the society it serves.

As the postindustrial society emerges and demands to produce more goods are replaced by demands to provide improved services, medicine is faced with yet another set of problems and related issues. Traditionally the physician has been taught to direct all his skills and attention to the individual patients who consult him. He receives his training in teaching hospitals, where the complaint-response system prevails and the focus is largely on acute, episodic illnesses that are usually serious and that can be cured or effectively palliated. This limited exposure of young physicians and their teachers to the full range of ordinary and complex health problems generated by large general populations, and their intense preoccupation with only those patients who are selected to obtain care in teaching hospitals, leave enormous qualitative and quantitative gaps in their experience and inevitably condition their views about the tasks of contemporary medicine.

The dimensions of the problem can be illustrated by considering the distribution of demand for medical care by a typical population of 1,000 persons in one year (Figure 43-4). As the illustration shows, the vast bulk of care is provided by physicians in ambulatory settings. Only 10 percent of the people are admitted to a hospital and only 1 percent to a university hospital where the young physician is trained. The discrepancies between the world of medical practice and that of medical education are more than those of town and gown. They are discrepancies of experience, responsibility, functions and scale.

A belated recognition in the U.S. of the issues confronting medicine with respect to both the overall content of medical practice and the related objectives of professional education is now broadening to a concern for the ways in which medical care is best organized to meet society's needs. Although the individual patient-physician relationship remains the central element in

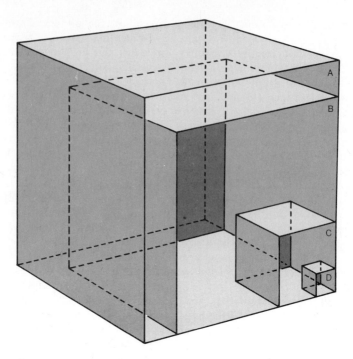

Figure 43-4. DISTRIBUTION OF DEMAND for medical care by a typical population in one year (1970), represented volumetrically in this illustration, points up the discrepancy in scale between the world of medical practice and the world of medical education in the U.S. Out of a total population at risk of 1,000 *(cube A)*, an average of 720 people visited a physician in an ambulatory setting at least once *(cube B)*, 100 people were admitted to a hospital at least once *(cube C)* and only 10 were admitted to a university hospital at least once *(cube D)*.

medical care, the profession is gradually acknowledging a larger collective responsibility for the health of the entire community — not the sole responsibility, but a major responsibility. If society has health problems, to whom should it turn if not to its health-care establishment? In former times an artificial dichotomy, professionally conceived, institutionalized and perpetuated, existed between "private medicine" and "public health." No longer does it appear sensible to separate preventive care from curative and restorative care, or the public's health from the individual's health. These are attitudinal, professional and institutional anachronisms for which there is no basis in contemporary knowledge or need.

How should the profession organize its efforts so that it can promote optimal health for all individuals within the limits of the resources society is willing to provide? Again we could come to grips more

successfully with the basic issues of priorities and value for money if we had adequate information about the distribution of problems in populations and communities. But experience and logic can at least suggest guides for sensible choices.

There are, broadly speaking, three categories of health problems. First there are those with a very low probability of being experienced by any one individual in his lifetime but with a relatively definable and predictable prevalence for large general populations of from 500,000 to several million. Examples include certain congenital abnormalities, unusual genetic and molecular aberrations, certain malignant neoplasms, catastrophic trauma, rare metabolic and endocrine disorders, acute poisonings, complex immune reactions and diseases acquired by travelers in areas remote from home. These problems require what is usually described as tertiary care: highly specialized, technologically based intensive care centralized in large medical centers and frequently located in universities.

Second, there are problems for which the probability is still low for a given individual but the prevalence is more substantial in general populations. It usually takes a population of from 25,000 to several hundred thousand to generate definable demands for health services. These problems include industrial, agricultural and traffic accidents, burns, fractures, tumors requiring radiation therapy, selected cardiac disorders, and emergencies needing uncommon types of blood or unusual laboratory tests. They require what is called secondary care: specialized consultant care that should be based in large-sized community hospitals (or district hospitals, to use the European term).

The third category of health problems includes those with a high probability of affecting any one individual at least once, if not frequently, in the course of a lifetime. They include respiratory infections, common forms of heart disease, arthritis, asthma, obesity, visual impairments, gastrointestinal disturbances, minor accidents and emotional problems. Comparatively small populations, ranging from 1,000 to 25,000, produce enough of these everyday problems to keep a general physician and his supporting personnel fully occupied. It is these problems, when they are not managed through self-care by the family, that require primary care: treatment based in offices, clinics, ambulatory facilities or health centers with a few "holding," or observation, beds close to where people live and work.

These three fundamentally different patterns of disease in general populations have important implications for the organization of health services, particularly in combination with the fact that most patients seek care initially not for specific diseases but for nonspecific health problems, complaints or symptoms. For the problems that require tertiary care both the low prevalence rates and the highly specialized and expensive resources required for effective management dictate the centralization of services. Only a fairly large community can afford the resources required and at the same time ensure reasonable equity of access for all its members to services of uniformly high quality. For many communities and regions the services are so specialized and expensive that only one source for such care is feasible; larger populations may be able to afford several sources, but even here unlimited choice is increasingly regarded as being wasteful. The same arguments apply to the secondary-care problems, but since they are more prevalent and the resources less costly, more choices are possible and greater dispersion is desirable.

For the class of primary-care health problems, however, multiple sources of care are possible and indeed essential if choice and constructive competition are values we want to preserve and encourage. For these common problems prompt and equitable access to a full range of health-care services is a matter of high priority in industrialized societies. This can be most readily achieved by numerous and widely dispersed health centers, clinics and physicians' offices, clustered around community or district hospitals and supported by links to sources of up-to-date information, consultation and highly specialized care. Recourse to the sources of primary care, in other words, should put a patient in reach of secondary and tertiary care promptly and reliably if it turns out to be necessary.

In countries where health services are regionalized there is a well-established hierarchical relation between the three levels of care (Figure 43-5). In many settings regional relations are based on statutory or centrally administered mandates and associated regulations.

In the U.S. we are faced with the difficult task of organizing our resources so that the economic and medical benefits of regionalization can be realized without sacrificing the equally desirable benefits associated with a reasonable choice of a primary physician. Somewhere between the extremes of a monolithic national health service and the fragmented arrangements that currently prevail in the U.S., with their consequent uneven quality and accessibility, a balance must be struck.

Similarly, some compromise must be reached between those who believe the

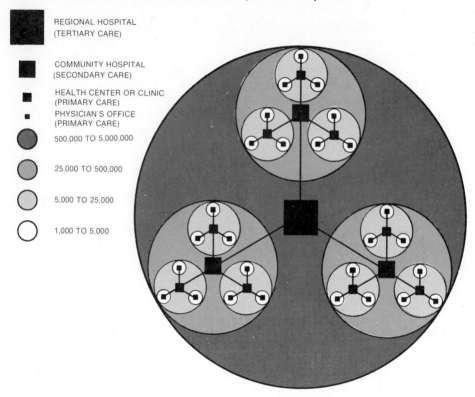

REGIONAL HOSPITAL
(TERTIARY CARE)

COMMUNITY HOSPITAL
(SECONDARY CARE)

HEALTH CENTER OR CLINIC
(PRIMARY CARE)

PHYSICIAN'S OFFICE
(PRIMARY CARE)

500,000 TO 5,000,000

25,000 TO 500,000

5,000 TO 25,000

1,000 TO 5,000

Figure 43-5. WELL-DEFINED HIERARCHY exists between the three levels of medical care (primary, secondary and tertiary) in countries where health services are regionalized. The effect of such regionalization is suggested by this illustration, which indicates the type of health-care facility associated with each level of care and the average population served by each facility *(key at left)*. Tertiary care is usually defined as highly specialized, technologically based intensive care centralized in large medical centers and frequently located in universities; secondary care is somewhat less specialized consultant care based in fairly large community, or district, hospitals; primary care is treatment based in physicians' offices, clinics, ambulatory facilities or health centers close to where people live and work.

only opportunity for the entrepreneur in health care is in solo, even isolated, clinical practice and those who consider a large national system to be the best way to organize and administer health care. New organizational patterns must emerge and there are many possibilities. They range from loose contractual affiliations among solo practitioners and small partnerships of primary physicians, community hospitals and subspecialty medical centers, on the one hand, and on the other, to large competitive local, regional or national systems — even "bureaucracies" — operating under government, voluntary, public or private auspices.

Among the possible options the one unique contribution of American medicine to the organization of health care deserves particular attention: prepaid comprehensive group practice. This arrangement constitutes the prototype for the health-maintenance organization (HMO) now espoused in many quarters. The essential elements of this organizational arrangement include prepayment of fixed annual premiums or taxes for each person or family enrolled, a contractual relation between the enrollees and the health-care plan or the providers for an agreed set of benefits, and an organized multispecialty group of physicians and other health professionals compensated by annual salaries and related incentives. The entire organization is at professional and financial risk for the provision of a full range of health-care services, including ambulatory and hospital care at all three levels.

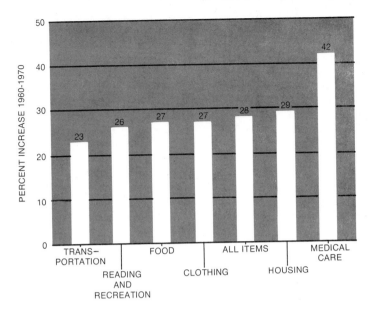

Figure 43-6. DRAMATIC RISE in recent years in the cost of supporting a health-care establishment in an industrialized society is put into perspective in this chart, which compares the percent increase in the cost of medical care in the U.S. with other major components in the consumer price index for the decade 1960-1970. The chart is adapted from one in a recently published book, *Dynamics of Health and Disease*, by Carter L. Marshall and David Pearson.

The trick in the U.S. will be to encourage the evolution of health-care arrangements and organizations that give reasonable choices to both consumers and physicians, that provide responsive and responsible services at reasonable rates and that meet established standards for quality and equity of access. It is difficult to see how we can achieve these new arrangements in the foreseeable future without some Federal leadership and financing. External monitoring of quality and some form of regulation through franchising and in some instances subsidy, depending on the form of national health insurance that eventually emerges, seem inevitable. The professional-standard-review organizations represent only the beginning of Federal, state and local monitoring of the quality of medical care.

In addition attention will have to be paid to the urgent need for adequate capitalization of new health-care organizations and institutions. The entire system is at present labor-intensive and undercapitalized. The possibilities for accomplishing its adequate capitalization include philanthropy, Federal and state grants or loans, debt and equity financing. Whatever its source, the new capital will have to be amortized over a couple of decades and must be paid for by the consumers and taxpayers. Although the notion of "profit" in medicine is confused with the concept of "incentive" and has been regarded as unwholesome if not unethical in some circles, the logical basis for this position is difficult to discern. As in the communications and transportation systems in the U.S., or even in the competitive national and private airline bureaucracies in Canada and the United Kingdom, there may well be a place for profit-making health-care systems. Such systems can mobilize private capital and can effectively take advantage of economies of scale while preserving some of the entrepreneurial spirit of solo practice. Of necessity they must undertake adequate "marketing" studies, assume "risks" and provide consumer satisfaction. Although privately owned, they probably have to be widely held public companies with expert management in order to generate adequate capital. If such systems cannot meet established standards for the quality and the distributional equity of services, or if they go bankrupt, they can always be taken over by nonprofit organizations or by local or state governments. In that event the health problems, the patients and the personnel will remain; only the ownership and the control will change.

At present we simply do not know whether particular forms of ownership, particular types of control or particular styles of management for health-care institutions or systems can be associated with differences in the health-care status of the patients who patronize them. Opportunities abound for comparison, experiment and creative innovation. This remains one of the challenges and opportunities for health care in the U.S. What is clear is that containment of our overall health-care costs within tolerable limits will be difficult without expert management of those systems. At present our hospitals and health-care institutions are largely run by amateurs with on-the-job training. For example, no more than a third of the country's 17,500 hospital administrators have had anything that can be regarded as formal training for managing these complex organizations.

New financial incentives, particularly the notions of prebudgeting based on fixed annual payments for each person enrolled in a health-care plan or system and of assigned risk or responsibility, should encourage needed changes. For example, prepaid group practices (such as the Kaiser Foundation Health Plan and the Health Insurance Plan of Greater New York) have already demonstrated that a large portion of the health-care dollar can be shifted from inpatient hospital care to other modalities of care, particularly to ambulatory care.

Although the eventual patterns of organization in the U.S. and the extent of Federal involvement are still obscure, there will undoubtedly be a growing need for quasipublic authorities on the regional, state or community levels to monitor the type and quality of care their citizens receive, to franchise, license or certify health-care organizations, services and facilities, and to review costs and approve premiums, rates, charges and benefit packages for health-care plans and institutions. That in turn is unlikely to happen without effective financial incentives and a combination of Federal regulation, surveillance and control.

Health-care systems in even the most developed countries are in a rudimentary stage of evolution compared with systems for the mass production of manufactured goods and agricultural products or even for the provision of services such as transportation, communications and defense. In most service systems one can identify examples where optimal mixtures of science, technology, capital, personnel and management are meeting the needs of defined markets or populations effectively and efficiently to the satisfaction of most people most of the time. In the U.S. the same can rarely be said for health care as yet.

One element that is clearly missing is a first-rate medical intelligence service to analyze quantitative information bearing on health-care issues in the light of political, social and economic factors. To accomplish this we need groups of policy analysts at Federal and state levels of government and in extragovernmental institutes and universities. To the extent that history and experiences here and abroad, together with information and critical thought, can illuminate health-care problems and issues, policy analysis should be encouraged, if not required. How else can we take advantage of the opportunities afforded by our traditions of diversity and pluralism, by the advances in science and technology and by the American talent for organization? There is no greater challenge in the realm of social services than the application of these powerful forces to improving our health-care arrangements.

In all our efforts we should not forget that health is a personal matter and an individual responsibility, that we are born alone and we die alone. There is a limit to the extent that collective action can reverse the ravages of time, ameliorate the human condition or forestall our ultimate death.

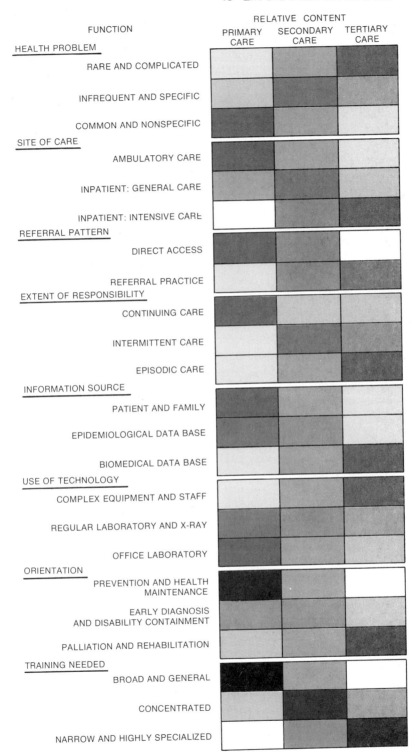

RELATIVE CONTENT

FUNCTION	PRIMARY CARE	SECONDARY CARE	TERTIARY CARE

HEALTH PROBLEM
RARE AND COMPLICATED
INFREQUENT AND SPECIFIC
COMMON AND NONSPECIFIC

SITE OF CARE
AMBULATORY CARE
INPATIENT: GENERAL CARE
INPATIENT: INTENSIVE CARE

REFERRAL PATTERN
DIRECT ACCESS
REFERRAL PRACTICE

EXTENT OF RESPONSIBILITY
CONTINUING CARE
INTERMITTENT CARE
EPISODIC CARE

INFORMATION SOURCE
PATIENT AND FAMILY
EPIDEMIOLOGICAL DATA BASE
BIOMEDICAL DATA BASE

USE OF TECHNOLOGY
COMPLEX EQUIPMENT AND STAFF
REGULAR LABORATORY AND X-RAY
OFFICE LABORATORY

ORIENTATION
PREVENTION AND HEALTH MAINTENANCE
EARLY DIAGNOSIS AND DISABILITY CONTAINMENT
PALLIATION AND REHABILITATION

TRAINING NEEDED
BROAD AND GENERAL
CONCENTRATED
NARROW AND HIGHLY SPECIALIZED

Figure 43-7. LEVELS OF MEDICAL CARE are characterized loosely in this illustration according to the relative importance of primary, secondary or tertiary care in dealing with a wide range of medical problems and functions. The more important the level of care, the darker the color in the appropriate box.

Insofar as knowledge can help, however, we should pursue it vigorously and use it sensibly — knowledge not only about our psychobiological system but also about ourselves and our relations to one another, knowledge about social, political and economic forces that shape our future, and knowledge about the health-care resources, professions and institutions that seek to improve our common lot. It is more science in medicine, not less, that will ultimately help to improve the quality of life and ease the perilous adventure from birth to death.

44   The Lower Class:

Health, Illness, and Medical Institutions

Lee Rainwater

Our concern is with ways in which the characteristics of lower-class persons influence their behavior in connection with the issues of health, illness, and the utilization of medical services. The group characterized below constitutes some 25 to 30 per cent of the population of the country. It includes that segment of the society usually referred to by the term "lower lower-class" or "lower working-class" (some 15 per cent of the population) and a portion of the stable working class just superior to them in social status. A considerable body of research suggests that this group at the bottom of the social-status, occupational, income, and educational hierarchy has certain distinctive ways of looking at the world and of relating to it, as well as distinctive problems of adaptation to the world. Inevitably, these distinctive world views and modes of adaptation influence the ability of working-class people to take advantage of the standard services of the society, whether these be in the private or public sector.

The particular institutional activities considered in this chapter, those of medical care, represent but a very small part of the total adaptive activity of individuals. In the case of the lower class, we must at all times remain aware that lower-class ways of coping with different kinds of problems are much less subject to the elaborate systems of specialized role behavior and concomitant cultural techniques that are so characteristic of the middle class. Lower-class people find it much less easy or sensible to maintain different ways of coping and reacting to different situations and are more likely to bring to any one situation much the same approach that they bring to any other.

The lower-class person's experience of himself and his world is a highly distinctive one in our society. It is distinctive for its qualities of pain and suffering, hopelessness, and concentration on the deadly earnest present. It is distinctive for its problem and crisis-dominated character — as S. M. Miller has commented, "Lower class life is crisis-life constantly trying to make do with string where rope is needed." Having many problems at any one time and being constantly either going into a crisis, trying to manage during a crisis, or coming out of a crisis mean that for lower-class people any one misfortune does not stand out sharply and does not tend to call forth a focused effort at combating the misfortune. Thus, any one problem that lower-class people have (which as middle-class persons we believe should be solved

Rainwater, L.: The lower class: Health, illness, and medical institutions. In Deutscher, I., and Thompson, E. J. (eds.): Among the People: Encounters with the Poor. New York, Basic Books, Inc., 1968.

immediately, if not sooner) appears to them as simply one among many fires that must be put out or controlled, or maybe just lived with.

This means that lower-class people (often with a considerable amount of realism on their side) will be inclined to slight health difficulties in the interest of attending to more pressing ones, such as seeing that there is food in the house, or seeking some kind of expressive experience which will reassure them that they are alive and in some way valid persons. The same kind of medical problem will stand out much more sharply to the middle-class person because he tends to conceive of his life as having a relatively even and gratifying tenor; his energies are quickly mobilized by anything which threatens to upset that tenor. (Studies of more stable working-class people who do not have the same chronic crisis situations suggest that the view of life as made up of a series of difficulties just barely coped with is not too far removed from their own impressions of the world they live in. While the overt character of daily life may seem quite stable, there is a constant theme of unease in stable working-class people, a constant sense that the world holds many potentialities for pushing them back into an unstable, highly punishing kind of existence.)

In the sections which follow we will take up particular aspects of the world view, belief system, and life style of the lower class. But it is important to keep in mind that behind any one particular orientation discussed is the problematic character of lower-class existence. This pervasive characteristic tends to make unreal the careful, meticulous, and solicitous attitude toward health which is held out by the health professions, and which is by and large subscribed to by middle class and perhaps by an increasing proportion of the better-off parts of the working class. Such concerns will often seem empty and minor to lower-class people, who feel they have much more pressing troubles.

Another very general characteristic of the lower-class situation relevant to its crisis character is that these households are much more often "understaffed" than are stable working-class or middle-class households.

That is, the complement of persons who normally maintain and run a household in our society, including at least a husband and wife, is much more often reduced. First off, households in which both husband and wife are present are less common in the lower class than in the middle and stable working class. For example, while in the St. Louis metropolitan area only 8 per cent of the white children under eighteen years of age do not live with both of their parents, 41 per cent of Negro children are in this position. If one looks at the census tracts inhabited mainly by poor Negroes, we find that well over half of the children under eighteen do not live with both of their parents. While marital dissolution among lower-class whites is perhaps not so common as it is among Negroes, it is certainly a great deal more common than in the white middle and stable working class. The understaffed households which result from this factor have many problems of coping with the normal pressures of daily living. Even when both the husband and wife are present, the typical patterns of lower-class marital relations have the result that husbands tend to be much less involved with what goes on in the home and to contribute less in the way of labor to maintain the family enterprise. Even when the household takes the form of a stem family in which there is some other relative present, our research suggests that the most frequent pattern is one in which one adult ends up having almost all of the internal family-maintenance responsibilities; the other adults see their role as either that of provider or of grown-up child who has a right to spend her time away from home engaged in activities for her own amusement.

This pattern of understaffed households in a situation of considerable family stress means that each individual's health receives relatively little preventive attention; when someone is sick, it is more difficult to care for him; and when the main adult is sick, she or he will be in a very poor position to care for herself properly or even to find the time to seek medical help. The attitude toward illness (even when it becomes chronic) in this kind of situation is apt to be a fairly tolerant one. People learn to live with illness, rather than use their small stock of interpersonal and psychic resources to do something about the problem.

THE LOWER CLASS AND THE BODY

In many ways lower-class people are heavily preoccupied with their bodies — a fact apparent in their heavy consumption of patent medicines, in the folk beliefs which researchers have documented as being common at this class level, and in the cultivation of various kinds of substances (alcohol, drugs) and activities (dancing, fighting) which have as one goal a heightened awareness of physical existence. Also frequently noted is that lower-class people tend to express their psychic difficulties somatically. It might be more correct to say that lower-class people do not differentiate psychic and somatic components of stress symptoms. For example, in our sample of some fifty intensively studied families, as many as one third indicated that at one time or another one member of the household had a "nervous" condition. It is usually apparent from the context that respondents are talking about some kind of undifferentiated state of unease which manifests itself both psychically, in terms of anxiety and confused feelings and cognition, and somatically, in terms of physical discomfort or other kinds of physical symptom. Considering all this, then, it would not be surprising to find lower-class people heavily preoccupied with issues of health and illness, and in a certain sense, they are. However, we know that rather seldom do lower-class people organize their lives around being ill, as in hypochondriasis; or, on a more constructive level, organize themselves instrumentally toward doing something about poor health.

Lower-class people perceive the world as a dangerous and chaotic place. This very primitive level of existential comprehension also carries with it a tendency to see the body as dangerous, or as potentially so. Thus, lower-class people seem fairly readily to think of their bodies as in some way injuring or incapacitating them. They view the body as mysterious, as not rationally understandable, and there is a tendency to relate to it in magical rather than in instrumental ways. When they talk about illness, lower-class people sometimes communicate a sense of alienation from their own bodies, a sense of distance from the illness processes going on in their bodies. They do not, like middle-class people, identify with their bodies and work toward a cure of physical difficulties in much the same way that they would work toward some lack in knowledge by discovering an appropriate solution to a problem.

This tendency to see the body as mysterious and potentially dangerous carries with it a rather poor differentiation of bodily parts and function. For example, in a study of how lower-class men and women think about the process of reproduction and about the bodily parts relevant to sexual relations, we found a rather low differentiation of the female sexual organs on the part of both men and women. A majority of lower-class respondents had very poor notions of the process of conception. This was found to be quite closely related to their inability to understand or trust chemical methods of contraception or feminine methods such as the diaphragm.

Another very general characteristic of lower-class persons is their tendency to have a low self-evaluation, to have as a chronic problem difficulties in maintaining a secure sense of self-esteem. Much lower-class behavior that appears flamboyant or deviant to middle-class people can be seen as an effort to compensate for lowered self-esteem. The reasons for this chronic lower evaluation of self are complex, involving a lifelong interaction between the symbolic communications others make and the more direct experiences of failure, punishment, and impotence that lower-class people have in striving to adapt to the harsh world in which they live. Lower-class people thus develop an attitude toward themselves characterized by a sense of being unworthy. They do not uphold the sacredness of their persons in the same way that middle-class people do. Their tendency to think of themselves as of little account is readily generalized to their bodies.

This is in sharp contrast to middle-class attitudes, which emphasize the intrinsic value and worth of the self and of the body. For the middle-class person, lowered body functioning is readily taken as an insult to both the body and the self, an insult which is intolerable and must be remedied as quickly as possible. For lower-class people, a body which does not function as it should, which has something wrong with it, simply resonates with the self that has these same characteristics. Just as lower-class people become resigned to a conception of themselves as persons who cannot function very well socially or psychologically, they become resigned if necessary to bodies that do not function very well physically. This is probably particularly likely to happen as lower-class people grow older and increasingly face a sense of failure because some of the adaptive techniques they have used to ward off a negative self-image begin to play out. Related to these interactions between self-concept and body image is a finding reported by Bernice Neugarten that lower-class people believe they become middle-aged at a much earlier chronological age than do working- and middle-class people. Thus, lower-class persons are likely to accept impaired functioning in the thirties as a natural consequence of aging, whereas working- and middle-class people are less likely to see impaired functioning at this, or even later ages, as "natural." Rosenblatt and Suchman's characterization of blue-collar attitudes toward the body takes on a special significance when related to the differential notions of aging that the classes have:

The body can be seen as simply another class of objects to be worn out but not repaired. Thus, teeth are left without dental care, and later there is often small interest in dentures, whether free or not. In any event, false teeth may be little used. Corrective eye examinations, even for those people who wear glasses, are often neglected, regardless of clinic facilities. It is as though the white-collar class thinks of the body as a machine to be preserved and kept in perfect functioning condition, whether through prosthetic devices, rehabilitation, cosmetic surgery, or perpetual treatment, whereas blue-collar groups think of the body as having a limited span of utility: to be enjoyed in youth and then to suffer with and to endure stoically with age and decrepitude. It may

be that a more damaged self-image makes more acceptable a more damaged physical adjustment.

The low "body esteem" which lower-class people have applies by extention to the persons under their care, including their children. Lower-class persons tend to develop rather negative images of their children as "bad" and/or "unsuccessful." This seems inevitable, given their conceptions both of themselves and of the nature of the world. The low esteem in which others are held as social beings easily extends to a minimal exercise of protectiveness and solicitude toward their physical needs and states. Thus we observe lower-class parents seemingly indifferent to all kinds of obvious physical illnesses their children have — particularly infections, sores, colds, and the like. Greater tolerance by their parents for children's physical disability or malfunctioning means that medical professionals cannot count on the parents to exercise careful observation or supervision of children's illnesses. And any program of treatment which does count on this is much more likely to fail than in the middle-class case.

The acceptance of something short of good health has implications both in terms of the care of people who are already ill and in terms of preventive medicine. Lower-class parents are much less likely to carry out a consistent preventive regimen in the way the household is maintained and the children's activities controlled. The much higher accident rate among lower-class individuals, particularly children, is not only a result of the greater objective danger of their environment (more broken bottles around, more dangerous housing) but also results from the lack of consistent circumspection on the part of parents.

Low body esteem carries an important secondary gain. If one can regard one's body as in some sense not working right, then one has a legitimate extenuating circumstance for many failures to live up to one's own standards and those expressed by others. We have noted in our work with lower-class families that an enormous number of health complaints come up both in participant observations of daily living and in interviews. While these complaints are obviously related to many of the factors discussed in this chapter, one important function or consequence of the developing conception of oneself as not in tip-top physical condition is that of warding off allegations of irresponsibility or failure based on "not caring."

At the risk of unnecessarily proliferating role terms, it may be worth while to distinguish here between the "sick role," the "patient role," and the "disabled role." As used by Parsons and others, the sick role involves basically a notion of withdrawal from all normal responsibilities because of physical incapacity; the "patient role" is superimposed when the individual brings himself within the purview of healing agents. It may be true, as some researchers have suggested, that higher-status persons find it easier to accommodate themselves to these two roles, whereas lower-status persons champ at the bit to shed the sick and patient roles. However, it is also clear that lower-class people much more commonly regard themselves as in minor or major ways disabled from functioning "normally" — disabled in the sense of their physical condition not allowing them to function as fully active adults. We would suggest that the difficulties of coping with situations in such a way that self-esteem can be maintained tempts lower-class people to assume the role of the partially disabled. This assumption of the disabled role was described in its most dramatic form by Halliday in his discussions of the psychosomatic diseases of English workers during the depression. We also see it in a more moderated but chronic form in lower-class individuals, particularly women, where the connection with unemployment and the possibility of compensation is not at all in question. Once impaired functioning is defined as a "normal" state of the body and self, expectations of what one can and cannot do are greatly modified. It is possible for the individual to counter claims on the part of other individuals by pointing to his physical condition. To the extent that the disabling condition is thus defined as "normal," the individual's motivation to seek treatment is considerably lowered. Self-medication can then become a ritual which symbolizes the disabled state.

THE LOWER CLASS AND MEDICAL TREATMENT

The implications of most of what has been said so far for the kind of treatment regimen that will be maintained, and the likelihood of seeking medical treatment in the first place are fairly obvious. Here we will simply focus the discussion on concepts of causality and initiative in connection with health and illness.

Lower-class notions of how things happen attribute a very great importance to good or bad luck — to "the way things are" — and tend to deemphasize one's ability to affect importantly the course of future events by self-directed action. These beliefs, plus the deep commitment to self-maintenance in a difficult present, mean that lower-class people concern themselves relatively little with the long-term aspects of their problems. They do not plan for the future (how can they?), but rather live from day to day or, at most, from week to week. Such future-oriented plans as they do develop tend to be held much less tenaciously and are much more readily dropped under the impact of immediate crisis. Lower-class people tend to feel that the difficulties they encounter are the result of bad luck, rather than of failing to take proper care — indeed, the extent to which by taking proper care lower-class people can significantly affect their life chances is a very open question. The intense preoccupation with the immediate maintenance of the self in a given and difficult world makes it very difficult to take out of this system energy for planful action toward some future goal. The readiness with which lower-class people are distracted by immediate dangers or prospects for immediate gratification reduces the likelihood of their carrying out carefully tailored regimens of treatment and sharply limits preventive activities directed toward the future goal of avoiding an illness.

Health and illness, therefore, tend to be dealt with in terms of crises. That is, when the impairment of functioning becomes so great or so obvious in the immediate situation that the individual feels this problem stands out above the rest, some action is likely to be taken. Until that time, the illness problem recedes into the background as more pressing issues are dealt with. The immersion in the immediate situation also probably accounts for the difficulties lower-class people have in observing schedules of all kinds. It is difficult for them to keep appointments because something that seems more important is always going on. Clearly, any program that requires lower-class people to be as observant of highly time-bound schedules as middle-class people are capable of being is going to have only modest success.

The lower class is motivated to obtain medical care when there is a breakdown of bodily functioning such that a crisis is presented and essential activities cannot be carried out. Therefore I would generalize a bit from Rosenblatt and Suchman's statement:

> For the blue-collar workers, with their greater distance from the whole medical-care system, illness is related to dysfunction in work, primarily related to incapacitating symptoms. Symptoms which do not incapacitate are often ignored. For the white-collar groups, illness will also relate to conditions which do not incapacitate but simply by their existence call forth medical attention.

In the middle class, any symptom that is obvious incapacitates because it takes away from the kind of more perfect person the middle-class individual likes to think of himself as being. The lower-class person cannot afford this conception of himself; he attends to physical symptoms, if at all, only when they pose a crisis in carrying out those activities he considers necessary.

THE LOWER CLASS AND MEDICAL INSTITUTIONS

Lower-class people tend to have mixed feelings about physicians. On the one hand, because of their involvement with their bodies as in some sense mysterious and unpredictable, they would like to be quite dependent on physicians and to have physicians behave in paternalistic, nurturant, and solicitous ways. On the other hand, the physician, representing middle-class views and a detached instrumental ap-

proach to problems, can be quite intimidating and difficult to understand.

Just as lower-class people tend to personalize all relationships, they tend to seek highly personalized relationships with physicians where this is possible. This is most likely when dealing with physicians in private practice. Women of the stable working class often develop close and trusting relationships with their private physicians, and are both heavily dependent on them and quite responsive to what the physicians tell them to do. This is less likely to be the case in the lower class. Persons here often must use public medical facilities, where it is difficult to form a relationship with one physician. In addition, the lower-class individual's distrust and uneasiness in dealing with middle-class persons often gets in the way of establishing the kind of dependent relationship he would like. Even so, despite the frequent difficulties lower- and working-class people have in paying high medical bills, we have found that seldom do women express hostility toward their own physicians as overcharging them or being unreasonable about payment.

It seems likely that the ability to form a trusting and dependent relationship with physicians increases as lower-class people grow older and feel a greater need for a nurturant figure because of increasing failure in managing themselves and their lives. In any case, even when dealing with private physicians, where the structure of the relationship allows greater personalization, it would seem that lower-class men and women have a good deal more difficulty in being really attentive to their physicians and in carrying out the regimens which the physicians prescribe.

The ability to form a close, trusting relationship with the physician is greatest in connection with the lower-class person's own medical needs. It would seem to be a great deal more difficult to develop this closeness when the patient is a child rather than the parent. The preoccupation with oneself and the touchiness that lower-class parents exhibit about somehow having failed their children make it difficult for them to sustain a relationship with a helping third party who is an authority and may make negative judgments about how one has behaved. In these situations, physicians need to be very careful that they do not alienate parents and make contact so uncomfortable that the parents cease to come back. For this reason, relationships with general physicians are much easier for lower-class people to sustain, since they count on the physician to treat both their problems and the problems of their children. Relating to pediatricians, uninterested as they are in the health needs of adults, will be much more difficult for the lower-class family.

When one shifts the focus of inquiry from the context of private practice to that of the large medical institution, the negative possibilities increase sharply. Many lower-class people are used to dealing with medical personnel only in the context of the large institution, and have had little opportunity to develop the kind of more personalized relationships that they would like to have with physicians. They are often inured to receiving poor service in low-cost or charity clinics and hospitals. They expect to have to wait long hours in order to receive medical service and to be shabbily treated by those with whom they deal. Because this is their experience and expectation, they tend to be rather docile and impassive in the face of such difficulties, but one should not be misled into thinking that these kinds of experiences have no effects. The lower-class person who must journey by public transportation for an hour to reach a public facility and then wait for several hours before receiving service is going to think two or three times before going for such service. The difficulty of receiving care serves to reinforce the tendency to seek it only when a crisis situation is reached. Clinic personnel who force patients to wait long hours in order to weed out the "poorly motivated" only deepen these tendencies.

One of the problems lower-class people have with bureaucratic organizations is that they are used to dealing with people in non-segmentalized ways. They expect a superior or someone with special knowledge to be able to cope with whatever problem is presented him, and they neither understand nor are tolerant of the great division of labor that obtains in such institutions. They want *someone,* rather than a *team,* to take care of them. It takes them quite a while to sort out the various functions represented by a team — whether this be a team of physician specialists or the nurse-physician-technician team.

While it is true that the middle class has a greater understanding of a division of labor, it should also be noted that because of their ability to purchase services they are better able to have someone inside the system represent them to the whole system. That is, middle-class people will turn to their own private physician to sort out any difficulties they have with the different specialties represented in the hospital. For the person who can afford his services, the private physician functions to moderate the impersonality of the medical division of labor. The lower-class person, in contrast, often feels he has no one person to whom he can rightfully turn with his gripes and have them listened to. In addition, middle-class people much more readily establish personalized relationships with many specialists, and can find pride and pleasure in having "my internist," "my pediatrician," "my obstetrician," and "my ophthalmologist." It takes a great deal of psycho-social energy for someone to form such relationships; lower-class people have enough trouble forming a trusting relationship with one middle-class professional, let alone several.

As many observers have noted, there are tremendous problems of communication between middle-class professionals and lower-class clienteles. One of the most striking aspects of this communication is the amount of derogation and hostility that is covertly (and often overtly) expressed by the middle-class professionals. From the professionals' point of view, lower-class people are by definition "problem" people. It seems that over time professionals build up a considerable store of hostility and blaming attitudes toward such persons. The understanding that middle-class professionals develop of the peculiar characteristics of their lower-class clientele seems more often used as a way of avoiding blame for failure than of gaining insight into problems of dealing with this clientele and developing techniques that allow them to be more successful at their jobs. When lower-class people perceive the middle-class professional as blaming, derogating, or hostile toward them, they withdraw quickly into an adaptation of resentful docility, and are then much less available for any real communication or learning. While a few lower-class people develop an amazing ability to manipulate these situations toward their own ends, most simply retreat and get out of the situation as quickly as possible.

Lower-class people appear particularly prone to a sense of pervasive anxiety during hospitalization. They do not know what is going on nor on whom they can count for help. As patients, they also are likely to feel quite isolated. Their families' realistic difficulties in visiting them are often great, and the family ties may be weak enough so that, despite the best intentions, relatives just do not manage to make frequent visits. Thus hospitalization can be a painful experience for the lower-class person who spends most of his time alone in a situation in which he is frightened. There would seem to be a great need for facilities to be planned in such a way as to maximize the chance of establishing casual relationships with other patients. Also, visiting arrangements should be flexible so that when visitors do turn up, even at inopportune times from the point of view of the hospital, they can visit the patient.

The connections between class-related life-style characteristics and medical settings are illustrated by Rosengren's study of obstetric patients:

Consider the blue-collar woman: the relative personal and social isolation in which she lives — isolated, at least, from the personal contacts and formal experiences by which one assimilates the meaning and significance of professional ministrations — the relatively minimal education she has achieved, and the life milieu in which she lives, where illness, incapacitation, and the like abound; and also the very real, heightened chances that either she or her baby may encounter either insult or accident during pregnancy — all of these factors and others combine to make the pattern of high sick-role expectations among this group particularly understandable. Considering also that the blue-collar woman is likely to be cared for in a clinic setting rather than by a private doctor, it is easy to see why she might regard herself as "ill." The middle-class woman chooses her own physician — normally, on the basis of word-of-mouth advice from friends and relatives. She appears for her prenatal care in a treatment setting which has little of the symbolism of sickness — a quite "living-room-like" waiting room, perhaps occupied by a nurse without a uniform. This is in dramatic contrast to the clinic-attending woman who experiences her treatment within the confines of a hospital, with ambulances going to and fro, with uniformed nurses and interns scurrying about, sometimes in apparent anxiety, with stainless steel, tile walls, and medicinal odors intermixed with medical machinery and equipment. Not only, then, does the life milieu and its attendant contingencies conspire to move the blue-collar woman toward the enactment of the role of the sick, but so, too, does the peculiar character of her obstetric-treatment episode.

The ecology of medical services can work to the disadvantage of the lower-class person. Such persons customarily organize their use of the resources of the environment in such a way that they do not have to go far to get the necessities of living. They tend to shop close at hand for food, clothing, furniture, and other items. While they do not mind going far on rare occasions for entertainment or visiting, traveling around the city is generally costly, uncomfortable, and inconvenient. This is particularly true of women who typically have several children to care for and who seem to develop a very special kind of anxiety about the outside world, particularly as they grow out of the late-adolescent and young-adult period.

In addition, there is the very real problem of the expense of traveling. Some lower-class people are so poor that even expenditures for carfare have to be carefully calculated. If emergencies seem to demand the use of taxis, there may just not be money available. For example, one woman in the housing project we are studying has a grandson with asthma. When he has attacks, she often has to spend precious time finding someone to drive her to the hospital or loan her money for cab fare. She cannot understand why the Well-Baby Clinic across the street from her building will not provide the necessary service at times like this. Again, middle-class people are often in a much better position to deal with the same problem.

They have the money that allows them to travel (to own a car, call a cab, call an ambulance), and their demand for medical services is such that they are more likely to have the decentralized services of a suburban clinic or a medical office near them.

45   The Family in Health and Illness: Some Neglected Areas

Clark E. Vincent

A considerable literature purports to emphasize, if not document, the importance of the family in the prevention, cause, and treatment of individual illness. This literature contains some very basic but largely neglected implications for research, education, and policy planning in the public-health and mental-health fields. The most obvious implication is the need for information about families qua families in relation to health and illness. Only within the past decade has a noticeable number of researchers given sustained and systematic attention to the role of the total family in individual illness,[1] and such researchers appear more often to have had medical-clinical than social-science backgrounds. The early and still predominant emphasis has been upon a given illness and/or the patient as the unit to be studied. This was and is consistent, of course, with the traditional focus of "problem research" upon the illness or disease to be eliminated and with the humanitarian concern for the sick individual. Such an emphasis reflects both the belief that relatives are antitherapeutic for the patient and the practice of making the patient's familial relationships secondary to institutional routines and treatment processes — a belief and practice which, as Lidz and others have noted,[2] are now slowly being modified.

ONE-WAY FOCUS ON SELECTED ASPECTS

Much of the considerable literature of the past two decades which emphasizes the importance of the family in illness may be seen upon closer inspection to be limited to a one-way focus upon how or in what way illness may be the result of certain selected aspects of family life such as child-rearing patterns, parental attitudes, and mother-child relationships. Only recently has there been more than passing interest either in what illness does to the family or in what the total family contributes to illness, and most such interest has concerned the more dramatic of illness and handicap categories.[3]

---

[1] See bibliography in J. P. Spiegel and N. W. Bell, "The Family of the Psychiatric Patient," in S. Arieti (ed.), *American Handbook of Psychiatry*, Vol. 1 (New York: Basic Books, Inc., 1959) and the bibliography in Yi-Chuang Lu, "Contradictory Parental Expectations in Schizophrenia," *Archives of General Psychiatry*, Vol. 6 (March 1962), pp. 219-234.

[2] Theodore Lidz, George Hotchkiss, and Milton Greenblatt, "Patient-Family-Hospital Interrelationships: Some General Consideration," in *The Patient and the Mental Hospital*, ed. Milton Greenblatt, Daniel J. Levinson, and Richard A. Williams (Glencoe, Ill.: The Free Press, 1957), pp. 535-543.

[3] See, for example, Bernard Farber, "Effects of a Severely Mentally Retarded Child on Family Integration," *Monographs of the Society for Research in Child Development*, Vol. 24, No. 2 (1959).

Vincent, C. E.: The family in health and illness: Some neglected areas. Ann. Am. Acad. Polit. Soc. Sci. *346:* 110–116 (1963).

A variety of questions await answers concerning what individual illness — physical or mental, temporary or chronic — does to families as social units. Is illness similar to the economic depression of the 1930's in that it further weakens weak families and strengthens strong families? What changes in familial roles and structure accompany illness? Are there familial patterns of response to illness? Does hypochondriasis or physical cultism run in families? If the ill health of some families is attributable to the low income of the breadwinner, is the low income of some families due to the breadwinner's ill health?

Such questions derive few answers from the one-way concern about what causes illness — a primary and worthy concern, but one which obscures the relevance of knowing what illness causes.

A schizophrenic child must have considerable impacts not only upon its mother but upon siblings and the total structure of intrafamilial relations. Even a colicky baby or frail infant must have some measurable impact upon a new mother. Yet the degree and kind of impact, as well as the effect such impact has upon subsequent mother-child relationships, have received very little attention. Nor do very many of the one-way, mother-child studies include examination of the mother's relationships with her other children — the nonsick siblings of the subject or patient studied.

The afamily bias of research on illness is perhaps most apparent in the fact that studies of the mother-child dyad and even the father-mother-child triad in schizophrenia have rarely used the other children within the same family as the control group of nonschizophrenics. Thus, the several hundred studies of patients with schizophrenic, psychosomatic, psychoneurotic, and given organic illnesses provide us few answers as to what proportion of the siblings of such patients were similarly afflicted. If a very small proportion, what was it within the family unit or the total network of intrafamilial relationships that would account for the structuring of the mother's relationships with only one of her several children in such a way as purportedly to contribute to that child's illness? The

failure to examine the totality of intrafamilial transactions in such research would appear, at least superficially, to be accompanied by a tendency to misinterpret dyadic correlations as familial correlations — in somewhat the same way, perhaps, as William Robinson[4] has endeavored to show that ecological correlations are confused with individual correlations.

Even the relatively recent studies of how a family member's mental illness and subsequent recovery are perceived and handled within the family are generally limited to the marital dyad — how the spouse contributes to and/or is affected by the patient's mental illness and how or in what way the spouse influences the patient's decision to receive help and/or influences the subsequent recovery process.[5] But how do the children's perceptions of and responses to a parent's illness influence such decisions and processes? What do we know about how the physical or mental illness of a parent affects children at different ages?

The predominantly one-way focus on selected aspects and dyadic relationships has produced much valuable information, insightful concepts, and promising leads for further research. The point here, however, is that, when such information, concepts, and leads are not explicitly recognized as having been derived from studying only selected aspects and dyadic relationships of the family, they tend to become the bases for policy, public planning, and future research questions concerning illness and families qua families. Thus, it is not simply an academic or semantic issue when the study of child-rearing patterns, dyadic relationships, and parental attitudes results in neglected areas and unrecognized gaps in information concerning families as integral social units.

---

[4] William S. Robinson, "Ecological Correlations and the Behavior of Individuals," *American Sociological Review*, Vol. 15 (June 1950), pp. 351-357.

[5] See pertinent articles in *The Patient and the Mental Hospital, op. cit.;* John A. Clausen and Marian Radke Yarrow (Issue Editors), "The Impact of Mental Illness in the Family," *Journal of Social Issues*, Vol. 11, No. 4 (1955); and references in Harold Sampson and Others, "The Mental Hospital and Marital Family Ties," *Social Problems*, Vol. 9 (Fall 1961), pp. 141-155.

SICK-CARE FUNCTIONS AND THE MODERN FAMILY

One such gap may be illustrated with reference to the widespread belief that the stability and harmony of the family are endangered by the presence in the home of old, sick, retarded, or handicapped family members. This notion is explicit in popular literature, it is at least implicit in many family textbooks and professional journals, and it has received tacit support from the writings of Parsons and Fox among others. Using the welfare of the patient as one of their reference points, Parsons and Fox have postulated that the social organization of the modern, urban, nuclear family makes it increasingly necessary as well as convenient for the family to surrender its traditional sick-care functions to the hospital. They have suggested " ... that the optimal balance between permissive-supportive and disciplinary facets of treating illness is peculiarly difficult to maintain in the kind of situation presented by the American family."[6]

But the notion that the sick-care functions are incompatible with the organization if not the goals and interests of the modern family is contradictory to a number of current developments and trends. And it is these trends which underscore the need for an understanding of how families as social units influence and are influenced by individual illness. One such trend is evident in the treatment setting which has almost completed a full cycle — having changed from the home to the office to the hospital-clinic, it is currently being ushered back into the home and community. This trend is part of a complex configuration of factors which deserve study and documentation but which are mentioned here only in passing: The inevitable increase in medical specialization is accompanied by lament

and post-mortems concerning the passing of the family physician with the bedside manner and intimate knowledge of the total family. There is growing dissatisfaction with the fragmentation of patient-physician, patient-family, and family-physician relationships. There is increased awareness of the potentially detrimental results of the patient's long-term separation from home and community life.[7] There are experimental programs to release mental patients to the care of their families, and an increasing number of day-care and night-care facilities are being developed to offset the spiraling costs and shortage of facilities for prolonged hospitalization and institutionalization. There is increased interest in "conjoint family therapy,"[8] in family-centered clinics and in treating the family as a unit. Medical schools are developing teaching programs in Family Medicine.[9] The "helping professions" are utilizing a team approach to foster identity with a given family as an integral unit. There is interest in and some borrowing from the ideas and programs of noninstitutional care in other countries where there also are evidences of the trend toward the family and community treatment-setting.[10]

FAMILIES — IDEAL OR REAL?

Although this trend currently involves considerable sums of money, architectural planning, and public-policy decisions, family specialists appear ill prepared to

---

[6] Talcott Parsons and Renée Fox, "Illness, Therapy and the Modern Urban American Family," in E. Gartly Jaco (ed.), *Patients, Physicians and Illness* (Glencoe, Ill.: The Free Press, 1958), pp. 234-245. See also Joseph Greenblum, "The Control of Sick-Care Functions in the Hospitalization of a Child: Family Versus Hospital," *Journal of Health and Human Behavior*, Vol. 2 (Spring 1961), pp. 32–38.

[7] The studies of Erich Lindemann, John Bowlby, and Gerald Caplan are examples.

[8] See the bibliography and review discussion of the work of L. C. Wynne, D. D. Jackson, J. E. Bell and Others in Irving E. Alexander, "Family Therapy," *Marriage and Family Living*, Vol. 25 (February 1963).

[9] See bibliography in Robert J. Haggerty "Family Medicine: A Teaching Program for Medical Students and Pediatric House Officers," *The Journal of Medical Education* Vol. 37 (June 1962), pp. 531-580, and Iago Goldston (ed.), *The Family: A Focal Point in Health Education* (New York: International University Press, Inc., 1961).

[10] See, for example, James Farndale, *The Pay Hospital Movement in Great Britain* (New York: Pergamon Press, 1961).

provide information concerning the implications and consequences of such a trend. A major reason for this may be that educators, researchers, and counselors in the marriage and family field have reified or taken too literally the ideal-type model of the small, isolated, nuclear family. In fact, the postulate that the sick-care functions are incompatible with the organization of the modern family and the notion that sick, aged, or incapacitated persons endanger family cohesion may only be applicable to such an ideal-type model.

Consideration of this possibility and its implications requires a short but pertinent digression. The failure to examine the reciprocal influences or "transactions" between individual illness and the total family is not simply a failure by default. It represents, at least in part, a blind spot fostered by some theoretical and methodologic shortcomings in family theory. Specifically, the heuristic use of paired concepts and ideal types such as "rural-urban" and "nuclear-extended" has ignored the social reality of continuums in the structure and function of families.[11] The ideal types existing nowhere in time and place have been accepted all too readily as descriptions of flesh-and-blood families.

A case in point is the generally accepted idea that the contemporary American family is predominantly an isolated, nuclear family — consisting of mother, father, and their immediate offspring. In fact, this idea would appear to be so well accepted in textbooks and journal articles as to be regarded as factual. Consequently, there appears to be a contradiction between (a) the current trend back toward the home and family treatment-setting and (b) the notion that the sick-care functions are incompatible with the organization, if not the goals, of the modern family.

The contradiction is more apparent than real, however, if, instead of the ideal model of the isolated, nuclear family, we consider data obtained by several investigators indicating that the extended-family or a "modified nuclear family" system is still very much in evidence in this country.[12] Sussman found that help during illness was the major form of assistance provided by kin-related families, found no significant difference between social classes in the amount of help given or received during an illness of a family member, and found that such assistance was given in 92 per cent of the reported illnesses occurring among kin-related families living in the neighborhood in the twelve-month period preceding his study.[13]

SOCIAL REALITY

The inadequacy of familial theory based on nuclear-extended ideal types is perhaps best summed up in a statement by Dennis Wrong: "Social theory must be seen primarily as a set of answers to questions we ask of social reality."[14] The recent developments indicative of a trend back to the family, home, and community treatment-setting may be quite consonant with a social reality which many professionals in the family field have overlooked or ignored — the existence of a modified but very viable extended-family system.

To what degree do data from oldsters indicating they would not choose to live

---

[11] See Reinhard Bendix and Bennett Berger, "Images of Society and Problems of Concept Formation in Sociology," in Llewellyn Gross (ed.), *Symposium on Sociological Theory* (Evanston, Ill.: Row-Peterson and Co., 1959), pp. 92–118.

[12] See Eugene Litwak, "The Use of Extended Family Groups in the Achievement of Social Goals: Some Policy Implications," *Social Problems,* Vol. 7 (Winter, 1959–1960), pp. 177–187; "Geographic Mobility and Extended Family Cohesion," *American Sociological Review,* Vol. 25 (June 1960), pp. 385–394; "Occupational Mobility and Extended Family Cohesion," *American Sociological Review,* Vol. 25 (February 1960), pp. 9–21; Marvin B. Sussman and Lee Burchinal, "Kin Family Network: Unheralded Structure in Current Conceptualization of Family Functioning,"*Marriage and Family Living,* Vol. 24 (August 1962), pp. 231–240.

[13] Marvin B. Sussman, "The Isolated Nuclear Family: Fact or Fiction," *Social Problems,* Vol. 6 (Spring 1959), pp. 330–340.

[14] Dennis H. Wrong, "The Oversocialized Conception of Man in Modern Sociology," *American Sociological Review,* Vol. 20 (April 1961), pp. 183–193.

with their relatives illustrate a "self-ful-filling prophecy" when such oldsters have been indoctrinated with the widespread but unvalidated notion that their presence in the home is harmful? What proportion of the 95 per cent of those aged sixty-five and older in this country who are not institutionalized or hospitalized live with or receive help from members of their extended families? Is it possible that a majority do and that, in a majority of such cases, this augments financial stability and family cohesion? If not, under what conditions is it harmful?

What proportion of mothers depend on and receive a temporary visit and help from female members of their extended families during hospitalization and/or immediately after returning home with their new-born babies? What proportion of the total non-institutionalized but chronically ill, handi-capped, or incapacitated population in this country is taken care of partially or com-pletely by some extended-family members? Is the proximity of their elderly and widowed parents with limited financial resources a factor in the decision of whether and where couples move? Given the telephone, car, and jet, extended-family members who today live in the same city or even 100 miles apart may be as accessible to each other as were extended-family members who several generations ago lived within the same neighborhood or on adjacent farms. How much support for the medical-care legislation has come from young couples with aged parents? Few questions have been asked of the social reality that may include a very effectual extended family in modified forms.

FAMILSOMATIC ILLNESSES

When not dependent on ideal or dichoto-mized family types, Parsons' writings on the normative structuring and the function-al aspects of illness and the sick role in our society contain many very insightful con-cepts and fruitful leads. He has suggested "that somatic illness may be defined in terms of incapacity for relevant task-per-formance in a sense parallel to that in which mental illness is thought of as

incapacity for role-performance." He also has postulated that to be ill is to "be in a partially and conditionally *legitimated* state."[15] The conditional nature of this legitimation refers to the requirement that the sick person reaffirm the valuation of health by recognizing that to be sick is undesirable and by accepting the obligation to try to get well as soon as possible and to co-operate with others to that end.

Application of these concepts within the family setting suggests a number of ques-tions, only a few of which may be noted here with particular reference to non-chronic illnesses. Are there "familsomatic" ailments or manifestations that accident-ally or purposefully, real or imagined are developed to avoid certain husband-father or wife-mother tasks? Familsomatic or task-avoidance ailments of the wife in relation to coitus are legendary, as is "housewife's fatigue," but what of task-avoidance ailments of the husband-father? And what is the impact upon marital relationships when the well spouse thinks the ill spouse is neither trying nor co-operating to get well? Do the familsomatic manifestations which may excuse the male from relevant father-husband task perform-ance on week ends and between 5:00 P.M. and 9:00 P.M. on weekdays gradually alter either the acceptance of or his capacity for role performance within the family?

Within the occupational group, reduced capacity for relevant task performance probably is tolerated only for a limited time without changes being made in role assignments and work relationships. Such changes presumably occur very quickly when the reduced or impaired task per-formance of one worker imposes increased tasks on coworkers. What realignment of husband-wife roles and rights accompanies reduced task performance due to illness — familsomatic or organic, temporary or chronic — of the spouse? That some and perhaps considerable such realignment does occur would appear even more probable

[15] Talcott Parsons, "Definitions of Health and Illness in the Light of American Values and Social Structure," in E. Gartly Jaco (ed.), *Patients, Physicians and Illness, op. cit.,* pp. 165–187.

when we consider that illness of the spouse directly increases the tasks of the other spouse.

SPOUSE OR PARENT AS THE INITIAL DIAGNOSTICIAN

Mechanic and Volkart[16] have used the concept of "illness behavior" to refer to "the ways in which given symptoms may be differentially perceived, evaluated, and acted (or not acted) upon by different kinds of people." They have attempted to demonstrate that various types of medical diagnoses are differentially related to two independent variables — the "tendency to adopt the sick role" and the degree of "perceived stress." Their work has considerable relevance for research on the family and individual illness, particularly if we assume that most individuals discuss their symptoms with a spouse or a parent before seeing a physician or therapist. The spouse's or parent's response to or evaluation of the pain or symptom undoubtedly has some influence upon whether the person even sees a physician and how soon. Presumably, it also influences the intensity, the manner, and the completeness with which given pains, complaints, and symptoms are communicated to the physician. Thus, many people may see their physician either too late or needlessly because their action decisions regarding their own symptoms have been influenced by the way in which such symptoms were perceived and evaluated by their initial diagnostician — their spouse or parent.

Differences in the "tendency to adopt the sick role" and in the degree of "perceived stress" have been investigated far more along class, ethnic, and cultural lines than in relation to intrafamilial relationships and family structure. Yet the structure of the family in relation to other social units may impose some sex differences which cut across class, ethnic, and cultural differences in one or both of these variables. The husband-father who is provided annual sick leave with pay may need not only to adopt but to accentuate the sick role if he is to obtain the physician's statement that will enable him to remain on the payroll while enjoying the secondary gains of the sick role represented by release from job tasks during a few days rest at home. While he is home, his wife will add his care and some of his father-performance tasks to her own performance tasks. The wife-mother is provided no sick leave with pay, however, and, at least during his working hours, cannot depend on her husband to take care of her or to assume any of her mother-housekeeping tasks.

To what degree and in what direction does the variable of sick leave with pay influence the wife's perception and evaluation of her husband's as well as her own symptoms? How does the absence of sick leave for the mother-housekeeper not only influence her "tendency to adopt the sick role" and her degree of "perceived stress" but also increase her reliance on extended-family members? It would also be informative to know the degree and direction in which the sick-leave variable influences male-female illness rates, when such rates are derived from reported visits to a physician or medical facility.

A LONG-OVERDUE EMPHASIS

The strengths of the family have long been glorified as bases for mental and physical health; its weaknesses have equally long been damned as sources of mental, psychosomatic, and even organic illnesses. Thus, it is encouraging that an increasing number of educators and researchers are emphasizing the total family — nuclear and extended — in relation to health and illness. Such emphasis is long overdue. With millions of dollars and man-hours being spent on medical research, we still lack such basic information as the distribution of most illness along blood lines for the total extended family over several genera-

---

[16] David Mechanic and Edmund H. Volkart, "Stress, Illness Behavior, and the Sick Role," *American Sociological Review,* Vol. 26 (February 1961), pp. 51–58; "Illness Behavior and Medical Diagnoses," *Journal of Health and Human Behavior,* Vol. 1 (Summer 1960), pp. 86–91.

tions. With a variety of proposed and enacted medical legislation, we know very little about how the different medical services in various countries influence and are influenced by family life. With considerable concern about the physical fitness of youth and the ills of old age, we remain largely uninformed concerning how the family, the schools, and mass media inculcate a philosophy that health is a by-product of health practices, versus a view that health is purchased via pills and the doctor.

Thus, the question remains as to whether the recent and growing interest in the reciprocal influences of illness and the total family will develop with sufficient speed and soundness to provide policy guidance and fruitful research concerning the implications of current developments in the public-health and mental-health fields, some of which may well pose long-run contraindications for health and family life.

XVI SOCIOBEHAVIORAL CORRELATES OF HEALTH AND DISEASE

Sociobehavioral events have been shown to be associated with both the incidence and character of most physical and mental disorders. The natures of these influences are many and varied. Some are simply linked to an increase in exposure to infectious agents; others play a role in shaping emotional responses to certain illnesses. Whatever the specifics, sociobehavioral conditions provide a context within which the course of a disease will unfold.

Social and class distinctions inevitably arise in all cultures. At a fundamental level, basic biological differences, such as those of age and sex, play a role. Distinctions of an ethnic, socioeconomic, and racial character are also drawn in some societies, often resulting in sharp demarcations of power and prestige among their members. Individuals are separated into fairly rigid "classes" in social strata, each with a characteristic life style that determines such diverse experiences as educational prospects, clothing preferences, and speech habits. These class "norms" are transmitted subtly, but powerfully, to the young and serve as an implicit blueprint for approved social behavior and future aspirations.

Social class norms are a major force, not only in shaping styles of thought and communication (Article 32), but also in influencing the way in which illness is experienced by a patient (Article 44). Our attention will turn in this chapter to a variety of other sociobehavioral correlates of health and disease, such as ethnic differences in the nature of patients' presenting complaints and minority group differences in response to experienced pain. It may be instructive, before reading these fascinating reports, to note some of the more prosaic findings that relate sociobehavioral characteristics to illness behavior and medical care.

Age is among the most obvious of correlates of disease incidence. Sociocultural theorists contend, however, that this covariation cannot be ascribed solely to the cumulative ravages of time. As Wilson has written (1970):

> Obviously, the risks of dying or becoming ill advance steadily with increasing age. Yet this heightened risk at older ages is not solely of interest as a matter of biological decay; the distribution of illness by age leads us as well into a series of social and psychological questions. What ordinary stresses in the wear and tear of living a life bear most heavily on the aging individual? What accumulations of pressures from family life, work, or the pace of an urban environment pile up on the person? Is the effect of air and water pollution, noise, smoking and drinking only demonstrably pathogenic after a cumulative exposure? Which specific hazards attached to the social role of the older person are most probably deleterious: loosening of interpersonal bonds with children, loss of friends, isolation, or retirement and attendant feelings of uselessness? Thus, to know the single characteristic, "age," seemingly the simplest of all categories for grouping population groups, is related to systematic differences in health rates implies a host of clues for etiological search.

Sex-linked correlates of health, illness, and death have been clearly established; as with age, however, their causal roots are complex and difficult to determine. For example, although women exhibit considerably greater longevity, surviving men at all stages in the life cycle, the web of influences that account for this fact — constitutional, stress, or social — is not easily disentangled; thus, complicating the interpretation, we find that women, despite their lower mortality rate, display a consistently higher frequency than men in reported illnesses.

One of the most striking relationships implicating sociobehavioral processes is the correspondence found between race and illness. For example, in contrast to whites, blacks suffer to a greater extent almost every variant of disease, both physical and emotional; these difficulties are exhibited in both sexes and at all ages. Thus, to add to the many other strains of social disadvantage and degradation, nonwhite minority groups carry the burden of increased illness and higher morbidity.

The disparity in health status between white and nonwhite populations can be attributed in great measure to differences in socioeconomic status. The evidence is overwhelming that those on the lowest rung of the social ladder suffer the highest risk of both mild and severe illnesses. Although there are exceptions, most notably the greater prevalence of coronary disease among middle-class males, epidemiologic data point convincingly to a consistent and clear-cut negative correlation between class ranking and health. To compound this disadvantage, the lower socioeconomic groups are not as accessible to medical services and utilize these facilities to a lesser extent than those of the middle and highest strata.

Turning to the first of the three papers making up this chapter, Saxon Graham, a distinguished medical sociologist, details a number of social factors associated with disease incidence. He provides several concrete illustrations and offers a scholarly introduction to the concepts and methods employed in epidemiologic study.

The papers by Irving K. Zola and Mark Zborowski report on the results of their studies into ethnic correlates of "presenting complaints" and "response to pain." Both articles are considered to be "classics," that is, exemplary in their procedures and illuminating in their results. The student-physician should gain considerable insight from these investigations, and knowledge of the special characteristics of "minority group" patients should aid him in providing more effective medical care.

REFERENCE

Wilson, R. N.: *The Sociology of Health: An Introduction.* New York, Random House, 1970.

46   Sociological Aspects of Health and Illness

Saxon Graham

Human biology and sociology deal with two aspects of the same organism; certainly human biology is the natural science most closely related to sociology. Sociologists and human geneticists use similar methods in studies of familial aggregation of disease, and it is always difficult to separate the sociological from the genetic factors in deducing from their results. It is hardly surprising that in those particular aspects of human biology dealing with the etiology, treatment, and prevention of illnesses, sociological factors such as individual roles and cultural patterns should play such an important part. The socio-biological relationships relating to the etiology, prevention, and treatment of illness will be the subject of this chapter.

DEFINITIONS OF HEALTH AND ILLNESS

As in other facets of science, definitions of pathological phenomena have been much circumscribed by the development of biological knowledge, the intellectual orientation of the culture, and the society's value system. Thus, in some underdeveloped societies, the malaise and apathetic approach to life associated with infestation by certain parasites is a normal condition of life and is not considered a state of disease as it would be in the urban middle and upper classes (but not necessarily in the rural lower classes) of the United States. Similarly, a "touch of the liver," a bacterial enteritis, is a common complaint, but not necessarily an illness, in

France. In the middle-class urban United States, where emphasis has been placed less upon the gastronomic delights of cuisine than upon its hygiene, the gastric and intestinal symptoms so loosely defined in France are unusual and avoided wherever possible. The mere question of the presence or absence of a diseased state is answered in terms of the expectations in the culture.

Once a condition of nonhealth has been recognized, the problem of the definition of the kind of illness, disease, or other abnormality involved arises. Here again, the medical orientation of the society plays a part. The host of diseases classified as "fevers" by nineteenth-century physicians have today resolved themselves into a number of separate disease entities which are not only identified but are amenable to preventive measures as well as therapy. Most recently, something similar has taken place with regard to cancer. Cancers may possess some common elements; they generally involve the growth of abnormal cells. They differ, however, with respect to the site of the body involved, the histology of the tumor cells, their relation to metabolic processes, the therapies which are effectual, and many facets of their etiology. Thus, the large group of diseases which the layman often conceives of simply as cancer has been found to comprise a number of entities as distinct as those which formerly comprised the "fevers."

Fortunately for students of cancer epidemiology considerable progress has been made in distinguishing the various neoplastic diseases. Equally reliable diagnostic

Graham, S.: Sociological aspects of health and illness. In Faris, R. E. L., (ed.): Handbook of Modern Sociology, Chicago, Rand McNally, 1968, pp. 311–316, 319–325.

procedures are available for many communicable diseases, but not for all diseases. In many pathological states, for example in some cases of coronary artery disease, the condition may not be discernible until its lethal effects have been shown. In these instances, the investigator is reduced to studying persons who have died of the disease, who constitute a significant proportion of those having single attacks. The material the student can gather on deceased persons is so limited and biased by the fact of death that he is hard put to generalize to the living.

Even in diseases where definition comes in time for adequate investigation, the details of diagnosis may be confused — as in the case of arthritis.[9] Again, in the definition of hypertension in an individual, confusion is generated by potentially great changes in blood pressure from time to time and from one set of examining circumstances to another.[13] In many of the various mental illnesses, definition is extremely difficult and even the most experienced clinicians differ greatly in diagnosis. Few areas of medical diagnosis find definition as hazy.

To this point, we have been discussing the definition of disease states from the point of view of the medical scientist. We have seen that his definition is at odds with the absolute biological reality in various degrees, and that the divergence is determined by the extent of medical knowledge and interest at any given time in any given culture. Definition is also relative to who does the defining within the culture. The layman's recognition or nonrecognition of what his physician conceives as illness determines the roles he will play, his relationships with others, his demands for medical care, and the medical facilities which must be made available to him. Consider the case of two men killed by a speeding ambulance. On autopsy, both are found to have had a mild coronary infarct earlier in life. One had felt chest pain and had experienced shortness of breath, sought medical advice, curtailed certain activities, and followed a prescribed regimen. He had taken six weeks off from work, followed the role of a cardiac patient, and his family and friends reacted

in kind. The other had passed his seige of pain off as a gastric disturbance of greater than usual intensity and continued business as usual, although he had wondered occasionally at his loss of breath. Both men had the same symptoms; neither died of the condition. But the demands for medical care and their relationships with family members and others were quite different because of their different conceptions of disease. Thus, the layman's conception of disease definition must also be considered.

In short, in the sociological study of epidemiology or medical care, the definitions made of case groups are always influenced to some extent by the varying recognition by the patient that something is wrong and by whether or not he seeks medical advice in answer to his symptoms. Research in a given disease of mild symptoms may show, for example, that the upper classes have a higher incidence than the lower. The question must then be considered as to whether this was because the upper classes have a higher standard of physical performance than the lower, and easier access to medical care for diagnosing even mild symptoms.

To this point, we have discussed the definition of illness. The other side of the coin, health, has often been thought of as simply the absence of illness. However, with the conquering of many of the traditional scourges of mankind, scientists thinking of the medical concerns of the future have conceived of health as implying optimum functioning of the individual and group, physically, mentally, and socially. Indeed, the definition of health given by the World Health Organization is that "state of complete physical, mental, and social well-being." The burden of this definition is that even comparatively minor physical and mental abnormalities will be of concern to the medical scientist and epidemiologist. Furthermore, social maladjustments also would be within their purview. It may be argued that this is carrying medicine into areas traditionally staked out by sociology for research and social work for action. It may also be argued that in view of the current social problems these disciplines need all the help they can get.

EPIDEMIOLOGY

Almost every branch of biology takes some part in developing knowledge of the etiology of pathological processes; these include sciences whose major source of research data is the controlled experiment and observation conducted in the laboratory on either animals, man, or tissue derived from them. Epidemiology, however, is the major science dealing with large masses of human population, their biosocial characteristics, and the way these relate to the distribution of disease in that population. Although epidemiology originated in the studies of etiology of epidemics in human populations it has developed interest in the etiology of all human diseases. Like medicine itself, epidemiology has, in quest of its answers, made a marriage of a variety of biological sciences. Thus, in the study of conditions ranging from measles to mongolism to atherosclerosis, contributions from virology, chromosome study, and the biochemistry of nutrition, among other disciplines, are used as they apply to masses of people.

The key phrase here, for sociologists, is "masses of people." Many of the genetic, virological, nutritional, and other biological characteristics of individuals in these populations are closely related to such demographic characteristics as race, socioeconomic status, ethnic background, and fertility. Confronted with these observations, the sociological intuition envisions the possibility that still other aspects of social behavior may be related to states of health, aspects such as occupational behavior, religious prescriptions, recreational patterns, dietary habits, and factors of family relationships.

The common observation of both the clinician and layman that various aspects of human behavior may predispose to or protect against illness is congruent with the sociological view. The result has been that sociologists recently have increased their work in the area of epidemiology. At the same time, imaginative physician-epidemiologists have been more frequently concerned with details of human behavior and relationships. Studies of sociological variables have been pursued in research on the etiology of such varied conditions as coronary disease,[32] hypertension,[6] ulcerative colitis,[37] alcoholism,[54] lung cancer,[16a; 30] congenital abnormalities,[44] neuroses,[31; 45; 53] and injuries from skiing[24] and automobile accidents.[39] Scientific method dictates that the investigated phenomenon be observed in detail and that relationships among the details be investigated to furnish explanations for the phenomenon. Application of this method has led epidemiologists from both medicine and sociology minutely to examine the characteristics of dietary, smoking, and driving behavior and of interpersonal relationships as they relate to various pathological states. Knowledge of the causes of a given condition provides suggestions as to various methods of prevention and therapy.

The Etiological Chain of Events

For the purposes of this discussion, we will define disease as a tissue change to a morbid state brought about by some endogenous or exogenous biochemical or biophysical agent. Most often, the tissue change is the last in a series of events or factors, many of which are social, that put the host in contact with the pathogenic agent.[21] The first might be membership in a particular social group — for example, watch dial painters; next, this group may exhibit a particular behavior pattern — e.g., its members may form a point on the brush with the lips; next, the host might be exposed to a vector or carrier of the agent — in this case, a paint for illuminated dials; and finally, an agent, a radioactive ingredient of the paint that in some still undiscovered way brings about sarcoma, a fatal malignant bone tumor.[41] The categories of factors leading to disease usually are membership in a social group engaging in a pathogenic behavior pattern, consequent exposure to a vector or carrier of the agent, and the agent itself which brings about the tissue change. Whether or not a disease is clinically evident may depend greatly upon host characteristics, inherited or acquired. Thus, some individuals appear to have a genetic predisposition to diabetes, which, together with certain dietary behavior, may result in this particular illness. The same diet in another individual will not produce the disease because these host characteristics are absent. Similarly, the tubercle bacillus may or may not bring about a clinically recognizable condition, depending on the state of the host, possibly including his genetic endowment, nutrition, and other factors relating to socioeconomic status.

All of the above steps in pathogenesis do not necessarily appear in the history of a given disease. Indeed, in a very few conditions, genetic predisposition plus time for the illness to manifest itself are the only factors which can be chronicled: mongolism and other congenital anomalies and probably sickle-cell anemia are examples. Sometimes a behavior pattern may be pervasive in a society, and not peculiar to any one social group. Thus, in the United States a majority of adult males smoke cigarettes; although the habit is less manifest in some occupational, ethnic, or other social groups (such as clergymen, Italian-Americans, or jet pilots), it is generally pervasive. The first in the chain of factors, membership in a group, is less important in distinguishing those exposed to this vector. Among adolescents, however, the chain of factors has a high probability of starting with group membership, such as belonging to a family in which most members smoke;[31a] the host is then introduced to the pattern which puts him in contact with the vector, cigarette smoke, and the agent in the smoke which produces lung cancer.

Occasionally, the social situation seems to be in itself the precipitating factor. This may occur in instances where, in susceptible hosts, a trying social situation brings about an endocrine disturbance in the body which might cause disease. Similar situations, in susceptible hosts, might contribute to development of neuroses through unknown mechanisms, perhaps biochemical. It is possible, too, that traumatic social situations operating together with other exogenous agents on susceptible hosts may help to produce certain cases of hypertension, peptic and duodenal ulcer, ulcerative colitis, asthma, or alcoholism.

From the point of view of prevention, the chain of factors leading to disease may

be interrupted at any stage, and the disease thereby controlled. Thus, Percival Pott prescribed bathing to eighteenth-century English chimney sweeps as a preventive measure against scrotal cancer. His prophylaxis worked even though he had not identified the agent in soot causing the disease. A century earlier, James Lind suggested the eating of limes by English sailors to prevent scurvy long before the properties of ascorbic acid were understood. Similarly, today, a large proportion of lung cancer deaths could be prevented through abandonment of the cigarette-smoking habit. This could be done even though it is not known which of the specific chemical fractions of cigarette smoke which produce tumors in animals are also carcinogenic to humans. It is not necessary, obviously, to recognize the agent that causes the tissue change in order to effect prevention.

Rather, if health is to be preserved, once a link in the pathogenic chain has been found, this knowledge must be applied. This problem, a social one, is very difficult. Lind's prophylaxis against scurvy is a case in point. Scurvy was a disease serious enough to kill 100 of 160 men accompanying Vasco da Gama on his voyage of 1498. Nevertheless, not until a century after Lind gave his recommendation did the British Admiralty institute use of citrus fruit among its sailors. In our own time, even though there is more evidence regarding the relationship between dental caries and fluoridation of public water than between most other diseases and their preventive measures, the prophylaxis, for obscure sociological reasons, is not being universally applied.

The strategy of epidemiological investigation devolves from the etiological chain of factors and events described above. In instances where there are hints as to the relationship between a behavior pattern and a disease, as in the case of cigarette smoking and lung cancer, the investigation may begin with the suggested behavior trait. In such instances, hunches are derived from knowledge of a close relation between the possibly pathogenic substance and the given organ, in this case, the inhaled smoke and the lung.

Where no correlational hypotheses suggest themselves, the strategy must be revised. The fact that, as we pointed out earlier, membership in particular social groups may be the first step in an etiological chain suggests that investigation of the presence of disease in occupational, ethnic, religious, regional, social class, recreational, racial, or other social groups may be profitable. If a given disease is found to occur with more or less frequency in a given social class, further investigation can look into the specific behavioral trait characterizing the group which might be responsible for fomenting or protecting against the disease. The first stage of epidemiologic investigation, therefore, may be that of isolating unusual incidence of disease in given subcultures in the society. Research into many of the chronic diseases has reached only to this stage today. Investigation of some other diseases has turned up other kinds of evidence, in addition to the demographic. In these instances, it is important for the development of a coherent and complete theory of the etiology of the given disease that the sociological findings be consistent with those of the other disciplines. Indeed, one function of sociological epidemiology is to investigate the extent to which relationships of behavior patterns to disease are consistent with what is known regarding biophysical and biochemical relationships.[21]

Inherent in this description of the etiological chain is the point made earlier that epidemiology must be a marriage of a variety of disciplines. Indeed, it must use whatever may shed light on the development of disease. The variety of scientific data utilized in this research is great. Geological studies of outcroppings of radioactive rock in the vicinity of homes where congenital anomalies occurred have proved useful.[19] Soil science has been referred to in studies of gastric cancer.[58] These data are used to supplement the more conventional epidemiological resources of biology, sociology, chemistry, and physics. An example of the variety of sources of data utilized in the epidemiology of some diseases is shown in the case of lung cancer.

Over a score of studies comparing smoking habits of lung cancer and control patients in hospitals have been undertaken.[35] These have consistently shown a relationship between lung cancer and smoking cigarettes. These have been retrospective studies based on hospital series, with the biases these populations entail. In addition, however, prospective studies have been conducted in which large samples of healthy people were asked about their smoking habits and were then followed through several years to determine the incidence of lung cancer in the various smoking categories. Three of the four prospective studies used a minimum of 180,000 individuals chosen from various populations in the United States, and the other used the physician population of Great Britain; for all, a result similar to those of the retrospective studies was obtained.[14; 16; 29; 30] It is noteworthy that, in these studies, a dose-response relationship was established; thus, the incidence of lung cancer increased with each increase in amount of cigarettes smoked per day. Similarly, the longer the period for which individuals had stopped smoking, the lower was their lung cancer risk.

Further investigations have been undertaken to determine whether the relationships exist in particular subpopulations which in themselves are more subject to lung cancer, such as urban groups. The smoking relationship persists even here. Multivariate analysis of a variety of other factors also associated with lung cancer indicates that, while a few others are etiologically related, the smoking factor is extremely large in comparison.[28a; 34]

In addition to these many population studies much laboratory research has been undertaken on histological and biochemical facets of the relationship between smoking and lung cancer. For example, pathologic studies have been done of the cells in the tracheobronchial trees of smokers of various amounts of cigarettes and of non-smokers. In the autopsy studies of Auerbach, the bronchial epithelium of non-smokers was usually normal, but only .2 per cent of heavy smokers and .1 per cent of lung cancer cases showed normal epithelium. Carcinoma *in situ* (a tumor of malignant characteristics which has not yet invaded surrounding tissues) was found in 75 per cent of heavy smokers as compared to none of nonsmokers.[2a]

Studies of the effect of tobacco smoke on the epithelia of freshly slaughtered cattle showed an inhibition of action of the cilia, the waving grasslike processes that waft foreign matter out of the respiratory passages. In many studies, the application of tobacco tars to the skin of mice resulted in the growth of many malignant and nonmalignant neoplasms. It is interesting that applications of tar from filter cigarettes resulted in less cancer to the mice than those from nonfilters.[5a] Also indicating a dose-response relationship is the fact that smoke condensate from cigarettes yielding large amounts of tar resulted in more tumors than that from cigarettes lower in tar. Applications of chemically isolated fractions of cigarette smoke to the skin of mice have indicated a large number of fractions which are carcinogenic. In short, many studies using the methodologies and knowledge of several disciplines — including sociology, biochemistry, and pathology — have been completed. It is interesting that the findings of each are consistent with those of the others. Equally important is the point that everything is grist for the epidemiological mill.

Sociological Factors Related to Disease

The discussion of the chain of factors leading to the clinical recognition of disease noted that membership in a social group often entails a behavior pattern which puts the host into contact with a pathogen. Thus, membership in given social class, ethnic, religious, occupational, or other group is often related to unusual risk of a given disease. Examinations of incidence in such gross demographic categories put the investigator further away from etiological knowledge of the agent causing the tissue change than he would be if he searched for the individual items of behavior which in themselves might set the stage for disease. Frequently, however, there is no suggestion as to what those items of behavior might be, so the demographic approach must be utilized. From the sociological point of view, the demographic relationships discovered stimulate speculations about behavioral characteristics of the social groups involved which might predispose to or protect against the disease. Several studies have shown, for example, that the highest incidence of tuberculosis[55] is in the lower classes. For some reason, although a very large proportion of the population of the United States is exposed to the tubercle bacillus, a very small percentage develops clinical symptoms and active disease. The fact that the lower classes have more than their share of the disease suggests that factors relating to the lower-class environment, possibly crowding, poor diet, bad ventilation, or air pollution may determine whether or not an individual exposed to the bacillus develops clinically recognizable symptoms.

Trachoma, a disease of the eyes, is apparently concentrated in members of the lower classes in certain non-Western societies, perhaps because hygienic precautions against infection are less easily applied in them.[42] Schistosomiasis is a similar case.[2] Poliomyelitis, on the other hand, has been found in a few studies to be more frequent in the upper classes than the lower. One theory[12, 28] to account for this is based on the assumption that infection in infancy allows the individual to develop protective antibodies to the disease without the dramatic symptoms exhibited by individuals exposed later in life. Infants in large families are likely to be exposed to the disease by reason of crowding and to develop antibodies at an early age. These, of course, are more likely to be lower-class individuals, and the disease, therefore, manifests itself (as paralytic poliomyelitis) at a greater rate in the upper classes.

Much is known about the etiology of the above-mentioned diseases. Nevertheless, to complete the understanding of their pathogenesis, the sociological relationships must be reconciled with the microbiological, and the theories available to account for the relationships between social environment and such diseases as tuberculosis and poliomyelitis, for example, must be further tested. In a large class of diseases, even less is known about potential agents. Frequently these are termed chronic or noninfectious to distinguish them from the infectious diseases discussed above. This is a slippery designation, however, because some of the infectious diseases can be chronic, and some of the illnesses discussed below may be infectious.

One theory of cancer etiology, for example, is that it may be caused by a virus, perhaps acting with a cocarcinogen which triggers the development of disease. This theory may apply even though the etiology of cancers at different sites is likely to be different: The virus and/or the cocarcinogen may vary from site to site. That the cocarcinogen for many sites of cancer may be associated with socioeconomic status is suggested by a number of studies in many parts of the world. These show, for example, that the decrease in socioeconomic status is associated with an increase in the incidence of cancers of the following sites: cervix uterus, stomach, esophagus, and lung. An increase in class status coincides with an increase in cancer of the breast, corpus uterus, and probably the testis.[8;10;22]

With reference to diseases of the circulatory system, there is some evidence that hypertension increases with decreases in socioeconomic status.[6] On the other hand, deaths from coronary artery disease have been found in a number of studies to be more characteristic of the upper classes than the lower.[7] Hospitalization for mental depression may be less associated with socioeconomic status than for neurosis and psychosis, which are found more frequently in the lower classes.[18] Alcoholism is another disease which may have higher rates in the lower classes.

Ethnic background has also been related to a variety of diseases. Thus, one study suggested that the prevalence of hyperthyroidism among Winnipeg school children was higher among those deriving from countries of Eastern Europe than from Western Europe.[1] It is interesting that the rates decreased from east to west, declining in regular fashion from a high among children deriving from Poland, to a somewhat lower rate among German-Americans, to increasingly lower rates in the French, English, Irish, and Icelandic children. It was hypothesized that this may have been related to dietary differences in the cultures of the peoples involved. A study of mortality among ethnic groups shortly after many of them arrived in this country suggested that Italian-Americans had especially high rates of death from pneumonia. German-Americans evidenced unusually low rates of pneumonia and of tuberculosis. These relationships with pneumonia and tuberculosis, of course, may reflect differences in the socioeconomic characteristics of the ethnic groups.

Interesting correlations between ethnic background and coronary artery disease have been found in Israel. There, the Oriental Jews (Yemenites) were found to have appreciably lower rates of mortality from this disease than were the European Jews (Ashkenazim).[57] The Yemenites were of lower socioeconomic status and ate less animal protein and fats. The intake of dietary animal fats is probably related to blood cholesterol levels. If it should be established that such levels are related to the development of the fatty plaques which contribute to the narrowing of coronary arteries and to myocardial infarction,[17;32] the low rates among the Yemenites may be explained. On the other hand, there are further behavior patterns which distinguish Yemenites from other Jews in Israel.

Still other relationships between ethnic background and coronary artery disease have been shown in work in the United States. Thus, the Irish may have lower rates of the disease than other Western European groups.[20] If this relationship is real, it may obtain because of some trait of the Irish, such as their high alcohol intake. Preliminary findings of Baedenkopf and associates[4] suggest that persons with low alcohol intakes have more thickening of the coronary artery wall and therefore perhaps higher risks of infarction than those with higher alcohol ingestion. If it should be found that the lower classes ingest more alcohol than the upper, their lower mortality from heart disease might thereby be explained. This is a hypothesis only, but the possibility must be considered that characteristics of ethnic and class groups other than or in addition to ingestion of animal fats may be related to coronary disease.

Whether or not alcohol ingestion is related to class, alcohol addiction appears to be correlated with ethnic variations. Thus, various researches suggest that there is less alcoholism among Italians in the United States than among other ethnic groups. Irish- and Scandinavian-Americans, on the other hand, appear to have unusually high rates.[27] The very permissive attitude of the Irish toward drinking as a recreation may be associated with this finding.[3] So might the Italian conception of alcohol as a food to be ingested mainly with meals. Such explanations, of course, are after the fact; nevertheless, the discovered ethnic relationships may point to variables which should be examined further as characteristics of drinkers with and without alcoholism.

Cancer at various sites has also been related to ethnic background. Cross-cultural studies, for example, have shown that the Japanese have unusually high rates of mortality from gastric cancer and unusually low rates of breast cancer.[50] The English and Americans have outstanding mortality rates from lung cancer.[60] Within the United States, evidence from two studies shows that cancers of the lung and esophagus have an unusually high rate among Polish-Americans; whereas cancers of the pharynx and colon occupy similar positions among Italian-Americans.[23; 25] The foreign-born population in the United States considered as a whole have been found to have higher risks of cancer of the lung, stomach, esophagus, and cervix than do the native born.

Potentially useful relationships have also been found between religion and some diseases. Although incidence of the disease is difficult to measure, Jews have been reported to have low rates of alcoholism as compared with Catholics and Protestants in the United States. The rate of alcoholism among Jews reportedly increases with generation after immigration and with decline in orthodoxy. Sociologists investigating this phenomenon suggest that the low rate among Jews may be related to the fact that Jews utilize wine in their religious services, giving it some sanctity. They have also

proposed that the permissive attitude toward male drinking to the point of befuddlement, present, for example, in the immigrant Irish culture, is not only absent but frowned upon in Jewish culture.[52]

Jews also have much lower rates of mortality from cancer of the cervix than Protestants or Catholics. This has been found both in cross-cultural comparisons between Israel and the United States and within the United States.[15] Some facet of Jewish culture may provide protection against the disease. In view of the superior hygiene associated with the practice of circumcision, investigators hypothesized that the Jewish practice of circumcising might furnish this protection.[61] Whether this is the case or not is problematical; the results of the few studies done on the subject are equivocal.[38]

Still other relationships exist among diseases and religion. Thus, Jews may have higher risks of leukemia.[40] This provocative finding suggests that some trait of the Jewish subculture in American society may be promoting the disease. A possible factor here is the greater exposure of Jews to diagnostic radiation which in some research has been shown to be related to the disease.[36a] Again, some findings indicate that Protestants may be particularly prone to testicular cancer: One series adjusted for differences in social class, rural-urban residence, and native or foreign birth, showed Protestant patients to have higher risks than Catholic ones (Graham, n.d.). Further research on this point is highly desirable.

Throughout this discussion of ethnic background and religion as related to diseases of various kinds, it has been assumed that some sociological characteristic of the groups under investigation is responsible for the relationship discovered. The hypothesis must be entertained, however, that the crucial trait is not wholly sociologic but, in part at least, genetic. There is some evidence, for example, to indicate a common gene pool among Jews, present among Jews of all nationalities,[49] and which may protect against or promote the diseases we have discussed. Similarly, genetic differences between Italians and Poles may account for their different risks for the various cancers; the same may be said for differences in alcoholism risks.

The Epidemiology of Gastric Cancer

An examination of the manner in which a variety of sociological variables are related to a number of different diseases provides an intimation of the potential of these relationships for suggesting hypotheses about the etiology of disease. It is also instructive to examine the epidemiology of a particular disease exhaustively. This kind of study indicates the way the discovery of one relationship suggests the possible existence of others, and it demonstrates the efforts to develop theories which can account for and make mutually consistent all of the relationships discovered. The epidemiology of gastric cancer is an especially useful example, particularly because sociological variables figure so prominently in its epidemiology.

Gastric cancer, like few other cancers, is declining in incidence almost yearly. Formerly, it was the cancer of highest incidence (and mortality) among males; its average annual incidence in New York State in 1942 was 26.8 per 100,000 among males, and 16.1 among females. By 1961, however, its incidence had fallen to 15.4 among males and 8.8 in females.[43]

A number of biological conditions, which are perhaps associated with its early phases or which perhaps set the stage for its later development, may be related to this disease. Thus, one biological factor, gastric, achlorhydria, has been found among approximately 70 per cent of cases but among only 10 per cent of controls.[5;11]

Another medical condition which, it has been hypothesized, may be related to the disease, is pernicious anemia.[47] Here again, it is difficult to obtain numbers of such patients large enough to contain sufficient individuals who develop gastric cancers. The hypothesis is reasonable, however, in view of the fact that the prolonged deficiency of vitamin B_{12} associated with pernicious anemia could result in damage to the gastric mucosa.

Gastric ulcers have also been hypothesized to serve as loci in which gastric cancers can develop. This suggestion is difficult to examine because the presence of an ulcer

in the stomach may be obscured by the subsequent development of cancer at the same site. From the epidemiological point of view, diseases such as gastric ulcers, if they are precursors, must be examined to discover the mechanism by which they could develop the cancer. In addition, the problems remain of discovering the epidemiology of these promoting conditions and of that large proportion of gastric cancers which is not related to them.

Another important hypothesis relating medical conditions to etiology of stomach cancer has to do with dentition; fortunately, the easy access to teeth makes large-scale surveys of this factor possible, if not inexpensive. The small studies of dentition to date are equivocal, but current large-scale investigations may shed more light on the problem.

In addition, some evidence suggests a modest familial aggregation in this disease. A fair number of studies of this factor have been completed.[23a] Usually these compare the incidence of gastric cancer among the kin of cases as compared with the kin of controls. These studies show approximately twice as much gastric cancer in the relatives of cases as among those of controls. Thus, some genetic predisposition to the disease may run in families. Also, some behavior pattern may run in these families, which accounts for the disease. One way of examining these possibilities is to look into the incidence among nonblood kin living in the households, as compared to that among the blood kin. Woolf tried this and found that spouses of the cases had rates like those of the kin of controls; the blood kin of the cases had higher rates.[59] Woolf's is the only such study of the problem, although a number are currently under way; nevertheless, it suggests that at least a small amount of gastric cancer may be related to a genetic predisposition.

A number of sociological characteristics may be associated with the disease. It was noted earlier that gastric cancer is inversely related to socioeconomic status. This relationship has been found in Denmark, England and Wales, New Haven, and Buffalo. In addition, occupational relationships have been reported — workers exposed to iron dust experience greater risks.[33] Controlling on age, rural-urban residence, smoking, color, and marital status, it has been found that 12.5 per cent of cases, as compared to 1.0 per cent of controls, worked at jobs involving exposure to iron dust. Other research shows higher risks with increasing age, urban as opposed to rural residence,[36] smoking,[16] and Negro as compared to white racial background.[26] Further studies controlling on residence, carcinogenic occupation, socioeconomic status, and smoking show that foreign-born have about two-and-one-half times the risk of native-born individuals among the Roswell Park Memorial Institute patient population. Polish-American females have unusually high risks.[23]

Intercultural data also show differences. Thus, the Japanese, Finns, Chileans, and Icelandic populations appear to have elevated risks of the disease. The Japanese relationship is reinforced by the finding that the Japanese in the United States have higher risks than other American ethnic groups. However, their risk in the United States is lower than that in Japan, suggesting (because they are probably genetically little different from Japanese in Japan) that their new culture must have introduced something to protect them against the disease. It is particularly interesting that the Japanese in Hawaii have rates intermediate between those in the United States and Japan.[51] The Japanese character of the Hawaiian-Japanese culture may be similarly intermediate. Another interesting ethnic relationship is the unusually high rates of gastric cancer among some of the Polynesian peoples. High rates have been suggested for the Samoans.[56] Investigation has also revealed higher than usual

rates among the native Hawaiians, part-Hawaiians,[46] and, particularly, the Maori of New Zealand.[48] Investigation is currently going on among other Polynesian groups to determine whether the relationship exists for them all. Research is needed to discover possible reasons for these relationships.

Because there apparently is a sociological as well as a genetic relationship with this disease, diet has suggested itself as a possibly relevant factor. Some item of diet, or perhaps the frequency or manner of eating, the temperature at which food and drink is taken, the use of alcohol, the type of cooking, or the use of condiments may be related to protection against or predisposition to this disease. Research could profitably begin by examining the diets of the groups of varying incidence noted above. Preliminary examination of dietary data already gathered at Roswell Park Institute suggests that higher risks of the disease may be related to frequent ingestion of potatoes, beer, animal fats and to irregular eating habits (Graham & Levin, n.d.). Sociological investigations suggest that the first, second, and last of the above mentioned variables are perhaps more characteristic of the lower than the upper classes; thus, this relationship is consistent with the marked socioeconomic gradient of gastric cancer incidence. It is obvious that much research must be done on the epidemiology of this disease. Nevertheless, it is quite possible that the leads furnished by the sociological aspects of this epidemiology will be among the most valuable in directing attention to factors bringing about the tissue change known as gastric cancer.

REFERENCES

1. Abbott, A. C. Simple goitre. *Canad. Med. Ass. J.,* 1932, 27, 236–239.
2. Affifi, M. A. *Bilharzial cancer.* London: Lewis, 1948.
2a. Auerbach, O., Stout, A. P., Hammond, E. C., & Garfinkel, L. Changes in bronchial epithelium in relation to cigarette smoking and in relation to lung cancer. *New Eng. J. Med.,* August, 1961, 265, 253–267.

3. Bales, R. F. Attitudes towards drinking in the Irish culture. In D. J. Pittman and C. R. Snyder (Eds.), *Society, culture and drinking patterns.* New York: Wiley, 1962. Pp. 167-187.
4. Beadenkopf, W. Personal communication, 1963.
5. Berkson, J., & Comfort, M. The incidence of development of cancer in persons with achlorhydria. *J. nat. Cancer Inst.,* 1953, 13, 1087.

5a. Bock, F. G., Moore, G. E., Dowd, J. E., & Clark, P. C. Carcinogenic activity of cigarette smoke condensate. *J. Amer. Med. Ass.,* August, 1962, 181(8), 668–672.
6. Boe, J., Hummerfelt, S., & Wedevang, F. *The blood pressure in a population.* Bergen: A. S. John Griegs Boktrykkeri, 1956.
7. Breslow, L., & Buell, P. Mortality from coronary heart disease and physical activity of working. *J. chron. Dis.,* 1960, II, 421–444.
8. Clemmesen, J., & Nielsen, A. Social distribution of cancer in Copenhagen, 1943–1947. *Brit. J. Cancer,* 1951, 5, 159–171.
9. Cobb, S., Warren, J., Merchant, W. R., & Thompson, D. J. An estimate of the prevalence of rheumatoid arthritis. *J. chron. Dis.,* 1957, 5(6), 636–643.
10. Cohart, E. M. Socioeconomic distribution of cancer of female sex organs in New Haven. *Cancer,* 1955, 8, 34–41.
11. Comfort, M. W., Butsch, W. L., & Eusterman, G. B. Observations on gastric acidity before and after development of carcinoma of the stomach. *Amer. J. Dig. Dis. Nutrit.* 1937–1938, 4, 673–681.
12. Corriell, L. L., Schaeffer, K., Felton, H. M., Fernandez-Moran, H., & Bierly, M. Z. A serologic and clinical survey of poliomyelitis in Caracas, Venezuela, and Galveston, Texas. *Amer. J. publ. Hlth,* 1956, 46, 1431–1438.
13. Diehl, H. D., & Lees, M. D. Variability of blood pressure, II. *Arch. Int. Med.,* February, 1929, 44, 229–237.
14. Doll, R., & Hill, A. B. Lung cancer and other causes of death in relation to smoking: Second report on mortality of British doctors. *Brit. med. J.,* 1956, 2, 1071–1101.
15. Dorn, H. F. Cancer morbidity survey: A tool for testing theories of cancer etiology. Paper read at Amer. Publ. Hlth. Ass., Buffalo, October 14, 1954.
16. Dorn, H. F. Smoking and cancer. Social Statistics Section Proceedings, Amer. Stat. Ass., 1958, Chicago.
16a. Dorn, H. F. Tobacco consumption and mortality from cancer and other diseases. *Publ. Hlth. Rep.,* 1959, 74 (7), 581–593.
17. Doyle, J. T., Heslin, A. S., Hilleboe, H. E., Formel, P. F., & Korns, R. E. A progressive study of degenerative cardiovascular diseases in Albany. *Amer. J. Publ. Hlth.* 1957, 47 (4), suppl., 25–32.
18. Faris, R. E. L., & Dunham, H. W. *Mental disorders in urban areas.* Chicago: Univer. of Chicago Press, 1939.
19. Gentry, J. T., Parkhurst, Elizabeth, & Gulin, G. V., Jr. An epidemiological study of congenital malformations in New York State. *Amer. J. publ. Hlth,* 1959, 49 (4), 1–22.
20. Graham, S. Ethnic background and illness in a Pennsylvania county. *Soc. Probs,* 1956 4 (I), 76–82.
21. Graham, S. Social factors in the epidemiology of cancer at various sites. *Ann. New York Acad. Sci.,* December, 1960, 84(17), 807–815.
22. Graham, S., Levin, M. L., & Lilienfeld, A. M. The socioeconomic distribution of cancer of various sites in Buffalo, N.Y., 1948–1952. *Cancer,* 1960, 13(I), 180–191.
23. Graham, S., Levin, M. L., Lilienfeld, A. M., & Sheehe, P. Ethnic derivation as related to cancer at various sites. *Cancer,* 1963, 16(I), 13–27.
23a. Graham, S., & Lilienfeld, A. M. Genetic studies of gastric cancer in humans: An appraisal. *Cancer,* 1958, II (5), 945–958.
24. Haddon, W. Jr., Ellison, A. E., & Carroll, R. E. Skiing injuries: Epidemiological studies. *Publ. Hlth. Rep.,* 1962, 77(II), 975–985.
25. Haenszel, W. Cancer mortality among the foreign-born in the United States. *J. nat. Cancer Inst.,* 1961, 26(I), 37–132.(a).
26. Haenszel, W. Incidence of and mortality from stomach cancer in the United States. *Acta Unio Int. Contra Cancrum,* 1961, 17 (3), 347–364.(b)
27. Haggard, H. W., & Jellinek, E. M. *Alcohol explored.* New York: Doubleday, 1942.
28. Hammon, W. McD. Comparative epidemiology of poliomyelitis in certain California cities. *Amer. J. publ. Hlth.,* 1947, 37, 1545–1558.
28a. Hammond, E. C., Smoking and cancer: Consideration of some statistical aspects. Paper presented at the Annual Meeting of the American Statistical Association, New York City, December 27, 1955.
29. Hammond, E. C. The effects of smoking. *Scient. Amer.,* 1962, 207(I), 39–51.
30. Hammond, E. C., & Horn, D. Smoking and death rates – report on forty-four months of follow-up of 187,783 men. *J. Amer. Med. Ass.,* 1958, 166, 1159–1308.
31. Hollingshead, A. B., & Redlich, F. C. Social stratification and psychiatric disorders. *Amer. sociol. Rev.,* April, 1953, 18, 163–169.
31a. Horn, D., Courts, F. A., Taylor, R. M., & Solomon, E. S. Cigarette smoking among high school students. *Amer. J. publ. Hlth,* 1959, 49(II), 1497–1511.
32. Kannel, W. B., Dawber, T. R., Kagen, A., Revotskie, N., & Stokes, J., III. Factors of risk in the development of coronary heart disease – 6-year follow up experience: The Framingham study. *Ann. int. Med.,* 1961, 55, 33–50.
33. Kraus, A. S., Levin, M. L., & Gerhardt, P. R. A study of occupational associations with gastric cancer. *Amer. J. Publ. Hlth,* 1957, 47(8), 961–970.
34. Levin, M. L. Smoking and cancer: Retrospective studies and epidemiological evaluation. In G. James and T. Rosenthal (Eds.), *Tobacco and health.* Springfield, Ill.: Charles C. Thomas, 1962. Pp. 163–171.
35. Levin, M. L., Goldstein, H., & Gerhardt, P. Cancer and tobacco smoking *J. Amer. Med. Asso.,* May 27, 1950, 143, 336–338.
36. Levin, M. L., Haenszel, W., Carroll, B. E., Gerhardt, P. R., Handy, V. E., & Ingraham, S. C., II. Cancer incidence in urban and rural areas of New York State. *J. nat. Cancer Inst.,* 1960,

24 (6), 1243-1257.

36a. Lilienfeld, A. M. Diagnostic and therapeutic x-radiation in an urban population. *Publ. Hlth Rep.,* 1959, 74(I), 29-36.

37. Lilienfeld, A. M. Personal communication, 1960.

38. Lilienfeld, A. M., & Graham, S. Validity of determining circumcision status by questionnaire as related to epidemiological studies of cancer of the cervix. *J. nat. Cancer Inst.,* 1958, 21(4), 713-720.

39. McCarroll, J. R., & Haddon, W., Jr. A controlled study of fatal automobile accidents in New York City. *J chron. Dis.,* 1962, 15 (8), 811-826.

40. MacMahon, B., & Koller, E. K. Ethnic differences in the incidence of leukemia. *Blood,* 1957, 12(I), 1-10.

41. Martland, H. S. The occurrence of malignancy in radioactive persons. *Amer. J. Cancer,* 1931, 15, 2435-2516.

42. May, J. M. *The ecology of human disease.* New York: M. D. Publications, 1958.

43. New York State Department of Health, Bureau of Cancer Control, *Ann. Rep.,* 1961.

44. Pasamanick, B., & Lilienfeld, A. M. Association of maternal and fetal factors with development of mental deficiency. I. Abnormalities in the prenatal and paranatal periods. *J. Amer. Med. Ass.,* September 17, 1955, 159, 155-160.

45. Pasamanick, B., Rogers, Martha E., & Lilienfeld, A. M. Pregnancy experiences and the development of behavior disorders in children. *Amer. J. Psychiat.,* 1956, 112 (8), 613-618.

46. Quisenberry, W. B. Sociocultural factors in cancer in Hawaii. *Ann. New York Acad. Sci.,* 1960, 84 (17), 795-806.

47. Rigler, L. G., Kaplan, H. S., & Fink, D. L. Pernicious anemia and the early diagnosis of tumors of the stomach. *J. Amer. med. Ass.,* 1945, 128, 426-432.

48. Rose, R. J., Personal communication, 1963.

49. Sachs, L., & Bat-Miriam, Mariassa. The genetics of Jewish populations: I. Fingerprint patterns in Jewish populations in Israel. *Amer. J.*

Hum. Genet., 1957, 9(2), 117-126.

50. Segi, M., Fujisaku, S., & Kurihara, M. Geographical observations on cancer mortality by selected sites on the basis of standardized death rate. *Gann,* June, 1957, 48, 219-225.

51. Smith, R. L. Recorded and expected mortality among the Japanese of the United States and Hawaii with special reference to cancer. *J. nat. Cancer Inst.,* 1956, 17, 459-473.

52. Snyder, C. R. Culture and Jewish sobriety. In D. J. Pittman & C. R. Snyder (Eds.), *Society, culture and drinking patterns.* New York: Wiley, 1962. Pp. 188-225.

53. Srole, L., Langner, T., Michael, S., Opler, M. K., & Rennie, T. A. C. *Mental health in the metropolis: Midtown Manhattan study.* Vol. I. New York: McGraw, 1962.

54. Straus, R., & Bacon, S. D. *Drinking in college.* New Haven, Conn.: Yale Univer. Press, 1953.

55. Terris, M. Relation of economic status to tuberculosis mortality by age and sex. *Amer. J. publ. Hlth,* August, 1948, 38, 1061-1070.

56. Thieme, J. C. Western Samoa, unpublished data, 1963.

57. Toor, M., Katchalsky, A., Agmon, J., & Allalouf, D. Atherosis and related factors in immigrants to Israel, *Circulation,* 1960, 22, 265-279.

58. Tromp, S. W., & Diehl, J. C. A statistical study of the possible relationship between cancer of the stomach and soil. *Brit. J. Cancer,* 1955, 9(3), 349-355.

59. Woolf, C. M. A further study on the familial aspects of carcinoma of the stomach. *Amer. J. hum. Genet.,* 1956, 8 (2), 102-109.

60. World Health Organization. Malignant neoplasms according to location in selected countries. *Epidemiological and vital statistics Rep.,* 1959, 12, 181-225.

61. Wynder, E. L., & Mantel, N. Statistical considerations on circumcision and cervical cancer. *Amer. J. Obst. Gynecol.,* 1960, 79 (5), 1026-1030.

47   Culture and Symptoms — An Analysis of Patients' Presenting Complaints

Irving Kenneth Zola

THE CONCEPTION OF DISEASE

In most epidemiological studies, the definition of disease is taken for granted. Yet today's chronic disorders do not lend themselves to such easy conceptualization and measurement as did the contagious disorders of yesteryear. That we have long assumed that what constitutes disease *is* a settled matter is due to the tremendous medical and surgical advances of the past half-century. After the current battles against cancer, heart disease, cystic fibrosis and the like have been won, Utopia, a world without disease, would seem right around the next corner. Yet after each battle a new enemy seems to emerge. So often has this been the pattern, that some have wondered whether life without disease is attainable.[1]

Usually the issue of life without disease has been dismissed as a philosophical problem — a dismissal made considerably easier by our general assumptions about the statistical distribution of disorder. For though there is a grudging recognition that each of us must go sometime, illness is generally assumed to be a relatively infrequent, unusual, or abnormal phenomenon. Moreover, the general kinds of statistics used to describe illness support such an assumption. Specifically diagnosed conditions, days out of work, and doctor visits do occur for each of us relatively infrequently. Though such statistics represent

only treated illness, we rarely question whether such data give a true picture. Implicit is the further notion that people who do not consult doctors and other medical agencies (and thus do not appear in the "illness" statistics) may be regarded as healthy.

Yet studies have increasingly appeared which note the large number of disorders escaping detection. Whether based on physicians' estimates[2] or on the recall of lay populations,[3] the proportion of untreated disorders amounts to two-thirds or three-fourths of all existing conditions.[4] The most reliable data, however, come from periodic health examinations and

[1] René Dubos, *Mirage of Health,* (Garden City, N. Y.: Anchor, 1961). On more philosophical grounds, William A. White, in *The Meaning of Disease* (Baltimore: William and Wilkins, 1926), arrives at a similar conclusion.

[2] R. J. F. H. Pinsett, *Morbidity Statistics from General Practice,* Studies of Medical Populations, No. 14 (London: H. M. S. O., 1962); P. Stocks, *Sickness in the Population of England and Wales,* 1944–1947, Studies of Medical Populations, No. 2 (London: H. M. S. O., 1944); John Horder and Elizabeth Horder, "Illness in General Practice," *Practitioner,* 173 (August, 1954), 177–185.

[3] Charles R. Hoffer and Edgar A. Schuler, "Measurement of Health Needs and Health Care," *American Sociological Review,* 13 (December, 1948), 719–724; Political and Economic Planning *Family Needs and the Social Services* (London: George Allen and Unwin, 1961); Leonard S. Rosenfeld, Jacob Katz, and Avedis Donabedian, *Medical Care Needs and Services in the Boston Metropolitan Area* (Boston: Medical Care Evaluation Studies, Health, Hospitals, and Medical Care Division, United Community Services of Metropolitan Boston, 1957).

[4] That these high figures of disorder include a great many minor problems is largely irrelevant. The latter are nevertheless disorders, clinical entities, and may even be the precursors of more medically serious difficulties.

Zola, I. K.: Culture and symptoms — An analysis of patient's presenting complaints. Amer. Soc. Rev. 31: 615–630 (1966).

community "health" surveys.[5] At least two such studies have noted that as much as 90 percent of their apparently healthy sample had some physical aberration or clinical disorder.[6] Moreover, neither the type of disorder, nor the seriousness by objective medical standards, differentiated those who felt sick from those who did not. In one of the above studies, even of those who felt sick, only 40 percent were under medical care.[7] It seems that the more intensive the investigation, the higher the prevalence of clinically serious but previously undiagnosed and untreated disorders.

Such data as these give an unexpected statistical picture of illness. Instead of it

being a relatively infrequent or abnormal phenomenon, the empirical reality may be that illness, defined as the presence of clinically serious symptoms, is the statistical *norm*.[8] What is particularly striking about this line of reasoning is that the statistical notions underlying many "social" pathologies are similarly being questioned. A number of social scientists have noted that the basic acts or deviations, such as law-breaking, addictive behaviors, sexual "perversions" or mental illness, occur so frequently in the population[9] that were one to tabulate all the deviations that people possess or engage in,

[5] See for example, Commission on Chronic Illness, *Chronic Illness in a Large City* (Cambridge: Harvard University Press, 1957); Kendall A. Elsom, Stanley Schor, Thomas W. Clark, Katherine O. Elsom, and John P. Hubbard, "Periodic Health Examination – Nature and Distribution of Newly Discovered Disease in Executives," *Journal of the American Medical Association,* 172 (January, 1960), 55–61; John W. Runyan, Jr., "Periodic Health Maintenance Examination – I. Business Executives, *New York State Journal of Medicine,* 59 (March, 1959), 770–774; Robert E. Sandroni, "Periodic Health Maintenance Examination – III. Industrial Employees," *New York State Journal of Medicine,* 59 (March, 1959), 778–781; C. J. Tupper and M. B. Becket, "Faculty Health Appraisal, University of Michigan," *Industrial Medicine and Surgery,* 27 (July, 1958), 328–332; Leo Wade, John Thorpe, Thomas Elias, and George Bock, "Are Periodic Health Examinations Worth-while?" *Annals of Internal Medicine,* 56 (January, 1962), 81–93. For questionnaire studies, see Paul B. Cornerly and Stanley K. Bigman, *Cultural Considerations in Changing Health Attitudes* (Department of Preventive Medicine and Public Health, College of Medicine, Howard University, Washington, D. C., 1961); and for more general summaries, J. Wister Meigs, "Occupational Medicine," *New England Journal of Medicine,* 264 (April, 1961), 861–867; George S. Siegel, *Periodic Health Examinations – Abstracts from the Literature,* Public Health Service Publication No. 1010 (Washington, D. C.: U. S. Government Printing Office, 1963).

[6] See Innes H. Pearse and Lucy H. Crocker, *The Peckham Experiment* (London; George Allen and Unwin, 1949); *Biologists in Search of Material,* Interim Reports of the Pioneer Health Center, Peckham (London: Faber and Faber, 1938); Joseph E. Schenthal, "Multiphasic Screening of The Well Patient," *Journal of the American Medical Association,* 172 (January, 1960), 51–64.

[7] Pearse and Crocker, *op. cit.*

[8] Consider the following computation of Hinkle et al. They noted that the average lower-middle-class male between the ages of 20 and 45 experiences over a 20-year period approximately one life-endangering illness, 20 disabling illnesses, 200 nondisabling illnesses, and 1,000 symptomatic episodes. These total 1,221 episodes over 7,305 days or one new episode every six days. And this figure takes no account of the duration of a particular condition, nor does it consider any disorder of which the respondent may be unaware. In short, even among a supposedly 'healthy" population scarcely a day goes by wherein they would not be able to report a symptomatic experience. Lawrence E. Hinkle, Jr., Ruth Redmont, Norman Plummer, and Harold G. Wolff, "An Examination of the Relation between Symptoms, Disability, and Serious Illness in Two Homogeneous Groups of Men and Women," *American Journal of Public Health, 50* (September, 1960), 1327–1336.

[9] See Fred J. Murphy, Mary M. Shirley, and Helen L. Witmer, "The Incidence of Hidden Delinquency," *American Journal of Orthopsychiatry,* 16 (October, 1946), 686–696; Austin L. Porterfield, *Youth in Trouble* (Fort Worth: Leo Potishman Foundation, 1949); James F. Short and F. Ivan Nye, "Extent of Unrecorded Delinquency," *Journal of Criminal Law, Criminology, and Police Science,* 49 (December, 1958), 296–302; James S. Wallerstein and Clement J. Wyle, "Our Law-abiding Lawbreakers," *Probation,* 25 (April, 1947), 107-112; Alfred C. Kinsey, Wardell B. Pomeroy, and Clyde C. Martin, *Sexual Behavior in the Human Male* (Philadelphia: W. B. Saunders, 1953); Stanton Wheeler, "Sex Offenses: A Sociological Critique," *Law and Contemporary Problems,* 25 (Spring, 1960), 258–278; Leo Srole, Thomas S. Langner, Stanley T. Michael, Marvin K. Opler, and Thomas A. C. Rennie, *Mental Health in the Metropolis* (New York: McGraw-Hill, 1962); Dorothea C. Leighton, John S. Harding, David B. Macklin, Allister M. MacMillan, and Alexander H. Leighton, *The Character of Danger,* (New York: Basic Books, 1963).

virtually no one could escape the label of "deviant."

Why are so relatively few potential "deviants" labeled such or, more accurately, why do so few come to the attention of official agencies? Perhaps the focus on how or why a particular deviation arose in the first place might be misplaced; an equally important issue for research might be the individual and societal reaction to the deviation once it occurs.[10] Might it be the differential response to deviation rather than the prevalence of the deviation which accounts for many reported group and subgroup differences? A similar set of questions can be asked in regard to physical illness. Given that the prevalence of clinical abnormalities is so high and the rate of acknowledgment so low, how representative are "the treated" of all those with a particular condition? Given further that what *is* treated seems unrelated to what would usually be thought the objective situation, i. e., seriousness, disability, and subjective discomfort, is it possible that some selective process is operating in what gets counted or tabulated as illness?

THE INTERPLAY OF CULTURE AND "SYMPTOMS"

Holding in abeyance the idea that many epidemiological differences may in fact be due to as yet undiscovered etiological forces, we may speculate on how such differences come to exist, or how a selective process of attention may operate. Upon surveying many cross-cultural comparisons of morbidity, we concluded that there are at least two ways in which signs ordinarily defined as indicating problems in one population may be ignored in others.[11] The first is related to the actual prevalence of the sign, and the second to its congruence with dominant or major value-orientations.

In the first instance, when the aberration is fairly widespread, this, in itself, might constitute a reason for its not being considered "symptomatic" or unusual. Among many Mexican-Americans in the Southwestern United States, diarrhea, sweating and coughing are everyday experiences,[12] while among certain groups of Greeks trachoma is almost universal.[13] Even within our own society, Koos has noted that, although lower back pain is a quite common condition among lower-class women, it is not considered symptomatic of any disease or disorder but part of their expected everyday existence.[14] For the population where the particular condition is ubiquitous, the condition is perceived as the normal state.[15] This does not mean that it is considered "good" (although

[10] As seen in the work of Howard S. Becker, *Outsiders* (Glencoe, Ill.: The Free Press, 1963); Kai T. Erikson, "Notes on the Sociology of Deviance," *Social Problems,* 9 (Spring, 1962), 307-314; Erving Goffman, *Stigma — Notes on the Management of Spoiled Identity* (Englewood Cliffs, N. J.: Prentice-Hall, 1963); Wendall Johnson, *Stuttering* (Minneapolis: University of Minnesota Press, 1961); John I. Kitsuse, "Societal Reaction to Deviant Behavior: Problems of Theory and Method," in Howard S. Becker, ed., *The Other Side* (Glencoe, Ill.: The Free Press, 1964) pp. 87-102; Edwin M. Lemert, *Social Pathology* (New York: McGraw-Hill, 1951); Thomas J. Scheff, "The Societal Reaction to Deviance: Ascriptive Elements in the Psychiatric Screening of Mental Patients in a Midwestern State," *Social Problems,* 11 (Spring, 1964), 401-413.

[11] Here we are dealing solely with factors influencing the perception of certain conditions as symptoms. A host of other factors influence a second stage in this process, i. e., once perceived as a symptom, what, if anything, is done. See, for example, Edward S. Suchman, "Stages of Illness and Medical Care," *Journal of Health and Human Behavior* 6 (Fall, 1965), 114-128. Such mechanisms, by determining whether or not certain conditions are treated, would also affect their over- or under-representation in medical statistics.
[12] Margaret Clark, *Health in the Mexican-American Culture* (Berkeley: University of California Press, 1958).
[13] Richard H. Blum, *The Management of the Doctor-Patient Relationship* (New York: McGraw-Hill, 1960), p. 11.
[14] Earl L. Koos, *The Health of Regionville* (New York: Columbia University Press, 1954).
[15] Erwin W. Ackerknecht, "The Role of Medical History in Medical Education," *Bulletin of History of Medicine,* 21 (March-April, 1947), 135-145; Allan B. Raper, "The Incidence of Peptic Ulceration in Some African Tribal Groups," *Transactions of the Royal Society of Tropical Medicine and Hygiene,* 152 (November, 1958), 535-546.

instances have been noted where not having the endemic condition was considered abnormal)[16] but rather that it is natural and inevitable and thus to be ignored as being of no consequence. Because the "symptom" or condition is omnipresent (it always was and always will be) there simply exists for such populations or cultures no frame of reference according to which it could be considered a deviation.[17]

In the second process, it is the "fit" of certain signs with a society's major values which accounts for the degree of attention they receive. For example, in some nonliterate societies there is anxiety-free acceptance of and willingness to describe hallucinatory experiences. Wallace noted that in such societies the fact of hallucination *per se* is seldom disturbing; its content is the focus of interest. In Western society, however, with its emphasis on rationality and control, the very admission of hallucinations is commonly taken to be a grave sign and, in some literature, regarded as the essential feature of psychosis.[18] In such instances it is not the sign itself or its frequency which is significant but the social context within which it occurs and within which it is perceived and understood. Even more explicit workings of this process can be seen in the interplay of "symptoms" and social roles. Tiredness, for example, is a physical sign which is not only ubiquitous but a correlate of a vast number of disorders. Yet among a group of the author's students who kept a calendar noting all bodily states and conditions, tiredness, though often recorded, was rarely cited as a cause for concern. Attending school and being among peers who stressed the importance of hard work and achievement, almost as an end in itself, tiredness, rather than being an indication of something being wrong was instead positive proof that they were doing right. If they were tired, it must be because they had been working hard. In such a setting tiredness would rarely, in itself, be either a cause for concern, a symptom, or a reason for action or seeking medical aid.[19] On the other hand, where arduous work is not gratifying in and of itself, tiredness would more likely be a matter for concern and perhaps medical attention.[20]

Also illustrative of this process are the divergent perceptions of those bodily complaints often referred to as "female troubles."[21] Nausea is a common and treatable concomitant of pregnancy, yet Margaret Mead records no morning sickness among the Arapesh; her data suggest that this may be related to the almost complete denial that a child exists, until shortly before birth.[22] In a Christian setting,

---

[16] For example, Ackerknecht, *op. cit.,* noted that pinto (dichromic spirochetosis), a skin disease, was so common among some South American tribes that the few single men who were not suffering from it were regarded as pathological to the degree of being excluded from marriage.

[17] It is no doubt partly for this reason that many public health programs flounder when transported *in toto* to a foreign culture. In such a situation, when an outside authority comes in and labels a particularly highly prevalent condition a disease, and, as such, both abnormal and preventable, he is postulating an external standard of evaluation which, for the most part, is incomprehensible to the receiving culture. To them it simply has no cognitive reality.

[18] Anthony F. C. Wallace, "Cultural Determinants of Response to Hallucinatory Experience," *Archives of General Psychiatry,* (July, 1959), 58–69. With the increased use of LSD, psychodelics, and so forth, within our own culture such a statement might have to be qualified.

[19] For the specific delineation of this process, I am grateful to Barbara L. Carter, "Non-Physiological Dimensions of Health and Illness" unpublished manuscript.

[20] Dr. John D. Stoeckle, in a personal communication, has noted that such a problem is often the presenting complaint of the "trapped housewife" syndrome. For detail on the latter see Betty Friedan, *The Feminine Mystique* (New York: Dell, 1963); and Richard E. Gordon, Katherine K. Gordon, and Max Gunther, *The Split-Level Trap* (New York: Dell, 1962). We realize, of course, that tiredness here might be more related to depression than any degree of physical exertion. But this does not alter how it is perceived and reacted to once it occurs.

[21] This section on "female troubles" was suggested by the following readings: Simone de Beauvoir, *The Second Sex* (New York: Knopf, 1957); Helene Deutsch, *The Psychology of Women* (New York: Grune & Stratton, 1944), and Margaret Mead, *Male and Female* (New York: Morrow, 1949).

[22] Margaret Mead, *Sex and Temperament in Three Primitive Societies* (New York: Mentor, 1950).

where the existence of life is dated from conception, nausea becomes the external sign, hope, and proof that one is pregnant. Thus in the United States, this symptom is not only quite widespread but is also an expected and almost welcome part of pregnancy. A quite similar phenomenon is the recognition of dysmenorrhea. While Arapesh women reported no pain during menstruation, quite the contrary is reported in the United States.[23] Interestingly enough, the only consistent factor related to its manifestation among American women was a learning one — those that manifested it reported having observed it in other women during their childhood.[24]

From such examples as these, it seems likely that the degree of recognition and treatment of certain gynecological problems may be traced to the prevailing definition of what constitutes "the necessary part of the business of being a woman."[25] That such divergent definitions are still operative is shown by two recent studies. In the first, 78 mothers of lower socioeconomic status were required to keep health calendars over a four-week period. Despite the instruction to report *all* bodily states and dysfunctions, only 14 noted even the occurrence of menses or its accompaniments.[26] A second study done on a higher socioeconomic group yielded a different expression of the same phenomenon. Over a period of several years the author collected four-week health calendars from students. The women in the sample had at least a college education and virtually all were committed to careers in the behavioral sciences. Within this group there was little failure to report menses; very often medication was taken for the discomforts of dysmenorrhea. Moreover, this group was so psychologically sophisticated or self-conscious that they interpreted or questioned most physical signs or symptoms as attributable to some psychosocial stress. There was only one exception — dysmenorrhea. Thus, even in this "culturally advantaged" group, this seemed a sign of a bodily condition so ingrained in what one psychiatrist has called "the masochistic character of her sex" that the woman does not ordinarily subject it to analysis.

In the opening section of this paper, we presented evidence that a selective process might well be operating in what symptoms are brought to the doctor. We also noted that it might be this selective process and not an etiological one which accounts for the many unexplained or overexplained epidemiological differences observed be-

---

[23] Mead, *op. cit.*, 1949. As far as the Arapesh are concerned, Mead does note that this lack of perception may be related to the considerable sefl-induced discomfort prescribed for women during menstruation.

[24] Reported in Mead, *ibid.* The fact that one has to learn that something is painful or unpleasant has been noted elsewhere. Mead reports that in causalgia a given individual suffers and reports pain because she is *aware* of uterine contractions and not because of the occurrence of these contractions. Becker, *op. cit.*, 1963, and others studying addictive behaviors have noted not only that an individual has to learn that the experience is pleasurable but also that a key factor in becoming addicted is the recognition of the association of withdrawal symptoms with the lack of drugs. Among medical patients who had been heavily dosed and then withdrawn, even though they experience symptoms as a result of withdrawal, they may attribute them to their general convalescent aches and pains. Stanley Schacter and Jerome Singer, "Cognitive, Social, and Physiological Determinants of Emotional State," *Psychological Review,* 69 (September, 1962), 379–387, have recently reported a series of experiments where epinephrine-injected subjects defined their mood as euphoria or anger depending on whether they spent time with a euphoric or angry stooge. Subjects without injections reported no such change in mood responding to these same social situations. This led them to the contention that the diversity of human emotional experiences stems from differential labeling of similar physical sensations.

[25] A term used by Drs. R. Green and K. Dalton, as quoted in Hans Selye, *The Stress of Life* (New York: McGraw-Hill, 1956), p. 177.

[26] John Kosa, Joel Alpert, M. Ruth Pickering, and Robert J. Haggerty, "Crisis and Family Life: A Re-Examination of Concepts," *The Wisconsin Sociologist,* 4 (Summer, 1965), 11–19.

tween and within societies.[27] (There may even be no "real" differences in the prevalence rates of many deviations.[28] Such selective processes are probably present at all the stages through which an individual and his condition must pass before he ultimately gets counted as "ill." In this section we have focused on one of these stages, the perception of a particular bodily state as a symptom, and have delineated two possible ways in which the culture or social setting might influence the awareness of something as abnormal and thus its eventual tabulation in medical statistics.

[27] For example, Saxon Graham, "Ethnic Background and Illness in a Pennsylvania County," *Social Problems,* 4 (July, 1956), 76–81, noted a significantly higher incidence of hernia among men whose backgrounds were Southern European (Italy or Greece) as compared with Eastern European (Austria, Czechoslovakia, Russia, or Poland). Analysis of the occupations engaged in by these groups revealed no evidence that the Southern Europeans in the sample were more engaged in strenuous physical labor than the Eastern Europeans. From what is known of tolerance to hernia, we suggest that, for large segments of the populations, there may be no differences in the actual incidence and prevalence of hernia but that in different groups different perceptions of the same physical signs may lead to dissimilar ways of handling them. Thus the Southern Europeans in Graham's sample may have been more concerned with problems in this area of the body, and have sought aid more readily (and therefore appear more frequently in the morbidity statistics). Perhaps the Southern Europeans are acting quite rationally and consistently while the other groups are so threatened or ashamed that they tend to deny or mask such symptoms and thus keep themselves out of the morbidity statistics.

[28] In studying the rates of peptic ulcer among African tribal groups Raper, *op. cit.,* first confirmed the stereotype that it was relatively infrequent among such groups and therefore that it was associated (as many had claimed) with the stresses and strains of modern living. Yet when he relied not on reported diagnosis but on autopsy data, he found that the scars of peptic ulcer were no less common than in Britain. He concluded: "There is no need to assume that in backward communities peptic ulcer does not develop; it is only more likely to go undetected because the conditions that might bring it to notice do not exist."

SAMPLE SELECTION AND METHODOLOGY

The investigation to be reported here is not an attempt to prove that the foregoing body of reasoning is correct but rather to demonstrate the fruitfulness of the orientation in understanding the problems of health and illness. This study reports the existence of a selective process in what the patient "brings" to a doctor. The selectiveness is analyzed not in terms of differences in diseases but rather in terms of differences in responses to essentially similar disease entities.

Specifically, this paper is a documentation of the influence of "culture" (in this case ethnic-group membership) on "symptoms" (the complaints a patient presents to his physician.) The measure of "culture" was fairly straightforward. The importance of ethnic groups in Boston, where the study was done, has been repeatedly documented;[29] ethnicity seemed a reasonable urban counterpart of the cultures so often referred to in the previous pages. The sample was drawn from the outpatient clinics of the Massachusetts General Hospital and the Massachusetts Eye and Ear Infirmary; it was limited to those new patients of both sexes between 18 and 50 who were white, able to converse in English, and of either Irish Catholic, Italian Catholic, or Anglo-Saxon Protestant background.[30] These were the most numerous ethnic groups in the clinics; together they constituted approximately 50 percent of all patients. The actual interviewing took place at the three clinics to which these patients were most fre-

[29] Oscar Handlin, *Race and Nationality in American Life* (Garden City, N. Y.: Doubleday, 1957); Oscar Handlin, *Boston's Immigrants* (Cambridge: Harvard University Press, 1959).
[30] Ethnicity was ascertained by the responses to several questions: what the patients considered their nationality to be; the birthplaces of themselves, their parents, their maternal and paternal grandparents; and, if the answers to all of these were American, they were also asked whence their ancestors originated. For details, see Irving Kenneth Zola, *Sociocultural Factors in the Seeking of Medical Aid,* unpublished doctoral dissertation, Harvard University, Department of Social Relations, 1962.

quently assigned (the three largest outpatient clinics): the Eye Clinic, the Ear, Nose and Throat Clinic, and the Medical Clinic.

In previous research the specific method of measuring and studying symptoms has varied among case record analysis, symptom checklists, and interviews. The data have been either retrospective or projective, that is, requesting the subject either to recall symptoms experienced during a specific time period or to choose symptoms which would bother him sufficiently to seek medical aid.[31] Such procedures do not provide data on the complaints which people actually bring to a doctor, a fact of particular importance in light of the many investigations pointing to the lack of, and distortions in, recall of sickness episodes. [32] An equally serious problem is the effect of what the doctor, medicine-man, or health expert may tell the patient on the latter's subsequent perceptions of and recall about his ailment.[33] We resolved these problems by restricting the sample to new patients on their first medical visit to the clinics and by interviewing them during the waiting period *before* they were seen by a physician.[34]

The primary method of data collection was a focused open-ended interview dealing with the patient's own or family's responses to his presenting complaints. Interspersed throughout the interview were a number of more objective measures of the patient's responses — checklists, forced-choice comparisons, attitudinal items, and scales. Other information included a demographic background questionnaire, a review of the medical record, and a series of ratings by each patient's examining physician as to the primary diagnosis, the secondary diagnosis, the potential seriousness, and the degree of clinical urgency (i.e., the necessity that the patient be seen immediately) of the patient's presenting complaint.

THE PATIENT AND HIS ILLNESS

The data are based on a comparison between 63 Italians (34 female, 29 male) and 81 Irish (42 female, 39 male), who were new admissions to the Eye, the Ear, Nose, and Throat, and the Medical Clinics of the Massachusetts General Hospital and the Massachusetts Eye and Ear Infirmary, seen between July, 1960, and February, 1961.[35] The mean age of each ethnic group

---

[31] The range of methods includes case research analysis — Berta Fantl and Joseph Schiro, "Cultural Variables in the Behavior Patterns and Symptom Formation of 15 Irish and 15 Italian Female Schizophrenics," *International Journal of Social Psychiatry*, 4 (Spring, 1959) 245-253; checklists — Cornely and Bigman, *op. cit.*; standardized questionnaires — Sidney H. Croog, "Ethnic Origins and Responses to Health Questionnaires," *Human Organization*, 20 (Summer, 1961), 65-69; commitment papers — John B. Enright and Walter R. Jaeckle, "Psychiatric Symptoms and Diagnosis in Two Subcultures," *International Journal of Social Psychiatry*, 9 (Winter, 1963), 12-17; interview and questionnaire — Graham, *op. cit.*; Mark Zborowski, "Cultural Components in Response to Pain," *Journal of Social Issues*, 8 (Fall, 1952), 16-30; interview and psychological tests — Marvin K. Opler and Jerome L. Singer, "Ethnic Differences in Behavior and Psychopathology: Italian and Irish," *International Journal of Social Psychiatry*, 2 (Summer, 1956), 11-12; observation — Clark, *op. cit.*; and Lyle Saunders, *op. cit.*

[32] See Jacob J. Feldman. "The Household Interview Survey as a Technique for the Collection of Morbidity Data," *Journal of Chronic Diseases*, 11 (May, 1960), 535-557; Theodore D. Woolsey, "The Health Survey," presented at the session, "The Contributions of Research in the Field of Health," 1959 AAPOR Conference, May, 1959, Lake George, New York.

[33] Charles Kadushin, "The Meaning of Presenting Problems: A Sociology of Defense," paper read at the 1962 annual meeting of the American Sociological Association.

[34] This particular methodological choice was also determined by the nature of the larger study, that is, how patients decided to seek medical aid, where the above-mentioned problems loom even larger. While only new admissions were studied, a number of patients had been referred by another medical person. Subsequent statistical analysis revealed no important differences between this group and those for whom the Massachusetts General Hospital or the Massachusetts Eye and Ear Infirmary was the initial source of help.

[35] Forty-three Anglo-Saxons were also interviewed but are not considered in this analysis. They were dropped from this report because they differed from the Irish and Italians in various respects other than ethnicity: they included more students, more divorced and separated, more people living away from home, and more downwardly mobile; they were of higher socioeconomic and educational level, and a majority were fourth generation and beyond.

(male and female computed separately) was approximately thirty-three. While most patients were married, there was, in the sample, a higher proportion of single Irish men — a finding of other studies involving the Irish[36] and not unexpected from our knowledge of Irish family structure. [37] Most respondents had between 10 and 12 years of schooling, but only about 30 percent of the males claimed to have graduated from high school as compared with nearly 60 percent of the females. There were no significant differences on standard measures of social class, though in education, social class, occupation of the breadwinner in the patient's family, and the occupation of the patient's father, the Irish ranked slightly higher.[38] The Italians were overwhelmingly American-born children of foreign parents: about 80 percent were second generation while 20 percent were third. Among the Irish about 40 percent were second generation, 30 percent third, and 30 percent fourth.

With regard to general medical coverage, there were no apparent differences between the ethnic groups. Approximately 62 percent of the sample had health insurance, a figure similar to the compar-

able economic group in the Rosenfeld survey of Metropolitan Boston.[39] Sixty percent had physicians whom they would call family doctors. The Irish tended more than the Italians to perceive themselves as having poor health, claiming more often they had been seriously ill in the past. This was consistent with their reporting of the most recent visit to a doctor: nine of the Irish but none of the Italians claimed to have had a recent major operation (e.g., appendectomy) or illness (e.g., pneumonia). Although there were no differences in the actual seriousness of their present disorders (according to the doctor's ratings) there was a tendency for the examining physician to consider the Irish as being in more urgent need of treatment. It was apparent that the patients were not in the throes of an acute illness, although they may have been experiencing an acute episode. There was a slight tendency for the Irish, as a group, to have had their complaints longer. More significantly, the women of both groups claimed to have borne their symptoms for a longer time than the men.

In confining the study to three clinics, we were trying not only to economize but

TABLE 47-1. DISTRIBUTION OF IRISH AND ITALIAN CLINIC ADMISSIONS BY LOCATION OF CHIEF COMPLAINT

Location of Complaint	Italian	Irish[a]
Eye, ear, nose, or throat	34	61
Other parts of the body	29	17
Total	63	78

Note: X^2 =9.31, p<.01.
[a]Since 3 Irish patients (two women, one man) claimed to be asymptomatic, no location could be determined from their viewpoint.

[36] Opler and Singer, *op. cit.*
[37] Conrad M. Arensberg and Solon T. Kimball, *Family and Community in Ireland* (Cambridge: Harvard University Press, 1948).
[38] In Warner's terms (W. Lloyd Warner, *Social Class in America,* Chicago: Science Research Associates, 1949), the greatest number of patients was in Class V. Only a small proportion of new Irish and Italian patients were what might be traditionally labeled as charity cases, although by some criteria they were perhaps "medically indigent."

also to limit the range of illnesses. The latter was necessary for investigating differential responses to essentially similar conditions.[40] Yet at best this is only an approximate control. To resolve this difficulty,

[39] Rosenfeld, *op. cit.*
[40] This is similar to Zborowski's method, in his study of pain reactions, of confining his investigation to patients on certain specified wards. *Op. cit.*

TABLE 47-2. DISTRIBUTION OF IRISH AND ITALIAN CLINIC ADMISSIONS
BY PART OF THE BODY CONSIDERED MOST IMPORTANT

Most Important Part of the Body	Italian	Irish
Eye, ear, nose, or throat	6	26
Other parts of the body	57	55
Total	63	81

Note: $X^2 = 10.50$, p<.01.

after all initial comparisons were made between the ethnic groups as a whole, the data were examined for a selected sub-sample with a specific control for diagnosis. This subsample consisted of matched pairs of one Irish and one Italian of the same sex, who had the same primary diagnosis, and whose disorder was of approximately the same duration and was rated by the examining physician as similar in degree of "seriousness." Where numbers made it feasible, there was a further matching on age, marital status, and education. In all, thirty-seven diagnostically matched pairs (18 female and 19 male) were created; these constituted the final test of any finding of the differential response to illness.[41]

---

[41] These pairs included some eighteen distinct diagnoses: conjunctivitis; eyelid disease (e. g., blepharitis); myopia; hyperopia; vitreous opacities; impacted cerumen; external otitis; otitis media; otosclerosis; deviated septum; sinusitis; nasopharyngitis; allergy; thyroid; obesity; functional complaints; no pathology; psychological problems.
To give some indication of the statistical significance of these comparisons, a sign test was used. For the sign test, a "tie" occurs when it is not possible to discriminate between a matched pair on the variable under study, or when the two scores earned by any pair are equal. All tied cases were dropped from the analysis, and the probabilities were computed only on the total N's excluding ties. In our study there were many ties. In the nature of our hypotheses, as will appear subsequently, a tie means that at least one member of the pair was in the predicted direction. Despite the problem, the idea of a diagnostically matched pair was retained because it seemed to convey the best available test of our data. Because there were specific predictions as to the direction of differences the probabilities were computed on the basis of a one-tailed sign test. This was used to retest the findings of Tables 47-1 to 47-6. See Sidney Siegel. *Non-Parametric Statistics for the Behavioral Sciences* (New York: McGraw-Hill, 1956), pp. 68–75.

LOCATION AND QUALITY OF PRESENTING COMPLAINTS

In the folklore of medical practice, the supposed opening question is, "Where does it hurt?" This query provides the starting point of our analysis — the perceived location of the patient's troubles. Our first finding is that more Irish than Italians tended to locate their chief problem in either the eye, the ear, the nose, or the throat (and more so for females than for males). The same tendency was evident when all patients were asked what they considered to be the most important part of their body and the one with which they would be most concerned if something went wrong. Here, too, significantly more Irish emphasized difficulties of the eye, the ear, the nose, or the throat. That this reflected merely a difference in the conditions for which they were seeking aid is doubtful since the two other parts of the body most frequently referred to were heart and "mind" locations, and these represent only 3 percent of the primary diagnoses of the entire sample. In the retesting of these findings on diagnostically matched pairs, while there were a great many ties, the general directions were still consistent.[42] Thus even when Italians had a diagnosed eye or ear disorder, they did not locate their chief complaints there, nor did they focus their future concern on these locations.

---

[42] For the prediction that the Irish would locate their chief complaint in eye, ear, nose or throat, and the Italians in some other part, 8 matched diagnostic pairs were in favor of the hypothesis, 1 against, 28 ties (p=.02); for the same with respect to most important part of the body there were 12 in favor of the hypothesis, 2 against, 23 ties (p=.006).

TABLE 47-3. DISTRIBUTION OF IRISH AND ITALIAN CLINIC
ADMISSIONS BY PRESENCE OF PAIN IN THEIR CURRENT ILLNESS

Presence of Pain	Italian	Irish
No	27	54
Yes	36	27
Total	63	81

Note: $X^2 = 10.26$, $p < .01$.

Pain, the commonest accompaniment of illness, was the dimension of patients' symptoms to which we next turned. Pain is an especially interesting phenomenon since there is considerable evidence that its tolerance and perception are not purely physiological responses and do not necessarily reflect the degree of objective discomfort induced by a particular disorder or experimental procedure.[43] In our study not only did the Irish more often than the Italians deny that pain was a feature of their illness but this difference held even for those patients with the same disorder.[44] When the Irish were asked directly about the presence of pain, some hedged their replies with qualifications. ("It was more a throbbing than a pain . . . not really pain, it feels more like sand in my eye.") Such comments indicated that the patients were reflecting something more than an objective reaction to their physical conditions.

While there were no marked differences in the length, frequency, or noticeability of their symptoms, a difference did emerge in the ways in which they described the quality of the physical difficulty embodied in their chief complaint. Two types of difficulty were distinguished; one was of a more limited nature and emphasized a circumscribed and specific dysfunctioning; the second emphasized a difficulty of a grosser and more diffuse quality.[45] When the patients' complaints were analyzed according to these two types, proportionately more Irish described their chief problem in terms of specific dysfunction while proportionately more Italians spoke of a diffuse difficulty. Once again, the findings for diagnostically matched pairs were in the predicted directions.[46]

Diffuse Versus Specific Reactions

What seems to emerge from the above is a picture of the Irish limiting and understating their difficulties and the Italians spreading and generalizing theirs. Two other pieces of information were consistent with this interpretation: first, an enumeration of the symptoms an individual presented — a phenomenon which might reflect how diffusely the complaint was perceived; second, the degree to which each patient felt his illness affected aspects of life other than purely physical behavior.

[43] William P. Chapman and Chester M. Jones, "Variations in Cutaneous and Visceral Pain Sensitivity in Normal Subjects," *Journal of Clinical Investigation,* 23 (January, 1944), 81–91; James D. Hardy, Harold G. Wolff, and Helen Goodell, *Pain Sensations and Reactions* (Baltimore: Williams and Wilkins, 1952); Ronald Melzack, "The Perception of Pain," *Scientific American,* 204 (February, 1961), 41–49; Harry S. Olin and Thomas P. Hackett, "The Denial of Chest Pain in 32 Patients with Acute Myocardial Infection," *Journal of the American Medical Association,* 190 (December, 1964), 977–981; Zborowski, *op. cit.*

[44] For the prediction that Italians would admit the presence of pain and the Irish would deny it, 16 matched diagnostic pairs were in favor of the hypothesis, 0 against, 21 ties (p=.001).

[45] Complaints of the first type emphasized a somewhat limited difficulty and dysfunction best exemplified by something specific, e. g., an organ having gone wrong in a particular way. The second type seemed to involve a more attenuated kind of problem whose location and scope were less determinate, and whose description was finally more qualitative and less measurable.

[46] For the prediction that the Italians would emphasize a diffuse difficulty and the Irish a specific one; there were 10 diagnostically matched pairs in favor, 0 against, 27 ties, (p=.001).

TABLE 47-4. DISTRIBUTION OF IRISH AND ITALIAN CLINIC ADMISSIONS BY QUALITY OF PHYSICAL DIFFICULTY EMBODIED IN CHIEF COMPLAINT

Quality of Physical Difficulty	Italian	Irish[a]
Problems of a diffuse nature	43	33
Problems of a specific nature	20	45
Total	63	78

Note: $X^2 = 9.44$, $p < .01$.
[a]Since 3 Irish patients (two women, one man) claimed to be asymptomatic, no rating of the quality of physical difficulty could be determined from their viewpoint.

The first measure of this specific-diffuse dimension — number of distinguishable symptoms[47] — was examined in three ways: (1) the total number presented by each patient; (2) the total number of different bodily areas in which the patient indicated he had complaints, e. g., back, stomach, legs; (3) the total number of different qualities of physical difficulty embodied in the patient's presenting complaints.[48] The ethnic differences were consistent with the previous findings. Compared to the Irish, the Italians presented significantly more symptoms, had symptoms in significantly more bodily locations, and noted significantly more types of bodily dysfunction.[49]

The second analysis, the degree to which a patient felt his illness affected his more general well-being, was derived from replies to three questions: (1) Do you think your symptoms affected how you got along with your family? (2) Did you become more irritable? (3) What would you say has bothered you most about your symptoms?[50] An admission-of-irritability scale was created by classifying an affirmative response to any of the three questions as an admission that the symptoms affected extraphysical performance. As seen in

TABLE 47-5. DISTRIBUTION OF IRISH AND ITALIAN CLINIC ADMISSIONS BY NUMBER OF PRESENTING COMPLAINTS*

Number of Presenting Complaints	Italian	Irish
Zero	0	3
One	5	21
Two	15	22
Three	14	16
Four	10	7
Five	9	7
Six or more	10	5
Total	63	81

Note: $p < .001$.
*The Mann-Whitney. U-test was used. Probabilities were computed for one-tailed tests. They are, however, slightly "conservative"; with a correction for ties, the probabilities or levels of significance would have been even lower. See Siegel, op. cit., pp. 116–127.

[47] This number could be zero, as in a situation where the patient denied the presence of any difficulty, but others around him disagreed and so made the appointment for him or "forced" him to see a doctor.
[48] Qualities of physical difficulty were categorized under nine headings.

[49] The distributions for these two tables closely resemble those of Table 47-5 (p=.018 for bodily locations; p=.003 for types of bodily dysfunction).
[50] For the latter question, the patient was presented with a card on which were listed eight aspects of illness and/or symptoms which might bother him. One of these statements was, "That it made you irritable and difficult to get along with."

TABLE 47-6.   DISTRIBUTION OF IRISH AND ITALIAN CLINIC ADMISSIONS BY
RESPONSES TO THREE QUESTIONS CONCERNING ADMISSION OF IRRITABILITY
AND EFFECT OF SYMPTOMS ON INTERPERSONAL BEHAVIOR

Response Pattern	Italian	Irish
No on all three questions	22	47
Yes on at least one question	41	34
Total	63	81

Note: $X^2 = 7.62$, $p < .01$.

Table 47-6, the Irish were more likely than the Italians to state that their disorders had not affected them in this manner. Here again the asides by the Irish suggested that their larger number of negative responses reflected considerable denial rather than a straightforward appraisal of their situation.

To examine these conclusions in a more rigorous manner, we turned to our subsample of matched diagnostic pairs. In general, the pattern and direction of the hypotheses were upheld.[51] Thus, even for the same diagnosis, the Italians expressed and complained of more symptoms, more bodily areas affected, and more kinds of dysfunctions, than did the Irish, and more often felt that their symptoms affected their interpersonal behavior.

The composite on p. 555 offers a final illustration of how differently these patients reacted to and perceived their illnesses. Each set of responses was given by an Italian and an Irish patient of similar age and sex with a disorder of approximately the same duration and with the same primary and secondary diagnosis (if there was one). In the first two cases, the Irish patient focused on a specific malfunctioning as the main concern while the Italian did not even mention this aspect of the problem but went on to mention more

diffuse qualities of his condition. The last four responses contrast the Italian and Irish response to questions of pain and interpersonal relations.

SOCIOCULTURAL COMMUNICATION

What has so far been demonstrated is the systematic variability with which bodily conditions may be perceived and communicated. Until now the empirical findings have been presented without interpretation. Most of the data are quite consistent with those reported by other observers.[52] Although no data were collected in our investigation on the specific mechanics of the interplay between being a member of a specific subculture and the communication of "symptoms," some speculation on this seems warranted.

---

[51] For the prediction that the Italians would have more symptoms in all instances, there were for total number, 24 matched diagnostic pairs in favor of hypothesis, 7 against, 6 ties (p=.005); for number of different locations, 16 in favor, 5 against, 16 ties (p=.013); for number of different qualities of physical difficulties, 22 in favor, 9 against, 6 ties, (p=.025). For the prediction that Italians would admit irritability and Irish would deny it, there were 17 in favor, 6 against, 14 ties (p=.017).

[52] The whole specific-diffuse pattern and the generalizing-withholding illness behavior dovetails neatly with the empirical findings of Opler and Singer, op. cit., Fantl and Schiro, op. cit., and Paul Barrabee and Otto von Mering, "Ethnic Variations in Mental Stress in Families with Psychotic Children," *Social Problems,* 1 (October, 1953), 48–53. The specific emphasis on expressiveness has been detailed especially by Zborowski, op. cit., and the several studies of Italian mental patients done by Anne Parsons, "Some Comparative Observations on Ward Social Structure: Southern Italy, England, and the United States," *Tipografia dell' Ospedale Psichiatrico,* Napoli, April, 1959; "Family Dynamics in Southern Italian Schizophrenics," *Archives of General Psychiatry,* 3 (November, 1960), 507–518; "Patriarchal and Matriarchal Authority in the Neapolitan Slum, *Psychiatry,* 24 (May, 1961), 109–121. The contrast on number of symptoms has been noted by Croog, op. cit., and Graham, op. cit.

Diagnosis	Question	Irish Patient	Italian Patient
1. Presbyopia and hyperopia	What seems to be the trouble?	I can't see to thread a needle or read a paper.	I have a constant headache and my eyes seem to get red and burny.
	Anything else?	No, I can't recall any.	No, just that it lasts all day long and I even wake up with it sometimes.
2. Myopia	What seems to be the trouble?	I can't see across the street.	My eyes seem very burny, especially the right eye . . . Two or three months ago I woke up with my eyes swollen. I bathed it and it did go away but there was still the burny sensation.
	Anything else?	I had been experiencing headaches, but it may be that I'm in early menopause.	Yes there always seems to be a red spot beneath this eye . . . .
	Anything else?	No.	Well, my eyes feel very heavy . . . at night they bother me most.
3. Otitis externa A.D.	Is there any pain?	There's a congestion . . . but it's a pressure, not really a pain.	Yes . . . If I rub it, it disappears . . . I had a pain from my shoulder up to my neck and thought it might be a cold.
4. Pharyngitis	Is there any pain?	No, maybe a slight headache but nothing that lasts.	Yes, I have had a headache a few days. Oh, yes, every time I swallow it's annoying.
5. Presbyopia and hyperopia	Do you think the symptoms affected how you got along with your family? your friends?	No, I have had loads of trouble. I can't imagine this bothering me.	Yes, when I have a headache, I'm very irritable, very tense, very short-tempered.
6. Deafness, hearing loss	Did you become more irritable?	No, not me . . . maybe everybody else but not me.	Oh, yes . . . the least little thing aggravates me . . . and I take it out on the children.

In theorizing about the interplay of culture and symptoms particular emphasis was given to the "fit" of certain bodily states with dominant value orientations. The empirical examples for the latter were drawn primarily from data on social roles. Of course, values are evident on even more general levels, such as formal and informal societal sanctions and the culture's orientation to life's basic problems. With an orientation to problems usually goes a preferred solution or way of handling them.[53] Thus a society's values may also be reflected in such preferred solutions. One behavioral manifestation of this is defense mechanisms – a part of the everyday way individuals have of dealing with their everyday stresses and strains.[54] We contend that illness and its treatment (from taking medicine to seeing a physician) is one of these everyday stresses and strains, an anxiety-laden situation which calls forth coping or defense mechanisms.[55] From this general reasoning, we would thus speculate that Italian and Irish ways of communicating illness may reflect major values and preferred ways of handling problems within the culture itself.[56]

---

[53] Florence R. Kluckhohn, "Dominant and Variant Value Orientations," in *Personality in Nature, Society, and Culture,* 2nd ed., Clyde Kluckhohn, Henry A. Murray, and David M. Schneider, eds. (New York: Knopf, 1956), pp. 342–357; Florence R. Kluckhohn and Fred L. Strodtbeck, *Variations in Value Orientations* (Evanston, Ill.: Row Peterson, 1961); John Spiegel, "Some Cultural Aspects of Transference and Counter-Transference," in *Individual and Family Dynamics,* Jules H. Hasserman, ed. (New York: Grune & Stratton, 1959), pp. 160–182; John P. Spiegel, "Conflicting Formal and Informal Roles in Newly Acculturated Families," in *Disorders of Communication,* 42 (Research Publications, Association for Research in Nervous and Mental Disease, 1964), pp. 307–316; John P. Spiegel and Florence R. Kluckhohn, "The Influence of the Family and Cultural Values on the Mental Health and Illness of the Individual," unpublished Progress Report of Grant M-971, U.S. Public Health Service.

[54] Anna Freud, *The Ego and the Mechanisms of Defense* (London: Hogarth, 1954).

[55] That illness is almost an everyday problem is shown by the data in our opening section on the prevalence of illness. That illness and its concomitants are anxiety-laden is suggested by the findings of many studies on patient delay. Barbara Blackwell, "The Literature of Delay in Seeking Medical Care for Chronic Illnesses," *Health Education Monographs,* 16 (1963), 3–32; Bernard Kutner, Henry B. Malcover, and Abraham Oppenheim, "Delay in the Diagnosis and Treatment of Cancer," *Journal of Chronic Diseases,* 7 (January, 1958), 95–120; *Journal of Health and Human Behavior,* 2 (Fall, 1961), 171–178.

[56] Speculation as to why the Italians and the Irish, with similar problems of hardship and poverty, should develop dissimilar ways of handling such problems is beyond the scope of this paper.

For the Italians, the large number of symptoms and the spread of the complaints, not only throughout the body but into other aspects of life, may be understood in terms of their expressiveness and expansiveness so often seen in sociological, historical, and fictional writing.[57] Yet their illness behavior seems to reflect something more than lack of inhibition, and valuation of spontaneity. There is something more than real in their behavior, a "well-seasoned, dramatic emphasis to their lives." In fact, clinicians have noted that this openness is deceptive. It only goes so far and then . . . Thus this Italian overstatement of "symptoms" is not merely an expressive quality but perhaps a more general mechanism, their special way of handling problems – a defense mechanism we call dramatization. Dynamically, dramatization seems to cope with anxiety by repeatedly overexpressing it and thereby dissipating it. Anne Parsons delineates this process in a case study of a schizophrenic woman. Through a process of repetition and exaggeration she was able to isolate and defend herself from the destructive consequences of her own psychotic breakdown. Thus Anne Parsons concludes:

rather than appearing as evidence for the greater acceptance of id impulses the greater dramatic expression of Southern Italian culture might be given a particular place among the ego mechanisms, different from but in this respect fulfilling the same function as the emphasis on rational mastery of the objective or subjective world which characterizes our own culture (U. S. A.).[58]

While other social historians have noted the Italian flair for show and spectacle, Barzini has most explicitly related this phenomenon to the covering up of omnipresent tragedy and poverty, a way of making their daily lives bearable, the satisfactory *ersatz* for the many things they lack.

---

[57] In addition to the references cited in footnotes 52 and 53, we have drawn our picture from many sociological, literary, and historical works. A complete bibliography is available on request. For the compilation and annotation of many of these references I am particularly indebted to Mrs. Marlene Hindley.

[58] Anne Parsons, *Psychiatry, op. cit.,* p. 26.

The most easily identifiable reasons why the Italians love their own show. . . . First of all they do it to tame and prettify savage nature, to make life bearable, dignified, significant, and pleasant for others, and themselves. They do it then for their own private ends; a good show makes a man *simpatico* to powerful people, helps him get on in the world and obtain what he wants, solves many problems, lubricates the wheels of society, protects him from the envy of his enemies and the arrogance of the mighty — they do it to avenge themselves on unjust fate.[59]

Through many works on the Southern Italian there seems to run a thread — a valued and preferred way of handling problems shown in the tendency toward dramatization. The experience of illness provides but another stage.

But if the Italian view of life is expressed through its fiestas, for the Irish it is expressed through its fasts.[60] Their life has been depicted as one of long periods of plodding routine followed by episodes of wild adventure, of lengthy postponement of gratification of sex and marriage, interspersed with brief immediate satisfactions like fighting and carousing. Perhaps it is in recognition of the expected and limited nature of such outbursts that the most common Irish outlet, alcoholism, is often referred to as "a good man's weakness." Life was black and long-suffering, and the less said the better.[61]

It is the last statement which best reflects the Irish handling of illness. While in other contexts the ignoring of bodily complaints is merely descriptive of what is going on, in Irish culture it seems to be the culturally prescribed and supported defense mechanism — singularly most appropriate for

their psychological and physical survival.[62] When speaking of the discomfort caused by her illness, one stated, "I ignore it like I do most things." In terms of presenting complaints this understatement and restraint was even more evident. It could thus be seen in their seeming reluctance to admit they have any symptoms at all, in their limiting their symptoms to the specific location in which they arose, and finally in their contention that their physical problems affected nothing of their life but the most minute physical functioning. The consistency of the Irish illness behavior with their general view of life is shown in two other contexts. First it helped perpetuate a self-fulfilling prophecy. Thus their way of communicating complaints, while doing little to make treatment easy, did assure some degree of continual suffering and thus further proof that life is painful and hard (that is, "full of fasts").[63] Secondly, their illness behavior can be linked to the sin and guilt ideology which seems to pervade so much of Irish society. For, in a culture where restraint is the *modus operandi*, temptation is ever-present and must be guarded against. Since the flesh is weak, there is a concomitant expectation that sin is likely. Thus, when unexpected or unpleasant events take place, there is a search for what they did or must have done wrong. Perhaps their three most favored

---

[59] Luigi Barzini, *The Italians* (New York: Bantam, 1965), p. 104.

[60] In addition to the papers in footnote 52, Arensberg and Kimball, *op. cit.*, remains the classic reference work.

[61] The ubiquitous comic spirit, humor, and wit for which the Irish are famous can be regarded in part as a functional equivalent of the dramatization by Italians. It is a cover, a way of isolating life's hardships, and at the same time a preventive of deeper examination and probing. Also, while their daily life was endowed with great restrictions, their fantasy life was replete with great richness (tales of the "wee folk").

[62] Spiegel and Kluckhohn, *op. cit.*, state that the Irishman's major avenue of relief from his oppressive sense of guilt lies in his almost unlimited capacity for denial. This capacity they claim is fostered by the perception in the rural Irish of a harmonic blending between man and nature. Such harmonizing of man and nature is further interpreted as blurring the elements of causality, thus allowing for continually shifting the responsibility for events from one person to another, and even from a person to animistically conceived forces. Thus denial becomes not only a preferred avenue of relief but also one supported and perhaps elicited by their perception of their environment.

[63] Their "fantasying" and their "fasting" might be reflected in the serious illness they claim to have had in the past, and the dire consequences they forecast for their future. We do not know for a fact that the Irish *had* more serious illnesses than the Italians, but merely that they claimed to. The Italians might well have had similar conditions but did not necessarily consider them serious.

locations of symptoms (the eyes, ears, and throat) might be understood as symbolic reflections of the more immediate source of their sin and guilt — what they should not have seen; what they should not have heard; and what they should not have said.

In these few paragraphs, we have tried to provide a theoretical link between membership in a cultural group and the communication of bodily complaints. The illness behavior of the Irish and the Italians has been explained in terms of two of the more generally prescribed defense mechanisms of their respective cultures — with the Irish handling their troubles by denial and the Italians theirs by dramatization.[64]

QUALIFICATIONS AND IMPLICATIONS

The very fact that we speak of trends and statistical significance indicates the tentativeness of this study. In particular, the nature of sample selection affected the analysis of certain demographic variables since the lack of significant differences in some cases may be due to the small range available for comparison. Thus, there were no Italians beyond the third generation and few in the total sample who had gone to college. When comparisons were made within this small range (for example, only within the second generation or only within the high school group) there were, with but one exception, no significant differences from previously reported findings. [65] Despite the limitations cited, it can be stated with some confidence that, of the variables capable of analysis, sociocultural ones were the most significant. When a correlational analysis (and within this, a cluster analysis) was performed on all the codable and quantifiable material (including the demographic data, the health behaviors, and attitude scales) the variable which consistently correlated most highly with the "illness behaviors" reported in this study was ethnic group membership.

There is one final remark about our sample selection which has ramifications, not for our data analysis, but rather for our interpretation. We are dealing here with a population who had decided to seek or were referred for medical aid at three clinics. Thus we can make no claim that in a random selection of Irish, they will be suffering primarily from eye, ear, nose, and throat disorders or even locate their chief symptoms there. What we are claiming is that there are significant differences in the way people present and react to their complaints, *not* that the specific complaints and mechanisms we have cited are necessarily the most common ones. (We would, of course, be surprised if the pattern reported here did not constitute one of the major ones.) Another difficulty in dealing with this population is the duration of the patients' disorders. Since the majority of these patients have had their conditions for some time, one may wonder if similar differences in perception would exist for more acute episodes, or whether the very length of time which the people have borne their problems has allowed for coloration by sociocultural factors. As a result of this we can only raise the issues as to whether the differences reported here between members of a cultural group exist only at a particular stage of their illness, or reflect more underlying and enduring cultural concerns and values.[66]

---

[64] The Anglo-Saxons complete the circle with an emphasis on neutralizing their anxiety.

[65] The previously reported ethnic differences with respect to presenting complaints did begin to blur. The Italian and the Irish males tended to "move" toward the "middle position" of the Anglo-Saxon Protestant group. In many of the major comparisons of this study, the Anglo-Saxon group occupied a position midway between the responses of the two other ethnic groups, though generally closer to the Irish. For example, when asked about the presence of pain some 70 percent of the Irish males denied it, as compared to almost 60 percent of the Anglo-Saxon males, and 40 percent of the Italian males.

[66] Such a problem was explicitly stated and investigated by Ellen Silver, "The Influence of Culture on Personality: A Comparison of the Irish and Italians with Emphasis on Fantasy Behavior," mimeographed, Harvard University, 1958, in her attempted replication of the Opler and Singer work, *op. cit.,* and was emphasized by the somewhat ambiguous findings of Rena S. Grossman, "Ethnic Differences in the Apperception of Pain," unpublished undergraduate honors thesis, Department of Social Relations, Radcliffe College, 1964, in her replication of Zborowski's findings, *op. cit.,* on a nonhospitalized population.

While there has long been recognition of the subjectivity and variability of a patient's reporting of his symptoms, there has been little attention to the fact that this reporting may be influenced by systematic social factors like ethnicity. Awareness of the influence of this and similar factors can be of considerable aid in the practical problems of diagnosis and treatment of many diseases, particularly where the diagnosis is dependent to a large extent on what the patient is able and willing, or thinks important enough, to tell the doctor.[67] The physician who is unaware of how the patient's background may lead him to respond in certain ways, may, by not probing sufficiently, miss important diagnostic cues, or respond inappropriately to others.[68]

The documentation of sociocultural differences in the perception of and concern with certain types of "symptoms" has further implications for work in preventive medicine and public health. It has been found in mental health research that there is an enormous gulf between lay and professional opinion as to when mental illness is present, as well as when and what kind of help is needed.[69] If our theorizing

is correct, such differences reflect not merely something inadequately learned (that is, wrong medical knowledge) but also a solidly embedded value system.[70] Such different frames of reference would certainly shed light on the failure of many symptom-based health campaigns. Often these campaigns seem based on the assumption that a symptom or sign is fairly objective and recognizable and that it evokes similar levels of awareness and reaction. Our study adds to the mounting evidence which contradicts this position by indicating, for example, the systematic variability in response to even the most minor aches and pains.

University Press, 1957); Howard E. Freeman and Gene G. Kassebaum, "Relationship of Education and Knowledge to Opinions about Mental Illness," *Mental Hygiene*, 44 (January, 1960), 43–47; Gerald Gurin, Joseph Veroff, and Sheila Feld, *Americans View Their Mental Health* (New York: Basic Books, 1960); Jum C. Nunnally, *Popular Conceptions of Mental Health* (New York: Holt, Rinehart & Winston, 1961); Glenn V. Ramsey and Melita Seipp, "Attitudes and Opinions Concerning Mental Illness," *Psychiatric Quarterly*, 22(July, 1949), 1–17; Elmo Roper and Associates, *People's Attitudes Concerning Mental Health* (New York: Private Publication, 1950); Shirley Star, "The Public's Ideas about Mental Illness," paper presented to the Annual Meeting of the National Association for Mental Health, Indianapolis, 1955; Shirley Star, "The Place of Psychiatry in Popular Thinking," paper presented at the annual meeting of the American Association for Public Opinion Research, Washington, D. C., 1957; Julian L. Woodward, "Changing Ideas on Mental Illness and Its Treatment," *American Sociological Review*, 16 (August, 1951), 443–454.

[70] This approach is evident in such works as Stanley King, *op. cit.*; Clyde Kluckhohn "Culture and Behavior," in Gardner Lindzey, *Handbook of Social Psychology*, Vol. 2 (Cambridge: Addison-Wesley, 1954), pp. 921–976; Walter B. Miller, "Lower Class Culture as a Generating Milieu of Gang Delinquency," *Journal of Social Issues*, 14 (July, 1958), 5–19; Marvin K. Opler, *Culture, Psychiatry, and Human Values* (Springfield, Ill.: Charles C Thomas, 1956); Marvin K. Opler, *Culture and Mental Health* (New York: MacMillan, 1959); Benjamin D. Paul, *Health, Culture, and Community — Case Studies of Public Reactions to Health Programs* (New York: Russell Sage Foundation, 1955); Henry J. Wegroski, "A Critique of Cultural and Statistical Concepts of Abnormality," in Clyde Kluckhohn, Henry A. Murray, and David M. Schneider, *Personality in Nature, Society, and Culture*, rev. ed. (New York: Knopf, 1956), pp. 691–701.

[67] Several examples are more fully delineated in Irving Kenneth Zola, "Illness Behavior of the Working Class: Implications and Recommendations," in Arthur B. Shostak and William Gomberg, eds. *Blue Collar World* (Englewood Cliffs, N. J.: Prentice-Hall, 1964), pp. 350–361.

[68] This may be done to such an extreme that it is the physician's response which creates epidemiological differences. Such a potential situation was noted using data from the present study and is detailed in Irving Kenneth Zola, "Problems of Communications, Diagnosis, and Patient Care: The Interplay of Patient, Physician, and Clinic Organization," *Journal of Medical Education*, 38(October, 1963), 829–838.

[69] The explanations for such differences have, however, more often emphasized negative aspects of the respondents' background — their lower education, lower socioeconomic status, lesser psychological sophistication, and greater resistance and antipathy — by virtue of their membership in certain racial and cultural minorities. See Bernard Bergen, "Social Class, Symptoms, and Sensitivity to Descriptions of Mental Illness — Implications for Programs of Preventive Psychiatry," unpublished doctoral dissertation, Harvard University, 1962; Elaine Cumming and John Cumming, *Closed Ranks: An Experiment in Mental Health Education* (Cambridge: Harvard

The discerning of reactions to minor problems harks back to a point mentioned in the early pages of this report. For, while sociologists, anthropologists, and mental health workers have usually considered sociocultural factors to be etiological factors in the creation of specific problems, the interpretative emphasis in this study has been on how sociocultural background may lead to different definitions and responses to essentially the same experience. The strongest evidence in support of this argument is the different ethnic perceptions for essentially the same disease. While it is obvious that not all people react similarly to the same disease process, it is striking that the pattern of response can vary with the ethnic background of the patient. There is little known physiological difference between ethnic groups which would account for the differing reactions. In fact, the comparison of the matched diagnostic groups led us to believe that, should diagnosis be more precisely controlled, the differences would be even more striking.

The present report has attempted to demonstrate the fruitfulness of an approach which does not take the definition of abnormality for granted. Despite its limitations, our data seem sufficiently striking to provide further reason for reexamining our traditional and often rigid conceptions of health and illness, of normality and abnormality, of conformity and deviance. Symptoms, or physical aberrations, are so wide-spread that perhaps relatively few, and a biased selection at best, come to the attention of official treatment agencies like doctors, hospitals, and public health agencies. There may even be a sense in which they are part and parcel of the human condition. We have thus tried to present evidence showing that the very labeling and definition of a bodily state as a symptom or as a problem is, in itself, part of a social process. If there is a selection and definitional process, then focusing solely on reasons for deviation (the study of etiology) and ignoring what constitutes a deviation in the eyes of the individual and his society may obscure important aspects of our understanding and eventually our philosophies of treatment and control of illness.[71]

---

[71] This is spelled out from various points of view in such works as Samuel Butler, *Erewhon* (New York: Signet, 1961); Rene Dubos, *op cit.,* Josephine D. Lohman (participant), "Juvenile Delinquency: Its Dimensions, Its Conditions, Techniques of Control, Proposals for Action," Subcommittee on Juvenile Delinquency of the Senate Committee on Labor and Public Welfare, 86th Congress, S. 765, S. 1090, S. 1314, Spring, 1959, p. 268; Talcott Parsons, "Social Change and Medical Organization in the United States: A Sociological Perspective," *Annals of the American Academy of Political and Social Science,* 346 (March, 1963), 21–34; Edwin M. Schur, *Crimes Without Victims – Deviant Behavior and Public Policy* (Englewood Cliffs, N. J.: Prentice-Hall, 1965); Thomas Szasz, *The Myth of Mental Illness* (New York: Hoeber-Harper, 1961); Thomas Szasz, *Law, Liberty, and Psychiatry* (New York: Macmillan, 1963); Irving Kenneth Zola, "Problems for Research – Some Effects of Assumptions Underlying Socio-Medical Investigations," in Gerald Gordon, ed., *Proceedings, Conference on Medical Sociology and Disease Control* (National Tuberculosis Association, 1966), pp. 9–17.

48   Cultural Components in Response to Pain

Mark Zborowski

This paper reports on one aspect of a larger study: that concerned with discovering the role of cultural patterns in attitudes toward and reactions to pain which is caused by disease and injury — in other words, responses to spontaneous pain.

SOME BASIC DISTINCTIONS

In human societies biological processes vital for man's survival acquire social and cultural significance. Intake of food, sexual intercourse or elimination — physiological phenomena which are universal for the entire living world — become institutions regulated by cultural and social norms, thus fulfilling not only biological functions but social and cultural ones as well. Metabolic and endocrinal changes in the human organism may provoke hunger and sexual desire, but culture and society dictate to man the kind of food he may eat, the social setting for eating or the adequate partner for mating.

Moreover, the role of cultural and social patterns in human physiological activities is so great that they may in specific situations act against the direct biological needs of the individual, even to the point of endangering his survival. Only a human being may prefer starvation to the breaking of a religious dietary law or may abstain from sexual intercourse because of specific incest regulations. Voluntary fasting and celibacy exist only where food and sex fulfill more than strictly physiological functions.

Thus, the understanding of the significance and role of social and cultural patterns in human physiology is necessary to clarify those aspects of human experience which remain puzzling if studied only within the physiological frame of reference.

Pain is basically a physiological phenomenon and as such has been studied by physiologists and neurologists such as Harold Wolff, James Hardy, Helen Goodell, C. S. Lewis, W. K. Livingston and others. By using the most ingenious methods of investigation they have succeeded in clarifying complex problems of the physiology of pain. Many aspects of perception and reaction to pain were studied in experimental situations involving most careful preparation and complicated equipment. These investigators have come to the conclusion that "from the physiological point of view pain qualifies as a sensation of importance to the self-preservation of the individual."[1, p. 23] The biological function of pain is to provoke special reactive patterns directed toward avoidance of the noxious stimulus which presents a threat to the individual. In this respect the function of pain is basically the same for man as for the rest of the animal world.

However, the physiology of pain and the understanding of the biological function of pain do not explain other aspects of what Wolff, Hardy and Goodell call the *pain experience,* which includes not only the pain sensation and certain automatic reactive responses but also certain "associated feeling states."[1, p. 204] It would not explain, for example, the acceptance of intense pain in torture which is part of the initiation rites of many primitive societies,

Zborowski, M.: Cultural components in response to pain. J. Soc. Issues 8: 16–30 (1952).

nor will it explain the strong emotional reactions of certain individuals to the slight sting of the hypodermic needle.

In human society pain, like so many other physiological phenomena, acquires specific social and cultural significance, and, accordingly, certain reactions to pain can be understood in the light of this significance. As Drs. Hardy, Wolff and Goodell state in their recent book, "... the culture in which a man finds himself becomes the conditioning influence in the formation of the individual reaction patterns to pain. ... A knowledge of group attitudes toward pain is extremely important to an understanding of the individual reaction."[1],p.262

In analyzing pain it is useful to distinguish between self-inflicted, other-inflicted and spontaneous pain. Self-inflicted pain is defined as deliberately self-inflicted. It is experienced as a result of injuries performed voluntarily upon oneself, e. g., self-mutilation. Usually these injuries have a culturally defined purpose, such as achieving a special status in the society. It can be observed not only in primitive cultures but also in contemporary societies on a higher level of civilization. In Germany, for instance, members of certain student or military organizations would cut their faces with a razor in order to acquire scars which would identify them as members of a distinctive social group. By other-inflicted pain is meant pain inflicted upon the individual in the process of culturally accepted and expected activities (regardless of whether approved or disapproved), such as sports, fights, war, etc. To this category belongs also pain inflicted by the physician in the process of medical treatment. Spontaneous pain usually denotes the pain sensation which results from disease or injury. This term also covers pains of psychogenic nature.

Members of different cultures may assume differing attitudes towards these various types of pain. Two of these attitudes may be described as pain expectancy and pain acceptance. Pain expectancy is anticipation of pain as being unavoidable in a given situation, for instance, in childbirth, in sports activities or in battle. Pain acceptance is characterized by a willingness to experience pain. This attitude is manifested mostly as an inevitable component of culturally accepted experiences, for instance, as part of initiation rites or part of medical treatment. The following example will help to clarify the differences between pain expectancy and pain acceptance: Labor pain is expected as part of childbirth, but while in one culture, such as in the United States, it is not accepted and therefore various means are used to alleviate it, in some other cultures, for instance in Poland, it is not only expected but also accepted, and consequently nothing or little is done to relieve it. Similarly, cultures which emphasize military achievements expect and accept battle wounds, while cultures which emphasize pacifistic values may expect them but will not accept them.

In the process of investigating cultural attitudes toward pain it is also important to distinguish between pain apprehension and pain anxiety. Pain apprehension relfects the tendency to avoid the pain sensation as such, regardless of whether the pain is spontaneous or inflicted, whether it is accepted or not. Pain anxiety, on the other hand, is a state of anxiety provoked by the pain experience, focussed upon various aspects of the causes of pain, the meaning of pain or its significance for the welfare of the individual.

Moreover, members of various cultures may react differently in terms of their manifest behavior toward various pain experiences, and this behavior is often dictated by the culture which provides specific norms according to the age, sex and social position of the individual.

The fact that other elements as well as cultural factors are involved in the response to a spontaneous pain should be taken into consideration. These other factors are the pathological aspect of pain, the specific physiological characteristics of the pain experience, such as the intensity, the duration and the quality of the pain sensation, and, finally, the personality of the individual. Nevertheless, it was felt that in the process of a careful investigation it would be possible to detect the role of the cultural components in the pain experience.

THE RESEARCH SETTING

In setting up the research we were interested not only in the purely theoretical aspects of the findings in terms of possible contribution to the understanding of the pain experience in general; we also had in mind the practical goal of a contribution to the field of medicine. In the relationship between the doctor and his patient the respective attitudes toward pain may play a crucial role, especially when the doctor feels that the patient exaggerates his pain while the patient feels that the doctor minimizes his suffering. The same may be true, for instance, in a hospital where the members of the medical and nursing staff may have attitudes toward pain different from those held by the patient, or when they expect a certain pattern of behavior according to their cultural background while the patient may manifest a behavior pattern which is acceptable in his culture. These differences may play an important part in the evaluation of the individual pain experience, in dealing with pain at home and in the hospital, in administration of analgesics, etc. Moreover, we expected that this study of pain would offer opportunities to gain insight into related attitudes toward health, disease, medication, hospitalization, medicine in general, etc.

With these aims in mind the project was set up at the Kingsbridge Veterans Hospital, Bronx, New York,[1] where four ethnocultural groups were selected for an intensive study. These groups included patients of Jewish, Italian, Irish and "Old American" stock. Three groups — Jews, Italians and Irish — were selected because they were described by medical people as manifesting striking differences in their reaction to pain. Italians and Jews were described as tending to "exaggerate" their pain, while

the Irish were often depicted as stoical individuals who are able to take a great deal of pain. The fourth group, the "Old Americans," were chosen because the values and attitudes of this group dominate in the country and are held by many members of the medical profession and by many descendants of the immigrants who, in the process of Americanization, tend to adopt American patterns of behavior. The members of this group can be defined as White, native-born individuals, usually Protestant, whose grandparents, at least, were born in the United States and who do not identify themselves with any foreign group, either nationally, socially or culturally.

The Kingsbridge Veterans Hospital was chosen because its population represents roughly the ethnic composition of New York City, thus offering access to a fair sample of the four selected groups, and also because various age groups were represented among the hospitalized veterans of World War I, World War II, and the Korean War. In one major respect this hospital was not adequate, namely, in not offering the opportunity to investigate sex differences in attitude toward pain. This aspect of research will be carried out in a hospital that has a large female population.

In setting up this project we were mainly interested in discovering certain regularities in reactions and attitudes toward pain characteristic of the four groups. Therefore, the study has a qualitative character, and the efforts of the researchers were not directed toward a collection of material suitable for quantitative analysis. The main techniques used in the collection of the material were interviews with patients of the selected groups, observation of their behavior when in pain and discussion of the individual cases with doctors, nurses and other people directly or indirectly involved in the pain experience of the individual. In addition to the interviews with patients, "healthy" members of the respective groups were interviewed on their attitudes toward pain, because in terms of the original hypothesis those attitudes and reactions which are displayed by the patients of the given cultural groups are held by all members of the group regardless of whether or not they are in pain although in

[1] I should like to take the opportunity to express my appreciation to Dr. Harold G. Wolff, Professor of Neurology, Cornell University Medical College, Dr. Hiland Flowers, Chief of Neuropsychiatric Service, Dr. Robert Morrow, Chief of Clinical Psychology Section, Dr. Louis Berlin, Chief of Neurology Section, and the management of the hospital for their cooperation in the setting up of the research at the Kingsbridge Veterans Hospital.

pain these attitudes may come more sharply into focus. In certain cases the researchers have interviewed a member of the patient's immediate family in order to check the report of the patient on his pain experience and in order to find out what are the attitudes and reactions of the family toward the patient's experience.

These interviews, based on a series of open-ended questions, were focussed upon the past and present pain experiences of the interviewee. However, many other areas were considered important for the understanding of this experience. For instance, it was felt that complaints of pain may play an important role in manipulating relationships in the family and the larger social environment. It was also felt that in order to understand the specific reactive patterns in controlling pain it is important to know certain aspects of child-rearing in the culture, relationships between parents and children, the role of infliction of pain in punishment, the attitudes of various members of the family toward specific expected, accepted pain experiences, and so on. The interviews were recorded on wire and transcribed verbatim for an ultimate detailed analysis. The interviews usually lasted for approximately two hours, the time being limited by the condition of the interviewee and by the amount and quality of his answers. When it was considered necessary an interview was repeated. In most of the cases the study of the interviewee was followed by informal conversations and by observation of his behavior in the hospital.

The information gathered from the interviews was discussed with members of the medical staff, especially in the areas related to the medical aspects of the problem, in order to get their evaluation of the pain experience of the patient. Information as to the personality of the patient was checked against results of psychological testing by members of the psychological staff of the hospital when these were available.

The discussion of the material presented in this paper is based on interviews with 103 respondents, including 87 hospital patients in pain and 16 healthy subjects. According to their ethno-cultural back-

ground the respondents are distributed as follows: "Old Americans," 26; Italians, 24; Jews, 31; Irish, 11; and others, 11.[2] In addition, there were the collateral interviews and conversations noted above with family members, doctors, nurses and other members of the hospital staff.

With regard to the pathological causes of pain the majority of the interviewees fall into the group of patients suffering from neurological diseases, mainly herniated discs and spinal lesions. The focussing upon a group of patients suffering from a similar pathologic condition offered the opportunity to investigate reactions and attitudes toward spontaneous pain which is symptomatic of one group of diseases. Nevertheless, a number of patients suffering from other diseases were also interviewed.

This paper is based upon the material collected during the first stage of study. The generalizations are to a great extent tentative formulations on a descriptive level. There has been no attempt as yet to integrate the results with the value system and the cultural pattern of the group, though here and there there will be indications to the effect that they are part of the culture pattern. The discussions will be limited to main regularities within three groups, namely, the Italians, the Jews and the "Old Americans." Factors related to variations within each group will be discussed after the main prevailing patterns have been presented.

PAIN AMONG PATIENTS OF JEWISH AND ITALIAN ORIGIN

As already mentioned, the Jews and Italians were selected mainly because interviews with medical experts suggested that they display similar reactions to pain. The investigation of this similarity provided the opportunity to check a rather popular assumption that similar reactions reflect

---

[2] Italian respondents are mainly of South Italian origin; the Jewish respondents, with one exception, are all of East European origin. Whenever the Jews are mentioned they are spoken of in terms of the culture they represent and not in terms of their religion.

similar attitudes. The differences between the Italian and Jewish culture are great enough to suggest that if the attitudes are related to cultural pattern they will also be different despite the apparent similarity in manifest behavior.

Members of both groups were described as being very emotional in their responses to pain. They were described as tending to exaggerate their pain experience and being very sensitive to pain. Some of the doctors stated that in their opinion Jews and Italians have a lower threshold of pain than members of other ethnic groups, especially members of the socalled Nordic group. This statement seems to indicate a certain confusion as to the concept of the threshold of pain. According to people who have studied the problem of the threshold of pain, for instance Harold Wolff and his associates, the threshold of pain is more or less the same for all human beings regardless of nationality, sex or age.

In the course of the investigation the general impressions of doctors were confirmed to a great extent by the interview material and by the observation of the patients' behavior. However, even a superficial study of the interviews has revealed that though reactions to pain appear to be similar the underlying attitudes toward pain are different in the two groups. While the Italian patients seemed to be mainly concerned with the immediacy of the pain experience and were disturbed by the actual pain sensation which they experienced in a given situation, the concern of patients of Jewish origin was focussed mainly upon the symptomatic meaning of pain and upon the significance of pain in relation to their health, welfare and, eventually, for the welfare of the families. The Italian patient expressed in his behavior and in his complaints the discomfort caused by pain as such, and he manifested his emotions with regard to the effects of this pain experience upon his immediate situation in terms of occupation, economic situation and so on; the Jewish patient expressed primarily his worries and anxieties as to the extent to which the pain indicated a threat to his health. In this connection it is worth mentioning that one of the Jewish words to describe strong pain is *yessurim*, a word which is also used to describe worries and anxieties.

Attitudes of Italian and Jewish patients toward pain-relieving drugs can serve as an indication of their attitude toward pain. When in pain the Italian calls for pain relief and is mainly concerned with the analgesic effects of the drugs which are administered to him. Once the pain is relieved the Italian patient easily forgets his sufferings and manifests a happy and joyful disposition. The Jewish patient, however, often is reluctant to accept the drug, and he explains this reluctance in terms of concern about the effects of the drug upon his health in general. He is apprehensive about the habit-forming aspects of the analgesic. Moreover, he feels that the drug relieves his pain only temporarily and does not cure him of the disease which may cause the pain. Nurses and doctors have reported cases in which patients would hide the pill which was given to them to relieve their pain and would prefer to suffer. These reports were confirmed in the interviews with the patients. It was also observed that many Jewish patients after being relieved from pain often continued to display the same depressed and worried behavior because they felt that though the pain was currently absent it might recur as long as the disease was not cured completely. From these observations it appears that when one deals with a Jewish and an Italian patient in pain, in the first case it is more important to relieve the anxieties with regard to the sources of pain, while in the second it is more important to relieve the actual pain.

Another indication as to the significance of pain for Jewish and Italian patients is their respective attitudes toward the doctor. The Italian patient seems to display a most confident attitude toward the doctor which is usually reinforced after the doctor has succeeded in relieving pain, whereas the Jewish patient manifests a skeptical attitude, feeling that the fact that the doctor has relieved his pain by some drug does not mean at all that he is skillful enough to take care of the basic illness. Consequently, even when the pain is relieved, he tends to check the diagnosis and the treatment of one doctor against the opinions of other specialists in the field. Summarizing the difference between the Italian and Jewish attitudes, one can say that the Italian attitude is characterized by a present-oriented apprehension with regard to the actual sensation of pain, and the Jew tends to manifest a future-oriented anxiety as to the symptomatic and general meaning of the pain experience.

It has been stated that the Italians and Jews tend to manifest similar behavior in terms of their reactions to pain. As both cultures allow for free expression of feelings and emotions by words, sounds and gestures, both the Italians and Jews feel free to talk about their pain, complain about it and manifest their sufferings by groaning, moaning, crying, etc. They are not ashamed of this expression. They admit willingly that when they are in pain they do complain a great deal, call for help and expect sympathy and assistance from other members of their immediate social environment, especially from members of their family. When in pain they are reluctant to be alone and prefer the presence and attention of other people. This behavior, which is expected, accepted and approved by the Italian and Jewish cultures often conflicts with the patterns of behavior expected from a patient by American or Americanized medical people. Thus they tend to describe the behavior of the Italian and Jewish patient as exaggerated and over-emotional. The material suggests that they do tend to minimize the actual pain experiences of the Italian and Jewish patient regardless of whether they have the objective criteria for evaluating the actual amount of pain which the patient experiences. It seems that the uninhibited display of reaction to pain as manifested by the Jewish and Italian patient provokes distrust in American culture instead of provoking sympathy.

Despite the close similarity between the manifest reactions among Jews and Italians, there seem to be differences in emphasis especially with regard to what the patient achieves by these reactions and as to the specific manifestations of these reactions in the various social settings. For instance, they differ in their behavior at home and in the hospital. The Italian husband, who is aware of his role as an adult male, tends to avoid verbal complaining at home, leaving this type of behavior to the women. In the hospital, where he is less concerned with his role as a male, he tends to be more verbal and more emotional. The Jewish patient, on the contrary, seems to be more calm in the hospital than at home. Traditionally the Jewish male does not emphasize his masculinity through such traits as stoicism, and he does not equate verbal complaints with weakness. Moreover, the Jewish culture allows the patient to be demanding and complaining. Therefore, he tends more to use his pain in order to control interpersonal relationships within the family. Though similar use of pain to manipulate the relationships between members of the family may be present also in some other cultures it seems that in the Jewish culture this is not disapproved, while in others it is. In the hospital one can also distinguish variations in the reactive patterns among the Jews and Italians. Upon his admission to the hospital and in the presence of the doctor the Jewish patient tends to complain, ask for help, be emotional even to the point of crying. However, as soon as he feels that adequate care is given to him he becomes more restrained. This suggests that the display of pain reaction serves less as an indication of the amount of pain experienced than as a means to create an atmosphere and setting in which the pathological causes of pain will be best taken care of. The Italian patient, on the other hand, seems to be less concerned with setting up a favorable situation for treatment. He takes for granted that adequate care will be given to him, and in the presence of the doctor he seems to be somewhat calmer than the Jewish patient. The mere presence of the doctor reassures the Italian patient, while the skepticism of the Jewish patient limits the reassuring role of the physician.

To summarize the description of the reactive patterns of the Jewish and Italian patients, the material suggests that on a semi-conscious level the Jewish patient tends to provoke worry and concern in his social environment as to the state of his health and the symptomatic character of his pain, while the Italian tends to provoke sympathy toward his suffering. In one case the function of the pain reaction will be the mobilization of the efforts of the family and the doctors toward a complete cure, while in the second case the function of the reaction will be focussed upon the mobilization of effort toward relieving the pain sensation.

On the basis of the discussion of the Jewish and Italian material two generalizations can be made: (1) *Similar reactions to pain manifested by members of different ethno-cultural groups do not necessarily reflect similar attitudes to pain.* (2) *Reactive patterns similar in terms of their manifestations may have different functions and serve different purposes in various cultures.*

PAIN AMONG PATIENTS OF "OLD AMERICAN" ORIGIN

There is little emphasis on emotional complaining about pain among "Old American" patients. Their complaints about pain can best be described as reporting on pain. In describing his pain, the "Old American" patient tries to find the most appropriate ways of defining the quality of pain, its localization, duration, etc. When examined by the doctor he gives the impression of trying to assume the detached role of an unemotional observer who gives the most efficient description of his state for a correct diagnosis and treatment. The interviewees repeatedly state that there is no point in complaining and groaning and moaning, etc., because "it won't help anybody." However, they readily admit that when pain is unbearable they may react strongly, even to the point of crying, but they tend to do it when they are alone. Withdrawal from society seems to be a frequent reaction to strong pain.

There seem to be different patterns in reacting to pain depending on the situation. One pattern, manifested in the presence of members of the family, friends, etc., consists of attempts to minimize pain, to avoid complaining and provoking pity; when pain becomes too strong there is a tendency to withdraw and express freely such reactions as groaning, moaning, etc. A different pattern is manifested in the presence of people who, on account of their profession, should know the character of the pain experience because they are expected to make the appropriate diagnosis, advise the proper cure and give the adequate help. The tendency to avoid deviation from certain expected patterns of behavior plays an important role in the reaction to pain. This is also controlled by the desire to seek approval on the part of the social environment, especially in the hospital, where the "Old American" patient tries to avoid being a "nuisance" on the ward. He seems to be, more than any other patient, aware of an ideal pattern of behavior which is identified as "American," and he tends to conform to it. This was characteristically expressed by a patient who answered the question how he reacts to pain by saying, "I react like a good American."

An important element in controlling the pain reaction is the wish of the patient to cooperate with those who are expected to take care of him. The situation is often viewed as a team composed of the patient, the doctor, the nurse, the attendant, etc., and in this team everybody has a function and is supposed to do his share in order to achieve the most successful result. Emotionality is seen as a purposeless and hindering factor in a situation which calls for knowledge, skill, training and efficiency. It is important to note that this behavior is also expected by American or Americanized members of the medical or nursing staff, and the patients who do not fall into this pattern are viewed as deviants, hypochondriacs and neurotics.

As in the case of the Jewish patients, the American attitude toward pain can be best defined as a future-oriented anxiety. The "Old American" patient is also concerned with the symptomatic significance of pain which is correlated with a pronounced health-consciousness. It seems that the "Old American" is conscious of various threats to his health which are present in his environment and therefore feels vulnerable and is prone to interpret his pain sensation as a warning signal indicating that something is wrong with his health and therefore must be reported to the physician. With some exceptions, pain is considered bad and unnecessary and therefore must be immediately taken care of. In those situations where pain is expected and accepted, such as in the process of medical treatment or as a result of sports activities, there is less concern with the pain sensation. In general, however, there is a feeling that suffering pain is unnecessary when there are means of relieving it.

Though the attitudes of the Jewish and "Old American" patients can be defined as pain anxiety they differ greatly. The future-oriented anxiety of the Jewish interviewee is characterized by pessimism or, at best, by skepticism, while the "Old American" patient is rather optimistic in his future-orientation. This attitude is fostered by the mechanistic approach to the body and its functions and by the confidence in the skill of the expert which are so frequent in the American culture. The body is often viewed as a machine which has to be well taken care of, be periodically checked for disfunctioning and eventually, when out of order, be taken to an expert who will "fix" the defect. In the case of pain the expert is the medical man who has the "know-how" because of his training and experience and therefore is entitled to full confidence. An important element in the optimistic outlook is faith in the progress of science. Patients with intractable pain often stated that though at the present moment the doctors do not have the "drug" they will eventually discover it, and they will give the examples of sulpha, penicillin, etc.

The anxieties of a pain-experiencing "Old American" patient are greatly relieved when he feels that something is being done about it in terms of specific activities involved in the treatment. It seems that his security and confidence increase in direct proportion to the number of tests, X-rays, examinations, injections, etc., that are given to him. Accordingly, "Old American" patients seem to have a positive attitude toward hospitalization, because the hospital is the adequate institution which is equipped for the necessary treatment. While a Jewish and an Italian patient seem to be disturbed by the impersonal character of the hospital and by the neces-

sity of being treated there instead of at home, the "Old American" patient, on the contrary, prefers the hospital treatment to the home treatment, and neither he nor his family seems to be disturbed by hospitalization.

To summarize the attitude of the "Old American" toward pain, he is disturbed by the symptomatic aspect of pain and is concerned with its incapacitating aspects, but he tends to view the future in rather optimistic colors, having confidence in the science and skill of the professional people who treat his condition.

SOME SOURCES OF INTRA-GROUP VARIATION

In the description of the reactive patterns and attitudes toward pain among patients of Jewish and "Old American" origin certain regularities have been observed for each particular group regardless of individual differences and variations. This does not mean that each individual in each group manifests the same reactions and attitudes. Individual variations are often due to specific aspects of pain experience, to the character of the disease which causes the pain or to elements in the personality of the patient. However, there are also other factors that are instrumental in provoking these differences and which can still be traced back to the cultural backgrounds of the individual patients. Such variables as the degree of Americanization of the patient, his socio-economic background, education and religiosity may play an important role in shaping individual variations in the reactive patterns. For instance, it was found that the patterns described are manifested most consistently among immigrants, while their descendants tend to differ in terms of adopting American forms of behavior and American attitudes toward the role of the medical expert, medical institutions and equipment in controlling pain. It is safe to say that the further the individual is from the immigrant generation the more American is his behavior. This is less true for the attitudes toward pain, which seem to persist to a great extent even among members of the third generation and even though the reactive patterns are radically changed. A Jewish or Italian patient born in this country of American-born parents tends to *behave* like an "Old American" but often expresses *attitudes* similar to those which are expressed by the Jewish or Italian people. They try to appear unemotional and efficient in situations where the immigrant would be excited and disturbed. However, in the process of the interview, if a patient is of Jewish origin he is likely to express attitudes of anxiety as to the meaning of his pain, and if he is an Italian he is likely to be rather unconcerned about the significance of his pain for his future.

The occupational factor plays an important role when pain affects a specific area of the body. For instance, manual workers with herniated discs are more disturbed by their pain than are professional or business people with a similar disease because of the immediate significance of this particular pain for their respective abilities to earn a living. It was also observed that headaches cause more concern among intellectuals than among manual workers.

The educational background of the patient also plays an important role in his attitude with regard to the symptomatic meaning of a pain sensation. The more educated patients are more health-conscious and more aware of pain as a possible symptom of a dangerous disease. However, this factor plays a less important role than might be expected. The less educated "Old American" or Jewish patient is still more health-conscious than the more educated Italian. On the other hand, the less educated Jew is as much worried about the significance of pain as the more educated one. The education of the patient seems to be an important factor in fostering specific reactive patterns. The more educated patient, who may have more anxiety with regard to illness, may be more reserved in specific reactions to pain than an unsophisticated individual, who feels free to express his feelings and emotions.

THE TRANSMISSION OF CULTURAL ATTITUDES TOWARD PAIN

In interpreting the differences which may be attributed to different socio-economic and education backgrounds there is enough evidence to conclude that these differences appear mainly on the manifest and behavioral level, whereas attitudinal patterns toward pain tend to be more uniform and to be common to most of the members of the group regardless of their specific backgrounds.

These attitudes toward pain and the expected reactive patterns are acquired by the individual members of the society from the earliest childhood along with other cultural attitudes and values which are learned from the parents, parent-substitutes, siblings, peer groups, etc. Each culture offers to its members an ideal pattern of attitudes and reactions, which may differ for various sub-cultures in a given society, and each individual is expected to conform to this ideal pattern. Here, the role of the family seems to be of primary importance. Directly and indirectly the family environment affects the individual's ultimate response to pain. In each culture the parents teach the child how to react to pain, and by approval or disapproval they promote specific forms of behavior. This conclusion is amply supported by the interviews. Thus, the Jewish and Italian respondents are unanimous in relating how their parents, especially mothers, manifested over-protective and over-concerned attitudes toward the child's health, participation in sports, games, fights, etc. In these families the child is constantly reminded of the advisability of avoiding colds, injuries, fights and other threatening situations. Crying in complaint is responded to by the parents with sympathy, concern and help. By their over-protective and worried attitude they foster complaining and tears. The child learns to pay attention to each painful experience and to look for help and sympathy which are readily given to him. In Jewish families, where not only a slight sensation of pain but also each deviation from the child's normal behavior is looked upon as a sign of illness, the child is prone to acquire anxieties with regard to the meaning and significance of these manifestations. The Italian parents do not seem to be concerned with the symptomatic meaning of the child's pains and aches, but instead there is a great deal of verbal expression of emotions and feelings of sympathy toward the "poor child" who happens to be in discomfort because of illness or because of an injury in play. In these families a child is praised when he avoids physical injuries and is scolded when he does not pay enough attention to bad weather, to drafts or when he takes part in rough games and fights. The injury and pain are often interpreted to the child as punishment for the wrong behavior, and physical punishment is the usual consequence of misbehavior.

In the "Old American" family the parental attitude is quite different. The child is told not to "run to mother with every little thing." He is told to take pain "like a man," not to be a "sissy," not to cry. The child's participation in physical sports and games is not only approved but is also strongly stimulated. Moreover, the child is taught to expect to be hurt in sports and games and is taught to fight back if he happens to be attacked by other boys. However, it seems that the American parents are conscious of the threats to the child's health, and they teach the child to take immediate care of any injury. When hurt the right thing to do is not to cry and get emotional but to avoid unnecessary pain and prevent unpleasant consequences by applying the proper first aid medicine and by calling a doctor.

Often attitudes and behavior fostered in a family conflict with those patterns which are accepted by the larger social environment. This is especially true in the case of children of immigrants. The Italian or Jewish immigrant parents promote patterns which they consider correct, while the peer groups in the street and in the school criticize this behavior and foster a different one. In consequence, the child may acquire the attitudes which are part of his home life but may also adopt behavior patterns which conform to those of his friends.

The direct promotion of certain behavior described as part of the child-rearing explains only in part the influence of the general family environment and the specific role of the parents in shaping responses to pain. They are also formed indirectly by observing the behavior of other members of the family and by imitating their responses to pain. Moreover, attitudes toward pain are also influenced by various aspects of parent-child relationship in a culture. The material suggests that differences in attitudes toward pain in Jewish, Italian and "Old American" families are closely related to the role and image of the father in the respective cultures in terms of his authority and masculinity. Often the father and mother assume different roles in promoting specific patterns of behavior and specific attitudes. For example, it seems that in the "Old American" family it is chiefly the mother who stimulates the child's ability to resist pain, thus emphasizing his masculinity. In the Italian family it seems that the mother is the one who inspires the child's emotionality, while in the Jewish family both parents express attitudes of worry and concern which are transmitted to the children.

Specific deviations from expected reactive and attitudinal patterns can often be understood in terms of a particular structure of the family. This became especially clear from the interviews of two Italian patients and one Jewish patient. All three subjects revealed reactions and attitudes diametrically opposite to those which the investigator would expect on the basis of his experience. In the process of the interview, however, it appeared that one of the Italian patients was adopted into an Italian family, found out about his adoption at the age of 14, created a phantasy of being of Anglo-Saxon origin because of his physical appearance and accordingly began to eradicate everything "Italian" in his personality and behavior. For instance, he denied knowledge of the Italian language despite the fact that he always spoke Italian in the family and even learned to abstain from smiling, because he felt that being happy and joyful is an indication of Italian origin. The other Italian patient lost his family at a very early age because of family disorganization and was brought up in an Irish foster home. The Jewish patient consciously adopted a "non-Jewish" pattern of behavior and attitude because of strong sibling rivalry. According to the respondent, his brother, a favored son in the immigrant Jewish family, always manifested "typical" Jewish reactions toward disease, and the patient, who strongly disliked the brother and was jealous of him, decided to be "completely different."

This analysis of cultural factors in responses to pain is tentative and incomplete. It is based upon only one year of research which has been devoted exclusively to collection of raw material and formulation of working hypotheses. A detailed analysis of the interviews may call for revisions and reformulations of certain observations described in this paper. Nevertheless, the first objectives of our research have been attained in establishing the importance of the role of cultural factors in an area relatively little explored by the social sciences. We hope that in the course of further research we shall be able to expand our investigation into other areas of the pain problem, such as sex differences in attitudes toward pain, the role of age differences and the role of religious beliefs in the pain experience. We hope also that the final findings of the study will contribute to the growing field of collaboration between the social sciences and medicine for the better understanding of human problems.

REFERENCE

1. James D. Hardy, Harold G. Wolff, and Helen Goodell, *Pain Sensations and Reactions*, The Williams & Wilkins Company, Baltimore, 1952.

XVII SOCIOBEHAVIORAL ISSUES IN THE PROFESSION OF MEDICINE

A profession, according to Freidson (1970) is "an occupation which has assumed a dominant position in a division of labor, so that it gains control over the determination of the substance of its own work." Simply stated, professions are distinguished from other occupations in that they have achieved a status that allows them to be the ultimate authority of the work they perform. Thus, when clients bring a problem to a member of a profession, he redefines the problem in accord with established professional practices and employs specialized, and often esoteric, techniques to resolve it.

On all grounds, medicine fulfills the criteria for a profession. Moreover, medicine is unique among the major professions. In contrast to law and the ministry, for example, medicine is firmly anchored in and constantly modified by advances in modern science and technology. Not only has it expanded its boundaries of competence over the past two centuries, but it has fostered the emergence of a large and diverse group of supportive occupations that aid in the diagnosis and treatment of illness.

Not the least of medicine's distinction as a profession is the extraordinary prestige attached to its services and the privileged status accorded its members, a consequence in part, no doubt, of its scientific "mystique," its responsibility for matters of life and death, and its dramatic success in healing the ills of its patrons. Further enhancing its high status is the substantial remuneration that physicians derive from their labors, as well as the tradition of an advanced education and general prosperity associated with its members.

Despite the recognition, rewards, and privileges granted the medical profession, doctors are rarely conceded status in the political and economic life of their communities. Not uncommonly, physicians are viewed by the general public with envy and suspicion, in part owing to what is claimed to be their unjustified high income and, in part, to their traditional resistance to "progressive" health and welfare legislation. In recent years, however, under pressure from a discontent public, programs initiated by federal agencies, and the agitations of "liberal" younger physicians, the "official" policies of the profession have begun to move more in accord with the desires of the general population.

Among recent developments characterizing the medical profession is the proliferation and dominance of specialty practice, an inevitable consequence of the vast growth of biologic knowledge and technology. As Roemer has written (1963):

> ... innovations are emerging at a geometric rate over the last century. The knowledge to be encompassed has grown rapidly beyond the competence of even the most exceptional human minds, so that the only answer was specialization. It has occurred along several dimensions: the organs of the body — opthalmology, cardiology, or dermatology; the techniques used — surgery, internal medicine, radiology; age groups served — pediatrics or geriatrics; even the physician's social role — public health, teaching, industrial medicine. Some twenty "specialty boards" have been established to certify qualifications in those fields — a form of superlicensure under nongovernmental

auspices. Specialization has occurred not only within the ancient medical art, that itself evolved from the priesthood, but it has led to the fragmentation of healing into a score of other separate occupations: pharmacy, an early offshoot of the middle ages; nursing, a much later offshoot of the nineteenth century; dentistry; laboratory technology; physiotherapy; dietetics; medical social work, a new comer to the health scene. And within each of these paramedical or auxiliary health professions are many further subspecialities to cope with the needs of an ever-expanding science.

Despite the advantages of specialization, it has engendered strong criticism from several quarters. Thus, medical generalists contend that specialists overlook the "whole person," and that they fail to recognize important clinical signs arising outside their narrow purview. Along similar lines, patients complain of the impersonal character of their specialists' treatment and their lack of interest in the full range of both their ills and their lives. It is increasingly evident that patients sorely miss contact with the largely romanticized "old family doctor."

Specialization has expanded, despite these criticisms and shortcomings. Numerous innovations have developed, however, to remedy the segmented approach to patients and the isolated character of specialty practice. Most notable is a marked upsurge in a new variant of "group practice," not one in which practitioners of the same specialty join together, but a collaborative practice of different specialists who coordinate their diverse talents. The recent advent of the "general practice" specialty signifies another solution in this direction; similarly, there has been a sharp increase in the number of comprehensive health centers and pre-care Health Maintenance Organizations (HMO). All of these, as well as other forms of health delivery service to be evolved in the future, seek to compensate for the deficiencies inherent in a proliferation of autonomous specialties.

The three articles that constitute this chapter touch on the major features of traditional medical practice and discuss in some detail the critical issues facing the young physician today. Oswald Hall, a prominent medical sociologist, addresses the topic of the informal structure of practice, drawing upon numerous interviews with both new and established physicians to illustrate how referrals, power, and prestige unfold among a community's practitioners. In his paper on conflicts associated with forming one's "medical identity," Wayne Menke, a well-known political scientist, outlines both the classical problems of assuming the physician's role and current stresses produced by the changing character of the medical profession. Richard Magraw, a distinguished internist and medical educator, focuses on the problems and issues of medical specialization in his informative paper. In it, he describes both the challenges and opportunities that flow from efforts to coordinate these services into effective clinical teams.

REFERENCES

Freidson, E.: *The Profession of Medicine.* New York, Dodd, Mead, 1970.

Roemer, M. L.: Changing patterns of health service: Their dependence on a changing world. *Ann. Am. Acad. Polit. Soc. Sci. 346:* 44–56 (1963).

49   The Informal Organization of the Medical Profession

Oswald Hall

The study of professions requires a manifold approach, one which corresponds to the various facets of the type studied.[1] In order to understand a profession one would need to know something about the following: (1) the institutions within which the members carry on their activities, (2) the characteristics of the clienteles which the members acquire, and (3) the groups into which the members of the profession are organized.

The successful practice of medicine requires access to a multiplicity of institutions. Of particular importance are the hospital, the clinic, and the established office practice. The successful career in medicine involves gaining admittance to these institutions, and maintaining connexion with them. Only the exceptional practitioner can survive without access to such institutions; the free-lance practitioner has gradually been supplanted by one whose career depends on his relationships with a network of institutions.

In order to succeed in medicine a practitioner must attract and acquire a clientele, and maintain the loyalty of that clientele. The development of specialization in medicine gets itself reflected in specialized clienteles. There are, however, other classifications of clienteles, such as that implied when one speaks of a "good" practice. Whether or not a doctor achieves a "good" practice depends on many factors other than his technical competence.

A clientele develops through the accumulated choices which patients make in selecting a doctor. By and large these choices are not made on a rational basis. In order to choose the most competent person for a given ailment the patient would need to know not only the type of ailment from which he suffered but also the relative competence of the various practitioners in that field of medicine. Such rationality of choice is beyond the patient.

It is a characteristic of our own type of society that a person chooses his doctor in large part on the basis of characteristics which are irrelevant to the competence of the practitioner. In general when one chooses a doctor he selects a person who is white, male, Protestant, of upper class tastes and standard of living. In a given community certain doctors are chosen more frequently than others merely because they are popular, or fashionable, or associated with a successful doctor. None of these characteristics has any direct bearing on the competence of the doctor chosen. However, it is just such choices that build up a substantial clientele for a doctor. It is not argued here that persons in need of a doctor's services consciously check such a list of characteristics before making a selection. All that is contended is that persons carry about with them preferences and biases of which they may be largely unaware, but which influence profoundly the careers of the medical practitioners in the community concerned. In the jargon of sociology, the status ascribed to a doctor, determines the status he achieves as doctor.

These apparently extraneous factors influencing a doctor's career are not mere

---

[1] For a penetrating analysis of the range of characteristics deserving attention see E. C. Hughes, "Dilemmas and Contradictions of Status" (*American Journal of Sociology*, vol. L, 1945, pp. 353–359).

Hall, O.: The informal organization of the medical profession. Can. J. Econ. Polit. Sci.; 12 30–44 (1946).

fortuitous circumstances. In so far as the doctors of a given community are established, and possess relatively loyal clienteles, they form a system. This system can effectively exclude the intruding newcomer. On the one hand they have control of the hospital system through occupying the dominant posts therein. On the other hand they tend to develop, in the course of time, through association, a sort of informal organization. Rights to position, status, and power become recognized and upheld; mechanisms of legitimate succession and patterns of recruitment become established.

The provision of medical facilities in a given community, in so far as a system or an order has been established, depends heavily on such an organization. As a matter of fact the two matters discussed above, i.e., institutions and clienteles, are intimately related to the working of the informal organization. The allocation of positions in the institutions, the pace at which one receives promotions, the extent to which one has patients referred to him, all hinge on the workings of the informal organization.

It is more or less a truism in sociology that the analysis of informal types of organization is more revealing than the analysis of formal structures. This is particularly the case in the matter of professional organization.[2] However, the observation of such organization may be exceedingly difficult.[3] On the one hand the habit of looking on the profession as a set of competing colleagues tends to divert attention from such organization, and keeps it out of view. And on the other hand the idealized fictions which have grown up, such as the insistence on the direct relationship between patient and practitioner, tend to hamper observation and discussion of the inner workings of a profession.

Hence the day to day working of such organization may be effectively concealed both from those within and without the profession.

The general problems deserving attention in the study of any profession can be readily indicated. They are related to the essential processes of the life of such a group. They concern, among other things, the service rendered, the way in which a profession recruits its new members, the means of acquiring a clientele, the means by which the profession prevents intruders from poaching on its territory, the different types of career lines within the profession, the techniques for tempering competition between colleagues, the sorts of controls exerted over its own members, and the relation of the profession to other social groups. All these are found in any profession; presumably the same set of questions could be raised with respect to law, medicine, the academic world, the ministry, and so forth.

The title of this paper calls attention to a neglected feature of professional life, and offers a basic concept for the study of professions. It is presumed here that the *established* members of the profession will in the course of time develop a sort of organization which functions to provide order, to ascribe and maintain status, to control the conduct of the members, and to minimize competition and conflict. In other words they will develop an orderly manner of incorporating new members into their community, of repelling the unwanted and the intruder, of allocating rights and privileges, of distributing clients among colleagues, of applying sanctions and penalties, and preserving their status.

To call such an organization "informal," implies that it does not originate by establishing a constitution. Actually it may possess no formal constitution. In this case the activity precedes the recognition of a purpose, and the group may have a well-defined pattern of action without any official apologia. It is an assumption of this paper that the working constitution of any established profession is something that has to be discovered. Moreover it is very likely to deviate significantly from the formal constitution. The latter is likely to present

---

[2] For a careful analysis of the inner workings of a formal group see O. Garceau, *The Political Life of the American Medical Association* (Cambridge, Mass., 1941).

[3] A critical and suggestive treatment of the problem of gaining access to information in such fields is found in E. C. Hughes, "The Study of Institutions" *(Social Forces,* vol. XX, 1940, pp. 307–310).

an idealized picture of what the members would like outsiders to believe, and should not be accepted uncritically as a description of the workings of the professional group.

The foregoing discussion has set forth some of the activities of the profession over which the informal organization exercises control. In this paper the informal organization of the medical profession is referred to as the "inner fraternity." The name connotes that the group has some of the characteristics of the secret society, some of the features of the primary group, and that the relationships are closer and more inclusive than those of sheer colleagues.

While the inner fraternity influences the practice of medicine in diverse ways it has one dominant method of functioning. Its basic activity is referred to here as "sponsorship." By sponsorship is meant simply that established members of the inner fraternity actively intervene in the career lines of newcomers to the profession. By so doing they influence the careers of those selected. The intervention may continue over very long spans of time and relate to many features of the professional career. Sponsorship is a dual process. It facilitates the careers of those selected, and relegates those not so selected to a position where they compete under decidedly disadvantageous terms. In this way it tends to keep the inner fraternity a stable, self-perpetuating group, and maintains its control over the profession in general.

Much of the assistance given by the sponsor to his protégé is of an intangible sort. It may be as nebulous as the help of an older person who encourages a younger person to define himself as a potential colleague. Since the professional ambition is, in its early stages, a fragile affair this aid is very important. However, the aid may be much more substantial. It may mean smoothing the path to easy acceptance to the right training school; it may mean appointments to positions within the appropriate institutions; it may mean deflecting clientele from the sponsor to the protégé; it may mean designating the protégé as successor to the sponsor.

Such sponsorship is not necessarily a

one-sided process. It permits the newcomer to share in the established system of practicing medicine, but it also imposes responsibilities upon him. It obligates him to fulfill the minor positions in the institutional system. Where he needs expert advice or assistance it obligates him to turn to his sponsor. And if he is designated as a successor to an established member of the profession he necessarily takes over the duties and obligations involved there. Hence the protégé is essential to the continued functioning of the established inner fraternity of the profession.

The assumption of the inner fraternity provides a frame of reference for observing the conduct of the members of the profession. It provides a sort of lens for drawing into focus types of facts which would otherwise escape the notice of the enquirer.

The next part of this paper presents condensations of a set of interviews with representatives of the medical profession in an eastern American city. The interviews were of an exploratory sort, planned to see what sorts of information could be secured about the members of the medical profession. The doctors were invited, as the leading members of their group, to discuss the factors leading to success in medical practice. Hence much of the material is autobiographical. An exhaustive set of interviews would sample the main ethnic and religious groups in the profession, as well as covering the important specialties represented. The seven[4] quoted below are not a representative sample; by their diversity they serve to emphasize the range of types of careers involved in the practice of medicine in a modern urban setting.

Dr. A. is a general practitioner, Irish, Catholic, who ranks high in the Catholic hospital. He lives in a relatively low-rent area and has his office in his home.

To start at the beginning we should consider how interns get selected. The main consideration is "personality." That's an intangible sort of thing, but it means partly the ability to mix well, to be humble to the correct degree to superiors and to act the dignified but definitely superior

------

[4] Only four of the original seven interviews are included in the present selection (Editor).

part towards patients. Because all medical schools are now Class A schools there is no longer any point in holding competitive examinations for internships. All the graduates know their medicine. The weeding out process has gone on at an earlier stage, and internship committees need not consider the medical abilities of interns. The main problem is one of selecting men who can fit into the particular hospital.

Not all interns can fit into a hospital. Some fellows are trouble makers who just can't help being that way. *You* know the kind I mean – just like these labour agitators in industry. If they get onto the staff they disrupt efficiency markedly.

Another reason for not holding competitive examinations for internships is that there are a lot of Jews in medicine. Did you know that? Now there is something about the Jew. Of course there is a prejudice against him, but there is something else; he seems to lack a sense of balance. He tends to overtreat his patients. He finds too many things wrong and too many symptoms. There are a lot of Jewish doctors in the city, but few of them have the respect of their colleagues.

But to get back to internships. What is the ideal type of internship? Well, by all means the doctor should come to the city where he intends to practice. This probably means he will have to take a general sort of training and get very little of the specialized kind of work he is interested in. However, it is more important to get to know the doctors with whom one is going to associate. After getting established in this way there is time to go away to a larger hospital for the specialized kind of internship which fits his interest.

I made a mistake and started off to a large hospital. I got to see a large number of the kinds of cases I was interested in. That was a blunder. I got to know cases instead of doctors. In spite of that I've been able to build up a moderate practice and live comfortably.

In medicine a person has to *build* a practice. The word "build" is the right one. A medical practice is like a piece of architecture. Some are grander than others. Some have a poor foundation and will not support the continued weight of the super-structure. Some of them mushroom upward and then taper off or perhaps decline. For instance there is a doctor in town who has a very large practice made up of race track people, people connected with the show business, gamblers and the like. Every doctor in town knows him, but that isn't a good kind of practice.

It isn't good to have a practice grow too rapidly. When that happens a doctor is likely to be criticized rather sharply by his colleagues. This is happening to three young fellows I know. None of them are Jewish, and none are unethical. It is just that they put an excessive amount of drive into their work. This seems to get the other doctors annoyed. I don't think the criticism is justified. Around the hospital we want to see young fellows really interested in their work, and I think the older doctors are always ready to go out of their way to help out such young fellows.

But to go back to building a practice. A mushroom practice can be developed simply by getting a lot of patients coming to your office. Success of that sort pyramids on success. That means haphazard treatment for the patient. But the doctor is inviting later pitfalls unless he builds the size of practice he can handle thoroughly. Some of the doctors around here practice cheap tricks in their efforts to go ahead. One doctor in particular has a habit of fishing a rosary or some emblem out of his pocket and toying with it while he talks to a patient or family. That works with certain people.

Dr. *B.* is of old Yankee stock, a specialist in internal medicine, who shares office space with six specialists on the East Side. He is about sixty years of age and is the leading man in his field. He is associated with the largest hospitals and holds major posts.

There are two distinct types of success in medicine. There are a lot of young men who come out who either need to start earning money, or are inclined that way, who go into general practice and take on any kind of work they think they can handle. They become immersed in their private practice, do no outside reading, and have no time to do ward or clinical work. They accumulate a large amount of real estate in many cases, have holidays in Florida, etc. On the other hand there are men who start off by getting attached to a hospital, spend long hours in the clinics where the older men can see what they are interested in, climb very gradually, but contribute something to the world of medicine. They turn over the difficult cases to reliable consultants and thus protect their patients.

Success comes in medicine from getting the respect of one's colleagues. It is from the convinced colleague that one gets his referred cases. Moreover there are no short cuts to such success. No one who is willing to go into the hospital and work hard need fear the eventual outcome.

In medicine as in all professional life a great deal depends on the personality of the doctor concerned. It is a kind of salesmanship which is required. One can assume that it is an essential and without it no combination of favorable factors would put a man ahead. Dr. C. I. was one of the best trained men who came here. He was smart but he offended the persons with whom he worked. Eventually he had to turn to radiology where he is more of a technician, and the personal relations are unimportant.

The goal of the good doctor in this city is to get associated with the leading hospital and work with the men there. There is a surprising amount of co-operation among these doctors. These men may have enemies over in other sections of the city. The Catholic and sectarian hospitals are possible sources of antagonism. Until recently the

Homeopathic had a very bad reputation. Some very poorly qualified men had done some atrocious surgery there. The good men in the city would go there to operate if it were necessary but much preferred not to.

Harmony and co-operation were more noticeable among the physicians of the city than among the surgeons. The latter have a propensity for bickering. I don't understand why. The pediatricians also seem a harmonious lot.

How would a new surgeon get into the setup? Well there is a case of that here now. A new surgeon practically unknown came here. He had very good recommendations from the school where he had been teaching surgery. Naturally there is a considerable waiting period. A person may have to wait a couple of years before he finds things coming his way. This man was reputed to be one of the best abdominal surgeons. Doctors waited to see. Some of them rate his work very high. Others have been a bit disappointed in what he can do.

Of course local conditions differ in such cases. In some cases the local doctors would advise a man to come in. For example, a man came here very well trained in psychiatry, intending to settle. He met some of the local men in medicine and they advised him not to come. The reason was the field was already pre-empted by a man who was not nearly as well trained as this man, but who would be hard on the man. He would be tough on him, and the man would have a very disagreeable time living here and might never catch on. The man coming had decided to go to another place and was eminently happy there.

[Dr. *B* expressed very democratic attitudes towards his Jewish colleagues.] With the exception I mentioned above I feel that they receive fair treatment. I recognize that the head of the hospital is wary of allowing too many to get on in any one service. As an example of their opportunities there is Dr. K. L. He has a typical Jewish face and a decided accent. He had to go to a poor school and take a second-rate internship at the Catholic hospital. However, he worked hard, came over to the big hospital and took an externship, and now is on the active staff there and has risen in other hospitals also. Anyone who really wants to work and will give the hours to the hospitals, can climb up in this system.

Dr. *C* is Irish, Catholic, extremely energetic and genial. He is a specialist in internal medicine and shares his office with two younger Irish colleagues. His chief hospital connexions are in the main hospital system. He has minor responsibilities in the Catholic hospital.

I am on the go all day and usually until eleven at night. It is between then and twelve-thirty that I get any professional reading done.

In this work the most important single factor is sincerity. By that I mean absolute sincerity with patients, colleagues, and everyone concerned. A successful doctor is a man of high character.

The art of salesmanship doesn't help in medicine. Other doctors would see through that in short order. However a doctor does need a sort of drive — it's the kind of thing we call surgical courage.

A doctor's career has an upgrade, a plateau, and a downgrade. Doctors don't talk much of what brings about or hastens the downgrade. Part of it is the competition of younger doctors coming along. But part of it is a matter of patients retiring the doctor. Many doctors end up with a very shrivelled practice. In a way their colleagues help retire them. In my earlier years here I sent a lot of surgery to Dr. Z. He was the busiest surgeon in town then. Even then he didn't specialize completely. He always kept a core of his old patients. He was the landlord of this office building so it didn't hurt to send him patients.

But every doctor has a few young fellows in whom he is interested. He needs to send them cases in order to get them launched. For this reason I had to withdraw most of my surgery from Dr. Z. In his good days he was making fifty thousand a year. But most fellows taper off badly after they reach sixty.

When a doctor gets into a position of head of a department over at the big hospital, he can do a great deal for his young friends. He can always give a good fellow a couple of kicks in the right direction. For example, take Dr. Y. who is sharing my practice now. I met him at a Medical Association dinner. He had gone from here to McGill Medical School. I met him there and was impressed by his character. He mentioned that he would like an internship at our large hospital. I was helping the internship committee, so it was easily arranged. [Mentioned two others whom he helped in similar fashion.] In helping these fellows I have to take cases away from older established doctors. I find helping young fellows very enjoyable; not all doctors like to take the time. But the young fellows show gratitude and probably attribute more of their success to me than I deserve.

I think a strong factor of loyalty runs through all the practice of medicine. There is a guild sense in the profession. See how large a proportion of the young doctors are doctors' sons. Much of their success is due to the friendship of their fathers' colleagues. I was the only doctor in our family. However, not all doctors' sons get into practice. The mortality in medical school is high. I hope some other doctor will do in the future for my boy what I've done for other men's sons.

Dr. *D.* is a young Italian surgeon, Catholic. He does much general practice besides. He has his office in his home in the Italian section. He has a post on the large general hospital, and lesser ones in the Catholic hospital.

Of course there is plenty of fee-splitting in the city. When old Dr. X. (a surgeon) died two years ago, Dr. Y. came to me and asked if I'd like to take care of his surgery. Previously he had sent all his cases to Dr. X. The arrangement was a straight 60-40 proposition. I had got started pretty well by then, so I turned it down. If I wanted to I could get lots of cases over at the Catholic hospital at $35 each. But I don't need to do that. No, I have no patients from the East Side. I've only had one. He was an executive and had contracted gonorrhea. He wanted to be anonymous, so he came to me. He paid my rent for six months. Usually such fellows go out of town.

There is plenty of discrimination against Italians at the large hospital. It is worse for the Jews, I guess. They don't take us on as interns, and if we get on the staff later, we don't climb up the way the Yankees do. The other doctors, especially the surgeons, don't like to see us taking over their Italian patients. The way things are going now we will pretty soon have a monopoly on surgery over here in the Italian section.

Medicine in this city is a clique affair. A big part of the clique is a set of old doctors who caught on during the last war. There's a lot of dead wood among them. That's one reason why they don't want the competition of us younger fellows. A few of the older men used to refer calls to me when I started up here, especially night calls. But so often they turned out to be patients who refused to pay that I gave up accepting such calls. I think some of the older doctors exploit newcomers that way. The big hospital here is a closed affair, with a lot of graduates of the local university holding the big positions. Lately they've tried a merit system in the place of the old seniority system. But very often the most competent man doesn't get chosen. Friendships are mighty important among most doctors. Of course, the hospital isn't just one big happy family. There are bitter squabbles between men who want the key positions and equally bitter fights to prevent certain men from getting those positions. It is very important for a doctor to catch on there. They have a system of ward specials by which a doctor may have his patients admitted, in certain cases, to the charity wards where there is no charge for medical care. That allows the doctor to do very nice favours for his patients.

Most of my patients are Italian. About twenty per cent are non-Italians who live around here. Most of those are referred to me by doctors for whom I have done favours in the past. I suppose the Italians, like all Latins, are more expressive and emotional than are other types. But I've heard lots of good Yankees squeal plenty when they are in pain. Italians have a poor reputation as patients, but that is partly because the hospital in Italy was the place you went to die. Besides, the whole hospital experience is often novel and usually terrifying because of the language barrier. The sensible doctor recognizes this and treats the patient accordingly. I usually spend half an hour with a surgical patient explaining carefully what

I'm going to do. Amputating a leg is a simple technique for a surgeon, but it may be a terrifying present and future experience for the patient.

You can't go far in medicine unless you learn how to deal with the patient. On the one hand you have to develop the gravity of the professional attitude in order to impress certain patients. But you also need to be a "good fellow" to get along with the bulk of them. That's one of the biggest assets in getting ahead — what you might call a positive personality. I can name you a lot of doctors who lack that. Some get into special sorts of specialization and by the use of the referral system get ahead in spite of their negative personalities. Of course they really have to know their stuff. Getting the patients is no more difficult than holding them. The young surgeon faces a sort of dilemma. He would like to get wealthy, important patients who can make his name known; but if he loses such a patient his reputation suffers a terrific blow. People then ask, "Why did you trust such a young surgeon?"

In the interviews quoted there is abundant evidence of the existence of an inner fraternity — in other words an informal sort of organization. It is not identified in this fashion. Different doctors pick out different aspects of it, and they view it in varying lights. Some see it as the stranglehold of an ethnic group. Others look upon it as control of the profession by a group of specialists. Some allude to it as a spatially segregated group. Others look upon it as a homogeneous religious group of practitioners. Still others look on it as an integral part of the profession, a control group necessary to administer the institutions and safeguard the ethics of the profession. Some see mainly the presence of disturbing cliques within the profession. They all agree in recognizing the existence of a group, one whose bonds and functions appear extraneous to the practice of medicine, but one which exercises a profound influence upon their careers.

In order to test the validity of this hypothesis a study was undertaken to discover whether or not there was a group, spatially segregated, homogeneous as to religion and ethnic characteristics, limited to the more important types of specialities, commanding the important hospital posts, and integrated into a system in which its members exchanged substantial favours. These five points will be considered in turn.

THE DISTRIBUTION OF DOCTORS

Spot maps were prepared to determine the spatial distribution of doctors within the community studied. Two heavy concentrations of offices appeared, comprising about one-third and one-sixth of the doctors of the community respectively. The rest of the doctors were distributed in random fashion throughout the remainder of the community. Interestingly enough there were very few doctors' offices in the central business section. Their absence from this area poses an interesting problem in human ecology. The smaller concentration of doctors' offices occurs in a low rent residential area, while the larger concentration occurs in the highest rent residential area of the city.

The offices in the area of heaviest concentration are unique in that doctors have grouped themselves in buildings housing from two to eight. A couple of the buildings involved were commercial ventures built especially to accommodate the medical or dental profession. In the main what has occurred is that one doctor has acquired a large residence and transformed it into a set of offices and gathered around himself a set of congenial colleagues. In general it can be argued that the spatial relationships of these doctors are an index to their technical relationships. Those with offices in the area of densest concentration are welded into a set of close working relationships, while the individual groups of doctors occupying the multiple offices discussed above maintain an even closer set of relationships.

ETHNIC AND RELIGIOUS COMPOSITION OF THE PROFESSION

The most important dividing lines in the medical profession in the community studied were ethnic and religious, and not technical. The large general hospitals can accommodate any type of case from maternity to brain surgery. The specialists in all the varied fields are able to work together to provide the range of services which a general hospital offers. However this is true only within the limits of separate ethnic groups and religious communions. By and large, Jewish, Catholic, and Protestant doctors are attached to hospitals of their own group. Unfortunately for purposes of research the lines of demarcation found in the profession are largely disregarded in official statistics. Locally the most important distinctions in the population concern four groups: the Old Yankee, the Irish, the Italian, and the Jewish. The first and the last are utterly disregarded in census figures, while only the first generation Irish are distinguished.

When spot maps were prepared of the ethnic distribution of doctors' offices it appeared that the small area of concentration was almost entirely Italian, the Irish doctors were scattered at random throughout the city, while the Yankee and Jewish doctors each had about half their numbers in the large area of dense concentration. The Italians and Irish had almost no representation in this area. Inspection of the multiple offices showed that each was restricted to one ethnic group.

SPECIALIZATION

Information on specialization can be found in the Medical Directory. By and large specialization is restricted to the Yankee and Jewish groups. Moreover the specialists have gravitated to the area of heavy concentration, the East Side. The multiple offices discussed earlier house specialists almost exclusively. It is fairly clear that the minute division of labour involved in specialization requires close spatial relationships in order for the specialist to deal effectively with his patients and colleagues.

HOSPITAL CONNEXIONS

It was indicated earlier that hospital connexions are almost essential to the present day practice of medicine. This is particularly true of the practice of a specialty. Information was obtained on all the hospital connexions of all the doctors of the community. These hospital connexions were classified in order of their importance. In the community studied the hospitals were almost all of the closed type – that is, doctors can practice only on the invitation of the men already on the staffs. Hence the doctors holding the positions of importance in the dominant hospitals of the community wield a peculiarly important type of power. Moreover the newcomer entering medicine is extremely dependent on the selection policy of those in positions of authority.

The hospital positions are of three main types: internships, externships, and positions on the active staff. Internships permit the young doctor to carry on his education under practical working conditions. It is in the hospital that one learns medicine. However internships do not give the young doctor access to paying patients. Externships permit the young doctor to carry on his education in the charity clinics of the hospital. While he may at the same time be accumulating patients in his private practice, the position as extern does not aid directly in accumulating a clientele. The positions on the active staff permit the doctor to take his patients into the hospital. This is the key privilege as far as hospital connexions are concerned. Until a doctor has this privilege he is seriously limited in the things that he can do for his patients.

The main hospital system of the community comprises about ninety positions above the rank of assistants. Of these approximately two-thirds are held by Yankee specialists occupying multiple offices in the area of concentration on the East Side. The heads of departments are still more heavily concentrated in the above group. The composition of the controlling group in the main hospital, the Staff Association, is more heavily weighted still.

The group of Yankee, East Side specialists occupies a position of pivotal importance. They are spatially homogeneous. They belong to the democracy of first names. They practice integrated specialties, and thereby share clienteles. They can designate the appointees to positions on the hospital system. By continually recruiting young men to their offices they maintain the stability of their group through time.

THE SYSTEM OF REFERRING

The practice of specialized medicine hinges around the referral system. No doctor can succeed unless he gets incorporated into the local system. One of the first questions that a specialist asks a new patient is "Who referred you to me?" Among specialists it is, of course, a reciprocal system, one on which they are mutually dependent. Moreover it is an autonomous system, and once established is secure from any competing group. Disloyalty to such a group by its members would be very costly. The rules of the referring game are unwritten, but extremely important in the eyes of those involved. Some measure of their importance can be gathered by noting the amount of emotion generated by such activities as "fee-splitting." The latter practice substitutes a monetary relationship for the established system, and in that sense constitutes a threat to the very system itself.

There are two types of referring. General practitioners find it necessary to send their difficult cases to the specialists. The latter have no occasion to send patients in the opposite direction, though they are under obligation to refrain from tampering with the loyalty of the patient to his general practitioner. On the other hand specialists are continually sending patients with an ailment outside their competence to other specialists. These favours are reciprocal. Hence there is a tendency for the inner fraternity to gather ever new elements to its collective clientele, and to preserve and maintain that clientele. Its members are thereby sheltered in the competition for patients in the practice of medicine.

The material gathered on the referring process was collected from a small group of patients who could recall their relations with different doctors. The evidence pointed clearly to the fact that the inner fraternity referred always towards its own members, and never toward outsiders. Outsiders were frequently obliged however to refer patients to the inner fraternity because of the concentration of important specialists within that group.

The above materials document the existence of an inner fraternity within the medical profession, a spatially segregated group, homogeneous with respect to ethnic and religious affiliations, involved in the lucrative specialized fields of medicine, occupying the dominant hospital posts, and having preferred claims on the good paying clienteles of the city. It maintains its existence, and controls the practice of medicine, by sponsoring new members.

The interview materials exhibit the ramifications of the sponsorship process. Six distinctive activities are worthy of note. (1) The selection of recruits to the profession. The members of the inner fraternity exercise an indirect control over the selection policies of medical schools by their recommendations of students. No significant studies have been made to date of the manner in which medical schools recruit and select their students. (2) The selection of interns. His internship is one of the most important status badges that the doctor wears. It can never be discarded, and serves immediately to categorize the doctor. It constitutes a persisting judgment on the young doctor, and represents a crucial turning-point in his career. By their institutional positions the inner fraternity controls the allocation of the better internships. (3) The appointment of externs. An externship is the legitimate avenue to progress in the hospital system of the community. It obligates the doctor to work in the charity clinics. It involves a heavy tax on time and energy. It is an index that the incumbent is in earnest about his medical career. The inner fraternity controls the allocation of these. (4) Appointment to staff positions. These are

an indication that the doctor has "arrived." Externships are both sifting devices and periods of probation. The inner fraternity decides which externs will be selected for staff positions, and how long the periods of probation will be. (5) Incorporation into the office practice. The durable medical practices of the community persist beyond the lives of the founders. The latter can invite younger men to share and inherit such practices. Such an invitation carries with it the prestige associated with the office itself, and with the name of the established doctor. It carries the endorsation and certification of the established doctor. The members of the inner fraternity have a monopoly over such favours. (6) Incorporation into the system of referrals. The practice of medicine is synonymous with the acquisition of a clientele. The chief vehicle for acquiring patients is the referral of another doctor. There is no speedy route to this goal. One must traverse the designated stages, and be vouched for at each stage by an established member of the fraternity. One maintains his position in such a system by remaining personally acceptable to the membership of the innergroup.

In conclusion it seems worthwhile calling attention to the type of knowledge that can be obtained concerning a profession by ignoring the techniques of the profession and focussing attention on the social organization. The concepts of the inner fraternity and the sponsoring process seem to offer a particularly fruitful lead to the study of any profession. They are useful tools for tracing the stages in the professional career, for understanding the mechanisms of control within the profession, and for interpreting the milieu within which professional life is carried on.

50   Medical Identity: Change and Conflict in Professional Roles

Wayne G. Menke

That medical practice is wracked by rapid changes in technology has become a cliché What is less obvious but at least as important are the stresses on the ethical system of medicine abetted by current economic, technological, and bureaucratic imperatives.

At the vortex of the medical profession's difficulties in adjusting to current organizational forms are the traditional values of professional practice. Both explicit and implicit value conflicts are induced and aggravated by the movement of physicians from entrepreneurial to organizational practice. A large percentage of the profession now practices within formal organizations; this percentage is increasing. The expectations of the organizations will of course vary; the group may be professionally organized or it may be formed by lay persons; it may be dominated by a labor union or a corporation; the physician may be salaried by a hospital, university, or government agency. The important point, however, is that medicine is at long last being subjected to the rational, bureaucratic imperatives of large-scale organization. Though the example is repugnant to the professional image, it is roughly analogous to the discipline workers undergo in a large industrial corporation. George Rosen has suggested that in experiencing its version of the Industrial Revolution, medicine brings physicians into the hospital "factory," where they are subjected to the bureaucratic[1] procedures of hierarchic organizations. No longer is the doctor's will accepted without question; his authority gradually yields before the medical team and the hospital bureaucracy. There are increasing pressures for revising physician roles in American life. The profession has resisted these pressures with mixed, though quite astonishing, success. That it has been eminently successful in resisting the forces of social change is a testament to the political power of the profession and to the validation of its unique social authority by the public.

Since medical care requires social interaction within institutional forms, it may be referred to as a social system. Both doctor and patient are members of other social systems, all of which comprise the social order. Participants have specified roles and behaviors as well as appropriate values which motivate them. Like other groups, the medical profession shares and institutionalizes certain ideas, values, and standards of behavior toward colleagues, patients, and the public. Explicitly or implicitly, these norms are generally accepted by physicians. In acquiring values, attitudes, and behaviors, doctors develop a conception of identity which defines the physician's role.

ASSUMING THE PHYSICIAN'S ROLE

During their medical education, students are initiated into the physician's role as its values and behavior become more explicit; however, even during the period of training, the medical role is not presented as a consistent pattern. Anticipating the difficulties that the young doctor will encounter when he begins his practice, the medical role is burdened with conflict. During the last two years of medical school and during

---

Menke, W. G.: Medical identity: Change and conflict in professional roles. J. Med. Educ. 46: 58–63 (1971).

his internship, a student physician works in the context of group practice. The work is cooperative, he is supervised, consultation and guidance are readily available and there is little need to consider the financial status of the patient, to secure a fee, or even to determine whether or not the service is desired by the patient. The medical subculture which he is absorbing, however, emphasizes the values and attitudes of private entrepreneurial practice.

As Michael Davis[2] has pointed out, medical students do not seem to be prepared for private practice. Years ago, before the widespread acceptance of professional standards in formal medical education, a student could go from house to house with a physician from whom he would learn medical practice, and he could absorb medical information and the methods of private practice simultaneously. Though much of the old value system persists today, the training has changed dramatically. The training of an academic physician is consistent with his subsequent practice; the training of a private practitioner is not. It is not surprising that the chasm between academic and private medicine is deep; each is likely to look down on the other.

Identity is by no means problematic only in medical education or in the medical profession. It is considered a pervasive problem of the modern world, particularly in technologically sophisticated social systems. A great many factors, some outside the bounds of personal control or even influence impinge upon a person's choice of roles. His status involves several roles which must be played out concurrently, though behavior appropriate to one role may be inconsistent with another. Resulting tensions can be disturbing, and such conflicts are especially marked in the professional role of the contemporary physician. During his medical training, he may receive both "verbal and nonverbal signals which prove confusing to him."[3]

When he becomes a physician, he must take into consideration not only what he personally decides his role should be but also what is expected of him by the public and by his medical colleagues.

In one sense, a role is what a man expects of himself, and what others expect of him in certain situations. People somehow expect miracles of physicians; the physician has to learn how to handle this expectation in such a way to give his patients both the best chance of getting well and the least chance of disillusionment. This is the eternal problem of helping people to face uncertainty, or unwelcome certainty (as the case may be), the problem of maintaining balance in the relations between the more skilled partner (the physician) and the less skilled, but more crucially affected partner (the patient).[4]

Roles may be highly charged with emotion or they may tend toward the elimination of emotion in the interests of objectivity. On occasion, they may also be ends in themselves rather than merely instrumental techniques toward some other goals.

Man of understanding, man of patience, confidante, advisor, pillar of strength — and their opposites — these are terms having to do with roles, rather than with techniques as such.[4]

SOURCES OF ROLES

Sources of medical roles vary. A student may emulate and identify with an older physician. His model may be a stereotyped image of a doctor derived from schools, literature, or television. He may also evince an emotional response to pain and base his ideal medical conception on a strong sense of compassion — or he may observe the high status, income, and prestige of practicing physicians. That resulting attitudes and behavior are inconsistent is hardly surprising.

The medical profession itself offers one concerted and professionally accepted means of identification for the young physician: the ethical statements and actions of the American Medical Association. This professional image of the physician is deeply related to the private entrepreneur, and the profession has found it difficult to modify the conception to meet changing circumstances, particularly the organizational forms of practice. The American tradition of individualism in medicine was "stronger, if anything, than it was in business."[5] It is thus irksome for doctors to find themselves increasingly dependent upon insurance organizations, especially since they are operated by laymen. Advertising, bureaucracy — with its infamous "red tape" — the declining prestige of physicians as they become "employees," and especially increased regulation of medical practice have been perceived by the professional physician as tending to "rob him of his freedom."

He came to fear the complete loss of his professional status, which involved not only his personal interest but the quality of his service as well. An ancient and honorable guild seemed about to be forced into the employee status of modern industrial society; and like other guilds in the same situation, it feared not only a loss of personal prestige but also the cheapening of its product.[5]

But even within historic prerogatives of medical diagnosis and treatment, physician roles change rapidly.

In the exercise of curative medicine the physician is becoming increasingly a middle man between the patient and the diagnostic laboratory (sometimes operated by the so-called specialists) on the one hand, and the pharmaceutical houses on the other — reflect on what changes have taken place in the task of diagnosing and treating such disorders as pulmonary tuberculosis, penumonia, and the venereal diseases. It is not an exaggeration to affirm that it is not the physician but the laboratory that makes the diagnosis; it is the pharmaceutical house that provides the treatment.[6]

NEW DEMANDS

New factors impinge upon the stereotyped conception of the family doctor in individual entrepreneurial practice which tend to alter his role. By 1957, a third of the profession had left traditional fee-for-service practice, and the proportion continues to rise. The physician's autonomy is curtailed by bureaucratic restrictions (both public and private), by the proliferation of medical specialties, and by an increasing demand for more and better medical care by the public. Accelerated by the technological development of medicine and narrower specialization, differentiation within the profession also increases.

The fee system is being challenged, the individual doctor-patient relationship is being severely modified if not actually threatened, and physicians are being hired as salaried employees in larger numbers.

Individual doctors seldom have the resources to furnish expensive and intricate equipment for the modern practice of medicine at its best, and treating one complex case often requires the cooperation of several physicians with different specialties as well as a host of auxiliary personnel to make the tests and operate the mechanical devices.

The traditional definition of professional role, developed in the medical code of ethics, internalized by students in medical schools, and popularized by the American Medical Association, is inadequate to the exigencies of modern medical practice. Its values are functional primarily within the context of private entrepreneurial practice. Not only does it fail to equip young physicians working within an organization with a workable definition of the professional role, but it also creates conflicts between traditional expectations and the possibilities posed by organization. Yet it is precisely the specialized techniques and the segmentation of both doctor and patient that are the imperatives of modern medical practice in the organizational context.

Wilson[7] describes three major forces producing changes in the physician's medical role. The first is medical science itself. The burgeoning growth of knowledge and techniques indicate that modern medical practice involves much more of both than the ability and application of any one man can encompass. The division of labor known as specialization, therefore, restricts a doctor's area of competence to realizable limits. Significantly, responsibilities and prerogatives are reduced by such limitations.

Now it is just this concept of limited performances and responsibilities, of technical skill which does not pervade the whole personality or color all of the physician's interpersonal relations, which is an essential mark of the bureaucratic role. Specialization also implies the bureaucratic corollary of well-defined sets of relationships among individual professionals.[7]

Secondly, as the hospital bureaucracy grows increasingly complex, the doctor must be integrated into its structure. As these pressures mount, the relative authority of individual physicians diminishes. It is no longer possible for the physician to command immediate and unquestioning assent to his demands upon the hospital.

Thirdly, as the hospital assumes a central role in medical practice, the organizational power of administrators increases. Furthermore, administrators gravitate toward the higher status of their own professional role, always an attractive one in American life.

PHYSICIAN-PATIENT RELATIONSHIP

Dictated by bureaucratic organizations and the increasing knowledge of medical science, the specialization of functions in medical practice is also reflected in pressures to modify the physician's traditional role. While the "family doctor" was presumed to be a whole, well-balanced person in order to treat other persons effectively, the physician is now under great pressure to limit his treatment to a particular bodily area or function and to divide the patient between himself and other specialists. The traditional family physician presumably enjoyed a close personal relationship with his patient which was heavily laden with magical and religious overtones of confidante and confessor. This intimate relationship is now undergoing great stress. Excepting marriage, it is probably the last area of modern life where such a relationship may still exist; this perception alone would indicate that the decay of the doctor-patient relationship is not only an interesting sociological phenomenon but also of important social consequence.

As the hiatus between ethical and organizational imperatives in medical practice widens, a satisfactory sense of identity for the physician becomes increasingly difficult to achieve. Yet if the doctor-patient relationship is to be improved, the physician must have a clear conception of his own identity.

... In the attempt to train future physicians for better doctor-patient relationships, one cannot teach only about the *other* (the whole patient) but also must know about the self (the student). Only thus can this self-other interaction be improved. [8]

This difficulty is complicated by many anxiety-inducing features in the rapidly changing society that "outlast the devices for resolving them."[9] Among other things, the doctor-patient relationship is one traditional device for the reduction of a patient's anxieties; the pressures of modern life often overtax its limited resources. Physicians tend to inherit "responsibilities formerly spread over many institutions,"[9] further straining the already overburdened doctor-patient relationship.

ROLE CONTROL

In the contemporary world, the physician has a wide "choice" of roles.[3] Although all of them are to some degree implicit in the conception of a practicing professional physician, the degree to which they have become polarized and abstracted from the original context of the professional relationship is unprecedented.

Professional roles are notably easier to control in some environments than in others. In his office, the doctor is subject "chiefly to the controls of the professional values and norms, to his concept of himself as a professional person, and to what he considers good practice."[1] The profession has sanctions, ranging from advice to expulsion from the medical society, with which it supports its definition of the physician's role performance, but in day-to-day activity it cannot scrutinize his work. Patients may do so, but they are hardly qualified to evaluate his technical procedures. As a doctor moves into the hospital or into the group, however, his performance of the professional role comes directly under the scrutiny of his professional colleagues and hospital personnel, who are capable of evaluating his behavior and who can readily compare it with others or with their own.

INDIVIDUAL AND ORGANIZATION

Now the role conception of various physicians may be quite different. The nature of the work environment, whether hospital or clinic organization, has certain imperatives of operation which may — and do — conflict with the role conception of individual physicians. There are mechanisms of control in any organization that subject personnel to pressures designed to further the institutional goals of the organizations; these strictures clearly apply to the labor union health center, the company clinic, or a group prepayment practice.[10] That physicians imbued with the traditional individualist ideology of the profession will find difficulty in adjusting to such organizations seems inevitable.

In becoming a physician, each doctor undergoes some process of socialization.[11, 12] As a student he internalizes medical attitudes and values which will guide his professional development. These values are neither accepted nor rejected lightly. Even when the physician "deviates from the dominant values, attitudes, and behaviors of his profession, he rarely breaks completely with them."[1] He would probably determine his relationship with patients and with colleagues at least in part by the norms of his profession, even though the imperatives of the organization in which he works may dictate other values and norms. This is by no means to imply that individual and group practice are diametrically opposed but merely that some of the traditional value system is inappropriate in new enviornments and that value conflicts will result.[13]

Specialization, group practice (whether public or private), and the government's role in the administration of medical care remain problematic within the profession. By virtue of changing work environments, a physician may be a healer, a scientist, a bureaucrat, an organization man, and a businessman as well as a professional. In some circumstances, he may even be a clerk, an auditor, a bookkeeper, and a bill collector. One of the difficulties of being a bureaucrat, if a doctor practices in a hospital environment, is that he is also a professional and a healer; he may be an administrator and a supervisor as well. As a professional, he cannot help but subscribe in some degree to the position of organized medicine; as a healer he is profoundly moved by the family doctor stereotype; as an administrator he is particularly susceptible to the imperatives of organization and rational bureaucracy. Conflicts between the expectations appropriate to these divergent goals will continue. Since differences may become irreconcilable within current organizational forms, a satisfactory solution is of deep significance to the individual practitioner, to the medical profession, and to the public at large.

REFERENCES

1. Rosen, G. Provision of Medical Care. *Public Health Prep.*, 74: 100–209, 1959.
2. Davis, M. M. *America Organizes Medicine.* New York: Harpers, 1941.
3. Mendel, W. M., and Green, G. A. On Becoming a Physician, *J. Med. Educ.*, 40: 266–272, 1965.
4. Hughes, E. C. The Making of a Physician — General Statement of Ideas and Problems. *Hum. Org.*, 14: 21–25, 1956.
5. Shyrock, R. H. *The Development of Modern Medicine. An Interpretation of the Social and Scientific Factors Involved.* New York: Knopf, 1947.
6. Galdston, I. *The Meaning of Social Medicine.* Cambridge, Massachusetts: Harvard University Press, 1954.
7. Wilson, R. N. Physician's Changing Hospital Role. *Hum. Org.*, 18: 177–183, 1959.

8. Bloom, S. W. Some Implications of Studies in the Professionalization of the Physician. In *Patients, Physicians and Illness. Behavioral Science and Medicine.* Jaco, E. G. (Ed.). Glencoe, Illinois: The Free Press, 1958.
9. Wolff, H. Disease and the Patterns of Behavior. In *Patients, Physicians and Illness. Behavioral Science and Medicine.* Jaco, E. G. (Ed.). Glencoe, Illinois: The Free Press, 1958.
10. Parsons, T. *The Social System.* Chicago: Free Press, 1951.
11. Clausen, J. A. Organism and Socialization, *J. Health Soc. Behav.*, 8: 243–252, 1967.
12. Levinson, D. J. Medical Education and the Theory of Adult Socialization. *J. Health Soc. Behav.*, 8: 253–265, 1967.
13. Menke, W. G. Professional Values in Medical Practice, *New Eng. J. Med.*, 280: 930–936, 1969.

51   Medical Specialization and Medical Coordination

Richard M. Magraw

The public admires specialists. The professions admire them. The so-called generalists are out of fashion if not out of date. Occasionally we do them homage as though recognizing an impossible ideal for old times sake. Now and again the medical profession will single out a general practitioner toward the close of an honorable career and give him public honors, but there is something sentimental and nostalgic about this gesture . . . We respect the man who tries within the short limits of a lifetime and the demands of an important field of activity to take all knowledge to be his province, but we are at the same time aware that, the more knowledgeable and effective a profession becomes, the more refined are its means, the more exacting its demands, and the more likely its drift toward increasing specialization . . .

A surprising and sobering fact about our culture is that while its total knowledge is vast and of extraordinary refinement, and the potential for more – and more recondite – knowledge is apparently inexhaustible, the area of individual ignorance is becoming correspondingly greater. As knowledge in every area increases and as the number of areas in which exact knowledge is possible multiplies, the individual's chances of knowing what there is to be known are radically reduced. This axiom applies not only to the man outside a particular field of learning but also the one in it. Every notable advance in physics, for example, renders not only the non-physicist more ignorant but also the average physicist as well. In every science we will find good men who modestly concede that concerning some significant phase of their subject they do not know enough to have an educated opinion. We are in a better position than any before us to realize that the pursuit of excellence demands specialization and that the pursuit of specialization creates problems.

Prior

THE TREND TOWARD SPECIALIZATION

Thirty years ago graduating medical students had before them in sharp focus a stable model of the practicing doctor, i.e., the general practitioner or "physician and surgeon" as he was called, which described more than 80 per cent of the practicing physicians of the time. Of doctors in private practice in 1931, only 17 per cent were *full-time* specialists, whereas by 1964, this percentage had risen to 61 per cent.[3] Today approximately 70 per cent of all active physicians outside the federal government (if we include doctors now getting specialty training) are full-time specialists. Consequently, for today's graduate there is no predominant, clearly defined channel to follow, and the mainstream of medicine has broken up into a bewildering raveling of ramifying channels, like those of the delta of the Mississippi, and as we will note, it is correspondingly difficult to navigate.

In 1964 there were 278,275 physicians in the United States.[16] This included 10,660 retired physicians, 2752 not in medical practice, 3133 in foreign countries or whose whereabouts were unknown, and 21,914 in government practice. There were then, exclusive of government service, 239,816 physicians in active practice. Of these almost 70 per cent, or 160,075, were full-time specialists. (In 1961, 45 per cent of these specialists were fully certified by the various specialty boards.)

The trend to both absolute and proportional gains in the number of specialists is well established and is dramatized in the accompanying graphs (Figures 51-1, 51-2, and 51-3).

As is apparent from Figure 51-1, there has been a striking increase in the number of full-time specialists in *private practice* from 22,158 in 1931 to 106,630 in 1964.

Magraw, R. M.: Medical Specialization and medical coordination. In Magraw, R. M.: Ferment in Medicine, Philadelphia, W. B. Saunders Co., 1966.

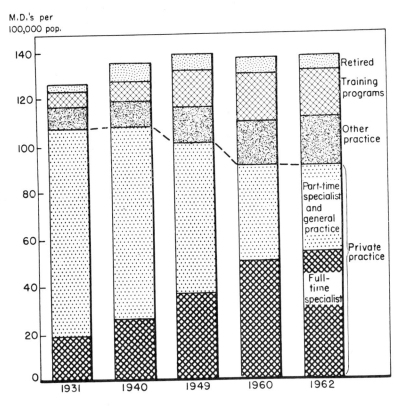

Figure 51-1. Types of medical practice of physicians. (From Peterson, P. Q., and Pennell, M. Y.: Health Manpower Source Book, 1962, published by the United States Government Printing Office, Washington, D. C.)

At the same time the number of general practitioners (including the so-called part-time specialists) declined from 112,116 to 68,344. In the same period the number of interns and residents increased from an estimated 5200 to 35,156. Similarly, physicians employed by the federal government on a full-time basis increased from 3551 to 21,914. Thus, in 1964, about 8 per cent of all active physicians were serving in the armed services, the public health service, or the Veterans Administration. The number of physicians outside the federal government who are full-time hospital staff members but not in training increased from an estimated 4500 to 11,021 in the same period.

Every one of the trends noted in the graphs in Figures 51-1, 51-2, and 51-3 indicates a move in the direction of increased specialization. In the face of what has been occurring in practice and in the light of the continuing tendency of students to supplement their medical-school training with an additional three years of graduate training in a specialty, there is little justification for predicting that the trend is likely to stop short of the specialization of virtually the entire physician population within another 15 to 20 years, if not sooner. In fact, a continuation of this trend seems incontestable. If so, further consequences are predictable.

First, the general practitioner who heretofore has been the main provider of first-line medical care and the main coordinator of medical care will gradually fade out of the picture of American medicine. As we will discuss later, there does not now exist in American medicine any consensus as to whether this function is essential to the medical care of tomorrow, much less is there any overall effort to provide the doctors to fulfill this function.

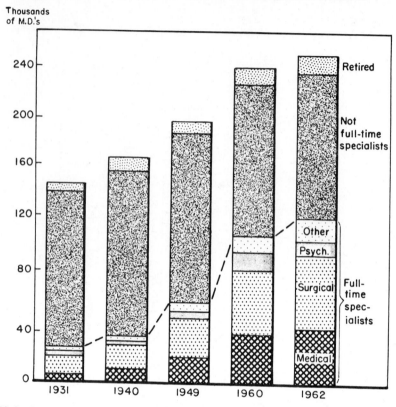

Figure 51-2. Types of specialty practices of physicians. (From Peterson, P. Q., and Pennell, M. Y.: Health Manpower Source Book, 1962, published by the United States Government Printing Office.)

Second, as graduate medical training becomes universal rather than exceptional, medical education and its institutions will change. Since all students will remain students for four years beyond medical school, medicine will become a 12 year course after high school. More accurately, it will be a variety of 12 year courses. What we now know as undergraduate training in the curriculum is likely to have a decreasing impact on the professionalization of the physician in relation to the years spent in specialty training. And since this shared undergraduate experience is one of the primary cohesive bonds now existing among American physicians, we may expect any lessening in importance of undergraduate training to weaken such bonds. What identity the individual specialist now has with a single medical profession will be further diluted.

Another predictable effect in medical education will be the increasing formalization of graduate training. At present there is no consistent academic supervision of training programs. Basically the educational aim and tone are set by the specialty boards themselves rather than by the universities or the medical profession as a whole. In a time of increasingly sophisticated social scrutiny of medicine, more formal supervision will be required and less autonomy of the specialty group will be permitted.

Third, at least in terms of training, everybody will come to be a specialist, and hence nobody will be "special." Consequently, a new round of exclusive definition of expertness is likely to occur and new and more stringent criteria for special accolades may develop. Part of the designation "specialist" derives from the idea of being special or extraordinary. A specialist among other specialists is simply a team member, but a specialist among generalists is unique and has an associated aura of superiority. It may be seen that in some measure a specialist, as we have often used

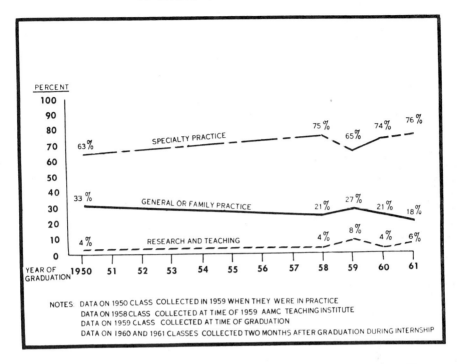

PERCENT

NOTES: DATA ON 1950 CLASS COLLECTED IN 1959 WHEN THEY WERE IN PRACTICE
DATA ON 1958 CLASS COLLECTED AT TIME OF 1959 AAMC TEACHING INSTITUTE
DATA ON 1959 CLASS COLLECTED AT TIME OF GRADUATION
DATA ON 1960 AND 1961 CLASSES COLLECTED TWO MONTHS AFTER GRADUATION DURING INTERNSHIP

Figure 51-3. Proportion of medical graduating classes in selected years making specific types of career choices in medicine.* (Courtesy of Association of American Medical Colleges, Datagram, March, 1962.)

the term in medicine, requires the presence of a generalist to define himself and is less of a specialist without the generalist for comparison. This is one manifestation of the complementarity of the specialist and the generalist, a theme to which we will return later.

THE EXTENT AND PROCESS OF SPECIALIZATION

Although each of these changes has important implications in medical care and practice, at present in many levels of American life there is a growing awareness of the modification if not the disappearance of the doctor who is concerned with the basic entities of medical

---

*It should be noted that since a career of research and teaching is essentially a choice of specialty practice as opposed to general practice, these percentages should be added to the specialty practice, which makes the figure more indicative of actual developments.

practice, the patient and his family. We will discuss this problem at greater length later. First let us take a closer look at the medical specialties and the process of specialization as they now exist in American medicine.

At present there are some 52 specialties recognized by the advisory board for medical specialists of the American Medical Association. These officially recognized specialties are certified by some 19 examining boards,[15] 12 of which were established in the mid-1930's.[2] As noted in Table 51-1, the first specialty board, that of ophthalmology, was established in 1915. Also in this table, the name of each certifying board, the date of its establishment, and the medical specialty (when it is not obvious from the name of the board) which it certifies are listed. In addition, the number of doctors now practicing their specialties and the number in training are included, together with the number of available positions for training. The figures listed *do not* denote the number of doctors certified by the boards.

TABLE 51-1.   SPECIALTY PRACTICE IN THE UNITED STATES*

	Number of Physicians in Full-time Specialty†		Residencies Available in 1963	Number Filled in 1963	Residencies Available in 1965–1966	Year of Founding of Specialty Board
	1963	1931				
Medical Specialties						
American Board of Dermatology	3,261	638		410	458	1932
American Board of Internal Medicine						1936
Allergy	831	(1)‡	(1)	(1)	(1)	
Cardiovascular disease	1,703	(1)	(1)	(1)	(1)	
Gastroenterology	561	(1)	(1)	(1)	(1)	
Internal medicine	34,334	4,003	6,408	5,129	6,713	
Pulmonary disease	1,137	465	(1)	(1)	(1)	
Pediatrics						
American Board of Pediatrics	14,077(5)	1,568	2,234	1,820	2,381	1933
Pediatric allergy	72(6)	(2)	33	17	39	
Pediatric cardiology	105(6)	(2)	38	33	40	
Psychiatry and Neurology						
American Board of Psychiatry and Neurology						1934
Child psychiatry	518 ⎫		450	343	546	
Psychiatry	15,569 ⎬	1,401	4,291	3,274	4,523	
Neurology	1,788 ⎭		634	503	654	
Surgical Specialties						
American Board of Anesthesiology	7,623	152	1,693	1,145	1,858	1938
American Board of Colon and Rectal Surgery (Proctology)	670	195	24	16	25	1940
American Board of Surgery (General surgery)	25,331	4,320	6,601	5,656	6,888	1937
American Board of Neurological Surgery	1,817		470	435	475	1940
American Board of Obstetrics and Gynecology	15,683	1,418	2,728	2,457	2,794	1930
American Board of Opthalmology	7,839 ⎰	6,410	1,017	969	1,054	1915
American Board of Otolaryngology	5,166 ⎱		713	621	769	1925
American Board of Orthopaedic Surgery	6,791	609	1,557	1,388	1,577	1934
American Board of Plastic Surgery	990	(3)	157	152	157	1938
Board of Thoracic Surgery	1,291	0	253	224	272	1949
American Board of Urology	4,630	1,346	851	712	912	1935
Other Specialties						
American Board of Administrative Medicine	3,329	0				
American Board of Pathology	7,321	518	3,281	1,944	3,457	1936
American Board of Physical Medicine and Rehabilitation	910	0	389	181	420	1947
American Board of Preventive Medicine						1948
Aviation medicine	688	0	79	76	87	
Occupational medicine	1,732	(3)	81	24	73	
General preventive medicine	708		47	24	47	
Public health	1,550	778	117	54	117	
American Board of Radiology	8,725	1,005	1,971	1,490	2,055	1934
Part-time specialists	(4) ⎱					
General practitioners	85,157 ⎰	125,599	783	370	808	
Retired or not in practice	14,747	5,981				
Total	276,477	156,406				

---

*Sources: see references 2, 4, 5, and 16 at the end of this chapter.
†The figures in this column do not denote the number of doctors certified by the boards.
‡Key to numbers in parentheses:

(1)	Included in Internal Medicine	(4)	The concept of part-time specialist has changed, and this category was not included in recent years.
(2)	Included in Pediatrics		
(3)	Included in General Surgery	(5)	Includes pediatric specialties
		(6)	These data are for 1964 and are not included in totals.

The list of official and fully certified specialties is not static. More specialties are continually evolving and are gradually added. This process is natural, irresistible, and shows no sign of slackening. Informal and de facto subspecialization within these fields constantly develops as a natural extension of new knowledge and new techniques. There are at least as many more existing but not officially sanctioned specialties as there are those now certified. The continual formation of new specialties threatens the preserve of the established, broader specialties. General surgery, for example, feels the encroachment of its subspecialties, e. g., thoracic surgery, urology, and in particular orthopedics, which is laying claim to the entire field of trauma.

Almost every defined medical specialty has one or several recognized subspecialties requiring special knowledge, skills, or perspective. These areas require a kind of expertness which necessarily precludes continuing general expertise in the parent area. Thus psychiatry has well-developed movements in social psychiatry, forensic psychiatry, psychopharmacology, and family therapy, all of which result in new and more or less exclusive specialists. Internal medicine has rheumatology, endocrinology, hematology, etc. True expertise in these fields, cannot be claimed by most internists and cannot now be obtained without relinquishing broad expertise in internal medicine. Indeed there are at least four varieties of hematologists, each of whom loses to some extent a claim of expertness in the "general" subspecialty of hematology, even though hematology itself has not matured to official specialty status. Thus, the modern tower of Babel grows. Since the use of the phrase "tower of Babel" emphasizes the problems of specialization and not its benefits, it is well to remind ourselves that scientific progress and specialization in knowledge are virtually synonymous. In the face of rapid change it is also natural that traditionalism and conservatism should increase, but standing still has its own problems. The continuing process of diversification in the special fields of expertise throughout society is necessary and desirable as much as it is inevitable.

THE EFFECTS OF SPECIALIZATION ON MEDICAL EDUCATION

One of the ways in which medical specialization has been affecting medical practice in America is by its effects on medical education. In the past decade an often-made charge regarding medical schools by general practitioners is that students are taught virtually exclusively by specialists, who are removed from the realities of medical practice. There is no gain-saying this fact. Almost all full-time medical educators are specialists, and in the nature of the academic research endeavor they tend to be "super-specialists." Thus, as more and more faculty members of the clinical departments of medical schools are developed from such a research-oriented background rather than from one of practice, the narrowing effects of specialization are accentuated. Correspondingly, medical students are increasingly taught clinical medicine by persons who had very little or no experience in what has heretofore been regarded as the basic medical experience, i.e., personal responsibility for the care of patients for a sustained period. The lack of coherent experience in overall patient care in his fulltime teachers cannot help but be apparent in the student's learning. It is perhaps for this reason that Scott comments:[21]

It is important therefore that every medical student, whatever his destiny should have a period of common training where he becomes imbued with the idea of the indivisability of medicine, with the need to know and understand the role of medicine in different settings, for example, in the hospital, in the community, in preventive and public health service, and in the academic field of research and advancement of knowledge.

To state this differently, it is increasingly true that whatever practice or patient care a medical school faculty member experiences is of a very specialized type. Aside from the limitations that this imposes on the teaching of students, it inevitably leads to a loss of perspective about the place of this special part of medicine in medicine as a whole. In terms of the politics of the medical schools, therefore, the specialties are apt to act like pressure groups.

Many authors have been concerned with this very aspect of medical education. Waldenstrom,[23] the great Swedish clinician, in discussing the impact of specialization on medical education, quoted from *The Training of a Doctor,* a publication of the British Medical Association, as follows:

The pressure of interested specialist groups to include more and more of their branches in the curriculum must be resisted for there is a limit to the burden which a student can be expected to sustain in any formal education programme.

Wolfle[24] points out:

... the tendency to include more and more within the compass of training of a professional man must inevitably break down.

Another reflection of the loss of perspective in the overall task of preparing medical students is the not uncommon circumstance of faculty members competing to present their material, i.e., material concerning their specialty, early in the clinical years so they can "get to" the student and thus recruit him for their specialty. Consequently as he passes through medical school the student is experiencing a variety of enticements, which at their best add enthusiasm for learning but which sometimes stop little short of seduction.

As suggested at the beginning of the chapter, when today's senior student approaches graduation he is faced with a decision about his own future in regard to specialization. It is not unusual for a student to have begun to make formal arrangements for specialty education before he leaves medical school for internship. More than anyone else in the medical educational center, the graduating senior student has an investment in broad medical knowledge. We should not be surprised then that he sometimes finds the choice he is confronted with difficult. Should he continue to attempt to work as a doctor with broad general capabilities, or should he limit his professional effort to a smaller, more manageable segment of medicine, which may be at once less demanding of his personal time and more prestigious and remunerative?

If he chooses general practice today, he does so in spite of the trends depicted in the earlier tables and in spite of the fact that most of his colleagues are going to get additional training. Ordinarily, in medical school he has no readily available model of the general practitioner with which to identify, although he usually knows some of these men and their work in consequence of the hospital "externship" at which he is moonlighting. He probably has two years of military service awaiting him, and this gives added poignancy to his choice. He feels he cannot afford the risk of time in a possible false start.

In the succeeding classes of medical students in the years since 1960, three factors appear to have entered into the choice of those who have planned to go into general practice: (1) indebtedness and the need for immediate income; (2) the student's personal characteristic of aggressive strivings for independence summed up in the phrase "rugged individualist," and (3) commitment to an ideal of personal or family medical care still nurtured after four years of medical school. Of these, the first two appear the more frequent motivations. In support of this view, an unpublished survey of the class of 1960 at the University of Minnesota Medical School which was conducted at the end of the internship year and again six months later indicated that over 60 per cent of the graduates entering or planning (at the conclusion of military service) to enter general practice listed as their second choice in medicine one of the surgical specialties, such as orthopedics or ophthalmology, instead of a broad medical field, such as internal medicine, pediatrics, or possibly psychiatry, usually considered as being more closely akin to general practice.

On the other hand, if the graduating student opts for a specialty, he often does so ambivalently and with some sense of loss and regret in turning his back on a part of medicine in which he painfully acquired expertness. As Jacob[14] says:

Undoubtedly deep in the heart of each specialist is the feeling that he has enlarged his knowledge on an increasingly narrow area of information and that he no longer has the temerity of his ancestors, who may have known less about more, to make judgments concerning the total situation or problem. There arises a strong desire to limit the area in which he feels himself competent and to address his remarks and judgment within these boundaries for he may feel that his knowledge gives him safety and good grounds for opinion.

In addition to his sense of regret in having to make the choice of either a broad overall competence or a limited competence in depth, the young doctor who takes specialty training must be resigned to a prolongation of his student status and a limited income. (It is a social paradox that the families of the resident physicians providing care to the medically indigent in charity hospitals in this country are themselves usually eligible as indigents for care in such hospitals because of their pay scale.) Thus, more time is added to an already protracted training, a period made lengthier for many by pending military service.

Once he has made the "big" decision, the graduate is spared many other small decisions. In a sense he has decided what medicine is, at least for him, but without special coaching he is not likely to recognize that although this decision simplifies things for him, it actually leads to increasing complexity in medicine as a whole and in the social logistics of medical care.

In making the choice of specialization, the graduate changes his identification or his professional citizenship. He asks now for a second set of papers so that while retaining his medical licensure he also becomes a citizen of a more restricted community. He thinks of himself increasingly as a psychiatrist or a surgeon, an ophthalmologist or pediatrician, and is less identified or concerned with the overall problems of medicine and medical care. It is particularly worth emphasizing that this kind of limited or exclusive identity in medicine develops under the very circumstances which must require a continuing awareness of the total medical job.

Failure to help the young specialist to recognize and to take into account the complexities which his decision to specialize brings to medical care must be laid to the door of the various specialty groups no less than to the medical educational institutions and the hospitals that provide the specialty training. The professional associations of specialty groups have understandably given priority to matters involved in defining and maintaining their own uniqueness rather than to those promoting the broad welfare of society. The members of the instructional staff of the training institutions simply do not conceive of the education of the specialist in terms of the overall social task of medicine.

THE NEED FOR SYNTHESIS

Specialization thus pervades American medicine today and shows every sign of increasing. Yet an individual (meaning literally indivisible or not dividable) is a whole, standing in persistent and perverse opposition to the focus of the specialty, which is by definition a fragment. Therefore, the effective utilization of this specialized knowledge requires an integration which year by year becomes increasingly difficult to accomplish in clinical medicine. We make an important mistake in emphasis when we talk of problems of specialization in medicine. Our real problems are those of coordination and integration.

As the reader well knows, one of the themes of this book is that the well-being of American society urgently requires that this synthesis be accomplished both at the philosophical and educational level and at the operational level in medical practice. To be sure, some of this synthesis has been accomplished in medicine through group practice in clinics and hospitals. An even larger portion occurs by way of the informal but pervading network of personal associations which each practicing physician builds with those colleagues whose expertness he frequently needs. However, it must also be acknowledged that the greater part of the synthesis has not been accomplished. For the most part, getting all opinions of potential value or bringing all available talent to bear on a clinical problem is a special and an out-of-the-ordinary effort in medical practice. More often than not such help is obtained incompletely or not at all.

Efforts to establish this synthesizing or integrating function have been more than offset by the disintegrating or fragmenting forces operating in medical care in a time of expanding knowledge. Sooner or later we will be asked what has prevented more complete resolution of the problem.

Undoubtedly the most important factor is the lack of definition of the problems and an associated lack of general agreement that specialization has raised genuine problems in the care of individual patients. Some patients and some physicians insist that patients can integrate their own medical care and that what is needed is a "cafeteria" of specialists from which patients can make a selection.

The physicians, the patients themselves, and the third-party payers all tend not to properly value the synthesizing effort of adapting medical knowledge and procedures to a particular patient. No one pays for it. As a matter of fact, doctors don't charge for it. It is not included in the fee schedule of Blue Shield plans. It does not even have a good professional label other than possibly "personal or comprehensive medical care" or "first-line medical care." Perhaps because it doesn't seem definable or glamorous enough, no professional group fully accepts the responsibility of providing it.

In a way this is rather surprising since one might expect that the very fact of specialization, with its implicit preoccupation with less than the whole problem, would automatically define a complementary integrating function. Undoubtedly, had the general practitioners been less beleaguered at this time, less involved in the rear-guard action of fighting the encroachment of specialists in areas of technical competence, they might have assisted in this definition, for it is an area of natural and special competence for them. Recently there is some indication that general practitioners will turn from battling with specialists on the specialist's own ground,[17] i.e., grounds of technical procedures, surgery, and the like, and will define their function more in Bower's terms as "doctors who concern themselves with the core of medical knowledge, those who specialize in the overall picture."[6]

In contrast, it is logical to suppose that medical care given solely by specialists is incomplete and therefore inadequate. Nevertheless, there have been few attempts to identify and measure any incompleteness or deficiencies in such care and fewer to define and provide whatever coordination is necessary. In fact many physicians differ with this view of care given by the specialist. We can understand much of this difference if we recognize that the term "specialist" embodies several different meanings for both the physician and society. When considered in relation to the actual needs of patients, these meanings are partly contradictory, and yet they are unavoidably present in everyday usage.

In America when we refer to a physician as a "specialist", we may be describing:

1. A consultant physician, a helper, one who performs special tasks to help the patient's doctor.

2. A physician who has had *additional* and different training beyond medical school.

3. A special doctor, a better doctor, a true medical expert, one who knows medicine as all doctors do, and something more besides.

4. A physician who undertakes to carry out only a limited part of medical care and is correspondingly expert in it.

It is the paradox involved in the last two meanings of the word that has given us the most trouble. The concept of a "better doctor" or a "special doctor" in the third definition derives from the additional and special training beyond medical education and also from the idea of a specialist as a court of last appeal (since at times both the doctor and the patient feel the need for some higher authority). Taken together these two definitions paradoxically ascribe both a superior general expertness and a highly focused special ability in one and the same person.

The fourth definition, that of the doctor who undertakes to carry out only a limited part of medicine, describes all doctors today.[1] Inasmuch as it is no longer possible for any one physician to provide more than a part of the entire spectrum of medical care, we may say that no doctors are truly generalists and that all are perforce specialists. But even if we grant that all doctors are specialists, there is an important distinction between the functions of physicians: some specialize by the *exclusion*[9] of all the patient's problems *except* those which fall into the area of the doctor's special competence, whereas other define their practice by the *inclusion* of all the patient's problems *except* those which others are more competent to handle. In the first instance, the definition of practice by excluding everything but problems in an area of special competence is firmly announced at the time the physician opens his office with the statement (an announcement), implicit in the name of his specalty, that his practice is "limited to" diseases of some organ or system, or to some age group, or to problems requiring a certain modality of treatment, as in surgery or radiology.

However, at the same time that the "specialist by exclusion or limitation" specifically undertakes a fragment or part of the whole, in a curious but understandably human way he also arrogates to himself expertness about the whole. This is a classic example of eating one's cake and having it, too. Several factors have fostered this specialist's view of his general competence.

For one thing, his announcement of himself as a certain kind of specialist necessarily "predetermines the kinds of clinical problem"[18] which the patient will bring to him. Inevitably, therefore, he gets a distorted view of the ailments of mankind, akin to the famous distorted map reflecting the New Yorker's view of the United States, since in the universe of patients presented to him, the specialist is superbly competent. The specialist does not escape censure for this. Sir Heneage Ogilvie[18] wrote bitingly:

No specialist has yet advanced the thesis that the part is greater than the whole, but all of them believe in their hearts that their own part is equal to the whole.

Moreover, since the specialist takes the same medical training as everyone else and then takes "additional training" (a phrase we still use), the natural assumption has been that he knows what ordinary doctors know and more besides. It is from this historical fact that the term "specialist" took on the special luster and aura immortalized by Thurber in *The Secret Life of*

Walter Mitty when "coreopsis set in." As Brenneman said, "Even death loses some of its sting when ushered in by a specialist."

The traditions of omnipotence and omniscience have died hard in medicine, but almost everyone now recognizes that special or exclusive attention to the part necessarily makes one less competent in dealing with the whole. (It is similarly true that the doctor who regularly gives attention to the whole of his patient has less capacity to develop a more narrow specialized expertness.) Nonetheless, there is no general acceptance that medicine, as it is now evolving, lacks a specialist in the whole patient. Perhaps it is more accurate to say that there is no general acceptance that this lack is important or consequential to the patient's well-being. To paraphrase Ben Franklin's admonition about savings, many of us in medicine appear to be operating on the assumption that if we "take care of the giblets the patient and his family can take care of themselves." When we look at it this way, it is clear that specialists have regularly excluded the total care of the patient or family from their responsibility. What we now must see is that, in consequence, much medical thinking has gone further and has even denied the need for any such care. Specialists have been inclined to define the patient's need in terms of what they themselves have to offer.

Of course, there are degrees of limitation or narrowness among the specialists in medicine, and by virtue of their relative breadth some of the specialists at times lay claim in the abstract to a broad responsibility for the care of the patient. As Jaco[13] states:

... it is not by accident today that specialists in psychiatry, pediatrics and internal medicine often proclaim to be the only physicians who treat the whole person or who are the new family doctors. It is also no mere coincidence that the decline in the percentage of general practitioners has been correlated to an increase in the number of and demand for psychiatrists and their services as well as for the internist who also treats psychophysiological disorders and "functional illness" in general.

General surgeons also lay claim, less by their words than by their actions, to broad general responsibility for the whole patient. But none of these specialists are really trained for such a role. Although the psychiatrist is clearly the most expert in dealing with the "whole man" or family unit, he has almost no competence in physical illness and specifically eschews involvement with it. The surgeon, although he ordinarily does not hesitate to deal with either the medical (i.e., nonsurgical) or psychosocial problems which arise in the course of his care of his own patients (at times he has a tendency to be a bull in a china shop in such instances), nevertheless does not want to be the first contact doctor for patients who have sore throats or depressions and the like.

The internist has a broad knowledge of medicine but has no knowledge of human development in infants or children, and with adult patients he has major deficiencies in training and in orientation; for example, he has no specific knowledge of the emotional elements in illness, since residencies in internal medicine do not ordinarily provide training in this area. Furthermore, he has little professional knowledge of family relationships or family medicine or other aspects of community care, and finally, he has not been trained to think in terms of preventive care or maintenance care but tends to regard the "real" medicine as that which he learned in training, namely, that of the hospital ward, which is both episodic and unrelated to family and community realities. In an important report on the patterns of American medical practice which the editor of *The Lancet*, T. F. Fox,[7] prepared for his British medical readers, the internist's functioning as a personal physician is characterized as follows:

At clinics where general medical care was given by internists, I sometimes asked two leading questions: These men having trained as specialists in internal medicine I asked them whether they would accept an opportunity of full time work in that specialty. Their answers usually, though not always, suggested that their hearts were still in hospital medicine rather than in personal medical practice.

Secondly, I asked members of the group whether they would like their clinic to form part of the buildings of the local hospital. Here the reply was in the words of *My Fair Lady* "wouldn't it be loverly?"

My own opinion therefore is that if, in any country, the general practitioner is replaced by a group of doctors trained to regard themselves as specialists, the result will eventually be provision of general medical care by and from the hospitals. The experiments I saw in the United States seemed to be leading in that direction; and, though they were atypical, they would probably not have existed if the American public had not accepted medical specialization more fully than the public here.

(Doctors in eastern United States are already familiar with the development of the hospital-based specialist care which Dr. Fox says is likely to occur. Elsewhere, notably in the Midwest and the West, group-practice clinics are a major vehicle for this development.)

Finally pediatricians, who have more of an understanding and appreciation of preventive and maintenance care than any of the other groups mentioned, except perhaps psychiatrists, are deficient in certain knowledge and skills necessary in caring for the whole person or family. For example, they are not specifically trained in adult medicine, they tend to lack adequate training in the community aspects of illness, and, with few exceptions, they have little training in the community aspects of medical care.

Hence it may be seen that even the "broad" specialists are not generalists by training or self-concept. Aside from the hampering effects of the deficiencies in training cited, there is no reason why such a specialist cannot undertake broad and continuing responsibility for providing first-line and personal medical care to individuals and families. But this requires a different *gestalt* of medical care and the doctor's job than that required when the practice is limited to some part or another of the whole. Moreover, aside from conceptual differences there is a definite difference between the functions a doctor carries out. Basically, in regard to patient care, the role of the specialist and the generalist are mutually exclusive. As stated earlier, this paradox has been obscured by our use of the term "specialist' in these contradictory ways.

What we need to define first is whether a specialist-based system of medical care such as America seems to be rapidly evolving can provide the expected quality of care to individuals without some special or formalized and institutionalized synthesis. To be sure there is an approach which assumes that the patient can effectively serve as his own prime contractor, selecting specialists a la carte as it were, and making his own synthesis. It was Fox's[7] observation that:

The more sophisticated and affluent American tends to bypass the general practitioner, making his own provisional diagnosis and going straight to the appropriate expert . . .

Friedson,[8] in his study on patient care, noted a related tendency in a different socioeconomic group for patients to take matters into their own hands.

Put somewhat oversimply, the people who use a general practitioner are less likely to be profoundly worried about their ailments than people who use a specialist after having seen a general practitioner. People distinguish between everyday simple ailments and "serious" illness, between seeking relief for temporary discomforts and care for unusually persistent pain.

In the episodic care of self-limited illnesses, this approach oftentimes works quite well. However, for the long pull, particularly with the chronic illnesses and the maintenance care now becoming characteristic of American medicine, as well as for the preventive aspects of medicine, such arrangements do not work well. In such instances there is almost invariably a lack of clearly defined and accepted medical responsibility, and the patient's care tends to fall between two stools. The patient cannot be expected to coordinate the often-conflicting elements in such care. A medical coordinator or programmer is probably required. This does not mean simply an authoritative "big brother is watching you" kind of relationship between doctor and patient. Rather it requires of doctors and other health workers and of society as a whole the definition of such a specialized medical orchestrating function. The patient is required to be no more trustful in engaging a doctor to assist him in making an appropriate synthesis of available skills and alternate choices than he is in submitting to a surgical procedure or an anesthetic. It is a mistake to regard this as authoritative or coercive, or to think that fundamentally doctors order patients about.

POSSIBLE SOLUTIONS TO THE PROBLEM OF SYNTHESIS

Although it is only now developing, it is likely that a sweeping consensus will rapidly mature to the point that some reintegration of specialized medical care must occur. There are really only two possible ways of obtaining this. One is to formalize collaboration through the structure, organization, and conditions of medical practice. The other is to extend the knowledge of the individual practitioner. One approach does not preclude the other.

It is important to recognize that the design and organization of medical instutions and the patterns of professional relationships can only facilitate (or hinder); they cannot accomplish synthesis of knowledge. Himsworth[12] points out that integration of knowledge only "occurs within a man, not between men." And Jacob[14] says:

This places on someone the extreme responsibility to tie the many ends together. The whole is more than the sum of its parts. A number of limited recommendations usually do not answer the problem, especially when dealing with people. This "someone" must put the pieces together and in doing so necessarily imparts to the recommendation his point of view of what is needed to answer the problem or to give the needy person the help he needs.

Implicit in Himsworth's assertion is the idea that either all physicians or certain physicians should be specially trained for the integration and adaptation of specialty knowledge and the care of the individual patient. We have already noted that although not everybody agrees that this is required for good medical care, there is growing opinion in support of this idea. Similarly, there is no agreement as to whether personal medical care requires the special role of personal physician or whether all physicians can and should fill this function. And finally, among those who think that there must be a special role of personal physician, there is no overall agreement as to who should fill it or how it should be accomplished.

Rather, there are four distinct lines of thought as to how this can be accomplished discernible in the welter of current professional opinion.[1,9,17,22] A discussion of each of these proposed solutions follows:

1. All physicians should provide this care. No special integrating role or coordinating personal physician is required. All physicians should become accustomed as students to the concept of medical teamwork and trained to assume broad responsibility for comprehensive care.

Discussion. This is a variant on the theme that all specialists become broadly knowledgeable, i.e., generalists. We can concur in the necessity of all students having this experience and understanding, but it is doubtful that the necessarily limited focus and expertness of the specialist can be regularly or effectively transmuted to the individual focus of the personal physician. In this solution, the assumption is made that no more than basic knowledge is required in providing personal medical care.

2. The function of the general practitioner or of the purveyor of first-line medical care should be frankly recognized as a lesser professional skill than that of the specialist. Medical training should be divided into two kinds, with differing lengths of training and differing levels of complexity for family doctors and for specialists.

Discussion. This proposition rests on the bold assumption that first-line medical care is less demanding intellectually and that personal medical care is less technically skillful than specialty care. This assumption is almost invariably made by specialists who have not had personal experience with broad medical practice. Such a suggestion makes one sympathetic with the caustic denunciation of specialists that Barker[3] made in the *Journal of the American Medical Association* in 1922 when he stated:

Specialists as a class are exposed to a particular set of dangers including those of the narrowness and monotony of "piece worker," those of loss of adaptability, those of objectionable aggressiveness, those of stubborn opinionatedness, those of boastful self-sufficiency, those of selfish materialism, and those of vanity and arrogance . . .

General physicians or specialists who have been in general practice do not accept such a proposal. Of course it is possible that a shortage of physicians might precipitate some arrangement such as this, or that because doctors decreasingly assume the integrated role some new kind of generalist, say a family nurse, might by default arrive on the scene.

3. The general practitioner should be replaced by a better-trained personal physician drawn from the ranks of current specialists.

Discussion. Earlier in this chapter the adequacy of the preparation of current specialists for the role of the new generalist was analyzed. There is at present little disposition to modify existing programs of training in order to tailor them to the needs of the coordinating personal physician or for family or community practice. But with appropriate modifications in training there is no reason why this approach could not be successful. However, there seems to be a disposition to assume that the skills required to do this job can be readily learned once the doctor is in practice. There is no absolute reason why this could not be done. Indeed surgery, E.N.T., and pediatrics can likewise be learned on the job. What usually happens under these circumstances, however, is that the doctor learns to muddle through or to get by somehow. Certainly, formal training for such a role should be directed to its central functions. Anything less is an evasion of teaching responsibility.

4. The general practitioner should be trained in a different way, upgrading his training in length and range to that of any other specialist.

Discussion. In effect, this would be a different way of approaching the same end as that suggested in the third solution. The practical difficulties of modifying existing patterns of residency training in pediatrics and internal medicine should not be under-emphasized. Training in those specialties appears to be moving much more in the direction of research, with a narrow interpretation of the respective specialty, than it does toward broadening to meet community needs. A major problem in getting recruits for training as general practitioners is the hesitancy of graduates to make a major investment of training time in a field which appears to be declining in status and in number. Efforts to provide attractive and effective residency training in general practice have not been notably successful. Only 47 per cent of the 783 residencies in general practice offered in 1963 were filled.[15] Of these, 52 per cent were filled by foreign medical graduates, who must take two years of hospital study to qualify for practice in this country.

It would seem that two things must occur if the role of personal physician or new generalist is to successfully play a part in the reintegration of medicine. Training for this function must be as extensive, lengthy, and rigorous as that of the other specialties, and the practice of medicine itself must be so structured that the role is recognized and the concept of the personal physician becomes a concrete reality. A massive educational campaign will be required to present the concept and the need to various sections of society, including patients, third party payers, lawmakers, and bureaucratic planners. But first of all, physicians themselves need to be effectively educated to an understanding of the "complementarity of the specialist and generalist." Pellegrino[19] sums up the whole matter in these words:

> Though we may deprecate specialization for the problems it may introduce, its growth is essential to the continued practice of medicine. To the extent that it does flourish, there is concomitant need for integration, interpretation and generalization. The value systems, methods and organization of medical education and practice have adapted well to the needs of society for training of specialists but have left largely unsolved the corollary development of equal stature for the integrating function of medicine. We now face the task of interweaving the benefits of specialization into general medical care. Neither the internist nor the general practitioner as presently constituted are equipped to perform optimally this integrating function. A new kind of generalist is required, not just the introduction of general practice into medical education.

In summary we may state with Galdston[10] that specialization "is here to stay, but that it will not stay the same." Year by year, modifications of the existing specialties will occur.

The issues of how specialized knowledge will be applied and adapted to the service of the individual patient are currently being worked out on a broad pragmatic basis in American medicine. If such an integration is not vested in persons, it is likely to be vested in institutions, most likely hospitals. For the moment a group of specialists working as a clinic sometimes serves as a composite personal doctor, as Fox points out, but it seems possible that a major new specialty, that of integrative or personal or comprehensive medicine, is going to evolve. If so, this would be a major adaptation of the medical profession to the growing medical knowledge and the flowering of specialized functions.

THE INTERDEPENDENCE OF THE HEALTH PROFESSIONS

Until very recently, neither organized medicine[29] nor medical schools have undertaken the needed study of the complex and evolving relationships among the various health professions, nor have they taken action to resolve existing problems.[30] Hospital administrators and medical sociologists have studied this partially, but physicians have little knowledge of or interest in such studies. Recently, organized medicine as a whole has initiated more egalitarian and less hierarchical approaches to interprofessional relationships. The goal of such efforts is to keep the organization of medical care geared to scientific advances and the addition of more and more special skills. In medical schools the clinical teaching program needs a new emphasis to help the medical student learn the functional interdependence of all these professions.

Without such training during their clinical experience most physicians do not practice the part of modern medicine which derives from systematic application of "paramedical" skills in patient care. The failure to apply such available skills in practice will materially detract from the health of many patients and may make a difference between incapacity and recovery. Nothing makes the lack of training more obvious than the striking fact that there is no out-of-hospital counterpart to the "institutionalized teamwork" found in the large metropolitan teaching hospitals. [31] Other than the three or four largest American clinics with staffs of up to 1000 doctors, the clinics or groups of doctors virtually never have social workers, psychologists, speech therapists, audiologists, etc., associated with them. Nurses and technicians are employed but only as medical assistants. There are a good number of otherwise exemplary groups of 20 to 80 or more doctors who need these persons to round out their clinic services but who have never even considered the possibility of adding such potentiating skills.

We have already recognized that no physician can provide all the needed medical care himself and that perforce every physician is in a kind of group practice. Although we are accustomed to think of group practice as solely an association of physicians, it is appropriate to recognize that we physicians are even now associated with these related professions in a wider kind of group practice. Of course physicians are unique in being the ones licensed to practice medicine, so that this wider group has different characteristics from the group composed only of physicians.

Even though we physicians are more nearly self-sufficient than any other group and in a pinch a physician could set up practice in a barn, we are not actually able to deliver modern medical care by ourselves. Most of these other professions now possess knowledge and skills which physicians, at least in any clinically usable way, do not have. We can be certain that an increasing number of such "paramedical" experts possessed of increasingly specialized skills will play an ever more important part in medical care teamwork.

THE ATTITUDES OF PHYSICIANS TOWARD OTHER HEALTH PROFESSIONS

The attitudes of physicians are important in determining the effectiveness of this teamwork. We need to understand these attitudes and then later consider their effect on the professions we are here concerned with. It is worth digressing briefly to emphasize these points since they are likely to be dismissed by the physician as trite and inconsequential.

We physicians understandably and, by this time, almost reflexly resist any development which might require us to relinquish an authoritative position in medicine. To recognize our need for the special skills of others is to acknowledge our limitations in medicine, and as we can then no longer lay claim to all medical knowledge, teamwork becomes the inescapable sequel. Hence, it may be more comfortable to avoid the full recognition of our growing dependence on the associated professions. Nascent professions, striving for status, sense this reluctance and assume that the doctor is selfishly unwilling to share the stage when he does not enthusiastically endorse their professional claims.

But this isn't the whole story. An important part of the doctor's resistance to any sharing of the mantle of expertness derives from his own professional role.

This role requires that the doctor be decisive, authoritative, and assertive (that is, both able and willing to decide). Harry Truman's motto for the presidency, "The buck stops here," depicts this part of the doctor's job. Also with many doctors, resistance to the idea of shared expertness derives from their own personality and way of relating to patients. Certain doctors may structure all patient contacts on an authoritarian pattern. This pattern is likely to spill over into all the doctor's professional work. In other words, because this is the way he does business with patients, he must continue it with others or become confused and powerless —hence his defensiveness. Such doctors don't want ancillary personnel to speak up anymore than they want their patients to talk back.

When the capabilities of a person in an allied field are known to the doctor, however, most physicians are happy to avail themselves of, or to have their patients make use of, the skills of such a trained person. The coworker (or sometimes a whole profession) is accorded the status of colleague.* But for the most part, we tend to consign the other allied health personnel to a nonprofessional limbo, regarding these persons as working for us rather than working for the patient. We make the further assumption that these skilled people are carrying out delegated functions; that is, functions which we physicians could perform but do not for reasons of efficiency and convenience. Thus, when the medical technologist performs a differential white blood count or serum potassium determination or an audiologist fits a hearing aid, we say that he is carrying out delegated duties of a licensed expert, the doctor. In the *legal* sense of the term, then, we consider these persons as our servants rather than as associates or colleagues. (Some of the problems that doctors have in hospitals are related to this attitude.)

In thinking this, are we honest about our ability? Moreover, are we correct in our intepretation of licensing and wise in our insistence on clinging to an older, relatively unchanging view of the functions of such professions in medicine?

Are we honest in implying that we can do the differential count or potassium determination when in fact we may not have done any work in hematology or chemistry since medical school? We do not lay similar claims to areas of "licensed" expertness in the medical or surgical specialties simply because we once may have had a smattering of it in medical school.

Are we correct in our assumption that society has actually licensed us, and only us, as physicians to perform laboratory hematology or chemistry for example? In a recent book which is generally expressive of the attitudes of organized medicine, the idea of the delegation of work is made explicit when various paramedical fields are

*Clinical psychologists have made particularly rapid progress toward professional acceptance in comparison to other groups. The length of their training, the fact that they had doctor's degrees (Ph.D.'s), the fact that their direct competition with physicians was restricted to psychiatrists (at that time a low status specialty), and that they were predominantly males may explain their relatively rapid acceptance in comparison to other health professions.

described "because they illustrate certain principles involved in the *delegation of responsibilities to non-physician workers* [the italics are supplied]." The idea that these functions are delegated, in the sense that they are given to workers by an authority who, by implication, could do it as well or better than they, is often not accurate in today's medicine. Furthermore, it probably is not the best way of obtaining the responsible and enthusiastic participation of those doing the work. Often a more realistic concept than that of master and servant is that of contractor and subcontractor.

Obviously some professions and occupations in this group are relatively independent of the work of a doctor, whereas others are less so. Since what is sought overall is the cooperative and enterprising contributions of each expert rather than any perfunctory performance, all reliable and independent expertness should be recognized.

SOME BENEFITS AND RESPONSIBILITIES OF PROFESSIONALIZATION

There can be little doubt that prestige and self-determination in any occupation are likely to foster greater pride in the work, and greater personal investment and initiative. This is perhaps the beginning of a pragmatic answer to the problem posed earlier as to how the health professions can best work together.

There is an immense gain for society when out-of-the-ordinary behavior, developed out of an attitude of service, can be bottled, as it were, for routine and dependable application. Of course such attitudes are notoriously hard to capture or to legislate (or it might be added, to measure in order to establish a pay scale). In designating an occupation as a profession, society seeks to perpetuate such out-of-the-ordinary behavior and thereby to prevail over the variations and vagaries in human personality. Merton describes this as an "institutionalized altruism."[28] It is the standards of behavior of a role, along with the implicit values behind it, which the individual "professes" when he or she enters professional training (as a nurse, physiotherapist, medical technologist, or physician). Since people tend to live up to their pretensions, the assumption of a *profession* by an individual or a group benefits society.[27] It is manifestly to society's advantage to have experts using their expertness reliably in the service of others instead of solely for their own gain. Society awards recognition and also autonomy in consequence of such effective self-discipline.

"Society gives the professions a mandate to do certain jobs and grants them autonomy in order to do these jobs," according to Merton.[28] He points out that the professions decide what the job is, how it is to be done, and who is qualified to do it, indicating that such autonomy brings self-respect and highly prized community status.

Granting such autonomy to powerful groups is risky, for as Merton[28] goes on to say:

What's to prevent an occupation that has been granted much autonomy from becoming self-centered and preoccupied with its own interests at the expense of others? With autonomy comes the ever present risk of irresponsibility. The profession must therefore be ultimately subject to social control . . . . The members of every profession know this as well. They try . . . to impose self-regulation partly in order to avoid regulation from without.

Obviously some of these occupations require more training and self-discipline than others. All of us involved in the care of patients ought to consider whether we are content to have any of them be "just jobs." The alternative is to encourage the conscious formation of professions and to help these professions acquire responsibility and prestige in the family of medical professions. Whether each occupation becomes what is called a profession is perhaps a matter for debate. But why should they not be? What are the reasons for not regarding them in this way? Are we fearful of somehow overrating the importance of these tasks?

One concern is whether acquisition of professional status and prestige by yet another group detracts from that of the already existing professions. At the beginning of this chapter we recorded Merton's comments about the "undeclared wars" which develop over professional boundaries. Another sociologist, Wilson,[32] is sure that a gain to one profession is a loss for another. He writes of the "excruciating struggle for the occupational prestige," and adds, "A struggle for a place in the hospital sun is unremittingly waged by most of the myriad occupational groups, especially those most closely tied to therapeutic tasks . . . . " He then goes on to state:

The doctor is bound to reshape his role . . . from a wise healer who often presents charismatic qualities and enjoys a very generalized respect, he is becoming more nearly a technical specialist who works as part of a close-knit medical team. As a team member, the physician sacrifices at least a certain portion of the autonomy of action and the unique prestige which have been traditionally attendant on his role.

If the new professions can gain prestige only at the expense of the existing professions, then physicians and to some extent nurses will be the principal losers. Of course, there is very little doubt that already some of the *mystique* of the doctor is being lost; but, in my opinion, more as a consequence of the increasingly rigorous educational requirements in other fields of knowledge and of growing public sophistication about science than because of the inroads of new professions.

THE HEALTH PROFESSIONS AND THE PHYSICIAN'S PRACTICE

The aim of this chapter in addition to presenting some facts about health professions is to consider the effects of these evolving disciplines on medical care and on the physician's practice. The sociologist's view suggests that the physician cooperates with these new professions only at his own risk.

There is another view, however. In the 1920's and 1930's the physician was the completely dominant figure in medicine and in the hospital. The nurse was in the picture, but only to carry out his instructions. The doctor's position could be compared to that of a piano virtuoso on the stage; the nurse was his page turner and maid of all work.

In the intervening time there have stolen in from the wings enough other instrumentalists to make up an orchestra of players. As an instrumentalist the pianist is now only one of many, although to be sure he carries the melody more often than anyone else. Now something else is needed — a conductor. But, if our doctor virtuoso is to conduct, he cannot begrudge the orchestra members their instrument parts or their solos. If he wastes time insisting either that they shouldn't play because they don't have union cards or else that they do homage to him as a better instrumentalist, he destroys the orchestra which he should be leading. At a simpler time there was one instrument and now there are many. Consequently our doctor has changed his function and carries less of the melody himself, but he has not necessarily diminished in stature in the change.

Perhaps the metaphor is overdrawn since few doctors are called on to lead the "full orchestra" at once, and maybe we should think in terms of a smaller grouping, as in chamber music. Whether orchestra or sextet, however, the necessity for adaptation is clear.

Dean Harlan Cleveland[25] may have had something like this in mind, as well as an added note of warning, when in 1958 he wrote:

> In our inter-dependent society . . . I suspect that those individuals will feel independent and self-confident who have learned how to survive and grow within a large scale organization, not how to escape into the interstices between them . . . . It is precisely by the development of

his administrative skills that man preserves and extends his freedom.

Dr. John Ellis[26] added a further note of warning:

> Yet is is abundantly clear that modern medicine demands a close interdependence of all its branches, and that too stubbornly maintained independence leads inexorably to frustrated isolation.

But to return for a moment to the metaphor — it is important that the change in function, i.e., from a virtuoso soloist to a conductor of the orchestra, not be misunderstood as a painless change from one kind of prestigious position to another. There is an inevitable dislocation in moving from a professional role centered solely in one's own virtuosity to one of coordinating the functions of others, in which a part of the task is to so structure things that an increasingly complex group of free professionals can work together. Do doctors really want to take on this function? Clearly somebody must, and somebody else will if we do not.

Here is another area in which physicians are being asked to change and quite clearly and understandably resist it. There is some tendency for those of us in medicine to assume that we have existed as a profession from the beginning of time and will always exist in our present form, in a kind of naturally ordained scheme of things like the divine right of kings. However, society grants autonomy to a profession only as long as it serves society's interests to do so and only as long as the profession genuinely continues to serve the interests of society.

REFERENCES

1. Adams, W.: Ground Rules of Specialization and Advanced Education in Medicine. *J.A.M.A., 185:* 445, 1963.
2. American Medical Association: Requirements for Certification for American Specialty Boards, June 30, 1964.
3. Barker, L. F.: The Specialist and the General Practitioner in Relationship to Teamwork in Medical Practice. *J.A.M.A., 78:* 776, 1922.
4. Commission on the Cost of Medical Care: General Report, Vol. 1. Chicago, American Medical Association, 1964, p. 13.

5. Department of Health, Education and Welfare: Health Manpower Source Book, Section 14 and 18, Washington, D. C., 1962, p. 9; 1964, p. 28.
6. Bower, A. D.: Medical Care: Its Social and Organizational Aspects. *New Eng. J. Med., 269:* 667, 1963.
7. Fox, T. F.: The Personal Doctor and His Relation to the Hospital. Observation and Reflections on Some American Experiments in General Practice by Groups. *Lancet, 1:* 743 (April 2) 1960.

8. Friedson, E.: Medical Care and the Public: Case Study of a Medical Group. *Ann. Amer. Acad. Polit. Soc. Sci., 346:* 57, 1963.

9. Galdston, I.: The Birth and Death of Specialties. *J.A.M.A., 167:* 2056, 1958.

10. Galdston, I.: The Natural History of Specialism in Medicine. *J.A.M.A., 170:* 294, 1959.

11. Health Information Foundation: Progress in Health Services. Chicago, University of Chicago Press, Vol. XIII, May-June, 1964.

12. Himsworth, H.: The Integration of Medicine: The Endeavor of Thomas Linacre and Its Present Significance (Linacre Lecture). *Brit. Med. J., 2:* 217, 1955.

13. Jaco, E. G.: Medicine and Behavioral Science. Introduction to *Patients, Physicians and Illness.* Glencoe, Ill., The Free Press, 1958, p. 4.

14. Jacob, W.: The Jig-Saw Assembler (editorial). *Train. Sch. Bull.,* Vol. 59, No. 1, May 1962.

15. Medical Education in the United States. *J.A.M.A., 190:* 625, 1964.

16. Ibid., p. 627.

17. Medical World News. *6:* 15, 1965.

18. Ogilvie, H.: Akinoia. *The Practitioner, 183:* 742, 1959.

19. Pellegrino, E. D.: Beehives, Mouse Traps, and Candlesticks. *The Pharos, 67,* 1964.

20. Prior, M. E.: Specialization and the Pursuit of Excellence. *J.A.M.A., 170:* 289, 1959.

21. Scott, R.: Education and Training of the Physician for Family Practice. Geneva, World Health Organization, Education 113, September 11, 1962.

22. Somers, H. M., and Somers, A. R.: *"Doctors, Patients, and Health Insurance."* Washington, The Brookings Institution, 1961.

23. Waldenstrom, J.: The Impact of Specialization on Medical Education. *J. Med. Educ., 38:* 644, 1963.

24. Wolfle, D.: The Implications of Specialism for University Education. *J. Med. Educ., 36 (12) pt. 2:* 35, 1961.

25. Cleveland, H.: Quoted in Somers, H., and Somers, A.: *Doctors, Patients and Health Insurance.* Washington, D. C., The Brookings Institute, 1961, p. 106.

26. Ellis, J.: Medical Care: Its Social and Organizational Aspects; The Regionalization of Hospital Service. *New Eng. J. Med., 269:* 953, 1963.

27. Fox, T. F.: The Greater Medical Profession, *Lancet: 271:* 779, 1956.

28. Merton, R. K.: The Search for Professional Status. *Amer. J. Nurs., 60:* 662, 1960.

29. The President's Commission on Heart Disease, Cancer and Stroke: *Report to the President. A National Program to Conquer Heart Disease, Cancer and Stroke.* Washington, D. C., 1964.

30. *Proceedings, First National Conference for Professional Nurses and Physicians.* Williamsburg, Va., February 13-14, 1964.

31. Somers, H., and Somers, A.: *Doctors, Patients and Health Insurance.* Washington, D. C., The Brookings Institute, 1961.

32. Wilson, R. N.: The Social Structure of a General Hospital. *Ann. Amer. Acad. Polit. Soc. Sc., 346:* 72, 1963.

XVIII SOCIOBEHAVIORAL TRENDS IN HEALTH CARE DELIVERY

It is not uncommon to hear that medical care in the United States is chaotic, inefficient and fast reaching a point of crisis. The rapid rise in hospital costs, the insufficient number and maldistribution of health personnel, the higher infant mortality rate and lower life expectancy than in economically less-advantaged countries, the overburdened emergency services in urban centers, have all led in recent years to a vigorous movement for health reform. What is puzzling to some, and disgraceful to others, is that these deficiencies persist despite the fact that the number of health personnel, the volume of services delivered, and the proportion of the nation's resources devoted to medical care have all grown considerably faster than the economy as a whole.

It would appear from the above that if health services are in a state of crisis today, then matters must have been worse decades ago. Recent commentators have noted, however, that the deficiencies in health that were catalogued 40 years ago are no different from those of today — understaffed hospitals, geographic maldistribution of personnel and insufficiency of funds. In summarizing the findings of a health study in a large metropolitan city, economist Eli Ginzberg (1971) reported that "While changes have occurred in response to emergencies, opportunities, and alternatives in the marketplace, the outstanding finding is the inertia of the system as a whole." Expanding on this theme that the established system of vested powers in the health business "swallow up" and effectively undermine innovative change, Robert R. Alford comments (1972):

> The overwhelming fact about the various reforms of the health system that have been implemented or proposed — more money, more subsidy of insurance, more manpower, more demonstration projects, more clinics — is that they are absorbed into a system which is enormously resistant to change. The reforms which are suggested are sponsored by different elements in the health system and advantage one or another element, but they do not seriously damage any interests. This pluralistic balancing of costs and benefits successfully shields the funding, powers, and resources of the producing institutions from any basic structural change.
>
> This situation might well be described as one of "dynamics without change." . . . both the expansion of the health care industry and the apparent absence of change are due to a struggle between different major interest groups operating within the context of a market society — professional monopolists controlling the major health resources, corporate rationalizers challenging their power, and the community population seeking better health care.

Apart from the consumer of health service, two opposing groups of medical reformers are active today, those following the traditional laissez-faire philosophy, dubbed the "market" reformers, and those espousing the European model of national medical programs, known as the "bureaucratic" reformers.

Market reformers seek to enlarge the number of physicians, invite increased participation of private insurance companies and, in general, diversify and encourage competition among all medical facilities. They assume that the public is able to evaluate quality service and, hence, should be free to choose among competing groups of health service providers. As would be expected in a laissez-faire market system, providers that are incompetent, inaccessible or highly priced will not survive, that is, they will be bypassed and driven out of practice.

Bureaucratic reformers doubt the feasibility of the laissez-faire model, contending that it merely makes more explicit the essential character of our current health care system. To them, medical services cannot continue in their present fragmented fashion, producing a system that allows health to be the incidental byproduct of crude economic motivations, the fortunes of chance, and some residual good intentions. As the prominent physician and public health educator, Milton Roemer, has commented (1971):

> . . . Our spectrum of health services in America has conventionally been described as pluralistic. More accurate would be to describe it as an irrational jungle in which countless vested interests compete for both the private and the public dollar, causing not only distorted allocations of health resources in relation to human needs but all sorts of waste and inefficiency along the way.

The specter of national health insurance has been vigorously resisted by the leaders of organized medicine, viewing any incursion on the freedom of the American doctor as an invitation to the decline of medical standards. Nevertheless, the dramatic surge in medical costs has forced the profession to accept recent inroads upon their autonomy. Rather surprisingly, as is evident in the aftermath of Medicare legislation — fought bitterly by organized medicine — the fear that physicians would suffer reduced incomes and lose their professional freedom and status has in no way materialized.

The three papers of this chapter address several of the issues and prospects for health delivery in this last quarter of the 20th century. The first article, by Barbara and John Ehrenreich, offers a powerful critique of contemporary medical services. Basing their appraisal on a series of extensive studies, they contend that health care has not only become increasingly scarce, fragmented, and expensive, but is typically offered in a "mysterious" fashion, that is, with few controls to assure quality evaluation and cost accountability.

In the second paper of the chapter, Charles Code, a distinguished medical researcher and educator, attacks the problems of medical service delivery by recommending an integrated system of health-care units. The foundation of his schema is medical regionalization. Within each region, a group of separate, but related, direct service units is carefully located and integrated with one or more major health centers; these larger centers serve to coordinate the units and to provide sophisticated medical functions, as well as carrying out the tasks of education and research.

Reporting on his experiences within the British Health system, Paul Beeson, an eminent American clinician at Oxford University, provides a thoughtful analysis of its strengths and weaknesses. Beeson compares the character of health delivery in the United States and England, as well as the distribution of physician services, and the relative dominance of specialty and general practice. He concludes that American physicians would do well to implement the virtues of the British system before the government imposes one that is less in accord with effective medical service.

REFERENCES

Alford, R. R.: The political economy of health care: Dynamics without change. *Politics and Society 3:* 1–38 (1972).

Ginzberg, E., et al.: *Urban Health Services.* New York, Columbia Univ. Press, 1971.

Roemer, M. I.: Nationalized medicine for America. *Trans-Action* 31–36, (September, 1971).

52   The System Behind the Chaos

Barbara Ehrenreich and
John Ehrenreich

The American health crisis became official in 1969. President Nixon announced it in a special message in July. Liberal academic observers of the health scene, from Harvard's John Knowles to Einstein College of Medicine's Martin Cherkasky, hastened to verify the existence of the crisis. Now the media is rushing in with details and documentation. *Time, Fortune, Business Week,* CBS, and NBC, are on the medical scene, and finding it "chaotic," "archaic," and "unmanageable."

For the great majority of Americans, the "health care crisis" is not a TV show or a presidential address; it is an on-going crisis of survival. Every day three million Americans go out in search of medical care. Some find it; others do not. Some are helped by it; others are not. Another twenty million Americans probably ought to enter the daily search for medical help, but are not healthy enough, rich enough, or enterprising enough to try. The obstacles are enormous. Health care is scarce and expensive to begin with. It is dangerously fragmented, and usually offered in an atmosphere of mystery and unaccountability. For many, it is obtained only at the price of humiliation, dependence, or bodily insult. The stakes are high — health, life, beauty, sanity — and getting higher all the time. But the odds of winning are low and getting lower.

For the person in search of medical help, the illness or possibility of illness which prompted the search is quickly overshadowed by the difficulties of the medical experience itself:

PROBLEM ONE: FINDING A PLACE WHERE THE APPROPRIATE CARE IS OFFERED AT A REASONABLE PRICE

For the poor and for many working-class people, this can be all but impossible. Not long ago it was commonly believed that sheer distance from doctors or hospitals was a problem only in rural areas. But today's resident of slums like Brooklyn's Bedford-Stuyvesant, or Chicago's south side, is as effectively removed from health services as his relatives who stayed behind in Mississippi. One region of Bedford-Stuyvesant contains only one practicing physician for a population of one hundred thousand. Milwaukee County Hospital, the sole source of medical care for tens of thousands of poor and working-class people, is sixteen miles outside the city, an hour and a half bus ride for many. A few years ago, a social science graduate student was able to carry out her thesis work on rural health problems in a densely populated Chicago slum.

After getting to the building or office where medical care is offered, the next problem which affects both poor and middle-class people is paying for the care. Except at a diminishing number of charitable facilities, health care is not free; it is a commodity which consumers purchase from providers at unregulated, steadily increasing prices. Insurance plans like Medicaid, Medicare, and Blue Cross helps soften the blow for many, but many other people are too rich for Medicaid, too poor for Blue Cross, and too young for Medicare. A

Ehrenreich, B., and Ehrenreich, J.: The system behind the chaos. In Health Policy Advisory Committee Center: The American Health Empire. New York, Random House, 1971.

total of twenty-four millon Americans have no health insurance of any variety. Even for those who are insured, costs remain a major problem: first there is the cost of the insurance itself, then there is the cost of all those services which are not covered by insurance. 102 million Americans have no insurance coverage for visits to the doctor, as opposed to hospital stays. They spend about ten dollars just to see a doctor; more, if laboratory tests or specialists are needed. Otherwise, they wait for an illness to become serious enough to warrant hospitalization. Hardly anyone, of course, has insurance for such everyday needs as dental care or prenatal care.

Supposing that one can afford the cost of the care itself, there remains the problem of paying for the time spent getting it. Working people must plan on losing a full work-day for a simple doctor's appointment, whether with a private physician or at a hospital clinic. First, there is a long wait to see the doctor. Middle-class people may enjoy comfortable chairs, magazines, and even coffee, while waiting in their doctor's anteroom, but they wait just the same. As busy private doctors try to squeeze more and more customers into their day, their patients are finding that upwards of an hour's wait is part of the price for a five- or ten-minute face-to-face encounter with a harried physician.

Not all kinds of care are as available, or unavailable, as others. In a city studded with major hospitals the person with multiple bullet wounds or a rare and fatal blood disease stands a far better chance of making a successful medical "connection," than the person with stomach pains, or the parents of a feverish child. Hospitals, at all times, and physicians, after 7:00 P.M. (if they can be located) are geared to handling the dramatic and exotic cases which excite professional interest. The more mundane, or less obviously catastrophic, case can wait — and wait. For psychiatric problems, which are probably the nation's single greatest source of disability, there are almost no outpatient facilities much less sympathetic attention when one finds them. Those of the mentally ill who venture forth in search of help are usually rewarded with imprisonment in a state

institution, except for the few who are able to make the investment required for private psychiatric care. Even for the wealthy, borderline problems, like alcoholism and addiction may as well be lived with — there are vanishingly few facilities of any kind to deal with them.

PROBLEM TWO: FINDING ONE'S WAY AMIDST THE MANY AVAILABLE TYPES OF MEDICAL CARE

Most of us know what buildings or other locations are possible sources of medical help. Many of us can even arrange to get to these buildings in a reasonable amount of time. But, having arrived at the right spot, the patient finds that his safari has just begun. He must now chop through the tangled morass of medical specialization. The only system to American health services, the patient discovers, is the system used in preparing the tables of contents of medical textbooks. Everything is arranged according to the various specialties and subspecialties doctors study, not according to the symptoms and problems which patients perceive.

The middle-class patient is relatively lucky. He has a private doctor who can serve as a kind of guide. After an initial examination, which may cost as little as five dollars or as much as fifty dollars, the patient's personal doctor sends him to visit a long list of his specialist colleagues — a hematologist, allergist, cardiologist, endocrinologist, and maybe a urologist. Each of these examines his organ of interest, collects twenty dollars and up, and passes the patient along to the next specialist in line. If the patient is lucky, his illness will be claimed by one of the specialists fairly early in the process. If he is not so lucky, none of them will claim it, or — worse yet — several of them will. Only the very wealthy patient can afford the expense of visiting and retaining two medical specialists.

The hospital clinic patient wanders about in the same jungle, but without a guide. The hospital may screen him for his ills and point him in the right direction, but, from then on, he's on his own. There's nobody to take overall responsibility for his illness. He can only hope that at some point in time and space, one of the many specialty clinics to which he has been sent (each at the cost of a day off from work) will coincide with his disease of the moment.

Just as exasperating as the fragmentation of medical care is the fragmentation of medical care financing. Seymour Thaler, a New York state senator from Queens, likes to tell the story of one of his constituents who came to Thaler's office, pulled out his wallet, and emptied out a stack of cards. "Here's my Medicaid card, my Medicare card, my Blue Cross supplementary card, my workmen's compensation card, and my union retirement health plan card." "So what are you complaining about?" Thaler asked. "I've got a stomach ache," the old man answered, "so what do I do?"

A family makes matters even more complicated and confusing. Grandparents have Medicare, children have Medicaid, the parents may have one or several union hospitalization insurance plans. No one is covered for everything, and no mother is sure just who is covered for what. If three members of the family came down with the same illness, they would more than likely end up seeing three different doctors, paying for it in three (or more) different ways, and staying in separate hospitals. In 1968, a New York father of six quit his job and applied for welfare, claiming he couldn't work and see to his children's health care. One child, diagnosed as retarded, had to be taken to and from a special school each day. All required dental care, which was free at a Health Department clinic on Manhattan's lower east side. For dental surgery, however, they went to a clinic a bus ride away, at Bellevue. The youngest children went to a neighborhood pediatrician who accepted Medicaid patients. An older child, with a rare metabolic defect, required weekly visits to a private hospital clinic a half hour's trip uptown. The father himself, the victim of a chronic back problem, qualified for care at a union health center on the west side. For him, family health maintenance was a full-time job, not as it is for most parents, just a busy sideline.

Doctors like to tell us that fragmentation is the price of quality. We should be happy to be seeing a specialist, twice as happy to be seeing two of them, and fully gratified to have everyone in the family seeing a special one of his own. In many difficult cases, specialization does pay off. But evidence is accumulating that care which is targeted at a particular organ often completely misses the mark. Take the case of the Cleveland woman who had both a neurological disease and a damaged kidney. Since the neurologist had no time to chat, and since she assumed that doctors know a good deal more than their patients, she never mentioned her kidney to her neurologist. Over a period of time, her urologist noted a steady deterioration of her kidney problem. Only after the kidney had been removed did the urologist discover that his colleague, the neurologist, had been prescribing a drug which is known to put an extra strain on the kidney.

The patient may have only one problem — as fas as his doctors are concerned — and still succumb to medical fragmentation. Recently, an elderly man with a heart condition was discharged from a prestigious private medical center, assured he was good for another decade or two. Four weeks later he died of heart failure. Cause? Overexertion. He lived on the fifth floor of a walk-up apartment — a detail which was obviously out of the purview of his team of hospital physicians, for all the time and technology they had brought to bear on his heart. Until human physiology adapts itself to the fragmentation of modern medical practice, it is up to the patient himself to integrate his medical problems, and to integrate them with the rest of his life.

PROBLEM THREE: FIGURING OUT WHAT THEY ARE DOING TO YOU

Many people are not satisfied to have found the correct doctor or clinic. They also want to know what is being done to their bodies and why. For most, this is not just idle curiosity. If the patient has to pay all or some of the bill, he wants to know whether a cheaper treatment would be just as efficacious, or whether he should really be paying for something much fancier. The doctors' magazine *Medical Economics* tells the story of the family whose infant developed bronchopneumonia. The physician who visited the home judged from the furnishings that the family could not afford hospitalization. With little or no explanation, he prescribed an antibiotic and left. The baby died six hours later. The parents were enraged when they learned the diagnosis and realized that hospitalization might have helped. They wanted to know the risks, and make the decision themselves.

More commonly, the patients fear they will be overtreated, hence overbilled, for a medical problem. A twenty-five-year-old graduate student, a victim of hayfever, was told by an allergist at prestigious New York Hospital that his case would require several years of multiple, weekly, antiallergy injections. When he asked to know the probability that this treatment would actually cure his hayfever, the allergist told him, "I'm the doctor, not you, and if you don't want to trust my judgment you can find another doctor — or be sick forever for all I care!" Following this advice, the patient did, indeed, find a new doctor. And when the limitations of the treatment were explained to him, he decided the treatment was probably worth the trouble after all. The important thing is that *he* decided.

Some people, perhaps more trusting of doctors, never ask for an explanation until they have to in sheer self-defense. Residents of Manhattan's lower east side tell the story of the woman who was admitted to a ward at Bellevue for a stomach operation. The operation was scheduled for Thursday. On Wednesday a nurse told her she was to be operated on that day. The patient asked why the change. "Never mind," said the nurse, "give me your glasses." The patient could not see why she should give up her glasses, but finally handed them over at the nurse's insistence. Inside the operating room, the patient was surprised when she was not given general anesthesia. Although her English was poor, she noticed that the doctors were talking about eye cancer, and looking at her eyes. She sat up and said there was nothing wrong with her eyes — her stomach was the

problem. She was pushed back on the operating table. With the strength of panic, she leapt up and ran into the hall. A security guard caught her, running sobbing down the hall in an operating gown. She was summarily placed in the psychiatric ward for a week's observation.

Even when confronted with what seems to be irrational therapy, most patients feel helpless to question or complain. A new folklore of medicine has emerged, rivaling that of the old witch doctors. Medical technology, from all that the patient has read in the newspapers, is as complex and mystifying as space technology. Physicians, from all he has seen on TV serials or heard thirdhand from other patients, are steely-nerved, omniscient, medical astronauts. The patient himself is usually sick-feeling, often undressed, a nameless observer in a process which he can never hope to understand. He has been schooled by all the news of medical "space shots" — heart transplants, renal dialysis, wonder drugs, nuclear therapy, etc. — to expect some small miracle in his own case — a magical new prescription drug or an operation. And miracles, by their very nature, are not explainable or understandable. Whether it's a "miracle detergent," a "miracle mouth wash," or a "miracle medical treatment," the customer can only pay the price and hope the product works.

PROBLEM FOUR: GETTING A BEARING IF THINGS DON'T GO RIGHT

Everything about the American medical system seems calculated to maintain the childlike, dependent, and depersonalized condition of the patient. It is bad enough that modern technology has been infused by its practitioners with all the mystery and unaccountability of primitive shamanism. What is worse is that the patient is given absolutely no means of judging what care he should get or evaluating what he has gotten. As one Washington, D. C. taxi driver put it, "When I buy a used car, I know it might be a gyp. But I go over it, test it, try to figure out if it's O.K. for the price. Then take last year when I got started getting some stomach problem. The doctor says I need an operation. How do I know I need an operation? But what can I do — I have an operation. Later I get the bill — $1700 — and Blue Cross left over $850 for me to pay. How should I know whether the operation should cost $50 or $1700? Now I think my stomach problem is coming back. Do I get my money back?"

Doctors and hospitals have turned patients into "consumers," but patients have none of the rights or protections which consumers of other goods and services expect. People in search of medical care cannot very easily do comparative shopping. When they're sick, they take help wherever they can get it. Besides, patients who switch doctors more than once are viewed by other doctors as possible neurotics. Health consumers know what they'd like — good health — but they have no way of knowing what this should entail in terms of services — a new diet, a prescription, or a thousand-dollar operation. Once they've received the service, the doctor, not their own perception, tells them whether it did any good. And if they suspect that the price was unduly high, the treatment unnecessarily complicated or drastic, there is no one to turn to — no Better Business Bureau or Department of Consumer Protection.

When something goes really wrong — a person is killed or maimed in the course of medical treatment — there is still no formal avenue of recourse for the patient or his survivors. Middle-class people, who know the ropes and have some money to spend, can embark on a long and costly malpractice suit, and win, at best, a cash compensation for the damage done. But this process, like everything else in a person's encounter with doctors and hospitals, is highly individualistic, and has no pay-off in terms of the general health and safety of the community. For the poor, there is usually no resource at all short of open resistance. A Manhattan man, infuriated by his wife's treatment in the emergency room of New York's Beth Israel Medical Center, beat up the intern on duty. Another man, whose child died inexplicably at a big city public hospital, solitarily pickets City Hall summer after summer.

PROBLEM FIVE: OVERCOMING THE BUILT—IN RACISM AND MALE CHAUVINISM OF DOCTORS AND HOSPITALS

In the ways that it irritates, exhausts, and occasionally injures patients, the American medical system is not egalitarian. Everything that is bad about American medicine is especially so for Americans who are not male or white. Blacks, and in some areas Indians, Puerto Ricans, or Mexicans, face unique problems of access to medical care, and not just because they are poor. Many hospitals in the south are still unofficially segregated, or at least highly selective. For instance, in towns outside of Orangeburg, South Carolina, blacks claim they are admitted to the hospital only on the recommendation of a (white) employer or other white "reference."

In the big cities of the north, health facilities are available on a more equal footing to blacks, browns, and poor whites. But for the nonwhite patient, the medical experience is more likely to be something he will not look forward to repeating. The first thing he notices about the large hospital — he is more likely to be at a hospital clinic than at a private doctor's office — is that the doctors are almost uniformly white; the nonskilled workers are almost entirely brown or black. Thus the nonwhite patient enters the hospital at the bottom end of its social scale, quite aside from any personal racial prejudices the staff may harbor. And, in medicine, these prejudices take a particularly insulting form. Black and Puerto Rican patients complain again and again of literally being "treated like animals" by everyone from the clerks to the M.D.'s. Since blacks are assumed to be less sensitive than white patients, they get less privacy. Since blacks are assumed to be more ignorant than whites, they get less by way of explanation of what is happening to them. And since they are assumed to be irresponsible and forgetful, they are more likely to be given a drastic, one-shot treatment, instead of a prolonged regimen of drugs, or a restricted diet.

Only a part of this medical racism is due to the racist attitudes of individual medical personnel. The rest is "institutional racism," a built-in feature of the way medicine is learned and practiced in the United States. As interns and residents, young doctors get their training by practicing on the hospital ward and clinic patients — generally nonwhite. Later they make their money by practicing for a paying clientele — generally white. White patients are "customers"; black patients are "teaching material." White patients pay for care with their money; black patients pay with their dignity and their comfort. Clinic patients at the hospital affiliated with Columbia University's medical school recently learned this distinction in a particularly painful way. They had complained that anesthesia was never available in the dental clinic. Finally, a leak from one of the dental interns showed that this was an official policy: the patient's pain is a good guide to the dentist-in-training — it teaches him not to drill too deep. Anesthesia would deaden the pain and dull the intern's learning experience.

Hospitals' institutional racism clearly serves the needs of the medical system, but it is also an instrument of the racist, repressive impulses of the society at large. Black community organizations in New York have charged hospitals with "genocidal" policies towards the black community. Harlem residents tell of medical atrocities — cases where patients have unwittingly given their lives or their organs in the cause of medical research. A more common charge is that, to public hospital doctors, "the birth control method of choice for black women is the hysterectomy." Even some doctors admit that hysterectomies are often performed with pretty slim justification in ghetto hospitals. (After all, they can't be expected to take a pill every day, can they? And one less black baby is one less baby on welfare, isn't it?) If deaths from sloppy abortions run highest in the ghetto, it is partly because black women are afraid to go to the hospital for an abortion or for treatment following a sloppy abortion, fearing that an involuntary sterilization — all for "medical" reasons — will be the likely result. Aside from their medical policies, ghetto hospitals have a reputation as racist because they serve as police strongholds in the community. In the emergency room, cops often outnumber doctors. They interrogate the wounded — often before the doctor does, and pick up any vagrants, police brutality victims, drunks or addicts who have mistakenly come in for help. In fact, during the 1964 riots in New York, the police used Harlem Hospital as a launching pad for their pacification measures.

Women are the other major group of Americans singled out for special treatment by the medical system. Just as blacks face a medical hierarchy dominated by whites, women entering a hospital or doctor's office encounter a hierarchy headed by men, with women as nurses and aides playing subservient, hand-maid roles. And in the medical system, women face all the male supremacist attitudes and superstitions that characterize American society in general — they are the victims of sexism, as blacks are of racism. Women are assumed to be incapable of understanding complex technological explanations, so they are not given any. Women are assumed to be emotional and "difficult," so they are often classified as neurotic well before physical illness has been ruled out. (Note how many tranquilizer ads in medical journals depict women, rather than men, as likely customers.) And women are assumed to be vain, so they are the special prey of the paramedical dieting, cosmetics, and plastic surgery businesses.

Everyone who enters the medical system in search of care quickly finds himself transformed into an object, a mass of organs and pathology. Women have a special handicap — they start out as "objects." Physicians, despite their supposed objectivity and clinical impersonality, share all the sexual hangups of other American men. The sick person who enters the gynecology clinic is the same sex as the sexual "object" who sells cars in the magazine ads. What makes matters worse is that a high proportion of routine medical care for women centers on the most superstitious and fantasy-ridden aspect of female physiology — the reproductive system. Women of all classes almost uniformly hate or fear their gynecologists. The gynecologist plays a controlling role in that aspect of their lives society values most, the sexual aspect – and he knows it. Middle-class women find a man who is either patronizingly jolly, or cold and condescending. Poorer women, using clinics, are more likely to encounter outright brutality and sadism. Of course, black women have it worst of all. A shy teenager from a New York ghetto reports going to the clinic for her first prenatal check-up, and being used as teaching material for an entire class of young, male medical students learning to give pelvic examinations.

Doctors and hospitals treat pregnancy and childbirth, which are probably among the healthier things that women experience, as diseases – to be supervised by doctors and confined to hospitals. Women in other economically advanced countries, such as Holland, receive their prenatal care at home, from nurses, and, if all goes well, are delivered at home by trained midwives. (The Netherlands rank third lowest in infant mortality rate; the U.S. ranks fourteenth!) But for American women, pregnancy and childbirth are just another harrowing, expensive medical procedure. The doctor does it; the woman is essentially passive. Even in large cities, women often have to go from one obstetrician to another before they find one who approves of natural childbirth. Otherwise, childbirth is handled as if it were a surgical operation, even to the point of "scheduling" the event to suit the obstetrician's convenience through the use of possibly dangerous labor-inducing drugs.

Most people who have set out to look for medical care eventually have to conclude that there *is* no American medical system – at least there is no systematic way in America of getting medical help when you need it, without being financially ruined, humiliated, or injured in the process. What system there is – the three hundred thousand doctors, seven thousand hospitals and supporting insurance plans – was clearly not designed to deal with the sick. In fact the one thing you need most in order to qualify for care financially and to survive the process of obtaining it is *health*, plus, of course, a good deal of cunning and resourcefulness. The trouble is that it's almost impossible to stay healthy and

strong enough to be able to tackle the medical system. Preventive health care (regular check-ups, chest X-rays, pap tests, etc.) is not a specialty or even an interest of the American medical system.

The price of this double bind – having to be healthy just to stay healthy – is not just consumer frustration and discomfort. The price is lives. The United States ranks fourteenth among the nations of the world in infant mortality, which means that approximately 33,000 American babies under one year old die unnecessarily every year. (Our infant mortality statistics are not, as often asserted, so high because they are "spoiled" by the death rates for blacks. The statistics for white Americans alone compare unfavorably to those for countries such as Sweden, the Netherlands, Norway, etc.) Mothers also stand a better chance of dying in the United States, where the maternal mortality rate ranks twelfth among the world's nations. The average American man lives five years less than the Swedish man and his life expectancy is shorter than for males in seventeen other nations. Many American men never live out their already relatively short lifetime, since the chance of dying between ages forty and fifty is twice as high for an American as it is for a Scandinavian. What is perhaps most alarming about these statistics is that they are, in a relative sense, getting worse. The statistics improve a little each year, but at a rate far slower than that for other advanced countries. Gradually, the United States is slipping behind most of the European nations, and even some non-European nations, in its ability to keep its citizens alive.

These are the symptoms: unhealthy statistics, soaring costs and mounting consumer frustration over the quality and even the quantity of medical care. Practically everyone but the A.M.A. agrees that something is drastically wrong. The roster of public figures actively concerned about the health care crisis is beginning to read like *Who's Who in America:* Labor leaders Walter Reuther of the Auto Workers and Harold Gibbons of the Teamsters, businessmen like General James Gavin of Arthur D. Little, Inc., politicians like New York's Mayor John Lindsay and Cleveland's

Mayor Carl Stokes, doctors like Michael DeBakey of Baylor College of Medicine, and civil rights leaders like Mrs. Martin Luther King, Jr. and Whitney Young, Jr. With the help of eminent medical economists like Harvard's Rashi Fein and Princeton's Ann Somers, these liberal leaders have come up with a common diagnosis of the problem: the medical care system is in a state of near-chaos. There is no one to blame — medical care is simply adrift, with the winds rising in all directions. In the words of the official pamphlet of the Committee for National Health Insurance (a coalition of one hundred well-known liberals): "The fact is that we do not have a health care system at all. We have a 'nonsystem.'" According to this diagnosis, the health care industry is, in the words of the January, 1970, *Fortune* magazine, a "cottage industry." It is dominated by small, inefficient and uncoordinated enterprises (private doctors, small hospitals, and nursing homes), which add up to a fragmented and wasteful whole — a nonsystem.

Proponents of the nonsystem theory trace the problem to the fact that health care, as a commodity, does not obey the orderly, businesslike laws of economics. With a commodity like bacon, demand reflects people's desire to eat bacon and ability to pay for bacon. Since the supply gracefully adjusts itself to demand, things never get out of hand — there is a *system* of bacon production and sales. No such invisible hand of economic law operates in the health market. First, people buy medical care when they have to, not when they want to or can afford to. Then, when he does go to purchase care, the consumer is not the one who decides what and how much to buy — the doctor or hospital does. In other words, in the medical market place, it is the supplier who controls the demand. Finally, the medical care suppliers have none of the usual economic incentives to lower their prices or rationalize their services. Most hospitals receive a large part of their income on a cost-plus basis from insurance organizations, and couldn't care less about cost or efficiency. Doctors do not compete on the basis of price. In fact, given the shortage of doctors (which is maintained by the doctors themselves

through the A.M.A.'s prevention of medical school expansion), they don't have to compete at all.

Solutions offered by the liberal viewers of the medical nonsystem are all along the lines of putting the health industry on a more "rational," i.e., businesslike basis. First, the consumer should not have to fish in his pocket each time the need for care arises; he should have some sort of all-purpose medical credit card. With some form of National Health Insurance, all consumers, rich or poor, would have the same amount of medical credit, paid for by the government, by the consumer, or both through payroll taxes. Second, the delivery of health services must be made more efficient. Just as supermarkets are more efficient than corner groceries, and shopping centers are more efficient than isolated supermarkets, the medical system ought to be more efficient if it were bigger and more integrated at all levels. Doctors should be encouraged to come together into group practices, and group practices, hospitals and medical schools should be gradually knitted together into coordinated regional medical care systems. Since they are the centers of medical technology, the medical schools should be the centers and leaders of these regional systems — regulating quality in the "outposts," training professional and paraprofessional personnel, and planning to meet changing needs.

There is only one thing wrong with this analysis of the health care crisis: it's based on a false assumption. The medical reformers have assumed, understandably enough, that the function of the American health industry is to provide adequate health care to the American people. From this it is easy enough to conclude that there is no American health *system*. But this is like assuming that the function of the TV networks is to give comprehensive, penetrating, and meaningful information to the viewers — a premise which would quickly lead us to believe that the networks have fallen into wild disorganization and confusion. Like the mass media, the American medical industry has many items on its agenda other than service to the consumers. Analyzed in terms of all of its functions, the medical industry emerges as a coherent, highly organized system. One particular function – patient care – may be getting slighted, and there may be some problems in other areas as well, but it remains a *system*, and can only be analyzed as such.

The most obvious function of the American medical system, other than patient care, is profit-making. When it comes to making money, the health industry is an extraordinarily well-organized and efficient machine. The most profitable small business around is the private practice of medicine, with aggregate profits running into the billions. The most profitable big business in America is the manufacture and sale of drugs. Rivaling the drug industry for Wall Street attention is the burgeoning hospital supply and equipment industry, with products ranging from chicken soup to catheters and heart-lung machines. The fledgling nursing home (for profit) industry was a speculator's dream in 1968 and 1969, and even the stolid insurance companies gross over ten billion dollars a year in health insurance premiums. In fact, the health business is so profitable that even the "nonprofit" hospitals make profits. All that "nonprofit" means is that the hospital's profit, i.e., the difference between its income and its expenditures, is not distributed to shareholders. These nonprofits are used to finance the expansion of medical empires – to buy real estate, stocks, plush new buildings, and expensively salaried professional employees. The medical system may not be doing too well at fighting disease, but, as any broker will testify, it's one of the healthiest businesses around.

Next in the medical system's list of priorities is research. Again, if this undertaking is measured in terms of its dividends for patient care, it comes out looking pretty unsystematic and disorganized. Although the vast federal appropriations for biomedical research are primarily motivated by the hope of improving health care, only a small fraction (much smaller than need be) of the work done in the name of medical research leaks out to the general public as improved medical care. But medical research has a *raison d'être* wholly independent of the delivery of health services, as an indispensable part of the nation's giant research and development enterprise. Since the Second World War, the United States has developed a vast machinery for R.&D. in all areas – physics, electronics, aerospace as well as biomedical sciences – financed largely by the government and carried out in universities and private industry. It has generated military and aerospace technology, and all the many little innovations which fuel the expansion of private industry.

For the purposes of this growing R.&D. effort, the medical system is important because it happens to be the place where R.&D. in general comes into contact with human material. Medical research is the link. The nation's major biomedical research institutes are affiliated to hospitals to a significant extent because they require human material to carry out their own, usually abstract, investigations. For instance, a sophisticated (and possible patentable) technique for investigating protein structure was recently developed through the use of the blood of several dozen victims of a rare and fatal bone marrow disease. Even the research carried out inside hospitals has implications for the entire R.&D. enterprise. Investigations of the pulmonary disorders of patients in Harlem Hospital may provide insights for designing space suits, or it may contribute to the technology of aerosol dissemination of nerve gas. Or, of course, it may simply lead to yet another investigation.

Human bodies are not all that the medical care system offers up to R.&D. The sociological and psychological research carried out in hospitals and ghetto health centers may have pay-offs in the form of new counterinsurgency techniques for use at home and abroad. And who knows what sinister – or benignly academic – ends are met by the routine neurological and drug research carried out on the nation's millons of mental hospital inmates?

Finally, an important function of the medical care system is the reproduction of its key personnel – physicians. Here, again, there seems to be no system if patient care is the ultimate goal. The medical schools graduate each year just a few more doctors than are needed to replace the ones who retire, and far too few doctors to keep up with the growth of population. Of those who graduate, a growing proportion go straight into academic, government, or industrial biomedical research, and never see a patient. The rest, according to some dissatisfied medical students, aren't trained to take care of patients anyway — having been educated chiefly in academic medicine (a mixture of basic sciences and "interesting" pathology). But all this is not as irrational as it seems. The limited size of medical school classes has been maintained through the diligent, and entirely systematic, efforts of the A.M.A. Too many — or even enough — doctors would mean lower profits for those already in practice. And the research orientation of medical education simply reflects the medical schools' own consuming preoccupation with research.

Profits, research and teaching, then, are independent functions of the medical system, not just adjuncts to patient care. But they do not go on along separate tracks, removed from patient care. Patients are the indispensable ingredient of medical profit-making, research, and education. In order that the medical industry serve these functions, patient care must be twisted to meet the needs of these other "medical" enterprises.

Different groups of patients serve the ends of profit-making, research and education in different ways. The rich, of course, do much to keep medical care profitable. They can afford luxury, so, for them, the medical system produces a luxury commodity — the most painstaking, super-technological treatment possible; special cosmetic care to preserve youth, or to add or subtract fatty tissue; even sumptuous private hospital rooms with carpeting and a selection of wines at meals. The poor, on the other hand, serve chiefly to subsidize medical research and education — with their bodies. City and county hospitals and the wards and clinics of private hospitals provide free care for the poor, who, in turn, provide their bodies for young doctors to practice on and for researchers to experiment with. The lucky poor patient with a rare or interesting disease may qualify for someone's research project, and end up receiving the technically most advanced care. But most of the poor are no more interesting than they are profitable, and receive minimal, low-quality care from bored young interns.

The majority of Americans have enough money to buy their way out of being used for research, but not enough to buy luxury care. Medical care for the middle class is, like any other commodity, aimed at a mass market: the profits are based on volume, not on high quality. The rich man may have his steak dinners catered to him individually; the middle-class consumer waits for his hamburger in the check-out line at the A&P. Similarly, the middle-class patient waits in crowded waiting rooms, receives five minutes of brusque, impersonal attention from a doctor who is quicker to farm him out to a specialist than to take the time to treat him himself, and finally is charged all that the market will bear. Preventive care is out of the question: it is neither very profitable nor interesting to the modern, science-oriented M.D.

The crisis experienced by the poor and middle-class consumer of health care can be traced directly to the fact that patient care is not the only, or even the primary, aim of the medical care system. But what has turned the consumer's private nightmare into a great public debate about the health care crisis is that the other functions of the system are also in trouble. Profit-making, research, and education are all increasingly suffering from financial shortage on the one hand and institutional inadequacies on the other. The solutions offered by the growing chorus of medical reformers are, in large measure, aimed at salvaging profits, research, and education as much as they are aimed at improving patient care. They are simple survival measures, aimed at preserving and strengthening the medical system as it now operates.

No one, so far, has seen through the proposed reforms. Union and management groups, who have moved into the forefront of the medical reform movement, seem happy to go along with the prescription that the medical system is writing for itself. The alternative — to marshall all the force of public power to take medical care out of the arena of private enterprise and recreate it as a public system, a community service, is rarely mentioned, and never considered seriously. To do this would be to challenge some of the underlying tenets of the American free enterprise system. If physicians were to become community employees, if the drug companies were to be nationalized — then why not expropriate the oil and coal industries, or the automobile industry? There is an even more direct antipathy to nationalizing the health industry: a host of industries, including the aerospace industry, the electronic industry, the chemical industry, and the insurance industry, all have a direct stake in the profitability of the medical care system. (And a much larger sector of American industry stands to profit from the human technology spun off by the medical research enterprise.) Of course, the argument never takes this form. Both business and unions assert, in their public pronouncements, that only a private enterprise system is capable of managing medical services in an efficient, nonbureaucratic, and flexible manner. (The obvious extrapolation, that all medical services, including voluntary and city hospitals, would be in better shape if run as profit-making enterprises, is already being advanced by a few of the more visionary medical reformers.)

For all these reasons, business and unions (and, as a result, government) are not interested in restructuring the medical care system in ways contrary to those already put forth by the doctors, hospitals, and medical industry companies. Their only remaining choice is to go along with the reforms which have been proposed, in the hope that lower costs, and possibly even more effective care, will somehow fall out as by-products.

For the health care consumer, this is a slim hope. What he is up against now, what he will be up against even after the best-intentioned reform measures, is a system in which health care is itself only a by-product, secondary to the priorities of profits, research, and training. The danger is that, when all the current reforms are said and done, the system as a whole will be tighter, more efficient, and harder to crack, while health services, from the consumer's point of view, will be no less chaotic and inadequate. Health care will remain a commodity, to be purchased at great effort and expense, and not a right to be freely exercised.

But there are already the beginnings of a consumer rebellion against the reformer-managers of the medical care system. The demand is to turn the medical system upside down, putting human care on top, placing research and education at its service, and putting profit-making aside. Ultimately, the growing movement of health care consumers does not want to "consume" health care at all, on any terms. They want to take it — because they have to have it — even if this means creating a wholly new American health care system.

53   Determinants of Medical Care — A Plan for the Future

Charles F. Code

Although I am licensed to practice in Minnesota, Canada and the British Isles, I have never really been a practicing physician. My life's work has been in research. I am a professional research worker earning my living by doing experiments.

The life of an experimenter is devoted to reviewing the known, to identifying rela-

Code, C. F.: Determinants of medical care — a plan for the future. New Eng. J. Med. 283: 679–685 (1970).

tions between segments of it, to constructing a hypothesis or a prospective working model and then to testing it. I have used this approach to medical care. What are the determinants of its course today? What factors are pushing and pulling it? Can they be drawn into a model, providing something better, something more workable than we have today?

We cannot design the ultimate; we can only struggle toward it. Thus, the system must have built into it testing programs, great flexibility to accommodate a wide variety of practice situations, and ready mechanisms to adapt and to improve.

Fine experiments are in progress in our country, some right here in Boston. My audience, however, is not the directors of these programs and their coworkers, but instead the doctors of my community or of yours, and the American public. I hope to influence the selection of the system of health care that they will support in the future.

DEFINING THE DETERMINANTS OF MEDICAL CARE

The Matrix Surrounding Medicine Today

The medical profession is no longer *the* determinant of its destiny. We have influence, but not the deciding vote. The voice of the American public is clear, and its message simple: "We want the best medical care, and we want ready access to it."

The public today regards adequate health care as essential to civilized living. Health care ranks with national defense, electric lights, highways, air travel and the water works; in short, medicine is looked upon as a public necessity — a public utility.

To achieve these goals, the public turns naturally to its means of implementation — its government. In response to such pressures, noteworthy steps have been taken and others lie ahead. Greater participation by the government in the delivery of health care is inevitable; for in a democracy, when a function becomes indispensable, controls are inescapable. Programs in the practice of medicine with public funds are being car-

ried out through Medicare and Medicaid and with private funds through health insurance plans. But the public must know that simply *paying the bill* for illness *will not* provide the system of superior care that it seeks and medicine can deliver.

The reason is that a superior health system has three vital components: delivery of care, or practice; education; and research. They must integrate and develop within the same system. They are not independent units.

Medical education provides the regenerative force of the system — it replenishes the system with new and improved human components and it revitalizes those already in the system. Medical care and medical education are inseparable, for the novice must learn from personal association with the experienced.

Unless research is included in the health system it will stagnate. A health system, like a good business, must have a research-and-development arm as an integral part of the enterprise. Where would great businesses like IBM, 3M, Eastman Kodak, DuPont, and General Motors be if they had not had strong research departments for years? If research in transportation had stopped years ago we would still have gravel roads between our cities, Model-T cars on them, and a few propeller biplanes in the air. If medicine had not had research during the last 60 years we would be back in horse-and-buggy days too. But during these years medicine has produced the equivalent of the superhighway, the jet aircraft and, I think, some accomplishments equivalent to man's reaching the moon.

The complexity of the practice of medicine today is forcing the development of a system that will more uniformly aid maintenance of health and provide care for the sick. The doctor traditionally has responded to the knock on his door, but today his service capabilities are more than he can deliver individually. His profession has grown beyond him. It has incurred community-wide responsibilities because of its delivery capability. These it cannot fulfill without greater integration and amalgamation, without in some way developing a system for the delivery of health care.

The situation seems like that which once existed in telephone communication. Each town, each city, had its own telephone company, sometimes more than one. Each did a reasonably good job. But the demand for uniform and widespread service forced amalgamation. The independent company could not provide the integrated service that the new technology made possible and public demand required.

The situation is frightening, even disagreeable, to many rugged, individualistic doctors, but it is also challenging. It offers the prospect of developing the best system for maintenance of health and for care of the sick yet devised. We have the facts. Can we build, from them, a feasible, improved system?

The Physicians' Response

With this matrix surrounding the physician, what is his reaction to it? This is difficult to measure. The plaintive cries of "Leave us alone," "Leave us as we are," have been heard clearly through the great guild or union of my profession, the American Medical Association, of which I am a member. This reaction is understandable; the strongest voice in the Association is that of generalists and solo practitioners. They now see the current trend to interdependence as a threat to the system to which they are devoted and intensely loyal. But things have changed around them, at least in America. The destiny of medicine no longer lies with them but with the irrepressible march of advancing knowledge and with the younger men and women who possess it.

Not all physicians are digging in for a last-ditch stand. Many have put their heads together and devised new programs to provide health care. Some of these are in the testing stage, and, fortunately, representatives of the AMA are participants in many. Doctors, young and old, in many cities, are giving some of their time to caring for those who cannot pay for health care. Such volunteer service is a tradition in medicine, and I believe it always will be, but the arrangement provides an emergency rather than a permanent solution to long standing problems.

The attitude of many recent graduates and medical students is heartening. My colleagues who teach these young people, who quell their riots and discern the basis of their unrest, recognize in the majority a strong social conscience — a sense of moral and personal obligation to provide care for those who cannot afford it as well as for those who can, and a willingness to serve a system of delivery designed to reach "everyone." I hope these attitudes will survive, because they are so relevant to the solving of present-day problems.

As I see the ferment, the public is demanding, the Government is responding, and the medical profession is beginning to stir. These are the attributes of a productive setting, a great opportunity, a time when something can be done. And if we physicians are not responsive it will be done by others.

But Why This Ferment?

Because the effectiveness of medicine today in the prevention of illness and the treatment of the sick has increased immensely during the last 60 years. We are doing a better job — 100 times better, by my estimate.

The horse-and-buggy doctor was independent because he was not really indispensable. In most serious situations there was little he could do. He could listen, look, give injections, hold the hand and calm concerns. No wonder he made house calls. He carried most of what he had to offer with him in his little black bag.

Today, the physician controls a vast array of testing and treating procedures, devices and skills that he, his medical colleagues and his associates in the health sciences can exercise. But he requires laboratory facilities, technical associates, physician colleagues skilled in special technics and knowledge to practice his profession. He is no longer independent. He requires an emergency admissions unit, an outpatient facility and a modern hospital and laboratory if he is to deliver his 1970 brand of care. He is almost helpless alone. No wonder he hesitates to make a house call, for by his standards, alone at the home, there is so little he can do. Is it worth the patient's money to have him come?

The public, I believe, has not come to realize that in terms of health care, today's doctors can deliver a Cadillac rather than a Model-T or a horse and cart. They are getting the equivalent of color TV but, remembering the past, hope to be billed for a crystal set!

This improvement in care reflects the expansion of medical knowledge over the last 60 years. It is said that over 80 per cent of the medical information applied in practice now was amassed in the past 60 years. More medical knowledge and more effective therapeutic programs have been established during these years than during all the other centuries of man's recorded history. This 60 years' accumulation is more than one man can possibly read, let alone hold in his head.

There are three important consequences to the explosion of medical knowledge. These are the doctor shortage, the decline in solo and general practice, and the increase in group or integrated practice.

The Doctor Shortage

Medical schools 30 years ago aimed to provide doctors at a density of about 1 per 1000 population or 100 doctors per 100,000 citizens. In Minnesota our medical school has kept pace with population growth; in our state we have somewhat more than 100 doctors in practice per 100,000 population, and this is just about the national ration.[1] Our medical schools have kept physician production in pace with the population increase but not with the expansion of knowledge. Today, physicians can do so much more in maintaining the health and treating the ailments of their patients than was possible years ago that the demands for their services have increased tremendously and now have exceeded their capacity to deliver.

The Decline of Solo And General Practice

Medical schools recruit from the top 20 per cent of the country's students. Such intelligent men and women know when they are spreading themselves too thin. They are unhappy when they are not doing all that might be done for their patients, and they seek means to correct it. One reaction is to abandon general practice. For example, in Minnesota, in 1910, 95 per cent of the doctors were in general practice (Table 53-1).[1] The percentage today is about 50.[1] Nationally, the trend is clear; increasing numbers of physicians are seeking the personal security and satisfaction of specialization (Fig. 53-1).[2,3] They look for a body of knowledge they can contain and can be highly skillful in applying. To be able to deliver what he knows is the best, the doctor today is forced to limit the breadth of his practice — to specialize. The trend has been fired by the demand of the American public for the ultimate in medical care.

The general practitioner, particularly the soloist, is not replenishing his ranks. He is overworked and overtaxed beyond his mental and physical capabilities; his plight has become recognized, and his numbers

TABLE 53-1. PERCENTAGE INCIDENCE OF ACTIVE PHYSICIANS IN MINNESOTA ACCORD-
ING TO TYPE OF PRACTICE, 1910–1965.*

Field of Practice	Incidence (%)						
	1910	1920	1930	1940	1950	1960	1965
General practice	95	70	64	62	59	41	52
Combined specialists	5	30	36	38	41	59	48

*Data reproduced from Health Manpower for the Upper Midwest by permission of the Louis W. and Maud Hill Family Foundation.

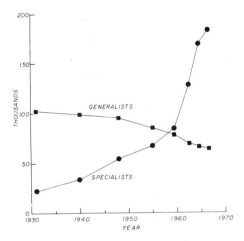

Figure 53-1. Numbers of Generalists and Specialists in Private Practice in the United States (Data from the United States Department of Health, Education, and Welfare[2,3].)

have diminished. This appears to me a natural physiologic — or psychologic — or sociologic — consequence of advance in medicine. I see no reason to fight this natural trend toward specialization.

The solo practitioner, like the one-room schoolhouse, is disappearing from the American scene — for many of the same reasons. In Minnesota the one-room school will vanish in 1970 (Fig. 53-2).[4] The decline in incidence of general practitioners is not so dramatic. One projection indicates that those in general practice will be reduced to inconsequential proportions in the 1980's (Fig. 53-3).[5] Soloists are disappearing more rapidly. Doctors, like teachers, know when they cannot do the whole job alone. The public is aware of it, too, though it is more reluctant to give up the solo doctor's office than the one-room schoolhouse!

Group or Integrated Practice

A third consequence of the explosion of knowledge is the banding together of physicians and surgeons into an integrated practice — groups of doctors with differing skills, organized, ideally, so that each ailment of each of their patients can have the care of an expert. Integration enables the patient to move freely within a framework of experts. The system pools intellectual resources in the resolution of patient prob-

lems. It fosters the development of specialists and superspecialists. It provides a shelter for the harassed physician because responsibilities can be shared — responsibilities for highly specialized knowledge, for round-the-clock service, for time spent on vacation and in continuing education. Most importantly, the system generally provides superior and more uniform care to the sick whether it is used in a private clinic, in the environment of a medical school, in a community hospital, in an industrial-health program or in a veterans or other military establishment.

In recent years some general practitioners, each having a special interest in one area of medicine or surgery, have banded together into a clinic, an integrated group. Together, they believe they deliver better care, more consistently, than as individuals. A slow but steady increase has occurred during recent decades in the number of doctors practicing in integrated groups (Table 53-2). Figures for 1968 from California show that a sixth of the doctors in private practice there are associated with a group,[7] and in Canada the fraction is nearly a third.[8]

The public has accepted the trend. The public likes health centers just as it likes shopping centers. Both offer advantages to the consumer and to those who deliver the goods. Both are here to stay.

Transportation and Communication

The final determinants of future health-care systems are transportation and communication. Highways and automobiles, airports and airplanes, have completely

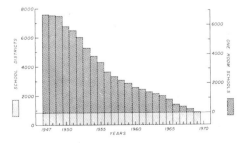

Figure 53-2. Disappearance of One-Room Schools in Minnesota (Data from the State Advisory Committee on School Reorganization.[4])

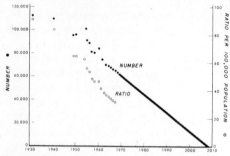

Figure 53–3. Numbers of General Practitioners in the United States, with Projection of Decline in Numbers in the Future (Reproduced from Fahs and Peterson[5] with the Permission of the Publisher.) Fahs, I. J., and Peterson, O. L.: The decline of general practice. Public Health Rep. *83*: 267 (April, 1968).

Information regarding the history of patients, data from testing procedures performed or analyzed within a co-ordinated laboratory system, and consultation with experts regarding the ailment suspected or identified are all at hand within an integrated system having an adequate communication network.

Reviews of medical topics, seminars and lecture courses can also be transmitted long distances without geographic displacement of the participants. We doctors need to learn more about using modern communications media. Experiments, particularly within regional medical programs, are in progress. Many more are needed.

altered the geographic requirements of health-care delivery systems. In the past, some people living in rural areas felt insecure if a doctor was not available within 10 miles. Today, these people can be better served by an adequate health-care unit within a radius of 100 miles or more. Even critically ill patients can be moved safely over these or greater distances by skilled attendants.

Today, having a doctor in every hamlet is wasteful. The physician realizes this and often will not stay alone, for he cannot deliver the care the public demands without the support of a health-care unit. To deliver superior care, much more is required in technical skills and professional attention than a lone practitioner can provide. Today, it is the patient, not the doctor, who is mobile.

Modern methods of communication can provide to each practitioner within a co-ordinated system more information than any one of them could retain or even file.

A PLAN FOR THE FUTURE – AN INTEGRATED REGIONAL HEALTH SYSTEM

With these as the determinants, can we identify the system most likely to deliver the best health care? As a professional researcher, I would say, "An improved system can be visualized, then tested, and by this means the best produced."

The basic principle is integration; the basic ingredients are regionalization, health-care units of integrated practice in the region and a health center integrated in practice, education and research with the units of the region (in large regions possibly two or more such centers).

The Region

The region consists of a network or grid of transportation and communication (Fig. 53-4). The overall dimensions, the dis-

TABLE 53–2. INCREASING PRIVATE GROUP PRACTICE*

Yr	Thousands in Private Group Practice	Private Practitioners In Groups (%)†
1946	3.5	3
1959	13.0	8
1965	28.4	12

*From data for total numbers of physicians in private practice[2,3] & for total numbers of physicians in group practice[8]; percentages calculated by author.

†These percentages would be larger if those practicing integrated medicine in medical schools & veterans and other military & industrial establishments were included.

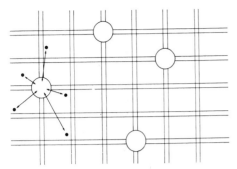

Figure 53-4. Modern Network of Transportation and Communication upon Which the Health-Care System is Superimposed; Dimensions Depend upon Density of Population.
The circles indicate placement of health-care units on the transportation and communication network. Patients and solo practitioners relate to units.

tances between the crossroads are not defined in miles or city blocks but in terms of density of population — the need for service.

Health-Care Units of Integrated Practice

These consist of groups of physicians and surgeons who accept joint responsibility for the patients who enter their unit and for the health care of all or a portion of those who live in their community. The doctors see that each patient is attended by the physician or surgeon in the group best qualified to render the required care. They specialize in the different branches of medicine and surgery.

Location of health-care units (HCU). These are placed strategically at the important crossroads of the regional transportation and communication networks (Fig. 53-4).

Composition of health-care units. A certain number of doctors and a certain pool of allied skills and facilities are necessary before a unit can function effectively and survive. It seems likely that the minimal requirements of a viable unit are as follows:

Medical specialists: an internist, a general surgeon, an obstetrician and gynecologist, a pediatrician and probably a psychiatrist.
Location: ideally these doctors will have offices to see their ambulatory patients in a clinic building immediately adjacent to the community

hospital to which they admit their patients and a laboratory facility serving their patients in the clinic and the hospital.

Additional personnel: there must be nurses and their assistants, allied health scientists and administrative assistants to aid the doctor in the delivery of care.

The size and complexity of such units depend ultimately upon the skills, cooperativeness and organizing abilities of the participants, the density of the population and the attitude and support of the public. The unit can provide superior health care to those within an area of 100 city blocks, or 100 rural miles.

Major Health-Care Centers

Each region, which may have many health-care units, requires one or more health centers. The region's grid of transportation and communication connects with the center (Fig. 53-5). The center energizes the grid. It is the complete health resource for the patients, physicians and allied health scientists of the area. It services the grid in patient care, medical education and research (Fig. 53-6).

Contributions to the Region by the Health-Care Center

Support in The Delivery of Health Care

At the center, the greatest concentration of medical knowledge can be devoted to baffling and difficult problems of maintaining health and treating sickness. The most complex and expensive tests and therapeutic procedures can be performed more

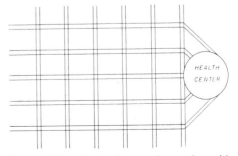

Figure 53-5. Health Center Connecting with Major Pathways of Transportation and Communication in the Health-Care Delivery Region.

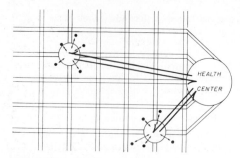

Figure 53–6. Health Center and Health-Care Units Interacting in Patient Care, Education and Research in the Health-Care Delivery Region.

efficiently and effectively in a major center, where they are done more often than at health-care units. But not all is esoteric at the center, for it assumes its share of delivery of care to the community surrounding it.

The health center of the future will, I am sure, provide laboratory services to the region. Laboratory medicine is the most rapidly growing branch of the health sciences. Specialists are emerging in its various divisions. The facilities that they man perform the most advanced and complex tests of health and illness, and because of large volume, they usually perform these, as well as the simpler procedures, at lowest cost.

Provision and Evaluation of New Knowledge, Research and Development

The major center provides a service to the region by developing, evaluating and applying new technics and procedures. The center is a major source of new knowledge to the region. To perform such functions, a substantial portion — one fourth to one third — of the effort of the center must be devoted to medical research, both basic and practical.

The center continuously revitalizes the health-care units by a flow of new information to improve the maintenance of health and the care of the sick.

Education

The third demand upon the center is teaching, the transmission of knowledge

from experts to students. Undergraduate, graduate and continuing education are thus offered by the center. Physicians and surgeons, research workers, allied health scientists and technicians are trained, and their knowledge renewed at the center — a tremendous undertaking.

Ideally, besides the major health centers, each health care unit will have programs of education and of research — self-generated programs of under-graduate, residency and continuing education integrated with those of the center. Trainees in the allied health sciences and in medicine need exposure to the most practical aspects of health-care delivery that health-care units can provide.

Thus, the center serves the region by providing advanced patient care, new knowledge and education to doctors, allied health professionals and medical technologists.

The center receives in return patients who require its skills and facilities, and financial support for its programs of patient care, research and education. A center without research and educational programs soon equilibrates with its region, rather than leading it. If Americans are to have the health care they demand, research and education must be a part of the system providing it, for they are basic to its superiority.

Items included in the cost to the public of a superior health system are, therefore, delivery of care to the sick, prevention of illness for the healthy, health education for the novice, continuing education for the expert and new information, through research, for the entire system.

Can physicians provide all this care, education and research? If we are short of doctors today, won't the public be more poorly cared for if more doctors assume these responsibilities?

Allied Health Scientists

Clearly, we must have increased numbers of doctors. Their multiplication is medicine's most acute need. But will their increased numbers alone correct the imbalance? Definitely not. Many of the skills that modern science has brought to medicine do not, in their application to patients, require the broad and deep knowledge of physicians and surgeons. Doctors should do only what they alone can do and train others for the rest.

In 1900, sick people were cared for by a doctor and a nurse, or by a doctor alone. Later, the doctor began to need technical assistance, and it was one patient, one doctor, a nurse and a technician in the laboratory or in the x-ray department. As scientific knowledge has amassed, greater skills have been demanded of those who help physicians, and more and more of them have been recruited.

In 1966 an average of about nine individuals, each with different skills and only one a medical doctor, were often involved in the care of one sick person in the United States (Table 53-3). By the end of the 1970's, if doctors and their helpers increase at the rates they have in the past, the ratio will be about 12 persons per patient, but I hope it will have reached 20 or more. None of the 20 persons will devote all his time to one patient or be necessarily in the service of one doctor. Each will be doing different tasks, providing service for many patients, and aiding a number of doctors. This development will further force the integration of practice, as many doctors and many patients use the skills of many individual experts in a co-ordinated fashion.

A great opportunity lies within this framework. The increased use of allied health professionals offers a means of improving and expanding health care more rapidly and more adequately than by increasing the number of doctors alone.

The Role of the Medical Doctor

The doctor must be located at the center, at the apex of the medical decision-making process. He must be willing to assign information-collecting to others, and must be satisfied with correlation of the data and with responsibility for the decisions based upon it.

He determines the diagnosis and prescribes the therapy, and at this point in the delivery process he establishes his relation with his patient.

The Logjam in the Present System

By this teamwork, I believe the ever worsening logjam in the delivery of health care can be broken. Three options are available. One is to curtail the advance of medical knowledge; another is not to use the information it provides. These are unacceptable. A third is to provide more help, more supporting personnel to perform tasks the doctor does not have to do, so that the application of new information to the maintenance of health and the care of the sick may be uninterrupted.

A change in the attitude of the public and of many doctors will be needed if this is to be accomplished. I see this change coming, quickly!

The Portal of Entry to the System

Where is the logjam in the delivery of health care today? It is in the doctor's office. This is the major portal of entry to our present-day delivery system: the doc-

TABLE 53-3. RELATION OF NUMBER OF PHYSICIANS TO TOTAL NUMBER IN HEALTH OCCUPATIONS

Yr	Persons In Health Occupations[9]	Physicians In Health Care[2,3]	Ratio of Health Workers To Physicians
1940	1,090,000	165,290	6.6
1950	1,440,000	194,052*	7.4
1960	2,040,000	230,762	8.8
1966	2,786,000*	297,097	9.4

*Estimates.

tor's office, where he spends so much time in the collection of data before he performs the task that only he can do — that of reaching decisions regarding the delivery of care. Of course, he is helped by laboratory aides and consultants. But does he need to collect all the other information himself? Why cannot others help him more?

We need a variety of portals of entry to our system. These may range from physician to nurse, from physician's assistant to questionnaires analyzed by a computer. We need better and cheaper ways to collect patient data than via the harassed, overworked physician.

The Challenge

Doctors need much help, and yet it is so hard to give it to them, for their security seems threatened when others perform their traditional tasks and the public loses the assurance of their presence. But unless doctors assign some of these tasks, they will not have time to acquire new skills or to deliver enough care to enough people to satisfy the health needs of the nation. And unless the public is willing to see the doctor in a new role and recognize that he is of more use to them when some of his traditional activities are performed by others, the delivery of care will not be quickly improved or increased.

This is a challenging time, full of prospects of improvement. Given a willingness on the part of doctors and patients to test new programs, I believe the best system for the delivery of health care the world has known can be developed here in America in the next decade.

REFERENCES

1. Peterson, OL, Fahs IJ, Health Manpower Study Commission: Health Manpower for the Upper Midwest. St. Paul, Minnesota, Louis W and Maud Hill Family Foundation, June, 1966, p 32.

2. Peterson PQ, Pennell MY: Health Manpower Source Book. Section 14. Medical Specialists. Washington, DC, Government Printing Office, 1962 (PHS Publication No 263), pp 2–3.

3. United States Department of Health, Education, and Welfare, Public Health Service, Health Services and Mental Health Administration: Health Resources Statistics Reported from the National Center for Health Statistics. Washington, DC, Government Printing Office, 1968 (PHS Publication No 1509), p 124.

4. State Advisory Committee on School Reorganization: Eleventh Report on the State Advisory Commission on School Reorganization to the Sixty-sixth Legislature of the State of Minnesota, January 1969, p 15.

5. Fahs IJ, Peterson OL: The decline of general practice. Public Health Rep *83:* 267–170, 1968.

6. Balfe BE, McNamara ME: Survey of Medical Groups in the U.S. 1965. Chicago, American Medical Association, 1968, p 81.

7. Characteristics and Distribution of Physicians in California, June-July 1969. California Medical Association, Division of Socio-Economics and Research, Bureau of Research and Planning. February, 1970, p 21, Table B-4.

8. Lyon EK: Group practice in Canada. Presented at the First International Congress on Group Medicine, Winnipeg, Manitoba, Canada, April 26–30, 1970. Canadian Medical Association: Group Practice in Canada. Toronto, Canada, Ryerson Press, 1967, pp 9–16 and 36.

9. United States Department of Health, Education, and Welfare, Public Health Service: Education for the Allied Health Professions and Services: Report of the Allied Health Professions Education Subcommittee of the National Advisory Health Council, Bureau of Health Manpower, Washington, DC, Government Printing Office, 1967 (PHS Publication No 1600), p 5

54   Some Good Features of the British National Health Service

Paul B. Beeson

I was glad to be invited to speak to this audience about the British National Health Service, in which I have been working during the last eight years. I shall not be describing it as a model we should copy here; nevertheless, there are some useful lessons to be learned from it. I must acknowledge that when I moved from Yale to Oxford in 1965 I did not quite realize that a professor in one of England's old universities would have to work in conformation with the guidelines of a huge nationalized industry, but indeed that is the case; and it soon showed me some sharp contrasts with the American way of doing things. I found myself having to take more interest in the problems of medical care from a national standpoint than I had ever done before.

THE BRITISH SYSTEM

Let me review briefly certain essential features of the British system. Its stated goal is to provide "a comprehensive medical health service, free and open to all." It started with a bang, so to speak, because on a given day in 1948 the government took possession of all the hospitals and put virtually all the doctors on its payroll. Measures were instituted to ensure a relatively even distribution of doctors over the entire country. Every man, woman, and

---

This paper was prepared for delivery at the November 6, 1973, plenary session of the 84th AAMC Annual Meeting in Washington, D.C.

Dr. Beeson is Nuffield Professor of Clinical Medicine, University of Oxford.

child was to be enrolled with a general practitioner, who would provide primary care and would arrange for specialist attention or hospital treatment as required.

Now, what is the situation after 25 years? About 50,000 doctors are active in Britian today. A relatively small proportion is engaged in industrial, military, or public health work. About half are in general practice; the other half are doing hospital work. In the hospitals are 15,000 junior staff, equivalent to our interns and residents, whereas only 8,000 are of the consultant grade, which includes specialists in all fields.

It is worth emphasizing that only 8,000 specialists staff all the hospitals in a country that has about one-fourth the population of the United States. Obviously, they have to be very carefully distributed. To achieve this, the country is divided into regions, each of which has its quotas. The Oxford region in which I work serves about 2,000,000 people in an area roughly 50 by 40 miles. Our quotas for a few specialties are as follows: general physicians, 46; general surgeons, 41: neurosurgeons, 3; pediatricians, 15; and psychiatrists, 70. For the nation as a whole, the numbers in certain types of specialties are as follows: general physicians, 927; general surgeons, 889; ophthalmologists, 348; pediatricians, 303; neurosurgeons, 74; obstetricians and gynecologists, 589. Compared with America, these numbers look very small indeed. To emphasize this point, note that there are only 927 general physicians for all the United Kingdom; yet by comparison Harvard's Department of Medicine alone has 500 full-time and part-time

---

Beeson, P.B.: Some good features of the British National Health Service. J. Med. Educ. 49:1: 43–49, January, 1974.

teachers, and the American College of Physicians has 24,000 members.

In Britain the distribution of posts for specialists is made on the advice of committees which appraise the current situation and try to foresee future developments. To avoid a surfeit of trainees in any one specialty, the Department of Health maintains firm control on the junior positions in the nation's hospitals. Thus it is very hard to establish a new house staff job in a popular field such as general medicine but comparatively easy to do so for certain undersubscribed specialties.

When any consultant post becomes vacant, the opening is announced in the weekly medical journals, and qualified trainees can apply for it. A local committee selects the new consultant from the applicants. It can be seen, therefore, that young British doctors are not free to choose the places in which they will practice their specialties; their options depend on the places that happen to fall vacant at the time they are nearing the end of their training.

While I am dealing with the relatively small number of specialist physicians in Britian. I should like to digress to its effect on clinical teaching in the medical schools. The size of clinical faculties in all British medical schools is fairly uniform, because the number of positions is dependent on government support in accord with national formulas, whether the salary comes via a university or the National Health Service. I have put in Table 54-1 the relative strengths of Oxford, Harvard, Ohio State, and the University of Washington. As we all know, the size of clinical departments in American medical schools expanded greatly during the past quarter century owing to the initiative of section heads who have secured research grants that

TABLE 54-1. STRENGTHS OF CLINICAL FACULTIES

	Full-time	Part-time
Oxford	69	114
Harvard	840	1,129
Ohio State	400	1,006
University of Washington	520	1,000

included salaries. I realize, of course, that the scale of research is far greater in this country and that there is also a large teaching responsibility for graduates because of the greater numbers of residents and research fellows. I want only to consider this matter of size from the standpoint of undergraduate teaching. As you can see from the Oxford figures, the senior staff strength simply does not allow for much individual or small group teaching. All the full-time people carry out some service work, and the part-time people are National Health Service consultants, each with a full hospital service to maintain. Medical students are, of course, assigned to the wards and outpatient clinics, but there is no possibility of attaining a one-to-one teacher-to-student ratio as can frequently be done in the outpatient clinic of an American school. British teachers have to place considerable reliance on such old-fashioned pedagogy as didactic lectures and text books. The surprising thing is that I do not find much difference in the products of the two systems. I had previously allowed myself to be persuaded that didactic lectures are a waste of time and that the more teachers one can have in the hospital the better the learning opportunity for the students. It would be an interesting experiment to give the same examination to a sample of the graduating classes of British and American schools and see how they do come out.

Now to return to the work of British doctors in the Health Service. As to the consultants, except for restrictions on choice of location, I have the impression that most are well satisfied with their jobs. Each has security and a good deal of autonomy — his own beds in the hospital, his own team of nurses and junior doctors. The patients he sees have been screened so that comparatively little of his time is spent inappropriately. His income at present ranges from $14,000 to $20,000. In addition, about one consultant in three receives a supplementary merit award, which in a few cases could bring the income up to as much as $36,000. These figures are small when contrasted with American professional incomes, but remember that there is no overhead for office expenses. Moreover, there is no compelling need to pile up capital for retirement because each will receive a government pension.

If we turn now to look at the general practitioner in Britain, we find that dispersal throughout the country is managed in a different way. The government pays each one an annual fee according to the number of patients on his list and aims to have about 2,500 patients per general practitioner. If too many GPs were to try to locate in one place, there would just not be enough income to go around.

In discussions of general practice, one has heard much about the unhappy plight of the British GP. He is described as isolated and forced to work with inadequate office equipment and staff. That did characterize the early days of the Health Service, and it was the principal reason for emigration of some thousands of British doctors. But the Department of Health has energetically set out to improve the conditions of general practice. Incomes have been brought up to a range similar to that of hospital consultants. Funds have been made available for equipping and staffing of offices. The formation of group practices has been encouraged, and many so-called health centers have been built. These are places in which small groups of general practitioners work together. Public health nurses and social workers have been provided. Laboratory services for general practitioners have been established. Post-graduate teaching centers, now over 200 in number, have been located all over the country. These are equipped with lounges, seminar rooms, and libraries, and GPs receive payment for attendance at post-graduate instruction.

As a result of these measures, their surroundings are more suitable, their isolation has been lessened, and they have predictable hours off duty. The British general practitioner is now far happier, and the problem of emigration no longer exists. A number of them have told me they regard their jobs as more rewarding and more challenging than any in the Health Service. The good ones enjoy the continuing relation with their own group of patients and look on themselves as leaders of small community teams. While at Ox-

ford I have seen a marked change in the career plans of our students. Right now the great majority of them intend to become general practitioners; this includes some of the top people who could undoubtedly survive the competition for good consultant posts. Incidentally, we have made no change in our teaching and have no department of general practice. What it all seems to show is that careers in family practice can be made attractive to young doctors if the working conditions are improved and the pay is comparable with that of specialists.

How well does the British Health Service really work? There are, of course, many unsolved problems, and there are frustrations from the restrictions of any nationalized business. Nevertheless, my feeling is that the system works surprisingly well. The goal of providing a good standard of medical care for every person without private cost has been achieved, and the health service has the approval of the British people. No politician would dream of suggesting that it be supplanted by something else. I have been interested to note, too, that people belonging to all social classes use it. We see some of Oxford's most distinguished citizens on our ward services, and they accept this quite naturally. But the thing I want to stress most of all is that British doctors themselves approve of the principle of the service. Several medical friends have told me they believe Britain has the best system of medical care in the world. And, when a young doctor returns after spending a year or two training in the United States, I have learned to expect a remark like this, "Well, it was interesting and worthwhile, but I certainly am glad to get back to the NHS."

Now, while talking about good features, I am going to venture to say something about attitudes toward patient care in the teaching hospitals of the two countries. I do so with trepidation, because it entails criticism in an extremely sensitive area. Let me just preface it by saying that I am still an American, proud of many accomplishments of American medicine, and am looking forward to coming back to a new job in this country within the year. But, in general, I have come to feel that more thought is given to the comfort and welfare of the patient in a British teaching hospital. There is less drive to be absolutely thorough, and no special credit comes from solving the diagnostic puzzle in record time. Not uncommonly a patient is sent home for a rest after some uncomfortable procedure. Due to the fact that each consultant controls a small unit throughout the year, it is accepted that house staff will clear important decisions with him. Consequently, the conduct of work seems a little less venturesome, especially if a procedure carries with it risk or discomfort. I have spent a week or two as a visiting professor in this country every year since 1965 and confess that now and then I have felt uncomfortable because of the relentless drive of the diagnostic work-up. Long before 1965 I remember being nettled by the comments of some British friends that our house officers have too much freedom. In rebuttal I used to describe all the checks in our system, but I have had to modify my view on this. While I was writing this paper, I received a letter from a former registrar, who is presently working in one of America's best medical centers. Here is a paragraph:

I have recently started teaching clinical students, which I am finding a fascinating experience. The students are remarkably keen, and by English standards work very long hours on the ward. The organization of the wards is very curious. The house staff take the attitude that every conceivable differential diagnosis has to be excluded, including all the possible tests, before a diagnosis can be reached. The patients get a pretty thin time, for not only do they have three ward rounds a day (one with the attending and two by the house staff), but they are also subjected to many unnecessary tests. It is not hard to see why medical costs are escalating so much.

In what I have just been saying, my illustrations were in the context of internal medicine, but I think they apply to other fields as well. Certainly, there are figures to show that about twice as much surgery is done in the United States as in Britain. And America seems to rush in all too rapidly with such procedures as coronary by-pass surgery. I tend to attribute these tendencies to the freedom of action that characterizes American medicine at every

level of its organization. I think that some constraints may be advantageous.

A national health service has great advantage over our free-enterprise system in terms of economy and avoidance of redundancy. For example, such expensive facilities as those for hemodialysis or cardiac surgery are distributed in Britain according to a national plan and not, as so often happens here, because groups of doctors would like to be able to have these things available in their hospitals. According to HEW figures, the American health industry cost about $83 billion in 1972. The bill for the British National Health Service will be in the neighborhood of $6 billion in 1973. I do not think this vast difference can be explained by higher wages and cost of supplies in the United States.

PERSONAL VIEWS

Now I am going to offer some personal views that I have developed as a result of working abroad for several years. I ought first to repeat what I said at the beginning, namely that the British system would not be suitable for us. It evolved from a different background of medical practice and is tailored to the needs of a small, densely populated country which is politically far more socialistic. Despite these and other dissimilarities, I believe we can make use of their experience in our search for a better American medicine.

As I see it now, the striking thing about the American medical scene is lack of overall regulation. There is no uniform planning and no top guidance. The federal government and several states have tried a variety of schemes to influence the training of medical students and residents, but these efforts have had little effect. Many medical schools and their teaching hospitals have inaugurated programs to involve themselves more in community medicine and to encourage young doctors to go into family practice in localities where they are needed, but these have all been more or less in the nature of experiments and limited in scope. I feel that time for experimenting is short. If we are to avoid a takeover such as that which happened in

Britain in 1948, we must achieve better organization.

I understand that a new top level body, the Coordinating Council on Medical Education, has been formed to take the lead in national planning. Any such agency will have to do more than issue hand-wringing statements; it will have to exert powerful pressure for there is much inertia. A real campaign of education and persuasion will have to be directed at the medical profession if its individual members and its various organizational units are to be convinced that changes are needed. And if one central issue is to characterize that campaign, I would aim at reversing the trend to specialty practice. I would go after it with all the passion we are giving to population control throughout the world. Data on specialty practice in America are given by Rousselot in the August issue of the *American Journal of Medicine.* They show that only 19 percent of America's doctors are now in family practice; and extrapolation of present trends indicates that this percentage will fall to six by 1990. Thoughtful students of medical care, such as John Knowles, William Longmire, Robert Ebert, Francis Moore, and Rosemary Stevens, have all issued warnings about the course we are on; nevertheless, our training mills seem to be running unchecked. Note, for example, the recent controversy about neurosurgery in the *New England Journal of Medicine.* This specialty is surely supersaturated in the United States today, yet there was strong objection to the suggestion that resident training be reduced. Let me remind you again how our organization of medical practice contrasts with that in Britain. There are 22,000 in family practice in the United Kingdom and 70,000 in family practice in the United States. There are 8,000 in specialist practice in the United Kingdom and 280,000 in specialist practice in the United States. Here is a country with one-**fourth the** population of the United States, where the current trends in health statistics are better than ours, where every person has access to a good standard of medical care, and where the total expenditure for medicine is far below ours. The striking difference is economy in the use of specialists. To me this is the most obvious reason why America has a badly distributed, excessively costly system. If we could begin to shift our ratio of specialists to primary physicians toward that of Britain, I think we would cease to hear about the need for more doctors or for training paramedical assistants. I have no doubt at all that a good family doctor can deal with the great majority of medical episodes quickly and competently. A specialist, on the other hand, feels that he must be thorough, not only because of his training but also because he has a reputation to protect. He, therefore, spends more time with each patient and orders more laboratory work. The result is waste of doctors' time and patients' money. This not only inflates the national health bill but also creates an illusion of doctor shortage when the only real need is to have the existing doctors doing the right things. We now have board-certified internists spending more than half their time with patients who have functional complaints and board-certified pediatricians checking well babies or treating the self-limited viral infections of childhood. Good family doctors can do these as well and sometimes better.

American professors of medicine often tell me that the well trained internist is the best answer to America's need for a family physician. I cannot agree with that. Today's well trained internist is hospital-oriented and wants to practice "big" medicine. He has had little training in such important branches as pediatrics, dermatology, or nonsurgical gynecology. If we really believe that the internist is the family doctor of the future, we ought to change our system of training and strengthen links between the American College of Physicians and the Academy of General Practice. The subspecialties of internal medicine have their own organizations, anyway.

Where should we begin our efforts to achieve better balance? Undoubtedly, it should be in our medical schools and teaching hospitals. Other places will follow that lead. Unfortunately, however, American medical schools and their associated residency training programs are overwhelmingly oriented toward certification by some board or other. Resistance to change springs from the fact that present systems of resident training are traditional and convenient. Clinical teachers rely on them in every phase of their work: patient care, research, and undergraduate instruction. If American clinical professors today are like I was in 1965 — and my guess is that many of them are — their main attention is on local hospital and medical school affairs and research. Although they may be somewhat troubled by criticism, they are loath to make radical changes. Many of the gestures that have recently been directed at a larger world seem to me quite inadequate. It is just not enough for a famous teaching hospital to organize a minor family practice training program by affiliation with some nearby community hospital. I feel we need to have our most respected teaching centers putting the highest priority on training programs suited to national needs. Perhaps we should try to break down some of the elaborate sectional barriers that we created during the lush 1950s and 1960s. This would not inevitably impair the quality of research or training.

Our profession is almost certainly going to have to give up a share of its traditional independence and free enterprise. Some kind of control of medical practice already exists almost everywhere else in the world. We must realize that we have a sort of monopoly on an essential service — a service that has lately become hugely expensive but still has major shortcomings. Admittedly, many of the difficulties relate to social and economic factors outside our sphere, but we must accept responsibility for excessive independence of action. I speak here of action at all levels — the house officer, the head of an academic section, the individual medical school, the certification board, the private practitioner. It would be miraculous if such an arrangement added up to a good system of health care for the country.

Some agency will have to take charge; and, of course, the federal government is the most likely one. Wouldn't it be gratifying, though, if we could exhibit the statesmanship and self-discipline to do it ourselves?